MAP A

CENTRAL AND EASTERN MEDITERRANEAN
JEWISH SETTLEMENTS OF THE FIRST TWO CENTURIES A.D.
PROVINCES UNDERLINED

WITH ACKNOWLEDGMENT TO ADOLF DEISSMANN
THE WORLD AS KNOWN TO SAINT PAUL

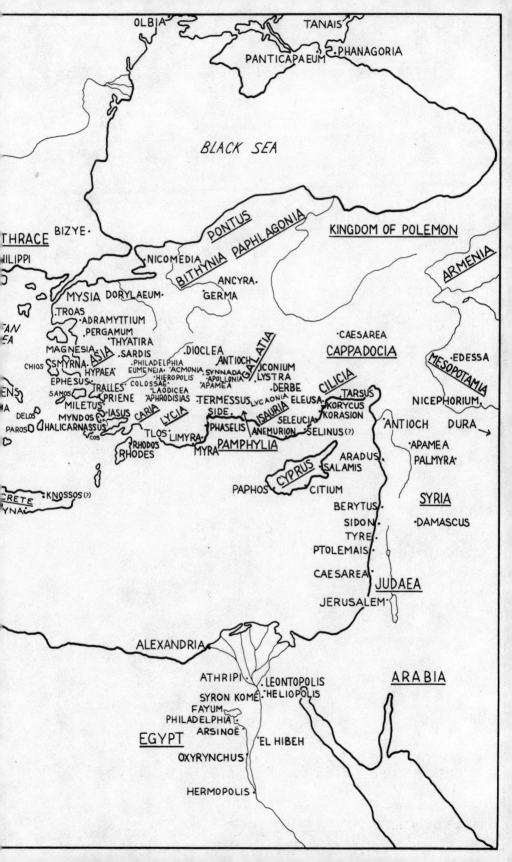

The Rise of
Christianity

The Rise of Christianity

W. H.C. FREND

FORTRESS PRESS   PHILADELPHIA

Published in the United States, 1984, by Fortress Press, Philadelphia.

Jacket design: Steven L. Zellers
Jacket photograph: Scala/Art Resource, Inc.
"The Trophy of the Cross," a panel of a fourth-century sarcophagus from
    the Domitilla Catacomb in the Lateran Museum, Rome.

First paperback edition 1985

Library of Congress Cataloging in Publication Data

Frend, W. H. C.
    The rise of Christianity.

    Bibliography: p.
    Includes indexes.
    1. Church history—Primitive and early church, ca.
30–600.   I. Title.
    BR.162.2F733   1984   270.1   84–3994
    ISBN 0–8006–1931–5

Printed in the U.S.A.   AF 1-1931

03   11   12   13   14   15   16   17

Contents

CONTENTS

PART 4: The Parting of the Ways

Illustrations

Covers: "The Trophy of the Cross," a panel on a fourth-century sarcophagus from the Domitilla Catacomb in the Lateran Museum, Rome. At left, Simon of Cyrene carries the cross; next, Christ is crowned with a victory wreath. The central motif (see also back cover) features a labarum with the Chi-Rho and two guards representing the sleeping guards at Christ's tomb. On the right, Christ, the victor, is escorted before Pilate (at extreme right) who turns away in confusion.

Frontispiece: "The Good Shepherd," a third-century fresco in the Vault of Lucina, Catacomb of San Callisto, Rome.

Egypt. Although from a later period, this tapestry illustrates the transition from the more human, earthly style of pagan art to the mythologically portrayed deities of Christian art.

Page 397: "Orante and Eucharistic Offering," a mid-third-century fresco in the Catacomb of San Callisto, Rome.

Page 439: "The Arch of Galerius," late third to early fourth century, erected in Salonika by Galerius to commemorate his victory over Narses. From top: the unarmored emperor addresses his troops in Sardica; Armenian envoys seek protection; Diocletian and Galerius attend the sacrifice to the imperial gods before the campaign; Persian peace envoys bring gifts and treasures.

Page 473: Coin portrait (c. 313) commemorates the meeting in Milan between Constantine and Licinius proclaiming religious peace and thus officially recognizing Christianity. The obverse (top), inscribed INVICTUS CONSTANTINUS MAXIMUS ("Unconquerable Constantine the Great"), shows Constantine and Licinius riding together. On the reverse (bottom), inscribed FELIX ADVENTUS AUGUSTORUM NOSTRORUM ("The auspicious entry of our Augusti"), Constantine is led by Victoria and followed by Virtus.

Pages 518–19: The great baptistery in the Christian quarter at Djemila (Cuicul), fourth century.

Page 521: "Constantine the Great," a fourth-century marble statue; originally located in the apse of Constantine's basilica, now at the Palazzo dei Conservatori, Rome.

Page 553: Christian treasures from the Water Newton site, mid to late fourth century: (top) Silver-gilt votive leaf with Chi-Rho; (bottom) Chalice.

Page 593: "Julian the Apostate," marble statue now in the Louvre, Paris.

Page 615: (left) "Ambrose of Milan," fifth-century mosaic from the basilica of San Vittore in Ciel d'Oro, adjoining Sant'Ambrogio, Milan; (right) "Valentinian I(?)," a fourth-century bronze statue at the Church of San Sepolcro in Barletta, Italy.

Page 651: (top) A sixth-century basilica at Haidra (Ammaedara); (bottom) A fourth-century Donatist chapel at Azrou Zaouia.

Page 699: Detail of boar hunt mosaic from a villa near Piazza Armerina, Italy, early fourth century.

Page 741: The Greek Fathers: Basil (left), John Chrysostom (center), Gregory of Nazianzus (right); a twelfth-century mosaic from the cathedral of Cefalu, Sicily.

Pages 786–87: "The Empress Theodora and Her Court," a sixth-century mosaic from the presbyterium of San Vitale, Ravenna.

Page 789: A page from the *Codex Argenteus* (*The Silver Codex*), a sixth-century Gothic gospel.

Page 827: (top) Byzantine cisterns in Constantinople; (bottom) A late-fifth-century mosaic from the narthex of the basilica at Knossos.

Page 869: (top) "Head of Christ in Glory," fresco, probably tenth century, originally from the central church at Abdallah Nirqi, Nubia, Egypt; currently located in the Coptic Museum at Cairo; (bottom) Gallarus's Oratory, sixth century, Dingle Peninsula, Ireland.

Page 903: (top) Haidra (Ammaedara)—south wall of a Byzantine fortress; (bottom) Sbeitla (Sufetula)—the last phase: From town to village. Remains of a seventh-century(?) olive press among ruined buildings near the forum.

PHOTO ACKNOWLEDGMENTS

Alinari/Art Resource, Inc.—11, 521, 741; Reproduced by Courtesy of the Trustees of the British Museum—553T,B; Hamish Brown, Scottish Photographer—869B; Courtesy of the Dumbarton Oaks Collection, Washington, D.C.—367; W. H. C. Frend—8–9, 85, 119, 193, 307, 337, 651T,B, 827B, 903T,B; HIRMER FOTOARCHIV MÜNCHEN—439, 473; Musée de Louvre—593; Courtesy of the National Museum of Antiquities, Netherlands—869T; Pontificia Commissione di Archeologia Sacra—frontispiece, 229, 268–69, 271, 397; Scala/Art Resource, Inc.—Covers, 161, 615L,R, 699; Courtesy Uppsala University Library—789.

TEXT PERMISSIONS

Material on pages 182, 184, 192, 194, 256, 289, 310, 321, 324–25, 342, 374, 444, 451, 479, 481, 486, 495–96: Reprinted by permission of the publishers and the Loeb Classical Library from ECCLESIASTICAL HISTORY, Eusebius, translated by Kirsopp Lake (vol. I) and J. E. L. Oulton (vol. II); Cambridge, Mass.: Harvard University Press.

Material on pages 317, 320, 327, 355, 385, 459, 476, 480 from J. Stevenson, ed., *A New Eusebius* (London: SPCK, 1963) is reprinted by permission of the publisher.

Material on pages 529, 538, 566, 572–73, 605–6, 624–25, 638, 675, 728, 748, 756, 757, 761–62, 767, 771 from J. Stevenson, ed., *Creeds, Councils and Controversies* (London: SPCK, 1966) is reprinted by permission of the publisher.

Material on pages 233, 238, 245, 247–48: From EARLY CHRISTIAN FATHERS, translated and edited by Cyril C. Richardson (Volume I: The Library of Christian Classics). Published simultaneously in Great Britain and the United States of America by the S.C.M. Press, Ltd., London, and The Westminster Press, Philadelphia in MCMLIII. Used by permission.

Material on pages 381, 399, 399–400: From ALEXANDRIAN CHRISTIANITY, edited by John Ernest Leonard Oulton, D. D. and Henry Chadwick, B. D. (Volume II: The Library of Christian Classics). Published simultaneously in Great Britain and the United States of America by the S.C.M. Press, Ltd., London, and The Westminster Press, Philadelphia in MCMLIV. Used by permission.

Abbreviations

AAMz	Abhandlungen der Akademie der Wissenschaften u. der Literature, Mainz
AAWB	Abhandlungen der (Preussischen) Akademie der Wissenschaften zu Berlin
ABAW	Abhandlungen der bayerischen Akademie der Wissenschaften
ABSA	*Annual of the British School of Archaeology at Athens*
ACIAC	*Actes du congrès international d'archéologie chrétienne/ Atti del congresso internazionale di archeologia cristiana*
ACW	Ancient Christian Writers
AGG	Abhandlungen der Gesellschaft (Akademie) der Wissenschaften zu Göttingen
AGJU	Arbeiten zur Geschichte des antiken Judentums und des Urchristentums
AJ	*Antiquaries Journal*
AJP	*American Journal of Philology* (Baltimore: 1880–)
AnBoll	Analecta Bollandiana
ANCL	Ante-Nicene Christian Library (British edition)
ANF	Ante-Nicene Fathers (American edition)
ANRW	*Aufstieg und Niedergang der römischen Welt,* ed. H. Temporini and W. Haase (Berlin: Walter de Gruyter)
ASOR	American Schools of Oriental Research
BAA	*Bulletin de l'archéologie algérienne*
BAC	*Bulletin archéologique du Comité des Travaux historiques et archéologiques*
BAR	*British Archeological Reports*
BASOR	*Bulletin of the American Schools of Oriental Research*
BhistTh	Beiträge zur historischen Theologie
BJRL	*Bulletin of the John Rylands University Library of Manchester*
BNTC	Black's New Testament Commentaries (= HNTC)
CCSL	Corpus Christianorum, series Latina
CH	*Church History*
CIG	*Corpus inscriptionum Graecarum*
CIHEC	Comité international d'histoire ecclésiastique comparée

CIJ	*Corpus inscriptionum Judaicum*
CIL	*Corpus inscriptionum Latinarum*
CNRS	Centre National de la Recherche Scientifique
CP	*Classical Philosophy*
CQ	*Classical Quarterly*
CQR	*Church Quarterly Review*
CRAIBL	*Comptes rendus de l'académie des Inscriptions et Belles-Lettres*
CSCO	Corpus scriptorum christianorum orientalium
CSEL	Corpus scriptorum ecclesiasticorum latinorum
DACL	*Dictionnaire d'Archéologie chrétienne et de Liturgie*, ed. F. Cabrol and H. Leclercq (Paris: L. Letouzey et Ané, 1903–50)
DCB	*Dictionary of Christian Biography*, ed. W. Smith and H. Wace, 4 vols. (London, 1877–87)
DCKAWW	Denkschriften der philosophisch-historischen Klasse der Kaiserlichen Akademie der Wissenschaften du Wien
DTC	*Dictionnaire de théologie catholique*, ed. A. Vacant, E. Mangenot and E. Ammann, 15 vols. (Paris: 1903–50)
EHR	*English Historical Review*
ET	*The Expository Times*
FIRA	Fontes Iuris Romani Ante-Iustiniani, ed. S. Riccobono et al., 3 vols. (Florence, 1940–43)
GCS	Die grieschichen christlichen Schriftsteller der ersten drei Jahrhunderten
HE	*Historia Ecclesiastica*, Eusebius
HNTC	Harper's New Testament Commentaries (= BNTC)
HNTSup	Handbuch zum Neuen Testament, Supplement
HTR	*Harvard Theological Review*
HTS	*Harvard Theological Studies*
ICC	International Critical Commentary
IEJ	*Israel Exploration Journal*
ILCV	*Inscriptiones latinae christianae veteres*
JAC	*Jahrbuch für Antike und Christentum*
JBL	*Journal of Biblical Literature*
JEA	*Journal of Egyptian Archaeology*
JEH	*Journal of Ecclesiastical History*
JHS	*Journal of Hellenistic Studies*
JJS	*Journal of Jewish Studies*
JRH	*Journal of Religious History*
JRS	*Journal of Roman Studies*
JTS	*Journal of Theological Studies*
KlT	Kleine Texte für Vorlesungen und Übungen
LCC	Library of Christian Classics

LCL	Loeb Classical Library
LQHR	*London Quarterly and Holborn Review*
LXX	Septuagint
MAMA	Monumenta Asiae minoris antiqua
MEFR (A)	*Mélanges d'archéologie et d'histoire*
MGH	*Monumenta Germaniae historica,* ed. G. H. Pertz and successors (Berlin: Hanover, 1826–)
NCBC	New Century Bible Commentary
NGG	Nachrichten der Gesellschaft (Akademie) der Wissenschaften zu Göttingen
NHS	Nag Hammadi Studies, ed. M. Krause, J. M. Robinson, F. Wisse (Leiden: E. J. Brill)
NPNF	Nicene and Post-Nicene Library of the Fathers
NT	*Novum Testamentum*
Ntsup.	Novum Testamentum Supplement
NTS	*New Testament Studies*
NV	*Nova et Vetera*
OECT	Oxford Early Christian Texts
OGIS	*Orientis Graecae inscriptiones selectae*
OrChrA	Orientalia Christiana (Analecta)
Pap. Lond.	*Greek Papyri in the British Museum*
Pap. Oxy.	*Oxyrhynchus Papyri*
PBSR	*Papers of the British School at Rome*
PG	*Patrologia graeco-latina,* ed. J. P. Migne
Ph. Hist. Kl	Philologische-historische Klasse
PhP	Philosophia Patrum
PL	*Patrologia Latina,* ed. J. P. Migne
PS	E. Schwartz, "Publizistische Sammlung zum acacianischen Schisma" (in *Abh. der Bayerischen Akademie, Phil-Hist Abt.* n.s. 10.4 [1934])
PSI	*Papiri greci e latini*
PW	Pauly-Wissowa, *Real-Encyclopädie der classischen Altertumswissenschaft*
1QH	*Thanksgiving Hymns (Dead Sea Scrolls)*
1QpHab	*Commentary on Habakkuk (Dead Sea Scrolls)*
4QpPs37	*Commentary on Psalm 37 (Dead Sea Scrolls)*
1QS	*The Community Rule (Manual of Discipline) (Dead Sea Scrolls)*
RAC	*Reallexikon für Antike and Christentum*
RB	*Revue Biblique*
RelS	*Religious Studies*
RelSRev	*Religious Studies Review*
RFIC	*Rivista di filologia e d'istruzione classica*
RGG³	*Religion in Geschichte und Gegenwart* (third edition)

RHE	*Revue d'histoire ecclésiastique*
RHPR	*Revue d'histoire et de philosophie religieuses*
RHR	*Revue de l'histoire des religions*
RIDA	*Revue international des droits de l'Antiquité*
RivAC	*Rivista di Archeologia Cristiana*
RP	*Revue de Philologie*
RQ	*Römische Quartalschrift für christliche Altertumskunde und Kirchengeschichte*
RSLR	*Rivista de storia e Letteratura religiosa*
RSR	*Recherches de science religieuse*
SAB	Sitzungsberichte der Deutschen (Preussischen) Akademie der Wissenschaften zu Berlin
SAH.PH	Sitzungsberichte der Heidelberger Akademie der Wissenschaften—Philologische-historische Klasse
SBAW	Sitzungsberichte der Bayerischen Akademie der Wissenschaften
SBT	Studies in Biblical Theology
SC	Sources chrétiennes
SCH	*Studies in Church History*
Scr. Hieros.	*Scripta Hierosolymitana*
SE	*Studia Evangelica*
SHA	*Scriptores Historiae Augustae*
SHAW.PH	Sitzungsberichte der Heidelberger Akademie der Wissenschaften—Philosophisch-historische Klasse
SIG	*Sylloge inscriptionum Graecorum*
SJ	*Studia Judaica*
SJ.FWJ	Studia Judaica, Forschung zur Wissenschaft des Judentums
SJLA	Studies in Judaism in Late Antiquity
SJT	*Scottish Journal of Theology*
SNTSMS	Society for New Testament Studies Monograph Series
SP	*Studia Patristica*
SPB	Studia Post-biblica
ST	*Studi e Testi*
T.B.	*Babylonian Talmud,* ed. I. Epstein, 35 vols. (London: Soncino Press, 1935)
Theophaneia	*Der Kirchenbegriff Novatians und die Geschichte seiner Sonderkirche* = Theophaneia, Beiträge zur Religious- und Kirchengeschichte des Altertums (Bonn: Peter Hanstein Verlag)
TRE	*Theologische Realenzyklopädie*
TU	Texte und Untersuchungen
VC	*Vigiliae Christianae*

xvi

WUNT	Wissenschaftliche Untersuchungen zum Neuen Testament
ZKG	*Zeitschrift für Kirchengeschichte*
ZNW	*Zeitschrift für die neutestamentliche Wissenschaft und die Kunde der älteren Kirche*
ZPE	*Zeitschrift für Papyrologie und Epigraphik*
ZTK	*Zeitschrift für Theologie und Kirche*

Preface to the Paperback Edition

I am glad that just a year after it was published *The Rise of Christianity* will be available to many more students through a paperback edition.

So far critics have been generous. I should perhaps have made clear that our evidence for the development of Christianity in the first three centuries of its history is very patchy. Eusebius of Caesarea apart, with all his prejudices as a historian, much of the surviving evidence has been the result of chance, such as the Nag Hammadi Gnostic library, or due to selection in accordance with orthodox patterns of Christian truth. The gaps as well as the survivals in the record should have been given prominence. Even so, the main structure of the work has survived. The arguments in favor of the diversity of Christian teaching and practice from the earliest days still hold, as does the view put forward that, in contrast to monasticism in the East, the ascetic movement in the West should be included among those symptoms of lack of confidence among the leadership there that resulted in the barbarian victory in the first half of the fifth century. Similarly, the ultimate division between Eastern and Western Christendom was likely from the moment of the appearance of a distinctive Latin Christianity in the last years of the second century. The length of the book could only be justified if it was about these and other major historical questions raised by the rise of Christianity.

The second (hardback) printing and the first paperback edition have eliminated a number of minor errors. For the long, hard grind of editorial work that resulted in these successive impressions I cannot praise too highly Fortress Press in the person of my book editor, Dr. John A. Hollar. The immense labor, too, of checking bibliographical references and making the style acceptable on both sides of the Atlantic has fallen to the capable and cheerful hands of Margret A. (Mimi) McGinnis. The book took ten years to write amidst the ordinary duties and, especially in the last years, the pressures of university work, and it is to the support of my wife at all times that I owe its completion.

W. H. C. FREND
Barnwell Rectory
Peterborough
U.K.

August 14, 1985

Introduction

This book arose largely from a chance meeting with an old student, Mr. Robin Baird-Smith, later a director of Darton, Longman & Todd. It was suggested that there was room for a work on the lines of J. Daniélou and H. Marrou's *The First Six Hundred Years* (1964), but devoted more specifically to the early Christians themselves and explaining how Christianity survived the hostile environments, first of Judaism and then of the Greco-Roman world, to become the civilization of Eastern and Western Europe.

The title, *The Rise of Christianity*, that I eventually chose is, of course, that of Bishop E. W. Barnes's work, published in 1947. Barnes, however, concentrated on the New Testament area and only extended his detailed research as far as the time of Justin Martyr (c. 100–165). The real inspiration for this work has come from Adolf von Harnack's *Mission and Expansion of Christianity in the First Three Centuries* (1902; Eng. trans. 1908). Harnack was among the first scholars to realize the overriding importance of the Jewish Dispersion (Diaspora), not only in molding the early Christian mission but in providing the basis for its steady expansion throughout the Greco-Roman world. By the end of the third century Christianity had penetrated to every corner of the empire and to almost every section of the population. Practically nothing had escaped von Harnack's eye. From his detailed examination of texts relating to Christianity in the first three centuries and the lists that he compiled of bishoprics in each Roman province, he concluded that the Great Persecution unleashed in 303 by the emperor Diocletian and his colleagues was foredoomed to failure. The church would have triumphed even without Constantine's conversion.

Von Harnack's conclusions remain valid. They can now, however, be tested and elaborated with the aid of evidence that was not available to him when he wrote more than three-quarters of a century ago. Harnack stood at the very threshold of the explosion of archaeological evidence that has characterized research into the ancient world during this century. Apart from work carried out by French scholars in North Africa (principally by Stéphane Gsell), and the continuous exploration of the Roman catacombs—the legacy of J. B. de Rossi (1822–94) and his predecessors—archaeological research into Christian origins had been concentrated on western Asia Minor. The possibility of checking the accuracy of Luke-Acts was the challenge that inspired the enormously fruitful journeys of W. M.

1

Ramsay through ancient Phrygia during the 1880s and 1890s. After reading *Cities and Bishoprics of Phrygia* (published in 1895 and 1897), no one could doubt anymore the strength of the Jewish Dispersion in those parts of Asia Minor which Paul visited. There was also the evidence of the visible remains of deserted Greek cities, many of which had been celebrated in the patristic period. A wealth of discoveries awaited excavation. Research was aided too by a quirk of European imperialism that led the Great Powers of the day to crowd their attentions on the Sick Man of Europe (that is, Turkey). Archaeological concessions accompanied foreign post offices as symbols of European influence in the Levant. In these early projects, the Austrians Josef Keil and Georg von Premerstein were the masters. They were tireless observers and collectors of information on their almost annual epigraphic missions through southern and western Asia Minor. These, with their recovery (with Wilhelm Heberdey) of the site of Ephesus and its theater where Paul may have faced his accusers in A.D. 53, remain monuments to that classic period of field research.

Ephesus had its temple of Diana (Artemis), where in Paul's time the age-old Anatolian fertility cult was becoming fused with the more sedate Romanized worship of Diana-Artemis and the imperial cult. He who attacked Diana of the Ephesians attacked the strongest links in the chain of belief and cult that held the loyalties of the varied inhabitants of western Asia Minor to the empire. He took his life in his hands. Diana's worship was that of a fertility and mystery cult. The cities of the Roman provinces in Asia Minor were among the centers where the mystery religions flourished most in the first two centuries A.D. It was tempting to ask how much Christianity owed to these; whether, for instance, the Christian's relation to his Savior was not akin to that which united the pagan initiate to the gods of the oriental cults. There was just enough evidence to suggest that, in the rites of Baptism and the Eucharist, the resemblances between Christianity and the mystery religions were influenced by the pagan mysteries. The rise of the "history of religions" school in the early years of this century owed much to the expansion of research from text to archaeology. It produced Alfred Loisy's masterpiece, *Les mystères païens et le mystère Chrétien* (1914; 2d ed., 1930), and Wilhelm Bousset's *Kyrios Christos* (1921; Eng. trans., 1970). Bousset stated his view that Irenaeus's belief, that the destiny of humanity was divinization, was rooted in the pieties of the Greek mystery religions (pp. 342–43).

Bousset was mistaken. Most, though not all, of the ideas and attitudes which the early Christians were believed to have derived from their pagan environment can be shown to have been mediated through Hellenistic Judaism. A finer balance between the Jewish and pagan influences on Christianity may now be struck. Since the Second World War an enormous quantity of new evidence, mainly archaeological, has become available. The *Gospel of Thomas,* completing the Oxyrhynchus *Logia* found in 1897, has suggested the existence of a new, independent Aramaic-based Gospel. It is even less easy than it was to claim that Jesus was a mythological figure. The *Dead Sea Scrolls* have provided for the first time the means of comparing his teaching, as recorded in the Gospels, with that of a contemporary pietistic Jewish sect—in every probability the Essenes. The discovery in 1945 of the library of the Gnostic texts (which included the *Gospel of Thomas*) at Nag Hammadi, and as of 1977 in English translation, also emphasizes the links that bound elements of early Christianity to Jewish models. As Ernest Renan had appreciated, there was no problem in Christianity in the first two centuries that was not already apparent in Judaism.

Added to these discoveries have been others almost as important. These include the cult center in a pagan cemetery beneath the Vatican dedicated in the second century to St. Peter, the rural churches and cemeteries of Numidia whose discovery has thrown so much light on the Donatist movement, and the Christian quarters that grew up outside the walls of the old cities in the fourth century, all of which emphasize the independence of the new Christian civilization. These and the very many inscriptions, mosaics, and individual objects including some from Britain are witness to the great change that overtook the Greco-Roman world as Christianity advanced.

A clearer picture of the rise of Christianity has been emerging, and a new attempt to chart its course may perhaps now be made. This book, however, is not designed as a textbook of church history. The great narrative histories of the past two generations, of Louis Duchesne, B. J. Kidd, Hans Lietzmann, and the contributors to the volumes of A. Fliche and V. Martin's *Histoire de l'église depuis les origines jusqu'à nos jours*, can hardly be repeated. Not only is the evidence too vast and complex for any single scholar to control and systematize, but our own day is more analytically inclined and less willing to see the victory of orthodoxy as inevitable and providential. Though it spans nearly 750 years of history from 140 B.C. to A.D. 600, the aim of this work is more restricted. It tries to answer specific questions: How and why did Christianity become the religion of the Greco-Roman world? What was Christian civilization, and how did it produce the divergent traditions that even within orthodoxy resulted in permanent divisions within the church? How did the church set the stamp of its values on Byzantine and medieval Europe and thus influence more profoundly than any other factor the life and thought of the world in which we live? However one looks at it, ideas derived from Christianity and Judaism lie at the root of modern European civilization even in the "countercultures" and in Marxism.

We start then, in Part 1, with the Jews, first in Palestine on the aftermath of the Maccabean Wars (167–142 B.C.) and then in the Dispersion. This was the environment in which Jesus was to grow up, minister, and die, and in which Paul and his friends preached the gospel. The Jews in the Roman Empire, however, were something like the Third World today. They made up a goodly proportion of the population of the empire—perhaps as much as seven million out of fifty million to adopt von Harnack's figures—but their interests and attitudes were different from those of their fellow provincials. They were self-proclaimed "sojourners" in the Greco-Roman cities, sharing the security and standard of life these provided, but indifferent to their future. They were in the empire but not of it; and they preserved sedulously their own way of life in accordance with the Law prescribed by God to Moses and interpreted by the authorized teachers of their race. They belonged automatically to the spiritual opposition to the empire. Greek monarch and Roman emperor alike were the representatives of one of the idolatrous world empires destined to dominate the world until the time for their destruction came at the hand of God. Many of the Jews hoped to see the world consumed by fire and brimstone.

The early history of Christianity unfolded amid the fervent hopes and expectations of the Jewish people. The Christians, too, accepted the legacy of the gathered community awaiting the coming of the Lord, though Jesus and Paul both regarded the empire as the legitimate de facto authority on earth. When the Jews clashed disastrously with Rome in the war of 66–74, Christianity survived. It became, however, a predominantly "Western" religion, its strength concentrated in the cities of western Asia Minor ("the seven churches that are in Asia"). The language of its liturgy, Scriptures, and mission was Greek. Failing to make good its claim to be the "true Israel," the church nonetheless began to expand its influence among the Gentile provincials who had no previous links with the synagogue. After the second capture of Jerusalem in 135 this development proceeded apace. Christianity gradually established its identity as "the third race" in the Greek-speaking world, a new and powerful religious force competing with Judaism and paganism and opposed to both. By 190 the Christian church was a closely organized and well-knit federation of communities extending from one end of the Mediterranean world to the other. It was governed by bishops among whom a certain precedence was being accorded to the bishop of the capital city of the empire, whose see could also claim to have been founded by the apostles Peter and Paul.

Even at this time, however, divisions were appearing. Successions of Gnostic teachers and Montanist prophets challenged the supremacy of episcopal successions. More important even than these movements was the emergence of distinctive interpretations of what became orthodoxy in each of the major cities where Christianity had taken root. Alexandria, Antioch, Rome, and Ephesus perhaps were all beginning to evolve particular theological outlooks associated with the growing importance of the Christian communities in their midst. At the same time, the emergence of a Latin-speaking Christianity at Carthage entailed a further and more far-reaching distinction, that between the Eastern and Western interpretations of the faith.

In Part 2, we follow these developments through the third century down

4

to the Constantinian revolution. This was a great period in the history of the early church. It witnessed the formation of distinctive Christian doctrine exemplified in the creative theology of Origen (c. 185–254). It saw the first flowering of Christian art at Dura-Europos and in the Roman catacombs, and the transformation of the Roman see from a Greek artisan and immigrant institution to a Latin church sharing with Carthage the leadership of Western Christianity. It witnessed also the steadfastness of Christian confessors in the face of the Decian, Valerianic, and Diocletianic persecutions. By the end of the century Christianity had become the most important single religious force in many parts of the empire, challenging the age-old supremacy of the immortal gods that had watched over the fortunes of the Roman state since its foundation. Only a small step was needed between Galerius's concession that the Christian God could not be left out of account in determining the fortunes of the empire (311) to Constantine's acceptance of Christianity as the religion of his empire. But by that time the incipient doctrinal traditions in the great Christian centers had diverged and led to increasingly incompatible interpretations of the faith.

These interpretations become a major theme of Part 3, spanning the patristic period from the Councils of Nicaea to Chalcedon (325–451). We follow first the triumph of Christianity in the Mediterranean world. How did it happen? On what grounds? Why were so many of the provincials willing to accept the new religion so eagerly? We see the emergence, for the first time (with the exception of Montanism) since Jesus' preaching, of a distinctive rural Christianity whose social and religious aspirations—expressed in Egyptian monasticism and the Circumcellion movement in Africa—differed profoundly from those of the settled urban communities. And with the triumph of Christianity came other movements, that of asceticism in the West, the short and brilliant period when educated Christian lay influence was exercised effectively on the thought of the church by men and women alike. Doctrine, however, was all-important. This was the age of the great theologians: Athanasius, Basil of Caesarea, Apollinaris of Laodicea, Augustine, Theodore of Mopsuestia, and Cyril of Alexandria. East and West, however, were now going their separate ways. For the East the question was how people were redeemed, ultimately to be restored to their true nature in the image and likeness of God. It was an optimistic outlook as one progressed from level to level, from education in the Greek classics towards an understanding of the truth of Christian philosophy and a rational appreciation of reality. For the West the function of the church was more restrictive and protective as the sole vehicle that could save humanity from the effects of the Fall and assure vindication at the Judgment. "No salvation outside the church" involved controversies over predestination and grace and over the church's nature as an institution and authority within it. Who had the last say, the successor to the apostles at Rome or a council of bishops?

At the Council of Chalcedon in 451, the conflict of regional theological

5

schools and the clash of disciplinary claims came to a head. The decisive moment in the relations between the churches in the eastern and western parts of the empire came when Pope Leo refused to accept canon 28 of the council which accorded Constantinople, as New Rome, ecclesiastical authority second only to Rome, confirming the decision of the Second Ecumenical Council at Constantinople in 381. Part 4 follows the consequences of this rejection of imperial and conciliar authority on the one hand, and, on the other, the rejection of the Chalcedonian christological definition by large numbers of Eastern Christians, particularly in Egypt and Syria. There a new, rival Monophysite church gradually emerged, eventually to extend its influence down the Nile Valley to the Nubian kingdoms and Ethiopia and in Armenia on the eastern frontier of the empire. If final schism between Constantinople and Rome was avoided during the sixth century, the gradual distancing of two incompatible systems of doctrine and discipline became more apparent, despite all efforts by the emperors from Justin I onwards to maintain communion between both Romes. Christianity was meaning different things to different people. With Gregory I (590–604), the papacy moved further towards its destiny as the authoritative center of Christianity in northern Europe as well as in the old Latin-speaking provinces of the empire. The early years of the seventh century effectively closed the era of the ancient world and foreshadowed the vast irruptive changes caused by the Arab and Slavonic invasions.

To trace the rise of Christianity in this long period of history would be challenge enough. During these last two decades, however, another need has come into being, that of preserving the study of early Christian civilization in the English language and handing the results on to one's successors. The decline in the study of the classics in schools, the lessening of the importance of the early church councils in theological education, and the fact that despite all the research carried out in the last fifty years the period 450–550 still remains a "Dark Age" in British history, have rendered the future study of early Christianity uncertain. University faculty boards, anxious to save what can be saved of the study of ancient history or medieval history, or to experiment in modern theology, have had no compunction in axing the early church from staff and syllabus alike. There is no equivalent in Britain of the Institut Lenain de Tillemont in the Sorbonne and the F. J. Dölger Institut für Antike und Christentum in Bonn devoted to advancing the study of early Christian literature and archaeology. So, while the evidence has become more abundant and the study flourishes in Europe, qualified students in Britain become ever fewer. A great tradition of British scholarship, claiming T. R. Glover, N. H. Baynes, F. C. Burkitt, P. R. L. Brown, and the ancient historian A. H. M. Jones among its exponents, faces the danger of extinction.

A word, finally, about method. My approach is chronological. It may be, as one critic has stated, that "the rise of Monophysitism" can be traced

6

back to John 1:14, but this does not help the student to understand why Monophysitism became a problem in the fifth and sixth centuries! For reasons set out in the previous paragraph, I have taken a wider canvas than I had intended at first, and since the expansion of Christianity involved decisions by countless individuals, attention to detail at some crucial moments in its history has been necessary. A description of the transformation of the Greco-Roman world during the reign of Constantius II (337–61) requires more than generalities. I have drawn some material from my earlier works, for the third century in particular from *Martyrdom and Persecution*, chaps. 12–15. Wherever possible, I have used my friend and former colleague James Stevenson's (ed.) *A New Eusebius* (1963) and *Creeds, Councils and Controversies* (1966), and hope my study may prove to be a useful companion to those well-chosen collections of early Christian texts in translation. At the end of each chapter is a short bibliographical note introducing the student to the main works he will need for further study. This is supplemented by a select bibliography of other works at the end of the book, and chronological guides. The arrangement of these last also owes much to James Stevenson's work. I am greatly indebted to the work of Henry Chadwick on the Alexandrians, to J. N. D. Kelly and R. V. Sellers on the development of early Christian doctrines, and to Peter Brown's *Augustine of Hippo* (1967), and his studies of the spread of Christianity among the lettered classes in the west.

In the preparation of this manuscript, I am grateful to Dr. Robert Gordon, now University Lecturer in Divinity at Cambridge, for help and advice on Judaism, to John Riches on chap. 2 (Jesus of Nazareth), to my former pupil, Kevin Clancy, for reading and checking chaps. 11 to 14 covering the Constantinian revolution. For the typing, I cannot praise too highly the devotion of Mrs. Blythe O'Driscoll and Mrs. Margaret White, and I am grateful to the directors and editors of Darton, Longman & Todd, London, and Fortress Press, Philadelphia, for their help, forbearance, and patience during the long period needed to prepare this manuscript. The mistakes only are mine.

W. H. C. FREND
Marbrae
Balmaha
by Glasgow

March 31, 1980

JEWS AND
CHRISTIANS

PART 1

The Jewish Background

Christianity arose from the life, preaching, and death of Jesus of Nazareth. It began as a renewal movement within Palestinian Judaism, and its first members regarded their faith in the risen Jesus not as a new religion but as a confirmation of God's promises to Israel. They were the people of the new covenant foreshadowed in Jer. 31:31. Their acceptance of Jesus as Messiah and Christ (the Anointed One) would have meant little outside the confines of Judaism. Saul or David could be "the Lord's Anointed," but anointing played no part in pagan religious rites. The earliest Christian confession of faith preserved in 1 Cor. 8:6, written in circa A.D. 53, opened with the assertion that there was one God, and conformed to the basic confession of Israel (Deut. 6:4). Indeed, Paul never envisaged a permanent breach with Judaism. The first generations of Christians inherited their Scripture and many of their characteristic attitudes and beliefs as well as much of their organization from the Jews. Their problems were also Jewish problems. One may ask how this came about. How was it that the new religion arose in Galilee, a semicolonial Jewish territory ruled by Herod Antipas, a client princeling dependent on Rome?

Judaism itself was not the monolithic religion it appeared to be to those outside its bounds. In Palestine at the time of Jesus, Sadducees, Pharisees, Herodians, and Essenes represented different interpretations of Judaism and jostled for predominance. Between them and the millions of Jews who remained in Babylonia or had settled in the Greek-speaking East there were great differences involving language, religious ideas, and attitudes toward pagan society. Yet for all these differences, there remained a certain unity of observance and the passionately held conviction that the Jewish way of life was inspired and directed by God. God had chosen Israel. Faithful to his promise to Abraham he had singled out the patriarch's descendants to be his own people. The Jews alone "saw God," claimed the Alexandrian Jewish philosopher Philo, circa A.D. 40.[1] Accepting the discipline imposed upon them by the divine ordinances, they were ready also to face the consequences. Near the end of the first century A.D., the Jewish historian Josephus explained to his pagan opponents: "There should be nothing astonishing in our facing death on behalf of our laws with a courage no other nation can equal." Furthermore, Josephus also noted that "it is an instinct with every Jew, from the day of his birth, to regard them [books of the Law] as the decrees of God, to abide by them, and, if need be, cheerfully to die for them."[2] Christian martyrdom, therefore, was preceded by Jewish martyrdom.

Jews, whether they spoke Aramaic or Greek, whether their life was centered on the Temple at Jerusalem, or on the synagogue in a town in Asia Minor, whether they were Palestinian peasants or Alexandrian philosophers, all formed part of a religious and cultural confederation extending throughout the Greco-Roman world, and beyond it among its enemies into

12

Parthia. They were dangerous to provoke. The Christians were to be their heirs to the steadfast attitudes, the worldwide organization, and missionary sense but not to the national ambitions that accompanied these.

What was the religion that held the Jews together? One may best follow Günther Bornkamm's description.[3] The Jewish religion was unique among the religions of the ancient world. As he says, in contrast with the Greeks and Orientals and indeed all other peoples of the time, the Jews worshiped a God that "had no image, no myth, and no cult practices whereby men might share in the natural-supernatural powers of the deity." Sacrifices might turn away his wrath, but could not identify the worshiper with him. Yahweh was lord of the universe with limitless power and he acted in and controlled history, imagined by the Jews in linear terms extending from creation to judgment and not as a cyclical process as understood by the Greeks. So, while the Jews were God's people, his authority was not confined to them or their territory. The record, however, of Jewish sacred history from the beginning of the world told how successive covenants had been made by God (Yahweh) with Noah, Abraham, and Moses, thus binding Israel to him. In return for obedience, God had delivered the people of Israel from their enemies and brought them into the land of Canaan. "The Lord has taken you, and brought you forth out of the iron furnace, out of Egypt, to be a people of his own possession, as at this day" (Deut. 4:20). Loyalty brought unity and victory, disobedience brought disintegration and defeat (cf. the Deuteronomic rationale of Judg. 2:11–23). But God's will could not be thwarted. Amidst every form of unrighteousness and wickedness, there was always a faithful remnant who would uphold his law, such as Gideon's three hundred razing Baal's altar (cf. Judg. 7:6–8). When defeat finally overtook the Jews with the fall of Jerusalem to the Babylonians in 587 B.C., their faith withstood the shock. Even as they bewailed their fate in Babylon, they were comforted by the conviction that God would send his representative who with supernatural power would overthrow the heathen oppressor and restore Israel to its former glory. The Messiah—Anointed One—would redeem and save Israel.

Yahweh's will was expressed in the Law (Torah). This, too, was more than a code of ethics or an ideology. It was a faith, a discipline, a guide to conduct, and a way of life that governed every Israelite from birth to the grave. It was the distinctive wisdom of Israel revealed by God. Jews, Josephus liked to point out, were members of a "theocracy."[4] The tradition of the Law handed down by Moses to his successors was not static, however. Its comprehensiveness and its application to all individuals and situations required constant interpretation by those skilled in this work and set apart in the community for this purpose. The scribes and Pharisees as interpreters of the Law were the intellectual leaders of the Jewish people in Jesus' day.

13

Moreover, the covenant between the Lord and Israel assumed similar covenant relations between Jew and Jew. Duty towards one's neighbor came second only to duty to God. "You shall open wide your hand to your brother" (Deut. 15:11), it was laid down. So, alone among the peoples of the ancient world, the Jews exhibited an uncompromising sense of social justice. To "trample upon the poor" (Amos 5:11) was as heinous in the eyes of the prophets as idolatry. To "put out . . . money at interest" (Ps. 15:5) was among the sins of the reprobate. In the sabbatical year—once every seven years—all debts owed by Jews to Jews must be cancelled. "Every creditor shall release what he has lent to his neighbor . . . because the Lord's release has been proclaimed" (Deut. 15:2). In the same way, labor with one's hands and good craftsmanship, along with right use of wealth, formed part of the way of righteousness which Jews must follow from youth up and teach their children to obey by precept and example (cf. Deut. 6:6ff.).

A religion that combined a universal view of humanity's relations with God with detailed practical rules for human conduct, and whose adherents knew why they believed as they did, was bound to attract attention and support. Judaism became a religion of mission in the Greco-Roman world. The history of conversion, in the sense of the transfer of allegiance from one set of religious and moral values to another, begins with Judaism.

At the same time, there were tensions and cross-currents within the Jewish theocracy. The story of King David and his successors as told in the books of Samuel and Kings does not hide tension between the authority of the king and the authority of the prophet. Even David was shown to have his weaknesses, while those of his successors were denounced mercilessly. Ahab's outraged protest to Elijah, "Have you found me, O my enemy?" (1 Kings 21:20), shows how far hostility might extend. The kings found themselves obliged to bend towards more powerful neighbors, to marry heathen wives and accept idolatry and priests of Baal, but for the prophet who spoke in the name of the Lord no compromise with idolatry in any form could be tolerated. Apart from their denunciations of backsliding into heathenism, one may detect an outspoken skepticism towards the value of the priestly cult and its sacrifices centered in the Temple of Solomon. "Bring no more vain offerings; incense is an abomination to me," so says Isaiah (1:13). Jeremiah, himself of priestly stock, also points to the uselessness of observing the ceremonial law unless the heart was pure also (Jer. 3:23 and 4:4). And he looked for a new covenant based on Israel's unfeigned love of God's law (Jer. 31:31–34). He accepted that he would be opposed by the kings of Judah, its princes, its priests, and the people of the land (Jer. 1:18–19). Future generations were to depict the great prophets as persecuted, despised, and even martyred, wandering about "in skins of sheep and goats, destitute, afflicted, ill-treated" (Heb. 11:37). They, however, maintained the heroic ideal of embattled Israel threatened by adversaries within

14

as well as without, an ideal which the early Christians were to inherit and develop for themselves.

FROM 587 TO 140 B.C.

Jerusalem fell in 587 B.C. In the Babylonian Captivity that lasted for the next fifty years, close contact with alien captors, combined perhaps with hopes of averting more of God's wrath, seems to have awakened the Jews to the consequences of adhering to a religion not restricted to territorial boundaries. As the prospects of deliverance and return to their homeland grew brighter, Jewish hopes became increasingly idealistic and universal. The poetry of Second Isaiah (c. 540 B.C.) breathes optimism and anticipation. "For behold, I create new heavens and a new earth . . ." (Isa. 65:17). "Arise, shine; for your light has come" (Isa. 60:1). A Messiah was promised, not a military conqueror, but a Servant whose suffering atoned for the sins of the people: "upon him was the chastisement that made us whole" (Isa. 53:5). "Therefore I will divide him a portion with the great, and he shall divide the spoil with the strong; because he poured out his soul to death, and was numbered with the transgressors; yet he bore the sin of many, and made intercession for the transgressors" (Isa. 53:12). Hope, however, was not to be confined to born Israelites. Proselytes ("the foreigner who has joined himself to the Lord" [Isa. 56:3]) were assured their place on the Lord's holy mountain, and Israel herself was to be "a light to the nations" (Isa. 49:6). Gentile nations and their kings and queens and their gods would bow to the Lord. Salvation would reach to the end of the earth. It was a universal ideal. Judaism was henceforth to appear to outsiders both as a missionary and a national faith, a combination with which the Greek successor states to Alexander's empire and the Romans would try to come to terms, and fail.

The deliverance promised in Second Isaiah turned out to be disappointing. By no means all the Jews chose to return to Judea in c. 537 B.C. after Cyrus the Persian had conquered the Babylonian Empire. Though Jerusalem became once more the focus of the Jewish nation and its religion, Babylonia remained the second largest center of Judaism for centuries. Moreover, the universal vision faded. The Temple might be restored, but the restricted area around Jerusalem granted to the Jews by the Persians took on the appearance of another Syrian temple-state. It was a small, close-knit community dominated by service to its God.[5] The Persians appointed the high priest and there was a Persian governor in the city. Jewish religion, under the influence of Ezra the scribe (c. 400 B.C.) emphasized the duty of following out the prescriptions of the Law with punctilious exactitude. This was the cult of a "gathered community," not the missionary and comprehensive ideal of Second Isaiah; and the two were not easily to be reconciled later. Yahweh became once more a tribal god, jealous of his authority over his people and opposed to association with outsiders. The Persians, however, were tolerant. They treated the Jewish religion with respect we are told (Ezra 1:2ff.), and in return the Jews accorded them a high place in the scale of values they applied to the Gentile world.[6]

Moreover the long association with Persia, which lasted until 332 B.C., did materially influence Jewish religious ideas. The relative dualism that existed already in Judaism became more pronounced through contact with Iranian Zoroastrianism.[7] Yahweh was thought of as opposed by externally active forces of spiritual wickedness. The concept of "idolatry" moves from the heathen gods of Israel's adversaries to cosmic forces or spiritual beings, eternal enemies of God and humanity. Satan, the roving tempter in the book of Job who acts according to God's will, evolves into the Devil of the Gospels and Antichrist of apocalyptic literature. Sheol, the vacuous abode of shades, becomes hell in whose fires those condemned at the judgment at the end of the age would groan in torment.

The overthrow of the Persian Empire by Alexander the Great in 332 B.C. brought further profound changes for the Jews. Judea, however, continued to exist as a political unit, but there was now greater opportunity to move out of the cramped conditions of Palestine, and trade and settle throughout the Hellenistic world. The movements were two-way. During the third century B.C., Greek settlements became established within the borders of Palestine, while Syria and Egypt attracted many Jewish settlers as did the Greek cities in Asia Minor. Generally speaking, Jews were welcomed as likely to provide a loyal and hardworking labor force against the ever-present threat from the unassimilated barbarian countryside. For a long time the Greek rulers were not disappointed. Moreover, Hellenistic civilization as it developed under the Ptolemies and Seleucids became increasingly attractive to the Jews. It was not merely that the great majority of those settled in Syria and Egypt became Greek-speaking (and to some extent Greek-thinking also), but in Palestine itself the prescriptions of the Law began to be watered down as Greek trade and Jewish interest in Hellenistic culture, at least in its outward forms, increased.[8] Thus, Jesus Ben Sirach's Ecclesiasticus, written in Hebrew (c. 200 B.C.) but translated into Greek, is in many ways an amalgam of traditional Jewish and Greek morality. The writer protested against those readers who were becoming ashamed of the Law of the Most High (Sir. 42:2) and reminded them that the Most High was a judge and would not delay his vengeance (Sir. 35:17–18). His appeal, however, was only partially successful. Seleucid domination replaced that of the Ptolemies in 200 B.C. The pace of Hellenization quickened. In the next generation Greek ways of life and thought had penetrated even among the guardians of the nation's religion and identity. Members of the high priesthood were among those who acquiesced in, or even favored, the establishment of pagan organizations such as the ephebate (2 Macc. 4:12–14) and gymnasium (1 Macc. 1:11–15). "Let us go and make a covenant with the Gentiles round about us'' (1 Macc. 1:11). Even circumcision, the sign of Israel's election as Yahweh's people, was becoming concealed or neglected (1 Macc. 1:15). Only in the country areas were the traditions of Judaism obstinately maintained.

Yet, as in other crises of Jewish history, that obstinacy prevailed. The Seleucid monarch Antiochus IV Epiphanes (175–163) tried—for reasons as much material as cultural—to move too far and too fast towards the complete Hellenization of the Jewish people. Both pagan and Jewish sources reflect the view that he did intend to bring some overall change in Jewish observance.[9] The reaction was bitter, profound, and lasting. The Maccabean revolt and the subsequent conflicts and diplomatic wrangles with the Seleucid rulers of Syria lasted for twenty-five years, from 166 to 142 B.C. The Jewish cause triumphed. For all Jews at the time of Christ these remained the decisive events that colored their thinking. The fight for freedom to worship Yahweh as they wished had been fought and won. If the main battles had been contested in a comparatively small area of Palestine around Jerusalem, the commitment displayed by the Jewish insurgents and the ferocity of this first religious war in the history of humankind left an indelible mark on the relations between Jew and Greek throughout the Mediterranean world.

The altar, which Antiochus IV had ordered to be set up in honor of Zeus in the court of the Temple at Jerusalem in 168 B.C., was regarded as a lasting insult to Judaism. Josephus, a friend of Rome and admirer of Roman values, writing in circa A.D. 75, or nearly 250 years after the event, recalled bitterly how Antiochus ''sacrificed swine upon the altars and bespattered the temple with their grease, thus perverting the rites of the Jews and the piety of their fathers'' (*Antiquities of the Jews* XIII.243). In contrast, he spoke admiringly of the forbearance of the emperor Titus towards the Jews even under the appalling provocation caused by the events of the Jewish revolt of A.D. 66. On the capture of Jerusalem in August 70, Titus promised to spare the lives of the rebel leaders (Josephus *The Jewish War* VI.2), and no attempt was made to suppress the Jewish religion. Unfortunately, Antiochus IV's rash actions resulted in lasting damage to the relations between the Jews and pagan kingdoms. The Jewish nation that emerged from the successful wars against him and his successors was self-conscious and intolerant towards all Gentiles whether friendly or unfriendly. It was imbued with a determination to build an even-higher ''barrier around Torah'' than before.[10] The proclamation of Simon Maccabeus in 140 B.C. as the ''great high priest and commander and leader of the Jews'' (1 Macc. 13:42) ushered in a century when Israel combined self-aggrandizement at the expense of its Gentile neighbors with factions at home. The yoke of the Gentiles was removed from Israel (1 Macc. 13:41), but Israel's was placed on inconveniently situated Gentiles.[11] The harvest of antipathy between Jew and Gentile that matured over these years was eventually to be reaped by the Christians in the form of popular pogroms and officially inspired persecutions.

PALESTINE IN THE LAST CENTURY B.C.

Simon Maccabeus was the last of the five sons of Mattathias of the house of Hasmoneus, the priest in the village of Modein northwest of Jerusalem, who had first taken up arms against Antiochus IV. He had declared that he and his sons would never abandon their native way of worship (Josephus *Antiquities* XII.269). So long as his descendants ruled, the aura associated with national liberation excused the worst excesses of their government. Revolt, even under the national and orthodox party of the Pharisees, stood little chance of success. At first, however, the priestly state of Judea survived largely through the dissensions and difficulties that confronted the Seleucids. Simon himself was murdered in 135 B.C. with two of his sons, but the dynasty survived under his other son John Hyrcanus I (135–104 B.C.).[12] Three years later the Jewish state nearly came to a summary end when Antiochus VII Sidetes (140–129 B.C.) besieged him in Jerusalem. However, worse dangers threatened the Seleucids from the Parthians in the eastern part of their dominions. A treaty was patched up. John paid an indemnity, offered hostages, and found himself a somewhat unwilling ally of Antiochus VII against the Parthians, but when Antiochus was slain in battle (129 B.C.), John exploited the situation. Soon he set out on a series of aggressive campaigns at the expense of his neighbors with the dual objectives of restoring the boundaries of "the promised land," that is, the boundaries of David's kingdom, and ensuring that only believers in the one God should dwell in it.[13] First, the Samaritans were defeated (128 B.C.), Shechem and Mount Gerizim with its temple destroyed, and Jerusalem rid of a challenge to its religious supremacy. The Samaritans claimed to be the original stock of Israel, but this claim was resisted by the Jews of Judea on the grounds that the Samaritans had intermarried with heathen peoples during the exile and had lost their racial purity. Soon after, the cities on the Phoenician plain were taken from the Syrians, then the kingdom of the Idumeans was conquered (c. 109 B.C.). Finally, Samaria itself was destroyed as retribution for its inhabitants having been allies of the Seleucids (c. 107 B.C.).[14] Little wonder Jews and Samaritans were not on speaking terms in Jesus' time (cf. John 4:9).

John Hyrcanus I died in 104 B.C., but his conquests were continued by his vigorous if short-lived son and successor Aristobulus I (104–103 B.C.). In a little over a year the latter had added parts of Galilee and Iturea to the Jewish state.[15] By this time Judea had taken on the character of an independent kingdom and the high priest the trappings of a king. Aristobulus may have assumed the royal title "king," though this cannot be confirmed before the coinage of his brother Alexander Janneus (103–76 B.C.).[16]

Janneus, despite revolts among his more religiously minded subjects and

18

severe defeats at the hands of the Arabs and Seleucids, brought his kingdom to a climax of prosperity. Pagan mercenaries were hired to fight his wars. The conquest of Galilee was completed and, moving across the Jordan, he subdued the Greek cities established there by the Seleucids. Just as important as these conquests was his development of relations with Parthia and the arrival of a Parthian embassy at his court.[17] Some understanding may have been reached that made the Jews allies of Parthia against any enemies on Parthia's western borders; such enemies would eventually include Rome. When Alexander died in 76 B.C., he left the Jews with a kingdom almost as extensive as Solomon's and greater than they were ever to possess until modern times.[18] They were an established power in the eastern Mediterranean holding a balance between the Ptolemies, the remnants of the Seleucid dominions, and Parthia. Rome was not yet involved in their affairs.

Janneus's kingdom proved a bad neighbor despite its veneer of cosmopolitanism. As Josephus stated, independence had enabled the Jews to practice separateness from other peoples (*Antiquities* XIII.247). When they came within the Jewish sphere, however, they were refused the right to continue their own traditions. The policy of the Hasmoneans towards their conquered subjects was consistent and harsh. Successively the Idumeans, Itureans, and the inhabitants of the Greek cities on the coast and across the Jordan were presented with the alternatives of loss of land or conversion to Judaism. Even the Greek cities seem to have submitted to this demand, Pella being the only city recorded to have withstood it.[19] Galilee with its fertile agricultural areas became a magnet for Jewish colonists and these gradually turned the minority Jewish population into a majority. The acquisition of these convert states on their borders proved a mixed blessing. Their non-Jewish inhabitants hated Jewish rule and were to welcome the coming of the Romans. From Idumea, the one state where Josephus says "they have continued to be Jews,"[20] the Jews acquired the house of Herod.

The Hasmoneans had always recognized the latent power of Rome and their policy had been one of watchful conciliation. While the relations between the Jews and their non-Jewish neighbors became increasingly hostile, those with Rome remained friendly. The early contacts between Rome and the Jews extended back to the era of the Maccabean Wars and had been based on mutual support against the Seleucids. In 161 B.C. Judas Maccabeus had sent an embassy to Rome and an alliance was concluded, a fact duly chronicled by the author of 1 Maccabees (1 Macc. 8:17ff.) some sixty years later. The treaty with Rome was renewed by his brother Jonathan, c. 144 B.C.[21] In 139 B.C., despite the expulsion of Jewish ambassadors from Rome for some actions deemed offensive to the Roman gods,[22] the alliance was extended. The Senate may have instructed autonomous rulers to respect Jewish territory.[23] Probably in 134 B.C. John Hyrcanus I sent a further embassy to the Senate aimed at renewing friendship with Rome (Josephus *Antiquities* XIII.9.2). Rome and the Jews began therefore as allies, a fact not forgotten by Jews of Josephus's period. Josephus goes out of his way to stress the tradition of friendship between illustrious leaders of the Roman Republic and the Jewish people. He had to do so, having changed sides during the revolt of 66–74.[24] Orthodox Judaism was not to be displaced in Roman eyes as *religio licita*—the recognized and acknowledged religion of the Jewish people—in favor of the rival claims of the rebel sect of Christianity.

Rome first became directly involved in the affairs of Palestine through the quarrels that broke out after the death in 67 B.C. of Alexander Janneus's successor, his widow Alexandra. Her two sons Hyrcanus II and Aristobulus II disputed the succession. At this moment, the Roman general Pompey, having defeated Rome's enemies in the East, was in Antioch and the rival claimants attempted to outbid each other for his support. Pompey at first inclined towards Aristobulus, but the latter proved troublesome and in 63 B.C. Pompey himself advanced on Jerusalem. The city fell after a three-month siege and though Pompey entered the Holy Places he committed no act of sacrilege in Jewish eyes similar to that committed by Antiochus IV, and he allowed sacrifices to be resumed. The Romans were preferable to the Seleucids as masters. In the ensuing peace, the Jewish state preserved some vestiges of independence. It was reduced to Judea and Idumea in the south and Perea and Galilee in the north. Samaria cut Galilee off from Judea and the Greek cities regained their independence. Those on the east side of Jordan formed a league of Ten Cities, the Decapolis, hostile to the Jews and a political factor in Jesus' time (Mark 5:20 and 7:31). Hyrcanus II was allowed to assume the title of high priest and ethnarch (not "king"), but the power lay with his protector Antipater II, a chieftain and governor of Idumea.[25] The real authority lay with Rome where it was to remain for the next seven centuries.

The Jewish kingdom now became a pawn in Roman politics in the East. In the civil war between Pompey and Julius Caesar that broke out in 49 B.C., Hyrcanus II and Antipater II maneuvered as best they might. Both survived Caesar's victory the next year, and in 47 B.C. Hyrcanus gained for the Jews a privileged status among Rome's subject peoples in the East. From then on he supported Caesar and so did the Jews in Egypt. In return for Hyrcanus's and Antipater's signal services the Jews were guaranteed full religious freedom, the walls of Jerusalem were rebuilt, and, more to the point, Caesar ordered that the Jews in the Greek cities of the Dispersion (Diaspora) should also enjoy complete religious liberty including the legalizing of their social and religious societies (*collegia*) at a time when some of those of their Greek neighbors remained banned.[26] Not surprisingly, when Caesar was murdered in 44 B.C., the Jews of all foreign nations mourned at his graveside.[27] Even so, many Jews in Palestine were only too well aware that their liberties had been accorded by grace of an idolatrous power. When Herod, one of Antipater's sons (Antipater had been murdered in 43 B.C.), was appointed governor of Galilee guerrilla warfare broke out. Herod captured the leader of the rebels, Hezekiah, and had him executed in 41 B.C., only to find himself summoned to Jerusalem by Hyrcanus to explain why he had inflicted the death penalty.[28] He escaped from his enemies in the capital and was appointed by the Romans as governor of Coele-Syria (between Galilee and Syria proper). He had become Rome's man[29] and the enemy of the majority of the Jewish religious leaders at Jerusalem. In 40 B.C. the Senate at Rome voted to make him king of Judea and he was allowed to extend his authority to Samaria.

Herod assumed possession of his kingdom as a client ruler under Roman protection in 37 B.C., after the Parthians had tried and failed to take over Syria and Palestine, and the last Hasmonean, Antigonus, had been removed at his instigation (Josephus *Antiquities* XIV.490). For most Jews he represented the worst combination of evils. Nominally a Jew, he was in reality a foreigner and a member of a subject people who had no love for the Jews (Josephus *Antiquities* XIV.491). He made no secret that his sympathies lay with the non-Jewish inhabitants of his kingdom. Yet his policy towards the Jews was just sufficiently accommodating to secure him from a national uprising. In 20 B.C. he began to rebuild the Temple on a grandiose scale with the finest masonry. In Jesus' time it had already taken forty-six years in building and was still not complete (John 2:20). "Look, Teacher, what wonderful stones and what wonderful buildings!" (Mark 13:1), reflects accurately a genuine wonderment at Herod's achievement.[30] While Herod's Temple increased vastly the power and prestige of the Sadducean priestly class (Herod had no possible claim to take the high priesthood himself as successor to the Hasmoneans), he still managed to keep on reasonable terms with the Pharisees. In almost every other way, however, he ruled like a Hellenistic monarch. Hebrew disappeared from his coinage. In 26 B.C., a Greek city named "Sebaste" ("Royal City") was built near the site of Samaria and equipped with a temple in honor of Augustus. Other cities, notably Sepphoris in Galilee, were given their trappings of Greco-Roman civilization: baths, colonnades, fountains, and temples. "Actian Games" in honor of Augustus's (Octavian's) victory at Actium were instituted, a deft compliment to the supplanter of Herod's former patron, Mark Antony. Roman emblems were placed over the gateway of the Temple, and on the coast sixty miles from Jerusalem a small port known hitherto as Strato's Tower became second only to Jerusalem in importance. Caesarea was endowed with temples and a fine harbor constructed there. When Judea became a province in A.D. 6 it was chosen by the Romans as their capital.[31]

Herod was an able soldier, a resourceful individual, and a shrewd ruler who may have had a vision of uniting Jew and Gentile, Hasmonean and non-Hasmonean, in a single state dependent on but not entirely subjected to Rome. His purposeful benefactions among the Hellenistic cities of Syria, western Asia Minor, and the Greek islands, that is, where there were strong Jewish settlements, suggest hopes for extending the ideal of Jewish-Greek unity to the Dispersion.[32] If this were so, circumstances were too strong for him and, as his reign went on, a cruel streak in his character came increasingly to the fore. His marriage to the Hasmonean princess Mariamne proved a catastrophe. Divided in his affections between his wife and his sister Salome who hated Mariamne, Herod moved from one atrocity to another in which his own family were the chief victims. The Massacre of the Innocents (Matt. 2:16–17) though perhaps a fragment of Christian *haggadah* nonetheless reflects accurately what his subjects believed him capable of.[33] His thirty-three years as ruler (37–4 B.C.) sharpened all the latent antagonism among the Jews against non-Jewish power in their land, and inflamed the imagination of some with the hope that the day of deliverance would soon dawn in a vast cataclysmic war.[34] Freedom would be gained through a warrior Messiah of the house of David.

SECTS AND PARTIES

Such was the political situation into which Jesus was born at Bethlehem in Judea in the last years of Herod's reign. While every Jew accepted the Law (Torah) and the hope of ultimate deliverance, capacity for action was blunted by social strife and sectarian rivalries. The New Testament names Herodians, Sadducees, and Pharisees as rival Jewish groups, while Josephus neglects the Herodians but adds the Essenes. For him the Sadducees, Pharisees, and Essenes were the "philosophic sects" into which the Jews were divided (*Antiquities* XIII.171–73). In the shadows stood the true revolutionaries, the Zealots.

The Herodians

The Herodians exercised little influence on the development of Christianity and as partisans and retainers of Herod's dynasty they had passed from the scene by the time Josephus wrote his *Antiquities* (circa A.D. 95). However, Palestine in New Testament times cannot be understood without reference to them. They represented the relatively strong current among the Jews, especially in Jerusalem and the larger centers, that were not averse to adopting many of the outward aspects of Hellenistic civilization. In this they were the successors to similar trends among the wealthier Jews in Jerusalem in the years preceding the Maccabean revolt, people stigmatized by Josephus as "godless Jews" who took advantage of the death of Judas Maccabeus in 161 B.C. to harass his supporters (*Antiquities* XIII.2). A degree of Hellenism, even at the height of the power of the Jewish kingdom, was an accepted fact. Greek was the second language to Aramaic and the existence of Greek names (Philip and Andrew are examples among

Jesus' disciples) and even words in ordinary use at the time of Christ testify to its continued penetrative power.[35] Herod's policy of striking a balance between Jew and non-Jew in Palestine did not lack a historical justification. The Herodians reflected this viewpoint.

The Sadducees

The Sadducees also were drawn from the same wealthier strata of society but represented the Jewish nationalist element within it. Their origins are not known. They may have taken their name from the word "doing right" (*zaduk/zadik*) or from some personage in the Maccabean revolt whose memory has perished.[36] They first appear alongside the Pharisees and Essenes on the embassy sent by Jonathan Maccabeus and the assembly of the elders to Rome and Sparta, c. 145 B.C.[37] As the Jewish state became more institutionalized and less fired by prophetic and nationalist aspirations, so their power grew. They were the priestly and aristocratic party in Judea and from the time late in his reign when John Hyrcanus I transferred his affections from the Pharisees to them, they provided the succession of high priests in the Temple. They supported the Hasmoneans loyally. Their religious and social attitudes were strict and conservative and they hated Herod's rule, but they lacked popular support.[38] The commands of Yahweh were to be found in the received text of Scripture alone.[39] They rejected the legalistic developments inspired by the scribes and Pharisees. They also rejected ideas—propagated by the Pharisees and accepted in the population as a whole—regarding the survival of the soul, the great judgment, and the revival of the body in a life to come as unscriptural.[40] Yet with the administration of the cult might also go the gift of prophecy; and in this as well as in their attachment to the concept of priestly succession, the Sadducean high priesthood formed a model for some features of the early Christian episcopate, especially that represented by Ignatius of Antioch (d. 107).[41] These were the men around the high priest Caiaphas at the time of Jesus' ministry. They were deeply conscious of their responsibility for maintaining the purity and survival of Judaism and were prepared to sacrifice an inconvenient individual if he appeared to endanger what they believed to be its true interests. Rome had to be accepted as a temporary affliction. Rebellion could not be tolerated and messianic enthusiasm was dangerous aberration.

The Pharisees

Their counterparts, the Pharisees, permeate the whole New Testament story, "Scribes and Pharisees, hypocrites"; and the nefarious—according to the Gospels—role they play in Jesus' ministry is known to every Christian. Yet, here if anywhere, the Gospel writers are misleading and partisan. The Pharisees, as Josephus makes clear, represented the religious leadership of the mass of the Palestinian Jewish people.[42] The position in popular estimation which they gained under the earlier Hasmoneans was never seriously challenged. In addition, they contributed to the formation of some of the beliefs of the early Christians and their adherents are named by the writer of Acts as members of the church in Jerusalem (Acts 15:5). After the catastrophe of A.D. 70, they rallied the survivors and established new institutions to safeguard the Law, centered on the academy at Jamnia. Without them, Judaism might hardly have survived as a national and religious force.

The origins of the Pharisees are as obscure as those of their Saducean rivals. Without entering into the scholarly discussion, two characteristics stand out. First, they were laypersons and considered themselves a godly elite among their fellow citizens. Josephus who had close ties with the Pharisees described them as "a body of Jews with the reputation of excelling the rest of their nation in the observances of religion and as exact exponents of the laws."[43] In this, they seem to have been militant rather than military. Their outlook if not their origins was akin to the *Hasidim* that appear, c. 165 B.C., at the beginning of the Maccabean Wars.[44] Jews of profound scrupulosity, the Hasidim would prefer to die rather than violate the Sabbath through defending themselves against attack (1 Macc. 2:34ff). Though not wholly out of sympathy with the armed revolt of the Maccabees, they regarded it as "a little help" (Dan. 11:34). They suspected the motives of some of the rebels ("And many shall join themselves to them with flattery" [ibid.]). They put their trust in God's judgment which would raise the righteous "from the earth" and let them "shine like the brightness of the firmament" (Dan. 12:3), whereas their opponents (the Hellenizers) would "awake . . . to shame and everlasting contempt" (Dan. 12:2). This was the first explicit reference to the resurrection of the body to be judged at the end of the existing age. It became one of the cardinal tenets of the Pharisees and of the early church. If the Hasidim were the first stage of the Pharisees, one can understand their suspicion of the Hasmonean monarchy. They supported it up to a point, but they disliked the trappings of royalty and were prepared to rebel against Janneus, c. 88 B.C. Though this failed disastrously, in the reign of his widow Alexandra (76–67 B.C.) they became the powers in the land. As Josephus put it, "she permitted the Pharisees to do as they liked in all matters" in order that "they would dispose the nation favorably toward her."[45] It was a decisive moment in Jewish history.

For the Pharisees the observance and understanding of the Law (Torah) was the object of human existence. It was "the precious instrument by which the world was created," the perfect expression of wisdom and knowledge.[46] They set out to comment, analyze, and interpret Torah to meet every possible case and contingency of life with an industry and persistence that would have done credit to medieval schoolmen. The result was a subtle and intricate web of case-law, which was also a terrible drag on ordinary human existence, and this feature seems to have impressed itself on Jesus and his disciples as the most glaring abuse of God's teaching. Nonetheless, the Pharisaic beliefs in the afterlife, in its rewards and punishments, in angels and demons, and also in the ability of each individual to repent of sins and earn forgiveness, and of the duty to die for Torah rather than compromise its prescriptions, were accepted by the people. Lazarus's sister Martha took it as a matter of course that her brother would rise again in the resurrection at the last day (John 11:24). Paul rallied Pharisaic support for himself when brought before the Sanhedrin by making a claim against the Sadducees: "Brethren, I am a Pharisee, a son of Pharisees; with respect to the hope and the resurrection of the dead I am on trial" (Acts 23:6).

Two other important features of Pharisaic teaching are found in early Christian thought. First, the Pharisees' opposition to kingship extended to placing the civil power on a far-inferior level to the sacred and priestly. Thus in the *Testaments of the Twelve Patriarchs*, usually attributed to the Pharisees in the last century B.C., one may read "As the heaven is higher than the earth, so is the priesthood of God higher than the earthly kingdom, unless it fall away through sin from the Lord and is dominated by the earthly kingdom" (*Test. of Judah* XXI.4). This qualification is aimed probably at the Hasmonean high priesthood which blatantly had become associated with "the earthly kingdom." The true relationship between the two is stated, however, in *Test. of Naphtali* (V.3), "Levi laid hold of the sun and Judah (the royal order) seized the moon." Peter's blunt statement in Acts 5:29 that "we must obey God rather than men" is in line with this tradition. One need hardly be reminded of the metaphors employed in the patristic and medieval periods in the West by those who sought to establish the superiority of church over state. Even in Herod's day these ideas could be applied dramatically. The two rabbis Judas and Matthias, who instructed their pupils to tear down the golden eagle which Herod had set up above the main gate of the Temple, explained their conduct to Herod: "Nor is it at all surprising if we believe that it is less important to observe your decrees than the laws that Moses wrote as God prompted and taught him, and left behind."[47] They went willingly to martyrdom. So would the Christians in their time.

In addition, the Pharisees systematized works of mercy and charity toward the poor. Tobit, for instance, begins with a recitation of his charities to the living and his care for the dead; this latter, including the burial of corpses and care of graves, was to become characteristic of Christian practice. The emperor Julian, commenting that it was acts such as these that attracted pagans towards Christianity, said: "No Jew ever has to beg, and the impious Galileans support not only their own poor but ours as well."[48] Relief of need by alms and charity was actively encouraged by the Pharisees. "Almsgiving and deeds of loving-kindness are equal to all the commandments of the law,''[49] it was said. The Pharisees, in theory at least, would have applauded the New Testament command to visit the sick, clothe the naked, comfort the mourner, and bind up the brokenhearted. Much of the social outlook of the early Christians was modeled on theirs.

The Scribes

Associated in popular imagination with the Pharisees, the scribes had become the leading laypersons in Palestine and enjoyed great prestige as people of learning and judgment. Since the restoration under Nehemiah and Ezra, the Jews had become the people of the Book and of the Law. As interpreters of both, those who followed in the wake of Ezra the scribe enjoyed the prestige belonging to a class that was learned in both secular and religious lore. Distinct from the priestly class and often exercising another calling for a livelihood, the scribes brought the knowledge and practice of Torah to wide sections of the population, and in the schools they established they guaranteed that that knowledge would be passed on to each generation. With the Pharisees they would supervise worship in synagogues and see whether what was said and done on the Sabbath accorded with the Law (cf. Luke 6:7). They were moralists, lawyers, and teachers combined, a nationally conscious and learned middle class which had no parallel elsewhere in the ancient world. Their prestige among the people was enormous. People rose and stood up as a scribe passed. The chief places at feasts and at synagogue were reserved for them.[50] Yet their faults as a class were evident enough. As Jesus is recorded as pointing out (Matt. 23:23), they gave more time to minute problems such as tithing dill, mint, and cumin than matters relating to justice, mercy, and faith.[51] They were responsible for many of the rigorous interpretations of the Law that provoked the wrath of the writers of the Gospels and probably of Jesus himself. It was against this "unwritten law" that Jesus turned his criticism (Mark 7:1-13; Matt. 15:1-20). Their association with the Pharisees strengthened this tendency and in the Sanhedrin the Pharisaic party was composed entirely of scribes. "Scribes, Pharisees, hypocrites," was a severe judgment on these representatives of the Jewish people, but any reform movement within Judaism which arose outside their ranks, especially if it aimed at lightening the burden of the Law on the individual, was likely to rouse their hostility.

The Sadducees, Pharisees, and scribes were all based in Jerusalem, and to a greater or lesser extent represented the outlook of the city, the Temple, and its connected institutions. Pharisees went up to Galilee from Jerusalem and listened to Jesus' teaching (Luke 5:17) just as they had sent emissaries from Jerusalem to test John the Baptist (when he was preaching and baptizing "in Bethany beyond the Jordan" [John 1:24-28]). Jesus' teaching, however, like that of John, was directed to the Palestinian countryside and his main support came from the "crowds," that is, unlettered country folk.

26

Important though the Pharisaic contribution to early Christian beliefs and attitudes was to be, a more immediate influence may have been that of the parallel nonurban reform movement within Judaism represented by the Essenes and more particularly by the Qumran community.

The Qumran Covenanters

There are still many unknowns concerning the origins and early history of the Qumran Covenanters. Here we accept the arguments of A. Dupont-Sommer and F. M. Cross in favor of identifying the Essenes and the Covenanters.[52] At Qumran itself the earliest coins date to John Hyrcanus I's reign and the Seleucid Antiochus VII, but the main buildings of the monastic settlement appear to be later, not before the time of Janneus.[53] This might suggest that the sect retreated into the desert as part of a protest against the perpetuation of the high priesthood in the Hasmonean family, coupled with opposition to the latter's policy of aping the ways of surrounding petty states and seeking closer ties with the Roman Republic. Israel's history was tending to repeat itself. This time the faithful remnant was represented by the Teacher of Righteousness and his followers, who went out into the wilderness to "prepare the way of the Lord, make straight in the desert a highway for our God" (Isa. 40:3) by studying the Law and the revelation of the Holy Spirit by the prophets.[54] They would prepare also for the final conflict between the Sons of Light and the Sons of Darkness, having separated themselves completely from idolatrous society and its influences ("the abode of perverse men").[55] The Teacher's probable martyrdom at the hands of the "Wicked Priest" (Janneus?) would have increased his followers' alienation from Jerusalem, its Temple, and the corruption for which they believed it stood.[56]

The sect survived for over a century. The main buildings at Qumran were severely damaged by an earthquake in 31 B.C., which left great cracks in the stonework of the stairway. The site may have been abandoned during Herod's reign and that of his equally tyrannical son and successor Archelaus (4 B.C.–A.D. 6). After that it was occupied continuously until A.D. 68–69 when it was stormed, probably by men of the Tenth Legion under Vespasian. Broken walls, arrowheads, and evidence of burning tell their own grim story. The possibility is that the Jewish revolt of A.D. 66 and its initial success seemed to the sectaries to be the opening of the great war, set out in the War Scroll, and for which they had been preparing for so long. Fragments of Qumran-type literature were found at Masada where the Zealot forces made their last stand between 70 and 74.[57]

The second period of activity at Qumran coincides exactly with Jesus' ministry and the establishment of the first Christian communities. It would be surprising if the two had held no ideas in common. Like Jesus himself and the early Christians, the Covenanters expected the rapid end of the age, they were concerned with membership of the future kingdom, and they shared with Jesus' followers a deep interest in discovering signs that might warn them of the approach of the end. Theirs, too, was a strongly social teaching favoring the poor, with whom they identified themselves. They were the "Community of the Poor."[58] They did not accept, however, that the Temple should be "a house of prayer for all the nations" (Mark 11:17 and compare Isa. 56:7) or that they should leave Qumran to carry their message into the world.

The Covenanters were a male sect, though probably not celibate on principle any more than were Jesus' disciples.[59] They resembled a strict Pharisaic brotherhood—and one may suspect that these contributed to their origins. Their basic aim was "to live according to the communal rule: to seek God . . . to do what is good and upright in his sight, in accordance with what he has commanded through Moses and his servants the Prophets."[60] Their way of life was monastic, with the strong sense of precedence that one finds in monastic institutions; they saw themselves "set apart and holy"; their routine of purificatory washings, of common meals, and their task of copying the Scriptures suggest an introspective community and, as we have seen, it was "in the wilderness" rather than at Jerusalem that they expected the coming. Then deliverance would be through a warrior Messiah of the house of David and a priestly Messiah of the house of Aaron.[61]

Given the difference of approach to interpretations of obedience to the Law and righteous conduct, there are nonetheless resemblances between the Covenanters and the early Christians.[62] Both regarded themselves as the true Israel, devoted exclusively to teaching and practicing the will of God. Some analogies can even be drawn between the place occupied by the Teacher of Righteousness and Jesus in the eyes of their immediate followers. The organization of each community after the deaths of their founders consisted of a leading triumvirate, of priests at Qumran and "pillars" in the church (Gal. 2:9) aided by a council of elders, and finally the congregation of the whole people.[63] In sect and church goods were held in common, and each new adherent turned over his property to the community and accepted in return a voice in its management. His property and the tools of his profession he committed to the custody of an officer of the sect, and even then he had another year of probation before admission to full membership.[64] The offense of Ananias and Sapphira was recognized at Qumran but the penalty was not so severe.[65] There was a greater immediacy of the power of the Spirit foreshadowing the end in the primitive church. In their ritual, each insisted on the bloodless character of their offering to God; even in their constant purificatory lustrations, the Covenanters might claim the Christian sect of Elkesaites or even perhaps the Mandaeans as imitators, if not successors.

Though there is nothing like the War Scroll in early Christian literature, the sect would have appreciated the radical either/or of Jesus' teaching.

28

The dominant psychology was that of the Two Ways, that of light and that of darkness, of truth and of lies and perversity.[66] "Now this God," so runs the sect's *Manual of Discipline,* "created man to rule the world and appointed for him two spirits he was to walk with until the final Inquisition. They are the spirits of truth and of perversity." Going back to the common source of Deut. 30:15 ("See, I have set before you this day life and good, death and evil"), one finds the same exposition of the Two Ways in the *Didache* (circa A.D. 70) and the *Letter of Barnabas* (circa A.D. 130), and it forms one of the themes of the Fourth Gospel. In all these the believer is the one who had chosen the true Way. A limited dualism is assumed because supreme power remained in the hand of God, but the "eternal enmity" ordained by him between the two spirits led effectively in both communities to ideas of eternal bliss and eternal damnation, and also to predestination to one or the other. These ideas were to have a long history in the Christian church.

The dualism reflected in the Light/Darkness symbolism also led to an apocalyptic sense of history. The Teacher of Righteousness was the one "to whom God made known all the mysteries of his servants the Prophets."[67] The emphasis was on the mysteries and their revelation. The Covenanters were not themselves the inventors of apocalyptic writing which aimed at revealing the secrets of the universe and, in particular, those events that signaled the end of the age. Daniel and the book of *Enoch* both represent apocalyptic writing independent of Qumran in the second and first centuries B.C. The Covenanters made use of these works and compiled a great many others themselves. They saw their world as governed by evil powers who had been granted a brief period of rule by God before the day of Israel's salvation and the great judgment. The world empires of apocalyptic history were set in descending order of merit, with that of Rome the last and worst. Current events were interpreted as signs of the end, and Scripture was read and commented upon with the same object. This, too, would influence the thought of the early Christians, especially in the West.[68] Hippolytus of Rome (circa A.D. 220) saw world history in much the same light as the people of Qumran.

Where Jesus and his followers parted company with the Covenanters was over the practical application of their understanding of Scripture. Signs of the end there might be, but for the Christian the new age had already arrived; for the sectary it was still to be. The new covenant would be concluded with the faithful at the end of the present era. In social terms the Christian agreed with the sect: the meek would inherit the earth, the rich would be brought low, property was suspect. The Christian, however, did not organize for war. There were no "camps" in the church, no preparation for battle, no Masada. Nor was the rigorous sectarian outlook attractive once the Christian mission moved out of Galilee and Jerusalem. Love for one's neighbors extended beyond the bounds of any elect group to publicans and to Samaritans, and though idolatry would be abominated in all its forms taxes would be paid and Caesar's due rendered. It would be by witnessing to the truth and dying for it that the works of Satan would be destroyed. The cross would become the symbol of the new religion.

The impression gained of Palestine in the last century B.C. is of a relatively prosperous and even an advanced society but one in which religious ferment was never far away. Even at the bottom of the scale many of the 'am ha'aretz or the "unlearned" country people would have attended a synagogue school and were far better instructed than their counterparts in any other part of the Mediterranean world. The general view that it was a poor and backward client state does not seem to be borne out by the evidence. Jerusalem was dominated by Herod's magnificent Temple: ". . . it appeared from a distance like a snow-clad mountain; for all that was not overlaid with gold was of purest white" (Josephus War V.223). It was only one among a number of fine buildings in the city which was, as J. Jeremias states, the citadel of theological knowledge and juridical authority in Judaism.[69] There was trade with Egypt in grain, with Arabia in spices, and with Babylonia in materials. There were local trades and manufacturers. The priestly aristocracy and traders benefited from the sums spent in the Temple and in the surrounding areas by the crowds of visitors that came from all over the Mediterranean for the great feasts (cf. Acts 2:8–13). Moreover, outside Jerusalem, especially on the coast and in parts of Galilee, there was excellent land that sustained a prosperous farming and fishing population, with the Greek cities providing markets for their wares.[70] Apart from material well-being, the peculiar nature of Judaism had encouraged the growth of a learned and well-to-do middle class which included the scribes and Pharisees—a middle class who had a knowledge of but little respect for Greek. The phenomenon of a large, well-educated class schooled in the institutions of their people and fanatically devoted to them, yet often carrying out other paid occupations which brought them into continuous contact with their neighbors, is unique in the Roman Empire. It provided the Jews of Palestine with a basis on which to build their hopes for the redemption of Israel and their ability to aspire to independence when they took up arms against Rome. In 66 and 132 the Romans were confronted not only by a priestly aristocracy and populace in arms but by an effective middle class also. The latter lacked an ability, however, to sustain a series of campaigns against disciplined troops. The messianic dream and the social revolution that accompanied it faded before the legions of the emperors Titus and Hadrian. Another way had to be found.

THE DISPERSION

The Jews in Babylonia[71]

Only a minority of the Jews transported eastwards first by Sargon in 722 B.C. and then after the fall of Jerusalem in 587 B.C. chose to return to

Palestine when they were offered the chance to do so by King Cyrus in 537 B.C. Their loyalty to Persia was rewarded, as we have seen, a century later by the restoration of the status of Jerusalem as a walled city and the capital of a temple-state. The good feeling these events brought about toward the rulers of Babylonia, whoever they might be, never evaporated entirely. The overthrow of the Persian Empire by Alexander the Great made little difference to the situation of the Jews settled there; indeed, the Jews benefited from it for wide areas to the west and north were open to their merchants. Tyre on the Mediterranean coast and Edessa in the upper valley of the Euphrates were two cities which contained groups of Babylonian Jewish silk merchants.[72] In contrast, too, to events in Palestine, the Jews in Babylonia found the Seleucids tolerant masters. In c. 220 B.C., Jewish forces fought alongside those of Antiochus III the Great against obscure but dangerous foes threatening the Seleucid domains from the north.[73] Some twenty years later the same ruler moved some two thousand families of Mesopotamian Jews to Lydia and Phrygia since he regarded them as loyal colonists who would uphold his cause against rebellious groups.[74]

The internal history of the Babylonian Jews in the Seleucid period is almost a blank. Greek became the predominant culture. A new capital, Seleucia, was founded by Seleucus I Nicator (c. 300 B.C.) and there, as in other parts of the Seleucid Empire, Greek political institutions, philosophies, and occupations connected with natural science and medicine flourished. The Jews were, of course, Aramaic-speaking, but trade, travel, and general intercourse spread a knowledge of Greek among them, seemingly with little of the friction that accompanied the progress of Hellenization in Palestine. The Jewish communities in this part of the Seleucid Empire thrived and multiplied.[75] In the north, Nisibis became the center for the collection and transmission to Jerusalem of temple offerings taken from a wide area—perhaps that originally settled by the Ten Tribes after their deportation in the eighth century B.C. South of Babylon, the town of Nehardea (in Mesopotamia) served a similar purpose for the Jews in the southern part of the country. This period also saw the establishment of Jewish communities in the Seleucid garrison towns such as Dura-Europos, Nicephorium, Circesium, and Carrhae, and ports such as Spasinou Charax (or Charax Spasinou) on the Persian Gulf; but of life within the communities little or nothing can be said.[76]

The Seleucid power crumbled after Antiochus VII's death in 129 B.C. in war with the Parthians. The latter were originally a nomadic people who from the late third century B.C. onwards gradually encroached on the Seleucid Empire from the east. The founder of a settled, orderly government, Mithridates I (171–120 B.C.) extended Parthian rule to western Iran, reaching Media in 155 and Seleucia in 141. The collapse of Antiochus VII's great effort at reconquest left the Parthians in full possession of the Euphrates Valley and the whole of the Seleucid Empire's one-time eastern provinces. The Parthians, however, were never more than a military aristocracy, and hence impinged little on the life of the Jewish settlements. Indeed, they preserved much of the Hellenistic forms of government, and Greek language and culture remained dominant in Seleucia. Greek served as their official language. The Jews accepted the Parthian regime, gave it loyal service including service in the army, and in return were able to exercise their religion with complete freedom. We can perceive dimly the beginnings of Jewish academies at Nisibis and Nehardea, represented by Judah ben Bathyra at the one and Nehemiah of Bet Deli at the other.[77] Some movement of learned Jews between Parthia and Jerusalem took place. One may detect perhaps the germs of the ''millet'' status they seem later to have enjoyed. In the later Parthian period Jewish authorities were also officials of the Parthian government and were empowered to administer justice, including the death penalty, over members of the community. Relations, however, between the Jews and their Parthian rulers remained good and, as already noted, the Parthians sought the alliance of the Hasmoneans in Palestine.[78]

The main event in Babylonian-Jewish history of the period that closes with the outbreak of the Jewish revolt in 66 was the conversion of the royal house of Adiabene, in circa A.D. 35. The story is told in Josephus's *Antiquities* XX of how both the queen mother Helene and her son Izates were converted separately by Jewish merchants with whom they had come into contact.[79] Adiabene was a client state lying on the upper reaches of the Tigris with its capital at Arbela, with a westward extension to include the city of Nisibis with its large Jewish population. Indeed, Adiabene was probably the most strongly Jewish area anywhere in the Greco-Parthian east and there was considerable friction between pro- and anti-Jewish elements among the ruling nobility. Izates, the heir to King Monobazus's throne, had been sent away in his youth to the port of Spasinou Charax to save him from possible injury from envious half brothers. There he was converted to Judaism by a merchant and, on his father's death in A.D. 36, returned to his own country to find his mother a Jewess. He was persuaded by yet another Jewish traveler that his conversion was not complete without circumcision and only with difficulty did he overcome his hesitations for fear of repercussions on the popularity of his dynasty. From then on his policy demonstrated his loyalty to Judaism. Like his contemporaries Paul and Barnabas, he sent relief to Jerusalem during the famine that befell Palestine in the reign of Claudius (41–54), and his ties with Jerusalem became increasingly firm. His death in A.D. 60 saw Adiabene as a pro-Jewish border state along the Romano-Parthian frontier. When the Jewish revolt broke out in 66, it supported the rebels. Two members of the royal house took part in the opening actions against Cestius.[80] In this they were doing the Parthians' work for them. Behind Izates' policy may have lain the same distant ambition as Herod harbored, namely to unite Judaism whether within or outside Palestine under their aegis, but within a Parthian and an anti-Roman context. To quote Neusner, "Adiabene might itself be the capstone of a Jewish alliance, based on Palestine to the west and Babylonia to the east and dominated by Adiabene itself to the north."[81] The specter of pan-Judaism hostile to themselves was one that the Romans rightly dreaded. Before the fall of Jerusalem in 70 it was practical politics.

Though many of the rabbis in Palestine believed that a great Parthian victory would usher in the messianic age, and messianism was a living force among the Jews there, Babylonian Jewry did not rise to the help of their Palestinian counterparts at the time of the revolt. A few individuals like "Silas the Babylonian" threw in their lot with the rebels and took a leading part in the early stages of the war, but the great majority of Jews remained quiet.[82] Rome was spared a concerted attack on its eastern frontier. The spread of Judaism northwards and eastwards into the debatable land between Rome and Parthia, however, proved a magnet for Christian missionaries with Adiabene itself one of the areas where the new faith took earliest root.

Jews in the Mediterranean World

The pattern of the Jewish Dispersion in the Parthian Empire was reproduced to a very much larger degree in the Greco-Roman world. It is difficult to overestimate the importance of Alexander's conquests in opening up the eastern Mediterranean to trade, colonization, and the movement of ideas. The Jews were able to take full advantage of the situation, and to their merchant communities such as at Delos were added colonists in Asia Minor attracted by land and the security offered by the earlier Seleucids. By the time of Christ there would hardly be a center of any importance in the eastern Mediterranean without its Jewish community, and there were Jews as far afield as the Greek colonies in the Crimea.[83] In the west also Judaism had spread to Rome, Carthage, and even to Volubilis in Morocco.[84] Strabo, cited by Josephus, was hardly mistaken when he wrote, "This people has already made its way into every city, and it is not easy to find any place in the habitable world which has not received this nation and in which it has not made its power felt."[85] (See map A.)

The Jewish communities of the Dispersion bore a family relationship to each other. They formed more or less autonomous groupings of resident aliens in the Greek cities where they existed. The majority of members were Greek-speaking though Hebrew and Aramaic were by no means unknown. The more educated would be deeply influenced by popular versions of Stoic and Platonic philosophy and would possess a smattering acquaintance with the Greek poets, but they would also be intent on adapting that acquaintance to the advantage of Judaism. Antioch and Cyrene were equally, with Jerusalem, centers of Jewish nationalism, the homes of the writers of 4 and 2 Maccabees respectively.[86] In almost every city there would be a synagogue or at least a meeting place for prayer. Torah would be spoken in Greek or Aramaic from memory. The writer of Acts provides evidence for regular Sabbath-day services. "For from early generations," he makes James say, "Moses has had in every city those who preach him, for he is read every sabbath in the synagogues" (15:21). In addition, the Jewish community would have their schools, cemeteries, financial trusts, courts of justice, and charitable institutions. Their graves would be marked *enthade keitai* (here lies) and end with the formula *en eirene* (in peace) and they would be segregated from the tombs of unbelievers.[87] The Jews would be organized in a manner parallel to their Gentile neighbors led by a "ruler of the synagogue," who would be advised by a council (*gerousia*) composed of elders. These would be responsible for the administration of the synagogue and for carrying out judgments. Such a body would have condemned Paul to beatings, the forty stripes minus one, of which he tells the Corinthians (2 Cor. 11:24). The new moon, the ceremonial law, and especially the regulations concerning food would be observed precisely; this punctiliousness contributed to the Jews' reputation not only for being members of a sad and cheerless cult but for a pedantic fussiness that alienated outsiders.[88]

Jerusalem remained the focus of the Jews' allegiance wherever they were. It was their capital as Philo said of the Dispersion Jews.[89] Since the synagogue service was not the Temple ritual and the due sacrifices could not be performed, thousands went to Jerusalem yearly on pilgrimage to participate in the great feasts and especially the Passover. The list given in Acts 2:9–11 shows Jews from places as diverse as Crete and Arabia, Parthia, Pamphylia, and Egypt, Phrygia, and Rome, "Jews and proselytes," attending the feast of Pentecost. Vast sums were collected also in the cities of western Asia Minor from the two drachmas subscribed by every male Jew over the age of twenty for transmission to the Temple. If there were lapses into degrees of pagan syncretism or into magic, it seems that the great majority of the Dispersion Jews were loyal to their traditions.[90] There was still a sense of belonging to a special community. If they looked sometimes like Greeks they remained Jews.

ALEXANDRIA

Alexandria was by far the most important center of the Dispersion. It was to exercise a greater influence on the development of a distinctive early Christian culture than any other center including Rome. In the first half of the first century A.D. the Jews were a majority of the population in two of the five districts into which the city was divided, and there were Jews elsewhere in the city. A very few possessed Alexandrian citizenship but the community formed a *politeuma*, meaning a corporation of resident aliens with its own self-governing institutions. There was a senate (*gerousia*), presided over by an ethnarch or genarch who held chief judicial and administrative power over the community. The latter had its own treasury and

34

record office and, one may presume, its own schools as well as its numerous synagogues, for its educated members were fully the equal of their counterparts in the intellectual life of the city.[91] From the second century B.C. onwards the Alexandrian Jews were consciously the mediators of Hellenistic-Jewish culture to the Greek world. In the Wisdom of Solomon, *The Letter of Aristeas* (to his brother Philocrates, c. 278–270 B.C.), the translation of the Hebrew Scriptures into Greek in the Septuagint (LXX), and through Philo and his school for whom Greek was "our language," they proved themselves the leaders of Jewry in the Hellenistic world.

The outstanding Alexandrian Jew is, of course, *Philo Judaeus* (20 B.C.–A.D. 50). His influence on what became Alexandrian Christianity was enormous. Much of the terminology which Origen used to explain his ideas of the Godhead was derived from Philo and so also was his use of the allegorical method to interpret Scripture. It has been said rightly that the history of Christian philosophy "began not with a Christian but a Jew," namely Philo of Alexandria.[92] Philo was a mystic, a Platonic philosopher, and a loyal Jew, but also loyal to Rome. Like Paul, he aspired to mystical experience. He described his soul as being "on fire" and his language, like Paul's, sometimes vibrated with emotion. But there was nothing of the rabbi and the Pharisee in his approach to Scripture. He was Greek to the core, in language, education, and manners, and his Bible was the Septuagint. For him there was no incompatibility between Hellenism and Judaism. While accepting the Law as the infallibly revealed will of God both to Jews and Gentiles, he attempted to interpret it exclusively through the mirror of Greek philosophy. He found the means at hand through his understanding of Stoicism and some of Plato's dialogues. The Platonic idiom dominated his thought. As had Plato, so he understood God as existence apprehensible by the human mind as abstract Perfection. Yet God was also the Creator, creating the universe out of Non-being, and stamping upon it the pattern of order and rationality, his own Reason or Logos. The Logos was interpreted in Platonic terms as "the Idea of Ideas," the first begotten Son of God, pattern and mediator of Creation and "Second God." Scripture was the word of the Logos to be understood by the same mystical process as that by which the human mind approached the Logos himself. The Bible, therefore, was to be interpreted allegorically, and the historical aspects, even the religious development of the Jewish people told in its pages, were lost among the spiritual and moral sentiments whereby Philo sought to demonstrate the harmony and rationality of the universe. Ultimately humanity itself was destined for deification, representing harmony and conformity with the Divine.[93]

The earthly ruler was the king, the godly monarch ruling in imitation of his Creator, the Word. Philo saw his ideal fulfilled by Augustus who gave peace to the war-torn peoples and established the empire. The concept, derived from contemporary Stoic thought,[94] proved to be of immense importance in the history of Christianity. It provided a means by which Christians from the second century onwards could identify with the empire, and later it formed the basis of East Roman and Byzantine theories of kingship. Philo became the forerunner of the whole succession of loyalist Greek Christian apologetic, from Justin Martyr to Eusebius of Caesarea. He may claim to have been the father of Christian political thought as of many aspects of Greek Christian theology.

Yet Philo was also a fervent missionary for his faith. He saw the Jews as the suppliants for the remainder of humanity, for which task they had been chosen by God.[95] By implication the Jewish faith was destined to become the faith of humankind. Conversion to Judaism was a sign of the individual's progress towards God, an illumination like initiates experience on entering a mystery.[96] Others before and after him thought similarly. The romance of *Joseph and Asenath* tells the story of the conversion of Asenath, the daughter of an Egyptian priest. Joseph prayed that God should grant her "refreshment," "newness of life,"[97] ideas we shall encounter in Christian baptismal terminology. In more general terms, the second century B.C. compilers of the Septuagint attempted to harmonize some of the crudities and anthropomorphic views of God contained in the Hebrew Bible with ideas borrowed from Greek philosophy. Behind this gigantic effort of interpretation was the desire to present Judaism in a favorable light to the pagan world. Jews, however Hellenized, believed in the superiority of the Law and their "theocracy" over Greek philosophy and secular constitutions. To Philo even Plato had been anticipated by Moses.[98]

The philosopher could also be a fighter when necessary. He warned the emperor Caligula after the destructive anti-Jewish riot in Alexandria in A.D. 38 that "the Jews living in Judea are infinitely numerous, physically strong, and mentally courageous, and prefer to die for the traditions in a spirit which some of their traducers would call barbaric but which is in actual fact free and noble."[99] Earlier he had said that "A glorious death met in the defense of the Law is a kind of life."[100] Philo and Josephus spoke the same language. There was an underlying hardness in Alexandrian Judaism that belied its seeming reasonableness. The grim conclusion of 3 Maccabees in which ten thousand apꞏ ꞏate Jews were supposed to be handed over for destruction by the Ptolemaic rulers could not have been lost on the Greek population of Alexandria.[101] Claims by the Jews to enjoy full citizen rights in the city were fiercely resisted.

Relations between the Jews in Egypt and the Palestinians were close. Jews from Cyrene, such as Simon who carried Jesus' cross (Matt. 27:32), were living in Judea. Jews at Jerusalem sent their greetings to "brethren in Egypt" (2 Macc. 1:1). Against this, Egypt served as a refuge for those for whom Judea was no longer comfortable, such as the deposed high priest Onias IV who attempted to set up a rival temple on Egyptian soil, or Jesus'

36

family as recorded by Matthew (2:14–15) when they were fleeing from Herod. It also attracted dissidents such as those referred to by the emperor Claudius who "sailed down [to Egypt] from Palestine to foment disorder."[102] These troublemakers, together with the riots and counterriots of 38 and 40, persuaded Claudius in 41 not to add to the existing privileges of the Alexandrian Jews. The "special relations" that had lasted since Julius Caesar's time between Romans and Jews in the eastern Mediterranean had ended.

THE SMALLER TOWNS OF EGYPT AND CYRENAICA

These towns fill out the picture of Egyptian Jewry. Philo's claim that there were "one million" Jews between the Cyrenaican border and Egypt's southern frontier may not be far from the mark.[103] Strabo, cited by Josephus, says that Jews formed one of the four main divisions among the nonindigenous people of Cyrenaica, namely citizens, resident aliens (*metics*), farmers, and Jews.[104] One example must suffice. Teuchira (Tokra) was a town, covering about 110 acres on the Cyrenaican coast, whose cemeteries of the Ptolemaic and early Roman periods provide a picture of the population as a whole. Of a total of 416 epitaphs published by 1960, no less than 103 appear to be Jewish, and of these about one-quarter were of people who had retained some link with Palestine, either by a Hebrew name or by recording a Palestinian birth-place.[105] The Greek-Jewish element was reinforced by immigrants from Asia Minor, Thessaly, and Thrace. There were also some proselytes indicated by the name "Sarra" (Sarah).[106] What sort of people were they? One may presume that, like those at Berenice (Benghazi), the Teuchira Jews formed their own *politeuma*, possessed meeting places, and in addition, to judge by the purely Jewish character of some funerary courts, some other communal organizations. Their members were drawn from almost every walk of life: there were peasants, holders of land granted by the Ptolemies (*klerouchoi*), freedmen, soldiers, slaves, and some Roman citizens.[107] Their families were no larger than those of their Gentile neighbors, consisting of two, three, or four children, but there is one grim indication that the majority remained at the lower end of the economic scale. No less than 47 percent of the funerary inscriptions were those of young people who had died before reaching the age of twenty, with the highest incidence between sixteen and twenty.[108] This must on any assessment seem extraordinary, for it means that marriage by sixteen would have been necessary for the community to have survived at all. Yet, when one visits the Jewish catacomb on the Via Torlonia in Rome and sees the rows upon rows of small anonymous graves that line its walls, one cannot say that this mortality among the young was exceptional. What caused it, however, remains unknown.

The last Jewish inscription from Teuchira is dated 116, midway through the great Jewish uprising in Cyrenaica of 115–17. How was it that so apparently Hellenized a community, who sometimes shared funeral courts with Gentiles and even named their children after the Muses like Euterpe daughter of Theodotus, should have risen in such savage and destructive fury? Again, one does not know. One might point to a change of attitude on the part of the Cyrenaican Jews after the Maccabean Wars. In the third century B.C. they were loyal to the Ptolemies and used the Ptolemaic calendar, and in return no let or hindrance was placed on their religion. The change of attitude is shown by Jason of Cyrene's account of the rising against the Seleucids (2 Maccabees), c. 120 B.C., and though this was not directed against the Ptolemies, it pointed the finger of accusation against a Hellenistic dynasty and gloried in the triumph of the Jewish cause. It could not have avoided inflaming suspicions between Jew and Gentile in Cyrenaica. The Jewish revolt of 66–74 had repercussions there, for the last flicker was kindled by Jonathan the weaver in Cyrenaica in 73. According to Josephus, Jonathan was a Zealot (*sicarius*). At this period, we may perhaps see Judaism and its converts as one focus of opposition to the empire and its institutions.[109] Tacitus's *exuere patriam* ("abandon one's fatherland, or native city")[110] concerning Jewish proselytes, circa A.D. 115, had a positive aspect, just as "abandonment of the Greek gods"[111] by Christian converts in the mid–second century indicated their rejection of the religion and culture of the Greco-Roman world. Recruits to both were seeking alternatives.

WESTERN ASIA MINOR

Western Asia Minor (the province of Asia) was to be the main center of Christianity for a century and a half after the Pauline mission. The Jews there, particularly in the cities, were numerous and relatively wealthy. Their situation was similar to that of the Jews in Alexandria and Egypt. Their language was Greek. Many would be acquainted at least with anthologies of the Greek poets and philosophers. They were well organized with their synagogues, craft guilds, courts of justice, treasuries, and cemeteries. As it did for the Egyptian Jews, Jerusalem still claimed their affection. Very large sums were sent yearly to the Temple out of a contribution of two drachmas a year from every Jew over the age of twenty.[112] This privilege was specifically safeguarded by the Roman administrators. Josephus preserves the text of a decree of Julius Caesar, addressed to the proconsul of Asia, C. Norbanus Flaccus, in favor of the Jews of Sardis that they "shall not be prevented from collecting sums of money, however great they may be, in accordance with their ancestral custom, and sending them to Jerusalem."[113] The casual mention also of the presence of John the Baptist's disciples at Ephesus (Acts 19:1), and Paul's own education in Jerusalem, show that links with the Palestinian homeland remained varied and strong.[114]

The Jewish communities themselves provide interesting examples of the life and organization of a religious minority which may be extended to early Christianity. With the probable exception of Jewry in parts of Phrygia, they were even more pronouncedly urban than those in Cyrenaica. This was to affect dramatically both the mission and organization of the church. Acts 13—17 indicate a core of Jews entirely committed to their faith, surrounded by an ever-wider circle of full proselytes and "God-fearers." The latter observed only parts of the Mosaic law and otherwise remained part of the Gentile population. The family of Timothy, for instance, was mixed Jewish and Greek. Timothy "from childhood [had] been acquainted with the sacred writings" (2 Tim. 3:15), but was not circumcised. At Miletus Jews were among spectators at games, which their stricter counterparts would shun, but they had their special seats.[115] Sardis provides an interesting example of the relations between Jew and Greek in the capital of the old Lydian kingdom.[116] What are the implications of the vast baths-gymnasium-synagogue complex near the center of the city begun sometime after the earthquake of A.D. 17? It may suggest a self-confident Judaism yet also a Judaism determined to apply its own rules for contact with its pagan neighbors. The synagogue did not communicate with the remainder of the complex though its worshipers were quite prepared to include "pagan imagery wholesale" within it.[117] It would seem that their position had improved considerably since Julius Caesar's time when they appealed to the Romans for help against threats from the Gentile population, and they were to continue to prosper for the next two centuries at least.

The Sardis Jews, however, reveal another aspect of the Jewish Dispersion. They considered themselves as much "men of Sardis" (*Sardianoi*) as the next man, but despite all their progress they failed to become a majority in the city.[118] They never converted Sardis as the Christians would convert Eumeneia or Orcistus.[119] Judaism remained a subculture, although an influential one. The situation at Sardis finds a parallel in that at Pisidian Antioch. There Judaism had attracted not only Greeks and native Phrygians but women who belonged to the ruling class of Italian-descended settlers. Crowds flocked to hear Paul and Barnabas; and they were treated to one of Paul's fullest justifications for accepting Jesus as Messiah. Some people were so committed to Judaism that they took sides in keen religious debate. The "devout women of high standing" in the congregation contributed to putting pressure on the city authorities and "stirred up persecution against Paul and Barnabas, and drove them out of their district" (Acts 13:50). The synagogue itself was located in a prominent place in the town at the foot of a wide street leading off the Platea Tiberia, one of the main squares of the city.[120] But for all this Jewish activity, Antioch at this period was one of the most Romanized cities of Asia Minor. It was a *colonia*, bearing the official name of Colonia Caesarea. Its leading citizens were descendants of veterans from the Fifth Legion (*Gallica*) and Seventh Legion.[121] The eight districts, or *vici*, into which it was divided all bore Latin names. The main square of the city was named the Platea Augusta, dominated on one side by the Temple to Augustus, and on the walls of the colonnade on each side were engraved in Latin "a record of his enterprises" (*Res Gestae Divi Augusti*). Latin was also the language of the local coinage and continued to be so down to the middle of the third century.[122] The tombstones of the local worthies included knights (*equites*) and even a sprinkling of men of senatorial rank, and were inscribed in Latin. The religious life of the city was characterized by the great number of priesthoods official and local. People grouped themselves into "brotherhoods" (*tekmoreiai*). The existence of the Jewish community seems to have affected little the popularity either of the imperial or Hellenistic cults, nor that of the powerful local god Mên Askaênos who appears on the city's coinage of the time of Philip (244–49) and in whose honor games were organized as late as the period of the Tetrarchy (285–305).[123] However active the Jews may appear to have been, they formed only one out of many communities into which the population of Antioch was divided. The flurry caused by the visit of Paul and Barnabas may have had little permanent effect on this outpost of Rome in Asia Minor.

The Jews, however, were too vigorous a minority to be ignored. However much they sought to sink their identity into that of their city, like those of Sardis or the Jews of Acmonia who recorded that they held public offices on tombstones that included clear evidence of their religion,[124] the problems of dual loyalty to their own cities and to Jerusalem found little sympathy among the Gentile inhabitants. Josephus preserves a long list of decrees[125] promulgated in the time of Julius Caesar and a few years later in which the Roman authorities sought to shield the Jews in the cities of Asia Minor from vindictive action by the Greek inhabitants.[126] At Ephesus, at Pergamum, and at Sardis, Jewish Sabbath worship was safeguarded; and at Sardis, the right of the Jews to have suitable food available for them in the marketplace. At Ephesus, Jews who were Roman citizens were released from the obligation to do military service.[127] These measures often produced bitter opposition from the Greeks. They might have asked a question similar to the one Apion asked Josephus, "why, then, if they are citizens, do they not worship the same gods as the Alexandrians?"[128] There was no satisfactory answer except that of political expediency. Rome found itself the heir to an intractable situation which the coming of Christianity was to intensify and prolong.

ROME

In Rome itself, the authorities could afford to treat the Jews as another foreign cult. The Jews at the time of the birth of Christ may have numbered as many as fifty thousand and were concentrated in the area across the Tiber from the forum around the Vatican hill. Their immigration had begun during the second century, as had that of other foreign groups in Rome, but their numbers had been reinforced strongly by thousands of prisoners of war whom Pompey brought back from Palestine in 61 B.C..[129] These Palestinians left their mark for posterity in four inscriptions recording the existence of "the synagogue of the Hebrews" that formed part of the large and wealthy Jewish community on the Monteverde. In 4 B.C. no less than eight thousand Jewish residents greeted a deputation of fifty Jews from Palestine that came to the capital and asked for the removal of Herod's son the tetrarch Archelaus.[130]

As in the east, the Jews flourished under Julius Caesar and Augustus. They had a limited part even in public life but enough to rouse Cicero's anger (*On Behalf of Flaccus* 60). They were regarded as an "allied nation"; they were free to adhere to their own religious observances, and they demonstrated their loyalty to Augustus by one of the groups who dedicated a synagogue calling itself "Augustesi."[131] The emperor in turn showed his good will by sending gifts to the Temple. The cessation of sacrifices to Yahweh in honor of the emperor marked the beginning of open revolution in Jerusalem in 66. The prosperity of the Jews in Rome, however, was brittle. They were tolerated rather than liked. Even when they were most useful to Rome in the east, antipathy came readily to the surface. Thus Cicero's defense of the extortionate proconsul of Asia Flaccus in 62 B.C. provides a clue. "The practice of their [Jewish] sacred rites was at variance with the glory of our empire, the dignity of our name and the customs of our ancestors."[132] *Mos maiorum* would be heard of again in connection with actions against both Jews and Christians. In Tiberius's reign an incident involving a noble Roman lady named Fulvia (who had become a proselyte) and an unscrupulous immigrant Jew resulted in action by the Senate. Egyptian and Jewish rites were banned from the city in A.D. 19 and four thousand Jewish freedmen dispatched to Sardinia on an unhealthy military campaign against bandits.[133] In Tiberius's minister Sejanus they found a determined enemy. By the end of Tiberius's reign opinion in Rome itself was becoming increasingly hostile towards Jews.

Proselytism had been a cause of Jewish unpopularity in Rome. This and the additional fact that the Jews were "friends and allies" of the Romans and appeared to bask in their favor provoked deep antipathy between Jew and Greek in the cities of Asia. Down to the end of Augustus's reign the Romans tended to take the side of the Jews and frustrate the efforts of the local authorities in the Greek cities to deny the Jews the right to worship as they chose and to live according to their own usages. All the time the Jews appear to be gaining ground. Apart from Acts there is abundant evidence in Josephus. Thus of the Jews in Antioch in Syria he says that they enjoyed there "an equality with the Greeks." He also notes, "they were constantly attracting to their religious ceremonies multitudes of Greeks, and these they had in some measure incorporated with themselves."[134] In Alexandria they offered a "friendly welcome" to Greeks, and this invitation was not always ignored.[135] By the time of Christ, Judaism was the single most vital religious movement in the Greco-Roman world. The focus of loyalty provided by the Temple and by Torah gave its adherents a strength greater than even the sense of an urban civilizing mission among the barbarian peoples that sustained the Greeks in Asia Minor and Syria. So far as worship was concerned, the latter were at a disadvantage when confronted with Judaism that could claim a documented and coherent history of salvation extending back to the beginning of the world. The *Antiquities of the Jews* and the Septuagint were alike missionary works on a vast scale aimed partly at vindicating to the Greek-speaking world the claim that Judaism as a philosophy and way of life was older and truer than anything the Greeks could offer. In Asia Minor and Parthia the missionary urge among the Jews was insatiable. The gibe at the Pharisees traversing "sea and land to make a single proselyte" (Matt. 23:15) signifies a great deal of purposeful propaganda by Jewish merchants or travelers in favor of their religion. Only the development of the imperial cult in Asia Minor gave the Greeks a sense of identity and focus for religion and loyalty strong enough to resist the pressures of a superior Jewish ethic and religion.

Yet the tensions within Judaism itself were mounting. There was a tendency among some of the more Hellenized to lapse or assimilate Yahweh/Sabaoth with a powerful local deity such as Jupiter/Sabazius in Anatolia. There was also the point of contact with the surrounding world through the lure of magic and necromancy which involved Jew and Gentile alike. When the crisis came in 66, the Dispersion did not join the Palestinian revolt and, after that had failed, by no means all the Hellenistic Jews were prepared to accept Pharisaism as normative Judaism. Christianity was the gainer from this situation. In the generation before, opinions ranged from uncompromising loyalty to Judaism, to despair and rejection. The Antiochene (?) writer of 4 Maccabees interpreted the Jewish ideal of martyrdom as the highest example of the Stoic virtues of fortitude and judgment, but others were less satisfied. Philo, we have seen, found his answer to the dilemma in an allegorical interpretation of Scripture that left nothing of the historical aspects of Israel's progress as God's people standing. But the Alexandrian thinker's solution had little general appeal. Yahweh as the jealous God of Scripture could not be so easily removed. Judaism was a national cult whatever its universal appeal. There were many more like Paul who experienced the anguish of attempting to balance loyalty to Torah with a realization that Torah was inadequate as a guide to life. Were all Gentiles doomed to destruction without opportunity of salvation? In contrast, another Pharisee, Rabbi Tarfon (circa A.D. 100), though convinced of the impossibility of total obedience to God's commands, came to a different conclusion. If it was impossible to complete the work of the Lord in his own lifetime nothing must be done to impede its completion. To follow deceivers (such as Jesus) invited destruction.[136]

By the time of Jesus' ministry, Judaism was becoming the melting pot of conflicting ideas all claiming to be the true interpretation of Torah. Everywhere there was vigor, growth, and expectation. At one end of the spectrum stood the conservative but nationalist high priesthood serving the Temple as the majestic symbol of surviving Jewish identity, at the other the incipient Zealot movement which cared little for the Temple but regarded social revolution as the proper accompaniment of uprising against the Romans. There was the apocalyptic prophecy of the Palestinian sects brooding in their wilderness settlements on the final conflict with the powers of idolatry, while at Alexandria Philo was affirming that Judaism was a universal faith in which all, be they ascetic monk or Platonist philosopher, would find their place. In the middle the Pharisees and their associates attempted to establish a normative Judaism reflecting the providential government of Yahweh over his people. To all this the Christians were to be to some extent heirs. While the Roman Empire provided their missionaries with ease of communications and a framework of law and order in which to work, the Dispersion communities were the magnet which drew them beyond the boundaries of Palestine. The more successful their mission was the more they attracted the hostility reserved previously for the Jews.

What direction Judaism would have taken without the coming of Jesus is anyone's guess. The Jewish world was ripe for upheaval. In Palestine itself social divisions reinforced cultural divisions that were to erupt under the stress of the war of 66. Both in Palestine and in the Dispersion, however, most Jews would have rated Roman rule only less oppressive than that of the Seleucids and equally idolatrous. In the veiled language of the Jewish *Sibylline Oracles* some Jews in Asia Minor anticipated Rome's decline with glee. Hatred of "the nations" they accepted. The risings of 66–74, 115–17 and 132–35 demonstrate the forces of violence and frustration in Judaism that were seeking outlet. The radical turn of events, however, created by the life, teaching, and death of Jesus of Nazareth could hardly have been anticipated.

BIBLIOGRAPHY

NOTE

The best guide to the development of Judaism in this period is Géza Vermès and Fergus Millar's new English translation of Emil Schürer's *The History of the Jewish People in the Age of Jesus Christ* (175 B.C.–A.D. 135), Organizing Editor Matthew Black, rev. ed., 2 vols. (Edinburgh: T. & T. Clark, vol. 1, 1973, and vol. 2, 1979). This covers history and institutions of Judaism in Palestine and the Dispersion. For the Jewish religion, and the respective parts played by the Pharisees, Sadducees, and scribes within it, see G. F. Moore, *Judaism in the First Centuries of the Christian Era, the Age of the Tannaim*, 3 vols. (Cambridge, Mass.: Harvard University Press, 1927–30). For the preeminent role of Jerusalem, see J. Jeremias, *Jerusalem in the Time of Jesus*, Eng. trans. F. H. Cave and C. H. Cave, 3d ed. (Philadelphia: Fortress Press, London: SCM Press, 1969).

The *Dead Sea Scrolls* have attracted an enormous literature. For the texts in English with a useful introduction, see T. H. Gaster, ed. and Eng. trans., *The Dead Sea Scriptures in English Translation*; and Géza Vermès's book, *The Dead Sea Scrolls in English*. An excellent short history of the monastery of Qumran and the scrolls and their significance is F. M. Cross, *The Ancient Library of Qumran and Modern Biblical Studies* (Garden City, N.Y.: Doubleday & Co.; London: Gerald Duckworth & Co., 1958). Their importance in New Testament study is discussed in a symposium edited by K. Stendahl, *The Scrolls and the New Testament* (New York: Harper & Brothers, 1957; London: SCM Press, 1958).

For the Dispersion, J. Neusner's *A History of the Jews in Babylonia*, 5 parts (Leiden: E. J. Brill, 1966–70) holds the field for the eastward expansion of Judaism. E. M. Smallwood's edition of Philo's *Legatio ad Gaium* (*On the Embassy to Gaius*), gives an excellent introduction to the Jews in Alexandria.

On Philo, see H. A. Wolfson's magisterial *Philo: Foundations of Religious Philosophy in Judaism, Christianity, and Islam*, 2 vols. (Cambridge, Mass.: Harvard University Press; London: Oxford University Press, 1947), and Henry Chadwick's chapter "Philo," in *The Cambridge History of Later Greek and Early Medieval Philosophy*, ed. A. H. Armstrong (New York and Cambridge: Cambridge University Press, 1967), pp. 137–57.

For the Jews in Asia Minor, A. T. Kraabel's account of the Jewish community in Sardis based on the American (ASOR) excavations there is essential, "Paganism and Judaism: The Sardis Evidence" in *Paganisme, Judaïsme, Christianisme: Influences et affrontements dans le monde antique. Mélanges offerts à Marcel Simon*, ed. André Benoit et al. (Paris: Boccard, 1978), pp. 13–34; and for Judaism in Rome, H. J. Leon, *The Jews of Ancient Rome* (Philadelphia: Jewish Publication Society of America, 1961), remains the best single-volume account.

SOURCES

Flavius Josephus. *Antiquitates Judaicae* (*Antiquities of the Jews*). *Books XII–XIV*, Eng. trans. and ed. R. Marcus (1943). *Books XV–XVII*, Eng. trans. and ed. R. Marcus; completed and ed. A. Wikgren (1963). *Books XVIII–XX*, Eng. trans. and ed. L. H. Feldman (1966). LCL. Cambridge, Mass.: Harvard University Press; London: William Heinemann.

———. *Bellum Judaicum* (*The Jewish War*). Eng. trans. and ed. H. St. J. Thackeray. LCL. Cambridge, Mass.: Harvard University Press; London: William Heinemann, 1927–28.

———. *Vita* and *Contra Apionem* (*The Life* and *Against Apion*). Eng. trans. and ed. H. St. J. Thackeray. LCL. Cambridge, Mass.: Harvard University Press; London: William Heinemann, 1926.

Philo Judaeus. *Legatio ad Gaium* (*On the Embassy to Gaius*). Eng. trans. and ed. E. M. Smallwood. Leiden: E. J. Brill, 1961.

———. *Supplements I* and *II*. Eng. trans. and ed. Ralph Marcus. LCL. Cambridge, Mass.: Harvard University Press; London: William Heinemann, 1953.

The *Dead Sea Scrolls:* T. H. Gaster, ed. and Eng. trans., *The Dead Sea Scriptures in English Translation* (Garden City, N. Y.: Doubleday Anchor Books, rev. ed.,

1964; London: Secker & Warburg, 1957); and G. Vermès, ed. and Eng. trans., *The Dead Sea Scrolls in English* (Baltimore: Penguin Books., rev. ed., 1970; Harmondsworth, Eng.: Penguin Books., 1963).

SECONDARY WORKS

Appelbaum, S. "The Jewish Community of Hellenistic and Roman Teuchira in Cyrenaica." *Scr. Hieros.* 7 (1961): 27–48.

———. *Jews and Greeks in Ancient Cyrene.* Leiden: E. J. Brill, 1979.

Baron, S. W. *A Social and Religious History of the Jews.* 7 vols. 2d rev. ed. Vols. 1 and 2. New York: Columbia University Press; London: Oxford University Press, 1952.

Bell, H. I., ed. *Jews and Christians in Egypt: The Jewish Troubles in Alexandria and the Athanasian Controversy.* New York: Oxford University Press, 1925.

Black, Matthew. *The Dead Sea Scrolls and Christian Doctrine.* London: University of London, Athlone Press, 1966.

———. *The Essene Problem.* London: Dr. Williams's Trust, 1961.

———. *The Scrolls and Christian Origins.* New York: Charles Scribner's Sons, 1961.

Bonsirven, J. *Palestinian Judaism in the Time of Jesus Christ.* Eng. trans. W. Wolf. New York: McGraw-Hill, 1965.

Dinkler, E. *Eirene: Der urchristliche Friedensgedanke.* SAH. PH (1973), vol. 1, pp. 7–47.

Dupont-Sommer, A. *Les écrits esséniens découverts près de la Mer Morte.* Bibliothèque historique. Paris: Payot, 1959.

Emerton, J. A. "The Problem of Vernacular Hebrew in the First Century A.D. and the Language of Jesus." *JTS* n.s. 24 (1973): 1–23.

Farmer, W. R. *Maccabees, Zealots and Josephus: An Introduction Into Jewish Nationalism in the Greco-Roman Period.* New York: Columbia University Press, 1956; London: Oxford University Press, 1957.

Flusser, D. "The Dead Sea Scrolls and Pre-Pauline Christianity." *Scr. Hieros.* 4 (2d ed., 1965): 215–66.

Foerster, W. *Palestinian Judaism in New Testament Times.* Eng. trans. G. E. Harris. Edinburgh: Oliver & Boyd, 1964.

Hengel, M. *Judaism and Hellenism: Studies in their Encounter in Palestine During the Early Hellenistic Period.* Eng. trans. J. Bowden. 2 vols. Philadelphia: Fortress Press, 1975; London: SCM Press, 1974; discussed by F. Millar, *JJS* 24 (1978): 1–21.

Lieberman, S. *Hellenism in Jewish Palestine.* New York: Jewish Theological Seminary, 1962.

Loewe, H. M. J. *Render Unto Caesar: Religious and Political Loyalty in Palestine.* New York: Macmillan Co.; Cambridge: At the University Press, 1940.

Milik, J. T. *Ten Years of Discovery in the Wilderness of Judaea.* SBT 26. Eng. trans. J. Strugnell. London: SCM Press, 1959.

Peterson, E. *Der Monotheismus als politisches Problem.* Leipzig, 1935.

Reicke, B. *The New Testament Era: The World of the Bible from 500 B.C. to A.D. 100.* Eng. trans. D. E. Green. Philadelphia: Fortress Press, 1968; London: A. & C. Black, 1969.

Rowley, H. H. *Jewish Apocalyptic and the Dead Sea Scrolls.* London: University of London: Athlone Press, 1957.

_____. *The Zadokite Fragments and the Dead Sea Scrolls.* New York: Macmillan Co., 1953; Oxford: Basil Blackwell & Mott, 1952.

Simon, M. *Recherches d'histoire judéo-chrétienne.* Études juives VI. Paris: Mouton Press, 1962.

_____. "Sur les débuts du prosélytisme juif." In *Hommages à André Dupont-Sommer*, pp. 509–20. Paris: Librairie d'Amérique et d'Orient Adrien-Maisonneuve, 1971.

_____. "Theos Hypsistos." In *Ex orbe religionum. Studia Geo. Widengren.* Vol. I, pp. 372–85. Leiden: E. J. Brill, 1972.

Tcherikover, V. A. "The Third Book of the Maccabees as a Historical Source of Augustus' Time." *Scr. Hieros.* 7 (1961): 1–26.

Werblowsky, R. J. Zwi. "Greek Wisdom and Proficiency in Greek." In *Paganisme, Judaïsme, Christianisme*, pp. 55–60.

Yadin, Y. *Masada: Herod's Fortress and the Zealots' Last Stand.* Eng. trans. M. Pearlman. New York: Random House; London: Weidenfeld & Nicolson, 1966.

NOTES

1. Philo *Embassy* 1.4; and compare Ps. 148:14 ". . . the people of Israel who are near to him."

2. Josephus *Apion* II.32.234 and I.8.42. Compare Philo *Embassy* 31.210, "For as they maintain that their Laws are God-given oracles and have been educated in this doctrine from their childhood, they bear images of the Commandments imprinted on their souls."

3. Günther Bornkamm, *Jesus of Nazareth*, Eng. trans. I. McLuskey and F. McLuskey (New York: Harper & Row, 1975; London: Hodder & Stoughton, 1973), pp. 34–35.

4. Josephus *Apion* II.16.165: "Our lawgiver, however, was attracted by none of these forms of polity, but gave to his constitution the form of what . . . may be termed a 'theocracy,' placing all sovereignty and authority in the hands of God."

5. For Judaism in this period, see J. Bright, *A History of Israel*, 2d ed. (Philadelphia: Westminster Press, 1972), chaps. 9–12; L. H. Brockington, ed., *Ezra, Nehemiah and Esther*, NCBC (Grand Rapids: Wm. B. Eerdmans; London: Marshall, Morgan, & Scott, 1969), pp. 13ff.; Baron, *Social and Religious History of Jews*, vol. 1, chap. 5.

6. For a favorable Jewish comparison of Persians as against the Romans, see *Abodah Zarah*, vol. 25 in *The Babylonian Talmud*, ed. I. Epstein, 35 vols. (London: Soncino Press, 1935), 2b, p. 4. The Persians "built the Temple" while the Romans destroyed it and the Persians "did not oppress Israel."

7. See W. O. E. Oesterley and T. H. Robinson, *Hebrew Religion: Its Origin and Development*, 2d rev. and enl. ed. (New York: Macmillan Co.; London: SPCK, 1937), pp. 344ff.

8. Against the apparent wishes of Antiochus III who issued a proclamation promising "all the members of the nation shall have a form of government in accordance with the laws of their country" and forbidding Gentiles and "unclean Jews" to enter the Temple. See Josephus *Antiquities* XII.138–48.

9. See F. Millar, "The Background to the Maccabean Revolution: Reflections on

Martin Hengel's 'Judaism and Hellenism,' " *JJS* 29 (1978): pp. 1–21, esp. pp. 13–14.

10. Compare *Pirke Aboth* 1.1 in C. Taylor, ed., *The Sayings of the Jewish Fathers* (Cambridge: At the University Press, 1897). The motto of the men of the Great Synagogue, "Be deliberate in judgment, raise up many disciples and build a barrier round Torah." For other examples of exclusive attitudes towards outsiders, see Ps. 147:19–20, and Bar. 6:4.

11. As when Simon captured Gazara, 1 Macc. 13:13–48, the "official" court line.

12. Josephus's admiration for John is shown by his summing up of his reign: "Now he was accounted by God worthy of three of the greatest privileges, the rule of the nation, the office of high-priest, and the gift of prophecy; for the Deity was with him and enabled him to foresee and foretell the future," *Antiquities* XIII.299. Note the association between the high priesthood and prophecy.

13. For John's political aims see Foerster, *Palestinian Judaism*, pp. 29–40. Josephus's account of John's conquests is given in *Antiquities* XIII.228–300.

14. Josephus *Antiquities* XIII.280 (Samaria).

15. Ibid., 318–19 (Iturea), and idem, *War* I.76 (Galilee).

16. Josephus *Antiquities* XIII.301, but see Marcus's (trans.) note, "The title 'king' (*melek*) does not appear on the Heb[rew] coins of Aristobulus" (p. 379). Strabo (XVI.2.40) attributes the innovation to Alexander Janneus.

17. See Neusner, *History of Jews in Babylonia, Part 1: The Parthian Period* (1969), pp. 25–26.

18. Josephus *Antiquities* XIII.395–97, for the area occupied by the Jews under Alexander Janneus.

19. Ibid., 397. Janneus had Pella demolished in consequence.

20. Ibid., 258, on Idumea.

21. Ibid., 163–65. Compare 1 Macc. 12:3.

22. Valerius Maximus 1.3.2; and, for Simon's embassy to Rome, see 1 Macc. 14:24. See Schürer—Vermès—Millar—Black, *History of Jewish People*, vol. 1, pp. 195–97.

23. 1 Macc. 14:24 and 15:15–24. For discussion see Schürer—Vermès—Millar—Black, *History of Jewish People*, pp. 195–96.

24. Josephus *Antiquities* XIV.185–86.

25. For Antipater's network of alliances among the Arab sheiks and with "the king of the Arabs," see ibid., 122. These alliances were important to Rome after Crassus's defeat by the Parthians in 53 B.C.

26. Ibid., 213–16 (Parium). The Jews are referred to explicitly as "our friends and allies."

27. Suetonius, *The Deified Julius*, Eng. trans. J. C. Rolfe (LCL, Cambridge, Mass.: Harvard University Press; London: William Heinemann, 1914), 84.5.

28. For a sketch of the political situation as it affected Herod, see S. G. F. Brandon, *Religion in Ancient History: Studies in Ideas, Men and Events* (London: George Allen & Unwin, 1973), chap. 18, and Schürer—Vermès—Millar—Black, *History of Jewish People*, pp. 275–86. Schürer dates the defeat of the Galilean rebels to 38 B.C.

29. While governor of Galilee Herod becomes pro-Roman. See Josephus *Antiquities* XIV.274.

30. See Jeremias, *Jerusalem*, pp. 21–25, on the construction of the Temple.

31. See C. T. Fritsch, ed., *The Joint Expedition to Caesarea Maritima*, Studies in the History of Caesarea Maritima I, ASOR, (Missoula, Mont.: Scholars Press, 1975), chap. 1, by Gideon Foerster.

32. For a list of Herod's benefactions extending from Tyre and Sidon on the Palestinian coast to Rhodes and Chios, see Reicke, *New Testament Era*, p. 101.

33. For a similar massacre in Judea by Ptolemy Lathyrus, in Janneus's reign, see Josephus *Antiquities* XIII.345–46.

34. See article by R. J. Bauckham, "The Great Tribulation in the Shepherd of Hermas," *JTS* n.s. 25 (1974): 27–40. The Qumran psalmist (like Hermas) seems to envisage "a period of cosmic distress which will both destroy the wicked and produce the eschatological community of the righteous" (p. 40). The six copies of the War Scroll found in Cave 4 seem to have been written in the first half of the first century A.D. See Maurice Baillet, ed., *Qumran Grotte Four, No. III*, Discoveries in the Judean Desert, vol. 7 (New York and London: Oxford University Press, 1982), 4Q482–4Q520.

35. See Lieberman, *Hellenism in Jewish Palestine*, pp. 100ff., and W. L. Knox, *Some Hellenistic Elements in Primitive Christianity* (New York: Oxford University Press, 1945; London: Oxford University Press, 1944), chap. 1; and Werblowsky, "Greek Wisdom." About one-third of inscriptions found in Palestine are in Greek (see Frey, *CIJ*, vol. I, Aramaic). For Aramaic as the normal language in Palestine at the time of Christ, see Emerton, "Problem of Vernacular Hebrew."

36. On the derivation of the name Sadducee from Zadok, see Moore, *Judaism*, vol. 1, pp. 68–69.

37. On three Jewish schools of thought, see Josephus *Antiquities* XIII.5.9.171–73.

38. On the Sadducees, see ibid., XIII.298.

39. The Sadducees held "that only those regulations should be considered valid which were written down [in Scripture]," ibid., 297.

40. See Moore, *Judaism*, vol. 1, pp. 66–68.

41. Ignatius *The Letter to the Philadelphians* VII.1, gift of "crying out in God's own voice." See over, p. 139.

42. Josephus *Antiquities* XIII.298. In contrast to the Sadducees, the Pharisees "have the support of the masses." Cf. XIII.401: in Janneus's reign they were said to have had "the complete confidence of the masses."

43. Josephus *War* I.110, on the Pharisees.

44. See W. H. C. Frend, *Martyrdom and Persecution in the Early Church: A Study of a Conflict from the Maccabees to Donatus* (Garden City, N.Y.: Doubleday Anchor Books, 1967; Oxford: Basil Blackwell & Mott, 1965), pp. 47–48, and Moore, *Judaism*, vol. 1, p. 59.

45. Josephus *Antiquities* XIII.408, and 400–401. Idem, *War* I.112, "But if she ruled the nation, the Pharisees ruled her."

46. *Pirke Aboth* III.19; see Moore, *Judaism*, vol. 1, chap. 4, pp. 263ff.

47. Josephus *War* I.650–53; idem, *Antiquities* XVII.159. For a similar attitude on the part of a Christian youth in Smyrna, c. 165, see Eusebius *HE* IV.15.5. See also G. Allon, "The Attitude of the Pharisees to the Roman Government and the House of Herod," *Scr. Hieros.* 7 (1961): 53–78.

48. Julian *Letter* 22. See over, p. 604.

49. Cited from Moore, *Judaism*, vol. 2, p. 171. Compare Josephus *Apion* II.29.

50. The ideal scribe is depicted by Sirach, a scholar widely traveled, rich in wisdom and understanding (Sir. 38:24—39:11): for his prestige, see Foerster, *Palestinian Judaism*, pp. 174–75.

51. See Foerster, *Palestinian Judaism*, pp. 169–74, and Jeremias, *Jerusalem*, pp. 233–45.

52. Cross, *Ancient Library of Qumran*, p. 37; Dupont-Sommer, *Les écrits esséniens*, chap. 2.

53. Cross, *Ancient Library of Qumran*, p. 43; and see also Milik, *Ten Years in Judaea*, pp. 51–52.

54. 1QS8, 13–15, taken from Gaster's translation, *Dead Sea Scriptures*, p. 65.

55. 1QS8, 12–13, Cross, *Ancient Library of Qumran*, p. 55.

56. Note 1QpHab 2:17, "The meaning of the city is 'Jerusalem,' where the Wicked Priest wrought abominations and defiled the sanctuary of God" (col. XII.7–9). Cited from Vermès, *Dead Sea Scrolls*, p. 242. Jerusalem priests as "plunderers of the peoples" (ibid., col. IX, Vermès, p. 240).

57. Yadin, *Masada*, pp. 172–74.

58. 4QpPs37 on Psalm 37:11, 21–22; see Gaster, *Dead Sea Scriptures*, pp. 244, 253. Note the statement in the Rule of the sect: "This is the rule of the men of the Community . . . that they separate from the men of perversion and become a community in doctrine and property" (1QS5, 1–2). Compare, of course, Acts 4:32 on the Jerusalem church. The Apostles, too, lived out of a common purse, entrusted to Judas (John 12:6 and 13:29).

59. See Cross, *Ancient Library of Qumran*, pp. 73–74, and Vermès, *Dead Sea Scrolls*, p. 30.

60. 1QS1, 2–4. See Gaster, *Dead Sea Scriptures*, p. 49.

61. See Black, *Scrolls and Christian Doctrine*, pp. 4–6; and K. G. Kuhn, "The Two Messiahs of Aaron and Israel," in Stendahl, *Scrolls and New Testament*, pp. 54–64.

62. See K. Stendahl's essay, "The Scrolls and the New Testament: An Introduction and a Perspective," in Stendahl, *Scrolls and New Testament*, pp. 1–17, and Gaster's comments, *Dead Sea Scriptures*, pp. 21–33.

63. Emphasized by Gaster, *Dead Sea Scriptures*, pp. 25–28.

64. 1QS6, 13–23.

65. 1QS6, 23–27 (Gaster, *Dead Sea Scriptures*, p. 61). Lying about one's wealth involved the loss of one-quarter of one's food ration for a year.

66. 1QS3, 13–14, 26 (Gaster, *Dead Sea Scriptures*, p. 53, and Cross, *Ancient Library of Qumran*, pp. 157–59). Cross compares the Qumran text with 1 John 3:7–19 and 4:1–6 (the Spirit of Truth versus the Spirit of Deceit).

67. 1QpHab 2.5–10. See Vermès, *Dead Sea Scrolls*, p. 236, and Cross, *Ancient Library of Qumran*, p. 83.

68. Cross's views, "We must now affirm that in the Essene communities we discover antecedents of Christian forms and concepts of eschatology," *Ancient Library of Qumran*, pp. 147ff.

69. See Jeremias, *Jerusalem*, pp. 74–75.

70. Ibid., pp. 31ff., "Commerce." For social strife in Palestine at this time, see Baron, *Social and Religious History of Jews*, vol. 1, pp. 276–80.

71. Neusner, *History of Jews in Babylonia, Part 1: Parthian* and note the reference to the Jewish population in Parthia in Philo *Embassy* 36.282.

72. Concerning Tyre, see *Genesis Rabba*, 77.2. in *Midrash Rabba*, ed. H. Freed-

man and Maurice Simon, 10 vols. (London: Soncino Press, 1939), p. 771. For Edessa, Jewish traders in fine raiment (silk?), see Cureton and Wright, eds., "The Teaching of Addaeus the Apostle," in ANCL, vol. XX, Syriac Documents, p. 23.

73. 2 Macc. 8:20, where they are, however, identified as Gaul/Galatians. See Neusner, *History of Jews in Babylonia*, p. 13.

74. Josephus *Antiquities* XII.147–53.

75. Philo's *Embassy* 36.282 speaks of Jews settled in fertile areas of Babylonia.

76. Neusner, *History of Jews in Babylonia*, pp. 47ff.

77. Ibid., pp. 48, 52–53.

78. See above, p. 19 and n. 16.

79. Josephus *Antiquities* XX.2–4.

80. Josephus *War* I.5; II.388, 520; IV.567; V.474; VI.356. King Agrippa tried to dissuade the Jews from rebelling by telling them that the Parthians would not allow the Jews of Adiabene to intervene significantly.

81. Neusner, *History of Jews in Babylonia*, pp. 63–64.

82. Josephus *War* II.520.

83. For Jews in the Crimea, see E. Schürer, SAB (1897): 204–25. Also A. D. Nock, *Conversion: The Old and the New in Religion from Alexander the Great to Augustine of Hippo* (New York and London: Oxford University Press, 1933), pp. 63–64 (syncretistic tendencies among these Jews).

84. For Carthage and North Africa in general, see P. Monceaux, *Histoire littéraire de l'Afrique chrétienne depuis les origines jusqu'à l'invasion arabe,* 7 vols. (Paris: Leroux, 1902), vol. 1, pp. 8–9; and Frend, "Jews and Christians in Third Century Carthage," in *Paganisme, Judaïsme, Christianisme*, pp. 185–94.

85. Strabo, cf. Josephus *Antiquities* XIV.115; and compare Philo *Embassy* 36.281–82, and Acts 2:9–11.

86. 4 Macc. 1.1; the Dispersion Jews were regarded as hostile to their Gentile neighbors. (See instances given by Frend in *Martyrdom and Persecution*, chap. 5). Philo himself had no sympathy for Greek "incomers" in Jamnia, *Embassy* 30.200–202.

87. See Dinkler, *Eirene*, for Jewish and Christian use of the *In pace* formula.

88. For the lugubrious nature of Judaism, see Tertullian *De Jejunio Adversus Psychicos (On Fasting)* 16, and later, Rutilius Namatianus *De Reditu* 1.383–98. For its "fussiness," see *The Letter to Diognetus* IV.6 (mid–second century A.D.).

89. Philo *Embassy* 36.281 (put into the mouth of Agrippa). Jerusalem was capital not only of Judea, but of "most other countries also," wherever there were Jews.

90. For a discussion of how the cults of Sabazios and Theos Hypsistos provided scope for Jewish tendencies towards syncretism with pagan cults, see A. D. Nock, C. Roberts, and T. C. Skeat, "The Gild of Zeus Hypsistos," *HTR* 29 (1936): 39–87; M. Simon, "Theos Hypsistos"; and Kraabel, "Paganism and Judaism," pp. 25–32.

91. I have followed Smallwood's description, Philo *Embassy*, Introd., pp. 5–7. For "genarch," see Philo *In Flaccum (Against Flaccus)* 74.

92. Thus, H. Chadwick, "The history of Christian philosophy begins not with a Christian, but with a Jew, Philo of Alexandria," "Philo," p. 137.

93. See H. Chadwick's account, "Philo," and other valuable comments in *Early Christian Thought and the Classical Tradition: Studies in Justin, Clement, and Origen* (New York and London; Oxford University Press, 1966), pp. 6–7, 44–46.

94. Philo on Augustus, see *Embassy* 21.143–44. Compare Plutarch *On the For-*

tune of Alexander 1.329a and 330d, where Plutarch describes Alexander "wishing to make the earth obedient to one law of reason (*Logos*) and to show that all men are one people under one polity." See also Peterson, *Der Monotheismus*, p. 78.

95. Philo *Embassy* 1.3.

96. Thus, Philo *De Specialibus Legibus* (*On the Special Laws*) 1.309; idem, *Ruth* 2.12; idem, *De Praemiis et Poenis* (*On Rewards and Punishments*) 152; idem, *De Migratione Abrahami* (*On the Migration of Abraham*) 18.201.

97. See M. Wolter, "Bekehrung I," *TRE* 5.3 (Berlin, 1980), p. 443.

98. See *De Opificio Mundi* (*On the Creation*) 8.12.131; and Colson, ed., *Quod Omnis Probus Liber Sit* (*Every Good Man Is Free*), LCL, 57 (Zeno borrows "from the law book of the Jews"). For a survey of the material, see K. Thraede, *RAC*, s.v. "Erfinder II."

99. Philo *Embassy* 31.215.

100. Ibid., 29.192.

101. For Egyptian resentment against the Jews, see Philo *Flaccus* 29, and for Jewish reputation for taking vengeance on backsliders and apostates, see 3 Macc. 7:10, and Tcherikover, "Third Book of Maccabees," p. 23.

102. Claudius's letter to the Alexandrians (*Pap. Lond.,* 1912), publ. by Bell, ed., *Jews and Christians in Egypt*, pp. 1–37.

103. Philo *Flaccus* 43.

104. Cf. Josephus *Antiquities* XIV.115.

105. Appelbaum, "Jewish Community," p. 30. Most of the inscriptions appear to be first century A.D.

106. Appelbaum, "Jewish Community," pp. 40–42.

107. Ibid., p. 47. For a *politeuma* at Berenice (Benghazi), *CIG* 5361.

108. Appelbaum, "Jewish Community," p. 43.

109. Josephus *War* VII.437–50. Also, an instance in the Dispersion of messianic expectations in the wilderness, combined with anti-Roman apocalypticism.

110. Tacitus *Histories* 5.5.3, "contemnere deos, exuere patriam, parentes, liberos, fratres vilia habere." For "cold war" between Jews and Greeks in Cyrenaica preceding the revolt of 115, see Appelbaum, *Jews and Greeks*, p. 240.

111. Lucian *De Morte Peregrini* (*On the Death of Peregrinus*) 13. See over, p. 176.

112. Cicero *Pro Flacco* (*On Behalf of Flaccus*) 28.67, and compare Philo *Embassy* 23.156.

113. Josephus *Antiquities* XVI.171. Cf. Philo *Embassy* 40.315 for a similar letter of Norbanus to Ephesus, dating perhaps to Augustus's reign. (See Smallwood for discussion, *Embassy*, pp. 309–10).

114. Note also the prayer written in Hebrew "for the peace of Jerusalem and Israel to the end of time," from the door of a Jewish place of worship at Acmonia, MAMA VI.334.

115. The translation of the inscription runs, "Place of the Jews who are also [called] God-fearers." See Adolf Deissmann, *Light from the Ancient East: The New Testament Illustrated by Recently Discovered Texts of the Graeco-Roman World,* Eng. trans. L. R. M. Strachan, rev. ed. (Garden City, N.Y.: Doubleday, Doran & Co.; London: Hodder & Stoughton, 1927), pp. 451–52.

116. See Kraabel's excellently documented account of the growth of the Jewish community in Sardis, "Paganism and Judaism."

117. Ibid., pp. 20–21. "Proximity appears to have produced clarity, and the enjoyment of a gentile culture did not automatically produce 'capitulation' to paganism," p. 32.

118. Ibid., p. 24, citing inscriptions from the synagogue. Yet Sardis also had its imperial cult, dedications to Cybele, and two gymnasia.

119. See over, chap. 14.

120. See W. M. Ramsay, "Anatolica quaedam," *JHS* 50 (1930): 263–87.

121. *CIL* III.293–94, 6824–48. See also L. J. F. Keppie, "Vexilla Veteranorum," *PBSR* 43 (1973): 13; and W. M. Calder, "Colonia Caesareia Antiocheia," *JRS* 2 (1912): 79–109.

122. Alexandra Kryzanowska, *Monnaies coloniales d'Antioche de Pisidie* (Warsaw: Travaux du Centre d'archéologie méditerranéenne de l'Académie polonaise des sciences, 1970), vol. 7, pp. 117–20 and Pl.30, a good survey of the evidence.

123. Ibid., p. 16.

124. Acmonia; see L. Robert, *Hellenica* X (1955): 249–53, and A. R. R. Sheppard, "Jews, Christians and Heretics in Acmonia and Eumeneia," *Anatolian Studies* 29 (1979): 169–80.

125. Though the Jews were obviously articulate enough to demand these decrees, their tenor is protective of minority rights rather than symbols of Jewish self-confidence (as suggested by Kraabel, "Paganism and Judaism," pp. 21ff.).

126. Josephus *Antiquities* XIV.185–267.

127. Ibid., 262–64, 259–61 (Sardis); ibid., 228–29 (Ephesus). For Jews in Ephesus, see also idem, *Apion* II.39, and Acts 19.

128. Josephus *Apion* II.6.6.

129. "The majority [of the Jews] were Roman freedmen." They had been brought to Italy as prisoners of war and manumitted by their owners. Philo *Embassy* 23.155. The standard work is Leon, *Jews of Ancient Rome*.

130. Josephus *Antiquities* XVII.300–301, and idem, *War* II.80.

131. For "Augustesi," six inscriptions, see Leon, *Jews of Ancient Rome*, p. 142; and cf. Philo *Embassy* 22.151 (similar synagogue in Alexandria).

132. Cicero *Flaccus* 28.69; see also Frend, *Martyrdom and Persecution*, chap. 5, pp. 139–41.

133. Tacitus *Annals* II.85.4; Josephus *Antiquities* XVIII.81–84; and Suetonius *Tiberius* 36.

134. On Antioch, see Josephus *War* VII.43–53.

135. Josephus *Apion* II.28.210 and 38.282; at Damascus, where in 66 the wives of most of anti-Jewish leaders were themselves proselytes; idem, *War* II.560. For proselytes in Rome, see Leon, *Jews of Ancient Rome*, pp. 254–56.

136. Thus, Tarfon cited in *Pirke Aboth* 2.19–20. See S. Ochser, *Jewish Encyclopedia*, s.v. "Tarfon"; and for more detail, J. Neusner, "A Life of Rabbi Tarfon, ca. 50–130 C.E.," *Judaica* 17 (1961): 141–67.

2

Jesus of Nazareth

It was into this unquiet Jewish-Greco-Roman world that Jesus of Nazareth was born in Bethlehem near the end of Herod's reign, about 6 B.C. Many aspects of his life can be interpreted only in the light of faith, but questions relating to his teaching as it is recorded in the Gospels, and the effect of that teaching on his contemporaries and on later generations, challenge the historian. Phrases such as "the Fatherhood of God" and "the brotherhood of man" have become trite through familiarity, but they were not trite when Jesus preached them. The God of Israel was feared as a "jealous God," and his wrath could smite his own people as well as their enemies. For Jesus, however, God was not only Lord, but a loving Father to be approached through prayer, through action and, above all, through submission to his will. God was not only the God of Israel and Creator of the universe, but one to be understood; in Paul's words, "God has sent the Spirit of his Son into our hearts, crying, 'Abba! Father!' " (Gal. 4:6). All believers could become "sons of your Father who is in heaven" (Matt. 5:45). The kingdom of heaven was seen in terms of a family with "little children" as the true members. The command also to "love your neighbor as yourself," though set down in Leviticus (19:18), for the congregation of Israel was given a new and universal application. Few if any Jews of Jesus' time would have included Samaritans among neighbors to be loved. Yet no one who read the Parable of the Good Samaritan could henceforth regard them otherwise. The lessons of mutual support, respect, and help taught by Jesus were to be among the hallmarks of his followers in the first centuries of the church. "See how they love one another" (Tertullian *Apology* 39) was a pagan, not a Christian observation.

Jesus' strongly individual and uncompromising teaching, however, made less impact than one might expect on the attitudes of his followers—before the rise of the monastic movement in the late third century. His utterances were collected by Christian communities so that these might direct their lives, although except in Aramaic-speaking eastern Syria their literal sense was removed from daily practice. The early Christian communities established in the cities of western Asia Minor and Greece accepted the interpretation put on them by "the good apostle Paul," and modeled their ethic on that of Jesus' Pharisaic opponents as set out in the Wisdom and other intertestamental literature.[1] If by dying Jesus renewed the Jewish ideal of the martyr-prophet and inspired his followers to imitate him, the crucifixion did not signal the onset of the last times as the disciples believed it would (Acts 2:16–17). The eschatological message, however, was not lost. Confessors of the first two centuries saw Jesus as "the true and faithful martyr," an assurance of the approaching end and of their own triumph;[2] by Rabbi Gamaliel's test (Acts 5:35–39) he was indeed "of God."

The cross was the culmination of Jesus' mission. The prophet had died in Jerusalem, but by contemporary standards that mission had failed. Jesus' final utterance, the despairing first verse of Psalm 22, was remembered and recorded in the Gospels. Why, then, was he accepted as unique? Unless he had been so regarded in his lifetime, the Easter story could not have come into being. The answer must lie in Jesus' personality alone. Its effect on those who heard him, as recorded by the Evangelists (especially Matthew, Mark, and Luke), was remarkable. He spoke "as one who had authority" and not (for example, by quoting precedents) as the scribes (Mark 1:22).[3] His word was "with authority" (Luke 4:32). "Elijah" or "John the Baptist" returned to earth was how his secular ruler Herod Antipas viewed him (Mark 6:14–16//Luke 9:7–9).[4] For the Galileans, he was "the prophet," foreshadowed in Deut. 18:15, greater than David and foretold by a succession of prophets. Such was Peter's interpretation of his life (Acts 2:34, 3:22), and thus he was in the eyes of those who heard him and experienced his cures (cf. John 9:17). "Even wind and sea obey him" (Mark 4:41), it was said. Whatever else may or may not be true, vivid memories of his words and work survived in Galilee long after the crucifixion.[5]

In their final form the Gospels are works reflecting the faith and attitudes of Christian communities some two generations after the crucifixion.[6] Their writers were concerned with "the gospel of Jesus Christ, the Son of God" (Mark 1:1) and not with historical biography. The story they tell, however, can hardly relate to a situation other than Palestine in the first half of the first century A.D. and to an individual who lived in those times. It was the period of Roman "direct rule," which even the Pharisees had at first preferred to that of Herod's descendants. The Romans themselves looked back to the reign of Tiberius (14–37) in which Jesus' ministry took place as one in which Palestine was quiet.[7] The Gospels leave the impression of the unstable equilibrium on which that quiet rested. Personal relations between Jew and Roman could be tolerably good (Luke 7:1ff.). If tribute to Rome was resented, Jesus' oblique answer to the searching question concerning it raised no immediate outcry. On the other hand, there was mutual fear and distrust. Occasional ugly incidents showed how menacing was the underlying situation. Brigandage was always in evidence. Barabbas was a "notorious prisoner" (Matt. 27:16) and those crucified with Jesus had been condemned as "robbers" and "murderers." Barabbas himself was named as one "who had committed murder in the insurrection" (Mark 15:7). It was remembered how Pontius Pilate, the prefect of Judea, had mingled the blood of the Galileans with their sacrifices (Luke 13:1). Messianism could not be taken lightly.

The Gospels also reveal many details of the social life of the time which can be confirmed from Josephus. They indicate, as he does, the relative prosperity of the fishing communities on the Sea of Galilee, with their family partnerships served by employees, the role of the Pharisees as roving guardians of orthodoxy, and the undercurrent of hostility against all non-Jews. No tears were shed for the Syrian landowners ruined by the destruction of their herds of pigs at Gadara (Mark 5:13–17). There is the overwhelming influence of the Temple represented by the constant round of journeys to and from Jerusalem to keep the feasts there. Local disasters like the fall of the tower of Siloam (Luke 13:4) are chronicled as though they were well-known facts. On the other hand, no tradition originating after the fall of Jerusalem in 70 would have recorded the position of Pilate's judgment seat (John 19:13), for the whole area in which the drama took place would have been buried under mounds of blackened debris. As for Jesus himself, we cannot agree with critics who reject the possibility of reconstructing the outlines of his personality and work.[8] Even without the additional information derived from the *Gospel of Thomas*[9] and Jesus' sayings recorded in sources other than the Gospels (that is, *agrapha*), and the comparison provided by the beliefs of the Dead Sea Covenanters, one would accept the view of C. H. Dodd, "The Synoptic writers give us a body of [his] sayings so coherent, and withal so distinctive in style, manner and content, that no reasonable critic could doubt that whatever reservations he might have about individual Sayings, we find reflected here the thought of a single, unique Teacher."[10]

Galilee, where Jesus grew up, was extraordinary even in terms of the patchwork of petty kingdoms and provinces composing the Roman east. It was essentially Jewish settler territory. It had been conquered by Aristobulus in his short and violent reign (104–103 B.C.) and had attracted an influx of Jewish families during the next century. In the resulting mixed population, tensions were never far absent. The Jews, once a threatened minority who had to be evacuated in time of crisis (1 Macc. 5:14–23), were now predominant and occupied the most fertile areas, such as the Plain of Esdraelon on the southern boundary with Samaria. Non-Jews remained numerous in some towns, such as Sepphoris (never mentioned in the Gospels, though barely five miles from Nazareth), while eastward across the Sea of Galilee the country was still known as "Galilee of the Gentiles" (Matt. 4:15).

Living in daily contact with people whom they once feared but now despised, the Galilean Jews had acquired something of a colonial outlook. They impressed contemporaries with their uncompromising and truculent nationalism combined with an execrable pronunciation of Aramaic.[11] They despised the Jews of Judea and their feelings were reciprocated. They also hated their Samaritan neighbors and were hated by them.[12] James and John, two of Jesus' leading disciples, thought that consumption by fire from heaven was no bad way to deal with inhospitable Samaritan villagers (Luke 9:52–54). On the other hand, few doubted the valor of the Galileans in the cause of Judaism. They were men "inured to war," and "always resisted any hostile invasion," according to Josephus.[13] The revolutionary tradition in the north of the country extended back to the days of Hezekiah's insurrection of the 40s B.C. On Hezekiah's execution by Herod, his son Judas took over his role, "an object of terror to all men," raiding Herod Antipas's capital Sepphoris in 4 B.C.,[14] and leading the bloody but futile revolt against the Roman census of A.D. 6.[15] Such were the inhabitants of this, the richest, most populous, but least stable part of Palestine, and when the great revolt broke out in 66, the Galileans were in the forefront.[16]

Jesus' family were apparently recent immigrants into Galilee. The census of 6 B.C., by whomsoever called, obliged them to travel south from Nazareth to Bethlehem to be registered in Joseph's home village.[17] Both Matthew and Luke trace Jesus' descent through Joseph back to Judah and David, not only an exclusively Jewish heritage but one which, as we learn from Zech. 12:12, was of a type carefully preserved by its possessors. Jesus was never taunted with being a "Galilean," and his family occupied a prominent place in the community. Joseph, even if "carpenter" is meant literally (and not as a synonym for a "learned man"),[18] would have been the provider of most of the technical wants of an agricultural locality. The family did not fare badly and seems to have had property in Capernaum as well as Nazareth. Mary's cousin Elizabeth is said by Luke to have been "of the daughters of Aaron" (1:5), that is, of priestly descent, and she was married to one of the Temple priests who took his turn of duty in Jerusalem. Mary and Elizabeth were firm friends, and Mary's first thoughts on conceiving Jesus were to undertake the long journey—presumably in some comfort—into Judea to break the good news to her (Luke 1:39–43). Jesus came therefore from a solid Jewish background in an area where the frontier with heathendom was an ever-present reality.

It is impossible to think of Jesus apart from Galilee. If as a child he "increased in wisdom and in stature" (Luke 2:52), he must also have appreciated events around him. His whole life was spent as the subject of Herod Antipas. The latter had been appointed tetrarch by Augustus as part of the settlement of the rival claims among Herod's heirs in 4 B.C. His long reign lasted until A.D. 39. Galilee was, therefore, not directly affected by the drastic change which took place in the remainder of Judea in A.D. 6. Archelaus, Herod's eldest son, had proved insufferable as a ruler, and Augustus, yielding to pressure from the Jews, stripped him of his title of ethnarch and exiled him to Gaul. His territories were organized as a Roman province with Caesarea as its capital. The first governor (*procurator*) entered on his duties at the same time as his superior, Publius Sulpicius Quirinius, became legate of Syria. Another census was taken; this time perhaps to assess the inhabitants of the new province for the poll tax. The repercussions were profound. The veteran insurgent Judas the Gaulonite raised the standard of revolt, claiming that the Jews owed service to God alone. His bid was for outright independence and he himself seems to have aspired to royal power. The insurrection which Josephus saw as marking the beginning of the Zealot movement is described by him in terms of Pharisaic extremism. It was crushed mercilessly.[19] As a boy of thirteen or fourteen, Jesus could hardly have avoided hearing of the deeds and dreadful end of the Galilean hero. Armed resistance to Rome was hopeless. He who took the sword would perish by the sword.

Others, however, drew different conclusions. Men of zeal, whether formally "Zealots" or not, delved into Israel's past determined to imitate the deeds of Phinehas (Numbers 25). Galilee had its share of such men. Simon "the Zealot" became one of Jesus' disciples.[20] The sons of Zebedee were Zealots at heart if not in name. How his own family stood in these years cannot be known. Luke, however, writes of a strongly religious household observing scrupulously the round of family and national feasts that characterized post-Maccabean Judaism. The household grew. Jesus had four brothers—James (Jacob), Joses, Judah, and Simon—and sisters (Mark 6:3). Judah and Simon bore good nationalist names. Jesus himself is recorded as sharing some of the Galilean distaste for Gentiles, their exaggerated manner of prayer (Matt. 6:7), and their rulers with their hypocritical claims to be "benefactors" (Luke 22:25). Only gradually does he accept that the Gentiles would be coheirs to the kingdom. Meantime, his education had been careful and thorough.[21] He succeeded brilliantly at his examination in the Law preceding his *bar mitzvah* (Son of the Law). Already he felt the call of his "Father's house" (Luke 2:49). Jerusalem and the Temple beckoned. Elsewhere, Luke records his ability to read and comment on Scripture, and implies that his sermon at Nazareth (Luke 4:16) was not his first.

Whatever was maturing in his mind along with his deep religious sense, it included compassion for the sufferings of others, a desire to champion them even to the extent of opposing the traditional leaders of Jewish opinion, a love of the Palestinian countryside and its natural beauties, and above all a sense, perhaps derived from meditation on the Psalms and Second Isaiah, of some special mission assigned to him by his Father. In some way, the Remnant would be embodied in himself.

BAPTISM

The silence of the "hidden years" was broken, perhaps in A.D. 26, by the sudden emergence of Jesus' cousin John as a preacher in the tradition of the great individualistic prophets of Judaism. The suggestion that John's message and way of life may have owed something to a connection with the Dead Sea Covenanters is not unreasonable.[22] John's parents were old. The Covenanters are known to have adopted children and also to have had a following among priestly families. One would have expected John to have followed his father's vocation but he did not, and the wilderness to which he was committed (Luke 1:80) may have been Qumran. He must have left the sect, however, before he emerged suddenly as a wild-looking and ascetic figure, a lonely but fearsome prophet proclaiming the imminent and catastrophic end of the existing age and calling on the people of God to

58

repent and be baptized before it was too late. Thus, Matthew's version reads, "In those days came John the Baptist, preaching in the wilderness of Judea, 'Repent, for the kingdom of heaven is at hand.' . . . 'Even now the axe is laid to the root of the trees; every tree therefore that does not bear good fruit is cut down and thrown into the fire' " (3:1–2, 10).

John had chosen Bethany "east of the Jordan," the country where Elijah had dwelt (1 Kings 17:5), to proclaim a baptism of repentance and forgiveness (Luke 3:3; compare John 1:28), a special act to meet a special situation (just as Jonah had described how the men of Nineveh "proclaimed a fast" [3:5]). His mission is one of the best attested in the Gospel story, appearing in very similar form in all four Gospels as well as in Josephus's *Antiquities*,[23] and the Jewish-Christian *Gospel of the Ebionites*. John, however, was by no means unique in first-century Palestine. Josephus himself describes how he became a devoted disciple of one, Bannus (c. 57) "who dwelt in the wilderness, wearing only such clothing as trees provided, and feeding on such things as grew of themselves, and using frequent ablutions of cold water, by day and night, for purity's sake."[24] The way of life and the purificatory ablutions are the same, but John's message was urgent and compelling. Purification would precede the coming of the end. Tradition records him fulfilling almost point by point Malachi chapter 3. His words sounded relevant enough to the religious leaders in Jerusalem for them to send a delegation of high priests and Pharisees to visit him and inquire whether he was indeed Elijah, who would be sent "before the great and terrible day of the Lord comes" (Mal. 4:5).

John's severity ("You brood of vipers! Who warned you to flee from the wrath to come?" [Matt. 3:7]) to his distinguished hearers is reminiscent of the scorn for Jerusalem and all it stood for felt by the followers of the Teacher of Righteousness. The wilderness prophet had little use for the religious leaders of the Jewish nation of his day. His concern was with the true Israelites (John 1:47) who repented sincerely and would be prepared to receive the true baptism by the one "mightier than I" (Luke 3:16). He would baptize with "the Holy Spirit" and with fire, and his purge would be thorough and drastic. The tree that failed to produce good fruit or those who turned out to be chaff would be consumed "with unquenchable fire" (Matt. 3:12).

In contrast, however, to other messianic prophets, John neither foretold cataclysmic signs of the end nor advocated political revolution. His requirements were moderate. Luke 3:10–14 preserves a fragment of his social teaching. Tax gatherers—persons unclean by Pharisaic standards—were accepted for baptism with the admonishment, "Collect no more than is appointed you." And to soldiers who were among the crowds he merely said, "Rob no one by violence or by false accusation, and be content with your wages." To all he urged a general sharing of wealth: "He who has two coats, let him share with him who has none; and he who has food, let him do likewise." John accepted the current political order. Any vengeance would be the Lord's.

Did John have Jesus in mind as he preached? It is not certain.[25] Mark's account (1:9–11) does not suggest it. John's words were directed at Judea and Jerusalem. Jesus was far away in Galilee and was not among the first Galileans to travel to Bethany. Andrew, his brother Simon Peter, and Philip, whose homes were at Bethsaida on the shores of the Sea of Galilee, had already become John's disciples when Jesus arrived (John 1:40–43). Why had he come? Was it to demonstrate a solidarity with sinners or his own submission to his Father's will?[26] One doubts a purely theological explanation. Had Jesus already been sure of the nature of his mission he would hardly have felt the need of accepting his cousin's baptism. But feel it he did. He made the long journey from Nazareth to Bethany alone and submitted to a rite which most contemporaries assumed to be one of purification.[27]

As he rose from the waters, he experienced what may legitimately be termed his call. The incident is recorded in all the earliest traditions.[28] The opening of the heavens, descent of the dove (the traditional bearer of a divine message as, for instance, in Gen. 8:8ff.), and the voice uttering words reminiscent of Isa. 42:1 ("Behold my servant, whom I uphold, my chosen, in whom my soul delights; I have put my Spirit upon him")[29] as Jesus came out of the water all show that the Evangelists and their sources attributed the highest importance to these events. Isa. 42:1 had a messianic significance. At least from now on Jesus felt himself to be in some way God's chosen instrument in an age in which God was speaking once more to his people.

TEMPTATIONS

What happened next? Not for the last time the synoptic (Matthew, Mark, Luke) and the Fourth Gospels give different and incompatible versions of events. Mark pushes the narrative on at breakneck speed. Immediately afterwards (*euthus*) the Spirit sends Jesus into the wilderness to be tempted (Mark 1:12–13), and he does not place his return to Galilee until after John's arrest. Matthew and Luke follow Jesus' baptism with the temptations, but with less urgency. The Fourth Gospel tells a different story. Jesus stays two days in the neighborhood of Bethany. His baptism is inferred rather than described. He is recognized by John on the afternoon of the first day as "the Lamb of God" (John 1:29) and calls Andrew and Simon Peter as his disciples. Before leaving for Galilee he also summons Philip and convinces a skeptical Nathanael that good things could come out of Nazareth after all.[30] The Gospel writer closes the passage with an assertion by Jesus: "Truly, truly, I say to you, you will see heaven opened, and the angels of God ascending and descending upon the Son of man" (John

1:51)—a reminiscence of Jacob's dream (Gen. 28:12). There are no temptations. The next incident is the wedding at Cana.

Here the synoptic order is accepted though the scene is more likely to be the Judean wilderness rather than near the fertile and populous lands of Galilee. Profound self-examination, alone and fasting, would be an expected sequel to the experience of the purificatory baptism. Fasting, as Josephus indicates, was related to expiation of sin and to atonement.[31] The first three Evangelists seem to have in mind a comparison between the travails of Israel in the wilderness and those of Jesus, for in the first and third temptations (Lukan version) quotations from Deut. 8:3 and 6:16 are put into Jesus' mouth. But however schematic, there is no reason to suppose that Jesus did not feel the temptations as recorded.[32] To break his fast by a wonderworking act would have placed him on a level with other Galilean magicians or with the Samaritan leader Simon Magus. It would have been abuse of his gifts, a failure to trust and obey God.[33] The second trial was more significant. The temptation to assume the role of a Galilean Judas Maccabeus must have been strong. Moreover, if judgment was to be exercised on the Gentiles (cf. Isa. 42:1), how else than by conquest? Was not Jesus greater than the Hasmonean priest-kings? Would it not fall to him to fulfill the prophecy in Zech. 14:9, "The Lord will become king over all the earth"? Had not his mother been told by the angel that he would be king over Israel forever (Luke 1:33)? How else would Israel be redeemed except by the reassertion of royal power? Nationalism forms the permanent background to Jesus' ministry. His disciples never freed themselves from it. "King of Israel" came readily to their lips (John 1:49), but Jesus rejected earthly kingship absolutely (cf. John 6:15). The third temptation, to display miraculous power in Jerusalem itself from "the pinnacle of the Temple," was regarded by Luke as an even-greater test. Perhaps at the outset of his ministry Jesus saw that it would be in Jerusalem and not the wilderness that the kingdom must come. How then would God's power be displayed? He did not share his cousin's evident hostility to Jerusalem and the Jewish leaders. The Temple itself was his "Father's house" (Luke 2:49) where his name dwelt (Deut. 12:21).

JESUS AND JOHN

On the other hand, the Fourth Gospel's account of Jesus' association with John before he began the Galilean mission is not to be dismissed.[34] Times and places are mentioned which could have no conceivable theological interest. The writer previously had Jesus returning to Galilee, not to begin his mission as Luke would have his readers believe (Luke 4:14), but to accompany his mother and family to a wedding feast at Cana (John 2:1–11). There, whatever the precise translation of his rebuke to Mary (John 2:4), he was in a profoundly introspective mood and uncertain of the future. Though he had disciples with him, his "hour had not yet come," and he went on with his family to their new home at Capernaum. It was the last recorded family reunion,[35] for shortly thereafter Jesus left finally to go up to Jerusalem for the Passover, and then to cooperate with John in a new baptismal mission in Judea (John 3:22—4:3). This phase must have lasted several months for Jesus returned to Galilee via Samaria[36] in January–February A.D. 28 ("There are yet four months, then comes the harvest" [John 4:35]). It is noticeable, too, that no miracles and no teaching were recorded. The work was purificatory, the baptisms being carried out by Jesus' disciples (John 4:2), and Jesus' reputation rising gradually at the expense of that of his cousin. John's reported statement, "No one can receive anything except what is given him from heaven. You yourselves bear me witness, that I said, I am not the Christ, but I have been sent before him" (3:27–28) sounds like a natural tribute to one that was greater than he.

Why did they separate?[37] Luke gives a hint of the differences of outlook which led to Jesus' return to Galilee. Pharisees pointed out that John's disciples fasted and prayed often, but Jesus did not (Luke 5:33–34). Jesus' reported reply—that it was unreasonable for the bridegroom's friends to fast while the bridegroom was with them, there would be time enough for fasting later—suggests a different approach from John's. Jesus did not dress nor act like an ascetic prophet.[38] He had been at Cana ensuring that the wedding feast was a success, and would be dining with Pharisees and rulers of synagogues. He would be attacked as "a glutton and a drunkard" (Luke 7:34) as well as a friend of notorious sinners. Moreover, while he believed that God's kingdom was approaching and saw the need for ritual preparation for this event, he was opposed to anything that looked like forceful assistance from below. His reported statement, that "from the days of John the Baptist until now the kingdom of heaven has suffered violence, and men of violence take it by force" (Matt. 11:12), was a criticism of the fevered emotions John had stirred by his preaching. John's fault was impassioned impatience and for this he was to be regarded as "the least in the kingdom of heaven," if he ever reached it at all. On John's side, too, there were doubts. He could not divorce denunciation of wickedness from denunciation of the individual wicked, however highly placed. Herod Antipas reacted to his criticism of his marriage, and John was imprisoned in the Machaerus fort in the extreme southeast of Antipas's dominions. He was becoming politically dangerous. From prison he sent disciples to Jesus in Galilee asking for reassurance. Jesus' reply that the blind received their sight and lepers were cleansed (Luke 7:18–23//Matt. 11:2–6) showed how he intended the battle against Satan's kingdom to be carried out in a way different from John's.

After some months, Jesus may have realized that the baptismal mission had served its purpose. Notice had been given of great events ahead. The lost sheep of the house of Israel must now be sought and saved. This involved return out of the wilderness areas to his native Galilee. The episode on his way through Samaria in which he spoke not only to a Samaritan, but a Samaritan woman (John 4:4ff.), showed how extraordinary the new mission was to be.

THE GALILEAN MISSION A.D. 28–29

Its opening phase was as dramatic as John's only two years before. "What is this? A new teaching! With authority he commands even the unclean spirits, and they obey him" (Mark 1:27). In fact, Jesus was starting where John had left off, only with an even-greater urgency. John had preached repentance to prepare for the coming of the kingdom. Jesus preached its imminent arrival. "The time is fulfilled, and the kingdom of God is at hand; repent, and believe in the gospel" (Mark 1:15).[39] The hour had struck, yet the event would not be marked by doom and destruction. To Jesus, the kingdom implied some supernatural event, the coming of the Son of man, but also the active rule of God, the implanting of his sovereignty in the hearts and minds of people now, not their hearers' consignment to the fire in the future. Eschatology, the concern for the end time, always included "realized eschatology."[40] The figure of the bridegroom was one of joy not doom.

Jesus, however, was building on John's foundation in other ways. Three of his disciples—Andrew, Peter, and Philip—had already been with the Baptist. The others who made up the Twelve were chosen slowly and with deliberation as likely to become "fishers of men" (Mark 1:17). John's relations with his disciples, so far as one can see, had been as friend and mentor without the formalism of a rabbinic regime.[41] Jesus' disciples also were his companions and, more specifically than John's, a group of healers and teachers (Mark 3:14–15), sent out with instructions on how to live and what to say. Matthew preserves a tradition of how they were told to go into Israel and proclaim fearlessly the coming of the kingdom (Matt. 10:7). Whatever happened they must go on, for so close was the event that they would "not have gone through all the towns of Israel, before the Son of man comes" (Matt. 10:23). Samaritans and Gentiles would have to be left to God's mercy (Matt. 10:5).

Meantime, Mark emphasizes the all-out character of Jesus' attack on Satan's kingdom.[42] The Galilean ministry was a ministry of healing and preaching. Sickness was the most obvious sign of Satan's activity (cf. Luke 13:16), and hence Jesus' first miracles were miracles of healing. As in the days of Elijah, the sick were healed and lepers cleansed. Jesus "went throughout all Galilee, preaching in their synagogues and casting out demons (Mark 1:39). The latter acknowledged defeat.

He did not court conflict with the religious authorities. A leper who had been cleansed was told to "go, show yourself to the priest, and offer for your cleansing what Moses commanded, for a proof to the people" (Mark 1:44//Matt. 8:4). Dispute arose, however, through the urgency Jesus attached to his work and the authority he claimed for himself. Given the alternative of observing the Sabbath and restoring a man's withered hand, Jesus unhesitatingly chose the latter,[43] and incurred the ire of both Pharisees and Herodians (Mark 3:1–6). Another time, his healing of a paralytic with the words, "My son, your sins are forgiven" (Mark 2:5), seemed to contradict the statement by the prophet Micah (Mic. 7:18) that God alone could forgive sins.

What brought the Pharisees and Herodians into uneasy coalition, however, was the probable effect of Jesus' words and actions on public opinion. "The ordinary people" heard him gladly (Mark 12:37; compare 1:33, 45; 2:2, 13; 3:7–12; 4:1), and there can be little doubt that he raised expectations (Luke 10:23). Mighty events, "greater than Solomon, greater than Jonah," were in the offing, and in the current mood of the people this could only lead to some violent eruption in which Antipas and Pharisaism itself could be swept away. As the Covenanters were showing, there were far too many people in Israel with vague but melodramatic ideas about the future. But what chance had they against Rome? Would Jesus succeed where Judas the Gaulonite had failed?

At this stage, however, Jesus was acting within the limits of Jewish prophetic tradition. That he was conscious of the latter becomes clear from the story told by Luke, and repeated in less detail in Matt. 13:54–58 and Mark 6:1–6. It records the one serious reverse Jesus suffered in Galilee near the outset of his ministry.[44] He had begun in Capernaum (Mark 1:21), but was returning to Nazareth where he had been brought up and his family had lived for many years. His fame preceded him. Mighty works were expected. "What is the wisdom given to him?" people were asking (Mark 6:2). On the Sabbath he attended the synagogue with some of his disciples and was invited to read from the scrolls of Scripture and expound the chosen passages.[45]

What happened now seems to have been Jesus' deliberate intention. The people of Nazareth wanted to see for themselves what they had heard of Jesus' work at Capernaum (Luke 4:23). He would not disappoint them. He opened the scroll and found Isa. 61:1–2. He read it in Hebrew and then repeated for his audience in Aramaic. "The Spirit of the Lord God is upon me, because the Lord has anointed me to bring good tidings to the afflicted; he has sent me to bind up the brokenhearted, to proclaim liberty to the captives, and the opening of the prison to those who are bound; to proclaim the year of the Lord's favor." He rolled up the scroll and sat down. Then, speaking deliberately, he told them, "This day is the Scripture fulfilled in your ears." This was not in the text. As at Capernaum, the audience was electrified. The year might be the Sabbatical year, when slaves were freed and debts forgiven, but was Jesus saying more? The text referred to messianic times. Were the poor, that is, the Elect of Israel, to receive their rights and be freed from Rome and from Herod? And was he claiming that the spirit of the Lord was upon him and that he had been anointed by God? His family had been worthy members of the community, but had he shown exceptional gifts before now? Jesus read the admiring yet skeptical mood of his hearers. At once his mind went back to the great prophets of Israel with whom he instinctively associated himself. "Truly, I say to you, no prophet is acceptable in his own country. But in truth, I tell you, there were many widows in Israel in the days of Elijah, when the heaven was shut up three years and six months, when there came a great famine over all the land; Elijah was sent to none of them but only to Zarephath, in the land of Sidon, to a woman who was a widow [1 Kings 17:9]. And there were many lepers in Israel in the time of the prophet Elisha; and none of them was cleansed, but only Naaman the Syrian" (Luke 4:24–28). He got no further. The congregation turned against him as one person. These people he was praising were heathens, Syrians! Were they better than people of Galilee? What sort of liberation was this? Jesus was driven out and nearly thrown over a precipice (Luke 4:29). The incident sheds light on his mind and theirs. The prophetic image was uppermost in Jesus' mind, but it was also linked with messianism and liberation as well as with healing and compassion. The opposition also was powerful.[46] People suspected some devilish (Beelzebub) inspiration (Mark 3:22//Matt. 12:24; Luke 11:15). One can understand why his family and friends thought he had lost his reason (Mark 3:21). And Jesus himself had not yet linked suffering with prophecy. He simply passed "through the midst of them [and] went away" (Luke 4:30), marveling "because of their unbelief" (Mark 6:6).

The prophetic role involved a teaching role. Healing the sick would help usher in God's kingdom, but repentance to fit Israel for it would result only from teaching and example. "Teacher" is the favorite description of Jesus in the Gospels, being used no less than fifty times, and his opponents paid tribute to his fearlessness and devotion to God in this role (Mark 12:14).[47] In many ways Jesus taught in the normal rabbinic manner—stating, as in the Sermon on the Mount, a proposition from the law and then commenting upon it. Some of his interpretations would have been accepted by the Essenes and Pharisees. His condemnation of oaths coincided with that of the former.[48] His extension of the commandment to do no murder so that it included anger of any sort also followed rabbinic teaching. "Thou shalt not cause thy brother's blood to boil with bitterness because of thine actions" (*Pesikta Rabbati* 25.1).[49] The teaching looks back to Sirach 27:30—28:1, but while Sirach confines forbearance and forgiveness to dealings with one's neighbor, Jesus extends it to include one's enemies.[50] Few Jews would have accepted this, and certainly not the Essenes.

On the other hand, the teaching of the Beatitudes finds its parallels in rabbinic, Qumran, and intertestamental literature, particularly the blessing of the poor, the meek, and the mourners.[51] An author of one of the hymns in the Scrolls thanks God for having appointed him to preach to the humble the abundant mercy of God, and salvation from his eternal fountain, and "to declare joy to the oppressed in spirit and to them that mourn."[52] This is very near to Jesus' message, but Jesus draws out implications which his contemporaries could not accept. He repudiates the current Jewish cult of prosperity and wealth as the reward of virtue.[53] The rich man in the story of Lazarus and Dives (Luke 16:19–31) "was buried" and found himself in torment. Jesus does not say he had done anything wrong except that he had lived well and treated Lazarus with condescension. Mammon (wealth) was always "unrighteous." Its interests were incompatible with God's (Luke 16:13). Possessions, where not an encumbrance to discipleship, attracted moth and rust (Matt. 6:20). It was more difficult for a rich man to enter the kingdom than for a camel to pass through the eye of a needle (Luke 18:25). Yet in the last resort it depended on the individual. Where one's heart was, there was one's treasure also (Matt. 6:21). Jesus "loved" the rich young ruler. He dined with synagogue rulers and the leaders of local society. He accepted the fact of wealth and commanded its right use (Luke 19:12–27), as he accepted the fact of war, battle, and violence. He did not seek to change the structure of society, but the people in it.

Jesus' parables bring this home. He used these as his main vehicle of instruction, and though in form and literary character they resembled at times those of his Pharisaic contemporaries, their nature and the lessons they taught differed. God could not be approached through rules and precedents but through prayer, the outpouring of the individual conscience. The parables aimed at leading their hearers towards an inevitable conclusion, an understanding of the nature of righteousness, and an example to be followed by themselves.[54] God's ways were not the same as humanity's. In the passage immediately following Jesus' rejection of the rich young man, Peter exclaims self-righteously, "We have left everything and followed you" (Matt. 19:27). Jesus replies with the Parable of the Servants in the Vineyard, and comments at the end, "The last will be first, and the first last" (Matt. 20:16). There was no bank of merit in the kingdom. The disciple had no legal claim on any reward; he had to rely wholly on God's unfailing goodness.[55] In contemporary society, the Prodigal Son would have received scant respect. In the sight of God, he was the sinner who repented.

Other radical departures from the norms of Jewish daily conduct followed from this. Holiness was no longer to be regarded as by nature exclusive.[56] The elaborate rules as well as the harsh punishments set out in Leviticus were to be revised in a new law. Far from separating himself from the ungodly, Jesus taught identification with human sin and weakness and the duty of going out to search for and bring in the sinner. There was "more joy in heaven over one sinner who repents than over ninety-nine righteous persons who need no repentance" (Luke 15:7). He did not praise the occupation of tax collector—far from it[57]—but he had no hesitation in eating with tax collectors and other sinners (Mark 2:16–17). Matthew would have been impossible among the disciples of a Pharisee. Jesus was ready to enter the house of the centurion, a Gentile, and heal his slave (Matt. 8:5–13//Luke 7:1–10). Lazarus, in the parable told in Luke 16:19–31, was ritually unclean because he had been licked by animals; yet he is pictured as reclining in Abraham's bosom. Similarly, Jesus accepted defilement of women, disregarding Lev. 15:19–32.

Indeed, his attitude towards women was revolutionary,[58] and may have contributed to his final break with the Pharisees. Jewish society was a male-dominated society. A woman had her marriage contract but otherwise was very much at her husband's mercy, divorceable by him without redress, and dismissed to lowly status within the synagogue or the Temple. She could not teach, had no right to bear witness, and could not expect credence to be given to anything she reported (cf. Luke 24:11, "an idle tale"). "Better burn the Torah than teach it to a woman" was a saying of the Rabbi Eliezer in c. 90, for "she was in all things inferior to a man."[59]

This situation Jesus found intolerable. Once again he may have learned from John, for Matthew records his telling the chief priests and elders at Jerusalem, "Truly, I say to you, the tax collectors and the harlots go into the kingdom of God before you. For John came to you in the way of righteousness, and you did not believe him, but the tax collectors and the harlots believed him" (Matt. 21:31–32). Jesus, however, pushed matters further. For him the sexes were equal. Marriage had been decreed by God. Divorce,[60] except because of adultery, was forbidden (Matt. 19:9). He had no hesitation in speaking to married women (John 4:7ff.); he healed the daughter of Jairus (Luke 8:40); and the Syrophoenician woman asked him to help her daughter (Mark 7:24–30//Matt. 15:21–28). Women accompanied him on his journeys. The rebuke to Simon the Pharisee (Luke 7:39–50) was severe and it was combined with an assertion of personal authority. "Therefore I tell you, her sins, which are many, are forgiven, for she loved much; but he who is forgiven little, loves little" (Luke 7:47). It is difficult to see how the Pharisees could have done other than oppose Jesus after this.

There was a tension between the demands of tradition and Law and those of the kingdom which Jesus could not resolve. The Law would indeed be fulfilled in every particular, but in ways different from those imagined by the Pharisees and scribes. If they also emphasized the need for inward purity,[61] they appeared to subordinate this to the exact performance of religious duties. Jesus does not refer to the typical just persons of the period, to Job or Tobit (unlike the early Christians). The kingdom, to be interpreted as "God's kingly activity manifested in a breaking into history and human experience,"[62] was based on different presuppositions. Everything depended on the heart and actions of the individual. The widow contributing her mites to the Temple treasury, the tax collector praying in the Temple, the prostitute who turned from sin, and even the rich young man if he would sell his possessions, all were worthy, but all who would enter must commit themselves without reserve. "Whoever does not receive the kingdom of God like a little child shall not enter it" (Mark 10:15). The kingdom, even if in the future, was also "in the midst of you" (Luke 17:21). It was now,[63] to be searched for diligently until found, and then treasured as a "pearl of great value" (Matt. 13:46). It worked secretly, like leaven, until it pervaded the whole body (Matt. 13:33; Luke 13:20), or like mustard seed (Matt. 13:31–32; Mark 4:30–32; Luke 13:18–19), that grew until it became a vast tree in which all humanity would find a place. Above all, it was an experience of joy. It was symbolized by harvest time or the marriage feast. There was gladness and activity as well as rest for the heavy laden (Matt. 11:28). The eternal refreshment (*refrigerium*) of the early church, symbolized by Jonah reclining in the shade of a gourd (cf. Jonah 4:5), was not Jesus' concept of the kingdom and its rewards.

How long the Galilean ministry lasted is uncertain. It must have been more than a year, and more likely two (A.D. 28–29). It was long enough for Jesus to visit much of northern Galilee and preach beyond its boundaries in Tyre and Sidon, to have made one journey at least to Jerusalem via Samaria (Luke 9:51ff.; 17:11) and to have left him time for silent solitary prayer in the hills. It was long enough, too, for opposition to consolidate and render much of Jesus' efforts fruitless. It ended from a combination of circumstances. Growing hostility from the Pharisees, Herod Antipas's fears,[64] and the inevitable political implications of Jesus' attraction to "the crowds" in Galilee all played their part. One can only follow the Gospel writers in seeing the feeding of the five thousand (perhaps in the early summer of 29) as a turning point.[65] Jesus is recorded as having "compassion on them, because they were like sheep without a shepherd" (Mark 6:34; cf. Num. 27:17), and the suggestion that for the moment Jesus thought in terms of Joshua, "who shall go out before them [the children of Israel] and bring them in," cannot be dismissed.[66] At least the people, after being set down in ordered groups, took the hint and tried to "take him by force to make him king" (John 6:14–15). Once again, Jesus recoiled from the political consequences of his position. He retired to the hills to pray. "For what does it profit a man, to gain the whole world and forfeit his life?" (Mark 8:36) may represent his thoughts on messianic power as understood in his time.

Herod Antipas, however, was not convinced. He regarded Jesus with mingled awe and suspicion. He wished to meet him we are told (Luke 9:9). At some stage, Pharisees still well disposed towards Jesus warned him: "Get away from here, for Herod wants to kill you" (Luke 13:31). Jesus' dislike of royal power came through in his reply, "Go and tell that fox," that is, the cleverest but among the least pleasant of animals, that after having done his work of casting out demons and performing cures, he would be leaving for Jerusalem, for "it cannot be that a prophet should perish away from Jerusalem" (Luke 13:32–33).

MARTYR PROPHET

The crisis had come. For a time Jesus was to withdraw from public teaching and concentrate on his disciples alone. They also must learn through prayer how to do the will of the Father. The battle against Satan was no longer to be one of all-out attack without personal sacrifice. Victory could be achieved only through suffering. From now on, the figure of the prophet becomes the suffering and martyr prophet of current Jewish tradition, and any messianic thoughts are subordinated to this overriding ideal.[67] The second turning point in Jesus' life was reached outside Galilee in the territory of Herod's brother Philip, which lay to the north. Mark follows Jesus' question, "Who do men say that I am?" (Mark 8:27), with Peter's confession and the transfiguration.[68]

Moses and Elijah were both associated with the theme of prophetic leadership, tribulations, and suffering at the hands of Israel itself. This portrayed Jesus' own role.[69] The concept of the Son of man,[70] the mysterious agent of God in the last times and Judge of humankind that he had applied to himself, was now combined with that of the servant-prophet, giving his life "as a ransom for many" (Mark 10:45).[71] The acclaim of "Messiah" he rejected with anger. As understood at the time, this could only have been a political move embodying a challenge against the Roman authority. This was never Jesus' aim.

Meanwhile the disciples, people who had truly left all to follow him, were to be built up as the nucleus of the new Israel. Membership was by faith. This, with love, was the primary virtue. "Fear not, little flock, for it is your Father's good pleasure to give you the kingdom" (Luke 12:32). The "flock" was always Israel. The "little flock" would be the faithful few.[72] They would be recompensed, sitting "on twelve thrones, judging the twelve tribes of Israel" (Matt. 19:28//Luke 22:30). Their role was to serve; "whoever would be great among you must be your servant" (Mark 10:42–44//Matt. 20:25–28). Once again current ideas, this time of rulership, had been turned upside down. Leadership in the new community would be quite unlike leadership in the secular world. Moreover it demanded commitment unto death.[73] "Are you able to drink the cup that I drink, or to be baptized with the baptism with which I am baptized?" (Mark 10:38//Matt. 20:22). The disciples replied, "We are able." Never before, even in Israel's troubled history, had so much depended on the Remnant and so much been demanded from it.

ON TO JERUSALEM

After another quick and secret journey through northern Galilee (Mark 9:30) including his old base Capernaum (Mark 9:33), Jesus, his disciples, and friends set out for Jerusalem.[74] This time they followed the pilgrim route down the east bank of the Jordan (Mark 10:1) avoiding Samaria.[75] The date was perhaps towards the end of A.D. 29. Once in Judea, Jesus resumed his public ministry. It is to this phase, perhaps, that one would assign the great parables that Luke alone preserves—the Good Samaritan (Luke 10:30–37), and the Prodigal Son (Luke 15:11–32)—parables that showed that the kingdom stood open for all to enter and that a Samaritan could have greater understanding of its demands than the Pharisee or Levite, the accepted religious leaders of Israel. Later, in Jerusalem, the story of the Wicked Husbandmen would foretell Jesus' rejection by his own people. Whatever his fate he was resolved to challenge a decisive response in Jerusalem.

The synoptic Gospels show that Jesus was well known and well received on his journey. At Jericho he was entertained by Zacchaeus, the chief tax collector (Luke 19:1–10). As he reached the city, there must have been many like the blind Bartimaeus who immediately identified him as the ''Son of David'' (Mark 10:47//Matt. 20:31; Luke 18:38), and they associated him with the restoration of the royal line of Judah.[76] Would the crowds of Jerusalem react differently?

The duration of Jesus' ministry in Jerusalem is a matter for debate. Mark's story is, as always, fast-moving and suggests only a few days of action and preaching before the Last Supper and Jesus' arrest and trial. John, however, indicates that Jesus was in Jerusalem for the Feast of Dedication, that is, mid-December (John 10:22), and that soon afterwards he retired across the Jordan into Perea (10:40; 11:54) and returned to the city ''six days before the Passover'' (12:1). This seems more likely.[77] The existence of friends in the city, as well as his relationships with Martha, Mary, and Lazarus, and his own claim ''day after day I was with you in the temple teaching, and you did not seize me'' (Mark 14:49), suggests a relatively lengthy ministry in Jerusalem. Certainly the scribes and Pharisees who came to question him did not treat him as some stranger from Galilee.

Following the chronology of John's Gospel and accepting the year as A.D. 30, this would bring Jesus to Bethany on 2 April. There, there took place the anointing of Jesus' feet by Mary, not necessarily a symbolic recognition of Jesus as Messiah but an act of love by one whose brother had been restored miraculously to health. For Judas, however, it was the last straw.[78] Whatever hopes, material or even military, he may have set on Jesus were now irretrievably disappointed. The next day Jesus entered Jerusalem in triumph. For the crowds already gathering in the city for the Passover, this was an event. ''Hosanna! Blessed is he who comes in the name of the Lord! Blessed is the kingdom of our father David that is coming! Hosanna in the highest!'' (Mark 11:9–10). Palms were strewn in the road to emphasize the regal character of the progress. Jesus had crossed his Rubicon. The crowd imagined that they were hailing at least a prophet (Matt. 21:11); and the references to the restoration of the kingdom of David suggest the prophetic forerunner of the messianic age—even the military leader the Davidic Messiah as understood by the Covenanters of Qumran.[79] Luke indeed says that even before Jesus entered Jerusalem some believed "that the kingdom of God was to appear immediately" (Luke 19:11). Jesus, too, must have recalled the prophecy in Zechariah: "Rejoice greatly, O daughter of Zion! . . . Lo, your king comes to you . . . humble and riding on an ass, on a colt the foal of an ass" (Zech. 9:9). The new age was to dawn, but far differently from what they or the Jewish rulers had imagined.

The latter were now given real cause for alarm. Supposing Jesus was "a trustworthy prophet," would that not mean the end of their own rule in Israel? (Cf. 1 Macc. 14:41; and, for the same theme of the Temple representing an interim before the coming of the Prophet, see 1 Macc. 4:46.) Jesus' actions moved swiftly toward a final crisis. He went to the Temple and what he saw indicated that it was unfit for the worship of God. The episode of the fig tree also suggests he felt his time was near. The tree would not bloom again before his return in glory; and he would speak similarly of the wine he was to drink with his disciples before the Passover.[80] The next day he returned to the Temple and, with a demonstration of authority, drove out the money-changers—a necessary but unpopular part of the Temple economy that required payment of dues in antique Tyrian shekels. For Jesus, such transactions were abhorrent. The Temple was to be the world's religious center. One sees no reason to doubt his quotation of Isa. 56:7, "Is it not written, 'My house shall be called a house of prayer for all peoples'? But you have made it a den of robbers" (cf. Mark 11:17).[81]

THE LAST PHASE

The delegation that called upon Jesus to justify his action represented the Jewish religious leadership: "chief priests and the scribes and the elders" (Mark 11:27–28). Jesus countered by recalling John's baptism to them. Was it from heaven or of men? They could not answer, but the die was now cast. It was either Jesus' authority or theirs. The synoptic Gospels indicate an increasingly hostile relationship. The Parable of the Virgins demonstrated that the Jewish leaders lacked good deeds, the essential oil for their lamps to greet the bridegroom.[82] The Parable of the Great Feast emphasized that the kingdom would be carried beyond the bounds of Judaism, into "the highways and byways." The parables and discourses attributed to this period are heavier with condemnations of the unrepentant. Jesus himself becomes more insistent:[83] "Heaven and earth will pass away, but my words will not pass away" (Matt. 24:35). The time for decision was very close. Jesus now distinguished clearly between his role and that of the prophets. The sending of the son is the king's last resort after his servants (that is, the prophets) had been rejected by the husbandmen (Mark 12:1–11). Many realized, according to Mark, that the parable was aimed at them. A final effort, this time by Pharisees and Herodians acting once more in common, to trap Jesus on the question of tribute to Caesar failed. Jesus, though from Galilee, was not another Judas the Gaulonite. What belonged to Caesar should be rendered to him. The high priests were desperate to strike before the Passover: "If any one knew where he was, he should let them know, so that they might arrest him" (John 11:57).

They were not acting without reason. Whatever "the insurrection" involving Barabbas may have been, relations between the Jews of Jerusalem and the Romans were tense.[84] The high priests knew that rebellion against Rome was out of the question. Ten years later, when threatened by Caligula with the prospect of the emperor's statue being set up in the Temple—"the abomination of desolation"—all they could do was to offer themselves for death at the hands of the Romans rather than obey.[85] Now this false prophet was rousing the people with messianic expectations. If he were allowed to continue, the Romans would come and "destroy both our holy place and our nation" (John 11:48). For the sake of Israel it was expedient that he die, so argued Caiaphas (John 11:49–51).[86] It was a desperate moment, relieved by the luck of Judas's disillusionment and readiness to betray Jesus.

Meantime, Jesus and his disciples prepared for the Feast of Passover. There can be little doubt that the Last Supper was a Passover meal. The reasons given by Joachim Jeremias seem irrefutable.[87] The eating of the meal at sundown, the numbers limited to the Twelve, the attitude of reclining instead of being seated, the drinking of wine, all have religious significance; and together with the subtle point that the disciples believed Jesus had indeed sent Judas out on an almsgiving mission as might be expected on such an occasion, all point to a Passover ritual. It was perhaps an anticipation of the messianic banquet over which Jesus believed he would soon be presiding. The covenant which he was initiating, offering full and final forgiveness as Jeremiah (31:31–34) had envisioned, had now come into being. The words and actions of Moses must be related to his own greater mission.

Gethsemane was within the area prescribed for those who had come to Jerusalem for the feast to stay. The story showing Jesus wracked with doubts seems authentic though there were no eyewitnesses, according to the synoptic Gospels. Was this to be the end? Was this the Father's will? Would the cup pass from him? In any event he would obey (Mark 14:36). The disciples failed him.[88] The suspense was broken by the arrival of Judas with members of the Temple guard. After a brief resistance the disciples scattered and Jesus was arrested. He must face his supreme ordeal alone.

Accepting that the Last Supper took place in the evening of Thursday, 6 April, and Jesus was dead by 3 P.M. on Friday, events happened at great speed. But here again Jeremias's explanation may be correct. The authorities charged Jesus with being a false prophet who had uttered blasphemy by claiming to be Messiah and Son of God.[89] The Sanhedrin could no doubt have organized a stoning as they did in the case of Stephen a few years later. The Romans neither intervened to save Stephen nor, so far as is known, took action against the perpetrators. But evidently the Jewish leaders wanted to go further and have the hated Galilean executed with as much publicity as possible. To be hanged from a tree (Deut. 21:22–23) was a death reserved for the accursed of God, but the Roman governor was the only authority that could order crucifixion, a death that could be interpreted, as it later was, as fulfilling the terms of the Deuteronomic curse.[90] Even so they took a risk, for in the eyes of many to die at the hand of the Romans on a political charge was an honorable end. Barabbas would have become a local hero. The risk, however, was taken. The Jewish leaders were incensed by Jesus' calm avowal of his messianic character to Caiaphas. "I am; and you will see the Son of man seated at the right hand of Power, and coming with the clouds of heaven" (Mark 14:62). The end of the age was therefore announced. For neither party could there be any retreat.

So Jesus was taken before Pilate early on the Friday morning. Pilate made a futile effort to transfer Jesus to the jurisdiction of Herod Antipas who happened to be in the city for the feast. It was a good diplomatic move, but the case came back to Pilate.[91] The judgment seat was probably set on a raised place in the courtyard of the Antonia fortress which occupied the northwest corner of the Temple enclosure (John 18:28ff). There the high priests gave their version of Jesus' answer concerning the tribute penny, suggesting to the reader of the Gospels perhaps that this question had been put as a means of collecting evidence against him. Pilate was not convinced. He turned to Jesus with the direct question, "Are you guilty or not?"—just as Pliny the Younger would question the Christians taken before him in Bithynia eighty years later[92]—"Are you the King of the Jews?" Jesus' reply gave him no help. Pilate procrastinated. Only when he was cornered and threatened with denunciation, that if he acquitted Jesus he would be "no friend of Caesar," and confronted with growing disorder, did he give way.[93] He also feared seditious outbreaks and had to play safe; but his contempt for the high priests was unbounded. The formal superscription, "This is the King of the Jews," was not to be altered by their protests and the "king" was crucified between two known robbers, probably revolutionaries—so much for the kingship over the Jewish nation.[94]

The final scene, so poignantly told in all four Gospels, suggests what seems to be the truth. Though he rejected explicitly the "times and seasons" of the coming, Jesus appears to have believed that crisis would follow his arrival in Jerusalem. The Son of man would appear in glory to inaugurate in the visible world the kingdom of God. The agonized doubts he experienced in Gethsemane, briefly laid aside as he faced Caiaphas, were reinforced as he was stretched on the cross.[95] The reconciliation with his mother and some of his relatives was complete. His enemies he forgave.[96] But what of his own mission? No legions of angels appeared. His enemies mocked him. The end had not come. Was he really the chosen witness of God?[97] His last recorded words were the despairing first line of Psalm 22, but in the Psalms despair never displaces trust in God and belief in deliverance by him. In the same Psalm, it is foretold ''posterity shall serve him'' (Ps. 22:30). In a little more than three years Jesus of Nazareth had influenced the course of history as none other. New directions had been given to humanity's quest for salvation and a new pattern offered for our relations with our fellows. ''Did not our hearts burn within us while he talked to us on the road?'' (Luke 24:32) was the reaction of disciples to the risen Christ. The symbol of the centurion's recognition of the justice of Jesus' cause (Mark 15:39) pointed to the Gentiles being the heirs to the kingdom. The Jews moved on toward the catastrophe of A.D. 70. Political messianism and zealotry were too strong to be shaken off. The new wine of Jesus' teaching could not, after all, be contained within the old wineskins of Judaism.

BIBLIOGRAPHY

NOTE

Since Reformation times, the bibliography on Jesus of Nazareth has become enormous. Here we have kept to the well-trodden paths mapped out by British and Continental scholars. First, A. Huck's (ed.) *Synopsis of the First Three Gospels*, rev. ed. H. Lietzmann, and Eng. ed. F. L. Cross (New York and London: G. E. Stechert & Co., 1936), is an essential tool for study. C. H. Dodd, *The Founder of Christianity* (New York: Macmillan Co., 1970), the fruit of the author's forty years of New Testament scholarship, is a starting point for a historical assessment of Jesus. Günther Bornkamm's *Jesus of Nazareth*, Eng. trans. I. McLuskey and F. McLuskey (New York: Harper & Row, 1975; London: Hodder & Stoughton, 1973), is a finely written account, and M. Grant's *Jesus: An Historian's Review of the Gospels* (New York: Charles Scribner's Sons; London: Weidenfeld & Nicolson, 1977) is a stimulating narrative written from a historian's point of view. All these indicate that the new quest for the historical Jesus is not vain.

On the special themes connected with Jesus' life, C. H. H. Scobie's *John the Baptist* (Philadelphia: Fortress Press; London: SCM Press, 1964) is full and convincing. On Herod Antipas, H. T. Hoehner's study, *Herod Antipas*, SNTSMS 17 (New York and Cambridge: Cambridge University Press, 1972), is comprehensive but heavy going. On the parables, Dodd's early work, *The Parables of the Kingdom* (New York: Charles Scribner's Sons, 1936; London: James Nisbet & Co., 1935), is inclined to be discursive. Norman Perrin's *The Kingdom of God in the Teaching of Jesus* (Philadelphia: Westminster Press; London: SCM Press, 1963) provides some good discussion of views of scholars of earlier generations. C. F. D. Moule's *The Origin of Christology* (New York and Cambridge: Cambridge University Press, 1977) is a masterly summary of views concerning descriptions of Jesus ("Son of God," "Son of man"), as well as a pioneering work. On Jesus' relations with the Pharisees, John Bowker's *Jesus and the Pharisees* (New York and Cambridge: Cambridge University Press, 1973) contains translations of original source material, and for the Last Supper, J. Jeremias, *The Eucharistic Words of Jesus*, Eng. trans. N. Perrin (Philadelphia: Fortress Press, 1977; London: Charles Scribner's Sons, 1965), remains the classic work. For the trial of Jesus, see E. Bammel, ed., *The Trial of Jesus* (London: SCM Press, 1970); A. N. Sherwin-White's discussion of the trial considered in the context of Roman provincial legal practice is strongly recommended: *Roman Society and Roman Law in the New Testament*, The Sarum Lectures 1960–1961 (New York and London: Oxford University Press, 1963), chap. 2. The Jewish view of Jesus is well represented in J. Klausner's pioneer work, *Jesus of Nazareth: His Life, Times, and Teaching*, Eng. trans. H. Danby (New York: Macmillan Co., 1929; London: George Allen & Unwin, 1925). The more recent G. Vermès, *Jesus the Jew: A Historian's Reading of the Gospels* (Philadelphia: Fortress Press, 1981; London: William Collins Sons, 1973) and D. Flusser, *Jesus*, Eng. trans. R. Walls (New York: Herder & Herder, 1969) also place Jesus in his Galilean context. Works on the New Testament background should be mentioned. J. Jeremias, *New Testament Theology*, vol. I, Eng. trans. J. Bowden (New York: Charles Scribner's Sons; London: SCM Press, 1972); E. Trocmé, *Jesus and His Contemporaries*, Eng. trans. R. A. Wilson (Philadelphia: Westminster Press; London: SCM Press, 1973)—direct and uncompromising as all his works; and M. Hengel, *Die Zeloten* AGJU, I (Leiden: E. J. Brill, 1961; 2d ed., 1976).

Finally, on the Gospel tradition, B. H. Streeter's *The Four Gospels: A Study of Origins*, rev. ed. (New York: Macmillan Co., 1930) still holds the field as a foundation work; while C. H. Dodd's two studies on John's Gospel, *The Interpretation of the Fourth Gospel* (New York and Cambridge: Cambridge University Press, 1953) and *Historical Tradition in the Fourth Gospel* (New York and Cambridge: Cambridge University Press, 1963), are indispensable for John and also for the rabbinic background of the Johannine presentation. For Mark, Dennis Nineham's commentary, *The Gospel of St. Mark* (New York: Penguin Books, 1964; Harmondsworth, Eng.: Penguin Books, 1963), seems to underestimate the historical value of this Gospel, and E. Trocmé, *The Formation of the Gospel According to Mark*, Eng. trans. P. Gaughan (Philadelphia: Westminster Press, 1975), is a useful corrective. For Luke, see A. R. C. Leaney's *A Commentary on the Gospel According to Saint Luke*, HNTC, BNTC, 2d ed. (New York: Harper & Row; London: A. & C. Black, 1967), and for Matthew, G. Bornkamm, G. Barth, and H. J. Held, *Tradition and Interpretation in Matthew*, Eng. trans. P. Scott (Philadelphia: Westminster Press; London: SCM Press, 1963).

SECONDARY WORKS

Argyle, A. W. "The meaning of ἐξουσία in Mark 1:22–27." *ET* 80 (August 1969): 343–44.

Banks, Robert. *Jesus and the Law in the Synoptic Tradition.* SNTSMS 28. New York and Cambridge: Cambridge University Press, 1975.

Barrett, C. K. "The Lamb of God." *NTS* 1 (February 1955): 210–18.

Best, E. *The Temptation and the Passion: The Markan Soteriology.* SNTSMS 2. New York and Cambridge: Cambridge University Press, 1965.

Boobyer, G. H. "The Eucharistic Interpretation of the Miracles of the Loaves in St. Mark's Gospel." *JTS* n.s. 3 (October 1952): 161–71.

Brandon, S. G. F. *Jesus and the Zealots: A Study of the Political Factor in Primitive Christianity.* New York: Charles Scribner's Sons, 1968; Manchester, Eng.: Manchester University Press, 1967.

Brownlee, W. H. "John the Baptist in the New Light of Ancient Scrolls." In *The Scrolls and the New Testament,* ed. K. Stendahl, pp. 33–53. New York: Harper & Brothers, 1957; London: SCM Press, 1958.

Burrows, E. W. "Did John the Baptist Call Jesus the Lamb of God?" *ET* 85 (May 1974): 245–49.

Cave, C. H. "The Parables and the Scriptures." *NTS* 11 (July 1965): 374–87.

Crossan, J. D. "Mark and the Relatives of Jesus." *NT* 15 (1973): 81–113.

Daube, D. *The New Testament and Rabbinic Judaism.* New York: Arno Press, 1973; London: University of London, Athlone Press, 1956.

Davies, W. D. *The Setting of the Sermon on the Mount.* New York and Cambridge: Cambridge University Press, 1964.

Dodd, C. H. "The Historical Problem of the Death of Jesus." In *More New Testament Studies,* pp. 84–101. Grand Rapids: W. B. Eerdmans; Manchester, Eng.: Manchester University Press, 1968.

Downing, J. "Jesus and Martyrdom." *JTS* n.s. 14 (October 1963): 279–93.

Dupont, J. "L'origine du récit des tentations de Jésus au désert." *RB* 73 (January 1966): 30–76.

Farmer, W. R. "An Historical Essay on the Humanity of Jesus Christ." In *Christian History and Interpretation: Studies Presented to John Knox,* ed. W. R. Farmer, C. F. D. Moule, and R. R. Niebuhr, pp. 101–26. New York and Cambridge: Cambridge University Press, 1967.

Feuillet, A. "La personnalité de Jésus entrevue à partir de sa soumission au rite de repentance du précurseur." *RB* 77 (January 1970): 30–49.

_____. "Vocation et mission des prophètes—Baptême et mission de Jésus. Etude de christologie biblique." *NV* 54.1 (1979): 22–40.

Flusser, D. "Blessed are the Poor in Spirit." *IEJ* 10 (1960): 1–13.

Ford, J. Massyngberde. *The Wellsprings of Scripture.* New York and London: Sheed & Ward, 1968.

Furnish, V. P. *The Love Command in the New Testament.* Nashville: Abingdon Press, 1972.

Hiers, R. H. *The Historical Jesus and the Kingdom of God: Present and Future in the Message of Jesus.* Gainesville: University Presses of Florida, 1973.

Hooker, M. D. *Jesus and the Servant: The Influence of the Servant Concept of Deutero-Isaiah in the New Testament.* London: SPCK, 1959.

_____. *The Son of Man in Mark.* Montreal: McGill-Queens University Press, 1967.

Lampe, G. W. H. "The Lukan Portrait of Christ." *NTS* 2 (February 1956): 160–75.

Lightfoot, R. H. *History and Interpretation in the Gospels.* New York: Harper & Brothers; London: Hodder & Stoughton, 1935.

Montefiore, H. W., "A Comparison of the Parables of the Gospel According to Thomas and of the Synoptic Gospels." *NTS* 7 (April 1961): 220–48.

_____. "Revolt in the Desert? (Mark VI:30ff)." *NTS* 8 (January 1962): 135–41.

Moore, A. L. *The Parousia in the New Testament.* NT Sup. 13. Leiden: E. J. Brill, 1966.

Robinson, J. A. T. "The Baptism of John and the Qumran Community." *HTR* 50 (1957): 175–91.

Stanton, G. N. "On the Christology of Q." In *Christ and Spirit in the New Testament,* ed. B. Lindars and S. S. Smalley, pp. 27–42. New York and Cambridge: Cambridge University Press, 1973.

Taylor, Vincent. *The Life and Ministry of Jesus.* Nashville: Abingdon Press; London: Macmillan & Co., 1955.

———. "The Origin of the Markan Passion-Sayings." *NTS* 1 (February 1955): 159–67.

Trocmé, E. "Is There a Markan Christology?" In *Christ and Spirit,* ed. Lindars and Smalley, pp. 3–14.

Winter, Paul. *On the Trial of Jesus.* SJ.FWJ I. Edited by T. A. Burkill and G. Vermès. 2d ed. New York: Walter de Gruyter, 1973.

NOTES

1. See over, chap. 4, p. 133.

2. Eusebius *HE* V.2.3.

3. See Argyle, "Meaning of ἐξουσία in Mark 1:22–27," and Trocmé, "Is There a Markan Christology?" esp. p. 4.

4. See J. Blinzler, *Herodes Antipas und Jesus Christus* (Stuttgart, 1947), the classic discussion; and the very comprehensive work by Hoehner, *Herod Antipas,* esp. pp. 184–91.

5. See Trocmé, "Is There a Markan Christology?" esp. p. 13.

6. See over, pp. 122, 135. In general, I follow Streeter, *Four Gospels,* part 2.

7. Tacitus *Histories* V.9, "sub Tiberio quies. . . . ."

8. Thus, Lightfoot's conclusion in his Bampton Lectures for 1934, *History and Interpretation,* and see H. Conzelmann's discussion of the conclusions of form-criticism in "Jesus Christus," *RGG*[3] (1959): 620 (*Jesus,* Eng. trans. J. R. Lord, ed. J. Reumann, rev. and expanded ed. [Philadelphia: Fortress Press, 1973], p. 8): "It is no longer possible to establish a sequence of events in the life of Jesus and to provide a picture of the figure of Jesus."

9. See Montefiore's "Comparison of Parables," among other works on these lines.

10. Dodd, *Founder of Christianity,* pp. 21–22.

11. Matt. 26:73. Concerning Galilean Jews, see Vermès, *Jesus the Jew,* pp. 53–57; and their nationalism, ibid., pp. 46–48. Their rigid orthodoxy is, however, indicated by Flavius Josephus, *Antiquitates Judaicae (Antiquities of the Jews),* LCL, XX.43.

12. Josephus *Antiquities* XX.118–20.

13. Josephus, *Bellum Judaicum (The Jewish War),* LCL, III.41.

14. Cf. ibid., II.56 on the raid on Sepphoris. On Judas, cf. idem, *Antiquities* XVII.272. Sepphoris remained loyal to Rome in 66. See idem, *Vita (The Life),* LCL, 30.

15. Joseph *Antiquities* XVIII.1–6; compare idem, *War* II.118, and Acts 5:37.

Judas upbraided his fellow countrymen for "consenting to pay tribute to the Romans and tolerating mortal masters, after having God for their lord" (*War* II.118).

16. Josephus himself raised a force of "a hundred thousand young men" in Galilee when he was Jewish commander of the area in A.D. 66–67 (*War* II.576). Galilee's prosperity at this time rested largely on olive culture. It was the "special home of the olive" (ibid., 592; and III.41–43).

17. The question of the two censuses bristles with difficulties, but the New Testament accounts of Joseph and Mary's journey to Bethlehem are too circumstantial to be dismissed. There would be no point, for instance, in describing Mary's stay in Jerusalem after Jesus' birth (Luke 2:22f.) if in fact it had never happened. Joseph had only to register (*apographein*) in Bethlehem, as he would if he had property there. Ten years later, however, Josephus (*Antiquities* XVIII.4) refers to an actual assessment (*timētēs/apotimesis*) of property which caused an uprising. It may be that Luke mistakenly associated Quirinius with the earlier instead of the later operation. See L. H. Feldman, ed., in Josephus, *Antiquities*, bks. XVIII–XX, LCL, pp. 2–3, and R. Syme, "The Titulus Tiburtinus," *Vestigia* 17 (Munich, 1974): 585–601, esp. pp. 599–600.

18. The suggestion is made by Vermès, *Jesus the Jew*, pp. 21–22. (On the other hand, people would hardly have asked, "Where did this man get his wisdom?" [Matt. 13:54], if the obvious answer was "From his father.")

19. Josephus *Antiquities* XVIII.3–8. See Hengel, *Die Zeloten*, chap. 3 on Judas the Gaulonite.

20. Luke 6:16 (cf. Matt. 10:4; Mark 3:18). For Jesus and the Zealots see Brandon's *Jesus and Zealots* with its many ingenious reconstructions, Hengel, *Die Zeloten*, pp. 72–76, and Morton Smith, "Zealots and Sicarii, their Origins and Relation," *HTR* 64 (January 1971): 1–19 (strong criticism of previous writers. He believes the Zealots only came into being as a party in the winter of 67–68 [p. 19], and they represented "Palestinian, principally Judean peasant piety" hostile to the rich of the city, the upper priesthood of the Temple, and foreign rulers).

21. Flusser's view is, "Jesus' Jewish education was incomparably better than that of St. Paul" (*Jesus*, p. 18).

22. Robinson, "Baptism of John and Qumran"; and Brownlee, "John the Baptist."

23. Josephus *Antiquities* XVIII.116–19; Josephus regards John's baptism not as a means of forgiving sins, but "as a consecration of the body implying that the soul was already thoroughly cleansed by right behaviour." See, however, Scobie's discussion, *John the Baptist*, pp. 110–16. Compare *Manual of Discipline* (1QS) 5:7–20 (T. H. Gaster, ed. and Eng. trans., *The Dead Sea Scriptures in English Translation* [Garden City, N.Y.: Doubleday Anchor Books, rev. ed., 1964; London: Secker & Warburg, 1957], p. 53), where baptism is designed not of itself to purify but to confirm repentance. It was valueless to one who "rejects the ordinances of God."

24. Josephus *Life* 2.11.

25. The Fourth Gospel records the Baptist saying, "I myself did not know him" (John 1:33). Instinctive recognition by John that Jesus was Messiah at the moment of his baptism has been suggested by Burrows, "Did John the Baptist Call Jesus Lamb of God?" See also Dodd, *Interpretation of Fourth Gospel*, pp. 230–38, and for an opposed viewpoint Barrett, "Lamb of God."

26. Thus Feuillet, "La personnalité de Jésus." Feuillet points out that Jesus is not said to have recalled his past sins as Isaiah (6:5) or Jeremiah (10:23–24; Jeremiah numbers himself among the guilty) did in similar circumstances. On the other hand, Jesus associated himself with the Baptist movement and approved of it.

27. Thus, John 3:25.

28. See Stanton, "Christology of Q." Stanton believes (p. 29) that the Baptist material belongs to the Q core.

29. The words attributed to the heavenly voice might, however, be Ps. 2:7, from a Davidic coronation chant. For the Spirit descending on other Israelite rulers, see Judg. 3:10, 6:34, 11:29, 13:25.

30. Nathanael is not named by Matthew or Luke among the disciples. Is he, perhaps, Nathanael of Cana of John 21:2, who was also a friend of Peter, and was among the disciples to whom Jesus appeared by the Sea of Galilee?

31. Josephus *Antiquities* XIV.487 (referring to the Feast of Atonement).

32. On the Temptations, see Best, *Temptation and Passion*, pp. 5ff.; and J. Dupont, "L'origine des tentations de Jésus," esp. pp. 58ff. (the author believes the account may go back to Jesus himself).

33. Thus Bornkamm, *Jesus*, p. 133; and for Jesus shown as triumphing over temptations similar to those experienced after the Exodus and thus inaugurating the eschatological era beginning with the return to conditions of life in the Garden of Eden (Mark 1:13), see J. T. Milik, *Ten Years of Discovery in the Wilderness of Judaea*, Eng. trans. J. Strugnell, SBT 26 (London: SCM Press, 1959), p. 115.

34. For Jesus and John's association, see Scobie, *John the Baptist*, pp. 53–56; and for the Johannine place-names being devoid of any symbolical meaning, see Dodd, *Interpretation of Fourth Gospel*, pp. 452–53.

35. The New Testament evidence indicates that Jesus' family originally rejected his mission, but later belonged to the church and its missionaries (Acts 1:14; 1 Cor. 9:5), see Bornkamm, *Jesus*, p. 53. John says explicitly that Jesus' brothers did not believe in him (7:5), and Jesus and they go separately to Jerusalem for the Feast of the Tabernacles (7:10). Jesus himself emphasizes the incompatibility of family ties and even filial duties with service to God (see Matt. 12:46–50; Luke 11:27–28; 12:52; 14:26; 18:28–30). See Crossan, "Mark and Relatives of Jesus," and for rejection of parent by the Dead Sea sectaries, 1QH 9, lines 34ff. (Géza Vermès, ed. and Eng. trans., *The Dead Sea Scrolls in English* [Baltimore: Penguin Books, rev. ed., 1970; Harmondsworth, Eng.: Penguin Books, 1963], p. 182, lines 34ff., "for my father knew me not. . . . Thou art a father to all [the sons] of Thy truth").

36. Aenon by Salim (John 3:23) would seem to be in Samaria. For Jesus abused in rabbinic tradition as a "Samaritan," see Tertullian *On the Spectacles* XXX.

37. See Scobie, *John the Baptist*, p. 156, "no evidence for violent break"; and Vermès, *Jesus the Jew*, pp. 31–33, "Jesus' disciples asserted the superiority of Jesus over John."

38. Thus, he wore a caftan with the prescribed fringes (Mark 6:56; Matt. 14:36), referring back to Num. 15:38–40 ("a tassel to look upon and remember all the commandments of the Lord"). See also Daube, *New Testament and Rabbinic Judaism*, p. 251.

39. Compare Ezek. 7:12 ("The time has come, the day draws near"), and Zeph. 1:12 and Dan. 12:4 for the Israelite prophet's prophecies of the approaching end.

40. Thus, Taylor's *Life and Ministry*, pp. 66–67. The future character of the

kingdom is shown in Matt. 6:10//Luke 11:2 (the Lord's Prayer); Mark 11:1; and Luke 13:29//Matt. 8:11, "Men will come from east and west. . . ."

41. See Bornkamm, *Jesus*, p. 145, "The disciples of John, however, are no longer mere pupils in the school sense of the word, but are the followers of the movement originated by John."

42. See Dodd, *Founder of Christianity*, pp. 126ff.; and Best, *Temptation and Passion*, p. 178, claiming that Jesus' main achievement (in the Galilean ministry) was his defeat of Satan.

43. Not wholly extraordinary at this time. The Sabbath could be broken in certain circumstances. For instance, circumcision was permitted on the Sabbath, and as Rabbi Eliezer ben Azariah stated (circa A.D. 100), "If circumcision that affects only one of our 248 members repels the Sabbath, how much more must the whole body repel the Sabbath" (*Yoma* 85a–b). Jesus argued similarly to justify healing on the Sabbath. See Dodd, *Interpretation of Fourth Gospel*, p. 79.

44. There was relative failure, too, in the Galilean centers of Capernaum, Chorazin, and Bethsaida (Matt. 11:21–23). The taunt, "Physician, heal thyself" is interesting. Why should the people of Nazareth quote this particular proverb? Does it indicate perhaps some physical defect from which Jesus suffered or had suffered in earlier years? Jesus was certainly taken aback at their unbelief (Mark 6:6).

45. For the incident as a whole, see Leaney, *Gospel According to St. Luke*, pp. 50ff. The quotation from Isaiah 61 is, in fact, a composite made up of Isa. 61:1; 58:6; and the first four words of 61:2 (Leaney, p. 53). It is certainly curious that Jesus felt able to conflate passages of Scripture, placing Isa. 58:6 *after* 61:1, and expound the resulting text.

46. For expectations of how the Messiah would act, current in the first century A.D., see *Psalms of Solomon* 17:21–31: "Lord, look down and raise up for them their king, son of David, at the time which Thou hast seen, O God, that he shall rule over Thy servant Israel. Gird him with strength that he may break in pieces the unjust ruler, Purge Jerusalem of the heathen who have trodden it underfoot. . . . He will judge the nations and the heathen in the wisdom of his righteousness and he will submit the heathen to his yoke and they shall serve him." (Translation cited from H. Lietzmann, *A History of the Early Church*, Eng. trans. B. L. Woolf, 4 vols. [New York: World Publishing, Meridian Books, 1961; London: Lutterworth Press, 1962], vol. 1: *The Beginnings of the Christian Church*, pp. 26–27.

47. See Grant, *Jesus*, p. 82.

48. Matt. 5:33–37. For the Essenes, see Josephus *War* II.135: "Swearing they avoid, regarding it as worse than perjury."

49. See Daube, *New Testament and Rabbinic Judaism*, pp. 56–58.

50. Thus, the injunction in *The Manual of Discipline* (1QS) 1:1–15 (Gaster, *Dead Sea Scriptures*, p. 44), "to love all that He has chosen and hate all that He has rejected . . . to love all the children of light . . . and to hate all the children of darkness" and in the Hymn of the Initiants at Qumran, "I will harbor no angry grudge against those that indeed repent, but neither will I show compassion to any that turn from the way" (ibid., p. 139). For a wider concept of forgiveness, more like Jesus', see Philo, *De Virtutibus* (*On the Virtues*), LCL, XXI.105–8.

51. See Flusser, "Blessed are the Poor in Spirit" (comparison between Beatitudes and *Dead Sea Scrolls*), and also Ford, *Wellsprings of Scripture*, chap. 14.

52. Cited from Flusser, *Jesus,* p. 77. See *Commentaries on Ps. 37* (Vermès, *Dead Sea Scrolls,* pp. 243–44) applied by the sect to themselves.

53. None of the Old Testament and intertestamental examples (even Abraham) are mentioned as showing how wealth and righteousness might be combined. For the prophetic tradition against wealth, see Amos 8:4–6, and among the Essenes, Josephus *War* II.122, "riches they despise." The result for them, however, was a balance between poverty and wealth.

54. See Jeremias, *New Testament Theology,* vol. I, pp. 108–18.

55. See Mark 4:10–12; Matt. 13:10–15; and Luke 8:9–10. See Farmer, "Humanity of Jesus," esp. pp. 119–21; and Cave, "Parables and Scriptures."

56. See T. Glyn Thomas, "The Unity of the Bible and the Uniqueness of Christ," *LQHR* 191 (July 1966): 219–27; and Grant, *Jesus,* pp. 52–59.

57. Thus, as recorded in Matt. 5:46 and 18:17 ("let him be to you as a Gentile and a tax collector"), but even these should not be excluded from God's mercy (Matt. 20:1–16; Luke 15:11–32; and 18:10–14). See Farmer, "Humanity of Jesus," p. 125.

58. See J. Jeremias, *Jerusalem in the Time of Jesus,* Eng. trans. F. H. Cave and C. H. Cave, 3d ed. (Philadelphia: Fortress Press; London, SCM Press, 1969), pp. 359–76.

59. *Babylonian Talmud Jer. Sotah* 19a. Also Josephus, *Contra Apionem* (*Against Apion*), LCL, II.201: "The woman, says the Law, is in all things inferior to the man." Compare the prayer in *Babylonian Talmud Berakoth* VII.18, 16: "Blessed [be God] that hath not made me a woman." See G. F. Moore, *Judaism in the First Centuries of the Christian Era, the Age of the Tannaim,* 3 vols. (Cambridge, Mass.: Harvard University Press, 1927–30), vol. 1, p. 128.

60. See Jeremias, *New Testament Theology,* vol. I, pp. 224–27.

61. *Tosefta Yadaim* 1–4; an alleged Pharisee's reply to an Essene sectary who had reproached him for pronouncing the Name in the morning without taking a ritual bath. Cited from A. Lukyn Williams, ed. and Eng. trans., *Justin Martyr. Dialogue with Trypho,* Translations of Christian Literature, series 1: Greek Texts (New York: Macmillan Co., 1931; London: SPCK, 1930), p. 170 n. 4. See also Ps. 119:1–4, for the Pharisaic ideal of purity.

62. Cited from Perrin, *Kingdom of God,* p. 187.

63. Ibid., pp. 176ff.

64. For Antipas's fear that Jesus was a political danger to him, see Grant, *Jesus,* pp. 129ff.

65. The miracle itself is reminiscent of Elisha's feeding of one hundred starving people (2 Kings 4:38–44). See Dodd, *Founder of Christianity,* pp. 131–35; for its lack of eucharistic significance, see Boobyer, "Eucharistic Interpretation of Miracles of Loaves," pp. 170–71.

66. See Montefiore, "Revolt in Desert?" The reference to "green grass" there (Mark 6:39) suggests early summer. Jesus could not have dashed his followers' hopes completely, for after the crucifixion in Luke 24:21 and Acts 1:6, the disciples are recorded as still thinking of Jesus restoring Israel. This aspiration was proclaimed on the coinage of the war of 66–74.

67. Matt. 20:25ff.

68. See Downing, "Jesus and Martyrdom." The transfiguration underlines Je-

sus' role as the prophet whom Israel "shall heed" (Deut. 18:15). See Flusser, *Jesus*, pp. 96–97.

69. Elijah is represented as suffering at the hands of Israel, Mark 9:13//Matt. 17:12, where Jesus is associated with Elijah (but not with the Suffering Servant of Isa. 53:1–12). See also C. K. Barrett, *Jesus and the Gospel Tradition* (Philadelphia: Fortress Press, 1968; London: SPCK Press, 1967, 1975), chap. 2.

70. On this concept see Moule, *Origin of Christology*, pp. 11–22 (references to recent discussion), and J. Emerton's, "The Origin of the Son of Man Imagery," *JTS* n.s. 9 (October 1958): 225–42.

71. See C. K. Barrett, "The Background of Mark 10:45," in *New Testament Essays: Studies in Memory of T. W. Manson, 1893–1958*, ed. A. J. B. Higgins, pp. 1–18 (Manchester, Eng.: Manchester University Press, 1959), esp. pp. 12–15 (equates this passage with Dan. 7:13ff., rather than Isa. 53).

72. Thus Dodd, *Founder of Christianity*, pp. 91–92.

73. The point was taken by early Christian writers, as Tertullian *On Baptism* XVI (CSEL 20.214), and Origen *Exhortation to Martyrdom* 28, "By 'cup' he means martyrdom"; and see Dodd, *Founder of Christianity*, pp. 94–95.

74. The contrast between Jesus' situation in his hours of success in Galilee and in this period as a semi-fugitive, is well drawn by Klausner, *Jesus*, pp. 299–306.

75. This, of course, conflicts with Luke's narrative 9:51ff. Luke, however, would have Jesus going to Jerusalem through Samaria and via Jericho, which is like traveling from York to London via Dover! "The journey cannot be satisfactorily traced on a map," Leaney's comment, *Gospel According to St. Luke*, p. 171. The account could be a conflation of several journeys which Jesus made to Jerusalem during his mission. Here we follow Mark 10:1ff.

76. For the Palestinian origin of this story, see Jeremias, *New Testament Theology*, vol. I, p. 90. Klausner (*Jesus*, p. 307) notes Jesus' approval of Bartimaeus's shouts, "Son of David, have mercy on me."

77. I prefer this dating to leaving a gap between October A.D. 29 and April A.D. 30 (compare Dodd, *Founder of Christianity*, p. 141).

78. Judas's anger was not wholly unreasonable; three hundred denarii would represent a year's good pay for someone lucky enough to earn a laborer's wage all the year round. So far as Judas's possible motives are concerned, see Klausner, *Jesus*, p. 325 and H. J. Schonfield, *Jesus: A Biography* (2d ed., London: Herbert Joseph, 1948), pp. 234–37.

79. On popular messianic expectations of the day, see above, n. 46. Hiers, *Historical Jesus*, pp. 78–83, draws attention to Jesus not rebuking those who tried to silence people who acclaimed him as Messiah (Luke 19:40). Bornkamm, *Jesus*, p. 158, dates Jesus' resolve to take the initiative against the Jewish leaders from this moment.

80. Hiers, *Historical Jesus*, p. 85 n. 28. The figs were not due to ripen for another eight weeks or so. Fig trees were sometimes associated with vines to represent the ideal life in the Promised Land and in the messianic age (1 Kings 4:25; Micah 4:4; Zech. 3:10).

81. Perhaps recalling also Zech. 14:21: "And there shall no longer be a trader in the house of the Lord of hosts on that day" (see Hiers, *Historical Jesus*, p. 86). See also Bornkamm, *Jesus*, p. 158–59, and E. Trocmé, "L'expulsion des marchands du Temple," *NTS* 15 (October 1968): 1–22.

82. See K. P. Donfried, "The Allegory of the Ten Virgins (Matt. 25:1-13) as a Summary of Matthean Theology," *JBL* 93 (September 1974): 415-28. "Oil serves as a symbol for good deeds" resulting from obedience to the Father. The same point is made by J. Massyngberde Ford, *A Trilogy on Wisdom and Celibacy* (Notre Dame, Ind.: University of Notre Dame Press, 1967), pp. 115ff.

83. Jesus shown as "being harried, spied upon and ready to sacrifice his life" in the pre-gospel tradition, see Trocmé, *Jesus and His Contemporaries*, p. 117.

84. For instance, Pilate had used money from the Temple treasury to build an aqueduct, and thereby had provoked a serious riot in which numerous Jews were killed. Josephus *Antiquities* XVIII.60-62, and *War* II.175-77 (cf. Matt. 27:6).

85. Philo, *Legatio ad Gaium* (*On the Embassy to Gaius*), Eng. trans. and ed. E. M. Smallwood (Leiden: E. J. Brill, 1961), 32.229-36: "No one is so senseless as to oppose his master when he is only a slave." See Josephus *Antiquities* XVIII.59, when on the occasion of Pilate's marching his standards and busts of the emperor through Jerusalem, the Jews were "casting themselves prostrate and baring their throats" and "welcomed death rather than make bold to transgress the wise provisions of the laws."

86. Jesus was not without supporters in the Sanhedrin; see Luke 23:51 and compare John 3:1 and 19:39. His enemies accused him primarily of being a "false prophet" (cf. Deut. 18:20-22) "leading the people astray" and "subverting the nation." See Dodd, "Historical Problem of Death of Jesus," p. 89.

87. The chronology of John and the Synoptists is impossible to reconcile (Bornkamm, *Jesus*, pp. 159-60). For the nature of the Last Supper, see J. Jeremias, "The Last Supper," *JTS* 50 (1949): 1-10, and idem, *Eucharistic Words*, pp. 41ff.

88. Particularly grossly, as they had just participated in a solemn Passover meal with him.

89. Matt. 26:63; Mark 14:61-64; Luke 22:70. See also Winter, *Trial of Jesus*, and his lecture on 19 February 1964, to "the Friends of the Kibbutz," "The Trial of Jesus" with bibliography. See also Dodd, "Historical Problem of Death of Jesus."

90. Thus, Trypho in his debate with Justin Martyr (c. 135), recorded by Justin *Trypho* 89.2.

91. For the procedure before Pilate, see Sherwin-White, *Roman Society*, chap. 2.

92. Pliny *Letters* X.96.3. Sherwin-White, *Roman Society*, pp. 25-26.

93. For the use of "a friend of Caesar's" and its high standing at this time, Philo, *In Flaccum* (*Against Flaccus*), LCL, VI.40.

94. For Pilate's contempt for the Jews, see Philo *Embassy* 38.301, "inflexible, stubborn and cruel disposition." Jesus' possible reflection of a Zealot outlook during his period in Jerusalem, see Trocmé, *Jesus and His Contemporaries*, pp. 118-19.

95. Despite the Evangelists' attempts to interpret as many as possible of Jesus' acts as fulfilling Old Testament prophecies concerning the Messiah.

96. Perhaps a reminiscence of Isa. 53:12, with the sense of the atoning power of his death. See Jeremias, *New Testament Theology*, vol. I, pp. 298-99.

97. See Barrett's analysis of Jesus' possible expectations, not least that messianic deliverance would take place in Passover night (*Jesus and Gospel Tradition*, pp. 46-53).

3

Paul and the First Expansion
30–65

The burial of Jesus in Joseph of Arimathea's rock-cut tomb marked his official death in the eyes of the authorities. As Tacitus stated eighty years later, he had been executed "by one of our procurators, Pontius Pilate."[1] While the events of the first Easter morning belong more to faith than history, it is evident that the tomb was indeed found to be empty.[2] The vivid impressions left by Jesus' appearances to his disciples in Galilee, added to memories of his life and character, kindled a flame of inspiration that quenched their doubts and sent them back to Jerusalem. There they would confront the high priests and the people with the news that Jesus had risen from the dead and was indeed the true Messiah of David's line but greater than David. The final chance for repentance followed by baptism and reception of the Holy Spirit was now. Some at least hoped that the day for the physical restoration of Israel's sovereignty had dawned also (Acts 1:6).

The decision, probably Peter's, to return to Jerusalem was among the most important made in the early history of the church. Ideas held by John the Baptist and the sectaries at Qumran that the kingdom was to be sought in the wilderness were tacitly abandoned for the more orthodox tradition that Jerusalem would be the scene of the great gathering in of the tribes of Israel. The wilderness tradition was also to become increasingly associated with revolutionary messianism as the crisis of the Jewish revolt approached.[3] For those, however, who would spread their message widely and quickly, Jerusalem was the only possible center, thronged as it was on feast days by Jews from every part of the Dispersion. The choice of Jerusalem as the headquarters of the infant church also involved a reorientation of Jesus' own ministry. While Jesus had been in Jerusalem for the great feasts of the Jewish year and had taught there, he had never made it his center. He had concentrated on rural Jewish folk, preaching and healing in the small towns and villages of Galilee, and in particular, he had left alone the Greco-Jewish cities of Palestine. This was to change radically. If John preserves an ancient tradition, Greek-speaking Jews may already have shown an interest in Jesus' teaching before the crucifixion (John 12:20). Almost at once members of the Greek-speaking synagogues in Jerusalem became attracted to the new community. This increased enormously the possible radius of the disciples' missionary activity. Within a short time after Pentecost, Samaria and the coastal towns of Palestine were the scene of missions and the word had spread as far as Damascus. A completely new dimension had been added to Jesus' mission not more than five years after the crucifixion. With the conversion of the Cypriot Levite—Barnabas—and finally of Paul, a move into the far-wider fields of Dispersion-Judaism became possible.

These developments focus, of course, on the personality of Paul. In the fifteen or so years, however, between the crucifixion and Paul's emergence from his long meditations in the Judean wilderness and his preliminary activities on behalf of the church in Syria and Cilicia, the way had already been prepared for the dramatic changes he was to bring to Christianity.

THE JERUSALEM COMMUNITY

Looking back from the vantage point of a generation or more after the crucifixion, Luke sees the events of his own lifetime in terms of a continuous and glorious advance of God's work, first through Jesus himself, then through the community at Jerusalem, and finally through Paul. All these phases reflected the ceaseless activity of the Holy Spirit working in Israel for the fulfillment of the promise to Abraham (Gen. 22:18; cf. 12:1-3) that "in your posterity shall all the families of the earth be blessed" (Acts 3:25). The Jerusalem community is portrayed in Luke in glowing terms of an ideal family, worshiping in the Temple, meeting in each other's houses for prayer and the breaking of bread (Acts 2:46)—an ideal that passed down to future generations of Christians, "Now the company of those who believed were of one heart and soul, and no one said that any of the things which he possessed was his own, but they had everything in common. . . . There was not a needy person among them" (Acts 4:32, 34). This was the true apostolic community. It resembled Philo's description of the Essenes (That every good man is free = *Quod Omnis Probus Liber Sit* 86).

The facts may have been more complex. In many respects the Christians living immediately after the crucifixion resembled other pietistic and messianic Jewish sects, especially that of Qumran, only they were situated in Jerusalem and were in no way opposed to the Temple cultus.[4] Indeed, the Christians were "assiduous in the Temple" and Luke casually mentions how Peter and John were on their way up to the Temple "at the hour of prayer, the ninth hour" (Acts 3:1). The apostles preached "in the temple" as well as in private houses (Acts 5:42) to relatively wealthy individuals and households. The sectarian character of the new movement is demonstrated, however, by the further statement that the apostles met "in Solomon's Portico" (in the Temple area) and that "none of the rest dared join them, but the people held them in high honor" (Acts 5:12-13). The Christians felt themselves to be a group distinct from their fellow Jews and immediately under the guidance of the Spirit whom they received in baptism. Like their Qumran contemporaries, they saw their life as the Way: they were the true congregation of Israel; their community of goods was complete but, looking forward to the speedy return of the Lord, they exercised a severer discipline over their members than did the Qumran sectaries. Ananias, as we have seen, would only have had to do penance with respect to one-quarter of his food and would have been excluded from fellowship for a year for deliberately withholding some of his goods from the common pool.[5] For the Christians no backsliding could be tolerated. The call, "Repent therefore, and turn again, that your sins may be blotted out" (Acts 3:19) and "repent, and be baptized . . . save yourselves from this crooked generation'' (Acts 2:38, 40), recalled the urgency and message of John the Baptist's preaching only three or four years before.

Even so, prophetic fervor was accompanied, as at Qumran, by elements of established leadership. Significantly, we are told that at this stage ''a great many of the priests were obedient to the faith'' (Acts 6:7). When he went to Jerusalem in 48, Paul knew of Peter, James, and John as the three ''pillars'' (Gal. 2:9), reminiscent of the three priests who appear to have presided at Qumran.[6] On his previous visit in c. 39, it was to James and Peter that he reported. Peter, as the first witness of the risen Lord (1 Cor. 15:5), was at first spokesman and leader but sometime in the A.D. 40s, James emerged as undisputed ruler of the church. How and why are not known. He is represented in later tradition as holy man, as Nazarite[7]—so constantly at prayer that his knees became hard like those of a camel—and also as high priest.[8] Peter and Paul became equated as chief missioners under his direction, the one to the Jews and the other to the Gentiles (Gal. 2:7-8). The keystone of the arch, however, was James, assisted by a council composed of the disciples at Jerusalem and elders subordinate to them.[9] It was to them that the all-important ''collections for the poor'' were sent from Dispersion churches and it was to them that the early missionaries reported. In one major particular, however, the church differed profoundly from Qumran. From the outset it was missionary. There was nothing parallel to the sectaries' obligation to ''cut themselves off from the sons of destruction'' (1QS8:12-13). The duty of making known the Lord's salvation to the heathen had been proclaimed by the psalmist (Ps. 98:2). A tradition (Acts 6:4) to be transmitted as widely as possible already existed. It was that of the risen Messiah, to be preached more urgently even than the teaching of the prophet of Nazareth. Jesus, proclaimed Peter, was a man singled out by God, who had performed mighty works and was the Messiah, foretold by David, who had been slain in ignorance by the Jews, but who would return and restore all things as had been announced by the prophets (Acts 2:22ff. and 3:12-26). Time for repentance was running out. Mission was among the believer's most important duties.

Not surprisingly, the ferment caused by this preaching spread to the network of Greek-speaking synagogues in Jerusalem. The choice, from Hellenistic Jews, of the seven ''deacons'' to serve at the common meals points to a growing Christian influence among them.[10] Suddenly in some of these synagogues, the latent discontents against the Temple found their focus. Stephen stressed the pedigree of Israel's salvation to Moses and the tabernacle rather than to Solomon's Temple ''made with hands'' (Acts 7:47-48). This intensely angered the Sadducean high priesthood and caused furious dissensions in the Hellenistic synagogues themselves. The Christians became caught up in a controversy—over the Temple and its cult—which they had done nothing to cause. Stephen was martyred—the anger he caused resulted in his ritual stoning. The opportunity may have been the interregnum in Roman authority occasioned by Pilate's recall in 36 (but equally it might be a year or more earlier). Among those prominent in the affair was a young Pharisee from Tarsus—perhaps from the synagogue of the Cilicians in Jerusalem—named Saul.

Saul was not to come into prominence in Christianity for another eleven years. Meantime, the outlines of the earliest Christian mission were emerging. First, the adherence of some of the Hellenists provided the Christians with what proved to be an all-important urban base for mission and organization. The rapid spread of Christianity beyond Palestine to Damascus must have been due to the news passing through the network of Hellenistic synagogues radiating from Jerusalem. From this time onward, Galilee and its associations with the historical Jesus lost importance and Christianity became transformed increasingly from a rural into an urban movement. Then the effect of the persecution against the Christians in Jerusalem following Stephen's murder was to scatter the leadership and spread the gospel still further in Judea and Samaria (Acts 8:1). Philip the Evangelist renewed the mission through Samaria preaching that Jesus was Son of God (that is, in the closest relation to God) and baptizing in the name of the "Lord Jesus," with the apostle's subsequent laying on of hands on converts (Acts 8:14). A token of Philip's success was his encounter with Simon Magus, a religious leader of some stature in the area. The latter's attempt to use the new preaching for his own ends received the full measure of apostolic wrath from Peter and John who followed up Philip's progress.[11] Philip himself then journeyed south to Gaza, baptized the first non-Jewish convert recorded—the Ethiopian eunuch—and finally moved into Caesarea, the capital of the Roman province of Judea. Having worked through the villages of Samaria—no mean feat for so pronounced a Galilean[12]—Peter undertook an even more important journey. He went to Lydda where there was already a Christian community, and thence to Joppa near Caesarea and where he stayed with a supporter Simon the tanner (another proof of the surprising spread of this first mission). There he heard of Cornelius, the semiproselyte ("devout"), a centurion in the Italian Cohort in the garrison at Caesarea. Not only did he baptize him, but he ate with him though from the Jewish point of view Cornelius was a Gentile and unclean. No other single act demonstrated the aim of the disciples within a few years after the crucifixion—to bear the Lord's name before the nations (Gentiles; cf. Pss. 98:2–3 and 96:10) in missions that far exceeded the scope of anything attempted by Jesus. The flame of universalism, looking back—beyond the time of the restoration of the Temple—to Second Isaiah, had been well and truly rekindled.

By 40 Christianity was established as a movement throughout Palestine. Beyond its borders a second important center was developing at Antioch. There the Christians were not known as "Nazarenes" as they were in Palestine, but as "men of Christ" (*Christianoi*). A Hellenistic church was

89

emerging whose members lacked direct experience or knowledge of Jesus himself. For them the risen Christ was their all-important guide to salvation, perhaps, if one may believe the account of the baptism of the Ethiopian eunuch, the fulfillment of the prophecy of the Suffering Servant (the Messiah) of Isaiah 53.

In 41–42 other significant events occurred. While the Christians were expanding their influence, Palestine had experienced a series of incidents that foreshadowed the breakdown of relations between Jews and Romans that took place a quarter of a century later. During the winter of 39–40 the Jews in Jamnia destroyed an altar erected by the pagan Greek minority in the town.[13] News of this event reached the emperor Caligula, and as a punishment he ordered that a gilded statue of himself should be set up in the Temple. Rome was moving away from the Jewish alliance, but for the Jews this step, reminiscent of a similar move by the Seleucid Antiochus IV Epiphanes, was intolerable. Very many (Philo suggests "thousands") were prepared to commit suicide or allow themselves to be killed by the Romans rather than acquiesce in this "abomination of desolation." They found a sympathetic advocate in Publius Petronius, the legate of Syria, who managed to postpone carrying out the order at some personal risk.[14] At Rome, Herod Agrippa, a grandson of Herod I, who in 37 had been appointed tetrarch of the dominions of Philip and Lysanias (Upper Galilee, Abilene, and parts of Lebanon) managed to get the order rescinded.[15] Caligula's murder on 24 January 41 prevented its renewal. Agrippa returned to Palestine determined to represent his people to the uttermost within the bounds of client-kingship. His territories had been enlarged to include Jerusalem and Judea and he had been granted the title of king. Jerusalem became his capital and the Sadducean high priesthood his allies. "No day passed for him without the prescribed sacrifice,"[16] commented Josephus. He appointed a new high priest, ordered those who had taken a Nazarite vow to display this by having their heads shorn,[17] and turned on the Christians. "He killed James the brother of John with the sword; and when he saw that it pleased the Jews, he proceeded to arrest Peter also" (Acts 12:2–3). The first organized persecution of the church had broken out.

Agrippa died suddenly in 44 and the persecution was not pressed home. Peter was enabled to escape from prison. John, if one understands Paul's reference in Gal. 2:9 aright, survived. The reason may be that, while the Christians found uncompromising opposition among the Sadducees, and while the Hellenists among them who attacked the Temple and proclaimed Jesus to be greater than Moses brought trouble on themselves, they had not by any means alienated all the Pharisees. The incident in which Gamaliel dissuaded the Sanhedrin from punishing the apostles severely (Acts 5:38) was a straw in the wind. Later, we find Pharisees among the active members of the church, representing the Jewish party at the apostolic council (Acts 15:5). At this stage there was some common ground between them and the Christians. Both believed in the resurrection of the dead and in angels, in opposition to the Sadducees.[18] Even in 58 Paul appealed successfully to Pharisaic support against the Sadducees on these grounds when brought before the Sanhedrin (Acts 23:6–7). That under James the church in Jerusalem was left in peace for nearly twenty years (42–62) may have been due partly to James's good relations with the Pharisees and other Jews "zealous for the law." For him, belief that Jesus was the Messiah and the national ideal of the Pharisaic brotherhood may not have seemed incompatible.[19] For Paul, one-time Pharisaic zealot, however, they were incompatible. The vision on the road to Damascus epitomized the dilemma facing a deep-thinking Pharisee when confronted by Christianity. Stephen, a Greek-speaking Jew fearlessly advocating a completely different direction for Judaism, found a responsive chord in Paul.[20] Neutrality was not possible.

THE EMERGENCE OF PAUL

Paul (Saul's Roman name) is one of the few individuals in history who merit the title "religious genius."[21] Some foundations for his achievement already existed before he set out with Barnabas on his first missionary journey in 46. The word was already being preached where it could be heard by the Gentiles, and Antioch was second only to Jerusalem as a Christian center. Paul, however, provided the church with that additional drive and inspiration needed to take it beyond any horizons imaginable by its Galilean leaders. Perhaps just in time, he shifted the orientation of Christianity away from Palestine to the centers of Greek and Hellenistic-Jewish culture in Asia Minor and on the European mainland.

The key date is somewhere about 48 when Paul and Barnabas traveled south from Antioch to Jerusalem to meet those same Galilean leaders there.[22] We have two near-contemporary accounts of this apostolic conference: Luke's, which suggests everything was settled happily by James's decision (Acts 15:19–20), and Paul's, contained in a letter to the Galatians (2:1–10) that is less reassuring. Both agree, however, that the issue was whether all converts to Christianity should be circumcised as well as baptized. This would have affirmed the character of Christianity as a reform movement within Judaism, attractive to both Hellenistic and Palestinian Jews, but whose membership could only be attained through the same processes as conversion to orthodox Judaism. It would have legitimized the Jerusalem Christians' claim to be the true Israel, but at the expense of the church's permanent expansion among the Gentiles. The Jerusalem case was therefore strong. Paul moreover had not treated the disciples at Jerusalem with courtesy, and deserved their opposition. Luke suggests that in the long debate, the running was made by Paul supported by Peter and Barnabas. Finally, James, mindful perhaps of Micah's prophecy that the nations would "turn in dread to the Lord" (Mic. 7:17), pronounced that Gentile converts need not be circumcised but should observe the prescriptions of the Law (Lev. 17:8ff.) concerning diet and sexual behavior, the terms of the so-called Noachian covenant traditionally binding on any "stranger within the gate" in Judaism. This was the "decision of the Holy Spirit," accepted unanimously and transmitted to the churches in Syria, Cilicia, and Antioch. There was to be a Gentile church.

Paul's account of the conference (Gal. 2:1–10) is far more abrasive. He was not interested in compromise, he was not prepared to concede unrestricted authority to the Jerusalem disciples, and he makes no reference to the "decision of the Holy Spirit," or James's right to pronounce it. He was carrying out God's mission and he had been opposed by "sham-Christians." The advocates of the circumcision party had been the stronger party; only his invincible determination to uphold the truth and freedom of the gospel had carried the day. Moreover, the battle was not over. Back at Antioch he had a public row with Peter over the right to eat meals with the Gentiles, and even Barnabas had gone over to the pro-Jewish party. This issue, Paul saw, would have been an equally serious barrier to the conversion of the Gentiles and to the establishment of the church as a new creation in which there was neither Jew nor Gentile but all were one in Christ.

As Luke appreciated a generation later Paul need not have fretted so much. The Jewish party had not gotten their way, and their cause was to fade. Meantime, the missions to the Gentiles and to the Jews were placed on an equal footing. The church did not split. The apostolic conference at Jerusalem marked a decisive moment in the expansion of Christianity. Gentiles were offered citizenship in the new order even if "by adoption." The way was open to recruit the considerable number of men and women in almost every Mediterranean town who had rejected polytheism, but could not accept the narrow limits of Judaism as an alternative. Paul had opened the way for the religion of Jesus to become the religion of the nations.

Only with reservations can Paul be called the interpreter of the religion of Jesus.[23] He believed that the end was approaching, but he did not preach that the coming of God's kingdom was to be prepared for by repentance. Salvation was already available to believers through the cross. It was a question of all having the chance to accept belief in Christ while there was time. For this purpose, however, Paul made no recorded attempt to explain Jesus' teaching, to prove from his words and deeds that he was the Messiah. He did not disavow the Jesus "born of woman" (Gal. 4:4), "descended from David" (Rom. 1:3), but he made no reference to the virgin birth, the miracles, or any salient incident in Jesus' ministry. Jesus remains implied rather than explicit throughout. He reminds the Corinthians of Jesus' command about divorce (1 Cor. 7:10) and the payment of ministers (1 Cor. 9:14), and he alludes to Jesus' words from an early tradition that has not survived: "It is more blessed to give than to receive" (Acts 20:35), but all this was secondary to him. The Lord Christ, the God-man to be known by faith, replaced the prophet of Nazareth experienced by the disciples. As he himself says, "Though we once regarded Christ from a human point of view, we regard him thus no longer" (2 Cor. 5:16). Perhaps there is some significance in Paul's comparatively full description of the institution of the Eucharist (1 Cor. 11:23–26) and Jesus' resurrection appearances (1 Cor. 15:5–9). These may have marked for him the reality of the crucified and risen Messiah and that Jesus was indeed he.[24]

There was, however, more than the difference between a pre- and post-Easter interpretaton of Jesus. Paul was inhibited by his urban and Hellenistic background from placing himself in the context of rural Palestine where Jesus had worked. His tart "Is it for oxen that God is concerned? Does he not speak entirely for our sake?" (1 Cor. 9:9–10) could be contrasted with Jesus' description of the lilies of the field surpassing Solomon in all his glory (Luke 12:23); similarly his concern to save an animal that had fallen into a pit on the Sabbath day (Luke 14:5). If Jesus taught the multitudes in the countryside and instructed his disciples to pray to God as a loving Father, Paul preached in towns to those who, like himself, spoke and read Greek and knew their Septuagint; and he sought to interpret the mystery of God's purposes, for the relative few who could comprehend such concepts.[25] He took up residence in provincial capitals—Corinth and Ephesus—and chose these as the centers from which Christianity could spread. He moved easily among the upper reaches of provincial society, to the governor's palace at Paphos or the Areopagus at Athens. He was not the man to feel compassion for crowds. In some ways, even his sense of the elite prepared the way for a Gnostic system of salvation.

Paul's strength lay in an ability to dictate immensely powerful letters which could not fail to impress their recipients. He was less happy as a preacher. While he could be effective, as the Thessalonians bore witness (1 Thess. 2:1ff.), he tended to bore or "rave" when uncertain of his audience. There was truth, however, in his Corinthian opponents' gibe that "his letters are weighty and strong, but his bodily presence is weak, and his speech is of no account" (2 Cor. 10:10). With the exception of Luke's composition of his speeches at Pisidian Antioch (Acts 13:16–41) and Athens (17:22–31), his missionary sermons have not survived.

His letters tell us a great deal about the man. He was vigorous, direct, and confident, sometimes arrogant and self-centered. He wrote for the occasion as he felt, not in the carefully studied literary style of the *Letter of Aristeas* or the *Letter to Diognetus*, and he could be biting and sarcastic as well as humble and pleading; but he was always genuine and utterly devoted to the task in hand which he believed was entrusted to him personally by God.[26] The letters to the Corinthians show him ranging from indignation and angry denunciation to personal reminiscence and judicial pronouncements and then—at the end of 1 Corinthians—poetry of great beauty. In

Philippians he was so overcome with sudden anger against the Jewish party that he lost all self-control (Phil. 3:2ff.), abandoning his previous line of argument and launching into a furious tirade against them. Even in Romans, theology was interrupted by what must be personal reminiscence, and finally by an effort to clear up a dispute in the congregation. Paul's influence on world history was to be immense, though his own life may have ended less successfully than he had hoped. He did not convert Gentiles en masse. The Jewish party was by no means done for in A.D. 60.

To strike a balance, it is worth remembering that his younger contemporary Epictetus the Stoic, starting far lower on the social scale than Paul, exercised a much-greater influence on his contemporaries than did Paul.[27] In the next century he was regarded as one of humanity's guides. Paul died obscurely in Rome and, though remembered with honor by the next generation of Christians, his name was not free from controversy (2 Peter 3:15–16). Yet the seed he sowed on his missionary journeys ultimately became the main stem of the Christian interpretation of Jesus' gospel.

Paul was born into a strict Jewish Dispersion (that is, Diaspora) household at Tarsus. It was bilingual Greek and Hebrew, but Hebrew-thinking. Paul was proud of his lineage "of the people of Israel" and "of the tribe of Benjamin"—hence his name Saul (Phil. 3:5). He never lost his pride of ancestry. "Are they Hebrews? So am I. Are they Israelites? So am I. Are they descendants of Abraham? So am I." So he responds to his Corinthian opponents (2 Cor. 11:22). Pride of race and his calling as a Pharisee remained fundamental throughout his life. His family, however, was one of the relatively few favored members of the Dispersion to acquire Roman citizenship. He was born a Roman citizen, one of the five million or so privileged inhabitants of the empire, a fact that safeguarded him from humiliating punishments, enabled him to take a high hand with local authorities and opened the way to levels of provincial society that would otherwise have been denied him.[28]

Dual status did not make his family less Jewish. It was to Palestine and not Tarsus that Paul was sent for his education, probably after the age of fourteen. His sister married and lived in Jerusalem with her family (Acts 23:16). He was trained in the Law under Rabbi Gamaliel the Elder. He became a Pharisee gaining, as he says, a reputation for precision and enthusiasm beyond his years, "so extremely zealous was I for the traditions of my fathers" (Gal. 1:14 and compare Phil. 3:5–6). How such a man could conceivably have been drawn towards the Gentiles to the extent that he spent his working life attempting to convert them to the gospel of the risen Christ remains a mystery. There is nothing in Paul's extant writings that suggests that he had any acquaintance, outside anthologies, with the Greek poets and philosophers.[29] His own reading seems to have been dominated by the Septuagint, especially the Psalms and the Wisdom literature. He shows not the slightest interest in harmonizing the Jewish scriptural heritage with Greek philosophy. Scripture he interpreted according to the rules and traditions accepted by the rabbis of his day. His attitude towards pagans as illustrated in Romans 1 was that of contemporary Pharisees.[30] The pagans had deserted God's natural order, they had fallen into idolatry, and from idolatry came the long catalog of vice and wickedness with which the Jew reproached them (thus Eph. 4:17ff.). "So they are without excuse; for although they knew God they did not honor him as God" (Rom. 1:20–21). "Gentile" and "sinners" were equated in his mind (Gal. 2:15). The "commonwealth of Israel" was always the model to which Gentiles must conform (Eph. 2:12).

Why then did he want to help them? The explanation that he was shocked at the prospect of their utter destruction at the coming judgment is unproven.[31] He never agonized over the prospective fate of Gentiles as he does over that of his own people (Rom. 9:1–5). He may perhaps have been rather more influenced by the native religions and the mystery cults of his city than he cared to admit, and as he grew older he came to hate the ritual demands of the Law. Why should Gentiles who accepted Christ be circumcised in order to be saved? Was not the whole Law fulfilled in "You shall love your neighbor as yourself" (Gal. 5:14). But this was a later development. Was it the belief that God must be God of the Gentiles as well as the Jews that influenced him originally? (Rom. 3:29). Did he once think of becoming a missionary to the Gentiles before his conversion, as suggested perhaps in Gal. 5:11? What trait in Paul's character that made him the obvious choice to accompany Barnabas into Gentile territory in 46 to preach the gospel remains a matter of speculation.

THE MISSION

By then Paul had been a Christian for about eleven years. After his conversion he stayed first in Damascus where he was baptized, then went into the wilderness of southeastern Judea, and returned to Damascus as a member of a Hellenistic church. Despite his preaching in the synagogues that Jesus was "Son of God" and "the Christ" (Messiah; Acts 9:20, 22) and the attempt by the Arab ethnarch in Damascus (the head of the Arab community there) to have him arrested, the disciples in Jerusalem remained skeptical. Only after three years did he venture thither, and he saw only the two leaders James and Peter. They accepted him on Barnabas's recommendation (Acts 9:27) but then packed him off as far away as possible, via Caesarea, to his native Tarsus where he remained until 43–44. Paul did not forget. His contempt for these men "who were of repute" (Gal. 2:6), his repeated and emphatic outbursts against those who questioned his apostolic authority, and his assertion of equality with the "superlative apostles" (2 Cor. 12:11) may have originated from these snubs. In any event he had started his work without reference to Jerusalem. We would give much to know, however, what he was preaching in Syria and Cilicia, because this first missionary venture must have molded his attitudes during the remainder of his career. From Antioch, Barnabas brought him out of obscurity. He sought him out at Tarsus and thenceforth Paul's cause flourished. Probably in 44–45 he accompanied Barnabas to Jerusalem with famine relief for their fellow Christians in Judea. Evidently by now the community life there had broken down. The mention of elders who made the distribution suggests the existence of a hierarchy there (Acts 11:27–30). On his return to Antioch, Paul was designated to accompany Barnabas on a mission beyond the borders of Syria. Like a Levite of the old Israel he was set apart and hands were laid on Barnabas and him (Acts 13:2–3).[32]

Cyprus may have been chosen as a proving ground because of Barnabas's associations with it. That, after preaching in the synagogue at Paphos, the governor Sergius Paulus should invite apostles to talk with him shows the level at which the mission was being carried out. Its primary aim was the interest (and conversion) of the literate Jewish and proselyte synagogue congregation, an educated audience. Moreover, no conflict was discernible between Roman authority and the preaching of Jesus as Messiah, even though Jesus had died a felon's death only fifteen or so years before.

Success in Cyprus was followed by even greater triumphs among the larger towns of southern Asia Minor. The chronology of the three or four Pauline missions through Asia Minor and thence to the provinces of Macedonia and Achaia may be set down as follows:[33]

46–48 First missionary journey to Cyprus, Galatia, Pisidia, including Antioch, Lystra, and Derbe.

48 Return to Antioch and thence to Jerusalem for the apostolic council presided over by James.

49–52 Second missionary journey. Paul visits and strengthens the churches which he and Barnabas had founded, before moving through Phrygia northwest to the coast at Troas, and leaving out the major Greek cities of the province of Asia and those in Bithynia, both areas where Judaism was strong. From Troas he moves into Macedonia, preaching at Philippi, Beroea, Athens, and Corinth. His eighteen-month stay in Corinth is dated by its coincidence with the proconsulship of Gallio in 51–52.

53–56 Paul in Ephesus. Further missions by himself and his close associates up the Maeander valley as far as Colossae and probably Laodicea also.

56–57 A tour of inspection, including a three-month stay in Corinth (Acts 20:2), touching Philippi and Thessalonica, thence to Troas, and the Aegean islands.

58 Miletus (not Ephesus) and by ship to Jerusalem. Arrested there.

58–59 Prison in Jerusalem.

59–60 Journey to Rome.

60-62   Paul in Rome.
         Date of death unknown.

It is a record of astonishing activity. The energy required for such a program ending with imprisonment, and preaching even in his semicaptivity at Rome, was enormous. Paul was conscious of his powers of endurance. Thus he writes to the Corinthians, "Five times I have received at the hands of the Jews the forty lashes less one. Three times I have been beaten with rods [that is, by the Roman authorities]; once I was stoned. Three times I have been shipwrecked; a night and a day I have been adrift at sea; on frequent journeys, in danger from rivers, danger from robbers, danger from my own people, danger from Gentiles, danger in the city, danger in the wilderness, danger at sea, danger from false brethren; in toil and hardship, through many a sleepless night, in hunger and thirst, often without food, in cold and exposure" (2 Cor. 11:24–27). From Rome, a generation later, the writer of *1 Clement* (c. 95) added his tribute to Paul's remarkable determination and enterprise.[34]

What lay behind it? Partly, there was a personal need to prove that he was truly an apostle of the Lord Jesus Christ as he claimed to be.[35] At Jerusalem Paul was accepted as a missionary and reporter, in charge of the mission to the Gentiles as Peter was to the Jews (Gal. 2:8), but not as one who had witnessed the death and resurrection of Jesus. Only such witnesses could claim the title of apostle. Moreover, he was not trusted. At the outset his sudden conversion was not understood; in the end he was suspected of having given too much of the Jewish heritage away in order to win over Gentiles. Bouts of ill health combined with petty irritation at such things as the ability of Peter and other apostles to travel with their wives (1 Cor. 9:5) made him more difficult. Hence, he was always struggling. "Am I not an apostle? Have I not seen Jesus our Lord?" he asks the Corinthians (1 Cor. 9:1). "I did not receive it [the gospel] from man, nor was I taught it, but it came through a revelation of Jesus Christ" (Gal. 1:12). This was the point. The vision of the risen Christ on the road to Damascus could be set against the experience of the earthly Jesus shared by Peter with the other disciples. At Jerusalem James himself had been the recipient of a vision of the Lord (1 Cor. 15:7), but had not been a disciple. In this respect, Paul and he were on the same footing.

Second, Paul was an apocalyptist, believing that the end was rapidly approaching. He imagined himself carrying the gospel as one of the messengers (Rom. 10:15) promised for the end times.[36] The Messiah had already come though the end of history was delayed, perhaps to give humankind one final chance to repent. Thus he felt himself "under obligation" to Greeks and barbarians as well as to Jews (Rom. 1:14). Very shortly the messianic age would be succeeded by the final age to come which the souls of the righteous would enter upon at death. For the remainder who might

97

be living at this time, the prospect could be terrifying. There was no question in his mind of humanity possessing some saving and eternal spark of the Divinity that would preserve them from the world. On the contrary, Paul fully believed in the disasters and tribulations described in Jewish apocalyptic that would precede the end. The Lord Jesus, he told the Thessalonians (2 Thess. 1:7–9) in c. 52, would be revealed from heaven "with his mighty angels in flaming fire." He would do justice upon those who refused to acknowledge God and who would not obey the gospel of our Lord Jesus. Paul himself looked forward to the coming (1 Cor. 16:22), and in a beautiful, poetic passage in the same letter he spoke confidently that "we shall not all sleep," but that "we shall all be changed, in a moment, in the twinkling of an eye, at the last trumpet" (1 Cor. 15:51). Those who accepted Christ would be saved. "God has not destined us for wrath," he assured the Thessalonians (1 Thess. 5:9). A few years later he gave a similar assurance to the Christians of Corinth (1 Cor. 11:32). Persecution and the suffering of Christians would not only hasten the end, but also mitigate the horrors accompanying that event.[37]

Paul's beliefs concerning the resurrection were Pharisaic, traceable back to Dan. 12:2 if not beyond. He was, as has been said "not altogether an innovator but an able and advanced expositor of some current Jewish views";[38] but his acceptance of Jesus as true Messiah provided these beliefs with a sense of utmost urgency. He must preach salvation as far afield as possible, to Rome itself, to Illyricum, and even to Spain if he could. Humanity was indeed responsible for its misdeeds. The time of "ignorance" was past, he warned his hearers at Lystra and Athens.[39] Christ had appeared "in the fullness of time." Judgment was at hand. Even near the end of his life, writing to the Philippians from prison at Rome, he pondered whether it was better to hope for release and so continue preaching (Phil. 1:23–26) or rejoice that soon he would be sharing the sufferings of his Lord (3:10).

What did he hope to achieve? People more Jewish-looking than Paul and his companions were evidently difficult to imagine (Acts 16:20). Some success, however, he must have had. He alludes to the time when his Corinthian converts were "heathen" (1 Cor. 12:2), and the Colossians similarly, as people who were once "estranged and hostile in mind, doing evil deeds" (Col. 1:21), that is, pagans, and specifically the Thessalonians, having turned to God from idols (1 Thess. 1:9–10). But for all his emphasis on the Gentiles and having "broken down the dividing wall of hostility" between them and the Jews (Eph. 2:14), his recorded thoughts in his letters and his actions in Acts show little evidence of insight into the workings of the non-Jewish mind that he needed in order to succeed. Thus, when confronted with the bizarre situation at Lystra (Acts 14:8ff.), he appears at a loss. He could not speak about the Old Testament or about Jesus' messianic claims. This would have meant nothing to the Lycaonians. His good news was to attack idolatry as any Jewish missionary might, which would scarcely endear him to the priests who were about to honor him with a sacrifice. Why, they could have asked, should so beneficial a God become impatient to the extent of destroying his own creation? There is no sign of a considered line of argument aimed at attracting the ordinary pagan provincials he might encounter on his journey.

At Athens, too, Paul was unsuccessful. This time (if Luke-Acts gives a reasonably accurate account) he had made some attempt to study and conciliate his audience.[40] He appeared in the Jewish synagogue and in the Agora, and argued in both places. That he was taken up by local Stoics and Epicureans seems more than likely, and by the time he addressed the Court of Areopagus he had a coherent case to present. The initial reference to the dedication to "the unknown God" (or more likely, "gods")[41] was promising, and Paul's claim to be able to reveal its nature would have guaranteed him attention to the proof of God's existence from what his hearers could see around them. God as universal giver of life, he who fixed the epochs of history and set each race in its own territory would have interested the Stoics among his audience. Then came the quotation from Aratus, "We are also his offspring"—a blend of Stoic and Jewish universalism.[42] So far so good. This was to be the missionary preaching of the next generation. But once Paul left monotheism and turned to specifically Christian themes, the mood of his audience changed. With his reference to the need for repentance before an appointed day of judgment, common ground disappeared. At the climax of his address, with reference to the resurrection of Jesus, there was open mockery or polite disbelief. "So Paul went out from among them" (Acts 17:33). It was an anticlimax. He had failed to gain adherents for the new, strange gods called "Jesus" and "the Resurrection" (*Anastasis*).

Paul's real impact was on the Hellenistic-Jewish and "God-fearing" communities that existed wherever he preached. On this matter there is no conflict of evidence between Acts and Paul's letters. We have already seen how, at Antioch in Pisidia, Paul's sermon presupposed a thorough acquaintance among his hearers with the Septuagint, with its prophecies concerning the Messiah, and even of John the Baptist's preaching.[43] The pattern of Paul's experience at Antioch was repeated throughout his first two missionary journeys. On arriving at a new center he went straight to the synagogue or, where the Jewish community was too small, to the place where it met for prayer. His debates and disputes were with local Jews, or with rival groups of Jewish Christians. The converts we hear most about are women, such as Lydia at Philippi and Damaris at Athens. At Thessalonica he won over some Jews but "a great many of the devout Greeks" and "leading women" (Acts 17:4). Except at Ephesus where his three-year stay eventually provoked local traders to blame him for a decline in business connected with the city's patron goddess Artemis-Cybele, there is little recorded pagan reaction. Once a Christian community had been established, Paul's letters to its members presupposed a synagogue background. He used the normal Jewish salutations to them. The content breathed the Septuagint and synagogue society. The Corinthians were reminded, for instance, "that our fathers were all under the cloud" (1 Cor. 10:1)—what would this have meant to a pagan? The Colossians were chided for their strife about new moons, fasting, and angel-worship, typical Jewish problems (Col. 2:16–18).[44] The Romans to whom he wrote would be expected to bear the name of Jew (Rom. 2:17). The problems of ethics, worship, and administration he discussed make sense only against the background of the synagogue. When in Corinth Paul declared that henceforth he would go to the Gentiles, his progress was as far as the house of Titius Justus, "a worshiper of God" who lived next door to the synagogue (Acts 18:7). Seen as a mission to the "God-fearers," Paul's activity and his successes become intelligible.

Paul transformed the Dispersion. Morality, mysticism, promise of salvation without the Law were what very many of its members wanted to hear. It seems incredible that within a decade (47–57) the Dispersion communities in large parts of Asia Minor and Greece had been shaken to their foundations. A growing series of Christian synagogues had been established at Antioch, Iconium, Lystra, Derbe, Philippi, and Beroea, to say nothing of the provincial capitals of Paphos, Ephesus, Thessalonica, and Corinth. Wherever the indefatigable little man and his companions went they left communities behind, with Athens the only known exception. Three years at Ephesus saw that community brimming over with enthusiasm and Paul's disciples making their way up the Maeander valley as far as Colossae and Laodicea. Even more remarkable is the obvious joy with which Paul's words were heard. The Galatians, he says, received him "as an angel of God, as Christ Jesus" (Gal. 4:14). The Thessalonians heard the word of God "with joy inspired by the Holy Spirit" (1 Thess. 1:6) though Paul and Silas arrived under the worst conditions. To the Corinthians he conveyed Spirit and power (1 Cor. 2:4) contrasting perhaps with the "lofty words of wisdom" (1 Cor. 2:1) with which he had wooed the Athenians. Paul, too, was not the only Christian missionary of his time. The prosperous community at Rome he did not found, and there was the work of the former follower of John the Baptist, Apollos of Alexandria and, of course, of Peter. The Dispersion had been more than ready for some such message as Paul and his fellow missionaries brought. Christianity never looked back.

Paul, too, shows that within the limitations of the interim, he was intending to found permanent communities on a worldwide scale. He organized ministries everywhere to carry on his work. His letters also show that he tried to see the problems that arose in the communities on a broad canvas and to be judged by what he considered to be the entire gospel of salvation.

He would not take sides in local quarrels though he would give advice to all.[45] Christ welcomed everyone, Jews and Gentiles, strong and weak to sing his praises in unison (Rom. 15:6–13). The vision was universal, and so was Paul's ambition. When he speaks of Philippi he includes all Macedonia in his view (Phil. 4:15). Ephesus is shorthand for Asia, and Corinth for Achaia (1 Cor. 16:1, 2 Cor. 1:1). His enthusiasm was boundless. Rome even was to be only a stopping place on the road further west to Spain— and beyond (Rom. 15:23).

THE OPPOSITION

Understandable too, is the unremitting hostility of the Jews and the pro-Jewish party. The latter were, after all, Christian missionaries themselves willing, like Paul, to work in Asia Minor and the Greek cities on the mainland. They were not opposed to the conversion of Gentiles, only they insisted that the church was Israel, and to enter one must become an Israelite.[46] To this there would be added the inevitable misunderstandings with Peter's mission to the Jews, as occurred at Corinth. For loyal Jews, Paul was a disaster. He had thrown into the open many of the unresolved tensions within the Dispersion. They were aghast at the consequences. The speech of their lawyer Tertullus (Acts 24:1–8), hired by them to accuse Paul in Jerusalem, tells of their anguish. Paul was "an agitator among all the Jews throughout the world." If he was right, Moses was wrong and the promises to Abraham were in vain. If Paul went free, the ideal of Jewish universalism was dead, and the communities of the Dispersion would be a prey to discord and schism.

The events of 58 in Jerusalem were merely the climax of their opposition. These Jewish opponents were often fair-minded enough to give Paul a favorable first hearing in the local synagogue. Once the significance of his message had been grasped they would react violently, their opposition confirmed by other Jews arriving from towns where Paul had been preaching. Then Paul and his friends would be assaulted, charged before the magistrates, beaten, imprisoned and left for dead. The experiences of Iconium and Lystra (Acts 14:19) were repeated on the second missionary journey (Acts 17:5–15), and from Corinth Paul wrote to the Thessalonians complaining of the Jews who persecuted him there and tried to prevent him preaching salvation to the Gentiles (1 Thess. 2:15–16). That Dispersion Jews should have thought it worthwhile to pursue him in Jerusalem shows the depth of feeling his preaching had aroused.

THE PAULINE CHRIST

Even in a Hellenistic-Jewish environment his message would have been startling enough. The majority of Jews in the Dispersion were, as we have seen, loyal to their religion.[47] They would have agreed with Simeon the Just that the world stood on three things: Torah, the worship of the temple, and acts of love (*Pirke Aboth* 1.2). Paul retained the last, but replaced Torah and Temple by Jesus Christ and faith in him.[48] Through faith in Christ the believer entered into the sphere of God's grace "in which we stand" (Rom. 5:1–2). A religion centered on the personality and love of Jesus could not be expressed in terms of the Law.[49] Law and grace were not compatible, as Marcion in the next century saw.[50]

Many of the intermediate steps to this fundamental proposition could, however, be taken within the framework of current Judaism. Thus, to have proclaimed the coming of the Messiah in synagogues during the 50s need not have caused opposition. That the Messiah should suffer, as many people believed the prophets had suffered, and that this should atone for Israel's collective guilt was also possibly acceptable.[51] Had not Abraham been ready to sacrifice his only son Isaac in obedience to the Lord's command?[52] (Cf. Isaiah 53 on the Suffering Servant.) Two things, however, made Paul's representation of Jesus as Messiah impossible: First, that Jesus had been executed as a criminal at the behest of the high priests at Jerusalem. Second, Paul associated this individual with the creative force in the universe, the *Logos* (Word) or *Sophia* (Wisdom) of Hellenistic-Jewish speculation, and proclaimed him redeemer of humankind. In addition, he was telling his audiences that the Law had been superseded by the new law of Christ and was useless for salvation. Instead, it was an occasion for sin.

The concepts of Davidic Messiah and divine creative power personalized in God's Word or Wisdom had run a parallel course in Judaism for more than a century. They had never been brought together and could not be without infringing on Jewish monotheism.[53] Paul's concept of the "Son of God" transcends the limits of Jewish messianism. "Christ is Lord" implied lordship over the universe. Jesus' claim was simply to a unique filial relationship to his Father. By the time he wrote to the Corinthians in c. 53, Paul had developed in his mind the equation of Christ with the divine Wisdom incarnate ("Christ the power of God and the wisdom of God" [1 Cor. 1:24]). When he wrote to the Colossians from prison in Rome (c. 60), he would speak of Jesus in terms of unequivocal divinity. He was the Being "in him all things were created." "All things were created through him." Like Wisdom in Prov. 8:22, Christ was "before all things," "the first-born of all creation"; "the image of the invisible God," in whom the whole fullness of the Godhead dwelt, and therefore supreme over the whole created order whether seen or unseen (Col. 1:15–19).[54] In his letter to the Philippians written at the same period, Paul describes Christ descending on earth "in the likeness of men" (Phil. 2:7). Bethlehem was far away. The germs of christological controversy had been sown. In the next generation Christians were worshiping Christ "as a God."[55]

Closely allied to these ideas was Paul's concept of Christ as second Adam, reversing the damage caused to humanity by the sin of the first

Adam. To Jews of the time Adam was conceived as a being embodying all the attributes of man in their perfection and possessing gigantic stature.[56] His fall involved all humanity in sin and death and, in some speculation, the animal kingdom as well.[57] In the messianic age, however, the evil consequences of the fall would be undone. Paul accepted this teaching, but transferred it to Christ. Just as death established its reign through the sin of one man, so God's grace and his gift of righteousness lived and reigned through one man Jesus Christ (1 Cor. 15:21; Rom. 5:17). Christ's resurrection had overthrown death. He was the sole means of reconciling "all things, whether on earth or in heaven" (Col. 1:20). In Christ the believer was both pardoned ("justified") and reconciled to God.

In these passages also, the emphasis lay on the heavenly Lord and Savior rather than the earthly Christ. As Christ was the second Adam, so believers were participants in this new creation, whose head was Christ.[58] Christ had indeed made all things new (2 Cor. 5:17). The Christian belonged to a new and restored humanity—the Jews in the first place by birthright, Gentiles afterwards by adoption (Rom. 11:17ff.). The rhetorical dualism of "flesh" (that is, material pleasures and hopes) versus "spirit," the "old man" to be replaced by "the new," emphasized the break with the past—whether Jewish or Gentile—required of the Christian. Just as the three phases of circumcision, baptism, and the offering in the Temple united the proselyte to Israel and freed him or her from the ignorance and blindness of paganism, so baptism was the sign of the Christian's sharing in Christ's death and resurrection and entering into a heritage of salvation. Once baptized, members formed a brotherhood (1 Thess. 4:9). They were all members of one another (1 Cor. 12:25–26), sealed and committed like Paul himself in every whit to Christ, nailed to the cross mystically "in Christ." Having accepted the new yoke the Christian was a new creation (Gal. 6:15). He or she was free, justified by the grace of Christ and redeemed by love, delivered from the Law, from the world rulers, the planetary deities, and from death.

Paul was preaching a revolutionary religion of conversion and commitment to Christ, a new exodus based on a new Torah.[59] While most of the individual features of his preaching originated in Judaism and might not be unfamiliar to an educated Hellenistic-Jewish audience, the total effect was novel. To be "in Christ," to share in the age to come, was not the same as being "in Israel" as proclaimed by Israel's prophets and teachers. The new remnant was "chosen by grace, . . . no longer on the basis of works" (Rom. 11:5–6). It was open to all. The urgency of Paul's universalism and his conviction that God's hidden purposes were being revealed through him at that very hour (cf. Col. 1:26)[60] resulted in his uniting, perhaps unconsciously, other strands of contemporary religious thought with Judaism. Paul's insistence on humanity's innate natural belief in God, his natural equality, the comparison he draws between the church and the human body, and even the "athletic" terminology he uses may point nonetheless

103

to a Stoic rather than a Jewish origin, even if one rejects the direct influence of Stoicism on his thought.[61]

Some elements also in Paul cannot be accounted for in Judaism alone.[62] It is not only phrases such as having "become slaves of God" (Rom. 6:22) that come near to the language of contemporary mystery cults, but ideas such as that of a salvation mystically achieved through baptism identifying the believer with the fate of a Savior who died and rose again (Gal. 3:27; Rom. 6:2ff.; and Col. 2:12), approximate to the beliefs instilled in converts to the mysteries, such as Isis-worship.[63] Their initiation was performed "ad instar voluntariae mortis et precariae salutis" (Apuleius *The Golden Ass* XI.24); and for Paul too, baptism was reserved as though it formed the final stage of initiation into the Christian mystery.[64] If Paul himself could interpret this with some reference to rabbinic teaching, it is doubtful whether his hearers always possessed this degree of sophistication. Baptism into the death and resurrection of Christ was not the same as being cleansed from sin through repentance. Again, the idea of the Savior rousing the believer from deep slumber, the heavy sleep of drunkenness (for example, in Eph. 5:14) seems more connected with the idioms of Iranian religion than with Judaism, and this concept continues in Gnosticism (for example, the Song of the Pearl).[65] Tarsus, at the crossroads of several religious ideas, left its mark on Paul. His opponents from Palestine, intent on preserving the word wherever it might be spread within the bounds of Judaism, had some justification for their attempts to refute the "Pauline heresy."

THE NEW RELIGION AND SOCIETY

If Paul's preaching through the synagogues of Asia Minor and Greece was revolutionary, his political and social outlook was more conservative.[66] The powers that be were of God. They were not to be resisted. Taxes were to be paid. Honor was to be given to those to whom honor was due (Rom. 13:1–7). There was not even the rider put by Luke into the mouth of Peter (Acts 5:29), "We must obey God rather than men." The work of the state and its officers to maintain peace and judge between good and evil was a necessary part of the world, even though that was destined soon to pass away.[67] For the interim, the social system also would remain as it was. The Christians of Thessalonica, who had drawn an obvious conclusion from Paul's preaching of the approaching end and abandoned their work, "living in idleness" (2 Thess. 3:11), were taken to task. The conventions of family life, "wives, be subject to your husbands, . . . husbands, love your wives, and do not be harsh with them. Children, obey your parents" (Col. 3:18–19), were to be maintained.[68] In particular, slavery would not be abolished. Everyone should remain in the state in which he or she was called, Paul told the Corinthians (1 Cor. 7:20). Not only in his letter to Philemon but also in Colossians (4:1), the continuance of slavery was assumed. "Masters, treat your slaves justly and fairly, knowing that you also have a

Master in heaven." Similar views are expressed in the letter to the Ephesians (6:5–6), and in the post-Pauline Pastorals (Titus 2:9) as well as in 1 Peter (2:18). The newfound love of Christ among the congregations might soften the distinctions between class and class, slave and free, but the institutions and conventions which resulted in these were not challenged.[69] The opposition of the Essenes to slavery and their praise of hard manual work—particularly agricultural work—were not repeated by Paul.[70] Neither he nor the first generations of Christians went much beyond the Pharisaic code of charity toward one's neighbor.

Paul's ideas suited his audiences, educated members of the synagogue like Aquila and Priscilla who could travel extensively or people like Stephanas (1 Cor. 1:16) with their own household and hence their servants and slaves.[71] Lydia, the immigrant to Philippi from Thyatira in Asia, was converted and "baptized, with her household" (Acts 16:15). At Beroea the Jews who listened to Paul were well read, and examined "the scriptures daily" to check whether he had a case, and believers there included "Greek women of high standing" (Acts 17:11–12). The list of twenty-six Christians in Romans 16 includes three with households and Erastus the city treasurer of Corinth (?; cf. Rom. 16.23). Though the Christians at Corinth may not have contained many wealthy or noble members (1 Cor. 1:26), Paul's letters to them suggest an articulate and not unprosperous community whose sins arose from greed and affluence rather than from poverty. Christian services were and continued to be held in the houses of the richer members.[72] Paul's message was not directed to the outcasts and misfits of society—the inhabitants of the highways and byways—or even primarily to slaves. In this respect the difference between him and his Lord was fundamental.

The effect of his fervent message combining the idealism of struggle of the new age emerging from the old (1 Cor. 2:6) and the vision of the glorious future in store for those redeemed in Christ was, however, electrifying. Freedom and release from fears, taboos, and restraints was the immediate result of his preaching: "All things are lawful" (1 Cor. 10:23) or as Paul notes in 1 Corinthians (4:8), "Without us you have become kings!" Paul had opened a Pandora's box among the Jews and God-fearers wherever he established Christian communities. His first letter to the Corinthians indicates that the proclamation of freedom from the Law through the love of Christ and the approaching end led to wild revivalist prophesyings in which men and women participated, to claims of possession of "knowledge" (that is, esoteric knowledge of the beyond), and to the ending of all previous restrictions on eating ritually impure food (such as meat offered to the pagan gods) or participating in meals held in a temple. Paul, attempting to instill a sense of propriety and discipline in the congregation, foreshadowed the problems that would confront the church in connection with the Gnostics in the next century. The strongly individualist libertine tradition in early Christianity may be traced back to the Pauline mission, but not beyond.[73]

PAUL AND JAMES

Paul's fantastic energy and his success in the Dispersion put severe strains on the unity of the church. Personal rivalries and schisms he foresaw, as he told the presbyters at Miletus (Acts 20:30). That rival groups formed quickly among the Christians there is shown in 1 Corinthians. In 2 Corinthians we find the church in actual rebellion against him (2 Cor. 2:5—7:12). In addition, Acts and Paul's letters show that there were quarrels between Paul and his colleagues. He parted from Barnabas. He does not seem to have liked Cephas. His relations with James were equivocal and pose serious problems of interpretation.[74] Paul's devotion to the Judean churches was sincere (thus, 1 Thess. 2:14). Gifts from his churches were to be sent to Jerusalem. This was the mother church. He himself insisted on going there despite forebodings and the warnings of friends and the prophet Agabus (Acts 21:11). Yet James and he would seem to disagree on the basic objectives of the mission. James was opposed to table-fellowship with Gentiles (Gal. 2:12), but had given way at the apostolic council of 48 on the primary issue of circumcision. His welcome for Paul on his arrival in Jerusalem in 58 to report on his mission to the Gentiles, however, was anything but warm (Acts 21:18–25). If Paul's concern was for spreading the word to Jews and Gentiles alike throughout the inhabited world, James's concern was for the "many thousands . . . among the Jews of those who have believed; . . . all zealous for the law" (Acts 21:20), and clearly he hoped that eventually Gentiles would listen to "Moses' spokesmen" in their cities and accept the Law. Paul had moved away from the Temple and Judaism's historic mission while James was moving back towards orthodox Judaism. He may have aimed at a new and reformed high priesthood based on the new covenant with himself as the Aaron to his brother's Moses. Other movements of reform, such as that of the Maccabees, had involved the removal of unworthy holders of the office; why not that inspired by his brother? If such were his hopes (and later generations believed he wore the high priestly insignia on his forehead),[75] they were frustrated by the growing forces of Jewish fanaticism to which Acts bears witness (Acts 21:27–28; 22:22).

THE PAULINE MINISTRY

Paul's ideas were different. In his lifetime his churches were moving away from the Jerusalem model. In Jerusalem, James seems to have presided over elders who formed a sort of Christian Sanhedrin. His power was authoritative if not absolute.[76] In 57–58 the Temple seems still to have been a dominating factor in the life of the community. Taxes were paid to it (cf. Matt. 17:24), and the performance by Christians of the obligations of the

Nazarite vow in the Temple seems not to have been unusual (Acts 21:23). Paul also had a strong authoritarian streak in his character. His was the only message. "If any one is preaching to you a gospel contrary to that which you received," he tells the Galatians (Gal. 1:9), "let him be accursed." In the Pauline churches, however, there was no high priestly succession but a wide range of office holders, apostles, prophets, teachers (1 Cor. 12:28; Eph. 4:11), who moved from place to place, alongside the presbyters and subordinate "helpers," "administrators," and "speakers in various kinds of tongues" who served a local congregation. All baptized Christians lived under the inspiration of the Spirit and all were equal in the sight of the Lord. That admitted, officers were being appointed in each community and the churches became centers of a fairly elaborate social structure based on the households of the converted as well as individual converts such as Philemon (Phlm. 1–3) or Gaius at Corinth (Rom. 16:23).[77] The earliest specifically Christian officials were the "prophets and teachers" mentioned in Acts 13:1. These continued throughout the period of Paul's mission and beyond. In the first missionary journey Paul and Barnabas left their newly founded congregations under the leadership of presbyters. "They had appointed elders for them in every church" (Acts 14:23). In his letter to the Philippians, however, Paul refers to "bishops and deacons" there (Phil. 1:1). The contradiction may be more apparent than real. The deacon was always the subordinate whether in the liturgy or dispensing works of mercy. The presbyter and bishop were one and the same individual, which Paul shows when he addressed the leaders of the church of Ephesus at Miletus in 58 (Acts 20:17, 28).[78] Outwardly, the Pauline churches were modeled on existing Jewish synagogues. The offices brought into being through the needs of the Spirit in the brief period before the end, however, would soon settle into more fixed molds of organization with clear-cut disciplinary rules when that event was delayed.

THE LITURGY

How the liturgy was developing in Jerusalem in the 50s and 60s is not known for certain. From James's attitude towards other matters (for example, the sanctity of the Nazarite vow), we may assume that Jewish feasts were celebrated and that Christian worship remained near to Jewish. Paul himself went to Jerusalem for Pentecost (Acts 20:16). His churches, however, were evolving their own forms of service, related to those of the Hellenistic synagogue, which were to set the pattern of the future Christian liturgy. A new Christian significance was being given to traditional feasts. Thus, on the Passover itself, Paul wrote to the Corinthians, "For Christ, our paschal lamb, has been sacrificed. Let us, therefore, celebrate the festival, not with the old leaven, the leaven of malice and evil, but with the unleavened bread of sincerity and truth" (1 Cor. 5:7–8). Other festivals, new moons, and even the Sabbath were being dismissed as "a shadow of what is to come" (cf. Col. 2:16–17).[79] For all Paul's attachment to Israel, church and synagogue were beginning to part ways.

BAPTISM AND EUCHARIST

The Christian ceremonies themselves, involving the coming of the Spirit into the believer, may have been accompanied by an elaborate liturgy. There was certainly sealing and anointing (Eph. 1:13; cf. 1 John 2:20). Water was used to symbolize the forgiveness of sins, and hands were laid on the convert to confer the Spirit on him (Acts 19:6). As A. D. Nock pointed out,[80] the Johannine baptism included remission of sins and "probably the eschatological significance of sealing the elect who should be members of the Kingdom." Paul's view of the rite stated to the community at Rome included both those aspects combined with new, mystical meanings which appear to reflect pagan rather than Jewish influences. "Do you not know," he writes (Rom. 6:3), "that all of us who have been baptized into Christ Jesus were baptized into his death? We were buried therefore with him by baptism into death, so that as Christ was raised from the dead by the glory of the Father, we too might walk in the newness of life." Baptism, therefore, was the token of the new covenant. It brought the convert into intimate relation with Christ's death, which provided not merely the forgiveness of sin but completely new horizons of personal existence under the Spirit. Unlike Jesus' teaching, he or she did not become "as a little child," but, more in keeping with Philo's interpretation of proselyte status,[81] advanced from immaturity to full adulthood, as one who was capable of putting "on the whole armor of God" (Eph. 6:11).

How was this new life interpreted in worship? Aside from the prophesyings and ecstatic utterances at Corinth (1 Cor. 14), important though these were (cf. 1 Cor. 12:28), regular services probably were being held each Sunday—the day of Jesus' resurrection. The Eucharist was a memorial of Christ's death offered to God and a sacramental communion of the celebrants with their Lord. It was celebrated in all Gentile churches; and its form, with the words "Do this in remembrance of me" (1 Cor. 11:24), had already become a matter of tradition when Paul wrote to the Corinthians.[82] The *agape*, the fellowship meal, was associated with it,[83] and, if we may trust Pliny's letter to the emperor Trajan written in 112, separate from it and held afterwards.[84] These services, repeated Sunday after Sunday with hymns and prayers in anticipation of the second coming, were becoming part of the institution of the churches.[85] The need for order and leadership in worship moved their organization steadily in the direction of a single resident leader in charge of each community.

RELATIONS WITH THE AUTHORITIES

The disorder throughout the Dispersion that Paul was accused of stirring up had been confined to the eastern half of the Mediterranean. Within a few years of Paul's return to Jerusalem it had spread to Rome with catastrophic results for the future relations of the Christians with the authorities. The writer of Acts portrays the latter as consistently sympathetic towards the Christians.[86] Sergius Paulus rebuffed Elymas the sorcerer who sought "to turn away the proconsul from the faith" (Acts 13:8). Gallio had driven the Jews, who were accusing Paul, from his court (Acts 18:17); in Caesarea, only Felix's hope for a bribe and Porcius Festus's attempt to use Paul as a pawn in a diplomatic wrangle with the Jews kept the apostle in bonds. On the long voyage to Rome in 59 and in the capital itself Paul is shown to be receiving every consideration except unconditional freedom. It is tempting to think of Acts as being completed by the end of 62 with Paul preaching and making converts "unhindered" among the freedmen in the service of the emperor and the senatorial aristocracy of the capital.[87] The success of the Christian mission to date was confirmed by the tragic sequel.

THE NERONIAN PERSECUTION A.D. 64

Why Nero attempted to make the Christians the scapegoats for the disastrous fire on 19 July 64 that gutted entire districts of the city is unknown. That the promptings of orthodox Jews in the capital had something to do with it seems possible. The Jews were sometimes associated in the popular mind at this time with conflagrations of Gentile cities. They would be glad to use their influence at Nero's court to push the blame onto a hated rival synagogue.[88] In the background, too, of official and popular thinking was the memory of the Bacchanalian conspiracy of 186 B.C., more than two centuries before—meticulously chronicled by Livy.[89] How a small association of women worshipers of Bacchus developed into a vast politico-religious conspiracy among the plebeians that aimed at setting fire to Rome was a reminder of what happened when a foreign cult got out of hand. The fate of those involved had been exemplary. "More were killed than were thrown into prison," Livy commented, but the cult was not abolished entirely. Dread of the effects of outrage to the Roman gods wrestled with the equal dread of vengeance from the god whose worshipers had been done to death. Individual worshipers might be proscribed, but not the god himself. In 64 Nero probably sought to confront the angry and suspicious Roman people with the specter of a new Bacchanalian conspiracy, with the Christians and their newfangled God as the perpetrators.

Whether Peter and Paul were among the victims is not known. Later martyrologies number the apostles with 977 other Christians among the martyrs.[90] Important for the future of Christianity was that while this was an isolated catastrophe with no sequel even in Rome, it was not forgotten. Sixty years later the events were recalled by Tacitus with scant sympathy for the Christians.[91] In the same period another senatorial historian Suetonius lists the suppression of the Christians—"a class of men given to a new and wicked superstition"—among Nero's better acts.[92] Christianity was

109

henceforth associated with "evil religion" (*prava religio*) in the eyes of the ruling classes of the empire. It was not "legal religion" (*religio licita*). Its members, if denounced, could be punished as Christians, regardless of whether they were otherwise law-abiding persons. For more than a century the church was condemned to the life of a suspected and unpopular Judaistic sect that had no legal standing.

This situation was to overshadow the church in the period after Paul and the apostles. By 64, however, the new religious movement had taken root. Without detracting from the work of Peter, John, and the other disciples in the decade following the crucifixion, the credit belongs to Paul. Jesus was indeed the very ground of his being, but Paul had never experienced Jesus' ministry, and his interpretation of it gave Jesus' message a new and unexpected dimension. He transformed the proclamation of God's kingdom to "the lost sheep of the house of Israel" (Matt. 15:24) into a world movement. Despite all handicaps, Paul judged precisely the prevailing mood of very many fellow Dispersion Jews. The Galatians, as we have seen, received him with rapture (Gal. 4:14). On the mainland of Europe the Christians of Philippi were devoted to him. He offered a religion which, though basically Jewish, was stripped of the encumbrances of the Mosaic Law and its Pharisaic interpretations, a religion that had sufficient in common with Stoic ethics and the worship of the mystery cults to attract adherents on the outer fringes of the synagogue and even beyond. The ideal of a community in which there was neither bond nor free, Jew nor Greek, but which was united through love in a Savior (cf. Gal. 5:6), and freed thereby from the Law, the power of fate, and the malevolent astral lords of time, could also become the ideal of many of the inhabitants of the Greco-Roman world. The Savior whom Paul preached was not a savior god of current pagan myth but a historical figure invested with deity.

Though it was not apparent in his own lifetime, Paul had brought together some of the most powerful forces in the religious life of the empire. He had also encountered other forces almost equally powerful. The opposition, consisting of Jewish orthodoxy and Jewish nationalism on the one hand, and of provincial loyalty focused on the imperial cult and its increasing association with traditional native religion on the other, would not be overcome easily. Not until the social and economic life of the empire, of which paganism was a part, was put under intolerable strain during the third century did the Pauline mission reap its full harvest.

BIBLIOGRAPHY

NOTE

For the relative value of Acts and the Pauline letters as sources, see J. Knox, *Chapters in a Life of Paul* (Nashville: Abingdon Press, 1950; London: A. & C.

Black, 1954), part I. The literature on Paul is abundant and informative. For Paul himself, I have taken Adolf Deissmann, *Paul: A Study in Social and Religious History* (Eng. trans. W. E. Wilson. 2d rev. ed. [Garden City, N.Y.: Doubleday, Doran & Co., 1927; London: Hodder & Stoughton, 1926]), as a starting point. Günther Bornkamm's *Paul* (Eng. trans. D. M. G. Stalker [New York: Harper & Row, 1971]) is as stimulating as his *Jesus*, but by not accepting the Pauline authorship of Colossians and Ephesians, he ends Paul's letters on a rather forced note of climax with Romans. M. Grant's *Saint Paul* (New York: Charles Scribner's Sons, 1976) is a fast-moving account of the apostle's career. For the development of Paul's thought and its relation to rabbinic Judaism, W. D. Davies's great work *Paul and Rabbinic Judaism: Some Rabbinic Elements in Pauline Theology* (4th ed. [Philadelphia: Fortress Press; London: SPCK, 1980]), and H. J. Schoeps's equally significant contribution *Paul: The Theology of the Apostle in the Light of Jewish Religious History* (Eng. trans. H. Knight [Philadelphia: Westminster Press, London: Lutterworth Press, 1961]) are essential. W. L. Knox, *St. Paul and the Church of the Gentiles* (New York: Macmillan Co.; Cambridge: At the University Press, 1939) and A. D. Nock's studies in A. E. J. Rawlinson, ed., *Essays on the Trinity and the Incarnation by Members of the Anglican Communion* (New York and London: Longmans, Green & Co., 1928) are also among the ageless. Renewed interest in the social background of the Pauline mission and its communities is furthered by E. A. Judge, *The Social Pattern of the Christian Groups in the First Century: Some Prolegomena to the Study of New Testament Ideas of Social Obligation* (London: Tyndale Press, 1960), and by A. J. Malherbe, *Social Aspects of Early Christianity,* Second Edition, Enlarged (Philadelphia: Fortress Press, 1983), this latter adding to its usefulness by its abundant references and discussion of other authors' views. The Pauline ministry is discussed by A. A. T. Ehrhardt, *The Apostolic Succession in the First Two Centuries of the Church* (London: Lutterworth Press, 1953), and by W. Telfer in *The Office of a Bishop* (London: Darton, Longman & Todd, 1962), chap. 1. Liturgy is referred to in G. B. Caird's *The Apostolic Age* (Toronto: Thomas Nelson & Sons; London: Gerald Duckworth & Co., 1955).

Students should consult the quarterly issues of *New Testament Abstracts* (Cambridge, Mass.) for current articles on the New Testament period.

For the Neronian persecution, see this author's *Martyrdom and Persecution in the Early Church: A Study of a Conflict from the Maccabees to Donatus* (Garden City, N.Y.: Doubleday Anchor Books, 1967; Oxford: Basil Blackwell & Mott, 1965), chap. 6, with the literature cited there.

SECONDARY WORKS

Andresen, C. and Klein, G., eds., *Theologia Crucis, Signum Crucis: Festschrift für Erich Dinkler zum 70. Geburtstag.* Tübingen: J. C. B. Mohr (Paul Siebeck), 1979.

Bammel, E. "Judenverfolgung und Näherwartung zur eschatologie des Ersten Thessalonicherbriefs." *ZTK* 56 (1959): 294–315.

Barrett, C. K. *From First Adam to Last: A Study in Pauline Theology.* New York: Charles Scribner's Sons; London: A. & C. Black, 1962.

Bruce, F. F. *Paul and Jesus.* Grand Rapids: Baker Book House, 1974.

Dibelius, M. *Paul.* Edited and completed by W. G. Kümmel. Eng. trans. F. Clarke. Philadelphia: Westminster Press; London: Longmans, Green & Co., 1953.

_____. "Paul in Athens." In *Studies in the Acts of the Apostles.* Edited by H. Greeven. Eng. trans. M. Ling and P. Schubert (chap. 4), pp. 78–84. New York: Charles Scribner's Sons; London: SCM Press, 1956.

Easton, B. S. *Early Christianity: The Purpose of Acts and Other Papers.* Edited by F. C. Grant. Toronto: Oxford University Press, 1954; London: SPCK, 1955.

Ehrhardt, A. A. T. "Jewish and Christian Ordination," *JEH* 5 (1954): 125–38.

Foakes-Jackson, F. J., and Lake, K., eds., *The Beginnings of Christianity: The Acts of the Apostles.* Reprint ed. Grand Rapids: Baker Book House, 1979.

Goguel, M. *The Birth of Christianity.* Eng. trans. H. C. Snape. New York: Macmillan Co., 1954; London: George Allen & Unwin, 1953.

Goppelt, L. A. *Apostolic and Post-Apostolic Times.* Eng. trans. R. A. Guelich. London: A. & C. Black, 1970.

Hunter, A. M. *Paul and His Predecessors.* New rev. ed. Philadelphia: Westminster Press; London: SCM Press, 1961.

Johnson, Sherman E. "The Dead Sea Manual of Discipline and the Jerusalem Church of Acts." In *The Scrolls and the New Testament,* ed. K. Stendahl, pp. 129–42. New York: Harper & Brothers, 1957; London: SCM Press, 1958.

Knox, J. *The Early Church and the Coming Great Church.* Nashville: Abingdon Press, 1955; London: Epworth Press, 1957.

Lebreton, J. "The Missions of St. Paul." Chap. 3 in *The History of the Primitive Church* by Lebreton and J. Zeiller, Eng. trans. E. C. Messenger, vol. 1, pp. 201–83.

Morrison, C. D. *The Powers That Be: Earthly Rulers and Demonic Powers in Romans 13:1–7.* SBT 29. London: SCM Press, 1960.

Nock, A. D. *St. Paul.* New York: Harper & Brothers, 1938.

Ste. Croix, G. E. M. de. "Early Christian Attitudes Towards Property and Slavery." In *Church, Society and Politics,* ed. D. Baker, pp. 1–38. Studies in Church History, vol. 12. Oxford: Basil Blackwell & Mott, 1975.

Schlatter, A. *Jesus und Paulus.* 3d ed. Stuttgart: Calwer Verlag, 1961.

Sevenster, J. N. *Paul and Seneca.* NT Sup. 4. Leiden: E. J. Brill, 1961.

Simon, M. *Le christianisme antique et son contexte religieux.* Scripta Varia. 2 vols. WUNT 23. Tübingen: J. C. B. Mohr (Paul Siebeck), 1981 (important essays).

_____. *Les premiers chrétiens.* Paris: Presses universitaires de France, 1952; 3d ed., 1967.

Unnik, W. C. E. van. *Tarsus or Jerusalem: The City of Paul's Youth.* Eng. trans. G. Ogg. Naperville, Ill.: Alec R. Allenson, 1962.

Wiles, M. F. *The Divine Apostle: The Interpretation of St. Paul's Epistles in the Early Church.* New York and Cambridge: Cambridge University Press, 1967.

NOTES

1. Tacitus *Annals* XV.44.

2. See Hans von Campenhausen, "The Events of Easter and the Empty Tomb," in *Tradition and Life in the Church: Essays and Lectures in Church History,* Eng. trans. A. V. Littledale (Philadelphia: Fortress Press; London: William Collins Sons, 1968), pp. 42–89, esp. pp. 54ff.

3. See Acts 21:38 on the Egyptian who led four thousand men (of the Assassins)

out into the wilderness. Cf. Flavius Josephus on the rise of the *Sicarii*, esp. *Bellum Judaicum* (*The Jewish War*), LCL, II.254–58, 261–63.

4. See S. E. Johnson, "Dead Sea Manual of Discipline," esp. pp. 136–37.

5. *The Community Rule* (1QS) 6.25 in G. Vermès, ed. and Eng. trans., *The Dead Sea Scrolls in English* (Baltimore: Penguin Books, rev. ed., 1970; Harmondsworth, Eng.: Penguin Books, 1963), p. 82 (see above, pp. 28 and 49 n. 65).

6. S. E. Johnson, "Dead Sea Manual of Discipline," p. 134. The Council of Twelve at Qumran may also be paralleled by the rule of the Twelve Apostles at Jerusalem (Acts 6:2).

7. For the obligations of a Nazarite, see Num. 6.

8. Hegesippus writing c. 175, cited by Eusebius *HE* II.23.5, and Epiphanius (circa A.D. 380) *Medicine Box* (*Panarion* = *Haereses*) 78.14.

9. For the existence of "the elders," see Acts 21:18. Even Peter had to justify himself before them (Acts 11:1).

10. The appointment of the seven, chiefly administrative officials, reminds one of Josephus's appointment of seven judges in each city of Galilee to adjudicate petty disputes during the Jewish revolt. See *War* II.569–71.

11. Acts 8:14ff. Another indication of the senior position held by Peter and John, and Peter's concern with mission rather than central administration. They were commissioned as apostolic delegates to Samaria.

12. For the hostility between Galileans and Samaritans, Josephus *War* II.232–40. (See above, p. 56.)

13. Philo, *Legatio ad Gaium* (*On the Embassy to Gaius*) Eng. trans. and ed. E. M. Smallwood (Leiden: E. J. Brill, 1961), 30.201–2. For a rather different account, omitting any reference to Jamnia, see Josephus *Antiquitates Judaicae* (*Antiquities of the Jews*) XVIII.261–72, and idem, *War* II.185–87.

14. Josephus *War* II.199–203; idem, *Antiquities* XVIII.302–5.

15. Josephus *Antiquities* XVIII.297–304.

16. Ibid., XIX.331. Josephus speaks highly of Agrippa, emphasizing his compassionate and forgiving nature. The pretext for the persecution is by no means clear.

17. Ibid., 294 (cf. Num. 6:5).

18. See above, p. 23.

19. For a good summary of James's position see Telfer, *Office of Bishop*, chap. 1.

20. "Paul was a natural extremist." Thus Nock, *St. Paul*, p. 73. I suggest a date A.D. 35–36 when Christianity had had a chance to take root outside Palestine.

21. See Deissmann's sketch of Paul to which I am much indebted: *Paul*, p. 82.

22. See Bornkamm, *Paul*, p. 31, "The assembly may very well be described as the most important event in the history of the primitive Church"; also Paul Johnson's stimulating pages, *The History of Christianity* (New York: Atheneum, 1976), pp. 3–5; and Schoeps, *Paul*, pp. 66–69.

23. Were the differences due only to "the time shift," as suggested by Bruce, *Paul and Jesus*, p. 21?

24. For a more positive assessment, see Schlatter, *Jesus und Paulus*, chap. 6.

25. Schlatter, *Jesus und Paulus*, p. 89.

26. Thus Deissmann, *Paul*, pp. 66–70.

27. For Epictetus's life and times, see W. A. Oldfather's (Eng. trans.) Introduction to *Epictetus* in LCL (2 vols., 1925, 1928). Origen writing in c. 248 (*Contra*

Celsum [*Against Celsus*] VI.2), shows that his influence remained strong among the provincials of the Roman east. He was admired "even by the common people," because "they perceive the improvement which his words effect in their lives"—a striking testimony to popular (pagan) aspirations even in this period of stress.

28. For a sketch and assessment of Paul's early life, see van Unnik, *Tarsus or Jerusalem*, pp. 17, 46ff.

29. The substance of Paul's thought is rabbinic through and through. He uses also traditions not found in Scripture but which belonged to Jewish oral tradition of the time, for example, 1 Cor. 10:4; Gal. 3:19, 4:29. (I owe these examples to my colleague, Rev. Professor Ernest Best.) At the same time, his view that every man "by nature" can apprehend God recalls current Stoicism, as occasionally does his idea of Law = Law of Nature, but determined by the Spirit of Christ (see C. H. Dodd, *The Bible and the Greeks* (2d ed. [Naperville, Ill.: Alec R. Allenson, 1954], pp. 6, 36). See further Schlatter's chapter "Paulus und das Griechentum," in *Jesus und Paulus*, pp. 127–41, on the lack of Greek influence on Paul's religious thought see over, pp. 103–4, and n. 59.

30. See Davies, *Paul and Rabbinic Judaism*, pp. 64–68 for current rabbinic Jewish attitudes towards the Gentiles that anticipated God's impending judgment on them.

31. Bornkamm, *Paul*, p. 12.

32. See Ehrhardt, "Jewish and Christian Ordination," and idem, *Apostolic Succession*, p. 32. The analogy with contemporary rabbinic ordination is, in Ehrhardt's view, unlikely ("Jewish and Christian Ordination," pp. 136–38).

33. Even today the chronology of Paul's missions is not agreed upon. Gallio's proconsulship of Achaia in 51–52 provides one of the few fixed points. Here I have followed mainly Grant, *Paul*, p. 223, though I have reduced the duration of the first mission from four to two years (that is, 46–48). For a similar scheme, see Lebreton, "Missions of St. Paul." He omits, however, Paul's tour of inspection in 56–57 as a separate event. For the letters, I accept Grant's dating and accept the ten Pauline epistles as genuine. If Ephesians is not authentic, then Colossians can hardly be either; but the idea that these were written by some unnamed disciple of Paul and subsequently found their way into the Pauline collection raises, at the moment, too many unproved and unprovable hypotheses. For the rejection of these two letters, however, see Bornkamm, *Paul*, pp. 241–42, 247, and the suggestion that Romans 16 (the greetings) forms part of a lost letter to the Ephesians.

34. *1 Clement* V:5–7. For Paul's physical endurance, see Deissmann, *Paul*, pp. 63–66.

35. See, on Paul's conflicts concerning the apostolate, Schoeps, *Paul*, pp. 70–74.

36. In Isa. 52:7. See Goppelt, *Apostolic and Post-Apostolic Times*, p. 89.

37. Thus, 1 Thess. 1:10; 1 Cor. 7:29; and Phil. 4:4–5. See Schoeps, *Paul*, pp. 101ff.; Davies, *Paul and Rabbinic Judaism*, pp. 285ff.

38. See C. H. Dodd, *The Apostolic Preaching and Its Developments* (New York: Harper & Row, 1962; London, Hodder & Stoughton, 1936), p. 79; and Bammel, "Judenverfolgung und Näherwartung."

39. Acts 14:16, 17:30–31. See Nock, *St. Paul*, p. 101.

40. See M. Dibelius, "Paul in Athens," "a Hellenistic speech about recognizing God," p. 81.

41. See Deissmann, *Paul*, Appendix "On the Altar to the Unknown God," pp. 261–64.

42. See Dibelius's analysis of Paul's speech in "Paul on the Areopagus," in Dibelius, *Studies in Acts*, pp. 26–78, esp. pp. 51–52 (Aratus), 54–57.

43. See above, p. 39.

44. Compare the mid-second century *Letter to Diognetus* IV.1 and V, showing continued Hellenistic-Jewish concern for these matters.

45. See Schoeps, *Paul*, pp. 74–77, particularly concerning the Jewish party working in opposition to Paul in Corinth.

46. As Peter himself seems to have implied when addressing Cornelius, Acts 10:35–37: Cornelius as a "God-fearer" and still a heathen in Jewish eyes.

47. Above, p. 34.

48. Davies, *Paul and Rabbinic Judaism*, pp. 171ff.

49. Thus, Rom. 7:4: "Likewise, my brethren, you have died to the law through the body of Christ." Compare also Schoeps's statement, "The old authority of the Law could not subsist alongside the new authority of the Messiah who had come in the flesh" (Schoeps, *Paul*, p. 200).

50. See below, p. 214.

51. Accepted in the second century by Trypho, Justin Martyr's Jewish interlocutor (*Dialogue with Trypho* 89.2): "The Scripture proclaims that the Christ is liable to suffering" (but not crucifixion!).

52. But the emphasis in most rabbinic teaching was on Abraham's obedience, not the possibility of his performing a human sacrifice. See also Schoeps, *Paul*, pp. 142–49, however, for parallels to Paul's doctrine of Christ's atoning sacrifice (Rom. 8:32) that existed in rabbinic interpretations of the role of Isaac as the type of the paschal lamb.

53. See Schoeps, *Paul*, pp. 149–58, "Judaism never knew a Messiah who himself possessed divine being, or was son of God except in a purely allegorical sense" (p. 158).

54. See W. L. Knox, *St. Paul*, pp. 162–64, and Schoeps, *Paul*, p. 153. Even in his letter to the Corinthians, Schoeps claims, "this heavenly Christ seems to have wholly absorbed the earthly Jesus into Himself." In 2 Cor. 3:1–7, Paul links Christ directly with the Spirit.

55. Pliny *Letters* X.96.7. See over, p. 141.

56. Davies, *Paul and Rabbinic Judaism*, pp. 45–47, quoting rabbinic sources.

57. Ibid., p. 39.

58. Ibid., pp. 55–57.

59. For this aspect of Paul's outlook, see ibid., chap. 4, "The Old and the New Israel: 'Nationalism'."

60. For the close connection of the "mystery" with Jewish apocalyptic, see Ernst Lohmeyer, *Die Briefe an die Philipper, an die Kolosser und an Philemon*, Kritisch-exegetischer Kommentar über Neue Testament 9 (Göttingen: Vandenhoeck & Ruprecht, 1964), Part II, pp. 81–83.

61. See, however, the discussions by A. D. Nock, "Early Gentile Christianity and Its Hellenistic Background," in Rawlinson, ed., *Essays on the Trinity*, pp. 51–156, esp. pp. 147–50, and Nock's generally negative position: "In general, we may also be sceptical as to any large measure of Stoic influence on the Pauline writ-

ings." Also Sevenster, *Paul and Seneca*, and his similar conclusion (p. 240) that the process by which the resemblances between Christianity and Stoicism were no longer restricted to a few words and expressions "was not ushered in by Paul."

62. One such would be the derivation of the Pauline *"Christus soter,"* from the savior god, such as the Heraclean deity Sandan celebrated in Tarsus (Schoeps, *Paul*, pp. 159–60).

63. See M. Simon, "The *Religionsgeschichtliche Schule*, Fifty Years Later," *RelS* 11 (June 1975): 135–44.

64. Simon, *"Religionsgeschichtliche,"* pp. 139–40.

65. See Geo Widengren, *The Gnostic Attitude*, Eng. trans. and ed. B. A. Pearson (Santa Barbara: University of California, Institute of Religious Studies, 1973), pp. 35–38, citing the Song of the Pearl (lines 34–35) and a Manichean text.

66. See C. D. Morrison's discussion in *Powers That Be*, and C. J. Cadoux, *The Early Church and the World: A History of the Christian Attitude to Pagan Society and the State Down to the Time of Constantinus* (New York: Charles Scribner's Sons, 1925), pp. 109–15.

67. See Malherbe, *Social Aspects of Early Christianity*, pp. 24–28. I think, however, the parallel drawn between the early Christians and the Epicureans should be treated with reserve.

68. On the importance of these lists of social duties in the household in both Hellenistic-Jewish and Christian ethic and mission, see Malherbe, *Social Aspects of Early Christianity*, pp. 50–54 (useful references).

69. See the important article by Ste. Croix, "Early Christian Attitudes," p. 19, and briefly in Cadoux, *Early Church and World*, pp. 133–35.

70. Josephus *Antiquities* XVIII.21: "They [the Essenes] neither bring wives into the community nor do they own slaves, since they believe that the latter practice contributes to injustice and the former opens the way to a source of dissension." The Essenes did necessary menial tasks for each other.

71. See the studies by Judge, *Social Pattern of Christian Groups*, chap. 6, and Malherbe, *Social Aspects of Early Christianity*, chap. 3, who stresses rightly the relations between the early church and urban society implied by the house churches.

72. Noted by Malherbe, *Social Aspects of Early Christianity*, pp. 68–70, 74.

73. See Morton Smith, *Clement of Alexandria and a Secret Gospel of Mark* (Cambridge, Mass.: Harvard University Press, 1972), pp. 259–64. I am not convinced, however, by his suggestion (pp. 178–83) that "the mystery of the kingdom" was concerned with secret or magical rites of baptism involving sexuality.

74. See Goguel, *Birth of Christianity*, pp. 143–44 (growing anti-Pauline attitude of the Jerusalem church between 44 and 58) and pp. 345–49; and Karl Holl, "Der Kirchenbegriff des Paulus in seinem Verhältnis zu dem der Urgemeinde," *Gesammelte Aufsätze zur Kirchengeschichte*, 3 vols. (Tübingen: J. C. B. Mohr [Paul Siebeck], 1928), vol. II, pp. 44–67.

75. Hegesippus (c. 175) cited by Eusebius *HE* II.23.6.

76. Epiphanius *Medicine Box* 78.14. Like Jesus himself, James is recorded in Ebionite tradition to have performed miracles, and was known simply as "The Just." See above, n. 8.

77. See Malherbe, *Social Aspects of Early Christianity*, pp. 71ff., discusses recent (to 1977) literature on the social composition of the early churches.

78. On the Pauline churches and their ministries, see Ehrhardt, *Apostolic Succession*, pp. 28–34 (problem of "successions"), and Telfer, *Office of Bishop*, pp. 29–36.

79. Compare also Gal. 4:10–11.

80. Nock, "Early Gentile Christianity," pp. 111–20.

81. For Philo's views, see above, p. 36.

82. Following Schoeps's interpretation, *Paul*, p. 117; and see also Hunter, *Paul and Predecessors*, pp. 65–78.

83. Thus, 1 Cor. 11:33. See K. G. Kuhn, "The Lord's Supper and the Communal Meal at Qumran," in *Scrolls and New Testament*, ed. Stendahl, pp. 65–93, esp. pp. 88–89.

84. Pliny *Letters* X.96.7. The origins may go back to the suppers for the poor associated with Israelite feasts (Deut. 16:13–15). See B. Reicke, *Diakonie, Festfreude und Zelos*, Uppsala Universitets Årsskrift 51.5 (Uppsala: Lundequist, 1951), pp. 25–32.

85. For early Christian hymns, see Caird, *Apostolic Age*, pp. 113–14. For each bringing "a hymn, a lesson, a revelation" at the service, see 1 Cor. 14:26.

86. Thus, Easton, *Early Christianity*, pp. 42ff.

87. Thus, Phil. 4:22. For the judicial aspect of Paul's trial at Rome, see A. N. Sherwin-White, *Roman Society and Roman Law in the New Testament*. The Sarum Lectures 1960–1961 (New York and London: Oxford University Press, 1963) pp. 108–19.

88. See Frend, *Martyrdom and Persecution*, pp. 163–65.

89. Livy, *History of Rome*, LCL, XXXIX.8.

90. See the lists or calendars of Christian martyrs, especially the best-known and oldest: *Martyrologium Hieronymianum* (*Acta Sanctorum*), ed. L. Duchesne and J. B. de Rossi (Brussels, 1894) under 29 June (hardly a possible date, as the fire did not occur until 19 July).

91. As a reading of *Annals* XV.44 shows.

92. Suetonius *Nero* 16.2. The author does not, however, connect the punishment of the Christians with the fire, which he records elsewhere (*Nero* 38.2). His words "nova et malefica" imply "revolution" and "black magic" as Pliny suspected of the Christians in Bithynia in 112 (see below, p. 150).

4

The Christian Synagogue 70–135

The Neronian persecution was only one of the crises that confronted the infant church between A.D. 60 and 70. In 62, two years after Paul had arrived in Rome, his superior and, to some extent, his rival James was judicially murdered by the Sadducean high priesthood supported by the fickle mob—the same combination that had proved fatal to his brother. The Christians in Jerusalem had not recovered from that blow when the great Jewish revolt of 66 overwhelmed them. Whether they emigrated to the Greek city of Pella in the Decapolis cannot be stated for certain, and for all intents and purposes they seem to fade from history.[1] They suffered the fate of many historical moderates. After the catastrophe of the fall of Jerusalem to Titus in 70 the Jewish people in Palestine rallied to the Pharisees, the traditional upholders of religion and nationality. Christians in Jesus' homeland had little to hope for. The succession of bishops in Jerusalem lost importance. No great personality arose to rival Rabbis Johanan ben Zakkai, Gamaliel II, and Akiba. Between 70 and 135 Christianity became a religion based very largely on the geography and organization of the Hellenistic synagogue. In this form it started its long challenge to the Greco-Roman world.

The sub-apostolic period, extending between the two Jewish uprisings of 66–74 and 132–35, is confused and difficult to disentangle. The fall of Jerusalem left the Christians without a central point of reference. They were ill-prepared for this. Paul had established churches ruled by their own officers, but had been less interested in any overall scheme of church authority for the interim period before the coming which he believed would be short. Apart from the shadowy figures of "the presbyter" Aristion and John of Ephesus, there is little evidence for authoritative leadership in this period. This lack showed itself in divergent and inconsistent attitudes towards society and differing interpretations of the faith even among communities that fell within the bounds of an emerging concept of orthodoxy. It is difficult to conceive of the book of Revelation and *1 Clement*, both written, it would seem, near the end of the first century A.D., as products of adherents of the same religion. Jesus was Lord, but as hopes of his immediate coming began to fade, outlooks that were less dominated by concepts of the direct sovereignty of the Spirit began to assert themselves. Spiritual power, prophets, and apocalyptic had now to compete with the emergence within Christianity of ideas imbued with the morality of the enlightened Pharisaism that had influenced so strongly the Hellenistic-Jewish communities in the past, and also a residential and hierarchical ministry.

Despite the many obstacles towards understanding this period, including lack of agreement over the dating and origin of many of the key documents, certain features emerge: First, the life, thought, and organization of the church can be understood only within the framework of Hellenistic Judaism. Were the Christians the true Israel, bearers of the new covenant, the holy Remnant, or were they rebels and outsiders? Second, as a corollary to this controversy, the expansion of the church was accompanied by counterattacks by orthodox Jews and the pro-Jewish party within the church that have left their mark on the later books of the New Testament and on some of the sub-apostolic writings. Jews and Christians were rivals for proselytes in the Gentile world. Third, within the constraints implied in "the faith which was once for all delivered to the saints" (Jude 3), there remained pronounced differences in organization and interpretation of belief in the large but disconnected areas where Christianity was taking root. Finally, despite introspective tendencies among the Christian communities (very few references to secular events are to be found in the sub-apostolic writings), Christians began to impinge on the life of the empire and come to the notice of the authorities independently of Judaism. We attempt to follow these developments in this chapter.

THE NEW ISRAEL AND THE OLD

Tentatively we may divide the sub-apostolic period into two phases, between c. 65 and 100 and from 100 to 135. The first phase sees the compilation of the four Gospels in their final form, the later books of the New Testament, probably also the *Gospel of Thomas*, and the sub-apostolic texts of the *Didache* and *1 Clement*. The second phase includes the bulk of the sub-apostolic literature, *2 Clement* (Rome, c. 100?), the *Letters* of Ignatius (c. 107), *The Letter of Polycarp to the Philippians* (c. 108), Papias of Hierapolis (c. 130), and the *Letter of Barnabas* (Alexandria, c. 135?). It may also have seen the emergence of those curious Egyptian non-canonical but non-Gnostic gospels, such as the "Unknown Gospel," *The Gospel of the Hebrews*, and *The Gospel of the Egyptians*. It saw also the first attempts at Christian apologetic literature in *The Apology of Quadratus* (written c. 125), of which Eusebius preserves a single fragment (*HE* IV.3).

Until the close of the New Testament period, the church claimed to be Israel and wrote to the synagogues of the Dispersion accordingly. Thus, the writer of the New Testament letter of James (c. 80?) addresses "the Twelve Tribes which are in the dispersion" (*en te diaspora*), and 1 Peter (about the same date?) "to those of God's scattered people who lodge for a while in Pontus, Galatia, Cappadocia, Asia, and Bithynia." Jewish communities would have been addressed thus. Churches were being thought of in the same terms. Again, John's Gospel (c. 90) has Jesus speaking of himself as "the true vine" (John 15:1) and his followers as the branches, the symbols of Judaism, as these appeared on the coinage of the revolutionaries of 66–74. For John himself, Jesus' teaching summed up the entire message of Israel ("Before Abraham was, I am" [John 8:58]), and his coming to execute judgment on believers and unbelievers would not be long delayed.

In this period churches were still regarded as synagogues, whose members prayed three times a day and fasted twice a week like Jews, only they

121

chose Wednesday and Friday to commemorate Christ's arrest and crucifixion and not the normal Jewish Monday and Thursday.[2] They professed monotheism in the same terms as did the Jews. They used the Hebrew Scriptures, and they took the messianism, the eschatology (even the angelology), and the ethics of Judaism for granted, and like the Jews they claimed to be the "saints" (Jude 3; 1 Tim. 5:10; Heb. 6:10), "the people of God" (Heb. 4:9), "a royal priesthood" and "holy nation" (1 Peter 2:9). Within individual congregations they continued to think, argue, and act like their Jewish counterparts. For instance, *1 Clement* contains a *haggadah* on Adam and his sons (*1 Clement* III–IV).[3] Though he was violently anti-Jewish, *Barnabas*—perhaps near the end of the sub-apostolic period—presented his case for the messiahship of Jesus in the same way as a rabbi would have done. He divided his tract into *haggadah* (chs. 1–17) and *halakah* (18–20) and included a commentary on the "Two Ways of Light and Darkness," such as one finds in the Jewish Ethiopian *Enoch* and in the sectarian literature of Qumran,[4] and he interpreted Scripture in the same manner as did the sectaries. He claimed, of course, that Scripture (LXX) and its prophecies were fulfilled by Jesus and Jesus alone, but nonetheless the influence of Essene or Essene-type Judaism remained strong in his outlook.

Luke-Acts, dating perhaps to c. 75–80 in its final form, shows how closely the Christians were following another type of Jewish model. Luke was an educated Hellenistic Jew, perhaps from Antioch, the interpreter of Paul, who aimed, if not at writing a definitive Gospel, at least in improving on the work of predecessors (Luke 1:1), "having followed all things closely for some time past" (Luke 1:3). He leaves the clearest impression of the church as the new Israel, like the old, universal in scope, Greek in its language, and retaining a real respect for the Law as observed and interpreted by Jesus. One notes that while Matthew, in many respects more Jewish than Luke, stresses the fulfillment by Jesus of messianic prophecies, Luke emphasizes Jesus' fulfillment of the Law.[5]

Thus, Jesus himself underwent all the prescriptions of the Law, including that of Law apprentice (*bar mitzvah*) and rabbinic disciple in the Temple (Luke 2:41ff.). His ministry fulfilled the essence of the religion of the Old Testament. The life of the early church described in the first chapters of Acts was determined by its unqualified adherence to the Law. Only Luke tells of Moses having "those who preach him" (Acts 15:21) and his passing on to the Jews the words of life (Acts 7:38; cf. Deut. 32:47). Circumcision remained an essential part of the Law, but Gentile Christians were guaranteed salvation through acceptance of the older covenant of Noah through which they would become associated with Israel. Luke might indeed have written to refute those Jews who denied the right of the Christians to call themselves "Israel."[6] If, as seems probable, his Gospel gained most currency of all the Gospels in the Hellenistic world, there can be little question of the members of the "new Israel" desiring to break all links with the old in the period from 75 to 100.

The debate, therefore, over the importance of "Judeo-" (or "Jewish") Christianity in the sub-apostolic era is to some extent misconceived.[7] All Christianity at this stage was "Jewish Christianity." But it was Israel with a difference. First and foremost, as we have already noted, no Jew could have accepted Jesus Christ "as God." Yet in 2 *Clement* and in Pliny's report on the Christians in Bithynia c. 112, this was what the Christians were doing. "Brethren, we must think of Jesus Christ as God, as of the Judge of the living and the dead,"[8] so the writer of 2 *Clement* opens his sermon and similar ideas permeate the *Letters* of Ignatius. Second, though the Christians expected the same signs and wonders to herald the coming of the Messiah as did the Jews,[9] it was Jesus Christ whom they awaited. The new covenant with the house of Israel and Judah foretold by Jeremiah (Jer. 31:31–34) was already in force and it was greatly superior to the old. God had spoken in times past in fragmentary and varied fashion through the prophets. Now he spoke in this final age through his Son. Thus, the opening words of the letter to the Hebrews. Christians had a sense of liberation from the real shackles of the Law. One can feel this as one reads the twelfth chapter of Hebrews, where, following the long *haggadah* on faith (chap. 11), the writer contrasts the palpable "blazing fire" of Sinai with its dreadful taboos, before which Moses and the Israelites trembled, with "Mount Zion and . . . the heavenly Jerusalem," with its "innumerable angels in festal gathering," and the "first-born who are enrolled in heaven." This would be the heritage in store for the Christian. This was the new covenant whose "sprinkled blood . . . speaks more graciously than the blood of Abel" (Heb. 12:18–25). This was an astounding claim, for all examples of righteousness in Israel's salvation history led back to Abel. Now the direction was changed and all were to look forward to the fulfillment of Israel's hopes in Christ. To tell the philosophic yet profoundly patriotic and traditional Jews who read 4 Maccabees[10] that Jesus' sacrifice was infinitely greater than Abel's and ensured that the worshiper had "confidence to enter the sanctuary" (Heb. 10:19), was to challenge orthodox Judaism and provoke the swiftest of reactions.

That appears to have happened. In this respect the story of Christianity in both phases of the sub-apostolic period continues that of Paul. One only needs to peruse the later books of the New Testament and the apostolic fathers to realize that the churches were being perpetually harassed by enemies who could only be orthodox Jews and their allies.[11] Thus, the Pastoral epistles compiled perhaps c. 65–75[12] refer directly to the "empty talkers and deceivers, especially the circumcision party" who, though claiming to be Christians, were disrupting the life of the community (Titus 1:10). In 1 Timothy, Timothy was instructed to remain at Ephesus to "charge certain persons not to teach any different doctrine, nor to occupy themselves with myths and endless genealogies" (1 Tim. 1:3–4). The "myths and genealogies" can only refer to Jews or Jewish Christians. Similar disputes had previously driven Paul to write to the Colossians, and, in the form of "new moons," were among the complaints made against Judaism by the writer of *The Letter to Diognetus* in the mid–second century.[13] Similarly, the "false prophets" denounced in 1 John 4:1 who denied that Jesus was Messiah could hardly be other than Jews. The struggle against these enemies was desperate, for 1 John makes an urgent call to faith. "It is the last hour; and as you have heard that antichrist is coming, so now many antichrists have come" (1 John 2:18). The "synagogue of Satan" (Rev. 2:9), those "who say that they are Jews and are not, but lie" (Rev. 3:9), were an ever-present adversary in the last decades of the first century. Loyal Christians were, as *1 Clement* asserted, "the true Israelites."[14]

In the next generation, perhaps in some way connected with the decisions of the Jewish academy of Jamnia and the expulsion of Christians from the synagogues (John 9:22), the issues between Jew and Christian became more clear cut. After circa A.D. 100 there was less of a tendency for Christians to claim to be Israel and more of a tendency to contrast Christianity and Judaism as separate religions. Christianity claimed to be heir to the universalist claims of Judaism. "Catholic" or "universal" was applied to the church for the first time.[15] One can recognize the transition in Ignatius's *Letters*. Ignatius was writing under emotional stress as he journeyed through Asia Minor to Rome where he expected to be martyred c. 107/8. He opened his mind to all the Christian communities through which he passed, denouncing heresies and urging the fullest respect for the episcopal office. He hated the Jews and rejected any identification between the church and Judaism, but he was also profoundly influenced by Judaism. It was "outrageous to utter the name of Christ and live in Judaism,"[16] he asserted. "Judaism" had been cast off as "tombstones and sepulchres of the dead," "ancient fables" that were profitless. The Lord's Day was to be lived for, not the Sabbath.[17] Yet he found his own inspiration "through the Hebrew prophets" who lived according to Jesus Christ, and for all his unreserved devotion to the cross, he thought of martyrdom in the same sacrificial terms as did the Antiochene Jews responsible (probably) for 4 Maccabees. He uses the rare word $\dot{\alpha}\nu\tau\acute{\iota}\psi\upsilon\chi o\nu$ found in 4 Maccabees, but not in the New Testament,[18] to express the idea of martyrdom as ransom.

There was obviously a good deal of fluidity between the Jewish and Christian communities in Antioch and in the cities of Asia according to Ignatius: "But if anyone interpret Judaism to you do not listen to him; for it is better to hear Christianity from the circumcised than Judaism from the uncircumcised."[19] The main issue between the two communities concerned the proof from Scripture that Jesus was Messiah. Qumran had had its Testimony literature in favor of the Righteous Teacher.[20] Testimonies and proof texts derived from the Old Testament indicating that Jesus was Messiah played a crucial part in the debate. Matthew's Gospel is dominated by such considerations. Jews and Christians accepted Scripture as the voice of God. His will and purposes were unchanging and hence his message as set down in Scripture must be self-consistent. Either Jesus did fulfill the prophecies and was Messiah, or he did not and was a fraud who suffered—a just reward for his deceit. For the Jew, a suffering Prophet Messiah was conceivable; however, one who had died as a felon on the cross was not.[21] No compromise was possible. At the end of the period, *Barnabas* was shrill in his anger against the Jews—"wretched men," he calls them—and mixed fanciful allegories with mosaics of testimony to prove his argument that Jesus was indeed Messiah, and that he had been destined to suffer. The Jews misunderstood their own Scriptures. Yet almost in the same breath he admitted that he was "one of yourselves and especially loving you all above my own life."[22] The sub-apostolic age is dominated by the love-hate relationship between members of the two "Israels." It was left to Marcion in the 140s to cut the Gordian knot and deny the relevance of the Old Testament to Jesus' saving work.

As the argument dragged on, both Jews and Christians were competing for converts. It would be a mistake to think that after the fall of Jerusalem Judaism turned in upon itself. In Palestine it reorganized itself quickly around the scholars of the academy at Jamnia under a leader (patriarch) of the house of Hillel. There is the tale of the Pharisee, Johanan ben Zakkai (d. 83?), sole survivor of the Jerusalem Sanhedrin, escaping from the Zealots during the siege of Jerusalem, making his way to the Roman lines, and asking permission to establish an academy at Jamnia.[23] The story indicates the character of the future leadership of Judaism and its acceptance of the protection of Roman power. Josephus himself, one-time Pharisee and commander of the Jewish armies in Galilee also became firmly pro-Roman, indicating in his story of the great revolt how time and again the forces of moderation among the Jews were overborne by fanatics bent on the destruction of Jewry. The defenders of Masada he respected, but he did not share their aspirations.

Josephus, like Philo a generation before, believed strongly in the universal mission of Judaism. In *Against Apion*, he tells the Alexandrians that they would receive a warm welcome from their Jewish brethren if they joined them.[24] His appeal to pagans was pitched high.[25] "Distinguish between piety and impiety," worship not in temples made with hands, but spiritually, as exemplified by the prophets. Jewish and Christian propaganda were following parallel lines. Josephus's contemporary, the writer of the *Sibylline Oracles*, Book IV, was more urgent. Perhaps inspired by the eruption of Vesuvius in 79, he told his hearers that God would burn the whole earth and consume the whole race of men. "He shall burn everything out and there shall be sooty dust," he asserted.[26] Time to repent was perilously short. On one ground or another Judaism, like Christianity, was presenting itself as a universal religion. It did not fall entirely on deaf ears. Juvenal, writing of Rome c. 125, shows that conversions to Judaism could be gradual but involve families over two generations.[27] But the results were thorough. Justin Martyr was to refer (c. 160) to these convexts being among Christianity's worst adversaries.[28]

The universalist trend in Judaism was not destined to prevail. Johanan ben Zakkai had established his reputation as a scholar in Torah before the outbreak of the Jewish War. He was now able to put into effect his belief that study of Torah was as important as sacrifices to the Temple. The latter had gone with the high priests. Torah and its interpretation remained. Some of the prescriptions of the Law, such as the Sabbath rules, were modified[29]—perhaps one single long-term effect of the feeling reflected by Jesus' teaching. Vows also were virtually excluded from the pious life, for one obvious reason that the Temple to which one might, for instance, dedicate one's property no longer existed. The canon of Scripture was closed. It was self-sufficient; there was no need to look forward to new books with so-called revelations of the fulfillment of God's promises through a spurious Messiah. To make doubly sure, a sentence was added, c. 90, to the twelfth of the *Eighteen Benedictions* (*Sh^emoneh ʿEsreh*) recited in the synagogues in which the "Nazarenes" and heretics (*minim*) were cursed.[30] From John's Gospel we learn that anyone who acknowledged Jesus as the Messiah was cast out of the synagogues with contumely (John 9:22; 12:42). For Christians, the "disbelieving Jew" had become the enemy, the persecutor, and defamer of the faith, a situation that was to continue until the middle of the second century and beyond. Proselytes too could expect no waiving of traditional demands. In 135 these could be summed up by Trypho the Hellenistic Jew, a refugee in Ephesus from the Palestinian-Jewish uprising: "If you are willing, therefore, to listen to me," he tells Justin, "first be circumcised, then as is commanded by the Law, keep the Sabbath feasts and God's new moons, and then perhaps you will find mercy from God."[31] Many who might have listened were repelled by this sort of preaching. The "general silliness, and deceit and fussiness and pride of the Jews,"[32] were Christianity's gain.

THE CHRISTIAN MISSION

If the sub-apostolic era saw Judaism's last great effort to proselytize the Greco-Roman world and its collapse amidst the trammels of the Law, it also saw its Christian rival consolidate and progress. The story of the church's mission in this period, however, is obscure. In the Pauline period, we can see missionaries at work, such as Paul preaching in the school of Tyrannus at Ephesus and the mission of Epaphras to Colossae. Now there is silence about such persons and even the details of the message or *kerygma* they proclaimed. All we know is that missions went on. First, the synoptic Gospels and Acts are themselves missionary documents. They contain detailed accounts of Jesus' instructions to his disciples, and all end on a missionary note. The disciples were commanded to preach Christ crucified everywhere "beginning from Jerusalem" (Luke 24:47; cf. Matt. 28:19–20; Mark 16:15) and are recorded as doing so (Mark 16:20). Acts continues the theme by stating that the disciples would be the Lord's witnesses "in Jerusalem and in all Judea and Samaria, and to the end of the earth" (1:8).

Such may have been the position down to c. 80 to 90 while Paul's immediate disciples were still alive. We know from the Pastoral letters that Timothy was active on tours of inspection in Asia, and Titus is recorded as appointing "elders in every town" in Crete (Titus 1:5). From the *Didache* (chap. 11) we hear of traveling teachers whose ostensible object was to "increase righteousness and knowledge of the Lord" in the communities they visited. To this time, also, must date the mission that established Christianity in Bithynia-Pontus on the Black Sea coast. This area is included among the addresses of 1 Peter (c. 80). Marcion's father was "bishop" of the Christians in Sinope in Marcion's youth (c. 85–95) and Christianity in Bithynia was sufficiently alive at this stage for converts to move in and out of it. Pliny learned in 112 that some Christians had abandoned their faith as much as "twenty years before."[33]

We may assume, therefore, an active and successful Christian mission within and beyond the radius of Paul's work north to Bithynia and east into Cappadocia. It may not be altogether fanciful to accept W. M. Ramsay's thesis that the "Seven Churches that are in Asia" were missionary centers.[34] Ephesus and Laodicea were Pauline foundations but Smyrna, Pergamum, Philadelphia, Sardis, and Thyatira were not. With Tralles in Caria and Hierapolis and Magnesia in the Maeander valley, their communities date to the second generation of Christian mission. The province of Asia emerged as the area where Christianity was strongest, with Ephesus as its radial point. Ephesus is the first of the seven churches addressed by the Seer of Patmos and it was the provincial capital of Asia. This was where one would have sought the Gnostic heretic Cerinthus as well as Paul's successors. After Timothy, the dominating figure there in c. 90 was John the mysterious Elder, still claimed by some critics as the "beloved disciple," and author of the Fourth Gospel.[35] The Palestinian background of the group that he led is suggested by the memory a century later that he (like James of Jerusalem) wore the *petalon*, the insignia of the Jewish high priest, on his forehead (Eusebius *HE* V.24.3).[36] That he had authority over other communities and individuals in the area is shown by the language of 2 and 3 John, again marking Ephesus as the directing center. Diotrephes seems to have been a "diocesan bishop" whose bad manners earned a merited rebuke from his superior.

With the passing of John, his contemporary Aristion, and the last survivors of the Pauline era, the missionary momentum seemed to flag. The period 100–135 may have witnessed a crisis within the Christian communities. Was the church to settle down as a messianic and mildly reforming movement on the fringes of Judaism content with its existing membership? Or was it to continue the urgency of Paul, and better equipped than he after a generation of experience, attempt to convince the pagan world that Christianity offered the sole means of salvation? The prevalent teaching was still that the coming was not far off.[37] "These are the last times," Ignatius declared (*The Letter to the Ephesians* 11.1). There were, however, doubters. In the first decades of the second century, there was a growing division between those who believed that the time of the second coming was desperately close—that the end of the world would come by fire just as "the world that then existed was deluged with water and perished" (2 Peter 3:6) and that Christ was tarrying only "that all should reach repentance" (2 Peter 3:9)—and those who were ceasing to believe in the coming at all. And if it did not, why hurry to proselytize the Gentiles? And what was the use of "being watchful" with "loins girded" awaiting the appearance of Jesus? There is plenty of evidence for slackness, feuds, and factions in the sub-apostolic communities. The writer of the letters to the seven churches (Rev. 1:4—3:22) does not mince words. "I know your works; you have the name of being alive, and you are dead," he tells the church at Sardis (Rev. 3:1). "I am rich, I have prospered, and I need nothing" was the prevalent attitude of Laodicea (Rev. 3:17). "You have abandoned the love you had at first" (Rev. 2:4) sums up his message. The classic writings of the sub-apostolic period do not suggest collective enthusiasm as the hallmark of Christianity and show small concern for mission. Ignatius (*Ephesians* 10) urged that Christians should "pray unceasingly" for other men, and show an example of Christian behavior, but neither he nor *Barnabas* suggests rapidly expanding churches. Nowhere do we find a church office of "missioner."[38] The term "Apostle" is confined to the Twelve and Paul. Both *1 Clement* and Polycarp's *Philippians* leave the impression of small self-contained and socially stable communities concerned for their own good order and holiness, but having little regard for the outside world. Rules of behavior had replaced the fullness of Christ's grace as a prerequisite of salvation. Being "blameless before the Gentiles" (Polycarp *Philippians* 10.2 and compare *2 Clement* XIII) like the Pharisees and separated from them did not involve the duty of seeking to save them. The writer of *1 Clement* did not tell the bickering Corinthians that they might forget their quarrels and follow the example of Peter and Paul, and carry the gospel to the ends of the world. Though he warned that the Lord might come into his temple "suddenly,"[39] no Christian at Rome or Corinth seemed destined to perish before his time.

Yet all the while, the church was advancing and by the outbreak of the

Second Jewish War (132–35) its progress outside Asia Minor may have been something like the following—

Syria

Antioch was the Christian center. Ignatius claimed to be the third bishop there and bishop of Syria. He was accompanied on his way to Rome in 107/ 8 by a deacon from Cilicia,[40] which suggests that Antioch was exercising some influence over Christian communities in that province.

Antioch was relatively isolated, however, and it was centuries before it made its influence felt in the areas to the south, dominated by the Hellenistic cities fervently attached to Greek and Syrian deities. To the east, however, where Aramaic remained the lingua franca, Christian-Jewish merchants may have been responsible for planting Christianity as far as Edessa, independent of Antiochene influence. Such activity may lie behind the legendary correspondence between Jesus and King Abgar of Osrhoene preserved in Eusebius.[41] Thence, from Edessa Christianity moved along the caravan routes into Parthia and by A.D. 100 had established itself in the Jewish-Parthian state of Adiabene. This must have happened around this date, for an entry in the *Chronicle of Arbela* puts the martyrdom of the second bishop Simeon as "seven years after the emperor Trajan's victory over King Osroes," that is, in 123. There had, however, been a six-year vacancy before Simeon's consecration.[42] Edessa seems to have been an autonomous church, its original links being with Jerusalem. *Thomas,* with its strongly ascetic bias and its retention of what appears to be a very early Aramaic-based tradition of Jesus' teaching, may be the gospel of the Christians at Edessa.[43] On the other hand, Christianity failed to take root in Nisibis or Seleucia-Ctesiphon where there were important Tannaitic Jewish academies. Where Judaism was self-confident and united, Christianity failed to attract converts.

Egypt

Except that there were Christian communities in Egypt before 135, practically nothing is known of their organization. John's Gospel was circulating among them by the reign of Hadrian (117–38) and also a variety of other gospels, including the "Unknown Gospel" which appears to be a mixture of Luke and John with some original and semilegendary tradition about Jesus.[44] As one would expect from the composition of the Jewish Dispersion in Egypt, Christianity seemed to have been developing in several directions at once. First, there was a philosophical interpretation that sought accommodation with Platonism following the example of Philo. This would form one of the main bases for Gnosticism. Basilides was already active in Alexandria c. 130.[45]

Second, there was a Christian-rabbinic element corresponding perhaps to the Sanhedrin and priestly element in Alexandrian Judaism. We have noted this in action against the Jews in *Barnabas*. Third, as C. H. Roberts has indicated,[46] one can detect the existence of what were to become Jewish-Christian sects, represented by the writer of the *Gospel of Hebrews*, and the *Gospel of Egyptians* cited by Clement of Alexandria near the end of the century, and the scrap of *The Shepherd of Hermas* discovered in a second-century setting in the Fayum.[47] Finally, *Thomas* was circulating alongside Matthew's Gospel in the Nile Valley by about 140–50.[48] The Egyptian towns provided a meeting place for many different interpretations of Christianity with the Jewish connection always strong.

The Aegean Islands and Greece

Crete may be assumed to have contained active congregations, with Gortyna and Knossos as the main centers. Later they became the metropolitan and senior bishopric (*proto-thronos*) respectively. On the mainland, Philippi was the recipient of Polycarp's letter forwarding copies of Ignatius's letter to the churches in Asia. We may assume Christian congregations in the other Pauline foundations. Nicopolis in western Macedonia is mentioned in Titus 3:12 as a place where Paul expected to winter and presumably had a community to receive him.

Rome

Along with the seven churches in Asia, Rome began to emerge as a leading Christian center. *First Clement* suggests the existence of presbyter-bishops rather than a single monarchical bishop; and the tradition that this latter had always been the form of church government cannot be traced beyond Hegesippus (c. 175).[49] To the writer of *1 Clement*, Peter and Paul were "good Apostles" whose deaths he hints may have taken place in Rome, but he does not mention them as founders of the see.[50] From Hermas we hear of various officials in charge of different tasks. Clement is mentioned as being concerned with "foreign correspondence,"[51] and we hear too of bishops or overseers charged with hospitality and charitable works. There may even have been a number of different Christian synagogues in Rome: that of Clement seems to have been composed predominantly of freedmen from the aristocratic Roman houses. Were they in the same organization as Hermas's prophecy-oriented community? Rome, however, was already showing a concern for communities beyond the city. Though the bearers of the letter to the Corinthians were primarily messengers, they brought warnings and recommendations to the Corinthian church. At least the advice of their church had been sought. Their function may have been rather more important than, for instance, that of the bearers of Polycarp's letter to the Philippians in 107/8.

Italy

That there were Christian communities in Italy c. 80–90 is evident from Hebrews (13:24); but claims for Christianity in the cities of Pompeii and Herculaneum, overwhelmed by the disaster of 79, seem less well founded than was once thought.[52] There is nothing inherently unlikely about Christianity penetrating thither as there were Christians in nearby Puteoli (Acts 28:14). However, suggestions that graffiti scratched or painted on house walls indicated the existence of a Latin liturgy and the use of the Chi-Rho as a Christian symbol at this time seem far-fetched. One inscription only, a sentence reading something like "Bovios audi(t) Christianos sevos o(s) ores" ("Bovios hearkens to the Christians, the cruel haters[?]") from a half-obliterated graffito is the most positive evidence and this demands a stretch of imagination to construct a meaning from it. Regarding the ROTAS word-square scratched on a pillar of the west wall of the wrestling school at Herculaneum, and also on the wall of a house at Pompeii, it must be conceded that the earliest certain Christian usage of the cryptogram dates to the sixth century, while its existence on a temple wall in the garrison town of Dura-Europos on the Euphrates suggests a non-Christian origin. It may be Jewish, connected perhaps with the wheels seen by the prophet Ezekiel (Ezek. 1:16); Jews there seem to have been in Pompeii. For good or ill, the words "Sodom" and "Gomorrah" also scratched on the wall of a house point in that direction.[53]

THE CHURCH AND SOCIETY

Little is known about the social level and outlook of these early congregations. Except in eastern Syria and Edessa, they were Greek-speaking, though retaining words and phrases of Aramaic in the liturgy.[54] The earliest extant Christian records, including Q, are in Greek. Papias of Hierapolis's statement that "Matthew first collected the oracles [*ta logia*] in the Hebrew language and each interpreted them as best he could" (Eusebius *HE* III.39.16) reflects a very early stage in the life of the church. By the time connected Gospel-narratives were being written down, the medium had to be Greek. Greek was to remain a binding force in the church of the eastern Mediterranean for generations. In addition, Matthew's Luke's, and John's Gospels presuppose a certain level of education, and in John an ability to follow the long discourses put into Jesus' mouth. Luke's aim was to write a Gospel-history based on accurate records, a Christian Thucydides. This style was designed for an educated audience, but one which could show concern for the poor, and if the correct significance is attached to the Magnificat, one whose members would associate the coming of the kingdom with great social change.

The theoretical revolutionary social message that underlay Christianity in this period should not be underestimated. The recitation of the messianic "woes," with famine and pestilence among them, coupled with denunciation of the merchants who traded between the East and Rome, that we find in Revelation (Rev. 18:11–19), could only appeal to those who saw the coming as the signal for upheavals in society.[55] Also, Papias's equating of the coming with millennial joys and huge material benefits for the Christians suggests that a generation later (c. 130) these ideas were still current in Asia Minor. It is interesting that Papias, diligent collector of oral and written traditions about Jesus, believed that this was what Jesus himself expected.[56] It was a poor man's dream. In Rome, Hermas (c. 120) explains that the ideal for catechumens was poverty, and that some wealthier individuals must remain outside the church "until this world and the vanity of riches were cut away from them."[57] The letter of James, too, indicates a poorish congregation looking for material benefits and envious of the status of their superiors (James 2:2). By implication as well as by the personal attitudes of many Christians, Christianity was opposed to many of the values accepted by the rulers of the Roman Empire and the majority of its inhabitants.

In practice, however, sub-apostolic Christianity was far from being a subversive cult. First, it was by now almost entirely an urban religion whose adherents accepted the very real privileges of Greco-Roman urban society. Pliny records Christians in rural Bithynia (*Letters* X.96.9), but he knows nothing of rural parishes at this period.[58] The church's language of mission was Greek, the language of the Macedonian conquerors. Not until the time of Irenaeus (c. 180) do we hear of any attempt to carry the word to "the wild and barbarous" peoples beyond the city walls. Within the towns, too, it attracted a considerable number of wealthy individuals who seemed also to have acquired positions of responsibility in the communities. At Sinope we have noted that Marcion's father was bishop and his son moved in wealthy ship-owning circles—the people denounced in Revelation (Rev. 18:11) and in *Thomas* (*Logion* 65). In Ephesus there is "the elect lady" and her children, to whom John wrote with such deference (2 John) and she was clearly not alone. Ignatius's journey through some of the larger churches in the province of Asia provided evidence for the comparative ease of some of their leading members. Those whom he greeted included a "steward" and his wife, with their children "and whole house,"[59] and there was also the "house of Tavia" in Smyrna whom Polycarp was asked to greet on Ignatius's behalf.[60] Polycarp himself was a well-known personage in Smyrna with servants even to tie the latches of his shoes.[61] At Rome, Christianity may have been the religion of the emperor Domitian's niece, Flavia Domitilla, as well as of some rich women such as Hermas's mistress, Rhoda. The most important members, however, seemed to have been freedmen in the houses of Roman aristocracy such as Clement and his friends Claudius Ephebus and Valerius Vito (*1 Clement* LXV.1). These formed part of an influential and conservative-minded class who lived in a society used to order and deference, and expected it themselves. The wide span of the Hellenistic-Jewish communities of the day, including wealthy, influential, and pious women on the one hand, and artisans and slaves on the other, was paralleled in the Christian churches, though among the latter a greater proportion of the less wealthy could be expected. Work with one's hands was considered normal. There were to be no idle Christians (*Didache* 13.4).

The code of conduct expected of Christians recalls the requirements of righteousness set out in intertestamental writings, more than the stark demands of Jesus. Social duties towards the less fortunate are summed up in Hermas: "To minister to widows, to look after orphans and the destitute, to redeem from distress the servants of God, to be hospitable, for in hospitality may be found the practice of good, to resist none, to be gentle, to be poorer than all men, to reverence the aged, to practice justice, to preserve the brotherhood . . ." and not to "oppress poor debtors."[62] Hermas mentions "bishops" in charge of dispensing hospitality and sheltering the destitute and widows.[63] Duties towards widows and orphans are stressed in *Barnabas*,[64] that of almsgiving in *2 Clement*,[65] as well as the burial of poor in Aristides' *Apology* (c. 145).[66] These were traditional duties laid on the pious Israelite, and the Christian did not go beyond them. In particular, in contrast to Jesus' teaching, there was no command to "sell all," to free the captives; or, in general, to strive to abolish slavery. On this point the Christian ethic contrasted also with that of the Essenes (see Philo *Every Good Man Is Free* 79). For the writer of the *Didache* the negative form of the Golden Rule was the first principle of the way of life to be observed by the catechumens.[67] They were also expected to lead an orderly moral life and generally be a good neighbor, but with no special duties outside those current in Judaism.

Regarding slavery, Ignatius of Antioch urged Polycarp "not to be haughty to slaves" but the slaves themselves were to "endure slavery to the glory of God."[68] They should not be set free at public cost "lest they become slaves of lust." In the *Didache*, the slave was also told to "serve his master in reverence and fear" as "counterpart of God,"[69] and slavery was accepted as a normal institution. Before God indeed there was neither bond nor free, male nor female (Gal. 3:28), but on earth, until the coming, social distinctions remained. The emphasis continued to be, as in Judaism, on "the household" with its servants and slaves as well as children and kinsfolk.[70] The prevalent ethic was that of Tobit or Ecclesiasticus. For all the apocalyptic hopes some may have had for grand upheavals associated with the coming, the churches in the sub-apostolic age were not centers of social revolution.

The one exception to the Christian's pietistic acceptance of the world was his attitude towards martyrdom.[71] Here we find two traditions uniting to produce confessors of the character of Ignatius of Antioch. First, there is

133

the heroic tradition enshrined in the Maccabean Wars whose martyrs believed themselves atoning for Israel's collective sin as well as vindicating the justice of the cause against idolatrous oppression. The second tradition consisted in imitation of the passion of Christ, involving complete communion with him, atonement for sin and hastening his coming. To change the world, however, the Christian like his or her master must be prepared to die to it also.

SOUND DOCTRINE AND ITS OPPONENTS

What was the message that was moving the church forward all this time and the tradition that all must hold fast? The lordship of Jesus, his approaching coming bringing judgment, the overthrow of Satan's kingdom, and the establishment of the "city which is to come" (Heb. 13:14) formed a vital part in Christian preaching. The first petition of the Lord's Prayer is "Thy kingdom come" (Matt. 6:10; Luke 11:2). The same ends the book of Revelation (Rev. 22:20); it is prominent in the *Didache* (9.2; 10.4). The prophecies and the parables attributed to Jesus in the last week of his life in Jerusalem looked forward to that event and the "wars and rumors of wars" that would precede it (Matt. 24:6). Other writings of the late New Testament and sub-apostolic period such as the letter of James and *1 Clement*, however, show less urgency. Side by side with the simple acceptance of Jesus as Messiah and the millennial hope for his return, there was also continued striving towards what may best be called a "normative Christianity." This was perhaps not wholly uninfluenced by the emergence of a rival normative Judaism. It was the result also of the church beginning to come to terms with the world, while lacking the outward rigor and sense of nationality that held the Jews together.

The call for "one Lord, one faith, one baptism" in Ephesians (4:5)—whether Paul's final letter or written by a disciple is not relevant here—is paralleled by an appeal in the Pastorals to take heed to the doctrine (1 Tim. 4:16), "follow the pattern of the sound words" (2 Tim. 1:13), and confirmed by the expulsion of various individuals described as having "made shipwreck" concerning faith (1 Tim. 1:19–20). The ideal was a single faith and an ordered church government. The crime of the innovators of Corinth was that they had sinned against a "fundamental order of Christian and of all right living, by dispossessing elders and exalting themselves over the flock of Christ."[72] The rules laid down in the Pastorals for the conduct of bishops and deacons, the deportment of widows, the consideration to be shown to older persons, were being applied a generation later in the Rome of *1 Clement* or Polycarp's Smyrna. Both these writers, together with Ignatius, were conscious of the oneness of the church, and distinction between belief and organization that was acceptable, and what was not.[73]

How was the "normative Christianity" to be defined? To judge from the sub-apostolic writings, and in particular Polycarp's *Philippians, 2 Clem-*

ent, and Ignatius, "sound doctrine" consisted primarily of the contents of the Gospels and Pauline letters together with credal-sounding statements concerning the birth, ministry, and death of Christ. This now formed the tradition of the church, which presbyters must teach and congregations accept. The Law, on the other hand, had no binding force, and the Old Testament served merely to confirm the Spirit-inspired message of the New. The Gospels and epistles were circulating in Asia, Syria, and Alexandria (less certainly in Rome), and being read and discussed in the Christian synagogues there by about 100.[74] In Polycarp's short letter there is an astonishing amount of direct and indirect quotation from the New Testament; Matthew, Luke, and John, Acts, the letters to the Galatians, Thessalonians, Corinthians, Ephesians, Philippians, Colossians, Romans, the Pastorals, 1 Peter particularly, and 1 and 2 John are all used; and "the blessed and glorious" apostle Paul's letters to the Philippians are recalled specifically.[75] Ignatius is influenced through and through by John and Paul.

The Christian Scriptures were quoted so familiarly as to suggest that they had been in regular use a long time. It is difficult therefore to place the final form of the Gospels or collection of Pauline letters much later than A.D. 80, with perhaps the Fourth Gospel a decade or so beyond.[76] The synoptic Gospels' object was to record the life, ministry, passion, death, and resurrection of Jesus, when the church had entered on its third generation and oral tradition was becoming confused. Communities needed an account of the life of the Savior for their edification and in order to refute those who denied that he was the Messiah or claimed that his ministry was not real. What they achieved was a new literary form, unlike any known Jewish Scripture, and never to be repeated. In their separate ways, Matthew and Luke both argue that Jesus did fulfill both the Law and the messianic prophecies, and that the Messiah was destined to suffer as Jesus suffered. In addition, Matthew indicated that Jesus was the second and greater Moses, promulgating like his predecessor his new covenant from the mountaintop, combining in himself spiritual and moral authority because God had given him "all authority . . . to the close of the age" (Matt. 28:18–20). To the certainty that Jesus was Messiah, John added the dimensions of drama and interpretation, reflecting also, in its "light-darkness" symbolism, pieties that had inspired the Covenanters of Qumran. Jesus (not the Righteous Teacher, however) was the historical figure to whom all Jewish life and thought—whether in terms of Scripture or in terms of the pietism of Qumran or elsewhere—was tending, and he was also Word and Wisdom of God, and Judge of humankind. The Christians were the only authentic witnesses of the truth of his message.

The Pauline letters, including the Pastorals, were also being collected and read throughout the Christian communities. But, much as Paul was admired as an individual and received without qualification as an apostle, his views were not accepted unconditionally. There is the criticism in

James 2:14–26 of some of the effects of Paul's doctrine of justification by faith alone. James, it has been pointed out, shows no comprehension of what Paul actually meant by his formula, but the formula was alien to him and he disliked it. He insisted that works, particularly charitable and social works, and right action were necessary to salvation. He considered Christianity as God-given Law.[77] He waś not the only Christian writer of his day who had doubts about Paul's views. For the author of 2 Peter, Paul was "our beloved brother" but one who combined inspired wisdom with things "hard to understand," liable to misinterpretation by "the ignorant and unstable . . . to their own destruction" (2 Peter 3:15–16). What aspects of Paul's teaching were being misinterpreted is not known, but the implicit dualism in some of his preaching combined with exaggerated hopes among his hearers of freedom from the constraints of the Law are possibilities, in view of Gnostic interpretations of Paul in the second century. In *1 Clement* also, we find praise for Paul himself "as a great example of the faith," who knew how to restore harmony among quarreling factions,[78] but it included no discussion of justification, no call to the errant Corinthians to put off the "old Adam" of strife and jealousy and renew themselves in the Spirit through Christ. The mystical side of Paul's teaching was simply ignored.

One can point to a third and equally important set of ideas underlying "normative Christianity," that were not derived primarily from either the Gospels or the Pauline letters. These may best be described as a Christian interpretation of Isaiah, the Wisdom, and other intertestamental literature; their influence on the future of Christianity was to be enormous. Over a wide field of late New Testament and sub-apostolic writings produced as far afield as Rome and Syria we find the same emphasis on the moral obligations of Christianity set down in exhortatory tones that resemble Proverbs or Ecclesiasticus. The church was recognized as a force for stability in an ordered and harmonious universe with no pressing expectation of doom to come (*1 Clement* XX). Christianity continued the religion of Israel but the faith had been given a new impetus and direction through Christ. As Moses knew that there should be no disorder in Israel to prevent the glorification of the name of the true and only God,[79] so there should be no contentions among Christians. It was a joyful and optimistic faith. "How blessed and wonderful, beloved, are the gifts of God," writes *1 Clement*, "life in immortality, splendour in righteousness, truth in boldness, faith in confidence, continence in holiness; and all these things are submitted to our understanding."[80]

In this faith, however, the impression was of Jesus Christ interpreted less in terms of the Gospels than in those of the messianic prophecies of Isaiah. Thus, both *1 Clement* and the *Didache* presented Christ as "the Servant," and when *1 Clement* wishes to draw attention to Christ's humility he cites Isaiah 53, and not his trial before Pilate.[81] In the *Didache*, Christ is also "the holy vine of David" (9.2), which would appear to owe its inspiration to Isaiah 11. In *1 Clement* immortality is proved by reference to the phoenix and not the empty tomb. The phoenix was used by the Alexandrian Jews as a symbol of the rebirth of Israel.[82] The ethical teaching of both writers seems also to owe less to the Sermon on the Mount, though the *Didache* was familiar with this, than to ideas drawn from the Two Ways combined with the wisdom of Job, Proverbs, and Ecclesiasticus. There is a lack of immediacy and fervor inspired by the Spirit in favor of abstract moral exhortation. Judith and Esther were chosen as models of self-sacrificing womanhood, not the Virgin or Mary Magdalene.[83] In *1 Clement*, Christianity meant moral duties, mutual love, tolerance, and forbearance, the intermingling of Jewish and Stoic ethics characteristic of Hellenistic Judaism. The "hard sayings" of Jesus were pushed into the background in favor of general commandments to love God and one's fellows in the beauty of holiness. Those who had vainly sought salvation from Judaism in the Dispersion turned with relief and conviction to Christianity. Let the new generation of Pharisees and their disciples concern themselves about "arbitrary distinctions between the changing seasons ordained by God."[84] Sufficient to know that the ocean kept its bounds and the seasons followed in due order,[85] for love was the bond between God and his universe, and Jesus was his Servant and the Messiah.

By c. 100, "normative Christianity" was beginning to emerge as a distinct religion within the general cultural framework of Hellenistic Judaism. A body of teaching was becoming established to which appeal could be made. Its authenticity could be guaranteed by reference to the apostles and to Christ himself. It was represented by an ordered hierarchy that could claim descent from apostolic times. Geographically, its strength lay in the main seaport towns of the eastern Mediterranean, where communications were relatively swift, and in cities such as Philippi that were situated on the main trunk routes of the empire. Bishops of these cities were already in communication with each other, ensuring thereby a certain uniformity of outlook within their congregations. Apart from Judaizers within the churches, the opposition was the now-dominant Pharisaism within Judaism on the one hand, and on the other, ideas circulating within and on the fringes of the Christian communities that sought to diminish the human activity of Jesus (Docetism) and to subvert the ethical teaching of the churches through various forms of libertinism.

Whatever the "foolishness of the crowd" in Polycarp's Smyrna may have been (*Philippians* 7.2), libertinism and docetic beliefs that were to be incorporated in Gnosticism a generation later were challenging the "normative faith." The libertine element in Christianity's break from Judaism had been prominent in some of the Pauline churches, notably Corinth. A generation later it was very much alive in the churches of Asia. The rage of the Seer of Patmos was directed against a plethora of antinomian schisms, and there are traces of the same in the vituperations of 2 Peter and Jude.

Whoever the Nicolaitans were in Pergamum (Rev. 2:15), or the prophetess "Jezebel" in Thyatira (Rev. 2:20), these rejected restrictions on their freedom. For them the Law and its shackles were truly dead. Gentile ways, such as eating sacrificial meat or attending banquets, were matters of indifference to the "saved" and could even be justified from Scripture (Rev. 2:14).[86]

Deviation in morals accompanied deviation in belief. Erroneous views about Christ's ministry were associated, by orthodox spokesmen, with lack of Christian charity. Ignatius and Polycarp found themselves opposing a Judaistic heresy whose proponents taught that Jesus could be worshiped as some angelic being, similar perhaps to the angels that appeared to Abraham at Mamre. Such a being might be a "savior" but he had no contact with humanity. The incarnation and birth narratives of the Gospels were rejected. Jesus "neither ate nor drank,"[87] and his earthly ministry was not that of the son of Mary. It was against beliefs of this type even when backed by "the charters" (that is, the Old Testament) that Ignatius reacted with such anger (*The Letter to the Philadelphians* VIII). Moreover, "for if it is merely in semblance that these things were done by our Lord," he wrote to the church in Smyrna, "I am also a prisoner in semblance. And why have I given myself up to death, to fire, to the sword, to wild beasts?" (*The Letter to the Smyrnaeans* IV.2). If Christ was a "phantom," he was not worth dying for (*The Letter to the Trallians* X). The duty of martyrdom in imitation of the living Christ was the cornerstone of Ignatius's faith; and he was not content to leave matters there. He accused his docetic opponents of failing to carry out elementary acts of charity. "For love they have no care, none for the widow, none for the orphan," he claimed.[88] If they did not accept the humanity of Christ and the reality of his ministry, they could not be expected to follow his example. And how could they celebrate a Eucharist if they did not "believe in the blood of Christ"?

Polycarp also was opposed by adversaries who quoted the Septuagint to prove their case. He castigates everyone "who does not confess that Jesus Christ has come in the flesh" (*Philippians* 7.1). Such a man was an "anti-Christ." Whosoever did not confess the testimony of the cross was a devil, and he who perverted "the oracles of the Lord for his own lusts and says there is neither resurrection or judgement, this man is the first-born of Satan" (*Philippians* 7.1). The last phrase was one of Polycarp's favorite descriptions of opponents, and he was said to have applied it to the young Marcion, perhaps already preaching his alternative interpretations of Christianity.[89] What this evidence suggests is that by the end of the first century these "alternative interpretations" were emerging as responses to assertions of Christian orthodoxies whenever the new religion was taking root. It would be hazardous to attempt to assess with Walter Bauer and his critics which came first.[90] The impact of the life and teaching of Jesus Christ mediated by Paul and his fellow missionaries was such as to evoke widely different responses among the Hellenistic-Jewish congregations which heard them. Some of these responses were rejected, others fell within the framework of orthodox belief and practice. "Orthodoxy" and "heresy" were thus simultaneous and ongoing developments throughout the sub-apostolic period. There were to be many shifts of emphasis from one side to the other before orthodoxy crystallized in the words of the Apologists and Irenaeus.

THE CHRISTIAN MINISTRY

Ignatius, and less explicitly Polycarp, saw a firm connection between orthodox Christian belief and orthodox Christian organization, liturgy, and conduct. The continued combination of these in the minds of its representatives made "orthodoxy" formidable during the second century. So far as concerns the emergent Christian ministry, all surviving documents of the sub-apostolic age presuppose the existence of "bishops," "presbyters," and "deacons," and assume a regular ministry in which these officers play a part, though not always an exclusive part. In the first phase down to A.D. 100, we may recognize differing patterns of ministry reflecting the influence of James's church at Jerusalem and the Hellenistic churches respectively. The continued influence of Jerusalem may be seen in the remains of Palestinian Christianity, where kinship with Jesus was a qualification for leadership (Eusebius *HE* III.20.6), and at Antioch. There Ignatius writes with such confidence that he must represent a longstanding tradition. He insisted on the mystical connection between the Christian bishop and the heavenly high priest in which the bishop was the essential link between the Christian community and the Lord.[91] He combined the roles of prophet and priest as the Jewish high priest once had done. Elsewhere, however, we find the continuance of two types of ministry that had grown up in the wake of Paul's missionary journeys and had also been accepted in some non-Pauline churches. The main division was not between "charismatic" or "non-charismatic"—all baptized Christians were potentially men of the Spirit—but the residential and the itinerant ministries. The latter group included Paul's disciples Timothy and Titus, who had major regional responsibilities, the one in Asia and the other in Crete, and Aristion and John of Ephesus, whose role was supervisory and itinerant. It included the Christian prophets and teachers whose continued eminence is shown in the *Didache*. The proven prophet "might celebrate the Eucharist as he would,"[92] ignoring if he wished the writer's precise directions how to hold the service.

In each Christian community, however, there was also a residential ministry, consisting probably of presbyter-bishops, each with an allotted function,[93] that administered its affairs, taught, and celebrated the liturgy. Rome, Corinth, and the churches in Crete provided examples of this form of government. Those appointed had to be "blameless," "the husband of

139

one wife," and so on (Titus 1:6–9), and "were not to be despised" (*Didache* 15.2), but clearly were inferior to the itinerant ministers who could expect sustenance in the form of first fruits of oil and wine from communities they visited.[94] In the last resort, the churches had been founded "by the apostles and prophets," who in Paul's mind were the interpreters of the Spirit and stood in immediate relation to the "cornerstone"—Jesus Christ (Eph. 2:20).

By the end of the century, however, there had been a marked move away from the collegial system of church government and a decline in the influence of the itinerants. The great men had died; prophecy was not being poured out as expected in the last times. We find communities now being governed by a single officer, whether known as "bishop," "presbyter," or simply as "chairman," as in Rome in Justin's time, c. 150. Even Philadelphia, the church most favored by the Seer of Patmos and later to be near the Montanist centers of the New Prophecy, was ruled by a bishop with presbyters and deacons under him.[95] Polycarp's congregation at Smyrna, a church of whom the Seer also approved, was a neatly graded hierarchical community centered on himself, with each grade in the church—the presbyters, deacons, widows, and "young men"—having its respective duties.

There may have been a number of reasons for this development. First, there was the natural tendency for leaders to emerge in any community, and in course of time for this to become fixed and traditional. We can see this happening in the Rome of *1 Clement*, where the presbyter-bishops were believed to derive their offices from the apostles, and then, in the celebrated and much-discussed text (*1 Clement* XLIV.1–5), "they [the apostles] then made a decree that when these died, other eminent men should succeed to their ministry," and having been appointed "with the agreement of the whole Church"[96] should not be removed while they "ministered to the flock of Christ blamelessly and in all humility, peacably and nobly." They were the men of the Spirit and would in practice hold their appointments for life.[97] The emergence of a single leader in each community, possessing par excellence the gift of the Spirit, may also owe something to the same evolutionary processes. Administration of discipline and refutation of heretical views needed a single responsible official. Thus, Polycarp wrote to the Philippians as a leader, referring to his duties of teaching, instructing, and refuting, and urged the recipients of his letter to "obey the word of righteousness" (*Philippians* 9.1), while he also expressed his sorrow, like any disciplinary official might, for the fall of the presbyter Valens (*Philippians* 11.1). Discipline apart, there were empire-builders like Diotrephes who were prepared to defy itinerant leaders whomever they might be (3 John 9–10). One might point, however, to the liturgy and, in particular, the Eucharist for the clue to the permanent emergence of the monarchical bishop. As the *Didache* shows (10.6), the Eucharist was the moment when the Lord himself would come "and this world pass away.'' The celebrant would therefore be in the position of representing the faithful to Christ and Christ to the faithful—the eucharistic community of the baptized. His position would be superior to that of his fellow presbyters, and this must have contributed powerfully to the establishment of monepiscopacy in the Pauline and post-Pauline areas of mission.

Ignatius of Antioch represented another trend, however. His assertion of monepiscopacy as the sole form of church government had nothing to do with "tradition" or apostolic succession. It was the product of a mystical theology in which he identified his office with that of Christ's high priestly role. The common ground between his concept of episcopacy and that of his contemporaries in Asia was the Eucharist. This played a decisive part in his theology, relating "breaking one bread" (Eph. 20) to immortality, and relating this also to his abhorrence of docetic heresy.[98] For him no valid Eucharist and no valid service could be held without the bishop's authorization.[99] Presbyters and deacons were subordinates. Ignatius's exalted view of the episcopate was to be paralleled in the Jewish-Christian Clementine literature of the third century and also in the monarchical episcopacy of Cyprian's church in North Africa.

THE LITURGY

The ceremonies over which the bishop or presbyter presided were expected to be the same in every Christian community. The writer of *1 Clement* states that "the Master commanded us to celebrate sacrifices and services, and that it should not be thoughtlessly or disorderly, but at fixed times and hours."[100] As in Paul's time, our authorities tell us of Baptism and the Eucharist, and in addition that Christians, like the Jews, prayed three times a day,[101] and that the Lord's Prayer was used. Baptism was the formal means of entry into the church. In the ceremony, described by the writer of the *Didache*, the convert was "sealed" in his faith, just as the proselyte was sealed by circumcision.[102] He fasted with his baptizer. Then, as Paul had preached, he went down into the water "dead" and came up "alive," mystically united with Christ and prepared to live and die to him. The water, we are told by Hermas, was the "seal."[103] The prescription of "running water," the most honorable of the six Jewish grades of water, also corresponded with Jewish usage.[104]

It is not easy to disentangle the ceremonies of the weekly Eucharist and the agape, except that these were reserved for baptized Christians and that the prayers and readings probably followed the pattern of the synagogue Sabbath liturgy.[105] Some idea of the praise offered to Christ "as a God" may perhaps be gleaned from Rev. 1:5–6, "To him who loves us and has freed us from our sins by his blood and made us a kingdom, priests to his God and Father, to him be glory and dominion for ever and ever. Amen."[106] Primarily then the Eucharist, as its name indicates, was a service of thanksgiving. Believers had been washed and redeemed by the

141

blood of the Lamb, and glorified God for Christ's saving act. "We give thanks to thee, our Father, for the Holy Vine of David thy child [or servant], which thou didst make known to us through Jesus thy servant. To thee be glory for ever." Thus the writer of the *Didache* quotes the prayer for the consecration of the cup (*Didache* 9.3). There was then a prayer following the breaking of bread, and the service concluded with the fervently expressed hope for the end. "Let grace come and let the world pass away. Hosannah to the God of David. If any man be holy, let him come! If any man be not, let him repent. Maran'atha. Amen" (*Didache* 10.6).

Pliny's letter to Trajan about the Bithynian Christians in 112 provides further information. There was a meeting "on a fixed day before daylight." There Scripture would be read, probably the Ten Commandments recited, and psalms or hymns sung antiphonally. Then, after dispersal and reassembly, there would be the fellowship meal, or agape, which the Christians abandoned after Pliny's order forbidding clubs and associations to meet.[107] This must be different from the solemn breaking of bread and drinking of the cup described in the *Didache*, and one must presume these acts took place with the reading of Scripture and prayer recorded by Pliny.

To the joyful thanksgiving of the Eucharist and agape were added prayers that show the strongly ethical (and even non–New Testament) character of the early Christian worship. We may quote the beautiful prayer from *1 Clement* LIX.4: "We beseech thee, Master, to be our 'help and succour.' Save those of us who are in affliction, have mercy on the lowly, raise the fallen, show thyself to those in need, heal the sick, turn again the wanderers of thy people, feed the hungry, ransom our prisoners, raise up the weak, comfort the fainthearted; let all 'nations know thee, that thou art God alone,' and that Jesus Christ is thy child, and that 'we are thy people and the sheep of thy pasture.' " Here we see a mosaic of ideas and phrases drawn from Psalms 78, 94, 99, 118, and 2 Kings and Ezekiel, brought together in a prayer to God, and then by the end of the first century transformed by the Christians into an invocation for aid through Christ that has endured to our own day. Thus church order, though in form derived from Judaism, was developing its own Christ-centered liturgy by the end of the first century designed to knit together Christians "from the four winds" (*Didache* 10.5).

DIFFERING INTERPRETATIONS

The case for the existence of uniformity in belief and practice throughout the Christian communities at this early period must not be exaggerated. Docetism and libertinism where recognized were rejected, as were Jewish calendrical and ceremonial prescriptions that Christians considered superseded. The "differing opinions" about which scholars, notably Helmut Koester, have written were, however, a reality. Christians apparently found it possible to live with at least three versions of the Lord's Prayer, and with gospels and Logia attributed to the Lord that were equally varied. Wherever one looks, whether Asia, Syria, or Rome, one finds differing and indeed contrasting interpretations of the faith among those who were accepted as members of the Christian community.[108]

Asia Minor

In Asia Minor, the contrast between the outlook of stable communities such as Polycarp's and the apocalyptic hopes of those for whom the writer of Revelation wrote is obvious. Polycarp's ideas continue those found in the Pastorals, concentrating on salvation through adhesion to an orthodox faith based on tradition and sober conduct.[109] The book of Revelation shows a violently different view of salvation and the means of attaining it. The heightened imaginings of John the Seer may owe something to Palestinian apocalyptic influences. When one remembers that there was a community of the followers of John the Baptist at Ephesus in the 50s (Acts 19:1), this would not be surprising, but millenarist and apocalyptic notions were also at home in communities well away from the coast and sea links with Palestine.

Papias, bishop of Hierapolis, combined a conscientious study of the oral and written traditions of the faith with millenarist hopes that he shared with Jewish and proto-Gnostic contemporaries. He believed in a millennium in which the messianic kingdom would be established and the saints would enjoy the fruits of the earth in magnificent abundance. Both the idea and the imagery in which it was expressed, such as the grapes producing a thousandfold, were paralleled in contemporary Jewish prophetic works, such as the *Apocalypse of Baruch*.[110] There, this imagery may have represented an attempt to provide eschatological fulfillment of national Jewish hopes dashed by the catastrophe of the Jewish War. That influential Christians accepted the millennium in these same terms as late as Irenaeus (c. 185) suggests that radical Jewish aspirations were not alien to them.

Another who shared these opinions was Cerinthus (c. 100) who maintained that Christ would establish a kingdom on earth, centered in Jerusalem, followed by the millennium "to be spent in wedding festivities," as the Roman presbyter Caius (circa A.D. 200) commented sarcastically.[111] Cerinthus has gone down in history as a "Jewish Gnostic" and an opponent of St. John. He may have been, but he is also the first recorded writer who tried to reconcile the implications of gospel accounts of Jesus as the son of Joseph and Mary, and the Prophet of Nazareth, and the Pauline preaching of the heavenly Christ. He concluded that the Christ that descended on Jesus at baptism in the form of a dove was distinct from Jesus himself, and he denied any miraculous element in his birth.[112] Inconsequential though his ideas were, Cerinthus shows how even at this early stage some Christians in Asia were trying to reconcile the traditional beliefs of Judaism with the impact of varied and hardly reconcilable teachings about Christ.

Syria

The churches in Syria provide evidence for an equal degree of ferment and contradiction. Along with organized congregations one can see the emergence of apocalyptic baptist sects, like the followers of Elkesai, who were proclaiming that a "new remission of sins" would take place in the "third year of Trajan" (that is, A.D. 100).[113] The tradition of John the Baptist was surviving. By general consent three key documents of the sub-apostolic period originated in the Syrian Christian communities—Matthew's Gospel, the *Didache*, and the letters of Ignatius. To these must now be added *Thomas*, as we have noted almost certainly East Syrian in origin and perhaps the product of Christians in Edessa in Osrhoene. Despite some degree of family resemblance, these works represent greatly differing interpretations of the Christian message. Matthew, as Hans von Campenhausen has pointed out, "was the last witness to a Christian faith that sought to follow Jesus and live by his promises, but was also sincerely loyal to the Law."[114] The latter remained, but a new faith was now confessed and the believer was being forced reluctantly to come to terms with the fact that the "new wine" of Jesus' teaching could not be retained within the old wineskins of Judaism. The process of separation was painful on both sides. Matthew lifts the veil on an incredible degree of strife between orthodox Jews and Christians that divided families and turned friends into enemies. The theme of the division of the worthy from the unworthy that dominates chapters 23—25 must have reflected a real situation. Scribes and Pharisees had now ceased to be the possible allies of Christianity that they were in James's time, and were now denounced in the refrain that has echoed down the ages, "Scribes, Pharisees, hypocrites."[115]

Matthew had ultimate confidence in victory, and this was shared by the writer of the *Didache*. He takes large parts of Matthew 24 to justify his hope that the coming was near. The Christian must be watchful, his "loins girded," his lamp lit, and he must be on guard against false prophets, indeed, "Antichrist himself who will commit crimes as never occurred before." But as in Matthew, though many would fall away, those who persevered would be saved by the Lord and his angels (*Didache* 16).

Didache, like Matthew and Revelation in Asia, reflects the empirewide strife between Jews and Christians at this time, but in other respects *Didache* and Matthew have little in common. If for the latter Christ is the Lawgiver of the new covenant, the *Didache* represents him as the Servant and Vine of David. Matthew sees the church as a hierarchical community (like Qumran) based on Peter as the rock on which it was founded; the *Didache* does not refer to Peter, but portrays a community in which there is no single monarchical bishop, but a number of officeholders among whom the prophet who proves his authenticity is the most important. In matters of church order too—whereas Matthew's presentation of Jesus rejects fixed forms for prayer and fasting, with the exception of the Lord's Prayer—the writer of the *Didache* lists precise rules for both in the manner of Jewish books' instruction.

In their spirit and in content it is impossible to reconcile the *Didache* with the letters of Ignatius. Ignatius accepts the Matthean view of the hierarchical nature of the government of the church, but also makes no reference to Peter in that connection. The *Didache*, as we have seen, accepts the existence of bishops, but regards them as "meek men," hardly the sort of people to dominate a congregation. For him, Christian morality was a matter of law following the intertestamental pattern of the contrasting Ways of Light and Darkness. For Ignatius, it follows directly from a correct understanding of the Eucharist and imitation of Christ's earthly ministry and passion. With Ignatius one can see the beginnings of the emergence of a speculative theology based on John and Paul. The still Hellenistic-Jewish world of the *Didache* was to continue in the mixed Greek and Syriac tradition that produced the church order contained in the third-century *Didascalia Apostolorum*.[116]

Thomas, also, shows how strong the Jewish legacy was to remain in Syrian Christianity. Though it is penetrated by later Gnostic influences, there is a core of early (that is, first-century) material, probably Aramaic in origin.[117] Not surprisingly, links may be established between *Thomas* and Matthew. Thus, *Thomas* reproduces all the Matthean parables of the kingdom (Matthew 13), while giving different interpretations to them. His concept of the church also is hierarchical, or rather monarchical, only that, instead of Peter being its foundation, that role is attributed to James. In *Logion* 12 the disciples are recorded as coming to Jesus and saying, " 'We know that thou wilt go from us. Who is to be great over us?' Jesus said unto them, 'Wherever you have come you will go to James the Righteous for whose sake Heaven and earth came into existence.' " The Jewish character of this statement needs no emphasis. The title "righteous" is reminiscent of the Teacher of Righteousness of Qumran, while the claim that "Heaven and earth had been created" for James's sake, echoes identical claims made on behalf of Israel in *4 Ezra* (= *2 Esdras* 3—14). In the view of the writer of *Thomas*, James was similarly to represent Israel, and the assumption that the disciples would be left with an undisputed leader recalls the hopes of the sons of Zebedee.[118] How it was that Matthew attributed the role to Peter whereas *Thomas* exalted James remains unknown, nor how the rival traditions of monarchical episcopacy arose within Syria.

The basic purposes of *Thomas* and Matthew also differed. Matthew's Gospel looked forward to the coming; *Thomas* makes no reference to such an event. The kingdom of the Father was to be gained by personal striving towards an ascetic life and if, as in Matthew (5:3), the poor were to be its heirs (*Logion* 55), to be among the elect required also to be a solitary (*Logia* 50, 75). The way to the kingdom was through the recesses of the individual's contemplation. For those who were perfected it had indeed come (*Logion* 38). The Wisdom sayings that comprise the majority of the 114 *logia* in *Thomas* speak less for the community than for the individual, and it may be that they have preserved this aspect of Jesus' teaching better than have the synoptic Gospels.[119] Whatever the solution, the encratism ("severe asceticism") of *Thomas* seems to look back to the encratism of Qumran though freed now from the ceremonial law of Moses (*Logion* 54). From East Syria *Thomas* gradually extended its influence southwards into the Nile Valley, also an area where Greek influence was weak and whence monasticism arose in the latter half of the third century.

Rome

Rome also shows wide differences of outlook among the Christians there. As we have noted already, there is no trace in the sub-apostolic period of the monarchical episcopacy attributed to it from the time of Hegesippus (c. 175). In *1 Clement*, however, there is already an association with Peter and Paul, who in the course of the next half-century become, in the mind of the community, the founders of the see. This was still in embryo, and other Roman documents portray little of the sense of uniformity and order found in *1 Clement*. Clement's church was loyal to the empire and expected to live in peace with it. The discipline of the Roman legions was held up for admiration.[120] The state was to be obeyed and its rulers were included in the church's prayers (*1 Clement* LXI). The Christian was not a free alien in the world but had an obligation to the order of creation which was endorsed and explained through Christ (*1 Clement* XX).[121] All disharmony was abhorrent. The picture was of ordered growth and natural progression from the old Israel, contrasting with the exaltation of Ignatius of Antioch or the virulence of the denunciations and vivid imaginings of Revelation.

First Clement, however, does not tell the whole story of Christianity at Rome. *Second Clement* (if Roman)[122] shows that all was not peaceful orthodoxy. There was a docetic faction there as elsewhere, and libertines as well. Judgment was indeed expected and the end of the world anticipated in terms as violent and spectacular as those found in 2 Peter. The atmosphere in both *1* and *2 Clement*, however, is that of the Hellenistic synagogue. In the latter there is the same predilection for moral precept, the New Testament quotations seem to be derived from Logia, and there is a recourse to current Jewish material such as the lost apocalypse of Eldad and Modad (cf. Hermas *Visions* 2, 3; also Num. 11:26). The idea, found also in *Thomas*, that the kingdom would come "when the two shall be one, and the outside as the inside and the male with the female, neither male nor female," suggests a *haggadah* on the creation passing into Christian usage.[123] The coming would involve the return of all things to the state when Adam was the sole representative of the human race in Eden.

The Shepherd of Hermas (c. 120) takes us into a different world again. This is a series of prophetic tracts with much eschatological speculation and expectation of persecution based largely on current Jewish ideas. The revelations Hermas receives are made by "the Church" in the form of a woman, and as in *2 Clement* the burden of his message is the need for repentance before the end. The individual visions which accompany her exhortations reveal much of the outlook of the semiliterate Greek-speaking immigrants that had found their way into the Christian synagogue at Rome. Christianity is the law of God, and the symbol of the vast willow tree whose branches cover the whole earth recalls a Jewish counterpart derived ultimately from Ezekiel 31.[124] Hermas's association, too, of Wisdom with the Holy Spirit and the role he attributes to "spiritual sisters" as "holy spirits" is reminiscent of the outlook of some Jewish ascetic sects.[125] The "great tribulation" in Hermas (*Vision* 4) also is derived from traditional late Jewish material, in this case perhaps the *Sibylline Oracles* Book III.187. Hermas provides evidence for the outer circles of the inquirers and catechumens attached to the church like "God-fearers" in the synagogue, the "round stones," not yet shaped for insertion into the Tower.[126] Though it is hazardous to suggest the prophet was the "son of a converted Essene,"[127] he shows how many features of the Roman Christian community could be found in the sect and synagogue life of orthodox Jewry.

Hermas, however, was a Christian in sentiment and more than most he emphasized the confrontation between the church and the secular order and the situation resulting therefrom. The law of the Son of God was not compatible with that of the "earthly city."[128] Tribulation and persecution were to be expected. "Stripes, imprisonments, great afflictions, crucifixions, wild beasts" must be endured for the sake of the Name.[129] Apostates, the worst offenders, would be subjected to double punishment hereafter.[130] Such views portray one section of the Roman Christians as members of a fervid and embattled Judaistic sect seething with ideas and with many adherents at odds with the Greco-Roman world which was now entering the period of its greatest prosperity.

THE CHRISTIANS AND THE EMPIRE

What is true of the situation at Rome is true of other Christian communities. Though we have no information about the internal life of pagan mystery cults at the turn of the second century for purposes of comparison, the Christians can hardly have failed to impress their neighbors as an active group filled with a belief in Jesus of Nazareth as Messiah and Savior. Despite their perpetual internal dissensions, they were also an expanding group and the persecutions to which some looked forward implied a hostility to the institutions of the world in which they lived. To anticipate the total destruction of all humanity except themselves was not to harbor feelings of love and charity towards the remainder of the provincials. "Hatred of the human race" was not too harsh a judgment so far as the apocalyptists were concerned.[131]

In the sub-apostolic period collisions between the Christians and the authorities were rare. Between 70 and 95 the story is a blank. Despite the reference in 1 Peter to persecutions, generally speaking the Christians were left in peace. Two events, however, were to undermine their security. First, since the fall of Jerusalem, the two-drachma tax payable yearly by each adult Jew to the Temple treasury in Jerusalem had been transferred to Rome for Jupiter Capitolinus. The authorities naturally tried to gain as much from the change as possible. Rigorous means were employed to establish who were born Jews and who merely "lived like Jews."[132] Second, the orthodox Jews were progressively more successful in establishing their claim to be the only people recognized as Israel. In 95 the visit to Rome of the Nasi, or patriarch, Gamaliel II, head of the school of Jamnia, set the seal on the good relationships between orthodox Judaism and Rome in the previous two decades. Gamaliel II was a strong opponent of heresy within the ranks of Judaism and the success of his visit to Rome boded ill for the Christians.[133]

It does not seem that the "persecution of Domitian" was a direct result of these two events; they are never associated. The executions of Domitian's cousin and father of the boys nominated as heirs to the throne, Flavius Clemens, and of Acilius Glabrio, the consul for the year 91, together with the exile of the emperor's niece Flavia Domitilla on charges of "lapsing into Jewish customs" and "atheism," seem to have been due to bitter factions at court and the emperor's pathological suspicion of anything but the most orthodox religion.[134] It was, however, a straw in the wind. Whatever connotation was being given to "atheism" (*atheotes*), conversion to Christianity, like conversion to Judaism, meant putting oneself outside the ambit of Roman religion. It could lead to a charge of "atheism." To opt for Christianity was also to opt for a religion that had no claim to acceptance by the standards of antiquity or as a national cult, such as Judaism had.

Meantime, Christian attitudes towards the empire were following paths parallel to those of Judaism. On the one hand, there was the obvious loyalty of King Agrippa II who was rewarded by his attitude during the Jewish War by the enlargement of his territories, which he held until his death in 92 or 93. His sister Berenice became Titus's mistress and she remained in Rome from 75 to possibly 79, the year Titus became emperor.[135] Their loyalty was shared by influential Jews such as Josephus, who exonerated the Romans from causing the catastrophe of the Jewish War, and they were content with the status of a client-people so long as the Jewish religion was respected. If Judaism were to realize its universal ambitions it would be by argument and persuasion, not force.[136]

These individuals had their counterparts among the Christians. In Luke-Acts the Roman authorities are depicted consistently in a friendly light, from Jesus' encounter with the centurion, who "loves our [the Jewish] nation" (Luke 7:1–10), to his account of Paul's treatment in Rome. In turn, Sergius Paulus, Annaeus Gallio, Claudius Lysias, and the procurator Felix are shown as taking the view that preaching Christianity was no offense. No Roman governor is described as hindering Paul's mission. In John the pro-Roman tendency is, if anything, stronger. He paints the most favorable picture of Pontius Pilate found in the Gospels. At the same time, Paul's own loyalist attitude to the state found disciples in the Pastorals, in the writer of 1 Peter and in *1 Clement*. "Fear God. Honor the emperor" (1 Peter 2:17) even in persecution, and submission to every ordinance of man for the Lord's sake (1 Peter 2:13) were characteristic of both. Yet, as we have seen in Asia Minor, these loyalist utterances were balanced by others strident in their hostility towards the Greco-Roman world. In Revelation the kingdom and power of the world "are represented as demonic agents deployed against Christ and his Church."[137] The Seer of Patmos's vision of martyrs crying out for vengeance, the overthrow of the whore of Babylon (Rev. 17), the lake of fire and brimstone, and the second and final death does not stand alone. In the *Apocalypse of Peter* (Alexandria, c. 120?), Rome is spoken of as "the capital of corruption whither Peter must go" and "drink the chalice that I [Jesus] have announced to you, from the son of him who is in Hades that the ruin may begin."[138] Ruin, not order, was the writer's hope. For the prophet Hermas the empire was represented by a devouring dragon and heathens "would be burnt because they did not know their Creator."[139] Christian prophecy and apocalyptic always tended to envisage the violent downfall of the existing order before its replacement by the millennium.

In this, Christian and Jew expressed many of the same thoughts. The Jewish *Apocalypse of Baruch* and *4 Ezra*, both c. 80–120, show strong antipathy towards Rome. The saga of the four empires drawn from Daniel is retold, with that of Rome as the fourth and worst, soon to be destroyed. "This age is hastening swiftly to its end." The Roman eagle would be struck down and "the whole earth freed from thy [Rome's] violence and refreshed again."[140] Some Christians were prepared to go to extreme lengths of personal defiance, to imitate even the attitude of the Essenes or the defenders of Masada towards the empire and its gods. Defiance (*contumacia*) was the attitude that impressed itself on Pliny's mind.[141] There could be no service except to Christ, just as Judas the Gaulonite had once proclaimed there could be no service except to Yahweh.[142] To die the martyr's death was to imitate Christ's death, that of "the true martyr."[143] But the Christian unlike the Essene made no recourse to arms. To die to the world was to overcome it.

All this fervor, these expectations, and frustrations teemed among small but articulate groups that had grown up almost exclusively within the confines of the Jewish Dispersion. As yet Christians had made little impact on the Roman authorities. Only incidentally, on the suspicion of possible revivals of the Jewish messianic kingship, were Christians harassed (Eusebius *HE* III.20.3–5). In 95 the punishment of recalcitrant Roman aristocrats suspected of turning to Judaism could have had little effect on official attitudes towards ordinary Christians. When in 112 the emperor Trajan's special commissioner Pliny wrote to his master concerning the Christians who had been brought before him near Amastris in eastern Bithynia, he knew that profession of Christianity was illegal, but he did not know why. He had never been at a trial of Christians, senator and lawyer though he was.[144] He found in the Christians another irritant, obstinate and recalcitrant, and for that reason alone worthy of punishment, but an irritant no worse than the swindling town council of Nicaea or their grossly careless counterparts at Nicomedia, people who were causing the province to fall into the mess of bankruptcy and disorder from which he had been commissioned to rescue it.[145] He was relieved when some recanted and when, on closer investigation which included the torture of two slaves whom the Christians called deaconesses, he found they ate normal food, had obeyed his order concerning associations, and were nothing more than "an extravagant superstition." He prided himself in his report to Trajan that the situation was already beginning to improve, thanks to his firm and tactful measures. Trajan agreed; Pliny had acted correctly. Christians were not to be sought out, like common criminals, but if denounced, and if they refused to recant "and worship our gods," they were to be punished.[146] Otherwise, by implication they could be left alone.

For Trajan (98–117), the orthodox Jews represented the monotheistic alternative religion and the danger to the empire. In the uprising throughout the Dispersion in 115, Judaism showed its strength. Theirs was a vast messianic[147] crusade and, like the revolts of 66 and 132, it failed hopelessly. As in the revolt of 66–74, there is no evidence that the Christians joined them. Nor did they suffer in their catastrophic defeat two years later. Indeed, the treatment they received from Trajan's successor Hadrian (117–38) shows that a clear distinction was now drawn between them and the Jews. In 124/25 the emperor, who was to demonstrate his distaste for Judaism a few years later, informed the proconsul of Asia that Christians were not to be harassed by informers and condemned through unsupported accusations. Any accusations against individual Christians must be made in the courts and if these failed, the accused had the right to cross-petition under the *calumnia* procedure.[148] This allowed him to claim against his accuser the same penalty that he would have suffered had the charge succeeded, namely death or scourging.

In practice, this was toleration, except for victims of popular hatred or private vendetta, and Justin Martyr attached a copy of the rescript to Caius Minucius Fundanus to the end of his *First Apology* in c. 155, as though it gave the Christians full protection. Hadrian was justified, for the Christians were a minimal problem to the empire and its authorities. Only in the province of Asia were their numbers noticeable. Indeed, through the whole of the second century only three imperial rescripts concerning them were thought worth preserving by the Christians themselves.[149] These rescripts, however, had their significance. The fact that the authorities were distinguishing officially between Jews and Christians showed that the latter had lost their battle to be recognized as Israel. Had they but known it, they had won for themselves the chance of gaining the world as followers of the Lord and Savior Christ.

BIBLIOGRAPHY

NOTE

In this lengthy and difficult period, the key work is that of J. Daniélou, *The Theology of Jewish Christianity*, Eng. trans. and ed. J. A. Baker, A History of Early Christian Doctrine Before the Council of Nicaea, vol. 1 (Philadelphia: Westminster Press; London: Darton, Longman & Todd, 1977). There is a difficulty, however, in that the author takes "Judeo-Christianity" as a theological system to be compared and contrasted with later orthodoxy, rather than accepted as the obvious expression of Christianity of this period.

Hans von Campenhausen's contributions, *The Formation of the Christian Bible*, Eng. trans. J. A. Baker (Philadelphia: Fortress Press; London: A. & C. Black, 1972), and *Tradition and Life in the Church: Essays and Lectures in Church History*, Eng. trans. A. V. Littledale (Philadelphia: Fortress Press; London: William Collins Sons, 1968), are as always thought-provoking and scholarly works, and the same remarks apply to L. A. Goppelt's *Apostolic and Post-Apostolic Times*, Eng. trans. R. A. Guelich (London: A. & C. Black, 1970). J. Dauvillier's *Les Temps apostoliques,* vol. 2 of *Histoire du Droit et des Institutions de l'Eglise en Occident,* ed. Gabriel LeBras (Sirey, Paris, 1970), provides an enormous amount of detailed information though somewhat uncritically. For the rise of the ministry, A. A. T. Ehrhardt's *The Apostolic Succession in the First Two Centuries of the Church* (London: Lutterworth Press, 1953), is stimulating and should be read as a foil to Dom Gregory Dix's essay, "The Ministry in the Early Church" in *The Apostolic Ministry*, ed. K. E. Kirk (New York: Morehouse-Gorham, 1947; London: Hodder & Stoughton, 1946), pp. 183–303. See also W. Telfer, *The Office of a Bishop* (London: Darton, Longman & Todd, 1962). For the relations between Jews and Christians, G. W. H. Lampe's article, " 'Grievous Wolves' (Acts 20:29)," in *Christ and Spirit in the New Testament,* ed. B. Lindars and S. S. Smalley (New York and Cambridge: Cambridge University Press, 1973), pp. 253–68, is important and so, too, are the same author's remarks on Baptism in *The Seal of the Spirit: A Study in the Doctrine of Baptism and Confirmation in the New Testament and the Fathers,* 2d ed. (London: SPCK, 1967). On the relations between the church and the Roman authorities, A. N. Sherwin-White's section (pp. 691–712) in his edition of *The Letters of Pliny: A History and Social Commentary* (New York and London:

Oxford University Press, 1966), is comprehensive and useful also for its notes on the liturgy at this time; see, too, the same author's discussion on the question of Christian "obstinacy" with G. E. M. de Ste. Croix in *Past and Present*, no. 27 (1964): 23–27. For the rise of sectarian tendencies and differences of interpretation in the faith, see the classic Walter Bauer, *Orthodoxy and Heresy in Earliest Christianity*, ed. R. A. Kraft and G. Krodel (Philadelphia: Fortress Press, 1971; London: SCM Press, 1972), and Helmut Koester's "GNOMAI DIAPHOROI: The Origin and Nature of Diversification in the History of Early Christianity," in *HTR* 58 (1965): 279–318, reprinted in J. M. Robinson and H. Koester, *Trajectories through Early Christianity* (Philadelphia: Fortress Press, 1971), pp. 114–57. On the development of the Christian view of martyrdom and the indications this provides for Christian attitudes towards society, my *Martyrdom and Persecution in the Early Church: A Study of a Conflict from the Maccabees to Donatus* (Garden City, N.Y.: Doubleday Anchor Books, 1967; Oxford: Basil Blackwell & Mott, 1965) may prove helpful.

SOURCES

Audet, J. P. *La Didaché: Instructions des apôtres*. Études Bibliques. Paris: J. Gabalda, 1958.

1 Clement and Ignatius = J. A. Kleist, Eng. trans. and annotator. *The Epistles of St. Clement of Rome and St. Ignatius of Antioch*. ACW no. 1. Westminster, Md.: Newman Press; Cork, Ire.: Mercier Press, 1946; London: Longmans, Green & Co., 1952.

Didache = W. Rodorf and A. Tuillier, eds. SC 248. Text commentary and French translation. Paris, 1978.

The Epistle of Barnabas = P. Prigent and R. A. Kraft, eds. SC 172. Paris, 1971.

Hennecke, Edgar. *New Testament Apocrypha*. Edited by W. Schneemelcher. Eng. trans. R. McL. Wilson. 2 vols. Philadelphia: Westminster Press, 1963, 1966; particularly useful commentary on the *Gospel of Thomas*, vol. 1, pp. 278–307.

Lake, Kirsopp. *The Apostolic Fathers*. 2 vols. LCL: 1912, 1913.

Polycarp and Ignatius = P. Th. Camelot, ed. SC 10. 4th ed. Paris, 1969.

The Shepherd of Hermas = (1) M. Whittaker, ed., GCS 48 (Berlin, 1956), with H. Chadwick's comments on "The New Edition of Hermas," *JTS* n.s. 8 (1957): 274–80. (2) R. Joly, ed., SC 53 bis. Paris, 1968.

SECONDARY WORKS: Commentaries on the books of the New Testament are not included. See also the Bibliography to 1964, in *Martyrdom and Persecution*, pp. 589–91.

Audet, J. P. "Affinités littéraires et doctrinales du Manuel de discipline." *RB* 60 (January 1953): 41–82.

Barnard, L. W. *Studies in the Apostolic Fathers and Their Background*. New York: Schocken Books; Oxford: Basil Blackwell & Mott, 1967.

Bauckham, R. J. "The Great Tribulation in the Shepherd of Hermas." *JTS* n.s. 25 (1974): 27–40.

Beyschlag, K. *Clemens Romanus und der Frühkatholizismus*. BhistTh. Tübingen: J. C. B. Mohr (Paul Siebeck), 1966.

Bickerman, E. J. "Trajan, Hadrian and the Christians." *RFIC* 96 (1968): 290–315.

Campenhausen, H. von. *Aus der Frühzeit des Christentums: Studien zur Kirchengeschichte des ersten und zweiten Jahrhunderts*. Tübingen: J. C. B. Mohr (Paul Siebeck), 1963.

_____. *Ecclesiastical Authority and Spiritual Power in the Church of the First Three Centuries*. Eng. trans. J. A. Baker. Stanford, Calif.: Stanford University Press; London: A. & C. Black, 1969.

Dinkler, E. "Älteste christlicher Denkmäler—Bestand und Chronologie." In *Signum Crucis. Aufsätze zum Neuen Testament und zur christlichen Archäologie*, pp. 134–78. Tübingen: J. C. B. Mohr (Paul Siebeck), 1967.

Donfried, K. P. "The Theology of Second Clement." *HTR* 66 (October 1973): 487–501.

Dugmore, C. W. *The Influence of the Synagogue Upon the Divine Office*. London: Faith Press, 1964.

Frend, W. H. C. "The Gospel of Thomas. Is Rehabilitation Possible?" *JTS* n.s. 18 (1967): 13–26.

Hare, D. R. A. *The Theme of Jewish Persecution of Christians in Matthew*. SNTSMS 6. New York: Cambridge University Press, 1968; Cambridge: At the University Press, 1967.

Jervell, J. "The Law in Luke-Acts." *HTR* 64 (1971): 21–36.

Keretzes, P. "The Emperor Hadrian's Rescript to Minucius Fundanus." *Phoenix* 21 (University of Toronto Press, 1967): 120–29.

Molland, E. "Besass die Alte Kirche ein Missionsprogramm und bewusste Missionsmethoden?" In *Kirchengeschichte als Missionsgeschichte*, vol. 1, *Die Alte Kirche*, ed. H. Frohnes and U. W. Knorr, pp. 51–70. Munich: Chr. Kaiser, 1974.

Montefiore, H. W. "A Comparison of the Parables of the Gospel According to Thomas and of the Synoptic Gospels." *NTS* 7 (April 1961): 220–48.

Neusner, J. *A Life of Yohanan ben Zakkai*. 2d ed. Leiden: E. J. Brill, 1970.

Parkes, J. W. *The Conflict of the Church and the Synagogue: A Study in the Origins of Antisemitism*. London: Soncino Press, 1934.

Peterson, E. "Die Begegnung mit dem Ungeheuer, Hermas, Visio IV." *VC* 8 (1954): 52–71.

Quispel, G. "The Gospel of Thomas and the New Testament." *VC* 11 (December 1957): 189–207.

Ramsay, W. M. *Letters to the Seven Churches of Asia*. Garden City, N.Y.: Doubleday, Doran & Co., 1904.

Richardson, P., and Shukster, M. B. "Barnabas, Nerva and the Yavnian Rabbis." *JTS* n.s. 34 (April 1983): 31–56.

Roberts, C. H. *Manuscript, Society and Belief in Early Christian Egypt*. New York and London: Oxford University Press, 1979.

Ste. Croix, G. E. M. de. "Why Were the Early Christians Persecuted?" *Past and Present* 26 (1963): 6–38.

Simon, M. "La migration à Pella: légende ou réalité?" *RSR* 60 (1972): 37–54.

_____. *Recherches d'histoire judéo-chrétienne*. Paris: Mouton Press, 1962.

_____. *Verus Israel: étude sur les relations entre Chrétiens et Juifs dans l'Empire Romain (135–425)*. Paris: Boccard, 1948; 2d ed. augmented, Paris: Boccard, 1964.

Speigl, J. *Der römische Staat und die Christen*. Amsterdam: Hakkert, 1970.

Suggs, M. Jack. "The Christian Two Ways Tradition: Its Antiquity, Form and

Function.'' In *Studies in New Testament and Early Christian Literature: Essays in honor of Allen P. Wikgren*, ed. D. E. Aune, pp. 60–74. Leiden: E. J. Brill, 1972.

NOTES

1. See the discussion in Simon, ''Migration à Pella.'' Simon points out the value of the tradition preserved by Epiphanius (*Medicine Box* [*Panarion* = *Haereses*] XXIX.7.8) that the migration took place before the outbreak of the war in 66.

2. Synagogues: see James 2:2; Hermas *Mandates* XI.9.13; and Irenaeus *Adversus Haereses* (*Against Heresies*) III.6.1. The Ebionites continued to use this term about their churches (Epiphanius *Medicine Box* XXX.18.2) and paradoxically so did the Marcionites in Syria in the early fourth century (see *OGIS* 618 from Deir el Ali near Damascus). Fasting: *Didache* VIII, and see Dugmore, *Influence of Synagogue*, pp. 37–41.

3. Thus, Beyschlag, *Clemens Romanus*, pp. 48ff.

4. See Suggs, ''Christian Two Ways Tradition''; and Barnard's essay, ''Judaism in Egypt, 70–135,'' in *Apostolic Fathers*, pp. 47–51.

5. Jervell, ''Law in Luke-Acts.''

6. Jervell, ''Law in Luke-Acts,'' p. 35: ''He [Luke] fights the Jews who charge Christian-Jews with apostasy and treachery to Israel, thus not being entitled to salvation.''

7. As in the form defined by J. Daniélou, *Theology of Jewish Christianity*, pp. 18–21, who nonetheless has shown more than any other previous scholar the scale and ramifications of Judaism and its influence on Christianity to circa A.D. 150.

8. *2 Clement* 1, and Pliny *Letters* X.96.7. See C. Mohlberg, ''Carmen Christo quasi Deo,'' *RivAC* 14 (1937): 93–123.

9. Thus, the resurrection of the dead saints recounted in Matt. 27:52, and compare the vision of the valley of dry bones in Ezek. 37:1–11. For the reconstruction of the Temple as accompanying the return of Christ, see M. Simon, ''Retour du Christ et Reconstruction du Temple, dans la Pensée chrétienne primitive,'' in *Recherches d'histoire judéo-chrétienne*, Études juives VI (Paris: Mouton, 1962), pp. 9–19.

10. 4 Macc. 18:11–18.

11. See the excellent article by Lampe, '' 'Grievous Wolves.' ''

12. I find myself unable to agree with von Campenhausen's thesis that the Pastorals were composed ''in the first half of the second century'' (*Ecclesiastical Authority*, p. 107), though the case for some connection between these and *The Letter of Polycarp to the Philippians* seems strong (von Campenhausen, *Polykarp von Smyrna und die Pastoralbriefe*, SHAW.PH 2 [1951]). See below, n. 109.

13. *The Letter to Diognetus* IV.1 and 5. Dating is uncertain but likely to be c. 150. See H. C. Meecham, ed. and Eng. trans. *The Epistle to Diognetus* (Manchester, Eng.: Manchester University Press, 1950), p. 19.

14. *1 Clement* XLV.1–7. The writer of *1 Clement* sees the Christians as lineal descendants of old Israel.

15. Ignatius *The Letter to the Smyrnaeans* VIII.2.

16. Ignatius *The Letter to the Magnesians* X.3. Compare *The Letter to the Philadelphians* VI.1.

17. Ignatius *Magnesians* IX.1.

18. Ignatius *Smyrnaeans* X.2, and *The Letter to the Ephesians* XXI.1. Compare 4 Macc. 6:27–29; and see O. Perler, "Das vierte Makkabaerbuch," *RivAC* 25 (1949): 47–72.

19. Ignatius *Philadelphians* VI.1.

20. On the whole question of Testimonia, see C. H. Dodd, *According to the Scriptures: The Sub-Structure of New Testament Theology* (New York: Charles Scribner's Sons, 1953; London: James Nisbet & Co., 1952); Daniélou, *Theology of Jewish Christianity*, pp. 102ff.; and Barnard, *Apostolic Fathers*, pp. 115–19.

21. See above, p. 102.

22. *Letter of Barnabas* IV.6. The tract was evidently written after a debate with Jews (I.4).

23. Recorded by Neusner, *Yohanan ben Zakkai*, p. 157; also, P. Schäfer, "Die Flucht Johanan b. Zakkais aus Jerusalem und die Gründung des 'Lehrhauses' in Jabne," *ANRW*, vol. 19.2, pp. 44–101.

24. Flavius Josephus *Contra Apionem* (*Against Apion*), LCL, II.39.280–86.

25. Note particularly Josephus's final exhortation stressing the benefits that flowed from the Law (ibid., II.291–95).

26. *Sibylline Oracles*, Book IV.78–80.

27. Juvenal *Satires* XIV, 96ff.

28. Justin Martyr *Dialogue with Trypho* 122.2.

29. On the development of Rabbinic Judaism, after A.D. 70, see J. Neusner, "The Formation of Rabbinic Judaism," *ANRW*, vol. 19.2, pp. 3–42, esp. pp. 32–42.

30. *Babylonian Talmud Berakoth* XXIXa. For cursing Christians in Palestine, see Epiphanius *Medicine Box* XXIX.9.2. For anti-Christian acts by Jews in the second century, see Justin *Trypho* 16.4, 47.4 and 117. In general, see Goppelt, *Apostolic and Post-Apostolic Times*, pp. 118–19.

31. Justin *Trypho* 8.4.

32. *Diognetus* IV.6.

33. Pliny *Letters* X.96.6.

34. Ramsay, *Seven Churches,* ch. 15, esp. p. 191. Ephesus was a magnet for Jewish movements (cf. Acts 19:1). In 1972, the writer found a Hebrew inscription engraved on the steps of the Library of Celsus in the town, that is, after A.D. 112.

35. Thus G. M. Lee, "The Presbyter John, a Reconsideration," *SE* 6, TU 112 (1973): 311–20. For John as high priest, see Polycrates of Ephesus, cited by Eusebius *HE* V.24.3, who believed that John of Ephesus was John the Apostle.

36. For the symbolic importance of the Petalon in first-century Jewry, see Philo *Questions and Answers on Exodus* II.124, in Philo *Supplement II*, LCL, pp. 175–76.

37. Thus, *2 Clement* XII.1, *Barnabas* IV, and Ignatius *Ephesians* XI.

38. See Molland, "Besass die Alte Kirche?" pp. 56–57.

39. *1 Clement* XXIII.5.

40. Ignatius *Philadelphians* XI.1.

41. Eusebius *HE* I.13.

42. See E. Sachau, ed., *Chronicle of Arbela*, AAWB 1915. Cf. the *Chronicle of Arbela* entry in B. Altaner, *Patrology*, Eng. trans. H. C. Graef, rev. ed. A. Stuiber (New York: Herder & Herder, 1961), p. 283. The most recent defender of its

authenticity is J. Neusner, "Conversion of Adiabene to Christianity," *Numen* 13 (August 1966): 144–50, esp. p. 144.

43. Quispel, "Thomas and New Testament."

44. H. I. Bell and T. C. Skeat, eds., *Fragments of an Unknown Gospel and Other Early Christian Papyri* (New York: Oxford University Press; London: British Museum, 1935), and discussed by C. H. Dodd, "A New Gospel," *BJRL* 20.1 (1936): 3–39: "We have here the same kind of material we have in the canonical Gospels" (p. 7).

45. See Eusebius-Jerome *Chronicle*, ed. R. Helm, GCS 24 (1913), p. 201. See over, p. 205.

46. See Roberts, *Manuscript, Society and Belief*, chap. 3, though he is inclined to play down the Gnostic element in early Egyptian Christianity.

47. Roberts, *Manuscript, Society and Belief*, p. 22, stressing the popularity of the *Shepherd* in provincial Egypt.

48. See Frend, "Gospel of Thomas," p. 25. Also, prophetic writings like those of Hermas were in circulation (*Pap. Oxy.*, 1172), and apocalyptic texts. See the collection of texts by C. Wessely, *Patrologia Orientalis* XVIII.3, pp. 371ff. Cf. Hennecke-Schneemelcher, vol. 1, pp. 91–116.

49. Thus, T. H. Klauser, *Gesammelte Arbeiten zur Liturgiegeschichte, Kirchengeschichte und christlichen Archäeologie*, ed. E. Dassmann (Münster: Aschendorff, 1974), pp. 132–38.

50. *1 Clement* IV and V.

51. Hermas *Visiones* (*Visions*) II.4.3. Not necessarily the same Clement to whom *1 Clement* is attributed. Grapte had the duty of "exhorting the widows and orphans."

52. See Dinkler, "Älteste christliche Denkmäler." Except for the shrine of St. Peter below St. Peter's, Rome, Dinkler does not believe that any Christian archaeological remains are earlier than the third century.

53. See *ILCV* 4935. Compare the reference in 2 Peter 2:6 to the fate of Sodom and Gomorrah.

54. For example, *Didache* 10.6; note the parallel of some European Mithraic communities retaining phrases from the original Iranian in their cult. See below, p. 276.

55. These presages of the end all envisage, at this period, the collapse of existing society. Rome is cast in the role of persecutor (*Ascension of Isaiah* 4–5 and *Apocalypse of Peter*), and the emperor himself is thinly veiled under the title of "Beliar" or "the Beast." See Frend, *Martyrdom and Persecution*, p. 182.

56. Papias, cited by Irenaeus *Heresies* V.33.3 and 4. Compare Eusebius *HE* III.39.11–12.

57. Hermas *Similitudines* (*Similitudes*) IX.31.2 and also IX.30.5.

58. The only exceptions would be some surviving Christians in Galilee and perhaps some Aramaic-speaking adherents in East Syria and Osrhoene.

59. Ignatius *Smyrnaeans* XIII.2.

60. Ignatius *The Letter to Polycarp* VIII.2.

61. Eusebius *HE* IV.15.30. Polycarp was on good terms with leading citizens of Smyrna.

62. Hermas *Mandates* VIII.10.

63. Hermas *Similitudes* IX.27.2.

64. *Barnabas* XX.2, following Isa. 1:23. Failure in these duties was equated to the "Way of the Black One."

65. *2 Clement* XVI.4.

66. *The Apology of Aristides* XV.7–8. For similar lists of duties in Judaism at this time, see Josephus *Apion* II.198ff.

67. *Didache* I. 2. The "second commandment" (ibid., II–IV) regarding behavior includes only one command from the Sermon on the Mount (Matt. 5:5), namely "be thou meek, for the meek shall inherit the earth."

68. Ignatius *Polycarp* IV.3. See Ste. Croix, "Early Christian Attitudes Towards Property and Slavery," p. 20.

69. Cf. *Didache* IV.11: *typos theou.*

70. Thus Ignatius *Polycarp* VIII.2, *Smyrnaeans* XIII.1; and Hermas *Mandates* XII.3.6 and *Similitudes* VI.3.9. Tobit (4:10 and 12:9) is cited in support of virtuous almsgiving in Polycarp *Philippians* X.2.

71. See Frend, *Martyrdom and Persecution*, pp. 199–201.

72. See von Campenhausen, *Ecclesiastical Authority*, p. 88; and cf. *1 Clement* XVI.1.

73. See Goppelt, *Apostolic and Post-Apostolic Times*, p. 176.

74. See von Campenhausen, *Formation of Christian Bible*, pp. 30–31ff., referring particularly to Paul and the Gospel writers.

75. Polycarp *Philippians* XI.2, and compare IX.2.

76. The emphasis is on "final form." I am inclined to follow C. F. D. Moule, *The Birth of the New Testament*, HNTC, BNTC (New York: Harper & Row; London: A. & C. Black, 1962), pp. 121ff., that there may be "extremely little of the New Testament" later than A.D. 70. For circa A.D. 80 as the date of Luke's Gospel, see B. H. Streeter, *The Four Gospels: A Study of Origins*, rev. ed. (New York: Macmillan Co., 1930), p. 540.

77. Thus, J. H. Ropes, *St. James*, ICC (New York: Charles Scribner's Sons, 1916), p. 35.

78. *1 Clement* V and XLVII.

79. Ibid., XLIII.6.

80. Ibid., XXXV.1–2.

81. Ibid., XVI. For Jesus as "Servant," see also LIX.1 and 3; *Didache* X.3.

82. For the phoenix and used in this sense in a Hellenistic-Jewish context, see W. Bauer et al., *Die apostolischen Väter*, HNT Sup. 1 (Tübingen: J. C. B. Mohr [Paul Siebeck], 1923), pp. 88–89 (many references).

83. *1 Clement* LV.3–8.

84. So, the writer of *Diognetus* IV.5. To him this was not piety but folly.

85. *1 Clement* XX, following Job 38.

86. A comprehensive account of the early Christian libertine tradition is to be found in Morton Smith, *Clement of Alexandria and a Secret Gospel of Mark* (Cambridge, Mass.: Harvard University Press, 1972), esp. pp. 258–64; and see above, pp. 105–6. Compare also W. M. Ramsay, "The Letter to the Church at Thyateira," *Expositor* (1906): 59–60.

87. Ignatius *The Letter to the Trallians* IX; and compare *Magnesians* XI and *Smyrnaeans* III–IV.

88. Ignatius *Smyrnaeans* VI.

89. Irenaeus *Heresies* III.3.4.

90. For a useful summary of the arguments and counterarguments which W. Bauer inspired, see Georg Strecker's supplementary essay, revised and augmented by R. A. Kraft as Appendix 2 of the English translation of Bauer's *Orthodoxy and Heresy*, pp. 286–316.

91. Ignatius *Smyrnaeans* VIII.

92. *Didache* X.7.

93. Thus, *1 Clement* 42–44. For the likelihood of presbyter-bishops at Rome at this time, see XLII.4–5 with its references to "bishops and deacons" appointed to govern the church, and a similar order in Corinth, XLIV.5.

94. *Didache* XIII. Is this the origin of payments to the clergy, or did it begin earlier with Paul's claim to be entitled to be supported by his converts (2 Cor. 11:7–9)?

95. Ignatius *Philadelphians* V. The prophets "we love because they have announced the gospel," but otherwise they have no duties except "hoping" and "waiting" for Christ.

96. *1 Clement* XLIV.2, and see Ehrhardt, *Apostolic Succession*, pp. 77–79.

97. See Dix, "Ministry in Early Church," pp. 246–47. On the ministry in general in this period, *see* J. Dauvillier, *Les Temps apostoliques*, pp. 303–20.

98. See J. Zizioulas, "Verité et communion dans la pespective de la pensée patristique grecque," *Irenikon* (1977): 463–67.

99. Ignatius *Smyrnaeans* VIII.

100. *1 Clement* XL.2.

101. *Didache* VIII.3.

102. *Didache* VII.1 for the ceremony. For the parallel with proselyte baptism, see J. Jeremias, *Infant Baptism in the First Four Centuries*, Eng. trans. David Cairns (Philadelphia: Westminster Press, 1961; London: SCM Press, 1960), pp. 29–40. Baptism as an eschatological sacrament, see ibid., p. 23.

103. Hermas *Similitudes* IX.16, p. 3–4. See Lampe, *Seal of Spirit*, p. 105.

104. *Didache* VII.1–3. For the Jews there were six degrees of water used for cult purposes, of which the "living water" was the most honorable. The origins of this may go back to Lev. 14:5 and Num. 19:17 (washing of the unclean). See H. L. Strack and P. Billerbeck, *Kommentar zum Neuen Testament aus Talmud und Midrash*, 4 vols. (Munich: Beck, 1922–28), pp. 108ff.

105. *Didache* IX and Pliny *Letters* X.96.7. See Sherwin-White, ed., *Letters of Pliny*, pp. 702–3, citing further relevant discussion, and Dugmore, *Influence of Synagogue*, pp. 9–10. There is another and perhaps less straightforward explanation of the oath taken by the Christians before the agape. Hippolytus, writing of the Essenes, says that before being allowed to partake of the sacred meal, a new member of the sect "was bound under fearful oaths." He promised to "worship the Divinity, observe just dealings with men, not to injure anyone, not to hate anyone who injured him, but to pray for him, to aid the just and to keep faith with all, especially those who are rulers." The analogy may be accidental but the mention of the oath in both cases is interesting (Hippolytus *Refutatio Omnium Haeresium* [*Refutation of All Heresies*] IX.18). Oaths of any sort were frowned upon by other Christians (James 5:12).

106. See R. Bauckham, "The Worship of Jesus in Apocalyptic Christianity," *NTS* 27 (April 1981): 322–41, "John's churches offered praise to Christ comparable with that offered by the angels in heaven" (p. 331).

107. Pliny *Letters* X.96.7.

108. Koester, "GNOMAI DIAPHOROI"; and see also Bauer, *Orthodoxy and Heresy*, pp. 61–94 (Asia).

109. Note the suggestion made by von Campenhausen, that Polycarp might be the editor of the Pastorals, so close are the parallels in some places between them and his *Philippians*, in "Polykarp von Smyrna und die Pastoralbriefe," in *Aus der Frühzeit des Christentums*, pp. 197–252. I think the case is overstated. Polycarp's favorite New Testament work seems to have been 1 Peter, which he cites twelve times in his short letter.

110. *Apocalypse of Baruch* XLI.29–30. See Daniélou, *Theology of Jewish Christianity*, pp. 346–47; *4 Ezra* 3:5 (*4 Ezra* = 2 Esdras 3—14) restricts the "millennium" to four hundred years and is less explicit about its joys.

111. Caius quoted by Eusebius *HE* III.28.4. See Daniélou, *Theology of Jewish Christianity*, p. 81.

112. According to Irenaeus *Heresies* I.26.1.

113. Hippolytus *Refutation* IX.8, and see H. Lietzmann, *A History of the Early Church*, Eng. trans. B. L. Woolf, 4 vols. (New York: World Publishing, Meridian Books, 1961; Lutterworth Press, 1962), vol. 1: *The Beginnings of the Christian Church*, p. 247.

114. Von Campenhausen, *Formation of Christian Bible*, p. 17.

115. See Hare, *Jewish Persecution of Christians*, chap. 3: "No reason for believing Matthew's portrayal of the conflict between synagogue and Church is greatly distorted" (p. 129).

116. See Barnard, *Apostolic Fathers*, chap. 8, pp. 101–2.

117. See Montefiore, "Comparison of Parables," p. 248.

118. Mark 9:34; 10:35ff.; Luke 9:46; 22:27. See R. M. Grant and D. N. Freedman, *The Secret Sayings of Jesus* (Garden City, N.Y.: Doubleday & Co., 1960), pp. 124–25.

119. See Quispel, "Thomas and New Testament," and Koester, "GNOMAI DIAPHOROI," pp. 290–306.

120. *1 Clement* 37. The difference of religious climate as between *1 Clement* and Hermas is noted by Daniélou, *Theology of Jewish Christianity*, p. 49.

121. Cited from Goppelt, *Apostolic and Post-Apostolic Times*, p. 113.

122. Donfried, "Theology of Second Clement," p. 487.

123. *2 Clement* XII.2; compare *Gospel of Thomas, Logion* 23 and Clement of Alexandria *Stromata* (*Miscellanies*) III.64.1. See Donfried, "Theology of Second Clement," pp. 491–92; and Grant and Freedman, *Secret Sayings*, pp. 136–37.

124. Hermas *Similitudes* VIII.3.2, though in Ezekiel 31 the tree is a cedar and not a willow as in Hermas.

125. Hermas *Similitudes* VIII.13, and compare Daniélou, *Theology of Jewish Christianity*, p. 49.

126. Hermas *Similitudes* IX.30.4.

127. As suggested by Audet, "Manuel de discipline," p. 82, though retaining "personal ties with Judaism."

128. Hermas *Similitudes* I.3ff.

129. Hermas *Visions* III.2.1.

130. Ibid., I.3.3 and 4.2., *Similitudes* IX.28.8 (apostates worthy of a double punishment).

131. Tacitus *Annals* XV.44.

132. Suetonius *Domitian* 12.2.

133. On Gamaliel II in Rome see Speigl, *Der römische Staat*, pp. 38–39.

134. Dio Cassius *Epitome* LXVII.14. Frend, *Martyrdom and Persecution*, pp. 212–17 and notes.

135. See E. M. Smallwood, *The Jews Under Roman Rule from Pompey to Diocletian*, SJLA 20 (Leiden: E. J. Brill, 1976), pp. 385–87.

136. For Jewish loyalism in the generation after the end of the first Jewish War, see Speigl, *Der römische Staat*, pp. 5–6. Josephus added "Flavius" to his name to emphasize his loyalty to the Flavian dynasty.

137. Cited from von Campenhausen, *Tradition and Life*, p. 152.

138. *Acts of Peter*, ed. C. Wessely, *Patrologia Orientalis* XVIII.3 ("Textes divers de la littératur chrétienne"), pp. 482–83, though from a third- to fourth-century papyrus, and compare, for Revelation, Ramsay, *Seven Churches*, p. 203.

139. Hermas *Similitudes* IV.4. For a similar Jewish hope, *Sibylline Oracles*, Book IV.678.

140. *4 Ezra* 10:60—12:35 = *Vision 5*. Cf. 11:45–46 (*4 Ezra* appears in translation in R. H. Charles, ed., *The Apocrypha and Pseudepigrapha of the Old Testament*, Eng. trans. G. H. Box [Oxford: At the Clarendon Press, 1913], vol. II, *Pseudepigrapha*, pp. 561–624 [*Vision 5* occurs on pp. 608–12]), and compare for the same sentiments, *Apocalypse of Baruch* XXXVI–XL.

141. Pliny *Letters* X.96.3. See Sherwin-White, "Why Early Christians Persecuted?: Amendment," p. 23–27.

142. Josephus *War* II.118. See above, p. 57.

143. As stated by the confessors at Lyons in 177, Eusebius *HE* V.2.3. For Christ as "true martyr" see Rev. 1:5.

144. Pliny *Letters* X.96.1. See Sherwin-White, *Letters of Pliny*, p. 694, and Ste. Croix's valuable article, "Why Early Christians Persecuted?" and subsequent discussion.

145. Pliny *Letters* X.31 and 33. See Sherwin-White, *Letters of Pliny*, pp. 603, 608.

146. Pliny *Letters* X.97.

147. Smallwood, *Jews Under Roman Rule*, chap. 15, esp. p. 397, "The revolt was almost inevitably a messianic crusade."

148. Keretzes, "Hadrian's Rescript"; text in J. Stevenson, ed., *A New Eusebius* (London: SPCK, 1963), pp. 16–17.

149. Bickerman, "Trajan, Hadrian and Christians," p. 292.

5

Opposition Cult
135–80

Simon Bar Kochba's attempt to restore the independence of the Jewish people failed disastrously. In the autumn of 135 the legionaries captured Beth-Ter, his guerrilla stronghold five miles south of Jerusalem. The emperor Hadrian felt justified in proclaiming himself imperator for the second time. At Jerusalem the marble statue of a pig was placed in front of the Bethlehem Gate.[1] More perished, however, than Jewish national pride. Bar Kochba had been hailed as the "Son of the Star," promised Messiah, a warrior and the restorer of Judaism by authorities as eminent as the Rabbi Akiba.[2] He and other leaders of the Academy of Jamnia perished in the aftermath of reprisal and repression. The center of gravity in Jewish intellectual life was pushed eastwards across the Roman frontier to Babylon. The schools in Babylonia became the transmitters of Jewish orthodoxy. For the remaining Christians in Palestine the uprising had been equally catastrophic. They were harried as renegades by Bar Kochba's men,[3] but the victory of the Romans brought them scant relief. The new city of Aelia Capitolina which arose out of the ruins of Jerusalem took no more heed of Christian holy places than it did of the Jewish. Hadrian covered the reputed sites of Calvary and the tomb of Jesus with the temples of Jupiter and Venus.[4] The succession of the "Bishops of the Circumcision" came to an abrupt end. Jerusalem for the time being was an entirely Gentile city. No Jew might enter.

The second and final defeat of Jewish political and religious hopes, however, had lasting effects on the Christians. The previous generation had already seen Christianity grow away from Judaism. Messianic hopes were becoming less urgent. There was less emphasis on the church as "Israel." Christians, such as the writer of the *Preaching of Peter* (Alexandria? c. 130?), were beginning to argue with Greeks on the validity of their philosophy and were also taking a more dispassionate attitude towards Judaism, pointing to its failings and virtues alike while asserting the truth of Christianity.[5] With Basilides (also Alexandria c. 130), one sees the opening phase of a serious and considered effort to reconcile Christianity with contemporary Greek philosophy. Pagans such as Justin were beginning to be converted to Christianity without previous contact with the synagogue.

The war and its outcome accelerated these trends. Between 135 and the end of the century, Christians attained a self-identity based on their sacred literature, the New Testament, their distinctive liturgy, their rule of faith, and their wide-ranging organization. All this clearly marked them out as the "third race" which in terms of religion they claimed themselves to be.[6]

These developments occupied the rest of the century. If, from now on, the church's external relations were involved increasingly with the Roman authorities and with the growing hostility of the ordinary provincials, the Jewish legacy remained in the background. Even in as important a center as Ephesus, a Christian version of the Jewish practice of making the office of "ruler of the synagogue" hereditary persisted down to circa A.D. 180 (Eusebius *HE* V.24.6).[7] Judaism was to be the one continuous theme through all the variations of Gnosticism. Marcion (*flor.* 130–60) cannot be understood outside the controversy between church and synagogue; nor indeed can Justin Martyr's debate with Trypho at Ephesus in c. 135. Two witnesses from the pagan world show how gradual was the church's emergence from the role of Judaistic sect during the second century. We shall discuss the temporary conversion of Peregrinus Proteus to Christianity, but Lucian of Samosata (c. 165), who preserves the account, describes how his hero became a "prophet" and "synagogue leader" in his new faith, which had been proclaimed by "their first lawgiver."[8] These terms are all reminiscent of Judaism and though the term "lawgiver" for Christ is not found in the New Testament the idea would not be strange to the readers of Matthew's Gospel. A little more than a decade later (c. 178), the Platonist Celsus wrote the first serious literary challenge, entitled *True Reason* (*Alethes Logos*), to the Christians. In this he used the device of introducing a Jew as a critic of details of the claims made on Jesus' behalf that he was the Son of God. Celsus does so since "not the shadow of a donkey" separated the ideas of Jews and Christians,[9] and further that for the Jews the Christians were simply people who had "deserted the laws of their [Jewish] forefathers," and been led astray by Jesus' teaching when they "were progressing in Judaism."[10] Jesus was a "mere man,"[11] and a deceiver.

None of this would make sense if the Christians did not appear to their neighbors during the second century as a close-knit Judaistic sect, and an increasingly noxious one. The Greco-Roman world was still confronted by two monotheistic creeds whose members, if allied in their repugnance of idolatry, were at odds in everything else. Judaism continued to show astonishing strength in the Dispersion despite the military catastrophes it had suffered. One of the most remarkable instances of its religious and cultural influence has been provided by the synagogue of vast proportions unearthed at Sardis, a city which could boast of the usual range of provincial and imperial priesthoods and an articulate and well-organized Christian community. Between 175 and 210, the first stages took place in the building of a complex that covered an area of 130 × 20 yards in a main thoroughfare of the city, surrounded by shops many of which were owned by Jews. Its benefactors included a high official in the imperial administration and several city councilors. Its members were completely Hellenized and proud of their city.[12] Judaism remained at home in the Hellenistic world. In Palestine, Caesarea became the center of rabbinic schools, and in the third century Origen would be debating with their learned members.[13] In the west, the Jews in Rome were established on the Caelian Hill as well as in their older settlement in Trastevere and six catacombs were in use.[14] In

Carthage, the vigorous Jewish community provided the extensive cemetery on the Gamart Hill, two miles north of the city, and burial grounds to the west, below what became the Christian complex of Damous el Karita.[15]

The Jews evidently made the most of Antoninus Pius's grant of limited freedom,[16] and it does not seem that Greeks determined to become Jews found intolerable hindrances in their way. The evidence adds up to a picture of Judaism accepted in the empire as the religion of a distinctive ethnic and religious minority at the cost of their universalist claims. The process of narrowing horizons, however, had begun. Rabbinic scholarship was moving into the phase of acute and learned textual criticism with no concessions to allegorical interpretation. Trypho, Justin Martyr's opponent at Ephesus, marked the last generation of an outward-looking Hellenistic-Jewish religion.

The church's destiny was gradually to move out of its Jewish environment into the pagan world, and in the course of the next two centuries to conquer it. What was this world and how did the Christians view it? What scope was there for accommodation between the two? Why was it that during the second century the Christians were able to make their presence increasingly felt?

THE ROMAN EMPIRE IN THE SECOND CENTURY

The second century saw the Greco-Roman world reach the climax of self-confidence and prosperity. Gibbon's view of the Antonine age as one of the great eras of human stability and well-being was not wholly mistaken. On any reckoning the succession of rulers from Nerva (96–98) to Marcus Aurelius (161–80) were men of more than average ability as soldiers and administrators. Their aims, set out on the coinage that circulated from end to end of their dominions, were justice, security, and well-being for all. "Not in keeping with the spirit of the age"[17]—Trajan's comment on anonymous denunciations of Christians by the provincials of Pontus—was typical of a self-confidence that extended to toleration of critical minorities whether these were Stoic philosophers or Christians. The concept of empire was widening to include the provinces and their elite on equal terms with Rome and Italy. Hadrian (117–38) emphasized the importance of the empire from the point of view of the provinces as well as that of Rome. The magnificent series of coin types struck in 134–35 reflects the emperors' ceaseless journeyings through the provinces and their role in the life of the empire.[18] The concept of "Roman" was embracing the whole race (of educated urban provincials), its well-wishers claimed. The empire's frontiers extended to cover nearly the entire inhabitable world north and south of the Mediterranean from the edge of the Sahara to the Highland glens of Scotland. There the reign of Antoninus Pius (138–61) saw advances from the Antonine Wall to control the exits from the valleys sixty miles north. Ardoch (Braco) in Perthshire became the base on which the Roman defenses hinged. Only the confederations of Germanic tribes across the Rhine and the Parthian Empire remained outside the empire's control. The fame of Antonine Rome reached even the Chinese, and in 166 direct if fleeting contact was established between the two empires.[19]

Within the empire's borders there was peace. In a remarkable statement c. 150, a man of letters like Aelius Aristides of Smyrna (c. 120–89) could say "Wars have so far vanished as to be legendary affairs of the past." "A man simply travels from one country to another as though it were his native land. We are no longer frightened by the Cilician pass or by the narrow sandy tracks that lead from Arabia into Egypt. We are not dismayed by the height of mountains, or by the vast breadth of rivers or by inhospitable tribes of barbarians. To be a Roman citizen, nay even one of your subjects is a sufficient guarantee of personal safety."[20] Rome had brought a freedom of movement, a uniform system of justice and peace where none had reigned before. The old division between Greek and barbarian had been replaced by "Roman" and "non-Roman." This might be construed as the flattery of a Greek for his Roman masters, but it is echoed by Christian writers of the next generation. Athenagoras (c. 177) refers to the "deep peace" that prevailed in the empire,[21] and a few years later Irenaeus of Lyons commented on the peace and security of the times that even the Christians were enjoying.[22]

Aristides was not exaggerating. A genuine loyalty to emperor and empire was developing, based on the obvious benefits of peace and prosperity. Some of the inland provinces of the empire, especially those bordering the Mediterranean, would experience nothing more violent in the whole of the century than a riot between rival cities or an imitation sea battle staged in the amphitheater. There might be the occasional raids by mountain tribes in North Africa and parts of Asia Minor, and perils of pirates and bandits were not to be discounted, but these were the hazards of life, interruptions in long periods of a quiet and not too imaginative existence.

The Greco-Roman world of the second century A.D. was a world of city-states. Everywhere cities were growing in wealth and magnificence, not only centers of trade and administration, but powerful agents in the process of fusing provincial and Roman together into a single Greco-Roman commonwealth. These were imitation Romes with their capitols dedicated to the Roman gods Jupiter, Juno, and Minerva; their baths, fora, colonnades, temples, and amphitheaters copying from afar the splendor of the imperial city. The ideal was reflected in the inscriptions in the vast Antonine bath building at Carthage, its size and unity of construction (dating to 145–62) making it a treadmill for archaeologists. It has been described as a "veritable center of propaganda for Latin civilization."[23] On the huge capitals of the columns, the emperor himself is shown as Zeus destroying the Titans, represented by snake-headed monsters. The provincials were expected to see him as their protector against evil and the forces of chaos that always threatened their existence; and this is exactly how Celsus described his role.[24]

The cities were governed by men who also believed in defending order (including religious order) against chaos and faction. The local aristocracies were composed of middle-ranking landowners who had prospered under Rome and felt a pride in the culture of Homer, Menander, and Virgil. Latin in the west and Greek in the east were their common languages, and the classics their common heritage. These were the men who managed the affairs of their cities without remuneration and lavished enormous sums on public buildings or benefactions for the amusement and sometimes for the permanent welfare of their citizens.[25] Twenty thousand donors of the decurial class in North Africa between 98 and 244 is an estimated figure.[26] The cities of the Greco-Roman world remained the monument to their achievement. *"Quantam vim reip(ublicae)"* scratched by someone on a dedication set up to some worthy in the country town of Bulla Regia in North Africa reflected their ideal.[27]

There was indeed a darker side to this picture. The cities lived off the countryside and the Romanized provincials off the backs of the peasants. These were the subject populations, such as the "Penestae" of Thessaly, the "Pedies" of Priene, the Helots of Sparta, peoples conquered in ancient wars and now paying poll taxes and whatever was demanded from them for the upkeep of the cities.[28] There were also occasional outbreaks of discontent in the cities themselves resulting in strikes such as that by bakers (shop-owners) at Ephesus.[29] But these manifestations of unease were remarkably few. They have left practically no trace on either the literature or the enormous body of second-century inscriptions found throughout the Greco-Roman world. Partly, no doubt, the hold of immemorial custom fortified by religious sanction kept the peasants from grumbling too loudly, but also as we know from the *Lex Mancia* that set out the terms of peasant-holding in North Africa, terms of tenure offered to native farmers by the authorities were not ungenerous.[30] In case of extortion there was a right of appeal, and if an imperial estate was involved the appeal would be to the emperor himself. The material benefits of Romanization were seeping down to every level of society. Better buildings, paved streets, luxurious public sanitation, easier ways of life, more use of money, more education, better pots and household utensils were changing lives from the barbaric to the civilized. For the time being the local deities rejoiced like everyone else in Greco-Roman fashions. They were assimilated to the nearest Roman equivalent. We find the peasants on the Saltus Burunitanus in proconsular Africa, who appealed to the emperor Commodus in 183 against extortion by bailiffs, were articulate individuals aware of their rights.[31] They believed they would get justice from the "Imperial Providence." As the Platonist Celsus told the Christians only five or so years before, "Whatever ye receive in this world ye receive from him [the emperor]."[32] At the end of the second century the mass of provincials believed this to be the case. There was no widespread discontent in the empire that would lead to a questioning of the benefits derived from traditional gods and ways of life. Until this happened a century later amid unparalleled military and economic disasters, Christianity would remain a minority sect in an urban setting.

Intellectual and Religious Life

In Rome and the provinces the ideal was to be an educated gentleman, and the intellectual life of the period shows that, as civilizations go, the age of the Antonines was neither debased nor morally degenerate. It could be dull and humdrum. Tombstones in the provinces reflect conventional pieties and the mutual affections. *Pudicitia* was the virtue of the emperor's consort; *pietissimus* was the memory one wished to leave behind. They are sometimes poignant and wistful but almost always hopeful. The "last journey" represented on elaborate funerary memorials was often a joyful one.[33] There were forces of good to counteract death's terrors, or if an Epicurean, one would believe that one simply dissolved into nothingness. The tombstone of Flavius Agricola, a second-century citizen of Tibur, spoke for many of the Italian petite bourgeoisie. His rather large and vulgar memorial was garnished with his life story:

> Tibur is my native place, Flavius Agricola my name. Yes, I'm the one you see reclining here, just as I did all the years of life fate granted me, taking good care of my little self and never going short of wine. Primitiva, my darling wife, passed away before me, a Flavian too, a chaste worshipper of Isis, attentive to my needs and graced with every beauty. Thirty blissful years we spent together; for my comfort she left me the fruit of her body, Aurelius Primitivus, to tend my house [*or* tomb] with dutiful affection. And so, herself released from care, she has left a dwelling place for me forever. Friend who read this, do my bidding. Mix the wine, drink deep, wreathed with flowers, and do not refuse to pretty girls the sweets of love. When death comes, earth and fire devour everything.[34]

Flavius Agricola holding his drinking cup provides a cheerful picture of the religion of one who was content with the ordinary pleasures of a none too exacting or monogamous life, and was not particularly worried about the hereafter. His wife, who no doubt had experienced the greater hardships, was a chaste devotee of Isis, the mother of the gods and savior of those who trusted in her.

The worship of the gods was deep-rooted in popular faith. Lucian of Samosata (c. 160) describes the feast of the Syrian Goddess at Hieropolis, whither pilgrims flocked from all over Syria.[35] The great festivals of the territorial deities were frequented by visitors from far and wide. There were sacrifices, games, and entertainments for the crowds of singers, musicians, jugglers, and dancers. The scenes described by Lucian at the shrine of the serpent-god invented by Alexander of Abonuteichos were hardly unusual.[36] In the larger cities the prestige of the priesthood drawn from the local aristocratic families was enhanced by their association with the imperial cult. To be a *neocorus* (custodian) of this worship in one's city was to be on the high road to local fame.

"All peoples," said the pagan speaker Caecilius in his debate with Octavius (c. 170), "were convinced firmly that there were immortal gods, however uncertain they were of their origin,"[37] an argument that carried conviction in the second century. Some aspects of religious life in the Antonine era were, however, less inviting and defied conventional wisdom. The ancient world was alive with goblins and evil spirits. It was a bold man who failed to throw a grain or two of incense on a wayside shrine or incline briefly before its patron as he passed. The argument between the pagan Caecilius and the Christian Octavius opened with Caecilius blowing a kiss to a shrine of Serapis, "like superstitious common people do," as the two friends were walking along the shore near Ostia.[38] Other "superstitious people" swore by a host of gods of equal power when annoyed.[39] In some African cities there would hardly be a street corner without some prophylactic symbol carved on a wall to protect the wayfarer from evil spirits. The mosaics that adorned the fine townhouses of Dougga or Thuburbo maius, to take two instances, were not there merely for decoration, but the vine tendrils, mixing bowls, and representations of a human eye were chosen through their special potency to ward off the attentions of the evil eye, the bringer of strange disease and calamity.[40] Humankind was helpless against germs and the disturbances of nature. Sudden death was an ever-present possibility. The making of horoscopes designed to foretell the exact hour when an individual's life was destined to end was a common occupation. At Dura-Europos on the Euphrates frontier, the excavators of the town found that practically every household must have had its own horoscope.[41] To appear to deny the power of the gods to act violently in human affairs was "atheism," and those guilty of such unnatural beliefs deserved death at the hands of authorities fully supported by public opinion.

One aspect of the unknown world of spirits in particular attracted the awesome attention of pagans and Christians alike. Dreams, believed to be a divine means of communication to worshipers or the work of evil spirits, became terrifying experiences, the subject of minute investigation. Aelius Aristides (c. 160) has left a vivid account of horrible anxiety dreams, in which he was either being poisoned, chased by a wild bull, or attacked by barbarians.[42] A hypochondriac and something of a megalomaniac, he found consolation in a unique and intense relationship with the god Asclepius, so that he spent a large part of his life at his sanctuary near Smyrna. But he was not alone in his fears. About the same time the writer of the Alexandrian (?) Gnostic tract *The Treatise on the Three Natures* also depicts the individual who has not been enlightened by Gnosis in terms of dream-experiences. He was like one who "flees blindly from he knows not what, commits murder, or falls helplessly from a great height into a bottomless abyss." This was the intolerable situation whence the initiate was rescued by Gnosis.[43] At N'gaous (Nicivibus) in Numidia, the parents of Concessus record their sacrifice of a lamb in substitution for a human being, thus obeying the dread command of the god Saturn, communicated to them in a dream.[44] Such visitations were the nighttime fears of countless inhabitants of the empire in the second century. The prayer for "sweet dreams" on a mosaic in a villa of Emporium (Ampurias, near Gerona) was not an idle request.[45]

Mystery Cults

Many turned to the traditional gods or to initiation into the mysteries of Isis, Attis, or Mithra, or one of the celebrated local cults. Often initiation was a conversion experience, involving observances which tested the zeal of the initiate and the completeness of his or her devotion to the deity. Juvenal's description (c. 125) of the initiate of Isis flinging herself into the icy Tiber and crawling round the temple of the goddess on her bleeding knees may not have been exaggerated.[46] The North African, Apuleius, describes in memorable terms the release of his hero Lucius from the witch's spell that had turned him into a donkey. Near the end of the story, Lucius invoked the aid of Isis and the goddess appeared to him in a dream promising him release from his donkey's skin provided he followed her precise instructions. She told him that from then on he was under her protection and that she alone had the power to prolong his life beyond the bounds appointed by his fate. Lucius obeyed, and was initiated into the Isiac mysteries. He was impatient, but his impatience was curbed by the priest to whom he had presented himself. He was sprinkled with holy water and instructed in the details of the cult of Isis. Then he fasted for ten days and, his time completed, he was clothed in a linen garment and led into the inner chamber of the shrine. There he had an awe-inspiring vision whose nature he could not reveal, but in the outline he disclosed he believed that he "made his way to the verge of death. I trod the threshold of Proserpine. I travelled through all the elements and I made my return. At midnight I beheld the sun ablaze with brilliant light."[47] Lucius was restored and saved.

Philosophies

Initiation into the Eleusinian or Isiac mysteries assured the believer of salvation. Fate and the astral deities might be outwitted, but it was no part of the mystery cult to provide knowledge of God or knowledge of self through which the individual might learn to live virtuously before he entered on his heritage. This knowledge was derived from the philosophies, notably the popular versions of Platonism, Stoicism, and Pythagoreanism.

All these systems had tended in the course of time to move towards religion. "Do not philosophers converse entirely about God and hold their discussions invariably about supreme government and providence?" Thus Trypho somewhat indignantly asked Justin in the prosperous times of Hadrian's reign.[48] This was possible, for in the unprogressive view of creation which prevailed in the last centuries of pagan antiquity the universe was seen as a harmonious whole (a *cosmos*) in which conformity to the divinely ordained pattern of existence was the highest goal in human life. The world itself was conceived as fixed in the center of the universe with the sun and moon and five known planets circling round it. There was an ordered community between the world of gods and the world of creatures. Time, too, was regarded as cyclical, repeating each event and situation after an infinite number of years. Man himself, composed of body, mind, and spirit, was a microcosm of creation (part or an imitation of the soul of the world, as Plutarch said),[49] endowed in his spirit with a spark of the divine light wherewith he might understand his true nature and so conform himself to the ideal values of the world beyond visible creation. The task of the philosopher was to ask the questions and find answers that would guide individuals towards their goals. The philosopher was as much concerned with practical ethical questions as with the quest for abstract truths. The means varied, but whether one was a Pythagorean or a Platonist, one moved through branches of human knowledge such as mathematics or music towards understanding the eternal harmonies that lay behind these studies. Study gave way to contemplation, indifference to bodily passions to asceticism; the body itself was regarded as a "tomb" from which the soul was liberated on death. The soul was immortal and could enjoy salvation; the body was mortal and destructible. Religious conversion was conversion to the effects produced by philosophy for the benefit of the soul.[50]

The individual's quest for union with God could be fulfilled through ecstatic vision as among the Platonists or, alternatively, through a life devoted to duty in which each situation could become the means of controlling earthly feelings and elevating the soul towards God. There would not be many like Justin's Stoic philosophers who assured their pupils that knowledge of God was unnecessary for the good life. More representative of Stoicism in the second century was Marcus Aurelius, whose *Meditations* (written probably between 170 and 180) provide, in the words of a critic, "evidence unique in antiquity, perhaps in any age, for the inmost thoughts of a ruler."[51]

Marcus was deeply religious and he found in Stoicism the means of uniting his sense of duty to his fellows, especially his army, with his conviction that the universe formed a harmony governed by a supreme ruler whom he must seek to know. Where he and his fellow Stoics differed from the Christians, apart from deep intellectual antipathy which regarded Christian self-sacrifice as so much exhibitionism,[52] was that they did not conceive that ruler in personal terms. God was not Yahweh; in a cyclical preordained time-scheme he could not be active in the lives of individuals or institutions in the universe. Divine providence (*pronoia*) immanent in the universe was concerned with the harmony of the whole rather than the specific well-being of its individual parts. Zeus, "the gods," nature, and God are terms all used apparently indifferently by Marcus to convey the same meaning. For him, "to live in accordance with nature" meant to live according to the will of the ruler of the universe. "There is," said Marcus, "one *cosmos* made up of all things, and one God that goes through all things, and one substance, one law, reason common to all intelligible beings."[53] Yet how far Providence or the gods were concerned with individuals and their problems was a mystery.[54] Prayer to them for human welfare was right. Sacrifices of hecatombs to the gods was an act of piety, but the end of it all remained uncertain. Marcus's quest after God was never finished. Unlike Augustine, he could never say he "rested in Thee."[55]

Marcus's philosophy might point towards answers to the final questions of human existence and conduct, but could not provide the answers themselves. By the mid–second century the various philosophical schools seemed to have reached the end of the road. Their debates led to endless questioning without the possibility of finding answers. Exasperation turned at times into mockery of their predicament. Thus Lucian of Samosata, writing c. 165, tells how Zeus described to Menippus, his visitor from earth, how "these people" (the philosophers) dividing themselves into schools and inventing word-mazes, have called themselves Stoics, Academics, Epicureans, Peripatetics, and other things more laughable than these.[56] Lucian regarded the situation as a joke, like Zeus's dilemma when confronted with two petitions both properly presented, backed by sacrifices duly promised, whose dedicants were demanding exactly the opposite favors from him.[57] Others, however, were less amused, and it was from among these angry and disillusioned individuals as well as from plebeians and educated but dissatisfied women that Christianity was beginning to draw its recruits.

THE OPPOSITION

Perhaps the foundations were not so stable as they looked. Cynics, Jews, and Christians were united in exposing and criticizing the weak points of the imperial system. Cynics had long denounced the institution of the emperor, and in 71 Cynic philosophers had been expelled from Rome for preaching antimonarchic, if not anarchic tenets. Jewish leaders also had their own tradition of hostility to Rome's ways of government. Many of them remained pro-Parthian, and looked forward to a Parthian liberation of Palestine, as a presage to the coming of the Messiah.[58] Gamaliel III (c. 190) complained that Rome's rule was purely self-centered and did nothing for the good of its subjects. Rome was like a snake. Its army was like flies feasting on a basket of fruit.[59] "Customs dues, baths, theatres and taxes," thus did Rome waste her provincials' substance, so spake Gamaliel II a century before.[60] Derogatory remarks[61] were dangerous but seldom suppressed. The Christians of the second century reflected these attitudes. They too were sojourners in their cities, in the Roman Empire but not of it. For some, acceptance of Christianity involved a deliberate acceptance of a "barbarian" teaching in preference to that of the Greco-Roman world.

The middle years of the second century provide three examples of striking conversions to Christianity. Justin Martyr (c. 100–165) and his pupil Tatian (*flor.* 170–80) were won over completely. The third, Peregrinus Proteus (d. 165), had a relatively long flirtation with Christianity before adopting the Cynic's mantle.

Justin

Justin tells his story in his three surviving works, *Dialogue with Trypho* written c. 160, and his *First Apology* and *Second Apology*, written c. 155 and 160 respectively. He was born of Greek settler parentage at Flavia Neapolis (ancient Sichem, modern Nablus) in Samaria. He had a strong religious sense, and in early manhood he left home on a quest through the philosophic systems to discover the one by which he might direct his life and arrive nearest to God. Significantly, he gives no hint of ever considering conversion to Judaism or to the Samaritans, though his knowledge of Judaism was exceptional for a pagan. To use his own words:

So at first, as I myself had the same desire to come into contact with one of these, I put myself into the hands of a certain Stoic, and as, after I had spent a fair time with him, I got no further with respect to God (for he did not know himself and he was continually saying that this learning was not necessary), I withdrew from him, and came to another, called a Peripatetic, a sharp fellow, as he supposed. And after bearing with me for a few days he thought that I ought to fix his fees, that our intercourse should not be without profit to us! So for this reason I left him, for I did not think that he was a philosopher at all. But as my soul was still painfully full of desire to hear the special note and the supreme excellence of philosophy, I addressed myself to a Pythagorean of great reputation, a man who devoted much thought to wisdom. Whereupon, as I began conversation with him, desiring to be one of his hearers and associates, "Well," he said, "have you paid attention to music and astronomy and geometry? For surely you do not suppose that you will get a clear vision of any of the things that contribute to happiness, if you were not first taught those which will draw the soul away from the visible, and make it fit for the intellectual, so that it may have a clear vision both of the noble and the good as they are in themselves?" And when he had greatly praised these branches of learning, and had insisted on the necessity of them, he dismissed me, for I confessed to him that I knew them not. I felt vexed, therefore, as might be supposed, at being thus disappointed of my hope, and the more so as I thought he did know something. Reckoning also once more the time I should have to spend on those subjects, I could not bear to put things off so long. Now in my distress I thought it well to have recourse to the followers of Plato, for their reputation also was high. Accordingly I had as much intercourse as I could with an intelligent man, a leading man among the Platonists, recently come to live in our city, and I was making good progress, advancing more and more every day. I was quite enraptured with the perception of immaterial things, and the contemplation of ideas added wings to my intelligence, and within a short time I supposed I had become wise, and in my obtuseness was hoping to have forthwith a clear vision of Good. For this is the aim of Plato's philosophy.[62]

In this frame of mind he met and conversed with an old man on the seashore at Ephesus.[63] The old man was exceptional. He was evidently a Christian with a God-fearer background and he either knew or had experienced enough Platonism (he cites *Philebus* and *Timaeus*) to put his finger on the weak points of the system. As R. M. Grant has shown,[64] he aimed at undermining the key Platonist doctrine of reminiscence, and he asked Justin whether or not the soul remembered the vision of God after returning to the body. Justin gave the wrong answer, and unmindful of *Phaedrus* (249c–d) said that it did not. The old man then asked pointedly, "What's the use?" given the axiom that God or nature does nothing without purpose.[65] Then he attacked the consistency of Plato himself, for if souls could not recall their previous existences, how could they know why they occupied the bodies they did. It was all useless. There was no possibility of the soul attaining direct communion with God. The aid of the Holy Spirit was necessary. Justin was shaken and ready to listen to the old man's view that knowledge of God could be attained from the writings of the Hebrew prophets. These were inspired by God: they discussed the deepest philosophical questions and theirs was the true answer.

Justin did not immediately become a Christian. In fact, the old man had only won the argument against the transmigration of souls. Justin's conversion came when, as he recounts in his *Second Apology*, he witnessed the serene bravery of Christians going to martyrdom.[66] Christianity combined truth with inspiration for moral reform. Without abandoning his respect for the Stoic ethic and Platonism or his philosopher's cloak—the incomplete systems to which he had previously adhered—he now accepted Christianity as the complete revelation of reality. He had missed, as he says, the feeling that God cared for individuals as well as the universe or species within it.[67] This he had now found and therefore he rejected the "philosophy of the Greeks" for the true philosophy he identified with Christianity.[68] He became the first orthodox Christian to work out a systematic theology which attempted, not altogether successfully, to integrate millenarianism, the arguments for the truth of Christianity derived from prophecy, and Stoic and Platonic ideas of creation into a single Christian system. He indicated, too, the possibility of a confluence of Hebrew prophecy and some Greek philosophy in Christianity. Less ambitious than his Gnostic contemporaries in his aims, he nonetheless was to have a greater influence than they as one of the founders of the orthodox doctrinal tradition. From Ephesus he migrated to Rome. There he set up a small school and entered into debate with the local run-of-the-mill exponents of philosophy and heresy. His philosophy was orthodox Christianity as against Cynicism, Gnosticism, and Marcionism. In the end, he was denounced to the authorities by an angry rival, the Cynic Crescens. Tried before the prefect of the city, Q. Junius Rusticus, he refused to sacrifice to the gods and went unflinchingly to his death in 165.[69]

Critics tend to concentrate on the heroism of Justin's martyrdom, and rightly so; but behind the categorical refusal to recognize the celestial powers that his contemporaries believed preserved the safety of the state, his writings show some ambivalence towards the society in which he lived. He felt loyalty towards the empire and sought to establish that Christianity could be harmonized with its institutions. He even saw the cross-shaped *vexillum* carried by the legionaries as a sort of representation of the Word "placed X-shaped over the universe."[70] But his loyalty was conditional. No hindrance must be placed in the way of the Christian's worship of God, and this could be extended even to disobedience if the law appeared to be unjust. In his *First Apology*, he comments how death had been decreed against "those who read the books of Hystaspes or Sibyl prophets." When this had been ordered is not known. These *Sibyllines* and *Hystaspes* may be Jewish writings propagating the perennial hope still nursed by many Jews, as we know from Celsus, for the coming of the Messiah at the head of armies led by Rome's enemies from the east.[71] Justin's attitude is instructive. Much as he disliked the Jews, he did not uphold the law. In a rather unguarded outburst (*1 Apology* 44) he denounces it as "the workings of the wicked demons," and declares his intention of consulting the books and encouraging others to do so. His attitude towards the emperor from whom he was asking toleration was arrogant, threatening him with divine judgment if he did not act justly towards the Christians. There was a streak of the unquiet rebel; the man who had wandered from one philosophic school to another and found all unsatisfying was not to abandon his radicalism when he became a Christian. The martyrs that so inspired him would have seemed to most onlookers to be rebels, utterly misguided and futile. Put to the test, Justin was prepared to join them rather than concede one iota to what he considered to be "the working of evil demons" and idolatry.

Tatian

His pupil Tatian (*flor.* 160–80) was a man of very different character. Where Justin was normally conciliatory, Tatian was uncompromising. Where Justin saw a relative value in the pagan philosophies, Tatian saw none; but both found themselves opponents of the established attitudes of their times. Tatian describes himself as "an Assyrian," that is, born in the frontier district between the Roman Empire and Parthia.[72] As many like him, he left his homeland to seek his fortune in the cities of the empire, including Athens and Rome itself. He hoped to learn something of the philosophy and wisdom of the Greco-Roman world which his own country lacked. He was initiated into one of the mystery cults, but in the end he was bitterly disillusioned by what he found and by the reception he himself received. "Things I have set before you," he wrote in his *Address to the Greeks*, "I have not learned at second hand. . . . We bid farewell to the arrogance of the Romans and the idle talk of the Athenians. I embraced our barbaric philosophy [Christianity]. I began to show how this was more ancient than your institutions."[73] The argument from prophecy had no doubt influenced Tatian as it had Justin, but Tatian was an angry man, and he found in the universality, apparent simplicity, and directness of the Christian message the means to belabor the civilization that had disappointed him. His attack was leveled not only at pagan religion, but at the Roman system of law and government. "On this account," he says, "I reject your legislation also; for there ought to be one common polity for all. But now there are as many different codes as there are states, so that things held disgraceful in some are honourable in others."[74] Origen was to make the same point against Celsus seventy years later (*Against Celsus* I.1), but Origen was loyal to the empire and saw its value in providing a framework within which the gospel could spread. Tatian was at heart a rebel, and had no place for the Roman Empire or its rulers in his scheme of values.

His acceptance after 165 of an extreme ascetic (Encratite) interpretation of Christianity involved also his rejection of the orthodox Christian moral values represented by his master Justin. He had been attracted to Christianity as a religion of protest, an effective counter to the emptiness, pride, and injustice of the Greco-Roman world as he had experienced it. He had scant use for a Christianity that was prepared even on its own terms to live with the world. He illustrates the underlying forces of alienation and discontent that sometimes existed below the calm surface of the Greco-Roman city-states of the Antonine era.

Peregrinus Proteus

Some of his ideals were shared by Peregrinus Proteus. Combined with the exhibitionism that eventually resulted in his public suicide was a streak of radicalism based on a serious reflection on the world around him. In some ways he is the most interesting of the three converts to Christianity. He went right through Christianity, achieving a position of local leadership and suffering imprisonment as a Christian. Then he thought better of it and found an equally radical outlet for his passion for notoriety, as Cynic debater, and finally by committing suicide as the crowning public spectacle of the Olympic games of 165. The main source for his life is Lucian of

175

Samosata's satire entitled *On the Death of Peregrinus*, but the Christian apologist Athenagoras also alludes to what must be the same incident, with the implication that Peregrinus's shortcomings were forgiven by his fellow townsmen who set up a statue in his honor.[75] A further confirmation of his existence, however, comes from Aulus Gellius who admired him and heard him make a speech at Athens on the subject, "Your secret sins will find you out."[76]

Peregrinus's Christian episode came fairly early in his life. He was born of wealthy parents at Parium on the Asiatic side of the Hellespont. He quarreled with his father and left his native city under the suspicion that he had murdered him. By and by he arrived in Palestine, fell in with Christians, was converted and accepted not only, as we have seen, as a "prophet" but as a "synagogue leader" (*synagogeus*). He made commentaries on Scripture and achieved fleetingly the reputation of being a "second Socrates."[77] Then he was thrown into prison where every form of attention was lavished upon him by Christians from near and far. Eventually he was released, but then he quarreled with them. Lucian may well be right in saying that the cause was Peregrinus's rejection of food taboos enforced by the Christians (*Peregrinus* 16). The compact Judaistic community which he had served no longer sufficed Peregrinus's ambitions. He asked for the return of his estates that he had made over to them, and when this was refused, he left in high dudgeon. He moved south into Egypt and there took up even more severe austerity, flagellating himself and adopting the way of life of a Cynic. Thence he sailed to Italy but was expelled for abusing the emperor. Finally he moved to Greece where, after insulting Herodes Atticus, the enormously wealthy patron of the arts and builder of monuments in Athens, he burned himself on a pyre at the end of the Olympiad of 165.

It is an extraordinary story which throws much light on Christianity as it was practiced c. 150 and the motives of those who joined it. The introverted and sectarian outlook is obvious. Food laws, probably those laid down at the original apostolic council were still being enforced, and the Christian community was known as a "synagogue."[78] It was bound to other similar bodies by the firmest of links for, when Peregrinus was imprisoned, people arrived to honor him, "even from the cities in Asia" hundreds of miles away. But it was also an opposition body. Lucian points out that

> the poor wretches have convinced themselves, first and foremost, that they are going to be immortal and live for all time, in consequence of which they despise death, and even willingly give themselves into custody, most of them. Furthermore their first lawgiver persuaded them that they are all brothers of one another, after they have transgressed once and for all by denying the Greek gods, by worshipping that crucified sophist himself and living under his laws. Therefore they despise all things indiscriminately and consider them

common property, receiving such teaching by [force of] tradition without any definite evidence.[79]

They were open therefore to the attentions of charlatans like Peregrinus. Like Tatian, Peregrinus found "the Cynic way of life" akin to Christianity. He accepted it and reverted to paganism.[80] He still needed to find an outlet for his opposition to authority; his absurd attempt to stir up the Greeks against the Romans[81] and his expulsion from Italy for insulting the emperor were in keeping with this. Yet he was not wholly a fool. Aulus Gellius found him a "serious and steadfast person," one who had "many profitable improving things to say."[82] His tragedy lay in his youth and upbringing. He was haunted no doubt by the memory of his relations with his father, but his career shows how this, combined with a radical outlook towards contemporary society, found in Christianity a possible alternative. Christianity, Judaism, and Cynicism were aspects of the "alternative society," challenging the apparently changeless world of the Antonines.

Celsus's True Reason

Lucian of Samosata did not take the Christians very seriously, but he did not like what he saw: Christianity was a "new-fangled cult." Its adherents were fanatics, but the authorities controlled the situation. The occasional flogging of their leaders was all that was required. Other more thoughtful observers judged differently. Celsus (*flor.* 170–80) we have mentioned already. He probably came from the area of Palestine-Phoenicia (he knew what was happening there apparently at first hand); he was an educated man, a Platonist, and he had taken the trouble to read some of the writings of the Christians and of late Judaism. He knew the Pentateuch, Matthew's Gospel, some apocryphal works—such as the *Preaching of Peter, Protevangelium of James*—and some Marcionite and Gnostic tracts.[83] Moreover, he did not share the irrational prejudices of many of his contemporaries against Christians. This makes his witness the more formidable.

Celsus accused the Christians of being a revolutionary sect, bound to each other by oaths, and intent on subverting the established order of society.[84] They were an offshoot of Judaism.[85] There was no question about Plato's having provided a bridge from pagan to Christian. In their essential doctrines of God and of man, Christians differed little from Jews.[86] Christ himself, according to Celsus, far from being a worker of miracles and a savior, was an impudent quack who learned his magic in Egypt and was unable to save himself from death at the hands of his enemies. If he had been genuine he ought to have appeared to those who had reviled and crucified him.[87] His followers formed an illegal association, a "disruptive movement" (a *stasis*) against the Jews themselves and the rest of the community. They were sacrilegious people who would stand up, strike an image of Zeus or Apollo, and then proclaim it had taken no revenge on them. Therefore, no doubt it was a "dumb idol."[88] Abandon it, and become a Christian! Their unquestioning faith provided them with a "trustworthy foundation for their unity in revolt."[89] Celsus, however, seldom threatened. He analyzed and exhorted. Christians owed a duty to the emperors; they should swear obedience to them "since not even they hold their position without the might of divine powers."[90] They should be prepared "to help the emperor with all their power, and so co-operate with him in what is right and fight for him. They should not refuse to serve in public office if this was necessary for the preservation of the laws and of piety."[91] Seventy years later, when he answered Celsus's tract, Origen could dismiss many of his statements as untrue or irrelevant. At the time they were written, however, Celsus's charges against Christianity as an introverted sect concerned with saving its own members at the expense of their neighbors were not short of the mark. The Christians might quarrel among themselves, but (like the Jews before them) they appeared to be hostile to everyone else.

The basic problem concerned Christians' attitudes towards the protecting deities of the world in which they lived. Marcus Aurelius could accept a plurality of gods as he could a plurality of men and peoples. The peace of gods and men rested on the maintenance of ancestral usages. In this Marcus was at one with the popular Platonist ideas that Celsus represented. Celsus claimed there was one God, named variously Zeus, Adonai, or Zen, but below this Being was a hierarchy of territorial gods, such as Attis the god of the Phrygians, or Osiris, god of the Egyptians. These could be regarded as "satraps" of the ruler of the universe. Below these were "daemons who have been allotted control over earthly things," and had a right to offerings and prayers.[92] Celsus's contemporary, Maximus of Tyre, pointed out that two truths were accepted by Greeks and barbarians, namely that there was only one God, King and Father of all, and that there were many gods, children of God, who participated in his power.[93] It was on this issue that Christians refused to compromise, despite the multitude of angels (or aeons) they acknowledged. The ties with Judaism were too strong to allow their acceptance of a divine order based on something other than strict Jewish monotheism. The emotional barriers were too great to assimilate the pagan deities to the angels of late Judaism. Michael and Mithras would never sit down together at the same messianic banquet.

CHRISTIAN ADVANCE

The actual missionary progress of the church from 135 to the end of the century is difficult to plot. Down to 150 it seems to have been slow. It is noticeable that Justin's school at Rome included no converts. All six members were immigrants from Asia and three had admitted to having Christian parents.[94] At Smyrna, Polycarp recoiled with horror at the very suggestion that he might try to persuade the pagan spectators in the amphitheater.[95] By 170, however, there were congregations in the Peloponnese and in Thessaly (Larissa) as well as at Athens and Corinth. About the same time, one would place the foundation of the Christian church at Lyons and Vienne in the Rhone valley. Eusebius's account of Dionysius of Corinth's correspondence with colleagues as far away as Amastris in eastern Pontus on the one hand, and Rome on the other, shows how Christianity was spreading through the whole of the Greek-speaking world.[96] Marcion, as we shall see,[97] tried to continue the Pauline mission, and his communities were established in areas as far separated as Rome, Nicomedia in Bithynia, Antioch, and near the Persian frontier. There were some wealthy Christians. Marcion gave two hundred thousand sesterces to the Roman community c. 140, and there was the steady trickle of Gentile converts for one reason or another who found in Christianity the true religion they were seeking. Nothing suggests, however, that Christianity was a formidable movement before the reign of Marcus Aurelius (161-80). Compared with the advance of Mithraism from 150 onwards, its progress must have seemed halting and slow.

Celsus, however, painted quite a different picture. Though the exclusive sectarian outlook still prevailed ("If all men wanted to be Christians, the Christians would no longer want them"),[98] the Christians "had spread to become a multitude,"[99] and were engaged in active mission. Their targets were artisans, slaves, the women and children in major households, and gullible and stupid people, prepared to be taken in by propaganda.[100] Going around from marketplace to marketplace dressed as beggars, the Christian missionaries were plying their disruptive trade. The charge was serious because to seek to undermine the authority of masters over slaves, and paterfamilias over his household was about the most subversive attack that could be made on established society. Moreover, Tatian and Athenagoras, writing from very different viewpoints at the same time as Celsus, confirmed the truth of Celsus's charge. "You pagans," taunted Tatian, "who assert we gossip among women and children and old women, and whom you reproach us with, because they do not accept you, listen to what absurdities there are among the Greeks"[101]—which he proceeded to relate. Athenagoras, too, contrasted the "ambiguities and confusions of the philosophers and their disciples" with the simple truths expounded by the Christians, which anyone could follow. He continued, "With us you will find unlettered people, tradesmen and old women, who cannot express in words the advantages of our creed, demonstrate by acts the value of their principles."[102] A year or two later in July 180 the Scillitan Martyrs, the earliest Christian martyrs in North Africa, showed themselves remarkably articulate in defying the orders of the proconsul of Africa to sacrifice to the gods and abandon Christianity. They preferred the works of the "just man, Paul," which they carried with them, and went to their deaths thanking God for the privilege.[103]

Between c. 170 and 180 a whole range of the less-privileged members of Greco-Roman society were beginning to move towards the new and clandestine religion of Christianity. The personal stories of the converts provide reasons for some decisions. More generally, there were features in Christian conduct and ethics that impressed them. Origen, writing his reply to Celsus (*Celsus* VI.2), provides one possible clue, for he points to the popularity of Epictetus in his own day. Epictetus preached the high moral ideals of Stoicism in simple ethical discourses designed for the ordinary provincials.[104]

The Christians went further along the same road. They claimed to be "brethren," and as Lucian indicated, gave surprising proofs of the reality of this claim. Another witness of the same period Dionysius, bishop of Corinth, writing to his colleague Soter of Rome (c. 170), praised the Roman church for sending contributions to less-wealthy churches and money for the relief of Christian prisoners condemned to the mines.[105] No one could feel an outcast in a Christian community. For many, including Justin, the adoption of Christianity also involved the moral reformation which some others were able to find through philosophy. "Tyrannical and violent dispositions" were reformed. Origen made much the same claim.[106] Christian morality, which earlier in the century had tended to degenerate into mechanical acts of charity on the Pharisaic model, was taking on new fervor and relevance. Gentile converts found in the ideal and sincerity of the Christians a practical fulfillment of the demand of the good life they had sought in vain elsewhere. Christianity offered personal salvation, based on proofs drawn from the undeniably ancient revelations of the Hebrew prophets, fulfilled for humankind by the life and work of Jesus, together with an appeal to a living idealism that all classes and men and women could share. What Judaism had attempted by absorbing Stoic values into its theology the Christians now achieved. The Gospels and the ultimate sacrifice of personal martyrdom went beyond Jewish particularism, and individuals were being increasingly attracted to this new dynamic creed. Celsus marks the watershed between the church as a sect and the church as a world mission.

Conflict and Martyrdom

Courage to face martyrdom was being increasingly demanded of the Christians. As the second century wore on, the enmity between the populace and the authorities increased. Most, if not all, provincial governors took their religion for granted and had a tendency to identify it with loyalty to the empire. Thus, Vigellius Saturninus, proconsul of Africa in 180, when confronted with the apparently subversive statements of the confessors from Scilli (probably near Carthage), put his own point of view: "We too are a religious people, and our religion is a simple one; we swear by the genius of our lord, the emperor, and we offer prayers for his health, as you also ought to do."[107] This is echoed more strongly by an official (perhaps legendary), who tried the confessor Procopius at Caesarea in the reign of Diocletian. "I, however, love the emperor, and the gods even more so, because they provide their benevolence for all men." Emperor and gods went together. *Romanitas* was not so much civic status as a way of life, guarded by the worship "handed down to us by our parents."[108] All this the Christians seemed set on destroying. Indeed, Irenaeus shows Christians regarded "Romans and other nations" as separate from themselves.[109] When, therefore, officials heard outbursts such as "I do not recognize the empire of this world. Rather, I serve that God whom no man has seen,"[110] they had not the slightest doubt that the Christians deserved punishment.

They were supported fully by public opinion. The well-known phrases of Tertullian (c. 197) sum up the fear and hostility the Christians were inspiring, as though they were able to disrupt the course of nature by their practices, as well as harboring disloyal views towards the empire. "If the Tiber reaches the walls, if the Nile does not rise to the fields, if the sky doesn't move or the earth does, if there is famine, if there is plague, the cry is at once 'The Christians to the lion. What, all of them to one lion?' "[111] Forty years before, Cornelius Fronto, a kindly and reasonable man, tutor to Marcus Aurelius, denounced the Christians in terms recalling Cicero's denunciation of the Catiline conspirators. They were a "sect that fled the light and conspired in the shadows" (*lucifuga et latebrosa natio*).[112] Their common feasts included the drinking of blood that had been heated, followed by sexual orgies. By 150 general ill-feeling against the Christians had outrun official policy towards them. "Out with the Christians"[113] was a popular cry whether on the lips of Alexander the charlatan of rural Paphlagonia or among the citizens of Smyrna.

Throughout the second century the authorities still followed the rulings of Trajan and Hadrian. The right of cross-petitioning their accusers conceded by the latter to the Christians would ensure that few charges would be brought. There was no protection, however, against mob violence backed by all sections of opinion. The charges of "atheism," "Oedipean intercourse" (incest) and "Thyestean feasts" (cannibalism) all carried the suggestion of conspiracy and black magic enacted under the guise of religion. The explosion came in the reign of Marcus Aurelius. First in Asia and then among the isolated Christians in Gaul, Christians became the object of terrible outbursts by the populace, which the authorities were unable or unwilling to control.

Smyrna in c. 165 and Lyons in 177 were the scenes of two of the most famous Christian martyrdoms. Between them they illustrate the strength and weaknesses of second-century Christianity, its heroism and its narrowness of vision. In each case the record of the events was preserved through a letter written by the survivors of the pogrom to another congregation. Polycarp was well known in Smyrna where he had been bishop for about sixty years; he was wealthy and was held in esteem by his fellow citizens, yet when the mob in the amphitheater at Smyrna shouted for his blood, nothing except a public recantation could have saved him from an immediate and cruel death. Contrary to official rulings, he was sought out and discovered on a farm outside the city. Thence, he was personally escorted by the police chief (*irenarch*) and his father to the amphitheater and there brought before the proconsul of Asia who was watching the games. On the way, the *irenarch* had attempted in vain to persuade him to do something to save his life, and then they tried to put words into his mouth which would have enabled him to escape punishment.[114] Thus an eyewitness recorded the scene:

> The Proconsul asked him if he were Polycarp, and when he admitted it he tried to persuade him to deny, saying: "Respect your age," and so forth, as they are accustomed to say: "Swear by the genius of Caesar, repent, say: 'Away with the Atheists' "; but Polycarp, with a stern countenance looked on all the crowd in the arena, and waving his hand at them, he groaned and looked up to heaven and said: "Away with the Atheists." But when the Governor pressed him and said: "Take the oath and I will let you go, revile Christ," Polycarp said: "For eighty and six years have I been his servant, and he has done me no wrong, and how can I blaspheme my King who saved me?" But when he persisted again, and said: "Swear by the genius of Caesar," he said: "If you vainly suppose that I will swear by the genius of Caesar, as you say, and pretend that you are ignorant who I am, listen plainly: I am a Christian. And if you wish to learn the doctrine of Christianity fix a day and listen." The proconsul said: "Persuade the people." And Polycarp said: "You I should have held worthy of discussion, for we have been taught to render honour, as is meet, if it hurt us not, to princes and authorities appointed by God; but as for those, I do not count them worthy that a defence should be made to them." And the Proconsul said: "I have wild beasts, I will deliver you to them, unless you change your mind." And he said: "Call for them, for change of mind from better to worse is a change we may not make; but it is good to change from evil to righteousness." And he said again to him: "I will cause you to be consumed by fire, if you despise the beasts, unless you repent." But Polycarp said: "You threaten with the fire that burns for a time, and is quickly quenched, for you do not know the fire which awaits the wicked in the judgment to come and in everlasting punishment. But why are you waiting? Come, do what you will."[115] [Eusebius, *HE* VI.15.18–25]

Such was the hearing. The proconsul immediately had Polycarp's confession proclaimed to the crowd by the herald. Then pagans and Jews banded together to ensure Polycarp was done away with, even though it could no longer be through the beasts as the proconsul had closed the games. Polycarp was burned, "the Jews being especially zealous as is their wont in preparing wood and faggots"[116] for the fire. Confronted by the threat posed by Christianity, the established religions made common cause against the newcomers. The odium which had once been the lot of the Jews in Asia now fell on the Christians.

Polycarp represented orthodox Christianity. The accounts of his martyrdom stress the parallel between his martyrdom and that of his Lord. No more than Jesus had done, did Polycarp set out to defy the authorities and thereby provoke his death. There was no self-glorification, only the acceptance of the results of an uncompromising commitment to Christ. Though this ruled out any accommodation with paganism, Polycarp's attitude was otherwise conformist and dependent on the prosperity of the city for his well-being. The spirit of the Christians at Lyons was like that described by Celsus.

The Christian community there had grown out of the colony of merchants from Asia and Phrygia that had established itself on an island in the Rhone below the original Celtic hill-fort of Lugdunum and opposite the federal area with the temple to Augustus.[117] Like other similar communities, they had brought their religion, which was Christianity, with them. They had prospered, acquired slaves, learned Latin, attracted some Gallic proselytes, and perhaps had stirred the envy of the population. By 177 the community included a wide cross section of society. It contained Roman citizens such as the Phrygian Attalus, a physician Alexander, and merchants, but significantly among its more prominent members were slaves. The slave girl Blandina stands out in the role of a heroine from the start of the persecution, and she and the fifteen-year-old youth Ponticus were the last to die. Nothing demonstrates better the prevalent equality within the second-century churches than the matter-of-fact way in which the survivors' narrative concedes her guiding example to the community, though her mistress was also among the confessors.

The persecution itself was a pogrom, starting with a series of social and semireligious sanctions against the Christians before they were rounded up and brought before the governor's tribunal.[118] The latter treated the Christians as though they were suspected of treason, torturing their slaves to secure proofs of their guilt. The slaves obligingly said that their masters indulged in incest and cannibalism,[119] but before passing sentence the governor followed the example of Pliny and asked Marcus Aurelius for his ruling. The emperor decided to act along the lines of Trajan's directive. Those who recanted were to be freed if they were not guilty of any criminal offense, but those who persisted were to be condemned to the beasts or, if Roman citizens, were to be beheaded.[120] In the end some forty-eight Christians perished in prison or in the amphitheater on 1 August 177.

The account of their martyrdom tells us much about their beliefs. It confirms the close-knit sectarian aspect of Christianity stressed by Lucian and Celsus and it confirms also their relative isolation in the population as a whole. But with this went an extraordinary fortitude. Persecution was to be expected and was accepted as a prelude to the coming of antichrist and the end of the age.[121] The Christians at Lyons were inspired by ideas derived from the book of Revelation and the saga of the Maccabees, especially as told in 2 Maccabees.[122] Blandina in particular was compared to the heroic mother of the youths who sacrificed her sons rather than see them or herself polluted by pagan meat. Like her prototype, she died last encouraging the youngest of the confessors to be steadfast. For her and the confessors, the Spirit was their guide and they were conscious of possessing the power of binding and loosing on the earth,[123] and they saw themselves in deadly conflict with antichrist represented by the torturers and executioners. Such indeed was the combination of conviction, self-sacrifice, heroism, and obstinacy that was confronting the pagan world. The theme that only religious steadfastness would save the people was well understood by both the old and the new Israel. The *Acta Martyrum*, too, served a missionary purpose to encourage their recipients to behave likewise.

Meantime, their influence on surrounding society was small. Paganism was not threatened. We do not hear of Christians in Lyons again until the mid–fourth century. Once the victims were condemned, the townsfolk found room for pity tinged with exasperation. Of Blandina herself, those who watched her first tortures in the amphitheater are reported to have said: "Never among them had a woman suffered so much for so long."[124] When it was all over others asked, "Where is their god, and what good to them was their worship which they preferred beyond their lives?"[125] For some few, like Justin, such apparently pointless heroism stirred the first inquiries into what manner of faith this was that had such a hold on its adherents' minds. Deeds rather than words made Christians. Such individuals were as yet few and far between. For most it was a token of madness. In the Antonine era the church seemed at once heroic and pathetic. In retrospect, it can still be seen wrestling with intractable elements in its Jewish heritage, divided against itself, and abhorred by people in all sections of the community. The *Acta Martyrum* provide a true insight into second-century Christianity.

Only near the end of the century did the clouds begin to lift. Some educated people, including the aged physician and philosopher Galen (d. circa 200), began to admit that though Christians accepted everything on trust their behavior gave them some claim to be regarded as philosophers.[126] Conditions in the second century had provided a test of survival which the Christians had surmounted. The "third race" had established itself as a fact of life in the cities of the Roman Empire.

BIBLIOGRAPHY

NOTE

This chapter opens the continuing theme of the church and the Roman Empire. The best short guide to the empire remains M. P. Charlesworth's *The Roman Empire*

(New York and London: Oxford University Press, 1951). Students will also find the essays in S. A. Cook, F. E. Adcock, and M. P. Charlesworth's (eds.) *CAH*, vol. 11, *The Imperial Peace, A.D. 70–192*, 2d ed. (New York: Macmillan Co.; Cambridge: At the University Press, 1936) helpful. For economic and social questions, M. I. Rostovtzev's great *Social and Economic History of the Roman Empire*, ed. P. M. Fraser, 2d ed. rev., 2 vols. (New York and London: Oxford University Press, 1957), chaps. 5–8 with Fraser's encyclopedic notes, is essential. For religion in the empire, see John Ferguson, *The Religions of the Roman Empire* (Ithaca, N.Y.: Cornell University Press; London: Thames & Hudson, 1970); R. E. Witt, *Isis in the Graeco-Roman World* (Ithaca, N.Y.: Cornell University Press, 1971); A. D. Nock, *Conversion: The Old and the New in Religion from Alexander the Great to Augustine of Hippo* (New York and London: Oxford University Press, 1933); and the important study by Ramsay MacMullen, *Paganism in the Roman Empire* (New Haven, Conn.: Yale University Press, 1981). For the grayer side of religious experience, E. R. Dodds, *Pagan and Christian in an Age of Anxiety: Some Aspects of Religious Experience from Marcus Aurelius to Constantine* (New York and Cambridge: Cambridge University Press, 1965). For the expansion of Christianity in the second century, see A. von Harnack, *The Mission and Expansion of Christianity in the First Three Centuries,* Eng. trans. J. Moffatt (Gloucester, Mass.: Peter Smith, 1963), book 4. My *Martyrdom and Persecution*, chap. 10, may also be useful on this period.

SOURCES

H. A. Musurillo, ed. and Eng. trans. *The Acts of the Christian Martyrs*. Oxford: At the Clarendon Press, 1972; and G. Lanata, ed., *Gli atti dei martiri come documenti processuali*. Milan: Guiffré, 1973.

Apuleius. *Metamorphoses (The Golden Ass)*. Eng. trans. W. Adlington. Rev. ed. S. Gaselee. LCL. Cambridge, Mass.: Harvard University Press; London: William Heinemann, 1915.

Eusebius. *Ecclesiastical History*. Vol. I, book IV. Eng. trans. Kirsopp Lake. LCL. Cambridge, Mass.: Harvard University Press; London: William Heinemann, 1926.

Justin Martyr, *1* and *2 Apology = PG* 6, cols. 328–469.
   1 Apology, Eng. trans. and ed. E. R. Hardy. In *Early Christian Fathers*, ed. and Eng. trans. C. C. Richardson et al. LCC I. Philadelphia: Westminster Press; London: SCM Press, 1953.
   2 Apology, Eng. trans. in ANCL, *Justin Martyr and Athenagoras*, by Marcus Dods et al. Edinburgh, 1867.
   Justin Martyr. Dialogue with Trypho. Edited and Eng. trans. A. Lukyn Williams. Translations of Christian Literature, series 1: Greek Texts. New York: Macmillan Co., 1931: London: SPCK, 1930.

Lucian of Samosata. *Alexander the False Prophet*. Vol. IV. Eng. trans. A. M. Harmon. LCL. Cambridge, Mass.: Harvard University Press; London: William Heinemann, 1925.
   De Morte Peregrini (On the Death of Peregrinus). Vol. V. Eng. trans. A. M. Harmon. LCL. Cambridge, Mass.: Harvard University Press; London: William Heinemann, 1936.
   De Syria Dea (The Goddesse of Surrye). Vol. IV. Eng. trans. A. M. Harmon.

LCL. Cambridge, Mass.: Harvard University Press; London: William Heinemann, 1925.
On Lucian's "Proteus" in the *Death of Peregrinus*, see J. Schwartz, *De Morte Peregrini*. 1951.
Marcus Aurelius Antoninus. *Ad se ipsum.* Libri XII. Edited by J. Dalfen. Leipzig: Teubner, 1979.
Origen *Contra Celsum (Against Celsus)* = ed. P. Koetschau, GCS 2 and 3; H. Chadwick, Eng. trans., Origen, *Contra Celsum*, New York and Cambridge: Cambridge University Press, 1953.
Tatian. E. Schwartz. *Tatiani Oratio ad Graecos.* TU 4, 1. Leipzig: Hinrichs, 1888.

SECONDARY WORKS

Andresen, C. *Logos und Nomos: Die Polemik des Kelsos wider das Christentum.* Munich: Walter de Gruyter, 1955.
Avi-Yonah, M. *The Jews of Palestine.* Oxford: Basil Blackwell & Mott, 1976.
Bardy, G. *La conversion au Christianisme durant les trois premières siècles.* Paris: Aubier, 1949.
Barnes, T. D. "Pre-Decian *Acta Martyrum.*" *JTS* n.s. 19 (October 1968): 509–31.
Brunt, P. A. "Marcus Aurelius in His *Meditations.*" *JRS* 64 (1974): 1–20.
Buckler, W. H. "Labour Disputes in the Province of Asia." In *Anatolian Studies Presented to Sir William Ramsay.* Manchester, Eng.: Manchester University Press, 1923, pp. 27ff.
Carcopino, J. *Aspects mystiques de la Rome païenne.* Paris: L'artisan du livre, 1941.
Chadwick, H. "Justin Martyr's Defence of Christianity." *BJRL* 47 (1965): 275–97.
Crook, J. A. *Consilium Principis: Imperial Councils and Counsellors from Augustus to Diocletian.* New York and Cambridge: Cambridge University Press, 1955.
Cross, F. M. "La lettre de Siméon Bar Kosba." *RB* 63 (1956): 45–48.
Festugière, A. M. J. *La révélation d'Hermés Trismégiste.* Vol. 1, *L'Astrologie et les sciences occultes.* Paris: J. Gabalda, 1950.
Frank, Tenney. "Commentary on the Inscription from Henchir Mettich." *AJP* 47 (1926): 153–70.
———. "The Inscriptions from the Imperial Domains of Africa." *AJP* 47 (1926): 55–73.
Frend, W. H. C. "Blandina and Perpetua: Two Early Christian Heroines." In *Les Martyrs de Lyon* (177), CNRS no. 575. Paris, 1978, pp. 167–77.
Glover, T. R. *The Conflict of Religions in the Early Roman Empire.* 3d ed. New York: Charles Scribner's Sons, 1909.
Hengel, M. "Die Synagogeninschrift von Stobi." *ZNW* 57 (1966): 145–83.
Joly, R. *Christianisme et Philosophie: études sur Justin et les apologistes grecs du deuxième siècle.* Brussels: Editions de l'Université Bruxelles, 1973.
Jones, R. Duncan. "Costs, Outlays, and *Summae Honorariae* from Roman Africa." *PBSR* n.s. 30 (1962): 46–115.
———. "Wealth and Munificence in Roman Africa." *PBSR* n.s. 31 (1963): 155–77.
MacMullen, Ramsay. *Roman Social Relations, 50 B.C. to A.D. 284.* New Haven, Conn.: Yale University Press, 1974.
Mattingly, H. *Christianity in the Roman Empire.* Dunedin, N. Z.: University of Otago Press, 1955.

Mattingly, H. and E. A. Sydenham, eds. *Roman Imperial Coinage.* Vol. 2, *Vespasian to Hadrian.* London: Spink & Son, 1926.

———. *Roman Imperial Coinage.* Vol. 3, *Antoninus Pius to Commodus.* London: Spink & Son, 1930.

Picard, Ch. "Quelques chapitaux historiés des Thermes d'Antonin à Carthage." *Karthago* 4 (1953): 97–118.

Piétri, Ch. "Les Origines de la Mission Lyonnaise: remarques critiques." In *Les Martyrs de Lyon*, pp. 211–31.

Walzer, R. *Galen on Jews and Christians.* New York and London: Oxford University Press, 1949.

Yadin, Y. *Bar-Kokhba: The Rediscovery of the Legendary Hero of the Second Jewish Revolt Against Rome.* New York: Random House, 1971.

NOTES

1. Eusebius-Jerome, *Chronicle,* ed. R. Helm, GCS 24 (1913), p. 201. Hadrian's Province-type coins show Judea sacrificing over an altar with a bull lying at its side, see H. Mattingly, ed., *Coins of the Roman Empire in the British Museum*, vol. 3: *Nerva to Hadrian* (London: British Museum, 1936), p. 512, and pl. 95, 3.

2. Num. 24:17 for the star as the symbol of the Messiah. For Akiba's involvement in the revolt, see L. Finkelstein, *Akiba: Scholar, Saint and Martyr* (New York: Covici Friede, 1936), pp. 260ff., and for the flight of many of his pupils to Babylonia, see J. Neusner, *A History of the Jews in Babylonia*, 5 parts (Leiden: E. J. Brill, 1966–70), *part 1: The Parthian Period* (1969), pp. 134ff.

3. Justin Martyr *1 Apology* 31, and Eusebius-Jerome, *Chronicle,* ed. Helm, p. 201. For a document signed by Bar Kochba indicating his hostility towards "Galileans" (Christians?), see F. M. Cross, "La lettre."

4. Eusebius *De vita Constantini* (*Life of Constantine*) III.26 (Venus), and Sozomen, *Historia ecclesiastica*, GCS, II.1.

5. See Clement of Alexandria, *Stromata: Excerpta ex Theodoto*, ed. O. Stählin and L. Früchtel, GCS, I.29.182; II.15.68.2; VI.5.39 and 6.48; in M. R. James, Eng. trans., *The Apocryphal New Testament* (New York and London: Oxford University Press, 1924; reprint ed., 1953), pp. 16–19; and also, Theophilus of Antioch (c. 180) *To Autolycus*, 1.14 (see G. Quispel and R. M. Grant, "A Note on the Petrine Apocrypha," *VC* [1952], 31).

6. Thus Tertullian *Scorpiace* X (Carthage); and see R. A. Markus, *Christianity in the Roman World* (New York: Charles Scribner's Sons, 1975; London: Thames & Hudson, 1974), chap. 2.

7. See T. W. Manson, *A Companion to the Bible* (New York: Charles Scribner's Sons, 1940; Edinburgh: T. & T. Clark, 1939), p. 460.

8. Lucian, *Peregrinus*, Eng. trans. Harmon (LCL). Josephus uses the same term *nomothetes* (lawgiver) for Moses, *Apion* II.15.154.

9. Origen, *Celsus* III.1, Eng. trans. H. Chadwick.

10. Ibid., II.1.

11. Ibid., II.79.

12. See A. T. Kraabel, "Paganism and Judaism: The Sardis Evidence," in *Paganisme, Judaïsme, Christianisme: Influences et affrontements dans le monde*

antique. Mélanges offerts à Marcel Simon, ed. André Benoit et al. (Paris: Boccard, 1978), pp. 13–34, esp. p. 24; and compare the situation at Acmonia where fifty magistracies were held by Jews during the third century. See A. R. R. Sheppard, "Jews, Christians and Heretics in Acmonia and Eumeneia," *Anatolian Studies* 29 (1979): 169–80. In general, Louis Robert comments *Hellenica* 3 (Paris, 1946), p. 93, that in the Dispersion of the second and third centuries, Judaism cannot be isolated from the life of the Greco-Roman world. The prosperity of some Jewish communities may be instanced by Ti. Claudius Polycharmus's munificent bequest to the synagogue at Stobi in Macedonia, though the date may be late third rather than second century. See Hengel, "Die Synagogeninschrift," and recently the Aphrodisias inscription (forthcoming). See above, p. 39.

13. "The Metropolis of Torah"; thus, I. M. Levey, "Caesarea and the Jews," in *The Joint Expedition to Caesarea Maritima*, Studies in the History of Caesarea Maritima, ed. C. T. Fritsch (ASOR; Missoula, Mont.: Scholars Press, 1975), I, pp. 43–49, esp. p. 59.

14. See H. J. Leon, *The Jews of Ancient Rome* (Philadelphia: Jewish Publication Society of America, 1961), p. 53. In all, eleven different synagogue-groups have been identified, but not all may have existed at the same time (pp. 165–66). The Jews were a tolerated community with full rights of worship, c. 185: see Hippolytus *Refutatio Omnium Haeresium* (*Refutation of All Heresies*) IX.12.8. The predominant language was Greek.

15. See P. Monceaux, *Histoire littéraire de l'Afrique chrétienne depuis les origines jusqu'à l'invasion arabe*, 7 vols. (Paris: Leroux, 1902), vol. 1, p. 9; and Frend, "The Early Christian Church in Carthage" in *Excavations at Carthage 1976, conducted by the University of Michigan*, vol. III, ed. J. Humphrey (publ. for ASOR 1977), p. 27.

16. See E. M. Smallwood, *The Jews Under Roman Rule from Pompey to Diocletian*, SJLA 20 (Leiden: E. J. Brill, 1976), pp. 467ff.

17. Pliny, *Letters* X.97. See above, p. 150.

18. Mattingly, *Coins of Roman Empire*, pp. 504–26, and note Mattingly's comment (p. CXLV), "The empire is a collection of nations capable of self-expression under Roman rule."

19. See J. Needham, *Science and Civilisation in China*, 7 vols. (New York and Cambridge: Cambridge University Press), vol. 1 (1954), p. 192 and vol. 3 (1959), pp. 174, 321. For other contacts with China, see Rostovtzev, *Social and Economic History of Roman Empire*, pp. 155, 604; and F. Cumont, "The Frontier Provinces of the East" in *CAH*, vol. 11, chap. 15, pp. 606–49, esp. pp. 628, 631–32.

20. Aelius Aristides, *Panegyric to Rome*, ed. B. Keil (Berlin, 1898), *Oratio* XXVI.70 and 100 = pp. 111, 121.

21. Athenagoras, *Legatio* and *De Resurrectione*, ed. W. R. Schoedel, OECT (New York: Oxford University Press, 1972), I.2.

22. Irenaeus *Adversus haereses* (*Against Heresies*) IV.30.3.

23. Ch. Picard, "Quelques chapitaux historiés," p. 99. The baths date from A.D. 145–62.

24. Origen *Celsus* VIII.67.

25. *CIL* VIII.1641 from Simitthu (grant of 1.3 million sesterces for *alimenta* for 300 boys aged between 3 and 15, donated c. 175–80.) See in general Jones, "Costs, Outlays, and *Summae Honoriae*"; and idem, "Wealth and Munificence." The

situation in North Africa does not seem to have been exceptional. See Rostovtzev, *Social and Economic History of Roman Empire*, chap. 6.

26. Jones, "Wealth and Munificence," p. 167.

27. *CIL* VIII.25523.

28. Subcultures: see Dittenberger *OGIS* 11 ("Pedies" at Priene); Aremachus, *Frag. Hist. Graec.* IV, ed. C. Muller (Paris, 1851), p. 315, on "Penestae" in Thessaly. For conflict between the Greek settlers around Pisidian Antioch and mountaineers, known as Homanadenses, see W. M. Ramsay, "Studies in the Roman Province of Galatia," *JRS* 14 (1924): 172, 176.

29. See Buckler, "Labour Disputes"; and Rostovtzev, *Social and Economic History of Roman Empire*, p. 621 n. 45.

30. *CIL* VIII.10570. See the classic articles by Frank, "Inscriptions from Imperial Domains"; and "Commentary on Inscription."

31. *CIL* VIII.10570, col. 3, lines 2-3. For Roman citizens among the *coloni*, see ibid., col. 2, line 14.

32. Origen *Celsus* VIII.67.

33. The present author's "Two Finds in Central Anatolia," *Anatolian Studies* 6 (1956): 95-100.

34. *CIL* VI.3.17985a, trans. J. M. C. Toynbee.

35. Lucian *Goddesse* 42-51: crowd scenes at her shrine at Hieropolis.

36. Lucian *Alexander* 26ff., and see Ferguson, *Religions of Roman Empire*, pp. 187-89.

37. Minucius Felix, *Octavius*, Eng. trans. G. H. Randall, LCL (in Tertullian volume) (Cambridge, Mass.: Harvard University Press; London: William Heinemann, 1931), VIII.1.

38. Ibid., II.4.

39. Thus Apuleius, *Golden Ass*, VIII.25, p. 386, imprecations of numerous deities. Also, MacMullen, *Paganism*, pp. 73ff.

40. See articles by L. Poinssot, "Mosaiques d'el Haouria," *Actes du Premier congrès des soc. arch. de l'Afrique du Nord* (Algiers, 1935), pp. 183-206; and A. Merlin and L. Poinssot, "Deux mosaiques de Tunisie," *Monument Piot* 34 (Paris, 1934): 129-76.

41. On astrology as queen of the sciences, see Stephen of Byzantium (*Catalogue Codd. astrol.*, II.235), 1.12. For Dura, see M. Rostovtzev, *Excavations at Dura Europos* (New Haven, Conn.: Yale University Press, n.d.), IV, 105-19 (illustrations in text). For a brief summary on religious life in the city, see my *Martyrdom and Persecution*, pp. 306-10. In general, see F. Cumont, *Les religions orientales dans le paganisme romain* (Paris: Paul Geuthner, 1929), chap. 7 and notes.

42. Aelius Aristides, *Oratio* XLVII.22, ed. Keil. See Dodds, *Pagan and Christian*, p. 41.

43. *The Gospel of Truth*, cited from F. L. Cross, ed. and Eng. trans., *The Jung Codex: A Newly Recovered Gnostic Papyrus* (New York: Morehouse-Gorham; London: A. R. Mowbray, 1955), p. 31. See below, p. 202.

44. Thus, J. Carcopino, "Survivances par substitution des sacrifices d'enfants," *RHR* 106 (1932): 592-99.

45. See E. Rippol Perello, *Ampurias, Official Guide and Itinerary* (publ. by Institute of Archaeology, Barcelona, 1979), Pl.6, and p. 30.

46. Juvenal *Satires* VI.522.

47. Apuleius *Golden Ass* XI.23. See Nock, *Conversion*, pp. 138–55.

48. Justin *Trypho* 1.3.

49. Plutarch, *De Virtutibus moralibus (On Moral Virtues)*, ed. D. Babut (Paris, 1969), 441f. Citing Plato, cf. *Timaeus* 69c.

50. See Nock, *Conversion*, chap. 2, esp. p. 179. "We can here use the word conversion for the turning from luxury and self-indulgence and superstition (another frequent object of philosophic criticism) to a life of discipline and sometimes to a life of contemplation, scientific or mystic." Also, MacMullen, *Paganism*, pp. 94ff.

51. See Brunt, "Marcus Aurelius," p. 1.

52. Marcus Aurelius *Meditations* XI.3.

53. Ibid., VII.9. See Brunt, "Marcus Aurelius," p. 15.

54. But note also Epictetus's view, *Discourses* III.24.16 (Eng. trans. W. A. Oldfather, vol. 2, LCL [Cambridge, Mass.: Harvard University Press; London: William Heinemann, 1928]): "Heracles knows no man as an orphan, but all have a father who cares for them."

55. Augustine *Confessions* I.5.5.

56. Lucian, *Icaromenippus or The Sky-man*, vol. II, Eng. trans. A. M. Harmon, LCL (Cambridge, Mass.: Harvard University Press; London: William Heinemann, 1915) 29 (p. 316).

57. Ibid., 25 (p. 312).

58. Thus, the remark attributed to Rabbi Simeon b. Yohai, c. 150: "If you see a Persian [i.e. Parthian] horse tethered in Israel, look for the coming of the Messiah" (Midrash *Lamentations Rabba* 1.13 and *Canticles Rabba* 8.10). For an earlier version of a similar story, compare the sayings of Yosi ben Kisma, recorded in the *Babylonian Talmud Sanhedrin* 98a–c. See Neusner, *History of Jews in Babylonia, part 1: Parthian*, p. 85, and Avi-Yonah, *Jews of Palestine*, p. 66.

59. See Smallwood, *Jews Under Roman Rule*, p. 486.

60. Cited from Günter Stemberger, "Rom in der rabbinischen Literatur," *ANRW* II.19.2, p. 386 n. 158.

61. See Smallwood, *Jews Under Roman Rule*, p. 464. "May his bones rot!" was the usual imprecation accompanying the mention of Hadrian.

62. Justin, *Trypho* II.2–7, trans. Williams.

63. See the thorough discussion concerning the old man, by Joly, *Christianisme et Philosophie*, pp. 42–79.

64. See R. M. Grant's valuable discussion, *Augustus to Constantine: The Thrust of the Christian Movement Into the Roman World* (New York: Harper & Row, 1970), pp. 111–43.

65. As pointed out by Grant, *Augustus to Constantine*, p. 111.

66. Justin *2 Apology* XII.2.

67. Justin *Trypho* IV.

68. Justin *2 Apology* XIII.

69. Text of his *Acta* in Musurillo, *Acts of Christian Martyrs*, pp. 42–61, and trans. in J. Stevenson, ed., *A New Eusebius* (London: SPCK, 1963), pp. 28–30.

70. Justin *1 Apology* LV.6. See H. Chadwick, "Justin Martyr's Defence," p. 287.

71. Origen *Celsus* II.29, and cf. *Sibylline Oracles* V.415.

72. Epiphanius, *Panarion Haeresium*, ed. K. Holl, 36; and Tatian *Oratio ad Graecos* (*Address to the Greeks*) 42.

73. Tatian *Address to Greeks* 35, and compare ibid., 29. See especially Ramsay MacMullen's "Two Types of Conversion to Early Christianity," *VC* 37 (1983): 174–91.

74. Tatian *Address to Greeks* 28.

75. Athenagoras *Legatio pro Christianis* (*Supplication for the Christians*) XXVI.3. See Harmon's editorial note *Lucian* V, pp. 2–3.

76. Aulus Gellius, *Attic Nights*, 3 vols., Eng. trans. J. C. Rolfe, LCL (Cambridge, Mass.: Harvard University Press; London: William Heinemann, 1927), vol. 2, XII.11.1, "philosophum nomine Peregrinum cui postea cognomentum Proteus factum est, virum gravem atque constantem vidimus."

77. Lucian *Peregrinus* XII.

78. Compare also Eusebius *HE* V.1.26 (Biblis's statement) and Minucius *Octavius* XXX.6. See above, pp. 121–22.

79. Lucian *Peregrinus* XIII. Compare Minucius *Octavius* XXXI.8, "We call ourselves 'brethren.' "

80. Lucian *Peregrinus* XV, XXIX, Proteus "noblest of Cynics."

81. Ibid., XIX; and compare ibid., XVIII, "he fell to abusing everyone, and in particular the Emperor."

82. Gellius *Attic Nights* XII.11.1, "multa hercle dicere eum utiliter et honeste audivimus."

83. See my *Martyrdom and Persecution*, p. 276.

84. Origen *Celsus* I.1.

85. Ibid., I.2; cf. II.1.

86. For example, ibid., III.1 and IV.22, 23, 38.

87. Ibid., II.63; cf. II.35.

88. Ibid., VIII.38.

89. Ibid., III.14.

90. Ibid., VIII.65, and cf. ibid., 55.

91. Ibid., 73.

92. Ibid., 33; cf. V.41.

93. Maximus of Tyre, *Philosophumena*, ed. H. Hobein (Leipzig: Teubner, 1910) XVII.5 (I owe this reference to Dodds, *Pagan and Christian*, p. 117 n. 2). A hierarchy of spirits extended from heaven to earth. Without demons (*Daimones*), Maximus claimed in *Oratio* XV, there could be no relation between God and man. For Maximus's belief that Apollo as the Sun was the leader of the harmony of heaven, reflected on earth through the harmonies of music, see J. F. Kindstrand, *Homer in der zweite Sophistik* (Uppsala: Studia graeca Upsaliensis, 1973), pp. 176–77.

94. *Acts of Justin and Companions* IV, in Musurillo, *Acts of Christian Martyrs*.

95. Eusebius *HE* IV.15.19.

96. Ibid., 23.6. The church in Rome was, of course, Greek-speaking at this time.

97. See below, p. 215.

98. Origen *Celsus* III.9.

99. Ibid., 12. Celsus associates the increase in the numbers of Christians with their divisions. See over, p. 194.

100. Ibid., III.52, 55, and cf. Minucius *Octavius* VIII.4.

101. Tatian *Address to Greeks* 33; cf. ibid., 32.

102. Athenagoras *Supplication* XI.2.

103. *Acta Scillitanorum*, ed. Musurillo in *Acts of Christian Martyrs*, pp. 86–89, 12 and 15.

104. See above, p. 94.

105. Cited by Eusebius *HE* IV.23.10.

106. Justin *1 Apology* XVI; cf. Origen *Celsus* I.43: "Even to this day the power of Jesus brings about conversion and moral reformation in those who believe in God through him."

107. *Acta Scillitanorum* 3.

108. *Passio Sancti Procopii*, 12, ed. F. Halkin, "Inédites byzantins d'Ochrida, Candie et Moscou," *Subsidia Hagiographica* 38 Brussels (1963): 111.

109. Irenaeus *Heresies* IV.30.2.

110. *Acta Scillitanorum* 6.

111. Tertullian *Apology* XL.2.

112. Minucius *Octavius* VIII.4, perhaps citing Fronto; and cf. IX.6 and XXXI.2 (Christian crimes). See J. Beaujeu, ed., *Minucius Felix, Octavius* (Paris: Collection Budé, 1964), pp. xxvii and 86–89.

113. Lucian *Alexander* 38.

114. For the earliest account of the martyrdom, see Eusebius *HE* IV.15.3ff. For the irenarch's efforts at persuasion, "But what harm is it to say 'Lord Caesar,' and to offer sacrifice, and be saved?" ibid., 15.15.

115. Eusebius *HE* IV.15.18–25, trans. Lake.

116. Ibid., 15.29; cf. 15.41. On the question whether this was a relatively isolated instance of pagan and Jewish cooperation against the Christians, see J. W. Parkes, *The Conflict of the Church and the Synagogue: A Study in the Origins of Anti-semitism* (London: Soncino Press, 1934), pp. 125–50.

117. See Ch. Piétri, "Les Origines de la Mission lyonnaise"; and chap. 1 of my *Martyrdom and Persecution.*

118. Recorded in Eusebius *HE* V.1 and 2.2–8.

119. Ibid., 1.14 (crimes), and 1.44 and 47 on the governor's correspondence with the emperor (Marcus Aurelius).

120. Ibid., 1.47.

121. Ibid., 1.10.

122. Ibid., 1.55; compare 2 Macc. 7:20–23, 26–29, 41. See my "Blandina and Perpetua."

123. Eusebius *HE* V.2.5.

124. Ibid., 1.56.

125. Ibid., 1.60.

126. From a lost summary by Galen (c. 180) of Plato's *Republic* preserved in Arabic quotations. Cited from Walzer, *Galen on Jews and Christians*, p. 15.

6

Acute Hellenization 135–93

Looking back from the vantage point of the triumph of Christianity under Constantine, Eusebius of Caesarea thus wrote of the church in the second century:

> Like brilliant lamps the churches were now shining throughout the world, and faith in our Saviour and Lord Jesus Christ was flourishing among all mankind, when the devil who hates what is good, as the enemy of truth, ever more hostile to man's salvation, turned all his devices against the church. Formerly he had used persecutions from without as his weapon against her, but now he was excluded from this he used wicked men and sorcerers for his purpose. [Eusebius *HE* IV.7.1]

These "sorcerers" were the Gnostic leaders "fabricating monstrous myths" (Eusebius *HE* IV.7.2) to support their "infamous heresy." In his eyes, destructive though the persecutions may have been, division was a worse menace than persecution, and the Gnostics were to blame. Celsus, writing as a contemporary, was more explicit. He saw Christians divided between "the great Church" which "had the same God as the Jews" and whose beliefs remained very similar, and a multitude of sects, such as Marcionists, Gnostics, followers of Martha, Marcellina, and "the Harpocratians who follow Salome." And these, he goes on, "slander one another with dreadful and unspeakable words of abuse. And they would not make the least concession to reach agreement; for they utterly detest each other." For the great church all these were "Circes and flattering deceivers"[1]—heretics to be abominated.

Both witnesses were right. Eusebius regarded the Antonine era as the period of the breakthrough, when Christianity shook off the Jewish millenarianism preached by "men of limited intelligence," such as Papias,[2] and began to enter on its true Gentile inheritance. Celsus, closer to events and an opponent, saw matters differently. The welter of confusion and the strife of warring sects accompanied the advance of Christianity, spelling danger to the traditional values of the empire. The two generations separating the second fall of Jerusalem in 135 and the accession of the Severan dynasty in 193 witnessed the gradual Hellenization of the church, as more and more provincials were attracted to it. Origen pointed to the increased interest of educated Greeks in Christianity as one of the reasons for the success of Gnosticism.[3] But the dissensions of which Gnosticism was the most obvious expression also reflected the continuation of some of the problems of late Judaism and of the Pauline era. Gnosticism itself can never be divorced from its Jewish background.

Amid the conflicts of the period, one may detect the emergence of a Christian orthodoxy representing a coalition of men and ideas almost as varied as it had been in the previous period. But it was identifiably a church, whereas its Gnostic opponents were leaders of schools whose teaching, though centered on Christ, accepted Scripture as only one source of revelation, which might be supplemented and even superseded by ideas drawn from Greek, Iranian, and Semitic mythology. At the other end of the scale, apocalyptic and prophetic tendencies survived to erupt in the Montanist movement in 172,[4] or to linger among small ascetic communities in Egypt that seem to have existed without any hierarchic government.[5] For neither orthodox nor unorthodox, however, were boundaries as fixed and defined in this period as Irenaeus of Lyon, writing c. 185, would have his hearers believe. Valentinus the Gnostic leader and Marcion both spent years among the orthodox community in Rome. In Alexandria, lines were still fluid by the end of the century and Gnostic and orthodox would be known to pray together.[6] Lasting divergencies, however, were opening up among the Christians. The transition from sectarian Judaism to potential world religion would not be accomplished smoothly. Through most of the second century orthodoxy stood on the defensive representing tradition against innovation. In this chapter we study its challengers, the Gnostics and the followers of Marcion.

THE GNOSTIC MOVEMENT

The middle years of the second century belong to the Gnostics. Between 130 and 180 a succession of teachers, working mainly in Alexandria, dominated Christian intellectual life and spread their influence to Italy and Rome, to Asia Minor and even among the Christians in the Rhone Valley. Basilides (*flor.* 130–50), Valentinus (*flor.* 140–60), and Heracleon (*flor.* 170–80) were among the pioneers of an authentic Gentile Christianity, a religion that had a place for all knowledge and experience, scriptural and pagan alike, in a scheme of salvation centered on a divine figure, Christ. It was a fantastic hope, but not the last of human endeavors to fuse all knowledge into a single pattern of truth. Even their opponents held the Gnostic leaders in high regard. Clement of Alexandria (*flor.* 180–200) linked Basilides and Valentinus with Marcion as outstanding personalities of the previous generation.[7] Origen's *Commentary on the Gospel of John* (c. 230) owes something to Heracleon's commentary on John's Gospel, written half a century before, and would hardly have been compiled without it.[8] Alexandrian Gnostics laid the foundation of much that became the Alexandrian school of theology in the next two centuries. Christian Platonism was indebted to a half century of Gnostic preparation.

The Alexandrians had been preceded by teachers in a similar tradition in Syria, whose activities extended far back into the first century A.D. There may be some justification for Justin Martyr and Irenaeus placing the origins of Gnosticism at the door of Simon Magus. "All sorts of heresies took their rise from him,"[9] Irenaeus claimed. The brief account in Acts (8:9–11) is suggestive: "But there was a man named Simon who had previously practiced magic in the city and amazed the nation of Samaria. . . . They all gave heed to him, from the least to the greatest, saying, 'This man is that power of God which is called the Great.' And they gave heed to him, because for a long time he had amazed them with his magic."

Simon, then, had been active "for a long time," and his teaching concerning "the Great Power"[10] was acceptable throughout the whole Samaritan people. This term passed without comment by the editor of Acts. It was evidently not a blasphemy to be rebuked by Philip the evangelist. If Simon himself was a disciple of a previous teacher named Dositheus, then the pre-Christian origins of the movement that came to be identified as Gnosticism would be evident, for Dositheus seems to have been connected at one time with Essenes.[11] As it is, behind the religious rivalry between Jews and Samaritans concerning the status of Jerusalem and Mount Gerizim as religious centers, one can see how an elaborate system of speculation was developing that included Jewish, other Semitic, and Hellenistic elements. Simon himself was accepted as a manifestation of the Great Power. At creation, the latter had emanated Thought and thence a succession of spiritual beings that made the universe.[12] Because of their desire to be regarded as supreme, these powers had then imprisoned their mother Thought in a succession of female bodies beginning with Helen of Troy and ending with a prostitute of Tyre, also named Helen, the true "lost sheep" (Irenaeus *Against Heresies* I.23.2). Simon's female companion was identified as Helen of Troy, as she was supposed to have emanated from God just as Athena had emanated from Zeus, or was identified with Selene the moon-goddess. In short, Simon's system was a conflation of many traditions. Among Semitic peoples at the time, the union of the high god Baal with his female counterpart, Astarte in Syria or Tanit in Punic Carthage, was believed to be the origin of the universe.

Simon had a disciple, Menander (*flor.* 60–100), and his movement was carried further by Saturninus (*flor.* 100–120), an Antiochene and contemporary of Ignatius. His views may perhaps be associated with those exponents of Jewish and Docetic ideas of Christ which so angered Ignatius. Both he and Menander shared a belief in a Supreme God, "one Father, unknown to all," and in creation by angels;[13] but Menander, like Simon, believed himself to be Christ, while Saturninus, a generation later, attempted to interpret the life and mission of Christ. He believed that the world was composed of evil matter and that the role of Christ was to free humankind from the nefarious work of the seven angels—one of whom was Yahweh—who created the universe. Here one touches on two of the essential tenets of the Gnostic credo, namely, the dualistic interpretation of reality and the association of the God of the Jews with the creation of an imperfect universe from which humankind must be freed. Christ had been sent "to destroy the God of the Jews, and to save them that believe on him."[14]

The teaching of Menander and Saturninus was ascetic—the human body belonged to the evil world of matter. In this their ideal corresponded to the

Gospel of Thomas and linked them to the Encratite (ascetic) tradition of Syria and Mesopotamia, represented by Tatian (c. 180) and Bardesanes (Bar Daisan; c. 220).[15] Theirs was an early attempt to integrate Jewish Scripture and angelology with speculations about Jesus Christ and borrowings from pagan mythology. That there may have been contact with the more influential tradition of Alexandria is possible, for *Thomas* circulated both in eastern Syria and the Nile Valley, as did another early Christian work known as *The Odes of Solomon*, sometimes called "the earliest Christian hymn book." These hymns resemble in outlook the psalms of Qumran and can hardly be later than the early second century A.D. Five, however, were incorporated in the Gnostic Coptic *Pistis Sophia* (Faith-Wisdom),[16] though the main area of circulation seems to have been eastern Syria.[17] The Nile Valley and eastern Syria share many common features in their religious history—Monasticism, Manicheism, and Monophysitism all took root there. How the connections were maintained remains for future research.

Despite their kaleidoscopic and often far-fetched beliefs that laid them open to destructive criticism by orthodox leaders, the Gnostics introduced novel and penetrating insights into the Christian faith. Christianity for the first time became a philosophical religion grappling with deep moral and intellectual problems, as well as being the Way preached by Jesus and Paul. Jesus' teaching had been practical, nearly always related to daily life in Palestine, possession of the kingdom being attainable by individuals through the integrity of their inner thoughts and the righteousness of their actions. Jesus made no attempt to discuss right and wrong on an abstract level. Moral issues were brought down to the events of real life. He pointed out to his hearers how it was obvious which of the two was justified, the Pharisee or the sinner, on the basis of their conduct and attitude towards God (Luke 18:14). Paul had provided an interpretation of the contrast between flesh and spirit, law and grace, Adam and Christ, and had preached salvation from evilly disposed astral powers. The writer of Hebrews had spoken of Christians being "enlightened," having "tasted the heavenly gift," and becoming partakers of the Holy Spirit, to "have tasted the goodness of the word of God and the powers of the age to come" (Heb. 6:4–5). At the end of the first century, the writer of *1 Clement* broached the subject of ultimate knowledge within the context of Monotheism and Christian conduct. "Let us consider from what matter we were made, of what sort and who we were when we came into the world, from what tomb and darkness he who formed and made us brought us into the world and prepared his benefits for us before we were born" (*1 Clement* 38.3). The argument, however, stopped there.

The Gnostics took these questions further. What were enlightenment and perfection, and how were they achieved? Theirs was a many-sided movement and not a single religion, but all the Gnostic sects shared a common view of the world in which they lived, its relation to God, and the means of human salvation. They believed that between God—incomprehensible to our thought but the ultimate cause of all things—and the visible world was insuperable division and antagonism. The "self" or "I" of the Gnostic, however, belonged to the divine world. It was a "spark of God." At some stage in its existence it had fallen into the visible world and had become imprisoned and drugged into slumber by it. It could be freed only by accepting the call of a "Divine Messenger" (Christ) and, thus enlightened and emancipated, would return to its true heavenly home at the end of time.[18]

The powers that ruled the universe—Yahweh, Lord of creation, and the goddess Fate (*Tyche*), and the astral powers (the Planets, the Sun and Moon, and the Twelve Signs of the Zodiac)—exercised a baleful influence on humanity. They constituted the hostile world into which each individual was born, but they could not withstand the power of grace brought by the Divine Messenger to those able to receive it. Illumined through knowledge of the true world of light, the Gnostic became a new being equipped to answer the basic questions that troubled humanity then as now: "Whence is man and what is his destiny?" According to Clement of Alexandria (c. 185), they sought to know "who we were and what we have become, where we were, and where we were placed [in time] and whither we are hastening, and from what we are redeemed and what is birth and re-birth."[19] Such knowledge freed its possessor from Fate, from Error (*Planē*), from Oblivion, and the dread chances of reincarnation, where one's lot might be that of the hapless Lucius in Apuleius's *The Golden Ass*.[20]

Gnosis had traditionally held a worthy if limited place in the Jewish and earliest Christian scale of values. To "know God" meant to acknowledge that Yahweh was God and to recognize the acts of God. In the Septuagint, God was indeed a "God of knowledge" (1 Sam. 2:3) and the word *gnosis* is used to denote this. The representative and teacher of Gnosis is the pious sage and Servant of the Lord (Isa. 53:11), while on the contrary, Gnosis is denied to the worldly minded and to sinners.[21] Following this tradition, Paul told the Colossians that "you have put off the old nature with its practices and have put on the new nature, which is being renewed in knowledge" (Col. 3:10). In his hymn to love (*agapé*) in 1 Corinthians 13, knowledge was a virtue on a par with prophecy (1 Cor. 13:2), but secondary when compared with faith, hope, and love. Knowledge of God, however, invited speculation about what God intended to do, and thus how prophecies and apocalyptic signs were to be interpreted. The Teacher of Righteousness in the Qumran sectaries was "the expositor of all the words of his servants the prophets."[22] God revealed to him the secrets concerning the final age concealed in their prophecies. To these speculations were added others connected with the origins of the universe and the nature of the "knowledge" acquired by Adam in the Garden of Eden, and what he had passed down to his children. Thus in c. 95, Josephus describes at the beginning of his *Antiquities* how Seth had been given power to teach the secrets of the Zodiac and of the stars (*Antiquities* I.2.3). The sectaries whose library was uncovered at Nag Hammadi seem to have been known as Sethites.

This was the secret knowledge that the Gnostics claimed to possess. It was acquired, however, not by perseverance in moral rectitude but by sudden illumination that enabled them to understand the ways of God, the universe, and themselves.[23] It was knowledge that freed, that revealed the mysteries of truth, that rent the veil that concealed how God controlled the creation.[24] Despite their reliance on the methods and attitudes of current philosophy, they claimed to have succeeded where philosophers failed. The latter they dismissed contemptuously as not "having the possibility" of understanding reality.[25] "We alone know the unutterable mysteries of the spirit," the Naassene ("Snake") sect claimed (c. 200).[26] Only its initiates could bring order into "the disorder of the world." Gnostics claimed they were the "true brothers" on whom love of the Father had been poured out.[27] In one of the Nag Hammadi documents called *The Stranger* (*Allogenes*), the candidate for initiation proclaims, "Now I am listening to these things [the speech of the "holy powers"]. I was filled with revelation . . . I knew the One who exists in me. . . . I saw the good divine Autogenes and the Saviour who is youthful, the perfect triple Male. . . . I sought the ineffable unknowable God . . . who subsists in stillness and silence and is unknown."[28] One is reminded, of course, of Apuleius's account of Lucius's initiation into the mysteries of Isis. (See above, p. 169.) In each case, knowledge of the beyond was also knowledge of self, and personal salvation was the reward for exclusive service to the deity.

The path to knowledge, however, might also be more prosaic. In practice, it could take the form of a study both of Scripture and the religions of reputedly ancient peoples, such as the Phrygians and Egyptians, traditionally endowed with wisdom and religious truth, with a view to harmonizing their beliefs with those they associated with Christ.[29] Gnostics attempted to prove, with the aid of some queer semantics and far-fetched analogies, that ancient pagan religious ideas, expressed in mysterious vocabulary and cult acts, corresponded with the truth which they as perfected beings claimed to possess. By assimilating and fusing together all existing religious knowledge they claimed to have arrived at the means of perfection which was knowledge of God. Such knowledge was not within the ken of all. The Gnostics, like Paul in some moments, believed in salvation for a spiritual elite, and they divided humankind accordingly (*Tripartite Tractate*).[30] The illumined or spiritual beings (*pneumatikoi*) were destined for salvation. They were those who had "made themselves free, awakened from drunkenness, returning to themselves," "knowing the knowledge of the Father and the revelation of his Son."[31] A much larger group, the Psychics (*psychikoi*) or ordinary Christians, were capable of receiving knowledge, but

199

the majority were earthbound, pagans, slaves of matter (*hylikoi*), and were destined to oblivion and death. The illumined soul, provided with spiritual baptism and the grace of knowledge, would wing its way through the seven spheres that surrounded the earth to the Ogdoad, the seat of immortality and perfection.

The Gnostics were organized like mystery sects.[32] Their leaders were teachers, both men and women, not ecclesiastics. These last were regarded as "servants of the Demiurge," and fit only to exercise authority over the mass of uninitiated Christians. Upon initiation the Gnostic received an entirely new relation to spiritual authority.[33] Each sect had its own baptismal ceremony, its passwords,[34] its sacred meal, its "ceremonies of the Bride Chamber,"[35] even its final instructions to the dying, how to outwit the powers the soul would encounter on its upward flight.[36] "The Lord has [done] everything in a mystery," they said, "a baptism and an anointing and a eucharist and a redemption and a bridal chamber" (*The Gospel of Philip* 68). The sacraments dispensed by orthodox clergy were limited in value, "psychic" as compared with "spiritual"; "anointing is superior to baptism,"[37] they claimed. Theirs were rites fit for the spiritual elite. These rites, moreover, must be kept guarded from the uninitiated. Gnostics would not provoke the authorities, but neither would they incur martyrdom by confession of the name.[38] As the *Apocalypse of the Great Seth* asserted, "These revelations are not to be disclosed to anyone in the flesh and are only to be communicated to the brethren who belong to the generation of life."[39] If called upon to sacrifice to the pagan gods, they would do so,[40] for such action would be a matter of indifference. Their freedom through knowledge gave them freedom from constraints, from ignorance, from the Law, and from fears of the coming, or of judgment. They were the true sons of the bridal chamber. And, in their social outlook, they were as elitist as in their spiritual. Slaves were excluded from salvation.[41]

Finally, they proclaimed fervently that they were Christians, and many of the Nag Hammadi writings are Christ-centered. Their understanding of Christ, of the Scriptures, and of man differed fundamentally, however, from that of members of the great church. The synoptic Gospels were only a partial revelation of Christ. "Jesus is a hidden name; Christ is a revealed name,"[42] they claimed. In *The Gospel of Truth*, Christ is "the shepherd who left behind the ninety nine sheep which were not lost. He went searching for the one which was lost. He rejoiced when he found it, for ninety nine is a number that is in the left hand which holds it; but when the one is found, the entire number passes to the right [hand]. Thus [it is with] him who lacks the one. . . . it is the sign of the one who is in their sound; it is the Father."[43] Scripture was a vast forest of mystic and secret teaching comprehensible only to the illumined. Basilides claimed, "Matthias communicated to them [Basilides and his son] secret discourses which, being specially instructed, he heard from the Saviour."[44]

200

The discourses, however, embraced all types of knowledge and religious experience. Gnostics drew easily and without inhibition on current philosophy and poetic wisdom in their search for truth. Homer ("the poet"), Plato ("the philosopher"), and Paul ("the apostle") were placed on the same level of authority and inspiration by them. Myth and Scripture alike had secret meaning that awaited discovery. Secular scientific theories might aid exploration of the secrets of the universe and, in particular, the cryptograms and number-symbolism used by the Pythagoreans, who believed that the mysteries of the universe could be solved by understanding numbers.[45] The Gnostic's hope of freeing one's fellows from Oblivion at death was reminiscent of that held out to initiates in the Orphic mysteries, that they would possess "the cold, flowing waters of the Lake of Memory."[46] Their explanation of natural phenomena, such as the existence of moisture, or the waters in the oceans, or the creation of plant life through the intercourse of Eros with the deities of Chaos,[47] may also be paralleled in the teaching of pagan mystery religions. Such "scientific theories" form part of the Gnostic legacy to influence the ideas of the Manicheans in the next century and to survive in the beliefs of the medieval alchemists.

REASONS FOR THE SUCCESS OF GNOSTICISM

Why did Gnosticism become so formidable a movement during the second century? One doubts whether any single event, such as the first or second capture of Jerusalem and the resulting decline in Jewish apocalyptic hopes, was really significant.[48] Gnosticism, as we have seen, had been progressing at least since the time of Christ, and Basilides, the earliest of the great Alexandrian teachers, evidently began his career before the defeat of Bar Kochba.[49] Origen's view,[50] that its success was due to the increasing interest taken by educated Greeks in the rising force of Christianity is true up to a point. Though the religious environment of Alexandria was probably the most important single factor in the rise of Gnosticism, it would seem also that a number of tendencies within paganism and Judaism throughout the Greek-speaking world were occupied with the same aspirations towards salvation and the same problems of the place of humanity in the universe. These found a common focus in the person of the Christ-Savior.

The problems the Gnostics were trying to solve were familiar enough in the second century. If God was Goodness, why was there crass evil in the world, unless the matter from which it was created was irredeemably bad? If the universe was not governed by Fate and its minions, how did one explain calamity, sickness, and sudden death? Many believed that their lives hung on Fate's decrees, and indicated their acceptance of these by including the exact hour of their death, as well as the day and month, on their tombstones. What was the use of attempting to practice moral excellence when one might be swept away overnight? Better listen to the Gnostic teachers and their claim to provide "spiritual resurrection that devours the psychical as well as the fleshly resurrection,"[51] and the promise, "If you have Christ you will conquer this entire world."[52]

Quotations from Plato's *Republic* that "God was not the cause of all things, but only of what is good"—for the causes of evil one could not look to God (*Republic* II.379)—or quotations from the pagan Hermetic Asclepius concerning "learning and knowledge" as the antidotes to the passions and evil,[53] had passed into the common language of the time by the middle of the second century. The text from Plato is quoted from memory in all probability and without any reference to its author by Basilides.[54] Hermetic works also found their way among Gnostic groups. These, which make no mention of Jesus or a redeemer-figure, ask the same question as the Gnostics did, why "man, unlike all the living things on earth, is twofold, mortal because of his body and immortal because of the essential Man,"[55] and explain through a vision how the man who recognizes his true self can strip himself of bodily passions and rise through the circles to be "in God."[56] Parallel, too, to the advance of Gnosticism went that of other religions—such as Mithraism—that held a dualistic view of the universe, promised deliverance from Fate, and also conceived salvation in terms of the orderly ascent of the soul through the successive spheres ruled by the planets to ultimate perfection. Other Indo-Iranian religious speculation penetrating the Roman east described the descent of the heavenly Savior into the world of matter, the awakening of the soul from "the slumber of ignorance," and its journey heavenward clothed in the garment of light.[57] The Gnostic teachers therefore stood in the mainstream of second-century religious speculation. They molded current ideas into their own systems, and associated them with Christ, the heavenly Messenger, who had appeared on earth in historical times.

Gnosticism, however, could never have become a threat to the existence of orthodox Christianity if it had been rooted primarily in pagan religious mysticism. It was formidable because it was steeped also in Jewish thought, both Hellenistic and Palestinian, which underlay the absorption of any pagan ideas and values that found their place in different Gnostic systems. One example may suffice. *The Apocryphon of John*, three copies of which were found at Nag Hammadi, sets the scene of the apostle John's vision of the secrets of the beyond in the wilderness not far from Jerusalem. John, the brother of James, meets a Pharisee called Ananias on the steps of the Temple. Ananias upbraids him, "Where is your master whose disciple you were? You followed a deceiver who estranged you from the tradition of your fathers." Then follows the vision of the risen Christ who revealed the secrets of creation and salvation in Valentinian Gnostic terms.[58] The Jewish setting is obvious. The accusation against Christians that they were lapsed Jews echoes Celsus,[59] and points to a second-century date of the original. Other features found in the secret teaching of John, such as the struggle between the two spirits for the control of the souls of individual men, are reminiscent of the beliefs of the Qumran sectaries. It is impossible to think of the emergence of Gnosticism in the second century without the background of the wisdom literature, of Philo, and the speculative preoccupation throughout Jewry with angelology, with the planets and the zodiac, and with mysteries connected with the sacred name of Yahweh. In these respects, it was one more successful manifestation of that extraordinarily vigorous Jewish culture that flourished at the time of Jesus, and of which Christianity was very largely the heir.

The Gnostics caught the tide of religious feeling, particularly in Alexandria. The importance of Alexandria as a center of interchange of religious ideas and as the intellectual meeting point between Jew and Greek cannot be overestimated. In this connection Origen's assessment of Gnosticism becomes significant. Though writing *Against Celsus* in Caesarea, he had had his main conflicts with the Gnostics earlier in his career at Alexandria, and hence it is probably the Alexandrian Greeks to whom he was referring. For three centuries Alexandrian Jews had been in contact with the representatives of Platonic-Stoic philosophy, and as a result Judaism there had undergone a profound change. There was, as Emil Schürer had pointed out, "a process of mutual internal amalgamations" between Judaism and Hellenism.[60] Yahweh ceased to be merely the God of Israel and became God of the universe, far removed from that guiding if erratic Being whose conduct of Israel's affairs was portrayed in the Old Testament. The God of the Alexandrian Jews approached the God of the Alexandrian Platonists. He existed without beginning and without end: he was describable only in negative terms and intelligible only through divine intermediaries. By the second century B.C., Wisdom had become identified with the principle of creation, the emanation of God's power and perfect reflection of his action. For Philo, however, it was God's Reason or Word, the Logos that interpreted God to the universe and man. The Word was less personal than Wisdom, and more akin to the Platonic Logos, while the angelic beings of Judaism came to resemble the "ideas" of Plato, the first offshoots of "the good."[61] One's salvation was seen as the ascent of the soul toward God and thus to become divine. On earth, the individual must break away from bodily passions and purify the self for the journey. Philo allegorized the story of creation in Genesis, and his treatise, *On the Creation*, resembled Plato's *Timaeus*, though Philo never lost contact with the narrative in Genesis.[62]

One result of this allegorization was the downgrading of Yahweh. Some of the Nag Hammadi documents appear to be pre-Christian, and in one, *The Apocalypse of Adam* which purports to be Adam's final words to his son Seth, Adam claims that originally "we were higher than God who had created us," and "we resembled the great eternal angels." Yahweh was not the "illuminator of knowledge," but a God of the aeons.[63] Elsewhere, Yahweh is reckoned a malevolent force who produced the world through a blunder. Such views foreshadowed those of both the Alexandrian Christian Gnostics and Marcion.

Alexandria also provided a forum for other aspects of Judaism that were to be absorbed by the Gnostics. Dualism was not the monopoly of the Greek and Iranian worlds. The Two Ways destined to life or death of Deut. 30:15 and the *Didache* I–V, provided scope for speculation as well as moral teaching. Philo, for instance, believed that through these powers, salutary or destructive, the world had been created and therefore reflected a precarious balance between good and evil.[64] Dualistic ideas of the universe interpreted in moral or cosmological terms of light and darkness were held in uneasy tension with the fundamental conviction that God was One. Qumran, the *Odes of Solomon* and the Fourth Gospel all show the existence of the problem during the first century A.D. Dualistic speculations were also affecting individual conduct. Philo inveighed against opponents, "the sons of Cain" as he called them, who claimed that as they understood the mysteries of the Law they could disregard its ordinances.[65] By A.D. 40 libertinism was beginning to claim an intellectual respectability for itself in Alexandrian Judaism and a century later it had established itself as one of the principal aspects of Gnosticism in Alexandria through Carpocrates' movement.

Finally, why was Jesus associated with the Great Illuminator of Jewish Gnosticism? One can point to the extraordinary power exercised by the name of Jesus by the end of the first century. Any reader of Acts could understand its efficacy for good in the hands of the apostles and the dire consequences of its misuse by unworthy people (Acts 19:13–16). Magical powers could not prevail against it, Ignatius claimed.[66] The Eucharist, too, was the "medicine of immortality, and the antidote for death."[67] Jesus himself was baptized in order to purify the water (not vice versa).[68] Ignatius was not a Gnostic and loathed Docetism, but there are Gnostic tendencies in his thought moving him towards an ever-increasing mystical glorification of Christ. In the next generation Justin Martyr had no doubt as to the power of Jesus' name to subdue and cast out demons.[69] "Jesus, God of the Hebrews," was becoming a name feared and coveted by anyone who aspired to understand and master the mysteries of the universe.[70] This is perhaps one possible line of inquiry. The second may be that by the end of the first century Christ was absorbing and replacing the Divine Wisdom as the creative force in the universe. The "Word [Logos] made flesh" (John 1:14) illumined the believer, the cross (rather than the moon, as in Simon Magus's system) marked the boundary between the visible world of sense and the world of ideas beyond, and it personified the element of suffering that pervades human affairs. The Messiah who rose from the dead moved easily into the role of the Savior who could conquer the archons. The name of Christ was becoming the focus of many currents of religious thought of which orthodoxy was only one. Gnostic and baptist schisms that had

204

hardly been held in check under Judaism[71] erupted under the influence of the new compelling movement of Christianity.

THE ALEXANDRIAN GNOSTIC TEACHERS

Basilides

Gnostic ideas therefore were already current by the time Basilides (c. 130) was teaching in Alexandria. Who his predecessors in Alexandria were is not known, nor the links through the first century that connected his thought with that of Philo and his school. Basilides' work fell within the reigns of Hadrian and Antoninus Pius, that is, c. 125–55. He and Isidore, his son and disciple, were prodigious workers. Basilides composed twenty-four books of exegesis on Scripture. Isidore produced a work on *Ethics*, another *On the Inseparable Soul*, and a curious-sounding *Expositions of the Prophet Parchor*.[72] Together they ranged widely through theology, exegesis, morals, and mysticism, discussing the relationship between God and creation, the possibility of sin in Jesus, the ethics of martyrdom, marriage and celibacy, and reincarnation. Basilides was the first recorded Christian who attempted to expound a philosophy of religion centered on Christianity but drawing from both Jewish and pagan sources, and not ignoring the problems of his day. He castigated Yahweh as an aggressive deity and the Jews as a people who took after him, aspiring to subjugate other nations,[73] an interesting comment perhaps on the feeling in Alexandria in the years between the Jewish rebellion of 115 and the rising of Bar Kochba in 132. Like his older contemporaries Ignatius of Antioch and the writer of *Barnabas*, Basilides was basically Jewish in his attitudes. His followers in Irenaeus's day are recorded as asserting that "while they were no longer Jews, they were more than Christians," as though for them Judaism was still a norm;[74] but Basilides hated Judaism as he knew it in his own time and makes no claim for his followers that they were a "new Israel."

Unfortunately, only fragments of his work survive, and his opponents Irenaeus and Hippolytus give different accounts of his thought.[75] These can be supplemented from passages preserved in Clement of Alexandria and by Epiphanius in the late fourth century which deal with different aspects of Basilides' thought from those found in Irenaeus. Both Irenaeus and Hippolytus, however, indicate that Basilides believed in a completely transcendent God who had no origin that the human mind could apprehend. ("There was a time when there was nothing at all.")[76] From God, according to Irenaeus's version, came Thought (*Nous*) and then Word or Reason (*Logos*), and thence in descending order Prudence, Wisdom, and Power; thus far, the Stoic virtues as found in Hellenistic Judaism. From these emanated the powers and angels that make the first heaven. Thence were emanated a succession of 365 heavens which separated God from the lowest group of angels who created the world. These angels apportioned the nations among themselves, an idea which Basilides shared with his pagan contemporaries. Basilides, however, made Yahweh the villain, and it was to liberate men from the strife Yahweh caused that God sent his Thought as Christ into the world. Naturally the crucifixion was not real as Christ could not suffer, but in what may have been a macabre gesture of hostility to the Jews, Basilides had Simon of Cyrene take on the appearance of Christ and Christ stand by and laugh his Jewish adversaries to scorn.[77] Their sin was ignorance which was also the characteristic condition of all the intermediate deities below the first heaven, each believing himself to be the Supreme God.[78]

Ignorance, therefore, becomes not merely a reproach leveled by Jews against pagans, and by Paul at the unconverted, but the condition of the whole universe. The answer was illumination through Gnosis imparted by inspired teachers. Basilides' concern, however, was moral as well as metaphysical. He aimed at explaining the paradox of divine goodness and human suffering—why a Christian who had supposedly been redeemed by Christ must undergo a martyr's death.[79] All suffering, Basilides asserted, was the result of sin. Individual confessors might not be grievous sinners but they possessed a capacity and desire to sin. Their sufferings might be regarded therefore as those of a child who suffered simply because of an innate sinful quality or perhaps through sin committed in a previous life. Suffering and death, therefore, were forms of atonement as they were in Jewish thought as represented by the writer of 4 Maccabees.[80] For Basilides, however, the aim of atonement was neither addition to a collective treasury of merit nor physical salvation but progress of the individual soul towards its perfection. Moreover, Basilides accepted the Platonic view of "providence," that in no sense could providence be held responsible for evil.[81] Evil, therefore, was independent of God and resulted from the actions of another deity, namely the God of the Old Testament Yahweh, the chief of the creator angels. True Christians, therefore, would reject the Old Testament and confess Christ, but not Jesus as crucified as that was merely material worship. They would identify themselves with the spiritual Christ as spirit to spirit. Similarly, Scripture was to be interpreted spiritually through the use of allegory in which the words of Homer "the poet" as well as of Paul "the apostle" could throw light on its true meaning. This demanded mastery of a range of Greek philosophy and poetry as well as of existing Jewish and Christian exegesis. Basilides reveals himself as a seminal thinker of great speculative power and sensitivity, who added a new dimension to the religious thought of his day, demonstrating at the same time the superiority of Christianity as a religion of salvation. It was not perhaps altogether just that he was remembered by future generations only for the dualistic aspects of his system and not, for instance, for his contribution to the interpretation of suffering. In the fourth century he was regarded as one of the founders of Manicheism.[82]

Valentinus

More influential, however, though equally subject to exaggeration and mis-understanding by his opponents was Basilides' younger contemporary Valentinus. Valentinus (*flor.* 140–65) was also an Alexandrian who, however, spent much of his life in Rome and by all accounts was an outstanding individual. Apart from Clement of Alexandria's tribute,[83] Jerome, by no means one of the kindliest of critics, wrote of him, "No one can bring heresy into being unless he is possessed by nature of an outstanding intellect, and has gifts provided by God. Such a person was Valentinus."[84] At Rome he was nearly chosen as bishop (probably c. 143) and is said to have worked there under Pope Anicetus (154–65).[85] His pupils Ptolemy, Heracleon, and Marcus all contributed to the spread and development of Gnosticism in Italy, Alexandria, and Gaul respectively, down to the end of the century.

Until the discovery of the Nag Hammadi library, Valentinus's ideas could be guessed only from accounts given by his opponents, especially Irenaeus.[86] Though no work actually bears his name, a group of four works from Nag Hammadi—the *Gospel of Truth*, the *Gospel of Philip*, the *Exegesis on the Soul*, and the *Treatise on Resurrection to Rheginus*—appear to have close affinities with each other and correspond to some extent to Irenaeus's account of Valentinus's ideas. Another important treatise, *The Teachings of Silvanus*, seems to have been contemporary with Valentinus and may also reflect an aspect of his thought. Valentinus, like Basilides, saw God as a single, transcendent, and utterly unknowable Being, but originating not in "absolutely nothing" but in the Primal Cause or Depth (*Bythos*). After countless ages Depth emanated Silence (*Sigē*) and eventually these two, representing Male and Female principles, emanate two other Beings—Understanding (*Nous*) and Truth (*Aletheia*). From these follow Word and Life, and Man and Church, and eventually thirty Aeons are produced, pair by pair, male and female (compare Gen. 1:27), representing Christian (or Jewish) concepts and virtues to complete the heavenly world or *Pleroma*. The last aeon was Wisdom (*Sophia*). She, desiring to know the unknowable Father, fell into the darkness of despair and gave birth to a premature and malformed infant Ialdabaoth (probably "Child of Chaos"), by whom the universe with all its imperfections was created. The subsequent struggle between Ialdabaoth and Wisdom was responsible for the mixture of good and evil, virtues and passions, in the world and in individuals. A Savior, Jesus, is sent to Wisdom. He "forms Wisdom according to understanding" and separates her from her passions, and thus sets in train the events that lead to similar processes of salvation in the visible universe.

207

While retaining a largely Jewish framework for their myth of creation, Valentinus and his disciples were moving towards more Gentile concepts of reality. Paradise, Satan, and the Garden of Eden recede before Platonic and Greek poetic ideas. The "psychic" elements in humanity are given scope to "know themselves" and be saved. *Silvanus* provides an example of the growing synthesis between Jewish and Greek elements on which all Gentile Christianity, whether Gnostic or orthodox, was to be based. The writing probably dates originally c. 160–200. Though it is written in the style of Ecclesiastes, it is also reminiscent of the contemporary pagan moral treatise known as the *Sentences of Sextus*, and draws its ideas from Stoic, Platonic, and Pythagorean thought.[87] Silvanus, Paul's companion, is the imparter of wisdom and education leading his hearers to spiritual perfection acquired through Gnosis, through which earthbound passions are tamed and the believer acquires a godlike nature. Silvanus shows how Gnosticism was offering a systematic theology and a coherent set of beliefs leading to the individual's salvation. Moreover, these were based on a canon of Scripture that included the Septuagint, and in the New Testament three Gospels (not Mark), the Pauline epistles, 1 and 2 Timothy, 1 Peter, 1 John, and Revelation.[88] In contrast, however, to the great church, Silvanus interpreted Scripture allegorically only; thus the merchants driven from the Temple by Jesus were not real merchants but "powers of Satan."[89] Christ himself was interpreted as Word incarnate in a way that looked forward to later Alexandrian Christology. The interweaving of Plato, Philo, and Scripture as the means through which Gnosis was acquired foreshadowed also the outlook of Clement of Alexandria. His ideal of the Christian Gnostic was not far removed from that of the teaching of Silvanus.

Apart from the means by which true Gnosis was identified and acquired, the Gnostics and their orthodox opponents were debating hotly any relationship between the Old and New Testaments. This went to the heart of the rival schemes of salvation. Was the Old Testament the prefiguration or introduction to the New, as in Hebrews 10, or was it wholly alien—the work of an inferior being or an evil archon? The existence of something resembling a Gnostic canon of the New Testament by 160 made the issue an actual one.

Ptolemy

In c. 170 the remarkable letter written by Valentinus's disciple Ptolemy, probably in Rome, to his friend Flora provides an insight into how an intelligent Gnostic Christian interpreted the relationship between the two Testaments.[90] The Law was not evil, Ptolemy explained, but it was inadequate: "It was not ordained by the perfect God, the Father, for it is secondary, being imperfect and in need of completion by another, containing (as it does) commandments alien to the nature and thought of such a God."[91] The Law contained in the Pentateuch had not been promulgated all at the same time nor by a single author. The Ten Commandments were God's law and were completed by the Sermon on the Mount. On the other hand, prescriptions such as "an eye for an eye" were abolished by the Savior, as these merely substituted one injustice for another. They were the work of an inferior god; not evil, but irreconcilable with the nature and goodness of the father of all. There remained the various Mosaic requirements such as sabbath-observance and fasting. These could be interpreted as types and prefigurations of laws laid down by the Savior (for example, sabbath-observance meant "rest from committing evil acts"). The Old Testament and the Law were the products then, of an "Intermediate Being, a distant image of the Father" but ignorant of the Father's existence.[92] This Being was responsible for the creation of the imperfect universe in which humanity dwelt and was inferior to the perfect God but superior to the Adversary.

Ptolemy does not discuss the New Testament, because Flora did not ask him to do so, but he presents with great clarity and intelligence a view of the world and an exegesis of Scripture which explain the situation of the Jews and the claims they made on behalf of the Law. He represents the type of educated provincial who was giving his adherence to Gnosticism. He sees Judaism as Irenaeus did, as a preparation for Christianity, and he has more in common with the Hellenistic synagogue than with the contemporary philosophic schools. Jewish practices were ordained "according to the image of the spiritual and transcendent things,"[93] but they were not necessarily wrong. Fasting, for example, could be observed "if it is engaged in reasonably," and not by habit nor imitation of others, nor because a particular day demanded it.[94] The Gnostic's gaze was always fixed on the spiritual, enlightened by the Savior Christ.

Flora, too, is interesting in the context of the religious attitudes which Gnosticism aimed at satisfying. She is articulate and literate; she has an inquiring mind and is dissatisfied with orthodox Christianity (or Judaism?). Her questions about the interpretation of Jewish Scriptures and the origins of the world ("one beginning of all things") were clearly among those frequently asked, and she found ready answers. The Gnostics had much to offer women such as Flora. Their mystical ceremonies were attractive to such women, as Marcus found among Christians in the Rhone Valley.[95] The logic of their teaching emphasized the part played by women in the process of salvation. Christ's female companions are given a major role in the Gnostic gospels. They are cast in the role of intermediaries between the divine and human. Mariamne is Philip's companion in the *Acts of Philip*. In the *Gospel of Philip*, Mary Magdalene is said to have been loved by Christ "more than [he loved] the disciples."[96] In the *Pistis Sophia* she plays a predominant role among the questioners of Jesus.[97] The earliest Mariolatry and the first assumption legends are Gnostic, and in the Gnostic Infancy Gospels that proliferated in the last quarter of the second century, Mary Magdalene, Joanna, Salome, as well as the Virgin, all feature largely.[98]

Religious-minded women who had chosen Christianity in preference to Isis-worship or other mysteries as their guide to salvation found themselves at home among the Gnostic sects. Among the strengths and weaknesses of the movement was that the Gnostics could be labeled "followers of Salome," or in Rome "followers of Marcellina."[99]

THE GNOSTIC LEGACY

Critics have tended to follow Irenaeus, Hippolytus, and Tertullian and to discuss Gnosticism as an aberration and its leaders as purveyors of ridiculous and impossible doctrines based on an ill-digested syncretism between Christianity and Greek philosophy. Basilides, Origen declared, "related the apostolic word to preposterous and impious fables."[100] From the standpoint of the victorious great church this was true. Basilides was trying to use Paul, Rom. 7:9, to support a Pythagorean belief in the transmigration of souls into different bodies! In general, the Gnostic interpretation of the immortality of the soul contradicted orthodox teaching concerning the resurrection of the body. Salvation through Gnosis was incompatible with salvation through grace and works. The Gnostics had no doctrine of the Spirit and did not baptize in the name of the Trinity. Though including many wealthy and educated in their ranks, they deprecated totally life in this world. The libertinism of sects such as the Carpocratians could not be reconciled with the views of those who regarded self-discipline and responsibility towards one's neighbor as the mark of a Christian. Christ the Divine Illuminator was not the Christ of the Gospels who would return as Judge.

Gnosticism, however, left a positive legacy for future generations of Christians. The Gnostics were the first to accept the logic of the Christian claim to be a "third race," and they asserted uncompromisingly their superiority over both paganism and Judaism. "A heathen man does not die," said the writer of the *Gospel of Philip*, "for he has never lived that he should die. The believer is only alive since Christ came."[101] Judaism was regarded an intermediate state between the Hylic (pagan-material) age and the Pneumatic (spiritual-Gnostic) age. Orthodox Christians were sometimes reproached with being "Jews." "In the days that we were Hebrews, we were orphans," and in the *Gospel of Philip* again, "We had [only] our mother, but when we became Christians we acquired father and mother."[102] "He who has not received the Lord is still a Hebrew."

Heracleon

Heracleon (c. 170–80) makes the same point. The "Psychics" (that is, orthodox Christians) were "worshipping as Jews," celebrating the Jewish Passover in the Eucharist, and making the mistake of interpreting the historical events typologically. Spiritual beings, on the other hand, "comprehend the passion of the Savior as the symbol of their restoration to the

Father."[103] Similarly, "Psychic" baptism was only bodily and imperfect, the "baptism of John," whereas that by the Gnostics was for perfection and spiritual.[104] The elect received imperishable grace as wealth furnished from above. The human was transformed into the divine, just as Christ transformed water into wine at Cana.[105]

The Gnostics also brought a sense of progression in religion, from ignorance and irrationality to knowledge and understanding, and in this they anticipated Clement of Alexandria and, above all, Origen. From the orthodox side, Irenaeus was to present an alternative view of Christian history. Salvation history, however, was implicit in all Alexandrian Gnosticism. Heracleon's commentary on John's Gospel sees humanity moving from a "material" to a "Psychic" period and finally to full spiritual revelation through Christ. Previous worshipers (including "orthodox Christians"), he says, "worshipped in fear and in error him who is not the Father."[106] For Heracleon as for the Christian Platonists of Alexandria, true Christianity represented "rational service" to God, the climax of human endeavor towards understanding reality. His commentary on John's Gospel was by far the most ambitious work of biblical exegesis accomplished in the second century and provided the inspiration for Origen's great commentary on the same Gospel forty years later.[107]

Finally, despite its ultimate fatalism and sense of predestination, Gnosticism appeared as a religion of release, of liberation and joy wherewith anguish, error, and fear of the grave were conquered. New converts, Irenaeus lamented, appeared to find out something new every day. The "perfect" were brimming over with often-contradictory ideas,[108] but ideas they were. The gladsome prospect held out to the believer is shown in the first lines of the *Gospel of Truth*:

> The gospel of truth is a joy for those who have received from the Father of truth the gift of knowing him, through the power of the Word that came forth from the pleroma—the one who is in the thought and the mind of the Father [and] who is addressed as the Savior, (that) being the name of the work he is to perform for the redemption of those who were ignorant of the Father, while the name [of] the gospel is the proclamation of hope, being discovery for all those who search for him.[109]

Ignorance is a slave, knowledge is freedom, and with knowledge went joy and hope. The world was a prison from which to escape. This was the way to salvation, and return of the soul to the divine world.

The Gnostics attempted too much. The challenge to the Christian faith presented by lively if discordant pagan philosophic schools could not be met by attempting to integrate all knowledge into an almost-as-discordant Christianity. The story of creation in Genesis could not be reconciled with the story in the *Iliad* of Ocean as Father of gods and men. Hermes, the messenger of the gods, could not be made into the demiurge that created the world, nor could Odysseus's exile be a convincing allegory of the exile of Israel in Egypt. In addition, their outspokenly antihierarchical stance put the orthodox on their mettle. Irenaeus's indignation was directed almost as strongly against Gnostic rejection of ecclesiastical discipline as against their perversion of Scripture and rejection of the earthly ministry of Jesus. Redemption was available to all through the church governed by its appointed leaders. Gnostic salvation was only for the few.

Nonetheless, Gnosticism may claim its place in the history of Christian civilization. Its dualism influenced directly the ideas of Priscillian in Spain near the end of the fourth century; his followers can best be described as "neo-Gnostics."[110] Manicheism and the religion of the medieval Bogomils and Cathari may also look back to Gnostic dualism as their ancestor. Its attempted harmonization of Jewish and Platonic ideas affected the whole range of Alexandrian theology and exegesis from the time of Origen onwards. Beyond the frontiers of Alexandrian orthodoxy, one may detect some Gnostic influence in the thought of Apollinaris of Laodicea (c. 310–90), as did his contemporaries.[111] Monophysites, such as James of Sarug in the sixth century, also accepted the Gnostic view of the wholly spiritual Christ whose flesh was a disguise aimed at deceiving the world rulers from whose servitude humanity must be freed.[112] The Monophysites also, like the Priscillianists and Manichees, made frequent use of the Gnostic apocryphal legends, particularly the Gnostic Infancy Narratives. Throughout the whole of the Christian East popular piety was sustained by these romances that proliferated in the second half of the second century. The most famous, the *Protevangelium of James* provided the inspiration and material for some of the beautiful frescoes seen on the walls of many medieval Byzantine churches. From Ethiopia to the Balkan principalities, the Gnostic tradition remained close to the hearts of devout Christian people. The early Christian romantic and mystical tradition owed much to the Gnostics.

MARCION

Some of the sense of release from the shackles of the Law and the inadequacies of current paganism provided by the Gnostics could be found in another opposition group whom Celsus contrasted with the great church, namely the followers of Marcion. Today, Marcion (c. 85–160) is not rated quite so highly as he was once by Adolf von Harnack.[113] He was neither the greatest Christian between Paul and Augustine, nor a forerunner of Wycliffe and Luther, but he was a considerable figure, one of the very few opponents of orthodoxy whom Greek and Latin theologians united in damning. For nearly a century after his death (c. 160), he was the archheretic, condemned in turn by individuals as different in outlook as Polycarp, Justin, Irenaeus, Clement, Tertullian, Hippolytus, the Latin writer known as Pseudo-Tertullian, Bardesanes, and Origen. He was distinguished in his age.

Information about his life and career is derived solely from his opponents, principally Irenaeus, Tertullian, and Hippolytus. He was born at Sinope, c. 85, the son of a Christian "bishop." He grew up, therefore, in Asia Minor in the generation before the full emergence of Gnosticism, when the conflict between Christians and Jews for the right to be "Israel" was at its height. He was wealthy, a shipowner, and a merchant—"sailor Marcion" as he was called by the orthodox—whose business took him far afield. Early in his career he had evidently pondered the religion of his father and particularly the problem of evil in the world.[114] He was beginning to preach a Christianity that made him suspect to Polycarp of Smyrna. The conflict in which Polycarp named Marcion "the first born of Satan" was memorable, for it was recalled vividly by Irenaeus towards the end of the century.[115]

Marcion eventually left Asia Minor and migrated to Rome c. 135. There he was accepted as a Christian and made the church a present of two hundred thousand sesterces. He also met a Syrian named Cerdo who, we are told, came to Rome in the episcopate of Hyginus (c. 137–45).[116] Cerdo seems to have been to some extent a Gnostic in the Simon Magus tradition—another instance of the extreme complexity of religious life in the Roman Empire in the second century. The teaching for which he was remembered, however, was that the God of whom the Law and the prophets spoke was not the Father of Jesus Christ, for that one is known, whereas the father of Christ was unknown.[117] There were two Gods, therefore; the God of the Old Testament, the Demiurge who created the world and presided over its destiny, who represented righteousness—that is, giving each his due reward and punishment, whereas the God himself was good. Cerdo is said to have provided Marcion with ideas, but Marcion may well have come to similar conclusions by another route, namely, by an attentive study of the Scriptures and in particular the key work for the Christians, Isaiah 39—66. There he found in 45:7 the claim made by Yahweh, "I make weal and create woe, I am the Lord, who do all these things," and this was fundamental to his interpretation of Christianity.[118] An evil tree, Marcion reminded, could not bring forth good fruit. Moreover, Yahweh's actions supported his statement. He had allowed his prophet Elisha to vent his rage on children who had teased him by having them eaten by bears (2 Kings 2:24);[119] he had stopped the sun in its path to allow Joshua to finish off the Amalekites (Josh. 10:13).[120] His ignorance was demonstrated by his having to ask where Adam was in the Garden of Eden.[121] His harshness was revealed in his prescription of "eye for eye" (Exod. 21:24).[122] Such a being could not possibly be the father of Jesus Christ who had said, "let the children come to me" (Matt. 19:14), and who through Paul had enjoined "do not let the sun go down on your anger" (Eph. 4:26), and "if any one strikes you on the right cheek, turn to him the other also" (Matt. 5:39). The promises of the Creator were earthly while those of Christ were heavenly. At every point the "judicial god" could be contrasted with the God of Goodness. Interpreting Paul in Romans and Galatians, Marcion recognized the Christian message in terms of contrasting Law and gospel, retributive justice against merciful love. The "newness" of Christian message was its glory.

While in Rome Marcion set down his thoughts in *The Contradictions*.[123] The opening words proclaimed his wonder at the majesty, might, and amazing promise of the gospel, to which nothing could be compared, and this he contrasted with Scripture (that is, the Old Testament). This latter was indeed a true historical narrative of Yahweh's dealings with his chosen people the Jews, but it had nothing to do with Christianity. The Messiah it foretold was the Messiah for the Jews and not the Christians, who would come in due course and reestablish their kingdom.[124] The father of Jesus Christ was the Unknown God of Acts 17:23, recognized by Paul and preached by him. Jesus represented the boundless and liberating grace of God as opposed to the bare justice reflected in the Law. He was sent by God to the whole human race for the saving of souls, what Marcion called "the inner man";[125] and he himself was "revealed as a man but not a man," a body only in appearance, subject to no nativity or passion, except in appearance.[126] Tertullian for once was being fair when he summed up Marcion's message:

> Marcion laid down the position that Christ, who in the days of Tiberius was, by a previously unknown god, revealed for the salvation of all nations, is a different being from him who was ordained by God, the Creator for the restoration of the Jewish state, and who is yet to come. Between these, he interposes a separation of a great and absolute difference as great as lies between what is just and what is good, as great as lies between the law and the gospel, as great as is the difference between Christianity and Judaism. [*Against Marcion* IV.6]

His "special and chief work was the separation of the law from the Gospel" (*Marcion* I.19).

The questions which Marcion had raised were not entirely novel. The supposed ignorance of Yahweh had been puzzling the Alexandrian Jews more than half a century before. Philo had seen the difficulty raised by Yahweh's reported questions in Genesis (3:9 and 4:9), "Where are you?" addressed to Adam, and "Where is Abel your brother?" addressed to Cain. He had as usual solved the problem by elaborate allegorization. These utterances were not to be taken literally, but as calls to repentance. Philo had also contrasted Yahweh with Elohim, and accepted the latter (*Theos*) as relating to God's creative power and goodness, while Yahweh (*Kyrios*) reflected his royal power and punitive actions. Jewish haggadic teaching too, had long made the same distinction. Yahweh was equated with God as judge and ruler, while Elohim was God as love and mercy.[127]

The new factor which Marcion introduced was that Scripture could not be understood allegorically. What was written must be accepted or rejected on its merits. Taken thus, there were too many occasions in which the New Testament contradicted the Old, or in which Yahweh's actions fell far short of the standards preached by Christ.

Marcion, as Tertullian shows in his five books of refutation, had made a most detailed and thorough study of Scripture to support his conclusions. These were revolutionary. For a Christian living in the first half of the second century to argue on the basis of Scripture against the church's attempt to wrest the title of "Israel" from the Jews was remarkable. Marcion proceeded on the same basis to deny the whole tendency of orthodox Christian apologetic, the assertion that the Old Testament prophecies referred to none other than Christ, and he rejected the orthodox system of interpreting Scripture typologically and allegorically to achieve this result. He went further: he was the first Christian to attempt to define a canon of Scripture embodying the gospel of salvation. Perhaps because this was the gospel used at Sinope, or because it appeared to promise most to those outside the Law,[128] he chose Luke's Gospel, beginning at chapter 3 and omitting references to Jesus' post-resurrection appearances. To this he added the Pauline epistles, excluding the Pastorals, but he purged these of material he believed to have been introduced by Jewish and Jewish Christian opponents of Paul. Thus Gal. 3:16—4:6 was cut because of its references to Abraham, his sons, and his promises, and 2 Thess. 1:6–8 because God was not concerned with "flaming fire" and punishment.[129] There was to be no "warrior Messiah" on the contemporary Jewish model. This was the good news, God's uncovenanted gift to man, preached within historical memory (Tertullian calculated 115 years and 6½ months) by "the saving spirit" Jesus Christ,[130] and now to be proclaimed everywhere.

All this was too much for the Roman community. In 144 Marcion was expelled and his donation was returned to him. For the remainder of his life (he was living when Justin wrote his *First Apology*, c. 155), he embarked on a vigorous series of missions just as his master Paul had done, founding churches that would preserve and extend his interpretation of the gospel. As Justin wrote in the 150s, he was making converts, "teaching men to deny that God is the maker of all things in heaven and earth and the Christ predicted by the prophets is his Son" (*1 Apology* 58).

As a missionary, Marcion was formidable and this also marks him off from the Gnostic teachers. He planted churches "as wasps make nests,"[131] declared Tertullian. His heretical tradition "filled the whole world."[132] In fact, apart from Rome and Carthage, we hear of Marcionite churches in Nicomedia[133] on the Asiatic side of the Sea of Marmara, at Smyrna,[134] in Phrygia, Gortyna, at Antioch,[135] and, above all, in northern and eastern Syria.[136] These churches were organized on a hierarchical basis;[137] martyrdom was accepted as among the hazards of a Christian's calling.[138] There was no refuge to be found in "protecting secret teaching." In sacramental teaching the Marcionites diverged from their orthodox colleagues in their use of water instead of wine at the Eucharist, but they baptized in the name of the Trinity.[139] By the end of the century, however, the strength and weakness of Marcion's message was becoming clear. If the good news was available to all and women as well as men might be fully the carriers of the Spirit, not many were worthy to receive it. Only those souls, according to Irenaeus, that had learned his doctrine would be saved.[140] It seems that the catechumenate in Marcion's churches was a long one, and baptism was granted only to those who were prepared to abandon the world and its joys, including family life.[141] To preach the kingdom demanded complete abandonment of family ties. No Marcionite would wish to fill a world made by the Creator-God (Clement *Miscellanies* III.3.12). Marcion's communities therefore tended to be small select groups, forming part of the Encratite movement within Christianity that exercised so powerful an influence in the latter part of the second century. This was, however, the way leading to the status of a respected sect, such as the Parsees in India, but not to that of world religion.

For some Christians, however, Marcion's rejection of the Law and all it stood for was attractive. Marcion was criticizing the Old Testament as fundamentally as Ptolemy did, but without the mumbo jumbo of Gnosticism. His interpretation of Christianity as a religion of insight and personal assurance of salvation through Christ was also relevant. The idea that God was to be feared and that the believer would fall an easy prey to temptation if he was not threatened with punishment was dismissed by Marcionites. As von Harnack wrote, "The amazingly simple 'Absit, absit' showed that believers perceived no necessity of adding a further foundation than trust in God for morality."[142] This is borne out in the record of the argument that took place in Rome (c. 190) between the Marcionite Apelles and the Catholic Rhodo. The latter challenged Apelles to expound his faith (there seems to have been little need for a Christian to hide his religious allegiance). Apelles said simply that he who placed his hope in Christ crucified would be saved if he persevered in good works. The prophecies in the Old Testament were false and inconsistent, and the writings of Moses were no guide towards Christ. Rhodo laughed at the apparent naiveté of these remarks, saying that a religious belief ought to be defensible by rational argument.[143] The great church had traveled far along the Gentile road since the beginning of the century. Philosophy was to be the guarantor of religion, but Apelles had a deeper insight into the true nature of Christianity.

Marcion's, however, was a subjective and exclusive view of Christianity, more sectarian in spirit even than the church which Celsus criticized. Its opponents realized that Christianity could not deny its origins in Judaism and must not be bereft of sanctions for the wicked. "Listen, you sinners," exclaimed Tertullian, "and any of you not yet so, that you may be able to become so. A better god has been discovered, one who is neither offended nor angry nor inflicts punishment, who has no fire warming in hell, no gnashing of teeth in the outer darkness."[144] To worship an unknown God, sending Christ as a "healthful Spirit swooping down from heaven" on an alien world[145] to guide humankind, was to make Christianity into another mystery religion with no roots in the past. Moreover, how could Marcion deduce Christ's divinity by calling in question his humanity? As Tertullian saw only too clearly, the resurrection of the body and the judgment formed part and parcel of the aspirations of the ordinary believer. The Christian needed the discipline of "fearing God" as the beginning of his wisdom just as did his Jewish contemporary. What was the use of a God who accepted humanity that he did not create? The good-natured spirit preached by Marcion was not one to inspire most would-be Christians to break from the world and accept the test of martyrdom.

LATER DEVELOPMENTS

There was a tendency, too, among Marcion's followers to go their separate ways and to blur the edges of his finely pondered message. Apelles, while accepting the idea of a single principle behind the universe, believed the world was created by an angel and that the prophecies came from "an enemy spirit."[146] His contemporaries, Potitus and Basilicus, went further introducing two opposite principles. Others were affirming the existence of three ruling powers—Good, Evil, and an intermediary force—though Marcion does not appear to have preached, like his Gnostic contemporaries, that Evil was coeternal with Good. By the third century, Marcionism was lapsing into the Gnostic dualism of Good and Evil. Between some of Marcion's followers and those of Ptolemy there could have been few matters in dispute.

In the end, Marcion's church took permanent root only in parts of Syria and toward the Euphrates frontier. There it found fertile ground in the existing ascetic Jewish Christian tradition, and it may have been the faith of the majority of Christians in those parts throughout the third century. The earliest dated inscription relating to a Christian church records "a synagogue of the Marcionites" near the village of Lebaba near Damascus, built by "a presbyter" in 318.[147] Controversies between Marcionites and anti-Marcionites were lively at this period, as is shown by a work once ascribed to Origen, the dialogue of Adamantius on *Right Faith in God*, but now dated to c. 325–30, where the orthodox speaker seeks to refute Marcionite arguments concerning creation and the Old Testament.[148] Even when orthodoxy eventually triumphed, Christians in eastern Syria retained much of the sternness of the Marcionite ethic; while marriage was lawful, their enthusiasm was for a life consecrated to Christ as a "single one" or a virgin. For Ephraem Syrus (d. 374) the church was the "assembly of those who watch and fast,"[149] and like the later generation of Marcionites he

217

divided the Christians into three groups, the "lower," the "middle," and "the perfect." These last abstained from marital relations and lived as ascetic a life as the full member of the Marcionite church. With "flesh" identified with evil and the dualist elements in Pauline teaching emphasized, the Marcionite legacy was perpetuated in Syrian monasticism. The frequent baptismal washings undertaken by its members linked its later development with the Mandaeans of the Euphrates Valley.[150] Its ideas underlay also much of Manicheism as this was interpreted in Syria. Indeed, Ephraem testifies to the absorption of the Marcionites by the Manicheans during the fourth century.[151] Christian communities found Marcion's teaching too restrictive. The Jewish legacy could not be shrugged off so easily. Orthodox Christianity moved on to new horizons without him.

BIBLIOGRAPHY

NOTE

Gnosticism, its origins and development, has attracted a huge literature. The decipherment and publication in English of the contents of the Sethite library of Nag Hammadi is a major advance. Unfortunately, the translations in J. M. Robinson, ed., *The Nag Hammadi Library* (New York: Harper & Row, 1978) sometimes do not read as smoothly as R. McL. Wilson's (ed. and Eng. trans.) in Werner Foerster, comp., *Gnosis: A Selection of Gnostic Texts*, 2 vols. (New York and London: Oxford University Press, 1972, 1974), which for its part suffers from providing a selection only of the Nag Hammadi texts.

The availability of the Nag Hammadi documents will require a new assessment of Gnosticism. Even so, some of the older works remain valuable. Hans Jonas's *The Gnostic Religion: The Message of the Alien God and the Beginnings of Christianity*, 2d ed. rev. (Boston: Beacon Press, 1963), though written originally in the 1930s, has been successfully updated, and is still the most comprehensive as well as being the best-written account. Also, Kurt Rudolph, *Gnosis: The Nature and History of Gnosticism*, Eng. trans. R. McL. Wilson (San Francisco: Harper & Row; Edinburgh: T. & T. Clark, 1983), is a fundamental study of Gnosticism, making full use of the Nag Hammadi materials and indicating its continuity with Manicheism and its links with the Mandaeans. R. M. Grant's *Gnosticism and Early Christianity*, rev. ed. (New York: Harper Torchbooks, 1966), has useful descriptions of the Gnostic systems, but suffers from being based on a theory of the development of Jewish apocalyptic which remains unproven. R. McL. Wilson's *The Gnostic Problem: A Study of the Relations Between Hellenistic Judaism and the Gnostic Heresy* (London: A. R. Mowbray, 1958) is sound, especially in the author's association of Philo with ideas behind Alexandrian Gnosticism. The Jewish background to Gnosticism is represented well in John Dart's *The Laughing Savior: The Discovery and Significance of the Nag Hammadi Gnostic Library* (New York: Harper & Row, 1976), a fast-moving and entertaining account of the Nag Hammadi publication, while Ugo Bianchi's *Selected Essays on Gnosticism, Dualism and Mysteriosophy*,

Numen Supplement 38 (Leiden: E. J. Brill, 1978) is another valuable addition to the ever-growing Gnostic library.

SOURCES

Acta Apostolorum Apocrypha, ed. R. A. Lipsius and M. Bonnet, Leipzig: 1891–1903. See also E. Klostermann, in K1T 3, 8, 11, and 12.

Adamantius. *Tyrannii Rufini librorum Adamantii Origenis adversus haereticos interpretatio*. Edited by V. Bucheit. Munich: W. Fink Verlag, 1966.

Basilides. Fragments cited in Clement of Alexandria, *Stromata*, ed. O. Stählin and L. Früchtel, GCS 15, 17, Berlin, 1960; and L. Früchtel and U. Treu, *Clemens Alexandrinus* III, Berlin, 1970, I.21, II.3, 8, 20, III.1, IV.12, 24, 26, VI.1, 6, and VII.17; Eng. trans. by S. G. Hall, *Gnosis*, comp. Foerster, vol. 1: *Patristic Evidence*, pp. 59–83.

Corpus Hermeticum. Edited by A. D. Nock and A. J. Festugière. Paris: Collection Budé, 1945–54.

Epiphanius. *Panarion Haeresium*, esp. chaps. 31–33. Edited by K. Holl. GCS 25, 31, 37. Leipzig, 1915–31.

Gospel of Mary. Eng. trans. G. W. Macrae, R. McL. Wilson, and D. M. Parrott. In *Nag Hammadi Library*, ed. Robinson, pp. 471–74.

Heracleon, fragments of a commentary on John's gospel preserved in Origen's *Commentary on St. John's Gospel*, ed. E. Preuschen, GCS 10, Origenes IV, Leipzig, 1903; and Eng. trans. D. Hill, *Gnosis*, comp. Foerster, vol. 1, pp. 162–83.

Hippolytus, *Refutatio Omnium Haeresium*. Edited by P. Wendland. GCS 26.

Irenaeus, *Adversus Haereses, PG* 7; also [*Sancti Irenaei. . .*] *Adversus Haereses*, ed. W. W. Harvey. 2 vols., Cambridge 1857. Books I and II, ed. A. Rousseau and L. Dontreleau, SC 263, 264, 293, and 294, Paris, 1979, 1982.

Odes of Solomon, *Die Oden Salomos*, ed. and Germ. trans. W. Bauer, K1T 64, Berlin, 1933; and Eng. text and commentary by J. R. Harris, Manchester, Eng., 1909.

Pistis Sophia and *Evangelium Mariae*, preserved on *Papyrus Berolinensis* 8502, *Papyrus John Rylands* 463, and *Pap. Oxy.* 1081, ed. W. Till, *Die gnostischen Schriften des koptischen Papyrus Berolinensis* = TU 60, Berlin, 1955.

Ptolemy (the Valentinian). *Ptolemée: Lettre à Flora*. Edited by G. Quispel. SC 24. Paris, 1949.

Sextus Pythagoraeus. *Sentences: A Contribution to the History of Early Christian Ethics*. Eng. trans. and ed. H. Chadwick. New York and Cambridge: Cambridge University Press, 1959.

Tertullian. *Scorpiace*. Edited by A. Reifferscheid and G. Wissowa. CSEL 20.

Adversus Valentinanos. Edited by A. Kroymann. CSEL 47, pp. 177–212. Leipzig: G. Freytag, 1906.

Adversus Hermogenem. Edited by A. Kroymann. CSEL 47, pp. 126–76. Leipzig: G. Freytag, 1906.

De Praescriptione. Edited by A. Kroymann. CSEL 70, pp. 1–58.

Adversus Marcionem (Against Marcion), Books I–V, ed. and Eng. trans. E. Evans, 2 vols. OECT, New York and London: Oxford University Press, 1972; analysis and commentary on Bks. I and II by E. Meijering, *Tertullian Contra Marcion*, PhP3, Leiden: E. J. Brill, 1977.

Theodotus. Fragments cited in Clement of Alexandria *Stromata*, ed. O. Stählin and L. Früchtel GCS 15, 17. (1) L. Früchtel and U. Treu, *Clemens* III, GCS. (2) G. Quispel, SC 23, Paris, 1970 (revision of F. Sagnard's *Extraits de Théodote*, Paris, 1948).

Secondary Works

Armstrong, A. H. "Gnosis and Greek Philosophy." In *Gnosis: Festschrift für Hans Jonas*, ed. B. Aland (Göttingen: Vandenhoeck & Ruprecht, 1978), pp. 187–224.

Betz, H. D. "The Delphic Maxim γνῶθι σαυτόν in Hermetic Interpretation." *HTR* 63 (1970): 465–84.

Beyschlag, K. *Simon Magus und die christliche Gnosis.* Tübingen: J. C. B. Mohr (Paul Siebeck), 1974.

Bianchi, U. "Marcion: Théologien biblique ou docteur gnostique?" *VC* 21 (September 1967): 141–49.

Blackman, E. C. *Marcion and his Influence.* New York: Macmillan Co.; London: SPCK, 1950.

Bultmann, R. *Gnosis.* Vol. 5 of Gerhard Kittel's *Bible Key Words,* Eng. trans. and ed. J. R. Coates. New York: Harper & Row, 1965; London: A. & C. Black, 1952.

――――. *Primitive Christianity: In Its Contemporary Setting.* Eng. trans. R. H. Fuller. Philadelphia: Fortress Press, 1980; London: Thames & Hudson, 1956.

Colpe, C. "Heidnische, jüdische und christliche Überlieferung in den Schriften aus Nag Hammadi I–IV." *JAC* XV (1972): 5–18.

Cornford, F. M., ed. *Greek Religious Thought from Homer to the Age of Alexander.* Boston: Beacon Press; London: J. M. Dent & Sons, 1950.

Cross, F. L., ed. and Eng. trans. *The Jung Codex: A Newly Recovered Gnostic Papyrus.* New York: Morehouse-Gorham; London: A. R. Mowbray, 1955.

Foerster, W. "Das System des Basilides." *NTS* 9 (April 1963): 233–55.

Frend, W. H. C. "The Gnostic Sects and the Roman Empire." *JEH* 5 (1954): 25–37.

Grant, R. M. "Notes on Gnosis." *VC* 11 (September 1957): 145–51.

Harnack, A. von. *Marcion, das Evangelium vom fremden Gott.* 2d ed. Leipzig: Hinrichs, 1921.

Hort, F. J. "Basilides." *DCB* 1, pp. 268–80.

Koschorke, K. *Die Polemik der Gnostiker gegen das kirchliche Christentum.* NHS 12. Leiden: E. J. Brill, 1978.

Layton, Bentley. *The Gnostic Treatise on Resurrection from Nag Hammadi.* Harvard Dissertations on Religion 12. Chico, Calif.: Scholars Press, 1979.

MacRae, G. "The Jewish Background of the Gnostic Sophia Myth." *NT* 12 (1970): 86–101.

May, G. *Schöpfung aus dem Nichts.* Berlin: Walter de Gruyter, 1978.

Nock, A. D. "Gnosticism." In *Essays on Religion and the Ancient World*, ed. Z. Stewart, vol. 2, pp. 940–59. Cambridge, Mass.: Harvard University Press, 1972.

Pagels, E. "The Demiurge and His Archons: A Gnostic View of the Bishop and Presbyters?" *HTR* 69 (1976): 301–24.

――――. *The Gnostic Gospels.* New York: Random House; London: Weidenfeld & Nicolson, 1979.

――――. "A Valentinian Interpretation of Baptism and Eucharist—and Its Critique of 'Orthodox' Sacramental Theology and Practice." *HTR* 65 (1972): 153–69.

Pearson, B. A. "Jewish Haggadic Traditions in the *Testimony of Truth* from Nag Hammadi (CGIX, 3)." In *Ex Orbe Religionum. Studia Geo. Widengren*, pp. 457–70. Leiden: E. J. Brill, 1972.

Peel, M. L., and Zandee, J. "The Teachings of Silvanus from the Library of Nag Nammadi." *NT* 14 (1972): 294–311.

Quispel, G. "Ezekiel 1:26 in Jewish Mysticism and Gnosis." *VC* 34 (1980): 1–13.

Robinson, J. M. "The Jung Codex: The Rise and Fall of a Monopoly." *RelSRev* 3 (1977): 17–30.

Scholer, D. M. *Nag Hammadi Bibliography 1948–1969.* NHS 1. Leiden: E. J. Brill, 1971, and kept up-to-date to 1980 in *NT*.

Simon, M. "Eléments gnostiques chez Philon." In *Studies in the History of Religions* XII, pp. 359–76. Leiden: E. J. Brill, 1967. (= pp. 336–55 of vol. 1 of Simon's *Collected Works*.)

Stead, G. C. "The Valentinian Myth of Sophia." *JTS* n.s. 20 (1969): 75–104.

Widengren, Geo. *The Gnostic Attitude*. Eng. trans. and ed. B. A. Pearson. Santa Barbara: University of California, Institute of Religious Studies, 1973.

Yamauchi, E. M. *Pre-Christian Gnosticism: A Survey of the Proposed Evidences.* Grand Rapids: Wm. B. Eerdmans; London: Tyndale Press, 1973.

Symposium: Barc, B., ed. *Colloque internationale sur les textes de Nag Hammadi* (Quebec, 22–25 August 1978). Louvain, 1981.

NOTES

1. Origen *Contra Celsum* (*Against Celsus*) V.62–63 and cf. ibid., 53.
2. Eusebius *HE* III.39.13.
3. Origen *Celsus* III.12.
4. See over, p. 253.
5. See E. Schweizer, "The Background of Matthew and Colossians" in *Jews, Greeks and Christians: Essays in Honor of W. D. Davies*, ed. R. Hamerton-Kelly and R. Scroggs (Leiden: E. J. Brill, 1976), pp. 247–48.
6. Eusebius *HE* VI.2.14.
7. Clement, *Stromata*, ed. Stählin/Früchte, GCS, VII.17.106.
8. Origen's *John's Gospel*, GCS 10, is our main source for Heracleon's commentary on John. See Foerster, comp., *Gnosis*, vol. 1, pp. 162–83.
9. Irenaeus, *Heresies*, *PG* 7, and Eng. trans. ANCL.23.2; and compare Justin *1 Apology* 26.1–3. The ANCL translation, ed. A. Roberts and J. Donaldson, has been used throughout, and the chapter and paragraph numbers are those of Migne (*PG* 7).
10. "The Great Power" is not unknown in late Jewish terminology. Philo calls God "the heavenly and greatest Power" (*De Vita Mosis* [*On the Life of Moses*] I.111), and the Logos was sometimes identified as "the power of God." See Beyschlag, *Simon Magus*, pp. 108–9 and references.
11. Epiphanius *Medicine Box* (*Panarion = Haereses*) XIII.1–2, supposedly a baptist preacher and rival of Jesus. See J. Daniélou, *The Theology of Jewish Christianity*, Eng. trans. and ed. J. A. Baker, A History of Early Christian Doctrine Before the Council of Nicaea (Philadelphia: Westminster Press; London: Darton, Longman & Todd, 1977), vol. 1, p. 84.

12. For the Simonian myth, see Foerster, *Gnosis*, vol. 1, pp. 27–32, and Yamauchi, *Pre-Christian Gnosticism*, pp. 58–62. Also, Jonas, *Gnostic Religion*, chap. 4.

13. Irenaeus *Heresies* I.24.1 (*PG* 7.674). See B. J. Kidd's brief description, *A History of the Church to* A.D. *461*, 3 vols. (New York: Oxford University Press, 1922), vol. 1, pp. 197–98, and Foerster, *Gnosis*, vol. 1, 27–33.

14. Irenaeus *Heresies* I.24.2 (*PG* 7.675A).

15. For Saturninus's asceticism as comparable with that of Tatian and Marcion, see Irenaeus *Heresies* I.28, cited by Eusebius *HE* IV.29.2–3. His tradition was carried on for another generation by Severus and the latter established the link with Tatian (Eusebius *HE* IV.29.5–6).

16. Solomon, *Odes* 1, 5, 6, 22, and 25. See Bauer, *Die Oden Salamos*, p. 1. In Gnostic legend, Pistis is representing as emanating Sophia the ruler of the Sixth Heaven; *On the Origin of the World*, Eng. trans. H.-G. Bethge and O. S. Wintermute, in *Nag Hammadi Library*, ed. Robinson, pp. 161–79, esp. pp. 162ff.

17. For the view that the *Odes* were based on Antiochene theology of the second century A.D. and contains "certain outspoken anti-Marcionite polemics and combats the congregation of Mani" (that is, are fourth-century documents, see H. J. W. Drijvers, "Early Syriac-speaking Christianity," *The Second Century* 2.3 (fall 1982): 157–75, esp. p. 167.

18. See Foerster, *Gnosis*, vol. 1, pp. 5–7 and Layton, *Gnostic Treatise on Resurrection*, p. 126.

19. Clement, *Excerpta ex Theodoto*, ed. Stählin/Früchtel, GCS, 78.2. Theodotus lived circa A.D. 160 and came from Asia Minor.

20. For Basilides's belief in reincarnation possibly even as animals on the basis of Deut. 5:9, see Clement *Stromata* (*Miscellanies*) IV.24.153.3 and *Excerpta ex Theodoto* (*Excerpts from Theodotus*) 28. For freedom from oblivion, see *The Gospel of Truth*, Eng. trans. G. W. MacRae, in *Nag Hammadi Library*, ed. Robinson, pp. 37–49, esp. p. 38.

21. See Bultmann's *Gnosis*, pp. 22–24.

22. 1QpHab 7:4–5. See F. M. Cross, *The Ancient Library of Qumran and Modern Biblical Studies* (New York: Doubleday & Co.; London: Gerald Duckworth & Co., 1958), p. 83, and cf. *The Manual of Discipline*, III.15, in T. H. Gaster, ed. and Eng. trans., *The Dead Sea Scriptures in English Translation* (Garden City, N.Y.: Doubleday Anchor Books, rev. ed., 1964; London: Secker & Warburg, 1957), pp. 44–65, esp. p. 53, "God of knowledge." See above, p. 29.

23. Thus, Basilides's followers claimed that faith was something "natural" and that teachings were revealed to them by "intuition" (Clement *Miscellanies* II.3.10.1). This is paralleled from Plato as understood in the second century. Thus Celsus (see Origen *Celsus* VI.3) quotes Plato *Letters* VII.341C: "the highest good cannot at all be expressed in words, but comes to us by long familiarity and suddenly like a light in the soul kindled by a leaping spark." Also, the pagan-Gnostic in Poimandres 4 (Foerster, *Gnosis*, vol. 1, p. 329), "and immediately everything became instantaneously clear to me."

24. *The Gospel of Philip*, in Foerster, comp., *Gnosis*, vol. 2: *Coptic and Mandean Sources*, p. 100 = Eng. trans. W. W. Isenberg in *Nag Hammadi Library*, ed. Robinson, pp. 131–51, paragraph 84, p. 150.

25. *The Treatise on the Three Natures* cited from F. L. Cross, ed., *Jung Codex*,

p. 59; and cf. *The Tripartite Tractate*, Eng. trans. H. W. Attridge, E. H. Pagels, and D. Mueller, in *Nag Hammadi Library*, ed. Robinson, pp. 54–97, esp. p. 85.

26. Hippolytus, *Refutatio*, V.8.27, GCS 26, p. 94.

27. *Gospel of Truth*, trans. MacRae, p. 49.

28. *Allogenes*, 58–61, Eng. trans. A. C. Wire, J. D. Turner, and O. S. Wintermute, in *Nag Hammadi Library*, ed. Robinson, pp. 443–52, esp. pp. 448–50. See Pagels, *Gnostic Gospels*, pp. 138–40.

29. Hippolytus *Refutation* V.7.28 and 8.31ff.

30. *Tripartate*, trans. Attridge, Pagels, and Mueller, p. 89.

31. *Gospel of Truth*, trans. MacRae, p. 43.

32. Bultmann, *Primitive Christianity*, pp. 169–71.

33. See Pagels, *Gnostic Gospels*, p. 38.

34. For Gnostic passwords, see Celsus in Origen, *Contra Celsum*, Eng. trans. H. Chadwick (New York and Cambridge: Cambridge University Press, 1953), VI.31, and Chadwick's notes, pp. 346–48; also Epiphanius *Medicine Box* XXVI.13.

35. Indicated in *Gospel of Philip* 126, Foerster, comp., *Gnosis*, vol. 2, 101 = Isenberg, trans., p. 151; and Irenaeus *Heresies* I.13.6.

36. Irenaeus *Heresies* I.21.5.

37. Thus *Gospel of Philip* 68, 95 (Foerster, comp., *Gnosis*, vol. 2, pp. 89, 93): "for from the anointing (chrism), we are called Christians, not because of the baptism" (p. 93).

38. Irenaeus *Heresies* IV.33.9; Clement *Miscellanies* III.13.92 and IV.16.3; and Tertullian *Scorpiace* VII.

39. *Apocalypse of Seth*, cited from H.-C. Puech, "Les nouveaux Écrits gnostiques découverts en Haute-Egypte," in *Coptic Studies in Honor of Walter Ewing Crum* (Boston: Byzantine Institute, 1950), pp. 91–108, esp. p. 108. Compare Tertullian, *Scorpiace* XV, ed. Reifferscheid and Wissowa, 178, and *The Apocryphon of John* 31, Eng. trans. F. Wisse, in *Nag Hammadi Library*, ed. Robinson, pp. 98–116, esp. p. 116.

40. Eusebius *HE* IV.7; and Irenaeus *Heresies* I.24.5.

41. *Gospel of Philip* 73, Foerster, comp., *Gnosis*, vol. 2, p. 90, "There is no bridal chamber for the beast, for the slaves," but for "free men and virgins."

42. *Gospel of Philip* 19, Foerster, comp., *Gnosis*, vol. 2, p. 81 = Isenberg, trans., p. 134.

43. *Gospel of Truth* 32, trans. MacRae, p. 44.

44. Hippolytus *Refutation* VII.20.1.

45. In the second century, see Justin *Trypho* II.4 (geometry and astronomy as a means of purifying the soul). For Philo's interest in the study of the same subjects and the influence of the number seven, *De Opificio Mundi* (*On the Creation*) XLII, 126–28.

46. Cornford, ed., *Greek Religious Thought*, p. 60, citing a fourth- to third-century B.C. inscription from Petelia in southern Italy.

47. See the Gnostic tract, *Origin of World*, trans. Bethge and Wintermute, pp. 168ff.

48. Grant's thesis, *Gnosticism and Early Christianity*, pp. 30ff., put it in moderate terms, "All I should claim is that the failure of apocalyptic (following Jewish military disasters) led to the rise of new forms of religious expression in which the old, while still present, was transposed and transformed" (p. 37).

49. Thus, Eusebius-Jerome, *Chronicle*, ed. R. Helm, GCS, p. 201; and Clement, *Miscellanies* VII.16.106.4.

50. Origen *Celsus* III.12. See above, n. 3.

51. *The Treatise on the Resurrection to Rheginus*, Foerster, comp., *Gnosis*, vol. 2, p. 73.

52. *The Teachings of Silvanus* 117, Eng. trans. M. C. Peel, J. Zandee, and F. Wisse, in *Nag Hammadi Library*, ed. Robinson, pp. 346–61, esp. p. 361.

53. *Asclepius 21–29* was included in the Gnostic library at Nag Hammadi; the quotation regarding learning and knowledge is at paragraph 67, Eng. trans. P. A. Dirkse and D. M. Parrott, in *Nag Hammadi Library*, ed. Robinson, pp. 300–307, esp. p. 301.

54. Cited from Clement *Miscellanies* IV.12.82.2; cf. Plato *Republic* II.379 Cornford, ed., *Greek Religious Thought*, p. 70).

55. Poimandres 15, cited in Foerster, *Gnosis*, vol. 1, p. 331.

56. Poimandres 25 and 26. In general, see Jonas, *Gnostic Religion*, chap. 7.

57. Widengren, *Gnostic Attitude*, points for instance to an Iranian prototype of the Song of the Pearl and its motif of the soul's exile and return to its true home (pp. 38ff.).

58. The entire text (Eng. trans. F. Wisse) is given in Robinson, ed., *Nag Hammadi Library*. For the Jewish connection with Gnosticism, see Dart, *Laughing Savior,* part 2.

59. Origen *Celsus* II.1. See above, p. 163.

60. Emil Schürer, *The History of the Jewish People in the Age of Jesus Christ (175 B.C.–A.D. 135)*, rev. ed., new English translation by Géza Vermès and Fergus Millar, organizing editor Matthew Black, 2 vols. (Edinburgh: T. & T. Clark, vol. 1, 1973, and vol. 2, 1979), vol. 2.3, pp. 157ff.

61. For this aspect of Alexandrian Judaism, see Wilson, *Gnostic Problem*, chap. 2; and Simon, "Elements gnostiques chez Philon."

62. Wilson, *Gnostic Problem*, p. 41.

63. Text translated by G. W. MacRae and D. M. Parrott, in *Nag Hammadi Library*, ed. Robinson, pp. 256–64.

64. Philo is not consistent. He is unwilling to admit any power limiting the agency of God, yet appears to believe that the body is not made by the soul but by Another (*De Migratione Abrahami* [*On the Migration of Abraham*] 193), and hence may be abandoned as the Self ascends to the Father-God. See Betz, "Delphic Maxim,"

65. Philo *De Posteritate Caini* (*On the Posterity and Exile of Cain*) 27, 39, and 53: some "impious people" asserting they had Cain for their master—much as did the Gnostic Cainites of the second century; also, idem, *Abraham* 83–90. See, however, Simon, "Elements gnostiques chez Philon" on the general nature of Philo's strictures (pp. 361–62).

66. Ignatius *The Letter to the Ephesians* XIX.

67. Ibid., XX.

68. Ibid., XVIII.2.

69. Justin *Trypho* LXXXV.2.

70. See lines 3019–20 of the *Paris Magical Papyrus*, ed. C. Wessely, *Patrologia Orientalis* V, pp. 187ff. Dating (originally late second century?) is discussed ibid., pp. 184–85.

71. Eusebius *HE* IV.22.7.

72. Clement *Miscellanies* II.20.113 and VI.6.53.2-5.

73. Irenaeus *Heresies* I.24.4; Epiphanius, *Medicine Box* XXIV.2; and Pseudo-Tertullian *Adversus omnes haereses* (*Against All Heresies*) I.

74. Irenaeus *Heresies* I.24.6. "More than" rather than "not yet," suggested by Hort, "Basilides," p. 279, 2.

75. Hippolytus was writing in Rome and twenty years later than Irenaeus. He tries to prove that Basilides derived his ideas from philosophers, especially Aristotle. Compare a similar line of attack by the Catholics in Rome, c. 200, against the Adoptionists (Eusebius *HE* V.28.14). Basilides was interested in man's salvation by Jesus from his hopeless situation on earth. For an evaluation of Basilides' theology and sources, see Foerster, "Basilides," and Hort, "Basilides."

76. Hippolytus *Refutation* VII.21, 2-4. Irenaeus represents Basilides as believing that God was "unoriginate" and "ineffable."

77. Irenaeus *Heresies* I.24.4.

78. Hippolytus *Refutation* VII.23.3 and cf. 25.3. The Great Archon was unable to penetrate into the realm of the "non-existent" God, and hence imagined himself to be the Supreme Being.

79. Basilides *Exegetica* XXIII, cited by Clement *Miscellanies* IV.12.81. Even the man, Jesus of Nazareth, had sinned, hence the crucifixion! See Foerster, "Basilides," p. 247.

80. 4 Macc. 6:29 and 18:4.

81. Cited by Clement *Miscellanies* IV.12.82.2. See above, p. 202.

82. Thus Clement *Miscellanies* IV.12.85.1 where Basilides is alleged to "deify the devil"; in *The Acts of Archelaus* (Syrian, late third century?), 55, where he is associated with Persian teachers of Mani; and ibid., 67, where he is alleged to imply belief in two absolutely contrary and eternal principles of light and darkness, while attributing such views to "the investigations of barbarians."

83. Clement *Miscellanies* VII.17.106.

84. Jerome *Commentary on Hosea* 11.10.

85. Irenaeus *Heresies* III.3.4.

86. Ibid., I.1 and 4.1; also, Epiphanius *Medicine Box* XXXI.9, 1-27.

87. See Peel and Zandee, "Teachings of Silvanus"; and as translators in Robinson, ed., *Nag Hammadi Library*: "[The Teaching] displays some eclectic tastes, with influences from the Bible, the exegesis of Philo of Alexandria, Middle Platonism and late Stoicism" (p. 346). Fragments of the *Sentences of Sextus* were found at Nag Hammadi (Eng. trans. F. Wisse, in *Nag Hammadi Library*, ed. Robinson, pp. 454-59).

88. See Peel and Zandee, "Teachings of Silvanus," pp. 302-3.

89. *Teachings of Silvanus* 109 (trans. Peel, Zandee, and Wisse, p. 357): "Let Christ alone enter your world and let him bring to naught all powers which have come upon you. Let him enter the temple which is within you so that he may cast out all the merchants." The way to God was "by Knowledge."

90. See Ptolemy *Ptolemée*, introduction.

91. Ptolemy *Ptolemée* (text preserved by Epiphanius *Medicine Box* 33. 3-8) 3.4 and cf. 5.3.

92. Ptolemy *Ptolemée* 7.7. The nature of the Adversary, on the other hand, was "corruption and darkness." The nature of the "ungenerated Father of all is incor-

ruption and self-existent, simple and homogeneous light" (as in Mani's system. See below, p. 316).

93. Ptolemy *Ptolemée* 5.8. For truth "entering the world in types and images," see *Gospel of Philip* paragraph 67, trans. Isenberg, p. 140.

94. Ptolemy *Ptolemée* 5.13.

95. Irenaeus *Heresies* I.13, and see Pagels, *Gnostic Gospels*, pp. 59–60.

96. *Gospel of Philip* paragraph 64, trans. Isenberg, p. 138. Compare also, paragraph 59, p. 135: "There were three who always walked with the Lord: Mary his mother, and her sister and Magdalene, the one who was called his companion." Mary Magdalene was "the companion of the Saviour" (p. 138).

97. In the *Pistis Sophia*, John shares the leading role with Mary Magdalene among Jesus' questioners (late third century). In *The Gospel of Mary*, trans. Macrae, Wilson, and Parrott, Mary Magdalene recounts to the disciples a vision of the resurrected Christ—much to Peter's chagrin: "Did he really speak privately with a woman [and] not openly to us?"

98. See the various Coptic and Syriac Gnostic texts of the assumption legend, published by M. R. James, Eng. trans., *The Apocryphal New Testament* (New York and London: Oxford University Press, 1924; reprint ed., 1953), pp. 194–227, and examples of Infancy narratives, ibid., pp. 38–39.

99. Origen *Celsus* V.62, and Irenaeus *Heresies* I.25.6.

100. Origen, *In Romans* V.1, *PG* 14, 1015A–B.

101. *Gospel of Philip* paragraph 52, trans. Isenberg, p. 132 = Foerster, *Gnosis*, vol. 2, p. 78.

102. Ibid.

103. Heracleon, cited by Origen *John's Gospel* X.19, pp. 190–91. See Pagels, "Valentinian Interpretation of Baptism and Eucharist," pp. 162–63.

104. The "baptism of John" = the "baptism of the demiurge." See Pagels, "Valentinian Interpretation of Baptism and Eucharist," pp. 156–57.

105. Ibid., p. 167.

106. Origen *John's Gospel* XIII.19 = Foerster, *Gnosis*, vol. 1, Frag. 22, p. 172, and Origen *John's Gospel* XIII.25.2 Frag. 24, where true piety is also equated with "rational service," citing Rom. 12:1.

107. See the Fragments of Heracleon published by Foerster, *Gnosis*, vol. 1, pp. 162–83. Origen sometimes praises Heracleon's interpretations, for example, *John's Gospel* XIII.10 = Foerster, *Gnosis*, vol. 1, Frag. 17, and cf. Frags. 6 and 8. At other times he thinks his interpretations "rash" (for example, *John's Gospel* XI.34 = Foerster, *Gnosis*, vol. 1, Frag. 14), or "does violence to the text" (!) (*John's Gospel* XIII.1 = Frag. 18).

108. Irenaeus *Heresies* I.18.1, "everyone of them generates something new"; and cf. I.21.5 (end) the "most modern 'Gnostics' make it their business to invent some new opinion."

109. MacRae, trans., pp. 37–38. Compare *Odes of Solomon* 23, stanzas 1–3, in *Die Oden Salomos*, ed. Bauer, p. 49:

> Joy belongs to the saints, and who shall establish it but they alone?
> Grace belongs to the elect, and who shall receive it,
> but those who trust in it from the beginning?
> Love belongs to the elect, and who shall put it on,
> but those who have possessed it from the beginning?
> Walk in the knowledge of the most high.

110. Below, p. 711. See the present author's review of H. Chadwick, *Priscillian of Avila: The Occult and the Charismatic in the Early Church* (New York and London: Oxford University Press, 1976), in *JTS* 28 (1977): 561–65.

111. Below, p. 635.

112. See R. C. Chesnut's description of James of Sarug's cosmology: "the human race grew up, progressively falling into the control of the 'Evil Archon,' the 'Ruler of the Air,'" *Three Monophysite Christologies: Severus of Antioch, Philoxenus of Mabbug, and Jacob of Sarug* (New York and London: Oxford University Press, 1976), p. 115.

113. Von Harnack, *Marcion*, is still a fundamental study, though criticized in its details by Blackman, *Marcion*.

114. Marcion's original interest in the problem of evil is stressed by Tertullian *Marcion*, I.2.

115. Irenaeus *Heresies* III.3.4.

116. Ibid., I.27.1 and cf. IV.17.11.

117. Ibid., I.27.1 and IV.17.11, and cf. Tertullian *Marcion* I.2, and II.24.

118. Tertullian *Marcion* I.2.

119. Ibid., IV.23, "a shameless contradiction." See von Harnack, *Marcion*, pp. 105–6 for other examples.

120. Origen *Homily on Joshua 12*, ed. W. A. Baehrens, GCS 30, Origenes VII, pp. 367–70 (Leipzig, 1921).

121. Tertullian *Marcion* II.25 and IV.41.

122. Ibid., II.18.1 and IV.16. See Meijering, *Tertullian (Marcion, I–II)*, pp. 135–36.

123. See von Harnack, *Marcion*, p. 81, second quotation.

124. Tertullian *Marcion* IV.6.3.

125. Hippolytus *Refutation* X.19.

126. Tertullian *Marcion* III.8. The probability that Marcion was equating Jesus' ministry with angelic appearances recorded in the Old Testament is suggested by Marcion's arguments derived from these appearances in the next section (III.9).

127. Philo *Legum Allegoriae (Allegorical Interpretation)* III.51–54, and *Quaestiones et Solutiones in Genesin (Questions and Answers on Genesis)* I.45.68. The same questions were also raised in *The Hypostasis of the Archons*, Eng. trans. R. A. Bullard and B. Layton, in *Nag Hammadi Library*, ed. Robinson, pp. 152–60, esp. p. 155. See R. M. Grant, "Notes on Gnosis."

128. Suggested by Tertullian's criticism of Marcion's argument centered on Jesus' call of the "outsider" (*profanum*) publican told in Luke 5:27–39.

129. Tertullian *Marcion* V.4, "Marcion's sponge!" and 16.

130. Ibid., I.19. See Meijering, *Tertullian*, pp. 56–57.

131. Tertullian *Marcion* IV.5.

132. Ibid., V.19.

133. Letter of Dionysius of Corinth, recorded by Eusebius *HE* IV.23.4.

134. Eusebius *HE* IV.15.46.

135. Suggested by Theophilus of Antioch, *Ad Autolycum* II.24, ed. and Eng. trans. R. M. Grant (Oxford: At the Clarendon Press, 1970), p. 66, probably answering Marcionite criticisms of God's dealings with Adam in Eden.

136. These in the third and fourth centuries A.D. See below, pp. 315, 765.

137. Metrodorus of Smyrna (cf. Eusebius *HE* IV.15.47) was described as a "presbyter."

138. Thus, the anti-Montanist writing c. 200, quoted by Eusebius *HE* V.16.21 (evidence also for Marcionites in Phrygia), and Metrodorus himself.

139. Cyprian *Letter* LXXV.3.

140. Irenaeus *Heresies* I.25.2.

141. Tertullian *Marcion* IV.11.8.

142. Von Harnack, *Marcion*, 135–36.

143. Eusebius *HE* V.13.5–7.

144. Tertullian *Marcion* I.27.

145. Ibid., I.19.2.

146. Eusebius *HE* V.13.2 and 5.

147. Commented upon by von Harnack, *Marcion*, pp. 263–66.

148. See Buchheit, ed., *Tyrannii Rufini Origenis,* Disputatio I.

149. See R. Murray, *Symbols of Church and Kingdom: A Study of Early Syriac Tradition* (New York and Cambridge: Cambridge University Press, 1975), pp. 12ff., and the chapter on "The Body of Christ," pp. 69ff.

150. See F. C. Burkitt, "The Mandaeans," *JTS* 29 (1927–28): 225–35, esp. p. 233.

151. Ephraem Syrus *Hymn Against Heresies* XXII.3, "Marcion divided the sheep of Christ, and Mani despoiled the despoiler. One madman bit another" (ed. E. Beck, CSCO, Script. Syri 76–77[Louvain, 1957]), p. 78. Ephraem Syrus emphasizes always the kinship between the Marcionites and Manicheans in his day.

7

The Emergence of Orthodoxy 135–93

The great church[1] was confronted by the same problems of adaptation to the pagan world as its Gnostic and Marcionite rivals. Its task, however, was more difficult than theirs. Its standpoint was different and less open to compromise. It was more influenced by Pharisaic norms and eschatological hopes, and its developing organization favored the guardian of tradition rather than the speculative thinker. In Asia Minor where it was strongest, the Jews had produced no school of philosophical theology, such as Philo's at Alexandria, which the Christians might inherit. As Paul's education showed, Greek philosophy was learned from anthologies, and pagan life and thought were caricatured in order to elevate pride in Judaism. For the Christian, biblical theology—accepting both Old and New Testament as self-consistent and divinely inspired—was hardly reconcilable with the ideas of current philosophic schools. A God active in history on behalf of his people had little in common with the God of Stoicism or Platonism who existed but did not come into contact with matter, let alone intervene in nature. For the orthodox Christian, however, the incarnation was the supreme example of such intervention, and the coming (Parousia) was at hand.

In New Testament times, Jews and Christians had linked pagan philosophy with pagan morality. Both were given a bad name. In Colossians (2:8) Paul associated philosophy with "empty deceit, according to human tradition," to be contrasted with the way of Christ. In 2 Corinthians (11:3) he pleaded with the Corinthians not to let themselves be corrupted "from a sincere and pure devotion to Christ." Luke-Acts had nothing complimentary to say about the Stoics and Epicureans whom Paul met in Athens. The Athenians' spirit of inquiry was not a point in their favor (Acts 17:18–21). The later books of the New Testament and the apostolic fathers show no change in this attitude. *First Clement* quotes no Stoic writer to support his convictions regarding the harmony and stability of the universe (*1 Clement* 20). His source is the book of Job. That Christians could have anything in common with pagans and their ideas was abhorrent to Polycarp. His pupil Irenaeus was not alone in believing that the heretics whom he abominated derived many of their notions from philosophy. Acknowledgment that the latter might possess truths and insights valuable for the deeper understanding of Scripture was always to be grudging. Even at the end of the patristic period, John of Damascus (c. 750) wrote, "Let us use whatever we can from the Greeks, for we receive many things from the Greeks that will enable us to fight against the Greeks,"[2] It was in this negative spirit that the theologians of the great church approached their task of living in the world.

The beginning was not promising. Although there were articulate, orthodox Christians even in Egypt, as Justin himself and early Christian papyri show,[3] nevertheless the Gnostics were intellectually superior and better attuned to the ideas of their age than were their orthodox rivals, and they were less bound to what was hardening into formal and legalistic tradition.

Orthodox Christianity appeared to outsiders as introspective, "frogs squatting around a marsh discussing who was the most sinful among them."[4] Celsus's parody was not wholly grotesque and orthodoxy produced no leaders of the intellectual range and status of its opponents. The orthodox were often of an administrative cast of mind, ones to whom rules of behavior necessary to win salvation seemed more important than the fullness of Christ's grace. Polycarp was a venerable figure, but of limited vision; Justin was a sincere and valiant debater, whose importance can be underestimated, but on his own admission he was no rhetorician;[5] Irenaeus possessed a robust common sense, a long memory, and flashes of theological insight, but between the memorable phrases his writing is prolix and tedious, and his ideas inflexible. Like his colleagues, he was encumbered with a millenarian legacy that frustrated all attempts to build a Christian philosophy with which to oppose paganism and Gnosticism. There could be no accommodation with the thought of the Greco-Roman world so long as millenarianism prevailed.

Even so, the second half of the second century witnessed the beginnings of the philosophic defense of Christianity, an apologetic that drew heavily on Jewish models and borrowed the methods but not the ideas of philosophers. The church also evolved a succinctly argued "rule of faith" that could be used as a test of orthodoxy from Gaul to Alexandria. Intellect apart, a century and a half of existence had enabled it to build up some solid defenses against its rivals. Against their speculation, the orthodox leaders could point to a tradition of teaching and organization that could demonstrably be traced back to the sub-apostolic period, and with a stretch of imagination to the apostles themselves. Tradition had once been "a fence for Torah" as Akiba had described it (*Pirke Aboth* 3.18). Now it served the great church well. Polycarp was able to confound Gnostic opponents, when on a visit to Rome in c. 154, by asserting that their views did not agree with those of John the Elder whom he had heard in his youth.[6] He embodied the appeal to tradition. Orthodoxy was now based, too, on established communities in many, if not most, of the larger cities of the Mediterranean. As we have noted, its leaders were in the habit of maintaining contact with each other by letter over considerable distances. The church of Smyrna recorded in detail the martyrdom of Polycarp (c. 165) and sent it to the church at Philomelium in Phrygia. Eusebius of Caesarea preserves a series of letters written during the 170s, between Soter of Rome and Dionysius of Corinth, and Dionysius to Pinytus of Knossos, to Palmas of Amastris in Pontus, and to the churches in Athens and Sparta, as well as the long account of the pogrom at Lyons by the survivors sent to the churches in Asia and Phrygia.[7]

Matters of common interest were being discussed and common policies accepted. In the 160s–70s, the main issue, judging from Dionysius's correspondence, seems to have been the excess of ascetic or Encratite practices in orthodox communities that threatened to erupt into schism. Justin mentions an orthodox youth at Alexandria because he had applied to the prefect of Egypt to be allowed to become a eunuch (*1 Apology* 29), and these tendencies persisted elsewhere. The existence of Encratism within the church indicates how much the views of Marcion's and Tatian's followers were those of their time. In a few years, bishops would also be acting in common against a new threat to their authority represented by the Phrygian New Prophecy. Their power was developing under the pressure of events. The second half of the second century provides the first information about the church councils since the apostolic age.

The church in Rome also was beginning to emerge as an authoritative center of Christianity. From about 130 onwards it had become a magnet for Christians of every persuasion. Cerdo, Marcion, and Valentinus representing the nonorthodox, Polycarp, Justin, Hegesippus, and Avircius Marcellus on the orthodox side, were among the many who frequented the city. At first, Rome was not conspicuously "orthodox." The fact that Marcion was well received and that Valentinus was nearly elected bishop suggests a certain elasticity in outlook as late as 150. The main body of Christians in Rome, however, belonged to a relatively wealthy church which was becoming increasingly conscious of its prestige through its foundation by the two apostles Peter and Paul, and was willing to extend its help and its influence on a wider scale. By the decade 160–70 a shrine (the *Aedicula*) commemorating what was believed to be the site of Peter's burial had been built into the wall of a pagan cemetery on the Vatican hill.[8] At the end of the century the "trophies" (that is, memorials) of the apostles were a well-known landmark for native Christians and an attraction for visitors.[9] The Roman church had an interest in maintaining the validity of apostolic tradition and threw its weight on the side of orthodoxy. Its bishops Soter (166–75) and Eleutherus (175–89) were men of standing from whom opinions could be asked and heeded. For Irenaeus in c. 185 Rome had become *the* example of a church where apostolic succession could be demonstrated, and in a significant if ambiguous sentence he pays tribute to its importance. "Each church must assemble at [or "be in harmony with"] this church because of its outstanding pre-eminence, that is the faithful from everywhere, since apostolic tradition is preserved in it by those from everywhere" (*Against Heresies* III.3.2). Unfortunately, only the Latin of this famous sentence has survived and the key words "convenire ad" can mean either "assemble" or, metaphorically, "agree with." Eusebius, writing from the Eastern point of view, omitted the sentence but cited the one immediately following in his *Ecclesiastical History* (V.6.1). Whatever its precise significance, Rome had become a formidable asset on the side of orthodoxy.

Liturgy, too, was providing a bond of unity between widely scattered communities, reinforcing the sense of brotherhood already mentioned as characteristic of the second-century church. As against the mysterious and theosophical nature of the Gnostic services, orthodoxy had been developing its own "mysteries" in the celebration of Baptism and the Eucharist.[10] The synagogue provided the framework of each but the focus was on Christ and Christ alone. Justin Martyr gives a detailed description of both ceremonies as he witnessed them in Rome c. 155. In fact, he describes the Eucharist twice over (*1 Apology* 65–66 and 67), once in connection with Baptism and a second time as following on the meeting (*synaxis*) of the brethren. He writes regarding the baptism of a convert:

> Those who are persuaded and believe that the things we teach and say are true, and promise that they can live accordingly, are instructed to pray and beseech God with fasting for the remission of their past sins, while we pray and fast along with them. Then they are brought by us where there is water, and are reborn by the same manner of rebirth by which we ourselves were reborn; for they are then washed in the water in the name of God the Father and Master of all, and of our Saviour Jesus Christ, and of the Holy Spirit. For Christ said, "Unless you are born again you will not enter into the Kingdom of heaven." This washing is called illumination, since those who learn these things are illumined within. The illuminand is also washed in the name of Jesus Christ, who was crucified under Pontius Pilate, and in the name of the Holy Spirit, who through the prophets foretold everything about Jesus.
>
> [Concerning the Eucharist] We, however, after thus washing the one who has been convinced and signified his assent, lead him to those who are called brethren, where they are assembled. They then earnestly offer common prayers for themselves and the one who has been illuminated and all others everywhere, that we may be made worthy, having learned the truth, to be found in deed good citizens and keepers of what is commanded, so that we may be saved with eternal salvation. On finishing the prayers we greet each other with a kiss. Then bread and a cup of water and mixed wine are brought to the president of the brethren and he, taking them, sends up praise and glory to the Father of the universe through the name of the Son and of the Holy Spirit, and offers thanksgiving at some length that we have been deemed worthy to receive these things from him. When he has finished the prayers and the thanksgiving, the whole congregation present assents, saying, "Amen." "Amen" in the Hebrew language means, "So be it." When the president has given thanks and the whole congregation has assented, those whom we call deacons give to each of those present a portion of the consecrated bread and wine and water, and they take it to the absent. This food we call Eucharist, of which no one is allowed to partake except one who believes that the things we teach are true, and has received the washing for forgiveness of sins and for rebirth, and who lives as Christ handed down to us.[11]

Pietistic and discreet in its phraseology though this is, Justin's description of these services tells us much about the spirit of second-century Christianity. Order and high ethical aspirations are associated with mystery necessary to consolidate the sense of brotherhood that was the feature of the sect. The baptismal liturgy, however, shows no traces of Pauline mysticism, of the convert's being baptized into Christ so that he might rise again with Christ. It is functional, obtaining for him remission of sins through illumination and rebirth. The Eucharist is rooted in the synagogue service with its readings from Scripture, psalms, sermon, and prayers, but it leads up to the solemn remembrance of the Last Supper ("This is my body. . . . Do this in remembrance of me [*anamnesis*]" [1 Cor. 11:25]),[12] and above all in Justin, to thanksgiving for the resurrection of Jesus and the salvation promised to believers. With the cult was developing a fixed hierarchy; Justin's "president" would soon be unequivocally the bishop and his assistant in the administration of the Eucharist, the deacon would become his right-hand man in other ways. The presbyterate charged with overseeing the community as such (see *The Letter of Polycarp to the Philippians* 6.1) would have to struggle hard to maintain its traditional seniority in the churches.

THE APOLOGISTS

Common liturgy, combining the arcane with the disciplinary, was to have an enormous effect in cementing the sense of community among the early Christians. In the second century their growing self-confidence and identity produced articulate defenders. The Apologists represented a movement contemporary with and parallel to Gnosticism and Marcionism. Like them, the Apologists were concerned with evolving a Gentile Christianity, and working out its relationship with the old Israel, with Greek philosophy, and with the Roman authorities. Like Gnosticism, too, the Apologetic movement had a history extending back into the first century and drawing on the legacy of Judaism before that. Luke-Acts and Matthew's Gospel were each in their own way apologies, the latter asserting that Jesus was indeed the Messiah who fulfilled the messianic prophecies, the former combining this claim with demonstrations from actual history that Christianity had been tolerated and even encouraged by the Roman authorities.

Between 130 and 200 the Christian Apologists tried to vindicate these claims against a combination of assailants.[13] Confronted by the growth of the Gnostic schools and Marcion's challenge, and by continual Jewish hostility and intermittent pagan persecutions, they sought to defend the orthodox position and convince their opponents. Often using the form of "open letters" addressed to the emperors or to pagan magistrates, their real target was literate provincial opinion. The amount they wrote suggests that there was a real market for these works of popular Christian philosophy among Christians and their opponents at this time.

The Apologists asserted that while they rejected idolatry—as cult and worship—in every form, they were loyal citizens of the empire which indeed benefited from their existence. They were not secretive adherents of an illegal and noxious society. If they were "atheists," they were atheists only in the sense that Diagoras, Heraclitus, and Socrates had been atheists. Against the claim by opponents, such as Lucian of Samosata, that Christianity was something of an imposture,[14] they claimed that theirs was the true and natural religion of humanity, and that even though Christ's appearance "had come so late in time," it had been foretold for centuries by the Hebrew prophets (the argument from prophecy). These were far earlier and therefore worthier of belief than the Greek philosophers.[15] Finally, the Apologists had to destroy the credibility of the Gnostics and Marcionites by demonstrating that God was the God of creation, whether in the Old or the New Testament, and that their church preserved the true tradition of faith handed down by Christ to the apostles and thence to the authoritative rulers of the church. Typical of their dexterity was the literary output of Miltiades, a lay orthodox writer in Phrygia (*flor.* 170–90). His work, unfortunately, has only survived in a fragment written against the Montanists. Eusebius, however, says that he wrote two books against the Gentiles, two against the Jews, and an apology addressed to the emperors.[16] This was defense against all comers. The Apologists mark an important stage in the transition from predominantly Jewish to predominantly Gentile Christianity.

The writings of five of the Greek Christian Apologists have survived, as well as the anonymous *Letter to Diognetus*; they are Aristides (c. 145), Justin Martyr (d. 165), Tatian (d. 180?), Athenagoras (c. 170–180), and Theophilus of Antioch (c. 180–85). In addition, a number of fragments have been preserved, mainly by Eusebius, including works of Quadratus, Melito of Sardis, and Apollinaris of Hierapolis (c. 170–80). They represent a wide and sometimes conflicting spectrum of orthodox Christian opinion.

Quadratus of Athens

Quadratus of Athens, who wrote an open letter to the emperor Hadrian in c. 125, was the father of the post-apostolic Apologists.[17] Jesus' miracles were put forward as proof of his claim to be Savior. Not long after, the writer of the *Preaching of Peter* (Alexandria?) outlined the first positive Christian apologetic aimed at both pagans and Jews. The latter was treated courteously. Their fault was their arrogance.[18] They believed they alone knew God, whereas they worshiped angels, as Paul claimed in Col. 2:18, "and the month and the moon," but pagans "sacrificed to corpses, not gods." They were "carried away by ignorance." (Quoted in Origen's *Commentary on the Gospel of John* XIII.17.)

Aristides

The earliest complete surviving *apologia*, that of Aristides (c. 145), is also the most Jewish-oriented and favorable to the Jews. In this respect, too, orthodoxy runs parallel to Gnosticism. The writer still breathes the world of late Judaism.[19] His religion is human-centered. The "beauty of the world" is "created for the Christians" ("Christianity" replacing "Israel"), and he follows Jewish tradition in dividing humankind into "races" according to their religion.[20] Paganism is dismissed in its cult and thought as hopeless error (as contemporary Gnostics would), but the Jews are praised. Like the Christians, they looked on themselves as mere sojourners in this world. Their only lapse from the truth was in their worship of angels:[21] "In the methods of their actions their service is to angels, not to God." The same reproach, as we have seen, is made by the writer of the *Preaching of Peter* and evidently formed part of standard Christian apologetic against the Jews at this time. On the contrary, the Christians alone worshiped God rightly and this worship was confirmed by their morality. The demands of Christianity quoted by Aristides—to look after the widow and orphan and to bury the dead—seem, however, to correspond to injunctions found in *2 Enoch* (*Book of the Secrets of Enoch* 51.1), *Sibylline Oracles*, Book III, or the book of Tobit.[22] The morality is still that of the Pharisees, but it is morality with a strong emphasis on action. Fasting was not merely ritual, but designed "to supply the needy with necessary food" (chap. 15).[23] Aristides thus continues the Christianity of *1 Clement* and of Polycarp's *Philippians*. It was the heir to the Hellenistic synagogue, but coordinated over wide areas in works of relief and mercy in a way which the Jewish Dispersion communities never seem to have attempted.

Letter to Diognetus

The attack on paganism contained in *Diognetus* (c. 150)[24] is similar to Aristides, but not necessarily dependent on it, and follows Hellenistic-Jewish apologetic found in Psalm 115, the book of Wisdom (13–15), and *Sibylline Oracles*, Book III. Pagans were "ignorant" (as in Aristides and in Jewish apologetic). They worshiped God's creation and not God. The idols were dumb and lifeless. They were made of wood and stone, and were helpless and useless.[25] The polemic, however, had a positive side for just as Philo had claimed that the Jews alone "saw God" and were a "race of suppliants" for the rest of humanity, so the anonymous writer claimed that the Christians had the responsibility of representing humanity to God. They were the soul itself of the human race.[26] Exploiting what appears to have been a philosophic commonplace originating from Plato, however, the writer gives one of the classic definitions of the role of the Christian in the world.

> Broadly speaking, what the soul is in the body, the Christians are in the world. The soul dwells in the body, but is not of the body, and the Christians dwell in the world but are not of the world. The soul, itself invisible, is guarded in the body that is visible. The Christians are known as being in the world, but their religion remains unseen.[27]

One may discern here that same blend of Hellenism and Judaism as in Aristides, but put much more elegantly by a writer of far higher skill and perception. In the first decades of the Christian era, the Jews had claimed to be the natural guides to the rest of humanity, and in the second century their religion also appeared to be "unseen" and needing "no temples made with hands."[28] Our author, however, rejected Judaism as decisively as he rejected paganism. He made no claim on behalf of the Christians to be "Israel" or "true Jews." That age had passed. The deadly hostility of Jews and pagans had to be accepted.[29] His was a Hellenistic Christianity based on a developing tradition and taking up the universalist role that only a generation or so before had been claimed for Judaism. If Christianity had come late, that was because God wanted to have no doubt as to humanity's inability to save the self.[30] Like Marcion, the author's reaction to the new religion was "amazement at God's love," but he believed that God had shown love from the beginning by making the world for humanity's sake and subjecting all living things to the first humans.[31] In this letter one may appreciate how Christianity had come to be accepted as the real fulfillment of Judaism by educated Greeks who accepted Jewish monotheism, ethics, and theology of history, but rejected Torah as a set of noisome irrelevancies. To such inquirers Christianity had come as a wondrous relief.

The writer of *Diognetus* was not original, but he systematized ideas that came to form the basis of the orthodox reply to Gnosticism. The Christian Gospels alone fulfilled the predictions of the Jewish prophets.

> Fear of the Lord is chanted and the grace of the prophets is recognized and the faith of the Gospels is established, and the grace of the Church has free and exulting course. And if you do not grieve this grace you will understand that the Word (Logos) speaks through whom he pleases and whenever he chooses.[32]

The argument from prophecy and the divine character of the Old Testament were part and parcel of his faith. At the same time, he emphasized the Christ-Word both as Savior and agent of creation, and said nothing about the Holy Spirit. His debt to current philosophy was deep if unavowed, and this, combined with his missionary purpose, places him (alongside his Gnostic rivals) among the forerunners of the Alexandrian tradition.

Justin Martyr

Compared with him, Justin Martyr was verbose, inconsistent, and not always convincing. A Platonist before he became a Christian, he never grasped the essential incompatibilities between Platonism and Christianity. He assimilated Jesus to the Logos of an eclectic Platonic and Stoic philosophy, arbitrarily and without understanding the implications either for the humanity of Christ or his relation within the Trinity to the Father. There is no evidence that he was influenced by any of the writers of the New Testament. He laid himself open to his Jewish opponent Trypho's well-directed thrust that the Christians "by receiving a worthless rumour, shape a kind of Messiah for themselves and perish for him blindly" (*Trypho* 8.4), and that they were trying to prove "impossibilities that God endured to be born and became a man" (*Trypho* 68.1). Yet Justin's importance is immense. He was the first orthodox writer to attempt an evaluation of the role of philosophy in Christian teaching. In his muddle-headed yet persistent way he succeeded in marking out the lines along which Christianity would seek to relate to philosophy and the Greco-Roman world, as well as to Judaism and the Old Testament, and to Gnostic and Marcionite unorthodoxy.

In *Trypho* (written c. 160) and the two *Apologies* (dating to c. 155 and 160 respectively), he elaborated with copious examples—sometimes enlightened by personal reminiscence—many of the arguments already set out in *Diognetus*. The argument from prophecy was the cornerstone of his defense of Christianity against all his opponents.[33] In his *First Apology*, his target was the pagans. After denying scornfully that Christians were guilty of cannibalism and incest, he claimed that Christ was the revelation of God in some ways analogous to the Stoic Seminal Word (that is, principle of growth),[34] but had enlightened humanity through the ages as a force. Thus all that had been good and valuable in the past, whether in the truths proclaimed by the poets and philosophers or by the Old Testament patriarchs, was implicitly Christian. "Those who lived in accordance with Reason (Logos)," said Justin, "are Christians, even though they were called godless, such as among the Greeks, Socrates, and Heraclitus and others like them; and among the barbarians, Abraham, Ananiah, Azariah and Mishael and Elijah and many others."[35] Through Jesus Christ, however, the Word had become fully revealed, and hence his followers the Christians participated in his revelation more completely than had the Jews and Greeks before them. Then, Justin went on, the prophets in the Old Testament were in a special way the conveyors of divine truths. Inspired by God through the Spirit, they taught the same truths as Christ subsequently taught, and they preceded the Greek poets in time. These had borrowed their wisdom from them.[36] Platonic philosophy had "plagiarized Moses," but like Philo and unlike Tatian, Justin did not hold this against the philosophers. It enabled him to take a more eclectic and critical view of the role of philosophy in Christianity. The Gnostics had criticized philosophers but had sought to integrate their teaching wholesale into Christianity, and had laid special emphasis on Homer. Justin, accepting fully Christianity's debt to the Old Testament and its prophetic revelation, was more wary. Elements in philosophy and particularly Platonism that could be harmonized with the latter were acceptable, but the remainder, along with the whole pagan cultus, must be rejected. Seeming similarities between some pagan and Christian ceremonies, as for instance in the offerings of bread and wine in Mithraism, were due to the evil work of demons.[37] These were the forces of destruction and confusion preventing humanity from accepting the truth represented by Christianity.

Against the Gnostics and Marcionites, Justin was equally severe,[38] though his works against them have not survived. Refuting Marcion, however, he claimed that all the events before Christ's appearance on earth, which were recorded in the Old Testament, had led up to the incarnation, the final act of God's self-revelation. Both Testaments were the work of one Creator God. In arguing thus, he set the pattern for abler exponents of orthodoxy than himself.

There was, however, another side to Justin. Alongside his philosophical arguments, he showed a strong emotional attachment towards an older stratum of Christian eschatology. He told his hearers that he believed that Christ and his angels would appear suddenly on the clouds of heaven, and there would follow the resurrection in which the souls of men and women would be reunited with bodies that had perished at death.[39] The Parousia (second coming) entailed both the coming of Christ, the renewal of heaven and earth, and the inheritance by the Christians of New Jerusalem.[40] Consciously Justin was reacting against Marcion, but also opposing the ideas of many whom he admits were of "pure and pious faith," and he also held to the idea of the earthly millennium in a rebuilt Jerusalem and the judgment thereafter. Just as Isaiah was sawn asunder,[41] so Christ would divide the Jews and the whole human race, and those who had done evilly in this life would suffer in eternal fire.[42] And those who (like the Gnostics) did not believe this would discover their mistake. In the last resort, as he showed in his final defiance at his trial, philosophy had not made his faith. His immediate reaction to Trypho's interest in his philosopher's gown was to ask him what could be gained from philosophy to equal that obtainable from Moses and the prophets.[43] Like Tertullian, he was a convert of the martyrs. "Isaiah sawn asunder" meant more to him than Plato's philosophy.

Justin's debate with Trypho at Ephesus (c. 135) is a reminder that, while the contestants may have shifted their ground, the argument between Jews and Christians continued as angrily as ever. Trypho was an educated Hellenistic Jew who had a knowledge of the Septuagint (LXX), Hebrew Scripture, and haggadic interpretation. He was not unrespectful of other religious outlooks, especially Platonism, but unbending when it came to the demands of Judaism.[44] He may have been a typical Jew of his time, Hellenistic but with a Palestinian background, and one who but for the catastrophe of Bar Kochba's rebellion might have continued to contribute much to the life of the Greco-Roman world. His discussion with Justin was courteous but unsparing. Justin showed that though he had ignored Judaism on his spiritual pilgrimage, he had picked up a wealth of knowledge of haggadic interpretations of Scripture at some stage of his life. As Trypho also used the Septuagint he found himself able to hold his own. While Trypho claimed that salvation had been promised to the Jews alone, Justin—like the writer of the *Letter of Barnabas* not long before—attempted to show that the Old Testament in its entirety belonged to the Christians. Salient events recounted therein, such as the appearance of the angels to Abraham at Mamre, referred to the preexistent Christ; the Passover lamb was a type of Christ's own sacrifice, the offering of the fine flour (Lev. 14:10) on behalf of those cleansed from leprosy a type of the eucharistic bread.[45] The ceremonial law too, on which Trypho laid so much stress, was secondary to the moral demands made in Scripture which were eternally binding. The Law should be understood spiritually, he urged, as Jeremiah had when he wrote of "the circumcision of the heart" (Jer. 4:4) rather than of the flesh.[46] Victory went to neither side, but one may sympathize with the Jews of the day having to listen to *Barnabas* and to Justin telling them that they did not understand their own Scriptures.[47]

Melito

Justin's younger contemporary Melito, bishop of Sardis (*flor.* 160–80), is also a Janus-like figure though, on the available evidence, recognizably Jewish-Christian in the way the term may be applied in the second century.[48] He argued with the Jews on their own terms, but he was equally ready to appeal to the emperors for toleration on the grounds of common interest between the Christian "philosophy" and the world monarchy founded by Augustus, in which Christ himself had grown up. Only "bad emperors" such as Nero and Domitian, persecuted the Christians.[49] For the rest, Melito seems to have stood in the loyalist tradition of Judaism and Christianity, accepting monarchy represented by the Roman emperor as the best (available) form of earthly government.

Melito was leader of a minority monotheist group in Sardis.[50] His main interest to historians lies in his attitude towards his orthodox Jewish neighbors. He was himself a Quartodeciman; that is, he accepted the Jewish computation of 14 Nisan as the date of Easter. Following in the footsteps of Babylonian rabbis, he undertook a study-tour in Palestine to satisfy the curiosity of one of his correspondents as to the "number of the ancient books [that is, the Old Testament], and the order in which they were placed."[51] Those who supplied him with the answers must have been Jews or Jewish Christians. All this suggests that Melito's community in Sardis was very much an offshoot of orthodox Jewry with little to offer pagan provincials. He himself was regarded in later tradition as a millenarian whose view of God tended toward the anthropomorphic.[52]

His surviving work, the *Homily on the Passion*, was probably preached as part of the Easter celebration of his church. The Quartodecimans began the commemoration with a fast extending from 14 Nisan to near dawn on 15 Nisan at which the celebrant commented at length on the deliverance of Israel told in Exodus 12. At cockcrow, the fast was interrupted by a love festival (*agape*) followed by the Eucharist. Baptisms were administered between these two events.[53] Melito's *Homily* is a long rhetorical sermon following the reading of Exodus 12 (the exodus of the Hebrews), and interpreting the events of the Passover typologically. The totality of the incidents refers to Christ and Christ alone. In agreement with Justin, but in contrast to Marcion, Melito interpreted the Old Testament, and the Passover narrative, as prefiguring the delivery of humanity from bondage through the sacrifice of Christ on the cross. Every incident in the Old Testament was oriented towards the New. Melito also drew on Jewish apologetic to show how Israel's righteous always suffered, from the time of Abel onward to the time of the prophets.[54] The lamb saved Israel with its blood; so Christ saved humanity.

Typology led to the concepts of progressive revelation perfected by Irenaeus. Here, however, it simply reinforced Melito's argument that the Old Testament was understood correctly only by the Christians and this served him as a weapon against the Jews. The second part of the *Homily* contains a violent attack against Judaism. "Why, Israel, did you commit this novel [*kainon*] injustice?"[55] The Jews and not Pilate were responsible for the crucifixion and thus for an unimaginable crime. The suffering Messiah was made to suffer at the hands of his own people. The Gentiles even treated him better, offering him vinegar and gall on the cross. Israel deservedly "lay dead."[56] The nations of the earth should come to Christ and receive remission from their sins. Melito's rhetoric almost reached hysteria as he lashed out at "ungrateful Israel." Thus the bitterness between the old Israel and new was increasing and becoming ever more permanent. Actions such as the incitement of the Jews in Smyrna against Polycarp were being answered in kind by Christian leaders in other towns in Asia Minor. In these years the seeds of Christian anti-Semitism were sown, and it would seem that the closer the two communities resembled each other the more deadly the enmity became.

Athenagoras

The last quarter of the second century saw some Christians turning from the endless bickering with the Jews. Athenagoras's *Supplication for the Christians* (written c. 176–80) was another "open letter" to the emperors.

His *Supplication*, addressed to Marcus Aurelius and Commodus, was written ostensibly to rebut the usual popular charges against the Christians. Athenagoras largely leaves "incest" and "cannibalism" on one side to concentrate on what he rightly assumed to be the real charge, namely, "atheism."[57] He argued, as Justin had, that Christianity was in harmony with the best of Greek philosophy. It reached nearer the truth than its rivals, and could be grasped by educated and uneducated alike. For him, God's existence and his unity could be proved by logical argument. Christians did not guess about his existence, like the poets and philosophers.

They learned from God's own witnesses, the prophets who were inspired by his Spirit.[58] Moreover, what was uncreated could only be one. God could not exist in or be derived from parts. Reason and Scripture, therefore, coincided to demonstrate the truth of Christianity, and hence its claim to respect and toleration.[59]

Athenagoras derived his arguments from current Middle Platonism. In attacking paganism he dispensed with the "dumb idol" charges favored by earlier Apologists and relied on those which, though used by the Hellenistic Jews, were shared with Cynic and popular Stoic preachers. The pagan gods existed, but they were originally humans.[60] He quotes Herodotus (*History* II.156) to demonstrate that "Apollo and Artemis were the children of Dionysus and Isis, and that Leto was their nurse who saved them [from death]." Osiris ("whom the Greeks call Apollo") himself had been declared a god through his discovery of grain. Prometheus was the first mortal to control fire. The arguments went back ultimately to the Sicilian philosopher Euhemerus (*flor.* c. 315 B.C.), and were taken up by the writer of the Jewish *Sibylline Oracles*, Book III, lines 108–13 (c. 150 B.C.). (Cf. Athenagoras, *Supplication,* chap. 30.) Their use at this period by Christians as well as Cynics is perhaps a further indication how both groups were competing for converts among confused or disillusioned East Roman provincials.

Athenagoras, however, was a man of the "establishment." He was a slave owner and took slavery for granted.[61] Like Justin, he had come to accept Christianity as the true philosophy and he regarded it as an entirely positive force in society.[62] He was loyal, even obsequious, to the empire and emperors, stressing the emperor's activity for peace, his love for his subjects (*philanthropia*), his establishment of justice and harmony throughout the empire and peace for the cities, and his personal love of learning.[63] Athenagoras links what he considers the best values of contemporary pagan society with his new faith, and incidentally anticipates the qualities expected of a Christian ruler in the early Byzantine age. Theodosius II was described by the Byzantine historian Socrates in much the same terms as those used by Athenagoras.[64] If Justin and Melito reflected both past and future attitudes towards the empire, Athenagoras set his face firmly towards the harmony of Christianity and the state. Christian Platonism could never be the philosophy of a rebel.

Athenagoras represents the beginnings of new trends within orthodox Christianity. From now on there would always be the risk of cleavage between educated Greek-speaking Christians who were prepared to think of philosophy as an aid towards apprehending Christian truth, and those to whom paganism in every form was simply "idolatry." Once again, tensions that had arisen within Judaism were emerging in its successor. When in c. 175 the Christians at Alexandria, the center of the Greek philosophical world, established a school of instruction under a converted Stoic named

Pantaenus aimed particularly at making converts among educated Greeks, the problem became actual.[65] Other pointers showed how Christianity was emerging from recognizably Jewish attitudes. Justin perhaps, and Irenaeus certainly, end the tradition of pseudonymity among Christian writers. Down to 135 at least, this had been the rule. Writings, including even apologetic writings, were placed under the names of apostles such as "Barnabas," "James," "Peter," "Jude," or "The Twelve Apostles" as demonstrating that these represented the true workings of the Spirit and therefore guaranteed orthodoxy.[66] In the same way the Jews recalled the names of great figures of their past such as Ezra and Baruch as the "authors" of their apocalyptic and prophetic works in the first century A.D. Now Christian authors, like their pagan contemporaries, set their own names to their works—a sign perhaps that they expected the church's stay in the world to be a lengthy one. In addition, they were beginning to preserve accurate records of their past.

Hegesippus

Hegesippus (*flor.* 175), probably a converted Palestinian Jew, was the first Christian who attempted to collect historical material concerning the church, notably the church at Jerusalem under James and his successors, and about the family of Jesus. His *Memoirs* (*Hypomnēmata*) survived to aid Eusebius of Caesarea compile his *Ecclesiastical History* in the first decades of the fourth century.[67]

Hegesippus is also a witness to a change taking place in the organization of the church. Down to 150 it seems that though episcopacy had become the normal form of organization there was still a certain flexibility in the status of the leadership, not least in major sees such as Rome. Both Justin Martyr and Dionysius of Corinth refer to the respective leaders of their communities as "chairman" (*proestos*).[68] This can hardly be mere carelessness. The term *episcopos* (bishop) had been in current use for a century, and Dionysius certainly knew of "bishops" elsewhere because he mentions those of Gortyna and Knossos in Crete and Palmas as bishop of Amastris in Pontus.[69] It looks as though in Rome and Corinth there was, as Robert Grant suggests, a "presiding presbyter" in charge, with other presbyters, deacons, and lectors (readers) to assist.[70] The first bishop of Rome who emerges clearly on the stage of history is Anicetus (c. 154–66) with whom Polycarp had discussions on the question of the date of Easter.[71]

Twenty years later, there can be no doubts. Monarchical episcopacy had become almost self-consciously the sole form of orthodox government in the churches. Hegesippus, traveling to Corinth and Rome c. 175, made it his duty to draw up lists of episcopal successions and trace these back to the foundation of the Christian community. He noted that the bishops he met all had "the same doctrine" (*didascalia*).[72] The tradition of monarchical bishops in Rome extending back to Peter and Paul and their successor Linus may perhaps be traced to one such list.[73]

IRENAEUS

In Irenaeus of Lyons (c. 130–200) these trends found forceful expression. Orthodoxy also found a champion, one who combined a relatively long life with a photographic memory and a determined character, and, though often verbose, possessed the ability to systematize ideas and sum up an argument in a few pungent sentences. Some of these have passed into the permanent heritage of the church. While Justin claimed to be a philosopher and treated philosophy as an ally, Irenaeus found he could not get on without it although he would have done so gladly. Some of his contributions to Christian thought were as indebted to contemporary philosophy as were those of his Gnostic opponents, but Plato was not welcome in his scheme. One suspects that he knew Plato's work at second hand only. No one who knew his Plato would speak of "Plato that ancient Athenian" and assert that he was the first to teach the doctrine of metempsychosis, confusing him with the Pythagoreans.[74] It would seem from Justin's experience with the old man at Ephesus that this aspect of Pythagorean and Platonic teaching had for a long time been attacked by Jewish and Christian Apologists. Irenaeus does not hide his antagonism toward any philosophic approach to Christianity that he blamed for providing the inspiration for the systems he so bitterly opposed and whose aims he so little understood.[75] For him, Christianity rested on revelation, on tradition, and on the power of the Holy Spirit. When he looked for theological proofs he went to the Bible.

Irenaeus (his name translates into Hebrew as "Solomon" or "Man of Peace," and Hebrew was not an unknown tongue to him)[76] was a native of Smyrna. As a young man he fell under Polycarp's spell and carried vivid early memories of him throughout his life.[77] He emigrated, probably to Rome. He was almost certainly acquainted with Justin's works and the supposition is that he may have studied under him in Rome.[78] Later, however, he moved to Lyons. He escaped the holocaust of 177, and accompanied members of the church to Rome to discuss the New Prophecy with Bishop Eleutherus there.[79] He had some sympathy with this as a movement of the Spirit. On his return, he was chosen by the survivors at Lyons to succeed the martyred bishop Pothinus, and found himself at odds with a Valentinian Gnostic movement which combined the approach to Scripture represented by Ptolemy's letter to Flora, Pythagorean number-symbols, and a strong mystical element.[80] Irenaeus's five books *Against the Heresies* (written c. 180–85) were his reply and they provide the classic statement of orthodoxy in the primitive Greek-speaking church. A decade or so later he wrote a smaller handbook of Christian apologetic, the *Proof of the Apos-*

tolic Preaching, addressed to one Marcianus who may have been hesitating between Judaism, Gnosticism, and orthodoxy as his spiritual home. In this, he first explained the teaching of Christianity and then set out to prove its truth from the writings of the prophets. In this proof philosophy played no part. About 195, near the end of his life, he found himself again mediating between contending parties. This time Victor of Rome was quarreling with the churches in Asia over longstanding differences about the dating and conduct of the Easter festival. He was threatening them with excommunication if they failed to obey his ruling: Easter should not be celebrated on 14 Nisan (the day on which the Passover lamb was slain), regardless of the day of the week, but rather the Easter fast should be observed from Friday until Sunday following 14 Nisan, when it would be succeeded by a joyful Eucharist celebrating the resurrection. Irenaeus wrote a courteous but forceful letter condemning his dictatorial act even if his views about Easter were correct.[81] Peace and unity must be maintained in the church above all else.

Against the Gnostics and Marcionites the main issue was authority. Irenaeus came straight to the point. Christianity was a faith "spoken with one voice" based on the tradition handed down to the churches by the apostles and accepted by Christians everywhere. In his words:

Now the Church, although scattered over the whole civilized world to the end of the earth, received from the apostles and their disciples its faith in one God, the Father Almighty, who made the heaven, and the earth, and the seas, and all that is in them, and in one Christ Jesus, the Son of God, who was made flesh for our salvation, and in the Holy Spirit, who through the prophets proclaimed the dispensations of God—the comings, the birth of a virgin, the suffering, the resurrection from the dead, and the bodily reception into the heavens of the beloved, Christ Jesus our Lord, and his coming from the heavens in the glory of the Father to restore all things, and to raise up all flesh, that is, the whole human race, so that every knee may bow, of things in heaven and on earth and under the earth, to Christ Jesus our Lord and God and Saviour and King, according to the pleasure of the invisible Father, and every tongue may confess him, and that he may execute righteous judgment on all.[82]

Elsewhere, he pointed out that the faith was based on the tradition of the gospels handed down to the apostles and "is guarded by the succession of the elders in the churches."[83] There were no "hidden mysteries" to which the Gnostic leaders could claim access. The Bible alone had authority.

This was the Rule of Faith observable everywhere and by Christians whatever their capacities and intelligence. If Irenaeus often failed to understand the problems the Gnostics were seeking to solve, he was clear about his own position. God was one; that unity penetrated the whole creation and all human history. Moreover, Irenaeus's monotheism was Hebraic rather than Greek and his sense of time was linear, not cyclical; God was active in creation which came into being at one point in time and ended at another. His "two hands" were the Son and Holy Spirit and they as "Word" and "Wisdom" were always with him.[84] There were indeed distinctions in their functions, but he would not speculate on these. "The Father is he that anoints, the Son is he who is anointed, and the Spirit is the unction" (*Heresies* III.18.3). He avoided the question put by so many of his contemporaries: *how* had God come to act in the beginning? He refused to identify the Son with the Reason or Mind of God emanated by him. If God was wholly Reason, he argued, then to attribute to God's mind an emanation could make God a composite being (*Heresies* II.28.5). Here, as Jean Daniélou has pointed out, the Gnostics had realized the problem existed even if they failed to solve it.[85] Irenaeus retreated into biblical formulas ("Who shall describe his generation?" [Isa. 53:8]), and one may suspect some rabbinical reminiscence, when he answered the Jewish schoolbook question—what was God doing before he made the world?—not by saying that he was preparing hell for philosophers, but by treating those who asked with scorn. "People should not try to force from him foolish, rash and blasphemous explanations" (*Heresies* II.28.3). There was a limit beyond which human intelligence could not and should not try to penetrate—an attitude which Western Christianity was to accept down to the period of the scientific revolution of the eighteenth century.

If God was one, then God who created the universe was the God of Israel in the Old Testament. Like Justin, either through his direct influence or because he was using a similar catena of *Testimonies*, Irenaeus attributed the appearances of God in the Old Testament to his Son, "showing God to man in many ways lest man wholly lacking God, should cease to exist."[86] Human being, therefore, was not the result of creation by an inferior God or by evilly disposed powers, but was made by God, through divine benevolence and for a set purpose. Like God, human beings also were one and their flesh would be saved as well as their souls. At the same time, they had been endowed with free will and, therefore, tendencies towards the carnal and spiritual. There was no contrast between the "spiritual man" who was the work of the Invisible God, and the "natural man" made by the Creator God. Man and woman had originally been created "in the likeness of God," but through the Fall that likeness had been obscured. The "image [*eikon*] of God" remained, but humans now needed the Spirit through which to regain the likeness (*homoiosis*) forfeited by Adam's disobedience.[87] United to the Spirit humans would be restored to the original state through faith in Christ who was the very image of God.[88] The Eucharist, "the Body and Blood of Christ" was the means through which the flesh was nourished and made incorruptible. The history of humankind told in the two Testaments was the story of that restoration, of humanity's gradual recovery of that likeness. The Old Testament recorded how humans moved from infancy towards maturity, each stage being marked by a covenant with God, that of Noah, of Abraham, and of Moses, leading through the prophets to the supreme manifestation of God through the Word, his Son, at the incarnation (*Heresies* III.11.8). Humanity moved slowly forward by its own free will towards reconciliation with God until "What we lost in Adam, we might regain in Christ, namely, the image and likeness of God."[89] The Spirit was continually renewing the church until the dispensations of God had been completed. Ultimately, humanity would be restored to its pre-Adam status by the abolition of sin and its effect, death, and raised to a higher form of being, "passing beyond the angels."[90]

Salvation, therefore, had been a process of education. Each covenant had been valid for its time but had been superseded when it had served its purpose. Scripture told the story. The apostles teach us, explained Irenaeus, that "the two Testaments were ordained by one and the same God" for the benefit of humankind.[91] The types and prefigurations of heavenly things characteristic of the Old Testament were shown by God, because humanity was not yet able with its own powers of sight to look upon the things of God, and those things were prefigured in images that now existed in the church, in order that our faith might be firmly established (*Heresies* IV.32.2).

Irenaeus could explain why standards in the Old Testament were obviously lower than in the New without recourse to Gnostic or Marcionite arguments contrasting the evil or bare natural justice of the Creator God with the love and goodness of God, the Father of Jesus Christ. Progress did not consist in passing from the authority of the one to the other, but in humanity gradually moving to a superior level of ability to accept God's revelation. The Law preceded Christ because humanity was not in a fit state to accept more at that time. Instead of Christ "suddenly appearing" at Capernaum, the messenger from an unknown God, the incarnation marked the climax in the ordered regularity of humanity's development. Now, the whole of humanity's previous progress towards salvation was summed up. Christian history both prolonged and fulfilled that of the Jews. Point by point, Christ as Second Adam had reversed the errors committed by Adam at the Fall. In well-known words, Irenaeus described how Christ triumphant "recapitulated" or summed up in himself the entirety of human experience.

So the Lord now manifestly came to his own, and, born by his own created order which he himself bears, he by his obedience on the tree renewed [and reversed] what was done by disobedience in [connection with] a tree; and [the power of] that seduction by which the virgin Eve, already betrothed to a man, had been wickedly seduced was broken when the angel in truth brought good tidings to the Virgin Mary, who already [by her betrothal] belonged to a man. For as Eve was seduced by the word of an angel to flee from God, having rebelled against his Word, so Mary by the word of an angel received the glad tidings that she would bear God by obeying his Word. The former was seduced to disobey God [and so fell], but the latter was persuaded to obey God, so that

247

the Virgin Mary might become the advocate of the virgin Eve. As the human race was subjected to death through [the act of] a virgin, so was it saved by a virgin, and thus the disobedience of one virgin was precisely balanced by the obedience of another.[92]

Moreover, in his earthly life Christ had sanctified each age of humankind from infancy even to old age itself, thus joining humanity to God and making it a partaker of incorruptibility (*Heresies* III.18.7 and 19.3).

Much of this, even to its details, was consciously Pauline, and interestingly the same theme is found later most forcefully expressed in the East Syrian tradition represented by Ephraem Syrus.[93] Others, including Luke, had had some sense of the reversal of the past brought about by Christ's coming. Pentecost, where all could understand each other though drawn from different races (Acts 2:7ff.), was the opposite to what happened at Babel. A historical sense of salvation, too, had become inevitable once the relationship of the two Testaments was seen in terms of typology, the lessons of the Old Testament foreshadowing the teaching of the New. To Irenaeus, however, belongs the credit of systematizing these ideas and welding them into a coherent theology, of applying the current concept of education (*paideia*) to the relation between the Old and New Covenant. Judaism, he could say, was superseded. It was "the first synagogue" whose "husband was the Law," but Christ was "Lord of the Law," and Christians had "no need of the Law as a tutor," when they "kept the sabbath perpetually" by serving God.[94] At this point the Gnostics, especially Ptolemy, and Irenaeus would have found much in common. Neither accepted the contemporary validity of the stark prohibitions of the Decalogue and the retributive justice of other parts of the Mosaic Law, but their solutions were radically different.

Irenaeus's solution was accepted by the church, but a price was exacted. Where Ptolemy encouraged inquiry and intellectual adventure, Irenaeus offered a closed system. He loved to contrast the unchanging church with the discordant and fissiparous sects. The faith was "ever one and the same" incapable of addition or diminution.[95] Salvation depended on the acceptance of set forms of belief, organization, and worship. The horror with which Irenaeus greeted the deviant beliefs of his old friend Florinus boded ill for those who stepped beyond permitted orthodoxy.[96] Christianity threatened to become as legalistic in its own way as the Judaism it repudiated. In detail, too, Irenaeus would have been hard put to answer Marcion's point by point attack on the Old Testament, for by no stretch of imagination could the stories of rape, slaughter, treachery, and adultery that it condoned be brought within even the broadest framework of "education." Yet Irenaeus must be credited with bringing a sense of history into the Christian concept of salvation, which Marcion's ideas lacked, while rejecting the bizarre features of the Gnostic systems. He preserved the church's continuity with the Jewish past which, however unwelcome, was indispensable at the time. Progress and change for the better became central to Christianity's missionary appeal in opposition to the pagan's undeviating acceptance of custom.

If Irenaeus was a pioneer in his theology, his concept of the church and its work followed more traditional lines. He was a pastor moved as in the prayer found in *1 Clement* (LXIX.6) to "reclaim the wanderers and convert them to the Church of God," and to "confirm the minds of the neophytes." The catholic, or universal church was the means through which salvation was obtained. Its teaching had been established by the apostles and "made clear in all the world."[97] The Eucharist united God and creation by imparting Christ's divine life to believers and guaranteed the regeneration of the flesh.

> Vain above all are they who despise the whole dispensation of God, and deny the salvation of the flesh and reject its rebirth, saying that it is not capable of incorruption. For if this [mortal flesh] is not saved, then neither did the Lord redeem us by his blood, nor is the cup of the Eucharist the communion of his blood, and the bread which we break the communion of his body (1 Cor. 10:16). For blood is only to be found in veins and flesh, and the rest of [physical] human nature, which the Word of God was indeed made [partaker of, and so] he redeemed us by his blood. So also his apostle says, "In whom we have redemption by his blood, and the remission of sins" (Col. 1:14). For since we are his members, and are nourished by [his] creation—and he himself gives us this creation, making the sun to rise, and sending the rain as he wills—he declares that the cup, [taken] from the creation, is his own blood, by which he strengthens our blood, and he has firmly assured us that the bread, [taken] for the creation, is his own body, by which our bodies grow. For when the mixed cup and the bread that has been prepared receive the Word of God, and become the Eucharist, the body and blood of Christ, and by these our flesh grows and is confirmed, how can they say that flesh cannot receive the free gift of God, which is eternal life, since it is nourished by the body and blood of the Lord, and made a member of him?[98]

In the Eucharist, therefore, believers participated in Christ and were redeemed. The distinctive marks of the church were the proclamation of the Word based on Scripture and the identification of the Christian with Christ through baptism and the Eucharist. Pauline mysticism, absent from the writings of second-century orthodox leaders, was being restored to a more central role in Christian thought by Irenaeus.[99]

The government of the church had been committed by the apostles to the succession of elders that continued to his own time. For Irenaeus, Polycarp was the outstanding example of an apostolic man,[100] just as Rome was the outstanding example of an apostolic see. Men such as he had received gifts of the Spirit and must be obeyed. "Therefore obedience," says Irenaeus, "is due to those presbyters who, as we have shown, are in the succession after the Apostles, having received, according to the will of the Father, a certain *charisma* of truth."[101] Succession, therefore, implied government and authority, but Irenaeus based this less on mechanical succession than on the fact that the Spirit had been present in the apostles and continued in these elders. However authoritarian in appearance, the church remained the church of the Spirit. Irenaeus mentions how he himself had encountered people raised from the dead by those with spiritual gifts.[102] It is interesting that the one non-canonical book that Irenaeus would admit as worthy to be read in church was the prophetic work *The Shepherd of Hermas.*[103] Finally, his hopes for the ultimate deification of the believer were combined with a strong belief in the joys of the thousand years' rule of the just. The general resurrection would be preceded by the millennium portrayed in terms derived from Papias as an extravaganza of prosperity. New Jerusalem would descend on a new earth. "The whole creation would obtain a vast increase."[104] To one thinking in such apocalyptic terms prophecy and the prophet still had a part to play.

EMERGENT ORTHODOXY

Irenaeus exaggerates the unity and singleness of purpose of the church in the late second century. He expressed a number of tendencies, however, that were converging to form a pattern of orthodoxy. The position it had achieved was impressive. Christianity in Irenaeus's time was more united than at any time before or since. Statements of belief were becoming standardized throughout the Christian communities. Irenaeus's Rule of Faith was not confined to Lyons. Similar documents were in use in Carthage and Alexandria. A recognizably early credal statement is contained in a Christian papyrus from Der Balyzeh (Dair Balaizeh) in Upper Egypt.[105] The church's liturgy was, as we have noted, evolving into a fixed pattern. The form of Eucharist described by Justin was a binding force celebrated wherever there were Christians. The Phrygian merchant, Avircius Marcellus, who became bishop of Hieropolis c. 200, found the same orthodoxies, the same Eucharist, and the same welcome among Christians all the way from Nisibis (on the Euphrates frontier) to Rome.[106] Pope Victor's instruction during the Easter controversy (c. 195) that councils, evidently provincial, should meet "from Rome to Osrhoene," was capable of being carried out.[107]

The New Testament Canon

Most important of all was the emergence of a fixed canon of Scripture that gave the church its own sacred book, different from that of the Jews and in no way dependent on any pagan or Gnostic literature. Marcion had made the earliest attempt to form a canon of Christian Scripture, but others also offered such guidelines. Irenaeus mentions how the Ebionites regarded Matthew as the only valid Gospel;[108] and combined with their use of Hebrew as the "language of Jesus" it long remained so.[109] It was not possible to refute opponents such as Ptolemy until a canon of Scripture had been defined, and between 170 and 200 there were efforts in many churches, especially in Asia Minor, to agree upon one. Dispute centered on the Johannine works. Were these the work of the apostle, or were they the work of another, even of the heretic Cerinthus? Some (the so-called *Alogi*) refused to accept John's Gospel as canonical, while on the other side of the Mediterranean in Egypt, it seems to have been in use since c. 125.[110] Other churches accepted apocryphal gospels, such as the *Gospel of Peter* read by the church of Rhossus in the Gulf of Issus.[111] In Alexandria the elite among the Christians may have used a "secret Gospel" of their founder Mark,[112] which included a story of the raising of Lazarus and baptismal rites supposedly initiated by Jesus himself. Episcopal authority prevented the widespread use of apocryphal literature in orthodox churches, reinforced by Irenaeus's robust (if whimsical) assertion that as there were only four winds there could only be four Gospels.[113] By about 200 the process of selection and rejection was almost complete. The early Latin (probably Roman) document listing books to be read and others to be rejected (known as the Muratorian Canon) shows that a New Testament had come into being very similar to our own, especially in its order of the books.[114] It included, however, the Wisdom of Solomon and the *Apocalypse of Peter*, but omitted 1 and 2 Peter, the letter to the Hebrews and 3 John. The *Shepherd* of Hermas might be read, but not publicly as Scripture, as it was not an apostolic document. As Adolf von Harnack pointed out, the Muratorian Canon was a document written with authority; it was intended as a guide to Christendom as a whole and to give an example that was expected to be followed. The Rome of Pope Victor might be an obvious place of origin. In any event, the canon of Scripture took its place with episcopacy, the Rule of Faith, and the liturgy to provide the basis for a disciplined and unified church.

THREATS TO UNITY

The measure of unity achieved in the church by c. 180 depended on its government staying in the hands of like-minded Greek-speaking bishops, whether resident in the cities of the Aegean or in Rome, able and willing to communicate with each other by letter or in council. This situation, however, was not to last. Among the Gnostics, Marcionites, and Ebionites[115] were a fair number of those who called themselves Christians. As the church succeeded in combating them other problems arose. There was first an incipient regionalism among the older established communities. An Aramaic-based Christianity in East Syria and Osrhoene centered on Edessa[116] continued to move toward an ascetic and self-renouncing outlook. Tatian's *Harmony of the Gospels* (*Diatessaron*) was read by at least some of the communities in the Euphrates garrison towns (a fragment was found at Dura-Europos).[117] Among the Greek-speaking churches, Antioch provides

251

evidence of a distinct theological direction which would be maintained into the fifth century. Second, the prophetic tradition, never entirely silent, revived explosively in the Montanist movement in Phrygia. Notice was being served that interpretations of Christianity in the countryside would not always coincide with those that satisfied Christians in the cities.

Theophilus of Antioch

Antioch was becoming the focus of a tradition, one that echoed Irenaeus's contempt for philosophy, including Plato, but which shows more obviously Jewish influences. Theophilus of Antioch (c. 180) may be contrasted with other Greek Apologists. His outlook resembles that of Tatian rather than the latter's master Justin. His letter addressed to the pagan Autolycus, though Christian in form and missionary in aim, was Hellenistic-Jewish in content, and written in a city where Judaism remained a powerful force.[118] Theophilus had nothing but indignant hostility for paganism. "Those who laid down such doctrines have filled the world with impiety," he cried. Greek literature was useless. Plato was held up to ridicule;[119] like Tatian, he scorned the immorality of the pagan gods and stigmatized the "theft" by otherwise discordant philosophers of truths enunciated by the Hebrew prophets.[120] All Greek writers were inferior to them. In this respect he was drawing heavily on the older streams of Hellenistic-Jewish apologetic, especially on the *Sibylline Oracles* (which he quotes no less than eighty-six times). For him, Moses indeed is "our prophet" who "delivered the law to the whole world, though especially to the Hebrews."[121] His quotations from Josephus's *Apion*, his elaborate chronologies and numerology, and his exegesis of Genesis betray a Jewish origin. Almost everything he says, R. M. Grant points out, could be paralleled in Jewish and Jewish-Christian writings.[122] Most important of all, his doctrine of the Word is derived from Hellenistic-Jewish sources "further developed in the light of Stoic and rhetorical refinements." The Word remained as Thought within God as his Counselor, Mind, and Intelligence as "innate" (*Logos endiathetos*). Before creation, however, it became the Word "expressed" (*Logos prophorikos*), "spoken" by God at the moment of creation, and represented by Spirit, Power of the Most High, Light, Voice, and Son.[123] In the last-named, it was to be identified with Jesus Christ, preexisting from all ages. Antioch was developing its own distinctive Christology and biblical exegesis, which when expounded by Paul of Samosata eighty years later would be denounced as "Jewish" and heretical by its opponents,[124] especially the Alexandrians.

Clement of Alexandria

Even now the real foil to Theophilus was to be his contemporary Clement of Alexandria (*flor.* 180–203). Clement was a convert to Christianity. Like Justin, he had been a wandering scholar, who had attached himself to an astonishing number of Christian teachers before settling in Alexandria. As he says, "One was in Greece . . . the next in Magna Graecia . . . others in the East, and in this region one was an Assyrian, the other a Palestinian, a Hebrew by descent"[125]—another indication of the spread of Christianity in the eastern provinces of the empire by the last quarter of the second century. Clement emerged from his teachers as successor to Pantaenus as head of the catechetical school at Alexandria. There he showed himself strongly missionary-minded. He valued the Hebrew legacy of Christianity that he found in Alexandria but also tended to push it into the background in favor of the greatest possible accommodation with Greek philosophy. In his three works, *Protrepticus* (*Exhortation*), *Paidagogus* (*Tutor*), and *Stromata* (*Miscellanies*), he described the Christian's progress toward perfection, elaborated a theology that, whether wittingly or not, substituted Philo's Logos for the Holy Spirit and conceived Christ in terms little different from those current among the Alexandrian Gnostics. Far from rejecting Greek philosophy as Theophilus did, he claimed that it formed an essential part of the Greek convert's grounding. "The law is for the Jew what philosophy is for the Greek, a schoolmaster to bring them to Christ."[126] Clement's objection to Gnosticism was that it lay outside the church and was offensive to human freedom of will and common sense. But like the Gnostics, his Christianity favored the formation of an intellectual elite, paralleled, he claimed, by Jesus' inner circle of favored disciples—Peter, James, and John—to whom he released his secret teaching, and to which Clement eventually added Paul.[127]

Here was an entirely different interpretation of Christianity, claiming to be orthodox and gaining predominance among the orthodox in the leading intellectual center of the Hellenistic world. Greek Christianity was already beginning to divide between Antioch, penetrated by Hellenistic Judaism and hostility to the pagan world, and Alexandria, where Greek intellectual values were respected and were being absorbed into a philosophic Christianity which owed much to Philo. Moreover, by the 180s the spread of Christianity to North Africa was beginning to confront the hitherto-dominant Greek churches with new problems. How was unity to be maintained with a Latin-speaking church whose members did not share the assumptions of and had few other affinities with the Greek-speaking East? Victor, the first Latin-speaking pope (189–99), and Tertullian (c. 160–240) were portents of a new age in church history.

The Montanists

The more immediate threat to Christian unity came from the Montanist movement in Phrygia. Christians in that province of Asia Minor, probably prior to 172, were startled by the appearance of Montanus, perhaps a onetime priest of Cybele, accompanied by two companions, Prisca and Maximilla, who claimed to be prophets inspired by the Paraclete.[128] They announced that the Parousia would take place near the villages of Tymion and Pepuza some fifteen miles east of Philadelphia.[129] The area is described as a "desert place," and Montanus's announcement represents a revival of the wilderness theory of the second coming accompanied by an outpouring of prophetic utterances. It was heard gladly. The prophets spoke of the millennium; people abandoned homes, families, and work, and streamed out into the countryside. Wars and rumors of wars were freely foretold, death as a martyr was accepted, and this was to be prepared for by fasting and abstinence as the command of the Holy Spirit.[130]

Discussion concerning the origins and inspiration of the movement has developed since Wilhelm Schepelern's study in 1929. Schepelern examined minutely, but ultimately discarded, the view that Montanism was in any way a revival within Christianity of the Phrygian cults of Mên, Cybele, and Dionysus.[131] He concluded that Montanism was a movement within the church that was inspired by the continuing Jewish-Christian apocalyptic tradition among the Christians in Asia Minor of which the book of Revelation and the writings of Papias were examples.[132] Others have also stressed the Jewish-Christian aspects of Montanism,[133] while still others have included the Fourth Gospel as well as Revelation in the Montanist line of descent.[134] All this is true, but the point might also be made that no contemporary author or ancient Christian writer claimed Montanus as a Jew or an Ebionite. Epiphanius of Salamis (d. 397), a former Jew and avid heresy-hunter, could hardly have failed to mention the fact. Prophecy, asceticism, and martyrdom, the hallmarks of Montanism, all belong to the second-century Christian tradition, but the public acknowledgment of sin, especially sexual uncleanliness in a sacred area, and admission of a penalty exacted by the gods were part and parcel of the religion of the provincials along the borders of Phrygia and Lydia-Mysia where Montanism was also strong.[135] Some interconnections cannot be ruled out. At the same time, there was nothing pagan about the Montanists' adherence to 14 Nisan as the date of Easter,[136] their prolongation of fasts until sundown instead of the ninth hour, as customary in the great church, and their practice of "dry fasts" (*xerophagia*). These must be of Jewish origin.[137] Equally, the place occupied by the Paraclete in Montanist theology, their hopes of martyrdom, and the coming of the millennium are surely Johannine. Their opponents in Asia Minor, the *Alogi*, refused to accept either the Gospel or Revelation of John ascribing both to Cerinthus, while anti-Montanist clergy in Rome, such as the learned presbyter Caius, also rejected the book of Revelation.[138]

Many elements contributed to Montanism, and this perhaps accounts for the movement's extraordinary tenacity in the face of persecution by orthodox Christians for centuries to come, and despite the failure of their prophecies to materialize. Prophecy in particular had a long history within and outside Christianity in Phrygia. Prophets of Cybele were part of the Phrygian scene, but there had also been a tradition of Christian prophets that had grown up alongside the bishops. The church of Philadelphia had been singled out by the Seer in Revelation on account of its zeal (Rev. 3:7–8). It was the church that he loved, and the "open door" before it suggests missions as well as prophetic enthusiasm. At Hierapolis in the same province, the evangelist Philip and his four daughters, all reputed prophetesses, were believed to have been laid to rest.[139] Later in the second century prophets such as Quadratus and Ammia (this a good Phrygian name) had flourished.[140] All told, with the large and long-established Jewish communities scattered around the province, the influence of an apocalyptic-minded church at Philadelphia, and a native religious tradition which tended towards violent and orgiastic religious manifestations, the emergence of Montanus's movement in Phrygia is not surprising. The orthodox clergy ran scared.

They were in a quandary. They could not deny that the Spirit was active in the church and manifested itself in prophecy, particularly with the approach of the last times—the Parousia. However outwardly normal their lives, this was what many Christians wanted to hear. At Lyons, those Christians who were arrested by the governor in 177 were, regardless of social status, described as "boiling over with the Spirit," and their leader Blandina in her zeal was praised as acting like a "Maccabaean mother." They believed persecution was a sign of the approaching end and they welcomed it.[141] In parts of Syria and Palestine also, Christianity was characterized by wandering prophets proclaiming that they were "God" or the "Son of God" and foretelling doom.[142] Montanism was a focus for a great deal of the latent apocalypticism, extreme ascetic practices, and yearning for martyrdom that characterized Christian protest not only in Phrygia during the reign of Marcus Aurelius. The church was still the church of the Spirit and no one in authority wished to be branded as a "slayer of the prophets"—as the Montanists branded their opponents.[143]

Women, too, had traditionally played a role in prophecy—extending back to Deborah and Huldah and sanctified in the New Testament by Anna (Luke 2:36). The writer of *l Clement* also (12.8) named Rahab, "not only as an instance of faith but also of prophecy" with the stress on prophecy. There was, however, always opposition from representatives of institutional religion. In the time of the Ezra/Nehemiah restoration, however, the representatives of the new orthodoxy had fought hard to discredit women prophets. Nehemiah classed the "prophetess Noadiah and the rest of the prophets" among his enemies (Neh. 6:14). Now, after six centuries, the new Israel was confronted with the same problem, either an organized urban and hierarchical church with set forms of worship and discipline and a set relationship with the outside world, or a church of the Spirit in which men *and* women participated equally as the vehicles of the Spirit. Once again, as in the old Israel, organization triumphed. The great church showed that it had little concern for the role of women in the church. Gradually, the forces of ecclesiastical law and order gained the upper hand. Before she died, c. 179, Maximilla complained that, "I am driven as a wolf from the sheep. I am not a wolf. I am word, spirit and power.[144]

Where exorcism had failed and episcopal councils were of little avail, sentiment and events aided the great church. First, schism "rending the seamless robe of Christ" was abominated, and the Lyons Christians, otherwise not unfavorable to the New Prophecy, rejected individualistic actions even of their own number that could lead to the destruction of unity.[145] Second, the parallel between the prophets of the Old Testament and the Montanists broke down. The former at least appeared to prophesy in their right minds and their words made sense. The Montanists apparently simply uttered, claiming that the Spirit worked upon them when they were in sleep or ecstasy, and thereby laid themselves open to objections by officials of the church. Their mode of prophecy was contrary to tradition. Was it not demonic possession and not genuine prophecy? The Montanists claimed that Peter knew "not . . . what he said" (Luke 9:33) under the impact of the transfiguration.[146] So the argument continued. They were also charged with avarice and arrogance, and some came to ignominious ends.[147] Above all, the world went on normally. The last days—the Parousia—did not come.

Unabashed, the Montanists began to organize themselves as a church. Their hierarchy differed from that of their orthodox rivals. Their grades included that of Patriarch and Companion (of the Lord) *Koinonos*,[148] an honored if informal title among Christians in Asia Minor, especially confessors. Polycarp had been so named. They set up a church treasury (for the first such treasury that there is evidence).[149] Even so, in the cities orthodoxy gradually gained the upper hand. Montanism, however, flourished among Christians in the countryside of Asia Minor. In the third century, the imperial estate in the Tembris valley of northern Phrygia was the site of a Christianity that openly proclaimed its identity and whose members styled themselves "soldiers" (of Christ).[150] Montanus's movement demonstrated that Christianity among the rural populations of the empire might retain a radical apocalyptic and prophetic outlook, long after the established communities in the cities were coming to terms with their environment. It also established a precedent as a regional movement "of the Phrygians." Most important of all, by 200 it was influencing the Latin churches of Rome and North Africa.

CONCLUSION

The two generations that separate the second fall of Jerusalem in 135 from the extinction of the Antonines (with the murder of Commodus on 31 December 192) witnessed great changes in the organization of the church and the outlook of its members. At the beginning of this period, many

Christians were still nonconformist Jews. In asserting that Jesus was Messiah and that the prophecies of the Old Testament referred to him alone, they might incur the enmity of orthodox Jews, but their tenacity of purpose and total rejection of idolatry, including the imperial cult, would have done credit to the Essenes. In 190 there was still an active Jewish Christianity, claiming Matthew's as the true Gospel, bitterly critical of Paul and the abandonment of Hebrew for Greek as the language of the church, but it had been reduced to the level of a sect, like the Elkesaites and Christian baptists, on the fringes of Christianity. Gradually, orthodox Christianity was moving toward more open attitudes to pagan society and pagan thought, though even now terms such as "authentic Gentile Christianity" or "Hellenization" are relative. The writings of Hegesippus, Theophilus, and Irenaeus himself still breathe the attitudes of the Hellenistic synagogue. A pagan citizen of Sardis might not have found much difference in religious outlook between the established Jewish community in the city and Melito's Christian sect. But, if Celsus's rhetorical association between Judaism and Christianity remained relevant, it was no longer the whole truth. Between 145 and 170 a shift of emphasis had taken place. The church now had a place for Athenagoras as well as for Theophilus of Antioch and Irenaeus. Christianity was making good its claim to be a "third race" independent of both Judaism and paganism. The first halting steps were being taken for the formation of Christian doctrine that would expound Christian truths in terms intelligible to those educated in Greek philosophy. How far would that process go? How far would Christianity be conditioned by the legalism of Irenaeus? What was to be its relation with the empire? These were questions confronting Christians in the next century. All the time, however, Christianity was gaining ground. The church of the Gentiles enters the age of the Severans already as one of the major religions of the Greco-Roman world.

BIBLIOGRAPHY

NOTE

The emergence of orthodoxy in the second half of the second century has long occupied historians of the early church. The student will find the established textbooks helpful, especially J. Lebreton's chapter, "The Catholic Reaction" (chap. 16, pp. 661–715 in vol. 2 of J. Lebreton and J. Zeiller's *The History of the Primitive Church*, Eng. trans. E. C. Messenger, 2 vols. [New York and London: Macmillan Co., 1949]), and B. J. Kidd's painstaking analyses of texts in this period, *A History of the Church to A.D. 461*, 3 vols. (New York: Oxford University Press, 1922), vol. 1, chaps. 10–13. In addition, Robert Grant's chapters on "The Apologetic Movement" (chap. 7) and "Christian Organization" (chap. 10) in *Augustus to Constantine: The Thrust of the Christian Movement Into the Roman World* (New York: Harper & Row, 1970) are stimulating. On the individual apologists and theologians,

L. W. Barnard's two works, *Justin Martyr: His Life and Thought* (New York and Cambridge: Cambridge University Press, 1967), and *Athenagoras: A Study in Second Century Christian Apologetic*, Théologie historique 18 (Paris: Gabriel Beauchesne, 1972), give a very fair picture of the encounter between philosophy and Christianity in this period. H. C. Meecham, ed. and Eng. trans., *The Epistle to Diognetus* (Manchester, Eng.: Manchester University Press, 1950) is a detailed analytical account of the letter and has not been superseded. For Theophilus of Antioch, R. M. Grant's edition and English translation of *Ad Autolycum* (Oxford: At the Clarendon Press, 1970) is strongly recommended. Irenaeus has been well served by Gustav Wingren's *Man and the Incarnation: A Study of the Biblical Theology of Irenaeus*, Eng. trans. R. Mackenzie (Philadelphia: Muhlenberg Press; Edinburgh: Oliver & Boyd, 1959) and J. Lawson's *The Biblical Theology of St. Irenaeus* (London: Epworth Press, 1949).

On the formation of the canon, see H. von Campenhausen, *The Formation of the Christian Bible*, Eng. trans. J. A. Baker (Philadelphia: Fortress Press; London: A. & C. Black, 1972), and for the creeds, J. N. D. Kelly, *Early Christian Creeds* (New York and London: Longmans, Green & Co., 1950).

On the Montanists, P. de Labriolle's *La crise montaniste. Les sources de l'histoire du Montanisme: Textes grecs, latins, syriaques* (Paris, 1913) remain the fullest account, as well as being excellently documented. See also W. Schepelern's study, *Der Montanismus und die phrygischen Kulte: Eine religionsgeschichte Untersuchung*, Ger. trans. from the Swed. by W. Baur (Tübingen: J. C. B. Mohr [Paul Siebeck], 1929), a thorough study of the possible Phrygian pagan background of Montanism.

SOURCES

Relating to Irenaeus and the Apologists, see Bibliography to chaps. 5 and 6.

Aristides. Edited by J. A. Robinson and R. Harris, *Cambridge Texts and Studies* I.1. Cambridge: Cambridge University Press, 1891.

Athenagoras. *Legatio* and *De Resurrectione*. Edited by W. R. Schoedel. OECT. New York: Oxford University Press, 1972.

Melito of Sardis. *Melito of Sardis: On Pascha and Fragments*. Edited by S. G. Hall. OECT. New York and London: Oxford University Press, 1979.

Montanist texts: see N. Bonwetsch. *Texte zur Geschichte des Montanismus*. KlT 129. Bonn: Marcus, 1914.

SECONDARY WORKS

Aland, K. "The Problem of Anonymity and Pseudonymity in Christian Literature of the First Two Centuries." *JTS* n.s. 12 (April 1969): 39–49.

Barnard, L. W. "The Philosophical and Biblical Background of Athenagoras." *Epektasis = Mélanges patristiques offerts au Cardinal Jean Daniélou*, pp. 3–17. Paris: Gabriel Beauchesne, 1972.

Calder, W. M. "Early Christian Epitaphs from Phrygia." *Anatolian Studies* 5 (1955): 25–38.

———. "Philadelphia and Montanism." *BJRL* 7 (1923): 309–54.

Campenhausen, H. von. *The Fathers of the Greek Church*. Eng. trans. L. A. Garrard. London: A. & C. Black, 1963.

Daniélou, J. *The Gospel Message and Hellenistic Culture*, Eng. trans. and ed. J. A. Baker. A History of Early Christian Doctrine Before the Council of Nicaea, vol. 2. Philadelphia: Westminster Press; London: Darton, Longman & Todd, 1973.

Dix, G. *The Shape of the Liturgy*. London: Dacre Press, 1945.

Drijvers, H. J. W. "Edessa und das Jüdische Christentum." *VC* 24 (1970): 4–33.

Ehrhardt, A. A. T. "Christianity Before the Apostles' Creed." *HTR* 55 (1962): 73–119.

Elze, M. *Tatian und seine Theologie*. Göttingen: Vandenhoeck & Ruprecht, 1960.

Ford, J. Massyngberde. "Was Montanism a Jewish-Christian Heresy?" *JEH* 17 (October 1966): 145–58.

Frend, W. H. C. "The Old Testament in the Age of the Greek Apologists, A.D. 130–180." *SJT* 26 (May 1973): 129–50.

Grant, R. M. "The Chronology of the Greek Apologists." *VC* 9 (1955): 25–33.

———. "Studies in the Apologists." *HTR* 51 (1958): 123–34.

Guarducci, M. "Die Ausgrabungen unter St. Peter." In *Das frühe Christentum im römischen Staat*, ed. R. Klein, pp. 364–414. Darmstadt: Wissenschaftliche Buchgesellschaft, 1971.

Hanson, R. P. C. *Allegory and Event: A Study of the Sources and Significance of Origen's Interpretation of Scripture*. Richmond: Board of Christian Education Presbyterian Church in the United States; London: SCM Press, 1959.

Harnack, A. von. "Über den Verfasser und den literarischen Charakter des muratorischen Fragments." *ZNW* 24 (1925): 1–16.

Joly, R. *Christianisme et Philosophie: études sur Justin et les apologistes grecs du deuxième siècle*. Brussels: Editions de l'Université de Bruxelles, 1973.

Klauser, T. H. "Die Anfänge der römischen Bischofsliste." In Klauser, *Gesammelte Arbeiten zur Liturgiegeschichte, Kirchengeschichte und christlichen Archäologie*, ed. E. Dassmann, pp. 121–38. Münster: Aschendorff, 1974.

La Piana, G. "The Roman Church at the End of the Second Century." *HTR* 18 (1925): 201–77.

Meijering, E. P. "Irenaeus' Relation to Philosophy in the Light of His Concept of Free Will." In *Romanitas et Christianitas (Festsch. J. Waszink)*, ed. P. G. van der Port, pp. 221–32. Amsterdam, 1973.

Nautin, P. *Lettres et écrivains chrétiens de IIe et IIIe siècles*. Paris: Les Éditions du Cerf, 1961.

Roberts, C. H. "An Unpublished Fragment of the Fourth Gospel in the John Rylands Library." *BJRL* 20 (1936): 45–55.

———, with Capelle, B. "An Early Euchologion. The Der el Balyzeh Papyrus." Enlarged and reedited. *Bibl. du Muséon* 23 (1949).

Schoedel, W. R. "Christian 'Atheism' and the Peace of the Roman Empire." *CH* 42 (September 1973): 309–19.

Schoeps, H. J. *Jewish Christianity: Factional Disputes in the Early Church*. Eng. trans. D. R. A. Hare (of *Das Judenchristentum* [Bern: A. Francke, 1964]). Philadelphia: Fortress Press, 1969.

Toynbee, J. M. C., and Ward-Perkins, J. B. *The Shrine of St. Peter and the Vatican Excavations*. London: Longmans, Green & Co., 1956.

Turner, H. E. W. *The Pattern of Christian Truth: A Study in the Relations Between Orthodoxy and Heresy in the Early Church*. London: A. R. Mowbray, 1954.

NOTES

1. The idea of the "great church" originates in Judaism. Thus, in Neh. 5:8 (LXX), "I [Nehemiah] appointed against them [malcontents] a great assembly [*ecclesian megalen*]"; and compare 1 Macc. 4:59 and 14:28, and Ps. 22:25.

2. John of Damascus, *De fide orthodoxa* 17 (De Scriptura), *PG* 94, 1177B. At the same time, Christians could "accept what was useful from authors outside [the church]." Like "good bankers," they should "collect the true and pure gold [pieces] and reject the dross."

3. Justin Martyr *1 Apology* 29.

4. Origen *Celsus* IV.23.

5. Justin *Trypho* LVIII.1. Trypho did not agree; see LVIII.2.

6. Irenaeus *Heresies* III.4.

7. Preserved by Eusebius *HE* IV.23; see above, p. 179. See also Nautin, *Lettres et écrivains*, pp. 16ff.

8. See Toynbee and Ward-Perkins, *Shrine of St. Peter*, pp. 135ff.

9. Eusebius *HE* II.25.7; and for Rome's wealth and influence, see Dionysius of Corinth's comments preserved in ibid., 25.8.

10. For the early development of the baptismal and eucharistic liturgy, see Dix, *Shape of Liturgy*, chap. 5 (Eucharist); and G. W. H. Lampe, *The Seal of the Spirit: A Study in the Doctrine of Baptism and Confirmation in the New Testament and the Fathers*, 2d ed. (London: SPCK, 1967), chap. 6 (Baptism).

11. Eng. trans. by E. R. Hardy in *Early Christian Fathers*, Eng. trans. and ed. C. C. Richardson et al., LCC I (Philadelphia: Westminster Press; London: SCM Press, 1953), pp. 285–86.

12. Dix, *Shape of Liturgy*, pp. 222–23; and S. G. Hall, "Paschal Baptism," ed. E. A. Livingstone, *SE* 6, TU 112 (1973): 239–51.

13. See Grant's excellent chapter, "Apologetic Movement." His dating of the Apologists is to be found in "Chronology of Greek Apologists."

14. Lucian *De Morte Peregrini* (*On the Death of Peregrinus*) XI: "wondrous lore of the Christians."

15. Thus Justin *1 Apology* 59–60, "Plato borrowed from our teachers"; Theophilus *Autolycus* III.26, "It is obvious how our sacred writings are proved to be more ancient and more true than the writings of Greeks and Egyptians and any other historiographers" (trans. Grant); Tatian *Oratio ad Graecos (Address to the Greeks)* 31; and Origen *Celsus* VII.28. The argument was derived from Hellenistic-Jewish sources, at least as far back as Aristobulus writing in the second century B.C. Compare also Philo *Quod Omnis Probus Liber Sit* (*Every Good Man Is Free*) 57, Zeno drew some of his ideas from "the law-book of the Jews."

16. Eusebius *HE* V.17.1–5. Compare IV.26.1, and 27, concerning an even-wider range of apologetic by Apollinaris, bishop of Hierapolis in Phrygia, 170–80.

17. Eusebius *HE* IV.3.

18. See extracts cited mainly from Clement *Stromata* (*Miscellanies*), in M. R. James, Eng. trans., *The Apocryphal New Testament* (New York and London: Oxford University Press, 1924; reprint ed., 1953), pp. 16–19, and above, p. 162.

19. Aristides, *Apology*, ed. Robinson and Harris; the editors point out (p. 13) that "if the Church was not in the writer's time any longer under the wing of the

Synagogue, it had apparently no objection to taking the Synagogue occasionally under its own wing."

20. *The Apology of Aristides* II: "There are four races of men in this world, barbarians and Greeks, Jews and Christians."

21. Ibid., XIV (Syriac version). See Robinson and Harris, p. 48, and compare Celsus in Origen *Celsus* V.6.

22. *Apology* XV. The editors point to the many parallels between the *Apology*, *The Preaching of Peter*, *Diognetus*, and *Sibylline Oracles*, Book III.

23. Compare Hermas *Similitudines (Similitudes)* V.3, for a similar attitude.

24. Meecham, *Diognetus*. Dating is difficult. *Diognetus* could have been written at any time between about 130 and 190. The use of Hellenistic-Jewish apologetic models, the absence of the Euhemerist argument against the pagan gods employed by the later Apologists, and parallels with Aristides, suggest a relatively early date, not later than A.D. 150.

25. *Diognetus* 2. Compare Ps. 115:4–8.

26. *Diognetus* 6. Compare Philo *Embassy* 1. 3–4.

27. *Diognetus* 6.1. See Joly, *Christianisme et Philosophie*, chap. 5, esp. pp. 218–20.

28. Thus, Juvenal *Satires* XIV.96ff., and Origen *Celsus* V.6.

29. *Diognetus* 5.16–17.

30. Ibid., 9; and Celsus in Origen *Celsus* IV.7, "Why did God think of judging mankind so late?"

31. *Diognetus* 10.2.

32. Ibid., 11.6.

33. Thus, Justin *1 Apology* 23; and *Trypho* 7.

34. The Stoics believed that the seeds from which things grew were contained in the basic structure of the universe. Human decisions were thus ultimately predetermined. See A. A. Long, ed., *Problems in Stoicism* (New York: Oxford University Press; London: University of London, Athlone Press, 1971), p. 178.

35. Justin *1 Apology* 46. Trans. in Richardson et al., *Early Christian Fathers*, p. 272.

36. Ibid., 59–60; see n. 15 above.

37. Ibid., 66.

38. Ibid., 26 and 28; and compare *Trypho* 80.3: "Christians in name but in reality are godless and impious heretics." See the valuable notes in A. Lukyn Williams, ed. and Eng. trans., *Justin Martyr. Dialogue with Trypho*, Translations of Christian Literature, series 1: Greek Texts (New York: Macmillan Co., 1931; London: SPCK, 1930), pp. 170–71.

39. Justin *Trypho* 120.4–5. Justin quotes Isaiah often as a witness that God called the Gentiles to salvation as the Jews had dishonored him. Thus, *Trypho* 12.1; 13.1–9; 14.4–7; 15.2–6; 19.8; etc. For Justin's ideas about the eternal punishment of the wicked ("Unquenchable fire on the unbelieving Gentiles"), see *Trypho* 120.5. See also Joly, *Christianisme et Philosophie*, p. 166.

40. Justin *Trypho* 80.5.

41. Ibid., 120.5, and see Williams's note *Trypho,* p. 249.

42. Justin *Trypho* 120.5.

43. Ibid., 1.3.

44. Ibid., 1.2, combined with 8.3, and 10.

45. Ibid., 56, 40 and 41.1.

46. Ibid., 28.2.

47. Ibid., 34.1, and see my "Old Testament in Age of Greek Apologists," pp. 139–45.

48. See Othmar Perler's views in *Melito de Sardes sur la Pâque et fragments*, SC 123 (Paris, 1966), introduction; Hall, ed., *Melito of Sardis*, introduction.

49. Melito, cited by Eusebius *HE* IV.26.9.

50. For the strength of Judaism in Sardis at this time, see above, p. 163.

51. Eusebius *HE* IV.26.12–14.

52. Gennadius of Marseilles (late fifth century), *Liber ecclesiasticorum dogmatum, PL* 58.4 and 55 (cols. 982 and 994).

53. Thus Perler, *Melito de Sardes*, p. 25.

54. Melito *Homily on the Passion* 59 in Perler, *Melito de Sardes*, p. 93.

55. Melito *Homily* 73 in Perler, *Melito de Sardes*, p. 101.

56. Melito *Homily* 99 in Perler, *Melito de Sardes*, p. 121, alluding perhaps to Israel's military disasters at the hands of the Romans.

57. "Atheism" occupies Athenagoras *Legatio pro Christianis* (*Supplication for the Christians*), chaps. 4–30; "incest" chaps. 32–34; and "cannibalism," chap. 35. On Athenagoras and his work, see Barnard, *Athenagoras*.

58. *Supplication* 7.2–3, ed. Schoedel. See also Joly, *Christianisme et Philosophie*, pp. 134–6, and Barnard, "Biblical Background of Athenagoras."

59. *Supplication* 8–9.

60. Ibid., 28ff. Cyril of Alexandria also uses the Euhemerist argument against the emperor Julian. *Contra Julianum* (*Against Julian*) *PG* 1028B–D.

61. *Supplication* 35.2.

62. See Schoedel, "Christian 'Atheism'," esp. pp. 316–18.

63. *Supplication* 1 and 2. (Much of this idealized portrait may have been drawn from Menander's *What Must Be Displayed* [*Peri Epideiknon*].)

64. Socrates *Ecclesiastical History* VII.22. The emperor's "humanity" and self-control are emphasized.

65. J. Lebreton, "Le désaccord de la foi populaire et de la théologie savante dans l'Eglise chrétienne du IIIe siècle," *RHE* 19 (1923): 481–506; and *RHE* 20 (1924): 5–37.

66. See Aland, "Anonymity and Pseudonymity": "the unknown men by whom they [the pseudonymous writings] were composed, not only believed themselves to be under the sign of the Holy Spirit, they really were" (p. 49).

67. Eusebius acknowledges his debt to Hegesippus in *HE* IV.22.1. See H. J. Lawlor, *Eusebiana* (New York: Oxford University Press, 1912), pp. 98–107.

68. Eusebius *HE* IV.23.2 (Publius of Athens). For Justin's use of the term *proestos*, see above, p. 233.

69. Eusebius *HE* IV.23.5, "Philip the bishop"; and also for Palmas and Pinytus "bishop of the diocese of Knossos," ibid., 7 and 8.

70. Grant, *Augustus to Constantine*, p. 151.

71. Eusebius *HE* V.24.16; and compare IV.22.3 where Anicetus (154–66) is the first to be called monarchical bishop of Rome. Klauser, *Gesammelte Arbeiten*, p. 139 (see below, n. 73), suspects that while the names of the earliest Roman bishops should be regarded as historical, their traditional dating is artificial and worthless.

72. Eusebius *HE* IV.22.1. A. A. T. Ehrhardt, *The Apostolic Succession in the First Two Centuries of the Church* (London: Lutterworth Press, 1953), pp. 63–66, draws attention to the parallel between the Jewish and early Christian concerns with the actual succession of the high priests. Hegesippus believed that James of Jerusalem had high priestly status, "being alone allowed to enter the sanctuary" (Eusebius *HE* II.23.4), another instance of the continued close connections in religious outlook between the old and new Israel during the second century.

73. See Klauser, in "Die Anfänge." In contrast to Ehrhardt, Klauser believes that, in early Christian writers, succession represented the handing on of apostolic tradition rather than the physical succession of one bishop to another (p. 139).

74. Irenaeus *Heresies* II.33.2 (Massuet's numbering in *PG* and the ANCL translation have been used throughout). Compare Theophilus *Autolycus*, ed. Grant, III.7 (equally critical of Plato).

75. Daniélou's point: the Gnostics "even if they are bad theologians are at any rate more of theologians than Irenaeus"; *Gospel Message*, p. 357.

76. Thus, Irenaeus *Heresies* II.35.3.

77. Eusebius *HE* V.20, and Irenaeus *Heresies* III.3.4.

78. As argued by the editor, St. Irenaeus, *Demonstration of the Apostolic Preaching*, Eng. trans. and ed. J. A. Robinson, Translations of Christian Literature, series 4: Oriental Texts (New York: Macmillan Co., 1920), pp. 6–23, Irenaeus cites a lost book of Justin's, *Heresies* V.26.2.

79. Eusebius *HE* V.4.1.

80. Irenaeus *Heresies*, preface to Book I, para. 3, and I.13.7 (Marcus and his disciples).

81. Eusebius *HE* V.24.11–18, "the disagreement in the fact confirms our agreement in the faith."

82. Irenaeus *Heresies* I.10; trans. by Hardy in *Early Christian Fathers*, Richardson et al., p. 360, and compare *Demonstratio apostolicae praedictionis (Proof of the Apostolic Preaching)* 32–34.

83. Irenaeus *Heresies* III.2.2. One believes that Irenaeus meant "presbyters," that is, holders of church office, of whom Polycarp was the prime example.

84. Irenaeus *Heresies* IV.20.3.

85. Daniélou, *Gospel Message*, p. 357.

86. Irenaeus *Heresies* IV.20.7 in *PG* 7.1037B.

87. Irenaeus *Heresies* V.6.1.

88. Ibid., 2.3. See Wingren, *Man and Incarnation*, p. 24.

89. Irenaeus *Heresies* III.18.1. At first sight a contradiction with the argument in Book V. See, however, Wingren, *Man and Incarnation*, pp. 45–47. The Fall involved "captivity" to sin rather than total loss.

90. Irenaeus *Heresies* V.36.3, Irenaeus's concluding words of faith and optimism.

91. Ibid., IV.32.1, Irenaeus quotes the views of a "presbyter," that is, Polycarp(?), described here as "a disciple of the apostles."

92. Ibid., V.19.1, trans. Richardson.

93. See R. Murray, *Symbols of Church and Kingdom: A Study of Early Syriac Tradition* (New York and Cambridge: Cambridge University Press, 1975), p. 84. An underlying Semitic element may be suspected in Irenaeus, but it is difficult to define this accurately.

94. Irenaeus *Apostolic Preaching* 96. Contrast Clement of Alexandria *Miscellanies* I.5.28, who regarded both the Law and philosophy as "tutors," to bring the Jew and Greek respectively to Christ.

95. Irenaeus *Heresies* I.10.2.

96. Eusebius *HE* V.20.4. Florinus was evidently a Valentinian Dualist (ibid., 20.1).

97. Irenaeus *Heresies* V, preface.

98. Ibid., V.2.2, trans. ANCL.

99. See Wingren, *Man and Incarnation*, pp. 164–70.

100. Irenaeus *Heresies* III.3.4. Polycarp, "who not only was taught by apostles but associated with many who had seen Christ, and was installed by apostles for Asia as bishop in the church in Smyrna."

101. Ibid., IV.26.2.

102. Ibid., II.32.4. Note, too, Irenaeus's high esteem of prophetic gifts.

103. Ibid., IV.20.2. Described as "Scripture."

104. Ibid., V.33.3–4, and 34.2–4. Irenaeus holds Papias in high regard (in contrast to Eusebius) and quotes him as "the hearer of John and companion of Polycarp," that is, a fully creditable witness to the truth of the church's tradition.

105. Found in 1907 by Flinders Petrie and W. E. Crum. The papyrus is a prayer collection, seventh century in date, but includes a simple creed at the end. Discussed by Roberts and Capelle, "Early Euchologion"; and by Kelly, *Early Christian Creeds*, pp. 88–89. Eng. trans. in Stevenson, ed., *A New Eusebius* (London: SPCK, 1973), p. 131, together with the early creed contained in C. M. Morris, *The Epistles to the Apostles* (Nashville: Abingdon Press, 1975), (circa A.D. 180–200).

106. Text in W. M. Ramsay, *Cities and Bishoprics of Phrygia* (New York: Oxford University Press, 1901), vol. 2, p. 723, and W. M. Calder, "The Epitaph of Avircius Marcellus," *JRS* 29 (1939): 1–4. See Stevenson's comments, *A New Eusebius*, pp. 143–44. Rome, described as a "queen golden-sandalled" may be taken from *Sibylline Oracles*, Book V's description of Babylon! (line 34).

107. Eusebius *HE* V.23.4.

108. Irenaeus *Heresies* I.26.2.

109. Epiphanius *Medicine Box* XXX.3.6 (and K. Holl's [ed.] note in *Panarion Haeresium*, GCS 25, 31, 37 [Leipzig, 1915–31], I.337).

110. For the *Alogi*, see Epiphanius *Medicine Box* LI.2, and Irenaeus's witness in *Heresies* III.11.9, to unnamed heretics who "set aside the Gospel [of John] and the prophetic Spirit." Regarding the Fourth Gospel in Egypt, see Roberts, "Unpublished Fragment of Fourth Gospel," p. 46. Also above, p. 129.

111. Eusebius *HE* VI.12.2.

112. See Morton Smith, *The Secret Gospel: The Discovery and Interpretation of the Secret Gospel According to Mark* (Harper & Row, 1973), pp. 39ff. I accept this part of the author's thesis.

113. Irenaeus *Heresies* III.11.8.

114. Eng. text in Stevenson, *A New Eusebius*, pp. 144–47. The omission of Hebrews might be on anti-Montanist grounds (von Campenhausen, *Formation of Christian Bible*, p. 232). It is rejected by the anti-Montanist presbyter Caius, Eusebius *HE* VI.20.3. The omission of 1 and 2 Peter is odd, if 1 Peter were composed in Rome. It was well known in Asia Minor. See von Harnack, "Über der Verfasser und den literarischen Charakter des muratorischen Fragments," pp. 7 and 15.

115. Briefly in Eusebius *HE* III.27; these were Jewish-Christians (their name translates from Hebrew "the poor men"), who continued to regard Christ as "the prophet," "righteous according to the Law," and a second and greater Moses. By this time they were tending towards an increasingly sectarian outlook, accepting vegetarianism and frequent lustral washings among their rites. It is difficult to see how they could have been numerous even at Edessa at the end of the second century. See Schoeps, *Das Judenchristentum*, chap. VI.

116. Regarding early Christianity in Edessa, see J. B. Segal, *Edessa the Blessed City* (New York: Oxford University Press; Oxford: At the Clarendon Press, 1970); also Drijvers, "Edessa," and W. Bauer, *Rechtglaübigkeit und Ketzerei im ältesten Christentum*, BhistTh, 2d ed. (Tübingen: J. C. B. Mohr [Paul Siebeck], 1964), p. 27.

117. *Dura Europos*, Final Report, vol. 1, Parchments and Papyri, 73–74 (New Haven, Conn.: Yale University Press, n.d.) (references).

118. Even in John Chrysostom's time (c. 380–90). See his *Adversus Judaeos* (*Against the Jews*), *PG* 48.844ff.

119. See n. 15. Theophilus *Autolycus* III.7. After saying "Plato contradicts himself," Theophilus goes on, "How is it possible that his teaching will not seem evil and unlawful for those who possess reason, when he holds that one formerly a human being will become a wolf or ass or some other irrational animal?" He "talks nonsense" with Pythagoras!

120. Ibid., II.37. See above, n. 15.

121. Ibid., III.9, 18 and 23.

122. Theophilus, *Autolycus*, ed. Grant, introduction, pp. xvii–xviii.

123. Theophilus *Autolycus* II.10 and 22. See Theophilus, *Autolycus*, ed. Grant, p. xv.

124. Epiphanius *Medicine Box* LXV.3, and for the opposition of the Alexandrians, see below, pp. 386–87.

125. Clement of Alexandria, *Stromata (Miscellanies)*, ed. O. Stählin/L. Früchtel, GCS, 1.11.1–2.

126. Ibid., 1.5.28.

127. Ibid., 1.11.3 and 14.2, "secret things not to be explained sufficiently." For Clement's teaching, see below, pp. 371–73.

128. Eusebius's date is preferred to A.D. 157 given by Epiphanius *Medicine Box* 48.2, on the grounds that for the martyrs of Lyons the movement was comparatively recent (Eusebius *HE* V.3.4). See the present author's "A Note on the Chronology of the Martyrdom of Polycarp and the Outbreak of Montanism," *Oikoumene: Studi paleocristiani pubblicati in onore del concilio ecumenico Vaticano II* (Catania: Università di Catania, 1964), pp. 499–506.

129. Eusebius *HE* V.16.6, and 18.2, and Epiphanius *Medicine Box* 48.14.1. See Calder, "Philadelphia and Montanism." For texts relating to Montanism, see Bonwetsch, *Montanismus*.

130. Eusebius *HE* V.16.18 (wars and revolutions), citing an anonymous tract against the Montanists, c. 190.

131. Schepelern, *Der Montanismus*, pp. 159–62, and compare pp. 129–30.

132. Ibid., pp. 160–64.

133. Ford, "Was Montanism a Jewish-Christian Heresy?"

134. See von Campenhausen, *Formation of Christian Bible*, pp. 221–23: "Mon-

tanism, considered as a whole, despite some peculiar ideas and practices, did not break out of the framework of earlier apocalyptic hopes and demands'' (p. 221).

135. Schepelern, *Der Montanismus*, p. 104; cf. Anonymous, cited by Eusebius *HE* V.16.6. Montanus's village of Ardabau was "in Phrygian Mysia."

136. Though this is first mentioned by the fifth-century historian Sozomen, *Ecclesiastical History* VII.12.18, he does not record it as an innovation.

137. Ford, "Was Montanism a Jewish-Christian Heresy?" p. 149.

138. Eusebius *HE* III.28.2. Caius as an anti-Montanist, ibid. II.25; and see E. B. Birks, "Caius" in *DCB* 1.384–86.

139. Eusebius *HE* III.31.

140. Ibid., V.17.3.

141. Ibid., V.1.9 and 55.

142. Origen *Celsus* VII.9.

143. Eusebius *HE* V.16.12.

144. Ibid., V.16.17. Also, Epiphanius *Medicine Box* XLIX.2 on the place of women in the Montanist church.

145. Eusebius *HE* V.3, concerning the ascetic way of life of the confessor Alcibiades.

146. Tertullian *Adversus Marcionem (Against Marcion)* IV.22. Also Eusebius *HE* V.17.2–3, and Epiphanius, *Medicine Box* XLV.3.4 (Adam in a trance), and 7.

147. Eusebius *HE* V.18.5–11, and 16.14.

148. Jerome *Letter* XLI.3, "habent enim primos de Pepuza Phrygiae patriarches, secundos quos appellant κοινωνούς." Bishops were ranked below these. See also Calder, "Early Christian Epitaphs," p. 37, in which a certain Paulinus is described as a [μο]ιστης κ(αι) κοινωνος, circa A.D. 500. For Polycarp as a κοινωνός, see *Martyrdom of Polycarp* in *The Acts of the Christian Martyrs*, ed. and Eng. trans. H. A. Musurillo (Oxford: At the Clarendon Press, 1972), 6.2.

149. Eusebius *HE* V.16.14: Theodotus, "the first steward [*epitropon*] as it were of their alleged prophecy."

150. Calder, "Philadelphia and Montanism," p. 35 and fig. 4.

CHRISTIANITY AND THE ROMAN EMPIRE

INVS
JRVM
O

Out of the Shadows 193–235

THE SEVERAN DYNASTY

The emergence of the Severan dynasty as rulers of the Roman world (193–235) ushered in a period of dynamic change and expansion for the Christians. Within a generation Christianity had moved from its self-proclaimed status of "third race," perched uneasily between Judaism and paganism, to the position of one of the major religions of the Roman world. Many pagans continued to point to the Jewish elements in Christianity and contrast "Judaism and Christianity" (and also occasionally "the religion of the Samaritans") with the "religion of the Romans,"[1] but for the Christians the main issue was now their relationship with the Roman world and its institutions, "the customs of our ancestors," as Tertullian declared.[2] The roles of Judaism and Christianity as monotheistic religions were becoming reversed. Judaism, despite the numbers and wealth of its adherents in the empire, was returning to the status of a national cult, leaving the role of world mission to the Christians. Origen characteristically dismissed it as "Christianity's little sister."[3]

Success, however, brought its own problems. Christians now had to define their place within society and also define their whole range of teaching, both disciplinary and doctrinal, in both Greek- and Latin-speaking parts of the Mediterranean. How would this teaching relate to contemporary non-Christian religious thought? What would happen if they did conquer the empire? Few besides Origen so much as envisaged the possibility. The attractive power of Christianity, and the church's ability to enforce relatively uniform beliefs among communities scattered over enormous areas rendered it formidable despite severe and continuous internal strains. The steady stream of converts in the Severan era laid the foundations for its triumph a century later.

Septimius Severus (193–211) won the empire through conquest. After four years of intermittent civil war his rivals—Pescennius Niger in the east, and Clodius Albinus, erstwhile commander of the Roman troops in Britain—had fallen in battle. Until his death at York in 211 Severus ruled like a military dictator; he was believed to respect none of his subjects apart from his troops. He was, however, a dictator with a religious cast of mind. His marriage to Julia Domna, the daughter of the hereditary prince-priest of the Baal of Emesa opened the way for the rule, for nearly forty years, of a Semitic dynasty whose members displayed a religiosity in character with their background. Julia Domna, her sister Julia Maesa, her daughter Julia Mamaea, and her nieces gave the imperial court the appearance of a highly articulate harem. There philosophers, lawyers, physicians, quacks, and literary men met on equal terms, and eastern travel tales set round the noble and ascetic career of Apollonius of Tyana vied for attention with less savory manifestations of religion, such as those of the emperor Elagabalus (218–22). Origen's description of Julia Mamaea, the mother of Alexander

Severus (222–35) who followed Elagabalus, as "a most religious woman"[4] was apt, and corroborated by Lampridius (so far as may be allowed this source).[5] Origen himself was accorded a military escort when he was summoned to her presence for a discussion of "divine things." In this environment orthodox Christianity shared the prosperity of its rivals, Gnosticism and the mystery cults.

Outwardly, the empire of Septimius Severus and his dynasty still resembled that of the Antonines. The title "Antoninus" appropriated by the Severans indicated that they meant it to be so. Territorially it now reached its furthest limits (except for Trajan's fleeting eastern conquests). The offensive-defensive strategy of Severus took Roman troops far south of the Chott el Hodna on the borders of the Sahara and north across the Tay in a final effort to crush the Caledonians. Within these boundaries peace prevailed as it had in the Antonine period. There were some severe local disturbances, like that caused by Bulla and his companions in Italy (Dio Cassius *Roman History* 77.10), but these were shrugged off amid the general well-being of the times. The Bithynian civil servant and historian Dio Cassius laid down his pen in 229 with no hint of the disasters which were to begin to crowd in on the empire within a decade, nor of the religious upheaval that was to accompany them.[6] Dio disliked Jews but never mentioned Christians. The empire itself continued to be governed by the same upright conservative administrators as he himself had been. In matters of religion un-Roman attitudes were punished, but offenders such as the Scillitan Martyrs were given plenty of time to come to their senses. The sovereign public virtue for a ruler remained *Liberalitas*.

The provincial cities, too, continued their upward road to prosperity. Where buildings had previously been half-timbered, they were now of stone. Baths, triumphal arches, temples, water fountains, amphitheaters of enormous size (such as at Thysdrus) characterized the Severan age. Sums were doled out by prominent citizens to entertain their poorer fellows, but little was done for the 90 percent or so who worked on the land. Some cities in Asia Minor were reputed to take the first cut of the yearly harvest and leave the wretched leftovers to the peasants.[7] Even so, these cities were sharing the prosperity of the times. In North Africa, native communities in Mauretania Sitifensis, for instance, were gaining the status of towns in this period.[8] Constitutionally, the remaining distinctions between Roman and non-Roman were almost entirely abolished by the *Constitutio Antoniniana* of 212 (or 214), promulgated by Severus's son and successor, Caracalla. Henceforth, nearly all free men in the empire could call themselves Roman citizens and this was remembered (rightly or wrongly) as a great and humane reform.[9] Christians, by no means favorable to the society in which they lived, could not withhold admiration for the security and obvious growth of material prosperity that the Roman world enjoyed.[10] In terms of institutions, ideas, architecture, and knowledge of the physical universe, the Severan age garnered the experience of previous centuries, and it was this, as Peter Brown has pointed out,[11] that was passed on as the legacy of the ancient world to the European and Arabian Middle Ages.

CHRISTIANITY'S RIVALS

Religious life reflected the cultural unification of the Mediterranean world. On the one hand, traditional religion had never seemed more deeply rooted. The great territorial deities presided unchallenged over their peoples, assisted by an army of lesser gods and demons. Even in Carthage one had to reckon with an enormous number of deities. Tertullian (in A.D. 197) mockingly enumerated "new gods and old, barbarian, Greek, Roman, foreign, captive, adoptive, private, public, male, female, rustic, urban, military and naval" that abounded there (*Apology* X.5). On the other hand, there was a great deal of assimilation and syncretism, as gods of one nation were associated with a similar god of another and worshiped together in the same city. A priest might find himself responsible for the worship of half a dozen different deities. In some towns, such as Dura-Europos, however, each community seemed to have kept to its own gods and shrines.[12] But everywhere the gods of Rome had precedence, demonstrated by the capitols dedicated to their worship in any city that claimed distinction. Provincials took pride in being associated with Rome and its gods. At Carthage, Tertullian preserved the note of shocked anger in the magistrates' charge against the Christians, "You do not worship the gods: you do not sacrifice to the emperors" (*Apology* X.1). The feeling was not confined to North Africa. At Dura-Europos, one of the most curious discoveries was that the local auxiliaries which formed a major part of the garrison solemnly kept the ancient feast days of the Roman people, extending sometimes into the mists of the early Republican period. The celebration of the imperial cult occupied a disproportionately large part of their religious observances. They were proud of their acquired *Romanitas*.[13]

In another important aspect the rule of the Severans followed that of the fallen Antonines. Commodus had exalted the imperial cult, with himself as its center, to exaggerated heights. Septimius Severus and his wife did the same, only more systematically and with less theatrical display. The divinization of the emperor had been implicit since the time of Augustus. Pliny had told Trajan that he had ordered the imperial effigies to be brought forward along with "our gods" for the Bithynian Christians to venerate.[14] Now the effigies themselves were regarded as endowed with divine power. Philostratus portrayed the imperial statues in a provincial town in Asia Minor as being "more dreaded at that time and more inviolable than the Zeus in Olympia."[15] He was not far wrong, for at Lambaesis, the headquarters of the Third Legion in central Numidia, statues and likenesses of the imperial house were mentioned before the guardian deities when a shrine was erected for the garrison.[16] The process by which the principate became associated with supreme power, and the office of chief magistrate of the Roman people transformed into that of an Eastern potentate took a long step forward under the Severans. The imperial statues were becoming the imperial icons of Byzantine times. The "advent of the emperor" became not simply the ceremonial entry of a ruler into his capital but the advent of an earthly savior. For the Christians the stakes had become higher, for where loyalty to the person of the emperor was involved, there could be no compromise between claims of the "immortal gods of Rome" and those of the Christian God to safeguard the fortunes of the Roman empire, its ruler, and its peoples.

Religious Syncretism

The first stage in this conflict was, however, masked by the all-embracing religious syncretism favored by the imperial house. In this system, Christianity could have claimed a place. The gossip told by Lampridius that Alexander Severus had a shrine set up for Abraham, Orpheus, Apollonius of Tyana, and Christ[17] must be nonsense, just as was Tertullian's claim in 197 that the emperor Tiberius intended to declare Christ a god;[18] but these stories may preserve something of the outlook of the times. Immature and dependent on his mother though Alexander was, he was also a man of letters and culture. He left behind a reputation of tolerance for both Jews and Christians.[19] Certainly, Julia Mamaea might have been expected to find a place for Christ, whom she admired so much, in her universal pantheon.

Philostratus's *Life of Apollonius of Tyana*—written, its author claimed, at the prompting of Julia Domna[20]—shows the positive ideals of the Severan court circle. Philostratus recounted the edifying life and activities of the first-century Pythagorean philosopher, Apollonius. What is remarkable is not so much the miraculous birth and miracles attributed to the hero—which could conceivably have been compared with the Christian gospels—as the author's recognition that a great deal was amiss with paganism, and his efforts to uncover and reform abuses. Wherever Apollonius traveled, he visited temples, hounded corrupt and laggard priests, and attempted to instill new life into their declining cults. In particular, he denounced the sacrifice of animals as derogatory to the gods and urged priests to abandon it.[21] At the end of the century, the Christian writer Lactantius was to make much of the blood-stained symbols of paganism.[22] Apollonius also drew attention to a whole range of other abuses, including merchants cornering markets and allowing the majority of the inhabitants of a town to starve. The earth's bounties were to be shared by all, he proclaimed.[23] He was portrayed as a disciplined ascetic, a vegetarian, who rejected marriage,[24] abhorred the frivolous, and insisted that religion was concerned with ethics and morality as well as with cult.[25] When he spoke, it was with authority "as a Lawgiver," and he saw paganism already in decline. Few engaged in philosophy. The temple of Apollo at Antioch was

275

graceful, but not the "home of serious studies."[26] One must approach God with a clear conscience and pray simply, "O ye gods, grant me that which I deserve."[27]

Philostratus recognized the religious needs of his time, and the romance marks the first real attempt to reform paganism by relating cult to morality in its worship. In this the *Life* anticipated the ideas of the emperor Julian by a century and a half. Had they been followed, paganism might have withstood the pressures of the next fifty years, and the victory of Christianity have been less convincing. As it was, the esoteric aspects of the *Life* attracted more interest than the sage's high principles. Shortly before the outbreak of the Great Persecution in 303, the governor of Bithynia, Sossius Hierocles, a confirmed enemy of the Christians, wrote a book to prove that Apollonius was not only a philosopher but a worker of miracles who expelled demons and was far superior to Christ.[28] Philostratus, however, never mentions Christianity, and there is no reason to believe that his aim was anti-Christian. He saw Pythagoreanism as a virile and convincing guide to life. The wellsprings of divine wisdom came from the East, and in particular from the Brahmins in distant India. Palestine did not enter into his reckoning.

Mithraism

Pythagoreanism was the cult of sophisticated and wealthy people at Severus's court and in the provinces. The religion, however, that bound emperor to slave, and commercial centers to frontier garrisons across the length and breadth of the empire was Mithraism. The Persian religion had been gaining adherents in the empire since the beginning of the second century. Between 170 and 240, however, it became probably the most important single cult in the Mediterranean world. Its prosperity and that of the empire coincided. To some extent, it fulfilled on a more popular level the religious aspirations outlined by Philostratus. The cult dramatized the eternal battle between good and evil, and it combined mystery and awesome ceremonial with a sense of comradeship and achievement. It promised salvation from evil and oblivion to all who would submit themselves to its discipline.[29] There was also something of the lure of the East that Philostratus found in Pythagoreanism. It is quaint to find Persian words like "unconquered" (*Nabarze*) addressed by Mithraists to their god in the Dacian capital of Sarmizegethusa.[30]

Mithras combined commitment to his worship with hospitality to other gods. He himself was worshiped as the Unconquered One, god of Time, superior to Fate, and lord of the planets. He was mediator between the worlds of light and darkness and revealer of the righteous way of life. On an inscription from the London Walbrook Mithraeum he promised "life to wandering humans." There, however, the god was associated with Hercules and Bacchus.[31] In Gaul he made Apollo, the god of healing, his companion.[32] In Spain (Emerita) his associates were Mercury and Oceanus.[33] Worship of the most varied origins was brought into harmony. Mithras answered prayers addressed equally to Zeus or Sarapis as well as to himself.

His worship was evidently organized on the basis of small conventicles like those of the Gnostics. The Mithraea were usually small, narrow, rectangular buildings with seats for twenty to twenty-five people on each side of a central aisle. One end would be dominated by a painted or carved representation of Mithras slaying the bull, but only seldom if ever would the initiate be sprinkled with the blood of a slain bull—the *taurobolium*. The worshipers were more concerned with acts that would enable the believer to move through the seven spheres, which surrounded earth, to salvation. In one Ostian Mithraeum there was a succession of seven doors on which had been painted the planetary deities and probably a prayer to be recited at each, just as Celsus described in 178.[34] There was also the imitation of the sacred meal eaten by Mithras and the Sun god, celebrated by the initiates in bread and wine; and the services gave scope for prophecy, ecstatic utterances, and the singing of hymns. Those who had accepted the service of the god (*militia*) had to undergo a fearsome initiation. Like the Gnostics whom they resembled in many ways, they swore to keep the mysteries secret; then, according to a wall painting in the Mithraeum of Capua, the convert would be propelled blindfolded by a master of novices, perhaps to be branded.[35] Thus, he was "born" or "sealed" and, like the initiate at Santa Prisca who scrawled the date of his "birth" on the wall ("at first light" on 20 November 202), could enter the lowest of the seven grades that ascended towards perfection.[36] Henceforth, his life was given over to service, for "Us too, thou [O, Mithras] hast saved by shedding the blood [of the bull] that grants eternity." "I have borne the greatest orders of the gods on my shoulders to the end."[37] Seventeen centuries later, the metrical inscriptions on the walls of the Santa Prisca Mithraeum preserve the ideals and hopes of the community that worshiped there before the Christians established themselves on the same spot in the next century.

In Rome more than one hundred inscriptions in honor of Mithras have been found. They come from all the seven regions of the city, except the Aventine where the Christians were traditionally strongest.[38] Seventeen miles down the Tiber at Ostia another sixteen Mithraea have been found, each apparently serving its own area, located sometimes in a shop, or a house, sometimes in its own building, but never prominently placed, preserving the religion's mysterious element in its buildings as well as in the cult.[39] Mithraism was at home in the capital, its port, and in the garrisons, but it had also won adherents in smaller country towns such as Capua. There the god was associated with a whole range of deities including Saturn as god of the harvest and Oceanus; and there was a magnificent early-third-century fresco showing the Moon-goddess being carried away into the night by her horses.[40] In the first half of the third century, Mithraism commanded the same devoted skills of craftsman and painter as the frescoes and mosaics of the Christian churches were to command in the next century.

Like Christianity, Mithraism drew its adherents from practically every walk of life. At the Mithraea in Ostia, of the twenty-one names identifiable, four probably were slaves, and others were freedmen. (One prominent individual in the Mithraea of the Animals and house of Diana was a member of the association of builders [*collegium fabrum tigsimarium*], but no official or magistrate has recorded his name for posterity).[41] On the other hand, in the Dacian capital, imperial officials seem to have been among the more prominent members of the cult, and with them was a priest of the temple dedicated to the imperial cult as well as freedmen.[42] In the frontier provinces senior officers often figured as dedicants, but at Carnuntum on the Danube, one of those who dedicated an altar to Mithras "the creator of light" was the slave Adlectus, associated in this act with a priest and a centurion.[43] Socially Mithras, despite his Persian origin, was a unifying force. His cult spanned the Greco-Roman pantheon bringing its different adherents together in a single moral and religious discipline.

Mithraism, however, was based on the acceptance of a myth, symbolizing the triumph of good over evil and the believer's progressive attainment to the knowledge of the rulers of the universe that would ensure salvation. These aims it shared with the Gnostics but it failed even more signally than they to sustain a coherent system of doctrine that might have ensured its permanency. Social religion though it was, it had little if any place for women, and while enforcing discipline on its members, there was no "Book of Mithras" to which reference could be made in case of disputes. Above all, Mithras was not a historical Savior who could inspire followers continuously from one generation to the next and who had left his gospels or sayings for them. Mithraic organization was diffuse. The *Pater Patrum* (Father of Fathers) in the Mithraeum at the Baths of Caracalla in Rome does not seem to have had a hierarchy beneath him. Each town or garrison had its Mithraea, but these depended for their upkeep on the enthusiasm of wealthy worshipers. In the 230s this was forthcoming freely enough. A generation later, the supply was drying up as the crisis of the empire deepened.

Under the Severans few could have foreseen this development. The authority of the pagan cults seemed unshakeable, and while they dominated the scene in every province, much of the religious life of the empire appeared to be moving along similiar lines towards similar goals. Educated provincials were coming to regard the Deity as one. "I think therefore, it makes no difference," Celsus had said, "whether we call Zeus the Most High, or Zen, or Adonai, or Sabaoth, or Ammon like the Egyptians or Papaeus like the Scythians" (*Celsus* V.41). Was God therefore an all-embracing Deity represented to humankind through a hierarchy of national and local gods and spirits, or was God exclusive, who required an exclusive awe and veneration from worshipers? Among the ranks of saviors, Mithras, Heracles, and Christ were being worshiped as conquerors of fate and benefactors of humanity,[44] and among humanity itself, while some proclaimed their cheerful ideal to posterity, "Drink that you may live,"[45] others stated their final message more soberly. "I have not had much wealth or money in my lifetime but I have practiced with diligence the words of metre and friendship as much as in my power."[46] Epicureans thus joined hands with Christians in praising the same ideals of moderation and brotherliness. The words too, of the great masters Plato and Zeno, and the Orphic poems, Hermetic writings, and the Chaldean Oracles were being venerated as inspired texts, a pagan "Scripture," that formed the basis of all discussion concerning the truth.[47] For the Christians, influential circles in Alexandria and Rome were regarding their faith in terms of Platonic or Aristotelian philosophy. A final touch of universalism was provided by the means through which the Deity was approached. However divergent their origins, an inhabitant of Severus's empire might have found the Mithraic and Christian meals of bread and wine, the ecstatic prophetic utterances of the participants, and the sealing ceremonies that prepared the initiate for the mysteries had intrinsically more in common than devilish parody.[48]

Gnosticism

The prosperity of the Gnostic sects in this period is another symptom of the coalescence of religious beliefs and attitudes throughout the empire. For Rome itself one has only to glance at Hippolytus's (c. 215) compendium of unorthodoxies. Naassenes, Valentinians, Carpocratians, Cainites, ascetic followers of Tatian and Marcion luxuriated. In Carthage c. 200, Tertullian painted an envious picture of the pulsating life of these sects, of their constant growth, division, decline, and reemergence, of the pert (Gnostic) women teaching and disputing, baptizing and exorcizing.[49] There were catechumens in plenty and pagans attended their rites. A real though unordered Gnostic ministry had come into being—confronting that of orthodoxy and, to Tertullian's outrage, "uniting in communion with all comers."[50]

Unconsciously, Tertullian provided a reason for the continuance of Gnostic prosperity; "Seek, and you will find" (Matt. 7:7) was, according to him, the Gnostics' favorite text.[51] They made no demand for simple or unquestioning faith. They accepted religion as a voyage of discovery, and in this final era of urban prosperity in the ancient world, reflected the fading, tenuous links that bound the educated individual to the age-old Greek spirit of inquiry. Vigorous minds were still attracted to Gnosticism. There was Prodicus of Alexandria, a libertarian who denied the need for prayer because God knew our needs anyhow.[52] Origen's wealthy patron Ambrosius was a Valentinian for much of his life. Another such was the

Athenian (?) Candidus, with whom Origen was invited to debate by the orthodox Christians of Achaia in c. 229. It was a long, overland journey from Alexandria, so that the occasion must have been important. Candidus was evidently a dualist and a determinist, and during the discussion argued that the devil, being wholly wicked, could not be saved. Origen swallowed the bait. Orthodoxy required acceptance of free will, he claimed, and hence even the devil could choose between right and wrong and ultimately achieve salvation. This utterance, perhaps touched up by Candidus, caused a furor in Alexandria and added to Origen's troubles with Bishop Demetrius.[53] But the debate highlighted the dilemma facing Christians who sought to harmonize current Platonist or Neo-Pythagorean philosophy with Christianity. If the body was a tomb whence the immortal soul must be liberated and saved, how could the conclusion be avoided that the material world was indeed evil? Or, if all living beings possessed free will and the means to return to God, how could it be that the devil alone could not be saved? The dilemmas were not all pointed against the Gnostics, especially among those who in their hearts suspected that the universe was indeed ordered on dualistic lines.

An example of the power, serenity, and beauty of artistic expression found in one Gnostic sect has been preserved in the magnificent frescoes discovered in 1919 in the Tomb of the Aurelii on the Viale Manzoni in Rome. These are third-century paintings dating probably to the period 220–40 and one of the earliest examples of Christian catacomb art.[54] They decorated the walls of the luxurious burial chambers built in honor of "the brethren and fellow-freedmen" (col[l]ibertis) of Aurelius Felicissimus, and show how in the apparent syncretism of Christian and Pythagorean themes, the pagan elements were being absorbed into Gnostic Christianity and furnished with a new Gnostic significance. The Gnostics had already embarked on a process discernible in the catacomb art of orthodox Christians in Rome by the end of the century. They were representing in art Orpheus charming the animals, the theme used by Clement in literature to demonstrate the superiority of the Logos, the inspirer of the true music of heaven.

The themes of the Creation, the Banquet (or Last Supper?), the Good Shepherd reading a scroll but also surveying his flock, and the triumphant entry of a leader into a city (Christ entering the heavenly Jerusalem?) portrayed in detail and delicacy by the artist, leave no doubt that Aurelius Felicissimus and his friends were Christians. The Gnostic element is shown more subtly. The heavenly light of the Pleroma bathes the Paradise where the "brethren" meet after death;[55] in the scene of the creation of the First Man by the Demiurge, the serpent also is not seeking to tempt Eve with the forbidden fruit but is curled round the tree, mouth open, as though speaking and teaching.[56] Two other frescoes, one above the other, depict the return of Ulysses to Ithaca, and Ulysses and Penelope with her suitors; but it is an ideal Ithaca, perhaps representing the beauty of the world of the divine Mind (*Nous*).[57] Hermes guides men's souls, represented by the suitors, to the heights of the firmament and not, as in pagan mythology, to the underworld of Hades.

The nonorthodox character of the Tomb of the Aurelii has long been recognized. It has been argued in detail by Carlo Cecchelli in his fine *editio princeps* of the paintings,[58] and reaffirmed by the more recent studies of Jerome Carcopino. But what heretics? The Carpocratians? Hardly, when one of the "brethren" was Aurelia Prima, described as a *virg(o)*. Montanists? But there was no reference to prophecy, and the Montanists hardly favored the use of pagan mythology. The evidence points to Valentinians, more specifically the Naassenes, both because of the presence of the "wise serpent" and Hermes identified by the sect as the redeemer who awoke souls to become "suitors" for salvation.[59] The frescoes show the explicit synthesis of Christian with Homeric and Pythagorean elements, characteristic of the Naassenes, each contributing towards an understanding of the mystery of the soul's progress towards salvation.[60]

At Rome, there was evidently still no clear-cut division between Gnostic sect and orthodox community. At Alexandria, this was true also. In Clement's time (c. 180–200) there may have existed an inner ring of orthodox initiates into "the greater mysteries." These studied a secret Gospel of Mark, longer than the canonical Gospel, and disputed the meaning of crucial passages with the Carpocratians who apparently had access to the same volume.[61] What was "the mystery of the kingdom" in which Jesus was supposed to have instructed a youth raised from the dead as Lazarus was raised in the Fourth Gospel? What was the significance of the "nakedness" of the youth on which the Carpocratians had evidently seized? The newly discovered text, perhaps included in a genuine letter of Clement, breaks off. Certain it is that at the turn of the third century there were Gnostic chaplains attached to wealthy Christian houses in Alexandria, and that orthodox and Gnostics attended services taken by these.[62] Origen was repelled, and his early writings show an obsession with the danger of Gnosticism. He wrote c. 230 in desperation,

> Today under the pretext of Gnosis, heretics rise against the Church of Christ. They pile on their books of commentaries. They interpret the Gospel and apostolic texts. If we are silent, if we do not oppose them, famished souls are fed with their abominations.[63]

The gigantic *Commentary on the Gospel of John* in which those sentences occur was aimed primarily at refuting Heracleon's commentary on the same Gospel, still influential half a century after its author's death.

ORTHODOXY

Thus in the Severan period dualistic syncretism, whether represented by an hospitable Mithraism or Neo-Pythagoreanism, or by an almost equally all-embracing Gnosticism, remained a powerful religious force among literate provincials in the Mediterranean provinces of the empire. Had this process continued, the supremacy of the immortal gods and of the cult of the emperor would never have been threatened. How then did the situation change so radically in favor of orthodox Christianity in the course of the third century? Partly, the orthodox "won the argument," first against the Gnostics, and then against paganism; partly their organization was proof against the disasters that befell the empire after the collapse of the Severan dynasty in 235; and partly they alone of the great religions of the time had the self-confidence backed by material power to support a prolonged missionary campaign.

Hippolytus of Rome, Tertullian of Carthage, and Clement of Alexandria all lived in the reign of Septimius Severus and wrote with the Gnostics as well as the pagans in mind. By their deliberate fusion of Paul with current interpretations of Plato, together with extravagant mythologies concerned with creation, the Gnostic schools had laid themselves open to varied forms of attack. The orthodox writers of the reign of Severus continued the work of Irenaeus. Hippolytus and Tertullian took their cue from their great predecessor and met the Gnostics head on. Both denied the possibility of a Christian debt to philosophy. Hippolytus's *Refutation of All Heresies* analyzed each Gnostic system in turn, in order to show how all led back to some Greek philosophical system, and hence were to be rejected. Tertullian was more direct and more pugnacious, combining his knowledge of legal procedure with a shrewd sense of gains to be won from confrontation. *On Prescription Against Heretics* (c. 200) claimed that the heretics had no right to use Scripture in any way. They were usurpers, latecomers whose sects had come into being long after the church had established itself and therefore held a possessory right over Scripture.[64] Heretics were automatically nonsuited. And if Scripture belonged to the church, what need was there of philosophy? Tertullian's outburst in the *Prescription*, "What has Athens to do with Jerusalem, the Academy with Christ? What have heretics to do with Christians? . . . Away with all attempts to produce a Stoic, Platonic and dialectic Christianity," was aimed at the Gnostics.[65] He gained the day. The majority of Christians in Roman North Africa followed him in accepting a religion based on the Bible and the activity of the Spirit, with the hope for martyrdom and anticipation of vengeance in a literal Day of Judgment. Not until Augustine's time was any attempt made in North Africa to harmonize the Latin classical heritage with Christianity.

In addition, the tradition of the goodness of God as creator of the universe was too firmly embedded in Jewish and Christian monotheism to be displaced by dualistic creeds, however well argued. The two stories of creation in Genesis had given rise to speculation for centuries, but to be acceptable any creation myth must bear some relation to tradition. Orthodox interpretations of Genesis eventually carried greater conviction than did the Gnostic. When the Manichees appeared on the scene in the fourth century and the same area was fought over, victory went once more to the orthodox. Clement of Alexandria's contribution to the debate was to show that Platonism and Scripture could be combined to demonstrate not dualism but the harmony and goodness of the universe. Its institutions, such as marriage, were good in themselves. Sin resulted not from defect of nature but defect of will. If wealth was used correctly, it benefited the community as a whole.[66] Unlike Tertullian and Hippolytus, Clement did not deny the Gnostics some insights into the truth, and like them he believed that "perfect knowledge" was the hallmark of the perfect believer. His interpretation of Christianity turned out to be as elitist as the Gnostics' but Gnostic sectarianism repelled him. He was determined to keep Christian Gnosticism within the framework of the church and its Rule of Faith.

Superiority, however, was won primarily on the plane of morality. Origen makes this clear in a response to Celsus. He pointed out how "in some respects the Greeks and those who believe our doctrines hold the same views, yet they have not the same power to win over souls and confirm them in their teachings" (*Celsus* VI.2). It was the "overwhelming power" of an individual at once divine and human and preached by "uneducated men" to educated and uneducated alike that proved the truth of Christianity for Origen. He himself was prepared to strain even the concept of monotheism, not shrinking from describing to a surprised audience the deity in terms of "two Gods," united however in love and power.[67] His definition, too, of the Holy Spirit as "the highest of the angels"[68] opened the way to a veritable galaxy of angelic beings to whom the lesser deities of paganism could be likened. Embarrassing concessions to polytheism were avoided only after a debate on the nature of the Trinity that began c. 200 and did not end until the Council of Constantinople of 381. That the debate did end, and that Christianity did not disintegrate in the process, is proof of its innate strength.

Orthodoxy was not only responding to the intellectual challenge of the times but was also developing a momentum of its own. It was strengthening its organization—not losing sight of its association with the forces of articulate opposition in the empire. Apocalyptic hopes, for instance, were no longer crucial. Orthodoxy, however, was beginning to scent victory in a world in which it must conquer or succumb. Christians, as heirs to the Dispersion, had for long tended to think of the church as worldwide in scope. The term "universal" or "catholic" church had been used by Ignatius of Antioch and Polycarp. Irenaeus paraded his knowledge of the geography of the empire to prove that Christians did speak the same language of belief everywhere.[69] Though Gnosticism and Montanism found adherents from one end of the Mediterranean to the other in a comparatively short time, episcopal Christianity had the edge on its rivals through its superior organization. In the reign of Septimius Severus, none but the orthodox

283

Christians would have contemplated holding councils "between Gaul and Osrhoene" to secure the uniform celebration of their chief feast, Easter, as did Pope Victor (c. 195).[70] In c. 210 Tertullian, sectarian Montanist though he was by then, envisaged "universal councils" (not Montanist) to discuss matters of general concern to Christians, and he mentioned councils in Greece as though he had some firsthand knowledge of these.[71] Even Tertullian felt the need to belong to a corporate body. Clement recognized this even more clearly when he admitted that "the sophists steal certain fragments of the truth for the injury of mankind and bury them in human systems of their own devising, and then glory at presiding over what is a school rather than the Church."[72] Both he and Origen preferred universality. Both were emphatically men of the church. In 200 though there were differences in detail, a single recognizable Rule of Faith, to which appeal could be made, circulated in the main centers of Christianity.[73]

Of these, Lyons was to fade from the scene after the death of Irenaeus, and Ephesus also was never quite able to assert its apostolic prerogatives. The other greater centers, including Antioch, were almost simultaneously able to produce capable episcopal leaders who could enforce collective decisions on recalcitrants. Victor of Rome (189–199), the first Latin-speaking pope, attempted to do this with the date of Easter.[74] Demetrius of Alexandria (189–232) established suffragan bishops in Egypt and consolidated the authority of the bishop of Alexandria over the rest of Egypt, at the expense of the Alexandrian presbyters who had apparently previously governed the church with the bishop.[75] Serapion of Antioch (190–209) enforced an orthodox canon of scripture on the churches under his rule. He forbade the congregation of Rhossus on the Gulf of Issus to read the apocryphal *Gospel of Peter* at services (Eusebius *HE* VI.12). Agrippinus of Carthage (c. 220) held a council—the first recorded in North Africa—and opened the baptismal controversy by declaring that those who had been baptized outside the church must be rebaptized on conversion to orthodoxy.[76] Together, these bishops represented a milestone in the history of the church. Its organization was becoming based on the major provincial capitals supervising the communities scattered over enormous contiguous areas, and foreshadowed the emergence of the archbishoprics of the fourth century and the patriarchates of the fifth. Rome, Antioch, Alexandria, and Carthage were already the leading sees in Christendom in the first quarter of the third century.

With the increase in the range of episcopal authority comes the first tangible evidence for the church holding property as a corporate body. The exact legal position continues to be disputed. It seems unlikely, however, that the church first acquired its property as a burial society for the poor. Its numbers in the larger centers would have prevented anything in the nature of a legal fiction. The alternative, that it formed a "society of the worshippers of the God Christ" (*cultores divinitatis Dei Christi*), as proposed by Charles Saumagne, is possible but has yet to be demonstrated.[77] Be this as it may, under Pope Zephyrinus (199–217) the church in Rome owned a catacomb which it placed under the control of a deacon, and the Severan period saw the first identifiable Christian catacombs in San Callisto and Calepodius.[78] In Carthage, Tertullian criticizes heretics for "not having churches" and speaks of the cemeteries (*areae*) as though they were typical of Christianity there. "Away with the *areae*," was as much an anti-Christian slogan as "Christians to the lion.'"[79]

REVIVAL OF MISSION

Strength of organization and growing wealth were accompanied by a revived sense of mission. Irenaeus, though claiming to have preached to "barbarian tribes" in Celtic,[80] was concerned mainly with thwarting the Gnostics, and there is no trace in his writings of any plan to translate the Scriptures into Celtic. In his time, Christianity had gained ground largely through natural growth, to which were added random conversions through example or through an individual lighting on the Scriptures and being convinced through them. The three-year catechumenate and introspective Jewish outlook of many Christians, such as those criticized by Celsus, were strong dissuasives. Much of this was to change. By 200 the church's "sojourn" in the empire was becoming a permanent stay. Montanism had shaken the authority of the episcopate momentarily, but at the end of the century established hierarchies were in firmer control of Christian communities than ever before. A Syrian bishop might send his flock out into the desert "to meet Christ" there,[81] while a colleague in Pontus averred, "if this [the Parousia] does not happen as I have said, believe the Scriptures no more, but let each one of you do as he will.'"[82] These voices, however, were ceasing to be representative. A new spirit was abroad. The appearance in 221 of a specifically Christian history, a synchronistic history of the peoples of the world, compiled by a wealthy Palestinian, Julius Africanus, was a further indication that the church was coming to terms with existence here below. Africanus's scheme did not envisage the millennium, "the Sabbath of the world," for another three hundred years.[83] Millenarianism was going quietly underground to provide a rallying cry and hope in times of crisis, but otherwise leaving the field clear for the church to discover its new destiny.

What could have been a profoundly discouraging prospect, as the bishop of Pontus realized, in fact coincided with Christianity's growing impact on the pagan world. "Nothing," the apostle Peter is alleged by the writer of the *Clementine Recognitions* (c. 240) to have complained, "is more difficult than to reason about the truth before a mixed multitude.'"[84] This, however, is what the Christians set about doing. First in Alexandria and then in Carthage and Rome there were serious and successful attempts to spread the faith to educated pagans, accompanied by a Christian apologetic compiled with an explicit missionary purpose. The success of this propaganda during the period 190–220 resulted in violent but sporadic persecution which in 202 may have received encouragement from the emperor.

Alexandria

Alexandria had already begun to be a center for the Christian mission by c. 180. The city was the main port for a varied trade between the eastern Mediterranean, the Red Sea, and beyond the Gulf of Aden across the Indian Ocean to the Malabar coast. There were also contacts with an important town just south of Pondicherry (Poduca) where quantities of fine Roman table ware (samian pottery) and amphorae have been found.[85] To undertake a voyage thither from Alexandria was something of a feat. There is no reason to doubt Eusebius's word that Pantaenus, the converted Stoic who had brought the Alexandrian catechetical school out of obscurity, should have "journeyed even to the land of the Indians" as "a herald of Christ even to the nations of the east."[86] There he is said to have found Christians who used the Gospel of Matthew, that is, Jewish Christians. Probably at about this time the writer of the Gnostic *Acts of Thomas* described a mission (probably from Edessa) to the court of King Gundaphorus somewhere in northern India, and the first missionary successes there due also to the welcome presence of a Jewish community among whom the gospel could be preached.[87]

Pantaenus handed over the leadership of the catechetical school to Clement and left Alexandria, never to return. Clement, as we have seen, was an immigrant, a convert to Christianity whose spiritual odyssey resembled Justin's.[88] He had fallen under the spell of Pantaenus, shared many of his ideals, and on his departure worked to establish the small catechetical school there as the center of Christian study and mission. His aim, however, was to convert members of the community of educated Alexandrian Greeks, who previously might have been attracted to a Judaism of the type represented by Philo. Just as Philo had presented Judaism as the highest form of wisdom and the means by which humankind would come to "see God," so Clement urged that Christianity was the end to which all current philosophy had been moving. He opens his *Exhortation to the Greeks* with a fine, challenging passage in which he compares the music of Amphion and Orpheus (which according to legend charmed the animals) with the true music of heaven—Christianity. Christianity was the new melody superior to that of Orpheus. Christ was both God and man, "becoming man in order that such as you [Gentiles] may learn from man how it is even possible for man to become a god [*theos*]."[89] Elsewhere (*Miscellanies*), he encourages Christians to become missionaries themselves. "The word of our teacher did not stay in Palestine as philosophy stayed in Greece, but was poured out over all the world persuading Greeks and barbarians alike."[90] To be a Christian and not to try to influence one's neighbor was to be an unprofitable servant.[91] Christians should become preachers and writers of the word, the latter a new development in itself.

Such was Clement's ambition. The *Exhortation*, the *Tutor*, and the *Miscellanies* seem to have been first aimed to convert, then to instruct the convert in Christian morality and etiquette, and finally to introduce this person to a number of separate themes, such as marriage, martyrdom, or those in which the Christian ideal of spiritual perfection could be explained and justified. The notes which have survived under the title *Extracts from Theodotus* are directed against the Gnostics. Clement owed much to Stoicism and its second-century expounders. His aim was to present the Christian as the truly virtuous person, who used God's gifts as they were designed to be used, and embodied the Stoic virtues of moderation and prudence. In thought and action the Christian excelled in the philosopher's way of life, just as his Lord perfected the harmonies expressed by the deities of pagan myth.

Unfortunately execution fell far short of aim. Despite its opening passage, the *Exhortation* is a disappointing work. Much of it follows the treadmill of Jewish apologetic against the pagan gods and their myths which most educated Alexandrians must have heard already. Only near the end does Clement develop an argument which marks a new and bold departure in Christian apologetic. He challenges his readers to examine their allegiance to custom. Custom strangles man. It turns him away from the truth. It leads him away from life. Perhaps thinking of his own experiences as a traveler, he wrote:

> Again in voyages by sea, deviations from the usual course may bring loss or danger, but yet they attract. So in life itself, shall we not abandon the old way, which is wicked, full of passion, and without God? And shall we not even at the risk of displeasing our fathers, bend our course towards the truth and seek after him who is our real Father thrusting away custom as some deadly drug.[92]

Custom was the reason why godliness was hated.

Here, Clement was right. Every aspect of religion and life in the ancient world depended on custom. "It was unreasonable to overthrow a way of life handed down to us by our forefathers"[93] was an argument used time and again against the Christians.[94] Celsus had even urged that, whatever one might believe, "there should be a formal acknowledgment of the gods," though he added, "so far as this is expedient."[95] For most people from officials downwards, the existence of the gods was a fact of life. The "immortal gods of Rome" were the "natural" and "saving gods." "Everyone knew them," affirmed the deputy prefect of Egypt, Aemilianus, addressing Bishop Dionysius in 257.[96] A late-second-century "cross-word puzzle" from Oxyrhynchus answers the clue "Isis" with "the great hope," and "Serapis" with "glory of Alexandria."[97] For anyone to claim openly that the abandonment of custom was "a great boon" was asking for

287

trouble. In c. 311 Eusebius of Caesarea at the beginning of his *Preparation for the Gospel* wrote of pagan charges against the Christians of his day: "How can men fail in every way to be impious and godless who have apostatized from their ancestral gods? To what kind of punishments would they not be justly subjected, who deserting their ancestral customs have become zealous for foreign myths of the Jews, which are of evil report among all men."[98]

This is what Clement was urging his converts to do, and he was not alone. In Syria, missionaries representing a very different Jewish-Christian tradition were using the same arguments combined with traditional exposure of the failings of the Olympian gods. Custom should be rejected, Christianity embraced—such is one of the principal themes of the *Clementine Recognitions*.[99] The Severan age saw Christianity emerge from the shadows as the main alternative religion and culture for those of inquiring minds to accept.

Clement, however, had other difficulties. Apart from his own streak of Jewish-Christianity and emotional rejection of paganism instanced by his admiration for Tatian, he was confronted in Alexandria by considerable numbers of Christians who wanted nothing to do with philosophy or philosophical Christians. Clement came to dislike and despise these people and their claims to orthodoxy. "The so-called orthodox," he declared, "are like beasts that work out of fear. They do good works without knowing what they are doing."[100] Such people "are scared of Greek philosophy as they are of [actors'] masks, fearing it would lead them astray."[101] The "orthodoxists" were "dumb animals that have to be driven by fear."[102] It was hopeless to tell the educated catechumen that the Greek poets were inspired by the Devil. "The earth is the Lord's and the fullness thereof, and anyone who seeks to help catechumens, especially if they are Greeks, must not shrink from scholarly study."[103] For these, the new religion could be presented as a natural progression from their past and its claims supported by reference to current philosophical speculation.[104] Christ was the true realization of the wise man of the Stoics, but his law was not merely advice but spoke of grace and with moral power.

By c. 200 Clement had built up a flourishing community of well-educated Alexandrians, orthodox in outlook and willing to defend themselves against pagans and Gnostics. Then in 202 savage persecution befell the Christians. He fled, but his place was taken almost immediately by Origen, a young man who was to leave his mark permanently on the history of Christianity. We reserve the contributions to Alexandrian theology both of Clement and Origen for another chapter. Here we are concerned only with Origen's early missionary work. He was born in 185 of mixed Alexandrian-Greek and Egyptian parentage. He was named "born of Horus" but by that time or shortly afterwards both his parents were Christians, and Origen developed as a zealot as well as a prodigy of learning. In 203 his father was martyred. Origen tried to share his fate, but he was frustrated. His mother hid his clothes, and modesty overcame valor.[105] In a year or two he set about continuing Clement's work and, as Eusebius of Caesarea says, "he won for himself an exceedingly wide reputation among all who were of the faith" by his encouragement of confessors.[106] Soon some of his own converts were among these and he was hounded from house to house. Years later, Origen looked back to those days as the heroic times of Alexandrian Christianity. Reminiscing in the midst of writing his fourth *Homily on Jeremiah*, sometime in the 240s, he wrote:

> Then one really was a believer . . . the catechumens were catechesized in the midst of martyrdoms and in turn these catechumens overcame tortures and confessed God without fear. Then, too, the faithful were few in numbers but were really faithful, advancing along the straight and narrow path leading to life.[107]

In Origen, the Alexandrian church found precisely the leader who could turn those influenced by Clement's teaching into convinced Christians. When in c. 225 he wrote *On First Principles* against the Gnostics, he pointed out that the more enterprising and thoughtful in "all Greece and the barbarous parts of the world," "the innumerable zealots," had deserted their ancestral gods and the laws of their fathers to embrace Judaism or Christianity.[108]

Origen saw Christianity as a movement of spiritual and moral reform, building sometimes on existing philosophy as well as on Scripture, but always leading the individual forward by its own merits toward a truer understanding of one's self and of the divine world. It was essentially an optimistic creed, designed for people "made in the image of God." Though there were times when laws, such as those that forbade the practice of Christianity, might rightly be disobeyed,[109] by the time he wrote *Celsus*, that is, about 248, he was already looking forward to the Christianization of the world and harmony between church and empire.[110]

In the West

The progress of Christianity had not been inspired by such ideals. What lay behind the angry protest of so much of Western Christianity during the third century is not fully known. Occasionally, an outburst by Tertullian in Carthage against the *leges dominantium* (that is, the laws of those in power, perhaps even conquerors),[111] a protest by a Christian woman in Corinth in 202/3 against the happy times,[112] a passage in Hippolytus of Rome comparing the Roman Empire to that of Nebuchadnezzar may have provided a clue.[113] Something was wrong. There was dissoluteness on the stage and gross cruelties in the amphitheater. There was a flatness and massive uniform vulgarity in the great buildings characteristic of the Severan age in Africa. Were these the customs of the Romans? Was their religion, at best antiquarian and more usually licentious and cruel, really worth following? There was a corresponding nostalgia for a pre-Roman Carthaginian past, for liberty of expression and integrity of thought, for the "natural religion of mankind" that Christianity seemed to offer. There was the spur, too, of living and dying for a cause whose triumph would assure the vindication of the faithful, the poor, and the deserving, and the destruction of all that represented demonic power and privilege in the existing world.

The first glimpse of the North African church shows this. The Scillitan Martyrs were seven men and five women brought in from the small settlements of Scilli near Carthage, and on 17 July 180 accused before the proconsul Vigellius Saturninus of being Christians and, perhaps in addition, of maligning the Roman gods. Proceedings were brief. The proconsul told the accused that if they returned to their senses they would be pardoned by "our lord the emperor." In reply Speratus, the Christian spokesman, asserted that they had done no wrong and when abused gave thanks "for we hold our own emperor in honor." Patiently, the proconsul explained that they too were a religious people. "Our religion is a simple one: we swear by the genius of our lord the emperor and we offer prayers for his health—as you also ought to do." No compromise was possible. Speratus refused to "recognize the empire of this world." He served God, who "is the emperor of kings and of all nations," and his fellow Christians agreed. A thirty-day reprieve was rejected with scorn, and the proconsul thereupon condemned them for "living in accordance with the rites of the Christians," refusing "the opportunity [thirty-days' respite] to return to the usage of the Romans," and having "persevered in their obstinacy." The confessors went cheerfully to their deaths. "Today we are martyrs in heaven. Thanks be to God!"[114] This was to be the spirit of North African Christianity. The conflict between the new religion and Roman customs was demonstrated here as political as well as religious. Like Pliny in Bithynia, Saturninus regarded the Christians as both "mad" and obstinate to the point of rebellion, and they deserved execution. Yet in the next twenty years, Christianity took off.

By early in 197 Tertullian, himself a convert with a Stoic background, was exultant over the progress his new faith was making. "Day by day," he told his pagan opponents, "you groan over the ever-increasing number of Christians. Your constant cry is, that your state is beset by us, that Christians are in your estates, your camps, your blocks of houses [insulas]. You grieve over it as a calamity, that every age, in short every rank is passing over from you to us" (To the Nations I.14). A few months later in his Apology, written as an "open letter" to the magistrates of Carthage, he repeated his claim. "Good and sensible men" as well as the trendy were becoming Christians; and Tertullian was not concerned so much with defending Christianity as with making a wholesale attack on every aspect of pagan religion and culture.[115] The contrast between "your camps" // "your state" and "we Christians" was unmistakable. He was thinking in terms of two rival ways of life, as the prophet Hermas had of rival "Laws," of which one only could emerge as victor.

This attitude was shared by one group of articulate Christians who were brought before the procurator Hilarianus during 202.[116] Vibia Perpetua was a young married woman of good family, twenty-two years old with an infant son at her breast. She was accompanied before the tribunal by her personal slave Felicitas and three other young Christians. Her catechist, Saturus, joined her voluntarily in prison. In Perpetua's family, her father, mother, aunt, and one brother were pagans, while she herself, her other brother, and her slave were Christian catechumens. How this family had become so irrevocably divided is unknown. It was precisely the situation that had worried Celsus, and the father's evident inability to control his daughter brought on him the procurator's anger. Whatever the reason, Perpetua was prepared to defy him, the authorities, and the world, and reject all the traditional pieties and loyalties in which she had been brought up. The diary which she kept in prison gives some idea of her hopes from Christianity and the instruction she had received. She believed that baptism by water was a preparation for martyrdom, that her status as confessor entitled her to vivid dreams and visions of paradise in which she could converse with the Lord. There is little trace of the teaching of the gospels or epistles in her account of her feelings. She was acquainted, however, with the Pentateuch, Revelation, the *Apocalypse of Peter*, probably *Enoch* and the Jewish-Christian *Gospel of Thomas*.[117] Her conviction was unshakable. Even after she had been badly hurt from being tossed by a maddened heifer in the amphitheater, she found strength to encourage her brother and other catechumens: "You must all stand fast in the faith and love one another and do not be weakened by what we have gone through."[118] It could be the utterance of an extremist leader; and just before this she had told off the warder for not looking after her companions and herself: "We are the most special prisoners, as we belong to Caesar, seeing that we are going to fight on his very birthday."[119] It was up to the authorities to see that they looked their best. Defiance could not be taken further. The joys of paradise awaited her, damnation her pagan enemies. Perpetua provides a link between religious and political discontent of the day.

Rome

Rome also produces interesting evidence of the pagan-Christian confrontation in these years. The *Octavius* of Minucius Felix probably incorporates fragments of a debate between a pagan and a Christian, perhaps in Cirta the capital of Numidia, in about 170 when Marcus Cornelius Fronto's attack on Christianity was still fresh in people's minds. In its final form, it dates after Tertullian's *Apology*, from which the author borrowed copiously, and may have been written as late as 240.[120] It shows that the debate between the two sides was well and truly joined, with the advantage turning towards the Christians. Minucius Felix himself was believed by Lactantius (c. 310) to have been a distinguished lawyer in Rome,[121] and his two friends, Octavius Januarius and Q. Caecilius Natalis, were men of the same standing.

The case for paganism argued by Caecilius was a fairly strong one. Caecilius's philosophic skepticism belied his deep loyalty towards the traditional gods of Rome. Human beings—limited in intelligence—were incapable of exploring the ways of God and nature, "how in shipwrecks the fates of the good and evil are confounded," and "in battle the better men fall first."[122] It was only sensible to accept the verdict of history and tradition in matters of religion. Rome had prospered under its gods.[123] The Christians had nothing tangible on which to base their assertions, while the horrid practices of their religion, their unproven and ridiculous beliefs regarding the future life, and their unsocial conduct in this life made their presumptions valueless.

Octavius's reply, though less aggressive than Tertullian's, attacked paganism in all its aspects—its irrelevance to Rome's success, the grotesque and barbarous origins of the gods, its lack of moral worth, and the lying nature of the wandering spirits that produced diseases and even madness in humans. Polytheism was a dangerous sham, responsible for human shame and degradation. The gods themselves were unclean spirits and demons, both deceiving and deceived.[124] God's providence, not these demons, ruled the fate of empires; for the individual, honor was a truer tribute to distinction than high office. Octavius was not making a plea for recognition on behalf of Christianity, but a demand that its truth be acknowledged. The debate revolved around the merits of polytheism versus a Christianized monotheism, argued mainly from Cicero's *On the Nature of the Gods*, with the image of Christian nobility adapted from Seneca's *On Providence*.[125] There is no quotation from the New Testament, and Christ is not mentioned once. The work shows that many members of the Roman professional classes were becoming disillusioned with ancestral paganism, and were seeking in Christianity a monotheist philosophy which could be combined with as much of the pagan classical heritage as possible. Caecilius admitted also to being won over by the "sincerity" of the Christian sect (*Octavius* XL), and Octavius's final thrust, "We do not preach great things but we live them" sounds like authentic argument.[126] There must also have been a growing skepticism regarding traditional ideas of Roman history. Livy's view of Rome's progressive and predestined advance to greatness was becoming unfashionable. There is a note of anger in Octavius's claim: "All that the Romans hold, occupy and possess is the spoil of outrage; their temples are full of loot, drawn from the ruin of cities, the plunder of gods and the slaughter of priests."[127] When these were not Roman gods and priests the Christians extended their sympathy.

Octavius triumphed, Caecilius confessed himself conquered and, like his two friends before him, ready to become a Christian. That such a work could be written speaks much of the advance of Christianity in the capital in this period but the ideals which Octavius represented were not to prevail. Only at the turn of the fifth century was there a possibility that the legacy of the classical past and of Stoicism in particular would be incorporated into Western Christianity. This hope foundered on the determination of Augustine and the North Africans that theirs would be the Christianity of the West.[128] Tertullian rather than Octavius set the pattern the West was to follow.

How far were the charges against pagan society in Rome and Roman North Africa justified? In some ways, quite sufficiently. Added to the account of the deaths of the martyrs of Lyons and of Perpetua and Felicitas in the amphitheater at Carthage in 203, a mosaic discovered in a villa at Zliten in Tripolitania contains a graphic and horrifying portrayal of the execution of condemned criminals by the beasts in the amphitheater.[129] All the details relayed with such anger by Latin Christian writers of the third century are present, and more. Against the background of an orchestra dominated by an instrument which looks like an organ and including trumpets and cornets, the prisoners are presented to wild beasts who in turn are provoked by *bestiarii* armed with long whips. The prisoners are either tied naked to stakes in the arena or mounted on a miniature chariot whose protective frontal shield, however, extended only as far as their knees, leaving their bodies free for the animals to attack. Lions and leopards were used as the executioners. It is not surprising that these bloodthirsty sights, which some liked to have on their dining room floors, should have revolted others. Christianity gained adherents. The insult to human dignity was too flagrant.[130]

PAGAN REACTION

Christianity meant different things to different individuals, but its progress from Lyons to the Euphrates frontier was sufficient to cause alarm among the pagan majority. Between 195 and 212, there were sporadic persecutions of varying degrees of violence in many parts of the empire. The events in Carthage have been immortalized by the account of the martyrdom of Perpetua and Felicitas in the amphitheater of Carthage on 7 March 203, and persecution continued intermittently at least until August 212, the approximate date of Tertullian's address to the proconsul Scapula. In Alexandria, Clement wrote of "roastings, impalings and beheadings" of Christians before he fled the city, probably during 203.[131] Under the prefect of Egypt, Q. Maecius Laetus (201–3), Origen's father was executed, and after Clement's departure some of his own converts were hunted down and executed likewise.[132] This second wave of persecution took place under the prefect Ti. Claudius Subatianus Aquila between 206 and 210.[133] In Rome, too, the presbyter Hippolytus has left a vivid description of the mob turning on the Christians—for the first recorded time since Nero "rid the earth of such like: they are not fit to live."[134] One Roman confessor of this period was the Monarchian heretic Natalius who eventually made his peace with Pope Zephyrinus. Persecution was real enough. For Corinth, Hippolytus instances a Christian woman denounced to the authorities on the grounds that "she had blasphemed both the times and the emperors and spoken ill of the idols."[135] Her indiscretions cost her her life. In Antioch, persecution resulted in Christians taking refuge with the Jews and the arrest of the future bishop Asclepiades.[136] In Cappadocia another future bishop, Alexander of Jerusalem, was imprisoned.[137] In faraway Britain, some have argued for the death of the soldier Alban in this period.[138]

What had happened? A clue may be provided by the fact that most of those confessors of whom we know anything were either catechumens or recently baptized converts. Perpetua and Felicitas in Carthage, Hero and his companions in Alexandria are examples, while influential bishops, such as Demetrius of Alexandria, Serapion of Antioch, or Zephyrinus of Rome remained unscathed. This is the opposite of what one would expect and contrasts with the situation in subsequent persecutions during the third century. One piece of evidence, much disputed, suggests both that the emperor Severus took some initiative, and that the aim of his measures was to discourage conversions. An alleged text of a rescript preserved by the author Aelius Spartianus in the *Scriptores Historiae Augustae* reads, "He forbade conversion to Judaism under heavy penalties and enacted a similar law in regard to the Christians" (*Severus* XVII.1). There are reasons to believe this to be derived from a good source,[139] and Eusebius himself independently speaks of "the persecution of Severus."[140] Christians "were made, not born," at this period, Tertullian tells his readers.[141] We learn from him as well as from Hippolytus and Clement that mobs often took the initiative against the Christians, and from Philostratus (*Life* 1.15) that mob outbreaks against the authorities on one or another pretext were among the hazards of life in the Greco-Roman cities of the time. It may be that the rescript that Spartianus preserves was the result of authorities reporting an outbreak against the Christians to the emperor, just as the governor of Lugdunum had done in 177, and Severus giving his orders accordingly.[142]

THE RETURN OF PEACE

Gradually, the wave of animosity subsided. Persecutions after 212 became more sporadic. Christians, in Lampridius's phrase, were "allowed to exist," and as this same phrase occurs in the edicts of Gallienus and Galerius ending persecutions, it may perhaps represent official thinking.[143] Some Christians attained influential positions in the household of Caracalla and Alexander Severus. In Aurelius Prosenes, who died c. 217, one may identify perhaps the first of a long line of Christians who held the office of chamberlain at the court.[144] Another Christian in an official position was Julius Africanus, Origen's correspondent in Palestine, a biblical scholar and chronographer who was appointed architect for the library which the emperor, Alexander Severus, established in the Pantheon at Rome.[145]

Osrhoene

One area that benefited from the long peace was the Euphrates frontier provinces of the empire where Christianity had been progressing slowly for the previous century. In the great area east of Antioch which included the client-state of Osrhoene and extended either side of the Euphrates, the lingua franca was Syriac and religion was traditionally connected with the worship of Bel and Atargatis (Astarte) with a strong predilection for astrology. Observation of the stars was, as J. B. Segal points out, the link between popular religion and the complex schemes of the philosophers.[146] Christianity, like Judaism before it, was often propagated by merchants moving in their groups along the desert caravan routes. We hear, for instance in the *Chronicle of Arbela*, of people "identified by their dress as merchants" taking Christianity further east across the Roman frontier into the Persian province of Adiabene.[147] Bishops and clergy seem often to have been itinerant, preaching from village to village traveling with merchant caravans. Addai (Thaddeus), the reputed evangelist of Edessa, came originally from Paneas (Banias) and stayed in the home of a Jewish merchant named Tobias.[148] If Christians regarded the "law of Christ" as universally binding, there does not seem to have been any firm "orthodoxy" such as was evolving in the Greek-speaking communities. The Marcionites seem to have been the predominant sect, and the Gnostic Valentinians also were numerous. Tatian's *Diatessaron (Harmony of the Gospels)* with its encratite overtones was probably read in Addai's congregations,[149] and its connections seem to have been strongest with the Christians in Adiabene. Orthodoxy, meaning in this case the church that depended on the "Western" bishopric of Antioch, was a newcomer in 200. Shortly afterwards in 201, the *Edessene Chronicle* records the destruction of the "temple of the Christians" by a flood.[150] The orthodox were one sect out of many.

The advance of Christianity in Edessa and the surrounding territory of Osrhoene between 200 and 235 may be associated with two developments. First, King Abgar VIII the Great (177–212) favored Christianity and, according to his friend Bardesanes (Bar Daisan), "believed." He symbolized his abandonment of tradition by forbidding any of his subjects to become eunuchs as a part of their worship of Atargatis.[151] Others are less definite about his conversion. Julius Africanus (c. 230) calls him a "holy man," and Epiphanius of Salamis in the next century "a most pious and reasonable man" (but not "a Christian").[152] His kingdom, however, did not survive

Caracalla's eastern campaign of 216. Edessa fell and was reduced to the status of a Roman *colonia*, but not before Christianity had been given an impetus as the religion favored by the old ruling house.

The second event was the emergence of Bardesanes (154–222) as the outstanding religious leader in Osrhoene. According to later tradition Bardesanes's family had emigrated from Parthia, but he was brought up in the court of King Abgar at Edessa where Julius Africanus met him in 195. He was a striking personality, "highly gifted in all fields," according to Epiphanius in the next century.[153] He was a skilled archer as well as being a philosopher, geographer, and man of science. What turned him to Christianity c. 179 from his original connection with the worship of the Dea Syra at Hierapolis (Mabbug) is not known—a chance encounter with the Christian bishop of Edessa was suggested later; his surviving work, *The Dialogue of Destiny, or The Book of the Laws of the Countries*, shows him to be a fervent Christian. For him the Christians were "the new people," to be found in every region and locality, and like his contemporary Origen he valued Christianity as the great solvent of dissonant and barbarous customs that divided people from people. All could now be left to the judgment of God.[154]

It is difficult, however, to be precise about his ideas. He opposed the Roman Empire because it suppressed freedoms, imposing its own laws on peoples such as the Arabs it had conquered.[155] His religious ideas, however, are recorded differently in Greek, Syriac, and Arabic sources. Some points seem clear and indicate why Bardesanes's influence was lasting, especially on the teaching of the Persian religious reformer Mani. Bardesanes opposed the powerful local Marcionites and, in particular, their teaching that God and the creator were not the same Being. Instead, he believed that originally there had been a universal harmony in which the four pure elements of Light, Wind, Fire, and Water existed in perfect equilibrium, separated from the fifth element, their enemy Darkness. The latter possessed no active qualities of its own, but as a result of some primeval catastrophe, "whether from some external body or by chance," became mingled with the pure elements, thus bringing them to movement and flux.[156] Out of this mixture the universe and humans came into being. Bardesanes's view of humankind was optimistic. Though as a mortal, one was under the domination of the planetary powers that controlled the material world, one's soul (*nous*) was divine in origin and capable of free choice and purification. One was able to accept the teaching of Christ, the Savior who came "from the bridal chamber of light," to show the way back towards the realm of Light.[157] Each generation would see the lessening of the elements of Darkness in the world, until after six thousand years the process of purification would be complete and the original harmony of the universe would be restored. Bardesanes's ideas belonged almost exclusively to the Semitic world, and Greek Christians such as Eusebius of

Caesarea were merely confused by them, writing their author off as a "Valentinian."[158] His imagery resembles that of the Song of the Pearl and some of the Nag Hammadi Gnostic writings, but no Gnostic asserted as he did the purifying nature of conception and birth.[159] At the same time, the ultimate dualism of Light and Darkness and the disturbance of original harmony through their mingling were notions that Mani was to take up and develop twenty years later. To that extent Bardesanes deserved the judgment passed on him by Ephraem Syrus (d. 374) that he was the "teacher of Mani,"[160] though he would have denied to Darkness the active qualities of evil that characterized the Manichean system. His career and ideas are another example of the extraordinary intellectual vigor and originality that was being expressed through Christianity in the first decades of the third century.

Dura-Europos

Further south, in the garrison town of Dura-Europos, Christianity was associated also with the overthrow of the powers of Darkness and Fate. In this polyglot city, which fell to the Persians in 256/57, the inhabitants seem to have been obsessed by their horoscopes and astrological predictions. The Christian community was mainly Greek-speaking and drawn from both the local citizenry and the garrison.[161] Their names were written in Greek or Syriac and contained no names that were necessarily Jewish. Thus, the community was parallel to rather than coincident with the Jews, though the church, constructed in 232 in a private house, was not far from the synagogue near the city walls and away from the center of the town.[162] It held a congregation of about seventy and on the walls of the assembly room were scratched apotropaic symbols and abecedaria designed to ward off evil.[163] One of the frescoes painted on the wall showed David overthrowing Goliath, the type or prefiguration of Christ destroying Satan. Christ himself was portrayed as the Great Physician and Athlete saving his followers from powers that reduced man to something less than human, condemned to do obeisance to idols as well as to secular rulers.[164] This interpretation of the paintings of Dura may be right. In the first thirty years of the third century Christianity emerged from the shadows as a liberating and renovating force when classical civilization had begun to seem to many provincials—especially in the eastern provinces of the empire—either oppressive or irrelevant.

BIBLIOGRAPHY

NOTE

Students will find a useful list of older works on the development of paganism in the Roman Empire on pp. 764–67 of *CAH*, vol. 12: *The Imperial Crisis and Recovery*,

A.D. 193–324, ed. S. A. Cook, F. E. Adcock, M. P. Charlesworth, and N. H. Baynes, 2d ed. (New York: Macmillan Co.; Cambridge: At the University Press, 1939). M. J. Vermaseren's studies of Mithraism should be consulted, including, in particular, his synthesis, *Mithras, the Secret God,* Eng. trans. T. Megaw and V. Megaw (New York: Barnes & Noble, 1963). For the religious policy of the Severans, see the present author's *Martyrdom and Persecution,* chap. 12, and "Open Questions Concerning the Christians and the Roman Empire in the Age of the Severi," *JTS* 25 (October 1974): 333–51. For the Roman Gnostics, J. Carcopino's *De Pythagore aux apôtres,* Etudes sur la conversion du Monde romain (Paris: Flammarion, 1956), is important, and for the cult of Heracles and its relationship to Christianity in the third century, see M. Simon, *Hercule et le christianisme* (Paris: Publications de la Faculté des Lettres de l'Université de Strasbourg, 1955). For a general picture of the relations between Christianity and philosophy, see the same author's *La civilisation de l'Antiquité et le Christianisme* (Paris: Arthaud, 1972), chap. 8.

For the Roman East, the reports on the excavations at Dura-Europos conducted by Yale University and the French Academy of Inscriptions and Belles Lettres, *The Excavations at Dura-Europos: Preliminary Reports* (1929–38), *Final Reports* (1953–58), ed. P. V. C. Bauer, M. I. Rostovtzev, A. R. Bellinger (New Haven, Conn.: Yale University Press), are essential. So, too, is J. B. Segal's *Edessa the Blessed City* (New York: Oxford University Press; Oxford: At the Clarendon Press, 1970).

For Minucius Felix and the Christian-pagan debate of the time, see J. Beaujeu, *Minucius Felix: Octavius* (Paris: Collections Budé 1964), and the final chapters of T. R. Glover's *The Conflict of Religions in the Early Roman Empire,* 3d ed. (New York: Charles Scribner's Sons, 1909). For the general history of the time see also F. Millar, *A Study of Cassius Dio* (New York and London: Oxford University Press, 1964).

Sources

Bardesanes. *Opera.* Edited by F. Nau. *Patrologia Syriaca,* Pars I, tom. II. Paris, 1907.
Chronicle of Arbela, ed. E. Sachau, AAWB, 1915. For opinions as to its authenticity, see B. Altaner, *Patrology,* Eng. trans. H. C. Graef, rev. ed. A. Stuiber (New York: Herder & Herder, 1961), p. 234.
Clement of Alexandria
  The Exhortation to the Greeks. Eng. trans. and ed. G. W. Butterworth. LCL. Cambridge, Mass.: Harvard University Press; London: William Heinemann, 1919.
  The Rich Man's Salvation. Eng. trans. and ed. G. W. Butterworth. LCL. Cambridge, Mass.: Harvard University Press; London: William Heinemann, 1919.
  Stromata (bks. I–VI), ed. Stählin/Früchtel, GCS; bk. VII, ed. O. Stählin, GCS (1909). Eng. trans. Book III by H. Chadwick and Book VII by J. B. Mayor, revised, in J. E. L. Oulton and H. Chadwick, eds. and Eng. trans., *Alexandrian Christianity,* LCC II (Philadelphia: Westminster Press; London: SCM Press, 1954); see also Clement of Alexandria, trans. W. Wilson, 2 vols. ANCL, Edinburgh, 1872.

Dio Cassius. *Roman History*. Eng. trans. and ed. E. Cary. LCL. 9 vols. Cambridge, Mass.: Harvard University Press; London: William Heinemann, 1914–27.

Hippolytus. *Commentary on Daniel*. Edited by N. Bonwetsch. GCS 1. Leipzig: Hinrichs, 1897.

Refutation. Edited by P. Wendland. GCS 26.

Minucius Felix. *Octavius* (in Tertullian volume). Eng. trans. and ed. G. H. Randall. LCL. Cambridge, Mass.: Harvard University Press; London: William Heinemann, 1931.

See also B. Kytzler, ed., Munich: Kösel Verlag, 1965.

Philostratus. *Life of Apollonius of Tyana*. Eng. trans. and ed. F. C. Conybeare. LCL. 2 vols. Cambridge, Mass.: Harvard University Press; London: William Heinemann, 1912.

SHA, ed. E. Hohl, Leipzig: Teubner, 1927, reprinted 1955; D. Magie, ed. and Eng. trans., LCL, 3 vols., Cambridge, Mass.: Harvard University Press; London: William Heinemann, 1922, 1924, 1932.

Tertullian. *Apology*. Eng. trans. and ed. T. R. Glover. LCL. Cambridge, Mass.: Harvard University Press; London: William Heinemann, 1931.

For various martyrologies, see H. Musurillo, ed. and Eng. trans., *The Acts of the Christian Martyrs*, Oxford: At the Clarendon Press, 1972; and G. Lanata, ed., *Gli atti dei martiri come documenti processuali*, Milan: Guiffré, 1973.

SECONDARY WORKS

Barnes, T. D. "Legislation Against the Christians." *JRS* 58 (1968): 32–50.

Burkitt, F. C. "The Christian Church in the East." *CAH*, vol. 12, chap. 14, pp. 476–513.

Carcopino, J. "Les *Castella* de la plaine de Setif." *Revue Africaine* 62 (1918): 1–22.

Cecchelli, C. *Monumenti cristano-eretici di Roma*. Rome: Fratelli Palombi, 1944.

Clarke, G. W. "Two Christians in the *Familia Caesaris*." *HTR* 64 (January 1971): 121–24.

Drijvers, H. J. W. "Bardesanes." *TRE* V 1/2, pp. 206–12. Berlin, 1979.

Fasola, U. M., and Testini, P. "I cimitiere cristiani." *ACIAC* IX (1975), pp. 103–39. Vatican: Pontificio Instituto di archeologia cristiana, 1978.

Fink, R. O., Hoey, A. S., and Snyder, W. F., eds. *The Feriale Duranum*. In Yale Classical Studies, ed. A. M. Harmon et al., vol. 7. New Haven, Conn.: Yale University Press; London: Oxford University Press, 1939–40.

Frend, W. H. C. "Blandina and Perpetua: Two Early Christian Heroines." *Les Martyrs de Lyon* (177). CNRS no. 575, pp. 167–77. Paris, 1978.

Laeuchli, S. *Mithraism in Ostia: Mystery Religion and Christianity in the Ancient Port of Rome*. Evanston, Ill.: Northwestern University Press, 1967.

Meiggs, R. *Roman Ostia*. 2d ed. New York: Oxford University Press; Oxford: At the Clarendon Press, 1973.

Mingana, A. "The Early Spread of Christianity in Central Asia and the Far East: A New Document." *BJRL* 9.2 (1925): 1–80.

Morris, J. "St. Alban and St. Albans." *Hertfordshire Archaeology* 1 (1969): 1–8.

Osborn, E. F. "Teaching and Writing in the First Chapter of the *Stromateis* of Clement of Alexandria." *JTS* n.s. 10 (1959): 335–44.

Simon, M. "Mithra, Rival du Christ." In *Études Mithraiques*, pp. 427–78. Leiden: E. J. Brill, 1978.

Smith, Morton. *Clement of Alexandria and a Secret Gospel of Mark*. Cambridge, Mass.: Harvard University Press, 1972.

_____. *The Secret Gospel: The Discovery and Interpretation of the Secret Gospel According to Mark*. New York: Harper & Row, 1973.

Turcan, R. "Ulysse et les prétendus prétendants." *JAC* 22 (1979): 161–74.

Vermaseren, M. J. *Mithraica I: The Mithraeum at S. Maria Capua Vetere*. Leiden: E. J. Brill, 1971.

_____, with Essen, C. G. van. *The Excavations in the Mithraeum in the Church of S. Prisca*. Leiden: E. J. Brill, 1965.

Wheeler, R. E. M. *Rome Beyond the Imperial Frontiers*. New York: Philosophical Library, 1955; London: G. Bell & Sons, 1954.

NOTES

1. Thus, the authors of the *Scriptores Historiae Augustae,* for instance, Lampridius, "Antoninus Heliogabalus" 3.4–5, ed. Hohl, vol. 1, pp. 223–50, esp. p. 225. See my "Open Questions," p. 345.

2. Tertullian *Ad nationes libri duo (To the Nations)* II.1 (ed. A. Reifferscheid and G. Wissowa, CSEL 20, pp. 59–133 [Vienna, 1890], p. 94).

3. Origen, *Commentarius in Cantica Canticorum*, Book II, ed. W. A. Baehrens, GCS 33 Origen (Leipzig: Hinrichs, 1925), pp. 168–69.

4. Eusebius *HE* VI.21.3.

5. Lampridius *Severus Alexander* XIV.7, "a woman greatly revered [mulier sancta], but covetous and greedy for gold and silver."

6. Thus, P. R. L. Brown, *The World of Late Antiquity* (New York: Harcourt Brace Jovanovich; London: Thames & Hudson, 1971), pp. 18, 22.

7. See Galen, *Peri euchymias kai kakokymias* I.1–7, ed. G. Helmreich, Corp. Medic. Graec. V.4.2, Galenus (Leipzig/Berlin, 1923), pp. 389–91 (I owe this reference to G. E. M. de Ste. Croix).

8. Carcopino, "Les *Castella*," pp. 1ff.

9. Two centuries later, Augustine praised the "humanity" of the *Constitutio Antoniniana* in his *De civitate Dei (City of God)* V.17.

10. Tertullian *De anima (Concerning the Soul)* XXX (ed. A. Reifferscheid and G. Wissowa, CSEL 20, pp. 298–396 [Vienna, 1890], p. 350).

11. Brown, *Late Antiquity*, p. 17.

12. See my summary of the religious situation in the third century there, in *Martyrdom and Persecution*, pp. 307–8.

13. A. S. Hoey in *Feriale Duranum*, ed. Fink, Hoey, and Snyder, p. 173.

14. Pliny *Letters* X.96.5. See above, p. 150.

15. Philostratus, *Life*, ed. and trans. Conybeare, 1.15, though allegedly referring to the reign of Tiberius.

16. *ILS* 2445. See for this and other examples W. Ensslin, "The End of the Principate," in *CAH*, vol. 12, chap. 10, pp. 352–82, esp. pp. 356–58, For a prayer of thanksgiving to "the gods" and the "saving Fortune of our lord the invincible

Severus Antoninus (Caracalla) which saved you. . . ," see *PSI* XII, 1261, lines 7–12.

17. Lampridius *Severus Alexander* XXIX.2.

18. Tertullian *Apology* V.2.

19. Lampridius *Severus Alexander* XXII.4, "Iudaeis privilegia reservavit, Christianos esse passus est."

20. Philostratus *Life* I.3.

21. Ibid., I.31–32 and IV.11, sacrifices of a bloodless and pure kind celebrated at the tombs of the Achaians at Troy; and cf. I.10, a sarcastic reference to a flood of blood from sacrifices on the altar.

22. Lactantius, *Divinae institutiones* (*Divine Institutes*), ed. S. Brandt and G. Laubmann, CSEL 19 (Vienna, 1890), VI.1.5 and 2.1 as examples.

23. Philostratus *Life* I.15.

24. Ibid., I.13.

25. Ibid., II.30.

26. Ibid., I.16.

27. Ibid., I.11.

28. Eusebius, quoting Hierocles in *Contra Hieroclem* 2 (*PG* 22. 797–800), and cf. Lactantius, *Divine Institutes* V.2–3.

29. The best survey of Mithraism in the Roman Empire is by Vermaseren, *Mithras.*

30. Ibid., p. 64; and in Rome, "Nama" (Hail), p. 65, found frequently in the dedications in the Santa Prisca Mithraeum.

31. "Hominibus bitam bagis" (= vitam vagis). See J. M. C. Toynbee, *Art in Roman Britain* (New York and London: Phaidon Press, 1962), pp. 128–29.

32. Vermaseren, *Mithras*, p. 1.12.

33. Ibid., p. 56.

34. See Laeuchli, *Mithraism in Ostia*, pp. 100–103; and cf. Celsus in Origen *Celsus* VI.22, and *CIL* V.5893 (Mithraism and astrology) and Chadwick's note, Origen *Contra Celsum* (New York and Cambridge: Cambridge University Press, 1953), pp. 334–35.

35. Vermaseren, *Mithraica I*, pp. 26ff. and Pl. xxi, xxv–viii.

36. See Vermaseren and van Essen, *Excavations in Mithraeum of Prisca,* p. 118 and Pl. xxi, 1–2.

37. "Nubila per ritum ducatis tempora cuncti" (Vermaseren, *Mithras*, p. 173); "Et nos servasti eternali sanguine fuso" (ibid., p. 177); and "Atque perlata humeris t[u]li m[a]x ima divum" (Vermaseren and van Essen, *Excavations in Mithraeum of Prisca*, p. 204).

38. See Meiggs, *Roman Ostia*, pp. 373–74; and Laeuchli, *Mithraism in Ostia*, chap. 2.

39. Laeuchli, *Mithraism in Ostia*, and Meiggs, *Roman Ostia*.

40. Vermaseren, *Mithraica I*, p. 15.

41. See Laeuchli, *Mithraism in Ostia*, p. 36.

42. Vermaseren, *Mithras*, p. 64.

43. Ibid., p. 61.

44. Regarding the cult of Heracles in this period, see Simon, *Hercule*, chaps. 2 and 3.

45. For the acclamation, see H. Leclercq, "Pie Zeses" *DACL* 14.1 (1939), cols.

1024–31, some of these invocations with the addition of "in deo" could be Christian.

46. The tomb of Gaius, a lawyer in Eumeneia = Insc. 232 from Eumeneia, publ. by W. M. Ramsay, *Cities and Bishoprics of Phrygia* (New York: Oxford University Press, 1901), p. 386 (early third century A.D.).

47. See Simon, *La civilisation de l'Antiquité*, p. 205.

48. Tertullian *De corona* (*Concerning the Crown*) XV; *De praescriptione Haereticorum* (*On Prescription Against Heretics*) XL; and *On Baptism* V. Compare Justin *1 Apology* 66. See Vermaseren and van Essen, *Excavations in Mithraeum of Prisca*, pp. 151–53.

49. *Prescription* XLI, and compare XLII for the vigorous life of the sects.

50. *Prescription* XLI.1. For the Gnostic challenge to the hierarchical system of the church of this time, see E. Pagels, *The Gnostic Gospels* (New York: Random House; London: Weidenfeld & Nicolson, 1979), chap. 2. Catholic clergy were described as "waterless canals" in the *Apocalypse of Peter* LXXIX (Eng. trans. J. Brashler, R. A. Bullard, and F. Wisse in *The Nag Hammadi Library*, ed. James Robinson [New York: Harper & Row, 1978], pp. 339–45, esp. p. 343).

51. *Prescription* XLIII.

52. For Prodicus, see Clement *Miscellanies* III.30 and VII.41.

53. See Chadwick's account in *Alexandrian Christianity*, ed. and trans. Oulton and Chadwick, pp. 431–32.

54. See the fine, beautifully illustrated account in Cecchelli, *Monumenti cristiano-eretici*, pp. 3ff.; and Carcopino, *De Pythagore*, pp. 85ff. Also J. Stevenson, *The Catacombs: Rediscovered Monuments of Early Christianity* (London: Thames & Hudson, 1978), pp. 111–17, and Turcan, "Ulysse" (bibliography).

55. Carcopino, *De Pythagore*, pp. 159–60; compare pp. 127–28.

56. Ibid., pp. 111–12.

57. Ibid., p. 182. For an alternative explanation, that the fresco represents the myth of Circe, interpreted as Circe instructing souls in process of reincarnation or transformation into animal species, see Turcan, "Ulysse," 168–73.

58. Cecchelli, *Monumenti cristano-eretici*, 92ff., though Cecchelli prefers Montanism to Gnosticism as the allegiance of the group.

59. Hippolytus, *Refutation*, ed. Wendland, V.7.30–37.

60. Thus Carcopino, *De Pythagore*, pp. 157ff., and 206–17. Hippolytus, *Refutation* V.7.30, 8.1, 8.34, leaves no doubt as to the esteem felt by the Naassenes for Homer. See also above, p. 201.

61. Morton Smith, *Clement of Alexandria*, pp. 46ff.; Eng. trans. of text of the fragment of Clement's (?) letter to Theodore, ibid., pp. 446–47; and note Origen's mention of privileged initiation of those able to receive it, *Commentary on St. John's Gospel* VI.3, ed. E. Preuschen, GCS 10, Origen (Leipzig, 1903), pp. 109–10.

62. Eusebius *HE* VI.2.14.

63. Origen, *John's Gospel*, GCS 10, V.8, p. 105.

64. Tertullian *Prescription* XXIX–XXX.

65. Ibid., VII.

66. The argument of Clement's *Rich Man's Salvation*, Eng. trans. and ed. Butterworth, pp. 13–14.

67. *Dialogue with Heracleides*, ed. and trans. H. Chadwick in *Alexandrian Christianity*, ed. and trans. Oulton and Chadwick, p. 438. See over, p. 381.

68. Origen *De principiis (On First Principles)* I.3:5. "The Holy Spirit is still less and dwells within the saints alone" (Stevenson, *A New Eusebius*, p. 216).

69. Irenaeus *Heresies* I.10.2; see above, p. 245.

70. Eusebius *HE* V.23.4; see above, p. 245.

71. Tertullian, *De ieiunio adversus psychicos (On Fasting)* XIII, ed. A. Reifferscheid and G. Wissowa, CSEL 20, pp. 274–97 (Vienna, 1890), p. 292.

72. Clement *Miscellanies* VII.15.92 and compare ibid., VII.17.107.

73. Compare the Rules in Irenaeus *Heresies* I.10.1, Tertullian *Prescription* XIII, and in the preface 4–8 of Origen's *On First Principles* (texts in Stevenson, *A New Eusebius*, pp. 115–16, 176, and 212–14), and for its existence in Alexandria in Clement's time, *Miscellanies* VII.15.90.2.

74. Eusebius *HE* V.24.9ff.

75. Jerome *Letter* CXLVI.1 for the Alexandrian presbyters being responsible for the appointment of the bishop, "choosing one out of their number" until "the episcopates of Heraclas and Dionysius." It looks as though the decisive change of authority from Alexandrian presbyters to suffragan bishops in Egypt took place in Demetrius's long episcopate (189–232).

76. Cyprian, *Letter* LXXI.4, ed. W. Hartel, CSEL 3.2, pp. 465–842 (Vienna, 1868), p. 774. Bishops from Numidia and proconsular Africa were present".

77. See C. Saumagne, *Saint Cyprien, Evêque de Carthage, "Pape" d'Afrique (248–258): Contribution à l'étude des "persécutions" de Dèce et de Valérien* (Paris: CNRS, 1975), p. 16, and in general, my *Martyrdom and Persecution*, pp. 324–26 (references).

78. Hippolytus *Refutation* IX.12.14; and for the dating of the earliest Roman catacombs, see Fasola and Testini, *I cimitiere cristiani*, p. 5 and pp. 106–7 in vol. I of *ACIAC*.

79. Tertullian *Apology* XL.2; *Ad Scapulam (To Scapula)* III.1, ed. V. Buhlart, CSEL 76, pp. 9–16 (Vienna, 1957), *(areae)*.

80. Irenaeus *Heresies*, preface 3.

81. Hippolytus, *On Daniel*, ed. Bonwetsch, IV.18.1ff.

82. Ibid., IV.19.1ff. Hippolytus blames both clerics for failing to understand scriptural passages about false prophets.

83. See Burkitt, "Christian Church in East," pp. 477–78. Hippolytus also seems to have thought the world would continue for some 270 years after he was writing. See R. Helm's (ed.) introduction to Hippolytus, *Chronicle*, GCS 46, Hippolytus (Berlin, 1955), p. ix.

84. *The Clementine Recognitions* III.1.

85. See Wheeler, *Rome Beyond Imperial Frontiers*, pp. 145–50, and Pl. xxi–xxiv.

86. Eusebius *HE* V.10.1–3.

87. See James, Eng. trans., *Apocryphal New Testament*, pp. 365ff. at p. 368; the flute girl who heard Thomas was "by race a Hebrew."

88. Clement *Miscellanies* I.11. 1–2. See above, pp. 252–53.

89. Clement, *Exhortation*, Eng. trans. and ed. Butterworth, p. 22, 1.

90. Clement *Miscellanies* VI.18.167, ed. Stählin/Früchtel, p. 518.

91. Ibid., I.1.3; and compare I.1.12: "Wisdom must be disseminated." See also Osborn, "First Chapter of *Stromateis*," concerning Clement's stress on writing as a means of proclaiming the Word.

92. Clement *Exhortation* X.73, Eng. trans. and ed. Butterworth, p. 196; compare ibid. XII.91, "custom strangles man."

93. Ibid., X.73, Eng. trans. and ed. Butterworth, p. 196, and compare Eusebius, *Praeparatio evangelica* (*Preparation for the Gospel*) IV.1.

94. For the same sentiment in the West, see (the pagan) Caecilius in Minucius Felix *Octavius* VI.1: "How much more reverent and better it is to accept the teaching of our elders as the priest of truth."

95. Origen *Celsus* VIII.62.

96. Eusebius *HE* VII.11.9.

97. *Pap. Oxy.* 3239 (later second century); Rome, on the other hand, is a "foreign city" (line 37).

98. Eusebius *Preparation* I.2 (*PG* 21.28D).

99. Especially in book IX.

100. Clement *Miscellanies* I.45.6. Were these the remnants of the Jewish-Christians in Alexandria?

101. Ibid., VI.80.5, and compare 162.1.

102. Ibid., I.45.6.

103. Ibid., VI.89.2.

104. For this aspect of Clement's mission, see W. W. Jaeger, *Early Christianity and Greek Paideia* (Cambridge, Mass.: Harvard University Press, Belknap Press, 1961; London: Oxford University Press, 1962), p. 67.

105. Eusebius *HE* VI.1.2–3.7.

106. Ibid., VI.3.3.

107. Origen, *Homily on Jeremiah* IV.3, ed. E. Klostermann, GCS 6, Origen (Leipzig: Hinrichs, 1901), pp. 25–26.

108. Origen *On First Principles* IV.1.

109. Origen *Celsus* I.1.

110. Ibid., VIII.72. See below, p. 311.

111. Tertullian *Nations* II.1.

112. Text of Hippolytus, preserved in Palladius's *Lausiac History* (c. 400), chap. 65, Eng. trans. W. K. Lowther Clarke, Translations of Christian Literature, series 1: Greek Texts (New York: Macmillan Co.; London: SPCK, 1918), p. 172.

113. Hippolytus *On Daniel* II.12 and IV.17. See my *Martyrdom and Persecution*, pp. 375–76.

114. *Passio Sanctorum Scillitanorum* (*Acts of the Scillitan Martyrs*), in *Acts of Christian Martyrs*, ed. and Eng. trans. Musurillo, pp. 86–89; and, with better bibliography and critical apparatus, G. Lanata, *Gli atti dei martiri come documenti processuali* (Milan: Guiffré, 1973), pp. 137–44. Both Vigellius and Pliny use the word *amentia* regarding Christian beliefs; cf. Pliny *Letters* X.96.4.

115. Tertullian *Apology* III.1; for "trendies," ibid., III.3.

116. *Passio Sanctarum Perpetuae et Felicitatis* (*The Martyrdom of Saints Perpetua and Felicitas*), in *Acts of Christian Martyrs*, ed. and Eng. trans. Musurillo, pp. 106–31. See also Lanata, *Gli atti dei martiri come documenti processuali*, pp. 158–61.

117. See my comments in "Blandina and Perpetua," pp. 172–73.

118. *Martyrdom of Perpetua* XX.

119. Ibid., XVI.

120. Thus, the editor, Beaujeu, *Minucius Felix, Octavius*, introduction pp. lxxff. and lxxix.

121. Lactantius *Institutes* V.1.22.

122. Minucius Felix *Octavius* V.10.

123. Ibid., 12: "Have not the Romans without your [the Christians'] God, empire and rule; do they not enjoy the whole world and lord it over you" (the "you" suggests a non-Roman origin for this part of the tract).

124. Minucius Felix *Octavius* XXVII.1ff. Christians at this period accepted that the pagan gods were real, but were malevolent demons.

125. See Beaujeu, *Minucius Felix, Octavius*, pp. xxxii–xxxiv; cf. Minucius Felix *Octavius* 36.5, 8, 9 and 37, 1, 3 (from Seneca *De providentia* [*On Providence*]).

126. Minucius Felix *Octavius* 38.6: "Non eloquimur magna, sed vivimus."

127. Ibid., XXV.5; cf. Tertullian *Apology* XXV.17.

128. See below, p. 673.

129. Now in the museum at Tripoli. Photographs to be seen in Simon, *La Civilisation de l'Antiquité*, Pl. 80–83, facing p. 213.

130. Thus Tertullian *Apology* XV.6, commenting on "the sheer contempt felt by those who do these things and by those for whom they do them."

131. Clement *Miscellanies* II.20.125. Regarding the persecutions in the reign of Severus, see my "Open Questions," pp. 334–43.

132. Eusebius *HE* VI.1–5.

133. See Barnes, "Legislation Against Christians," esp. pp. 40–41, and my note in "Open Questions," p. 340.

134. Hippolytus, *On Daniel* I.23, Bonwetsch, p. 35.

135. Hippolytus(?), cited in Palladius *Lausiac History* 65, see above, n. 112.

136. Eusebius *HE* VI.12 (refuge with the Jews) and ibid., XI.4 (Asclepiades). See my "Open Questions," p. 337.

137. Eusebius *HE* VI.8.7.

138. Morris's view, argued in "St. Alban," p. 3.

139. T. D. Barnes, "The Family and Career of Septimius Severus," *Historia* 16 (1967): 87–107, esp. pp. 91 and 95.

140. Eusebius *HE* VI.1.1.

141. Tertullian *Apology* XVIII.4, "De vestris sumus. Fiunt non nascuntur Christiani."

142. Frend, "Open Questions," p. 349.

143. Lampridius *Severus Alexander* XXII.4 (see above, n. 19).

144. "Prosenes receptus ad Deum" = *CIL* VI.8498 = Dessau *ILS*.1738 = *ILCV* II.3332). See Henri Grégoire's note, "Les Persecutions dans l'empire romain," *Mémoires de l'Académie royale de Belgique* 46.1 (1951), pp. 108–9; and Clarke, "Two Christians." Compare also Eusebius *HE* VI.28.

145. See Burkitt, "Christian Church in East," p. 477 (references).

146. Segal, *Edessa*, p. 50.

147. Sachau, ed., *Chronicle of Arbela*, p. 43. One bishop was recorded as away preaching in Ctesiphon, p. 64; another, Noah, spent his time in a hamlet, p. 53. For references to the discussion about the authenticity of the *Chronicle*, see Altaner, *Patrology*, p. 234, I accept the *Chronicle* as genuine.

148. For the legend of Addai and King Abgar and the introduction of Christianity in Edessa, see Segal, *Edessa*, chap. 2.

149. *The Teaching of Addai* (Eng. trans. ANCL 20, at p. 25); and see Burkitt, "Christian Church in East," pp. 493–95.

150. *Edessene Chronicle*, ed. I. Guidi, CSCO III.4 (Paris, 1903), p. 3.

151. Thus, Bardesanes in his *The Dialogue of Destiny, or The Book of the Laws of the Countries*, chap. 45, ed. F. Nau, *Patrologia Syriaca* I.2 (1907), probably early third century, and hence contemporary, writes, "when King Abgar the king believed [in Christ], he decreed that anyone who castrated himself should have his hand cut off."

152. Epiphanius, *Panarion* LVI.1, ed. Holl, p. 338, "aner hosiotatos"; and see also Julius Africanus, *Chronicle* LIII, in *Reliquiae Sacrae*, ed. M. J. Routh, 5 vols. (Oxonii: Academico, 1846), vol. 2, p. 193, "hieros aner."

153. Epiphanius *Panarion* LVI. For a concise life of Bardesanes, see Drijvers, "Bardesanes," (abundant references), and compare Burkitt, "Christian Church in East," pp. 496–99, and Segal, *Edessa*, pp. 35–45.

154. *Laws of the Countries*, ed. Nau, chap. 46.

155. Ibid., chap. 43.

156. Moses bar Kephor, cited from F. C. Burkitt, *The Religion of the Manichees* (New York: Macmillan Co.; Cambridge: At the University Press, 1925), 76–77. See also Drijvers, "Bardesanes," p. 209.

157. Burkitt, "Christian Church in East," p. 497.

158. Eusebius *HE* IV.30. For Valentinian communities in Roman Mesopotamia, see Ambrose of Milan *Letter* XL.6.13 (see below, pp. 623–24).

159. Moses bar Kephor, cited from Burkitt, *Religion of Manichees*, p. 77.

160. See *Ephraem's Prose Refutations*, ed. C. W. Mitchell (London, 1912–21), vol. 2, pp. xxxiiff.

161. *Excavations at Dura, Final Report* VIII.2. "The Christian Church," p. 114 (no certain Jewish names, p. 108).

162. Photographs of the baptistery, assembly hall, and some of the frescoes have also been reproduced in F. van der Meer and C. Mohrmann, *Atlas of the Early Christian World*, Eng. trans. and. ed. M. F. Hedlund and H. H. Rowley (New York: Thomas Nelson & Sons, 1958), 46, and in Marcel Simon, *La civilisation de l'Antiquité*, Pl.63 (see also Pl.62 for the Dura Mithraeum).

163. *Excavations at Dura, Final Report* VIII.2, pp. 109–10.

164. Ibid., p. 123.

9

Struggle and Advance 235–60

The Severan dynasty fell victim to a military revolution in March 235. In a mere half-dozen years the relative peace and prosperity of the reign of Alexander Severus had been irreparably shattered. That emperor had lost his life through his inability to crush the attacks by Germanic tribes on the Rhine frontier. In addition, there were threats by the Goths towards the Danube and the long-exposed border of the province of Dacia, but most serious of all were the objectives of the new Sassanid dynasty in Persia. Its founder Ardashir and his son Sapor I aimed at reconquering Darius's dominions, and hence driving the Romans from practically all they held east of the Bosporus. Ardashir joined Darius's name to his own as though to proclaim his intent. Between 232 and 298, the eastern frontier was seldom quiet. The catastrophic defeat inflicted by Sapor on the Romans in 260, commemorated in stone on the cliff of Naqsh-e-Rostam,[1] affected the social and religious life of the empire as well as its military prestige.

Between 235 and 270, the Roman Empire was in the gravest peril. Emperor followed emperor in rapid succession as each army, temporarily victorious over some barbarian foe, raised its general to the purple. There was an autonomous Gallic empire for fifteen years (259–74). The frontiers were devastated: Cities such as Athens and Milan, which for generations had seen nothing more violent than brawls, experienced the horrors of invasion and siege. The provinces of Asia Minor were overrun by Persians and Goths. The emperor Valerian was captured by the Persians near Edessa in June 260, eventually, it was said, to be flayed alive and his skin displayed on the gates of Ctesiphon. Military disaster accelerated economic collapse. Between 240 and 260 the *antoninianus*, the normal current coin, had been debased from a silver content of between 15 and 20 percent silver to 2 percent—a miserable silver-washed metal circle with an emperor's head decorating one side and a pious aspiration the other. Cities declined. After 244 (the death of Gordian III), it is noticeable that in many provinces inscriptions commemorating new buildings or individual beneficence become rare, not least in North Africa where they had previously been so numerous.[2] Aqueducts, fountains, markets, baths—all fell into disrepair. Municipal office, once sought after for its prestige, was avoided. There were plagues and famines on a worldwide scale. Agrarian discontent, justified by exploitation by city-dwellers and foreshadowed by incidents such as Bulla's revolt in Italy, increased. Even so reasonable a man as Dionysius of Alexandria, Origen's pupil, believed that the human race was destined to disappear through plague and civil war.[3] In Carthage, pagan magistrate and Christian bishop alike thought that the end of the world was approaching, but through whose fault?[4]

Gloom, however, should not be exaggerated. Not everyone was a pessimist. The Neo-Platonist philosopher Plotinus (204–70), who influenced the emperor Gallienus (253–68), was a man of robust intellect who dreamed of founding an ideal "Platonic city" (Platonopolis) in Campania. He attacked the dualistic and negative theology of the Gnostics who attended his lectures in Rome. He certainly preached withdrawal from the world, but he was also a practical man of affairs, believing that it was his duty to give others the benefit of an enlightened judgment. "What is the truth about this?" was his basic question to those who sought his advice, and truth required inquiry and the acceptance of intellectual challenge.[5]

Despite a desperate military situation, morale did not collapse as completely as it did in the western provinces of the empire in the first decade of the fifth century. Emperors might come and go but the administration at the center and in the provinces held firm. Senior officials were proud of their grades. *Ducenarius*, that is, an official with a salary of two hundred thousand sesterces a year, was a title to reckon with. Trade and sea routes, generally speaking, remained open. For all his gloom about the world he lived in, Cyprian of Carthage assumed that he could communicate with Bishop Firmilian of Cappadocia without difficulty, or with the Spanish congregations at Leon and Mérida who had appealed to him; the contacts between Rome and Carthage during his ten-year episcopate were frequent, rapid, and close.

Nevertheless, the foundations of society as it had evolved in the previous two centuries had been shaken. Cities were impoverished and less healthy places to visit. One was more likely than before to be struck down by plague or carried off by barbarians or Persian invaders. Christian refugees in Egypt during the Decian persecution were enslaved by nomad Saracen marauders;[6] a similar fate befell others at the hands of Kabyle rebels in North Africa in 253 (Cyprian *Letter* LXII). *Ubique pax* ("Peace everywhere") proclaimed on the coinage of successive emperors was a myth. If one is correct in placing the Latin Christian poet Commodian in the decades 250–70, there were Christians who rejoiced at the prospect of the destruction of Rome by the Goths and the overthrow of existing society.[7] The welcome given by some Cappadocian Christians to the Gothic invaders of their province in 254–55 cannot be dismissed as an aberration.[8] Christianity still meant in some cases the abandonment of the social as well as the religious values of the ancient world. It was still an opposition cult, and it was beginning to feed on agrarian as well as urban discontent.

CHRISTIAN PROGRESS

Maximin (C. Julius Maximinus), a camp-made emperor who supplanted Alexander, opened a new era of greater hazards and greater opportunities for the church. Christianity was now moving to the forefront of the empire's internal problems. Maximin was quick to single out the Christians as responsible for Severus Alexander's failures. Like other military dictators he tried to make a clean sweep of the former ministers and "disregarded his [predecessor's] directions."[9] Christians had prospered at the emperor's court, in Rome, and in some of the provinces. Eusebius refers to the execution of the Christian members of the fallen emperor's household, followed by an order "that the leaders of the Church alone should be put to death as being responsible for the preaching of the gospel."[10] It looks as though Maximin was striking at proselytism as Severus may have done at the beginning of the century. In any event, rumors of persecution in store inspired Origen to write his defiant *Exhortation to Martyrdom* in distant Caesarea. Nearer home, Pope Pontian and his rival Hippolytus, both of whom would qualify as leaders, were exiled to the notoriously unhealthy Sardinia where they died (late 235–early 236).[11]

Maximin's threats coincided with a more traditional form of persecution by Serenianus, the governor of Cappadocia, remembered twenty years later on as "a bitter and terrible persecutor." Churches were burned and Christians fled to neighboring provinces. Then a strange thing happened, suggestive of an underlying Christian apocalyptic tradition. "Suddenly," wrote Bishop Firmilian of Cappadocia,[12] "a certain woman arose among us, who in a state of ecstasy announced that she could actually cause earthquakes which had been occurring in the province, maintained that she was inspired by sources as far away as Judea, and Jerusalem," and as if to prove her authenticity "walked about barefoot over frozen snow during a hard winter." The story is interesting. There were many Christians in Cappadocia, and they owned their buildings. The Holy Land was still the center of inspiration and authority. Under stress, prophetic and apocalyptic forms of Christianity commanded a ready hearing.

This time the crisis passed quickly. Its author was murdered in 238, and in the reigns of Gordian III (238–44) and Philip the Arabian (244–49) Christianity made remarkable progress. "The faith was increasing and our doctrine was boldly proclaimed openly in the ears of all"—thus Eusebius.[13] The church not only gained massively, but from Origen's information it is clear that it was attracting large numbers of educated and ambitious people into its ranks. In a dozen years between 238 and 250, one can see the beginnings of a major change in the religious history of the Mediterranean and Near Eastern worlds—the change from the dominance of the territorial and national gods, which had lasted thousands of years, to that of personal religions claiming universal allegiance. The question—who won the debate, Celsus or Origen?—is meaningless, for though separated by only seventy years the two antagonists were already living in different worlds.

The extent of the transformation in Christianity's fortunes is shown by an exchange regarding numbers of Christians initiated by Celsus. Celsus affirmed that "if all men wanted to be Christians, the Christians would no longer want them"—a fair indication of the sectarian outlook of Christians in the reign of Marcus Aurelius. Origen, however, answered:

> I admit that at the present time perhaps when on account of the multitude of people coming into the faith even rich men and persons of position and honour

and ladies of refinement and high birth, favourably regard the adherents of the faith, one might venture to say that some become leaders of the Christian teachers for the sake of a little prestige.[14]

In the main cities, though Origen was careful not to claim that the Christians formed a majority, the "assemblies of the Christians" lived beside the assemblies of the people in each city, and set an example of uprightness that these would do well to follow.[15] They did not dominate them yet. Similarly, in his *Commentary on Matthew* (c. 248) he speaks of the continuous flow of convinced and dedicated individuals into the church. "Neither the recent date of their conversion," he writes, "nor their heathen parents are obstacles to those who struggle vigorously to ascend through obedience beyond those who have grown old in the faith."[16] Traditional gods had begun to fail, as the cities they were believed to protect declined.

Origen was thinking in worldwide terms. In Caesarea he had the leisure to write and could survey the prospects for the church. He makes much of the universal character of the Christian mission from its outset. Christ had commanded the apostles to "go and teach all nations," and they had done this. Their way had been smoothed providentially through the work of Augustus by uniting a host of warring peoples and discordant kingdoms into one empire "reducing to uniformity, so to speak, the many kingdoms on earth so that he had a single empire. It would have hindered Jesus' teaching from being spread through the whole world if there had been many kingdoms."[17] Church and empire were destined to work together sometime in the future. Meanwhile, he saw Christianity as the great solvent of discordant and barbarous pagan cultures. God was God, not Zeus, or Ammon, or Papaeus, each with different attributes.[18] Laws of cities and nations had to bow to natural law which God gave and his Christian worshipers upheld. He looked forward to the time when all (even those who appeared to be outside) "may become absorbed in the word of God and the divine law." "One day it will be the only one to prevail since the word is continually gaining possession of more souls."[19]

Why were people turning to Christianity? The decline of the cities, depressing their cults with them, is one reason. The local aristocracies and magistrates were the staunchest supporters of their gods, and the upkeep of the temples and the sacrifices depended heavily on them. That these were not always being performed is shown by an interesting papyrus that records that an Egyptian village temple was being used as a piggery, and that in 249 Myron the deputy high priest ordered its cleansing and removal of the pigs within fifteen days.[20] In Egypt, carelessness and formalism were creeping into the outward symbolism of the age-old religion, and the knowledge of the sacred script of the hieroglyphics was dying out.[21] The heart had been knocked out of the old national religions. One would contrast, too, the poverty of pagan writing at this time with the intellectual vigor displayed by the Christians: the stream of letters and treatises from Origen, Cyprian, and Dionysius. Apart from Dexippus, the Athenian soldier and historian, one finds no historian of the times once Dio Cassius (d. 229) and Herodian (d. circa 240) passed from the scene. Plotinus himself had few peers in the era of Valerian and Gallienus. Somehow the Severan age had sapped the originality and force of traditional institutions; Christianity filled the vacuum.

That something like this was happening may be gathered from accounts of conversions at this time. Becoming a Christian was often a matter of gradual decision, and eventually occurred when the convert was convinced that Christianity answered questions that pagan philosophies could not, and was a superior and more relevant faith. The classic evidence comes from the letter which Gregory the Wonderworker (Thaumaturgus) sent to Origen in 243 on his return to his native Cappadocia after five years as Origen's pupil at Caesarea. Gregory was a member of a Cappadocian noble family. At the age of fourteen, however, after his father's death he had been strongly attracted to Christianity.[22] Already Christianity seemed to offer more hope and consolation than traditional pagan worship. The phase passed, however, and Gregory embarked on his career as a lawyer and public speaker. In c. 236 he and his brother were on their way to the famous school of Roman law at Berytus (Beirut). They were not destined to arrive. Their sister had married a lawyer on the staff of the governor of Palestine and her two brothers found themselves ordered by the governor of Syria to form part of her escort to Caesarea. There Gregory met Origen. His former leanings towards Christianity reasserted themselves and he became a devoted pupil. For him, however, Christianity had nothing to do with protest, except against the errors, confusions, and swindles of current paganism. It was "true philosophy." Conversion was a matter of education and moral progress. Secular philosophy must be studied as a preparation in order to make the soul ready "to advance towards understanding things divine."[23] Far from Athens and Jerusalem being contrasted, Gregory believed with Origen that "true religion was impossible to one who did not philosophise."[24] And beyond philosophy lay the proper understanding of the word of God contained in Scripture. Christianity enabled the convert to imitate in his or her soul "the great Paradise of God"[25] (cf. Gen. 3:23 on Eden), and to understand rationally what he had only been able to admire irrationally.[26] Conversion led not necessarily towards martyrdom, but rather to a true regard for God's commands achieved by control of body and mind alike.[27] The ultimate ideal was that of the ascetic, who practiced as well as preached the virtues of Christianity. In later ages the "true philosopher" was the monk.

Origen, like Justin Martyr before him, always stressed the moral superiority of Christianity over its rivals. Comparing the claims of Judaism and Christianity, he asks, "Should we believe Isaiah and Ezekiel or Jesus? No work of theirs [the Jews] is to be found of comparable importance [with the

Gospels], whereas the goodness of Jesus towards men was not confined to the incarnation only, but even to this day the power of Jesus brings about conversion and moral reformation in those who believe in God through him."[28] Not only intelligent and educated people were being converted, "but there are also some of the most irrational people, and those most subject to passions, who on account of their lack of reason are changed to a more self-controlled life with greater difficulty."[29] Such was the power of Christ that this was accomplished. Origen himself contributed to this silent but irrevocable move towards Christianity that was taking place in the eastern provinces of the empire. He proclaimed a religion which was acceptable to the intellectuals of his day, yet at the same time was one for which simple believers were prepared to die. Christian Platonism in Origen's hand was a way of life as well as a creed. Paganism was thrown on the defensive.

In the West, Christianity was also gaining ground, though perhaps not so spectacularly. By c. 245 North Africa could at least boast of ninety bishops and a well-organized disciplinary system that could bring about the deposition of Privatus, bishop of Lambaesis (the military capital of Numidia) on a variety of charges involving scandal and error.[30] In Rome, Pope Cornelius (251–53) claimed that he had 155 clergy of all grades and more than fifteen hundred widows and distressed persons on the payroll of his church, backed by a "multiplying" congregation.[31] Cyprian confirmed this last statement by calling the Roman congregation "very abundant" (*amplissima*). After the Decian persecution, Cornelius was also able to bring together sixty-one bishops for a council to condemn Novatian.[32] There is no doubt that the church in Rome and in the cities of central Italy was flourishing.

Conversion, however, was less a matter of steady transition from one form of philosophical belief to another which seemed to transcend it than utter rejection of one's past and escape from sin, which only Christianity could bring. Cyprian, Gregory's contemporary, writing in c. 245 to his friend Donatus of his conversion, recounted his past almost in the manner of Augustine. It was a story of gloom and guilt. He "seconded his vices, despaired of improvement," regarded his faults as "natural" and "even favoured them." Conversion brought release. Baptism involved a complete rebirth and restoration to a new manhood in which doubts disappeared as if by magic. "I was able to recognize that what was born of flesh and lived under the rule of sin was of earth, earthly, while that which was animated by the Holy Spirit began to belong to God."[33] In a few short lines Cyprian summed up the role of conversion in a world dominated by sin. Baptism was regeneration by the Holy Spirit. Could he ever deny its sovereign power, even when in 255 he was confronted by the tradition of the Roman church which placed a greater emphasis on reception of the Spirit by the laying on of hands?

Different though the meaning of conversion was tending to become among Latin- and Greek-speaking Christians, both were contributing to the advance of the church. The Gnostics, so influential a generation before, were visibly fading. They never figure in Cyprian's voluminous correspondence, though Marcionites and Jews do. In writing *Celsus*, Origen mentions that some sects such as the Simonians had become practically extinct.[34] Others were by now "very undistinguished," so that even with his prodigious memory he could not place a "Passion Narrative" attributed by Celsus to one group.[35] Within the ranks of Christians, Monarchianism had replaced Gnosticism as the main threat to Origen's Word-flesh theology. Little did he think as he wrote to Beryllus,[36] bishop of Bostra, or debated with Bishop Heracleides in the 240s that Gnosticism was about to reappear in a new and deadlier guise, as a rival universal religion molded by a genius equal to himself, Mani (Manicheus).

MANICHEISM

Mani (216–77) had a gift for precise statement and synthesis, grafting aspects of Zoroastrianism, Buddhism, and ideas taken from Bardesanes and Marcion onto his own sectarian dualist Christianity. He also realized that in order to succeed, he must have worldwide appeal. A papyrus discovered among the Köln collection and published in installments in 1970, 1975, and 1978, throws new and unexpected light on his upbringing and formative years.[37] Mani was born in 216 near Basra into a Christian sect of Elkesaites which his father Fatah (Pittakios) had joined. The Elkesaites had communities on both sides of the Roman and Persian frontier, a sign of how cultural and religious frontiers were no longer coinciding with those between the rival empires. They were active enough to be noticed by Origen.[38] They may relate to the Jewish/Jewish-Christian "baptist" sects of the first century, for they professed a mixture of Jewish/Christian and Mandaean ideas. Like the Ebionites they accepted the Gospel of Matthew only, and they were "baptists," spending much time in purificatory ablutions. They believed that there were two primary natures, male and female, to which all creation was related. Vegetables belonged to the male, but weeds to the female. Hence, they were keen gardeners and growers of plants. The community in which Mani grew up was self-supporting, and its meals were sacramental occasions.[39]

Mani recounts two religious conversions, the first at the age of twelve (in 228). This directed him to separate from the sect in spirit but remain with them. The second conversion, in April 240, completed his rejection of the sect and his resolve to preach his own religion. Of his second conversion, he says:

When I was twenty-four years old in the year in which the King of the Persians, Ardashir, subdued the town of Hatra and in which King Sapor, his son, took for himself the greatest diadem, in the month of Pharmuthi on the 8th Day of the Moon, my all-holiest Lord showed mercy to me and called me to his grace and sent to me [. . .] my companion.[40]

The date was 23 April 240, the second and successful Persian attack on Hatra, and when Ardashir's son, Sapor, was crowned as heir-presumptive. The "Day of the Full Moon" indicates the astrological tendency in Mani's thought, and the "companion" is his "guardian angel," the twin-spirit from the world of Light who acted as guide and protector, a personal Paraclete and revealer of truth. The conversion was sudden, breaking away from the last remnants of his father's religion, and was due to grace—like Augustine 150 years later breaking suddenly but finally from the influence of overt Manicheism and skepticism.[41] Mani's environment was Persia. He traveled eastward to India to study Buddhism. The Roman Empire and its (Marcionite) Christianity was "the West." He went there as an envoy of Sapor's staff probably on his victorious campaign of 256/57.[42] The focus of his mission was on the Sassanid court. For much of his life he was favored by Sapor but the Zoroastrian priesthood realized he was a threat to their authority, and Sapor's successor Bahram ordered his execution in 277.[43]

The Jewish-Christian sect of the Elkesaites, however, provided the anvil against whom he hammered out his own ideas.[44] Mani recounted in his didactic style how, while still a member of the sect, he refused to accept the Elkesaite belief that purity concerned the body. The sect's frequent ablutions were a waste of time. One had no right to make water dirty. Anyhow, the body was destined to destruction and not eternal refreshment (*anapausis*). He was also contentious on ritual matters, from not taking vegetables from the communal garden but only accepting them as "a pious gift," refusing to bake his own bread to insisting on washing his food before eating it, and "eating the bread of the Greeks," an interesting sidelight showing how in the 200s sectarian Christians abominated Greek civilization just as much as the Greeks abominated them. Even Paul they despised as "a Greek."[45] Mani, however, insisted that a truly religious life was that of an ascetic, unworried by transitory matters. Jesus did not send forth his disciples equipped with mills and ovens.

Against the Elkesaites, Mani asserted that purity concerned the soul only, and came only from Gnosis. Gnosis, he believed, freed the soul from death and destruction.[46] Baptism was once and for all and provided the seal of illumination. The connection between Mani's ideas and those of most Gnostic sects is clear, but Mani went on to define Gnosis as knowledge of the division between light and darkness, the two primary entities in the universe. In most Gnostic systems dualism was assumed rather than defined, and in defining the division between God-Light and Evil-Darkness in detailed material terms which could be described in myth, he must have been—as Ephraem Syrus claimed—drawing upon the current interpreta-

315

tions of Marcion and Bardesanes. These were his teachers.[47] With Mani dualism reached its logical conclusion.

Mani was a systematizer as well as a preacher and prophet. Complex and arcane though the ramifications of the Manichean mythology became, the essential credo was simple. Following F. C. Burkitt,[48] Mani believed there were two Principles or Roots (Light and Darkness) and three Moments (the Past, the Present, and the Future). Light and Darkness were eternal contrasting realities. In the beginning they were separate, but in the Past the Dark invaded the Light and as a result became mingled with it, as it was in the Present, that is, in the world around us. The purpose of all existence was the refining and distilling of the Light from the Darkness, and the Light from further molestation by the Darkness, so that in the Future, Light and Darkness would be separate again and the original equilibrium of the universe restored. "Good is refined little by little and goes up."[49] The Moon was the ship of life, bearing the purged souls on their way towards the home of life (the Sun). Mani's theory of the process of salvation followed the Gnostic systems of his day including ideas derived from Bardesanes, but with some original elements. Light and Darkness were intermingled at the outset of creation, but for him Darkness was an active, material force. It "passionately desired and ate the light."[50] Christ was incarnate in Adam, and in the prophets as well as in Jesus, and in all creation. He was the Messenger, Bringer of Light, and its liberator from the clutches of Darkness. There was light not only in humans, but in all creation, in animals and vegetables. One did not kill animals; otherwise, one injured the light particles within them. The true Manichee (the Elect), existed on a diet consisting of the most light-bearing vegetables, for example, melons and radishes. One would take no part in the preparation of food, for that also involved the destruction of the light within the food. One did no work for that prolonged the existence of the Present and delayed the distillation of the Light. One was an ascetic; bodily needs were attended to by followers who would be taken from among the second grade of Manichee, the Hearers. The latter, while accepting the tenets of Mani and attending the great yearly festival of the *Bema*, were free to continue in their professions and even to marry.[51]

Mani accepted that the message of salvation had been proclaimed to humankind by a succession of prophets and teachers that included Plato, Hermes Trismegistus (in Poimandres), Moses, Buddha, Zoroaster, Jesus of Nazareth, and Paul, each for his own times and to different peoples.[52] Now, it was time to bring these different proclamations together and proclaim a single gospel from one end of the earth to the other and in all the languages of the day. In a book addressed to King Sapor, Mani wrote:

Wisdom and deeds have always from time to time been brought to mankind by the messengers of God. So in one age they have been brought by the messenger called Buddha to India, in another by Zaradusht [Zarathustra] to Persia, in another by Jesus to the West. Thereupon this revelation has come down, this prophecy in this last age, through me, Mani, messenger of the God of truth to Babylonia.[53]

Mani grasped that these great religious systems, which he had experienced, had more in common than their members realized. It was possible, therefore, to fuse them into a single system of universal validity. This system depended on "knowledge of salvation" achieved by understanding the secrets of the universe. "The truths and the secrets I proclaim . . ." were the truths of Gnosticism brought together into a synthesis and announced to humankind as revealed truth. While the basis of Manichean organization was always the individual Elect, named as the "son" of some distinguished spiritual predecessor, Mani's religion had of necessity to be practiced among communities. His book of Principles (*Kephalaia*)[54] which circulated in Egypt in the fourth and fifth centuries shows Mani thinking in terms of organizations of believers and churches, rivals to the "incomplete" institutions of the Christians. As he claimed with such confidence,

He who has his Church in the West he and his Church have not reached the East: the choice of him who has chosen his Church in the East has not come to the West. . . . But my Hope, mine, will go towards the West, and she will go also towards the East. And they shall hear the voice of her message in all languages, and shall proclaim her in all cities. My Church is superior in this first point to previous Churches, for these previous Churches were chosen in particular countries and in particular cities. My Church, mine shall spread in all cities, and my Gospel shall touch every country. [*Kephalaion* CLIV][55]

With this mixture of arrogance, shrewd calculation, and idealism, Mani aimed at embracing the whole of human religious experience into a single complete and universal system. The intellectual syntheses of some of Valentinus's followers were combined with missionary zeal imitating Paul, and a sense of publicity. Manichean missions to the West began between 244 and 262. Edessa and parts of the Nile Valley were among the earliest Manichean centers.[56] "The Teacher's" or "The Illuminator's" words were set down on the finest papyrus—written in the best script. Contemporaries quickly realized that this new universal faith was different from other Eastern cults or heresies. In the bitter debate in the late third and fourth centuries between champions of Mani and the church, pagan magistrates found themselves chosen as umpires.[57] They were uninvolved in their struggle for preeminence. Perhaps their ideas already belonged to the past.

Mani struck a responsive chord. The hymns and poetry sung by his followers show that for all its strangeness and complexities, the Manichean religion evoked deep religious feeling among those who hitherto had been content with traditional cults.[58] With Judaism, Manicheism was a formi-

317

dable rival and provided a system of doctrine which orthodox Christianity both had to refute and avoid at all costs.

THE DECIAN PERSECUTION

Such was the situation as the thousandth year of Rome's foundation approached. The "Millennial Celebrations" of 247 were the last great festivals of pagan Rome unchallenged by Christianity. Rome had prospered for a thousand years under the protection of the gods. There were three days and nights of celebrations. No one got any sleep, it was remembered.[59] The coinage of the emperor Philip (M. Julius Philippus) proclaimed "the happiness of the age."[60] The clash with the Christians could hardly be postponed. With his usual clarity Origen saw that it must come and that when it did it would match the church on a world scale. He wrote in *Celsus*, "God, who sent Jesus, destroyed the whole conspiracy of demons, and everywhere in the world in order that men might be converted and reformed. He made the Gospel of Jesus to be successful, and caused churches to exist in opposition to the assemblies of the superstitious, licentious and unrighteous men."[61] To date, all that the empire, its representatives, and its people had done against the Christians was in vain. Now, however, persecution that had hitherto been partial would be worldwide.

As he wrote, Philip's reign was drawing to an inglorious close. To Gothic invasions were added the rise of usurpers, brigandage, and the oppression of local populations by officials and soldiers.[62] People were on the lookout for scapegoats. Christians, Origen admitted, were regarded as responsible for "the rebellion that is so strong at this moment" (c. 248). It was regretted that provincial governors were not persecuting them as in "the good old days."[63]

Such hopes were soon fulfilled. Christians were liable to be as unpopular in the reign of Gordian as they had been at the beginning of the century. The *Acts of Pionius* records how a certain mistress in Smyrna (?) had driven out her slave and left her bound on the mountains because she was a Christian, and she had been looked after secretly by "the brethren."[64] But the serious trouble took place in Alexandria. The city had for centuries been a nerve center of religious (and to some extent, racial) tensions. In 248 the storm broke. It was like the anti-Jewish pogrom of 38 recorded by Philo,[65] but now directed against the Christians. Stirred up by a priest, the mob set upon them. Dionysius, who had been elected bishop the year before, wrote an eyewitness account to his colleague Fabius of Antioch a year or two later. He described how some Christians were lynched and others dragged to temples and forced to sacrifice; then how the mob rampaged through the streets looting, burning, and destroying property belonging to Christians. The rioters behaved instinctively as if their gods were in danger, and the Christians had become too powerful to be tolerated.[66]

Meantime, Philip had turned to the best soldier and administrator of the

318

day, C. Messius Quintus Decius, the prefect of the city of Rome. Decius was an Illyrian by birth, but married into the Roman aristocratic house of the Herennians and he was loyal to Philip. He promised to defeat the Goths invading the Danube provinces and kept his word. The troops, however, intervened and at the end of 248 proclaimed Decius emperor. Months of negotiation followed before the two sides confronted each other at Verona. Philip was defeated and committed suicide. Decius took over the government of the empire at a time of crisis, October 249.

For the Christians, history repeated itself. Philip had shown them as much toleration as had Alexander Severus. Otacilia Severa, his wife, was believed to have corresponded with Origen, and in the fourth century Eusebius portrayed him as the first Christian emperor.[67] Decius's ideas ran in the opposite direction. Eusebius said flatly that Decius raised a persecution against the churches on account of his enmity towards Philip.[68] A more contemporary writer, the compiler of the *Sibylline Oracles*, Book XIII, suggests the same.[69] Decius was inspired by the vision of the past military virtues of Rome and its emperors. He was hailed as the new Trajan, and he added the name of the "best of emperors" to his own. His coins celebrated the restoration of Pannonia and the memory of his "divine" predecessors, and he revived the republican office of censor.[70] His portraits depict him as a stern if noble figure, seemingly endowed with inflexible willpower and courage, the epitome of the tradition he pledged himself to restore.

The citizens of Ansedonia (Cosa) showed some insight by praising him as "the restorer of the sacred rites and liberty" (*restitutor sacr[o]rum et libertatis*),[71] the title bestowed on the emperor Julian a century later.[72] Decius took little time in justifying this. On 3 January 250, he solemnly performed the annual sacrifice to Jupiter on the Capitol and presented the imperial supplications (*vota*) for the year. This time, however, he ordered his example to be followed in the capitols of every city in the empire.[73] Contrary forces disrupting concord between the gods and humankind were to be eliminated.

Action must have followed immediately. By 20 January, Bishop Fabian of Rome had been arrested, tried before the emperor himself, condemned to death, and executed.[74] A similar fate befell Babylas his colleague at Antioch, perhaps on 24 January. Alexander of Jerusalem died in prison. Dionysius of Alexandria barely escaped arrest; he was aided by local peasants who disliked authority but cared little about Christianity. Cyprian of Carthage went into hiding.[75] In Pontus, Gregory the Wonderworker fled.[76]

However one interprets subsequent events, the arrest of the leaders of the church in the first weeks of 250 marked one phase in Decius's campaign against Christianity. Decius appears to have followed the tactics of Maximin's short-lived effort fifteen years before, striking down prominent Christians whether bishops or simple activists, who included otherwise obscure people such as Celerinus,[77] and letting the rest be. Subsequent

319

events are more difficult to interpret.[78] The orders that all should associate themselves with the imperial *vota* took varying times to reach different provinces. The authorities in Asia, reached mainly by an overland route, seem to have had their instructions by mid-February, for one has to fit in the recalcitrant presbyter Pionius's arrest, the preliminary hearing at Smyrna, the subsequent trial before the proconsul and the execution on 12 March.[79] Sea routes were hazardous, however, and that between Carthage and Rome was usually closed between November and March. It must have been after that date when commissions were established in each town to supervise the sacrifices. Even so, the lapse of nearly six months between the edict and its implementation in the Egyptian towns seems extraordinary, for Egypt usually received news from Rome quickly. Decius had been proclaimed emperor in Alexandria before the end of November 249.[80]

Officials, however, saw that the emperor's orders were obeyed on every level of society. Those who sacrificed received a certificate (*libellus*) and the sacrifice was registered as a formal, judicial act by the individual. Forty-three *libelli* have been found in the Fayum, dating between 14 June and 12 July 250.

One striking and well-known example reads:

> To the commission chosen to superintend the sacrifices. From Aurelia Ammonous, daughter of Mystus, of the Moeris quarter, priestess of the god Petesouchos, the great, the mighty, the immortal, and priestess of the gods in the Moeris quarter. I have sacrificed to the gods all my life, and now again, in accordance with the decree and in your presence, I have made sacrifice, and poured a libation, and partaken of the sacred victims. I request you to certify this below.[81]

The sacrifice was performed by all, not merely by suspected Christians,[82] and was accompanied by a libation to the deity and eating the sacrificial meat. In Carthage the commission consisted of the magistrates and five prominent citizens (*primores*) and there as elsewhere sacrifice was made on the capitols to the specifically Roman gods and the emperor's genius, rather than to local gods.[83] As an inscription from Aphrodisias, the capital of Caria, shows, the idea transmitted by the emperor and his advisers was that the provincials should show "solidarity with the Romans" and support "our empire" with their "just sacrifices and prayers."[84] Penalty for refusal was committal to the authorities in the provincial capitals, who had the power to inflict the death penalty on the recalcitrant.

These powers do not seem to have been used consistently.[85] Even so, the Christian church practically collapsed. In every large center for which evidence survived, the story was one of immediate obedience to the emperor's orders. Christians joined with their pagan neighbors in a rush to sacrifice. At Carthage the superintendents of the ceremonies were so overworked that they begged would-be worshipers to come back the next day.[86]

For Alexandria, Dionysius described with his usual flair the scenes he witnessed.

And what is more, the edict arrived, and it was almost like that which was predicted by our Lord, wellnigh the most terrible of all, so as, if possible, to cause to stumble even the elect. Howsoever that be, all cowered with fear. And of many of the more eminent persons, some came forward immediately through fear, others in public positions were compelled to do so by their business, and others were dragged by those around them. Called by name they approached the impure and unholy sacrifices, some pale and trembling, as if they were not for sacrificing but rather to be themselves the sacrifices and victims to the idols, so that the large crowd that stood around heaped mockery upon them, and it was evident that they were by nature cowards in everything, cowards both to die and to sacrifice. But others ran eagerly towards the altars, affirming by their forwardness that they had not been Christians even formerly; concerning whom the Lord very truly predicted that they shall hardly be saved. Of the rest, some followed one or other of these, others fled; some were captured, and of these some went as far as bonds and imprisonment, and certain, when they had been shut up for many days, then forswore themselves even before coming into court, while others, who remained firm for a certain time under tortures, subsequently gave in.[87]

It was almost total disaster. The effective staff of this important community was reduced to Dionysius and "four presbyters who were in hiding," secretly visiting the brethren, while two others "who are better known in the world are wandering about in Egypt."[88]

The authorities suddenly seem to have become aware of the latent strength of loyalty to the emperor and to Rome. It was the first time an emperor had promulgated such an edict, and left to them the task of enforcing it.[89] Their response where recorded was firm and even enthusiastic. At Smyrna the events leading up to the trial and execution of Pionius have been recorded in detail. A miscellaneous group of Christians was arrested, including a Catholic presbyter, a Montanist, a woman from Macedonia, and Pionius and his group.[90] Once Bishop Euctemon of Smyrna had sacrificed, those who held out could be treated like misfits and cranks. The pagan magistrates openly laughed at Pionius's worship of "the crucified one," and asked him and his companions to what sect they belonged.[91] Everyone tried to save them from what they believed acts of useless folly. Jews invited Christians into their synagogues. The crowd bewailed the prospect of Pionius's death as being unnecessary.[92] Someone shouted, "Well, if they don't sacrifice, they ought to be punished."[93] Pionius was warned, "it would be wise for you to obey and offer sacrifices like everyone else, so that you may not be punished."[94] The proconsul told him that "he would accomplish very little by hastening to his death."[95] Martyrs were a nuisance ("Why could not Sabina die in her own city?"), but in the end it was all in vain. Pionius was burned alive in the company of a Marcionite.

What had happened? Throughout the empire the church had been accepting a large number of nominal converts as well as committed individuals such as Cyprian. Behind its monolithic exterior all was far from well. Origen writes of congregations full of chattering women more concerned with household affairs than worship.[96] The gap between educated and uneducated, cleric and laity was widening. He describes how "some bishops, by no means examples of high-mindedness or knowledge of the truth were despising the mites and waifs of the Church who praised God and Christ, as though they were sinning."[97] Origen could be anti-ecclesiastic, but it is clear that the more important churches had become in the nature of administrative machines whose clergy felt themselves superior to their laity. Moreover, some were combining their clerical office with lucrative secular work, which included acting as bailiffs on imperial and private estates or as trustee (*tutor*) for family pension funds.[98] One bishop, Martialis of Mérida, was ready to step into the office of procurator ducenarius, once the persecution had begun.[99]

The church for all its gains remained an urban organization, its leaders well known but not, it seems, well liked, and its strength rooted among artisans and small traders. At Carthage in 251, Cyprian described Soliassus the mule-keeper and Paula the mat-maker as influential in the church.[100] Side by side with some traditionally militant families like that of Celerinus—a Carthaginian immigrant to Rome, a confessor like his uncle and grandmother who had been martyred for their faith—there were thousands who thought nothing of performing sacrifice in the temple and presenting themselves for Eucharist the next Sunday. No one disobeyed an imperial edict lightly. When confronted with the choice of empire or Christian church in 250, the great majority of Christians played safe and sacrificed.

In the end, the persecution cost relatively few lives, though nineteen Alexandrian victims can be counted.[101] By the end of 250 it was, to all intents and purposes, over. Christians who had lain low came out into the open again, some claiming the title of "confessors." Others, including the lapsed, awaited events. Decius had fallen in his last impetuous fatal campaign against the Goths (June 251). Even Cyprian lost only some of his possessions to public auction, but when he returned to Carthage near Easter 251, he found the church there disorganized and his personal standing low.

The penitential and disciplinary system built up over a generation lay in ruins. There were "thousands" of renegades, including clergy. The system of imposing individual penance and maintaining at all costs the integrity of the elect that was the church on earth was no longer possible. Moreover, the lapsed were clamorous and undisciplined. They were not prepared to apply to Cyprian for the church's remission of sins. In his absence the leadership of the church in Carthage had been taken over by the confessors, men and women of humble birth, often laypeople. Their leader recommended Cyprian himself "to have peace with the holy martyrs."[102] Cyprian might nominate penitents for forgiveness, but the confessors believed the right of forgiveness was theirs alone. Did the Holy Spirit rest upon them, as it had been believed seventy-five years before it rested on the martyrs of Lyons, or were the clergy and especially the bishops its repository? The question could not be avoided; the issue was fundamental to clerical authority.

In North Africa and Rome the decisive factor against the confessors proved to be the power now concentrated in the person of the bishop. Once validly consecrated, by neighboring bishops with the assent of the people, the bishops of Rome or Carthage were the possessors of great authority over the Christian community.[103] Carthage controlled the bishops of the rest of Roman North Africa, that is, Numidia and the two Mauretanias.[104] In 252, Cyprian could write without any fear of contradiction to his friend Cornelius of Rome in terms that would have become the emperor himself. He speaks of "the faithful and incorruptible majesty" and also "priestly authority and power" concentrated in the church catholic of which he was the leader in North Africa.[105] In Rome, Decius's alleged remark that he would rather face a usurper than another bishop of Rome reflected the gossip of the capital in 250, and shows the awe in which the bishop was held.[106] Majesty, authority, and power, such were the prerogatives of the bishops of Rome and of Carthage. Not in the darkest moments of his exile in 250 did Cyprian act as though he thought otherwise. The unity (or "uniqueness") of the church catholic was vested in him as bishop.[107] Jerusalem had indeed been transferred to Carthage, and Cyprian's opponents were made aware of the authority concentrated against them.

On his return, the church of Carthage recovered rapidly. The council he held sometime after Easter 251 decided that no one should be wholly or permanently excluded from penance.[108] Each case of lapse must be examined by the clergy on its merits, but clergy who had themselves lapsed were not to be readmitted to their orders. Those who had been certified (with *libelli*) as having sacrificed to the pagan idols, though they actually had not (*libellatici*), were to be allowed back into the church after periods varying with the amount of pressure to which they had been subjected before giving way. Those who had actually sacrificed (*sacrificati*) might be admitted only on their deathbeds. Apart from being a milestone in the formation of the penitential code of the early church, the council demonstrated Cyprian's strength. Decisions lay with him and the clergy alone. The confessors, who only a few months before had been asserting their right to grant peace to the lapsed with only cursory reference to Cyprian, were discomfited. While some joined Cyprian's opponents, most accepted the situation, and found themselves in due course elevated into the ranks of the Carthaginian clergy and made aware of their promotion.[109]

A month or two later, Cyprian's position was further consolidated. At last, the church in Rome was able to elect a successor to Pope Fabian. The choice was a surprising one. Cornelius, elected on 4 June 251, was mediocre but he was preferred to Novatian, the presbyter who had held together the Roman clergy in the previous eighteen months and was a pastor as well as a theologian.[110] But he was also apparently an invalid, and his failure to distinguish between various degrees of lapse (just as for Stoics one sin was essentially as serious as another) would have made him a hard taskmaster. Though Fabius of Antioch clearly preferred him to Cornelius, he stood alone.[111] Cyprian's support, at first hesitant, was probably decisive for Cornelius. Once given it was irreversible. The vigorous tract *On the Unity of the Catholic Church* was written, it would seem, in direct support of Cornelius. It gave Cyprian yet another opportunity to reiterate the integrity of the church, resting on the unity of the episcopate centered on its Petrine origin at Rome.[112] Apostates and schismatics must be abandoned by their flocks; for any who remained with them would share in their guilt. From Cyprian, through Donatus to Pope Gelasius, belief in guilt by association was to be a powerful weapon in the hands of orthodox rigorists against their opponents.

So long as Cornelius lived (he died in exile during Gallus's brief persecution in 253), Carthage and Rome were on the best of terms. Never again was the correspondence between the bishops of the two leading sees in the West so full and uninhibited. Within a few years Cyprian had restored the North African church to the powerful position it had held before the Decian persecution. When plague and barbarian raiders (Kabyles) ravaged Roman North Africa in 252–53, the church stood firm. One hundred thousand sesterces were collected to ransom captives.[113] No wonder schismatics were reconciled and converts came in in droves. Cyprian speaks of the "new population of believers."[114] In these years, the battle between "Church and Capitol" as Cyprian saw it, turned decisively in favor of the church.

For Alexandria, Dionysius's correspondence unfortunately says less about the recovery of the church's position. Disciplinary problems were evidently less serious; but congregations seem to have been reorganized and clergy recruited when in 252 the plague struck.[115] Here, too, the Christians stuck to their posts when all others had fled. The church's credit was restored. Alexandria was to share with Rome and Carthage the brunt of the next onslaught.

VALERIAN

At first Valerian (P. Licinius Valerianus, 253–60) who had been Decius's censor and succeeded to his heritage after a civil war, was friendly to the Christians. We cannot ignore Dionysius's statement:

> Valerian was mild and friendly to the men of God. For not a single one of the emperors before him was so kindly and favourably disposed toward them, not

even those who were said to have been openly Christians, as he manifestly was, when he received them at the beginning in the most intimate and friendly manner; indeed all his house had been filled with godly persons, and was a church of God.[116]

Allowing for Dionysius's desire to flatter Valerian's son and successor, Gallienus, it is obvious that Valerian did not pursue the same policy towards the Christians as Decius and his short-lived successors. Cyprian's correspondence reveals no further tensions with the authorities. Between 254 and 256 he held five episcopal councils in Carthage at the last of which, on 1 September 256, no less than eighty-seven bishoprics were represented. The emperor as Pontifex Maximus was being confronted with a rival religious confederation growing in authority as each year passed, and whose leaders were beginning to reflect opinion throughout the Mediterranean provinces of the empire better than the traditional authorities. They also pronounced with authority and could command obedience; "law of God" (*mandatum Dei*) confronted "rule of the Emperor" (*praeceptum imperatoris*) in earnest.

As the church emerged in these years as a world authority and state within a state, so did its internecine divisions. To the rumbling feud between Cyprian and his Carthaginian opponents, originating with his sudden elevation to the episcopate, were added disputes arising out of the Decian persecution. Supporters of opposite factions combined in efforts to overthrow Cyprian. At Carthage he was confronted by two rivals.[117] No sooner had he got the better of these than Cornelius's successor Lucius died, and after a short interlude the vacancy had been filled by an uncompromising prelate Stephen (12 May 254–2 August 257). On three occasions, each more serious than the last, Stephen and Cyprian were to clash, and their churches supported their leaders.[118] The issues will be discussed later, but the question whether baptism given by a cleric outside the church (in this case, Novatianist) was valid, caused an open rift between Rome and Carthage. Stephen may even have excommunicated Cyprian and informed churches in Asia Minor of his decision.[119] Death fortunately removed him from the scene on 2 August 257. These few years of peace foreshadowed the graver schisms in the West following the Great Persecution. A victorious church was unlikely to be united.

The causes of Valerian's change of policy during the summer of 257 are not known. Persecution began in July of that year and lasted intermittently until news of the emperor's defeat and capture by the Persians reached Rome in July 260. It was a creeping repression. It started with the summons of Cyprian and Dionysius of Alexandria before the proconsul and vice-prefect of Egypt respectively. (We know nothing of similar action taken against Stephen's successor Sixtus II [257–58] at Rome.) Both Cyprian and Dionysius went to the official *secretarium*. There they were told in slightly different words (based perhaps on a common rescript) that "the emperors had ordered that those who did not practise the Roman religion should acknowledge [*recognoscere*] the Roman ceremonies."[120] What was meant? Probably some token recognition of the "saving power" of the immortal gods was implied, not a great deal to ask at a time of peril, but unacceptable to a Christian leader. The antithesis "Roman" and "Christian" was recognized on both sides. The issue was already, as Origen had appreciated, worldwide and total.

Both leaders refused to comply. Cyprian's interview on 30 August 257 indicated that the death penalty was not envisaged except in the last resort for disobeying imperial orders. The emperors had forbidden "conventions" (*conciliabula*) to be held anywhere, and no one was "to enter the cemeteries."[121] Cyprian's reply was, "Do what you are ordered. . . . I am a Christian and a bishop, I know no other gods but the one true God. . . . We Christians render service to this God, and we pray for the safety of the emperors." Dionysius's discussion with the vice-prefect Aemilian was more courteous, but there, too, an unbridgeable chasm separated the two sides. Both Cyprian and he were exiled, Cyprian to a pleasant enough "assigned residence" on the Gulf of Hammamet, Dionysius to the isolation of the oasis of Kufrah.

Cyprian's year at Curubis stands in contrast to his self-imposed exile during the Decian persecution. His flock now knew him as a pastor passionately committed to their welfare. He was also a respected citizen, visited by members of the Carthaginian aristocracy, and for Christians no longer a hireling who had fled from danger but a prophetic example filled with the Holy Spirit. In this spirit he wrote to Numidian bishops who had been sent to the mines, and awaited his own fate.[122]

In early August 258, Valerian acted again. This time his eye may have been on the church's wealth as well as its leadership. An analysis of his message to the senate is preserved in Cyprian's letter to Successus, bishop of Abbirgermaniciana(?). Bishops, presbyters, and deacons were to be punished immediately. Senators, men of distinction (*vir egregii*), and knights were to lose their dignities and be deprived of their property. If they continued to profess Christianity they were to be executed. *Matronae* would lose their property and be banished. Imperial civil servants (*Caesariani*) would be reduced to slavery and sent in chains to work on the imperial estates.[123]

Valerian's edict gives a glimpse of how Christianity was penetrating all classes in Rome. The *matronae* and the *Caesariani* are particularly significant. Both would play their parts in the conversion of their city in the next century. In Africa, Cyprian's fate could not be long delayed. Whether the incident of Utica on 18 August 258 (in which as many as three hundred Christians were believed to have been killed) hastened it is uncertain.[124] On 13 September, however, he was summoned before the proconsul at his residence, perhaps at Ager Sextii just northwest of the city walls of Carthage. Galerius Maximus was a sick man but summoned enough strength to conduct a brief examination of the prisoner. It ran:

Galerius Maximus: "Are you Thascius Cyprianus?"
Cyprian: "I am."
Galerius: "The most sacred Emperors have commanded you to conform to the Roman rites."
Cyprian: "I refuse."
Galerius: "Take heed for yourself."
Cyprian: "Do as you are bid; in so clear a case I may not take heed."
Galerius, after briefly conferring with his judicial council, with much reluctance pronounced the following sentence: "You have long lived an irreligious life, and have drawn together a number of men bound by an unlawful association, and professed yourself an open enemy to the gods and the religion of Rome; and the pious, most sacred and august Emperors, Valerian and Gallienus, and the most noble Caesar Valerian, have endeavoured in vain to bring you back to conformity with their religious observances;—whereas therefore you have been apprehended as principal and ringleader in these infamous crimes, you shall be made an example to those whom you have wickedly associated with you; the authority of law shall be ratified in your blood." He then read the sentence of the court from a written tablet: "It is the sentence of this court that Thascius Cyprianus be executed with the sword."
Cyprian: "Thanks be to God."[125]

Once again, the sentencing throws into relief the issue between the Roman Empire and the Christians. Christianity was a "nefarious conspiracy," the church an "unlawful association," Cyprian himself "principal and ringleader in these infamous crimes."[126] The charges echo those leveled at Christians by Celsus eighty years before, and Cyprian did not deny them. Valerian, like Diocletian after him, had come to the conclusion after leaving the Christians be that church and empire could not survive together.

In the East, Dionysius and his clergy remained in exile, where they converted some of the inhabitants of the Kufrah oasis.[127] There were executions of Marcionites as well as catholics in Palestine (Eusebius *HE* VII.12); but this time the full force of the persecution fell on the West. In North Africa and in Spain executions continued into 259.[128] The threat to individual Christians was lifted only when disaster struck Roman arms near Edessa in June 260. When the news of the emperor's capture arrived, his son Gallienus wasted no time in reversing his father's policy. By 20 July a new bishop of Rome, Dionysius, had been consecrated, and a series of edicts (*mandata*) returned cemeteries and other property to the Christians and freed them from molestation.[129] The text of one such, addressed to Dionysius (of Alexandria) and two of his suffragans, has survived. It arrived at Alexandria two years later, after the end of a civil war in which Gallienus's forces emerged victorious, and it speaks of measures "already long" in force elsewhere.[130] Gallienus evidently intended to return to the policies of Alexander Severus and Philip. Christianity was not formally a "lawful association" (*religio licita*), but its existence, its right to hold property and conduct its own affairs were tacitly accepted. It had acquired a position of strength. Valerian's failure marked the beginning of the end of Greco-Roman paganism.

We have followed the fortunes of the Christians in the dozen years 248–60 in more detail than usual in this survey. Contemporary documentation for East and West is abundant. Moreover, these years were a watershed in the church's fortunes. In retrospect, the Decian persecution emerges as the real testing point between the church and the empire. Had the church collapsed, it could scarcely have recovered. As it was, the combination of military and economic disasters took a heavier toll on traditional pagan society than they did on the church. The latter proved triumphantly resilient. Its worldwide organization, its economic power, and its martyr-tradition were proof against persecution and mass temporary apostasies. By 256 it had become stronger than it had been before persecution broke out. The "unlawful association" (*religio illicita*) was now a rival to the empire itself. By the time Diocletian threw down the final challenge in 303, the battle had been lost.

BIBLIOGRAPHY

NOTE

The main event is the Decian persecution. There are three separate accounts of this in *CAH*, vol. 12, *The Imperial Crisis and Recovery, A.D. 193–324*, ed. S. A. Cook, F. E. Adcock, M. P. Charlesworth, and N. H. Baynes, 2d ed. (New York: Macmillan Co.; Cambridge: At the University Press, 1939), by A. Alföldi (chap. 6, "The Crisis of the Empire [A.D. 249–270]," pp. 165–231), H. Lietzmann (chap. 5, "The Christian Church in the West," pp. 515–43), and briefly, W. Ensslin (chap. 2, "The Senate and the Army," pp. 57–95), while R. M. Grant has a valuable short chapter (Part III.1) in his *Augustus to Constantine: The Thrust of the Christian Movement Into the Roman World* (New York: Harper & Row, 1970). On the documentation of the persecution, see L. Duquenne's *Chronologie des lettres de S. Cyprien (Le dossier de la persécution de Dèce)*, Subsidia Hagiographica 54 (Brussels: Société des Bollandistes, 1972); and for Egypt, J. R. Knipfing's classic publication of the *libelli* from Oxyrhynchus in "The Libelli of the Decian Persecution," *HTR* 16 (1923): 345–90 (texts of *libelli* begin on p. 363). For the legal aspects of the persecution, C. Saumagne's *Saint Cyprien, Évêque de Carthage, "Pape" d'Afrique (248–258): Contribution à l'étude des "persécutions" de Dèce et de Valérien* (Paris: CNRS, 1975) combines erudition with speculative flair. For Cyprian's career, E. W. Benson's monumental *Cyprian: His Life, His Times, His Work* (London: Macmillan & Co., 1897) remains usable, while a lighter touch will be found in P. B. Hinchliff's *Cyprian of Carthage and the Unity of the Christian Church* (London: Geoffrey Chapman, 1974).

For Valerian, see P. Keresztes, "Two Edicts of the Emperor Valerian," *VC* 29

(1975): 81–95, and for the restoration of toleration, see C. Andresen's "Der Erlass des Gallienus an der Bischöfe Aegyptens (Eusebius *HE* VII.13)," *Studia Patristica* XII (Berlin: Akademie Verlag, 1975), pp. 385–98.

For Manicheism, the standard work remains H. C. Puech, *Le Manichéisme: Son fondateur, sa doctrine* (Paris: Publications du Musée Guimet, 1949). A valuable short summary of Manichean beliefs is given by F. C. Burkitt in "The Christian Church in the East," *CAH*, vol. 12, pp. 504–12, and since 1971 there has been a growing literature resulting from Henrich and Koenen's publication of the Mani-Codex (see Sources, below).

SOURCES

Acta Archelai. Edited by C. H. Beeson. GCS 16. Leipzig: Hinrichs, 1906.

Acta Martyrum, texts and translations taken from Musurillo, *Acts of Christian Martyrs.*

Cyprian, *Opera omnia*, ed. W. Hartel, CSEL 3, Vienna, 1868; Eng. trans. ANCL, vols. VIII and XIII.

———. *De Lapsis* and *De Ecclesiae Catholicae Unitate.* Edited by M. Bévenot. OECT. 2d ed. New York and London: Oxford University Press, 1971.

———, *Acta proconsularia*, ed. W. Hartel, CSEL 3.3, pp. cx–cxiv, Vienna, 1868; *Acta Proconsularia Sancti Cypriani (The Proconsular Acta of St. Cyprian)* in *Acts of Christian Martyrs*, ed. Musurillo, pp. 168–75.

Dionysius of Alexandria. See Eusebius *HE* VI.40–VII.26; and W. A. Biernert, ed., *Dionysius von Alexandrien, Das erhaltene Werk*, Bibliothek der griechischen Literatur Bd. 2 (Stuttgart: Hiersemann, 1972); *Letters and Treatises*, Eng. trans. and ed. C. L. Feltoe, Translations of Christian Literature, series 1: Greek Texts, New York: Macmillan Co., 1918.

Gregory the Wonderworker (*Thaumaturgus*), *Panegyric to Origen*, ed. H. Crouzel, SC 148; *Address to Origen*, Eng. trans. and ed. W. C. Metcalfe, Translations of Christian Literature, series 1: Greek Texts, New York: Macmillan Co., 1920.

———, *Canonical Epistle* in J. D. Mansi, *Sacrorum Conciliorum Collectio nova et amplissima* I, 1023–30, Florence, 1759; Eng. trans. A. Roberts and J. Donaldson, ANCL XX.30–36.

———. *Life.* By Gregory of Nyssa. PG 46.893–958.

———, in *Le Liber Pontificalis*, ed. L. Duchesne, 2 vols., Paris: Bibliothèque des Écoles Françaises d'Athènes et de Rome, 1886–92; and ed. T. Mommsen, *MGH* Gesta Pontificum Romanorum, vol. 1, Berlin, 1898.

Mani (Manichean writings)

Recently recovered text of early *Life*, ed. A. Henrichs and L. Koenen, "Ein griechischer Mani-Codex," *ZPE* 5.2 (1970): 97–216; 19 (1975): 1–85; 32 (1978): 78–199.

Manichean texts, A. Adam, ed., *Texte zum Manichaismus*, KlT 175, Berlin, 1954; enlarged ed., 1969.

Origen, *Contra Celsum*, ed. P. Koetschau, GCS 2, Origen; Eng. trans. and ed. Chadwick, Origen, *Contra Celsum.*

———, *Protreptikus eis Martyrion (Exhortation to Martyrdom)*, ed. P. Koetschau, GCS 3, Origen, Leipzig: Hinrichs, 1899; Eng. trans. and ed. H. Chadwick in *Alexandrian Christianity*, ed. J. E. L. Oulton and H. Chadwick, LCC II, Philadelphia: Westminster Press; London: SCM Press, 1954, pp. 393–429.

Pontius, *Vita Cypriani*, ed. W. Hartel, CSEL 3.3, pp. xc–cx, Vienna, 1868; Eng. trans. ANCL, Cyprian, vol. 1, pp. xiii–xxxi.
For the imperal coinage of the period to 253, see H. Mattingly, E. Sydenham, and C. H. V. Sutherland, eds., *Roman Imperial Coinage*, vol. 4, part 3: *Gordian III to Uranius Antoninus*, London: Spink & Son, 1936.

Secondary Works

Alföldi, A. "Der heilige Cyprian und die Krise des römischen Reiches." *Historia* 22 (1973): 479–501.
Armstrong, A. H. "Plotinus." In *Cambridge History of Later Greek and Early Mediaeval Philosophy*, pp. 195–210. New York and Cambridge: Cambridge University Press, 1967.
Babcock, C. L. "An Inscription of Trajan Decius from Cosa." *AJP* 83 (1962): 147–58.
Barnes, T. D. "Pre-Decian *Acta Martyrum*." *JTS* n.s. 19 (October 1968): 509–31.
Bell, H. I. *Cults and Creeds in Graeco-Roman Egypt*. New York: Philosophical Library; Liverpool: University Press of Liverpool, 1956.
Bévenot, M. "*Primatus Petro datur*." *JTS* n.s. 5 (April 1954): 19–35.
Brown, Peter. "The Diffusion of Manichaeism in the Roman Empire." *JRS* 59 (1969): 92–103.
Clarke, G. W. "The *Collegium funeraticum* of the Innocenti." *Antichton* 1 (1967), pp. 45ff.
———. "Double Trials in the Persecution of Decius." *Historia* 22 (1973): 650–63.
———. "Prosopographical Notes on the Epistles of Cyprian." I: "The Spanish Bishops of Epistle 67," *Latomus* 30.4 (1971): 1141–45; II: "The Proconsul in Africa in 250 AD," *Latomus* 31.4 (1972); 1053–57; and III: "Rome in August 258," *Latomus* 34.2 (1975): 437–48.
———. "Some Observations on the Persecution of Decius." *Antichton* 3 (1969): 63–76.
Dodds, E. R. "Tradition and Achievement in the Philosophy of Plotinus." *JRS* 50 (1960): 1–7.
Gagé, J. "Le paganisme impérial à la recherche d'une théologie vers le milieu du iiie siècle." *Sitzungsberichte der Akademie der Wissenschaften und der Literatur du Mainz* 12 (1972): 587–604.
Grégoire, Henri. "Les persecutions dans l'empire romain." *Mémoires de l'Académie royale de Belgique* 46.1 (1951).
Jones, R. Duncan. "Costs, Outlays, and *Summae Honorariae* from Roman Africa." *PBSR* n.s. 30 (1962): 46–115.
Keresztes, P. "The Decian *libelli* and Contemporary Literature." *Latomus* 34.3 (1975): 761–81.
Klauser, Th. "Bischöfe als staatliche Procuratoren im dritten Jahrhundert." *JAC* 14 (1971): 140–49.
Macdermot, B. C. "The Roman Emperors in Sassanian Reliefs." *JRS* 44 (1954): 76–80.
Olmstead, A. T. "The Mid-Third Century of the Christian Era." *CP* 37 (1942): 241–62 and 398–420.
Rostovtzev, M. I. *Social and Economic History of the Roman Empire*. 2 vols. 2d

ed., rev. P. M. Fraser. New York and London: Oxford University Press, 1957. Chaps. 10 and 13.

Ste. Croix, G. E. M. de. "Why Were the Early Christians Persecuted?" *Past and Present* 26 (1963): 6–38 (the best short study of the persecutions).

Vogt, H. J. *"Coetus Sanctorum." Theophaneia* 20 (1968): 37–182.

NOTES

1. See Macdermot, "Roman Emperors," for the view that Valerian's capture is commemorated on the relief at Bishapur, while that at Naqsh-e-Rostam represents the surrender of the emperor Philip to Sapor, and also, M. L. Chaumont, "Conquêtes sassanides et propagande mazdéenne," *Historia* 22 (1973): 664–710.

2. For North Africa, see Jones, "Costs, Outlays, and *Summae Honorariae*," p. 53, after the death of Gordian there are very few dated African inscriptions in any reign until the time of the Tetrarchy. The improvements to the water supply at Tiddis in the reign of Gallus were undertaken "per populum." See A. Berthier, *Revue Africaine* 89 (1945): 1–11.

3. Eusebius *HE* VII.21.10, citing Dionysius of Alexandria's letter to Hierax (Festal letter), "the human race upon earth is thus ever diminishing and consuming away before our eyes." Its "total disappearance draws nearer and nearer."

4. See Cyprian's *Ad Demetrianum*, ed. W. Hartel, pp. 351–70, CSEL 3.1, and Alföldi, "Der heilige Cyprian." Christians alone were optimistic "inter ipsas saeculi labentis ruinas" (*Ad Demetrianum* XX).

5. See Dodds, "Tradition and Achievement," and Armstrong, "Plotinus."

6. Eusebius *HE* VI.42.4.

7. See below, p. 418.

8. For the raid, see Zosimus *Historia Nova* 1.31.3 and 32.1; and for a contemporary witness, see Gregory, *Canonical Epistle*, Canons V–IX, pp. 30ff. There can be no doubt that the Christians to whom he is referring did "enrol among the barbarians" (canon VI), that is, the Goths and Borani, and acted as guides on their expeditions of pillage and destruction, and even murdered their fellow provincials (canon VII). Motives can only be guessed at, but apocalyptic hopes, including perhaps the commencement of the rule of antichrist, heralded by a destructive onset of "powers from the east" or "Nero redivivus" cannot be excluded. This aspect of third-century Christianity calls for further research. For Cyprian's concern that the end of the world was approaching during the 250s, see *De bono patientiae* (*On the Benefit of Patience*) XXI, *Letter* LXVII.7, and Alföldi, "Der heilige Cyprian," pp. 486–90.

9. Julius Capitolinus on Maximinus Thrax, "The Two Maximini," in *SHA*, ed. and Eng. trans. D. Magie, vol. 2, LCL (Cambridge, Mass.: Harvard University Press; London: William Heinemann, 1924), IX.

10. Eusebius *HE* VI.28.

11. *Liber Pontificalis*, ed. Mommsen, p. 24.

12. Firmilian of Cappodocia to Cyprian, in Cyprian *Letter* LXXV.10.

13. Eusebius, *HE* VI.36.1, J. E. L. Oulton, ed. and Eng. trans., vol. II (Books

VI–X), LCL (Cambridge, Mass.: Harvard University Press; London: William Heinemann, 1932).

14. Origen *Celsus* III.9.

15. Ibid., III.29–30.

16. Origen, *Commentary on Matthew* XV.26, ed. E. Klostermann, GCS 40, Origen (Leipzig: Hinrichs, 1935), p. 426.

17. Origen *Celsus* II.30.

18. Ibid., V.46: "We hold that there is nothing divine about Zeus at all . . . we will rather die than call Amon God. . . ."; and compare I.1.

19. Ibid., VIII.68. See above, p. 289.

20. *OGIS*.210. The village was Talmis in southern Egypt.

21. The last hieroglyphic inscription is dated to 251. See Bell, *Cults and Creeds*, p. 64.

22. Gregory, *Panegyric to Origen*, ed. Crouzel, 5.50. The Greek *(katenanekasmenos)* could mean that Gregory was actually coerced into Christianity at this stage, but as he says (5.48) that both of his parents were pagans and brought him up as such, I prefer a more metaphoric meaning. For literal coercion, possibly by Christian relatives, see T. D. Barnes, *Constantine and Eusebius* (Cambridge, Mass.: Harvard University Press, 1981), p. 85.

23. Ibid., 11; and compare 15.182, a leading theme in the *Letter*.

24. Ibid., 6.79.

25. Ibid., 15.183.

26. Ibid., 8.111.

27. Thus Origen, *Homily on Jeremiah* IV.6, ed. E. Klostermann, GCS 6, Origen (Leipzig: Hinrichs, 1901), p. 29; and Gregory, *Panegyric to Origen*, ed. Crouzel, p. 9.

28. Origen *Celsus* I.43.

29. Ibid., II.79.

30. Cyprian, *Letter* LIX.10, ed. W. Hartel, CSEL 3.2, pp. 465–842 (Vienna, 1868), p. 677.

31. Eusebius *HE* VI.43.10. See over, p. 405.

32. Eusebius *HE* VI.43.2. It was a "very large council"; cf. Cyprian *Letter* LII.

33. Cyprian, *Ad Donatum* 4, ed. W. Hartel, CSEL 3.1, pp. 3–18 (Vienna, 1868), p. 6. See my *Martyrdom and Persecution*, pp. 399–401.

34. Origen *Celsus* VI.11.

35. Ibid.

36. See over, p. 380.

37. Henrichs and Koenen, "Mani-Codex."

38. Eusebius *HE* VI.38, and also Hippolytus *Refutation* IX.13.

39. Henrichs and Koenen, "Mani-Codex," pp. 133ff.

40. Ibid., p. 120 with references.

41. See below, pp. 665–67.

42. See Puech, *Le Manichéisme*, p. 47. If the campaign in which he took part is that against Gordian in 242–43, there would be the extraordinary coincidence of two great religious figures, Plotinus and Mani, confronting each other in opposing armies!

43. Ibid., p. 53. Probably 26 February 277 is the date of Mani's execution.

44. Henrichs and Koenen, "Mani-Codex," pp. 141ff.

45. Their rejection of Paul is referred to also by Origen, cited by Eusebius *HE* VI.38.

46. Henrichs and Koenen, "Mani-Codex," p. 137.

47. Ephraem Syrus, *Ephraem's Prose Refutations*, ed. C. W. Mitchell, vol. 2, p. xxxii. See above, p. 297, and compare John of Ephesus, *Lives of Eastern Saints*, ed. and Eng. trans. E. W. Brooks, *Patrologia Orientalis* 17–19 (Paris, 1923–26), 17.1, pp. 138–39.

48. Burkitt, "Christian Church in East," pp. 504–12.

49. Ephraem, citing Mani, in *Ephraem's Prose Refutations*, Mitchell, vol. 2, p. ci.

50. See Burkitt, "Christian Church in East," p. 506, and above, p. 296.

51. Augustine, himself nine years a "Hearer" in the sect, describes the Manicheans, *Enarrationes in Psalmos* 140.12 (*PL* 37.1823); and see also the anonymous writer of the *Acta Archelai*, ed. Beeson.

52. See Puech, *Le Manichéisme*, p. 61, and note on pp. 144–45, detailing references to "the prophets of humanity" who had preceded Mani.

53. Cited from F. C. Burkitt, *The Religion of the Manichees* (New York: Macmillan Co.; Cambridge: At the University Press, 1925), p. 37.

54. Sensationally discovered in 1931 by C. Schmidt, and reported by Schmidt and H. J. Polotsky, "Ein Mani-Fund in Aegypten," *SBAW* (1933): 24–90.

55. Cited from Stevenson, ed., *A New Eusebius*, p. 282.

56. See Brown, "Diffusion of Manichaeism." Dating, see A. Henrichs and L. Koenen, "Berichtigungen zu der Kölner Mani-Codex," *ZPE* 32 (1978): 78ff. in *ZPE* 34 (1979): 26.

57. *Acta Archelai* XIV, "religione gentiles."

58. See below, pp. 568, 663.

59. Eusebius-Jerome, *Chronicle*, ed. Helm, GCS 24, ad ann. 247 (p. 217).

60. For the coinage of this period, see Mattingly, Sydenham, and Sutherland, eds., *RIC*, vol. 4, pt. 3: *Gordian III to Uranius Antoninus*, pp. 54ff.

61. Origen *Celsus* III.29; see also II.79; and cf. *Sermo 39 on Matthew XXIV.9*, ed. E. Klostermann, GCS 38, Origen (Leipzig: Hinrichs, 1933), p. 75.

62. Note the two inscriptions of this period, from Scaptopare in Thrace, *SIG* 3, 888 (depopulation largely due to official extortions), and Araguë in Phrygia (depredations of soldiers); see Rostovtzev, *Social and Economic History of Roman Empire*, vol. 2, p. 741 n. 26.

63. Origen *Celsus* III.15.

64. *The Martyrdom of Pionius the Presbyter and His Companions* 9, in *Acts of Christian Martyrs*, ed. Musurillo, pp. 136–67, esp. p. 147.

65. Philo *In Flaccum (Against Flaccus)* IX.58–72.

66. Eusebius *HE* VI.41. (Dionysius's letter to Fabius of Antioch).

67. *HE* VI.34, but Eusebius covers himself by stating, "It is recorded that . . . ," which usually means mere suggestion.

68. Eusebius *HE* VI.39.1.

69. *Sibylline Oracles* Book XIII.79–88 (dated not much later than 265). See Olmstead, "Mid-Third Century," p. 398, "But straightway there shall be sudden pillage and murder of the faithful because of the former king [Philip]."

70. Zonaras *Epitome historiarum* XII.20. For Decius's coins, see Mattingly, Sydenham, and Sutherland, eds., *RIC*, vol. 4, pt. 3: *Gordian III to Uranius An-*

toninus, pp. 107ff.; and in general see my *Martyrdom and Persecution*, pp. 405–13, and notes on pp. 433–34.

71. *Année épigraphique*, no. 235 (1973): 63. See Babcock, "Inscription of Decius," p. 149.

72. Julian was hailed as "templorum restitutor" on a site near the kibbutz of Maᶜayan Barukh, in the upper Jordan valley (A. Negev, "The Inscription of the Emperor Julian at Maᶜayan Barukh," *IEJ* 19 [1969]: 170–73). See below, pp. 447, 602.

73. I have followed C. Saumagne, *Saint Cyprien*, p. 26; and see J. M. Reynolds, "Vota pro salute principis," *PBSR* 30 (1962): 33–36, publishing two inscriptions from Cyrenaica recording *vota pro salute principis*, suggesting a civic ceremony.

74. *Liber Pontificalis*, ed. Mommsen, p. 27.

75. Eusebius *HE* VI.39.4. For dating, see *Syrian Martyrology = Die drei ältesten Martyrologien*, pp. 7–15, esp. p. 8, ed. H. Lietzmann, K1T 2 (Bonn, 1911) For the trial and imprisonment of Alexander of Jerusalem, see Eusebius *HE* VI.39.2 and 46.4; for Dionysius's escape, Eusebius *HE* VI.40; for Cyprian in hiding, Roman presbyters' letter included in Cyprian's correspondence *Letter* VIII.1.

76. Gregory of Nyssa, *De vita Gregorii Thaumaturgi* (*Life of Gregory Thaumaturgus*), *PG* 46.949A.

77. He was tried before the emperor in Rome (Cyprian *Letter* 37.1), despite his lack of any exalted rank, and was imprisoned for nineteen days before release. He returned free and unharmed to Carthage. Also Clarke, "Observations on Decius," pp. 66–67; and for Celerinus's background as a confessor, see my "Open Questions Concerning the Christians and the Roman Empire in the Age of the Severi," *JTS* 25 (October 1974): 333–51, esp. p. 350.

78. There was probably no more than one edict requiring sacrifice to the gods. See Clarke, "Observations on Decius," p. 68 n. 38. For the chronology of Cyprian's letters 5–43 written during the persecution, see Duquenne, *Chronologie de Cyprien*, and my *Martyrdom and Persecution*, pp. 406–13.

79. *Martyrdom of Pionius* 23, in *Acts of Christian Martyrs*, ed. Musurillo, p. 167. For the authenticity of this dating, see Barnes, "Pre-Decian *Acta Martyrum*," pp. 529–31.

80. *Pap. Oxy.* XII.1636.

81. Cited from Stevenson, ed., *A New Eusebius*, p. 228.

82. "Liberti" and "domestici" were involved (even in Christian households these need not have been Christians), as Cyprian *Letter* XV.4 shows. For the view that Christians only were obliged to sacrifice, see Keresztes, "Decian *libelli*," p. 774.

83. Cyprian *Letter* XLII.3, ed. Hartel, p. 592. For the rites, see Cyprian, *De Lapsis* (*The Lapsed*) VIII (eager apostates taking "hostia" and "victima" to the smoking altars).

84. Inscription from Aphrodisias, the capital of Caria, MAMA VIII.424, dated October–November 250.

85. I accept Clarke's correction ("Observations on Decius," p. 73 n. 76) of my earlier view that "the penalty for refusal was death" (*Martyrdom and Persecution*, p. 407). Sometimes, as in Alexandria or in Asia, it was (Eusebius *HE* VI.41.14ff., and *Martyrdom of Pionius*), but in North Africa it seems seldom to have been so and even in Rome the policy was not consistent.

86. Cyprian *Lapsed* VIII.

87. Cited by Eusebius *HE* VI.41.10–12, ed. and Eng. trans. Oulton.

88. Dionysius, cited by Eusebius *HE* VII.11.24 (I assume that he is referring back to the Decian persecution); and for similar flights in other parts of Egypt, *HE* VI.42.2–4. The populace was still bitterly hostile to the Christians.

89. Thus, Barnes, "Pre-Decian *Acta Martyrum*," p. 531.

90. *Martyrdom of Pionius* 11. The Acta are accepted by G. Lanata, ed., *Gli atti dei martiri come documenti processuali* (Milan: Giuffré, 1973), p. 177, as an extremely important source on the Decian persecution.

91. Ibid., 16.5.

92. Ibid., 10.7. For Jews inviting Christians to convert to Judaism, ibid., 13.1.

93. Ibid., 10.4.

94. Ibid., 15.2; 16.1; 17.1: "Cease, Pionius, don't be a fool."

95. Ibid., 20.6. For Sabina, ibid., 18.7.

96. Origen *Homily on Exodus* XIII.3, ed. W. A. Baehrens, GCS 29, Origen, pp. 145–279 (Leipzig: Hinrichs, 1920), p. 272.

97. Origen, *Matthew* XVI.25, 8, ed. Klostermann, p. 558.

98. For example, Cyprian *Letter* I, and *Lapsed* VI; see Klauser, "Bischöfe als staatliche."

99. Cyprian *Letter* LXVII. See Clarke, "Prosopographical Notes, I: Spanish Bishops."

100. Cyprian *Letter* XLII.

101. Eusebius *HE* VI.41.4ff.

102. Cyprian *Letter* XXIII (from Lucian the confessor).

103. Cyprian's view of Cornelius's authority is instructive. He had had a long career in the church ("promoted through all ecclesiastical offices"). He was made bishop "by very many of our colleagues then present in the city of Rome." He was approved by the testimony of "almost all clergy," and "by the vote [*suffragio*] of the people" (*Letter* LV.8, ed. Hartel, p. 629).

104. Cyprian *Letter* 48.3.

105. Ibid., LIX.18, ed. Hartel, p. 687.

106. Cyprian *Letter* LV.9.

107. Ibid., LIV.4, "sed et catholicae ecclesiae unitatem quantum potuit expressit nostra mediocritas" (ed. Hartel, p. 623).

108. Cyprian *Letter* LV.6–7.

109. Ibid., XXXIX.4, ed. Hartel, p. 584, concerning Celerinus and Aurelius: "virtutum pariter et morum singulis exempla praebentes, et congressioni et paci congruentes, illic robore hic pudore laudabiles," that is, they had behaved themselves and hence deserved promotion to the priesthood.

110. On Novatian, see G. T. Stokes, "Novatian," in *DCB*, vol. 4, pp. 58–60, and A. d'Alès, *Novatien: Étude sur la théologie romaine au milieu du troisième siècle* (Paris: Gabriel Beauchesne, 1924), also Vogt, *"Coetus Sanctorum"* and bibliography in B. Altaner, *Patrology*, Eng. trans. H. C. Graef, rev. ed. A. Stuiber (New York: Herder & Herder, 1961), pp. 171–72.

111. Eusebius *HE* VI.43.3ff.

112. *Unity*, ed. M. Bévenot, OECT (New York and London: Oxford University Press, 1972); and on the two versions of chap. 4, see Bévenot's successive statements in *Analecta Gregoriana* IX (1938), and *"Primatus Petro datur,"* and in his

edition of Cyprian's *Unity*. My own view of the "first edition" is that this *could* be a fourth-century Roman interpolation. There were not two versions of this chapter circulating in North Africa during the Donatist controversy (see *Modern Churchman* n.s. 1 [1957]: 197–99, reviewing Bévenot's [ed.] *De Lapsis* and *De Ecclesiae Catholicae Unitate*, ACW 25, 1st ed. [Westminster, Md.: Newman Press; London: Longmans, Green & Co., 1957]), and see below, p. 352.

113. Cyprian, *Letter* LXII.4, ed. Hartel, p. 700.

114. Cyprian *Letter* LXVI.5, "novus credentium populus" (ed. Hartel, p. 730).

115. Eusebius *HE* VII.21.9; and 22.1ff. for Egypt. Compare Cyprian *De Mortalitate* (*On the Mortality*) for North Africa.

116. Eusebius *HE* VII.10.3.

117. Cyprian *Letter* LV; and see Benson's patient unraveling of the conflicts in Carthage 251–54, in *Cyprian*, chap. 5.

118. See over, pp. 353–57.

119. Firmilian of Cappadocia, cf. Cyprian *Letters* LXXV.25.

120. Eusebius *HE* VII.11.3ff.; Cyprian *Acta proconsularia* 1 (ed. Hartel, pp. cx–cxi).

121. Cyprian, *Acta proconsularia*, ed. Hartel, p. cxi, "nec coemeteria ingrediantur."

122. *Letter* 76; and compare 79; also, the fervent language of the Numidians' reply, 77.

123. *Letter* LXXX.

124. Related by Saumagne, *Saint Cyprien*, pp. 178–83; the idea that Cyprian was in some way inculpated in the incident that led to the massacre of Christians at Utica seems far-fetched, but there must have been some pretext for Cyprian's removal to Carthage for trial.

125. *Acta proconsularia* 3, ed. Hartel, pp. cxii–xiii. Cited from Stevenson, ed., *A New Eusebius*, pp. 261–62.

126. See Ste. Croix, "Why Early Christians Persecuted?" pp. 27–31.

127. *HE* VII.11.12–14.

128. See my *Martyrdom and Persecution*, pp. 427–29. The bishops of Hippo and Tarragona were probably among the victims.

129. Eusebius *HE* VII.13. See Andresen, "Der Erlass des Gallienus," pp. 385–98, and my "Which Dionysius?" *Latomus* 36 (1977): 164–68, replying to Clarke, "Prosopographical Notes, III: Rome," pp. 437–38.

130. Eusebius *HE* VII.13.

10

The Third Century: The Western Churches 190–260

Christianity had survived the persecutions of Decius and Valerian. For the next forty years the churches enjoyed almost unbroken peace. There were now four (or five) main centers of Christianity—Rome, Carthage, Alexandria, (Antioch), and Ephesus—long-established communities whose bishops dominated their subordinates over very wide areas. These were the leading sees of Christendom and during the third century each, with the possible exception of Ephesus (of which too little is known), came to reflect its individual interpretation of Christianity. By this time, too, the church was a mature institution whose leaders were the acknowledged representatives of one of the main religious traditions in the Roman Empire. The Parousia had not taken place, and hence Christians were not only beginning to develop their distinctive culture parallel to that of pagan and Jewish society, but were also confronted with growing theological problems. Underlying differences between the far-flung centers of the new religion were beginning to assert themselves, and tensions were accentuated by the alternations between peace and persecution. The Rebaptism controversy of 255/57 between Rome and Carthage was part of the aftermath of the Decian persecution and foreshadowed the more serious Donatist schism sixty years later, following the Great Persecution. In the 260s the rival theologies of Antioch and Alexandria clashed over the theology and personality of Paul of Samosata, bishop of Antioch by grace of Queen Zenobia of Palmyra.

Of the major churches, Alexandria, Antioch, and Ephesus were Greek-speaking; Carthage and Rome (after c. 240) were Latin-speaking. There were times, particularly during the Rebaptism controversy, when the leaders in both parts of the empire cooperated readily, but there were long intervals in which contacts seem to have been minimal. An episode like the appeal by the Cyrenaican bishops to Dionysius of Rome between 261 and 264 against the judgment of Dionysius of Alexandria seems to have been rare. Greek Christian writers, including even Origen to judge from Cyprian's correspondence, were practically unknown in the West and vice versa. At a vital stage in their formation, Greek and Latin theologies had little to prevent them from growing apart.

In the East, Origen spoke for many when he wrote, "For Christians see that with Jesus, human and divine nature began to be woven together, so that by fellowship with divinity human nature might become divine. . . ."[1] The immortality of the soul was designed for "friendship with God and fellowship with Jesus."[2] It was a positive hope achieved by human choice. God did not give people salvation, Origen reminded his hearers, he set it before them; it was for each one to make the choice,[3] and life in the world was not devoid of good things. Clement of Alexandria's and Origen's were optimistic views of humanity and its relations with God. They owed much to the legacy of the Greek philosophical tradition that taught that an individual should "know thyself" and live "according to

338

nature" in order to attain the good life. Eschatology and apocalyptic played little part in this thought, and the eternal leaping and destructive fires of hell, none. In the West on the other hand, more material views of the destiny of body and soul prevailed. God's anger was accepted as a literal fact, and so too, the virtue of imitating the passion and death of Jesus through martyrdom. Whether in Rome or Carthage, one took one's stand on the word of Scripture. All parties in the Novatianist dispute would have accepted the term "evangelical" for themselves. They simply disputed Novatian's sole right to it.[4] Attitudes towards the empire continued to be influenced by the Maccabean tradition of triumphant resistance to idolatrous powers. Church and world represented contrasting cities of Jerusalem and Babylon, each directed by their characteristic laws and ideals.

LATIN CHRISTIANITY

In this chapter, we concentrate on Latin Christianity; in practice, this means Rome and Carthage. Though there were communities in southern Gaul and in the cities of Spain, the Rhineland, and Britain, these seem to have shared the outlook of the two churches that were emerging as power-houses of Christendom. Southern Spain in particular seems to have shared the rigorist outlook and Jewish background of the church in Rome and North Africa.[5] Rome and Carthage with their large Christian populations were in continuous contact, but relations were more often correct rather than friendly, and each generation was marked by fundamental disagreement in theology and church order.

Rome

Rome, despite Irenaeus's respectful praises, remains a curiously obscure see. The end of the second century saw Christianity beginning to win adherents among some Roman families (possibly some women converts),[6] but the Roman Christians formed a mosaic of ethnic groups, mainly eastern Mediterraneans, often reflecting rival theological ideas, held together by an increasingly powerful episcopal leadership. The see was renowned for its wealth. Its faithful contributed, on a scale remembered a century afterward, to the relief of Christians sent to the mines in distant provinces.[7] In the city itself its prosperity was becoming increasingly evident. The period 200–260 was crucial for the development of its property, represented by the catacombs, and its organization. To the cemetery over which Callistus presided as deacon (c. 200) were added "the Crypt of the Popes" in the cemetery of St. Callistus (c. 230) and that of Calepodius (which housed the tomb of Pope Callistus (d. 222) and probably others.[8] Places associated with the founding apostles were often thronged with pilgrims, whose faith and petitions have survived as graffiti after seventeen hundred years.[9] Successive bishops were beginning to base claims for an authoritative status in Christendom on their see's apostolic and, in particular, Petrine foundation.

The third century saw the first conflicts in East and West over these claims, and also the earliest attempts by the Western sees to come to terms with them and, at the same time, to defend their independence.

In contrast to its increasing wealth and administrative authority, Rome failed to develop a characteristic theological tradition, such as that emerging at Alexandria, Antioch, and even Carthage. Only Dionysius (260–69) among its bishops has left any record of theological ability. Others, such as Zephyrinus (199–217) and Cornelius (251–53), were not regarded by contemporaries as skilled in Christian dialectic.[10] Fabian, successful organizer though he proved to be, found himself propelled into the bishop's chair without the least preparation and apparently still a layman.[11] Lack of competence among the leaders apart, one reason for theological backwardness was the problem of language. In 200, it seems as though a somewhat pragmatic Aristotelian form of theology may have been developing at Rome,[12] but if so it had no chance of taking root. Of the Roman theologians, Hippolytus (d. 236) wrote in Greek, while Novatian (*flor.* 250) wrote in Latin. Apart from the repudiation of the ideas of their foremost scholars, the gradual change from Greek to Latin as the predominant language of the Roman church could not have made theological discussion easy. All through the third century one may see from the mute witness of the catacomb inscriptions the continued competition of Greek and Latin for dominance. Sepulchral inscriptions tended to be in Greek (such as those of the popes, except Cornelius) until the end of the century and in many one finds Latin words and names written in Greek letters.[13] Well after the middle of the century the names of a significant number of the Roman clergy remained Greek. Popes Stephen (254–57), Sixtus II (257–58), and Dionysius (260–69) are examples over a period of fifteen years. Cornelius (251–53) and Lucius (253–54) represent Latinity. Philemon, Sixtus's presbyter with whom Dionysius of Alexandria corresponded,[14] must also have been Greek-speaking. The Christians in Rome, like their Jewish predecessors, retained many characteristics of an outpost of Hellenistic culture in the West for some time.

Some traditions of Jewish influence also survived. Conversion of pagans through Judaism to Christianity was not unknown and Minucius Felix seems to have borrowed from Jewish apologetic works in compiling his *Octavius.*[15] Like other Christian communities, that at Rome had grown largely out of Judaism. The earliest-known phase of Roman-Christian literature, represented by the anonymous work *De Aleatoribus (On the Dice-Players),* perhaps late second century, shows the influence of Jewish apocryphal writings on the community's thought.[16] It is interesting that the list of Novatian's works (c. 250) compiled by Jerome (*Concerning Illustrious Men* LXX) should be overwhelmingly concerned with Judaism and include *On the Passover, On the Sabbath, On Circumcision, On the Priesthood,* and *Concerning Jewish Foods.* In the letter addressed to his congregation on the latter, allegedly during the Decian persecution, he reminded them that while the new Law surpassed the old in moral demands, there was no requirement to observe Jewish food laws—as though some of its members did.[17] Jewish names also continued in fashion in the Roman Christian community. The last bishop in the fourth century, Siricius (384–99), shared his with a contemporary, the leader of the Samaritans at Thessalonica.[18] Members of his community still fasted on the sabbath. Themes from the Old Testament figure prominently in the catacombs, while much of the exegetical work of Hippolytus, especially his commentary *On the Song of Songs*, relies on rabbinic methods of argument and indicates a more than usual interest in and acquaintance with Judaism.[19]

Hippolytus himself raises difficult questions of identity. Writings attributed to him (we assume that we are dealing with a single author), such as *Benedictions of the Patriarchs, On the Passover, On Daniel* and his writing *On Antichrist*, are all examples of an interest in themes derived from a Judaism of the period of the Second Temple. In addition, analysis of some of the *Dead Sea Scrolls* compared with his own writings reveals that he must have possessed a detailed and accurate knowledge of the Essenes.[20] How did he come by this, except by close contact with members of the synagogue? Yet Hippolytus also represents the Jews in Rome as persecutors, "this people who today as well, lays traps for and calumniates Christians"—an interpretation he derived from the *Benedictions of Reuben*.[21] His adversary Callistus (217–22), too, had relationships for good or ill with the Roman Jews.[22] Finally, the intricate discussions over the date and computation of Easter, associated with the details of rival Johannine and synoptic Gospel calendars, are reminiscent of discussions among the Jews over the celebration of Jubilees. They breathe a Jewish environment. They lend credibility to Celsus's opinion that "the discussions which [Jews and Christians] have with each other regarding Christ differ in no respect from what is called in the proverb, 'a fight about the shadow of an ass.' "[23] This situation remained true well into the third century. The future of Roman Christian legalism may owe more to a heritage of rabbinic rather than to Roman civil law.

THE EASTER CONTROVERSY

The Easter controversy, followed by those relating to Monarchianism, reflects the heterogeneous character of the Roman community and the rivalries within it. For fifty years before Pope Victor's time (189–99), as we have noted,[24] the church of Rome and the churches in Asia Minor had differed as to whether Easter should be celebrated on 14 Nisan or whether the day of resurrection (Sunday) should also be taken into account. In c. 154 Polycarp and Anicetus had failed to agree, and there the matter had rested. The Christians from Asia residing in Rome continued to celebrate Easter on 14 Nisan, regarding the slaying of the paschal lamb and the consequent deliverance of Israel from Pharaoh as the pattern and prototype of the crucifixion and salvation assured to Christians through Christ's sacrifice. Pope Victor, an Afro-Roman and the first Latin-speaking pope, was unsympathetic towards this interpretation. He insisted that the Easter fast should be maintained from the Friday to the Sunday following 14 Nisan when a joyful Eucharist would be celebrated. His task was made easier by opinions held by some of his opponents. Among the leading Asians was a certain presbyter named Blastus, who seems to have been connected both with the Gnosticism attributed to Florinus, and with Judaism, Montanism, and strongly Quartodeciman views concerning Easter. "The Passover," he claimed, "ought to be observed according to the Law of Moses on the fourteenth day."[25]

If Blastus represented current Asian opinion within the Roman Christian community, Victor had some justification for attempting to enforce his own view. He summoned a council and in the name of his church required synods to be held from one end of the Greco-Roman world to the other to agree to accept the Roman dating. He had his way except in the all-important provinces of Asia Minor. In a moment of arrogance he excommunicated the recalcitrant churches. From Ephesus came a dignified letter from Polycrates: "Therefore we keep the day undeviatingly, . . . for in Asia great luminaries sleep . . . Philip . . . John . . . Polycarp. . . . All these kept the fourteenth day of the passover according to the gospel. . . . [I] am not afraid of threats."[26] Irenaeus of Lyon attempted to mediate, for while he accepted the Roman dating of Easter he considered Victor's attitude overbearing and told him so.

The crisis blew over, but the dispute remained. In the East, Firmilian of Cappadocia stated in 256 that the Roman dating of Easter was wrong, and demonstrated that the opinions of Rome's bishops were not always in accordance with tradition.[27] In the West, however, there was a growing feeling that Easter should not be tied to the Jewish Passover, and in c. 224 Hippolytus worked out a calculation of the times of Easter for the years 222 to 233 according to a cycle of sixteen years, and this was inscribed with a complete list of his works on a marble chair erected in his memory. He insisted that Sunday, the Lord's Day, gave the rule, the solemn Eucharist being celebrated on that day, and that Christ's death fell on the Friday. The equinox was taken to be 18 March.[28] Another writer, perhaps an anonymous North African, wrote a treatise on the calculations of Easter in 243— also with the object of freeing Christians from dependence on the Jews but correcting his unnamed predecessor's cycles. In c. 260 Dionysius of Alexandria worked out a cycle of eight years and in c. 277 another Alexandrian, Anatolius, calculated another cycle of nineteen years, but related it to an equinox on 21 March. This became the official Alexandrian use. The controversy rumbled on. In 325 Constantine believed that the fixing of the date of Easter independent of 14 Nisan was second in importance only to the settlement of the Arian controversy on the agenda of the Council of Nicaea.[29] For the first time in the history of the church, two traditions separated by geography and Christian heritage had come into conflict. Rome and Ephesus could both claim the presence of tombs of apostles and apostolic authority to uphold their case, but this time schism had been avoided.

THE MONARCHIAN CONTROVERSIES

In the Monarchian controversies between 200 and 230 a somewhat similar situation arose, with the disputes taking place both in Rome and in the cities of the province of Asia. Their importance lies in the fact that with them began the Trinitarian and christological controversies that dominated the history of Christian doctrine in the next two centuries. To some extent their emergence was a reaction to the dualism implicit in Gnosticism and Marcionism. There was only one God in the universe; and in asserting this Irenaeus had stated no more than most Christians believed.[30] But with the ever-lengthening delay in the Parousia the question had to be answered: How was Christ to be worshiped "as God"? What was his relation to the Father? How could the Trinity of Father, Son, and Holy Spirit, in whose name the catechumen was baptized, be reconciled with monotheism? How did Christianity differ from speculative Judaism? These were theoretical and practical questions arising within expanding Christian communities. Their emergence in the first decades of the third century shows Christianity gaining in self-confidence and self-sufficiency. Metaphysical questions could be answered as well as asked.

Once again, the immigrant Christians in Rome from Western Asia found themselves on the losing side. Noetus, a native of Polycarp's see of Smyrna, had been proclaiming (c. 200) that "Christ was the Father himself and the Father himself was born, suffered and died." He was reprimanded by the presbyters at Smyrna, but expostulated, "What evil then am I doing in glorifying Christ?"[31] He left for Rome where a similar reception awaited him. Yet he had voiced what many Christians in the East felt and continued to feel, namely that in some way God really suffered on the cross for humanity. "The Word of God died for us" remained the belief of the populace, as Nestorius found to his cost two centuries later.[32] Not surprisingly then, Noetus found willing disciples—Polemon and Praxeas—in Rome, the latter pushing his ideas to a logical conclusion in denouncing the New Prophecy of the Montanists that had gained a foothold in Rome and Carthage at this time.[33] Most important of all was Sabellius "the Libyan" (c. 220) who attempted to reconcile Monarchian and Trinitarian theology. He claimed that the Trinity was a reality, but consisted of modes or aspects of one God: God as Father in the creation, as Son in redemption, and as Holy Spirit in prophecy and sanctification.[34] There was one substance (*hypostasis*) but three activities (*energeiai*)—loaded words as they proved to be in the Arian controversy a hundred years later.

Victor's successors, Zephyrinus (199–217) and Callistus (217–22), were apparently not unfavorable to this type of thinking. Though we must rely mainly on the word of their enemy Hippolytus, it would appear that Zephyrinus, "an uneducated simpleton,"[35] believed in his heart that God and Jesus Christ were undifferentiated and one, and though he realized that God could not "suffer" and "die," he had no idea how to distinguish the persons of the Trinity. His protegé and successor, Callistus, seems to have been a friend of Sabellius and, according to Hippolytus, actually developed the latter's system by affirming that the Godhead consisted of a single *prosopon*, that is, individual or person.[36] There is some independent testimony, however, that the pope (whether Victor or Zephyrinus) in fact leaned towards Praxeas's views,[37] and Modalism remained deeply ingrained in Roman Trinitarian thought.

The other brand of Monarchians, however, were less well received at Rome. These Dynamic Monarchians, like the Modalists, insisted on the biblical oneness of God, but taking the synoptic account of Jesus as it stood, believed that he was a man on whom the Godhead as divine power (*dynamis*) had descended at baptism, and that he was ultimately adopted into the Godhead. This was, generally speaking, the view of another group of Asian immigrants to Rome between 200 and 230. These included two individuals named Theodotus, one a leather merchant from Byzantium and the other a banker—good examples of the middle-class Greek-speaking provincials who were influencing Christian thought at this time.[38] Later (c. 230) there was Artemon, and contemporaries were ready to link his views with those of Paul of Samosata, bishop of Antioch from 261 to 272.[39] All these stressed the completeness of the humanity of Christ. God sent his Spirit to descend on the man Jesus, enabling him to work miracles. The perfect harmony between the human and divine wills led to Jesus' adoption into the Godhead after his resurrection. There is no denying that this view embodies elements of primitive Christology, linked to Jewish angelology. Christ was the last and greatest of the prophets, the "high priest after the order of Melchizedek" on whom the Spirit descended.[40] At Rome the prophet Hermas had held similar views.[41]

The danger in both these viewpoints was that each could lead back to Judaism. On analysis, the Modalist view of Christ allowed little difference between Jesus' ministry and the theophanies related in the Pentateuch (Genesis—Exodus). In the fourth century this danger was to be emphasized by Basil of Caesarea, explaining why the views of Sabellius were abhorrent to the Eastern bishops.[42] With the Adoptionists the legacy from the Old Testament prophets was more obvious, but at the cost of denying the divinity of Christ,[43] as Origen was to point out.

In the West, the task of solving the problems raised by the Monarchians fell on two strongly individualistic theologians, Hippolytus and Tertullian of Carthage. Hippolytus (c. 160–236) reached back to the Wisdom literature to argue that God could never be without his reason, wisdom, and power, and that his created Word became Christ at the incarnation, part of the Godhead but distinct from the Father. He was able therefore, to divide the Trinity according to function. There is indeed one God, he tells his audience in *Against Noetus*, for "the Father commands, the Son obeys, the Holy Spirit gives understanding. The Father is over all, the Son is by all, and the Holy Spirit is in all."[44] Hippolytus was concerned to demonstrate the distinction between the Father and the Word, but in so doing emphasized also the role of the incarnation in making the Word "son" and thus showing forth the love of God for humanity.[45] Through the incarnate Word, God raised humanity to the dignity of his own rank. Though something of the christological language of the future emerges from this it would seem that, on analysis, Jesus Christ was simply a created being to whom divinity had been arbitrarily and temporarily assigned. Callistus's charge of "ditheism" against him could hardly be refuted,[46] but Callistus's own solution was no more satisfactory.

Tertullian (c. 160-240?), on the other hand, was a man to whom the inspiration of the Spirit was everything. His Christology, as shown in his *Apology* XXI, written in 197, was unoriginal and unconvincing when presenting the current assimilation of Christ to the Word and defining his relation to God as "a ray projected from the sun" (XXI.12). The Word was derivative ("a portion of the whole") and subordinate, and equally liable to Modalist interpretations. In reality, he believed in the whole truth of the New Testament story, whose details he rammed home relentlessly against Marcion, and in Jesus as Savior and Judge, mediator between God and humanity; and these ideas, combined with the ever-continuing work of the Spirit as inspirer of prophecy and the teaching (*disciplina*) of the church were infinitely more real to him than metaphysical discussion on the nature of Christ. It is noticeable in his work *Against Praxeas* (c. 213) that he puts the "expulsion of prophecy" even before "the introduction of heresy" as the heinous results of Praxeas's views and intrigues with Zephyrinus.[47] He coined the term Patripassian to describe his Modalist opponents. "Only fools," he pointed out with reference to John 10:30, could not see that "I and the Father" meant two persons but that in unity, likeness, conjunction, and mutual love, Father and Son were one.[48] It was he rather than Hippolytus, in suggesting the possibility of community of substance between the persons of the Godhead, combined with distinction in "personality," who was to have the greater impact on the Trinitarian thought of the West.

Hippolytus and Callistus had quarreled before. The latter was a sordid character with a suspect past, but was also a skilled administrator. When he became pope in 217, in opposition to Hippolytus, he had a clear idea of the practical needs of the church. As we have seen,[49] the church was expanding, reaching out to new groups in society, to the womenfolk of senatorial families and to well-to-do lawyers. It could no longer be held

345

within the straitjacket of sectarian life. The three-year catechumenate must have been a strong brake on growth. Faced with the problem of whether the church was to remain a body of the elect on earth, hedged about by Judaistic taboos of purity derived from Leviticus, or whether it was to be a school for sinners bound together by the sacraments administered by an ordered hierarchy, Callistus chose the latter. He decided to break with part of the disciplinary legacy of Judaism. The church had to be accepted as a "mixed body," containing unworthy as well as worthy members. "Let the tares grow along with the wheat," he is said to have urged;[50] and not for the last time this text (Matt. 13:30) was to be quoted to support an antirigorist position. According to Hippolytus, he went on to declare that the church might absolve any sin, and he accepted into his communion gross sinners whom even Gnostics and Marcionites had rejected.[51] There is probably salacious exaggeration in this, but judging from Tertullian's indignation, it would seem that he may have allowed adulterous clergy or those who were twice married to retain their orders.[52] While Hippolytus relied on arguments drawn from Old Testament tradition with which to denounce his opponent, Tertullian wrote *On Modesty* (c. 220), the classic statement of the gathered community contrasted with the institutional church. In so doing he opened up the latent conflict between the churches in Rome and North Africa.

In Rome there was always to be a strong rigorist minority, of which Hippolytus and Novatian were the third-century representatives, and the honor reserved for Peter and Paul as martyrs was perhaps the visible expression of it. Its influence, however, was destined to be outweighed, partly by the growing authority of the Roman bishops and partly because of the lack of cohesion within the Roman community itself. In North Africa, on the other hand, the rigorists were always to be in a majority, for whom the church symbolized protest against and alienation from the secular world. Despite Tertullian's thrust against Praxeas, Trinitarian theology never had a high priority in the thought of the North African church leaders. There was to be no equivalent to Novatian's *On the Trinity* until Augustine's time. God, Father and Christ, judge (*Deus pater et Christus judex*), the definition provided by the deacon Pontius in his biography of Cyprian (c. 260),[53] found ready acceptance. Fourth-century inscriptions if anything emphasize the subordination of Son to Father. God was "Omnipotent," Christ was "Saviour." In this period, few African Christians showed much concern regarding the accusation that Donatus was an Arian.[54]

North Africa (Carthage)

The theological interest of the North African Christians lay in another direction, namely in the nature of the church and its membership: who was saved and who damned, what was the role of martyrdom, what of predestination and grace? Far from subscribing to the universalist ideas of the church in Rome, the North Africans affirmed the absolute value of the purity of the church and integrity of its membership, however exclusive that might be. In Tertullian's time, they rejoiced in the name of "sect" (or "school"). "We are a society with a common religious feeling, a unity of discipline and common bond of hope,"[55] wrote Tertullian in 197. Baptism by water they considered merely a prelude to the true baptism of blood.[56] They were men and women of the Spirit, impatiently awaiting the end of the age and judgment and retribution on the pagan world.

How did the North African church come to accept and retain these ideals? To date, there can be no sure answer. There are two possible directions in which the origins of the church may be sought. As in Rome, Carthage had its strong Jewish population, and in both cities Hebrew was still used. Carthage had some reputation as a rabbinic center, and its schools produced three rabbis whose opinions are preserved in the Babylonian Talmud.[57] Its members included some relatively distinguished citizens. It was also an active and proselytizing community, as Tertullian's work *Against the Jews* shows.[58] Jewish Carthage is represented on the ground by the great cemetery covering the hill of Gamart about two miles north of the city. This was almost completely honeycombed with Jewish catacombs and graves that surround and dwarf the by-no-means small French war cemetery on the summit. The tombs appear to comply with traditional Jewish prescriptions. It was believed that Christians were also buried there, but the evidence comes from a period of excavations when such results could not be checked.[59] However, at Damous el Karita, the imposing Christian complex just outside the north wall of the city, the Christian *area* seems to have succeeded a Jewish (as well as a pagan) cemetery. An imposing second- and third-century Jewish bilingual Greek and Hebrew memorial to "Annianus son of Annianus" has been found there, near the Jewish (?) catacomb on which the first Christian church seems to have been aligned. Two other Christian centers have also produced seemingly Jewish burial inscriptions (*enthade keitai*).[60] In addition, the suspected translation of the Bible from Hebrew into Latin and the use of the Jewish-Christian *Gospel of Thomas* in the North African New Testament, point to Jewish influences.[61] It has been pointed out that the emphasis placed by the North Africans on the legal penalties involved in transgressing the law of God, and in almsgiving as well as martyrdom as part of "satisfaction," may also indicate a Jewish background. North African Christianity, too, was a religion which attached importance to the treasury of merit.[62] When in addition, the Carthaginian Jews in Tertullian's day labeled the Christians "Nazarenes" (not "Chrestiani" as did the pagans),[63] one may suspect that one impulse leading to the formation of a sectarian

347

biblical and legal-minded Christian community in Carthage c. 170 came from Judaism, perhaps even from some upheaval within the existing Jewish synagogue.

A second influence is easier to trace. The cult of Saturn (Baal-Hamon) which dominated religious life in Roman North Africa was part of the Carthaginian legacy. It was a Semitic religion in origin with a strong expiatory element. People felt they were under the direct influence of the god; for good or ill they were his slaves, obeying commands received in dreams and nightmares, subject to his inscrutable decrees. Human sacrifice even seems to have given way finally to substitutionary animal sacrifice only in the second century.[64] Sacrifice both saved the life of a threatened victim and assured salvation of the worshiper after death. Saturn was essentially a nonclassical deity, and his most articulate worshipers in the first two centuries were drawn from the lower classes in the towns and the countryside.[65] It is noticeable that temples in Greco-Roman style began to replace open courtyard shrines in his honor towards the end of the second century, and the god himself, the dread old man (*senex*) of popular lore, became an ill-tempered, bearded figure robed in a toga. Clearly, one cannot say without irrefutable literary or archaeological evidence that the Romanization of their chief god alienated some of his worshipers and made them think of a Christian alternative,[66] but subject peoples have been known to reject violently the deliberate modernization of traditional religious practices by their conquerors.[67]

The people of Carthage may have been no exception, and those who joined the growing Christian community brought with them a profound belief in blood sacrifice as expiation of sin and an implicit opposition to the massive vulgar imitations of Rome that were becoming characteristic of the cities of proconsular Africa. Perpetua and her companions represented that opposition. Tertullian's *On the Pallium* speaks for the indignation of the people of Carthage in these times and their nostalgia for the "good old days when Carthage was Carthage."[68]

TERTULLIAN

It was, of course, Tertullian who gave direction and form to the vigorous movement of protest that North African Christianity represented in the first decade of the third century. Though thirty-eight of his tracts have survived, they tell us little about his life, and the difficulty of dating some of his more important works (*Scorpiace* and *On Idolatry* are examples) prevents a definitive tracing of the development of his ideas. It would be advisable not to reject[69] out of hand Jerome's evidence that he was a son of a centurion in the proconsul's guard, a Carthaginian presbyter, possessing a "sharp and violent talent" (this, at least, is true); that he influenced Cyprian (also true); and that "because of the envy and insults of the clergy of the church of Rome he lapsed into Montanism and refers to the New Prophecy in

348

many treatises'' (this would not be an obvious detail for a romancer to fabricate). He died at an advanced age. The other certainties are his astonishing erudition in everything the current classical education could offer, a surprisingly detailed acquaintance of current Jewish arguments and practices, a strongly combative nature and belief in the approaching end of the current age. As T. D. Barnes points out,[70] he triumphantly paraded knowledge of at least thirty literary authorities in his *Apology*, from Herodotus to Varro and Pliny the Younger, not to mention King Juba of Mauretania, Hermippus, Apion and his adversary Josephus. But a deep knowledge of pagan literature and probably a long adherence to Stoicism before his conversion did not make him a bridge or a mediator between paganism and Christianity and ''a resolver of the antithesis between Athens and Jerusalem, the Academy and the Church.''[71] Indeed, it was he more than anyone who emphasized the cleavage between the two, and if he took a large part of his pagan intellectual inheritance with him into Christianity, he did so not to build bridges, but to turn that heritage against its adherents, and to make more effective and more telling his defense of the Christian sect.

Tertullian hated Romano-African pagan society and his warfare against it is reflected throughout his active career. The fifteen years between the *Apology* and the address to the proconsul Scapula (in 212) did not mellow him. He was equally opposed to those whom he regarded as unorthodox or lax Christians, who did not take the promptings of the Spirit seriously enough. Up to 207 he remained within the bounds of the church in Carthage. He relied on Irenaeus, the only contemporary Christian leader he singled out for praise,[72] for his arguments to refute the Valentinians and Marcionites in Carthage; he upheld the principle of ordered church government against the Gnostics, while his Rule of Faith seems to have been accepted from Irenaeus almost verbatim. Between 197 and 207 he was emphatically a man of the church, representing the starkest opposition to paganism and Gnosticism and expounding a morality which though harsh was no more demanding than that of some of his contemporaries.

The challenge of Marcion and his follows seems to have worked a gradual but profound change in Tertullian.[73] He disliked ''the sailor from Pontus'' for his denial of the true humanity and ministry of Jesus and for watering down the physical judgment hereafter. No manger and swaddling clothes, no angry God, no hell that bubbled; that was not Christianity. In his final drafts of his five-volume work against Marcion in c. 207, however, one may detect a new influence in his life, that of the New Prophecy.

The Montanists were strong in Carthage. They certainly influenced Perpetua, Felicitas, and their circle.[74] They have left their trace on an inscription opposing second marriages,[75] and Tertullian adopted this puritanical and uncompromising strand in his later theology. By so doing he provided the church in Carthage and in the West, in general, with directions it never lost. From 207 he began to quote the New Prophecy as having the same authority as Scripture. It may have been the final straw of the quarrel with the Roman presbyters that turned him into a schismatic. For the next thirteen years he lashed out at the lax but orthodox members of the church in Carthage, "the Psychics" as he called them, insulting them with Gnostic rhetoric. The period 207–20 is vintage Tertullian: the period of *Concerning the Crown, On Flight in Persecution, Praxeas, To Scapula, Modesty* (or *Purity*), all tracts for the times, hard hitting, topical, controversial works, brilliant expositions of the aims of an alternative Christian society accepting the example of Jesus, inspired by the Holy Spirit. This church was set irrevocably against paganism and against a Christianity that would compromise with the pagan world.[76]

Thanks to Tertullian the North African church was and remained a gathered church concerned with the maintenance of its integrity. How were its members to be recognized and, indeed, chosen? Could one who had lapsed grievously be restored by penance? How did the Spirit act within the community? Were the sacraments dispensed by a priest who was no longer in a state of ritual purity valid? And in all the discussions there was the issue of judgment, terrible and unsparing to the damned, glorious for the saved. All these issues were already on the minds of North African Christians in Tertullian's day.

Carthage was diverging from Rome on two main issues. First, there was no sympathy with the Monarchian tendencies at work in the capital. Tertullian proclaimed Christ as the Jesus of the Gospels. He did love humankind: for its sake he humiliated himself and died on the cross. "It is immediately credible because it is foolish. He was buried and rose again. It is certain, because it is impossible."[77] Tertullian loved paradox and contrast. He had thrown all his abilities into the debate with the Marcionites to prove Christ was indeed born, ministered, and died in the flesh, so that humanity also might rise to be judged in the flesh. The full humanity of Christ atoning for human sin was a cardinal doctrine in the North African church. It was to remain so as long as that church existed, whether in the time of Callistus or Justinian.

The main disagreement between Carthage and Rome, however, was over discipline. Here the vital difference between Hippolytus's and Tertullian's attacks on Callistus was that Tertullian's was founded on a concept of the activity of the Holy Spirit worked out over twenty years of experience, whereas Hippolytus relied on the tradition of the Old Testament and his contempt for Callistus's past. In *Modesty*, however, Tertullian, while implying also that his opponent was worthless, anticipated some of the arguments used by succeeding generations of African puritans. The church, he pointed out, was "the bride of Christ," having "neither spot nor wrinkle," and therefore could not allow the presence of the impure, the adulterer, and other demon-inspired sinners in its midst, least of all if they had been clergy.[78] These same proof-texts and attitudes were to be found again on the puritan-African side during the Rebaptism and Donatist controversies. One should not communicate with the works of darkness. A bishop was empowered to dispense discipline, but not to attempt to usurp the powers reserved only to God at the judgment.[79] The three capital sins of idolatry, adultery, and bloodshed were "unpardonable." As for Callistus himself, let him exhibit his own apostolic powers if he wished to speak in the names of the apostles.[80]

Tertullian spoke for the majority of Christians at Carthage, just as Callistus spoke for the majority at Rome. On each side, however, there were considerable minorities: In Africa some were not averse to attending pagan shows occasionally, some believed voluntary martyrdom to be a mistake, and some pointed out that the church as Noah's Ark should contain all types of people.[81] In Rome, as we have seen, there was a puritan minority under Hippolytus that would have accepted the North African views though for rather different reasons. This pattern would persist throughout the third century, emerging once more in the aftermath of the Decian persecution, and represented by Novatian.

CYPRIAN

By then, Tertullian and Callistus had passed from the scene. Thinking in Carthage had moved on, for the rapid increase in the numbers of Christians made Callistus's case acceptable. It was by now generally agreed in the West that the church had power to forgive sins, and "the remission of sins" by the church formed part of the creed in Carthage.[82] Cyprian, too, held views of church authority adapted to the age. In Tertullian's time it was possible to think of the church existing "where [two or] three were gathered together,"[83] groups however small who would claim possession of the Spirit, and for whom clerical authority was secondary to readiness for martyrdom. For Cyprian, such ideas were impossible, and demonstrably so, when the confessors attempted to assert their spiritual powers during the Decian persecution. The church was an institution led by bishops who were the successors of the apostles and to whom absolute obedience was due. While accepting much of Tertullian's eschatology, and himself believing that the last days were at hand, Cyprian grafted onto this a logical scheme of church government based on his understanding of the unity of God. God was one, and hence his church must be one and each community must have one leader, the bishop, maintaining peace and unity with his colleagues. The oneness of the church, however, implied its integrity, and though "through the necessity of the times" backsliding laity had to be tolerated as they were in the old Israel, those who held office, the Christian Levites, must be free from sin against God, able, therefore, to receive his Spirit.[84] The church was in the bishop and the bishop was in the church. There was an all-pervading unity in its theology, organization, and sacrament.

On nearly all these points, Carthage and Rome were as one, though as in the previous generation the Carthaginian scheme rested on the more logical foundations. The Roman bishop claimed his monarchical power not on any deduction from old Israel, but on his claim as Peter's heir to the authority of the chief of the apostles, to bind and loose and to be obeyed by other bishops. Cyprian acknowledged the Roman see as the "source" of episcopacy.[85] The origin of the unity of the church, as he stressed in *On the Unity of the Catholic Church*, began from one apostle. He went on to point out, however, that "other apostles were also the same as was Peter, endowed with an equal partnership both of honor and of power, but the beginning proceeds from unity so that the Church of Christ may be shown to be one."[86] This was a clear statement written in 251 when the relations between Rome and Carthage were of the best. One version of this same passage emphasized the primacy (*primatus*) of Peter and lessened the role of the other apostles.[87] Cyprian never doubted the need for communion with the church in Rome as "the origin" of episcopacy, and the *primatus* ("elder brother") status of its bishop.[88] But as he pointed out especially with reference to Paul's dispute with Peter over circumcision, Peter made claim neither to primacy nor to obedience from his colleagues.[89] The body of bishops were equal members of a "college" (*co-sacerdotes*). The episcopate "is one, of which each holds his part in its totality," that is, indivisibly.[90]

Cyprian had taken care to keep Cornelius informed on each stage of the debate over the readmission of the lapsed after the Decian persecution. The stream of letters which he dispatched to his friend near the end of 251[91] is as good evidence as any of how he regarded Cornelius's status. Cornelius himself he admired as a "peaceful and just priest."[92] Whatever his merits, his rival Novatian had put himself out of the church catholic by his schism.[93] The early death of Cornelius, however, resulting from Gallus's tentative renewal of the persecution in the spring of 253, followed by the death of Lucius, his successor (May 254), enhanced Cyprian's position as the most experienced bishop in the Western world. His was the advice to be sought in cases of difficulty and his verdict would be accepted. The clashes that developed almost immediately between him and the new bishop of Rome, Stephen (12 May 254–2 August 257), concerned both their personal authority as bishops and fundamental ideas as to the nature of the church. Two headstrong individuals were at odds.

Both would have agreed on the government of the church by monarchical bishops and in its unique claim to the activity of the Spirit within it. The disputes were over how that activity was exercised. Cyprian believed that the Spirit worked through the concord and unanimity of bishops consulting together in council. No single bishop could dictate to his colleagues. All were empowered to forgive and remit sins as successors of the apostles on whom Jesus after the resurrection had "breathed" and said "Receive the

Holy Spirit."[94] Second, for Cyprian each sacrament formed a unity that could not be broken. It could not be dispensed validly by one from whom the Spirit was absent, that is, outside the church. A man could not be born of God and sanctified unless each part of the rite of baptism was present, which could only be within catholic unity. Stephen, like Callistus before him, was more pragmatic in his outlook.[95] So far as baptism was concerned, the status of the minister was irrelevant, the efficacy being derived from the faith of the convert and the majesty of the name of Jesus.[96]

The first crisis came in 254 not long after Stephen had become bishop. Marcianus, bishop of Arles, the chief see in Gaul, had joined Novatian—an indication that rigorism was not confined to North Africa.[97] The matter had been reported to Cyprian by Faustinus, bishop of Lyons, who had apparently been keeping him posted on events in the province. Cyprian wrote to Stephen urging action against Marcianus on the grounds that he "had separated himself from our communion." The letter was written in some urgency, as one bishop to another, for Cyprian asserts a right "to advise and aid" as one "who, holding a just balance in the government of the Church, does so exercise towards sinners a vigorous authority, as yet not to deny the medicine of Divine goodness and mercy in raising the fallen and curing the wounded."[98] He goes on to ask Stephen to write to "our fellow bishops in Gaul" to appoint another bishop in Marcianus's place and to formalize his expulsion by excommunicating him ("because he seems as yet not to be excommunicated by us"). As Cyprian evidently had the confidence of the Gallic bishops he believed he was within his rights to urge Stephen to act, and in so doing acknowledged implicitly the latter's seniority over himself. However, the suggestion that Stephen had not been willing to do so (or perhaps resented his interest in affairs outside of Africa), could hardly have been lost on the recipient of his letter.

Stephen's reply has not survived. The next case, also arising from the Decian persecution, underlined the differences between the two sees more clearly. The bishops of Leon and Mérida in Spain, Basilides and Martialis, had lapsed and had accepted testimonials to their adherence to paganism, and of the two, the conversion of Martialis seems to have been complete. Basilides had repented and gratefully accepted the position of a layman, and both sees had been filled. Both exbishops had then had second thoughts. Basilides had gone to Rome (already therefore a place where appeals could be lodged by bishops) and persuaded Stephen to allow him and his colleague to be restored to their sees and they had returned to their indignant congregations. These now acted on their own, placing their case before Cyprian who summoned a council of thirty-seven bishops to decide the issue in the autumn of 254.[99]

While Stephen may have followed Callistus's precedent and allowed ostensibly penitent clergy to resume their orders, Cyprian had made his own view of such cases clear directly after the Decian persecution. A cleric who had become apostate was in a ritually impure state. "Flee from the pestilential contact of these men," Cyprian urges in *The Lapsed.* "Their speech is a cancer, their conversation is a contagion, their persuasion more deadly and poisonous than the persecution itself."[100] These ideas were supported unanimously by the council and applied to the case of the Spanish bishops. Stephen's recommendation was overturned. In a remarkable letter to their congregations, the people of Leon and Mérida, Cyprian gave his correspondents an insight into the thinking of the North African Christians. Their exbishops were apostates, and tested by an appeal to Scripture, especially to Exod. 19:22 and 28:43 and Lev. 21:17 dealing with the Levitical order, they were unfit to minister. The most they could hope for was restoration to lay communion after penance, and Cyprian referred to his agreement with Cornelius that lapsed clergy should not be restored to office. Moreover, if the congregations accepted them they would be involved in their damnation. "Let not the people flatter themselves as if they can be free from the contagion of the offence, when communicating with a sinner and lending their consent to the unrighteous and unlawful episcopate, since divine censure threatens by the prophet Hosea, and says, Their sacrifices shall be as the bread of mourning and all that eat thereof shall be polluted. . . ."[101] This was guilt by association which we shall find likewise in the theologies of Donatus, Augustine, and Pope Gelasius.[102] It was part and parcel of Cyprian's theology. The congregations were urged to separate themselves from their abandoned clerics and choose worthy pastors in their stead. Cyprian's council was declaring that evil was contagious, the worth of a sacrament depended on the state of the minister, and that separation from a minister in deadly sin was not only justifiable but necessary. The opponents of Caecilian of Carthage were to take their cue from this decision sixty years later in the aftermath of the Great Persecution.[103]

In this case also, Stephen's reaction to the verdict of the African council is not known, but the next year he showed how profoundly he disagreed with the entire Cyprianic view of the church. This time the problem was not lapsed bishops, but the status of those who had been baptized by Novatianist missionaries in North Africa. For a few years these had been active, but as Cyprian's authority grew theirs declined. By 255 many of their converts were clamoring to be admitted to the church led by Cyprian. Once again, Cyprian himself had no doubts. "Whoever," he had written in the *Unity*, "parts company from the Church and joins himself to an adulteress [for example, Novatian's party], is estranged from the promises of the Church."[104] He would receive none of Christ's rewards but "would be an alien, an outcast and an enemy." Thus, no sacrament given by anyone outside the church could be valid. Again, there was the notion of ritual impurity derived from Old Testament prescriptions. Like his Donatist successors, Cyprian affirmed, "he who is baptized by one dead, what availeth his washing."[105] When he was asked his opinion about schismatic or heretical baptism, Cyprian did not hesitate with his reply:

> But if any here object [he told a council of bishops in 255], and say that Novatian holds the same rule that the Catholic Church holds, baptizes with the same Creed wherewith we also baptize, acknowledges the same God the Father, the same Son Christ, the same Holy Ghost, and therefore can claim the power of baptizing because he seems not to differ from us in the baptismal interrogatory—whoso thinks that this may be objected, let him know in the first place that we and schismatics have not one rule of the Creed, nor the same interrogatories. For when they say, "Dost thou believe remission of sins and eternal life by the holy Church?" they lie in their interrogatories, since they have no Church. Then, moreover, they themselves confess with their own mouths that remission of sins can only be given by the holy Church; and, not having this, they shew that sins cannot be remitted with them.[106]

This passage shows that the North Africans accepted as a matter of faith the power of the church to remit sins for eternal life, in contrast to Tertullian's view a generation before. The ground had shifted, but not the fundamentals of North African theology. Long before Cyprian appeared on the scene, Bishop Agrippinus of Carthage, in c. 220, with council of seventy bishops (that is, the Christian "Sanhedrin"), had determined that baptism given by someone outside the church was invalid and must be renewed when the convert came into the orthodox community. Cyprian consciously followed his predecessor.[107] Moreover, baptism was of the greatest importance in the eyes of the North African Christian. It symbolized the complete renunciation of the pagan world and its associations. The gifts of the Spirit conveyed at baptism could not be isolated from each other. The convert "put on Christ" not this or that part of him, and was thereby destined to salvation.[108] In the great and richly decorated hexagonal baptismal fonts of many fourth-century North African churches, the convert literally went down into the waters and emerged a new being. Baptism was "the seal"; the Holy Spirit was believed to hover over the baptismal waters.[109] So how could one who did not possess the Spirit mediate the Spirit to the convert? Such was the view of the majority of the North African clergy.

A minority, however, were prepared to agree with Stephen. The case for accepting Novatianist baptism was prima facie fairly strong. The Novatianists were not heretics. They baptized in the name of the Trinity. They were no worse than the Marcionites in this respect. The letter that the Mauretanian bishop Jubaianus sent to Cyprian for his comments may perhaps have survived under the title "Auctor de Rebaptismate." In it the writer urged that the work of God through baptism could not be confined even within the bounds of the true church. It must be conceived of as inherently able to flow outside it.[110] Stephen was more explicit. So long as baptism had been given in the name of the Trinity, it was valid. Even a Marcionite could baptize validly, and for good measure he quoted Phil. 1:18, "whether in pretense or in truth, Christ is proclaimed."[111] Clearly in Rome baptism did not have the same profound significance that it had in Africa. The rite of confirmation, the laying on of hands, had begun to take on an equal importance with baptism itself.[112] Baptism was the means of entry (like circumcision for the Jews). Only confirmation involved reception of the Spirit. Thus, those who had been baptized outside the church needed the conveyance of the Spirit through the laying on of hands. This had evidently been the Roman tradition in respect of Marcionites.

This time, however, the quarrel between Rome and Carthage became bitter. Stephen denounced Cyprian as a "false Christ" and a "deceitful worker."[113] He refused to see a North African delegation. Unabashed, Cyprian held a major council of the North African church on 1 September 256. Eighty-seven bishops signified their support and eighty-five attended from Mauretania and Tripolitania as well as the nearer provinces of Numidia and proconsular Africa.[114] Cyprian opened proceedings with a short, trenchant speech, stressing the collegiality of the episcopate and denouncing him who would exercise "tyrannical terror" over his colleagues. Correspondence with Jubaianus and a letter to Pope Stephen were read. Then beginning with the senior, every bishop was invited to give his views. With remarkable unanimity they supported Cyprian. "One Lord, one faith, one baptism" (Eph. 4:5) admitted of no compromise. "Heretics," said one of the rank and file, "can either do nothing or they can do all. If they can baptize they can also bestow the Holy Spirit; but if they cannot give the Holy Spirit because they have not it themselves, neither can they spiritually baptize. Therefore, we judge heretics must be baptized." The bishop of the small town of Abbirgermaniciana spoke for his colleagues, demonstrating the reality of the unanimity of view regarding the nature of the church that prevailed among the Christians of third-century North Africa.[115]

Meantime (the precise date of Firmilian's letter is unknown), Cyprian had received support from the church in Cappadocia, for Firmilian had acted similarly towards converted Montanists and had been supported by councils at Synnada and Iconium in Phrygia.[116] He had little patience with Stephen and his follies. Custom was no answer to truth. Stephen, too, had been actively threatening excommunication to bishops in the East if they listened to Cyprian. There was general alarm.[117] The Alexandrian church tried to mediate,[118] and its task was made easier by Stephen's death on 2 August 257. His successor, Sixtus II, was a more equable character. Schism was averted. From Dionysius's letters to Sixtus, it is clear that, like Cyprian, he regarded the sacrament as an indissoluble unity and the acceptance of heretical baptism as heinous. Nonetheless, Dionysius's predecessor Heraclas had received heretics with laying on of hands,[119] and degrees in heresy might be allowed for. One had at times to temper the strict law. What of someone who had accepted such baptism years ago in a moment of folly? Was he to be regarded as forever outside?[120] For Dionysius baptism was illumination, the gateway to further progress towards perfection (rather than the exclusive connotation implied in the term "seal"), and there could accordingly be greater and lesser degrees of defect. The Council of Nicaea was to agree. Dionysius inclined towards Sixtus's and the Roman view that Novatianist baptism having being given in the name of the Trinity need not be repeated.[121] Reintegration into the church could be through penance followed by laying on of hands. His mediation was interrupted by the Valerianic persecution. It shows, however, how the worldwide character of the church was allowing opinions to be sounded among those not directly involved in a dispute between two major communities. In the informality of this procedure lay its strength. By 260 the Christian leaders were showing powers of statesmanship as well as of survival.

For the next forty years Rome and Carthage remained at peace. Their bishops were relatively obscure men who left little mark on history, but neither see abandoned its position. In Carthage, Cyprian's martyrdom seemed to set the seal on his leadership of a church that put its integrity above all else. Yet, even as he died, his deacon Pontius wrote his life to defend his reputation. His "moderation" did not suit all. Many lay people preferred the example of Perpetua and Felicitas to his.[122] At the other end of the scale, there were many who were ready to abandon Cyprianic puritanism. Attitudes leading to voluntary martyrdom were discouraged. Even martyrs themselves had to be authenticated before their relics might be honored. There was little scope for the traditional North African teaching about the Spirit here. Cyprian, his biographer argued, would have achieved glory even without martyrdom.[123] Deep rifts were forming in the North African church between the puritan and moderate wings, which the Great Persecution would force into the open.

Rome, on the other hand, could face the prospect of any future confrontation with confidence. Its bishops, however obscure, were indispensable. Peter's see was acknowledged in the West as the source of episcopal unity. If individual bishops lapsed, then someone else must be sent to represent Peter in Rome. This is what the Donatists had in mind when in c. 314 they sent the Numidian, Victor of Garba, as rival to Pope Miltiades (311-14), so that through him communion with Rome could be maintained.[124] Carthage had no such advantages. The Cyprianic tradition could only be maintained at the cost of North Africa's virtual isolation from the remainder of the Christian world.

BIBLIOGRAPHY

NOTE

In this chapter we have traced the beginnings of a specifically Western interpretation of Christianity. For the development of the Roman see and the important doctrinal controversies that occupied the period 190–230, the traditional textbooks, in particular L. Duchesne, *The Early History of the Christian Church: From Its Foundation to the End of the Third Century*, 3 vols. (London: Longmans, Green & Co., 1909–24), vol. 1, chap. 17, and B. J. Kidd, *A History of the Church to A.D. 461*, 3 vols. (New York: Oxford University Press, 1922), vol. 1, chap. 14, provide useful summaries of the evidence. For the Jewish-Christian character of the Christian community in Rome in the second and early third centuries, see J. Daniélou, *The Origins of Latin Christianity*, vol. 3 of A History of Early Christian Doctrine Before the Council of Nicaea, Eng. trans. J. A. Baker (Philadelphia: Westminster Press; London: Darton, Longman & Todd, 1977). Concerning individuals, for Noetus, see Robert Butterworth's *Hippolytus of Rome Contra Noetum*, Heythrop Monographs 2 (London, 1977), a convincing piece of detective work. There is no good book in English to date on Hippolytus, though the problems raised by the differing character and styles of writings attributed to him is examined acutely but perhaps somewhat perversely by P. Nautin, *Hippolyte et Josipe: Contribution à l'histoire de la littérature chrétienne du troisième siècle* (Paris: Edition du Cerf, 1947); the same lack of adequate work in English applies to Novatian, though the edition and translation of Novatian's *Treatise on the Trinity*, by Herbert Moore, Translations of Christian Literature, series 2: Latin Texts (New York: Macmillan Co.; London: SPCK, 1919), is a useful introduction. A. d'Alès's *Novatien: Étude sur la théologie romaine au milieu du troisième siècle* (Paris: Gabriel Beauchesne, 1924) still retains value.

On Tertullian, the study by T. D. Barnes, *Tertullian: A Historical and Literary Study* (New York and London: Oxford University Press, 1971), is a vigorous advocacy of Tertullian as a seminal thinker who was also a bridge between the pagan and Christian worlds. A similar theme is developed by J. C. Frédouille, *Tertullien et la Conversion de la culture antique* (Paris: Études augustiennes, 1972). I believe this approach is mistaken, and the more traditional treatment by P. Monceaux, *Histoire littéraire de l'Afrique chrétienne depuis les origines jusqu'à l'invasion arabe*, vol. 1 (Paris: Leroux, 1902), and C. Guignebert, *Tertullien: Etude sur ses sentiments à l'égard de l'empire et de la société civile* (Paris: Leroux, 1901), should not be neglected. Cyprian has attracted rather less literature than he deserves. E. W. Benson's monumental *Cyprian: His Life, His Work, His Times* (London: Macmillan & Co., 1897) remains a key work, and P. Hinchliff, *Cyprian of Carthage and the Unity of the Christian Church* (London: Geoffrey Chapman, 1974) is a lively and readable account. R. F. Evans's essays on Tertullian and Cyprian in his *The One and the Holy: The Church in Latin Patristic Thought* (Naperville, Ill.: Alec R. Allenson, 1972), to my mind, give the most convincing short account of the resemblances and contrasts in the ideas of these two North African Christians. G. W. H. Lampe, *The Seal of the Spirit: A Study in the Doctrine of Baptism and Confirmation in the New Testament and the Fathers*, 2d ed. (London: SPCK, 1967), is indispensible on the Baptismal controversy.

Sources

Anonymous. *Ad Novatianum*. Edited by W. Hartel. CSEL 3.3, pp. 52–68. Vienna, 1868.

———, *De Pascha computus*, ed. W. Hartel, CSEL 3.3, pp. 248–71; ed. and Eng. trans. G. Ogg, London: SPCK, 1955.

———. *De rebaptismate.* Edited by W: Hartel. CSEL 3.3, pp. 69–92. Vienna, 1868.

———, *Sententiae episcoporum de haereticis baptizandis (Opinions of the Bishops Concerning the Baptizing of Heretics),* ed. W. Hartel. CSEL 3.1, pp. 435–61, Vienna, 1868–71; ed. H. von Soden, *Nachrichten der Kgl. Gesellschaft der Wissenschaften zu Göttingen* (1909), pp. 247–307.

Cyprian. *Opera omnia.* Edited by W. Hartel. CSEL 3. Vienna, 1868–71.

Hippolytus. *Refutation.* Edited by Wendland. GCS 26.

Novatian. *De Cibis Judaicis (Concerning Jewish Foods). PL* 3, pp. 953–64.

Pseudo-Tertullian. *Adversus omnes Haereses (Against All Heresies).* Edited by A. Kroymann. CCSL 2:1 & 2, pp. 1399–1410. Turnhout, 1954.

Tertullian, *Adversus Marcionem (Against Marcion),* Books I–V, Eng. trans. and ed. E. Evans, 2 vols., OECT, New York and London: Oxford University Press, 1972; and for commentary on Books I–II, see E. Meijering, *Tertullian Contra Marcion,* PhP 3, Leiden: E. J. Brill, 1977.

———. *De baptismo.* Edited by A. Reifferscheid and G. Wissowa. CSEL 20, pp. 201–18. Vienna, 1890.

———. *De Baptismo liber; Homily on Baptism.* Eng. trans. and ed. E. Evans. London: SPCK, 1964.

———. *De pudicitia.* Edited by A. Reifferscheid and G. Wissowa. CSEL 20, pp. 219–73. Vienna, 1890.

———. *Treatise on the Incarnation.* Eng. trans. and ed. E. Evans. New York: Macmillan Co., 1957; London: SPCK, 1956.

———. *Treatise against Praxeas (Adversus Praxean liber).* Eng. trans. and ed. E. Evans. New York: Macmillan Co.; London: SPCK, 1949.

There are also ANCL translations of Tertullian's works by S. Thelwall, 3 vols. (Edinburgh, 1869–70).

SECONDARY WORKS

d'Alès, A. "Le diacre Pontius." *RSR* 8 (1918): 319–78.

Bardy, G. "L'autorité du Siège romain et les controverses du IIIe siècle (230–270)." *RSR* 14 (1924): 255–72, 385–99.

Barnes, T. D. "Tertullian's *Scorpiace.*" *JTS* n.s. 20 (April 1969): 105–32.

Bickel, E. *"Protogamia." Hermes* 58 (1923): 426ff.

Black, M. "The Account of the Essenes in Hippolytus and Josephus." In *The Background of the New Testament and Its Eschatology: Studies in Honour of Charles H. Dodd,* ed. W. D. Davies and D. Daube, pp. 172–75. New York and Cambridge: Cambridge University Press, 1956.

Bray, G. L. *Holiness and the Will of God: Perspectives on the Theology of Tertullian.* Atlanta: John Knox Press, 1980.

Brisson, J. P. *Autonomisme et Christianisme dans l'Afrique romaine de Septime Sévere à l'invasion vandale.* Paris: Boccard, 1958. Chap. 1.

Carpenter, H. J. "Popular Christianity and the Theologians in the Early Centuries." *JTS* n.s. 14 (October 1963): 294–310.

Chadwick, H. "St. Peter and St. Paul in Rome: The Problem of the *Memoria Apostolorum ad Catacumbas.*" *JTS* n.s. 8 (April 1957): 31–52.

Chappuzeau, G. "Die Auslegung des Hohenlieds durch Hippolyt von Rom." *JAC* 19 (1976): 45–81.

Ferron, J. "Epigraphie juive." *Cahiers de Byrsa* 6 (1956): 99ff.

———. "Inscriptions juives de Carthage." *Cahiers de Byrsa* 1 (1951): 175–206.

Frend, W. H. C. "Jews and Christians in Third-Century Carthage." In *Paganisme, Judaïsme, Christianisme: Influences et affrontements dans le monde antique. Mélanges offerts à Marcel Simon*, ed. André Benoit et al., pp. 185–94. Paris: Boccard, 1978.

Glover, T. R. *The Conflict of Religions in the Early Roman Empire.* 3d ed. New York: Charles Scribner's Sons, 1909. Chapter on Tertullian.

Guarducci, M. "Die Ausgrabungen unter St. Peter." In *Das frühe Christentum im römischen Staat*, ed. R. Klein, pp. 364–414. Darmstadt, 1971.

Labriolle, P. de. *Histoire de la littérature latine chrétienne.* 3d ed. Paris: Société d'Edition "Les Belles-Lettres," 1947. Chaps. on Tertullian, Minucius Felix, and Cyprian.

La Piana, G. "Foreign Groups in Rome During the First Centuries of the Empire." *HTR* 20 (1927): 183–403.

———. "The Roman Church at the End of the Second Century." *HTR* 18 (1925): 201–77.

Mohrmann, Chr. "Les origines de la latinité chrétienne." *VC* 3 (1949): 67–106, 163–83.

Monceaux, P. *Histoire littéraire de l'Afrique.* Vol. 2: *Cyprien.*

Powell, Douglas L. "Tertullianists and Cataphrygians." *VC* 29 (1975): 33–54.

Quispel, G. "The Discussion of Judaic Christianity." *VC* 22 (June 1968): 81–93.

———. "A Jewish Source of Minucius Felix." *VC* 3 (1949): 113–22.

Sage, M. M. *Cyprian.* Patristic Monograph Series, no. 1. Cambridge, Mass.: Philadelphia Patristic Foundation, 1975. Useful bibliography.

Sider, R. D. *Ancient Rhetoric and the Art of Tertullian.* New York and London: Oxford University Press, 1971.

Simon, M. "Melchisédech dans la polémique entre juifs et chrétiens et dans la légende." In *Recherches d'histoire judéo-chrétienne*, pp. 101–26. Études juives VI. Paris: Mouton Press, 1962.

Simonetti, M. "Due note su Ippolito." *Ricerche su Ippolito: Studia ephemeridis'. Augustinianum* 13 (1977).

Spanneut, M. *Tertullien et les premiers moralistes Africains.* Paris: Gembloux, 1969.

Toynbee, J. M. C., and Ward-Perkins, J. B. *The Shrine of St. Peter and the Vatican Excavations.* London: Longmans, Green & Co., 1956.

Wiles, M. F. "The Theological Legacy of St. Cyprian." *JEH* 14 (October 1963): 139–49. Cyprian "not an original theologian."

Zizioulas, J. D. "Councils and the Ecumenical Movement." *World Christian Union Studies* 5 (1968).

NOTES

1. Origen *Celsus* III.28.
2. Ibid.
3. *Dialogue with Heracleides*, ed. and Eng. trans. H. Chadwick, in *Alexandrian*

Christianity, ed. and Eng. trans. J. E. L. Oulton and H. Chadwick, LCC II, pp. 430–55 (Philadelphia: Westminster Press; London: SCM Press, 1954), pp. 454–55.

4. The writer of *Ad Novatianum* accused the Novatianists of reading the Scriptures more than understanding them and of interpolating them (Anon., *Ad Novatianum*, ed. Hartel, p. 54); and note Cornelius's sarcastic description of his opponent as "this vindicator of the gospel," Eusebius *HE* VI.43.2, and Cyprian's complaint, "si [Novatiani] se adsertores evangelii et Christi esse confitenture . . ." (*Letter* XLIV.3, ed. W. Hartel, CSEL 3.2, pp. 465–842 [Vienna, 1868], p. 599).

5. As shown by some of the canons of the Council of Elvira c. 309 (?). See below, p. 468 n. 66.

6. Eusebius *HE* V.21. See also La Piana, "Roman Church."

7. Recalled in c. 371 by Basil of Caesarea, *Letter* LXX, relating to Cappadocia.

8. See J. Stevenson, *The Catacombs: Rediscovered Monuments of Early Christianity* (London: Thames & Hudson, 1978), pp. 28–29; and above chap. 8 n. 74.

9. The *Memoria* "ad Catacumbas" was already in use as the site of a yearly celebration in honor of the apostles by 29 June 258—see Toynbee and Ward-Perkins, *Shrine of St. Peter*, pp. 178, 192. On the graffiti, see Guarducci, "Die Ausgrabungen unter St. Peter," pp. 411–14. See also Chadwick, "St. Peter and St. Paul in Rome."

10. On Zephyrinus's failings in this respect, see Hippolytus *Refutation* IX.11.1. On Cornelius, Cyprian praises his character, but does not venture a comparison of his theological ability with that of his rival Novatian.

11. Eusebius *HE* VI.29.3–4.

12. Ibid., V.28.14.

13. For the gradual move from Greek to Latin in the Roman church, first via a Greco-"Latin" koine, then through the use of Latin as the ordinary language of the church and finally in the liturgy, see Mohrmann, "Les origines de la latinité chrétienne," pp. 67, 163.

14. Eusebius *HE* VII.7.1. Dionysius of Alexandria wrote, of course, in Greek.

15. See Quispel, "Jewish Source of Minucius." It is not necessary to accept Quispel's additional thesis that Tertullian's *Apology* depended on Minucius Felix.

16. Thus, Daniélou, *Origins of Latin Christianity*, p. 96.

17. *De Cibis Judaicis* 1, PL 3.981–83. Novatian pointed out that the animals forbidden to Jews were clean, but that moral lessons should be drawn from each individual dietary prohibiton.

18. B. Lifshitz and J. Schiby, "Une synagogue samaritaine à Thessalonique," *RB* 75 (July 1968): 368–78. Probably fourth-century date.

19. See Chappuzeau, "Die Auslegung des Hohenliedes," pp. 68ff.

20. See Black, "Account of Essenes."

21. Hippolytus *Benedictions of Reuben* frag. 8 (II.56). See Simonetti, "Due Note su Ippolito," p. 124; see also *Commentary on Daniel* I.14 (ed. N. Bonwetsch, GCS 1 [Leipzig: Hinrichs, 1897], p. 24).

22. Hippolytus *Refutation* IX.12.7–10—a biased presentation but the basic facts must be correct.

23. *Celsus* III.1.

24. See above, pp. 245, 284.

25. Pseudo-Tertullian *Adversus omnes Haereses* VIII: "(Blastus) qui latenter Judaismum vult introducere." See Kidd, *History of Church*, p. 355.

26. Eusebius *HE* V.24.2–8, Kirsopp Lake, ed. and Eng. trans., vol. I (Books I–V), LCL (Cambridge, Mass.: Harvard University Press; London: William Heinemann, 1926).

27. Firmilian, letter to Cyprian, cf. Cyprian, *Letter* LXXV.6, ed. Hartel, p. 813.

28. For details, see Kidd, *History of Church*, pp. 376–78. For the *De Pascha computus*, see Ogg, ed. and trans. The author placed the equinox on 25 March, and the "first month" (Nisan) from 17 March to 15 April.

29. Socrates *Ecclesiastical History* I.9.

30. Expressed in a treatise sent to Florinus, a senior official in the province of Asia who may have gone over to Valentinian Gnosticism, and entitled "Concerning Monarchy, or concerning the [fact that] God is not the creator of evils." Cited by Eusebius *HE* V.20.1.

31. *Hippolytus, Noetus*, ed. Butterworth, vol. 1, *Refutation* IX.7–12, and Epiphanius *Medicine Box* LVII.

32. See below, pp. 755–58.

33. With their emphasis on the work of the Spirit, the Montanists were, of course, Trinitarians. Praxeas himself, according to Tertullian, had once been a confessor in Asia, and emigrated to Rome where he became a friend of Pope Victor (indicating that the latter was not exclusively pro-Latin). Tertullian *Adversus Praxean Liber* (*Against Praxeas*) I, and Pseudo-Tertullian *Adversus omnes Haereses* VIII.4.

34. For Sabellius's views, see Epiphanius *Medicine Box* LXII.1, and Dionysius of Alexandria, cited by Eusebius *HE* VII.6. See J. N. D. Kelly, *Early Christian Doctrines*, rev. ed. (New York: Harper & Row, 1978; London: A. & C. Black, 1977), pp. 121–23.

35. Hippolytus *Refutation* IX.11.1.

36. Ibid., 12.15–19. See Kelly, *Early Christian Doctrines*, p. 123.

37. Pseudo-Tertullian *Adversus omnes Haereses* VIII.4.

38. Eusebius *HE* V.28.6. Epiphanius *Medicine Box* LIV.1; Pseudo-Tertullian *Adversus omnes Haereses* VIII.2–3.

39. Eusebius *HE* VII.30; condemnation of Paul. See over, pp. 385–86.

40. Hippolytus *Refutation* VII.36, Pseudo-Tertullian *Adversus omnes Haereses* VIII.3, and compare Heb. 7:1–11. See the valuable article by Simon, "Melchisédech."

41. Hermas *Similitudines* (*Similitudes*) V.6.4–7, and note Kidd's comment, "Hermas anticipated the adoptionists," *History of Church*, vol. 1, p. 148.

42. Basil *Letter* CCX. See over, p. 632.

43. *Heracleides*, trans. Chadwick, p. 439.

44. Hippolytus *Contra Noetum* (*Against Noetus*) XIV.5. See A. Grillmeier, *Christ in Christian Tradition: From the Apostolic Age to Chalcedon (451)*, Eng. trans. J. S. Bowden (New York: Sheed & Ward; Oxford: A. R. Mowbray, 1965; 2d rev. ed. [Atlanta: John Knox Press; London: A. R. Mowbray, 1975]. All page references in this volume apply to the first edition.), pp. 134–40.

45. Hippolytus *Noetus* XV.5–XVI.5, ed. Butterworth, pp. 78–83.

46. *Refutation* IX.12.16 and for the justification of the charge, X.33.

47. *Praxeas* I.

48. Ibid., XXII.10.

49. See above, p. 292.

50. Hippolytus *Refutation* IX.12.22–23. Such teaching, Hippolytus admitted, was popular.

51. Ibid., 21, "rejected even by numerous heresies."

52. Ibid., 21–22, and compare Tertullian *De pudicitia* (*On Modesty*) 1 (ed. Reifferscheid and Wissowa, p. 222).

53. Pontius *Vita Cypriani* X.3 (ed. W. Hartel, CSEL 3.3, pp. xc–cx [Vienna, 1868], p. c).

54. Jerome *De Viris Illustribus* (*Concerning Illustrious Men*) XCIII. Inscriptions from Oued R'zel and Sbikra in Numidia. See A. Berthier, M. Martin, and F. Logeart, *Les Vestiges du Christianisme antique dans la Numidie centrale* (Algiers: Gouvernement Général de l'Algérie, Direction des Antiquités, 1942), pp. 207–8.

55. *Apology* XLIX.1. Another difference between Tertullian and Hippolytus who contrasted "the school" founded by Callistus with "the Church," *Refutation* IX.12.20.

56. Thus, *Passio Sanctarum Perpetuae et Felicitatis* (*The Martyrdom of Saints Perpetua and Felicitas*) 3.5, in *Acts of Christian Martyrs,* ed. Musurillo. After baptism, "et mihi [Perpetua] Spiritus dictavit non aliud petendum ab aqua nisi sufferentiam carnis." Compare Tertullian *Apology* L.16 on martyrdom as the sole human remedy for post-baptismal sin; and also *De baptismo* (*On Baptism*) XVI.

57. See Barnes, *Tertullian*, p. 284; and my summary of the evidence in "Jews and Christians."

58. Tertullian *Adversus Judaeos* (*Against the Jews*) 1.

59. See Leclercq's summary of the material from Gamart in his article "Gamart," in *DACL*, VI.1, cols. 604–10. His conclusion, however, that Gamart was "a poor Jewish cemetery" is not justified.

60. J. Ferron, "Inscriptions juives de Carthage," pp. 183–86.

61. See Quispel, "Discussion of Judaic Christianity," an additional note, esp. p. 93.

62. R. F. Evans, chapter on Tertullian in *One and Holy*, pp. 40–41; and compare Cyprian *Letter* XVI.3 on the idea that martyrs and confessors accumulated merit for the benefit of the community as a whole.

63. Tertullian *Marcion* IV.8.

64. See J. Carcopino, "Survivances par substitution des sacrifices d'enfants," *RHR* 106 (1932): 592–99.

65. See J. Toutain, *Les cultes païens dans l'empire romain*, vol. I: *Les provinces latines*, part 3 (Paris: Leroux, 1920), pp. 101–2; and see my summary of the evidence in *The Donatist Church: A Movement of Protest in Roman North Africa* (Oxford: At the Clarendon Press, 1971), pp. 78–84.

66. The issue is taken up by T. D. Barnes in his short study, "The Goddess Caelestis in the *Historia Augusta*," *JTS* n.s. 21 (April 1970): 96–101, against views expressed by G. Ch. Picard and the present writer.

67. Such as the Kikuyu in the "female circumcision" controversy with the Presbyterian church in Kenya during the 1920s.

68. Thus, "Sit nunc aliunde res, ne Poenicum inter Romanos aut erubescat aut doleat," *De Pallio* (*On the Pallium*) II.1.

69. Jerome *Illustrious Men* LIII. The case for rejection is argued by Barnes, *Tertullian*, chap. 2.

70. Barnes, *Tertullian*, p. 196; compare Glover, *Conflict of Religions*, pp. 308–9.

71. Barnes, *Tertullian*, p. 231. But see, for instance, *Apology* XLIV.18, "What have the philosopher and Christian in common, the disciple of Greece and the disciple of heaven . . . ?"

72. *Adversus Valentinianos* (*Against the Valentinians*) V.1. "Irenaeus, omnium doctrinarum curiosiosissimus explorator." He had used very similar words about the emperor Hadrian (*Apology* V.7). See Barnes, *Tertullian*, p. 49; and concerning his anti-Marcionite arguments, see Meijering, *Tertullian*, in commentary passim.

73. This seems evident from the numerous sympathetic references to Montanist tenets found in the text completed between April 207 and April 208. For instance, at I.29.4 he agrees with the Montanist prohibition of second marriages, in III.24 he claims that millenarian expectations of the New Prophecy were confirmed by a recent vision of the New Jerusalem, and his assertions that the New Prophecy did not contradict the tradition of the apostolic churches (see E. Evans's [trans. and ed.] Tertullian, *Marcion*, p. xviii). Compare *De Resurrectione Carnis* (*Concerning the Resurrection of the Flesh*) XI (quotation from the prophetess Prisca), also c. 207.

74. See my *Donatist Church*, pp. 117–18.

75. *CIL* VIII.25045; see Bickel, *"Protogamia,"* p. 426ff., and other references in Diehl, *ILCV* I, p. 191. Bickel suggests a fourth-century date and possible Donatist origin. Having seen the inscription, I incline to an earlier, third-century date.

76. See my remarks in *Martyrdom and Persecution*, pp. 366ff.

77. *Incarnation* V, trans. and ed. E. Evans: "Prorsus credibile est, quia ineptum est. Et sepultus resurexit: certum est quia impossibile," directed against Gnostics and Marcionites, c. 206.

78. *Modesty* XVIII, "non habentem maculam aut rugam." Compare Cyprian *Letter* LXIX.2, the church as a "hortus conclusus."

79. *Modesty* XXI.

80. Ibid.

81. *De Idololatria* (*On Idolatry*) XXIV, and see above, n. 50, for Callistus's view.

82. Cyprian *Letter* LXIX.7.

83. Tertullian *On Baptism* VI, and *De Exhortatione Castitatis* (*Concerning the Exhortation to Chastity*) VII, "Sed ubi tres, ecclesia est licet laici."

84. Cyprian *Letter* I, draws the analogy that just as Levites were sustained by the tithes of the other eleven tribes of Israel, so must Christian priests abstain wholly from secular affairs and receive tithes from the brethren.

85. *Letter* XIV, "ad Petri cathedram atque ad ecclesiam principalem unde unitas sacerdotalis exorta est . . ." (ed. Hartel, p. 683).

86. *De ecclesiae catholicae unitate* (*On the Unity of the Catholic Church*) IV and V.

87. See above, chap. 9 n. 112.

88. Thus, *Letter* 59.10; but for the *primatus* as something that could be lost by misconduct, see *Letter* 73.25.

89. Cyprian *Letter* LXI.3 (ed. Hartel, p. 773).

90. *Unity* V, accepting M. Bévenot's (ed.) translation, *De Lapsis* and *De Ecclesiae Catholicae Unitate*, OECT (New York and London: Oxford University Press, 1971), p. 65. See also R. F. Evans, *One and Holy*, p. 51.

91. *Letter* XX, covering *Letters* V–VII and X–XIX. Discussed by L. Duquenne,

Chronologie des lettres de S. Cyprien (*Le dossier de la persécution de Dèce*) Subsidia Hagiographica 54 (Brussels: Société des Bollandistes, 1972), chap. 2.

92. *Letter* LXVII.6; compare *Letter* XLV.1 and LV.8.

93. *Letter* LV.8, "nec habeat ecclesiasticam ordinationem qui ecclesiae non tenet unitatem." Note also, the paradigm of unity in Tertullian *Chastity* VII, "Unus Deus, una fides, una et disciplina" (*PL* 2.971).

94. *Letter* 69.8 and 11; 70.1; 73.1; and 74.4 and 5. R. F. Evans, *One and Holy*, pp. 61–62. The best summary of the significance of Cyprian's sacramental theology is Lampe, *Seal of Spirit*, pp. 170–78.

95. Stephen's ideas may be traced in Cyprian *Letter* LXXII, addressed to Stephen; and in Firmilian's *Letter* LXXV to Cyprian.

96. Cyprian *Letter* 75.20 and compare ibid., 73.14 (use of the same argument).

97. Ibid., 68.

98. Ibid., 68.1.

99. Ibid., LXVII.

100. *De lapsis* (*The Lapsed*) XXXIV.

101. *Letter* LXVII.4.

102. See over, pp. 654–57, 672–73, 810–12.

103. See over, p. 489.

104. *Unity* VI.

105. *Letter* LXXI.1. Compare Augustine, *Contra litteras Petiliani* (*Answers to Letters of Petilian*) I.5.10. The quotation is from Sir. 34:25, and was used by the Donatists.

106. *Letter* LXIX.7, cited in Stevenson, ed., *A New Eusebius*, p. 251.

107. *Letter* LXXI.4. The council included bishops from proconsular Africa and Numidia.

108. *Letter* LXXIV.4. See Lampe, *Seal of Spirit*, p. 172.

109. Tertullian *On the Spectacles* IV; and *On Baptism* V.

110. *De rebaptismate* (ed. Hartel). The authorship is discussed by H. Koch in the *Internationale Kirchliche Zeitschrift* (Berne, 1924), pp. 134–64. See also Frend, *Donatist Church*, p. 137.

111. Cyprian *Letters* 73.14 and 75.20.

112. The first reference to a ceremony of laying on of hands as distinct from baptism for the reception of the Spirit comes in Hippolytus *Apostolic Tradition* XXII (c. 220); and this could well have formed part of the tradition which Stephen claimed to follow.

113. Firmilian of Cappadocia to Cyprian *Letter* LXXV.25 (ed. Hartel, p. 827).

114. One bishop stood proxy for two absent colleagues. The proceedings have been edited by von Soden, *Opinions of Bishops,* and Hartel.

115. *Opinions of Bishops,* no. 16; see von Soden, p. 257, and Hartel, p. 443.

116. *Letter* LXXV.7.

117. Eusebius *HE* VII.5.4.

118. Ibid., 7.4.

119. Ibid., 9.1–5.

120. Ibid.

121. This seems clear from the lessons drawn from the correspondence by Severus of Antioch in c. 518. See Severus, *The Sixth Book of the Select Letters of Severus Patriarch of Antioch in the Syriac Version of Athanasius of Nisibis,* ed.

and Eng. trans. E. W. Brooks, 2 vols. (London: Williams & Norgate, 1902–3), *Letter* V.6, pp. 296–97.

122. Pontius *Vita Cypriani* I (ed. Hartel, p. xc), the derogatory reference to martyrdom of "plebeiis et catecumenis"—already the aristocratic bias in the church in Carthage is evident.

123. Ibid. (ed. Hartel, p. xci).

124. Optatus of Milevis, *De Schismate Donatistarum*, ed. C. Ziwsa, CSEL 26 (Leipzig: G. Freytag, 1893), II.4.

11

The Third Century: Christian Platonism of Alexandria and Its Opponents 190–275

Dionysius of Alexandria and his friends were in a good position to mediate between Stephen and Cyprian. They also faced a continuing problem of the validity of baptism given by heretics. For them, however, there were degrees of heresy and they were less preoccupied with the doctrine of the church and its earthly membership. Their concern was with the harmony and the beauty of the universe, and within that with how human beings might achieve fellowship with the Christ-Logos, and they were prepared to envisage the possibility that even those cut off from the visible church might be true brothers in Christ. There was a difference, too, in their attitude towards the secular world. In the West, Rome, its institutions, and its language had been imposed, whereas the cities in the Greek East had tended to absorb Roman values and to transform them into a common Greco-Roman culture in which the Greek element predominated. In much the same way, we find Christianity tending to absorb Greek philosophical values, until by the end of the third century the line between the beliefs of educated Christian and educated pagan in the East would often be hard to draw.[1] After the conversion of Constantine, the empire now directed from New Rome (Constantinople) moved with astonishing ease from the patronage of the immortal gods to that of the Supreme God.

CHRISTIAN PLATONISTS

In all these developments, the Christian Platonists of Alexandria played a crucial role. For two centuries the relations between Platonism and Christianity oscillated between attraction and repulsion. Basically, nothing could be more opposed than the Jewish and Greek views of God, of creation, of time and history, and of the role of humanity in the universe. Celsus was at his best in pouring scorn on Jewish-Christian claims to monopolize divine favor. Philo and his school, however, had already attempted a synthesis between Platonism and Judaism in Alexandria. The same work was taken up by the Gnostics, especially Basilides and Valentinus and their followers in the second century. It was to be brought to fruition in the interests of orthodoxy by Clement and Origen.

The need was real enough, for the contradictions between biblical and Platonic-oriented Christianity were already being exposed by the pagan opposition in the last quarter of the second century. To quote Celsus again, Christians were guilty of sophistry: "In proclaiming the Son of God to be Logos we do not bring forward as evidence a pure and holy Logos, but a man who was arrested most disgracefully and crucified."[2] This was the nub of the problem that was to haunt Christian Apologists in both parts of the empire until the disastrous failure of Julian's attempt to restore paganism as the religion of the empire had discredited that cause permanently. Celsus, however, perhaps unwittingly also began building a bridge from the Platonist side towards Christianity. At the end of the same section (*Celsus* II.31) he put into the mouth of his Jewish opponent of Christianity the

368

concession that "he would approve if the Logos in your [Christian] view is the Son of God." As Henry Chadwick indicates,[3] the passage shows that Celsus was aware of the Logos-theology of Hellenistic Judaism. As in Philo's time, the concept of the Logos would prove the most hopeful means of establishing common ground between Greek and biblical ideas of the universe.[4] To succeed in Alexandria and indeed in much of the Greek-speaking world, Christianity would have to be articulated in Platonic terms.

Clement and Origen's successful acceptance of the challenge of Platonism was followed up in the fourth century by the Cappadocian fathers. To a great extent the Christian understanding of the mystery of the Trinity depends even today on their interpretation. Platonism also helped formulate the theory of church-state relations on which the stability of the Byzantine Empire rested. But it also had its disadvantages. A gulf was opened up between the beliefs of the learned and the less-learned Christian in the East, between the theologies of the Greek- and Latin-speaking worlds, and between the dominant theology of Alexandria and that of the more biblically minded Antiochenes. Eastern and Western theologians did not confront each other until the Council of Sardica in 342/43. The first phase, however, of the two-century-long conflict between the theologies of Alexandria and Antioch arose within a decade of Origen's death in 253.

Gnosticism had dominated Alexandrian Christianity during most of the second century. In the last two decades, however, its position had become threatened by the emergence of a strong orthodox party loyal to the bishop of Alexandria. The catechetical school which Bishop Demetrius (189–232) controlled provided the orthodox with an intellectual focus and a means of spreading their faith among educated Greek catechumens. Pantaenus (c. 180), its first known leader, had related his philosophic interpretation of Christianity to traditional biblical teaching. His successor, Clement (*flor.* 180–203), was to do the same with greater effect.

Clement

Clement was not a systematic thinker. His writings, and in particular, the *Miscellanies* often betray an undigested amalgam of ideas gleaned from the variegated teachers he encountered before he settled in Alexandria. He was enormously erudite, perhaps even more widely read than Tertullian. Some 360 classical texts are to be found in the *Miscellanies*, many of which have not survived elsewhere.[5] Unlike Tertullian he did not use his learning to batter down the ideals of contemporary society but used the writings of poets and philosophers constructively to build his case for Christianity. He was inclined, however, to parade his knowledge artlessly like a collector, rather than as one who had meditated on the authors he had studied, and was ready to draw some new, Christian significance from their works. At heart, too, he was far from being a "liberal puritan."[6] He lacked a genuine appreciation of classical art, and dismissed the great masterpieces of that

369

age as "idolatrous" or "immoral."[7] Tatian, and not the latter's master Justin whom he never mentions, commanded his respect.[8] Another sign of his basically anti-Hellenic stance was his interest in the Jewish-Christian substratum of Alexandrian orthodox Christianity. Before the discovery of the complete text of the *Gospel of Thomas* in the Nag Hammadi library, Clement's *Miscellanies* was one of the main sources for our knowledge of the Jewish-Christian gospels circulating in second-century Egypt; it provided texts from *The Gospel of the Hebrews* and *The Gospel of the Egyptians*.[9] For all his appreciation of Plato, he repeated the Neo-Pythagorean Numenius's (*flor.* 150–80) gibe, "What is Plato but Moses in Attic Greek?"[10] and (following Philo) he never doubted that Moses provided the essentials of Plato's religious ideas. He heartily despised lesser practitioners of philosophy. Sophists were like "old shoes, worn out except for the tongue."[11]

Two factors, however, ensured that Clement would achieve more than compilations of anthologies (*florilegia*) of classical texts for the use of Christian Apologists. First, he realized from what he read that his missionary task would be hopeless unless he was able to interpret Christian truth in terms which educated inquirers could accept.[12] Second, he was an optimist in his outlook. He believed that humans were reasonable and reasoning beings. Christianity had to be interpreted in terms of the ultimate harmony between Scripture and philosophy. Therefore, Gnostic dualism, libertinism, and fatalism could not be the true Christian revelation.

Early in the *Miscellanies*, he admits that there were coincidences between Christian truth and the beliefs of Greek philosophers. Even if these hit on the truth accidentally, this suggested that God had revealed himself to them also.[13] His wisdom was not confined to the Hebrews. No race was deprived of the opportunity of apprehending God, and so philosophy must be God-given. It ranked "among the good things of Providence."[14] Plato, plagiarist though he may have been, also prepared the way for the Greeks to accept the Christian faith. Philosophy shared with the Law "in making ready the way for him who is perfected in Christ."[15] Its role, however essential, was still merely preparatory. Of itself it was "too weak to do God's commands." Its duty was "to prepare the way for the teaching that is royal in the highest sense of the word, by making men self controlled, by moulding character and making them ready to receive the truth."[16] Faith remained the foundation of Christianity, but the Christian advanced from faith towards knowledge, that is, an ever-deeper understanding of the Word of God, not achieved in a sudden flash of illumination, but through a life dedicated to obedience to God's will. Thus it was that the believer became "like God" enjoying a freedom from all passions that hindered the soul's ascent to perfection and deification.[17]

Few could attain this state. Clement's Gnostic was as much the member of a spiritual elite as the Gnostic's counterpart and shared the latter's

370

ultimate aim. The differences between Clement and the Alexandrian Gnostics were, however, equally important. Clement's religion was monotheist as well as being church-oriented and he was profoundly influenced by Philo's Platonism. For him also, God was absolutely transcendent, "unity but beyond unity, transcending the monad,"[18] and embracing all reality and infinitely greater than all his works. He could be known, however, through his Son, or Word (Logos), not a Demiurge or lesser creator-god, but his image, mind, and reason, inseparable from himself.[19] As J. N. D. Kelly pointed out, "the Word was like the *Nous* of middle-Platonism and Neo-Platonism; the Word was at once unity and plurality, comprising in Himself, His Father's ideas and also the active forces by which He animates the world of creatures."[20] He reflected God rather than contrasted with God, while the Spirit was light issuing from him, to illuminate the faithful (through the prophets and philosophers) pervading the world and drawing humans towards God. There was no dualism in Clement's religion. For him, the Trinity consisted of a hierarchy of three graded Beings, and from that concept—derived from Platonism—depended much of the remainder of his theological teaching.

In addition, Clement had an optimistic view of human beings and their relation to God. The world was created by God and therefore was good. Man and woman had been made in the image of God, and had the means within themselves to progress toward God. There was no "natural evil" and no impassible categories of Spiritual Men, Psychics, and Hylics as in the Gnostic systems. Christ was Teacher (*paidagogos*) of humankind rather than Illuminator of the few. Understanding—itself the fruit of moral progress—was true Gnosis.

> A man of understanding and perspicacity [he wrote] is then a Gnostic. And his business is not abstinence from what is evil (for this is a step to the highest perfection), nor the doing of good out of fear . . . nor is he to do so out of hope of a promised reward . . . but only the doing of good out of love and for the sake of its own excellence is to be the Gnostic's choice.[21]

All action leads towards perfection or towards negation. It was up to the individual to use free will rightly "training oneself for impassibility."[22] Heretical Gnostic systems belied their adherents' claims to love and freedom. Nor were exaggerated strivings after perfection necessary. Encratism was as bad as Gnosticism. The body also belonged to the divinely created order and therefore was good. Birth was not evil as some Gnostics proclaimed.[23] He emphasized marriage and the moderate use of things, such as wine, that made life pleasant. There was no need to be a teetotaller or vegetarian. God gives us all things richly to enjoy.[24] A Christian should not imitate Indian gymnosophists and rush forward to suicidal martyrdom.[25] "Nothing in excess," the Stoic maxim, was also Clement's bon mot. Riches were neutral gifts, depending on how they were used. In *The Rich*

Man's Salvation Clement adopted a pragmatic standard that effectively spiritualized away the point of the Lord's command to sell all that one has and give to the poor. "We must not fling away riches that benefit our neighbours as well as ourselves,"[26] he argued. One who lacked life's necessities could not rise to higher things. Here the contrast with Tertullian was obvious. For the North African, wealth was bad of itself and a gross hindrance to Christian progress.[27] To Clement, however, wealth was a matter of stewardship and the church was a school (*didaskaleion*) for the imperfect where the soul was trained for the ladder of ascent towards God.[28] It was not a sect of those already illumined and saved. The advice of the Stoic sage had replaced the absolute commands of the New Testament. After Clement, Alexandria could never be a center of biblical Christianity.

Clement loathed the Gnostics, not least the Carpocratians, for their fatalism and libertinism. Emotionally he recoiled from Docetism. But he, like the Christian philosophers of the second century, whether Valentinus or Justin, failed to harmonize the Jesus of the Gospels with the Word incarnate. Jesus had a true human nature, he asserted, but "was wholly without passion and into him there entered no emotional movement, neither pleasure nor pain."[29] He even quoted with approval the letter of Valentinus to his disciple Agathopus, that Jesus "ate and drank in a manner peculiar to himself and that the food did not pass through his body."[30] There was no element of corruption in him—again, one contrasts his Christology with that of Tertullian's *Against Marcion*. By accepting this view (and, incidentally, anticipating the Monophysitism of Julian of Halicarnassus in the 520s)[31] and agreeing that the Word itself was the "inner man" in Jesus, Clement committed the Word-flesh Christology to a permanent tendency to undervalue Christ's humanity.

Clement won his argument and his place in Alexandrian Christian theology. He demonstrated that Christianity could be an optimistic and rational creed that made the highest demands on human morality, while requiring acceptance of the rule of the church and its essential articles of faith.[32] Platonism had been gained for orthodoxy. Nonetheless, Clement's ideal would not have been unacceptable to his Gnostic opponents and seemed even to be more Buddhist than Christian. His knowledge of Indian religion, shown by his numerous if critical references to Indian customs and the correct distinction he made between the Brahmins and Sarmanians,[33] may be more relevant to his outlook than is sometimes admitted. The early third century saw strong links being made between the Roman Empire and India and these links affected thought as well as trade.[34] Meanwhile, except in moments of dire stress, the prophetic and apocalyptic elements of Egyptian Christianity—a strong if latent force throughout the second century—were destined for the time being to the role of a subculture, preserved on papyri but not in the annals of theological debate.[35] Representative Greek Christians were already moving towards radically different understandings—of the Trinity, eschatology, and Christian ethics—from those held in the West. Even Origen would be unable to reconcile history and revelation. Those who founded their faith on Jesus of Nazareth and his saving example would find scant support among the intellectual Christians of Alexandria.

Origen

Origen (185–253) we have met already. His *Against Celsus* was a sustained piece of theological writing even though hardly relevant to Celsus's charges made seventy years before. He shared with Paul and Augustine the honor of being one of the few early Christian leaders who have deserved their reputation—unquestionably. For more than a century after his death in 253, few theologians were immune from his influence. All sides in the Arian controversy could claim him as their master. He influenced the direction of Eastern Orthodox Christianity. We have seen him arguing the superiority of Christianity over its rivals. Now we see him equally forthright as a critic and theologian. In character he was quite unlike Clement. The latter was a quietist, his passivity towards the secular authorities contrasting with his missionary zeal. Origen was fearless and outspoken, and always a fighter. He could also be prolix and a bore to those who had to listen to the intricacies of his arguments.[36] He was at his best as a writer and scholar, not as a public speaker. The *Hexapla* and *On First Principles* would have sufficed most men, but added to these works was the massive *Commentary on the Gospel of John*, the homilies and commentaries on practically every book of Scripture, the eight books comprising *Celsus*, detailed learned correspondence with contemporaries, and teaching that could fire pupils with enthusiasm and turn them into missionaries as zealous as himself. His mind could never have been at rest,[37] and, despite all the envy and unreason he encountered, he remained loyal to the church.

To his contemporaries he was an enigma. Pagans as well as Christians failed to understand him. Porphyry (c. 232–304) gave an interesting sketch of the great man whom he must have known when he himself was very young.[38] He says (wrongly) that Origen was brought up as a Greek in Greek letters, but became a protagonist of barbarous religion, that is, Christianity. But while he lived as a Christian he held Greek views about everything, including God, and gave the "foreign myths" a Greek meaning. He had read the entire literature of the Platonists and Pythagoreans and read the mysteries of the Greeks into the Jewish writings (that is, in his commentaries on books of the Old Testament). For some Christians, Origen's insistence on the immortality of the soul and denial of its material substance seemed to make too great a concession to current philosophical ideas. He was persecuted by Bishop Demetrius, cold-shouldered by his old pupils Heraclas and Dionysius, and towards the end of his life was constantly fighting in defense of his own orthodoxy.

What Origen tried to do was to interpret Christian beliefs from a recognizably Platonic angle, and thus far Porphyry was right. Eusebius added the testimony that he "was proclaimed as a great philosopher even among the Greeks themselves."[39] Plato and philosophy were powerful allies for Origen in his fight against the Gnostics. But emotionally Origen was a Christian through and through. Whereas Clement would quote extensively from the classics and call "the city of Plato a copy of that founded in heaven,"[40] Origen would have none of such language. He seldom quoted Plato directly; at no time did he place the ideas of philosophers on the same level as those of Scripture. When he cited examples of courage and integrity it was to the Maccabees that he turned, not to Regulus or other classical heroes. He encouraged his patron Ambrose to face death in 236 with a verse of Psalm 116, "Precious in the sight of the Lord is the death of his saints."[41] Yet he had absorbed Platonism. He told his pupils to acquaint themselves with every Greek philosophy. "Know thyself," the advice of the Delphic oracle, was elevated to a fundamental of Christian conduct.[42] He raised problems taken from earlier philosophers as well as from Scripture, and his understanding of the latter depended on his understanding of Plato. His was the decisive influence that brought Greek philosophy and Christianity together at a crucial moment when Christianity was becoming second only to the religion of the immortal gods themselves.

One can best follow Eusebius, who devoted much of Book VI of the *Ecclesiastical History* to him, and approach Origen's unending quest for knowledge and experience in the service of the church through the recorded events of his life. He was recognized as a prodigy from earliest years with an amazing command of secular works and Scripture.[43] In 203, when he was about eighteen, Bishop Demetrius appointed him head of the catechetical school after Clement's flight from Alexandria. He had already shown his intellectual rigor. His father had died a martyr. He refused to pray with his patroness' Gnostic chaplain, Paul, emphasizing the contrast between church and sect.[44] He sold his father's library for an annuity to enable him to instruct students without fee. His asceticism and extremism showed themselves in his literal acceptance of Matt. 19:12, an act not unknown among Christian zealots in Alexandria,[45] but a disastrous handicap to his own ultimate fulfillment.

Intolerance and missionary fanaticism had characterized his early efforts. At some stage in his early manhood, however, an interest in his father's secular and philosophic studies returned. He seems to have attended the lectures of the mysterious but celebrated Neo-Platonist, Ammonius Saccas, and as it did with Augustine later, Neo-Platonism struck a responsive chord.[46] From this time on, his interpretation of Christianity was Platonic. He inclined toward a zeal for knowledge. In c. 210 he visited Rome to hear Hippolytus and "see the most ancient church of the Romans."[47] Hippolytus was strongly hostile towards the Jews, and it may not be accidental that Origen's next move was to place himself under a Jewish-

Christian tutor to learn Hebrew so as to better refute the Jews. This led to the beginnings of his first great scriptural work, the compilation of the *Hexapla*. He was now freed from the teaching routine in which Bishop Demetrius was interested. He made his friend Heraclas responsible for preliminary studies in the catechetical school, while he taught the more experienced pupils.[48]

Origen believed that the Jews must be met on their own ground, that is, Scripture. Some knowledge of Hebrew and an accurate text of it were necessities. The *Hexapla*, on which he started c. 212 and worked on for the next forty years, was a vast synopsis of the various extant editions of the Old Testament. It was arranged in six columns; hence, its title. In the first was the Hebrew text; next was a transliteration of the Hebrew into Greek characters. Why is uncertain. It may be, as Chadwick has suggested, "that some churches had preserved the old synagogue practice of having the Old Testament read in Hebrew even if its hearers did not understand it,"[49] another indication of how close church and synagogue still stood in the 240s. In the third column was the Septuagint, and the remaining three contained different versions by the learned Jewish proselyte Aquila, Symmachus, an Ebionite, and Theodotion, another Jewish-Christian. For the Psalms, Origen added two extra columns, one containing the precious find he had made at Jericho—a scroll of the text hidden in a pot.[50] The work of compilation was stupendous. His friend and patron, Ambrose, testified to the pressure put on his staff and himself. "The work of correction," he recorded, "leaves us no time for supper, for exercise or for rest. Even at these times we are compelled to study and to emend manuscripts."[51] The labors of the staff began at dawn! It was like work on the *Dead Sea Scrolls* themselves when they were first discovered.

This was not simply scholarship for its own sake. As in almost everything else Origen did, there was an argumentative edge. Origen believed that the Jews had altered their texts of Scripture when it suited them and these changes could now be brought to notice and checked.[52] More innocently, different churches found themselves with different texts of Scripture. Now, there was to be one authoritative text, with symbols showing where one version differed from another. Christians henceforth had a sound basis from which to preach the faith and to defend it.

Already by about 214, Origen was becoming known outside Alexandria. Around that year the Roman governor of Arabia sent an officer to Alexandria with letters addressed to both Bishop Demetrius and the prefect of Egypt, asking the latter to send Origen to him for an interview. The reason is not stated by Eusebius, but it is interesting that the governor recognized especially Demetrius's position and his authority over the movements of his subordinate, Origen.[53] It is another indication of the quasi toleration the Christians enjoyed under the Severans and the first direct friendly contacts between a Christian representative and the authorities since Paul.

In the following year, however, his life was in danger. Roman policy in Egypt was "racist," that is, rigorous efforts were made to keep the various ethnic groups in the country, and particularly in Alexandria, apart. No Greek might knowingly marry an Egyptian woman. Christianity broke through these barriers (as Leonides may have found) and provided a further reason for its unpopularity.[54] In 215 the emperor Caracalla, angry with the Alexandrians for satirizing him for his murder of his brother Geta in 212, strictly enforced the rules. There were massacres in Alexandria. All Egyptians were ordered out of the city. Origen was included, but by now he had powerful friends in Palestine—the bishops of Caesarea and Jerusalem—and, though a layman, was invited to preach before them. Demetrius was irked, complaining that such a thing was unheard of, and demanded Origen's return to Alexandria.[55]

This rift was healed. Origen returned to Alexandria about 219 and worked there for the next ten years. He was now at the height of his powers, and the period saw him complete *On First Principles* and begin his *Commentary on John*. As in the *Hexapla* the aim was debate, this time with the Gnostics. Origen's object was to "bring clarity among those who profess to believe in Christ but differ from each other not in small and trifling subjects, but also on matters of the highest importance, for instance, about God, or the Lord Jesus Christ, or the Holy Spirit; and not only regarding these, but also regarding others which are created existences, that is powers and holy virtues."[56] He constantly attacked heretics for failing to understand the message of Scripture.[57] It was a superhuman task, something attempted only by Augustine in *De Trinitate (On the Trinity)* and by Thomas Aquinas in *Summa Theologica*. Moreover Origen noted at the outset that he would not diverge from the Alexandrian Rule of Faith, only that he would set down "a connected series of truths agreeably to reason" to elucidate the statements contained in it.[58] A few gaps needed to be filled!

The result showed, once again, the immense difficulty of fitting a revealed religion based on Scripture into a philosophic framework based on Plato. Origen's system was in some ways as mythological as those of the Gnostics, though seeking (like Clement) to avoid their dualism, determinism, and, above all, their antinomianism. His *Principles* begins with God, absolute and immutable substance, the original source of life, and "beginning of all things."[59] In place of the passive qualities of beauty and goodness of the Platonic or Hermetic monad, Origen, on the basis of Prov. 8:22–25 (LXX) and Col. 1:15 asserted that God could never be without the active qualities of Wisdom, Word, and Power.[60] Wisdom was "a kind of breath and power of God," coeternal with him, intelligible to humanity as ever-begotten Son, eternal image of the Father. Again relying on Scripture, Origen defines the Son as reflecting "the glory of God and [bearing] the very stamp of his nature" (Heb. 1:3). His generation then, was "as eternal and everlasting as the brilliance produced by the sun."[61] He belonged to the very nature of

God and revealed himself to humankind as such. He was joined to God through the perfection of love (*Principles* II.6.4). And in his *Homily on Ezekiel*, Origen attributed the "passion of Love" to the Father himself.[62] The Son, therefore, was "a second God," mediator between God and the divine powers, images, and aspects of God. He was less than God himself, therefore, but superior to all created beings, as he alone knew God and knew his will.[63] The Holy Spirit, the first Being created by the Word, was followed by the creation of the world of spirits. "Before all the ages, minds were all pure, both demons and souls and angels, offering service to God and keeping his commandments."[64] The original Golden Age must have appeared very similar to Valentinus as to Origen. But for Origen there was nothing predetermined about creation nor, indeed, did he have any place for Adam and Eve. In his *Commentary on Genesis*, begun about this time (c. 227), the first chapter is allegorized away.[65] Origen insisted that the Fall was not due to Adam's guilt but through a misuse of free will by the powers themselves. Their love towards God had cooled. They had become bored and rebellious, and as a result they were driven from the divine presence—falling in concentric circles, some a greater distance, some less, according to their fault. Hence the world came into being, God "binding souls to bodies as a punishment."[66]

Creation, however, was always sustained by God who destined it for ultimate restoration. Humankind was in this world to be educated in the love of God. None of God's creatures therefore could be so depraved as to be incapable of any goodness. The sending of the Word, Christ, united to the one soul that had remained pure and undefiled in the rebellion of the angels was the decisive step in the process of restoration. Even so, all creation moved forward to that goal; "for there was no part of creation entirely out of harmony with that final unity and concord."[67] Only the good element in nature truly existed. Evil, like death, was not a positive force, and so even the blackest devils and Satan himself could be restored.[68] The fires of Hell, said Origen elsewhere, were purging and refining fires.[69] "Everlasting fire" was not to be taken literally. Humanity was educated and prepared for salvation and this was the destiny of all. Some souls would "endure severe punishment" on the way.[70] There was no final damnation, only an endless vista of worlds and existences. All penalties were ultimately remedial and all things would one day be restored to their original harmony.

Origen had indeed evolved a system with which to refute the Gnostics—at considerable cost. Basically it reflected the outlook of contemporary Platonists.[71] Plotinus's concept of the Divine existing in three separate hypostases or entities was paralleled by Origen's concept of the Trinity as three distinct and graded beings. Moreover, the cyclical sense of time accepted by both led to a predetermined end, for Origen (as for Plotinus) an optimistic one; instinctively Christians recoiled at the very idea of Satan being saved. And if divine harmony was destined to be restored, what purpose had the incarnation? What role was there for the Spirit? Origen was never quite clear about its role in the heavenly or the secular order. The Spirit could hardly display the same active power in human events as the Western Christians believed, entering into prison with confessors, the agent of the church's daily inspiration. But was the Spirit's action confined to the saints alone?[72] Yet if Platonism and biblical Christianity were to merge to form the basis for universal religion, how else were the foundations to be laid? If Origen's attempt was adjudged a failure, who could succeed?

Origen did not see the contradictions in his system. He lived in the Bible, but the Bible had to be understood in a way that would lead the Christians to God, that is, spiritually. He would have agreed with Marcionite and Gnostic critics that, taken literally, the Bible contained impossibilities and absurdities. "Who is so silly," he asked, "as to believe that God after the manner of a farmer" planted a paradise eastwards of Eden and set in it a visible and palpable tree of life so that anyone who tasted it with his bodily teeth would gain life.[73] Even the Gospels were full of passages of this kind. Christ could not possibly see "all the kingdoms and the glory of them" at one and the same time.[74] Injunctions such as "salute no one on the road" (Luke 10:4) were absurd,[75] or to have neither two coats nor two pairs of shoes was ridiculous when applied to people living in cold climates.[76] No one had seen griffins or stag-goats even if they were positively mentioned in Scripture among clean and unclean beasts.[77] Christians, too, would have to admit the superiority of Greek and Roman laws over the laws of the Old Testament if this was to be accepted as it stood.

The answer, however, was not the destructive criticism of the Marcionites nor the even more fanciful allegorizations of some of the Gnostics. Using, as he customarily did, the Platonic analogy that individuals consisted of body, soul (*psyche*), and spirit, he affirmed that Scripture also had to be understood in three senses, the literal, moral (or "psychic"), and the spiritual. The Christian must aim at penetrating to the heart of the meaning of each passage by intense thought and contemplation (*theoria*) and so understand the mysteries implicit in any Word of God.[78] In fact, Origen used much the same method of allegorical interpretation as that employed by his pagan contemporaries in the study of Homer. He would then search for a key word or idea in the passage under review, which could be understood more profoundly by linking it with passages taken from other parts of Scripture. The Old Testament always provided "an example and shadow of heavenly things."[79] The expositor had to show how that shadow helped to reveal spiritual truth. One studied "the profundities of meaning contained in the words to become a participator of all the doctrines of God's counsel."[80] Although Origen often had useful things to say about the texts he was studying (for example, about the authorship of Hebrews),[81] nevertheless he was not primarily interested in historical data. All words, including names such as Moab, Hebron, or Jerusalem, had spiritual meanings as part of revelation. They ceased to be places, but under Origen's imaginative erudition became mirrors of heavenly truth. Every word of Scripture meant something, he argued; otherwise it would not be there. Similarly, what was not in Scripture was not the Word of God. Fanciful though most of his exegesis seems today and fraudulent to some of his pagan contemporaries,[82] he committed his followers to a purely scriptural view of reality, however Scripture might be understood. This was to be tested a century later in the Arian controversy.

Significantly, Origen's first major commentary was on John, to him as to Clement "the spiritual Gospel." Until Origen started writing in c. 228, Heracleon's commentary, compiled a half century before, held the field. Origen, as we have noted,[83] was prepared to accept something of Heracleon's method while avoiding his conclusions. Thus, his interpretation of John 4:1–42, the woman at the well of Samaria, agrees with Heracleon's that the woman's husband represented unregenerate human nature, but the woman's former worship was not regarded as false, but as a type giving way to the spiritual reality of her new life.[84] His long debate with Heracleon, with its often fine points of difference, demonstrated how substantial was the element of continuity between the Valentinian Gnostics and the Christian Platonists of Alexandria. Concerning the nature of Christ, Origen met Heracleon more than halfway and moved into the shifting sands of christological speculation. "By nature Christ is divine [*theoteta*], but we being able only to grasp truths concerning him in material terms, regard him as man, although to know Christ crucified thus is the knowledge of babes."[85] Belief in Christ as Redeemer also belonged to the lower life. "Blessed is he who wants the Saviour no longer as Physician, Shepherd or Redemption."[86] To be fair to Origen, his "high" Christology followed from his meditation on the meaning of the Eucharist. To believe that Christ was corporeally present in the Eucharist was also the work of the inferior intellect, which failed to move beyond the letter of Scripture. Christ was present spiritually at the solemn moment, just as he must be conceived only in spiritual and divine terms.[87] In arguing thus, Origen laid the foundation of Greek liturgical belief and anticipated Cyril two centuries later.[88]

By the time he had finished the fifth book of his commentary in 229, tension was mounting once more with Demetrius. Why is not known, but the gap between Origen's teaching and the beliefs of the simpler members of the community was becoming obvious, while the question of the bishop's control of the catechetical school may also have been a contributing factor. Origen noted that he was glad of a respite from the threatening storm by an opportunity to leave Egypt.[89]

As we have seen, there arose a dispute among the churches of Achaia over Gnosticism. Origen was invited to debate with Candidus, the Gnostic leader, and went without Demetrius's permission. To make matters worse, Candidus claimed that Origen had said that the devil could be saved.[90] There was consternation at Alexandria. Moreover, traveling overland, Origen had allowed himself to be consecrated presbyter by his friends the bishops of Caesarea and Jerusalem. Demetrius was furious. "The enemy," said Origen, "redoubled his violence through his new writings truly alien to the gospel and raised against us all the blasts of iniquity in Egypt."[91] Successive synods at Alexandria censured Origen, and proclaimed a sentence of degradation against him. In this instance, the presbyters of Alexandria were outvoted by Demetrius's newly created suffragan bishops. Synods at Rome and elsewhere supported Demetrius, but not in Phoenicia, Palestine, Arabia, and Achaia where Origen had friends.[92] He settled in Caesarea in 231, temporarily bereft of his shorthand writers, and when Demetrius at last died in 232 after forty-three years as bishop, his successor was Heraclas. Even so, Origen was not recalled, nor by another pupil, Dionysius, who became bishop on Heraclas's death in 247. Perhaps there were more than personalities at issue.

For more than twenty years Origen was in exile at Caesarea. He was protected there by the bishops "from the fiery darts of the enemy." Most of his theological ideas had already been set out in his *Principles*. From this point on he concentrated on the Bible, on his exhaustive commentaries and sermons, and his teaching and mission. Whatever Alexandria may have thought, Origen was a famous man outside Egypt. Probably in 232 he was summoned to meet the empress-mother at Antioch and traveled with a military escort.[93] The advent of Maximin in 235 and the threat of persecution brought forth the ringing *Exhortation to Martyrdom* to Ambrosius, who had been imprisoned, to take courage and imitate the Maccabees and other Jewish and Christian heroes. The danger passed, and from Gregory the Wonderworker we learn of the scholar and teacher of the years 237–42: Origen demonstrated that only through Christianity could the unanswered riddles of philosophy be solved, and that, in arriving at this truth, conduct was more important than precept.[94] He now became a sort of roving ambassador for Christianity. In the 240s he seemed to have been engaged in particular with sorting out problems in the province of Arabia. Eusebius records two separate visits to the province in this period.[95] Gnosticism was fading into memory. The issue was now Monarchianism which was beginning to impinge on Origen's thinking c. 230.[96] Beryllus, bishop of the capital city Bostra, was accused of holding Monarchian views, and the *Dialogue with Heracleides* was concerned largely with the same group of controversies.[97] Contacts with the great and influential continued to come Origen's way. He corresponded with Otacilia Severa, the wife of Philip the Arabian, and tried to clear charges of unorthodoxy against him with Pope Fabian and "a great many other rulers."[98] He crowned his career in 247–48 with the two great works, *Against Celsus* and the *Commentary on Matthew*. He was imprisoned and tortured in the Decian persecution, but his iron constitution survived the ordeal and he died four years later in 253 at Tyre at the age of sixty-nine.

In these years of exile, study, and writing, his ideas matured. An example of Origen at work in this later period is his dialogue with Heracleides, held probably at a synod in Arabia ''of no small dimensions.'' (The chance find, in the summer of 1941 in the caves of Tura south of Cairo, of a small library of the works of Origen and Didymus the Blind produced an unscripted and apparently unrevised record of his examination of the views of Bishop Heracleides).[99] As in his *Principles*, Origen first took his stand on the Rule of Faith and then proceeded to draw some surprising conclusions from it. The quick-fire question and answer made Heracleides appear like an unsatisfactory student:

Origen: I charge you, father Heracleides: God is the almighty, the uncreated, the supreme God who made all things. Do you hold this doctrine?
Heracleides: I do. That is what I also believe.
Origen: Christ Jesus who was in the form of God, being other than the God in whose form he existed, was he God before he came into the body or not?
Heracleides: He was God before.
Origen: Was he God before he came into the body or not?
Heracleides: Yes, he was.
Origen: Was he God distinct from this God in whose form he existed?
Heracleides: Obviously he was distinct from another being and, since he was in the form of him who created all things, he was distinct from him.
Origen: Is it true then that there was a God, the Son of God, the only begotten of God, the firstborn of all creation, and that we need have no fear of saying that in one sense there are two Gods, while in another there is one God?
Heracleides: What you say is evident. But we affirm that God is the almighty, God without beginning, without end, containing all things and not contained by anything; and that his Word is the Son of the living God, God and man, through whom all things were made, God according to the spirit, man inasmuch as he was born of Mary.
Origen: You do not appear to have answered my question. Explain what you mean. For perhaps I failed to follow you. Is the Father God?
Heracleides: Assuredly.
Origen: Is the Son distinct from the Father?
Heracleides: Of course. How can he be Son if he is also Father?
Origen: While being distinct from the Father is the Son himself also God?
Heracleides: He himself is also God.
Origen: And do two Gods become a unity?
Heracleides: Yes.
Origen: Do we confess two Gods?
Heracleides: Yes. The power is one.[100]

There was evidently a gasp from the assembled bishops. Was Origen preaching polytheism? Quickly he explained in detail what he meant. Characteristically, he started from the fact of duality (God and creation). The Scriptures taught how several things were two and also were one. Man and woman were two but were also "one flesh." In prayer a righteous person was united with Christ in spirit; but Christ was united with the Father, not in flesh nor spirit, "but more honourable than these, God." "That is why we understand in this sense 'I and the Father are one.' . . . In this way we avoid falling into the opinion of those who are separated from the Church and turned into the illusory notion of monarchy, who abolish the Son as distinct from the Father, and virtually abolish the Father also. Nor do we fall into the other blasphemous doctrine that denies the deity of Christ."[101] This latter form of Monarchianism, of which the Antiochenes were to be accused, was infinitely more obnoxious to him.

It was familiar ground by now. In this one paragraph, however, Origen summed up the theological problem that had been developing over the previous twenty years. The Word-Flesh (Logos-Sarx) theology triumphant over the Gnostics was being confronted by a more formidable alternative. The ideas of Sabellius the Libyan were to survive and taunt Origen's disciples for more than a century. Despite condemnations, Monarchianism in both its forms corresponded to the instinct of many Eastern Christians, and Origen's own ideas were not without their weaknesses. The Monarchians started from Jewish and Christian monotheism, Origen from the Platonic division between God and creation. The Word or Son was the logical link between the two. There was never when he was not. Only the fact of "eternal generation" distinguished him from the Father, who alone was unbegotten and the source of his divinity.[102] As Origen's Eusebian successors at the Council of Antioch in 341 found, all the scriptural definitions of Christ involved the Son's subordination to the Father. The absolutes of Goodness, Power, and Love belonged to God alone.[103]

In the long, involved explanation that Origen found himself giving the assembled bishops, one may sense the beginning of a new phase of theological controversy in the Greek-speaking church, and Origen was well aware that the last word had not been spoken.

Yet Christianity's debt to Origen is immense. No Christian writer had attempted so thorough and complete a statement of this religion. No one before him had defended it so thoroughly against its opponents, and with such success. The demolition of Gnostics and Marcionites had resulted in the formulation of an optimistic faith in which humankind might mount step by step towards knowledge of God through Christ. "Let us take up eternal life," Origen exclaimed at the end of *Heracleides*; "Let us take up that which depends on our decision. God does not give it to us. He sets it before us. 'Behold, I have set life before thy face.' "[104] That life was Christ who by uniting human and divine enabled humanity to rise towards ultimate glorification. It was a religion without material heaven or hell, and in which education replaced vindictive punishment. It was also a universal religion whose adherents could truly be called "the race of Christians," without distinction of nation or class. With Origen, Alexandria assumed the intellectual leadership of the Christian world just as it had previously ruled the minds of Jews and Greeks.

Dionysius of Alexandria and His Opponents

Dionysius of Alexandria (247–64) continued Origen's work by combining it, however, with the role of statesman in mediating between the antagonists in the civil war of 261–62, and bringing Egypt and Cyrenaica under the effective control of Alexandria. The intellectual problems left over from Origen's day reemerged during his episcopate. First, there was the problem of millenarianism. He opposed this as much as Clement and Origen had before him. Dionysius rebuked Bishop Nepos of Arsinoë sternly for millenarianist teaching,[105] and he attempted the most thorough and perceptive piece of biblical criticism that has survived from the early church, to demonstrate that the book of Revelation could not have been written by the author of the Fourth Gospel.[106] While careful not to reject Revelation out of hand or attribute it to Cerinthus, he affirmed that it could not be accepted in its literal sense, and that differences of style and vocabulary ruled out a common authorship. The Gospel and epistles of John were written in faultless Greek, "and were literary works constructed with great skill and sound reasoning." Revelation contained "inaccurate Greek usages" and "downright solecisms."[107] Whether or not Dionysius was right in equating the "two tombs at Ephesus" with two leading Christians called John, this work demonstrated yet again the strength of the Christian intellectual leadership after the middle of the third century.

The second problem was Monarchianism yet again, this time among the Christians of Cyrenaica. The dispute rumbled on from c. 255 until interrupted by the Valerianic persecution. Cyrenaican bishops were teaching the identity of Father and Son and even inventing a technical theological term (huio-pator = Son-Father) to make their point, but Dionysius needed no such precision of heresy.[108] He was outraged, refused to hear the Cyrenaican explanations, and wrote to Pope Sixtus II in 257 warning him of their error. Dionysius, however, pushed his reasoning too far. Describing the relationship of Father and Son in the Philonic terms concerning the Word of boat-builder to boat and affirming that the Son was "a creature,"[109] Dionysius moved Origen's Trinitarian teaching further along the road towards Arianism. Indeed, with Dionysius's letter in mind, Arius becomes explicable.

The Cyrenaicans took their cause to Sixtus's successor Dionysius (260–69). At Rome they could expect a fair reception in view of the Monarchian tradition of its bishops in the early part of the century. The resulting correspondence (preserved by Athanasius) between Dionysius of Rome and Dionysius of Alexandria always had the makings of a comedy of errors.

Neither was fluent in the other's language (though it is difficult to think of Dionysius of Rome knowing no Greek). The meaning of the technical terms for "substance" (*ousia* and *substantia*) became obscured. Dionysius of Rome thought his colleague believed the Trinity consisted in three different substances while Dionysius of Alexandria regarded his namesake as an ally of the Cyrenaican Modalist Monarchians. The Roman bishop's letter showed the razor edge on which orthodoxy was now resting.[110] A new word had made its appearance in the theological vocabulary of the East. The resourceful Cyrenaicans had employed "of the same substance" (*homoousios*) to define the relationship between Father and Son.[111] Dionysius of Alexandria had rejected this as nonscriptural, but his colleague at Rome had not followed suit. Nor would the bishops at Nicaea sixty years later.

The third problem was even more serious. Some of the questions raised with Origen by the Arabian Christians suggest more than clashes between intellectuals drawing different conclusions from the same synthesis of Christianity and philosophy. Jean Daniélou has pointed to the possibility of a Semitic background to the questions—whether, for instance, the soul survived the death of the body, and the debate on the immortality of the soul and whether the soul had blood.[112] Origen's interlocutors in his dialogue with Heracleides were perhaps basing themselves on the literal reading of the Old Testament while Origen was answering them from the basis of philosophy.

Paul of Samosata

The difference between the two approaches to Christianity became clear in the next two decades. The history of the church at Antioch is only less obscure than that of Ephesus among the major sees of third-century Christendom. It is evident, however, that the contrasting outlooks between its leaders and those of Alexandria that we noted at the end of the second century persisted. Eusebius is reticent about developments at Antioch. He mentions Serapion's suppression of the reading of apocryphal material at the church of Issus (*HE* VI.12), the names of his successors, the martyrdom of Babylas in 250, and the correspondence between Fabius of Antioch and Dionysius of Alexandria mainly over the recognition of Novatian, but, except that the church at Antioch must have been rigorist-inclined, gives no hint of its theological leanings. There are, however, two other facts we know about Antioch. First, it was divided into Greek- and Syriac-speaking sections. When Antioch fell to the Persians in 261, its inhabitants along with its bishop Demetrian were transported to southern Persia, and in Yaranšahr, which became an episcopal city, the congregation divided themselves into Greek- and Syrian-speaking groups.[113] Second, Jewish influence remained strong and, so far as one can see, relations between the two monotheistic communities were reasonably harmonious. A century later, John Chrysostom complained that Christians were saying there was "only a small difference between us and the Jews."[114] In the third century, the church in Antioch still celebrated Easter on the Sunday following the Jewish Passover whose date was accepted from the Jews.[115]

Down to the removal of Demetrian, relations with Alexandria were friendly enough. A change took place, however, with the election of the new bishop, Paul of Samosata. Paul has always had a bad press. The description which Eusebius, at his least scrupulous, gave of his character—loud-mouthed, dishonest, brash, and adulterous—has stuck.[116] The fact that he also served as a senior financial officer of Queen Zenobia of Palmyra, who recaptured Antioch from the Persians, made the pro-Roman bishops of Alexandria and Asia Minor ready to condemn him as the worst of heretics. In fact, despite the difficulties of the evidence, Paul's religion was obviously based on a literal understanding of the New Testament and acceptance of its historical account of Jesus' life and ministry. He asserted that the Virgin Mary gave birth to a man and that the Spirit who anointed him was the same Spirit that had inspired the prophets, but in Jesus' case that inspiration was complete. At his baptism the Spirit took up his abode in him as in the Temple (cf. John 2:21). To Paul Jesus was a complete human being to whom the Word or Spirit had joined himself. As he said in a surviving statement that appears genuine:

A human being is anointed: the Word is not anointed. The Nazarene our Lord is anointed. For the Word is greater than the anointed one [that is, Christ], since the anointed one became great through Wisdom. For the Word is from above, Jesus Christ is from hence. Mary did not give birth to the Word; she was not before the ages. And Mary is not older than the Word, but she gave birth to a man like us though better in every way since he was of the Holy Ghost.[117]

This is an interesting statement. The association of Word and Wisdom looks back to Theophilus of Antioch and the late Jewish apologetic that he represented.[118] Second, Word and Wisdom are represented not as "personalities" or "subsistences" but as activities, Wisdom as thought, Word as speech. The word spoken (for example, by God at creation) was essentially part of God. Hence, Paul's use of the term *Homoousios* to describe the relationship between God and the Word was proper,[119] though it was not at all what the Cyrenaican Monarchians had meant by the term. Third, the Spirit occupied a central role in Paul's theology as the source of grace and of Christ's redeeming power, and here Antioch and the West were saying the same things.[120]

Finally, Paul's ideas were those of a numerous section of Christian leaders in Syria and Arabia. Beryllus of Bostra, for instance, was accused of teaching that "the Lord did not pre-exist in an individual existence of his own before the incarnation, nor did he have a divinity of his own but only his Father's indwelling in him."[121] This is what Paul was saying. Also, in the *Acts of Archelaus* (probably early fourth century), which record a debate between the bishop of Carrhae(?) and Mani c. 270, the former asserted, as did Paul, that Mary bore a man who was not made perfect until the dove descended on him at baptism. The bishop further stated that the Christian was also saved through redemption from sin at baptism and by following a Christ-like life thereafter.[122] Antiochene theology, if strongly influenced by Judaism as its detractors declared, was also being forged in conflict with Manichean missionaries who preached the Docetic nature of Christ as well as a radically dualist view of the universe and of man.

Whether the Logos-Sarx Christology of Alexandria would have clashed with the Logos-Anthropos Christology of Antioch had Paul been an exemplary bishop in other ways cannot be said. The two interpretations of Christ were held by Christians over wide areas in the East, yet both could not be orthodox. If, for Paul, Christ was "from below" and "the Nazarene," for Origen and Dionysius he was the Word-incarnate, preexistent from before all ages. In commenting on the key text Luke 2:52, Origen explained that the body was assumed by the Word for the purpose of humanity's instruction and salvation. It was an "envelope" that expanded as Jesus "grew in stature."[123] The Word, he replied to Celsus, "suffers nothing of the experience of the body or the soul."[124] The reference to the soul implied that the human soul in Christ, like the body, could be regarded as an adjunct, necessary because Christ's humanity would not be complete without it, but wholly passive.[125]

The clash broke out in 264, and Dionysius wrote to the community at Antioch condemning Paul after having put a series of searching questions to him. There must have been a synod at the same time for Eusebius mentioned the presence of Firmilian of Cappadocia at Antioch on two occasions, 264 and 265(?). Paul's "new-fangled" ideas might be condemned, but he stuck to them. There were, however, enemies in his own camp. Antioch had its schools of Greek philosophy, and Malchion, the leader of the school of rhetoric, was also a presbyter. In 268 he played a leading part in securing Paul's downfall. In that year there was a third synod, this time composed of numerous bishops from Asia Minor and Syria with priests and deacons, and Paul was interrogated by Malchion. Paul rejected any idea of essential unity between Christ and the Word. Substance (*ousia*) and participation were not alike. Godhead and humanity were utterly different in constitution. Christ was not preexistent.[126] The difference was now clear-cut. For the Alexandrians, the Word was present in Christ "substantially," and not "from without," and occupied, as Malchion said, the same place as the inner human being. Logically, therefore, Christ was not true man, but representative of humanity.

The Alexandrians, however, prevailed. The council held in 265(?) pronounced that whoever did not accept the preexistence of Christ was "alien to the catholic church."[127] Symbolic of the ecclesiastical structures beginning to take shape, that of 268 addressed its synodal letter to "all our fellow-ministers throughout the world, bishops and presbyters and deacons, and to the whole Catholic Church under heaven" starting with Dionysius of Rome and Maximus of Alexandria.[128]

Already, too, if one may accept as genuine the extracts of the synodical letter preserved by Leontius of Byzantium in the sixth century, some of the charges raised by the Alexandrians against the Antiochenes in the fifth century were foreshadowed. Paul was preaching "two Sons" (that is, Jesus of Nazareth, and the Divine Wisdom who inhabited him). Participation in the Godhead through "will" and "conjunction" was not true union.[129] Above all, Antioch was revealed to be profoundly divided against itself, a situation which Cyril of Alexandria would exploit unmercifully.

It was easier to condemn Paul than to remove him. So long as Zenobia held Antioch, he was safe and retained the "bishop's house." In 272 Aurelian retook the city and captured Palmyra, restoring the eastern frontier of the empire. The problem of the rival Christian congregations in Antioch was one of the administrative problems that came his way in the aftermath of victory. Why should the Christians approach him? The simplest explanation is that Paul's opponents regarded him as excommunicate and outside the church, and the matter in dispute was how to resume holding property that legally belonged to them. The church in Antioch was exercising openly the rights and responsibilities of a property-holding corporation, and this was accepted by the authorities. Aurelian's decision was interesting. He told the petitioners that the building would be "assigned to those with whom the bishops of the doctrine in Italy and Rome should communicate in writing."[130] Eusebius comments that this was "an extremely just decision." Italy and Rome were not directly involved and still represented the heart of the empire. In no sense was this a recognition by the emperor that "legitimate ecclesiastical authority was communion with the Roman Church."[131] The aim had been impartiality, just as Constantine sixty years later was to delegate his powers as chief magistrate of the Roman people to bishops in the West who did not appear to be directly concerned with the quarrel between Caecilian and Donatus at Carthage.[132] The episode of Paul of Samosata had shown how near the surface were the tensions between the major sees now that the church was firmly established in the world. In this situation Christians were quite prepared to approach the emperor for justice. Any other community within the empire could do the same.

BIBLIOGRAPHY

NOTE

The Christian Platonists of Alexandria have been the subject of a number of outstanding works. Charles Bigg's Bampton Lectures of that title, though preached in 1886, are still a key work on both Clement and Origen (2d ed., ed. F. E. Brightman

[New York: Oxford University Press, 1913]). For Clement, too, Henry Chadwick's *Early Christian Thought and the Classical Tradition: Studies in Justin, Clement, and Origen* (New York and London: Oxford University Press, 1966) is a fine piece of writing, drawing attention to both Clement's debt to Philo and his seminal qualities in Alexandrian theology. The same author's edition of Origen's *Contra Celsum*, and his translation of some of Clement and Origen's work in *Alexandrian Christianity*, ed. and Eng. trans. Oulton and Chadwick, LCC II, add up to an outstanding contribution to the study of the Alexandrian theology.

For Origen himself, J. Daniélou's *Origen*, Eng. trans. W. Mitchell (New York and London: Sheed & Ward, 1955), remains without rival, though E. de Faye's work, *Origène, sa vie, son oeuvre, sa pensée*, 3 vols. (Paris, 1923–28), and Hans von Campenhausen's essay in *The Fathers of the Greek Church*, Eng. trans. L. A. Garrard (London: A. & C. Black, 1963), are also valuable studies.

As noted (chap. 9 Bibliography, p. 369), Dionysius's works have been collected and translated into English by C. L. Feltoe, ed., *Letters and Treatises*, Translations of Christian Literature, series 1: Greek Texts (New York: Macmillan Co., 1918). For Paul of Samosata, see H. de Riedmatten, *Les Actes du procès de Paul de Samosate: Etude sur la christologie du III⁰ au IV⁰ siècle* (Fribourg: Editions St. Paul, 1952); and the discussions in J. N. D. Kelly, *Early Christian Doctrines*, rev. ed. (New York: Harper & Row, 1978; London: A. & C. Black, 1977), pp. 158–60; H. J. Lawlor, "The Sayings of Paul of Samosata," *JTS* 19 (1918): 20–45, and G. L. Prestige, *God in Patristic Thought*, 2d ed. (London: SPCK, 1952), pp. 197–211, are useful.

SOURCES

Clement. *Opera*. See above, chap. 8.

———. *Stromata (Miscellanies)*. Eng. trans. rev. J. B. Mayor. In *Alexandrian Christianity*, ed. Oulton and Chadwick, pp. 93–165.

Dionysius of Alexandria. See above, chap. 9.

Gregory the Wonderworker. *Panegyric to Origen*. Edited by H. Crouzel. SC 148. 1969.

Origen, *De principiis*, ed. P. Koetschau, GCS 22, Origen, Leipzig: Hinrichs, 1913; *Origen on First Principles: Being Koetschau's Text Translated Into English*, ed. and Eng. trans. G. W. Butterworth, New York: Macmillan Co.; London: SPCK, 1936; and also ANCL.

———. *Commentary on St. John's Gospel*. Edited by E. Preuschen. GCS 10, Origen. Leipzig: Hinrichs, 1903.

———. *Commentary on Genesis*. Edited by W. A. Baehrens. GCS 29, Origen. Leipzig: Hinrichs, 1920.

———. *Homily on Jeremiah*. Edited by E. Klostermann. GCS 6, Origen. Leipzig: Hinrichs, 1901.

———. *Homily on Ezekiel*. Edited by W. A. Baehrens. GCS 33, Origen. Leipzig: Hinrichs, 1925.

———. *Homily on Luke*. Edited by M. Rauer. GCS 49, Origen. Leipzig: Hinrichs, 1959.

———, *Dialogue with Heracleides*, J. Scherer, ed., *Entretien d'Origène avec Héraclide et les evêques ses collègues sur le Père, le Fils, et l'Âme*, Cairo: Publications de la Société Fouad I de Papyrologie, 1949; Eng. trans. Chadwick, *Alexandrian Christianity*, ed. Oulton and Chadwick, pp. 430–55.

———, *Letter to Africanus*, PG.11, pp. 47–86; ANCL trans., pp. 371–87, Origen, vol. 1.

Early Christian Egyptian papyri are listed and commented upon by C. H. Roberts, *Manuscript, Society and Belief in Early Christian Egypt*, New York and London: Oxford University Press, 1979, pp. 13–14.

SECONDARY WORKS

Bardy, G. "Paul de Samosata." In *DTC*, vol. 12, part 1, pp. 46–51.

Bethune-Baker, J. F. *An Introduction to the Early History of Christian Doctrine to the Time of the Council of Chalcedon*. 8th ed. New York: British Book Centre, 1950. Chap. 8 on Dionysius of Rome and Dionysius of Alexandria.

Capelle, B. "L'Entretien d'Origène avec Héraclide." *JEH* 2 (1951): 143–57.

Dihle, A. "Indische Philosophen bei Clemens Alexandrinus." *Mullus: Festschrift Theodor Klauser*, pp. 60–70. Münster: Aschendorff, 1964.

Floyd, W. E. G. *Clement of Alexandria's Treatment of the Problem of Evil*. New York and London: Oxford University Press, 1971.

Frend, W. H. C. "Some Cultural Links Between India and the West." *Theoria to Theory* 2 (1968): 306–11.

Grant, R. M. *The Earliest Lives of Jesus*. New York: Harper & Row; London: SPCK, 1961.

Grillmeier, A. "Christus licet vobis invitis deus: Ein Beitrag zur Diskussion über die Hellenesierung des christuskerygmas." In *Kerygma und Logos*, Festschrift für Carl Andresen, ed. A. M. Ritter, pp. 226–57. Göttingen: Vandenhoeck & Ruprecht, 1979.

Jaeger, Werner W. *Early Christianity and Greek Paideia*. Cambridge, Mass.: Harvard University Press, Belknap Press, 1961; London: Oxford University Press, 1962.

Kettler, F. H. "Origenes, Ammonius Sakkas und Porphyrius." In *Kerygma und Logos*, ed. Ritter, pp. 322–28.

Lebreton, J. "Le désaccord de la foi populaire et de la théologie savante dans l'Eglise chrétienne du IIIe siècle." *RHE* 19 (1923): 481–506, and *RHE* 20 (1924): 5–37.

Lilla, S. R. C. *Clement of Alexandria: A Study in Christian Platonism and Gnosticism*. New York and London: Oxford University Press, 1971.

Meijering, E. P. "Wie platonisierten Christen? Zur Grenzziehung zwischen Platonismus, kirchlichem Credo und patristischer Theologie." *VC* 28 (1974): 15–28.

Osborn, E. F. *The Philosophy of Clement of Alexandria*. New York and Cambridge: Cambridge University Press, 1957.

Völker, A. *Der wahre Gnostiker nach Clemens Alexandrinus*. TU 57.2. Berlin: Akademie Verlag, 1952.

Wiles, M. F. *The Christian Fathers*. London: Hodder & Stoughton, 1966, esp. chap. 2, "The Divine Christ."

———. "Eternal Generation." *JTS* n.s. 12 (October 1961): 284–91.

———. *The Spiritual Gospel: The Interpretation of the Fourth Gospel in the Early Church*. New York and Cambridge: Cambridge University Press, 1960.

NOTES

1. Thus P. R. L. Brown, "Approaches to the Religious Crisis of the Third Century A.D.," *EHR* 83 (1968): 542–58, esp. p. 553; reprinted in *Religion and Society in the Age of Saint Augustine*, pp. 74–93 (New York: Harper & Row, 1972), p. 89.
2. *Celsus* II.31. Also, Jesus not free from blame, ibid., II.42, and VI.75 (nothing divine in Jesus' life).
3. Chadwick, ed., *Contra Celsum*, p. 93 n. 3.
4. See J. Zizioulas, "Verité et communion dans la perpective de la pensée patristique grecque," *Irenikon* (1977): 451–510, esp. pp. 456–67.
5. For the figure, see Altaner, *Patrology*, p. 191.
6. Thus Chadwick, *Early Christian Thought*, chap. 2.
7. *Protrepticus* (*Exhortation to the Greeks*) IV.41 and X.78 (relating to Phidias's Zeus), and IV.47 concerning the statue of Aphrodite at Cnidus.
8. *Stromata*, ed. Stählin/Früchtel, I.21, 101–7, where he relies on Tatian's chronological calculations to prove the antiquity of Moses and his priority over the earliest Greek philosophy and the Trojan War itself (Tatian *Oratio ad Graecos* [*Address to the Greeks*] 38–40).
9. Thus *Miscellanies* II.9.45 (*Gospel of the Hebrews*) and III.9.63, 13.93 (*Gospel of the Egyptians*). These and other passages are arranged conveniently in James, ed., *Apocryphal New Testament*, pp. 2, 10, though his references seem to be mistaken.
10. *Miscellanies* I.22.150.4. Numenius himself demonstrates the eclectic nature of second-century Platonism, with its absorption of ideas derived from the Stoics, Pythagoreans, and even Philo, as well as its bedrock of Plato. For the plagiarism of them in Clement, see Chadwick, *Early Christian Thought*, pp. 44–45, and Jaeger, *Early Christianity*, p. 61.
11. *Miscellanies* I.3.22.5.
12. See above, p. 288.
13. *Miscellanies* I.19.94.1.
14. Ibid., I.5.28.
15. Ibid.
16. Ibid., I.16.80.6, and compare VII.20. For Clement, the maxim, "Know thyself," meant "to know for what purpose we were made." He adds (VII.21) it was "for submission to God."
17. The key text is *Paedagogus* (*Tutor*) I.6: "Being baptized we are illumined; being illumined we are made sons; being made sons, we are perfected and being perfected we become immortal." See C. Lattey, "The Deification of Man in Clement of Alexandria: Some Further Notes," *JTS* 17 (1916): 257–62, esp. p. 260.
18. *Tutor* I.8.71. Compare also *Miscellanies* II.2.6.1, V.11.71, 12.81, and VI.18.166. See Bigg, *Christian Platonists*, pp. 91–94.
19. *Miscellanies* IV.25.156, where Clement also states that the Son is "wisdom and knowledge and truth."
20. Kelly, *Early Christian Doctrines*, p. 127.
21. *Miscellanies* IV.22.135.1–136.1.
22. Ibid., VI.13.105.1.
23. Ibid., III.17.102. Clement refers to the Gnostics, Cassian and Valentinus,

and to Marcion, and points rightly to the association of the view that birth was evil with a blasphemous, Docetic view of Christ. For Clement's strong defense of marriage throughout *Miscellanies* Book III, see F. Bolgiani, "La Polemica di Clemente alexandrino contro gli Gnostici libertini nel iii libro degli Stromati," *Studi Materiali di storia della religioni* 38 (Rome, 1967): 86–136.

24. See Chadwick, *Early Christian Thought*, p. 63.

25. Ibid., IV.14.17–18. See also *Martyrdom and Persecution*, pp. 354–55.

26. *The Rich Man's Salvation*, Eng. trans. and ed. G. W. Butterworth, LCL (Cambridge, Mass.: Harvard University Press; London: William Heinemann, 1919), 14. Poverty was no great gain if one was "rich in passions," ibid., 15.2.

27. Tertullian *De patientia* (*Concerning Patience*) VII, and compare *Ad uxorem* (*To His Wife*) II.8, ed. Kroymann, CSEL 70, p. 122, "Difficile in domo Dei dives . . . ," and *De cultu feminarum* (*Concerning the Deportment of Women*) II.9, CSEL 70, pp. 85–86.

28. *Tutor* III.98.1, and compare Justin *2 Apology* II.13. See Chadwick, *Early Christian Thought*, p. 63.

29. *Miscellanies* VI.9.71.1–2.

30. Ibid., III.7.59.

31. See below, p. 841.

32. *Miscellanies* VII.90.2.

33. Ibid., I.71.3–6. See Dihle, "Indische Philosophien."

34. See Frend, "Some Cultural Links."

35. See Roberts, *Manuscript, Society and Belief*, pp. 13–14, 71.

36. See *Dialogue with Heracleides*, where Origen after a long exposition on the meaning of "the life of the flesh is in the blood" (cf. Lev. 17:11) suddenly breaks off to accuse his hearers at great length and with considerable venom of not paying enough attention. See *Alexandrian Christianity*, Oulton and Chadwick, pp. 445–47. Origen's contempt for high standards of public speaking (*Ezekiel* III.3) may be "sour grapes."

37. Relays of stenographers relieving each other at set intervals as Origen composed his treatises—see Eusebius *HE* VI.23.2.

38. Cf. Eusebius *HE* VI.19.5.

39. Ibid., VI.18. See Chadwick, *Early Christian Thought*, pp. 111–16.

40. *Miscellanies* IV.26.172.

41. *Exhortation to Martyrdom*, Eng. trans. Chadwick, in *Alexandrian Christianity*, ed. Oulton and Chadwick, pp. 388–429, 29 (end). For the Maccabees' example of heroism, ibid., 22 and 23.

42. Thus, *Commentarius in Cantica Canticorum* II, ed. W. A. Baehrens, GCS 33, Origen (Leipzig: Hinrichs, 1925), pp. 141ff.; and in Gregory the Wonderworker's *Panegyric to Origen* 6 and 11. For Origen's debt to Plato, see Jaeger, *Early Christianity*, p. 65.

43. Eusebius *HE* VI.2.1 and 9–10.

44. See above, p. 281.

45. Eusebius *HE* VI.8.2; and for previous occasions as a mark of zeal by youthful Christians, see Justin *1 Apology* 29.

46. For Origen's contacts with Ammonius and Porphyry, see Kettler, "Origenes."

47. Eusebius *HE* VI.14.10.

48. Ibid., VI.15.

49. See Chadwick, *Early Christian Thought*, p. 70.

50. Eusebius *HE* VI.16.4, another instance of Origen's spirit of inquiry beyond his times.

51. Cited from Ambrose's letter to a friend in C. H. E. Lommatsch, ed., *Origenis opera omnia* (Berlin, 1831–44), vol. 17, p. 5. See Bigg, *Christian Platonists*, p. 157.

52. See especially Origen *Letter to Africanus* (esp. paragraphs 4 and 5).

53. Eusebius *HE* VI.19.15, and see Grant, *Augustus to Constantine*, p. 233.

54. I owe this information to Professor C. Youtie at a lecture given to the Fourteenth International Congress of Papyrologists at Oxford in July 1974. On the actual reasons (or obscurity concerning them) for Caracalla's action, see F. Millar, *A Study of Cassius Dio* (New York and London: Oxford University Press, 1964), pp. 156–58.

55. Eusebius *HE* VI.19.17.

56. *De principiis*, ed. Koetschau, GCS 22; and *Origen on First Principles*, ed. Butterworth, Prologue 2.

57. For example, *De principiis* (*On First Principles*) III.5.7.

58. Ibid., Prologue 10, and even then backed up by a biblical quotation, Hosea 10:12 (LXX), "Enlighten yourselves with the light of knowledge."

59. *Principles* I.1.6.

60. Ibid., I.2.1–2.

61. Ibid., I.2.4.

62. *Ezekiel* VI.6, ed. Baehrens, GCS 33, pp. 384–85. Origen's Hermetic contemporaries attributed "goodness" as the "passion of God," Poimandres 14.9.

63. See *Celsus* V.39 ("second God") and other references in P. Koetschau, ed., GCS 2, p. 30. See Daniélou, *Origen*, pp. 249–52.

64. *Principles* I.8.1.

65. *Genesis* I.15: "Videamus autem etiam per allegoriam quomodo ad imaginem Dei homo factus masculus et femina est" (ed. Baehrens, GCS 29, p. 19); and *Celsus* IV.40, Origen claims his understanding of the descent of the soul was superior to that found in Plato (*Phaedrus* 246b and c).

66. *Principles* I.8.1 (ed. Koetschau, p. 96).

67. Ibid., I.6.3.

68. Ibid., I.8.3: "Not even the Devil himself was incapable of good"; and cf. I.6.3: Could "any portion of the creation be utterly and entirely out of harmony even with final unity and concord . . . ?" and *Celsus* VIII.72.

69. *Celsus* IV.13, citing as scriptural warrant, Mal. 3:2.

70. *Principles* I.6.3, and II.10.3. On the remedial aspect of divine punishment, see Daniélou, *Origen*, p. 277.

71. See Wiles, *Christian Fathers*, pp. 34–35.

72. *Principles* I.3.5.

73. Ibid., IV.3.1 (ed. Koetschau, p. 323).

74. *Principles* IV.3.1.

75. Ibid., IV.3.3. See Grant, *Earliest Lives of Jesus*, chap. 4.

76. *Principles* IV.3.3 (ed. Koetschau, p. 327).

77. Ibid., IV.3.2.

78. He defines the three types of scriptural interpretation in ibid., IV.2.5–6. The "psychical" seems to be valuable mainly for interpreting Pauline figures of speech.

He describes *theoria* as the mind "burning with an inexpressible desire to know the reason of those things implanted within us by God," ibid., II.11.4 (ed. Koetschau, p. 187).

79. *Dialogue with Heracleides*, in *Alexandrian Christianity*, Oulton and Chadwick, p. 454. This whole passage provides a good example of Origen's method of establishing a truth from a mosaic of scriptural quotation taken equally from Old and New Testaments.

80. *Principles* IV.3.1.

81. Cited by Eusebius *HE* VI.25.11–13.

82. So Porphyry, cited by Eusebius *HE* VI.19.4.

83. Above, chap. 6 n. 106. See also Daniélou, *Origen*, pp. 190ff.

84. *John's Gospel* XIII.9, ed. Preuschen, GCS 10, pp. 233–36. See Wiles, *Spiritual Gospel*, p. 47, and in general, M. Simonetti, "Eracleone e Origene," *Vetera Christianorum* 3 (1966), and 4 (1967): 23–64.

85. *Commentary on John* I.20. See Bigg, *Christian Platonists*, p. 212 n. 1.

86. *John's Gospel* I.22 (ed. Preuschen, p. 25), but adds Origen "as Wisdom, Word and Righteousness." See Bigg, *Christian Platonists*, p. 212.

87. *John's Gospel* XXXII.24(16), ed. Preuschen, p. 459. See Bigg, *Christian Platonists*, pp. 264–67, with references.

88. See below, p. 756.

89. *Commentary on John* VI.2.8. Eusebius *HE* VI.8.4–5, suggests that Demetrius was actuated by jealousy and now held Origen's act of self-mutilation against him. There may, however, have been more in it than this, as Origen was never recalled to Alexandria.

90. See above, p. 280.

91. *Commentary on John* VI.2.9.

92. Thus Jerome *Letter* 33.4 (*PL* 22.447).

93. Eusebius *HE* VI.21.3. "Origen's fame," adds Eusebius, "was now universal."

94. Gregory *Panegyric to Origen* 9 and 11.

95. *HE* VI.33, 37.

96. Thus in *Commentary on John* X.37(21), Origen implicitly criticizes Noetus's views, especially his failure to differentiate properly between the Father and the Son.

97. See Chadwick's discussion of the background to *Heracleides*, in *Alexandrian Christianity*, ed. Oulton and Chadwick, pp. 432–44, and J. Scherer in his edition, *Entretien d'Origène*, and the discussion by Capelle, "L'Entretien d'Origène."

98. Eusebius *HE* VI.36.4. On Origen's death, see R. M. Grant, *Eusebius as Church Historian* (New York and London: Oxford University Press, 1980), pp. 78–79.

99. Also a tract by Origen, *Pascha*, fragments of a *Commentary on Romans*, a *Homily on the Witch of Endor*, and the first six books of *Celsus*. See the brief description in Altaner, *Patrology*, p. 199, and H. C. Puech's "Nouveaux écrits d'Origène et de Didyme découverts à Toura," *RHPR* 31 (1951): 293–329.

100. Cited from Oulton and Chadwick, *Alexandrian Christianity*, pp. 437–38.

101. Ibid., p. 438.

102. *Jeremiah* IX.4, ed. Klostermann, GCS 6, 70. See Wiles, "Eternal Generation."

103. *Principles* I.2.12: "Primal goodness is to be understood as residing in God the Father, from whom both the Son is born and the Holy Spirit proceeds . . ." (*ANCL* trans.).

104. Cited from Oulton and Chadwick, *Alexandrian Christianity*, pp. 454–55.

105. Eusebius *HE* VII.24.1. For millenarianism as an issue in Origen's lifetime, see his *De oratione* (*On Prayer*) XXVII.13, with its sarcastic reference to "this is perhaps the famous period of thousand years" (Eng. trans. in Oulton and Chadwick, *Alexandrian Christianity*, p. 303), which he then explains allegorically.

106. Cited by Eusebius *HE* VII.25.

107. Ibid., VII.25.25.

108. Ibid., VII.26., and Athanasius *Epistula de sententia Dionysii episcopi Alexandrini* (*Dionysius*) V (*PG* 25.485–88). See Bethune-Baker's interesting and whimsical chapter on "The Correspondence Between Dionysius of Rome and Dionysius of Alexandria," in *Introduction to Early History*, chap. 8, pp. 113–18; and Kelly, *Early Christian Doctrines*, pp. 135–36.

109. Cited by Athanasius *Dionysius* IV–VI. Theologians have tended to characterize Dionysius's definitions as "unfortunate." In fact, they follow from Origen's teaching, and the metaphors may owe their origin to Philo.

110. Fragments preserved in Athanasius *Epistula de decretis Nicaenae synodi* (*On the Decrees of the Synod of Nicaea*) XXVI (*PG* 25.461–65), Eng. trans. in Stevenson, ed., *A New Eusebius*, pp. 268–69.

111. Athanasius *Dionysius* XVIII. The term *Homoousios* had begun to become current with Heracleon who had claimed that those who worshiped God in spirit and in truth were themselves spirit and "of the same nature as the Father" (cf. Origen *Commentary on John* XIII.25.148). Origen himself uses the term as an illustration of the community of substance between Father and Son, but not as a definition. Compare Prestige, *God in Patristic Thought*, pp. 199–200; and Kelly, *Early Christian Doctrines*, pp. 133–36.

112. See J. Daniélou in Daniélou and H. Marrou, *The Christian Centuries: A New History of the Catholic Church*, vol. 1, *The First Six Hundred Years*, Eng. trans. V. Cronin (New York: McGraw-Hill; London: Darton, Longman & Todd, 1964), pp. 185–88.

113. Thus, the *Chronicle of Séert*, ed. A. Scher, *Patrologia Orientalis* 4 (Paris, 1908), p. 222.

114. John Chrysostom *Adversus Judaeos* (*Against the Jews*) IV.3 (*PG* 48.875).

115. See the letter of Constantine to Bishop Alexander of Alexandria after Nicaea, with his reference to "all the Oriental brethren [that is, Antiochenes] who have hitherto kept the [Paschal] feast when the Jews did" (Socrates *Ecclesiastical History* I.9.18).

116. Eusebius *HE* VII.30.6–16.

117. Eng. trans. in Stevenson, *A New Eusebius*, p. 278. See Leontius of Byzantium, *Contra Nestorianos et Eutychianos* (*Against the Nestorians and Eutychians*) III, *PG* 86.1.1267–1398, esp. p. 1392B. Published with other probably genuine statements by Paul by Riedmatten, *Les Actes de Paul de Samosate*, p. 153. The authenticity of this statement is suggested by the reference to Jesus Christ being a "man from hence," quoted by Eusebius *HE* VII.30.11.

118. See above, p. 252.

119. Leontius of Byzantium suggests that Paul applied the title "Word" to God's

commandment and ordinance (*On the Sects* III.3, *PG* 86.1216); but see also the discussion of Paul's meaning in Prestige, *God in Patristic Thought*, pp. 201–9.

120. The Spirit "bestowed grace on the apostles" (in Leontius *On the Sects* III.3). One hesitates to accept Kelly's view here (*Early Christian Doctrines*, p. 118) that Paul used a Trinitarian formula "but only as a veil to cover a theology that was nakedly unitarian." As Tertullian, Paul believed that the sanctifying agent of the Godhead was the Spirit. "Word and Spirit were always in God as reason was in the heart of man," Epiphanius *Medicine Box* LXV.1. His theology was genuinely Trinitarian, whereas that of his Alexandrian opponents was not.

121. Eusebius *HE* VII.33.1.

122. *Acta Archelai*, ed. C. H. Beeson, GCS 16 (Leipzig: Hinrichs, 1906), 58.11–12 and 60.3.

123. *Luke* XIX, ed. Rauer, GCS 49, pp. 114–15.

124. *Celsus* IV.15.

125. For Origen the Logos was "completely in control" of the incarnate Christ. See A. Grillmeier, *Christ in Christian Tradition: From the Apostolic Age to Chalcedon (451)*, Eng. trans. J. S. Bowden (New York: Sheed & Ward; Oxford: A. R. Mowbray, 1965), p. 170.

126. Taken from the record of Malchion's examination of Paul (Eng. trans. cited from Riedmatten, ed., *Les Actes de Paul de Samosate*, p. 158, in Stevenson, *A New Eusebius*, pp. 278–79). For Malchion himself, see Jerome *De Viris Illustribus* (*Concerning Illustrious Men*) LXXI.

127. J. D. Mansi, *Sacrorum Conciliorum Collectio nova et amplissima* (Florence, 1759), I, pp. 1033ff., and F. Loofs, *Paulus von Samosata* (Leipzig: Hinrichs, 1924), pp. 108ff., 265ff. Also J. N. D. Kelly, *Early Christian Creeds* (New York and London: Longmans, Green & Co., 1950), p. 207. The text of part of the bishops' letter has been reproduced in Eusebius *HE* VII.30, but important doctrinal statements are preserved in Leontius of Byzantium's *Against Nestorians and Eutychians* III (*PG* 86.1.1358–96) and reproduced in M. R. Routh, ed., *Reliquiae Sacrae*, 5 vols. (Oxonii: Academico, 1846), vol. 2, pp. 465ff., and by Lawlor, "Sayings of Paul."

128. Eusebius *HE* VII.30.2.

129. Dionysius's primary accusation against Paul in his *Letter* (Mansi, *Sacrorum Conciliorum*, I, p. 1040).

130. Eusebius *HE* VII.30.19.

131. As suggested by Daniélou in Daniélou and Marrou, *Christian Centuries*, vol. 1, *First Six Hundred Years*, p. 208.

132. See below, p. 490.

12

Church and People in the Third Century

By the last quarter of the third century the church had become part of the landscape, if not part of the urban establishment, over much of the Mediterranean world. In 303 the cathedral at Nicomedia, Diocletian's headquarters, stood on high ground in full view of the imperial palace, a sign of things to come.[1] Bishops, such as Dionysius of Alexandria and his namesake at Rome, were regarded by the authorities as important leaders with whom negotiations sometimes had to be conducted. They and their colleagues had secured de facto the right of free assembly as well as that of free expression. The councils held in the 250s and 260s in the West and East, respectively, required a high degree of organization, and the acquiescence at least of numerous local and imperial authorities. The Christians had obtained what might be described as a "millet" status. They were recognized as a separate community with its own institutions and leaders, but whose security depended on the good will of the authorities of the day. How was this great religious movement organized and what did its members expect from their faith? How did they regard their duties to God and their neighbor? How did they express themselves in art and writing? Beyond the walls of the cities, Christianity had at last begun to make an impact in the countryside. What of these new Christians drawn from provincials who enjoyed few advantages from the empire? Between Antony and his monastic followers, and many urban bishops, there was little in common except the name of Christian.

AUTHORITY AND CHURCH ORDER

One of the most interesting surviving documents of the late third century is the letter of the synod of Antioch of 268 which finally condemned Paul of Samosata.[2] It throws light on questions of authority and precedence as well as on what the dominant Alexandrian party in the church regarded as heresy. The letter recounts how this council "was attended by bishops, presbyters and deacons in the adjacent cities and provinces" and that it had announced its decision to "our fellow-ministers throughout the world and the whole Catholic Church under heaven," beginning with Dionysius of Rome and Maximus of Alexandria.[3] This gathering, when compared with those summoned by Cyprian in the previous decade, shows not only how authority in the church was being exercised collegially everywhere but the effective, worldwide range of that authority as well. In imitation perhaps of the apostolic council, the undoubted vehicle of the Spirit, the council of bishops—accompanied by presbyters and deacons, and in the presence of the Christian people[4]—is shown to be the means by which decisions of the church were arrived at and communicated to the new people of Israel.

Individual councils and communities were jealous of their authority. The church at Antioch (or a large faction within it) had called in senior bishops, such as Dionysius of Alexandria and Firmilian, to strengthen their hand against Paul, but their role had only been advisory. Not until a full council assembled could Paul be condemned to deposition. Collective opinion was not to be subordinated to that of any one bishop. All bishops belonged to one sacerdotal body, Cyprian had reminded his colleagues (*Letter* LXVII.4). At the same time, accepted patterns of leadership were emerging. Once assembled, bishops would not usually step out of line from the policy of their chief. At Cyprian's council of 256, every bishop had his say, but their speeches read like a roll call of arguments in favor of Cyprian's standpoint on baptism and the issue was never in doubt. A century later, the catholic councils of Carthage presided over by Bishop Aurelius provided unanimous "placets" for the bishop of Carthage's suggestions.

In Alexandria, too, universal pretensions by any one bishop were questioned. Origen may have had his own reasons for repudiating clerical claims, but what he wrote during his exile at Caesarea may also have been representative:

> Certain persons, I know not how, arrogating to themselves powers beyond the priestly office, perhaps because they have no accurate grasp of the knowledge that a priest should possess, boast that they are able to pardon even idolatry and to forgive adultery and fornication, on the ground that by means of the prayer offered for those who have committed these deeds even "the sin unto death" is absolved. For they do not read the words: "There is a sin unto death: not concerning this do I say that he should make request" (1 John 5:16). [*On Prayer* 28.10][5]

This sounds like an echo of the controversy between Hippolytus and Tertullian on the one hand and Pope Callistus on the other, some fifteen years before. Origen had no doubt where in such matters the right lay, and, as always, he was ready to prove his point from Scripture. In the next century, Eastern bishops were as suspicious of the claims of New Rome (Constantinople) as they were of its counterpart on the Tiber.

Tests of orthodoxy resided in collective documents. The creeds of the early church combined the christological affirmations of the Rule of Faith with the formal interrogations put to the convert at baptism.[6] By the middle of the third century many major communities had their own statements of belief set out in credal form. These were being used increasingly as tests of orthodoxy where deviation was suspected. Origen himself was careful to set out the accepted statements of belief held in the church of Alexandria, at the beginning of *On First Principles*.[7] Bishop Heracleides, whose views were being examined by Origen, opened the discussion with a statement of belief which he shared with his colleagues.

> I also believe what the sacred Scriptures say: "In the beginning was the Word, and the Word was with God, and the Word was God. He was in the beginning with God. All things were made by him, and without him nothing was made." Accordingly, we hold the same faith that is taught in these words, and we believe that Christ took flesh, that he was born, that he went up to heaven in

the flesh in which he rose again, that he is sitting at the right hand of the father, and that thence he shall come and judge the living and the dead, being God and man.[8]

Origen, like Malchion when confronting Paul of Samosata, then probed whether Heracleides meant what he appeared to say. In 265, three years before he underwent that ordeal, Paul had been confronted with a long "statement of faith," affirming belief that the Son of God was God and condemning those who disagreed as being "outside the ecclesiastical rule," which he was invited to sign.[9] The road to the Council of Nicaea (325) was being marked out by the events in Antioch sixty years earlier.

Rome

Though councils were the final authority, an order of precedence was evolving among the senior bishops which would be confirmed in its turn at Nicaea.[10] In the Antiochene letter, Dionysius of Rome precedes Maximus of Alexandria. Rome, therefore, was regarded as the senior bishopric in both East and West,[11] though with rather different significance in each. Here, differences of biblical exegetical method were as important as ideas of episcopal precedence. This was an instance where Platonism or lack of it played a crucial part in contrasting Eastern/Western attitudes. In the West, Matt. 16:18 was being interpreted literally, as the Lord's will, and we have seen how Peter's see was regarded by Cyprian as the origin and seat of episcopacy with which communion must be maintained.[12] He never went back on this principle, even in the heat of the Rebaptism controversy. Rome, he would add, was a larger city than Carthage and therefore should be accorded precedence.[13] At the same time, acceptance of Rome as the "leading see" (*principalis*) implied no jurisdictional rights for its bishop. If Stephen could be expected to discipline Marcian of Arles for his lapse into Novatianism, he could equally stand rebuked by Cyprian's council summoned to hear the complaints of the Spanish congregations against his decision to restore lapsed bishops to their sees. Stephen and his church could also be in error, appealing to "human tradition, not legitimate" and persisting in their mistaken views.[14] In the minds of many North African Christians, Peter and Paul were "pillars of discipline," "spiritual men," martyrs, and with whom North African martyrs could be associated.[15] Their episcopal successors had no particular claim to obedience. Nonetheless, the Roman church was coming to be considered in the West as the pivot of episcopal government. It is surprising perhaps that more was not heard of its bishops in the half century after the Rebaptism controversy.

In the East, while some bishops were simply embarrassed by Stephen's claims, others were as forthright in their denunciation of them as the North Africans. For Firmilian, Stephen could be "blind and in error," a prey to wrongheaded custom and on the way to excommunicating himself. Ideas based on his succession to Peter were fallacious.[16] In calmer moods, how-ever, the Petrine texts were interpreted allegorically, leading to a more general sense being attributed to them than in the West. They were referred by Origen and his successors to "the Church," or "the faithful," and not to Peter himself. Commenting on Matt. 16:18, Origen stated that "the rock" was "every imitator of Christ from whom they drank, who drank from a spiritual rock that followed them."[17] The church and its constitution were built on such a rock. The passage referred to the apostles as a whole and not only to Peter. Elsewhere, Peter is seen as the pattern of all who had a right disposition for the church to be built upon. The "keys of the king-dom" were given to all who believed in the confession Peter made and repented their faults.[18] Origen's lead was followed. In the fifth century, we find the Alexandrian Monophysite patriarch, Timothy Aelurus (454–77), writing to the church of Constantinople and referring to Peter's rock as "meaning the orthodox faith," and not Peter's successors.[19]

For some Easterns, including the historian Eusebius, James rather than Peter was preeminent as a bishop, as "brother of Christ," who received the episcopate at Jerusalem "from the Saviour and the apostles."[20] Respect for the Roman see, as Origen shows (Eusebius *HE* VI.14.10), was connected with its antiquity and perhaps also with the primacy of the city of Rome as capital of the empire.

In Rome itself, however, the third-century bishops were consolidating their authority over the Christian community in the city and its surround-ings. Fabian (236–50) is credited with the assignment to the Regions of the city of seven deacons and seven subdeacons, whom he created, probably to supervise the distribution of relief.[21] Under Dionysius (260–69) the city was organized into parishes (later *tituli*) under their own presbyters.[22] From Fabian's time, the anniversary of the bishop's enthronement was kept as a solemn feast. All the while new catacombs and new churches were being built. Calepodius's and Domitilla's c. 230, the shrine to the apostles on the Appian Way c. 245, Novatian's c. 260, and that of Peter and Marcellinus near the end of the century, are examples of the successive extensions of the property of the church in Rome during the third century.[23] By the end of the century there were believed to be no less than forty churches in the city.[24] Beyond its boundaries, the Roman see was acquiring estates (*fundi*) perhaps by bequest before the outbreak of the Great Persecution in 303.[25]

The bishop's authority was extending throughout the whole hundred-mile radius, administered by the prefect of the city. Cornelius held a coun-cil of sixty bishops with priests and deacons in 251, who must have been drawn from that area.[26] Dionysius was credited with the establishment of further bishoprics.[27] Not surprisingly, the Council of Nicaea (canon 6) recognized the pope's direct authority over bishops and clergy in the "sub-urbicarian area." By this time, Rome had become the point of reference for the West as a whole. The Council of Arles (1 August 314) was careful to inform Pope Miltiades of its decisions and was flattering in its praises of him.[28]

Alexandria

The same canon of Nicaea accorded primatial rights to Alexandria and Antioch. In the synodical letter of 268 Maximus of Alexandria was addressed second after Dionysius. Maximus (264–82) apparently had profitable trading as well as ecclesiastical connections with Rome,[29] and the authority of his see was second only to that of the capital. In Alexandria itself, the church was well organized on a parochial basis, and Maximus's predecessor Dionysius (247–64) was already claiming disciplinary rights over the churches of Cyrenaica in the Monarchian affair. His rebuke to Nepos of Arsinoë for teaching millenarist doctrines shows that his writ extended down the Nile Valley.

The ecclesiastical unity of the Nile Valley under Alexandria in the fourth and fifth centuries is a commonplace, but in Dionysius's time this could not be taken for granted. Alexandria was not popular even among Greek-speaking Egyptians. For the writer of the Oracle of the Potter, it was a "foreign city" whose wealth and power was envied.[30] On the other hand, for educated Alexandrians Libya was the back of beyond. Dionysius was particularly angry at the prospect of exile far from Alexandria.[31] Two factors helped Dionysius change these attitudes. First, he showed great courage and political savvy during the civil war of 261–62 between the forces of the prefect of Egypt, Aemilian, and forces loyal to the emperor, Gallienus. Dionysius was conspicuously loyal to the latter and was rewarded by rescripts of toleration which allowed Christians rights of worship and property-holding.[32] The second factor concerned Easter. The church of Alexandria, like Rome and probably Carthage also, was intent on calculating the date of Easter independently of the Jewish calculation of 14 Nisan. Dionysius, by circulating an annual Festal Letter, kept his suffragans informed of the Alexandrian calculation based on an eight-year cycle.[33] Perhaps partly as a result of the chaotic situation in Alexandria in 260–62, it contained also "words specially suited to a solemn occasion" (Eusebius *HE* VII.20.1) including news of important events with his own reactions and decisions. During Dionysius's lifetime, the Festal Letter became an important means of centralizing the organization of the churches in Egypt and Cyrenaica under Alexandrian leadership. By 300 this hegemony extended from the First Cataract in the south to the Altars of Philene marking the boundary between Cyrenaica and Tripolitania.

Antioch

Antioch might have rivaled Alexandria. It was the "mother see" of the East, where the earliest Christian missions had been established, and it possessed a vague authority over territories vaster than those under Alexandria. The affair of Paul of Samosata brought bishops from Pontus, Cappadocia, and Cilicia to Antioch for meetings in 264 and 265(?).[34] Was this accidental? One notices, first, that the sees of Asia and Bithynia—such as might be expected to depend on Ephesus—were not represented, while on the other hand, in 314 Vitalis, bishop of Antioch, presided at a council at Ancyra in Galatia. The same city was chosen by the Antiochene council of 325 as the place where Eusebius of Caesarea was to appear to exculpate himself from a charge of heresy.[35] Is it legitimate, therefore, to suggest some form of Antiochene suzerainty over the bishoprics of northern and eastern Asia Minor as well as Syria and Mesopotamia? Unlike the power of Alexandria, however, that of Antioch was not based on any geographic or ethnic unity and, in addition, its Trinitarian and christological doctrines conflicted with those of Alexandria. Moreover, the counterattraction of Edessa in the east and Jerusalem in the south further prevented consolidation of Antiochene authority. Already Jerusalem was beginning to assert its claims to special status as the site of the Holy Places, and to chafe at the authority of Caesarea, and more distantly at that of Antioch. The memory of James and his episcopal chair could not be wished away.[36]

Other Bishoprics

Beyond the "great sees" of Christendom, one can discern three or four bishoprics which would become influential in the next century. Ephesus, looking back to its apostolic foundation by John, was to dispute the primacy over the sees of western and northern Asia Minor with Constantinople for nearly two centuries. Carthage could claim the unchallenged leadership over the rapidly growing numbers of bishoprics throughout North Africa.[37] Arles had outstripped Lyons and Vienne in importance as the center of Gallic Christianity. Edessa would never lose its role as the focus for the Aramaic-based church in eastern Syria and Mesopotamia. While the importance of bishoprics tended to match the secular importance of cities, there were some exceptions. By the end of the third century, the senior bishop of Numidia was the senior in terms of consecration, not the bishop of the capital city, Cirta. Why primacy should devolve on the old man (*senex*) of the Numidian church is not known.[38]

BISHOPS AND CLERGY

The bishop was chosen by the clergy and with assent of the people, just as the whole people of Israel was summoned to witness Eleazar succeed Aaron (Num. 20:22–28). Cyprian clarifies the procedure by stating (*Letters* LV.8) that the worthiness of Cornelius had been attested by the bishops who came together, the majority of the clergy, and the votes of the people.[39] Once elected, his authority was practically unchallengeable. He was the high priest (*sacerdos* in North Africa), descendant of the apostles, and endowed with apostolic powers.[40] He represented the church on earth, and the white cushion on the episcopal chair seems to have symbolized this.[41] At Rome and Antioch, the bishop's chair was placed on a dais, perhaps already within the apse of the cathedral.[42] At Aquileia, however, where no apse can be traced in the church of Bishop Theodore (c. 300–320), it may have occupied a special space marked out within the mosaic that covered the floor.[43] In the art of the fourth and succeeding centuries the bishop is often shown seated on a chair, holding a Bible against his breast, and his left hand outstretched in the gesture of a teacher.

Apart from presiding over the liturgy, ordaining clergy, and preaching, the bishop's life in the mid–third century was a busy one. Dionysius of Alexandria's letters show a continuous round of negotiations with authorities, of organizing charity and relief, theological debate, disciplining errant subordinates, as well as action on major questions affecting relations with other important sees occasioned by the heresies of Paul of Samosata. Other senior bishops might also find themselves overburdened. Their churches had become considerable charitable institutions with buildings and estates to maintain.[44] At the beginning of the century, Tertullian referred to church funds being used for the relief of the poor,[45] and at the end, the house-church of Cirta (Numidia) was a veritable storehouse for clothes, shoes, and sundry articles for the needy.[46]

By 250 the church's charitable work in the West had become centralized under the control of the bishop. In the letter of Pope Cornelius denouncing Novatian, Cornelius mentions "more than 1500 widows and persons in distress" supported by the church in Rome.[47] Cyprian is not so precise but he adds some details as to what was entailed. While he was in hiding during the Decian persecution, he reckoned his first duty was to find funds to maintain the poor on the church's roll, and he instructed clergy who had stayed in Carthage to act as almoners.[48] Then came hospitality for travelers and refugees. A few years later (in 253), he had to raise a massive sum of one hundred thousand sesterces and more to ransom prisoners taken by the Kabyle raiders.[49] The church, as the Jewish synagogue did, acted as trustee for widows and was responsible for maintaining orphans.[50] Even before the Decian persecution Cyprian reveals that bishops were doing the same type of work in the secular world. He refers to a canon of an unnamed synod that forbade clergy to act as executors or guardians of an estate, even though it belonged to a close relative. Cyprian took the drastic step of excommunicating the testator! This letter is interesting, because it shows how, from the outset of his episcopate, Cyprian compared the situation of clergy to that of Levites in the old Israel.[51] They were a people apart. They must abstain from secular business and rely on tithes, the same point made by the Syriac *Didascalia Apostolorum* of like date.[52] In fact, monthly payments based perhaps on tithes from the faithful seem to have been the normal form of salary from the bishop downwards in the church in Carthage and in parts, at least, of the East as well.[53] The bishop's responsibility for making these payments increased his disciplinary powers over his clergy, as some found to their cost.

We do not know the amount of these clerical salaries. The first existing figure for a bishop's salary is 150 denarii a month paid by the Theodotian Monarchians in Rome, c. 200, to the confessor Natalius, while he was their bishop.[54] It was not a great deal by the standard of the time, seventy-two hundred sesterces a year compared to one hundred thousand sesterces paid to a professor of rhetoric and the same to a middle-grade official. Bishops had a long way to go before their pay was equated to that of provincial governors.

Nonetheless, episcopal power for good or ill was formidable. Origen says some, "especially in the largest cities," behaved "like tyrants, imitating officials and terrorizing the poor."[55] Paul of Samosata was said to have come to his see penniless and emerged a rich man from his multifarious activities.[56] Certainly, Cyprian exercised severe discipline over his flock, though not so complete and absolute as that credited to the Jewish patriarch of the time. He suspended from pay, pending their trial, two subdeacons and an acolyte who had disappeared from Carthage during the persecution.[57] He told a colleague, Bishop Rogatian, to deal with an insubordinate deacon "with episcopal vigour."[58] He laid down the law on a variety of moral questions. An actor who had been converted would have to abandon his profession and, if necessary, be sustained from church funds until he found a new calling, and if the local church could not manage, then the church in Carthage would take him on.[59] The deacon who slept with dedicated virgins must be disciplined with full penance and confession (exomologesis).[60] By the middle of the third century the foundations of the church's canon law were being laid.[61]

Clericalization of Church Life

Cyprian's comparison of the clergy with the Levitical priesthood was apt. The clerical career was already becoming specialized and stereotyped. Since the 240s, at least, the increase in miscellaneous administrative commitments inside and outside the dioceses was resulting in an increase in the number of those in minor orders. These were not technically members of the clergy, but in every other way were associated with the church as an institution.[62] Pope Cornelius was proud of the numbers on his staff. There were, he declaimed, 46 presbyters, 7 deacons, 7 subdeacons, 42 acolytes, 52 exorcists, readers, and doorkeepers, 155 clergy in all,[63] requiring revenues for their upkeep and duties to occupy them. It was a formidable civil service.

The exorcists, readers, and janitors (gravediggers, as well), remained functional.[64] The janitors were a legacy from Judaism (cf. Neh. 7:45 and 73, where they are associated with "singers" and "temple-servants"). The readers were often children, but it would seem that some could continue as such into mature years. They were not ordained but appointed by the bishop's handing the Scriptures to the reader.[65] The exorcists are recorded as expelling demons and tackling female heretics, and in general acting as healers of mental disorders,[66] but subdeacons and acolytes were often used as clerks and messengers. Cyprian, for instance, sent Mettius the subdeacon and Nicephorus the acolyte to Rome carrying mail and also to support the presbyters Caldonius and Fortunatus in their negotiations.[67]

Promotion went partly by age (a presbyter in the early fourth century had to be thirty years old), but always depended on the bishop. Cyprian promoted the confessors Celerinus and Numidicus as loyal and moderate individuals. Celerinus became a reader. Apparently he could not be promoted straight into the presbyterate because of his youth, while the reader Numidicus was ordained presbyter. Both, however, were to receive a presbyter's stipend.[68] The presbyter's office was a distinguished one. He sat with the bishop during the liturgy.[69] People were expected to stand up at his approach as at that of the bishop.[70] At Antioch, Malchion was clearly a leader and a theologian far better equipped than most of the bishops under the jurisdiction of his see. At Rome, a council of presbyters administered the bishopric for fifteen months between the execution of Fabian and the election of his successor Cornelius, and the presbyters corresponded directly with other major sees, such as Carthage.[71]

The main sphere of the presbyter's authority was his parish. He might, with the bishop's consent, ordain deacons to aid him. But the latter, though subordinate, were beginning to become the presbyter's rival, especially in the central administration of the see. The traditional restriction of the deacon's numbers to seven and the close personal association of members of the order with the bishop tended to increase their influence at the expense of the more amorphous presbyterate. The deacon was "not ordained for the priesthood, but for the service of the bishop to do [only] the things commanded by him."[72] These could, however, be important. In Gaul, it would seem that a dependent community, such as that of Vienne in relation to Lyons, was administered by a deacon as bishop's deputy. Sanctus was known as "the deacon of Vienne."[73] In Rome by the end of the second century, the deacon was the administrative officer, and as shown by the example of Callistus, a strong contender for succession to the see. Pope Stephen (254–57) was his predecessor's "archdeacon."[74] Rome was not alone in this. Elsewhere, the deacon was also the administrative officer. At Carthage, the rebel deacon Felicissimus had apparently been in charge of church funds and had abused his trust. He had embezzled funds set aside for widows and minors.[75] Administrative and financial experience resulted in deacons undertaking further responsible duties. Cyprian and Cornelius both used members of the order as negotiators, and in the Rebaptism controversy, Rogatian was Cyprian's confidential agent with Firmilian of Cappadocia.[76] Another deacon, Pontius, was his biographer. By the end of the century, the senior deacon at Carthage had acquired the title of "arch-deacon."[77] In the person of Caecilian, the diaconate outwitted the presbyters after Bishop Mensurius's death in 311 and secured the succession for itself, at the cost of precipitating the Donatist schism.

Clericalization of church life was being emphasized in two other directions. The liturgy was becoming more formal and the penitential system more exact. The administration of both had become a clerical preserve. At the beginning of the century the laity in the church at Carthage might still expect to take an individual part in the service, to "prophesy," or sing something of one's own composition.[78] The laity could also baptize, and this seems to have been the tradition in Rome also.[79] By mid-century this had changed. Cyprian never speaks of baptism by laity in his many references to the subject. The celebration of the mysteries was the prerogative of priests alone. "We priests," he told Cornelius in 252, "who celebrate the sacrifices of God, prepare sacrifices and victims [that is, martyrs] for God."[80]

Liturgy

In Greek-speaking congregations, the Eucharist seems to have developed by the first half of the century into an approximation of its later form. Hippolytus (*Apostolic Tradition*, composed about 215) and Origen complement each other. Origen indicates that there were two parts of the service anticipating the "mass of the catechumens" and the "mass of the faithful." At the former, all, including inquiring pagans, might be present. The bishop or presbyter presided. There would be prayers and readings from Scripture, now arranged in lections taken from the Old and New Testaments, followed by a sermon based on a selection of the readings. On one occasion, Origen records asking the bishop, probably Theotecnus of Caesarea, which reading he should take,[81] and to judge from some of his *Homilies*, he preached for up to an hour sometimes to the boredom of congregations.

The sermon marked the end of the mass of the catechumens.[82] Catechumens and penitents, except the highest grade, the "Co-standers" (*consistentes*), would then depart, the doors would be closed and the celebration of the Eucharist begin. Here Hippolytus provides a contemporary picture. After the kiss of peace, the deacons would place the offerings of bread and wine on the altar. The bishop or presbyter would lay hands on them. Later, there would be prayers for the church, but at this date the celebrant began with "Lift up your hearts" (*Sursum Corda*) followed by a long prayer of commemoration and thanksgiving. There were thanks to God for sending "thy beloved Servant, Jesus Christ, whom in the last times thou hast sent as Saviour and Redeemer and Messenger of thy Counsel, the Logos who comes from thee, through whom thou hast made all things. . . ." The institution of the Eucharist itself was commemorated in the words of Paul's letter to the Corinthians (1 Cor. 11:24–25), and the offering of the loaf and the cup in thankful remembrance. There followed the invocation of the Holy Spirit (*Epiclēsis*):

> And we beseech Thee, that Thou send down Thy holy Spirit upon this offering of the holy church. Unite it, and grant to all the saints who partake of it to their fulfilling with holy Spirit, to their strengthening of faith in truth, that we may praise and glorify Thee through Thy Servant Jesus Christ, through whom to Thee be glory and honour to the Father and the Son with the Holy Spirit in Thy holy church now and forever. Amen.[83]

After this, came the solemn moment of the participation by the congregation in the sacred elements now touched by the Holy Spirit. The duty of passing the cup belonged to the deacons. Further prayers would follow, and finally a hymn and the words of dismissal, "Go in peace," spoken by a deacon. Inevitably, the role of the laity was restricted in the service to making the responses. Extempore activity as envisaged by Tertullian had no place. The celebrant indeed included a prayer of thanksgiving that "Thou hast counted us worthy to stand before thee and to do thy priestly service." He was already more than a delegate; he was representative of the body, a pastor offering the gifts presented by the people and thanking God on their behalf for all the benefits that they had received at his hands, and especially for the coming of Jesus Christ. Elaboration of the liturgy which would tend to enhance his status, however, would be inhibited so long as the normal place of prayer was a house-church whose assembly room varied in shape and size.[84] There was still a partnership in prayer and reception of the Spirit, though an increasingly unequal one.

In North Africa, however, a new element was being introduced. The strongly sacrificial nature of the church there, with its glorification of confession and martyrdom, was affecting the interpretation of the Eucharist. Cyprian defined the act of the priest as an imitation of the sacrifice of Christ in which he offered a full and true sacrifice in the church to God the Father.[85] This change of emphasis was to be very important. In the medieval Latin church greater stress would be laid on the sacrificial rather than the purely spiritual and recalling element in the Eucharist. One can see now how this could have originated with the African church as a consequence of the bishop's and especially Cyprian's appropriation of the glory of the martyrs' sacrifice as belonging to the bishop.[86] The bishop alone represented the people's virtues to the Lord. He alone made the eucharistic sacrifice. He was the "great priest and martyr."[87] Not surprisingly, personal acts of devotion at the liturgy also came under scrutiny. In Carthage c. 300, the archdeacon Caecilian rebuked a wealthy member of his congregation for kissing a martyr's bone before receiving the Eucharist. The martyr, he claimed, had not been authenticated by the church. The lady was a Spanish grande dame named Lucilla.[88] Caecilian was not forgiven.

In contrast, the agape survived in the West at least, and retained its

408

primitive character of a communal meal, sometimes perhaps connected with a wake in honor of the dead or with a martyr's anniversary. Tertullian described how all, rich and poor, joined in. A prayer was said standing and then all reclined and a "modest meal" began (*Apology* XXXIX.16–17). The banquet was the principal theme in paintings on three semicircular recesses (*arcosolia*) of the catacomb of Peter and Marcellinus, dating probably to the last years of the third century. On yet another similar scene the artist depicts a family(?) meal at which children as well as adults were present. There was food on the table, probably bread and chicken, and the diners were helping themselves, leaning over each other to get at it.[89] These scenes suggest the owner's wealth or at least his comparative ease, and they are reminiscent of the banquet depicted on a mosaic in a wealthy villa at el-Djem (Thysdrus).[90] In North Africa itself, the agape survived through the fourth century, some rural churches—Morsott is an example[91]—producing great quantities of communion vases—fragments of which survive. These suggest communal feastings, perhaps on the anniversary of a local martyr, a custom of which Augustine complained at least at the outset of his clerical career.[92]

Penitential System

Penitential discipline, partly because it was connected with purging ritual faults, and partly because it afforded a significant means of exerting control within a congregation, was also a fiercely contested area between episcopal and nonepiscopal forms of leadership within the church. In the West, where the issue was interwoven with rival ideas concerning the nature of the church, victory went once more to the bishop. In the second century, the confessors were still believed by the writer of the *Acta* of the martyrs of Lyons in 177 to have power to "bind and loose," and they used these powers to restore Christians who had lapsed under intolerable pressure.[93] In Tertullian's time, the penitents prostrated themselves before "those dear to God" (confessors?) as well as before the presbyters (*On Penance* VII). Forty years later, the confessors still made up a formidable group and during the Decian persecution challenged Cyprian for the leadership of the Carthaginian community. They lost, and the main issue was the right to absolve penitents. By the end of 251 Cyprian was telling Pope Cornelius that while laity would be present at the ceremony, confession and penance must be performed before the clergy.[94] They alone had the right to absolve where absolution was possible. The *Didascalia* shows that in Syria the bishop had the same prerogative of "teaching, refuting and loosing by forgiveness."[95]

Congregational control of penance tended to be either too severe or too lax. Before the Decian persecution, argument concentrated on the ability of the church to forgive the three deadly offenses inherited from Judaism—apostasy (idolatry), bloodshed, and adultery. These were distinguished from other crimes such as theft or embezzlement, serious though these might be. How could these dread offenses be absolved? Both at Rome and Carthage opinions were divided. Tertullian's early work (c. 200, *Penance*) agreed with Hermas at Rome, that a "second plank after shipwreck" should be permitted.[96] Even then, penance was a grim enough ordeal. Derived from practices prescribed in the Pentateuch such as Num. 19:7 (the use of ashes of a heifer to purify uncleanliness), and reinforced by references in prophecies concerning the last times, as to fasting, weeping, and rending garments (Joel 2:12), the penitents would be dressed in sackcloth; they would undergo stringent fasts, confess their faults in public, and roll at the feet of the presbyters imploring forgiveness. "Wretched is he who comes thus to exomologesis,"[97] commented Tertullian in a rare moment of sympathy. At heart, however, he contested the value even of this lifeline. Sins against God could only be forgiven by God. Only martyrdom could assure forgiveness of (deadly) sin committed after baptism.[98] Display of remorse might aid the sinner, but the debt incurred by the sin could only be repaid at the judgment. Only then would "satisfaction" be accepted.

The acceptance of this view, however, would have condemned Christianity permanently to the life of a strict brotherhood of the elect. First Callistus and then, grudgingly and ambivalently, the North Africans accepted the right of the church to forgive deadly sins.[99] By the 240s, penitential discipline was becoming as stereotyped as other forms of ecclesiastical administration. Cyprian refers twice to the sequence of penance followed by exomologesis as representing the separate steps the sinner must take towards rehabilitation, "at the hands of the bishop and clergy."[100] The Decian persecution threw this carefully constructed scheme into confusion. There was lapse into apostasy on a massive scale. Confronted with thousands rather than scores of penitents, however, and with Cyprian absent, the Carthaginian confessors handed out "certificates of peace" (*libelli pacis*) wholesale.[101] This was also recognized as an abuse ("no breast is to sigh, no tears to flow"), and in the end Cyprian had no serious difficulty in reasserting the bishop's and, in disputed cases, the episcopal council's control over penitential discipline. Henceforth it would remain in their hands though, as the Great Persecution was to show, the authority of the lay confessors could not be gainsaid in times of crisis.

The East took a less legalistic view of sin and penance. Clement of Alexandria interpreted the commandment against adultery allegorically: "It was leaving the true knowledge found in the Church for vain opinion." Theft was plagiarism, "the imitation of true philosophy."[102] Not surprisingly, we know nothing of the administration of exomologesis in the East, but the tendency was to exclude the sinner from various degrees of participation in the mysteries, rather than to inflict physical punishment upon him. Third-century councils indicate the existence of four classes of penitents. The lowest, known as the Mourners, were allowed only to hear the mass of the catechumens from the porch (atrium?) of the church. Otherwise, they were excluded totally from its ministrations. The Hearers and Kneelers were equated with grades of catechumens. After up to ten years of exclusion, the penitent might gain a place in the ranks of the Co-standers. One could then be present at the eucharistic ceremonies and prayers without participating in the enactment of the mysteries.[103] Punishment consisted in exclusion from the mysteries, and as Dionysius discloses in a description of a longstanding penitent he knew well, who had once submitted to heretical baptism, of consciousness of wrongdoing and bitter remorse.[104]

Celibacy

As yet, however, the ultimate barrier between clergy and laity had still to be established. All through the century a debate was continuing on whether clergy should be celibate or not. The logic of the Levitical tradition, the stubborn legacy of encratism in the church, and the profound distaste for sexual activity as preeminently the work of Satan, favored enforcement of celibacy. Practical and perhaps also pastoral considerations told against it. After all, Paul had instructed Timothy that a bishop was to be the husband of one wife (1 Tim. 3:12). Marriage of another wife after the death of one's spouse (digamy) might be forbidden, but there was no call for the enforcement of celibacy. This seems to have been widely accepted during the third century.[105] Some senior bishops, such as Demetrian of Antioch (251–61) were married with families. Demetrian's son, Domnus, succeeded his father as bishop after the deposition of Paul of Samosata.[106] In Egypt, the Decian persecution saw Bishop Chaeremon of Nilopolis fleeing into the desert with his wife.[107] In the West, Martialis, apostate-bishop of Mérida, had a numerous family whom he evidently brought up as pagans(!), but he is not reproached for his marital state.[108] Nor was the heroic Numidicus, left for dead after being burned and stoned but found by his daughter and revived. Marriage was no bar to his elevation to the presbyterate.[109] Cyprian also refers without comment to Novatus, one of his opponents, except that he grossly abused his wife.[110]

On the other hand, the ascetic tradition was deeply rooted. Virgins were always esteemed ("voluntarily separated and named," as the *Apostolic Tradition* stated [chap. 13]). Widows, similarly, had been registered as an order within the congregation since sub-apostolic times (1 Tim. 5:3–16). In some Eastern churches they exercised the authority of deacons, but in others, by the time the *Didascalia* was compiled, the order was falling into disrepute. Widows were being criticized as "being like wallets, always roaming around the houses of Christians hoping to pick up cash" (*Didascalia* XV). They should stay home and pray. For Origen, women lacked the *imago Dei* ("image of God") possessed by males. They might be admired for their virtues, but they must keep quiet in church; otherwise they could be an occasion for sin (*Commentary on First Corinthians* XIV.34).[111] Origen himself had taken drastic steps to avoid temptation. He was not alone. Some clergy, such as the Roman priest Hyacinthus (c. 185), were specifically described as "eunuchs" (*spado*).[112] Origen, for once on the illiberal side, expressed abhorrence at clergy, the true Levites, enjoying normal family life, but he did not indicate the existence of a rule enforcing celibacy.[113] In the West, Tertullian was similarly outspoken though he was married, and he claimed that many men and women in the "orders of the church" practiced continence.[114]

Only gradually, however, did the arguments in favor of celibacy come to prevail. On the eve of the Great Persecution, there were still family men among the clergy. Saturninus, presbyter of Abitina in the west of proconsular Africa, was accompanied to prison in Carthage by his four children.[115] In Egypt, Bishop Phileas was reminded by his judge of his family responsibilities before he committed himself to martyrdom.[116] Nevertheless, one can see from the (late third century?) tract, *On the Particularity of the Clergy*, that pressures were building up. Women, the writer claimed, were the source of eternal temptation, quoting Genesis and Sir. 42:13 in support. Service to Christ involved leaving parents and observing complete abstinence.[117] The commands of the Lord were beginning to be taken literally. Such was the tradition on which the Council of Elvira was drawing when it forbade clerical marriage,[118] while in the East, Methodius, bishop of Olympus in Lycia (c. 300) glorified the virginal and celibate state as the Christian ideal.[119] But, equally Paphnutius the confessor praised marriage.

THE *SENIORES*

One institution proves the survival of an element of lay control in the churches of the West. The *seniores* or lay elders were believed by some in the late fourth century to be of Jewish origin. Though they are first mentioned in connection with events in Carthage at the time of the death of Bishop Mensurius in 311, it is difficult to imagine them as a recent creation. Their duties were varied and responsible. At Carthage, the *seniores* cooperated with the bishop in administering and safeguarding church property, particularly its movable wealth.[120] In the East this work was already being done by deacons.[121] In other African sees, they seem to have acted as watchdogs over the conduct of the clergy on behalf of the congregation, and they continued to exist and make their presence felt in both the Donatist and catholic churches. In the sixth century they survived as administrative officers in North African monasteries.[122]

The *seniores* are something of an anomaly, for in the third century the drift towards hierarchical government in the church, whether in East or West, was irresistible. At the beginning of the century bishops could be looked upon mainly as the church's disciplinary officers. "Correct thy people" was the angel's command to the bishop whom Perpetua saw in her dream waiting outside the gates of Paradise.[123] In the course of the century this situation changed irreversibly. As fears of persecution waned and the church became established in the empire, so the power of the bishop and clergy increased. The long peace that followed the Valerianic persecution ensured that church government would be in the hands of those who represented administrative and sacramental continuity. Within the urban community, bishop, priest, deacon, and minor orders had already anticipated the organization of the medieval church.

THE PEOPLE

What of the "people of Israel" who provided the background for the great occasions in the church? For Rome the early catacombs provide some answer. That on the Via Latina, whose maximum use seems to span the period 250–350, shows a comparatively rich community, descended from Greek-speaking freedmen, but now thoroughly Romanized and distinctive only by their adherence to Christianity. Their relative wealth contrasts with the obvious poverty of parts of the Jewish community at the same period. The Jewish catacomb in the Villa Torlonia belonged probably to the Siburesians who are mentioned twice on grave-niches (*loculi*). Most of the inscriptions are in Greek with a few in Hebrew and appear to date to the third century. What strikes the visitor, however, is the hundreds of simple tile graves stacked from floor to ceiling on each side of the narrow passages, and the very large proportion of infants and children among them.[124] Poverty and high infant mortality coupled with scrupulous care for the dead, however young, would appear to have been the rule among them.

Rome perhaps was exceptional. Already by the middle of the third century there were ladies of high social standing (*matronae*) and civil servants (*Caesariani*, who often had their own slaves) among the Christians there.[125] The relationship between the Christians and their rivals, however, did not always weigh so heavily in their favor. At Sardis, for instance, the Jews were obviously the more important of the two monotheistic sects throughout the third century, with their enormous and well-supported synagogue implanted in the midst of a commercial area.[126] It is difficult to build up a convincing overall picture of the social level of Christian congregations. Artisans were prominent in Cyprian's congregation at Carthage and some of the confessors "did not know letters."[127] There were some upper-class ladies also,[128] but Cyprian himself seems to have forfeited part of his standing when he became a Christian. He retained respect and support of former friends, but seems to have been rejected by Carthaginian society in general. Behind his back he was called "Dung-head" (*Koprian*) by local wits.[129] The churches in southeastern Spain, for whom the Council of Elvira legislated, included moneylenders and slave owners, people who had clothes to spare to give to those organizing public shows, and women used to relative independence and the management of their own affairs.[130]

Throughout the West, the relative lack of explicit evidence for slaves and freedmen among classes whose occupations were recorded is interesting. In the course of the century, Christianity had ceased necessarily to be associated with the lowest rungs of society.

In the East, the Alexandrian Christians were often wealthy, as shown by Clement's *Rich Man's Salvation*, and they were not necessarily sympathetic to the poor. Origen may have been irritated when he wrote, "Not even the most stupid person would praise the poor indiscriminately; the majority of them have very bad characters."[131] In calmer moments, he was moved by the obvious inequalities of life, the differences between one legal system and another, how some "from the very hour of their birth" were slaves, and how others were born deaf or blind.[132] Even so, the Christian Platonism of Clement and Origen was not a religion for those of simple faith, whose level of education allowed them no alternative. Origen admits it was the Marcionites and followers of Valentinus and Basilides who worried about the nature of God's providence in allowing gross inequalities in this world. Origen himself could give no answer except "the justice of God."[133]

While no statistics whatsoever exist, Christianity would seem to have made most progress among an urban middle class that did not aspire in general to official positions. The money-lenders and wool-workers employed by the government at Cyzicus in the fourth century, who defended Christianity so staunchly in the reign of Julian,[134] probably had their counterparts in the previous century.

ART, LITERATURE, AND ETHICS

Other features of third-century Christianity point toward the same conclusion. If we look now at the art, writing, and ethical code of the Christians, we are left with the impression of a culture that derived its strength from the middle rather than lower orders of Greco-Roman society. It was vigorous and articulate, opposed to the religious and often to the political values of that society. It was no longer the product of a "third race" but of an "alternative society," able and ready to impose its own values on the empire if paganism were to falter. It also harbored contradictions. In its art it showed a tendency to absorb and harmonize with what could be absorbed of pagan culture. Old Testament scenes and non-Christian mythology confront the beholder in adjacent tombs in some Roman catacombs. Christian writing, however, was often intransigent in the extreme, and, if this had been the only survival of third-century Christianity, would have indicated a revolutionary character of the faith. Though the thesis that the Christians especially in the West evolved an arcane language corresponding to their position as a "secret society" remains unproved, many words used by Christians were given a nonclassical meaning, akin to usages current in Dispersion Judaism.[135] But when one examines the church's ethic one finds once more a desire to conform and adapt to the ways of existing society. The ideals of Tertullian and Perpetua had evidently little practical effect among the stolid urban Christians at the end of the century.

Christian Art

The origins of Christian art remain a mystery.[136] Ostensibly, both Judaism and Christianity rejected pictorial art on religious subjects. The second commandment had forbidden Israel to make any graven image, and Christian leaders in East and West alike, including Tertullian, accepted this. Clement and Eusebius, showing rare unanimity, considered this prohibition absolute and binding on Christians.[137] The principal crime of the human race, the highest guilt charged upon the world, the whole procuring cause of judgment, is idolatry,[138] and for once Tertullian commanded almost universal assent. The Syriac *Didascalia* laid down that no offerings were to be received from those who painted with colors, nor from those who made idols or worked in silver and bronze.[139] At the other end of the Mediterranean world, canon 36 of the Council of Elvira stated without qualification that there should be no paintings in church "lest what was painted on the walls should be worshiped and venerated" (*ne quod colitur et adoratur in parietibus depingatur*).

This ban was explicit. There was no satisfactory means of reconciling it with the flowering of Christian art during the third and fourth centuries. It may be that this actually began with the Gnostics. Irenaeus refers to the Carpocratians' inclusion of Christ with Pythagoras, Plato, and Aristotle in their iconography.[140] The frescoes in the Gnostic tombs on the Viale Manzoni suggest that a tradition of painting had become established.[141] The gradual Hellenization of the church through the second century could have contributed to the development of Christian motifs on sarcophagi as well as in funerary painting. Clement of Alexandria had to advise Christians drawn from a wealthy Greek background what was permissible and what was not as images engraved on their seals and jewelery. The themes he chose, such as the dove, fish, ship, and lyre, were selected to remind Christians of "the apostle and the children fished from the water," and were adapted to fit with their previous ideas.[142]

Some Christian motifs, such as the ship, may be derived from Judaism, for in *The Testament of Naphtali* the ship is the symbol of Israel.[143] The anchor appears on the "widow's mite."[144] Other early themes, such as the fish or Good Shepherd, must be Christian in origin.[145] The development of the Jewish and Christian artistic tradition in the first half of the third century exemplified by the paintings on the walls of the synagogue and church at Dura-Europos, respectively, may be seen as a parallel movement in the two monotheistic religions rather than conscious borrowing of one from the other.[146] For both, the frescoes were illustrated Bibles, but though the Christians drew heavily on the Old Testament, their choice and treatment

415

of themes differed from the Jews. The latter told the story of Israel's salvation. They emphasized the role of Moses, portrayed larger than life-size delivering the Israelites from bondage, or Abraham receiving the promise from Yahweh, Dagon the Philistine god lying shattered in his temple, and the resurrection of Israel portrayed by Ezekiel's vision of the revival of the dead in the valley of dry bones (Ezekiel 37).[147] The Christian usage of the Old Testament scenes almost invariably pointed towards the New. Adam and Eve, David slaying Goliath, or the Jonah sequence all had significance in terms of fall and deliverance or triumph over temptation and evil as universal truths. In addition, the Christian at Dura-Europos saw representations of Christ's miracles, his healing of the paralytic, Peter and Christ on the water, and over the baptistery, the Good Shepherd, the woman at the well (cf. John 4:9), and, associated with this, the three women at the tomb, reminders of the links between baptism, sanctification, and the resurrection.[148]

The same ideals, though often with varieties of biblical scene, are found in the catacombs. The art of the Roman catacombs is not a poor person's art, like that of the crude third-century figurines and steles associated often with the worship of the African Saturn. It was the work of individuals, probably lay people, who felt an assurance in the promises of their religion and had the means and skills to depict their beliefs in vigorous and arresting form. It was a beautiful, figurative art illustrating the life of the Christian from conversion to reception into Paradise. In probably the earliest cata-comb (San Callisto), baptism is illustrated as the convert stands naked while a cleric pours the baptismal water over him. We see him at prayer, standing alone in a white tunic, his arms outstretched. The forgiveness of sins is symbolized by the healing of the paralytic taking up his bed and walking. Christ is represented as Teacher and Savior. Representations of the agape and Eucharist show Christ seated with his disciples or at a banquet served with bread and wine.[149]

Old Testament incidents recalling scenes from the period of the Judges and Kings evidently had little place in Christian art.[150] The history of the Jews was valued in terms of its prefiguration of Christian salvation history. The crossing of the Red Sea could be interpreted as the type of the catechu-men's deliverance from the world. The crossing of the Jordan foreshad-owed one's entry into the Promised Land. Messianic expectations are well represented. Balaam, renowned as a seer and prophet of the star that "shall come forth out of Jacob" (Num. 24:17), is portrayed in the catacomb of Peter and Marcellinus; also the ass finds its way blocked by an angel, as in the catacomb on the Via Latina.[151] Jonah resting under his pergola after deliverance from the whale also reflects the idea of rescue from danger and peaceful triumph. Jonah's repose portrays the Christian's refreshment (re-frigerium) in Paradise.[152] Christ himself is represented in terms of youth, as a shepherd and a teacher, sometimes with a scroll in his hand and a sheep

416

across his shoulders (as *moscophorus*) or as Orpheus charming the animals and leading them to the peaceful enjoyment of Paradise.[153] In contrast, neither the crucifixion nor the judgment are portrayed. However vividly that day had impressed itself on the mind of the believer, in death one wished only to be reminded of the reality and joys of the resurrection. The raising of Lazarus represented his unity with the Lord. The idyllic pastoral scenes, the birds, garlands, browsing sheep, fish, and parklands, depicted a serene world beyond where cares were unknown.[154] "Go and play," the command of the elders to Saturus and Perpetua in Saturus's vision, illustrates these hopes. So, too, does Perpetua's reply, "Thanks be to God, I am happier here than I was in the flesh."[155]

There was assurance also of deliverance from the powers of the present world. Daniel in the lion's den, and the Three Holy Children in the fiery furnace preserved in painting and in text show that Christianity still rejected and defied the world. These were prefigurations of Christian steadfastness, while Nebuchadnezzar was regarded as a fitting type for secular rulers. In a prayer of the last half of the third century, there is the same sequence, praying for deliverance of the soul as Daniel was delivered from the lion's den, the youths from the fiery furnace, and Susanna from false accusations.[156] "The enemies of the Church," namely Jews and pagans, remained. The voice of protest was not completely silent.

Christian Literature

It was more in evidence in Christian literature of the third century. This was a period of great creative activity, uninhibited by constraints due to Christianity being the religion of the empire. Letters, apologetic tracts against pagans and Jews, commentaries on Scripture, sermons, homilies, exhortations, and epic tales of the courage of Christian confessors all find their place in the works of Christian authors of the time. One result of the severe but intermittent persecutions was the creation of the popular literature of "the Acts of the Martyrs." In the midst of the advance of hierarchies towards an ever-increasing measure of control of the church, the folk heroes remained the "plebs and catechumens" who had defied the imperial authorities.[157] And while hopes of an immediate Parousia faded, few Christians doubted that the life of the present world would end comparatively shortly, or that persecution itself heralded the approach of antichrist and the onset of the last times. What eventually became Christian historiography began with speculations on the meaning of the prophecies in the book of Daniel. The first Christian chronographer, Judas (c. 200), linked his record of events to the framework of Daniel's prophecy of the seventy weeks allowed for the reconciliation of God's people (Dan. 9:24), and ended it in 202, a year of persecution "when there was much talk of the coming of Antichrist."[158] Third-century Christian historiography was an extension of apocalyptic, universal in scope and periodized to fit preconceived ideas of the destiny of the world.[159] And the Christian's view of the latter left no scope for the eternity of Rome.

Judas's younger contemporary, Hippolytus, also drew his inspiration from the book of Daniel, but his message was more political in content. The vision of the four beasts representing the four godless empires that had dominated humanity (Daniel 7) was applied to his own day. The first three beasts—interpreted as the Babylonian, Persian, and Macedonian empires—had grown out of single kingdoms, and, horrible though they were, were more tolerable than Rome. The Romans had prospered at the expense of other peoples whom they held in subjection with feet of iron. Yet like Nebuchadnezzar's statue that empire had its weaknesses. The "toes," claimed Hippolytus, "are meant to represent the democracies that are to come, and which will separate from each other, like the ten fingers of the statue in which iron will be mingled with clay."[160] The empire would fall and be replaced by "the [liberated] peoples." Hippolytus, therefore, despite some aristocratic connections, represented an astonishingly radical outlook among the Roman Christians. With him begins the tradition in the West of associating Rome with Babylon in contrast to the heavenly city, Jerusalem.

His was not an isolated voice. Tertullian and Minucius Felix, as we have seen,[161] were both strongly critical of the Roman Empire. Tertullian regarded the Romans simply as another foreign people like the Phrygians.[162] Cyprian denied that the world (and by implication, the empire) was in any sense eternal.[163] Augustine, like Hippolytus, was to state his preference for small kingdoms as against great empires.[164] Finally, whether one places the poet Commodian in the late third or early fifth century, his writing reflects the underlying hostility of many Western Christians towards the political and social institutions under which they lived. For Commodian, persecutions would be avenged by Rome's fall. "She was rejoicing, but the whole world was groaning. Soon will come worthy retribution. She who boasted herself eternal would mourn eternally." The Goths preferred the Christians to the pagans and treated them as brothers.[165] The rich, too, would be punished. In the millennium roles would be reversed. The great of this world would serve the saints.[166] The church also would not be justified by its numbers but by the few who persevered to the end.[167] Despite all obscurities surrounding Commodian, here was an authentic voice of Western Christendom. The various strands of hostility to the empire and to the riches and estates of the great, the glorification of martyrdom, and welcome to the barbarians were to find their exponents in the outraged protests against the times by the Donatist martyrologists in the fourth century, and by Salvian of Marseilles, and even by Augustine, and Paulus Orosius in the fifth.

In the East, while the Jewish tradition of chronological writing was accepted, and with it rejection of any authority claimed by pagan philosophers, there was not the same intensity of anger and frustration. Origen's friend, Julius Africanus (c. 240), seems to have written his *Chronicles* in much the same spirit as Origen himself compiled the *Hexapla*. He wanted to prove the antiquity of the history of the Hebrews, from whom the Christians claimed descent, and the truth of the prophecies concerning Christ as Savior found in the Old Testament.[168] The Old Testament was demonstrably more accurate than pagan histories and antedated them. Africanus's was basically a work of apologetic in the tradition of Theophilus of Antioch. Its register of events in the histories of the Jews, Parthians, Greeks, Macedonians, and Romans, however, served the more expert chroniclers of the next century. For his part, Origen, critic of the empire's anti-Christian measures though he was, accepted that the empire had received divine sanction through Christ's birth in the reign of Augustus.[169] That it could be compared to the tyrannies of the Babylonians and Medes did not enter his reckoning. Dionysius of Alexandria's correspondence shows complete loyalty to the empire and its legitimate sovereign (Eusebius *HE* VII.23.3). His praise of Gallienus (260–68) foreshadows the even-stronger praise of Constantine by Eusebius and prepares the way for the integration of the church in the East with the Constantinian state.

Christian Ethics

The revolutionary edge of Christian writing during the third century was never translated into practice. However much their propagandists despised the pagans as "nations" outside God's community, the great majority of Christians, whether orthodox or sectarian, conformed to society. The reversal of fortunes would take place after the world had come to its appointed end (Africanus calculated this event as about 250 years into the future). Persecutions meantime were to be expected as events that preceded salvation.[170] In addition, Christian morality tended to be individual, and concerned with avoiding sin rather than attempting a collective reform of society. Public life was to be shunned.[171] Only Clement of Alexandria took an opposite viewpoint.[172] Church councils of the period spent an enormous amount of time castigating sexual misdemeanors and defining degrees of idolatry.[173] At Elvira lapse of a penitent guilty of adultery was accounted more heinous than the murder of a slave.[174]

Slavery and war, however, were two issues which no one living in the third century could avoid, and Christianity might be expected to have pointed the way toward changed attitudes.[175] But no; Christians in both East and West accepted slavery. The Christian mission was indeed directed toward slaves, and with their masters' consent they could be baptized. There is one instance in Asia of a runaway Christian slave being aided by Christians, but the asides dropped by writers show that the institution with its cruelty and repression was accepted.[176] Thus, Methodius of Olympus (c. 311) compares the sea to a slave obeying his master "unwillingly and with angry mutterings."[177] Throughout the century, one hears of Christian households where the treadmill, prison, and scourges remained the rule.[178] Slaves who sought freedom were regarded as "wicked," "most worthy of stripes and chains and prison and cross and every evil," though apostates, Lactantius affirmed also, deserved worse.[179] Slavery and the sale of slaves was accepted as part of society. The relative cheapness in which the life of a slave was held is shown by the canons of the Council of Elvira, especially canon 5, which laid down that a mistress who beat her slave to death in a fit of rage should undergo seven years penance if death was premeditated, but only five years if not—the same as the first offense of adultery.[180]

Attitudes to war were more complicated. In the West, they were connected with the same requirement to avoid bloodshed which forbade Christians to undertake magistracies, on the assumption that a magistrate's duties would almost always involve bloodshed.[181] No one raised the point that a Christian magistrate might contribute by a sense of justice and mercy to the well-being of his fellow citizens. Similar inability to think out any positive evaluation of the soldier's role in a Christian state resulted in inconsistent and impractical notions. Cyprian and Lactantius condemned wars as crimes and calamities, but Cyprian's true conservatism in outlook comes out in his praise of generals "who maintain the standards entrusted to them,"[182] while Lactantius eulogized Constantine for his "diligence in military matters" as well as for his moral uprightness.[183] Attitudes were influenced, too, by a tendency toward simplistic naturalism which maintained that nothing should be used for purposes other than those originally intended by God. Isaiah and Micah had prophesied that nations would turn their swords and spears into plowshares and sickles.[184] Therefore, Cyprian argued, God wished iron to be used for the cultivation of the earth and not to commit acts of homicide. A generation before, Tertullian had warned his readers that if God had meant them to wear highly colored garments, he would have provided sheep with bright blue or scarlet wool![185]

The attitude, however, of the Western leaders was not consistent. They were too imbued with the Maccabean tradition, and their idea that Christian service was itself like warfare (*militia*) with its oath of duty (*sacramentum*), stations, and camp to adopt pacifism. Personally they were often individuals of combative and uncompromising temperament. It was not perhaps an accident that the family of the confessor Celerinus included members who had both served in the legions and been martyred for their faith.[186]

The East also exhibited confusion of thought. Here there was no condemnation of war on the basis of Christian law, but typically one finds Clement of Alexandria condemning it as contrary to the Christian spirit.[187] While Origen saw no place for Christians in the imperial armies, he was prepared for Christians to pray for these,[188] and he was by no means opposed to violence. A would-be martyr, he accepted the necessity for tyrannicide, approving Judith's murder of Holofernes.[189] Important in the development of a theory of the right use of force was his justification of Augustus's enforced pacification of the Mediterranean world, for only in a world united under the Roman Empire could Christianity spread.[190] This view prevailed. The Constantinian monarchy accepted Origen's theories. The antimilitarism of the West gradually faded. The Council of Arles (314) excommunicated soldiers who threw away their arms (in time of peace?).[191] In the fourth century, East and West alike accepted the theory of a just war when confronted with the fact of barbarian invasions of the Christian empire.

The more active virtues practiced by Christians also delved back into the heritage of a late Jewish past. Visiting the sick and captives, securing a decent burial for the dead, care of orphans, love for the brethren, and frequent giving of alms were all included in the Pharisee's as well as the Christian's search for righteousness. The difference in Christianity was that these virtues were now practiced on a worldwide stage by individuals drawn from every level of society and highly organized as church. They were, however, sometimes carried out in a legalistic manner with an eye toward banking personal merit for the Christian hereafter. "Let us give to Christ our earthly garments, so that we may receive a heavenly raiment," urged Cyprian in support of alsmgiving.[192] For him, too, Tobit "always at prayer or work, and an upright father" was the model of Christian conduct.[193] (Jesus' example in his Nazareth home is not mentioned.) Almsgiving, prayer, and fastings purged sin and opened the way to Paradise.[194] Martyrdom even was no longer necessary.[195]

Christians in the "long peace" that preceded the Great Persecution were carrying on daily occupations in trade and commerce like other provincials, but they were nonconformists, and when the final crisis came in 303, they were unpopular more on account of what they failed to do than for what they did. The empire, however, had nothing to fear from the social teaching prevalent among the urban churches. Any threat to its equilibrium would come from elsewhere.

RURAL CHRISTIANITY AND THE FIRST MONKS

Christianity had been slow to make an impact on the rural populations of the empire. When it began to do so, however, it was the literal message of the New Testament that appealed, combined with hopes for the reversal of fortunes between rich and poor that apocalyptic literature sustained. The period of the Decian persecution marked a watershed in Christianity's progress into the countryside. Dionysius of Alexandria's letters show that in Egypt, while Christians risked being "torn to pieces by the heathen" in town and village alike,[196] there were now native Egyptians among the faithful; and he mentions six Egyptians and a Libyan among the martyrs of that

421

time.[197] In the 260s there were "presbyters and teachers" in villages in the Arsinoite nome,[198] and from the life of Antony of Egypt (251–356) we know that some villages in Upper Egypt possessed churches and even convents (*parthenaia*).

Phrygia

The most articulate rural Christian communities, however, were to be found in Phrygia. Montanism had survived all the pressure that orthodoxy could exert against it, and from 250 onward the puritanical strain in Phrygian Christianity was being reinforced by Novatianism, which was destined to retain a hold there for centuries to come. While Montanism was by no means extinct among urban communities,[199] it had advanced spectacularly in some of the remoter parts of the province. On an imperial estate in the Tembris valley in the northern part of the province, the cultivators proclaimed their faith openly as "Christians for Christians." These inscriptions date from 248/49 to 313. They belonged to relatively prosperous farming communities, literate in Greek, and capable of producing large, finely decorated inscriptions. These depict many aspects of their daily life, the plow, sickle, and large weaving comb, spindle, and distaff. One records a bequest of plots of land, a tool chest, a sheep, and thirty measures of barley.[200] They are, however, explicitly Christian. One refers to baptism and perhaps to confirmation. It praises the deceased as "hospitable to strangers," just and compassionate. Another commemorates a neophyte, and a third elaborate monument describes its owner as a "great and illustrious soldier," terminology reminiscent of Tertullian or the *Acta Martyrum*.[201] For these Christians also, religion was a *militia*, allegiance to which was to be proclaimed. "We are also soldiers," Tertullian had stated, "our discipline being firmer in such degree [as befits] so great an Emperor."[202] In the 240s, Christianity in rural Phrygia was developing a similar spirit, and as we have seen earlier on, Gregory the Wonderworker reveals that among the Christians of the Black Sea province of Pontus the arrival of barbarian raiders in 254 and 255 was a signal for revolutionary actions aimed against established society. Perhaps apocalyptic expectations had been referred to the immediate situation. The North African Circumcellions were to do just this a century later.

Egypt

It was in Egypt, however, that the aftermath of the Decian and Valerianic persecutions had the most startling results. Persecution on the one hand and economic stress on the other were forcing individuals to abandon settled communities for a precarious livelihood in the desert, "Shall I flee?" "When shall my flight end?" "Am I to become a beggar?" were questions put to an oracle by despairing peasant-farmers in this period.[203]

Some Christians who had fled into the desert during the persecutions stayed there, providing examples of ascetic life which others might follow. In c. 270 Antony, a young Egyptian Christian farmer, had just inherited a considerable holding from his parents. One Sunday he was at a service in his village church in the nome of Heracleopolis. The lesson he heard read was from Matthew 19 and contained the Lord's command to the rich young man, "Go, sell what you possess and give to the poor, and you will have treasure in heaven; and come, follow me" (Matt. 19:21). There was no allegorical interpretation for Antony. He acted at once. He placed his sister in a convent (*parthenaion*) and left his home to establish himself as a solitary on the edge of the village where the desert would come to the very edge of the cultivated land.[204] There he remained until fifteen years later when he forsook the sparse company even of the local hermits for the Arabian mountain on the east side of the Nile. There, at Pispir, he remained in an abandoned fort until the outbreak of the Great Persecution in 303.

Antony's motives were partly religious, to live entirely by literal obedience to Scripture, but there was also a social motive. "Why do the rich grind the faces of the poor?"[205] he is alleged by Athanasius to have asked. Hard work for his own subsistence needs was his practice. He himself had been a failure in early life and had little use for the ways of secular society. His settlement of ascetics in the mountains became a refuge for those fleeing from extortions of tax collectors, whose "grumbles" he records.[206] This social motive was combined with an ascetic tradition that reached back to the dawn of Christianity, to John the Baptist, and to Jesus' example of seeking out a solitary place for prayer in the mountains or wilderness. Almost for the first time in three centuries the Lord's commands were being accepted literally by Christ's followers.

Syria

A similar movement, even more individualistic in character, was beginning in parts of Syria. Jerome probably correctly believed the origins of Syrian monasticism extended back to the mid–third century, and from then on Syrian and Egyptian monasticism were destined to run on parallel courses. Some links seem to have existed between the two areas by way of desert routes. We have already noticed that the ascetic-inspired *Gospel of Thomas*, while originating probably in Edessa, found its way to sites in the Nile Valley.[207] Similarly, by 270 missionaries preaching the equally ascetic gospel of Mani were arriving in Egypt via Syria. Syriac Manichean fragments have been found alongside the Coptic Mani documents.[208] For once the dominant Greek cultural influences were being bypassed, for the ascetic movement in the Syrian and Egyptian countrysides owes little or nothing to them. Antony suspected all philosophy as heretical, and he spoke to Greeks through an interpreter.[209] Only in the second half of the fourth century do the ascetic ideals of Clement and Origen contribute to

Egyptian monasticism, while in Syria the movement remained strongly anti-Hellenistic.

In Syria the association between asceticism and Christianity was long-standing. It was not accidental that the Marcionites continued to be influential throughout the third century, and even when orthodoxy eventually triumphed, baptism involved sexual abstinence by the baptized Christian. The "spiritual sisters" (*subintroductae*) of Antioch that aroused the ire of Eusebius[210] were also symbols of ascetism paralleled by the spiritual virgins in Hermas,[211] with whom one slept "like sisters." The institution reached far back into Jewish-Christianity as a reminder of the sexless life that was required of those who would dedicate themselves wholly to God's service.[212]

North Africa

Far to the west, Roman North Africa was becoming a third area where Christianity was spreading beyond the city boundaries. One notices in Numidia in particular the existence of some up-country bishoprics represented at Cyprian's council in 256 that were to feature in the Donatist schism in the next century. Octava, for instance, was to be a center for Circumcellions in the 340s.[213] In its own way the religion of this new generation of rural Christians was to be as much inspired by the literal word of the Bible as that of Antony, but it was to associate this with an apocalyptic which regarded the world and its rulers as representatives of Satan. Cyprian's martyrdom was more appreciated than his "moderation" and "works and merits."

The full significance of these developments within Christianity could hardly have been recognized at the time. When Diocletian seized power in 284, the church was still overwhelmingly an urban institution. Only when after nearly twenty years of rule, Diocletian and his colleagues tried to wring religious conformity as well as conformity in other fields from his subjects, did the strength of the nonurban Christians in North Africa and Egypt become apparent. Their reaction to the Great Persecution confronted both church and empire with the gravest of crises.

BIBLIOGRAPHY

NOTE

This chapter falls into two distinct halves, the first being devoted to the church's organization and the second to its cultural life. For development of the hierarchy in the third century, W. Telfer's *The Office of a Bishop* (London: Darton, Longman & Todd, 1962), chap. 7 onwards, is an excellent introduction; and specifically for Rome, see T. G. Jalland, *The Church and the Papacy: A Historical Study* (New York: Morehouse-Gorham; London: SPCK, 1944), pp. 124–80. On the evolution of the liturgy, Dom Gregory Dix's classic *The Shape of the Liturgy* (London: Dacre Press, 1945), may be supplemented by Hans Lietzmann's chapter 15, part 2, "The Christian Church in the West," in *Cambridge Ancient History*, vol. 12, *The Imperial Crisis and Recovery*, A.D. 193–324, 2d ed. (New York: Macmillan Co.; Cambridge: At the University Press, 1939). For exegesis, especially Origen's, see R. P. C. Hanson, *Allegory and Event: A Study of the Sources and Significance of Origen's Interpretation of Scripture* (Richmond: Board of Christian Education Presbyterian Church in the United States; London: SCM Press, 1959), part 5.

On the church's cultural life in the third century, the most important work is the Acts of the Ninth International Congress of Christian Archaeology (*ACIAC*; Rome: Pontifical Institute of Christian Archaeology, 1978), and devoted to pre-Constantinian Christian archaeology. It may be difficult of access, however, and students will find J. Stevenson's *The Catacombs: Rediscovered Monuments of Early Christianity* (London: Thames & Hudson, 1978) a good scholarly introduction to the catacombs in Rome and elsewhere. The Christian attitude to social problems has been documented by C. J. Cadoux's monumental *The Early Church and the World: A History of the Christian Attitude to Pagan Society and the State Down to the Time of Constantinus* (New York: Charles Scribner's Sons, 1925), and very readably in R. M. Grant, *Early Christianity and Society* (New York: Harper & Row, 1977), and also in part 5 of *Augustus to Constantine* by the same author, to whom I am much indebted.

SOURCES

Didascalia apostolorum. Edited and Eng. trans. by R. H. Connolly. New York and London: Oxford University Press, 1929.
Gesta apud Zenophilum. In Optatus of Milevis, *De Schismate Donatistarum*, ed. C. Ziwsa. Appendix I, pp. 185–96. CSEL 26. Leipzig: G. Freytag, 1893.
Hippolytus. *Church Order*. In R. H. Connolly, *The So-Called Egyptian Church Order and Derived Documents*, Texts and Studies: Contributions to Biblical and Patristic Literature, ed. J. A. Robinson, vol. 8, no. 4. New York: Macmillan Co., 1916.
——. *Treatise on the Apostolic Tradition of St. Hippolytus of Rome, Bishop and Martyr*. Edited and Eng. trans. by G. Dix. New York: Macmillan Co.; London: SPCK, 1937; 2d ed., 1968.
Lactantius. *De Mortibus Persecutorum (On the Deaths of the Persecutors)*. Edited by J. Moreau. 2 vols. SC 39. Paris, 1954.
——. *Divinae institutiones (Divine Institutes)*. Edited by S. Brandt and G. Laubmann. CSEL 19. Vienna, 1890.

SECONDARY WORKS

Brandenburg, H. "Überlegungen zum Ursprung der frühchristlichen Bildkunst." *ACIAC* IX (Rome, 1978). 2 vols. Vol. I:330–60.
Breckenridge, J. D. "The Reception of Art in the Early Church." *ACIAC* IX (Rome, 1978). 2 vols. Vol. I:361–69.
Brisson, J. P. *Autonomisme et Christianisme dans l'Afrique romaine de Septime Sévère à l'invasion vandale*. Paris: Boccard, 1958. Concerning Commodian.
Bruyne, L. de. "La peinture cemetériale constantinienne." *ACIAC* VII (Rome, 1969): 159–214.

Calder, W. M. "Leaves from an Anatolian Notebook." *BJRL* 13 (1929): 254–71.

_____. "Philadelphia and Montanism." *BJRL* 7 (1923): 309–54.

Caron, M. "Les *Seniores Laici* de l'Église africaine." *RIDA* 6 (1951): 7–22.

Deissmann, A. *Light from the Ancient East: The New Testament Illustrated by Recently Discovered Texts of the Graeco-Roman World.* Rev. ed., Eng. trans. L. R. M. Strachan. Garden City, N.Y.: Doubleday, Doran & Co.; London: Hodder & Stoughton, 1927.

Duval, N. "Les Edifices de Culte des origines à l'époque constantinienne." *ACIAC* IX (Rome, 1978). 2 vols. Vol. I:513–37.

Ehrhardt, A. A. T. *Politische Metaphysik von Solon bis Augustin.* Vol. 2. Tübingen: J. C. B. Mohr (Paul Siebeck), 1959–69.

_____. "Quäker Latein," *Existenz und Ordnung (Festschrift Erik Wolff)*, pp. 111–16. Frankfurt, 1962.

Frend, W. H. C. "The *Memoriae Apostolorum* in Roman North Africa." *JRS* 30 (1940): 32–49.

_____. "The Roman Empire in Eastern and Western Historiography." *Proceedings of the Cambridge Philological Society* 194 (1968): 19–32.

_____. "The 'Seniores Laici' and the Origins of the Church in North Africa." *JTS* n.s. 12 (October 1961): 280–84.

Gibson, E. "The 'Christians for Christians' Inscriptions of Phrygia." *HTS* 32 (1978): 116–19. Useful bibliography; overcautious regarding Montanism.

Gryson, R. *Les origines du célibat ecclésiastique.* Gembloux: Duculot, 1970.

Hanson, R. P. C. *Christian Priesthood Examined.* London: Lutterworth, 1978.

Hinchcliff, P. B. "Church and Society Before Nicea." *CQR* 165 (Jan.–Mar. 1964): 39–51.

Kraeling, C. H. "The Christian Building." *The Excavations at Dura-Europos: Final Report* VIII.2. New Haven, Conn.: Yale University Press, 1967.

_____. "The Synagogue," *Excavations at Dura: Final Report* VIII.1. New Haven, Conn.: Yale University Press, 1956; 2d ed., New York: Ktav Publishing, 1979.

McArthur, A. A. "The Office of Bishop in the Ignatian Epistles and in the *Didascalia Apostolorum* Compared." *SP* 4, TU 79 (1961): 298–304.

Marschall, Werner. *Karthago und Rom.* Päpste und Papstum, vol. 1. Stuttgart: Hiersemann, 1971. Chaps. 1 and 2.

Murray, C. "Art and the Early Church." *JTS* n.s. 28 (October 1977): 303–45.

Ramsay, W. M. *Cities and Bishoprics of Phrygia.* New York: Oxford University Press, 1901.

Turner, H. E. W. *The Pattern of Christian Truth: A Study in the Relations Between Orthodoxy and Heresy in the Early Church.* London: A. R. Mowbray, 1954.

Williams, G. H. "The Ancient Church, A.D. 30–313." In *The Layman in Christian History,* ed. S. C. Neill and H.-R. Weber, chap. 1, pp. 28–56. Philadelphia: Westminster Press; London: SCM Press, 1963.

NOTES

1. Lactantius, *Deaths of Persecutors*, ed. Moreau, XII.3.
2. Eusebius *HE* VII.3.2–17. See above, p. 387.
3. Ibid., 30.2.
4. *Sententiae episcoporum de haereticis baptizandis (Opinions of the Bishops*

Concerning the Baptizing of Heretics), ed. W. Hartel, CSEL 3.1, pp. 435–61 (Vienna, 1868), p. 435; cf. H. von Soden (ed.), in *Nachrichten der Kgl. Gesellschaft der Wissenschaften zu Göttingen* (1909), pp. 247–307, esp. pp. 247–48.

5. Eng. trans. by J. E. L. Oulton in *Alexandrian Christianity*, ed. Oulton and Chadwick, pp. 180–387, esp. p. 310.

6. On the development of the creeds from these two roots, see J. N. D. Kelly, *Early Christian Creeds* (New York and London: Longmans, Green & Co., 1950), pp. 94–99.

7. Origen *De principiis* (*On First Principles*) preface 4–8.

8. *Dialogue with Heracleides*, trans. Chadwick, in *Alexandrian Christianity*, ed. Oulton and Chadwick, p. 437.

9. Text in J. D. Mansi, *Sacrorum Conciliorum Collectio nova et amplissima* (Florence, 1759), I, 1033ff. See above, p. 386, and compare Kelly, *Early Christian Creeds*, p. 207.

10. Canons 6 and 7.

11. Not a completely justified conclusion, since in the same letter Jerusalem precedes Caesarea, but Caesarea remained the senior see. Nicaea (canon 7) attempted a compromise between their rival claims.

12. Above, p. 352.

13. Cyprian *Letter* LII.2.

14. Ibid., 73.4, "Quae ista obstinatio est quaeve praesumptio humanam traditionem divinae dispositioni anteponere. . . ."

15. See Tertullian *De pudicitia* (*On Modesty*) XXI ("pillars of discipline"); and my "*Memoriae Apostolorum*."

16. Firmilian (in Cyprian *Letter* LXXV, especially para. 16), "Qualis vero error sit et quanta caecitas eius."

17. Origen, *Commentary on Matthew* XII.10, ed. E. Klostermann, GCS 40, Origen (Leipzig: Hinrichs, 1935), pp. 85–86, and similarly, idem, *Jeremiah*, p. 134). All imitators of Christ were "rocks." See Hanson, *Allegory and Event*, p. 330.

18. Origen, *Matthew* XII.14 (ed. Klostermann, pp. 96–100). Apparently Bishop Demetrius of Alexandria tried to justify his authority on the basis of this text. Origen is skeptical (ibid., pp. 98–99).

19. See R. Y. Ebied and L. R. Wickham, "A Collection of Unpublished Syriac Letters of Timothy Aelurus," *JTS* n.s. 21 (October 1970): 321–69, esp. p. 351. Severus of Antioch also takes Matt. 16:18 to mean "the Church that is founded on the true faith," *The Sixth Book of the Select Letters of Severus Patriarch of Antioch in the Syriac Version of Athanasius of Nisibis*, ed. and Eng. trans. E. W. Brooks (2 vols., London: Williams & Norgate, 1902–3), p. 295.

20. Eusebius *HE* VII.19.

21. *Liber Pontificalis*, ed. T. Mommsen, *MGH*, Gesta Pontificum Romanorum (Berlin, 1898), vol. 1, p. 27 (ed. L. Duchesne, 2 vols. [Paris: Bibliothèque des Écoles Françaises d'Athènes et de Rome, 1886–92], vol. 1, p. 148).

22. Ibid., ed. Mommsen, p. 36 (ed. Duchesne, vol. 1, p. 157), and see L. Duchesne's "Notes sur la topographie de Rome au Moyen-Age" II (Les listes presbytéraux et les diaconies), *MEFR* 7 (1887), pp. 218–43.

23. See the useful brief summary of the Roman catacombs of known pre-Constantinian date in A. Ferrua, "L'epigraphia cristiana prima di Constantino," *ACIAC* IX (Rome, 1978), I:583–613.

24. Optatus, *De Schismate Donatistarum*, ed. Ziwsa, II.4. Pope Felix (269–74) is credited with building a church on the Via Aurelia (*Liber Pontificalis*, ed. Mommsen, p. 37).

25. *Liber Pontificalis*, ed. Duchesne, vol. 1, p. 182. The estate belonged at one time to a certain Ciriaca, described as a "femina religiosa," which had been seized by the authorities during the persecution.

26. Eusebius *HE* VI.43.2.

27. *Liber Pontificalis*, ed. Mommsen, p. 36. Felix also consecrated five bishops "per diversa loca."

28. Letter of the bishops to Miltiades in Optatus, *De Schismate Donatistarum*, ed. Ziwsa, Appendix IV, pp. 206–8, "gloriosissime papa" and pherhaps more to the point, "te qui maiores dioceses tenes." What was the precise significance of this?

29. See Deissmann, *Light from Ancient East*, pp. 192–201. Maximus and an unnamed lector act as the link between Christian corn merchants in the Fayum and Roman merchants, and they expect their profit from these transactions.

30. *Pap. Oxy.* 2332 (third century); and see C. H. Roberts's and E. Lobel's commentary, pp. 89–94: "These prophetic texts may convey the feelings of the humbler Greek-speaking population, who were no longer conscious of any common bond with the Greek upper class, let alone with their Roman governors, in spite of the *Constitutio Antoniniana*" (p. 94).

31. Eusebius *HE* VII.11.15–16.

32. See C. Andresen, "Der Erlass des Gallienus an der Bischöfe Aegyptens (Eusebius *HE* VII.13)," *SP* 12 (1975): 115 (1973): 385–98, and above, p. 388.

33. Eusebius *HE* VII.20–21.

34. Ibid., VII.30.3.

35. See below, p. 497.

36. Jerusalem's prestige was undoubtedly enhanced during the distinguished episcopate of Alexander (d. 251); see Eusebius *HE* VI.11 and 46.4; but it was still "Aelia" and dependent on the civil capital of the province, Caesarea (see above, n. 11). It is noticeable that Jerusalem and Antioch thought differently over the date of Easter at the time of Nicaea.

37. Cyprian *Letter* 48.3 (ed. Hartel, p. 607).

38. See my *The Donatist Church: A Movement of Protest in Roman North Africa* (Oxford: At the Clarendon Press, 1971), pp. 12 and 102 n. 4.

39. *Letter* LV.8; and compare X.8 and LXVII.4. For the same requirements in the East, see Origen, *Homily on Leviticus*, ed. W. A. Baehrens, GCS 29, Origen (Leipzig: Hinrichs, 1920), III.2 (the presence of laity was essential in episcopal elections).

40. Cyprian *Letter* XLV.3, and note the same view expressed in 256 by the relatively obscure Bishop Clarus of Mascula in Numidia, "quibus (apostolis) nos successimus eadem potestate ecclesiam Domini gubernantes et credentium fidem baptizantes" (ed. Hartel, p. 459).

41. Pontius, *Vita Cypriani* XVI, ed. W. Hartel, CSEL 3.3, pp. xc–cx (Vienna, 1898), p. cviii. The white cushion is associated with episcopal honor. A century before, Hermas (*Visiones* [*Visions*] I.2.2) refers to the chair of "holy Church" as "white cushioned with wool," corresponding to the white covering of the cushions on the presbyteral bench. See Telfer, *Office of Bishop*, p. 203.

42. Eusebius *HE* VII.30.9: Paul seated "on a tribunal and lofty throne."

43. See Duval, "Les Edifices de Culte." Duval remarks on the scantiness of liturgical material in Theodorus's church.

44. Church buildings in the 240s, apart from Dura, see Origen, *In Jesus Nave Hom.* II.1, ed. E. Klostermann, GCS 38, Origen (Leipzig: Hinrichs, 1921), p. 296, and *Sermo 39 on Matthew XXIV.9* (ed. E. Klostermann, GCS 38, Origen [Leipzig: Hinrichs, 1933], p. 75).

45. *Apology* XXXIX.6, "egenis alendis humandisque et pueris ac puellis re ac parentibus destitutis. . . ."

46. *Gesta apud Zenophilum*, p. 187, "82 women's dresses, 47 pairs of women's shoes."

47. Eusebius *HE* VI.43.11.

48. *Letter* VII.

49. Ibid., LXII.4.

50. Ibid., LII.1. For a Phrygian Jewish community maintaining an orphanage in Hierapolis, see Ramsay, *Cities and Bishoprics*, Insc. 412. The reference to "unleavened bread" and "pentecost" suggests Judaism rather than Christianity.

51. *Letter* I, analyzed by Telfer, *Office of Bishop*, pp. 173–74.

52. *Didascalia*, ed. Connolly, chap. 8, pp. 78ff. (also references to the "revenues of the Church" from which the bishop must live).

53. Cyprian *Letter* XXXIX.5. At Rome, Callistus seems to have been paid monthly as deacon (Hippolytus *Refutation* IX.12.13). Origen, *Homily on Numbers* 11:2, ed. W. A. Baehrens, GCS 30, Origen [Leipzig: Hinrichs, 1921], pp. 78–79) also refers to payments to the clergy through tithes. See Grant, *Early Christianity*, pp. 137–38.

54. Eusebius *HE* V.28.10. Montanist preachers were also paid a salary from offerings; Apollonius in Eusebius *HE* V.18.2.

55. *Matthew* XVI.8 (ed. Klostermann, p. 494), a very strong attack on episcopal arrogance and injustice.

56. Eusebius *HE* VII.30.6.

57. *Letter* XXXIV.4.

58. Ibid., III.

59. Ibid., II.

60. *Letter* IV. Because their crime was against Christ, whose bride the virgin was. How cohabitation between deacons and virgins was even connived at is not clear. Were the virgins in this case a North African version of the *subintroductae* who attended Paul of Samosata? See below, nn. 210, 211.

61. For the Syrian bishop judging cases between Christians, see *Didascalia*, ed. Connolly, pp. 110–17.

62. Compare Cyprian *Letters* VIII, IX, XXIX, and XXXIX. *Letter* XXIX shows clearly that lectors were not part of the clergy and would have to be promoted into it (ed. Hartel, p. 548).

63. Eusebius *HE* VI.43.1. Pope Gaius (284–96) is recorded (*Liber Pontificalis*, ed. Mommsen, p. 39) to have laid down that a bishop should have passed through all clerical orders from doorkeeper to presbyter before consecration as bishop.

64. With the extension of catacombs, the "diggers" (*fossores*) became a close organization, proud of their membership, who not only dug but also sold spaces to applicants. See *ILCV* 2126, 2128, 3782, 3811–13, Stevenson, *Catacombs*, pp. 20–23, and de Bruyne, "La peinture," vol. 2, fig. 149.

65. For lectors, see H. Leclercq, "Lector" in *DACL* 8.2, cols. 2241–69, and

Frend, "The Church in Carthage" (Michigan University Excavation III, Ann Arbor: ASOR, 1977), pp. 27 and 29 (references). They acted not only as readers but as servers at the altar and existed in the North African church at least from A.D. 200 (see Tertullian *De praescriptione Haereticorum* [*On Prescription Against Heretics*] XLI).

66. For example, Cyprian *Letters* LXIX.15, and LXXV.10 (combating inconvenient spirit-manifestations in Pontus and Cappadocia during the persecution of 235–36).

67. Ibid., XLV.4.

68. Ibid., XXVII.3. Cyprian praised Celerinus as "moderatus et cautus." For his and Numidicus's promotion, see *Letters* XXXIX.3, 5; and XL. For the promise that Celerinus "would find a seat among the presbyters," see ibid., XXXIX.5, and for another promotion to presbyter, see ibid., XXIX. In Hippolytus's *Treatise on Apostolic Tradition*, ed. Dix, the confessor "possessed the honour [*timé*] of the presbyterate by his confession" (p. 18).

69. *Letter* XL.1.

70. Cyprian, *Ad Quirinum* (*Testimoniorum libri tres*) III.85, ed. W. Hartel, CSEL 3.1, pp. 35–186 (Vienna, 1868), p. 174. Cyprian justifies the practice by reference to Lev. 19:32.

71. For instance, in Cyprian *Letter* XXX (letter from the presbyters and deacons in Rome).

72. Thus, Hippolytus, *Treatise on Apostolic Tradition*, ed. Dix, IX (p. 15).

73. Eusebius *HE* V.1.17.

74. *Liber Pontificalis*, ed. Duchesne, vol. 1, p. 153, "Archdeacon" could be an anachronism here, but Lucius is recorded as having treated Stephen as his coadjutor.

75. Cyprian *Letter* LII.2.

76. Ibid., LXXV.1.

77. Optatus *De Schismate Donatistarum*, I.16, "archidiaconus."

78. Tertullian *Apology* XXXIX.16–19. See also Williams, "Ancient Church," pp. 45–46.

79. Tertullian *On Baptism* VIII. For Rome, Ambrosiaster, *Commentary on Ephesians* IV.12.3 (ed. H. I. Vogels, CSEL 81 [Vienna, 1969]), "Everybody used to baptize" (though referring to apostolic times).

80. Cyprian *Letter* LVII.3 (ed. Hartel, p. 652).

81. The problem concerned 1 Sam. 25—28 that had been included in the lesson before the sermon. Origen asks which incident he should discuss and the bishop told him, "The Witch of Endor." See C. Bigg, *The Christian Platonists of Alexandria*, ed. F. E. Brightman, 2d ed. (New York: Oxford University Press, 1913), pp. 166–67.

82. Clear from Origen's statement at the end of his thirty-ninth *Homily on Luke*, ed. M. Rauer, GCS 49, Origen [Leipzig: Hinrichs, 1959], p. 231). He says, "Let us arise and pray to God, that we may be worthy to offer him the gifts, so that he may restore to us and may bestow heavenly gifts for earthly ones in Jesus Christ." See Grant, *Augustus to Constantine*, p. 302.

83. Hippolytus, *Church Order*, in Connolly, *So-Called Egyptian Church Order*, p. 176. Extract cited from Lietzmann's chapter, "Christian Church in West," pp. 524–26 (references) and Dix, *Shape of Liturgy*, chap. 7. I consider the "recalling

element" ("Remembering therefore his death and resurrection . . .") still predominant over the sacrificial in the Eucharist.

84. Even at the end of the century a congregation as numerous and wealthy as that of Cirta met in a "house" (domus). See Gesta apud Zenophilum, p. 186.

85. Cyprian Letter LXIII.14, and compare ibid., 4, the "sacrament of the sacrifice of the Lord" prefigured in Melchizedek. See Lietzmann, "Christian Church in West," p. 527. I prefer, however, to see the connection with the martyr's sacrifice rather than a reminiscence of the ideas behind cult acts in the mystery religions of the day.

86. Letter XIII.1, and see also Letter LVIII.1, "drinking the blood of Christ in order to be able to shed blood for him." Eucharist prepares for martyrdom.

87. Pontius Vita Cypriani (Life of Cyprian) I, "Cypriani tanti sacerdotis et tanti martyris."

88. Optatus, De Schismate Donatistarum, I.16. For this incident contributing to the outbreak of the Donatist schism, see V. Saxer, Morts, martyrs, reliques en Afrique chrétienne aux premiers siècles, Théologie historique 55 (Paris: Gabriel Beauchesne, 1980), pp. 233–35.

89. See de Bruyne, "La peinture," p. 209 and fig. 157. Compare also p. 186 and fig. 145. Conveniently illustrated in Stevenson, Catacombs, p. 95.

90. Housed in the Bardo Museum, Tunis. See M. Yacoub, Le Musée de Bardo (Tunis: Ministère des affaires culturelles, 1970), pp. 70–71 and fig. 75.

91. For Morsott, see "Morsott" in DACL, 12.1, p. 13.

92. Augustine Letters XXI and XXIX.

93. Eusebius HE V.2.7.

94. Cyprian Letter LVII.1.

95. Didascalia, ed. Connolly, VII, p. 55. Connolly points out, pp. 54–55, that while the writer seems to be consciously an opponent of the older regime, it is not certain that he would concede rehabilitation to those who had committed a deadly sin even if they had done penance.

96. The actual phrase is in Jerome Letter CXXX.9, but it seems to have been derived from Tertullian De paenitentia (On Penance) IX, "Paenitentiae secundae et unius."

97. Tertullian Penance X, "Miserum est sic ad exomologesin pervenire." In Rome, in c. 200, Natalius, the confessor who had accepted an Adoptionist form of Monarchianism, was obliged to humiliate himself before Pope Zephyrinus before being restored to communion (Eusebius HE V.28.8–12).

98. Tertullian Apology L.16 (c. 197).

99. Ambivalence—see Cyprian's remark in Letter LV.21 concerning adultery. A provincial council before his time had decided that the peace of the church could not be restored to adulterers. That had now changed. Cyprian, however, never quite reconciled himself to penance being open to apostates. His utterance in De lapsis (The Lapsed) XVII came from the heart, "Let no man deceive himself. Let no one be misled. Sins committed against him can only be cancelled by him alone who bore our sins and suffered for us. . . . Man cannot be above God." Even Moses prayed on behalf of the people without securing pardon for the sinners he was pleading for (ibid., XIX). At the same time, no one should be denied the chance of contrition, and the church's ability through its ministers to remit sins was a canon of faith.

100. *Letters* XV.1 and XVI.2. In both these letters the system was designed for "minor sins." "Full penance" (*plena paenitentia*) followed by exomologesis before restoration to the church was the penalty for graver sins, for example, sexual misdemeanors (*Letter* IV.4). Restoration was by episcopal laying on of hands.

101. See above, p. 322.

102. Clement *Miscellanies* VI.146 and 147.

103. The three lesser grades are referred to in canon 11 of Gregory the Wonderworker's *Canonical Epistle*, chap. XI (c. 255). See also Peter of Alexandria's *Canons* issued during the lull in the Great Persecution in the East (May 305–April 306) (in *Reliquiae Sacrae*, ed. M. J. Routh, 5 vols. [Oxonii: Academico, 1846], vol. 3, pp. 321–43), canon 11 of the Council of Nicaea, and canon 9 of the Council of Ancyra (c. 314).

104. Quoted in Eusebius *HE* VII.5.2–5.

105. See the discussion of the evidence in Gryson's *Les origines du célibat ecclésiastique*, chap. 1.

106. Eusebius *HE* VI.30.17.

107. Ibid., VI.42.3.

108. Cyprian *Letter* LXVII.6.

109. Ibid., XL.1.

110. Ibid., LII.2. Caecilian, the priest who converted Cyprian, was also a family man, who placed his children under Cyprian's care when near death; see Pontius *Life of Cyprian* IV.

111. Cited from C. Jenkins, "Origen on 1 Corinthians," *JTS* 10 (1909), fragment 74, pp. 41–42.

112. Hippolytus *Refutation* IX.12.10.

113. Origen *Leviticus* IV.6 (ed. Baehrens, p. 324): "Ante omnia enim sacerdos, qui divinis assistit altaribus, castitate debet accingi." See Gryson, *Les origines du célibat ecclesiastique*, pp. 14–22.

114. *De Exhortatione Castitatis* (*Concerning the Exhortation to Chastity*) XII.4.

115. *Acta Saturnini* 2 (*PL* 8.688–715, esp. p. 694): "Saturninus presbyter cum filiis quattuor."

116. *Acta Phileae* (*The Acts of Phileas*) VIII, in *Acts of Christian Martyrs*, ed. Musurillo, pp. 328–53. This detail is confirmed in Eusebius's account of Phileas's trial and death, *HE* VIII.9.8.

117. *De singularitate clericorum* (*On the Particularity of the Clergy*), ed. W. Hartel, CSEL 3.3, pp. 173–219 (Vienna, 1868), 19 and 33.

118. Canon 33. Compare canon 27 which forbids virgins to sleep under the roof of a cleric, and also Cyprian *Letter* IX.4—another possible instance of *subintroductae* in the West.

119. Regarding Methodius, see Altaner, *Patrology*, pp. 215–16.

120. See Caron, "Les *Seniores Laici*," and my " 'Seniores Laici.' "

121. Origen, *Matthew* XVI.22 (ed. Klostermann, p. 553).

122. For instance, in Byzacena, mentioned in the dispute between Abbot Peter and Bishop Liberalis at the Council of Carthage in 525; see E. Munier, *Concilia Africae* (CCSL 149), p. 276.

123. *Passio Sanctarum Perpetuae et Felicitatis* (*The Martyrdom of Saints Perpetua and Felicitas*) XIV.6.

124. As observed by the author during a visit in September 1975. See also H. J.

Leon, *The Jews of Ancient Rome* (Philadelphia: Jewish Publication Society of America, 1961), pp. 60–65, 214–18. The catacomb has some three thousand feet of galleries.

125. Cyprian *Letter* LXXX. Compare also Tertullian's claim that Christian "men and women of the highest rank" were to be found in circles close to Septimius Severus (*Ad Scapulam* [*To Scapula*] IV.6).

126. See above, p. 39.

127. *Letter* XLII.1 (artisans); ibid., XXVII.1 (illiteracy).

128. *De habitu virginum* (*On the Dress of Virgins*) VIII.

129. Lactantius *Institutes* V.1.24–27. Cyprian's friends, however, repurchased the property he had given away; see Pontius *Life of Cyprian* XV, and E. W. Benson, *Cyprian: His Life, His Times, His Work* (London: Macmillan & Co.,1897), p. 18.

130. Canons 19 and 20 (usurious clerics); 5 and 41 (slave owners); 57 (providers of clothes); 81 (women not to write in their own names to lay Christians).

131. *Celsus* VI.6.

132. *Principles* II.9.3.

133. Ibid., II.9.5.

134. Sozomen *Ecclesiastical History* V.15.4–10.

135. For some examples, see Ehrhardt, "Quäker-Latein"; and also Chr. Mohrmann, *Augustinus Magister* (Paris: Études Augustiniennes, 1954), vol. 1, pp. 111–16. The *Sondersprache* school is criticized strongly by G. L. Bray, *Holiness and the Will of God: Perspectives on the Theology of Tertullian* (Atlanta: John Knox Press, 1980), pp. 26–30.

136. See the examination of the evidence by Murray, "Art and Early Church," and Th. Klauser, "Erwägungen zur Entstehung der altchristlichen Kunst," *ZKG* 76 (1965): 1–11.

137. Thus Clement *Miscellanies* VI.16.147, and Eusebius's letter to Constantia (quoted at the Council of Nicaea, 787, in Mansi, *Sacrorum Conciliorum*, XIII.313), discussed by Murray, "Art and Early Church," pp. 326–36.

138. *De idololatria* I.1, ed. A. Reifferscheid and G. Wissowa, CSEL 20, pp. 30–58 (Vienna, 1890), p. 30; and see Breckenridge, "Reception of Art."

139. *Didascalia*, ed. Connolly, XVIII (p. 158).

140. Irenaeus *Heresies* I.25.6. See P. Corby Finney's "Gnosticism and the Origins of Early Christian Art" in *ACIAC* IX, vol. I:391–405 (useful references).

141. Above, p. 280. This school of highly expressive and technically excellent design could not have developed overnight. If dating could be more precise one of the origins of Christian art could perhaps be established.

142. *Paedagogus* (*Tutor*) III.11.59.2 and 12.1.

143. *The Testament of Naphtali* VI, a storm-tossed ship as on some Carthaginian Christian marble *memoriae*.

144. For the anchor on the widow's mite, see P. Romanoff, *Jewish Symbols on Ancient Jewish Coins* (New York: Numismatic Review, 1944), p. 63. The influence of symbols on the Jewish coins, especially of the periods of the two revolts, on Christian art, needs further research. The lyre, cornucopia, and grapes are common to the art of both religions in the second and third centuries A.D.

145. For the fish as the symbol of baptism at this period, see Tertullian *On Baptism* XIII. For the Good Shepherd, see "Pasteur (Bon)" in *DACL* 13.2, 2272–

2390; and F. W. Deichmann, "Repertorium der christliche antiken Sarkophage" *Rom und Ostia*, vol. 1 (Wiesbaden, 1967)—no less than sixty-three examples of the Good Shepherd motif dating before c. 300.

146. See Brandenburg, "Überlegungen zum Ursprung."

147. See Kraeling, "Synagogue," esp. pls. li–liii, lvi, and lxix–lxxi (2d ed.), and Brandenburg, "Überlegungen zum Ursprung," p. 25.

148. See Kraeling, "Christian Building," pls. xxxiv, xxxvi, xli, and xliv, and pp. 180–88.

149. I have taken these examples from the illustrations in F. van der Meer and C. Mohrmann's *Atlas of the Early Christian World*, Eng. trans. and ed. M. F. Hedlund and H. H. Rowley (New York: Thomas Nelson & Sons, 1958), pp. 42–43.

150. See Stevenson, *Catacombs*, p. 74, and his chapter on "The Old Testament and the Catacombs," discussing what themes were used and what were disregarded in the Roman Christian catacombs.

151. Cited from Stevenson, *Catacombs*, p. 73 (Balaam).

152. On the popularity of the Jonah-cycle in Christian art during the late third century, see W. Wischmeyer, "Die vorkonstantinische christliche Kunst in neuen Licht: Die Cleveland-statuetten," *VC* 35.3 (1981): 253–87, and idem, "Das Beispiel Jonas," *ZKG* (1981): 161–79.

153. The Christ/Orpheus is one of the favorite early motifs, being found in the catacombs of Domitilla and Priscilla; see "Orphée" in *DACL*, 12.2, 2735–55.

154. For the association of inviting landscapes with meadows and green woods and streams with Paradise, in the late third century(?), see *Passio Sanctorum Mariani et Jacobi* (*The Martyrdom of Saints Marian and James*), 6, 12–15, in *Acts of Christian Martyrs*, ed. Musurillo, pp. 194–213.

155. *Martyrdom of Perpetua* 12.

156. See "Défunts," *DACL* 4.1, 435–38 (*commendatio animae*, extending back to third century), and for examples in the Priscilla and Peter and Marcellinus catacombs, see Stevenson, *Catacombs*, pp. 78–79. As Stevenson says, "the image [which the youths were refusing to worship] looks suspiciously like a bust of a Roman emperor and the king wears Roman uniform" (p. 79).

157. Pontius *Vita Cypriani* I (ed. Hartel, p. xc): "Certe durum erat, ut cum maiores nostri plebeiis et catechumenis martyrium consecutis tantum honoris pro martyrii ipsius veneratione tribuerint. . . ." The *Acta of Perpetua and Felicitas* were "not Scripture," Augustine warned his congregation, *De natura et origine animae* I.10.12 (CSEL 60, p. 312).

158. Eusebius *HE* VI.7.

159. Compare Tertullian *De pallio* (*On the Pallium*) II.5, "[pagan] history extends only from the Assyrians. We who read divine [works] possess history from the birth of the world."

160. Hippolytus, *Commentary on Daniel*, II.12, ed. N. Bonwetsch, GCS 1 (Leipzig: Hinrichs, 1897), p. 68, and compare IV.5.6, 8, and 9. See Ehrhardt, *Politische Metaphysik*, vol. 2, pp. 127–30; and Santo Mazzarino, *The End of the Ancient World*, Eng. trans. George Holmes (London: Faber & Faber, 1966), pp. 39–40.

161. Above, pp. 289, 292.

162. *De pallio* II.6, "Scythae exuberant Persas, Phoenices in Af[f]ricam eructant, Romanos Phryges pariunt . . ." (ed. V. Buhlart, CSEL 76, pp. 104–28 [Vienna, 1957], p. 109).

163. *Ad Demetrianum* (*To Demetrianus*) III and IV, and *De Mortalitate* (*On the Mortality*) XXV–XXVI—the world not merely aging, but approaching its end.

164. Indicated in Augustine *De civitate Dei* (*The City of God*) IV.5.7, and XIX.21; and see N. H. Baynes, *Byzantine Studies, and Other Essays* (New York: John De Graff; London: University of London, Athlone Press, 1955), p. 302.

165. Commodian, *Carmen apologeticum*, lines 921–23, ed. B. Dombart, CSEL 15, pp. 113–88 (Vienna, 1887). I would choose late third century for Commodian's period, as Mazzarino does (*End of Ancient World*, pp. 6–7). The emphasis on martyrdom, vivid apocalyptic, and millenarianism derived from Papias and 4 Esdras point to an early rather than later date. The statement about Gothic/Christian fraternization was in fact true as Gregory the Wonderworker shows. Commodian's use of the term "summus deus" for God and his concern with "the wrath of God" (cf. Lactantius *De ira Dei* [*The Anger of God*]) also point towards late-third-century dating. It would be difficult for an African or even a south Gallic writer of the fifth century writing like Commodian not to refer to the Donatists and Circumcellions, whether as examples of true or false martyrs. See, however, Brisson, *Autonomisme et Christianisme*, pp. 378ff. for a defense of the fifth-century date.

166. Commodian *Instructiones* (*Instructions*) I.29.14ff.

167. *Carmen*, line 987: "Quorum qui pri(m)ores, praepositi sive legati/ in loco servorum rediguntur sancti(s) inqui." cf. *Instructions* II.39.12–17 (rich and nobles to be burnt eternally after the end of the millennium). See Brisson, *Autonomisme et Christianisme*, pp. 396ff.

168. Surviving text preserved in Routh, ed., *Reliquiae Sacrae*, vol. 2, pp. 124–95. See F. C. Burkitt, "The Christian Church in the East," *CAH*, vol. 12, *Imperial Crisis*, pp. 476–514, esp. pp. 477–78.

169. *Celsus* II.30, though the church was the earthly reflection of the heavenly Jerusalem, ibid., II.29.

170. Thus Tertullian *Marcion* IV.39.4.

171. Thus Tertullian *Apology* 38.3; *De Idololatria* (*On Idolatry*) XVII; and *On the Spectacles* XXIX; and compare Cyprian *De dominica oratione* (*On the Lord's Prayer*) XIII.

172. *Tutor* III.11.78.3.

173. At the Council of Elvira particularly, about one-quarter of the eighty-one canons were concerned with combating sexual misdemeanors.

174. Elvira, canons 5 and 75.

175. See the collection of texts assembled by Cadoux, *Early Church and World*, and discussion, pp. 402–25, 452–56, 564–93, and 605–9; also, Grant, *Augustus to Constantine*, pp. 269–70 and 273–74; and idem, *Early Christianity*, pp. 91–95.

176. *The Martyrdom of Pionius* IX.3–4. See above, p. 318.

177. *Concerning Free Will* (*PG* 18.244).

178. Callistus's fate for embezzlement, see Hippolytus *Refutation* IX.12.4. Beating slaves, see Eusebius *Praeparatio evangelica* (*Preparation for the Gospel*) 244c; and Christians with private prisons, *Didascalia* IV.6.1. Even Tertullian finds rebellious slaves an apt comparison for demons (*Apology* XXVII.7).

179. Lactantius *Divinae Institutiones* (*Divine Institutes*) V.18.14–16. See Cadoux, *Early Church and World*, p. 607.

180. Canon 5, compare canon 68.

181. Thus Lactantius *Institutes* VI.20.10; though in *Anger of God* he exculpates judges who visit their wrath on wrongdoers.

182. Cyprian *Letter* 73.10, and compare *Ad Fortunatum* (*De exhortatione martyrii*) XIII (ed. W. Hartel, CSEL 3.1, pp. 317–50 [Vienna, 1868], p. 346), where earthly military triumphs are not condemned as such but regarded as inferior to triumphs over Satan.

183. *De mortibus persecutorum* (*The Deaths of the Persecutors*) XVIII.10.

184. Cyprian *Dress of Virgins* XI; "ferrum esse ad culturam terrae Deus voluit, nec homicidia sunt idcirco facienda."

185. Tertullian *De cultu feminarum* (*Concerning the Deportment of Women*) II.10.1.

186. Cyprian *Letter* XXXIX.3.

187. *Miscellanies* IV.8.61.

188. *Celsus* VIII.73.

189. *De oratione* (*On Prayer*) XIII.2. Cadoux, *Early Church and World*, p. 416.

190. *Celsus* II.30.

191. Arles, canon 3.

192. *De opere et eleemosynis* XXIV (ed. W. Hartel, CSEL 3.1, pp. 373–96 [Vienna, 1868], p. 392): "Demus Christo vestimenta terrena indumenta caelestia recepturi"; and cf. ibid., XIII; "fac tibi possessionum terrestrium Christum participem, ut et ille te sibi faciat regnorum caelestium coheredem."

193. *On Lord's Prayer* 33; and cf. *De opere* V.

194. *De opere* II; and cf. *On Lord's Prayer* XXXII.

195. See Pontius *Life of Cyprian* I for this view: Cyprian would have gained glory by his merits even without martyrdom.

196. Eusebius *HE* VI.42.

197. Ibid., VI.41.17–21.

198. Ibid., VII.24.6.

199. Thyatira became largely Montanist apparently in the 260s—see Epiphanius, *Panarion* LI.33 (ed. Holl, p. 307).

200. Published by Calder, "Philadelphia and Montanism," pp. 28–41 (page numbers of offprint); and for a similar inscription from an estate south of Thyatira, see ibid., pp. 36–37. Also Gibson, " 'Christians for Christians' Inscriptions."

201. See Gibson, " 'Christians for Christians' Inscriptions," pp. 33–36.

202. *Chastity* XII.

203. *Pap. Oxy.* 1477. See M. I. Rostovtzev, *Social and Economic History of the Roman Empire*, 2d ed., rev. P. M. Fraser, 2 vols. (New York and London: Oxford University Press, 1957), pp. 479, 742.

204. Athanasius *Vita S. Antonii* (*Life of St. Antony*) II.

205. *The Sayings of the Fathers* XV.1, in *Western Asceticism*, ed. and Eng. trans. O. Chadwick, LCC XII (Philadelphia: Westminster Press; London: SCM Press, 1958), p. 156.

206. *Life of Antony* XLIV.

207. See above, p. 146. For an example of more direct connections see the letter of Taré written from Apamea in Syria to her aunt in Coptos in Egypt (*DACL* 12.2, 2756–57).

208. See Peter Brown, "The Diffusion of Manichaeism in the Roman Empire," *JRS* 59 (1969): 92–103, esp. p. 96 (references).

209. *Life of Antony* 72, 74, 77.

210. *HE* VII.30.13.

211. Hermas, *Similitudes* IX.11.3 (in *The Apostolic Fathers,* vol. 2, ed. Kirsopp Lake, LCL [Cambridge, Mass.: Harvard University Press; London: William Heinemann, 1913]), "You shall sleep with us as a brother and not as a husband."

212. A good example from the Tembris valley in the third- to fourth-century. Ammia receives baptism at the hands of a presbyter and joins the "Novatian saints." She sees her baptism as "virginity's lawful prerogative." (See Calder, "Anatolian Notebook," pp. 260–63.)

213. *Sententiae episcoporum* 78 (ed. Hartel, p. 459); and for Circumcellion activity there in the fourth century, see Optatus, *De Schismate Donatistarum,* III.4 (ed. Ziwsa, p. 82): "In loco Octavense occisi sunt plurimi" (Circumcelliones).

13

The Age of Diocletian 270–305

Gradually, the barbarians were beaten back. In 269 the Goths were defeated heavily near Naissus (Nish) and cleared from Illyricum. Under the emperor Aurelian (270–75), the empire found a commander who knew the value of rapid movement and decisive action. Within five years the empire was restored to its "natural boundaries" of the Rhine, Danube, and Euphrates rivers, and the Sahara. The suzerainty of the kingdom of Palmyra over the eastern provinces was ended (272), the Gallic empire was reabsorbed (273/74), and only the great trans-Danubian salient of Dacia and the settlements between the Rhine and Danube were given up. Even Britain was retained. Outstanding defensive successes had been won. The army and administration had found strength to ward off disaster, the currency was stabilized, and in 274 the city of Rome itself was protected by a girdle of walls twenty feet high. The immortal gods still deserved their worshipers and the emperor his claim to be "the restorer of the world."[1]

THE PAGAN FRONT

These years of recovery also witnessed a consolidation of traditional paganism and its more active defense against Christianity. Victory over Palmyra may have become associated in Aurelian's mind with the favor of the Sun god at Emesa, near where he won a decisive engagement.[2] In the last years of his reign the Sun god was hailed as "Lord of the Roman empire." Together with Jupiter, from whom Aurelian is shown on his coins as receiving the orb of majesty, he takes his place among its protecting gods.[3] In 274 Aurelian built a magnificent temple in Rome in honor of the Sun and established a new college of senators called "priests of the Sun-god." This was to be the universal faith of the empire. Significantly, before he was cut down in an ill-starred military conspiracy (April 275), Aurelian is recorded by both Lactantius and Eusebius as being pressed to persecute the Christians.[4]

The ensuing senatorial interlude of 275–76 was ended by the death of the emperor Tacitus, followed three months later by the removal of his half brother Florianus. Another Illyrian soldier-emperor, Probus (276–82), continued Aurelian's work. His coins show a growing self-confidence in Rome, its institutions, and religion. *Roma aeterna* and *Soli invicto comiti* (the "unconquered Sun" as the emperor's "companion") are accompanied by inscriptions exalting the person of the emperor—his "virtue" (*virtus*), his "coming" (*adventus*). Probus, too, was praised not only for his military prowess, but for his "mildness and sense of justice," and *Clementia Temp(orum)* is well represented on his coins. He was the pagan godly monarch exemplifying philosophic and military virtues and ruling over subjects devotedly loyal to him. With the gods as his helpers he would reestablish the golden age of peace.[5] Each in their way, Aurelian and Probus foreshadowed the ideals of the Tetrarchy of 305/6 and of Constantine himself before his conversion to Christianity.

Much of the credibility of these hopes depended on the emperor himself and the success of his armies. Paganism, however, was at last finding able intellectual defenders. The half century between Plotinus's death in 270 and the middle of Constantine's reign was dominated by the figures of Amelius, Porphyry of Gaza (d. 304), both Plotinus's pupils, and the Syrian Iamblichus (d. circa 326). Western Syria appears to have become a focus for this movement and there were centers of Neo-Platonist study in some of the Greek-Syrian towns, such as Apamea.[6] By this time Neo-Platonism had become the residuary legatee of the great philosophical systems of the past. Their representatives were steeped in the theories of Pythagoras and the Stoics as well as of Plato. They looked back to Socrates and the Seven Sages represented on a fourth-century mosaic from Apamea. Theirs, too, was a religious movement, sharing many of the ideals of the Alexandrian Christians. Like them, they believed in the essential harmony of a providentially guided universe and that the goal of human life was the divinization of the soul, but they also found scope in their system for the gods and heavenly powers of paganism. Mystical union with the One and release from the bonds of Fate was to be achieved by mystical experience, often associated with clairvoyance, and semimagical practices connected with the so-called Chaldean Oracles. The sacred art of the "theurgist" enabled the believer to speak with meaning about the gods and to know how to conduct one's own life.[7] Little may have divided the Neo-Platonists from the Christians in terms of religious philosophy. For all his passionate Christianity, Origen had shown that. Both he and Porphyry would have agreed that "the true philosopher is a priest of the supreme God, and by his abstinence he is united to the God he serves" (Porphyry *On Abstinence* II.49). Differences, however, even if largely emotional, remained unbridgeable over the meaning of "idolatry," one's duties to one's city and the state, and as always, the evident inconsistencies between the facts of the New Testament story and the Christian claims based upon them. As it had been a century before, the Jewish heritage prevented Christians from equating angels with the heavenly powers and protecting spirits of paganism, while their legalistic morality was alien to the intuitive piety of the Neo-Platonists. The latter also believed in the empire and a citizen's duty towards it. They were loyal to its traditional religion. Jupiter was their Supreme God. The result was a long and increasingly bitter debate between Christians and Neo-Platonists which lasted through the second half of the third century. When the crunch came near the end of Diocletian's reign, Neo-Platonist influence was thrown unreservedly on the side of the enemies of Christianity.

Porphyry

In the earlier phase (c. 260–70), the tone of controversy was conciliatory and even constructive. Eusebius quoted Amelius (c. 270) approvingly in his

441

Preparation for the Gospel, written on the aftermath of Christian victory c. 313–15. Despite his prejudice against its "barbarian origin," Amelius had seen value in the Christian explanation of the Logos contained in the Fourth Gospel. He could accept an incarnation manifesting divine majesty and in some way representing the perpetual and universal incarnation of the Heavenly Reason that enlightened every creature.[8] Porphyry's early work *On the Return of the Soul*, which influenced Augustine and helped free him from Manichean dualism, also conceded the exemplary character of Christ's life[9] while criticizing the disciples harshly. Peter in particular he described as a dabbler in the black arts.[10] Christians, too, were in error in their belief in the resurrection of the body, and they were blasphemers who showed their contempt for their fellows in their arrogance, credulity, and hopes for the cataclysmic end of the world.[11] Celsus's criticisms of a century before were dying hard.

In this earlier work, Porphyry had shown a considerable knowledge of the New Testament and an ability to pick out some weak points in Christianity. If Christ, he asked, was the sole way of salvation, what happened to the innumerable souls that had existed before his coming? What had they lacked?[12] The argument in *Return of Soul* led on to the severer judgments of *Against the Christians* (c. 270). This was a great book of fifteen volumes, a scourge of the Christians, abominated by Constantine, and judged as a formidable apologetic for more than a century, until 448 when the emperor Theodosius II ordered the burning of every copy that could be found along with the works of the hated heretic, Nestorius.[13] The fragments that survive show that Porphyry's was a far better informed and altogether more telling work than Celsus's. Once more, Jesus himself emerges as a worthy figure, though open to criticism for some of his acts and his pusillanimous behavior before Pilate. Why, for instance, choose the unfortunate pigs as a haven for freshly exorcized demons?[14] And anyhow, was the story possible? The apostles and evangelists are condemned as unworthy characters, Peter as unreliable, Paul as a shallow-minded exhibitionist. Porphyry's attack on the literal truth and consistency of Scripture was as old as Marcion and had been given a fresh lease on life by Origen. Origen, however, had used allegorical interpretation to uphold the general credibility of the Gospels, properly understood through philosophical and allegorical exegesis.[15] Now these same weapons were turned against the Christians. Porphyry would take an incident, such as the death of Judas Iscariot, compare the accounts given in Matt. 27:5 and Acts 1:18, and point out the inconsistencies between them.[16] Or he would fasten on observable facts of geography, such as the small area of the Sea of Galilee, easily traversible by a man in a boat in a couple of hours and hence not subject to storms of the violence described in Mark 4:37–39.[17]

Gradually, the picture was built up of the Evangelists as purveyors of fantasy, and the disciples as simpletons or malcontents. Some of Porphyry's criticism of Scripture was true. Evidently he devoted the whole of Book XII to a discussion of the book of Daniel, and showed that it was not the work of a seer in the remote past, but a Jewish compilation dating from the Maccabean Wars.[18] Hence, it had no merit as prophecy. Any Christian claims relying on it, such as those set out in Julius Africanus's *Chronicles*,[19] were worthless.

Porphyry laid less emphasis than Celsus on the need for a citizen to serve the emperor and the Christians' failure in this regard. Though he made fun of them, he also had no doubt that they had put themselves outside the law and deserved persecution. Like other pagan leaders, he was at heart profoundly conservative, viewing traditional usages as sacrosanct. The highest virtue was to honor the divine powers in the ancestral manner. Christianity was a "barbarian adventure" and a threat to established institutions.[20] Others in official positions felt likewise. Those who read Porphyry's works, like the able and energetic governor of Bithynia in 302, Sossius Hierocles, derived justification for their hostility towards the Christians from them.[21] Porphyry also found imitators in unlikely places. The "new men" attacked by Arnobius of Sicca (c. 300) were almost certainly Platonists, and they were bringing a new aggression into pagan polemic.[22] Christian doctrine was empty, Christ was not even an extraordinary magician, but on a par with Apollonius of Tyana, Zoroaster, or Julian the Chaldean. And if he did descend from heaven to save the human race, why did he not free all men with equal generosity? Why should people be obliged to become Christians in order to be saved?[23] Too many, however, were doing that. Tensions were mounting before the Great Persecution as they had before Decius.

In one important respect Porphyry followed Celsus. He was deeply perturbed at the spread of Christianity. In one expressive passage, he describes how the Christians "were building up great houses where they could assemble for prayer, no one preventing them from doing this, and the whole world had heard of the fame of the Gospels"[24]—an interesting comment on the spread of Christianity and the evolution of the church as a property-holding institution. In particular, Porphyry pointed to the influx of educated women, especially in Rome, into the church. A passage preserved by Augustine[25] contains the remark that in his work entitled *Philosophy from Oracles*, written c. 263, he puts into the mouth of Apollo the lament that it was practically impossible to reconvert any who had gone over to Christianity. It was easier to write letters on the surface of a pool of water. The liquid closed over each stroke. Better let the victim come to realize the folly of worshiping a "God" who had been condemned to a shameful death as a criminal.

Porphyry was observing the situation accurately. The last quarter of the third century saw what must be regarded as the decisive thrust of the church into the pagan world. Writing now of events in his lifetime, Eusebius cannot hide his enthusiasm at Christianity's prosperity in the years before the Great Persecution. "It is beyond our powers," he wrote, "to describe in a worthy manner the measure and nature of that honor as well as freedom which was accorded by all men, both Greeks and barbarians, before the persecution in our day, to that word of piety towards the God of the universe which had been proclaimed through Christ to the world."[26] He goes on to mention Christian leaders who held high positions in the imperial service, such as Adauctus who was a senior financial and administrative officer at Diocletian's court, and Dorotheus, a eunuch whom Diocletian appointed as superintendent of the imperial dye works at Antioch, and Philoromus, a senior official in Alexandria.[27] These were examples that struck the observer, but the advance of Christianity was quickening and, perhaps even more significant than any gain in numbers, Christianity was absorbing part of the heritage of paganism without any serious weakening of its own attitudes—in the city and the countryside alike.

THE ADVANCE OF CHRISTIANITY

For the expansion of Christianity, in terms of establishing new bishoprics and congregations, Adolf von Harnack's work remains fundamental.[28] Here and there it may be supplemented by new discoveries while some of the evidence based on later *Acta Martyrum* may perhaps be discounted. The main results, however, stand. From the map, "Christianity at the End of the Third Century" (see map D), one can see how Christianity was advancing strongly if unevenly. Its expansion may be divided into three main zones:

- The original missionary area covered by Paul and his immediate successors, where the Jewish Dispersion provided the foundation for the growth of Christianity, such as western Asia Minor, Cyprus, Crete, Greece (Achaia), the coast towns of southern Italy, and Rome.
- Territories outside the early missionary area, but where there were also strong Jewish communities, notably some parts of eastern Syria and Mesopotamia, parts of North Africa, and southeastern Spain.
- The remaining territories of the empire, especially the great areas of the Celtic and Germanic provinces extending from Illyricum to Britain and including northern Italy.

Original Missionary Area

Where evidence exists, for instance from Thyatira, it is clear that there continued to be strong Christian communities in the "Seven Churches" during the third century, and Christianity had made progress inland in Asia Minor both in the cities and countryside. In c. 260 Dionysius of Alexandria refers to "very populous" Christian communities in parts of Phrygia, whose vigorous activity was reflected in the synods of Synnada and Iconium (c. 230–40), debating problems relating to the rebaptism of schismatics and heretics.[29] Forty years later, both Eusebius and Lactantius record that an anonymous town in Phrygia, which was entirely Christian at the time of the Great Persecution in 303, was destroyed by the authorities on account of this.[30] Two other towns, Orcistus[31] and Eumeneia,[32] seem to have become Christian by 300 or not long afterward. Eumeneia had produced an openly Christian inscription bearing a cross, dating to 242/43.[33] With large concentrations of Christians around Synnada and Iconium in the south, and in the Tembris valley in the north, Phrygia must have been one of the most Christianized provinces of the empire by the end of the third century.

For some the Persecution must have come as a great shock. Even in towns where they were most numerous, we find Christians sharing fully in Greco-Roman culture, taking part in city life as councilors, and not averse to references to Hades and the Muses on their tombstones.[34] In the last quarter of the third century the process of absorbing and assimilating pagan values had gathered pace, and among urban congregations much of the sectarianism even of Origen's time was becoming outmoded. In Bithynia on the Black Sea coast, Christians were also numerous. When in 311 the emperor Maximin entered the capital, Nicomedia, he found that "nearly all" the inhabitants were Christians.[35] In the east of the province, Amaseia near where Pliny had encountered Christians in 112 there were "numerous churches."[36] In the great inland province of Cappadocia, Gregory the Wonderworker (Thaumaturgus) had returned to his native country in c. 243 and carried out a series of successful missions, designed to wrest the leadership of local communities from the pagan priestly families, and convert the inhabitants to a Christianity which did not involve too sharp a break from the past. His was an intelligent and successful enterprise, one of the few for which any record survives. In Neocaesarea, the capital city of Pontus, he left the reputation of having found only seventeen Christians on his arrival there, but leaving only seventeen pagans when he died thirty years later![37] In the east of the province, another Gregory, "the Illuminator," was setting out (c. 300) to the independent kingdom of Armenia to further the conversion of a significant part of the Armenian nobility. When King Tiridates (274–314) became a Christian, the effect on the political and religious balance in this sensitive area between the Roman and Persian empires was profound. A decisive obstacle was placed in the way of the emperor Maximin's effort to destroy Christianity in his dominions in the years 311 and 312, while Christianity became for the first time a factor to be considered in the empire's external relations.

Territories Outside Early Missionary Area

In parts of North Africa also, Christianity was spreading fast. In Cyprian's time there must have been about 130 to 150 bishoprics all told. We hear of

90 bishops assembled at Lambaesis in c. 245.[38] At Cyprian's council in 256 there were 87 bishops who voted.[39] For the situation half a century later, Optatus of Milevis, discussing the origins of the Donatist schism in 312, mentions 17 bishoprics, but only 8 of these are found in Cyprianic lists. Another 7 hitherto unrecorded bishoprics can be added from good literary sources. While no episcopal councils are recorded in the half century after Cyprian's death, that assembled by Donatus of Carthage in c. 336 included 270 bishops and these were only from his party. We should probably not be far wrong in estimating about 200 bishoprics in North Africa by the time of the Great Persecution in 303.[40]

Much of the success had been gained in the countryside, especially in Numidia. Many of the new bishoprics were in that province and the Numidians had become much more important in North African Christianity, to the extent that by 300 the primate of Numidia had gained the right of consecrating the bishop of Carthage.[41] Opinion, too, was changing in favor of the Christians in that province. During the persecution under Valerian in 259, the confessors Marianus and James were hounded by the local population of Cirta before the magistrates.[42] In 305, the townspeople, quarryworkers, and countryfolk outside the city were devotedly Christian. An artisan is recorded as having paid twenty folles to be ordained priest even in the immediate aftermath of persecution.[43] This movement toward Christianity may perhaps be associated with a decline in interest in the traditional all-powerful national deity Saturn and other local gods. In the second and early part of the third centuries, Saturn enjoyed enormous prestige throughout North Africa, especially among the poorer classes. His shrines, both within the towns and on high places such as the conspicuous twin-peaked mountain, the Bou Kournein south of Carthage, were the scenes of sacrifices and pilgrimages. After the mid–third century, this devotion seems to slacken. In Numidia and Mauretania no inscription in his honor is dated later than 272, and in the next century his cult had faded to such an extent that memorials dedicated to him were turned face down and used as paving slabs in the town of Cuicul.[44] In proconsular Africa his cult lasted longer. Two inscriptions dated to 323 have been found in western Tunisia, but interestingly both were set up by upper-class members of the community possessing the threefold Latin name (*tria nomina*), not by rustic provincials as was usual in the previous century.[45] Like the Gallic Druids of the same period, Saturn was beginning to be associated with an antiquarian past, though as "the old man" he long retained a hold over the subconscious allegiance of many North Africans.[46] Among local gods, the grotto of Bacax near the Numidian town of Aquae Tibilitanae saw its last recorded annual visit by the magistrates of the town in 283.[47] The heir to these gods was Christianity.

If paganism was losing contact with the people, it was nonetheless to retain the allegiance of the traditional local governing class for another century. In the middle of the fourth century, Timgad, an urban and garrison center in southern Numidia, was one of the most Christianized cities of Roman North Africa. It was a Donatist stronghold, with a cathedral and several churches and thousands of Christian graves laid out row on row on the slopes of a hill west of the town, among which there were also churches and *martyria*.[48] But the album of Timgad, a list of *curiales* or members of the city council, dated to A.D. 365, records no fewer than forty-seven out of seventy-two who held pagan priesthoods,[49] and in the emperor Julian's pagan restoration of 362–63, the city council of Timgad with other Numidian cities hailed the emperor as "restorer of liberty."[50] One has a clear impression of division on social lines, originating long before with most of the traditional landowning rulers of the towns remaining loyal to the gods while the mass of the inhabitants were steadily won over to Christianity. Even at the end of the fourth century Augustine mentions the city councils of Calama in Numidia and Sufes in Byzacena as still militantly pagan.[51] As though to confirm this, in the Great Persecution in 303–5, while some well-to-do patresfamilias were said to have perished, there is no tangible evidence for more than one decurion, Dativus of Abitina, being arrested as a Christian.[52] Ardent confessors in 303–4 were more likely to be individuals who found themselves behind with their taxes and hoped at least to end their lives in a blaze of glory.[53]

For Egypt, Antony's monasticism gathered strength among the Coptics as the century wore on, and the same tendencies were reinforced by other nonorthodox ascetic movements, such as that represented by Hieracas and by the Manichees.[54] In tune with this, a similar change in public opinion in favor of the Christians was taking place in Egypt as it was in North Africa. During the Decian persecution, Christians had been hounded into the desert to suffer death or capture by the Saracens;[55] now, worship of the traditional gods seems to have become ever more formal and sometimes aroused outright resentment, as is shown by the story of the youthful Pachomius refusing to join in his parents' sacrifice at the local temple, long before he became a Christian.[56] Villages with churches were increasing in number.[57] The way was being prepared for the great surge towards Christianity that took place during the era of the persecutions and gave the Coptic a permanent sense of identity through adherence to Christianity. Meantime, the cities were also moving in the same direction. By 300 Oxyrhynchus had its bishop, and more remarkable, a core of enthusiasts, dubbed *Philoponoi*, who were assisting the clergy to hold together the community when Peter of Alexandria visited them during his flight from his city "from fear of Diocletian and his persecution."[58]

In Syria evidence is more fragmentary and conflicting. Christian inscriptions before c. 370 are rare.[59] Edessa was strongly Christian, and by 300 Nisibis, which had resisted Christianity for a long time perhaps through the strength of its Jewish schools, had a bishop.[60] Antioch, on the other hand, remained relatively isolated from Jerusalem and Edessa by strongly pagan Greek cities and their territories. As late as 385, the intrepid western traveler, Egeria, records concerning Carrhae that apart from a few clerics and monks, "I found absolutely nothing Christian, but everything pagan."[61] In the countryside, however, the situation may have been different. Syrian monasticism, we have seen, arose about the same time as Egyptian.[62] By the end of the third century there were some *chorepiscopi*, that is, bishops appointed for country areas but subordinate to the urban episcopate.[63] There were Marcionite communities in some villages, such as Lebaba south of Damascus, where one of the earliest Christian inscriptions (dated 318) was found, while in the north of the province, the Marcionite villages encountered by Theodoret of Cyrrhus in the 420s and 430s could hardly be recent importations.[64] Around Edessa in many villages, such as that of Habib, the deacons were largely Christian. By c. 320 Zeus, along with the traditional Semitic deities of the sky and stars, Bel and Nebo, were being ousted by Christ.[65]

Other Territories

In the western provinces, apart from North Africa, southeastern Spain (Baetica) was the most Christianized area. At the Council of Elvira (c. 309?), Baetica and Carthagena accounted for nineteen and nine bishops respectively, leaving only five from the remaining Spanish provinces. Here the process may have been aided by the existence of a strong Jewish population, and the council shows that links between the Jews and Christians were still embarrassingly close.[66] The cities in other parts of Spain where there were Christian communities included Emerita (Mérida) and Legio (Leon), garrisons on the great military highways, which helped to set a pattern for the early distribution of Christianity in other parts of the West. In Gaul in 314 there were nine bishoprics, four of which were in the valley of the Rhone where Christianity had first penetrated, and Vaison within striking distance. Elsewhere, communities were confined to established commercial centers such as Bordeaux, or nodal points of communications such as Autun and Rouen.[67] And these, as has been pointed out, were "just isolated points in a pagan desert."[68] In the Rhineland (Germania inferior), Trier and Köln, both important garrisons, were bishoprics. In Britain, the legionary center of Caerleon produced early martyrs,[69] while the three bishoprics at London, York, and Lincoln (or Colchester) were all military and commercial centers. On the Danube frontier, Pannonia had a bishop in the fortress city of Sirmium, a young man whose relatives were pagan in 303.[70] In the neighboring province of Moesia, Eusebius alluded to "the young Christian community" there in Constantine's reign.[71] In Scythia, Christianity is represented by the beginnings of the episcopal list at Tomi in c. 290.[72]

All in all, the impression—and it can only be an impression in the present state of the evidence—is that by the end of the third century in the western and Danube provinces, Christianity had hardly progressed beyond the situation of an immigrant religion with roots particularly in major cities and garrison towns. From the names of bishops and of martyrs, such as Felix at Nola[73] and Aaron and Julius at Caerleon, it would seem to be associated also with Jews and immigrants, perhaps merchants from the eastern Mediterranean. Agroecius of Trier and Adelphius of Lincoln(?), who attended the Council of Arles in 314, are representative of bishops with names of Greek origin,[74] while at Salona on the Dalmatian coast, the first recorded bishop was a certain Domnio who seems to have come from the frontier city of Nisibis.[75] His stay was not unprofitable, for the Christian settlement that grew up some six miles north of Salona itself became one of the largest Christian centers in Illyricum. For the moment, however, the little church in the *area* outside the city of Cologne sums up the extent of Christian penetration in the Celtic and Germanic provinces of the empire.

Even in these unfavorable areas, Christianity was organized uniformly, and as Constantine was to find, its bishops were able to assemble rapidly and make collective decisions. It could discipline its members severely, and could direct their daily conduct in detail. It knew where it stood regarding the outside world. Its underlying position was infinitely stronger than that of Mithraism at the beginning of the century. Where it was more numerous, an observer might have noted other signs of strength, an attractive power and ability to absorb some elements of surrounding culture to its own advantage, significant portents for the future.

Assimilation and Absorption

We return to Rome and the catacomb in the Via Latina for an example. As we have seen, it must have belonged to a wealthy community descended from Greek-speaking freedmen, but now thoroughly Romanized, and it contained a greater than usual proportion of painted tombs.[76] In the same passageway only feet away from each other, the visitor can see two representations of Christ at the Last Supper, scenes from the Old Testament, Balaam and his donkey, Jacob's dream, Lot's wife, Rachel at the well, and Samson belaboring the Philistines with the jawbone of an ass; but most extraordinary of all is a group of sepulchres with purely pagan symbols: Medusa, and Hercules performing his labors. But were they really pagan? Hercules' labors could symbolize those of Christ the Savior doing mighty works on earth and the scene of Hercules rescuing Alcestis from Hades could perhaps symbolize the resurrection of Lazarus. But what of Medusa? What part could she play in overthrowing death? There is no cut-and-dried solution, any more than for the peacocks, dolphins, and lions that appear in Jewish funerary art of the time; but just as these symbols were accepted by Jews, so a similar process of absorption and reinterpretation of pagan symbols by Christians may have already begun.[77] On the other side of the city, in the Vatican cemetery, the tombs of the last period before its destruction to make room for the Constantinian St. Peter's in 322, provide a further illustration of the same process of development. Some are obviously Christian, but on one (Tomb M) Christ is represented as Helios drawing a miniature chariot with a horse looking up at him. Was Christ associated in some way with the Sun at this moment?[78] Is this the clue to Constantine's "dual religion" between 312 and 323? The names of the owners show a fairly even division between descendants of Greek-speaking forebears and owners of originally free, Roman stock, and they were converting to Christianity.[79]

The canons of the Council of Elvira show a similar phenomenon. There were still far more women among the Christians than men,[80] but the canons indicate a belief that the families brought up by Christian brides would be Christian. Six canons suggest conversions to Christianity.[81] The problems demanding regulation were those of conversion rather than lapse or apostasy. As more and more pagans from the ruling classes became Christians the question arose whether these Christians could hold nominal pagan councilorships and remain Christian. The assembled bishops decided with a greater show of liberality and common sense than in many of their canons that, provided they had not offered sacrifice nor contributed to pagan sacrifices in any way, the catechumens among them should be admitted to baptism after three years.[82]

On a personal level in the West we find a continuation of the same development that we noted with Minucius Felix. Philosophically minded individuals were turning to Christianity when confronted with aspects of paganism they disliked and were not seeking remedy from the opposite school of philosophy. Arnobius of Sicca in proconsular Africa (*flor.* 290–303) had built up a reputation as an anti-Christian polemicist, but he despised various superstitious practices he saw around him, designed to win divine favor. He noted the confusion and decline into which the pagan cults were falling, and, to judge from his sarcasm, he had probably quarreled with his fellow philosophers in Sicca. At heart he was a pious, if abrasive, Epicurean. He disliked Plato and he rejected Platonic proofs of the immortality of the soul put forward by Cicero in the first book of the *Tabletalks at Tusculum*; but he believed that somehow the soul possessed enough divinity to gain immortality by the gift and grace of God. Arnobius should have been a follower of Lucretius.[83] Instead, he converted to Christianity much to the surprise of the local bishop, and during the Great Persecution wrote his seven books, *Against the Pagans*, defending Christianity from the growing pagan charge that it was responsible for the ills of the world.[84] His pupil, Lactantius (*flor.* 290–320), was a convert a little later on, perhaps shortly after his arrival in Nicomedia c. 300; only he was to plunge deeper into the waters of now-traditional Western Christian hostility to pagan society. His work *On the Deaths of the Persecutors* was a piece of apocalyptic with Maccabean overtones, snobbish in its contempt for the lowborn emperors of the Tetrarchy, yet concerned for those who suffered injustices through their attempted reforms.[85] His great work *Divine Institutes*, modeled on Cicero in thought and style, sought to reconcile philosophy, including Epicureanism, with Christianity to the latter's advantage. Quotations from the (Jewish) *Sibylline Oracles* are as much in evidence as those from the Scripture. The utopianism is philosophic rather than Christian. Lactantius, however, accepted the ethical superiority of Christianity over its rivals and he hated the paraphernalia of blood sacrifices. For him Christianity meant integrity, sincerity, and justice to whose truth it was the role of pagan authors to bear witness. He wrote as one who was disillusioned with the injustices of the time and the vanished vision of the Golden Age.[86] The work of assimilation and absorption which he was performing in literature resembles what the unknown painters in the catacomb on the Via Latina were attempting in art.

In earlier times, Arnobius might have been an African Varro, a narrator of outlandish superstitions in which he himself did not believe, and Lactantius a Stoic with an interest in Eastern oracle literature. In the 290s both became Christians, and as Arnobius commented, "droves of educated people" did likewise.[87] But prosperity brought its own problems for the church as it had in the past. What precisely were the exacerbating disputes is not known. Christian sources for the last thirty years of the third century are tantalizingly sparse. Despite the progress its followers were making, the church produced no outstanding leader, as though from the point of view of organization it was content with the position it had won for itself and saw no danger ahead. Qualities of greatness were not called for. Arnobius and Lactantius were scarcely interested in doctrinal questions and ecclesiastical disputes. Eusebius for some reason is studiously vague about the actual controversies among which he was growing up. From Methodius of Olympus and Pamphilus's defense of Origen, one may guess that Origenism was one issue, tendencies towards Manicheism were another, as shown by a letter probably of Bishop Theonas of Alexandria (282–300) condemning the Manichees for preaching against marriage.[88] Sabellianism, to judge from the fear it was to provoke in the next century, must also have been a continuing threat.

Of the growing ferocity of the disputes within the church there can, however, be no doubt. Introducing Book VIII of his *Ecclesiastical History*, Eusebius, after extolling the prosperity of the church, wrote as follows:

> But when, as the result of greater freedom, a change to pride and sloth came over our affairs, we fell to envy and fierce railing against one another, warring upon ourselves, so to speak, as occasion offered, with weapons and spears formed of words; and rulers attacked rulers and laity formed factions against laity, while unspeakable hypocrisy and pretence pursued their evil course to the furthest end.[89]

The great religious revolution in the Mediterranean world was about to occur, and the church would not emerge unscathed from its victory.

DIOCLETIAN AND THE GREAT PERSECUTION

The Reorganization of the Empire

Meanwhile, the empire itself was evolving toward a constitution far different from that which had prevailed since the time of Augustus. In the decade 275–85 revival of senatorial choice of emperor, renewed military dictatorship, and restoration of dynastic government had all been tried and had failed. The last alternative, Carus's attempt to found an imperial dynasty based on his sons, Numerian and Carinus, had broken down after less than two years (283–85). Was yet another Illyrian soldier, Diocles, who seized power in November 284 and emerged as victor over his rivals in the spring of 285, to fare better? No one could have foretold that, as the emperor Diocletian, he would rule for twenty-one years, abdicate, and survive as an elder statesman in his palace at Salona (Spalato or Split) for another decade. He was one of the great conservative reformers of history.

Precisely why Diocletian launched the Great Persecution against the Christians throughout the empire on 23 February 303 will probably never be known. Of contemporary witnesses, Lactantius gives a convincing circumstantial account of events leading up to the promulgation of the first edict, but has nothing to say about the deeper causes.[90] Eusebius fails to find a rational explanation, except for the need of God's disciplining a church grown slack and quarrelsome after years of peace.[91] To Constantine, who was at Diocletian's court, it was an act of madness. The pagan emperors, his predecessors, he declared, had stirred up civil wars "when affairs human and divine were enjoying peace."[92] If one looks back to Diocletian's reforms and the spirit that animated them, however, one may arrive at some approximation of the truth.

The emperor himself was dour and autocratic by nature, "determining all by his word," and he went further than Aurelian and Probus in surrounding himself with the trappings of religion.[93] Everything to do with the emperor was invested with sanctity, so that the word *sacer* became synonymous with "imperial." The emperor himself, dwelling in his *sacrum palatium* must be approached reverently with a threefold prostration (*proskynesis*), ideas and actions previously current at times during the third century, but now made the rule. *Dominus* ("Lord") became the normal mode of address. The emperor had become an autocrat.

Recent history had shown, however, that the burden of office was too great for one man. Diocletian established his headquarters at Nicomedia on the Asiatic side of the Bosporus, and he imitated Carus by placing the Western provinces under their own ruler, subordinate to himself. The dynastic principle, however, which had failed so miserably, was abandoned.

Faced with a widespread peasant rising in Gaul (the Bagaudae) and raids by Kabyle tribesmen in North Africa, he appointed an Illyrian soldier like himself, named Maximian, first as Caesar and then, probably in March 286, Augustus in the West. Maximian proved himself, defeating the Bagaudae easily and the Kabyles at the end of three strenuous campaigns in c. 289. He carried out what Diocletian planned, declared the court panegyrist in 290.[94] His effectiveness and loyalty as a second in command was reflected in the religion of the age. The empire was committed to the care of Jupiter and Hercules, the supreme god and his faithful lieutenant. Diocletian represented the one and Maximian the other, and the elite troops recruited in Illyricum bore the names of *Jovii* and *Herculii*.

One untoward series of events threatened to ruin the slow recovery of the empire. Britain had become the prey to bands of Saxon pirates operating from the low-lying coasts of Holland and northern Germany. Defenses provided by a channel fleet based on Boulogne (Gesoriacum) and the massive fortresses set up at intervals between The Wash and The Solent had been committed to a single officer with the title of "Count of the Saxon Shore." In 286 Carausius, who held this command, rebelled and established himself as an autonomous ruler in Britain. The British empire that he governed for seven years could not be subdued. Perhaps to guard against its spread as well as for administrative reasons, in 293 each Augustus nominated a deputy or Caesar to share his burdens, adopting him as his heir as had the Antonines. Again, military men were chosen, Galerius for the East and Constantius for the West. The Tetrarchy, "four rulers of the world" interconnected by a web of marriage alliances, had come into being.

Security and restoration of past values were the hallmarks of this administration. In the next decade the existing forty-three provinces were gradually subdivided into 120 units, administratively and economically viable but too small to support an ambitious general in search of an empire. At the same time, however, the army and the administration were greatly increased in numbers, and the frontiers defended with massive fortifications. These typified the siege mentality that seems to have taken hold of the empire's rulers. The watchword was *disciplina*, replacing the *liberalitas* or even *clementia* of earlier reigns. The empire came to resemble a vast fortified camp; even the Alexandrian corn-dole was named "military bread" (*panis castrensis*). Tendencies for classes to become hereditary castes intensified with occupations passing ineluctably from father to son. All were expected to perform their duties for the benefit of the empire, and not least to look after the needs of "the honourable soldiers." A woman who could not supply two animals for corvée duty because one was sick had to write a formal report outlining the circumstances and asking to be excused.[95] All over the empire corvées were demanded, for no effort was spared to repair the cities after nearly half a century of neglect. From Londinium to the

Numidian towns of Lambaesis, Macomades, and Timgad, inscriptions tell of the restoration of temples, aqueducts, fountains, and public buildings "collapsed from decay," or "for a long time neglected."[96] The emperor's own building programs were on a vast scale. Galerius's palace at Thessalonica, Maximin's at Antioch, or Diocletian's at Spalato, or Maxentius's Baths at Rome were huge buildings; the palaces have frontages extending up to half a mile, while Diocletian's retreat at Spalato, a mere villa, was capacious enough to house an entire urban population during the Middle Ages. While not lacking in real distinction, and to judge from Spalato,[97] even grace in proportions, the cost of these public works must have been enormous, and the labor requirements presume a degree of regimentation of society to an extent hardly imaginable. Lactantius's criticism of the Tetrarchy's building schemes as "mania" was justified.[98]

The restoration of Roman virtues was to be under the aegis of the Roman gods whose worship was encouraged everywhere. This implied the suppression of local customs where these were thought to be noxious. The emperors seem to have been genuinely surprised as well as shocked at the survival in Egypt of marriage between brothers and sisters. The edict dating probably to c. 295 *Concerning Marriages* (*De nuptiis*) returns time and again to the theme of the example of Roman antiquity and the need for religious uniformity. The Roman people had prospered thanks to their respect for traditional morality. That favor could be lost if some of the inhabitants of the empire, through ignorance or "through some prescription of barbarian savagery," behaved otherwise. The "discipline of our times" compelled the emperors to intervene. "Our laws protect nothing that is not holy and venerable, and thus Roman majesty has attained so great a plenitude by the favor of the divine powers."[99] Less than twenty years later Constantine and Licinius were to invoke the same divine favor from the Supreme God worshiped by the Christians.

Uniformity was expressing itself in other, more material ways. Currency, taxation, and finally in 301, prices were all reorganized in the sense of a single, ostensibly simple system designed to operate throughout the empire. Between 294 and 296 the local mints, which were maintained by the larger cities of the empire and were a source of civic pride, were closed down. The multitude of virtues and pieties were banished from the reverse sides of the coinage. They were replaced by a new, uniform coinage in gold, silver, and silvered bronze, furnished with a few designs aimed at the widest possible appeal. On the new gold coin (*aureus*) stood the Roman gods, guardians of the state and the lives of its peoples. On the silver, reintroduced perhaps as a deliberate counterblast to Carausius's fine silver issues, the first seen in the empire since 244, were the military virtues of loyalty and concord, and the sacrificial cult, but on the new, handy, silvered bronze coin (the *follis*), minted in hundreds of thousands, read a single inscription, "To the genius of the Roman people" (*Genio populi Romani*), bearing Jupiter standing with a sacrificial dish in one hand and holding the horn of bounty in the other.[100] Unity was to bring peace and abundance, under the providence of the gods and their earthly representatives.

The imperial biographers (*Scriptores Historiae Augustae*), or their sources, were to present the emperors as "courageous and wise, benign and open handed, concerned for the welfare of the state, respectful to the senate, friends of the people, serious-minded and pious towards the gods," the sort of men one would pray to have as rulers.[101] The coins added the suggestion of massive strength, their bull necks and closely cropped hair hardly differentiating one from another. Even Valeria, wife of Galerius and Diocletian's daughter, did not escape from a Junoesque portrait. Yet for all the display of embattled force, there was a conscious effort to promote well-being even for the meanest of the provincials. The ill-fated Edict on Maximum Prices of November 301 was aimed at hoarders and profiteers, the curse of the lives of the ordinary subjects, as Philostratus showed so eloquently.[102] Every imaginable item from Celtic cloaks to the proper price of a donkey's load (four denarii!), the same price as a measure of beer, was arranged under subject heading and tariffed exactly. The terms of the edict were proclaimed in stone covering the walls of entire buildings in the main provincial cities. At least one provincial governor, Fulvius Asticus, the *praeses* of Caria, went further, declaring:

> This also is a sign of the divine foresight [of the Emperors] namely that a fair and fixed price has been laid down in respect of everything, since our uncon-quered and all-conquering masters, the Augusti and Caesares, proclaim [that there must be] a plentiful livelihood [for all], in order that by the establishment of a [plentiful supply] of things for sale in a context of just prices and [..?..] the same may be available to all men, and [that there must be] a state of affairs in which no one lacks the things which are necessary for use because of the excessive ambition and greed of some, all desire for wrong-doing having been eliminated. The divinity of the Emperors has provided that this measure may be preserved and last for ever.[103]

The edict, drawn up in a spirit reminiscent of the efforts of the medieval church to enforce a "just price," was to last "for ever." The Jovian dicta-torship was to be paternal.

This was the ultimate in the attempt to enforce uniformity in life and attitudes throughout the empire, and it was a radical departure from any known practice by the emperors in the past. Fifteen years later, Lactantius criticized this as well as many other acts "of that pious man" (Diocle-tian).[104] While Lactantius may merely have been reflecting the opinions of Constantine's court after the Edict of Milan, the measures he picked out and the knowledge he showed of their results suggest personal feelings and experiences. The hordes of tax gatherers, "more numerous than the tax-payers," that descended on the population as a result of the subdivision of the provinces, and the injustices that resulted from the rough and ready tax assessments impressed him vividly.[105] So, too, did the continued degradation of the laborer to the advantage of the rich.[106] He regarded Diocletian not as a restorer of the Roman world, but as a malign destructive force; though his own career as teacher of rhetoric in a North African provincial town, but with access to a range of Latin translations of uncommon Greek works, is an unconscious testimony to the restoration of cultural as well as material well-being to some of the cities.[107] In his protests, however, we see the Christians emerging as the main opponents of the Tetrarchy, casting doubt on the whole system of government and mocking even the military successes of the emperors. The fact was that, in some obvious respects, paganism and the government's oppressive measures could become associated. In Egypt the local temple, the center of the social life of the village might also be an agent for gathering and forwarding taxes.[108] In North Africa government property was sometimes stored in temples. The subdeacon Silvanus admitted stealing vases containing vinegar belonging to the fisc, that had been deposited in the temple of Sarapis at Cirta.[109] Such usages might have passed unnoticed in prosperous times, but in the dislocations and massive requirements in terms of labor and resources demanded by the Tetrarchy, protest could not be stilled. Christians showed themselves to be the most aware of the situation and, in individual cases, attempted to alleviate its rigors, and they gained accordingly.

The Outbreak of the Persecution

Seen thus, the Great Persecution becomes less of an aberration. Its timing, too, in terms of the military successes (Britain had been regained in 296 and the Persians defeated by 298) and economic policies of the empire, becomes intelligible. After 301, Lactantius's account of Galerius's relentless pressure on Diocletian could be true. There were personal tensions at court also, as Diocletian's wife and daughter were suspected of pro-Christian leanings. The crisis developed slowly, and long and anxious were the debates before the emperors decided on their fateful enterprise.

There had, however, been one dress rehearsal. In 296 the Persian War had been renewed and in its early stages had gone badly for the Romans. Galerius was defeated at Callinicum on the Euphrates and returned to Antioch to be publicly humiliated by Diocletian himself. More dangerous, however, than the Persian army appeared to be the spread of Manicheism through the empire. By 282 Manichean missionaries were working in Egypt, and a dozen years later there were evidently cells as far west as Carthage. The threat was almost certainly overestimated. The strict asceticism of the Manicheans and their mournful psalms and prayers won converts, but by and large the cult seemed to outsiders such as Alexander, the Neo-Platonist of Lycopolis (c. 300), to be overcomplicated, especially when compared with the simplicity of orthodox Christianity.[110]

To Diocletian and his advisers, however, Manicheism looked like a deadly Persian weapon. The rescript which he sent to Julianus, proconsul of Africa, on 31 March 297 when the Persian War was nearing its climax shows that he was prepared to crush a proselytizing creed if it appeared to be hostile to the state. Manicheans were ordered to hand over their sacred books for burning, and their leaders would be treated similarly. Once again, the emperor stressed "the wickedness of attempting to undo past tradition," and affirmed his determination "to punish the obstinacy of the perverted mentality of these most wicked men."[111] Similar thoughts must have gone through Pliny's mind as he dispatched the Bithynian Christians to execution in 112.

Galerius's decisive victory over the Persians by the end of 297 increased the possibility of a confrontation with the Christians. The Caesar was a convinced pagan and his star was in ascendance. A series of minor incidents now began to rouse Diocletian's own suspicions about the Christians. At Antioch in 298 auguries proved unsatisfactory because, claimed the pagan priests, of the disturbing presence of Christians at the sacrifices. A process began in which full-scale persecution was a logical outcome. Christians found themselves being dismissed from the army and imperial service. "Little by little persecution began against us," Eusebius records under the year 301.[112] As the *Chronicle* is one of his earliest works and Eusebius was writing almost contemporaneously, this is probably correct. Pressure gradually increased until, following the visit by the two emperors to the oracle of Apollo at Didyma, the irrevocable decision was taken at the end of 302. On 23 February 303, a date chosen deliberately by Diocletian and Galerius as being that of the feast of Terminalia, the final struggle for the allegiance of the empire began.[113]

The persecution resembled Valerian's more than Decius's. It had been carefully planned and the consequences had been weighed. Diocletian recognized the danger of making Christians martyrs. No blood, he insisted, must be shed.[114] The aim was to recall the Christians to their duty of recognizing the majesty of the Roman gods. The edict he promulgated on 24 February ordered that throughout the empire churches were to be destroyed, and the sacred books of the Christians handed over to be burned. Christians in public offices were to be removed from them. In private life Christians in the upper classes (*honestiores*) were to lose their privileges. In particular, they could not act as plaintiffs in cases of injury, adultery, or theft. Christian slaves might not be freed. But there was no requirement for universal sacrifice. The attack was concentrated on the organization of the church, its life as represented by the Scriptures and buildings, and on its influential members.[115]

Despite the inroads Christianity had been making into pagan society, Diocletian's edict commanded a fair measure of support. There may have been no great differences in the beliefs of an educated pagan and an educated Christian, but there was a depth of cleavage in terms of ultimate allegiance. However impatient pagans may have been with superstitious practices, blood sacrifices, and temple ceremonies, they accepted the value of ancestral customs and tradition, and they were prepared to blame every disaster, from barbarian invasions to unseasonable weather, on the Christians. The latter remained dangerous atheists, worshiping a man who had died a violent death as a rebel. "Serve them right," was the reaction of one of Lactantius's philosopher acquaintances at Nicomedia as they reached for their pens to attack their enemy while they had the advantage.[116] As the persecution took its course, there were plenty of others who justified the right of the authorities to have Christian books destroyed as they undermined respect due to the old national traditions. In 311 Galerius's Edict of Toleration made clear that the burden of complaint against Christians was that they had abandoned the religion of their forefathers; and this reflected opinion in the eastern provinces of the empire. Eusebius adds that hostility was rife against those who accepted "Jewish myths" at their face value, and made a criminal into a cult-hero.[117] In every town of the empire the temples to the Roman gods still dominated the scene. An inhabitant of Dougga or Sufetula, both medium-sized North African towns, would always have been aware, wherever she or he walked within the city walls, of these monuments to the immortal gods. Those who actually tried the Christian leaders, such as the mayors (*curatores*) of the North African cities, were often men of substance who had been benefactors of their communities.[118] For all their efforts to live at peace with their pagan neighbors, urban Christians could still be unpopular. In Nicomedia, the mob completed the destruction of the church begun by the emperor's troops. The fanatic who tore down the imperial edict with a mocking, "More victories over the Goths and Sarmatians," was seized and roasted alive.[119] Whatever respect might have been felt for individual Christians, no one in an official position in any part of the empire is recorded to have failed to carry out the emperor's orders.

Nonetheless, it is difficult to see how even with that measure of support the persecution could have achieved lasting results. The Christians were too well organized, too widespread, and too numerous to be destroyed. And, as Lactantius rubbed home, they had a case. At first, however, matters went well for the emperors. During 303 the pattern of events resembled that of the Decian persecution. The first reaction of the Christians of Cirta was flight. Many made for the Chettaba hills (Mons Bellona) about five miles south of the city.[120] In Egypt Bishop Peter of Alexandria left his city for Oxyrhynchus.[121] Meantime, all over the empire the authorities set about burning down Christian churches and collecting copies of the Scriptures. In proconsular Africa, for which there is good documentation, the first thing people knew of the emperor's orders was the sight of churches going up in flames (probably late April).[122] The edict was executed immediately and without question. The following oft-quoted dialogue between Bishop Paul

458

of Cirta and the mayor (*curator*) of the city may be cited as probably a typical instance. It took place on 19 May 303.

In the eighth and seventh consulships of Diocletian and Maximian, 19th May, from the records of Munatius Felix, high priest of the province for life, mayor of the colony of Cirta. Arrived at the house where the Christians used to meet, the Mayor said to Paul the bishop: "Bring out the writings of the law and anything else you have here, according to the order, so that you may obey the command."

The Bishop: "The readers have the scriptures, but we will give what we have here."

The Mayor: "Point out the readers or send for them."

The Bishop: "You all know them."

The Mayor: "We do not know them."

The Bishop: "The municipal office knows them, that is, the clerks Edusius and Junius."

The Mayor: "Leaving over the matter of the readers, whom the office will point out, produce what you have."

Then follows an inventory of the church plate and other property, including large stores of male and female clothes and shoes, produced in the presence of the clergy, who include three priests, two deacons, and four subdeacons, all named, and a number of "diggers."

The Mayor: "Bring out what you have."

Silvanus and Carosus (two of the subdeacons): "We have thrown out everything that was here."

The Mayor: "Your answer is entered on the record."

After some empty cupboards had been found in the library, Silvanus then produced a silver box and a silver lamp, which he said he had found behind a barrel.

Victor (the mayor's clerk): "You would have been a dead man if you hadn't found them."

The Mayor: "Look more carefully, in case there is anything left here."

Silvanus: "There is nothing left. We have thrown everything out."

And when the dining-room was opened, there were found there four bins and six barrels.

The Mayor: "Bring out the scriptures that you have so that we can obey the orders and command of the emperors."

Catullinus (another subdeacon) produced one very large volume.

The Mayor: "Why have you given one volume only? Produce the scriptures that you have."

Marcuclius and Catullinus (two subdeacons): "We haven't any more, because we are subdeacons; the readers have the books."

The Mayor: "Show me the readers."

Marcuclius and Catullinus: "We don't know where they live."

The Mayor: "If you don't know where they live, tell me their names."

Marcuclius and Catullinus: "We are not traitors: here we are, order us to be killed."

The Mayor: "Put them under arrest."[123]

In fact, they weakened and revealed the name of one reader, for the mayor moved on to his house, but the whole incident shows how when the issue was fairly joined the pagan authorities were still in command, and their administration of the edict fair but firm, and in the last resort the death penalty for disobedience was in the background.

Sometimes the authorities would accept a formal act of obedience. In the capital, Carthage, they allowed themselves to be fobbed off with "heretical" (Manichean?) works produced by Bishop Mensurius, and at Calama in Numidia the bishop got away with handing over medical works.[124] Resistance was minimal. Only Felix, Bishop of Thibiuca (Bou Cha?), is recorded as having refused to surrender anything. He was sent to Carthage and martyred probably on 15 July 303.[125] In Palestine, where Eusebius of Caesarea witnessed the events, only the scattered actions of real fanatics such as Procopius of Gaza (executed on 7 June), who compounded political with religious nonconformity,[126] interfered with the smooth carrying out of the emperor's orders.

During the summer these were reinforced by a second edict, ordering that all bishops and other heads of Christian communities should be arrested and forced to sacrifice. Prisons in the empire, however, were not designed to house numerous, potentially long-term inmates. The situation soon became impossible. Real criminals, says Eusebius, were being crowded out.[127] A third edict was promulgated perhaps as an amnesty in anticipation of the Vicennalia, ordering that the imprisoned clergy should be forced to sacrifice and should be freed. Grotesque scenes followed. The aim of the previous edicts had not been punishment so much as the enforcement of some recognition of the gods; and now every inducement was applied. Some gave way, but more seem to have resisted. Lactantius describes how he "saw in Bithynia the prefect [Hierocles?] wonderfully elated as though he had subdued some nation of barbarians, because one who had resisted with great spirit appeared at length to yield."[128] Eusebius describes a case in Palestine "of one man, others held him fast with both hands, brought him to the altar, and let fall on it out of his right hand, the hated and polluted sacrifice: then dismissed him as though he had sacrificed. . . ."[129] Others yielded more quietly, "shamefully hiding themselves here and there" before being produced at the altars for public mockery.

Diocletian felt sure enough of the situation that in the autumn he left Nicomedia for Rome to celebrate his twentieth salutation as emperor (*Dies imperii*), which fell on 20 November. The emperor's stay in the old imperial city was short and discouraging. Like Constantine and Constantius II after him, he found the Roman populace turbulent and unwelcoming, especially when he economized on the games. But at this time, it would seem, he resolved to carry out the act for which he is most remembered, abdication, and wrung a promise to do the same simultaneously from Maximian.[130]

Then, he left without regret on 20 December, and made for Ravenna—a portent of the future role of this city as an imperial headquarters in the West. At some point a lingering malady (malaria?) laid him low. His return journey through the Balkan provinces was painfully slow. One public appearance in Nicomedia on 1 March 305 sufficed to convince those who saw him that he was a dying man. For the last year, the reins of government had fallen to his more thrusting colleague, Galerius.

Galerius

During 304, Galerius had turned the persecution from a sharp reminder to the Christian clergy that the immortal gods still protected the empire, and required acknowledgment even from those who ordinarily turned their backs on them, to all-out war on Christians whether lay or clerical. Up to that time, Eusebius remarked, "the presidents of the Church alone had been menaced" (*On the Palestinian Martyrs* III.1). The fourth edict, promulgated probably in the early spring of 304, ordered Christians to sacrifice to the gods on pain of death. This was enforced in the provinces under Galerius's control immediately, but only towards the end of the year, it appears, in Diocletian's. In the West, there is some dispute whether the edict was enforced there at all. Certainly, in Constantius's provinces, that is, Britain, Gaul, the Rhineland, and Spain, there is no evidence for any mass obligation to sacrifice, and Lactantius suggests the contrary.[131] In North Africa and Italy, Maximian's territories, the problem is more difficult. The dating of various administrative changes affecting Numidia make it difficult to fit the alleged persecuting governor of the province, Valerius Florus, into that role. On the other hand, Optatus of Milevis, who was well informed of events of the time, distinguished clearly between handing over Scriptures (*traditio*) and the day of sacrifice (*dies thurificationis*).[132] In the proceedings at Cirta in May 303, Bishop Paul was not required to sacrifice as well as surrender the Scriptures (at some other places, in proconsular Africa, both were performed apparently at the same time).[133] On the other hand, Eusebius described the sufferings of the Africans as comparable with those of the Egyptians.[134] This was hardly the case during 303 and as persecution was not recommenced after the abdication of Diocletian and Maximian on 1 May 305, the real terror could only have occurred in 304. For Eusebius to record it, terror it must have been. A stone balustrade and an elaborate mosaic forming the focal point of a martyrium within a church at Ammaedara in western Tunisia record the names of thirty-four victims who "suffered persecution under the divine laws of our lords, Diocletian and Maximian."[135] The names of the men and women are those of laity, native provincials. The fourth edict tested the real strength of Christianity over much of the empire. What previously had been only a nuisance to ordinary Christians became a direct challenge to their faith.

Even before the fourth edict, there were stirrings among Christian laity that boded ill for either the successful vindication of the immortal gods or the future peace of the church. Again, an important piece of evidence comes from North Africa. We have already seen how, alongside the rather sedate and quiescent Christianity of the well-established communities, an idealism based on a literal understanding of the New Testament and Jesus' commands was inspiring a new generation of Christians. In the late autumn or winter of 303 a single, long-remembered incident lit the flame. While Christians had not been ordered to sacrifice to the gods, they had been ordered to stop celebrating their own services. At Abitina, a few miles west of Membressa (Medjez el Bab) on the Medjerda plain, the bishop had dutifully handed over the Scriptures on demand. His congregation disowned his act, and carried on with services in the house of the lector Emeritus. The latter subsequently told his interrogators, who asked whether he left copies of the Scriptures in his house, that he "had the Scriptures engraved on his heart." He was joined by young idealists from Carthage anxious to be "with brethren who kept the precepts of God" and, if necessary, suffer with them. The authorities also heard what was going on, and one day they struck. Forty-seven Christians, including the leader, the presbyter Saturninus, and his four children, were arrested, brought to Carthage, and imprisoned.[136] Through the winter months the confessors had time to think over the implications of their stand. The Donatist, but probably near-contemporary, writer of the *Acta* of their martyrdom, records that they held a meeting and condemned the *traditor* clergy in the strongest terms. Even to alter a single letter of Scripture was sacrilegious and an insult to their author, and it followed that "to destroy the testaments and divine commands of Almighty God and our Lord Jesus Christ" by handing them over to be burned merited lasting damnation in unextinguishable fire.[137] No one, therefore, who maintained communion with *traditores* would participate in the joys of paradise reserved for themselves. In claiming thus to bind and loose, the Abitinian confessors were walking in the footsteps of the confessors of the Decian persecution, and more so, because they were claiming to judge any clergy who had collaborated with the authorities and not merely to dispense deserving cases agreed with the bishop. Could *traditor* clergy be deemed true ministers of the Word they had betrayed?

The widespread arrests and executions could not have been welcome to Diocletian at last recovering from his sickness. As Aurelius Victor suggests, Diocletian may have been plagued with forebodings for the future peace of the empire. He may have been under pressure from Galerius and have felt that the present was the right time to put into effect his plan to abdicate.[138] He chose 1 May 305 and at a great parade at Nicomedia he bade his troops a solemn farewell, claiming in a short but moving speech to have saved the civilized world, and stepped off the rostrum as a private citizen; Galerius was acclaimed as his successor. Then came a surprise. All eyes had been turned on the young Constantine, son of the Western Caesar Constantius, who was staying at the court of Diocletian. He was about thirty and had already given promise of future achievement.[139] But he was now thrust aside, and the two new Caesars, Severus and Maximin, were military men and friends of Galerius. Dynastic arrangements which would have favored him and Maximian's son, Maxentius, had been rejected in favor of others which might eventually bring Galerius's young son, Candidian, to the fore.[140]

Meantime in Milan, Maximian had abdicated, but for fear of Galerius dared not proclaim Maxentius as Caesar. Thus, the first Tetrarchy ended with the empire rent by religious upheavals and deep dynastic quarrels. Galerius had emerged supreme, but there were two able and malcontent princes whose ambitions could not be realized without destroying the new overlord's settlement. For the immortal gods the die was cast, and Constantine remembered that he had once heard the Christians called ·"righteous men."[141]

BIBLIOGRAPHY

NOTE

N. H. Baynes's two chapters, "The Great Persecution" (chap. 19, pp. 646–77) and "Constantine" (chap. 20, pp. 678–99), concluding *CAH*, vol. 12: *Imperial Crisis*, remain the most convincing account of the period of the Great Persecution. Useful also for full bibliographies of older works to 1939. For the expansion of Christianity in this period, see first and foremost, A. von Harnack, *The Mission and Expansion of Christianity in the First Three Centuries*, Eng. trans. J. Moffatt (London: Williams & Norgate, 1908; reprinted, Gloucester, Mass.: Peter Smith, 1963), vol. 2. Some additional information may be found in my *Martyrdom and Persecution*, chap. 14.

For Porphyry and pagan propaganda against Christianity in the period 270–300, see P. de Labriolle, *La réaction païenne: Étude sur la polemique antichrétienne du Ier au IVe siècles* (Paris: L'Artisan du livre, 1934; 2d ed., 1950), pp. 223ff. For Lactantius, *De Mortibus Persecutorum (On the Deaths of the Persecutors)*, see J. Moreau, ed., 2 vols., SC 39 (1954), especially the introduction. For Diocletian's reforms, see A. H. M. Jones, *The Later Roman Empire, 284–602* (2 vols., Norman: University of Oklahoma Press; 4 vols., Oxford: Basil Blackwell & Mott, 1964), chap. 2.

SOURCES

Acta Habib. Ed. and Eng. trans. A. Roberts and J. Donaldson. ANCL 20, Syriac Documents, 91–105.

Acta Saturnini. PL 8.688–715.

Other *Acta Martyrum* in Musurillo, ed., *Acts of Christian Martyrs*; and see also Baynes, bibliography to "Great Persecution," pp. 789–95.

Arnobius. *Adversus nationes*. Edited by A. Reifferscheid. CSEL 4. Vienna: Geroldi, 1875.

Canons of Elvira, in Mansi, *Sacrorum Conciliorum*, vol. 2, 1–19.
Eusebius, *Contra Hieroclem*, PG 22.797–800; Eng. trans. F. C. Conybeare in
Philostratus, vol. II, pp. 483–605, LCL, Cambridge, Mass.: Harvard University
Press; London: William Heinemann, 1912.
_____. *Ecclesiastical History*, vol. II, book VIII. Eng. trans. J. E. L. Oulton. LCL.
Cambridge, Mass.: Harvard University Press; London: William Heinemann,
1932.
_____, *Martyrs of Palestine*, ed. E. Schwartz, GCS 9, Eusebius, pp. 907–50; Eng.
trans. and ed. H. J. Lawlor and J. E. L. Oulton, *The Ecclesiastical History and
the Martyrs of Palestine*, New York: Macmillan Co., London: SPCK, 1927–28.
_____, *Praeparatio evangelica* (*Preparation for the Gospel*), ed. K. Mras, GCS 43,
Eusebius, Berlin: Akademie-Verlag, 1954–56; Eng. ed. and trans. E. H. Gifford,
London: Oxford University Press, 1903.
Gesta apud Zenophilum. In Optatus of Milevis, *De Schismate Donatistarum*,
ed. C. Ziwsa, Appendix I, pp. 185–96. CSEL 26. Leipzig: G. Freytag, 1893.
Lactantius, *Divinae Institutiones* (*Divine Institutes*), ed. S. Brandt and G. Laub-
mann, CSEL 19, Vienna, 1890; Eng. trans. ANCL.
Mamertinus. In *Panegyrici Latini* II. Edited by E. Galletier. Paris: Edition Budé,
1949–55, French trans.
Porphyry, *Contra Christianos*, book XV, see A. von Harnack, *Porphyrius "gegen
die Christen," 15 Bücher, Zeugnisse, Fragmente und Referate*, AAWB 1916.1.
_____. *Philosophy from Oracles* and *De regressu animae* (*On the Return of the
Soul*), fragments found in Augustine, collected by J. J. O'Meara, *Porphyry's
Philosophy from Oracles in Augustine*, Paris: Études Augustiniennes, 1959.
Scriptores Historiae Augustae (for *Vita Cari et Carini*), ed. E. Hohl, reprint ed.,
Leipzig: Teubner, 1955; Eng. trans. and ed. D. Magie, vol. 3, pp. 416–52, LCL,
Cambridge, Mass.: Harvard University Press; London: William Heinemann,
1932.
Aurelius Victor. *Caesares*. Edited by F. Pichlmayr. Leipzig: Teubner, 1911.
For coinage, see *Roman Imperial Coinage*, vol. 5, pt. 1, *Valerian to Florian* (1927),
pt. 2, *Probus to Allectus* (1933), ed. H. Mattingly and P. H. Webb, London:
Spink & Son; and vol. 6, *From Diocletian's Reform* (A.D. 294) *to the Death of
Maximinus* (A.D. 313), ed. C. H. V. Sutherland. London: Spink & Son, 1967.
For inscriptions from Asia Minor, see MAMA; from North Africa, see *CIL* VIII.
For law, see S. Riccobono et al., eds. *Fontes Iuris Romani antejustiniani*
(= *FIRA*), 3 vols., Florence, 1940–43, esp. vol. 2 of 2d ed., pp. 544–89.
For Manichean texts, see Alfred Adam, *Texte zum Manichäismus*, KlT 175, Berlin:
Walter de Gruyter, 1954.

SECONDARY WORKS

Balty, J., and Balty, J. C. *Apamée de Syrie: Bilan de recherches archéologiques
1969–71*. Brussels, 1972.
Baynes, N. H. "Two Notes on the Great Persecution." *CQ* 18 (1924): 189–93.
Beschaouch, A. "Les stèles à Saturne de 8 novembre 323." *BAC* mono. ser. (1968):
252–68.
Calder, W. M. "The Eumeneian Formula." In *Studies Presented to W. H. Buckler*,
pp. 15–21. Manchester, Eng.: Manchester University Press, 1926.

Courcelle, P. "Anti-Christian Arguments and Christian Platonism: From Arnobius to Ambrose." In *The Conflict Between Paganism and Christianity in the Fourth Century*, ed. A. Momigliano, chap. 7, pp. 151–92. New York and London: Oxford University Press, 1963.

Crawford, M. H., and Reynolds, Joyce. "The Publication of the Prices Edict: A New Inscription from Aezani." *JRS* 65 (1975): 160–64.

Fennelly, J. M. "Roman Involvement in the Affairs of the Egyptian Shrine." *BJRL* 50 (1968): 317–35.

Frend, W. H. C. "A Note on the Great Persecution in the West." *SCH* 2 (1965): 141–48.

———. "A Note on the Influence of Greek Immigrants on the Spread of Christianity in the West." In *Mullus: Festschrift Theodor Klauser*, pp. 125–29. Münster: Aschendorff, 1964.

Gaiffier, B. de. "Palatins et eunuques dans quelques documents hagiographiques." AnBoll 75 (1957): 17–46.

Jones, R. Duncan. "An African Saint and His Interrogator." *JTS* n.s. 25 (1974): 106–10.

Kirsten, E. "Chorbischof." *RAC* II, 1105–14.

Lebreton, J. "The Pagan Opposition." In *The History of the Primitive Church*, ed. J. Lebreton and J. Zeiller, chap. 22, pp. 875–90. Eng. trans. E. C. Messenger. New York and London: Macmillan Co., 1949.

Leglay, J. "Les stèles à Saturne de Djemila-Cuicul." *Libyca* 1 (1953): 37–76.

Lloyd, A. C. "Porphyry and Iamblichus." In *The Cambridge History of Later Greek and Early Medieval Philosophy*, ed. A. H. Armstrong, chap. 18, pp. 283–301. New York and Cambridge: Cambridge University Press, 1967.

Mattingly, H. "The Imperial Recovery." In *CAH*, vol. 12, *Imperial Crisis*, chap. 9, pp. 297–351.

Rand, E. K. "The Latin Literature of the West from the Antonines to Constantine." In *CAH*, vol. 12, *Imperial Crisis*, chap. 17, pp. 571–610.

Rousselle, A. "Aspects sociaux du recrutement ecclésiastique au ive siecle." *MEFR(A)* 89 (1977): 333–70.

———. "La chronologie de Maximien Hercule et la mythe de la Tétrarchie." *Dialogues d'Histoire ancienne* 2 (Besançon, 1976), pp. 466ff.

Ste. Croix, G. E. M. de. "Aspects of the 'Great' Persecution." *HTR* 47 (1954): 75–113.

Sickle, C. E. van. "The Public Works of Africa in the Reign of Diocletian." *CP* 25 (1930): 173–79.

Warmington, B. H. *The North African Provinces from Diocletian to the Vandal Conquest*. New York and Cambridge: Cambridge University Press, 1954.

NOTES

1. *Restitut[or] Orbis*. See Mattingly and Webb, *RIC*, vol. 5, pt. 1, *Valerian to Florian*, pp. 297–98, and for *Pacator Orbis* featuring Sol, see ibid., p. 265, nos. 4 and 6.

2. See J. Gagé's interesting study, "Le paganisme impérial à la recherche d'une théologie vers le milieu du iiie siècle," AAMz 12 (1952): 587–607, esp. p. 600.

3. Mattingly and Webb, *RIC*, vol. 5, pt. 1, *Valerian to Florian*, p. 270, no. 48; and p. 279, no. 129.

4. Lactantius, *Deaths of Persecutors*, ed. Moreau VI, and Eusebius *HE* VII.30.20: Aurelian "changed his mind towards us" (Christians).

5. *RIC*, vol. 5, pt. 2, *Probus to Allectus,* for example, pp. 119–20 (Antioch). Also, Zonaras *Epitome historiarum* XII.29. For Probus's ideas see Mattingly, "Imperial Recovery," pp. 297–319.

6. On Apamea as a famous center for Neo-Platonism in the late third and early fourth centuries, see J. Balty, "Archéologie et témoignages littéraires," in *Apamée de Syrie*, ed. Balty and Balty, pp. 209–12. Libanius's grandfather visited the city to try to find an able philosopher to teach his sons, suggesting that Apamea was continuing to be a center for pagan letters c. 320 (Libanius *Orations* II.11 and XXXII.21).

7. See Lloyd, "Porphyry and Iamblichus," pp. 293–97.

8. Cited by Eusebius, *Preparation* XI.19, ed. Mras, p. 45.

9. Cited by Augustine, *De consensu evangelistarum* (*On the Agreement of the Evangelists*) I.32.49 (*PL* 34.1066). On the question whether Porphyry's work *Return of Soul* is not in fact the same as *Philosophy from Oracles*, see O'Meara, *Porphyry's Philosophy*, pp. 1–2 and argued throughout the book. However, the evidence does not seem watertight—too little survives for detailed comparisons to be made. I have treated them as separate works written at about the same period, c. 263–65.

10. Cited by Augustine *De civitate Dei* (*City of God*) XVIII.53, "Petrum autem maleficia fecisse subjugunt." See also ibid., XX.24.

11. Porphyry, cited by Augustine *City of God* XX.24, and cf. XIX.23. See O'Meara, *Porphyry's Philosophy*, pp. 50–51 and 64–67.

12. Cited from Augustine *Letter* CII.8.

13. *Codex Justinianus* I.1.3. See also *Codex Theodosianus* XVI.5.66 of 3 August 435 (quoting Constantine's law); and Socrates *Ecclesiastical History* I.9.31.

14. Porphyry, Fragment 49, in A. von Harnack, *Porphyrius "gegen die Christen."* "Why should not the demons have been consigned to the abyss?" asked Porphyry.

15. See above, pp. 378–79.

16. Fragment 17. See Labriolle, *La réaction païenne*, p. 252.

17. Fragment 55. See Labriolle, *La réaction païenne*, pp. 252–53.

18. Fragment 43. See Labriolle, *La réaction païenne*, pp. 266–68.

19. Thus, Julius Africanus, *Chronicle* (in Routh, ed., *Reliquiae Sacrae,* vol. 2, pp. 190–92).

20. Porphyry implies this in the passage quoted by Eusebius concerning Origen's "defection to Christianity," *HE* VI.19.2; and for his patriotic traditionalism, see the fragment of the *Letter to Marcella*, published by U. von Wilamowitz-Möllendorf in *ZNW* 1 (1900): 101–5.

21. Fragments preserved by Eusebius *Contra Hieroclem* (*Against Hierocles*) (*PG* 22.797ff.); and see Lactantius *Divinae Institutiones* (*Divine Institutes*) V.2–3. See Frend, *Martyrdom and Persecution*, pp. 497–98.

22. Arnobius *Adversus nationes* (*Against the Pagans*) II.12–15. See Courcelle, "Anti-Christian Arguments," p. 155. For Christ as a magician, see *Against Pagans* I.52–53.

23. *Against Pagans* II.63–64.

24. Porphyry as the heathen spokesman cited by Macarius Magnes *Apocriticus* IV.21 (= von Harnack, *Porphyrius "gegen die Christen,"* frag. 76, p. 93).

25. Augustine *City of God* XIX.23. See O'Meara, *Porphyry's Philosophy*, pp. 49–61.

26. *HE* VIII.1.1 and compare *Preparation* I.5.1 (ed. Mras, p. 19).

27. *HE* VIII.11.2 (Adauctus); ibid., 6.1 (Dorotheus); and ibid., 9.7 (Philoromus).

28. Von Harnack, *Mission and Expansion*, book 4.

29. Dionysius, cited by Eusebius *HE* VII.7.5.

30. Eusebius *HE* VIII.11.1; Lactantius *Institutes* V.11.

31. Orcistus's claim that "everyone was Christian" in Constantine's reign (c. 325) in its petition for promotion to *civitas* status. This could hardly have happened overnight. See W. M. Calder, MAMA VII, 305, and introd. p. xxxviii.

32. See Calder, "Eumeneian Formula." This formula, which invoked the aid of "the living God" to avenge violation of the dedicant's tomb could, however, be Jewish as well as Christian in the third century.

33. Published by E. Gibson, "The 'Christians for Christians' Inscriptions of Phrygia," *HTS* 32 (1978): 116–19.

34. See ibid., p. 140.

35. Eusebius *HE* IX.7.9. See von Harnack, *Mission and Expansion*, pp. 333–34.

36. Eusebius *De vita Constantini* (*Life of Constantine*) II.12.

37. Gregory of Nyssa writing a century later, *De vita Gregorii Thaumaturgi* (*Life of Gregory Thaumaturgus*) (*PG* 46.909C and 954D). Also Socrates *Ecclesiastical History* IV.27.

38. Cyprian *Letter* LIX.10.

39. Only eighty-five were actually present. Two Tripolitanian bishops mandated their colleagues to vote for them.

40. See von Harnack's discussion of numbers in *Mission and Expansion*, pp. 423–24.

41. When is uncertain, but the right was accepted by Augustine when he first took up the struggle against the Donatists in 393. See *Psalmus contra partem Donati* (*Psalm Against the Donatist Sect*) lines 44–46 (*PL* 43.26).

42. *Passio Sanctorum Mariani et Jacobi*, in *Acts of Christian Martyrs*, ed. Musurillo, pp. 194–213, 2.2.

43. *Gesta apud Zenophilum* in Optatus *De Schismate Donatistarum*, p. 194.

44. Leglay, "Les stèles à Saturne," p. 37; and compare 70–76. The temple was in ruins by 366–67 when it was replaced by a civil basilica, but some steles could be early fourth century. See also *CIL* VIII.6960 where a dedication to Saturn has been obliterated by the sign of the cross.

45. Publ. by Beschaouch, "Les stèles à Saturne."

46. See. A. Beschaouch, "Saturne à la barbe fleurie," *Africa* (1970): 315–17. For continued awe of Saturn in the early fifth century, especially in Carthage, see Augustine, *Agreement of Evangelists* I.21.29 (*PL* 34.1055–58); and I.23.36; and compare Leglay, "Les stèles à Saturne," p. 71.

47. *CIL* VIII.18828–57.

48. Based largely on own observations 1938–39. See also E. Albertini, *CRAIBL* (1939): 100 (the Donatist cathedral); and H. I. Marrou, "Sur une inscription concer-

nant Optat de Timgad,'' *Christiana Tempora*, Collection de l'Ecole française de Rome 35 (Rome: Palais Farnese, 1978), pp. 145–48.

49. Discussed by Warmington, *North African Provinces*, pp. 41–45. For the maintenance of the city-state ideal among the North African pagans in the late third century, see Pontius *Vita Cypriani* (*Life of Cyprian*) 2: "Illis [that is, the pagans] extra civitatem vivere gravis poena est.''

50. From Thibilis, *Année épigraphique* (1893): 87, and Casae where paganism is described as "Romanae religionis,'' *CIL* VIII.18529; and for Timgad itself, *CIL* VIII.2387 (a dedication by the *res [publica] et ordo* of the *colonia*).

51. *Letters* L and XC.

52. *Acta Saturnini* II.

53. Augustine, *Breviculus collationis cum Donatistis* (*Summary of the Conference with the Donatists*) III.13.25, *PL* 43.637.

54. For Hieracas as a Coptic and leader of an ascetic sect, see Epiphanius *Medicine Box* LXVII.

55. Eusebius *HE* VI.42.

56. Theodore, *Vita Sancti Pachomii* III, *PL* 73, pp. 227–82, esp. pp. 231–32.

57. For instance, a village church existed in Mareotis, where there was fierce rivalry between Melitius and Athanasius, by 330; and also churches in the nome of Oxyrhynchus, at the time of the Great Persecution.

58. Carl Schmidt, "Fragmente einer Schrift des Märtyrerbischof Petrus von Alexandrien,'' *TU*, Neue Folge 5.4 (1901): 6–7.

59. K. Liebeschutz, "Epigraphic Evidence on the Christianisation of Syria,'' *Akten der XI internat. Limes Congresses* (Budapest: Hungarian Academy of Sciences, 1978), pp. 485–505; and on the slow conversion of the province of Coele-Phoenicia, Sozomen *Ecclesiastical History* VI.34.4.

60. See J. Neusner, "Conversion of Adiabene to Christianity,'' *Numen* 13 (August 1966): 144–50, esp. 149–50.

61. *Peregrinatio Etheriae*, Eng. trans. and ed. John Wilkinson, *Egeria's Travels* (London: SPCK, 1971), 20.8.

62. See above, p. 423.

63. For *chorepiscopi*, see canon 13 of the Council of Ancyra in 314 (not to ordain priests and deacons); and Kirsten, "Chorbischof.'' On the whole this evidence tends to contradict K. Liebeschutz's view (in *The Church in Town and Country*, ed. Derek Baker, Studies in Church History, vol. 12 [Oxford: Basil Blackwell & Mott, 1979], p. 17) that there was little rural Christianity in Syria before Constantine.

64. *OGIS* 608; see A. von Harnack, *Marcion, das Evangelium vom fremden Gott*, 2d ed. (Leipzig: Hinrichs, 1921), p. 263*–66*. For Marcionites in eastern Syria in the third century, see Eusebius *HE* IV.30 (Bardesanes writing against them). For Theodoret's missions to Marcionite villages, see Theodoret, *Letters* LXXXI and CXLV.

65. *Acta Habib*. Habib was a village deacon and traveling missionary. The villagers are recorded "as crying out spontaneously, 'We are Christians': and they were not afraid of the persecution (in Licinius's time, 321–24), because those who were persecuted were more numerous than those who persecuted them'' (p. 91).

66. Council of Elvira, canons 16, 49, 50, and 70, designed to prevent Christians from associating with Jews and even having their first fruits blessed by them!

67. See Rousselle, "Aspects sociaux,'' pp. 334–36. The author gives the total

as eleven bishoprics, including Trier and Cologne (Köln) among the Gallic sees. In addition, there were communities led by a presbyter at Orange and Apt and by a deacon at Gabalis in Aquitania, the only community outside the main lines of communication.

68. Rousselle, "Aspects sociaux," p. 336, "quelques points dans un désert païen."

69. Bede, *Ecclesiastical History of the English People*, ed. Bertram Colgrave and R. A. B. Mynors (New York: Oxford University Press; Oxford: At the Clarendon Press, 1969), I.7; and see my "*Ecclesia Britannica*: Prelude or Dead End?" *JEH* 30.2 (April 1979): 129–44.

70. *Passio Sancti Irenaei Episcopi Sirmiensis* (*The Martyrdom of Saint Irenaeus Bishop of Sirmium*), in *Acts of Christian Martyrs*, ed. Musurillo, 3. Everyone joined with his relatives to try to persuade Bishop Irenaeus to sacrifice and yield to the authorities.

71. Eusebius *Constantine* IV.43.

72. I owe this information to Professor I. Ramureanu of the University of Bucharest.

73. Paulinus of Nola, *Carmen XXI*, ed. W. Hartel, CSEL 30, pp. 158–86 (Leipzig: G. Freytag, 1894), lines 367ff.

74. See my "Influence of Greek Immigrants."

75. Ibid., p. 128, citing Rudolf Egger's research.

76. See above, p. 416, and J. Fink, *RivAC* 56 (1980): 133–46.

77. See M. Simon, "Les rivaux du christianisme dans le monde romain" (Allocation prononcée à la séance publique annuelle des Cinq Académies, le 25 octobre 1976), *Publications de l'Institut de France*, 1976, 15, pp. 8–9.

78. Illustrated in J. M. C. Toynbee and J. B. Ward-Perkins, *The Shrine of St. Peter and the Vatican Excavations* (London: Longmans, Green & Co., 1956), Pl. 32.

79. Ibid., pp. 116–17.

80. Elvira; canon 15. At Cirta it is interesting that the church stocked far more female than male clothes and shoes.

81. Elvira; canons 4, 10, 39, 42, 44, and 62.

82. Canon 4. They were more severe towards *flamines* who had been baptized, (ibid., 2 and 3).

83. I have accepted the views of Rand in his chapter, "Latin Literature," pp. 607–8.

84. Arnobius, *Adversus Nationes* (*Against the Pagans*) I.13, ed. Reifferscheid; and compare Lactantius *Institutes* V.13.1.

85. Lactantius *Deaths of Persecutors* IX, concerning Galerius, "efferitas a Romano sanguine aliena."

86. For instance, the collapse of "the golden age of justice" through violence, *Institutes* V.6.

87. Arnobius *Against Pagans* II.5; and compare I.55.

88. *Papyrus John Rylands* 469, publ. also by A. Adam in *Texte zum Manichaïsmus*, KIT 175 (Berlin, 1954), pp. 52–54.

89. Eusebius *HE* VII.1.7.

90. *Deaths of Persecutors* XI and XII (Galerius mainly responsible).

91. *HE* VIII.1.7.

92. Eusebius, *Vita Constantini* II.49, ed. I. Heikel, GCS 7, pp. 1–148 (Leipzig: Hinrichs, 1901), p. 62.

93. Aurelius Victor, *Caesares*, XL.36, ed. Pichlmayr, and *Carus, Carinus* X, in *SHA*, described as "vir reipublicae necessarius"—respected but not loved.

94. Mamertinus, *Panegyrici Latini* II, chap. XI.6, ed. Galletier, p. 34: "Diocletianus initium facit, tu (Maximianus) tribuis effectum."

95. *Pap. Oxy.* 2849, dated 21 May 296.

96. For Britain, see *Britannia* VII, 1976 (repair to a temple). For North Africa, see van Sickle, "Public Works."

97. A useful description translated into English is by T. Marasovic, "The Basement Halls of the Palace of Diocletian at Split" (Split, 1970). See also Vulic, "Salona," in *PW* Supplement 1a2 (Stuttgart, 1970), cols. 2005–6.

98. Lactantius *Deaths of Persecutors* VII and XXIII.

99. *Codex Gregorianus* V = *Legum Mosaicarum et Romanarum Legum Collatio* VI.4, ed. S. Riccobono, *FIRA* II, 558–60.

100. See C. H. V. Sutherland, "Flexibility in the 'Reformed' Coinage of Diocletian," in *Essays in Roman Coinage Presented to Harold Mattingly*, ed. R. A. G. Carson and Sutherland (New York and London: Oxford University Press, 1956), p. 179.

101. *Carus, Carinus* XVIII.4, in *SHA*.

102. See above, pp. 275–76.

103. See Crawford and Reynolds, "Publication of Prices Edict"; and for individual items see K. T. Erim and Joyce Reynolds, "Diocletian's Edict on Maximum Prices" (the Aphrodisias Copy) *JRS* 63 (1973): 99–110.

104. *Deaths of Persecutors* XXIII.8, "homo pius."

105. Ibid., 7.1 and 23. For an assessment of Diocletian's fiscal reforms, see Jones, *Later Roman Empire*, chap. 11.

106. *Institutes* V.6.

107. See R. M. Ogilvie, *The Library of Lactantius* (New York and London: Oxford University Press, 1978), esp. chaps. 4 and 8.

108. See Fennelly, "Roman Involvement," pp. 333ff.

109. *Gesta apud Zenophilum*, in Optatus, *De Schismate Donatistarum*, p. 193, "Nundinarius dixit, de cupis fisci, quis illas tulit . . . in templo Serapi fuerunt."

110. *De Placitis Manichaeorum* II (*PG* 18.413).

111. *Legum Mosaicarum* XV.3, ed. Riccobono, *FIRA* II.580–81. Text also in Adam, *Texte zum Manichäismus*, pp. 82–83. Despite recent criticisms, I accept the date 31 March 297. For the alternative of 31 March 302, see F. Décret, *L'Afrique manichéenne (IVe–Ve siècles). Étude historique et doctrinale* (Paris: Études Augustiniennes, 1978), pp. 162–67.

112. Eusebius-Jerome, *Chronicle*, ed. Helm, GCS 24, p. 227. For the view that the *Chronicle* and the first seven books of *HE* were compiled by 276/77 and "reflect the optimistic assumptions of Christian writing before the Persecution," see T. D. Barnes, *Constantine and Eusebius* (Cambridge, Mass.: Harvard University Press, 1981), pp. 145–46. For my doubts, see my review in *JEH* 33.4 (1982): 590–95. I find it curious also that Eusebius should have delayed mention of the Manichees (*HE* VII.31) until his second edition of *HE*, when Manichean missionaries were active in Syria and Egypt from the 270s (see Barnes, *Constantine and Eusebius*, p. 355 n. 166).

113. For the events leading up to the persecution, see *Martyrdom and Persecution*, pp. 489–90.

114. Lactantius *Deaths of Persecutors* XI.8.

115. Eusebius's view, *Martyrs of Palestine* III.1, ed. and trans. Lawlor and Oulton, p. 339.

116. Lactantius *Institutes* V.2. Lactantius had been appointed to a chair of rhetoric in Diocletian's capital and was an eyewitness of the events of 303 as well as being very well informed about their antecedents.

117. *Preparation* I.2, *PG* 21.28.

118. Such as Magnilianus, the *curator* of Thibiuca (Hr. Bou Cha?) where Bishop Felix was tried and sent to Carthage for execution. See R. Duncan Jones, "African Saint." (I accept the correctness of the author's identifications.)

119. *Deaths of Persecutors* XIII.3.

120. *Gesta apud Zenophilum*, in Optatus, *De Schismate Donatistarum*, App. 1, p. 186.

121. Schmidt, "Petrus von Alexandrien," p. 7.

122. Recorded in *Acta purgationis Felicis episcopi Autumnitani* (*Record of the Exculpation of Felix Bishop of Aptunga*) in Optatus, *De Schismate Donatistarum*, Appendix II, pp. 197–204, esp. p. 199. The inquiry into these events took place in 314–15.

123. *Gesta apud Zenophilum*, Eng. trans. in Stevenson, *A New Eusebius*, pp. 287–89.

124. Augustine *Contra Cresconium grammaticum* (*Against Cresconius the Grammarian*) III.30, citing the *Acta* of the Council of Cirta in 305; and for Mensurius, see Augustine *Breviculus collationis cum Donatistis* (*Summary of the Conference with the Donatists*) III.13.25.

125. *Passio Sancti Felicis Episcopi* (*The Martyrdom of St. Felix the Bishop*), ed. Musurillo, *Acts of Christian Martyrs*, pp. 266–71. See also R. Duncan Jones, "African Saint."

126. He denounced the Tetrarchy itself. Quoting *Iliad* II.204 at his persecutors, he claimed "the rule of many is inferior to the rule of one." The Tetrarchy and polytheism were associated as twin evils in his mind: see Eusebius *De martyribus Palestinae* (*On the Palestinian Martyrs*) I.1.

127. *HE* VIII.6.9.

128. *Institutes* V.11.

129. *Palestinian Martyrs* I.4.

130. See G. S. R. Thomas, "L'Abdication de Dioclétien," *Byzantion* 43 (1973): 220–47. Diocletian assumed his ninth consulship at Ravenna on 1 January 304 and was back in Nicomedia by 28 August (see *Codex Justinianus* III.28.26).

131. *Deaths of Persecutors* XV.7.

132. *De Schismate Donatistarum* III.8. For the case against enforcement in the West, see Ste. Croix, "Aspects of 'Great' Persecution," pp. 84ff.

133. *Acta purgationis Felicis*, in Optatus, *De Schismate Donatistarum*, pp. 198–99.

134. *HE* VIII.6.10.

135. See Y. Duval, *Loca Sanctorum Africae*, Collection de l'Ecole française de Rome 58 (Rome: Palais Farnese, 1982), pp. 105–15.

136. *Acta Saturnini* (*PL* 8.695ff.). Interestingly, Saturninus's son was not asked

whether he was a Christian, but whether he had been present at the service. Of Saturninus's children, two were lectors in the church and his daughter, Maria, was a *sanctimonialis* (col. 705).

137. *Acta Saturnini* XVIII (col. 701). See Frend, *The Donatist Church: A Movement of Protest in Roman North Africa* (Oxford: At the Clarendon Press, 1971), p. 10.

138. *Caesares* XL.48.

139. He was already a senior *tribunus* in the army. See Lactantius *Deaths of Persecutors* XVIII.10.

140. See Rousselle, "La chronologie de Maximien," p. 466.

141. Constantine's reminiscence in his edict to the eastern provinces in 324, cited by Eusebius *Constantine* II.51.

14

The Constantinian Revolution 305–30

The quarter of a century that followed the abdication of Diocletian and Maximian witnessed a religious revolution in the Greco-Roman world. In particular, between 311 and 325, the short period separating Galerius's Edict of Toleration and the Council of Nicaea, the age-old protectors of the Roman Empire had been dismissed and replaced by the God of the Christians espoused by Constantine. Traditions that had governed ideas and actions of rulers and subjects alike for hundreds if not thousands of years were yielding to new values hitherto regarded as dangerous to the state. In their turn these were to endure in the eastern Mediterranean until the fall of Constantinople in 1453, and beyond that in the empire of the czars before being swept away in the cataclysm of the Russian Revolution.

TETRARCHY AND DYNASTY

The ceremonies at Nicomedia and Milan took place as the persecution was already faltering in the West. Two months before, in March 305, Christians at Cirta had met in tumultuary assembly and declared the subdeacon Silvanus their choice as successor to the *traditor* bishop Paul. Persecution was never renewed in the West though the aftermath shattered the unity of the church in its principal territory, North Africa, for more than a century. In the East, it was a different story, and Eusebius pointed to the divergence in the history of the two halves of the empire during the next eight years, and the calamity resulting from the wicked policies of the Eastern rulers.[1] There Galerius and his Caesar, Maximin, pressed on against the Christians. Maximin, probably no older than Constantine, was to prove himself as devoted a believer in the powers of the immortal gods as Constantine was of the Supreme God worshiped by the Christians. To Eusebius he was "the bitterest enemy of piety" of all (*HE* IX.1.1).

After a respite of eleven months lasting until just after Easter 306, Maximin issued an edict calling on all, regardless of age or sex, to sacrifice.[2] The new Caesar already showed himself a thorough planner and executive whom Christian adversaries underrated at their peril. Heralds called everyone to the temples, and the names of those who sacrificed were checked by soldiers against entries on taxation rolls. Atrocious punishments were meted out to defaulters. Through 307 and 308 anti-Christian measures continued, though in most cases Maximin substituted imprisonment or forced labor in the mines for death. There was another respite from the summer of 308 to November 309 when the executions started again. The execution of the scholar and fervent admirer of Origen, Pamphilus of Caesarea, on 16 February 310 marked the close of this phase.[3] While it lasted, however, a new element had begun to emerge, namely a popular resistance to the persecution inspired and led by Egyptian Christians. In these years their fanatical opposition to the pagan empire and its works was to be a milestone in the history of the Nile Valley.[4]

In the West persecution had ceased, but the second Tetrarchy (Constantius, Galerius, Maximin, and Severus) was coming under a different type of threat. The principle of collegiate government was being challenged successfully. Constantius had died at York on 25 July 306. The same day, his troops had hailed Constantine as "Augustus" and not merely Caesar. Loyalty to a father's son outweighed all other considerations. On 26 October 306 Rome witnessed similar scenes. Severus had ruled just long enough to make himself unpopular. Taxes had been raised, and the populace and troops turned to Maxentius, Maximian's son, for remedy. With more prudence than he is usually credited, Maxentius accepted the title of "princeps," reviving proud memories of republican times. He was seemingly not opposed to the system of the Tetrarchy, and hoped no doubt for his promotion. With his father's troops he defeated Severus (early 307) and Galerius himself had to beat a retreat from Italy. The rebuff stung, for while Constantine was acknowledged reluctantly by Galerius as Caesar, Maxentius was left out on a limb, to Constantine's advantage.

Maxentius's eventual downfall, victim of Constantine's overweening ambition, has guaranteed him a bad press from both Christian and pagan writers. To the one he was a pagan and to the other a usurper.[5] A closer look at his actions, however, reveals a more balanced policy that upheld the prestige of the gods while restoring to the Christians the liberties they had possessed before the persecution. Sixty years later, the African Optatus of Milevis, stated that "Maxentius restored liberty"[6] to the Christians. That this was true is suggested by an inscription dated to 309 from the military settlement of Altava in western Mauretania (northwest Algeria) recording the building of "a church of the Lord" (*basilica domenica*).[7] In Rome, he sent two successive bishops into exile, not for being Christians, but for being involved in partisan disorders. The *Liber Pontificalis* relates that Pope Marcellus (304–7?) instituted the *coemeterium novellae* and organized the city into twenty-five separate "parishes" (*tituli*), "on account of the baptism and penance of numerous heathen who were converted at this time."[8] In 311 Pope Miltiades is recorded as receiving back church property confiscated during the persecution.[9] Maxentius while focusing attention on *Roma Aeterna* and building a temple in honor of his deceased son Romulus in 309–10, accepted the fact of Christianity and tolerated it.

By the time he confronted Constantine at the northern approaches to Rome in October 312, the situation had altered radically to his disadvantage. Each stage in the bewildering kaleidoscope of events that punctuated the efforts of the heirs to the second Tetrarchy (Galerius, Constantine, Licinius, and Maximin) to survive saw Constantine emerge slightly stronger. When toward the end of 306 Maximian himself came out of retirement to support his son, Constantine had attached himself to his cause. Probably in the autumn of 307 he married Maxentius's sister, Fausta, was invested with the title of Augustus by Maximian, and assumed the government of Britain, Gaul, and the Germanies. In November 308 when Galerius made a supreme effort to salvage the legacy of Diocletian, by calling the latter out of retirement to a conference at Carnuntum on the Danube, Constantine was granted the title "son of Augustus" (*filius Augusti*), intended as sort of halfway between "Caesar" and "Augustus." The luckless Maximian was forced back into retirement and, instead of his son being recognized, the government of the key Balkan and Danube areas of the empire was committed to Licinius, Galerius's old comrade in arms.

The "Herculians" had been decisively worsted, but not Constantine. He had gained much-needed recognition from Galerius. He now shifted his ground. The year 310 proved decisive for his fortunes. The old Maximian had become jealous of his power and took up arms against him. Constantine turned the tables and it was Maximian who had to surrender after being besieged in Marseilles.[10] Then he plotted against Constantine, failed, and was forced to commit suicide. On his return from Marseilles to his capital at Trier on the Moselle, Constantine paused to visit the temple of Apollo at Autun. Then, to quote his panegyrist:

> O Constantine, you saw, I believe, your protector Apollo, in company with Victory, offering you laurel crowns each of which bears the presage of thirty years. . . . But why indeed do I say, "I believe"? You really saw the god and recognized yourself in the appearance of one to whom the prophecies of poets have declared that the rule of the whole world should belong."[11]

The panegyrist had caught the emperor's mood. Constantine was already interpreting his title "son of Augustus" literally, and casting back in history to claim descent from the great Illyrian soldier emperor Claudius II who had died of plague in 270 after destroying the Goths in Illyricum.[12] The Tetrarchs were upstarts and, as if to emphasize his distancing from them, he substituted the legend on his coins "To the Unconquered Sun my companion" (*Soli Invicto Comiti*) for the Tetrarchy's "To the Genius of the Roman people" (*Genio Populi Romani*). The sun was his preserver and intimate. This was the message he wished to convey on the tens of thousands of folles struck at his mints at London, Trier, and Lyon.[13] The huge imperial palace at Trier, the ninety-foot-high brick walls of the one wing forming the present evangelical church in the city, symbolized his rising ambitions. When Spain transferred its allegiance from Maxentius to him in the same year, he was on the way toward fulfilling his ambitions.[14] The next obstacle was Maxentius himself, and after that perhaps Licinius.

Maxentius lacked Constantine's administrative skills and perhaps his ambitions also. In 308 he faced a revolt in North Africa led by his praetorian prefect, L. Domitius Alexander. Constantine saw his chance and inscriptions from Numidia and Sardinia link his name with that of Alexander. There was no pro-Christianity in the alliance, merely a claim to be "restorers of public liberty" in traditional Roman style.[15] There is little to show that before 311 Constantine considered playing the Christian card. In the

East, however, a crisis was approaching. During the spring of that year, Galerius became seriously ill.

THE PROPAGANDA WAR

Events in Galerius's domains had been moving toward a climax. The years 310–13 saw each side put forward their supreme effort. To physical pressure on the Christians was added a war of words. The initiative had first lain with the pagans. Lactantius, as we have seen, mentions two pagan propagandists active in Nicomedia while he was there from 303 to 305, both evidently basing themselves on Porphyry, pointing out inconsistencies in the Gospels, vilifying the apostles, and comparing Jesus' activities and miracles with those of Apollonius to the obvious advantage of the latter. True majesty belonged solely to God. Jesus was a futility tarnished by revolutionary activities.[16] The dual themes—that Jesus was at best a local magician and that he deserved his fate—were followed up in the *Acts of Pilate* which purported to be a report written by Pilate of his trial and crucifixion of Jesus. It was used by Maximin (who assumed the title of Augustus in 310) to discredit the Christians on the popular level. Children were taught to recite passages in school.[17] In addition, a drastic if belated effort was made to put the pagan house in order. Temples were built in towns and sacred groves restored. The office of provincial high priest was instituted to stand against the Christian hierarchy.[18] All this added to the continuous barrage against Christians as "deserters of the religion of their fathers" and "atheists," people who "preferred the ways of barbarians," and merited punishment.[19] Points such as these were made not only in pamphlets but by pagan trial judges, especially when confronted by intellectual confessors, such as Bishop Phileas of Thmuis.[20]

Eusebius of Caesarea

This time, however, the Christians rose to the occasion. In Eusebius of Caesarea they produced a leader who was not only an immensely hardworking and able propagandist, but a historian in the tradition of Josephus, and a bishop who evolved a political theology that after 325 was to guide Constantine and his successors for centuries to come.

Eusebius was probably born in Caesarea in Palestine about A.D. 260 and died as bishop of that city about 339.[21] His life, therefore, spanned the great transition from the pagan to the Christian empire and he chronicled the main stages by which the revolution was accomplished. He had an inborn love of history and one aim of his earliest work, the *Chronicle*, compiled shortly after the outbreak of the persecution, was to provide him with an accurate chronological framework for future historical work.[22] Not for nothing, however, was he an admirer of Origen, sharing his zeal for Christianity, his Logos theology, but not his disdain for history. He worked closely with Origen's defender, the presbyter Pamphilus, whose *Apology*

477

for Origen was completed in 309, not long before his martyrdom. Eusebius would assuredly have developed into a Christian propagandist in any event, but the increasing violence of the persecution under Galerius and Maximin stung him into action. He hated the Tetrarchy, not least because it had introduced the principle of division into imperial government. His hero, after Constantine, was Augustus, who ended the civil wars and united the empire. The success of the *Acts of Pilate* to which he refers in the first book of the *Ecclesiastical History* may have inspired him to begin writing the first eight books of that work by 311. At that time, the "Palinode of Galerius" was the symbol of Christian triumph, "due to the manifestation of the Divine Providence itself" (*HE* VIII.16.2). Next year he had greater triumphs and a hero to celebrate—Constantine.

Like his opponents, he was also profoundly influenced and stimulated by Porphyry's attack on Christianity. In the *Preparation for the Gospel*, written c. 312–20, he quotes him no less than ninety-six times—more than any other single author.[23] The *Preparation* formed part of a systematic and comprehensive defense of Christianity, which had opened with the *Chronicle*, continued with the two books *Against Hierocles*, and included the *Prophetic Extracts* (the justification of the Christian argument from prophecy), the *Ecclesiastical History*, and finally, the *Proof of the Gospel*. This gigantic task of antipagan apologetic was to occupy some twenty years of Eusebius's life from c. 302 to 320 and in this time he witnessed the victory of his cause. He felt he was on the winning side. The *Preparation* was aimed at inquirers, showing the nature of Christianity to "those who know not what it means";[24] it ran into fifteen books. The *Proof* was aimed at "proselytes" (the retention of the Jewish term even by Eusebius is interesting), "who had passed beyond elementary knowledge of the faith" and were ready to receive higher truths, a self-confident assertion of the progressive nature of a Christian's understanding of the faith and of the supreme rationality of the faith itself, worthy of Origen.

Eusebius attacked on all fronts and with immense and, as it proved, justified confidence in his cause. As he wrote in the *Proof* about the progress of Christianity in his day, prophecies *had* been fulfilled. "Yea, these very things which we see even now after long ages in process of fulfillment. In the power of the Holy Spirit, they [the Hebrew prophets] all with one voice foretold a light of true religion would come to all men, purity of mind and body, a complete purging of the heart. . . ." At the end of Constantine's reign Eusebius could merely marvel how "churches of tens of thousands of men" had been converted by the "rustic and very deficient men" who were the apostles. It must be by divine power.[25] The positive advantages for humanity in terms of politics as well as religion, rather than in terms of the "seed of martyrs" or fear of judgment, were for Eusebius the cause of Christianity's advance. And thus he saw Origen's hopes for a Christian world fulfilled. For him the faith was a dynamic and liberating

478

faith, freeing people from age-old, demon-inspired superstitions. He realized he was breaking new ground in undertaking a history of Christianity from creation to his own times, "because I am not aware that any Christian ["ecclesiastical"] writer has until now paid attention to this kind of writing."[26] The starting point—creation—was significant, for Eusebius wished to prove that, far from being new or novel, Christianity was the "primitive, unique and true religion of mankind,"[27] the only novelty being the emergence of the "race of Christians" who were able truly to interpret and guide humankind toward it. True, Christians might use the Jewish Scriptures which Christ fulfilled, but they were not Jews. Rather, they could claim descent from the "Hebrews," the ancient patriarchs whose virtues were recorded in Genesis, stretching back to creation itself. Scripture, indeed, demonstrated the superiority of Jesus to Moses, let alone to Apollonius of Tyana. Like Origen in his time, Eusebius towered above his pagan and Jewish opponents. But now was the moment of victory.

Eusebius, however, did not regard the victory as being won at the expense of the empire. The events of 312-13 had been brought about by the emperors themselves. Drawing heavily on Philo and summing up the arguments of two centuries of Greek apologists, Eusebius pointed out that the coming on earth of the divine Word coincided exactly with the unification and pacification of the world by Augustus, and the creation of the Roman Empire.[28] Church and empire were designed to work in harmony frustrating the designs of "the envious demon," whose jealousy of increasing human enlightenment and prosperity was the prime cause of persecutions.[29] Between 311 and 320 Eusebius founded the political philosophy of the Constantinian state, based on the unity of the church and empire under the providence of God. He lived through its triumph and helped to guide it to permanence. Ironically, he himself was to face censure and threat of oblivion in the year immediately before the church's final victory in the Council of Nicaea. His Achilles' heel was that he had no claim to be a confessor.[30] He lacked the common touch.

THE HINGE OF FATE 311-13

As the spring of 311 advanced, Galerius's health became worse. By April it was clear that he was dying. Licinius was with him at Sardica (Sofia) and on 30 April may have aided his colleague in drawing up his Edict of Toleration, often referred to as the "Palinode of Galerius."[31] It is a revealing statement of the Tetrarchy's thinking on religion and the safety of the state. It runs:

> Among other steps which we are always taking for the profit and advantage of the state we had formerly sought to set all things right according to the ancient laws and public order [*disciplinam*] of the Romans and further to provide that the Christians too who had abandoned the way of life [*sectam*] of their own fathers should return to sound reason [*ad bonas mentes*]. For the said Christians had somehow become possessed by such obstinacy [*read (mala) volun-*

tas] and folly that, instead of following those institutions of the ancients which perchance their own ancestors had first established, they were at their own will and pleasure making laws for themselves and acting upon them and were assembling in different places people of different nationalities. After we had decreed that they should return to the institutions of the ancients, many were subjected to danger, many too were completely overthrown; and when very many [or most—*plurimi*] persisted in their determination and we saw that they neither gave worship and due reverence to the gods nor practised the worship [*observare*] of the god of the Christians, considering our most gentle clemency and our immemorial custom by which we are wont to grant indulgence to all men, we have thought it right in their case too to extend the speediest indulgence to the effect that they may once more be free to live [*sint*] as Christians and may re-form their churches [*conventicula componant*] always provided that they do nothing contrary to [public] order [*disciplinam*]. Further by another letter we shall inform provincial governors [*iudicibus*] what conditions the Christians must observe.

Christians were asked "to pray their god for our good estate, and that of the state, and their own, that the commonwealth may endure on every side unharmed, and they may be able to live securely in their habitations."[32] The emperor's hopes for the Christian God's aid were unavailing for he died on 5 May, but his last act turned out to be perhaps the most important in his career. The edict formally ended the persecution, freed imprisoned Christians, and restored Christianity to the de facto situation which it had enjoyed for a generation prior to 303. It went further admitting that, while the empire was sustained by its ancient laws and discipline, it could not dispense with the favor of the Christian God—one with great authority. This God could exercise a veto on the policies of the emperors and indeed had done so, as Galerius's illness showed. For the first time a power other than the immortal gods was accepted as an influence on the destiny of the empire.

The empire, however, could not be sustained by two rival deities and two sets of religious values; in city and country its peoples were now bitterly divided by religious allegiance. In the end politics as well as the strength of the convictions of the Christians decided the issue. At first victory eluded them. Maximin was senior Augustus, determined that the Christians should not profit from Galerius's dying wishes. With lightning speed he advanced into Asia Minor and took over the lion's share of Galerius's dominions including his capital, Nicomedia. The "fine print" of the edict was examined. Christians "might exist," so long as they did nothing against public order. Supposing they did, what then? In the autumn of 311 local councils and assemblies throughout his dominions were encouraged to petition the emperor against the Christians. The inscription from Arycanda in Lycia preserves the petition of the provincial councils of Lycia and Caria demanding that "the atheists" (Christians) should be made to sacrifice or be expelled from their midst.[33] The same tone was adopted by the city councils of Nicomedia, Antioch, and Tyre.[34] At Damascus, the military commander rounded up prostitutes and coerced them to confess to having witnessed disgraceful scenes in Christian churches.[35] Eusebius himself wryly admitted his zeal and that of some of his officers.[36] For Maximin "the benevolent exertions of the gods" maintained the precarious harmony of the universe on which humanity's survival depended (*HE* IX.7.8). Without any new edicts, prominent Christian leaders were seized, tried, and executed. The savage outbreak of killing between November 311 and January 312 deprived the Christians in the East of some of their foremost leaders.

The worst tragedies took place in Egypt. On 25 November, Bishop Peter was executed, but it was in the villages of the Thebaid that the full horror of the situation unfolded. In these years, "thousands" were killed, as Coptic peasants deserted the old gods in droves for Christianity. To quote Eusebius, who was an eyewitness of events in 311–12:

> We ourselves also beheld, when we were at these places, many all at once in a single day, some of whom suffered decapitation, others the punishment of fire; so that the murderous axe was dulled and, worn out, was broken in pieces, while the executioners themselves grew utterly weary and took it in turns to succeed one another. It was then that we observed a most marvellous eagerness and a truly divine power and zeal in those who had placed their faith in the Christ of God. Thus, as soon as sentence was given against the first, some from one quarter and others from another would leap up to the tribunal before the judge and confess themselves Christians; paying no heed when faced with terrors and the varied forms of tortures, but undismayedly and boldly speaking of the piety towards the God of the universe, and with joy and laughter and gladness receiving the final sentence of death; so that they sang and sent up hymns and thanksgivings to the God of the universe even to the very last breath.[37]

The Era of the Martyrs was justly named.

Time, however, was running out for Maximin. In the winter of 311–12 he attempted unsuccessfully to force the Armenians to renounce Christianity. His failure demonstrated anew the impossibility of destroying the faith, and the peril to Rome's alliances against Persia in trying to do so. Too late he recognized the danger posed by Constantine. An alliance was patched up with Maxentius; it proved ineffective. Constantine had laid his plans well. The menace of the Franks was removed by a great victory in 311 and by the dispatch of three of their kings to the beasts in the amphitheater at Cologne. An understanding may have been arrived at with Licinius, smarting at his humiliation at Maximin's hands—though this is by no means sure, for Licinius's presence on the northeastern frontiers of Italy in 312 suggests that he might have been preparing to anticipate Constantine for the battle for Rome. All was ready for a decisive campaign against Maxentius. Through his panegyrist Constantine declared Maxentius a bastard and hence no true ruler.[38] In the spring of 312 he entered northwestern Italy with his army. Maxentius, expecting an attack by Licinius from the north-east, had deployed the bulk of his forces around Verona. They fought well, but not well enough to avoid defeat and slow retreat on Rome. Even so, Constantine was thwarted through the summer and early autumn. It was not until 26 October that he reached a point five miles north of the city on the Via Flaminia, and the autumn rains were due. The fickle Roman crowd turned their scorn on Maxentius as he celebrated the seventh anniversary of his successful revolution. The oracles of the Sibyl seemed favorable, and foolishly he left the protection of the walls of Aurelian to meet his enemy in the field, "led by the response to hopes of victory," Lactantius records (*On the Deaths of the Persecutors* XLIV). In vain; his army was defeated by Constantine's numerically inferior forces. In the retreat across the Milvian Bridge he was borne down into the Tiber among a mob of fugitives and perished. On 29 October Constantine entered Rome in triumph and the Senate declared him senior Augustus. All success was due to a heavenly protector. For Constantine the question was "Which one?"

Had he entered Italy as the champion of the Christian cause? Granted that he had been directed by a dream and/or heavenly vision, as recounted by Eusebius and Lactantius respectively, why should Constantine have accepted a Christian interpretation so readily when such heavenly phenomena, through the sun's action on a misty cloud in the Italian autumn, were not unknown? Moreover, the ☧ (Chi-Rho) symbol was as yet unused by the Christians. As early as 320–22 Christians in Rome believed that he had seen a vision with a cross of light inscribed "in hoc (signo) vinces," as described by Eusebius.[39] There were Christian influences in Constantine's life; his half sister had been named Anastasia, not absolutely conclusive, but suggestive at least of favor toward Christianity. Years later, he claimed that his father worshiped "the Supreme God."[40] What mattered to Constantine, however, was Constantine, and like other egotistical generals such as Wallenstein or Napoleon, he believed completely in his star, whether this was represented now by the Sun god or by the Christian God.

His recorded actions in Gaul show him continuing his father's tolerant policy toward the Christians, but the latter were not numerous. After Galerius's death, he is said by Lactantius to have written to Maximin to dissuade him from reopening the persecution.[41] But only the year before, Apollo had promised him victory and a reign of thirty years, and so far he had kept his word. Constantine's coins proclaimed his allegiance to the Sun god and under his aegis he had entered Rome as "liberator of the world" (*Liberator Orbis*).[42] His panegyrist considered him specially favored by the Divine power and "religious" as against Maxentius's *superstitio* and *impietas*.[43] Yet he had been accompanied on his campaign against Maxentius by Hosius, bishop of Córdoba, a confessor, though for some reason at Trier and an exile from his diocese.[44] He had persuaded Constantine to commit his fate to the Christian God and the latter had responded. After the victory of the Milvian Bridge, Christianity was never again to lack an imperial patron.

Events during the winter of 312–13 favored Constantine and the Christians. The North Africans had not forgotten his support for their revolt against Maxentius, nor the latter's savage measures of repression, and they surrendered without a blow. Corn supplies for Rome were thereby assured during the crucial winter months, and Constantine was in a position of unexpected strength when he met Licinius at Milan, probably in February 313. The alliance between the two emperors was cemented by Licinius's marriage to Constantine's half sister, and together they set their seals on decisions that have gone down in history as the Edict of Milan.[45]

The edict (we have Lactantius's text and that of Licinius's proclamation on his entry into Nicomedia on 13 June) marks the end of the era of the persecutions. It also marks the first step towards the establishment of Christianity as the religion of the empire. Nominally it proclaimed complete religious freedom beginning, ''Since we saw that freedom of worship ought not to be denied, but that to each man's judgment and will the right should be given to care for sacred things according to each man's free choice. . . .'' Hence, unrestricted freedom was granted to the Christians along with complete and free restoration of all church property still remaining in the hands of the state or of individuals. Whereas Galerius had preserved the precedence of ''Roman traditions,'' Constantine and Licinius named the ''Christian religion'' first, and pagan traditions were referred to simply as ''any other cult.''[46] An attentive reader might have caught an echo of the demands for complete toleration for all religions made by Western Apologists from Tertullian to Lactantius. ''It is not in the nature of religion to compel religion,'' Tertullian had urged, and Lactantius had claimed that ''to worship as one pleased was a privilege of nature.''[47] Now, the emperors were saying the same. All were to have ''free choice of following whatever form of worship they pleased.''[48] Was Constantine already under Lactantius's spell?

The use of *Summus Deus* for the deity was also not usual in traditional Roman religion.[49] The change of emphasis can be seen more readily when the phrasing of the edict is compared with Maximin's belated Edict of Toleration (late 312) in which, while ''allowing the Christians to follow their own worship,'' that emperor states his aim ''to recall our provincials to the worship of the gods rather by exhortation and persuasive words.''[50] There was no question of this in the minds of the framers of the Edict of Milan. Both emperors believed they were beholden in varying degree to the Christian God, made evident in the ''reason given for the Edict''—''that the divine favour that we have experienced in a crisis of our fortunes may for all times prosper our undertakings and serve the common weal.'' Licinius's use of a monotheistic prayer addressed to the *Summus Deus*, to raise the morale of his troops when they confronted Maximin at the decisive battle near Heraclea (30 April 313),[51] appeared to have committed himself also to Constantine's developing religious revolution.

FROM MILAN TO CHRYSOPOLIS 313–24

Events, of course, were to prove otherwise. Acceptance of the fact of Christians and the power of the *Summus Deus* was one thing, adherence to their sect or even favor towards them was another. Licinius was a friend of Galerius and a traditionalist with a deserved reputation for harshness. He regarded himself as a legatee of the Jovian tradition and so long as he governed, the man in the street was made aware that he owed his welfare to "Jupiter the Preserver" (*Iovi Conservatori*).[52] Moreover, Licinius had good reason to suspect Constantine's intentions. In 314–15 (some say 316–17) he lost the Balkan provinces to Constantine after a war.[53] In 320–21, it seems that Constantine may have been meddling in the affairs of the Christian kingdom of Armenia.[54] Too late he came to the conclusion that Diocletian had been right after all. The new God of the Christians could not be assimilated into the Roman pantheon. Licinius's efforts to purge the civil service of Christians and make life unpleasant for them without declaring a new persecution were futile. They merely alienated a large and influential proportion of his subjects once Constantine decided to march against him. Eusebius declared in retrospect that the eastern provinces of the empire resembled murky night compared to "brightest day" prevailing in Constantine's dominions.[55] The battle of Chrysopolis on the east side of the Bosporus on 18 September 324 made Constantine sole ruler of the Roman world, and sealed the fate of the immortal gods under whose banner Licinius had belatedly fought.[56]

And what of Constantine during these years? The evidence points to a consistent if stormy progress toward accepting the Christian God as the one to whom exclusive service must be given. In his passionate, turbulent, and superstitious nature, there was never any place for a syncretistic philosophy centered on the *Summus Deus* holding a balance between Christianity and paganism.[57] However, until his preparations for his final campaign by 323, he did not abandon his allegiance to the Sun god, even though he regarded himself as a servant of the Christian God. The Christian clergy were the true ministers of the latter. For twelve years the two allegiances were held in uneasy tension until the "God of Battles" claimed his own. Constantine's public image remained—the Sun god was the emperor's "companion."[58] The liberation of Rome was attributed to the Sun on a medallion struck at the time. *Soli Invicto Comiti* continued to dominate the coinage, while other Western issues show the Sun's orb resting on an altar. The protection of the gods of the empire (*Providentia Deorum*) did not disappear from the coins until after c. 319. The senate saw Constantine, if specially favored by the divine powers, as legitimate successor to the Tetrarchy.[59] Outward manifestations of the emperor's Christianity, 312–22, are few.[60] For public officials in North Africa the reverence (*pietas*) shown by the two emperors toward the Christians indicated that the latter were not corrupting (traditional) discipline, but Christians need not expect privileges, such as immunity from torture, on that account.[61] The sources (or more probably, the actual writers) of the *Scriptores Historiae Augustae* take a similar view. Christianity in their eyes was still associated with Judaism and the religion of the Samaritans, a legitimate *devotio*, but radically different from Roman religion. The alleged attitude of toleration shown to the Christians by Alexander Severus was held up as a model of what the emperor should observe.[62]

One writer had no doubt, however, which way the emperor's mind was turning. Lactantius's peregrinations between the court of Nicomedia, an unknown resting place in Gaul, and renewed close association with Constantine as tutor to his son Crispus are baffling.[63] But he remained amazingly well informed both of events and even of motives. When he finished the *Divine Institutes* and sat down to write *Deaths of Persecutors* (c. 314), he had a very good idea that Christians had a friend in Constantine and should rely on him alone.[64] Constantine was for him "the first of the Roman emperors" who having "repudiated errors [that is, had already done so] acknowledged and honoured the majesty of the unique God." Licinius, in contrast, is represented merely as a butcher, massacring the children of his one-time colleagues in the Tetrarchy.[65] Lactantius, too, stressing the upstart nature of the Tetrarchy and the degradation of their morals, knew how to touch Constantine's weak spot, his vanity and his consciousness of his own dubious origins. In addition, the awful warning of the fates of the persecutors from Nero onward and the unfailing reality of God's justice visiting punishment on the guilty, which form the main theme of Lactantius's work, struck a responsive chord. This also showed tendencies in Western Christian historical writing that looked back to Jewish traditions of unrelenting enmity against idolatrous rulers. Whether Constantine was a convert or not, church-state relations for Lactantius would be based on separation and not integration. On this point, his propaganda parts company from Eusebius. Moreover, Eusebius had no thought of the empire falling to enemies from the East within the next two hundred years.[66]

Constantine's recorded words and deeds in the period following the Edict of Milan support Lactantius's view. By the end of 312, he had instructed the proconsul of Africa, Anulinus, to see that the catholic church in North Africa received back in toto possessions forfeited in the persecution, even if these were now in the hands of private citizens.[67] He set aside three thousand folles from the imperial estates in North Africa for Bishop Caecilian's use, and wrote direct to the latter informing him of this and promising him support against his opponents.[68] At the same time, he wrote to Anulinus, the proconsul, instructing him that clergy "in the Catholic Church over which Caecilian presides, were to be granted immunity from state burdens."[69] This he did apparently as a reward to those who "with due holiness and constant observance of the law, bestow their services on the performance of divine worship." Honor to "the most holy and heavenly [Power] . . . had bestowed the greatest good fortune on the Roman name and singular prosperity on all the affairs of mankind."[70] In the following year he had come to identify that power with the Christian God and align himself unequivocally with the Christians. He ended a letter to Aelafius, a Christian official in North Africa:

> Since I am informed that you too are a worshipper of the Highest God, I will confess to your gravity that I consider it absolutely contrary to the divine law that we should overlook such quarrels and dissension [that is, between rival parties in the North African church], whereby the Highest Divinity may be moved to wrath not only against the human race, but against me myself, to whose care he has by his heavenly will committed the government of all earthly things.[71]

This is a highly significant utterance; the "immortal gods" had now been displaced as the protectors of the empire. Constantine revealed his ambition of universal rule and placed his destiny in the hands of the Christian God. Justinian could have said no more.

If the whole letter Constantine sent to the bishops assembled at Arles on 1 August 314 is genuine—and the balance of probability is that it is—it also throws a great deal of light on Constantine's personal religion.[72] In this document, he impulsively claims that he had not believed that "there was any heavenly power that could see into the secrets of my heart." Now he believes that the "Almighty God, who sits in the watchtower of heaven has bestowed on me what I did not deserve." He speaks of him as "our God." He begins, too, to associate himself as "servant of God" (*famulum Dei*) with the "holy bishops of the Saviour Christ." His obedience to what he believed to be "the will of God" was absolute, and he allowed himself scant respect for the past. His aim was to discover which of the quarreling African parties were the true "ministers of God." Rebels were to be dispatched to the imperial court for punishment.

At this stage, too, Lactantius's influence was growing and the relations between the two men were becoming close. Constantine, as mentioned, had appointed the Christian philosopher to be tutor to his young son Crispus (b. circa 306), and he appeared also to adopt as his own the details of Lactantius's descriptions of the fate reserved for the persecuting emperors. In his address to "the assembly of the saints" (perhaps Easter 317), he, or his speech writer, included Aurelian among the villains, "a fierce perpetrator of every wrong," who died miserably, murdered on the public highway.[73] This was not the usual view of Aurelian, preserved in the *SHA*, and symbolized by the majestic walls of Rome, a city for which Constantine still declared his love, but it was that of Lactantius. It is tempting to see the emperor's curious mixture of respect for and criticism of the great classical philosophers and the appeals to the (Jewish) *Sibylline Oracles* as prophecies about Christ which he included in this speech as inspired from the same source. If this is true, Constantine was to undergo a second and even more lasting transformation in his thought when he reached the East and came under the spell of Eusebius.

Meantime, the Constantinian revolution was proceeding apace. Years later Julian the Apostate was to denounce his uncle as a "wicked innovator and disturber of the time-hallowed rites and sacred traditions of our fathers" (Ammianus Marcellinus XXI.10.8), and as a pagan he was justified: First, the immense material benefits imperial patronage was able to shower on the church. Second, the transformation in the situation of the Christian clergy. Third, a number of decrees between 315 and 323 designed seemingly to take Christian sensibilities into account and place Christianity in a morally privileged position.

First, of the imperial largess which started almost from the time Constantine entered Rome, there can be no doubt. The gift of his wife Fausta's palace on the Lateran to the church in 313 was followed by the grant of the rent of lands listed in the *Liber Pontificalis* to various churches in Rome, amounting to 26,370 gold solidi a year, or more than four hundred pounds of gold,[74] followed in c. 322 by the building of a monumental church in honor of St. Peter on the site of the *memoria* raised in his honor a century and a half earlier. Liberal benefactions were made also to other Italian churches. Churches thus entered the ranks of the empire's institutional architecture.[75] In 321 Constantine issued a constitution legalizing and encouraging bequests to the church, and as "the Church does not die," thereby laid the foundations for the church's enduring wealth in later centuries.[76]

Second, equally dramatic were the changes brought about in the status of the clergy. Throughout the third century this had been improving, but now from being merely a tolerated body, their members suddenly became favored and privileged. The immunity granted from the financial burdens of municipal administration and from all municipal levies[77] was very valuable and it was recognized immediately as such. The church became besieged by indigent city counselors (*curiales*) anxious to take advantage of the emperor's benevolence. Constantine's hazy notions that clergy were drawn from the lower orders (*tenuiorum*) of society received a jolt. Strenuous efforts were made to prevent *curiales* from escaping their lot and gaining the privileges of the clergy.[78] "The rich in this age [*saeculi*] must accept their burdens: the poor may be sustained by the wealth of the churches." The latter continued to receive massive benefits. Significantly, in January 314 Constantine wrote directly to Bishop Chrestus of Syracuse informing him that the public post was being put at his disposal when traveling to the council the emperor had summoned to meet at Arles. This privilege had been reserved hitherto for imperial messengers and high officials.[79] The direct correspondence, too, with Christian leaders on administrative matters was a new departure.

Third, in 318 Constantine went further by assigning to the jurisdiction of bishops the same validity as that of magistrates, while in 321 and in 325, the manumission of slaves by clergy in a church was declared as binding as that performed before magistrates.[80] An individual could also take his case to be heard before an episcopal instead of a secular tribunal, even though the case had been opened before the latter. The deliberate extension of the jurisdiction of church courts shows how far the church was moving beyond the "millet" status that it had de facto acquired in the third century. Clergy were being recognized as civic as well as religious leaders and accorded a corresponding status.

Other enactments through the years 315–23 tell the same story. Crucifixion and branding on the face were banned as punishments,[81] though it may not have been much solace to a criminal who could still be forced to drink boiling oil or molten lead. The disabilities imposed by Augustus on celibates of both sexes were removed in 320.[82] On the other hand, Jews were regarded with contempt and, to the restrictionist legislation of the Antonines and Severans, Constantine added the current Christian reproach of Jews being a "gloomy sect." If any Jew sought to punish apostates (in most cases, converts to Christianity), he would be burned alive, while the same penalty was invoked against proselytes to Judaism.[83]

Constantine was still only ruler of the West. The cross remained something of a personal talisman and occasionally appeared on the emperor's helmet depicted on coins and similarly on milestones. Officially, the Sun god was not dethroned, and when in 321 Constantine ordered that Sunday should be a day kept free from legal proceedings, he called it "the day celebrated by the veneration of the Sun," and not "the day of the Lord."[84] Even eighteen months after Chrysopolis, the veterans he discharged shouted "the gods preserve you, Constantine Augustus."[85] Personal religion could only be transformed into exclusive official policy after Licinius had been removed and Constantine had achieved his ambition of sovereign authority in the Roman world.

THE DONATISTS: PANDORA'S BOX

Constantine's victory over Maxentius brought peace to the church but not to the churches. In 312–13 both Constantine and Licinius had assumed that there was a single, united body of Christians, "the corpus Christianorum," distinguishable from the "worshippers of other cults." They were quickly undeceived. Forty years of prosperity before the Great Persecution had sharpened differences within the church; now its victorious survival together with its rapid change of status gave free rein to latent tensions within its ranks. Between 312 and 318–19, issues concerning the fundamentals of discipline and doctrine, that had been dormant for half a century, forced their way to the surface, first in the West and then in the East.

The schisms in Rome between 308 and 311 that originated from events in the Great Persecution should have warned any Western ruler of similar possibilities in North Africa. Constantine, however, seems to have been taken by surprise by events there, but immediately, probably on Hosius's advice, gave his full support to the new bishop of Carthage, Caecilian. He even advised him to bring his opponents before the magistrates for correction. This impulsive behavior was to cost him dearly.[86]

For the reasons, we need to return to the year 304 and the Abitinian martyrs in prison in Carthage. The threats they uttered at that time against the "betrayers" (*traditores*) were not empty, nor was their resentment against Caecilian, then archdeacon. Persecution ended, but not long after a dispute broke out between the bishop of Carthage, Mensurius, and his colleague the primate of Numidia, Secundus of Tigisis. Neither's record during the crisis had been unblemished, but whereas Mensurius seems to have been satisfied with his ability to trick the authorities with an offer to surrender heretical works, Secundus, quite unjustifiably, took his stand on the example of the martyr-priest Eleazar in 2 Maccabees and claimed to have defied them.[87] The choice is interesting, for it showed that whatever their personal unworthiness, the Numidian bishops would be likely to assert a hard line against *traditores*, while at Carthage excuses might be found for them.

No schism broke out over this exchange, which took place probably in 305 shortly after the end of the persecution, but feelings were stirred. Some clergy were taking the law into their own hands against colleagues they believed had betrayed the Scriptures and the cause of the martyrs. Among these activists was Donatus of Casae Nigrae, a Numidian agricultural settlement near the borders of the Sahara. He was said to be rebaptizing clergy who had lapsed and "causing a schism" at Carthage, while Mensurius was still bishop (that is, before 311).[88] In addition, there were tensions among the clergy resulting from the war between Maxentius and the North African rebels, and rivalry between the presbyters and deacons in Carthage. All this came to a head on the death of Mensurius in 311 on his way back from a meeting with Maxentius in Rome in connection with the alleged disloyalty of one of his clergy.[89] Amid intrigue and dispute, and before the Numidians could arrive in Carthage to exercise their right of consecrating a successor, Caecilian was elected bishop of Carthage and consecrated by three neighboring bishops. One of these, however, Felix of Aptunga, was regarded popularly as a *traditor*. The Numidians arrived. Opposition coalesced round them and, sometime during 312, they held a council. There they formally condemned Caecilian on the grounds, first, that he had been consecrated by a *traditor* (and hence his consecration was invalid), and second, he had denied food to imprisoned confessors (the Abitinians).[90] The council declared Caecilian deposed and elected in his stead Majorinus, a deacon and the chaplain to Lucilla, the Spanish grande dame whom Caecilian had offended a decade or so before. Thus, to use Optatus of Milevis's phrase, "altar was raised against altar."[91] The outbreak of the Donatist schism provides a classic example of a crisis caused by the interweaving of trivial with the more profound causes. Each generation of African Christians had experienced tension and schisms. Now, conflicts concerning the basic nature of the church and interprovincial rivalries—between Numidia and its richer neighbor—were complicated by intrigue and personal bickering so as to cause a lasting division.

This was the situation that confronted Constantine in 312. The detail of his handling of it cannot be retold here,[92] but some essential features for understanding the development of the new relationship between church and state may be noted. At first the anti-Caecilianists bided their time, but when Constantine followed his recognition of Caecilian by granting immunity from municipal burdens to his clergy, they protested. On 15 April 313 the proconsul of Africa, Anulinus, was confronted by a crowd whose leaders thrust two packages into his hands. One listed charges against Caecilian, the second petitioned the emperor to appoint judges from Gaul "which had been immune from this curse" (the persecution) to arbitrate.[93]

Constantine acted not unlike Aurelian forty years before in the dispute between the church of Antioch and Paul of Samosata. As chief magistrate of the Roman people, he also delegated his powers to arbitrators appointed from within the Christian community. For Aurelian these had been "the bishops of Italy and Rome"; for Constantine, the bishop of Rome, Miltiades (311–14), an African, seemed eminently suitable to head a tribunal with four Gallic episcopal assessors. There apparently was also no objection to Miltiades' widening the scope of the inquiry and adding fourteen Italian bishops to those from Gaul.

Miltiades' verdict, given on 5 October after three days' discussion, went against Caecilian's opponents, now represented by the far more formidable Donatus—the first of many and equally futile legal decisions rendered against the Donatists. The latter had no difficulty in finding grounds for appeal. Caecilian had been deposed by a church council, and in addition, ten years before, the bishop of Rome, Marcellinus, was alleged to have sacrificed for all to see on the Capitol. One of his deacons had been Miltiades.[94] He was, therefore, a *traditor* by association, and unfit to judge a case involving *traditio*. Constantine accepted the argument reluctantly but, perhaps to grant the appellants as much as he could, ordered a more representative tribunal, staffed also by judges designated by himself, superseding Miltiades' verdict. This tribunal took the form of a council representing the church throughout the prefecture of the Gauls to assemble at Arles on 1 August 314. Thirty-three bishops attended, including three from Britain, and thirteen other clergy.[95] It was a significant meeting, the first interprovincial council ever held in the West and the first assembled under imperial patronage. Again, the Caecilianists won, the bishops being horrified at the fanaticism of their opponents—not for the last time religious attitudes in North Africa were to be alien from those in the remainder of the West. Then, sitting as a council, they went on to show that some of the puritanism characteristic of church discipline in the third century had become out of place. Christian soldiers were not to throw away their arms in protest against their calling;[96] and even more important, those who rebaptized reconciled heretics were condemned.[97] The keystone to the arch of discipline and doctrine created by Cyprian had been removed.

Constantine missed the import of such finer points. With some justification he was angry that even this decision brought no peace among those whom he believed should be united "in brotherly love." He tried to keep both Donatus and Caecilian out of the way in northern Italy. Even when Felix of Aptunga was formally cleared of the accusation of being a *traditor* (February 315), he felt obliged to take the complaints against Caecilian into his own hands. On the occasion of his *decennalia*, celebrated in Rome on 21 July 315, Constantine told the Donatists that if they could prove anything against Caecilian he would treat this as though they had won their case. For some reason Caecilian failed to appear for the hearing. In the autumn the emperor sent an episcopal commission to Carthage to report. The bishops encountered anti-Caecilianist riots but reported once more in Caecilian's favor. It was useless, and what was worse, Donatus escaped from custody and by February 316 both he and Caecilian were back in Africa.[98]

Constantine now made a supreme effort to settle the issue. The letter which he sent to Domitius Celsus, the deputy prefect in Africa, throws much light on his views concerning the church and is one of the key documents for understanding his religious outlook. He announced that, "with the favour of the divine piety I shall come to Africa and shall fully demonstrate to all with an unequivocal verdict as much to Caecilian as to those who seem to be against him just how the Supreme Deity should be worshipped. . . ." There was no mention of Miltiades' council, of Arles, of Felix of Aptunga or the bishops' findings in Africa. Constantine, as supreme magistrate and chief priest (*pontifex maximus*) would judge the case on its merits. "What more," he goes on, "can be done, more in accord with my constant practice and the very office of a prince, than after expelling error and destroying rash opinions to cause all men to agree together to follow true religion and simplicity of life and to render to Almighty God the worship that is his due."[99]

The "servant of God" had now become God's representative, his vicar. Combining in his person the sacred authority accorded to his predecessors with the traditional powers of magistrate and high priest, Constantine showed that he intended to wield these powers in the service of "Almighty

God." Religious unity centered on the religion of the Christians was already his ideal. By 316 Christus-Sol had effectively displaced Jupiter as the divine power under whose providence the Roman Empire would prosper.

Constantine never went to Africa, but on 10 November 316 he decided finally at Milan that Caecilian was in the right. In the spring of 317 he followed up his decision by publishing a "most severe" edict against the Donatists, confiscating their property and exiling their leaders. Within four years, the universal freedom of conscience proclaimed at Milan had been abrogated, and the state had become a persecutor once more, only this time in favor of Christian orthodoxy. The effect, however, was only to exacerbate the differences between the African parties. The majority of the North Africans remained loyal to the ideals of Tertullian and Cyprian. They neither understood nor cared about Constantine's conversion. For them it was a case of the Devil insisting that "Christ was a lover of unity," of inspiring the use of money and gifts to undermine the faithful, and having failed in open persecution now falling back on guile.[100] In their view, the fundamental hostility of the state toward the church had not been altered.

Constantine's resort to force failed. By 320 the Donatists were so secure that they were able to ride out a major scandal in their stronghold of southern Numidia. A quarrel between Silvanus, the ex-subdeacon and now bishop of Cirta/Constantine, and one of his deacons, Nundinarius, flared into a major row. Nundinarius had evidently foreseen trouble and had kept dossiers on Silvanus and his principal colleagues. In December 320 these were read in open court at Thamugadi (Timgad) before the *Consularis*, Zenophilus. They did not make for happy reading. Silvanus and other principal bishops in Numidia were revealed as *traditores* themselves, adulterers, simoniacs, and even murderers.[101] Nonetheless, they remained popular heroes, no better sign that the Donatist schism was the expression of the continued loyalty of North Africa to the theology of Cyprian combined with profound social and regional grievances, for which the person of Caecilian was symbolic. In May 321 Constantine gave up coercion. He was beginning to have wider plans—a bid for universal rule. The lesson, however, had been learned. Never again did he seek to beat into submission a movement within the church. Meantime, in Africa Donatus and his church prospered while Rome and the other Western provinces continued to uphold Caecilian. The unity of Western Christendom was no more.

ARIUS

One of the reasons Constantine gave for wanting to invade Licinius's dominions was to secure the aid of Eastern bishops to help heal the Donatist schism.[102] Since 318, however, the church there had been torn by dispute which, like the Donatist schism, had its roots in the third century. Here the question was as doctrinal as the controversy in North Africa had been disciplinary.

Like the Donatist dispute, the origins of Arianism dated back to events in the Great Persecution. In Egypt the clergy had been divided between those who wanted a mild policy towards the lapsed, and those who insisted on harsher penances. The scene was a prison in Alexandria in 304. A number of confessors were incarcerated together. They included Peter, bishop of Alexandria, and Meletius, bishop of Lycopolis in Upper Egypt. None doubted eventual victory for the Christian cause, but a dispute broke out on how the lapsed were to be treated after the end of the persecution. Peter stood for a mild policy, Meletius for severity. The quarrel grew bitter. A curtain was hung across the cell dividing the two parties. Meletius's was the more crowded and included the majority of imprisoned bishops, presbyters, and, significantly, monks.[103] Diocletian's abdication on 1 May 305 brought a respite. The prisoners were released and returned to their homes. At Easter 306 Peter published his canons. Those who had given way under torture were to be readmitted to the church after a forty-day fast. Other penances matched degrees of culpability, but ultimate forgiveness was denied to none. Spontaneous martyrdoms were deprecated; a liberal interpretation was placed on the definition of "lapsed" clergy.[104]

Peter's canons fitted the situation, for up to then the persecution in Egypt had not been severe.[105] There followed the rule of Maximin and the gradually increasing horrors of the period 306–11. Meletius's cause gathered support, including that of a learned Alexandrian Christian named Arius. To date the situations in Alexandria and Carthage had run closely parallel, but on 25 November 311 Peter himself was martyred, a victim of Maximin's final defiant flourish. Though the schism did not end, the moderate cause benefited. Arius was one of those who changed sides, and the Meletians regarded him as a traitor, despite his having been excommunicated twice for defending Meletius. They now waited their chance for revenge. Meanwhile Arius had been ordained presbyter by Peter's successor, Achillas (311–12). He prospered and gained the reputation of being a fine dialectician, but in 318 his self-confidence betrayed him and his enemies were able to bring him down on a charge of heresy.

How? As we have seen, controversy over Origen and his teaching had never died down. None of the alternative theories regarding the relations between the persons of the Trinity was free from difficulty. If Adoptionism and Sabellianism were both unsatisfactory, Origen's ideas derived from the identification of the Son with the Divine Logos, the creative force in the universe linking God and creation, were also open to question. Apart from the arbitrary character of the Word's identification with Jesus, there was a profound philosophical difficulty. Logically, the Word could be interpreted as a "creature," unlike the Father subject to eternal generation. Though forever with the Father and sharing his essence, the fact of generation rendered the Word both different and subordinate to him.[106] Moreover, since Origen's death, the leaders of the Alexandrian church had moved further along the subordinationist road. Distaste for popular Sabellianism and horror of the newly entrenched Manichees may have contributed, and we may also detect a widening division between the intellectual Christianity of Alexandria and the beliefs of the majority of the Egyptian faithful.

These divergences were not new, but the development of the monastic movement reinforced pressures from those who saw salvation in physical terms as salvation from the corruption of death, and demanded a fully divine Savior who could redeem sinful humankind without any need of redemption himself. The Word incarnate was the entire Word and suffered on the cross. Such was the instinctive popular belief.[107] To these latent tensions, Arius seems to have introduced another element. Before the persecution he had been a pupil of Lucian, the learned presbyter of Antioch who had been martyred on 7 January 312. On the basis of his meager surviving writings it seems that he did indeed hold the curious mixture of Alexandrian and Antiochene theology with which Bishop Alexander credited him.[108]

The heart of his system was the complete transcendence of God and the application of a rigorous logic to the relationship of the Son to God. We acknowledge, he wrote to Bishop Alexander of Alexandria (312–28), "One God who is alone unbegotten [*agennetos*] alone eternal and alone without beginning."[109] From that premise he went on to assert that the Word was not only subordinate to the Father, but being begotten must have had a beginning of existence. Hence, it was clear that there was when the Son was not. Logically, therefore, "he had his existence from the non-existent." And if he was "made from nothing," he must be a "creature." Arius proceeded to weld this Platonic view of the Word onto the biblical understanding of Jesus Christ he had gained while a pupil of Lucian. He accepted the idea of Christ's ethical development, his "growth in wisdom and stature," and the harmonization of his will with his Father's will, but he attributed this to the Divine Word itself. The latter entered a human body taking the place of the soul. In a piece of popular verse known as the *Thalia* or *Banquet*, Arius wrote:

> The Logos is capable of change, as are we all, but of his own free-will he continues good so long as he wishes. He is capable of change even as we are, but God foreknowing that he would remain good, gave him in anticipation the glory which as man and in consequence of his virtue he afterwards possessed. God from foreknowledge of his works made him what he afterwards was.[110]

If Arius's definitions were correct, Christ could not have been fully God nor fully man. As Alexander said, Arius's Son was neither truly of the nature of the Father nor truly of his Wisdom.[111] He could neither create nor redeem. A Logos "capable of change" and an adopted "God" who had neither communion with nor knowledge of God could hardly be an object of worship. It is extraordinary that Arius was apparently able to hold and to teach these ideas in his wealthy parish in Alexandria without hindrance for at least six years. But for the Meletians Arius might have continued to prosper. In 318, however, Alexander held what one may suppose to have been a periodic theological discussion with his clergy, and chose the "Unity of the Holy Trinity" as the subject. Arius thought he had caught his bishop propounding Sabellian views and contradicted him flatly. "If the Father begat the son, there must be when he was not." He could not therefore be coeternal with the Father.[112] Resulting recriminations need not have spread. Alexander was himself an Origenist, who believed in the distinction of the Unbegotten Father and the Word eternally generated by him, but with attributes parallel to those of the Father and sharing his nature. The Meletians, however, who held Sabellian views themselves, threatened to denounce him as a heretic unless he acted against Arius.[113] Alexander gave way, and in 318–19 convoked a council of a hundred bishops at which Arius was condemned and exiled. Before long he arrived in Licinius's capital, Nicomedia.

Licinius's anti-Christian measures, particularly those designed to hinder episcopal councils, prevented further action. When these lifted after Constantine's victory we see that the dispute had widened. Though Alexander had canvassed opinion throughout the East, Arius had friends among other pupils of Lucian, such as Eusebius, bishop of Nicomedia, while Eusebius of Caesarea also took his part. In Egypt itself each side worked vigorously for support. The East was becoming divided into two camps, with the pro-Arian party strongly represented in the important provinces of Bithynia, Asia, and Cyrenaica,[114] when Constantine's victory at Chrysopolis on 18 September 324 opened a new and triumphant era for the church.

Chrysopolis was one of the few big battles fought on Roman soil during the fourth century. The long periods of peace that marked the Constantinian era stand in contrast to the successive military crises of the previous century. Constantine and his sons reaped the benefit of some of the reforms of the much-despised Tetrarchy. Down to 350 wars with Germanic tribes and Persian armies were restricted to the frontiers. Away from these provinces there was peace, and in the Greek-speaking world a view of humanity based on the optimism of Christian Platonism was not out of place. Constantine's victory over Licinius was hailed with unconcealed delight by the Christians. It would seem that almost as soon as the news reached him at Caesarea, Eusebius wrote his final book of the *Ecclesiastical History*. His joy was unrestrained. If the Edict of Milan and the end of Maximin had been greeted with dancing in the streets, Constantine's victory seemed to fulfill the agelong hopes of humankind. Eusebius ends on a note of triumph:

> Thus was Licinius cast down prostrate. But Constantine the most mighty Victor, resplendent with every virtue that godliness bestows, together with his son Crispus, an Emperor most dear to God and in all respects like unto his father, recovered the East that belonged to them, and formed the Roman

Empire, as in the days of old, into a single united whole, bringing under their peaceful rule all of it, from the rising sun round about in the two directions, north as well as south, even to the uttermost limits of the declining day. So then there was taken away from men all fear of those who formerly oppressed them; they celebrated brilliant festivals; all things were filled with light, and men, formerly downcast, looked at each other with smiling countenances and beaming eyes; with dancing and hymns in city and country alike they gave honour first of all to God the universal King, for this they had been instructed to do, and then to the pious Emperor with his sons beloved of God; old ills were forgotten and oblivion cast on every deed of impiety; present good things were enjoyed, with the further hope of those which were yet to come.[115]

In his optimism Eusebius was mistaken. He himself was to suffer humiliation within a month or two. If restored to favor at the Council of Nicaea, he was never to experience peace and harmony he hoped for in the church. In less than two years Crispus was judicially murdered (8 March 326) and Fausta asphyxiated in one of the steam rooms of the emperor's gigantic bath building at Trier, followed, we are told, by the murder of "innumerable friends."[116] Constantine's court became as perilous as that of Henry VIII. Before these terrible events took place, Constantine was in a buoyant mood. He hastened to inform his subjects in the eastern provinces of the new events to come and in two long letters he revealed his inner convictions to them.[117] The Tetrarchy and all its works were repudiated. "The former emperors I have been accustomed to regard as those with whom I could have no sympathy, on account of the savage cruelty of their character." The persecutions had been in the nature of unnecessary civil war.[118] But now "the perpetrators of this dreadful guilt are no more"; and Constantine pointed the moral of his victory. "Who could obtain any good who neither recognizes God, the author of good things, nor pay him proper reverence?" His own great success "starting from the sea that laps distant Britain" had been directly due to the guidance of the supreme power. Constantine believed in his star and was grateful. "Never can I ungratefully forget the gratitude I owe, believing this to be the noblest service, this the gift granted to me as I advanced to the regions of the East, which consumed by more grievous ills, called aloud for the greater healing care of my hand."[119] The pagans were granted a contemptuous toleration, "Let them have if they wish their temples of lies. We have the glorious edifice of the truth." Constantine, however, made the concession that "they too might enjoy the same degree of peace and tranquility as they who believe" (Eusebius *Life of Constantine* II.56), but henceforth the empire was to be Christian, ruled by an emperor imbued with missionary zeal. The city of Nicomedia had seen the wheel come full circle since the fateful day that Diocletian opened the persecution twenty-one years before.

Constantine had left Nicomedia on a tour of his new provinces when news reached him of the situation in Egypt. The letter which he sent immediately to Alexander and Arius at the hand of Hosius of Córdoba reveals more of his mind. Like all great conquerors from Alexander to Napoleon (or even Hitler) his aim was unity and unification on a worldwide scale. "My design then was, first," he claimed, "to bring the diverse judgements formed by all nations respecting the Deity to a condition, as it were, of settled uniformity; and, second, to restore a healthy tone to the system of the world, then suffering under the power of grievous disease."[120] Christianity, then, was to be the single religion of the Constantinian world-state as well as a gateway to individual immortality. But while paganism was to be abominated, Constantine reveals that his notion of Christianity was of a superior philosophy backed by the invincible power of the Supreme Deity. The questions at issue between Alexander and Arius he regarded as points of debate between rival philosophers. Under the new dispensation, they were frivolous and should never have been raised at all. The disputants should learn to live in harmony with each other and return to the emperor his trouble-free days and nights of repose![121] Once in Alexandria, Hosius for the second time supported the authority of the bishop against his opponents.

The scene now shifts to Antioch, where on 20 December 324, Bishop Philogonius had died. He had been one of Alexander's supporters, and so too, but for entirely different reasons, was his successor Eustathius. Again, Hosius appeared on the scene. The new turn of events nearly ended Eusebius's career. Hosius seems to have known nothing and cared less about Eusebius's role as spokesman for Christianity. Hosius left Eusebius in no doubt that he disliked his teaching and his friendship with Arius. For Eusebius, an Origenist to the core, Christ was the incarnate Logos, creator of the universe and of humanity, but "secondary to God" and ministering to the Father's commands, and he was unwilling to attempt to define the divine and human natures of Christ.[122] Such ideas may have been unexceptional in most of the East, but were regarded as heretical by the combination of Western and Antiochene influence that dominated the council of January 325 held on the occasion of Eustathius's election. Alexander's position was upheld, but far more serious than any condemnation of Arius was Eusebius's excommunication along with two of his colleagues for their alleged sympathies with Arius's views. All they were left to hope for was an acceptance of their defense at the forthcoming "great and hieratic synod at Ancyra" (Ankara), where Eustathius's influence would also have dominated.[123] Origenism itself was coming under attack as never before.

Fortunately Constantine did not accept Hosius's report without reservation. Maybe Eusebius's loyalty already counted with him. In any event, he decided to act as mediator (*Constantine* II.68.2). He retained the idea of a universal council but one where not only Arius's but every other problem afflicting the church would be settled, from the dating of Easter to the terms to be offered to Novatianist and Meletian schismatics. Unity was Constantine's watchword. The location of the great concourse was moved from Ankara to Nicaea in Bithynia which was far more favorable to Arius and was also near Constantine's headquarters at Nicomedia. The emperor would be taking his share in the proceedings.

About 230 bishops arrived, nearly all from the eastern part of the empire, though Caecilian of Carthage was there and Bishop Sylvester (314–35) was represented by two presbyters. Greek was the language of the assembly and so were the problems. Constantine meant it to be a memorable occasion and opened proceedings himself on 20 May 325. Symbolic of the way in which Christianity was now moving, there were only four bishops with biblical Jewish names and these came from near the Persian frontier, where the normal language of Christians would be Aramaic, and Jewish-Christianity had remained strong.[124]

COUNCIL OF NICAEA

Unlike other great ecumenical occasions in the fourth and fifth centuries, there is no contemporary record of the debates at Nicaea. Characteristic of the confusion into which theological ideas had been falling was that, apart from the conviction that Arius's teaching was unacceptable, much turned on personality. Socrates, a perceptive lay historian of the next century (380–450) wrote, "The situation was exactly like a battle fought by night for both parties seemed to be in the dark about the grounds on which they were hurling abuse at each other."[125] Some features stand out. First, very few were prepared to listen to Arius's arguments. Some bishops stopped their ears at his blasphemies. The real debate was over Origenism, with the council chaired by an imperial neophyte whose ideas of Christianity seem to have been derived mainly from Hosius and Lactantius; and Eusebius of Caesarea being technically under censure, the going was rough for the Origenists. In the fifth century, the Syrian historian Theodoret, bishop of Cyrrhus (d. 466), claimed that the newly consecrated bishop of Antioch, Eustathius, took a prominent part in the proceedings.[126] Eustathius was strongly anti-Origenist, a Trinitarian theologian, whose concept of the relationship of the persons of the Trinity had more than a passing resemblance to that of Paul of Samosata. Theodoret tells how he exposed ruthlessly the heresies of Eusebius. It may be assumed, though with reservation, that Eusebius of Caesarea is intended.[127] Eusebius, however, was a convinced Christian and a resilient individual. He produced the creed of his own church at Caesarea and this was hailed as "orthodox," not least, according to himself, by the emperor.[128] The question then revolved around how to define the faith in such a way that Arius's views were unquestionably unorthodox, and then how to paper over the cracks between the great majority of the Eastern bishops whose beliefs resembled those of Eusebius and the powerful Antiochene and Western representatives. It is against this background that we may accept Eusebius's testimony that the controversial term, defining the Son as "Consubstantial with [*homoousios*] the Father" was introduced by Constantine.[129]

The term was objectionable to any Origenist bishop and had, as we have seen, been rejected by Dionysius of Alexandria when used by the Libyan bishops, and by the Council of Antioch when used by Paul of Samosata. It could cover both Sabellian and Adoptionist theology and was not scriptural, and hence could not be accounted as the Word of God. Arius had condemned it as "Manichean."[130] On the other hand, Westerners since Tertullian's time had spoken of the Trinity as subsisting in "Three persons in one substance," without probing into the meaning of these terms (merely "numbering the Trinity," it was complained later), and now Constantine had spoken. The great majority of the Eastern bishops were placed in a false position. They dared not challenge the emperor or his obvious desire for unity, while Arius's views were impossible. Their embarrassment is shown by Eusebius's letter to his congregation trying to explain why he had accepted the terms *homoousios* and playing down its significance.[131]

The text of the creed that emerged was sacrosanct. It read:

We believe in one God the Father All-sovereign, maker of all things visible and invisible; and in one Lord Jesus Christ, the Son of God, begotten of the Father, only-begotten, that is the substance of the Father, God of God, Light of Light, true God of true God, by whom all things were made, things in heaven and things on the earth; who for us men and for our salvation came down and was made flesh, and became man, suffered, and rose on the third day, ascended into heaven, and is coming to judge living and dead. And in the Holy Spirit. And those that say, "There was when he was not," and "Before he was begotten he was not," and that, "He came into being from what-is-not," or those that allege, that the Son of God is "of another substance or essence" or "created" or "changeable" or "alterable," these the Catholic and Apostolic Church anathematizes.[132]

The emperor exerted all his influence toward winning unanimous acceptance and nearly succeeded. Only two bishops stood out against it; but two other senior bishops—Eusebius of Nicomedia, Constantine's capital, and Theognis of Nicaea, where the council was being held—refused to sign the anathemas against Arius and were exiled. The loss of such individuals could not be accepted permanently and compromises would have to be sought.

The council then turned to other questions likely to cause or perpetuate division. Independence from Judaism lay near to the emperor's heart. The Jews for him were "a hostile people" and a "nation of parricides" who "slew their Lord."[133] The fixing of the date of Easter, independent of Jewish calculations of 14 Nisan, was the emperor's second reason for summoning the council. He told the Alexandrians that the council had decided that the East (that is, Antiochenes) should conform to the date acceptable "to the Romans and to us who from the earliest time have observed our period of celebrating Easter," and abandon the Jewish date.[134]

A fair deal was attempted for the Meletians and Novatianists. Like the opponents of Caecilian, Meletius was allowed to retain the title of bishop and his ordinations were pronounced valid. His bishops were subordinate to Alexander's and strict regulations were established for their appointment to a bishopric.[135] Adherents of Paul of Samosata in Antioch were not so fortunate. Alone of deviationists dealt with by the council they had to submit to rebaptism on conversion to orthodoxy.[136] Other canons dealt with the organization of the church. The special status of Rome, Alexandria, and Antioch was confirmed and Aelia became "Jerusalem" possessing special honor, but with the saving administrative clause, without prejudice to the metropolitan status of Caesarea.[137] Bishops were not to move from see to see, thus effectively banning promotions but upholding the principle that a bishop was wedded to his see as Christ was wedded to his church.[138]

At the end, Constantine might be forgiven for believing that all the church's problems had been solved. After two months' work, he sent the bishops home in high style, celebrating his *vicennalia* with them at a banquet.[139] To the Alexandrians he wrote in unrestrained optimism:

> Beloved brethren, hail. We have received from divine Providence the blessing of being freed from all error, and united in the acknowledgement of one and the same faith. The devil will no longer have any power over us. . . . Wherefore we all worship the one true God and believe that he is. But in order that this might be done, by divine will I assembled at the city of Nicaea most of the bishops; with whom I also, who am but one of you, and rejoice exceedingly in being your fellow-servant, undertook the investigation of the truth.[140]

This was the euphoria we find at the end of Eusebius's tenth book of his *Ecclesiastical History*, Constantine acting as "friend of God" and living in a haze of flattery. To some extent, he was justified. The Creed of Nicaea stood the test of time. The council's decision became the touchstone of orthodoxy, its members being equated with the 318 servants of Abraham and regarded therefore as a type (in the Old Testament) of the highest sanctity. At Nicaea, too, Constantine had accomplished the rare feat, not only of a total repudiation of the empire's pagan past, but by open (not to say ostentatious) reconciliation with Egyptian confessors, especially Paphnutius, also winning over that important group for loyalty to the empire.[141] On the other hand, this creed was to raise as many questions as it solved. Was the seeming compromise between Alexandrian and Antiochene and Western theologies really possible? In this respect was not Nicaea to anticipate Chalcedon with the same disappointments in store? *Homoousios* with God, but in what way *homoousios* with man? And just emerging was a new representative of clerical power. It was at Nicaea that

Athanasius, Alexander's deacon, began his career as a zealous opponent of Arius and all he stood for, and a radical man of action as well.

CONSTANTINOPLE: *NOVA ROMA*

Five years separated Nicaea from the final act of the Constantinian revolution, the transfer of power from Rome to Constantinople. It was a step as important as the dethronement of the gods of old Rome, and it accompanied Constantine's own transformation from a Western to an Eastern ruler.

In 312 Constantine had entered Rome, the representative of the aspirations of the Roman nobility and their provincial counterparts. Carthage hastened to establish a cult of the *Gens Flavia* in the new Augustus's honor.[142] It was not only in religion that Constantine's views diverged from those of the Tetrarchy. If the latter had deprived the senatorial aristocracy, so far as possible, of power, Constantine to a large extent restored it. Eusebius says he was liberal in his granting of senatorial rank and those who held it were employed in the higher ranks of the administration.[143] One may see perhaps in Constantine's currency reform—involving the striking of a new gold coin (*solidus*) and silver (*siliquae*) while letting the value of the bronze *follis* depreciate—ideas exactly opposite to those of his predecessors. Diocletian's *follis* was the poor person's coin. Few would have handled the gold and silver issues. Constantine "substituted gold for bronze" to the benefit of the already wealthy.[144] Yet it must be granted that the Constantinian *solidus* remained the currency of the Mediterranean world for centuries, buttressing the military power of Byzantium. It must be ranked among Constantine's major claims to fame.

The Senate and the Roman aristocracy in general, however, stood for Rome and paganism. Already in 325 Constantine was thinking in terms of creating at Byzantium a *Nova Roma*, a seat of government for his son Crispus, a complement rather than a rival to the imperial city.[145] Next year, however, a series of events altered the emphasis of the emperor's plans.

Precisely what precipitated the crisis that struck the imperial family in 326 is not known. As mentioned, Crispus, whose daring leadership had paved the way for Constantine's victory over Licinius, found himself implicated in a charge of adultery and was judicially murdered at the imperial villa(?) at Pola. Fausta's end at Trier followed not long after. There seems to have been no connection between their deaths. As Ramsay MacMullen states, "a discreet or horrified silence settled on their memories."[146] Constantine's mother, Helena, emerged as chief of the imperial ladies, the irreproachable champion of the new religion, soon to travel to the Holy Land distributing gifts and to be credited with finding the true cross beneath a mound of earth and the Temple of Aphrodite.[147] Meantime, in July 326, the emperor paid what was to be a final visit to Rome to celebrate his twentieth anniversary as Augustus (*vicennalia*). It was a fiasco. The fifth-century historian Zosimus, drawing on earlier sources, records the sudden gust of passionate loathing for paganism that Constantine demonstrated as the customary sacrifices were being performed on the Capitol, and the effect the scene had on the onlooking members of the Senate and people.[148] There was no longer "eternal glory of the Senate and the people of Rome," proclaimed on gold coins struck in an anticipation of the jubilee,[149] nor of the emperor hymned as "the restorer of the golden age."[150] Critics noted that these crimes and manifestations of hostility to the gods accompanied Constantine's transition to Christianity. A generation later, the facts were recalled by the emperor's nephew, Julian the Apostate.[151]

Rome then could no longer satisfy Constantine. Nicomedia was associated with the Tetrarchy. Byzantium, with its superb natural position and proven strength as a fortress, must become the new capital. The mania for building that Constantine had once shared with other members of the Tetrarchy was now given full rein. The emperor's agents, we are told by Libanius two generations later,[152] began to sweep in the gold and silver treasures of the old gods to adorn the new capital, where Christianity would reign supreme, and the East would retain its predominant role in the religion of the Greco-Roman world.

Meantime, events were demonstrating Constantine's personal evolution from a Western- to an Eastern-oriented sovereign. The imperial diadem of pearls and jewels replaced the bayleaves and radiate crown of his predecessors. After Nicaea we hear no more of Hosius at Constantine's court. His place as the emperor's mentor was taken by Eusebius. The reasons for the transfer are obscure. Despite the censure he suffered at the Council of Antioch, Eusebius must have already stood high in the emperor's favor by the time the Council of Nicaea opened. One thing should be remembered. He may already have been in contact with the emperor's half sister, Constantia, who was Licinius's wife. He had told her that Christ could not be represented in pictorial form.[153] Like his namesake of Nicomedia, he had known when to change sides, even though he had always been an admirer of Constantine. The tenth book of the *Ecclesiastical History* would otherwise be inexplicable. Shortly after the end of the council, Eusebius received two fulsome letters from Constantine, the first to organize the building of churches and the second to order the compilation of the Scriptures for use in churches in Palestine, all at public expense.[154] No man had done more for the cause of Christianity in the East, and from that time on he was seldom far from the emperor's side.

Whether by Eusebius's advice or not, Constantine's handling of Arius and his friends after Nicaea was in marked contrast to his dealings with the Donatists. The appellation of "Porphyriani" directed against them was quietly dropped. Conciliation became the order of the day. By 327 Eusebius of Nicomedia and Theognis of Nicaea were back in their sees and those consecrated in their place were stepping down. The same year the emperor had a further success. Arius ("the Arius" as Constantine called him) presented a confession of faith on his urgent prompting agreeing that "the Lord Jesus Christ, his Son who was made of him before all ages . . . was incarnate, suffered, rose again, ascended into the heavens and will come to judge the quick and the dead."[155] It sounded fine, but in fact Arius had given nothing away, Christ was still a "creature." There was still "when" he was not, even if he was "made before all the ages." Constantine was satisfied. The penitent could be received into communion once more. But what of his return to Alexandria? Never, if Athanasius could help it.

Meantime, Constantine's ardor for Christianity was unbounded. Churches were built with imperial funds in the major cities of the empire. In the city of Constantine in Numidia where the Donatists had seized the main basilica, Constantine wrote to the Catholics telling them to apply to the financial officer (*rationalis*) for funds to build another (February 330).[156] Self-styled "brother of the bishops,"[157] he now regarded himself as "bishop of those outside," seemingly as a sort of universal herald and propagandist for his faith.[158] In 326 he wrote to the young king Sapor of Persia (309–79) extolling the Christian religion to him and commending the Christians in Persia to his benevolence.[159] Already Constantine seems to have been thinking of himself as the protector of Christians even though these might be outside the boundaries of the empire. In his hands the faith was becoming a weapon of foreign as well as domestic policy.

The year 327 marks the climax of Constantine's achievement. Apart from the Donatists, all dissenting groups of Christians seemed on the way to being reintegrated into the great church. The wounds temporarily caused by Nicaea were being healed. Origenism plus lip service to the emperor's catchword *homoousios* was becoming the official religion of the Greco-Roman world. Its opponents, such as Eustathius of Antioch, would soon experience this. Yet there was still some room for the old pagan religion. The emperor was superstitious. The Neo-Platonist philosopher Sopater found himself welcome at court and given the task of consulting the omens for a favorable day for the dedication of the emperor's new capital.[160] This was still two years away, when Alexander of Alexandria, the lynch-pin of Constantine's hopes for the settlement of the Arian Meletian quarrels, died in April 328. After six weeks of jockeying for power, the choice of a majority of Egyptian bishops fell on Athanasius, "a good man and a pious and an ascetic" (8 June 328).[161] The last epithet is significant. Monks were by now a major power in Egypt. Alexandria was to challenge the Meletians for their allegiance. No quarter was to be given to the schismatics. Within a few months Athanasius was making the first of his tours among the monasteries of Upper Egypt.

Meanwhile, work on Constantine's new city went on apace. It was to be a complete *Nova Roma* with its own senate and senate house and its citizens were to have the title of *populus Romanus*. At last all was ready.

On 11 May 330, two months before his twenty-fifth anniversary as Augustus, he dedicated the new capital. He forbade the offering of sacrifices in the pagan temples that had been restored or erected there since the city had fallen to him in 324. There was to be no idolatrous worship and no pagan festivals. The revolution had been accomplished.

The Christian Triumph

The century leading up to this event had been one of almost unbroken progress for Christianity. Like Judaism, it aimed at being a missionary and conquering religion, and it had succeeded where Judaism had failed. In the 230s the first recorded Christian churches, forming part of dwelling houses, had been built. Now, with the emperor's patronage there would hardly be any major cities without them, and new dedications, as Eusebius shows (*HE* X.3–4), would be magnificent spectacles. The transformation was due partly to the worldwide organization of the church and its steady accumulation of property, which helped to insulate it from the economic blizzard of the mid–third century. The Christian Dispersion was based on the firm foundation of Jewish tradition. Christians, however, were to be found in every race—guaranteeing diversity and change, and embracing a confidence in their own immortality. Partly, however, its success was guaranteed by the weaknesses of paganism. Despite the logic of the divine hierarchy expressed by the Neo-Platonists, the pagan gods were too local, too specialized and diffuse to sustain the ideal of a universal autocratic state such as developed during the third century. What was there in common between the Roman gods and even Sol or Isis or Bacax? Once the traditional guardians of peoples and territories began to lose credibility during the military and economic disasters of the third century, a vacuum was created into which Christianity stepped. Nor despite their elevated teaching were the philosophers able to compete. Iamblichus and Sopater were noble figures, but like the Gnostic teachers of the second century, they led schools and not churches. The pagan propaganda offensive that accompanied the Great Persecution was fifty years too late. Too many of the younger generation in the age of Diocletian were won over to the idealism of ascetic Christianity. This religion provided the new vision that they sought.

But what of the influence of Constantine himself? By 311 the Great Persecution had failed, and in some great territories of the empire, Christianity was already triumphing. In Egypt, North Africa, Mesopotamia, and parts of Syria and Asia Minor, the policies of Maximin and Licinius had no chance of success. The conversion of Constantine only set the seal on the Christian victory. Elsewhere, however, the patronage of the emperor, successful in war and forceful in government, proved to be a decisive influence. Instead of the empire dividing into Christian and non-Christian halves, its unity was maintained under a ruler increasingly dedicated to the service of the Christian God, with epoch-making results. A Westerner

504

himself, Constantine prepared the ground for the advance of Christianity in provinces which it had hitherto scarcely touched. By summoning the Council of Arles in 314 he gave the Western bishops an importance they had previously lacked. Within a generation, by the time the Council of Sardica met in 342 or 343, the number of known Gallic bishoprics had increased from nine to thirty-four,[162] and the church's progress was irreversible. Constantine's massive benefactions enhanced the power and prestige of the papacy and the churches in Italy with the same result. Without his restless energy and sense of purpose, the Council of Nicaea, which established the Christian episcopate as a force on a world scale, could not have taken place. Henceforth bishops became men of power and influence in political as well as religious life, advisers to the emperor like Eusebius of Caesarea and Eusebius of Nicomedia, or prestigious representatives of their people such as Athanasius. The "Age of the Fathers" would have been impossible without Constantine's conversion. The church's councils under the emperor's guidance became assemblies where the new, binding relationship with the Christian God, on which the safety of the empire depended, was established.

As such, these gatherings, in which rival theologies and individuals wrestled for supremacy, had political as well as religious importance. There could only be one orthodoxy. The ministers of the Supreme God would speak with one voice only.

This was the other side of the coin. In practice, the ancient world had exchanged the guardianship of one set of divine masters, capricious but generally benevolent, for another that would brook no opposition. There were already signs that the church which had suffered persecution for so long would soon be persecuting its opponents. The movement of protest could not be tamed overnight—to the victors belonged the spoils. Ecclesiastical decisions were to be enforced by the secular power. Within a few years of the Edict of Milan, heretics were being denounced in unequalled terms and denied the right of assembly.[163] The dynamic of change that had favored the triumph of Christianity did not favor its unity. The arrival of a Christian emperor of Constantine's dedication and political stature fanned the flames of division.

BIBLIOGRAPHY

NOTE

The best guide through this decisive period of European and Mediterranean history remains N. H. Baynes's classic Raleigh Lecture on History, *Constantine the Great and the Christian Church* (British Academy, 1929), 2d ed., preface by H. Chadwick (New York and London: Oxford University Press, 1972). It combines lucidity with an understanding of Constantine's policy based on a depth of study and information. A. H. M. Jones, *Constantine and the Conversion of Europe* (New York:

Macmillan Co., 1949; London: English Universities Press, 1948) is a succinct account of the period from the Great Persecution to Constantine's death. A. Alföldi, *The Conversion of Constantine and Pagan Rome*, Eng. trans. H. Mattingly (Oxford: At the Clarendon Press, 1969), is excellent for Constantine's legislative program and the events leading to the foundation of Constantinople. Another fast-moving narrative of Constantine's reign, strong on the political aspects, is Ramsay MacMullen, *Constantine* (New York: Dial Press, 1969). For Constantine's legislation relating to Christianity, see P. P. Joannou's *La législation impériale et la christianisation de l'empire romain (311–476)*, Orientalia christiana analecta 192 (Rome, 1972). On Eusebius of Caesarea, R. M. Grant, *Eusebius as Church Historian* (New York and London: Oxford University Press, 1980), provides a detailed analysis of *HE*, enabling the author to point to the different strata of redrafting and reedition. T. D. Barnes's *Constantine and Eusebius* (Cambridge, Mass.: Harvard University Press, 1981) offers a comprehensive survey of the period 285–337 in which he claims that Eusebius was a reluctant controversialist, and that the *Chronicle* and the first edition of *HE* reflect the attitudes of the era of peace in the early years of the reign of Diocletian—an original and controversial study.

The beginnings of the Donatist controversy may be studied in my *Donatist Church*. The theological origins of Arianism are discussed by G. C. Stead, *Divine Substance* (New York and London: Oxford University Press, 1977). J. Stevenson's *A New Eusebius* (pp. 297–396) includes translations of a considerable number of the key documents of the reign.

SOURCES

a. Constantine and the Victory of Christianity

Constantine. *Ad Coetum Sanctorum*. Edited by I. Heikel, in GCS 7, Eusebius, pp. 149–92. Leipzig: Hinrichs, 1902.

———, *Letters*—see Eusebius *HE* X.5–7; Optatus *De Schismate Donatistarum* App. III, V–VII, IX, X. For texts included by Eusebius in the *Vita Constantini*, see Heikel, ed., GCS 7, Eusebius, pp. lxxi–lxxii.

Eusebius. *Demonstratio evangelica*. Edited by I. Heikel. GCS 23, Eusebius. Leipzig: Hinrichs, 1913.

———. *HE*. Vol. II (Books VI–X). Eng. trans. J. E. L. Oulton. LCL. Cambridge, Mass.: Harvard University Press; London: William Heinemann, 1932.

———. *Praeparatio evangelica (Preparation for the Gospel)*. Edited by K. Mras. GCS 43, Eusebius. Berlin: Akademie-Verlag, 1954–56.

———. *Vita Constantini*. Edited by I. Heikel. GCS 7, Eusebius, pp. 1–148. Leipzig: Hinrichs, 1902.

English translations of the *Vita* in NPNF; of the *Vita* and Constantine's *Ad Coetum Sanctorum* in *The Greek Ecclesiastical Historians of the First Six Centuries of the Christian Era*, vol. 1, *Eusebius Pamphili. The Life of the Blessed Emperor Constantine* (London: S. Bagster & Sons, 1845); of the *Demonstratio* by W. J. Ferrar in *Proof of the Gospel, Being the Demonstratio Evangelica*, Translations of Christian Literature, series 1, Greek Texts (New York: Macmillan Co., 1920); and the *Preparation* by E. H. Gifford (London: Oxford University Press, 1903).

Lactantius. *Institutes*. Edited by Brandt and Laubmann. CSEL 19.

———. *De Mortibus Persecutorum (On the Deaths of the Persecutors)*. Edited by J. Moreau. 2 vols. SC 39. Paris, 1954.

Panegyrici Latini, VI (7)–X. Edited by E. Galletier. Vol. 2. Paris: Edition Budé, 1952.
For Constantine's coinage, see *Roman Imperial Coinage*, ed. C. H. V. Sutherland and R. A. G. Carson, vol. 7, *Constantine and Licinius*, A.D. *313–337*, ed. P. M. Bruun (London: Spink & Son, 1966).
For Constantine's legislation, see *Codex Theodosianus*, ed. Th. Mommsen and P. M. Meyer (Berlin, 1905; reprinted 1962), esp. XVI, 2, 1–7; 5, 1–2; 8, 1–5; 10.1.

b. The Outbreak of the Donatist Schism

Acta Saturnini, PL 8.688–703, and *Passio Donati et Advocati*, PL 8.752–58 (Donatist *Acta Martyrum*).
Eusebius *HE* X.5–7.
Optatus *De Schismate Donatistarum*, Book 1, 13–26, and Appendixes (part of a Catholic dossier on the origins of the schism).
Texts have been grouped conveniently by Hans von Soden, *Urkunden zur Entstehungsgeschichte des Donatismus*, KIT 122. Bonn: Marcus, 1913.
The Council of Arles = J. Gaudemet, ed., *Conseils gaulois de ive siècle*, SC 241. Paris, 1977.
For the careers of the Donatists and their opponents, see A. Mandouze, *Prosopographie chrétienne du Bas-Empire*, vol. 1, *Afrique 303–533*, CNRS, Paris, 1982.

c. The Outbreak of the Arian Controversy

Epiphanius. *Panarion*. Edited by Holl. GCS 69.
Gelasius of Cyzicus. *Church History*. Edited by G. Loeschcke and M. Heinemann. GCS 28. Leipzig: Hinrichs, 1918.
Socrates, *Ecclesiastical History* I, *PG* 67.29–872; Eng. trans. in NPNF.
Sozomen, *Ecclesiastical History* I, ed. J. Bidez and G. C. Hansen, GCS 50, Berlin: Akademie-Verlag, 1960; Eng. trans. in NPNF.
Theodoret, *Ecclesiastical History* I, ed. L. Parmentier and F. Scheidweiler, GCS 44, Leipzig: Hinrichs, 1954; Eng. trans. in NPNF.
For a collection of texts see H. G. Opitz, ed., *Urkunden zur Geschichte des arianischen Streits: 318–28*, vol. 3 of *Athanasius Werke*, Berlin: Walter de Gruyter, 1934.
For the episcopal list of the Council of Nicaea, see *Patrum Nicaenorum Nomina*, ed. Gelzer and Hilgenfeld and Cuntz. Leipzig: Teubner, 1898.

d. The Meletian Schism: See Epiphanius, *Panarion* 68, GCS 37; and sources listed by N. H. Baynes in *CAH*, vol. 12: *Imperial Crisis*, Bibliography to chap. 19, "The Great Persecution," pp. 789–95, esp. pp. 789–90.

SECONDARY WORKS

Alföldi, A. "The Helmet of Constantine with the Christian Monogram." *JRS* 22 (1932): 9–23.
____. "On the Foundation of Constantinople." *JRS* 37 (1947): 10–16.
Bardy, G. "La *Thalie* d'Arius." *RP* 53 (1927): 211–33.
Barnes, T. D. "The Emperor Constantine's Good Friday Sermon." *JTS* n.s. 27 (October 1976): 414–23.

———. "Lactantius and Constantine." *JRS* 63 (1973): 29–46 (excellent bibliographical notes).

Chadwick, H. "Faith and Order at the Council of Nicaea: A Note on the Background of the Sixth Canon." *HTR* 53 (1960): 171–95.

———. "Ossius of Cordova and the Presidency of the Council of Antioch, 325." *JTS* n.s. 9 (October 1958): 292–304.

Doerries, H. *Constantin der Grosse*. Stuttgart: Kohlhammer, 1958.

———. *Constantine and Religious Liberty*. Eng. trans. R. H. Bainton. New Haven, Conn.: Yale University Press, 1960.

Grant, R. M. "Religion and Politics at the Council of Nicaea." Inaugural lecture of Carl Darling Buck Professor in the University of Chicago. Chicago, 1973.

Gregg, R. C., and Groh, D. E. *Early Arianism: A View of Salvation*, Philadelphia: Fortress Press; London: SCM Press, 1981.

Jones, A. H. M. "Notes on the Genuineness of the Constantinian Documents in Eusebius's Life of Constantine." *JEH* 5 (1954): 196–200.

Momigliano, A. "Pagan and Christian Historiography in the Fourth Century A.D." In *The Conflict Between Paganism and Christianity in the Fourth Century*, pp. 79–99. New York and London: Oxford University Press, 1963.

Nesselhauf, H. "Das Toleranzedikt des Licinius." *Historisches Jahrbuch* 78 (1955): 33–61.

Nock, A. D. "The Emperor's Divine *Comes*." *JRS* 37 (1947): 102–16.

Parkes, J. "Jews and Christians in the Constantinian Empire." In Studies in Church History 1, pp. 69–79. Oxford: Basil Blackwell & Mott, 1964.

Pflaum, H. G. "L'alliance entre Constantin et L. Domitius Alexander." *BAA* 1 (1962–65): 159–66.

Salama, P. "Le plus ancien chrisme officiel de l'Afrique romaine." *ACIAC* 1962 (Rome, 1967): 537–43.

Schwartz, E. *Kaiser Konstantin und die christliche Kirche*. 2d ed. Leipzig and Berlin, 1936.

Seston, W. "Constantine as a 'Bishop.' " *JRS* 37 (1947): 127–31.

Stead, G. C. " 'Eusebius' and the Council of Nicaea." *JTS* n.s. 24 (April 1974): 85–100.

———. "The Platonism of Arius." *JTS* n.s. 15 (April 1964): 16–31.

Straub, J. "Kaiser Konstantin als ἐπίσκοπος τῶν ἐκτός" *SP* 1: 678–95; and in H. Ruhbach, ed., *Die Kirche angesichts der konstantinischen Wende*, pp. 187–205. Wede der Forschung 306. Darmstadt: Wissenschaftliche Buchgesellschaft, 1976.

Thomas, G. S. R. "Maximin Daza's Policy and the Edicts of Toleration." *L'Antiquité classique* 37 (1968): 172–85.

Vogt, J. "Die Bedeutung des Jahres 312 für die Religionspolitik Konstantins des Grosses." *ZKG* 61 (1942): 171–90.

Ziegler, J. *Zur religiösen Haltung der Gegenkaiser in 4 Jhr. n. Chr.*" (= Fas, Heft 4, Frankfurt, 1970), pp. 9ff. and 35–52 concerning Maxentius.

NOTES

1. Eusebius *HE* VIII.13.1.
2. Probably towards the end of April 306. Easter that year was on 18 April. For

the contents and implementation of the decree, see Eusebius *De martyribus Palestinae* (*On the Palestinian Martyrs*) IV.8.

3. For Pamphilus and his companions, see ibid., II, and the persecution's abatement c. 309-10, idem, *HE* VIII.16.1.

4. *Palestinian Martyrs* XIII.1. Also, VIII.1 and XI.1 and *HE* VIII.9.4-5. See my *Martyrdom and Persecution*, pp. 516-17.

5. See Ziegler, *Zur religiösen*, pp. 9ff. and 35ff.

6. Optatus *De Schismate Donatistarum* I.16 and 17.

7. Dated A.D. 309; see J. Marcillet-Jaubert, *Les Inscriptions d'Altava* (Aix en Provence: Publications des Annales de la Faculté des Lettres, 1968), reviewed by J. C. Mann, *JRS* 60 (1970): 234-35.

8. *Le Liber Pontificalis*, ed. L. Duchesne, 2 vols. (Paris: Bibliothèque des Écoles Françaises d'Athènes et de Rome, 1886-92), vol. 1, p. 164.

9. See *Gesta Collationis Carthaginensis* (of A.D. 411) III, 489-514 and the more explicit extract, cited by Augustine, *Breviculus collationis cum Donatistis* (*Summary of the Conference with the Donatists*) III.18.34.

10. Lactantius, *Deaths of Persecutors*, ed. Moreau, XXIX.7. See Barnes, "Lactantius and Constantine," pp. 41-43, on Lactantius's vilification of Maximian compared with his dispassionate treatment of Maxentius.

11. *Panegyrici Latini* VII.21.3-6, ed. Galletier; Eng. trans. Stevenson, *A New Eusebius*, pp. 297-98.

12. *Panegyrici Latini* VII.2, "Ab illo divo Claudio manat in te avita cognatio, qui Romani imperii solutam et perditam disciplinam primus reformavit." Constantine would do the same. Written shortly after 25 July 310, the date of Constantine's *dies imperii*. Note the continuance of the ideal of *disciplina* as the means of preserving the empire.

13. On the significance of this legend on Constantine's coins, see Nock, "Emperor's Divine *Comes*."

14. Barnes, "Lactantius and Constantine," p. 44 (with references) on the question whether Constantine was always ruler of the Spanish provinces.

15. See Pflaum, "L'alliance"; and A. Berthier, "Constantina; raisons et répercussions d'un changement de nom," *Receuil des notices et des mémoires de la Soc. archéol. de la Wilaya de Constantine* 71 (1969-71): 79-88.

16. Lactantius *Institutes* V.2-5 (ed. Brandt, pp. 403-11). See P. de Labriolle, *La réaction païenne: Étude sur la polemique antichrétienne du Ier au VIe siècles* (Paris: L'Artisan du livre, 1934; 2d ed., 1950), pp. 304-15, and above, p. 458.

17. Eusebius *HE* IX.5.1; compare also I.9.3 and I.11.9. He claims these *Acta* were "of recent origin."

18. Ibid., VIII.14.9.

19. Reproaches against the Christians are preserved in Eusebius, *Praeparatio evangelica* I.2.1-4, ed. J. Sirinelli and E. des Places, SC 206 (Paris, 1974).

20. By the prefect of Egypt, Culcianus, in c. 307. See G. Lanata, "Note al Papiro Bodmer XX," *Museum Philologum Londiniense*, ed. E. Giangrande (Vithoorn, 1977), pp. 207-26.

21. There is a useful sketch of Eusebius's career and suggestions for the dating of his writings in Sirinelli and des Places, *Preparation*, chap. 2; and Barnes, *Constantine and Eusebius*, pp. 81-190.

22. See Kirsopp Lake's introduction to Eusebius, *Ecclesiastical History*, vol. I,

LCL (Cambridge, Mass.: Harvard University Press; London: William Heinemann, 1926), pp. xvii–xxii.

23. Thus, Sirinelli and des Places, *Preparation*, p. 31. The long dialogue with Porphyry may be traced in the *Chronicle*, the two books *Contra Hieroclem* (*Against Hierocles*), c. 307–8, and above all, in the *Preparation* and the *Eclogae propheticae* (*Prophetic Extracts*).

24. *Preparation* I.1 (*PG* 21.28A–B).

25. *Demonstratio evangelica* (*Proof of the Gospel*) V.208 (Ferrar's trans., slightly altered). Cf. *Theophania* (*Divine Manifestation*) V.49. For the argument in this passage see Origen *Celsus* I.43.

26. *HE* I.1.5 (taking up even if unconsciously the tradition of Josephus).

27. *HE* I.4.15. See also Momigliano, "Pagan and Christian Historiography."

28. Eusebius *Proof* VII.2.

29. *HE* IV.7.1, "Demonic forces" continued to be the agents of disharmony among the Christians and any acts that appeared to disturb the harmony of church and empire; cf. Evagrius *Ecclesiastical History* II.5 on Monophysitism: "a device of the envious and God-hating demon."

30. Thus, at the Council of Tyre, the Egyptian bishop Potammon, who was also a confessor, refused to accept Eusebius as a judge of Athanasius. (Athanasius *Apologia contra Arianos* [*Apology Against the Arians*] 8 and Epiphanius *Medicine Box* 68.8. He accused him of lapsing during the persecution.)

31. Text in Lactantius *Deaths of Persecutors* XXXIV.1–5 and Eusebius *HE* VIII.17.6–11. The edict was published in the names of Galerius, Licinius, Constantine, and also Maximin (though his name is omitted deliberately by Eusebius). For discussion, see *Deaths of Persecutors*, ed. Moreau, pp. 388–95; and J. P. Knipfing, "The Edict of Galerius, 311 A.D., Reconsidered," *Rev. belge de la Philologie et d'Histoire* 1 (1922): 695ff. There is no need to follow E. Schwartz, "Zur Geschichte des Athanasius IV," *NGG* (1904), p. 527, and attribute any major influence in its drafting to Constantine.

32. Eng. trans. in Stevenson, *A New Eusebius*, p. 296.

33. *ILCV* 1a, and see Th. Mommsen's comments, "Die Zweisprächige Inschrift aus Arycanda," *Gesammelte Schriften* 6, pp. 555–65.

34. Eusebius *HE* IX.7.10–11; and compare IX.9.18 (Christians in Nicomedia). Nicomedia appears to provide another example of a city council remaining loyal to the gods, while the bulk of the townsfolk accepted Christianity.

35. Ibid., IX.5.2.

36. Ibid., 4.2. The final spasm of persecution seemed the worst of all (see ibid., 6.4).

37. Ibid., VIII.9.4–5 (Eng. trans. Oulton).

38. *Panegyrici Latini* IX.4, ed. Galletier.

39. For the vision, see Eusebius, *Vita Constantini*, ed. Heikel, I.28 (Eng. trans. NPNF); and the dream, Lactantius, *Deaths of Persecutors* XLIV (Eng. trans. ANCL). For the discovery of the "oc signo" graffito, see M. Guarducci, *I graffiti sotto la confessione di San Pietro in Vaticano*, 3 vols. (Libraria editrice Vaticana, 1958), II.2 and 27, and P. M. Fraser's discussion in *JRS* 52 (1962): 217.

40. Eusebius *De vita Constantini* (*Life of Constantine*) II.49.

41. Lactantius *Deaths of Persecutors* 37.1. Probably early 312, after petitions against the Christians had begun to be acted upon (see ibid., 36.3–7).

42. "Liberator Orbis," see H. Cohen, *Médailles impériales* VII (Paris and London, 1888), no. 317. On the Arch of Constantine the emperor's soldiers bear the symbol of the sun on their shields.

43. Nazarius(?) *Panegyricus Constantini* II and IV (*PL* 8.656 and 657).

44. Augustine suggests that Hosius was an exile having been condemned by a council in Spain for some unspecified offense, *Contra epistolam Parmeniani* (*Against the Epistle of Parmenianus*) I.4.7.

45. For the Eng. trans. of the so-called Edict of Milan, see Lactantius, *Deaths of Persecutors* 48 (ANCL, pp. 207–9) and Eusebius *HE* X.5 (ed. Oulton, pp. 447–53), and the Greek trans. in Eusebius *HE* X.5. Whether there ever was an actual edict has been questioned since Otto Seeck's article, "Das sogennante Edikt von Mailand," in *ZKG* 12 (1891): 381ff. See J. R. Palanque, "Apropos du prétendu édit de Milan," *Byzantion* 10 (1935): 607ff., and Nesselhauf's study entitled, "Das Toleranzedikt des Licinius."

46. For this translation of the text, see N. H. Baynes's chapter "Constantine," pp. 678–99 of *CAH*, vol. 12: *Imperial Crisis*, pp. 689–90, and comments in *Constantine*, pp. 72–73.

47. *Ad Scapulam* (*To Scapula*) II.2, "Sed nec religionis est cogere religionem quae sponte suscipi debeat"; and Lactantius *Divinae Institutiones* (*Divine Institutes*) V.20 for the same view.

48. Lactantius *Deaths of Persecutors* 48.6; Eusebius *HE* 10.5.8.

49. It was used, however, by pagans at the end of the century, see Nectarius to Augustine (cf. Augustine *Letter* CIII.4: "Deus summus te custodiat"), but for Christians it could be synonymous with "Theos Hypsistos" and in Lactantius's time used as such. See M. Simon, "Theos Hypsistos," in *Ex orbe religionum. Studia Geo. Widengren* (Leiden: E. J. Brill, 1972), I: 372–85, esp. pp. 384–85.

50. Eusebius *HE* IX.9a.1ff.

51. Lactantius *Deaths of Persecutors* XLIV.6.

52. For Licinius's coinage and its significance, see Bruun, *RIC*, vol. 7: *Constantine and Licinius*, pp. 266f.

53. The usual date for the first war between Constantine and Licinius has been challenged by Barnes (following P. Bruun), "Lactantius and Constantine," p. 36. If 316 is correct as the date of the civil war, Constantine's decision in favor of Caecilian of Carthage in November 316 could have been taken on the victorious aftermath of the war.

54. E. Honigmann's view. He connects the Licinian persecution and execution of Basil of Amaseia (cf. Eusebius *Constantine* II.1) with Licinius's discovery that Constantine had entered into a treaty relationship with the Armenians and was using clergy as agents against him; see his "Basileus of Amasea (314, about 320 A.D., Patristic Studies," *ST* 173 (1953): 6–27.

55. Eusebius *Constantine* II.16: "Licinius confident in the aid of a multitude of gods."

56. Eusebius *HE* X.8.19; and compare *Constantine* II.19.

57. The view of Otto Seeck, Edward Schwartz, and Henri Grégoire criticized by Baynes, *Constantine*, pp. 7ff.

58. See Nock, "Emperor's Divine *Comes*."

59. Constantine's victory over Maxentius is ascribed to "nutu divino" on the Arch of Constantine which the Senate had voted (see MacMullen, *Constantine*, p.

81). For Constantine's "special relation" with divine powers as seen by contemporaries, see Nazarius(?), *Panegyricus Constantini* II (*PL* 8.656A)

60. See Salama, "Le plus ancien chrisme."

61. Thus, the proconsul Aelianus at the trial of Ingentius in 315, who had made a false accusation that one of the bishops who consecrated Caecilian as bishop of Carthage was a betrayer (*traditor*), *Acta purgationis Felicis episcopi Autumnitani* (*Record of the Exculpation of Felix, Bishop of Aptunga*) (App. II of Optatus *De Schismate Donatistarum,* pp. 197–204, esp. p. 203).

62. For my view that the passages in the *SHA* referring to Christianity date most probably to the early fourth century, see "A Severan Persecution. The Evidence of the *Historia Augusta,*" *Forma Futuri* = Studi in onore de Cardinale Michele Pellegrino (Turin: Bottega d'Erasmo, 1975), pp. 470–80.

63. See *Deaths of Persecutors,* ed. Moreau, pp. 31–33, and Barnes, "Lactantius and Constantine," pp. 40–41. Lactantius must have been in Nicomedia 302(?) to 305, when Diocletian abdicated, and again in 311 for the publication of Galerius's edict. Also, to be Crispus's tutor, he must have been at Constantine's court at Trier from 315 onward. Otherwise, the options between Gaul, Italy, and even Sardica remain open for the intervening years.

64. *Institutes* I.1.13. In *Deaths of Persecutors* XXIV.9, he emphasizes Constantine's immediate legislative aid ("Haec fuit prima eius sanctio") in favor of restoring to the Christians their right to worship God (Edict of Milan or the emperor's instructions to his officials in Africa?).

65. Thus *Deaths of Persecutors* L.

66. *Institutes* VII.15; and the destruction that would precede this event, see ibid., 16.

67. Eusebius *HE* X.5.15–17.

68. Ibid., X.6.

69. Ibid., 7.2.

70. Ibid., 7.1.

71. Preserved in Optatus *De Schismate Donatistarum,* App. III, pp. 204–6, Baynes's translation.

72. Ibid., App. V, pp. 208–10. I now accept Baynes's view, *Constantine,* pp. 13–14; "Famulus Dei" was to recur often in Constantine's vocabulary. Note also Baynes's comment on the significance of "our God" in this letter, ibid., pp. 13, 78–79.

73. *Oratio ad Sanctos* 24, ed. I. Heikel, GCS 7, Eusebius (Leipzig, 1902), p. 190; compare Lactantius *Deaths of Persecutors* IV–VII, XVII. See Barnes, "Constantine's Good Friday Sermon." One may not agree with Barnes's precise dating, but the authenticity of the address seems evident enough.

74. They included *latifundia* in Italy, Sicily, and North Africa. See the list preserved in *Liber Pontificalis,* ed. Duchesne vol. 1, pp. 177–88, and discussed by A. H. M. Jones, *The Later Roman Empire, 284–602* (2 vols., Norman: University of Oklahoma Press; 4 vols., Oxford: Basil Blackwell & Mott, 1964), pp. 89–91, also by Duchesne, *Liber Pontificalis,* vol. 1, pp. 187–201, and Charles Piétri, *Roma christiana* I (Bibliothèque des Écoles Françaises d'Athènes et de Rome, 224, Rome, 1976), pp. 79–90. As Piétri points out, the income made the Roman church "comfortable" but not rich in comparison with even the wealthy members of the senatorial order (p. 90).

75. See Joseph Vogt, "Bemerkungen zum Gang der Constantinforschung," *Mullus: Festschrift Theodor Klauser* (Münster: Aschendorff, 1964), pp. 378–79.

76. *Codex Theodosianus* XVI.2.4., ad Populum, and compare Eusebius *Constantine* II.36. The church became the residuary legatee of those who died without heir.

77. *Codex Theodosianus* XVI.2.1 and 2 (31 October 313 and 21 October 319). Both interesting as suggesting immediate opposition to the status granted by Constantine to Catholic clergy.

78. Ibid., XVI.2.3 (18 July 320) to Bassus, the praetorian prefect; and compare for Constantine's intentions, ibid., XVI.2.6 of 1 June 326 to Ablabius (the Christian) praetorian prefect.

79. Eusebius *HE* X.5.23.

80. *Codex Theodosianus* I.27.1 (episcopal tribunals); and ibid., IV.7.1 (addressed to Bishop Hosius on 18 April 321).

81. *Codex Theodosianus* IV.40.2 of 21 March 315.

82. Ibid., VIII.16.1 (31 January 320).

83. Ibid., XVI.8.1 (13 August 315). See Parkes, "Jews and Christians." For Diocletian's policy, see M. Simon, *Verus Israel: étude sur les relations entre Chrétiens et Juifs dans l'Empire Romain (135–425)* (Paris: Boccard, 1948; 2d ed. augmented, Paris: Boccard, 1964), p. 135.

84. *Codex Theodosianus* XVI.8.1 (3 July 321).

85. Ibid., VII.20.2.

86. On the date of the outbreak of the Donatist schism in 311–12 see the present author and K. Clancy, "When Did the Donatist Schism Begin?" *JTS* n.s. 28 (April 1977): 104–9. For a date immediately following the end of the persecution, see T. D. Barnes, "The Beginnings of Donatism," *JTS* n.s. 25 (April 1975): 13–22, esp. pp. 18–20.

87. Augustine *Conference with Donatists* III.13.25 (*PL* 43.638).

88. Ibid., "adhuc diacono Caeciliano schisma fecisse Carthagine" (Donatus).

89. Optatus *De Schismate Donatistarum* I.1.7.

90. Augustine *Conference with Donatists* III.14.26: "tamquam a traditoribus ordinatus, et quia cum esset diaconus, victum afferri martyribus in custodia constitutis prohibuisse dicebatur."

91. Optatus *De Schismate Donatistarum* I.15 and 19, "et altare contra altare erectum est."

92. See my *Donatist Church*, chaps. 1, 11.

93. Optatus *De Schismate Donatistarum* I.22, and Augustine *Letter* 88.2. For Miltiades' role as "judex datus," conducting a *cognitio* to establish the fact of the situation, on the emperor's order, see Piétri, *Roma christiana*, pp. 160–66.

94. For the Donatist argument, see the *Acta* of the Council of Carthage in 411 (*Gesta Collationis Carthaginensis*), III.489–514 (*PL* 11.1255–56).

95. For the form of the council as primarily a legal tribunal set up by Constantine, using the bishops as assessors, see Gaudemet, *Conseils gaulois du ive siècle*, pp. 35–37. For the canons, see ibid., references. For the British bishops and their sees, see J. C. Mann, "The Administration of Roman Britain," *Antiquity* 35 (1961): 316–20.

96. Canon 3.

97. Canon 9.

98. For the events of 313–16, see *Donatist Church*, chap. 11, following in the main Baynes, *Constantine*, pp. 12ff.

99. Constantine to Domitius Celsus, *Vicarius Africae* in Optatus *De Schismate Donatistarum*, App. VII, pp. 211–12.

100. See the Donatist tract, *Passio Donati et Advocati* III (*PL* 8.754). "Christus inquit (Diabolus) amator unitatis est"—a good example of the extreme suspicion that greeted any rapprochement between church and empire, among Donatus's following.

101. *Gesta apud Zenophilum* in Optatus *De Schismate Donatistarum*, App. I, pp. 185–96.

102. Eusebius *Constantine* II.66 quoting Constantine's letter to Alexander and Arius.

103. Epiphanius *Medicine Box* 68.3. For 3d century monasticism see Socrates I.11.

104. Publ. in Routh, ed., *Reliquiae Sacrae*, vol. 3, pp. 321–43.

105. For instance, *Pap. Oxy.* 2601, showing that though litigants had to offer sacrifice before entering the court at Oxyrhynchus, a Christian had little difficulty in finding someone to act on his behalf.

106. A point on which Origen and Plotinus agreed. Both regarded the Second Principle as generated by the First; see Origen *Principles* I.2.4. and Plotinus *Ennead* V.2.1, 7–9.

107. See H. J. Carpenter, "Popular Christianity and the Theologians in the Early Centuries," *JTS* n.s. 14 (October 1963): 294–310, esp. pp. 309–10.

108. See Alexander's circular letter of 324, addressed to Philogonius of Antioch and others, preserved in Theodoret *Ecclesiastical History* I.4.35. For Arius's Platonism, see Stead, "Platonism of Arius," "Among Christian Platonists Arius probably owes most to Methodius" (p. 31). For his soteriology, see Gregg and Groh, *Early Arianism*, pp. 50–70.

109. Arius's letter is preserved in Athanasius, *De Synodis* XVI (*PG* 26.708ff) and Epiphanius *Medicine Box* LXIX.7. Written from Nicomedia, c. 320 in Stevenson, *A New Eusebius*, pp. 346–47.

110. Preserved, not in consecutive order, by Athanasius *Orationes adversus Arianos (Apology Against the Arians)* I.5 (*PG* 26.216), *De Synodis* XIV (end) and XV (*PG* 26.705ff.), and compare Socrates *Ecclesiastical History* I.6.11–12. See Stead, "Platonism of Arius," pp. 19–20, and the extracts quoted in Stevenson, *A New Eusebius*, pp. 350–51, and by Bardy, "La *Thalie* d'Arius."

111. *Depositio Arii* in Opitz, ed., *Urkunde zur Geschichte*, 4b, citing Socrates *Ecclesiastical History* I.6.4–13.

112. Socrates *Ecclesiastical History* I.5.

113. Sozomen *Ecclesiastical History* I.15, emphasizes Arius's links with the Meletians.

114. Ibid., I.5.10, reports a Bithynian synod convened by Eusebius of Nicomedia that found in Arius's favor.

115. Eusebius *HE* X.9.6–8 (Eng. trans. Oulton).

116. Eutropius, *Breviarum* X.6.3 (ed. G. Santini [Leipzig: Teubner, 1979]).

117. Eusebius *Constantine*—(a) II.25–42: to the provincials of Palestine ordering the complete restoration to the Christians of goods and property confiscated

during the persecution (b) II.48–60: to the "eastern provincials" affirming the emperor's complete dedication to God's service (II.55), granting a scornful toleration to the pagans and praying that all may become Christians, though voluntarily (II.60).

118. Ibid., II.49.

119. Ibid., 29. The question of authenticity seems settled by the discovery of a contemporary copy of the letter (*Pap. Lond.* 878). See Jones, "Genuineness of Constantinian Documents."

120. *Constantine* II.65; cf. II.56, "the general advantage of the world and all mankind."

121. Ibid., II.72. For the events of 324–5, see Grant, "Religion and Politics at Nicaea" and Chadwick, "Ossius of Cordova." For what was probably the credal statement of the Council of Antioch, see Kelly, *Early Christian Creeds*, pp. 208–11.

122. Thus Eusebius *HE* I.2; he accepted that the Word was a "secondary divine being," but unlike Arius, he believed also that "he alone knew the Father."

123. Text in Stevenson, *A New Eusebius*, pp. 354–57; see also Chadwick, "Ossius of Cordova," p. 303. Was Hosius's summons of the Council of Antioch really a "sudden decision" (p. 304)?

124. Thus G. D. Kilpatrick in a review of *CIJ* II, III, ed. V. A. Tcherikover, A. Fuks, and M. Stein, 3 vols., in *VC* 22 (1968): 137. Eusebius *Constantine* III.8 estimated total numbers as "more than 250," Constantine in his letter to the Alexandrians (Socrates *Ecclesiastical History* I.9) as 300.

125. Socrates *Ecclesiastical History* I.23 (*PG* 67.144), referring in particular to the controversy over the term *homoousios*.

126. Theodoret *Ecclesiastical History* I.27.

127. Which Eusebius? On the whole, I favor Eusebius of Caesarea as Eustathius's target. See Stead, " 'Eusebius' and Nicaea."

128. Opitz, ed., *Urkunde zur Geschichte*, 22. See Kelly, *Early Christian Creeds*, 220ff. for the relation between Eusebius's creed and the eventual Creed of Nicaea.

129. Opitz, *Urkunde zur Geschichte*; Socrates *Ecclesiastical History* I.8 states that only after mature reflection did Eusebius sign the creed and then wrote explaining his position to his congregation.

130. Arius to Alexander, c. 320; cited by Athanasius, *De Synodis* XVI. For the *homoousios* in previous debate, see J. N. D. Kelly, *Early Christian Doctrines*, (rev. ed., New York: Harper & Row, 1978; London: A. & C. Black, 1977), pp. 130, 135–37 and 233–37; and Stead, *Divine Substance*, pp. 216ff.

131. Text in Socrates, *Ecclesiastical History* I.8, *PG* 67.69. See Kelly, *Early Christian Creeds*, pp. 220–26.

132. Socrates *Ecclesiastical History* I.8, Eng. trans. in Henry Bettenson, ed., *Documents of the Christian Church* (New York: Oxford University Press, 1947; London: Oxford University Press, 1943), pp. 35–36.

133. Constantine, "To the Churches," preserved in Socrates *Ecclesiastical History* I.9, *PG* 67.89C and D. Compare Eusebius *Constantine* III.17–20.

134. Constantine, "To the Alexandrians" = Socrates *Ecclesiastical History* I.9, *PG* 67.81–84. Opitz, *Urkunde zur Geschichte*, 23.12.

135. Ibid., col. 80, and Sozomen *Ecclesiastical History* I.24.

136. Council of Nicaea, canon 19.

137. Canons 6 and 7 (Jerusalem).

138. Canon 15.

139. Eusebius *Constantine* III.15.

140. Socrates *Ecclesiastical History* I.9 (trans. NPNF).

141. Ibid., I.11.

142. Aurelius Victor *Caesares* XL.28, "tum per Africam sacerdotium decretum Flaviae genti."

143. *Constantine* IV.1, inflation of higher appointments in almost Gilbertian style, "in numberless instances the title Most Illustrious and many other distinctions were conferred."

144. See Bruun, *RIC*, vol. 7: *Constantine and Licinius*, general introduction, and for the effects, *De Rebus Bellicis. A Roman Reformer and Inventor*, Eng. trans. and ed. E. A. Thompson (New York and London: Oxford University Press, 1952), p. 94.

145. For Constantine's gradual alienation from pagan Rome, see Alföldi, *Conversion of Constantine*, chap. 7. In 325 Publilius Optatianus Porfyrius refers to what appears to be the site of Constantinople as "altera Roma" (*Carmen* IV.6, ed. J. Polara, 2 vols. [Turin: J. B. Paravia, 1973]).

146. Eutropius *Breviarum* X.6.3 suggests a conspiracy involving both Crispus and Fausta. Jealousy between Fausta and Helena may also have been a factor. Only Helena wore an imperial diadem on her coins though both had been declared "Augusta" at the end of 324. See Bruun, *RIC* vol. 7: *Constantine and Licinius*, p. 45.

147. MacMullen, *Constantine*, p. 188.

148. Zosimus *Historia Nova* II.27.5 and 30.

149. Alföldi, "Foundation of Constantinople."

150. Porfyrius *Carmen* VII, "reddens . . . aurea saecula," written before Crispus's death.

151. Julian, *The Caesars*, Eng. trans. and ed. W. C. Wright, vol. 2, LCL (Cambridge, Mass.: Harvard University Press; London: William Heinemann, 1913), 336A and B.

152. Libanius *Oratio* XXX.6 (*Libanii Opera*, ed. R. Foerster, 12 vols. [1909–27], vol. 3, p. 90). See Alföldi, *Conversion of Constantine*, p. 97.

153. Eusebius *Letter to Constantia* = *PG* 20.1545. Addressed as "Augusta" and hence presumably while she was Licinius's consort.

154. *Constantine* IV.35 and 36.

155. Gelasius of Cyzicus, *Church History* III.15, ed. Loeschcke and Heinemann, p. 164. Addressed to "Father Alexander the bishop" and received shortly before he died (15.7), that is, late 327 or early 328. For Arius's confession, see Socrates *Ecclesiastical History* I.26.

156. Reproduced in Optatus, *De Schismate Donatistarum*, App. X. Also, *Codex Theodosianus* XVI.2.7, issued on 5 February 330 from Sardica.

157. Eusebius *Constantine* II.69.

158. Ibid., IV.24. See Seston, "Constantine as 'Bishop,' "; and J. Straub, "Constantine as κοινος επισκοπος: Tradition and Innovation in the Representation of the First Emperor's Majesty," in *Dumbarton Oaks Papers* 21 (1967): 39–55, esp. pp. 51–53.

159. *Constantine* IV.9–13.

160. Alföldi, *Conversion of Constantine*, p. 105.

161. Athanasius, *Apology Against Arians* VII, *PG* 25.247–410. See E. R. Hardy, *Christian Egypt: Church and People; Christianity and Nationalism in the Patriarchate of Alexandria* (New York and London: Oxford University Press, 1952), p. 55.

162. Athanasius, *Apology Against Arians* XLIX.1, *PG* 25.337B, preserves the names but not the sees.

163. *Constantine* III.64 and 65.

FROM CONSTANTINE
TO CHALCEDON

PART 3

Toward
Byzantinism
330–61

At the dedication of Constantinople, Constantine still had another seven years to reign. From York, where he had first been acclaimed Augustus, he had traveled far, and now in his new capital he did not look back again to the West. Even Trier, which he had embellished first with a great palace and then with a magnificent church, seems only to have come into his mind as a place of exile for Athanasius. His interests—and we may trust Eusebius in this—developed towards theology, as the East understood it, and the achievement of unity in the church. His mind was occupied with his own city of Constantinople, with Jerusalem and the massive basilica he built over the spot identified with the Holy Sepulchre, and beginning the destruction of paganism. The mystic with heavenward gaze and zeal for prayer described by his biographer[1] also became an astute missionary, taking advantage of the almost fortuitous Christianization of the Black Sea kingdom of Iberia[2] to strengthen Rome's influence in this sensitive area where Roman and Persian interests clashed. Christianity was to serve the cause of the emperor's diplomacy. Even as he aged, Constantine remained hardheaded enough to establish his kinsman Hannibalianus as king of Armenia in 335, an insurance against the growing threat from Persia.

The emperor's policies need not be viewed too cynically. The Mediterranean world was now entering a completely new phase in its history, in which members of the "race of Christians" would be playing a predominant role. Their interest and ideas were to prevail and their leaders would direct affairs of state, accompany the emperor on campaigns, and act as his chief advisers at home. Indicative of the new state of affairs is the survival of the names of no less than eleven hundred bishops and other clergy who lived in the reign of Constantine and his sons.[3] The army, too, previously the symbol of the protecting power of the gods, now carried the sacred monogram on its shields.[4] After Constantine's death, his sons would faithfully, if unimaginatively, continue his policy. More and more of the emperor's and his advisers' time would be taken up with theological debates. Between 337 and 361 more than a dozen major councils attempted to define the faith of the empire in the way best calculated to secure the favor of the Supreme Divinity. In the thirty years between the dedication of Constantinople and the proclamation of Julian the Apostate as Augustus at Paris (Lutetia) in February 360, the Greco-Roman world had taken a long and irreversible step towards its transformation into the Byzantine church-state.

The herald of this new age was, once more, Eusebius of Caesarea. With his namesake of Nicomedia his was the most powerful influence in the empire during the decade 330–40 (not excluding Athanasius). While Eusebius of Nicomedia, one-time friend of Licinius, banished after Nicaea, mastered the art of survival and became Constantine's adviser and confidant, Eusebius of Caesarea set out the ideal of the godly monarch which was to influence Byzantine political thought for centuries to come. When

Constantine celebrated his thirty years of rule (*tricennalia*) at Jerusalem in 335 in splendid style, Eusebius was on hand to crown the occasion with theories of Christian imperial kingship.

Drawing on the traditions of the Hellenistic monarchy and its apologists as well as Philo, the enthusiastic tone of his panegyric dwarfed all previous praises. The emperor was hailed as "imitator and representative on earth of the Divine Word himself." He ruled as "vice-gerent of God." The world was filled with the doctrine of salvation and had become a likeness or imitation of the heavenly kingdom. Constantine, its ruler, reflected the divine virtues of wisdom, goodness, justice, and strength. His character was formed after the divine original of the Supreme Divinity.[5] Constantine was crowned in the image of the heavenly kingship and he steered and guided people on earth according to the pattern of his prototype, confirmed by the example of monarchical authority.[6] Monarchy was the best of all governments, and Constantine, the "friend of God," had been appointed by him as a brilliant example to carry out the divine plan for humankind.

Combined with the mystique that already belonged to the emperor under the Tetrarchy, and the traditional authority of the Pontifex Maximus, the Constantinian monarchy approached the godlike in its conceptions. Since Chrysopolis the jeweled diadem had become commonplace on the coinage. The emperor from now on was typed as a hieratic figure. The long face, high forehead, and fixed eyes denoted the image of majesty rather than the likeness of the individual emperor. Constantius II was entirely at home in this role. On Constantius's visit to Rome in May 357 the historian Ammianus Marcellinus described him as an impassive godlike figure, "keeping his eyes straight ahead as though he were a clay figure" (*tanquam figmentum hominis*). He never stirred but showed himself calm and imperturbable "as always, amid the plaudits of the crowds."[7] His bearing suggested that he regarded himself as an impersonal embodiment of monarchy, ruler of all people, and supreme arbiter over their destinies whether secular or religious. And in this he was supported by the army. At the siege of Amida in 359 the troops cheered and praised the power of the emperor as "lord of the world and the universe."[8] Unfortunately, in this encounter his great rival the Persian "king of kings" and "victor in wars" prevailed.

CONSTANTINE AND ATHANASIUS

These theories were already being tested while Constantine reigned. In North Africa the Donatists had gained the upper hand. "Nearly all Africa" accepted Donatus, Jerome was to say,[9] and in c. 336 Donatus assembled a conclave that outnumbered Nicaea. Some 270 bishops came together for seventy-five days to discuss the implication of relaxing the rule that no baptism given outside the church (that is, the Donatist communion)[10] was valid. An attempt in the same year to curb Donatus's activities cost the praetorian prefect Gregorius a sharp rebuff. Donatus addressed him as "pollution of the senate and disgrace of the prefecture."[11] He showed that Constantine's conversion altered not one whit the basic North African hostility to secular power.

Constantine's main problems, however, centered on Athanasius and the church of Alexandria. Judgments on Athanasius have tended to be harsh. Certainly his Meletian opponents had good cause to complain of his bullying tactics. A less-committed observer, the historian Ammianus Marcellinus, described Athanasius as "a man who exalted himself above his calling," one who "tried to pry into matters outside his province."[12] Throughout his forty-five-year episcopate (328–73), he aroused an uncommon degree of opposition from the most varied sources. Worse than that, he seemed to revel in controversy. He seldom spared an opponent. As a pamphleteer, he outdid the emperor Julian himself.

There is, however, much to be said in Athanasius's favor. He believed passionately in the validity of the Council of Nicaea and its Creed. Nicaea for him proclaimed the church's tradition against the personal theories of his opponents.[13] How could sinful humanity be redeemed if Christ was not fully God? As he put it during his third exile in c. 358, "the Word would never have made us divine if he were merely divine by participation and not himself the essential Godhead, the 'Father's veritable image.' "[14] However expressed, the unity of Christ with God must be acknowledged in such terms—Athanasius does not use *homoousios* before c. 350—that guaranteed Christians of the sureness of their faith. "How is the Son equal to the Father?" a monk is once said to have asked him. "Like the sight of two eyes,"[15] came the answer.

Without that assurance, orthodox Christianity in Egypt might not have prevailed at all. The massive popular movement away from devotion to the traditional deities had tended towards the enthusiastic acceptance of differing forms of asceticism, of orthodox and Meletian monasticism, or Gnosticism and Manicheism. For all their rivalries, these groups had important factors in common. They emphasized the divine nature of Christ, the wholeness of his manifestation of the Godhead, and the complete character of salvation to the believer illumined by faith in or knowledge of him. Any compromise with doctrines that could be interpreted as Arian would have damaged irreparably the credit of Athanasius and the see of Alexandria.

At the same time, his opponents could not give way. The Eusebians represented what had become the traditional Origenism of the majority of the Eastern bishops. They did not admire Arius, but they regarded what they believed to be the Sabellianism of Athanasius and Marcellus of Ancyra as an even worse menace. If Athanasius's problem lay with the monks and the Manichees, the Eastern bishops were confronted by large Jewish communities with whom relations were often unhealthily close. In addition, the *homoousios* formula was unscriptural and hence ultimately unacceptable. It did not accord with the truth that Christ was the agent of creation through whom one might come to know God; hence, he must in some way be separate from God. In fact, the two sets of ideas were by no means completely opposed. In *Against the Heathen* (written probably during his exile in Trier, c. 336) Athanasius uses the same biblical descriptions of the Son—"express image," "door," "shepherds" and "way"[16]—as his opponents used in the Second Creed of Antioch (341). Not altogether surprisingly after a generation of argument and under the stress of Julian's pagan reaction, the parties came to realize that "like in all respects" and "veritable image" must imply, as Athanasius argued, oneness (*henotes*) between Father and Son, and that *homoousios* could be used if combined with an explicit recognition of the distinction between the persons of the Trinity. But up to that point, truths tended to be obscured by personalities. Athanasius was regarded as ecclesiastically undisciplined as well as the champion of views dangerous to the church. After the Council of Tyre in 335, the opposition believed they had every reason to prevent his return to Alexandria.

Athanasius rightly assessed the danger from the Meletians as the most immediately pressing. John Arcaph, Meletius's successor, may have lacked the heroic stature of the bishop of Lycopolis, but his following was still formidable. In 327, the year before Athanasius's election, a list of supporters showed that there was one Meletian bishop in every six episcopal towns in the Delta, but one in every second or third city in the more purely Coptic-speaking provinces of the Thebaid.[17] The Meletian mission extended as far south as Coptos (Qift). Meletianism was thus not quite the force in Egypt that Donatism had already become in North Africa, but it was strong in Coptic Egypt and there were already organized Meletian monasteries. If Athanasius hoped to maintain the position of Alexandria as primatial see for all Egypt, he had to crush the Meletians quickly, and to do this he could not afford to appear to compromise with Arius, let alone restore him to his presbyterate in Alexandria.

Therefore within eighteen months of his consecration Athanasius was in the Thebaid. Antony may well have been his supporter already. We are told by Sozomen that he "showed unlimited friendship for him,"[18] but on this tour he won the respect of the far more important Pachomius, the founder of cenobitic (community) monasticism. Pachomius is said by his biographer to have avoided ordination as presbyter by Athanasius at this time, but remained his lifelong friend.[19] Unfortunately, Athanasius did not confine himself to charm and persuasion. By 330 complaints against him were reaching Constantine. Athanasius was summoned to the emperor's court. This time his obduracy regarding Arius was the main issue, and Constantine with characteristic impetuosity told him that if he did not restore Arius "he would come himself and depose him."[20] To be proclaimer of God's word involved a general oversight at least over his "fellow-ministers." He had restored pro-Arian bishops to their sees in 327.

Now he would act against the overmighty bishop of Alexandria. Athanasius did not protest. Indeed, as he shows in his actions and in his work, in *Against the Heathen*, he shared the main tenets of Eusebius's politico-religious theories. For him also, polytheism was atheism and "the government by many would be anarchy" (*Against Heathen* 38). He saw the emperor's rule on earth as parallel to God's government in the heavens—that of the essential leader who brought harmony into a multitude of different tasks in which citizens of a state would be engaged.[21] Disagreement with Eusebius and other theologians at Constantine's court concerned the doctrinal but not the political implications of this concept.

Unfortunately for Athanasius, by the 330s the two separate issues—that of the Eusebian campaign against the most outspoken defenders of Nicaea, and that of the Meletian resistance to himself—were coming together. An unlikely alliance formed between the two anti-Athanasian groups. In the East generally the Eusebians were on the offensive. Asclepas of Gaza, Eustathius of Antioch, Marcellus of Ancyra (Eusebius of Caesarea's particular enemy) all fell by 330. Paul of Constantinople would go the same way before the reign of Constantine ended.[22]

Athanasius, however, was becoming the real target. By 334 his enemies believed they had a case against him. Eusebius and his colleagues confronted him with a series of charges relating to his dealings with the Meletians. His presbyter, Macarius, had desecrated a Meletian church and broken a sacred chalice, he had levied a tax in Egypt to provide linen garments (that is, he had appropriated the right that had belonged previously to the pagan priesthood), he had sent a purse of gold to a former high official now disgraced, and, worst of all, he had organized the kidnap and murder of a Meletian bishop named Arsenius and used his severed hand for magical purposes. This time Athanasius had an answer. Arsenius had only been kidnapped and Athanasius was able to produce him in dramatic circumstances, safe and well, at an inquiry at Antioch.[23]

Unabashed, his opponents pressed the remaining charges. In 334 Athanasius refused to attend a council at Caesarea, Eusebius's see, on the grounds that it would be stacked against him. Constantine was patient, but he desperately wanted a settlement as he prepared to celebrate his long-anticipated thirty-year anniversary (*tricennalia*) in July 335. He was now leaning towards Eusebius of Caesarea and his friends as those most likely to "restore the blessings of peace" to the church.[24] Another council was summoned, this time to meet at Tyre (July 335). He appealed for peace and unity and upbraided those who sought to throw everything into confusion (Athanasius!). After long hesitation (revealed by a papyrus) Athanasius decided to attend. A Meletian presbyter, writing to a colleague who was a monastic leader, describes how "Athanasius is very despondent. . . . They have come to fetch him and so far he has not started. He put his luggage aboard as if he was starting and again he took the luggage off the ship a second time.''[25] Like Cyril before the Council of Ephesus in 431, he feared for his position once he left Alexandria. He took the precaution of having forty-eight Egyptian bishops accompany him, but this time his enemies were even better prepared.

For the future relationship between church and state in the East, the Council of Tyre was as important as that of Nicaea. It had been summoned by the emperor and organized like a court of justice but, unlike Arles (assembled to hear the Donatists' petition), it was presided over by an imperial official, the count Dionysius, a former consul. The emperor had intervened directly in a matter of church discipline and though sentence would be pronounced by the bishops, their proceedings would be supervised by a layman.[26] This was to be the pattern for all the great councils in the patristic age. At Chalcedon, the papal legates themselves had to address their speeches to a bench of lay assessors, and the emperor Marcian himself guided the deliberations of the bishops at the crucial sessions of the council.[27] In appointing Count Dionysius president of the council, Constantine had moved further along the road toward imposing state control on the victorious Christian church than when he had appointed Pope Miltiades as his delegate to judge between the parties in the Donatist dispute. Athanasius, however, never questioned the rightness of the presence of the lay element there, even when the case went against him. He was condemned on disciplinary grounds, that his consecration as bishop had been uncanonical, that he was guilty of sacrilege (a point of particular concern to the emperor), and that he had used violence against his opponents. He was sentenced to deposition and forbidden to return to Alexandria.

It is interesting that the bishops of Syria and Asia Minor had attracted the support of young and vigorous clergy from the Balkan provinces of the empire. Theirs was not merely conservative protest. Valens of Mursa and Ursacius of Singidunum (Belgrade) had taken part in one on-the-spot inquiry into the affair of Ischyras's broken chalice. Their support was valuable to the Eusebians, for these Balkan clergy were often bilingual in Greek and Latin, and thus a vital link between the churches in the eastern and western parts of the empire.

Constantine progressed triumphantly onward to Jerusalem. On 17 September 335 he inaugurated the new Church of the Holy Sepulchre before a great concourse of bishops from all over the empire. Athanasius, meantime, set out for Constantinople to meet the emperor on his return and make one last appeal to him. Once again, his enemies were ahead of him. An equally dramatic charge—that he had held up the sailing of the corn fleet from Alexandria to Constantinople—convinced the emperor. On 7 November 335, Athanasius was sentenced to exile in Trier, but Constantine also banished his Meletian rival, John Arcaph. Preparations were made for the complete restoration of Arius to his office of presbyter at Alexandria.

This never happened. In 336, it is said, the day before the ceremony of restoration was due to take place in Constantinople, Arius was struck down by a deadly malady, poison some believed.[28] At Easter next year the emperor, robed as a catechumen, was baptized by Eusebius of Nicomedia, now his personal chaplain. He did not survive long, for he died on 22 May 337. He was buried in his own city, in a splendid mausoleum he had prepared for himself, surrounded by effigies of the twelve apostles, himself represented as the thirteenth.[29] He left a Christian empire and, except for Donatus's powerful organization in North Africa, an almost united church.[30] In the provinces, particularly in the West, the Constantinian era had a deserved reputation for prosperity. The promise made by Apollo at Autun more than three decades before had been richly fulfilled.

THE COUNCIL OF SARDICA 342/43

In his last years, Constantine had looked beyond the sons of his disgraced and murdered wife, Fausta, for the government of the empire. His half brother, Delmatius, an experienced administrator, had presided at the inquiry conducted in Athanasius's absence at Caesarea in 334, and the next year his son was promoted Caesar. Fearing an attack by the Persians on the eastern frontier, another nephew, Hannibalianus, had been made king of Armenia about the same time and married the emperor's daughter, Constantina. As a final stroke, he had betrothed his youngest son Constans to Olympias, daughter of his trusted Christian prefect Ablabius. Constantine apparently aimed to combine lineage with administrative skill to sustain the future government of the empire. If so, he had miscalculated. Once again, the troops showed that loyalty to the dynasty outweighed other considerations. On 9 September a military coup in Constantinople saw the three sons of Constantine—Constantine II, Constantius, and Constans—proclaimed Augusti, and the remaining members of the imperial house massacred, unless, as in the case of Julian and his half brother Gallus, they were thought to be either too young or politically harmless.

Of the three brothers, Constantine II and Constans adhered to Nicaea while Constantius, guided by the two Eusebii, leaned toward Origenism. Though Constantinople was the de facto capital of the empire, the West still claimed the senior Augustus. The division of power left Constantine the West, while Constans had Illyricum and Africa, and Constantius the East. Constantine II almost at once ordered the return of Athanasius from exile (late 337). This was a fateful move, for it began a train of events destined to set Eastern and Western Christendom at loggerheads. When Athanasius returned to Alexandria on 23 November 337, his opponents pointed to his deposition by a council. The see was therefore vacant. They also accused him of embezzling corn set aside by the emperor for the poor in Egypt. Constantius threatened Athanasius with death. After fruitless haggling, a cleric from Cappadocia named Gregory was installed as bishop with the aid of the prefect of Egypt who was also a Cappadocian. Athanasius withdrew (19 March 339) and this time he trekked to Rome. His patron Constantine II passed from the scene in an ill-judged attack on his brother Constans's Balkan dominions (April 340), but Athanasius found even more effective support from Pope Julius (337–52). Constans now became ruler of two-thirds of the Roman world with power far superior to his brother's portion. The balance had swung dramatically in favor of Nicaea.

With Julius, the papacy quite suddenly emerged from the obscurity that had shrouded it since Miltiades' council in 313. Legend has made Pope Sylvester (314–35) a friend of Constantine and recipient of the famous "Donation." In fact, his long reign is an enigma. Hilary of Poitiers (c. 360) believed that he had intervened on the side of Alexander in his quarrel with Arius, but this cannot be known for certain.[31] His representatives played little recorded part at Nicaea. Yet Julius took up Athanasius's cause with a self-assertion and confidence suggesting a see which was used to having its orders obeyed. Late in 340 or in 341 a council of bishops held in Rome cleared Athanasius of the charges made against him at Tyre, and admitted him to communion as lawful bishop of Alexandria with his allies, Marcellus of Ancyra and Asclepas of Gaza. The long letter, preserved by Athanasius,[32] that Julius then sent to the Eastern episcopate, speaks outraged complaint in every line:

> Let us grant the "removal" as you write of Athanasius and Marcellus [of Ancyra] from their places, yet what must one say of the case of other bishops and presbyters who, as I said before, came here from other places and complained that they had been forced away and had suffered the like injustices? . . . And why was nothing written to us concerning the church of the Alexandrians in particular? Are you ignorant that the custom has been for word to be written first to us, and then for a just sentence to be passed from this place? . . . What I write is for the common good. What we have received from the blessed Apostle Peter, that I signify to you.[33]

This is by any test an extraordinary document. No trace of the custom claimed by Julius has been preserved in the previous history of the church. Even Pope Dionysius (260–69) had not arrogated to himself the right of overturning a disciplinary decision by his colleague of Alexandria. Moreover, though nominally reporting a decision of a Roman council, Julius speaks from his own episcopal position. He took no serious account of the findings of the Council of Tyre. Thus, while the rest of Christendom was accepting a council of bishops, judicial or otherwise, as the voice of the Holy Spirit, the papacy was staking its claim to speak to colleagues on the authority of Peter and nothing else. Though Julius ended on a more conciliatory note, inviting the Easterners to reopen their case, two rival theories of church authority were already beginning to take shape no more than fifteen years after Nicaea.

Not surprisingly, the Easterners replied in kind. They met at Antioch in the autumn of 341, nominally to celebrate in the presence of the emperor the dedication of the Church of the Golden Dome, begun under Constantine and now the symbol of the Christian triumph in this rich and pleasure-loving city. The ninety-seven bishops told Julius that East and West had previously respected each other's verdicts against Novatian on the one hand, and Paul of Samosata on the other,[34] and that it was novel and unheard-of for Eastern bishops to be judged by Westerners.[35] They denied they were followers of Arius. Why should "we being bishops follow behind a priest?" If he wished to remain in amity with them, he must condemn to deposition the bishops they had expelled. Not content with that, the council proceeded to issue a number of disciplinary canons, and more important, to lay down exactly what they conceived the faith of the church to be.

The Second Creed of Antioch is the first of a dozen creeds that were compiled during Constantius's reign to rid the church of the *homoousios* formula, and it is one of the more important. It came close to the Nicene position, and improved on the latter by insisting on the Trinity of Divine Persons in a way not achieved at Nicaea,[36] but it confined itself strictly to the terms used of Christ that could be found in Scripture. The Son, therefore, was "begotten before the ages from the Father, God from God, whole from whole, sole from sole, perfect from perfect . . . Living Word, Living Wisdom, True Light, Way, Truth, Resurrection, Shepherd, Door, both unalterable and unchangeable, exact Image of the Godhead, Substance, Will, Power and Glory of the Father. . . ." After anathematizing specific Arian teachings, the statement concluded, "For all that has been delivered in the Divine Scriptures, whether by the Prophets or Apostles, do we truly and reverentially both believe and follow." It may have been a creed written a generation before Nicaea by Lucian of Antioch (martyred January 312), as the fifth-century historian Sozomen says it was claimed to be,[37] and if slightly touched up by Eusebian supporters such as Asterius the Sophist, it represented fairly the scriptural rock on which the Eastern bishops took their stand. Interpreting Matt. 28:19, the mystery of the Trinity was represented as three individualities (*hypostases*) united by mutual harmony (*homonoia*) in a single will and each with its own function in the Godhead. If accepted, this formula could have had a profound and beneficial effect on the future history of the church, for it represented a meeting of Origenist and Antiochene ideas which could have led also to a rapprochement with the West.

As it was, there was deadlock between East and West, and for once the situation turned against the East. First, their leaders, the two Eusebii, had disappeared from the scene, and no outstanding figure replaced them. Second, Constans as emperor in the West ranked as the senior Augustus, and he favored Julius and Athanasius. In October 342 (or 343) he forced his reluctant brother to assemble a conference at Sardica (Sofia) just inside the

boundary of the Western empire. For once the Western bishops outnumbered the Eastern, by 96 to rather more than 70. In addition, the West had
as their leader the immensely experienced Hosius of Córdoba. There was
another difference between the two sides, for the Eastern bishops were
accompanied by two imperial officers (counts) and stayed in the imperial
residence in the city, thus emphasizing the progressive integration of
church and state in the Eastern provinces of the empire.[38]

There was no agreement. The Easterners refused so much as to sit with
Athanasius and Marcellus as these had been duly deposed by councils.
Indeed, they could not have done so without denying the validity of their
ideas and actions over the previous decade. They took the first opportunity
to withdraw over the frontier to Philippopolis on the grounds that Constantius had won a victory over the Persians and they must congratulate him.
There they renewed anathemas against Athanasius, Marcellus, and their
Western supporters including Pope Julius and Hosius. Persons were not
respected. Long after the council, Basil of Caesarea commented bitterly on
Western "double standards," anathematizing anything that sounded Arian, yet turning a blind eye to the worse impieties of Marcellus.[39]

The Western bishops carried on at Sardica. Athanasius and Marcellus
were vindicated again. The Easterners, it was declared, "were infatuated
with false doctrines" and were guilty of injustice and improprieties.[40] A
creed (or better, "statement of belief") was drawn up. Leaning heavily on
John 1:14, they asserted "the oneness of the hypostasis and unity of the
Father and the Son"—open therefore to a Sabellian interpretation. The
canons which they agreed upon tacitly rejected any intervention by the
emperor in church affairs, as well as the practice in the East of channeling
appeals from a smaller to a larger synod for decision. They attributed
instead to the bishop of Rome an important if limited appellate jurisdiction
in the event of disputes between bishops. A deposed bishop might appeal to
the pope, who would then pronounce a final judgment himself or through
his presbyters.[41]

On the face of it, the first meeting between Eastern and Western bishops
had ended in schism. Differences on a host of matters relating to doctrine
and discipline had erupted into irreconcilable dispute. To the Easterners,
as their letter to their supporters preserved by Hilary of Poitiers shows, the
Western bishops were "associates of men condemned for the worst of
heresies" compounded by Sabellianism and the teaching of Paul of Samosata, and they were disturbers of Eastern peace.[42] To the West, the Easterners were also heretics, Arians, and even murderers. The impression of
mutual antipathy and disagreement was lasting; nearly a century later the
lay historian Socrates wrote, "from that time on, the western Church was
severed from the eastern, and the boundary between them was the mountain called Soucis that divides the Illyrians from the Thracians."[43] Thus, to
this observant and fair-minded critic, Sardica had produced dramatic

531

results indicative of the gulf that separated Eastern and Western theologies.

THE SEARCH FOR EQUILIBRIUM 343–53

For the moment, however, both sides seem to have recoiled from the possibility of schism. Within two years the Easterners had met at Antioch and drawn up a lengthy document spelling out their position, which has gone down in history as the Creed of the Long Lines (*Macrostichos*). Christ was to be acknowledged as "like in all things to the Father"—a crucial phrase, for it might allow in the last resort that "likeness" be expressed as involving being of the same substance. But that time had not come. Instead, the Easterners explained in detail why they rejected the views of Marcellus of Ancyra and his following as Monarchian and Jewish, and for the same reasons were utterly opposed to any confession of faith which was open to Sabellian interpretations. In this long document (fourteen hundred words), however, Athanasius was not mentioned,[44] and when it was taken to the West in 345, other possibilities of compromise were beginning to appear. Gregory, Athanasius's supplanter in Alexandria, died on 25 June of that year, leaving the see vacant. How far would each side go for the sake of agreement?

The answer was: quite a long way. A convenient scapegoat appeared on the scene in the person of Photinus, bishop of Sirmium (c. 344). Photinus had been a deacon of Marcellus of Ancyra, and was accused of holding a medley of Sabellian and Adoptionist views concerning the Son. At the incarnation, the Divine Word became Son and dwelt in Jesus and, hence, his critics argued, the Son was neither preexistent nor eternal. It was a doctrine recognizably similar to that of Paul of Samosata and invited instant condemnation from Origenist bishops, while the West could hardly be expected to support so flagrant a deviation from orthodoxy. The Council of Antioch condemned him and by implication renewed the condemnation of Marcellus, though it was not until 351 that Photinus was formally deposed by an imperial consistory composed of laity and bishops. The West also accepted his condemnation at councils at Milan in 345 and 347.[45] There were further reconciliations, even Marcellus being allowed back to Ancyra, and in 345/46 Constantius authorized members of the imperial council (*Consistorium*) to write to Athanasius inviting him to return to court and thence to Alexandria. The act of restitution was to be an act by the imperial government and not by the church. In April 346 Constantius and Athanasius were formally reconciled at Antioch, and Athanasius passed by way of Jerusalem to the greatest reception given to any ecclesiastic in the fourth century. The people and authorities alike streamed out of Alexandria "like another Nile" to meet him at the hundredth milestone from Alexandria[46] (emperors usually had to be content with a ten-mile reception). There was feasting and rejoicing in the city which Athanasius entered on 21 October to begin his "Golden Decade."

Relative harmony reigned for more than three years, with Constantius engaged in bitter conflicts on the Persian frontier. Events there also showed in a different way how Christian attitudes had changed now that the church was triumphing. Gone was the idea that Christians and even clergy should not take up arms in defense of the empire. In the three sieges of Nisibis by the Persians in 338, 342, and 349, successful defense owed much to the inspiration of Bishop James, and monks joined the civilian population in urging the Roman troops to ever-greater efforts. James's prayers were believed to have resulted in the Persian forces being assailed by swarms of gnats and forced to retreat in disorder.[47] Whatever Constantius's doctrinal deviations, he was regarded by the Christian leaders in the Persian frontier area as their champion, and the hymns of Ephraem Syrus (c. 306–73) tell of the excellence of his virtues.[48] Christianity under the emperor was proving itself to be the common factor that linked all classes together in defense of their homes against external attack.

It was well that this was so for, in the years 350–52, Constantius faced a supreme test involving the future of the Constantinian house. In February 350 his brother Constans was murdered in southern Gaul as the result of a successful military uprising led by a semi-barbarian *laetus* (tributary), Magnentius. Other enemies of Constantius took their chance. On 1 March Illyricum acknowledged another usurper, also a senior officer, Vetranio, as emperor. At Rome Nepotian, a nephew of Constantine, seized power at the instigation of Constantine's daughter Constantina. Her husband Hannibalianus had been cut down in the military revolution in 337. Constantius, however, proved equal to the challenge. This strange, enigmatic figure was a mixture of gallantry and inertia, sound judgment and superstition, shrewdness and stupidity.[49] On the one hand, he continued his father's policy of maintaining the unity of the church on the basis of the widest measure of agreement; on the other, he allowed military force to be used against Paphlagonian Novatianists,[50] whom his father would have ignored good-humoredly. He was a resourceful commander with a sound technical sense yet he lacked confidence and relied on visions to confirm his judgment. He was an administrator who realized that the foundation of Constantinople provided a chance to create a new, powerful, higher administration based on talent rather than birth,[51] yet he was a prey to the influence and flattery of court eunuchs of whom the grand chamberlain, Eusebius, was the most powerful.[52] He gave free rein to sycophantic informers, such as the notorious Paul "the Chain," so called from his ability to enmesh his opponents in inextricable webs of calumny.[53] The deadly court intrigues and trials as well as the theological hairsplitting that characterized the last decade of his reign justify the verdict that Constantius was the founder of Byzantinism.

Yet in the crisis of 350 the emperor's combination of firmness and deviousness succeeded. Argument, perhaps backed by gold, won over Vetranio's troops near Sardica, and their commander was "cashiered like a common soldier," as Ammianus says,[54] and pensioned off in retirement. Nepotian was removed by Magnentius (30 June 350), and Magnentius himself was beaten in a desperate but decisive battle at Mursa on 28 September 351. A month or so before, the emperor had consolidated the good will of the Illyrian bishops towards himself by hearing the case against Photinus and ordering his removal from Sirmium into exile.

The battle of Mursa cemented the alliance between Constantius and the Illyrians for the remainder of his reign. Valens, bishop of the town, was devoted to Constantius's cause. He had a good intelligence service that kept him informed as to how the battle was going. When it at last turned in Constantius's favor, he was the first to announce the fact to the emperor, adding that he had a vision of an angel bringing the news to him.[55] As his father before him at the Milvian Bridge, Constantius accepted the vision as a sign of divine favor. But it was the semi-Arian god of Valens of Mursa that had shown his approval of the emperor's cause. The enemies of Athanasius and of Nicaea were to be ascendant as long as Constantius lived.

CONSTANTIUS AS SOLE EMPEROR 353–61

It took Constantius two more years to dispose of Magnentius. On 10 August 353, the usurper was cornered and committed suicide at Lyons. Constantius had emerged, like his father, as sole ruler of the Roman world, and like him was confronted with the problems posed by Athanasius. Rightly or wrongly, the latter was suspected of receiving an emissary of Magnentius. The duel between emperor and bishop therefore recommenced. First at Arles in 353 and then in Milan in 355, Constantius tried to bring the Western bishops into line against his adversary. The importance he attached to the issue may be gauged by his vain attempt to have the condemnation passed at Milan confirmed by Pope Liberius.[56]

The long-drawn-out conflict with the Western bishops underscored the difference between Eastern and Western attitudes to the Christian empire. What was said now played its part in forming the Western standpoint that was to prevail to the end of the European Middle Ages. Ostensibly the Western bishops were concerned about justice for Athanasius and for the sanctity of the *homoousios* formula. Both factors stiffened their attitude toward the emperor, but when one of Constantius's most influential opponents admitted that, before he reached his place of exile in Phrygia, he had never read the Nicene formula,[57] one may suspect that "Nicaea" was simply a rallying call of support for Athanasius. It masked the more basic differences of the Western church's relationship to the Christian empire.

Some catholics, like Optatus, bishop of Milevis in Numidia, were profoundly grateful for the emperor's support for the catholic cause against the Donatists. He declared that the "State [*res publica*] is not in the Church but the Church is in the State, that is the Roman empire which Christ in the

Song of Songs calls Lebanon."[58] The empire protected the virtues of the priesthood. Curiously, the Syrian writer Ephraem Syrus took a similar view. "From the empire [come] laws and from the priesthood propitiation. May our priesthood be gentle and our empire strong."[59] He saw, as did Optatus, the empire ("our empire") and the clergy as two distinct powers but working in harmony. Why North Africa and Mesopotamia should take the same approach to imperial-church relations remains a mystery.

Optatus's opponents, the Donatists, of course took the opposite view. "What has the emperor to do with the church?" Donatus asked Constans's emissaries who visited him at Carthage in 346.[60] His question was repeated by his successor Parmenian,[61] while in the 370s the Donatist theologian Tyconius taunted the Catholics with the charge that they "had no other king but Caesar."[62]

In this respect, however, the Donatists were not so remote from other Western opinion. Few if any bishops openly took the standpoint of Optatus of Milevis. Their outlook was conditioned—as almost always—by their reading of Old Testament history. The Roman emperor, like the king of Israel, might be the Lord's anointed, but his powers were limited. He was responsible for maintaining peace and providing conditions under which service to the Lord might be performed, but he could not usurp the place of the priests and offer sacrifice himself. Moreover, evil kings like Ahab and Manasseh had been subject to denunciation by priest and prophet, whatever prosperity they appeared to enjoy. This could be applied to a Roman emperor.[63] On this point Athanasius came to agree with his Western colleagues.

The problem which Constantius posed for the Western bishops, and eventually for Athanasius, was that while he was a Christian, he was, in their view, not orthodox. They accepted that he had the power to summon councils and to legislate to protect the church against pagans and heretics. What they objected to was Constantius's efforts to integrate the church with the state, with resulting imperial intervention in church law and ecclesiastical decisions, and they viewed with dismay his increasingly open rejection of Nicaea. During and following the Council of Milan these feelings were expressed forcefully. The bishops there spoke to Constantius of divine judgment. The royal will was not canon law even if the Syrian bishops accepted it as such.[64] Recalcitrant bishops were summoned to the emperor's headquarters. Hilary of Poitiers and Rhodanus of Toulouse were exiled to the provinces of Phrygia and Asia respectively for their refusal to condemn Athanasius. Liberius was approached personally and he defied Constantius, guardedly comparing him to Nebuchadnezzar and demanding the confirmation of the Creed of Nicaea and recall of exiled bishops. He himself was exiled to Thrace and a replacement sought in the person of the deacon, Felix.[65] Then it was Hosius of Córdoba's turn. At the age of ninety-nine he sent a letter to the emperor, a copy of which somehow found its way to Athanasius. It was a remarkable document, enunciating in classic form the doctrine of the Two Swords on which Western teaching about church-state relations would be based down to the Reformation.

> Do not use force [he says], write no letters, send no Counts. . . . When was any such thing done by Constans? What bishop suffered banishment? When did he appear as arbiter of an ecclesiastical trial? When did any palatine of his compel men to subscribe against anyone? . . . . Cease these proceedings, I beseech you, and remember that you are a mortal man. Be afraid of the day of judgement and keep yourself pure thereunto. Intrude not yourself into ecclesiastical matters, neither give commands unto us concerning them; but learn from us. God has put into your hands the kingdom; to us He has entrusted the affairs of His Church; and as he who would steal the empire from you would resist the ordinance of God, so likewise fear on your part lest by taking upon yourself the government of the Church, you become guilty of a great offence. It is written, "Render unto Caesar the things that are Caesar's, and unto God the things that are God's." Neither therefore is it permitted unto us to exercise an earthly rule, nor have you, Sire, any authority to burn incense.[66]

This statement was to be repeated by Ambrose of Milan during his conflict with the emperor Valentinian II in 385–86.[67] It was to be restated even more forcibly by Pope Gelasius to the emperor Anastasius in 493 during the Acacian Schism.[68] It represented a view far removed from that of the Syrian and indeed the great majority of Eastern bishops. It symbolized the difference of outlook that prevailed between Eastern and Western Christianity in the Christian empire.

Meantime, Constantius continued his father's policy of establishing religious unity around a creed acceptable to as many as possible and upheld by bishops loyal to him. Both aims involved the removal of Athanasius from Alexandria. The finale was dramatic.[69] After two years of intermittent harassment, Constantius decided to use force. On 6 January 356, the new military commander, the *Dux* Syrianus, arrived at Alexandria. At first it seemed that crisis could be avoided. Athanasius produced letters sent by Constantius to him at the beginning of the war with Magnentius assuring him of his protection. These did not prove Athanasius's own loyalty but they might have provided a basis for an attempt to restore confidence. They did not. On the night of 7/8 February, Athanasius was presiding at a vigil in the church of St. Theonas in Alexandria. The *Dux* had the church surrounded. Athanasius seated on his episcopal throne ordered the deacon to read Psalm 136, and the people to respond, "For his mercy endureth for ever." Then the soldiers broke in. There was utter confusion, but when order was restored Athanasius was not there. He had been spirited away to spend the next five years among the monasteries in Upper Egypt writing a series of memorable tracts against his tormentor.

Between 356 and 361 Constantius developed the full scope of his religious policy. Ammianus detected a hint of megalomania in these years. The emperor would sign himself "My eternity" and call himself "Lord of the whole universe.''[70] With this, and his demeanor during his visit to Rome in 357 in mind, it is not beyond belief that he styled himself "Bishop of bishops" as Lucifer of Cagliari asserts and not merely "general bishop" as his father had done.[71] His aims were, however, clear enough—the prevalence of orthodoxy as he approved it, its acceptance by all peoples both within and without the empire, and the ending of his father's contemptuous toleration for paganism. In this process the clergy were his aides and as a reward were fast developing into a new privileged caste.

Paganism had already been assailed by his brother Constans in 341, who had ordered the end of sacrifice and the closure of shrines in Italy, but this had had to be modified so far as it concerned rural shrines which were traditionally centers of festivities and sports.[72] In February 356 Constantius, however, published a comprehensive edict that forbade pagan sacrifice by ordering the closure of pagan temples, and practically speaking, disestablished pagan worship.[73] At the beginning of his reign, the priesthood ranked with the law and the "long-haired philosophers" as a respectable academic profession.[74] In Constantius's final years, Ammianus tells of the harrying of philosophers who dared to worship the gods openly.[75]

The new elite was composed of the Christian clergy as well as the emperor's officials. Some of the most prominent, such as George of Cappadocia and Aetius, were the gifted sons of traders and artisans. In the decade 349–59, their situation as clerics was improved dramatically. In 349 clergy and their children (note the latter!) were exempted from all fiscal obligations in regard to their cities.[76] There was aid to widows and virgins. The church was granted a share of the taxes in kind (*annona*) paid by the provincials.[77] Its clergy were allowed to use the public post in the same way as imperial officials, until by the end of his reign they had almost wrecked it and ruined the rural population whose carts and animals supplied it.[78] Other exemptions included that of providing supplies in kind to soldiers and officials or doing corvées (*sordida munera*).[79] Clergy might engage in trade. In 359 a demand by the bishops at the Council of Ariminum for exemption from all forms of taxation was refused but the church was exempted from all "new taxes."[80] Whatever the theoretical reservations of the Western Christian leaders, church and state were blending rapidly in these years, and the church itself was emerging as a vast, privileged corporation, the connection of many of whose leaders with the lives of the provincials was becoming increasingly tenuous.

At the same time Constantius continued another aspect of Constantine's policy, that of furthering the cause of Christianity whenever and wherever possible. It cannot be certain that Eusebius of Nicomedia's ordination of Ulphilas the Goth (c. 339) was intended to initiate a mission among the pagan Goths, rather than primarily to serve the Christians among them in the ex-Roman province of Dacia.[81] Ulphilas's great contribution to Christian civilization, his translation of the Bible into Gothic, must have been intended in the first place for Goths already Christian. There is no doubt,

537

however, about the intention of Theophilus "the Indian's" embassy to the Red Sea kingdom of the Himyarites (southeastern Arabia). The Arian (Eunomian) historian, Philostorgius, says Theophilus was sent "in order to induce them to come over to the true religion."[82] There is a hint at rivalry with Judaism, as well as with the Persians, that was to continue for two centuries in the southeastern corner of the Arabian peninsula, and there were Roman commercial interests to protect. In 356/57 there was a similar intervention by the emperor himself in the affairs of the Kingdom of Axum (northern Ethiopia). There, as recorded by Rufinus and Philostorgius, Frumentius—a sometime captive who had accompanied a Syrian philosopher on a visit to Christians in Axum (c. 330) and had been captured by a hostile band on their return journey—had gradually risen in royal service until he became a sort of prime minister to King Ezana. He had worked among the Roman merchant colony, propagating the cause of Christianity. By about 355, Ezana himself seems to have been converted to Christianity, perhaps fortified in this by a victory over the Blemmyes, the great confederation of tribes dwelling astride the Nile in the wilderness between the Roman and Ethiopian frontiers.[83] Unfortunately, Frumentius was a loyal supporter of Athanasius, and had returned to Alexandria for consecration as bishop at his hands. Constantius protested angrily and in a remarkable letter to the princes of Axum stated in unmistakable terms his theory of the religious unity of humankind under the guardianship of the Roman emperor.[84] He wrote:

> It is altogether a matter of greatest care and concern to us to extend the knowledge of the supreme God, and I think that the whole race of mankind claims from us equal regard in this respect, in order that they may pass their lives in accordance with their hope, being brought to the same knowledge of God, and having no differences with each other in their inquiries about justice and truth. Therefore considering that you are deserving of the same provident care as the Romans, and desiring to show equal regard for your welfare, we bid that the same doctrine be professed in your churches as in theirs.[85]

The princes were ordered to dispatch Frumentius to be reconsecrated by Bishop George (Athanasius's supplanter at Alexandria) and were told of the wickedness of Athanasius, "a man guilty of ten thousand crimes." Here we can discern the origin of the assertion by the Byzantine emperors of sovereignty over all Christians whether they lived within the boundaries of the empire or not. The Constantinian dynasty was preparing the way for the universalist theory of a world Christian empire associated with Justinian, and even the patronage of all Eastern Christians claimed in the nineteenth century by the czars.

CONSTANTIUS AND THE QUEST FOR A UNIFYING CREED

The keystone of this arch was an interpretation of Christian doctrine which avoided controversial terms, kept close to the scriptural definitions of

Christ, and hence might hope to command the widest support among the clergy. From 356 onward, the search for the right formula was complicated by the emergence of a genuinely Arian movement, whose leaders were Eunomius of Cyzicus, and the "godless" deacon Aetius. Constantius enjoyed debate over theological minutiae, the "old wives' tales" aspect of Christianity in the view of his pagan critic, Ammianus Marcellinus.[86] He was, however, to find Aetius's argument—that if the Son was a "creature" and did not share the Father's substance he must be "unlike" (*anomoios*) the Father—too much even for his breadth of comprehension. Between Athanasius on the one hand, and Aetius on the other, the emperor and the majority of the Christians found themselves engaged in an ever more exasperating quest for a formula on which they could agree. With hindsight one can see that in 357 the creed that has gone down in history as the Blasphemy of Sirmium nearly supplied the formula. It was the first example of Byzantine consensus religion, and it received more support in the West than is usually credited.[87]

In August of that year Constantius was at that Danube frontier fortress, and Sirmium for the next eighteen months was to be the center of theological activity. The occasion demonstrated the importance of the Illyrian episcopate, now the cornerstone of Constantius's religious policy. A small but powerful council was assembled under the leadership of Valens of Mursa, his inseparable colleague Ursacius of Singidunum, and a third Illyrian, Germanicus of Sirmium. This time the Westerners were well represented, and most remarkable of all, Hosius of Córdoba may have taken a leading part.[88] The bishops made a supreme attempt to cut through the thicket of arguments surrounding the use of *ousia* (= substance) either as *homoousios* or *homoiousios*. The "Second Creed of Sirmium" (in reality a declaration) set down the propositions that "there is one God Almighty and Father, as is believed throughout the whole world; and his only Son Jesus Christ, the Lord, our Saviour, begotten of the Father himself before all the ages." But there were not "two gods"; what can best be described as a prudent agnosticism was the only proper attitude toward the relation between the two divine *beings*. "Who shall declare his generation?" (Isa. 53:8, KJV) the framers quoted with satisfaction. Thus, there was to be no mention of *homoousios* or *homoiousios* nor should they be preached in church. All one could say was "that there is no question but that the Father is greater than the Son in honour, dignity, splendour and majesty," as the Son himself testified: "The Father is greater than I" (John 14:28).[89] So the Son was subordinate to the Father and God only, it could be argued, in a secondary sense. But this very lack of formula, and reliance on Scripture plus Origenist common sense gave the declaration its attraction.[90] Moreover, there were no anathemas attached to it. Hosius signed it, and more surprisingly, eventually Pope Liberius may have also.[91] So convinced was the former that he had at last found the talisman of truth that he returned to

Córdoba to spend his final months of a long life trying to force it on reluctant colleagues. For the orthodox, his lapse at the age of 101 cost him his title to sanctity and the world the survival of his writings. (Thanks to that loss, Constantine's religious odyssey in the years before the Milvian Bridge can never be fully traced.) The fall of Liberius from a strict *homoousian* confession grieved Athanasius and fueled many a controversy as to the precise nature of papal infallibility.

Events in the next two years showed that such forms of comprehension could not bring peace once people had time to consider their implication. The eventual triumph of Athanasius was assured by the splits that appeared in the ranks of his opponents. By the spring of 358, the traditionally minded Eastern bishops, heirs to Eusebius of Caesarea, had found a leader in Basil, bishop of Ancyra. At a council held in Ancyra in April of that year, *ousia* was restored to respectability and anathemas were aimed alternately at Aetius and Marcellus (whom Basil had supplanted as bishop of Ancyra).[92] The third synod at Sirmium accepted this statement and both Hilary and Athanasius himself indicated assent, though Hilary remained profoundly suspicious of "eastern heresies."[93] The bishops clearly favored *homoiousios* as the correct definition of the Father-Son relationship and they condemned *homoousios* when used, as they feared, in a Sabellian sense.[94] The explanation is interesting for it shows that, when confronted with the prospect of toleration for Arianism, many of the Eastern bishops began to move towards Athanasius's views.

Basil of Ancyra was to prove as intolerant as Athanasius himself. *Homoiousios* showed itself to be a stick with which to beat the Anhomoeans. Sentences of exile against them mounted,[95] but the emperor was not satisfied. He turned again to those who were prepared simply to accept that the Son was "like" the Father (the Homoians). Yet another Creed was worked out at Sirmium. Whatever its merits, in once more avoiding the term *ousia* as unscriptural, it stood condemned by its first lines. These started with a precise date, 22 May 359, asserting that on this day "the Catholic faith was published in the presence of our Master . . . Constantius Augustus"[96]—as though the faith had not originated with creation itself! Nonetheless, the essentials of the creed without the offending date were placed before assemblies of bishops that the emperor now summoned in East and West respectively.

Ariminum and Seleucia

The twin councils of Ariminum and Seleucia in Isauria were intended to be vast affairs and finish what Nicaea had set out to do, namely to define the creed of Christendom. The conclave easily exceeded that at Nicaea— more than 400 bishops being present at Ariminum and about 160 at Seleucia.[97] The choice of separate meeting-places showed how great had been the progress of Christianity in the previous twenty years. In 342/43, Sardica

540

had sufficed to house a joint council of Eastern and Western bishops. This was now impossible. The very success of Christianity was contributing to the division between East and West. The imperial presence was much in evidence through Taurus the praetorian prefect who supervised proceedings at Ariminum. There the bishops were kept in cramped quarters through a stifling Italian summer until their morale collapsed. They signed. Christ was "like the Father" (*homoios*) without any attempt to define how. The words "in all things" originally included were struck out. In October 359 also, the bishops at Seleucia reached the same conclusion, though amid deepening discord and division. Both synods were confirmed by a further meeting at Constantinople in January 360. It was a triumph for Valens and Ursacius. The world, wrote Jerome some twenty years later, "awoke with a groan to find itself Arian,"[98] a jaundiced view, for Constantius had at last brought East and West together to agree on a creed, though one which no conscientious Nicene could have recited. After every combination had been tried, Ariminum and Nicaea had emerged as the real alternatives as statements of faith. Was unity to be secured through comprehension or precision? Constantius and his Illyrian advisers favored Arminum. Extremists on all sides were to be rendered harmless. Aetius was judged by Constantius himself, stripped of his humble rank of deacon, and dispatched to share the fate of Hilary and Athanasius as an exile. Aristotle was unacceptable as a philosophic basis for the faith.[99]

The opposition, however, had not been inactive, nor as it proved, ineffective. If Basil of Ancyra and his friends were prepared to keep quiet, Athanasius and Hilary were not. For Athanasius the years 356–61 nourished a steadily growing conviction that Constantius was indeed the forerunner of antichrist, and that his previous unequivocal loyalty to the throne must be revised. We are able to follow the slow but irrevocable development of his thought. His immediate reaction to his renewed exile was to blame *Dux* Syrianus rather than the emperor. The tone of his first pamphlet, the *Defense Addressed to Constantius* (356/57), is deferential. Constantius was a longstanding Christian, he had never leveled calumny against him; he had never supported Magnentius whom he regarded as a murderer and a demon; he would address himself to Constantius as emperor, as Paul had done in his day. Disobedience was far from his mind. "God forbid," he concluded, "I am not the man to resist even the Quaestor of the city, much less so great a prince."[100]

By 358, however, the tone had changed. The *History of the Arians* that he sent to his monkish friends was for their eyes only. It was not to be copied; in it Athanasius proceeded to denounce Constantius as an Old Testament prophet might chastise a delinquent king of Israel. He was "worse than Saul," "worse than Ahab," and the "forerunner of Antichrist."[101] In this tract Athanasius preserves Hosius's famous utterance at the Council of Milan. Finally, in *On the Synods* Athanasius provides an apparently up-to-the-minute commentary on Ariminum and Seleucia. The emperor is characterized as most "irreligious" and the implication is left that Athanasius felt no further loyalty to him. In these years he had moved far toward espousing the dualistic theory of church-state relations that prevailed in the West. But this was less out of doctrinal principle than from desperation when confronted by a hostile and heretical autocrat. Other Eastern clerics, including John Chrysostom, would follow him in time of stress, but such times were few and far between. More often the emperor would be regarded, as John admitted, as "having no peer in the world";[100] other bishops would revere him as a sacred personage, a priest as well as king. It was no accident that in 452 in announcing the results of the Council of Chalcedon, the emperors Valentinian III and Marcian included the term "renowned priest" (*pontifex inclytus*) among their titles in their joint edict.[103] Athanasius's brush with Constantius failed to alter the basic political theory of the East focused on the emperor as the godly monarch.

In the West, opposition was more deeply rooted and directed against the emperor himself. It is reflected in the writing of Hilary of Poitiers during his exile, and in the stream of polemical tracts from Lucifer, bishop of Cagliari. Hilary's *Against Constantius*, written in 360/61, breathes defiance: "You distribute episcopal sees to your partisans and substitute bad bishops for good. You imprison priests and use your army to terrorize the Church, assembling councils. . . ."[104] Constantius was "Antichrist" himself and his rule an extension of that of the persecuting pagan emperors. Like the Donatists of a generation before, Hilary claimed that through Constantius the Devil was persecuting the church but using guile rather than force.[105] No wonder Hilary's writings found their way into Donatist episcopal libraries in the early years of the fifth century. Freedom of speech was not lacking to Western Christians of the day whether persecuted or not.

Lucifer of Cagliari attacked in similar vein. He never tired of justifying his attitude by reference to the rebellion of the Maccabees against Antiochus. That tradition had run deep in the Western church, inspiring the martyrs of Lyons, Cyprian, and Lactantius, and coming quickly to the tongue of the hypocritical Numidian, Secundus of Tigisis, after the Great Persecution. The limited monarchy bestowed on the Israelite kings by the Lord was the most that Western theologians were prepared to concede to the Christian emperor. If he fell into heresy, Jewish history provided precedents enough for justified rebellion.[106]

It is remarkable that Constantius seems to have taken Lucifer's threats in good part. He had reigned quite a long time, he reminded him.[107] He could hardly be characterized as an apocalyptic beast. If he had been a heretic, God would have punished him. The debate, however, was not to be pressed to a conclusion. In the autumn of 359 and 360, Constantius had even more urgent affairs to deal with than the utterances of angry and disillusioned bishops, however powerful. The Persian campaign had gone badly. Amida fell on 5 October 359. The campaign of 360 was grinding to stalemate with yet another Roman failure in that harsh theater of limited warfare. More troops were needed, but the reply of the Gallic legions was not to march to the emperor's aid. In February 360, they declared as emperor their Caesar, Constantius's cousin Julian. Julian was a convert to a mystical paganism, a disciple of the final flowering of Neo-Platonism.

BIBLIOGRAPHY

NOTE

There is no comprehensive survey in English of the reign of Constantius II, a serious gap in British scholarly studies. A number of useful studies deal with individual aspects of the reign. A good factual guide is G. Bardy's "Les Variations de l'Arianisme," chapter 3 (pp. 69–176) in part 2 of *De la paix constantienne à la mort de Théodose*, ed. P. de Labriolle, Bardy, and J. R. Palanque (Paris: Bloud et Gay, 1947), vol. 3 of *Histoire de l'église depuis les origines jusqu'à nos jours*, ed. A. Fliche and V. Martin. This provides an account of Arianism and the numerous church councils that followed Nicaea. For Athanasius also, there is no biography in English to date, but readers are recommended to E. P. Meijering, *Orthodoxy and Platonism in Athanasius: Synthesis or Antithesis?* (Leiden: E. J. Brill, 1968), R. W. Thomson's edition of Athanasius, *Contra Gentes* and *De Incarnatione* (New York and London: Oxford University Press, 1971), and my "Athanasius as an Egyptian Christian Leader in the Fourth Century" chapter 16 in *Religion Popular and Unpopular* (London: Variorum Books, 1976).

The theme of church and state in this period is treated in S. L. Greenslade, *Church and State from Constantine to Theodosius* (Toronto: Ryerson Press; London: SCM Press, 1954), and K. M. Setton, *The Christian Attitude Towards the Emperor in the Fourth Century* (New York: Columbia University Press; London: P. S. King & Staples, 1941). Attention is drawn also to the learned contributions in H. Ruhbach, ed., *Die Kirche angesichts der konstantinischen Wende*, Wege der Forschung 306 (Darmstadt: Wissenschaftliche Buchgesellschaft, 1976).

SOURCES

Ammianus Marcellinus. Edited and Eng. trans. J. C. Rolfe. 3 vols. LCL. Cambridge, Mass.: Harvard University Press; London: William Heinemann, 1935–40.

Athanasius. *Apologia ad Constantium imperatorem (Defense Addressed to Constantius). PG* 25.595–642.

———. *Apologia contra Arianos (Apology Against the Arians). PG* 25.247–410.

———. *Apologia de fuga sua (In Defense of His Flight). PG* 25.643–80.

———. *Historia Arianorum ad monachos (History of the Arians Addressed to the Monks). PG* 25.691–796.

———, *De Synodis, PG* 26.681–794; Eng. trans. in NPNF.

Also published by H. G. Opitz, ed., *Athanasius Werke*, vol. 2.1. Berlin: Walter de Gruyter, 1935.

Ephraem Syrus. *Carmina Nisibena.* Vol. 1. Edited by G. Beck. CSCO Script. Syri 92–93. Louvain, 1961.

Eusebius, *De Laude Constantini,* ed. I. Heikel, GCS 7, Eusebius, pp. 193–262, Leipzig: Hinrichs, 1902; Eng. trans. H. A. Drake, *In Praise of Constantine,* California University Publications: Classical Studies, vol. 15, Berkeley and Los Angeles: University of California Press, 1976.

Hilary of Poitiers. *Contra Constantium imperatorem. PL* 10.577–603.

——. *Opus historicum.* Edited by A. L. Feder. CSEL 65 (fragments). Leipzig: Freytag, 1916.

——. *De Synodis. PL* 10.479–546.

Jerome, *De viris illustribus, PL* 23.602–70; and ed. W. Herding. Leipzig: Teubner, 1879.

Lucifer of Cagliari. *De non conveniendo cum hereticis (On Not Coming to an Agreement with Heretics). PL* 13.767–94.

——. *De non parcendo in Deum delinquentibus (On Not Sparing Those Who Sin Against God). PL* 13.935–1008.

Philostorgius. *Ecclesiastical History.* Edited by J. Bidez and F. Winkelmann. GCS 21. Berlin: Akademie-Verlag, 1972. Books III–VI.

Optatus of Milevis. *De Schismate Donatistarum.* Edited by Ziwsa. Book III.

Socrates. *Ecclesiastical History.* Books II–III, chaps. 1–9.

Sozomen. *Ecclesiastical History.* Books II–IV.

Sulpicius Severus. *Chronicorum.* Edited by C. Halm. CSEL 1. Vienna, 1866.

Theodoret. *Ecclesiastical History.* Book II.

Aurelius Victor. *Caesares.* Edited by F. Pichlmayr. Leipzig: Teubner, 1911.

Zosimus, *Historia Nova,* Book II, ed. L. Mendelssohn, Leipzig, 1887, reprinted Hildersheim, 1963; Eng. trans. R. T. Ridley, Canberra, 1982.

Conciliar *Acta,* see Mansi, *Sacrorum Conciliorum,* vols. 2 (to 346), and 3 (347–409); C. H. Turner, *Ecclesiae Occidentalis Monumenta Iuris antiquissima* I, London: Oxford University Press, 1939; C. J. Hefele—H. Leclercq, *Histoire des Conciles,* Paris, 1907, 1.2.

Legislation, see *Codex Theodosianus* XVI.

Letters of Popes Julius and Liberius, see *PL* 8 and 13; and P. Jaffe and W. Wattenbach, *Regesta Pontificum romanum,* vol. 1, Leipzig, 1885.

SECONDARY WORKS

Anfray, F., Caquot, A., and Nautin, P. "Une nouvelle inscription grecque d'Ezana d'Axoum." *Journal des Savants* (1970): 260–73.

Arnheim, M. T. W. *The Senatorial Aristocracy in the Later Roman Empire.* New York and London: Oxford University Press, 1972.

Barnard, L. W. "Athanase et les empereurs Constantin et Constance." In *Politique et théologie chez Athanase d'Alexandrie, actes du colloque de Chantilly, 23–25 Septembre 1973,* ed. C. Kannengiesser, pp. 127–43. Théologie historique 27. Paris: Gabriel Beauchesne, 1974.

——. "Athanasius and the Meletian Schism in Egypt." *JEA* 59 (1973): 181–89.

Baynes, N. H. "Eusebius and the Christian Empire." *Annales de l'Institut de Philologie et d'histoire orientale (= Mélanges J. Bidez),* pp. 13–18. Brussels, 1933.

Berkhoff, H. *Kirche und Kaiser*. Zurich, 1947.

Chadwick, H. "The Fall of Eustathius of Antioch." *JTS* 49 (1948): 27–35.

Dinkler, E. "König Ezana von Aksum und das Christentum." *Schriften zur Geschichte und Kultur des alten Orients* 13, Aegypten und Kusch = Festsch F. Hintze (Berlin, 1973), pp. 121–32.

Ehrhardt, A. A. T. *Politische Metaphysik von Solon bis Augustin*. Tübingen: J. C. B. Mohr (Paul Siebeck), 1959–69. Vol. 2, chap. 7.

Frend, W. H. C. "The Roman Empire in the Eyes of the Western Schismatics During the 4th Century." *Miscellanea Historiae Ecclesiasticae* (Louvain, 1961): 9–22.

Girardet, K. M. "Constance II, Athanase et l'édit d'Arles (353)." In *Politique et théologie*, ed. Kannengiesser, pp. 63–92.

———. "Kaiser Constantius II als 'Episcopus episcoporum,' und das Herrscherbild des kirchlichen Widerstandes." *Historia* 26 (1977): 95–128.

———. *Kaisergericht und Bischofsgericht*. Antiquitas 1. Bonn: Rudolf Habelt, 1975.

Hardy, E. R. *Christian Egypt: Church and People; Christianity and Nationalism in the Patriarchate of Alexandria*. New York and London: Oxford University Press, 1952.

Hess, H. *The Canons of the Council of Sardica, A.D. 343: A Landmark in the Early Development of Canon Law*. New York and London: Oxford University Press, 1958.

Klein, Richard. *Constantius II und die christliche Kirche*. Darmstadt: Wissenschaftliche Buchgesellschaft, 1977. An excellent survey with bibliography.

Linder, A. "The Myth of Constantine the Great in the West: Sources and Hagiographic Commemoration." *Studi Medievale* 3a Serie XVI.1 (1975): 43–95.

MacMullen, Ramsay. "Social History in Astrology." *Ancient Society* 2 (1971): 105–16.

Meijering, E. P. "Athanasius on the Father as the Origin of the Son." *Nederlands Archief voor Kerkgeschiedenis* 55 (1974): 1–14.

Moreau, J. "Constantius II." *JAC* 2 (1959): 178ff.

Peterson, E. *Der Monotheismus als politisches Problem* (Leipzig, 1935); and the critique by A. Schindler, *Der Monotheismus als politisches Problem? Studien zur evangelischen Ethik* 14, Gütersloh, 1978.

Piétri, C. "La question d'Athanase vue de Rome (338–360)." In *Politique et théologie*, ed. Kannengiesser, pp. 93–126.

Roldanus, J. *Le Christ et l'homme dans la théologie d'Athanase d'Alexandrie: Étude de la conjonction de sa conception de l'homme avec sa christologie*. Leiden: E. J. Brill, 1968.

Schneemelcher, W. "Athanasius von Alexandrien als Theologe und als Kirchenpolitiker." *ZNW* 43 (1950/51): 242–56.

Thompson, E. A. "Christianity and the Northern Barbarians." In *The Conflict Between Paganism and Christianity in the Fourth Century*, ed. A. Momigliano, pp. 56–78. New York and London: Oxford University Press, 1963.

Vogt, J. "Constantinus der Grosse." *RAC* III (1957), cols. 306–79.

Attention is also drawn to the old but still valuable series of articles on Athanasius by E. Schwartz in *NGG* 1904–11, and in his *Gesammelte Schriften* III (Berlin, 1959), "Zur Geschichte des Athanasius," pp. 267–339.

For the whole period covered by Part 3, Frances M. Young's *From Nicaea to Chalcedon: A Guide to the Literature and Its Background* (Philadelphia: Fortress Press; London: SCM Press, 1983) will be found to be a very useful tool for study.

NOTES

1. Eusebius *Vita Constantini* IV.15, ed. I. Heikel, GCS 7, pp. 1–148 (Leipzig: Hinrichs, 1902), p. 123.
2. Socrates *Ecclesiastical History* I.20.
3. I owe this information to Dr. J. H. Chandler's thesis: "Imperial Politics and the Church in the Reign of Constantius II—Prosopographical Appendices" (Bristol University, 1978).
4. Eusebius *Constantine* IV.21.
5. Eusebius, *De Laude Constantini* V, ed. Heikel, pp. 203–4; and see Drake, *Praise of Constantine*, pp. 83–102; and Ehrhardt, *Politische Metaphysik*, vol. 2, chap. 7.
6. Eusebius *Laude Constantini* I.6. See H. Ruhbach, "Die politische Theologie Eusebs von Caesarea," in *Die Kirche angesichts*, ed. Ruhbach, pp. 236–59; and Baynes, "Eusebius and Christian Empire."
7. Ammianus XVI.10.9, ed. Rolfe.
8. Ibid., XIX.2.2.
9. Jerome *De Viris Illustribus* (*Concerning Illustrious Men*) LIII.
10. Augustine *Letter* XCIII.10.43, quoting Tyconius writing c. 380.
11. Optatus, *De Schismate Donatistarum*, III.3.
12. Ammianus XV.7.7.
13. Athanasius *De Synodis* V (*PG* 26.688C and D).
14. Ibid., LI (*PG* 26.784B).
15. Athanasius, in *Apophthegmata Patrum*, publ. in F. Nau, "Histoires des solitaires égyptiens," *Rev. de l'Orient Chrétien* 12 (1907), p. 48 n. 1.
16. *Oratio contra gentes (Against the Heathen)* XLI and XLVII for these definitions. For the dating of *Against Heathen*, see *Contra Gentes* and *De Incarnatione*, ed. Thomson, p. xxiii. For the more traditional date of 318/19, see Kidd, *History of Church*, vol. 2, p. 13.
17. Athanasius, *Apology Against Arians*, LXXI (*PG* 25.376); see Hardy, *Christian Egypt*, p. 53.
18. Sozomen, *Ecclesiastical History* II.17, ed. J. Bidez and G. C. Hansen, GCS 50 (Berlin: Akademie-Verlag, 1960), p. 74.
19. Theodore, *Vita Pachomii* 28, ed. L. Th. Lefort, CSCO *Script. Coptici* III.7 (Louvain, 1936). Did he eventually accept ordination, as suggested by Kidd, *History of Church*, vol. 2, p. 105? For Pachomian monasticism, see below, pp. 576–77.
20. Cited by Athanasius, *Apology Against Arians* LIX (*PG* 25.357).
21. Athanasius, *Contra Gentes*, ed. Thomson, chaps. 38–43. Like Eusebius, he saw the ideal of human society as order and harmony with each performing his allotted task. Change, let alone revolutionary social change, never entered his calculations.
22. Marcellus, however, may have survived until the Council of Constantinople in 336. He wrote to Pope Julius asserting his orthodoxy (Epiphanius *Medicine Box*

LXXII.2) in c. 338, an unexpected step, perhaps, if he had been in exile a considerable time.

23. Socrates *Ecclesiastical History* I.27; Sozomen *Ecclesiastical History* II.25. In fact, Arsenius later joined Athanasius, a tribute to the latter's powers of persuasion. See *Apology Against Arians* LXIX.

24. Eusebius *Constantine* IV.42.

25. *Pap. Lond.* 1913–14. See H. I. Bell, ed., *Jews and Christians in Egypt: The Jewish Troubles in Alexandria and the Athanasian Controversy* (New York: Oxford University Press, 1925), pp. 45ff.

26. For the council, see Socrates *Ecclesiastical History* I.28, and Sozomen *Ecclesiastical History* II.25. For the significance of Count Dionysius's role, see K. H. Girardet, *Kaisergericht*, pp. 67–68.

27. See below, pp. 770–71.

28. For Athanasius's account of Arius's end, see *De Morte Arii* III.3 (*PG* 25, pp. 685–90, esp. p. 688), "split in pieces in a public lavatory."

29. See H. Doerries, "Das Selbstbezeugnis Kaiser Konstantins," *Abhandlungen Göttingen* III.34 (1954), pp. 413ff.

30. As indicated by Sozomen *Ecclesiastical History* II.32.1; Marcionites, Valentinians, Montanists, and Paulianists alone were outside.

31. Hilary, *Fragmenta historica* VII.4, ed. A. Feder, CSEL 65 (Leipzig: Freytag, 1916), pp. 91–92. The account is secondhand, but suggests that those links between Alexandria and Rome were being maintained.

32. *Apology Against Arians* XX–XXXV: another instance of Athanasius's sense of telling propaganda, and also of his links with the West.

33. Translated by J. Stevenson, ed., in *Creeds, Councils and Controversies* (New York: Seabury Press; London: SPCK, 1966), p. 8.

34. Sozomen *Ecclesiastical History* III.8.7; and compare Socrates *Ecclesiastical History* II.15.5. This particular point comes in the Eastern encyclical at the Council of Sardica itself.

35. Quoted by Hilary of Poitiers, *Fragmenta historica* IV.1.12 (ed. Feder, p. 57): "Novam legem introducere putaverunt, ut Orientales episcopi ab Occidentalibus iudicarentur."

36. See Kelly, *Early Christian Creeds*, pp. 268–71. Nicaea dismissed the Holy Spirit in a single phrase.

37. Sozomen *Ecclesiastical History* III.5.9. Asterius was one of the most brilliant minds of the day but disqualified from orders through having lapsed during the Licinian persecution (Socrates *Ecclesiastical History* I.36).

38. Socrates *Ecclesiastical History* II.20.7–11. Another weakness in the Eastern camp was that some of the Palestinian bishops supported the Western view. See Bardy, "Les Variations de l'Arianisme," pp. 131–38.

39. Basil *Letter* LXIX. For the Easterners, Marcellus was a "Sabellian" (cf. Eusebius *Contra Marcellum* [*Against Marcellus*] I.8). He was, if anything, even more disliked than Athanasius. See L. W. Barnard, "East-West Conciliatory Moves and Their Outcome, 341–51." *Heythrop Journal* 20 (July 1979), pp. 243–56, esp. p. 249.

40. Theodoret *Ecclesiastical History* II.8.1ff.

41. Canons 3, 4, and 7. See Turner, *Ecclesiae Occidentalis*, II.3, pp. 452ff. Commentary by Hess, *Canons of Sardica*, chap. 6.

42. *Fragmenta historica*, Ser. A. IV.1 (ed. Feder, pp. 48–67). The Westerners who came to Sardica were called "an assembly of the lost" (p. 62).

43. Socrates *Ecclesiastical History* II.22. Compare Sozomen *Ecclesiastical History* III.13.1.

44. Texts in Socrates *Ecclesiastical History* II.19.7–28, and Athanasius, *Epistula de synodis Arimini in Italia et Seleuciae in Isauria celebratis* (*On the Synods of Ariminum and Seleucia*) XXVI; Eng. trans. in Stevenson, *Creeds, Councils and Controversies*, pp. 22–26.

45. For details of this period, see Bardy "Les Variations de l'Arianisme." And for discussion of Photinus's views, see L. A. Spellar, "New Light on the Photinians," *JTS* n.s. 34.1 (1983): 99–113.

46. The scene is described with some fine oratorical exaggeration by Gregory of Nazianzus, *Oration* XXI.27–29, *PG* 35.1113–16.

47. Theodoret *Ecclesiastical History* II.30. James had been present at Nicaea and was typical of the patriotic episcopate of the Persian frontier provinces.

48. Ephraem Syrus, *Carmina Nisibena* II and VI (anti-Persian), ed. Beck. See R. Murray, *Symbols of Church and Kingdom: A Study of Early Syriac Tradition* (New York and Cambridge: Cambridge University Press, 1975), pp. 244–45.

49. An example of Constantius's good sense is given by Libanius (*Oration* XIX.48–49). He did not react violently when a mob at Edessa rioted and threw down his statues.

50. Socrates *Ecclesiastical History* II.38. For Constantine's attitude to the Novatianists, see ibid., I.10.

51. One of his best-known administrators, Flavius Philippus, consul and praetorian prefect, was son of a pork butcher, but entered the civil service as a secretary (*notarius*). See A. H. M. Jones et al., *The Prosopography of the Later Roman Empire*, vol. 1: A.D. *260–395* (New York and Cambridge: Cambridge University Press, 1971), pp. 696–97 for his career, and *The Later Roman Empire 284–602* (2 vols., Norman: University of Oklahoma Press; 4 vols., Oxford: Basil Blackwell & Mott, 1964), p. 546.

52. For Eusebius, see Ammianus XIV.10.5, and XVII.4.3–7. The support of the imperial eunuchs was regarded as essential for the success of any project, Athanasius affirmed (*History of Arians* 37). Eusebius was reputed to be strongly pro-Arian.

53. Ammianus XIV.5.8, and XV.3.4. Another notorious character was Mercurius "Count of Dreams," so called for his ability to construe treason from the dreams of his colleagues.

54. Ammianus XV.1.2. Socrates *Ecclesiastical History* II.28.

55. Sulpicius Severus *Chronicorum* II.38.4–7 (ed. Halm).

56. Ammianus XV.7.10.

57. Hilary, *De Synodis* XCI, *PL* 10.545: "Fidem Nicaenum numquam nisi exsulaturus audivi." Hilary says (ibid.) that Scripture permitted both *homoiousios* and *homoousios*—but the fathers preferred the latter.

58. Optatus, *De Schismate Donatistarum* III.3 (ed. Ziwsa, p. 74). Optatus bases his loyalism on Paul, 1 Tim. 2:2.

59. Ephraem Syrus, *Carmina Nisibena* 21 and 22, ed. Beck, pp. 68–69; written to the emperor Jovian (363–64) evidently before his surrender of Nisibis to the Persians became known.

60. *De Schismate Donatistarum* III.3 (ed. Ziwsa, p. 73).

61. Ibid., I.22 (ed. Ziwsa, p. 25).

62. Tyconius, cited from *Tyconius-Studien*, ed. T. Hahn (Leipzig, 1900), p. 71.

63. Best exemplified by Lucifer of Cagliari (*flor.* 355–65), who deemed himself within his rights even as a provincial bishop to attack Constantius II directly as a "heretic" and imitator of Satan "destined to God's punishment." See K. Aland, "Kaiser und Kirche von Konstantin bis Byzanz," in *Die Kirche angesichts*, ed. Ruhbach, pp. 42–73, esp. pp. 52–53; and Girardet, "Kaiser Constantius II."

64. Constantius's reported dictum, "What I will, let this be considered a canon. For when I make such pronouncements the bishop of Syria accept it; obey therefore or you will go into banishment." comes from Athanasius's reportage, *History of Arians* 33, *PG* 25.732.

65. Sozomen *Ecclesiastical History* IV.11.9–12.

66. Athanasius *History of Arians* XLIV; translated by Greenslade in *Church and State*, p. 45.

67. See below, p. 622.

68. See below, p. 810.

69. Athanasius's account is contained in *Defense of Flight* 24–25, and *Defense Addressed to Constantius* 24–25.

70. Ammianus XV.1.3.

71. See Girardet, "Kaiser Constantius II," pp. 95ff.

72. *Codex Theodosianus* XVI.10.2 (following an unnamed edict of Constantine).

73. Ibid., 10.6.

74. Thus Firmicus Maternus, *Matheseos libri VIII* (*Learning*), IV.10.9, and V.1.3. See MacMullen, "Social History in Astrology," pp. 112–13.

75. Ammianus XIX.12.12; and victims of Paul "the Chain."

76. *Codex Theodosianus* XVI.2.9.

77. Sozomen *Ecclesiastical History* V.5.1–3, an important passage listing the privileges abrogated by Julian.

78. Ammianus XXII.5.4; Julian *Letter* XXXI.4.

79. *Codex Theodosianus* XVI.2.15.

80. Ibid., XVI.2.8.

81. See Philostorgius *Ecclesiastical History* II.5, "propter Christianorum in gente Gothorum consecratus [by Eusebius]," and Thompson, "Christianity and Northern Barbarians," pp. 62–63. Ulphilas may have been descended on his mother's side from Cappadocian Christians captured by the Goths in the raids of 255–56.

82. Philostorgius *Ecclesiastical History* III.4.4; Sozomen *Ecclesiastical History* II.24; and Rufinus, *Ecclesiastical History* I.9 (*PL* 21, col. 478). The merchants themselves trading in southern Arabia do not seem to have propagated their religion to any extent. See Klein, *Constantius II*, pp. 238–50 (discussion).

83. See E. Dinkler, "New Questions Concerning King Ezana of Axum," *Études et Travaux* 9 (Warsaw, 1976): 1–15; and for the "Jewish" and Christian inscriptions of the Ezana period, see E. Littman, *Deutsche Axoum Expedition* I (Berlin, 1913), p. 48, and Anfray et al., "Une nouvelle inscription grecque."

84. Athanasius *Defense Addressed to Constantius* XXXI.

85. Translated by Stevenson in *Creeds, Councils and Controversies*, p. 34.

86. Ammianus XXI.16.18. "Anilis superstitio" contrasted with the "absoluta" or "simplex religio" of authentic Christianity in Ammianus's view.

87. For instance, from the important Fortunatianus of Aquileia who is blamed by Jerome (*Illustrious Men* XCVII) for persuading Pope Liberius of its acceptability and Restitutus, Catholic bishop of Carthage, who was prominent in the Council of Ariminum (Rimini) in 359.

88. Hilary, *Contra Constantium imperatorem* XXIII (*PL* 10.599, "deliramenta Osii"), a contemporary if biased view. For a more merciful view of Hosius's "Fall," see Socrates *Ecclesiastical History* II.31.

89. Text in Hilary *De synodis* (*Concerning the Synods*) XI; Athanasius *On the Synods* 28; and Socrates *Ecclesiastical History* II.30.

90. Shown, in addition, by the attitude of Acacius of Caesarea and his followers at the Council of Seleucia in 359, where they rejected the terms *homoousios, homoiousios,* and *anhomoios* as "unscriptural" and the cause of incessant trouble, while taking their stand on the faith as set out in the Second Creed of Antioch (Socrates *Ecclesiastical History* II.40). See Kelly, *Early Christian Creeds*, pp. 290–91.

91. Hilary, *Fragmenta historica* VII.9 (ed. Feder, p. 170); Athanasius *History of Arians* XLI, and *Apology Against Arians* 89; Jerome *Illustrious Men* XCVII. See Bardy, "Les Variations de l'Arianisme," pp. 154–55; and Charles Piétri, *Roma christiana* I, Bibliothéque des Écoles Françaises d'Athènes et de Rome 224 (Rome, 1976), pp. 258–63. It seems clear from Hilary, *Fragmenta historica* VII.10.1 and 2 (ed. Feder, pp. 170–71), that Liberius at least acquiesced in the condemnation of Athanasius at this stage. Sozomen, *Ecclesiastical History* IV.15.3, thought that he was a *homoiousian*, believing, like Basil of Ancyra, that Christ was "like God in all respects," and condemning those who affirmed that he was "dissimilar to the Father." Altogether, his signature to Third Sirmium (attested in Hilary *Fragmenta historica*) seems as likely as his acceptance of "Blasphemy."

92. Sozomen *Ecclesiastical History* IV.13.4. Bardy, "Les Variations de l'Arianisme," pp. 156–57.

93. Hilary *De Synodis* 89 and 90, *PL* 10.541–42. See Bardy, "Les Variations de l'Arianisme," pp. 159–60.

94. As they believed it had been used by Paul of Samosata.

95. Thus Philostorgius *Ecclesiastical History* IV.8–9. On the other side of the fence, Pope Liberius returned to Rome on 2 August 358.

96. Sozomen *Ecclesiastical History* IV.17.10, on the absurdity of the date and Athanasius's comment that it was ridiculous to call Constantius "the eternal emperor," yet refuse the same title to the Son of God! For the text, see Socrates *Ecclesiastical History* II.37 and Athanasius, *De Synodis* VIII, *PG* 26.692–93.

97. For the numbers at Ariminum, see Athanasius *On the Synods* VIII, and at Seleucia, see ibid., XII. Rome, curiously enough, was not represented at Ariminum.

98. Jerome, *Dialogus adversus Luciferianos* (*Against the Luciferians*) XIX (*PL* 23.172C). Even more pointedly in *Chronicle* ad ann. 359: "Omnes paene toto orbe Ecclesiae, sub nomine pacis et regis, Arianorum consortio polluuntur" (ed. Helm, GCS 24, p. 241).

99. For Aetius's debt to Aristotelianism, see Socrates *Ecclesiastical History* II.35.

100. *Defense Addressed to Constantius* XIX; see Greenslade, *Church and State*, p. 47.

101. *History of Arians* 3 and 77.

102. John Chrysostom, *Homiliae 21 de statuis* (*21 Homilies on the Statues*) II.2 (*PG* 49.36) though a bishop might claim an even greater dignity (ibid., III.2).

103. *Codex Justinianus* I.1.4.

104. Hilary, *Contra Constantium imperatorem* VII, *PL* 10.584.

105. Ibid., 5.8 and 9 (*PL* 10.581–86), written c. 360 or 361. Lucifer, *Not Coming to Agreement with Heretics* (*PL* 13.781 and 783); and for the Donatists, see *Passio Donati et Advocati* II, *PL* 8.753.

106. Lucifer, *Not Coming to Agreement with Heretics*. See Frend, ''Roman Empire in Eyes of Western Schismatics,'' p. 19.

107. Lucifer, *Not Sparing Those Who Sin, PL* 13.963 and 1001.

16

From Pagan
to Christian Society
330–60

The reign of Constantius II saw the beginning of the Christian, and indeed the Byzantine eras of European history. The emperor's preoccupation with the teaching and affairs of the church reflected the outlook of an increasing number of his subjects. The great transition from pagan to Christian society was taking place through the length and breadth of the empire. In the last years of his reign Constantine had dealt a massive blow to paganism. Starting with the looting of some of the famous shrines of the Aegean to embellish his new city, the emperor had proceeded to vent his spleen on the gods he now despised and rejected. Celebrated temples, such as that of Asclepius in Agis in Cilicia and of Venus Ourania (Venus of the Heavens) near Mount Lebanon, were demolished or ransacked.[1] Eusebius records the beginning of the collapse of the old religion (*Constantine* IV.39). A century later, the Constantinopolitan historian Sozomen, writing c. 440, preserved the memory of bands of Christian youths going from town to town allegedly armed with letters from the emperor, ordering obedience to his antipagan decrees and browbeating the population into abandoning the priests. The latter were forced to display images and sacred objects to public gaze. Anything of precious metal was seized and melted down. Statues were destroyed or brought out into the streets, stuffed with straw, and the people were encouraged to ridicule what their ancestors had venerated.[2]

The emperor, to anticipate a phrase of Ambrose of Milan, was now "in God's service" (*militans pro Deo*).[3] Once imperial patronage was withdrawn, the old religion had little but tradition to sustain it. Pagan cults could not, as Maximin had found, be organized into a pagan "church." There were no recorded pagan martyrs under Constantine. In the reigns of his sons, paganism became irrevocably associated with the past. Temples were becoming museums, as the young Julian discovered on his stay in Troy in 354, to be visited by the great, but neglected as places of worship. In Rome untidy private dwellings were built against their walls, emphasizing their decay.[4] Constantius might set up an obelisk in the Circus Maximus to commemorate his visit in 357, but he also sent the relics of apostles from there to Constantinople, and he removed from the Senate house the altar of Victory, on which senators had offered incense at the beginning of each year since the time of Augustus.[5] Popular religious feeling in many parts of the empire was now Christian. The ecstatic triumph of the return of Athanasius to Alexandria on 21 October 346 symbolized the spirit of the new age.

THE NEW SYNTHESIS

The old order, however, was not swept away. Looked at carefully, the age of the sons of Constantine witnessed its survival in an uneasy synthesis with the new. People and institutions and much of cultural life were still rooted in the pagan past. Constantius II's ideal—"the restoration of prosperous times" (*Fel[icitas] Temp[orum] Reparatio*)—that dominated his coinage between 348 and 358, was far from revolutionary. Nor were the "new men" on whose ability the administration of the empire rested.[6] The imperial legislation, with the exception of *Codex Theodosianus* Book XVI, which was devoted to the multifarious problems resulting from the empire's acceptance of Christianity, showed little change in spirit from the past.[7] The church failed to win acceptance for its views regarding the sanctity of marriage which remained a contract in the eyes of the state, dissoluble by either party on traditionally approved grounds.[8] Punishments in criminal cases continued to be severe and cruel. Those who displeased an emperor risked being condemned—to be burned at the stake or eaten by bears.[9]

The most fruitful synthesis was in the cultural life of the period. Many find the mid–fourth century the most satisfying period of early Christian art, where the new generation of artists drew on the traditions of the pagan past to portray Christian teaching. The great increase in Christian sarcophagi, particularly in the West in this period, indicates how Christianity was becoming increasingly the religion of the upper classes, but these sarcophagi show an astonishing mixture of Christian and non-Christian themes. That of Junius Bassus—who was baptized in 358, became prefect of Rome the next year, and died in office—illustrates the way in which biblical subjects such as Adam and Eve were simply substituted for pagan motifs, while the traditional arrangement of the funeral procession accompanying the soul of the deceased to blessedness remained the same.[10] On pottery and lamps, Genius arising from the mixing bowl—by dint of a play on the word *lacus* ("mixing bowl," or "pit")—becomes Daniel emerging triumphant from the lion's den.[11] Education continued, as it had been in the past, to be wedded to a thorough mastery of the classics, leading to careers that demanded a high proficiency in public speaking. Trade and commerce were rejected as "ungentlemanly" careers.

The combination, however, of the classical with the biblical in an age which was still relatively secure, produced a degree of education and awareness among the Christian leadership unparalleled before the Renaissance in the fourteenth and fifteenth centuries. The age of the fathers required, apart from a Christian empire, an education based on Virgil, Cicero, and Seneca in the West, and on Platonism in the East. For the first and last time in Christian Europe for many centuries to come, the laity were able to take a full share in formulating church teaching and contributing to its cultural life. Each in their own way, Marius Victorinus, "Ambrosiaster," Cresconius Aper, and Tyconius, Paula, and Eustochium, Jerome's pupils, represent the active lay element in the Christian empire that emerged during the reigns of Constantius II and his immediate successors.[12]

Overshadowing changes in religious allegiance, however, were economic and social developments. These also would exercise an influence, lessening the impact of Christianity on the conditions of the time and failing to satisfy expectations and grievances. Constantine had attempted to temper the demands of the tax collector, but a generation later, critics were pointing out how his prodigal generosity to a few had come at the expense of the remainder of the provincials.[13] The fortunate had been able to pile up their wealth until noble families such as the Anicii (mainly Christian) possessed huge incomes derived from vast estates scattered throughout the entire Western empire. "Whether justly or unjustly is not a question for my humble judgment," wrote Ammianus Marcellinus, concerning its wealthiest member, Petronius Probus.[14] The minting of large quantities of gold and silver coinage, it was pointed out, also increased the gap between rich and poor and added to the discontent of the latter.[15] The poor, an observer stated "were bound to eternal toil, forever hiring out their bodies to some task."[16] The 340s saw the emergence of a revolutionary movement within Christianity, that of the Circumcellions in North Africa, which with other forms of extremism was calculated to drive the majority of Christians towards accepting the social and institutional status quo. Few looked beyond the traditional interests of their class.

While the church as well as the imperial administration provided some scope for social mobility—the gifted son of poor parents could become a bishop, just as a son of a pork butcher could become a praetorian prefect[17]— the mass of the provincials followed their fathers' callings amid perpetually rising taxes and growing official corruption. Few could have had the luck or the nerve or the sheer zest for life that characterized the "godless" deacon Aetius.[18] For the majority "the bitterness of the times," wrote Ammianus Marcellinus forty years later, "was increased by the insatiate extortion of the tax-collectors who brought him [Constantius] more hatred than money."[19] Honesty, as Augustine's friend Alypius of Thagaste discovered during a short career in the civil service in Rome (c. 382), was not expected of an assessor in the finance department.[20] A visit to a community by a member of the imperial messenger service (the *agentes in rebus*) struck deadly terror into the hearts of its inhabitants.

Though wealth and influence were flowing irrevocably into the hands of the landed aristocracy, the mid-fourth-century emperors continued to pour exhortations and resources into an ever more futile effort to restore the cities to the role they had occupied two centuries before. The prosperity created for them under the Tetrarchy had evaporated. The economic basis, depending on the prosperity of the urban upper class who owned lands around the city itself, was too fragile. There was too much imperial estate, too much church land, and too much in the hands of powerful landowners who could defy the city's agents. In the West, for every Bordeaux with its fine schools and jealously guarded tradition of classical learning there was an Aventicum (Avenches), the cantonal town of the Helvetii and once a *colonia* but described by Ammianus as abandoned and full of half-ruined buildings.[21] In the East, decay may have been less obvious. Antioch was praised by its foremost son, the philosopher and writer Libanius (310–90), as a splendid city, drawing crowds from the countryside to its markets, a trading center on the intersection of five routes, enriched by customs fees and able to supply lavish amusements for its inhabitants.[22] Athens, too, had recovered from the scourge of the Heruli raids in the previous century to become a fine university town where Christians and pagans met and debated on even terms.[23] Edessa enthralled the Spanish pilgrim Etheria with its churches and fountains when she visited it in 385.[24] But where there was no longer an obvious economic or cultural attraction, the Eastern cities shared the decline of their Western counterparts. Even Nicomedia, Diocletian's and Licinius's capital, was half in ruins, its walls "a heap of ashes," when Julian passed through it in the late spring of 362. Carnuntum, the great Danube fortress, was in a similar state.[25] The once-prestigious orders of city councilors sought any chance to migrate to the civil service or the clergy rather than remain the unpaid tax collectors of the government.[26]

Surprisingly, however, some local patriotism survived. From Augustine we learn of close-knit elites of "fellow-citizens" (*concives*) who still regarded their city with pride. At Timgad also, there were local worthies in the 350s and 360s who were proud of their status and prepared to accept traditional titles even if these were only ceremonial (and expensive).[27] The evidence of the *Codex Theodosianus* cannot be taken as the whole truth. It is clear, however, that the city councils had lost much of their power to imperial officials, and above all, to the bishop.

Christian Centers

The bishop was the rising star of authority symbolized by the fact that new buildings in the cities were becoming predominantly Christian. Nicomedia received a cathedral replacing that destroyed in the Great Persecution.[28] The dedication of the Church of the Golden Dome at Antioch in 341[29] provided an excuse for the emperor to preside over an important council. Athanasius saw a great new church being built in Aquileia when he visited there in 345. At Edessa and Jerusalem churches may well have outnumbered public buildings, but most significant of all for the change in popular mood was the development of large and exclusively Christian centers, generally on the outskirts but sometimes within the towns themselves.[30]

These Christian districts, dominated by the basilican churches, typified the new order. They took little account of earlier pagan buildings. In North Africa, where they have been most extensively studied, their gradual development kept pace with the progress of the Christian population. West of Tipasa on the Algerian coast, a great complex grew up around a church dedicated to the memory of the martyr Salsa, a tombstone originally that of an elderly matron of the third century being adapted to fit the legend of the youthful martyr. Tipasa became a center of pilgrimages from all over the

Mediterranean.[31] At Djemila there were two churches, a monumental baptistery (see photo, pp. 518–19), and a crypt for episcopal burials. At Timgad, the cathedral dominating the city from the south with its baptistery and barrackslike buildings covered five acres. This, too, was a pilgrim center—for the Donatists.[32] Perhaps the most impressive of these centers was that at Hippo Regius. There the Christian quarter was within the city walls, gradually extending from a rectangular room in a house to a church, thence to an area covering 5460 square meters, including a large basilica (built probably c. 350) and 120 separate rooms.[33] The scale of these Christian buildings contrasts with the shoddy repairs carried out on secular structures and the huddle of mean shacks and native-type dwellings of much of urban development in fourth-century North Africa.

What were these rooms for? Some were used to store goods for charitable purposes, like the store attached to the church at Cirta in 303.[34] Others would be for administration, perhaps housing the growing clerical staff in each church. Arbitration and judicial procedures took up much of a fourth-century bishop's time. There were charitable funds to be administered and so, too, the growing property of the church. Augustine's church at Hippo possessed property, twenty times what his father had owned as a *curialis* (that is, at least six thousand solidi a year).[35] He himself administered five large churches and he speaks (*Sermon* CCXIX) of the great size of his cathedral. Not surprisingly, the episcopate in both East and West was attracting the middle classes, with a preference for former lawyers and men trained in administration. Augustine's friends and opponents at the end of the century were drawn from these classes. Only one bishop mentioned in his correspondence, Samsucius of Turres, could be described as "illiterate."[36]

The churches themselves emphasized the status carved out by their articulate and educated leaders. Augustine as a presbyter wrote (c. 395) how, in the little town of Sinitum within the Catholic diocese of Hippo, a flight of steps led to the Donatist bishop's throne in the sanctuary; Augustine reminds his correspondent of the canopied episcopal chair (*cathedra*), the processions, and chants of consecrated virgins that greeted him (*Letter* XXIII.3), but none of these would avail him at the judgment seat of Christ where final sentence would be pronounced. Even in the mid–third century, the African clergy had been conscious of their authority, but so long as house-churches were the rule, the congregation would have had its say.[37] The emergence of the basilica by the mid–fourth century from the Euphrates frontier to Silchester presented the church as a solid, uniform institution governed exclusively by the clergy.

In North Africa, if one were to arrive in the morning on any Sunday or feast day one would be able to participate in the celebration of the Eucharist. Entering the church one would find the bishop or presbyter seated, his clergy ranged about him on either side. As in other Western churches, he would address the congregation or read from Scripture from this vantage point. In front of the raised apse would be the altar, beneath which might be housed the relics of martyrs. After the ministry of the Word at which catechumens would be present, the celebrant would stand at the altar and bless the offerings brought by the faithful and perform the bloodless sacrifice of the Body of Christ. The Alleluia would be sung; then he would administer the communion to the congregation and dismiss them with a benediction.[38] The people whose gifts had been blessed were assured, as Optatus of Milevis wrote (c. 365), of "eternal salvation, preservation of faith and hope of the resurrection."[39] In many places, in town and countryside alike, the agape would still be celebrated, and there it would seem the names of the martyrs were recorded.[40]

The people would face the clergy down the "court of the people" (*quadratum populi*), divided into three, five, or even seven naves in some great churches. Augustine tells us that men and women would be separated, divided by the wide expanse of the central nave.[41] They would stand, arms at each side, but hands open in gestures of supplication.[42] The floors would be paved with mosaic, parts given by pious donors. On the walls would hang tiles or plaques recalling biblical scenes. Above the clerestory would be a shallow penthouse roof.[43] The baptistery would be at the side, and sometimes a separate building. Outside in the courtyard leading to the church might be a pool (*piscina*).[44] In the East, the general plan of churches in this period was the same, with the difference that the altar would be nearer the apse and a pulpit would often stand halfway down the central aisle. Good sermons would be cheered. John Chrysostom sometimes preached, and was applauded, three times a week. He was a tireless speaker but sometimes he wished that people would give more attention to Scripture reading. Augustine had the same problems.[45] To learn about the Bible and the love of God revealed in it was the object of the sermon.[46]

There can be no doubt about the fervor and devotion that the liturgy aroused. While for the West minute-by-minute descriptions of the rite may be reconstructed largely from Optatus's and Augustine's works, the intrepid pilgrim Etheria has left an eyewitness account of the details of the services she attended at Jerusalem (c. 385). At Easter people would become exhausted by their all-night vigil before Easter Day, for the distinctive ceremonies of the Great Week began "six days before the Passover." Etheria recalls a merciful instruction from the bishop: "Now off you go home and sit down for a bit until the next service. Then all be back here at about 8 o'clock so that you can see the holy wood of the Cross, that as everyone believes helps us attain salvation."[47] Practice of the liturgy could become almost full time.

From one end of the Mediterranean to the other, the same rites were performed in similar buildings. The clergy themselves were conscious of the unifying effects of the spread of Christianity. Gone were the days when "there were thousands of different cults and each had its own idol," claimed Athanasius.[48] But much of local value was perishing also. Standardization of organization and liturgies worked in favor of the predominance of the two languages—Latin in the West and Greek in the East—with a frontier based on culture and belief between them. Coptic survived and flourished in the Nile Valley, and Syriac—a development of Aramaic—became the language of Christian Mesopotamia and lands further east. Other languages were less fortunate. The Bible was not, so far as is known, translated into Berber or Celtic, and as Etheria found at Jerusalem where Greek predominated as a liturgical language, there was only a condescending translation into Syriac.[49] Even among so African-conscious a church as that of Donatus, Latin was the language of the liturgy. The Berber element was expressed only in the revival of Berber art in a Christian setting.[50] The effect of the church's use of the official languages of the empire was to ensure the survival of these long after the empire itself was only a memory. Gaul and Spain in the West may owe their final Latinization and Romance linguistic heritage to the spread of Christianity among its peoples in the period after Constantine's death.[51]

The churches built during this period did not stand empty. Constantine, Sozomen recounts, "succeeded to the utmost of his anticipation" (*Ecclesiastical History* II.5.6). The numbers of Christians were increasing by leaps and bounds. In Phoenicia, whence Sozomen's family came, "the inhabitants of many cities embraced Christianity spontaneously without any edict of the emperor and overturned adjacent temples and statues, and erected houses of prayer in their stead." He names some towns which suddenly abandoned traditional cults for Christianity.[52] In the West, developments were similar if more haphazard. It has been pointed out that while some Christian buildings were erected by wealthy individuals, no instance is known so far of a dedication by a municipal council. Collectively these remained standard-bearers of pagan tradition.[53] Even so, Hilary of Poitiers, writing c. 365, near the end of his life, described how expagans were flooding into the church. "Every day the believing people increases, and professions of faith are multiplied. Pagan superstitions are abandoned together with the impious fables of mythology, and the altars of the demons and the vanity of idols. Everyone is moving along the road to salvation."[54] This was optimistic but not untrue. Despite the obscurity that surrounds the origins of bishoprics in Gaul, it is clear that Christianity had established itself as a political force during the 340s. Thirty-four Gallic bishops are mentioned by Athanasius as having attended Sardica in 342/43.[55] The usurper Magnentius, driven from the Balkans and Italy, hoped at least to hold Britain and Gaul. In 352 his mint at Amiens (Ambiani) struck a large copper coin whose reverse was filled entirely with the Chi-Rho symbol, while on other Gallic issues Constantine's banner of the cross (*labarum*) was prominent.[56] Magnentius himself was reputed a pagan who had legalized nocturnal sacrifices once again, but driven on to the defensive, he appealed to the Christian sentiment of the Gallic provinces, realizing perhaps that his best chance of defeating Constantius lay in portraying himself as the more devout and orthodox Christian.[57]

THE PROCESS OF CHRISTIANIZATION

How did this transfer of allegiance from paganism to Christianity take place? Success certainly bred success. To quote Athanasius, "Or why, if Christ is a man as they claim and not God the Word, is not his worship prevented from passing to the region where they are, by their gods? But rather the Word himself came and by his teaching destroyed their religion and put their illusion to shame."[58] Essentially, this was the same argument that Origen had used a century before,[59] but in the hundred years it had become even more relevant. Christianity had spread and survived a succession of persecutions. Its martyrs and their memory were now its glory, and as anyone could see, it was becoming the predominant civilization of the Constantinian empire.

That said, in general terms, the process of change is obscure. One factor was that mixed marriages between Christian and pagan tended to move in a Christian direction. Of Augustine's parents in Thagaste (Souk-Ahras) in Numidia in c. 350, Patricius, the pagan pater familias, found that he was no longer master in his own house so far as his wife's religion was concerned, and it was Monica's views that prevailed.[60] "I was a believer like all the household," said Augustine, "except my father; but he could not cancel in me the rights of my mother's piety" (*Confessions* I.10.17). Amid all the religious alternatives he explored, a return to traditional pagan worship and animal sacrifice was not one. Another example would seem to be that of the consul for the year 328, Flavius Ianuarinus, who had a sarcophagus (found at Arles) prepared for his Christian wife, Marcia Romana Celsa, featuring the raising of Lazarus.[61] In 328, a consul would hardly have been born a Christian. A third instance may perhaps be recognized from a mosaic inscription in the catacomb at Sousse (Hadrumetum) of the "Epicurean" Eustorgius who had inscribed on his grave his seven precepts, including "Drink young man while ye are able," and "God hates a wife of ill morals and a son plunged into senselessness and debt," but praises his own wife as "the most rare and unique [*unica*] lover of wisdom [*filosofa*] and "wondrous example of charity," and on her grave adjacent was a Constantinian monogram and the words *In pace*. As Stevenson comments, "Here is a family in the process of becoming Christians."[62] Christ had displaced Isis in the affections of the female line, and it was through the women of the family that Christianity was triumphing.

The influence of the women, especially educated women, on the religious life of the time was very considerable. That influence was often strong on the side of Christianity. This was ruefully admitted by Julian during his stay at Antioch in 363. "Every one of you," he told the citizens, "allows his wife to carry everything out of his house to the Galileans" to support charitable works for the poor (*The Beard Hater* 363A), and this, of course, redounded to the favor of Christianity. Rome itself provides some well-known examples. Theodoret, writing in the fifth century, records how in 357 Constantius was pestered by Roman aristocratic women, adorned in their finery, with demands that Pope Liberius should be recalled from exile. When next year he returned, his credit tarnished, he was received in triumph and Constantius's decree that he and Felix should share the bishopric was hooted down in the Circus Maximus by the spectators with the cry, "There is but one God, one Christ, one bishop."[63] One such supporter may have been the *matrona* Celerina who commemorated him on the elaborately painted niche (*arcosolium*) of her funerary chamber in the catacomb of Praetextatus. Liberius appears to be associated with the Roman martyrs, Laurentius and Pope Sixtus, while his persecutors, Constantius and Felix, are represented as wolves (just as the *matronae* described Felix to Constantius II).[64] Representing quite different grades of society, strong-minded women such as Celerina and Monica were the backbone of the fourth-century church. They were not only more open to Christian teaching than their husbands evidently were (see Sulpicius Severus *Life of St. Martin* VI), but they used their influence to dissuade their husbands from any lingering pagan sympathies. Libanius described the situation. "When the men are out of doors," he wrote to a friend, "they listen to your plea for the only right course and they come to the altars. But when a man gets home, his wife and her tears and the night plead otherwise, and they draw him away from the altars."[65] Christian womenfolk in the family played a great part in forming the outlook of Basil of Caesarea, John Chrysostom, and Ambrose of Milan. Each owed his later, strongly held views to the influence of a mother or sister in the decade 350–60.

Often, however, we know tantalizingly little how the conversion of pagan to Christian came about. How, for example, the family of Ausonius (c. 310–90), the Gallic poet who was tutor to the emperor Gratian from c. 367 to 378, became Christian is a mystery. One may suspect maternal influence,[66] but this is quite uncertain. Nothing could be more traditional than the family background. Ausonius's father was a physician and a *curialis* of Bazas in southwestern Gaul. His maternal grandfather had been a member of the Druidic order, and so loyal did he feel towards Rome that he actually fought against the secessionist Gallic emperor Victorinus in 269. Yet at some point, perhaps not long after Constantine's conversion, the family became Christian and Ausonius lived and died a convinced if irregular worshiper at the Easter services at Bordeaux. He occasionally put on his Sunday best as one critic has said.[67] Jerome's parents at Stridon in Dalmatia were eastern immigrants, to judge from the name (Eusebius) of his father, and are easier to understand. Theirs also was the complacent type of Christianity that drove Jerome toward disgruntled asceticism.[68]

The New Conformity

Conforming Christianity was replacing conforming paganism as the mark of an educated provincial. In the West, outside Donatist North Africa, one accepted Nicaea, but otherwise faith was comfortable rather than zealous. Christianity in the 350s and 360s was combined with love for the classical past. The one implied no exclusion of the other. Christian or pagan, a man of culture, as Peter Brown describes, still sat in his teacher's chair with a cupboard full of ancient scrolls of the classics close at hand.[69] The provincial schools, which Augustine and Jerome were attending at this time and at which Ausonius and his friends were teaching, still resembled those of Horace's or Quintilian's day. In Roman Britain and Roman Africa alike, scenes from the *Aeneid* could be found depicted on the mosaics or wall frescoes of a gentleman's house.[70] But even into this stronghold of Roman patriotic verse and feeling, Christianity was penetrating. Faltonia Betitia Proba, the Christian wife of a pagan prefect of Rome, wrote a Virgilian cento to celebrate "Christ's holy gifts announced in Virgil."[71] Jerome himself witnessed this culture in transition when he described his own youth in Rome (c. 350–55), how while being educated in the liberal arts, he used on Sundays to visit the tombs of the apostles with his friends. He remembered the "crypts dug deep in the earth with their walls on either side lined with the bodies of the dead, so dark that it seemed almost as though the words of the psalmist were fulfilled: 'Let them go down alive into hell.' [Ps. 55:15]."[72] It was a world in which the Christian was slowly absorbing the pagan classical past into a new imperial Christianity. Just occasionally, a striking public conversion to Christianity, like that of Marius Victorinus (c. 360) would set tongues wagging,[73] but generally the transition was smooth, unobtrusive but irreversible.

Curiously, Roman Britain provides some of the most interesting evidence for the gradual though only partial Christianization of society during the mid–fourth century. Lack of literary evidence prevents the process being traced with the same accuracy as is possible in some other provinces. Even the date of Alban's martyrdom at Verulamium is uncertain.[74] There were three British bishops at Arles in 314 and at Ariminum in 359, and they were poor so that they had to accept Constantius's offer of the posting service for their return to Britain.[75] Colchester (Camulodunum), the island's one *colonia*, may also have been the primatial see, but there are no personalities, such as Martin of Tours, around whom the story of the conversion of the British provinces can be told. Against this, some outstanding archaeological discoveries show how Christianity was penetrating the wealthier sections of the population in the countryside as well as making headway in the towns. The cemetery near Poundbury Rings outside Dorchester suggests a relatively large Christian population there in the mid–fourth century, though in the 370s a new Romano-Celtic temple and priest's house were to be built within the ramparts of Maiden Castle in full view of the town, three miles to the south.[76] At Lullingstone, the owner of the great villa was turning one of the rooms into a chapel. Busts of emperors(?) which had once held pride of place were being buried, their place taken by frescoes showing the Chi-Rho, a painting of a youthful Christ, and a church.[77]

In the living room, however, was a mosaic showing Bellerophon killing the Chimera. The myth had now become Christian, a parable of the overthrow of evil powers through Christ. This blend of pagan with Christian motifs is the feature of the transition. The Mildenhall treasure, buried perhaps c. 360, is dominated by the splendid Oceanus platter, showing Oceanus with large staring eyes, broad nose, and seaweed beard accompanied by dolphins. But buried with this and other silver dishes and goblets were five spoons marked with the Chi-Rho which could have been used for mixing the wine at the Eucharist.[78] A similar mingling of pagan and Christian was discovered on the Constantinian-period mosaics in the Dorset villas at Frampton and Hinton St. Mary, the latter depicting one of the earliest representations in the West of a youthful head of Christ, but associated with the Four Seasons and also, as at Lullingstone, with Bellerophon slaying the Chimera.[79] Most remarkable of all is the silver treasure from Water Newton, dating also to the mid–fourth century and containing not only the earliest-known communion chalice found in the West (see p. 553), but also small triangular plaques with leaf patterns of a type used as *ex voto* offerings in Romano-Celtic temples, but these were marked with the Chi-Rho.[80] The association of Christian and pagan is reminiscent of the art of the Roman catacombs earlier in the century. Pagan mythology was being retained but given perhaps a new Christian significance. Christ was being accepted as a new and powerful member of the Romano-Celtic pantheon.

Why was this happening at this time? Again, the historian must try to penetrate the mind of individuals whose decisions collectively made up the trend. For the urban middle classes of whom we have been speaking, we may discount rejection of the gods on economic grounds, as sometimes happened in the countryside. Part of the change was due to the Christianization of the state and the considerable zeal shown by Constantine and his sons against paganism. Some people were simply greedy for temple lands, like one landowner who turned a temple on his estate into a house for himself.[81] Other motives were more reputable. There are suggestions of the same steady penetration of the Christian message to individuals, much as Gregory the Wonderworker (Thaumaturgus) had experienced as a youth in the 220s. Sozomen tells how in Phoenicia, "prominent individuals were converted after conversations with bishops" and after signs and dreams,[82] that is, after a period of cogitation brought to a head by some event. More people had come to accept the strength of an argument used by Athanasius—that if God was all-powerful "and by nature incorporeal and invisible," it was ridiculous to "worship with honour due to God things which we see with our eyes and touch with our hands."[83] If the Word and the Creator of the universe was indeed Christ, then Christ must be the sole object of worship.

This obviously was the inspiration behind much of Christian funerary art. If one looks at the sarcophagi and catacomb paintings of the period one can see that the hope of resurrection through Christ was an abiding influence. The raising of Lazarus, prominent on a number of Roman sarcophagi, was the type of the individual's own resurrection, while the Three Holy Children symbolized his deliverance from malevolent powers. Refreshment (*refrigerium*) and peace (*pax*) anticipated a blessed life in Christ. "Januaria take thy good refreshment and make request for us,"[84] sums up the convictions of many ordinary people who were turning to Christianity at this time.

Another factor was the romance of the church's heroic past, the long-term influence of the martyrs of the previous generation. In Egypt and North Africa vivid memories of those days persisted and were turned to the benefit of the Christians.[85] Others were hastened in their decision by some apparently miraculous event. Sozomen relates how his grandfather was among the first in their village of Bethelea near Gaza to become Christian in c. 330. The village had a large temple sanctified by remote antiquity, but when his grandfather's friend Alaphion became ill, nothing that either the priests or the local Jews could do availed. Just as he was despairing of recovery, a monk named Hilarion arrived in the village and expelled the demon simply by calling on the name of Christ. Alaphion and Sozomen's grandfather were converted at once and many pagans followed their example.[86]

Superstition

Miraculous cures such as these, whether by Martin of Tours in Gaul or by monks in Syria, were among the best-documented reasons for conversion.[87] Here perhaps one puts one's finger on yet another major factor in the transition from paganism. From one end of the empire to the other, from top to bottom of society, demons with their accompaniment of magic, divination, and sorcery were feared as nothing else, and astrology was accepted as a science. Basil of Caesarea relates how (c. 375) his own town was thrown into a state of panic through the activities of those who claimed to be able to interpret dreams.[88] Use of magic was a deadly accusation to bring against one's enemies.[89] Ammianus Marcellinus tells how in Constantius's reign people who wore amulets around their necks as protection against the quartan ague might find themselves accused of necromancy.[90]

The same fate could await the unsuspecting who asked a soothsayer about a squeaking fieldmouse or a chance meeting with a weasel.[91] Denunciation and execution could follow.

The ordinary provincials, less under the eye of Paul the Chain and his companions, protected their houses against sudden disaster through the practice of both pagan and Christian rituals. One could not rely, however, on one power alone. The great number of prophylactic designs on fourth-century mosaics bear witness to an overwhelming concern felt by the inhabitants of both the eastern and western parts of the empire about the activities of malevolent spiritual powers. Few disbelieved what Augustine later called "the lying divinations" of the astrologers.[92] Many Christians would have agreed with a member of Augustine's congregation (c. 400): "To be sure, I visit the idols, I consult magicians and soothsayers, but I do not forsake the church of God. I am a Catholic Christian."[93] Centuries were to elapse before the unknown, dominated by unseen and hostile powers, would yield to the sign of the cross.

The process of change, however, was beginning. By word and deed the Christians showed that Christ was stronger than all these malevolent powers. "At the sign of the cross all magic ceases, all witchcraft is rendered void, all idols are abandoned and repudiated, all irrational desires cease, and everyone raises his eyes to heaven." Thus, Athanasius; and again, one need "only say the name of Christ, and he will see how thereby the spirits flee, augury is silent and all magic and sorcery are brought to nothing."[94] Bold claims from one who was himself believed to have used magic powers, and was once (falsely) accused of the murder of an opponent and of cutting off his hand for magical purposes!

The fear of magic and the sense of both liberation and revulsion from past servitude to demonic powers may account for the one piece of aggressive Christian propaganda against paganism that has survived from the period of Constantius II. Firmicus Maternus (*flor.* 330–50) was a Sicilian teacher of rhetoric. In Constantine's reign he wrote eight books on *Learning*—mainly horoscopes and the interpretation of prodigies. Sometime later, he became a Christian, and in his *On the Error of Profane Religions* (written c. 345–48) demanded that the emperors should cease from tolerating paganism, destroy the temples, and take over their wealth and revenues. This was as angry an antipagan rant as pagan attacks against Christianity a century before. "Pagan practices," he demanded, "must be completely excised, destroyed and corrected, Most Worshipful Emperors, by your legal pronouncements in the harshest terms, lest the dire error of pagan folly stain the Roman world any longer."[95] "Away with those temple treasures. Let the fire of your mints or the flames of your smelting works roast the gods. Transfer all the gifts to your service and control."[96] The underlying fear of the old gods was combined with Roman patriotism that looked ahead to a Christian empire. Half a century later Firmicus would not be alone in his demands. So far as melting down the temple treasures was concerned, his advice was being taken, and no doubt he was himself spending the fine Constantinian gold *solidi* and silver *siliquae* derived from this source.

Pilgrimages

What of the new Christian civilization that was replacing the traditions of the pagan world? How did it differ from what had gone before? Already, one begins to sense the arrival of new ideals, of pilgrimages, of the ascetic life, and the massive almsgiving that would characterize Christian religious life for the next thousand years. Rome and Palestine were the main centers of pilgrimage in the mid–fourth century. In Rome the pilgrims were simply continuing the tradition of visiting the tombs of the apostles established since the beginning of the third century. Rome was thronged with pilgrims making their way to these sites, around which Constantine's great basilica was rising. Ammon, Athanasius's companion in exile in 341, was proud that he had never visited the famous monuments of the past in the city but only the Martyrion of Peter and Paul.[97] Jerusalem, however, with its holy places had become the magnet, the symbol of the new Constantinian era. Eusebius describes, as early as c. 320, how crowds coming from all quarters of the earth were coming to Jerusalem and the Mount of Olives.[98] By 333 there was a pilgrim route that shepherded the traveler all the way from Bordeaux to Jerusalem. Many of those who traveled by it may have hoped to emulate the empress Helena's exploit and discover yet another relic of Christ's life. Some of the smaller towns in Palestine were quick to exploit popular credulity. The site, between Tyre and Caesarea, of the baths of the centurion Cornelius were singled out as a center where one gave alms.[99] This movement coincided with the first monastic settlements in Palestine, and from now on monks drawn from all parts of the empire would be installed in the main pilgrim sites in Palestine to serve and be served by the visitors.

Asceticism

Asceticism drew on the same sources of Christian piety as pilgrimages. In Palestine the tradition of the prophetic solitary in the wilderness had never died out. Eusebius, living in Caesarea, held up the ascetic as the representative of the true philosophical life which for him was Christianity's goal. He believed that the Therapeutae—the Jewish ascetics who had set up communes near Alexandria (circa A.D. 40), were in fact Christians, a further bizarre indication of the continuity of the ascetic tradition in the area familiar to him.[100] In many Eastern cities one might find apartments set aside in Christian houses for the practice of the ascetic life under the eye of the clergy. Eusebius's namesake, the maverick bishop of Emesa (*flor.* c. 340), who was accused in his time both of sorcery and Sabellianism, wrote eloquently about the splendors of the virgin life. He inveighed against the troubles and sorrows of matrimony, exemplified by the pains of childbirth and the nuisance of bringing up children.[101] Such views, however, were not always acceptable. A council held at Gangra in Paphlagonia about this time condemned any who lived unmarried for any reason other than the beauty and holiness of virginity.[102]

Another aspect of the strength of the attraction of asceticism in the mid–fourth century was the survival of nonorthodox sects dedicated to its practice. The Gnostics maintained small but identifiable communities within the general body of Christians in some Eastern cities, notably Edessa and Callinicum on the Euphrates frontier.[103] In the Nile Valley a thriving and literate community of "Sethites" was responsible for assembling the Coptic Gnostic texts (c. 370) that formed the Nag Hammadi library, buried not far from Pachomius's monastery at Chenoboskion north of Luxor.[104] Marcionites, too, remained a force to be reckoned with in Syria. One of the earliest-dated Christian inscriptions (found at Lebaba near Damascus), erected in 318, names Paul as "presbyter of the synagogue of the Marcionites"—a paradoxical though revealing title for a follower of Marcion a century and a half after his master's death.[105]

And behind the Gnostics and Marcionites were the Manichees, already making inroads into the Marcionite communites. They were emerging as the threat to Catholic Christianity in East and West alike. Their success shows yet again how the attraction of the ascetic ideal was penetrating all classes, from the highest officials such as Sebastianus,[106] prefect of Egypt in 356–57, to Coptic farmers, to middle class and shopkeepers alike in North Africa, including even Catholic clergy in that province.[107] Their hymns to the Virgin and to Jesus breathe hope and trust in salvation and the ideals of purity, poverty, and sacrifice.

> The poison of sin, even Mammon, I repulsed.
> I received and put on blessed poverty.
> I wavered not in going forward. I turned not
> back, though they call me pauper and stranger.[108]

> I rejoice as I ascend to my Father with whom
> I have conquered in the land of the Darkness. O my
> Great King, ferry me to the city of the gods,
> the angels. . . . The peace of the Father of
> Greatness be on you all, my brethren.[109]

> Be like a jar of wine
> Firmly set on its stand.
> Outside, it is pottery and pitch
> But inside it is fragrant wine.[110]

Refrain:
Glory and Victory to our Lord, our Light Mani.
And his holy Elect and the soul of the blessed Mary, Theona.
[*Psalm* 244]

Something of the days of persecution was being recaptured in the call to idealism, joyful service, and self-renewal. Manicheism would continue to flourish as Christianity became the religion of the state.

The Church and Society

The church had adapted itself too well to its new conditions. If one looks for fundamental social reforms resulting from its victory one will look in vain. Even in Gaul, where Christianity had come late and where one might have expected a certain level of idealism, many of its bishops were snobbish and worldly individuals. There were objections to Martin's consecration as bishop of Tours (c. 370) on the grounds of lowly birth and that he looked dirty.[111] With such leaders nothing would be done to upset the status quo. Others like Pope Damasus were wealthy men who handsomely endowed the churches they built.[112] Almsgiving was a duty inherited from an earlier age, but now in the period of Christian triumph it became systematized and helped to saturate the church with property. This in its turn discouraged the donors and recipients from questioning too closely institutions retained from pagan society. As in the third century, the church was mainly concerned with the improvement of the lot of individuals within the already-established order. The donors of churches and properties were looking to the world beyond. Constantine's law of 321 allowing unrestricted bequests to the church led lay people to bequeath part of their wealth to it as an insurance against the flames of hell. There was a certain formality about such transactions. Even Augustine would be treating almsgiving as a sort of business transaction, the transfer of capital from this unsafe world to the security of the next.[113] Some wealthy individuals gave lavishly. The exconsul Flavius Gallicanus left 869 solidi as a yearly income to the churches of Saints Peter and Paul and John the Baptist at Ostia.[114] Others less opulent would contribute a mosaic pavement to their church. In the 370s the Cappadocian fathers taught that all should leave a certain percentage of their estate to the church for the benefit of the poor. This would amount to as much as one-third, for "the poor" could be regarded as an additional heir, or even as a second "eldest son."[115] As Basil pointed out, "children who do not succeed to the estate of their fathers (through almsgiving by the latter) can often acquire wealth by their own industry, but if you abandon the care of your soul, who will have pity on you?"[116]

There was also the temptation to improve on the situation. Priests would search out rich widows and try to obtain legacies. Valentinian I, severe on clerical abuses as on all else, prohibited "ecclesiastics and ex-ecclesiastics and those who wished to be called by the name of continents [*continentes*]" from visiting widows and female wards and soliciting legacies.[117] Alongside such abuses, the church retained in Constantius's reign an enviable reputation for relieving distress, as Julian found when he tried to reorganize paganism as a "Church."[118]

There was, however, little that the church was able or willing to do to change society. Its leaders would wax eloquent and sarcastic in denouncing the worst abuses of power and wealth,[119] but its victory brought no end either to slavery or to official extortion and corruption. Naboth's vineyard might be an old story, Ambrose of Milan told his hearers, but it was being repeated every day.[120] Slavery was still accepted as an institution and justified alike from theology and reason. Few would have disagreed with the canon of the council of Gangra (c. 340): it declared anathema anyone who taught a slave under pretext of piety to despise his master and forsake his service.[121] Ordination of a slave without his master's consent was regarded as a serious matter and justified complaint even from a heretic.[122] But as in so many aspects of church life at this period one can detect signs of divergence between the thinking of Eastern and Western Christian leaders. In the East, there was a tendency, represented in Gregory of Nyssa's *On the Making of Man* (c. 380) to emphasize that human beings, "created . . . in the image of God" (Gen. 1:27) were by nature free and independent, the sovereign inhabitants of a world which God had prepared as a "royal lodging" for them.[123] Differences in status arose from the natural mutability of affairs that characterized the created order. Basil of Caesarea (c. 375) pursued a similar line of thought.[124] No one was a slave by nature, but how much better it was for those who had no natural principle of rule within themselves to serve those who had. In the fifth century, Theodoret of Cyrrhus (c. 435) defended slavery on grounds that had nothing to do with theology, namely that the master took all the risks and might face dire economic consequences through mistakes, while the slave could eat well without a care in the world.[125]

Slavery was disliked but not repudiated, but there was some room for gradual improvement in the slave's lot as one moved closer toward the divine image. Slaves, however, should not be sold.[126] There was less inclination than there was in the West—an exception being John Chrysostom— to associate slavery with the immutable penal consequence of the Fall. For Augustine, the relations between master and slave were as divinely ordained as those between husband and wife. They were part of a natural order whose disturbance was forbidden. Nothing justified a slave seeking to change his or her lot by violence.[127] Jerome would have agreed. Becoming a Christian did not excuse a slave from duties.[128] Indeed, there was now a double obligation based on religion as well as status. The Western fathers were thus impervious to ideas of social change. Radicalism henceforth would be linked to schism and heresy, and liable to religious as well as secular penalties. Even the epic martyrdoms now circulating in the West tended to emphasize the high birth and noble antecedents of the hero. Slaves such as Blandina, the heroine of Lyons, were no longer the subject of praise.[129]

A final point. Whereas in the East, church and state were increasingly integrated—with diocesan and civil boundaries coinciding—and the church was accepting the arbitration of the laity, not least of the emperor himself in its disputes, in the West the continued separation of powers inhibited the church's active concern for secular reform. Christians were still discouraged from accepting judicial and administrative appointments for fear of pollution by association with bloodshed.[130] This was of greater moment than the chance given to a Christian magistrate to temper the letter of the law and set an example of fair dealing and mercy. Thus the church failed to accept the challenge, provided by the relative security of the Constantinian age combined with its obvious injustices, to initiate reforms in society. The weight of its traditions were against any such attempt. These were reinforced by doctrinal considerations. Therefore it condescended rather than understood. Not surprisingly, the inhabitants of the countryside vastly outnumbered town dwellers and bore the main burden of the empire's needs. There Christianity took on more radical—in the West destructively unorthodox—forms.

CHRISTIANITY AND THE COUNTRYSIDE

The solid citizens of Aquileia who have left their portraits to posterity in the roundels on the mosaic floor of the city's cathedral may typify urban Christianity in the mid–fourth century, a worthy, moral, but intrinsically conservative religion.[131] Other ideas more akin to the stark imperatives of the gospels were stirring among the Christians of the North African, Egyptian, and Syrian countrysides.

The latter did not experience the same progressive decline that had befallen many of the empire's cities. Where investigations have taken place, these show a relative prosperity of villages in both halves of the Roman Empire. In Britain, the twenty years or so before the "Barbarian conspiracy" of 367 represent something of a golden age for the villa-owners of the lowland zone, and the period of maximum expansion of many of the villages in southern England and in the Fens.[132] In North Africa there were large farms owned by self-confident individuals like Constantius who proclaimed—on a mosaic in his villa at Ain Bessem (near Auzia in Mauretania Sitifensis)—that he had built baths, estate houses (*rura*), and dwellings, that he had bathed well and treasured the memory of his incomparable wife.[133] Another proprietor near Zaghouan (south of Carthage) welcomed all humans to his board, but not dogs![134]

The villages in North Africa also prospered. The olive oil they produced was being exported to Rome and elsewhere in the Mediterranean. Population was ever-increasing and occupied areas expanding.[135] But despite the security of tenure and status which tenants on imperial estates enjoyed under the provisions of the *Lex Mancia*, their lot was not as envious as it might have been. Contemporaries recognized that rural occupations were laborious and ill-rewarded.[136] The brunt of the increases in taxation that took place in Constantius's reign fell on the cultivators. Rents had to be paid and the enormous bureaucracy sustained. Good harvests were feared even more than bad, for signs of prosperity attracted the eye of venal and extortionate tax collectors.[137] Debt was an ever-present concern. The vagaries of the weather as well as human causes could put the less successful at the mercy of richer neighbors.[138]

By the mid–fourth century the North African countryside was overwhelmingly Christian. Villages in Numidia could boast as many as half a dozen chapels, often dedicated to uncanonical martyrs and displaying Donatist watchwords. Here, however, as elsewhere, the organization of the church had not kept pace with its expansion. It was still urban-based; its bishops were bishops of urban communities. The villages were not deemed worthy of a bishopric, and sometimes the bishop could not speak the language of his rural congregations. The barriers were to have far-reaching consequences. African Catholicism had little following in the countryside. Reaction to social injustices took the form of protest within the framework of Donatist Christianity,[139] unlike the peasant movement of the Bagaudae in Gaul and Spain, which had no similar known religious basis.[140]

The Circumcellions

The North African Circumcellions, and their leaders Fasir and Axido, self-styled "leaders of the saints," are described by Optatus of Milevis as emerging about 340. Milevis was on the edge of the thickly populated high plains of Numidia, and Optatus had the chance of gleaning his information at firsthand. What he says about them has attracted an enormous literature.[141] It is clear that theirs was a movement of protest reflecting a tradition of martyrdom that harked back to Maccabean examples. They were Donatists, though they despised the Donatist episcopate and the latter feared them. Indeed, alarmed at the activities of the Circumcellions in 340, the Donatists appealed to the military commander, Count Taurinus, to bring them to heel.[142] Optatus described the situation:

> For when men of this sort were, before the attainment of unity, wandering about in every place, and in their insanity called Axido and Fasir "Captains of the Saints," no man could rest secure in his possessions. Written acknowledgements of indebtedness had lost their value. At that time no creditor was free to press his claim, and all were terrified by the letters of these fellows who boasted that they were "Captains of the Saints." If there was any delay in obeying their commands, of a sudden a host of madmen flew to the place. A reign of terror was established. Creditors were hemmed in with perils, so that

they who had a right to be supplicated on account of that which was due to them, were driven through fear of death, to be themselves the humble supplaints. Very soon everyone lost what was owing to him—even to very large amounts, and held himself to have gained something in escaping from the violence of these men.

Even journeys could not be made with perfect safety, for masters were often thrown out of their own chariots and forced to run, in servile fashion, in front of their own slaves, seated in their lord's place. By the judgement and command of these outlaws, the condition of masters and slaves was completely reversed.[143]

The text leaves no doubt regarding the connection between the extreme wing of the Donatist movement and forces of economic and social discontent. The activities of the Devil, long identified with persecuting Roman authorities, were now extended in the minds of these latter-day "Champions" (*Agonistici*) to include other oppressors, the landowners, creditors, and indeed the possessing classes as a whole. We see also how the basic grievance was agrarian debt and its consequences of forced sales, destitution, and even slavery. In response, Axido and Fasir were social revolutionaries, but would no doubt have justified their actions from the Old Testament. "Captains of the Saints" would recall Gideon's small force of three hundred (Judg. 7:1–22) and other heroic examples drawn from Israel's history. And though the Circumcellions recruited their strength from the local populations that crowded into the traditional markets (*nundinae*), they also had a religious aim whence they got their name. In the 380s the Donatist writer Tyconius characterized them as "superstitious folk" who spent their time visiting the tombs of martyrs for, as they believed, the salvation of their souls.[144] They also gained their supplies from the chapels (*circum cellas vagantur*) dedicated to the martyrs. In more than one central Numidian chapel a silo for storing grain has been found in a small chamber adjoining the apse or in a suite of rooms associated with the church itself.[145]

The Circumcellions were the first Christian group to aim openly at the overthrow of the existing social order and a complete reversal of its values. Even the Jewish Zealots with whom they might be compared seem only to have included despoliation of the rich among their proclaimed ideals under the stress of the revolt of 66. They point the way to other agrarian-biblical movements in Western Europe in the Middle Ages, to the ideas behind the Peasants' Revolt in England in 1381 and the Peasant Rising in Germany in 1524.

From the Byzantine historian Zosimus (c. 450), one learns that over-taxation was a prime cause of the native revolt led by the Kabyle chieftain Firmus in 372.[146] The rising seems to have attracted some Donatist support.[147] Donatism, too, preserved latent inflammatory views concerning relations between church and state. When in 347 the emperor Constans determined to rid himself of Donatus and exiled him to Gaul, the Donatist

573

pamphleteers in Carthage assailed his government in unmeasured terms. The emperor's commissioners, Paul and Macarius, were "forerunners of Antichrist," and Constans's court was described as "an abode of Satan."[148] On the other hand, to the Catholics the emperor was "most religious," his emissaries "the servants of God," and Macarius himself as good as his name, "Blessed."[149] Fires of hatred against the state needed only to be stirred into life. These feelings united the Circumcellions and the Donatists in Carthage.

In the last resort, however, the fury of the Circumcellions was directed less against the Roman Empire as a political institution than against "the world" (*saeculum*) dominated by Satan, of which the empire was the visible representative. They would have regarded their aims as religious. Not even Augustine denied the title of "nun" (*sanctimonialis*) to the women who accompanied the Circumcellion bands. Their personal goal was martyrdom, attained by uncompromising opposition to all aspects of contemporary life that could be associated with Satan's kingdom and its allies, the pagans and Catholics. Their opponents, whether wealthy citizens or magistrates, might be ambushed and confronted with the choice of acting as their executioners or being killed themselves.[150] At the bottom of the steep cliffs at Nif-en Nisr in central Numidia was found a large number of loose stones and rocks each marked with a name, a date, and the word *nat[alis]*, that is, "anniversary," or *r* (= *redditio* or "rendering" of the soul). A Circumcellion unable to find martyrdom had taken a short cut by throwing himself down to certain death[151]—a mute testimony to the fanaticism that gripped religious life in North Africa during the fourth century.

The Monks

Monasticism in the East was also born out of a combination of religious and social causes.[152] Yet the monks were not Circumcellions, and the monastic movement provided an example of nonrevolutionary reform, the byproduct of its primary aim of personal salvation which the West eventually followed.

Antony's monks at the turn of the fourth century had taken on themselves the "whole yoke of the Lord." They had gone out to fight the demons that were thought to have infested the deserts, and they were joined by many a small landholder who had thrown up his farm as a hopeless proposition, and even by fugitives from justice. In the 350s, Athanasius described Antony's community as one in "which was heard neither the evil-doer, nor he who had been wronged [by the magistrates] nor the reproaches of the tax-gatherer."[153] Egypt and Syria were experiencing much the same conditions as prevailed in North Africa.

Both territories had a large class of peasant proprietors.[154] In parts of Syria also, the fourth, fifth, and sixth centuries saw a steady increase in the area of land utilized and the population maintained by it. As in North

Africa, economic expansion was based on olive plantations, particularly in the area of Antioch itself and in the limestone hills east of the city. These were also areas of large villages rather than towns,[155] and there, as in North Africa, if left to themselves the villagers would have been reasonably well off. However, increasing taxation, in Egypt especially, supplemented by extortion and the violence of the soldiers, forced many individuals out of their holdings and communities to seek the protection of a powerful patron, to whom they risked becoming virtual serfs.[156] In Syria between 370 and 440, Libanius on the one hand, and John Chrysostom and Theodoret on the other spoke in stark terms of the conditions endured by the farming population. An urban patron of a Syrian village was no more kindly disposed toward the inhabitants than his Egyptian counterpart. Peasants were driven into flight from chronic debt due to excessive rates of interest and taxation. Their animals were seized for public transport, they were oppressed by billeting and requisitioning officers.[157] John Chrysostom (c. 380) described how "landowners were more cruel than the barbarians because they imposed intolerable and unending taxes and corvées on the working population on their lands."[158] Yet there was a basic prosperity. The peasants did well out of trading in Antioch. They preferred cash for their wares. Other areas—Syria and Palestine—were beginning to flourish in a way which in the sixth century would make them the most prosperous areas of the eastern Roman Empire.

Similar conditions had turned many a Numidian peasant into a Circumcellion, and yet, socially aware and intellectually vigorous though the monks often were, they never advocated violent opposition to the authorities. Partly this may have been due to the tact of the emperors themselves. Both Constantine and Constantius were assiduous in their attention to Antony and other ascetics, and they reciprocated.[159] The monks were regarded as individuals able to work miracles; they had contact with the divine powers who could interpret their will. Hence Antony spent much time forwarding petitions to officials and to the emperor himself, sure that they would receive favorable response.[160] A bond of respect and loyalty was established, which was completely lacking in North Africa between the Circumcellions and the administration.[161] Second, the existence of demons was taken literally and these could be held responsible for social and economic ills, while martyrdom, the prize of the Circumcellion's fortitude, was regarded as a figurative goal to be accepted "in intention" by the monks fighting spiritual rather than temporal foes.[162] No scorn sufficed for pagans and Arian heretics and contact with Meletian spiritual ascetics (anchorites) was avoided,[163] but the monks followed the tradition of the Egyptian and Syrian bishops, of loyalty to the imperial house. Indeed, grumbling against any form of authority was discouraged. Orthodoxy was upheld at all times. In the *Sayings of the Fathers*, it is related of the abbot Sisoe, "that at one time there came certain Arians to him and they began to speak ill of the orthodox, but the old man kept silence. Then calling a disciple, Abraham, he said, 'Bring me a book of the holy Athanasius and read.' The heretics were silent and then acknowledged their faults and Sisoe sent them away in peace.''[164] Loyalty, above all to Athanasius and his memory, silent dignity, and complete assurance of their position and way of life made the Coptic monks a formidable influence in the eastern Roman Empire.

In the Nile Delta and southwest of Alexandria (Wadi Natrun), Antony had many imitators. Amoun was a Coptic and close friend. In c. 325, he left his wife, with whom he had been living in celibate union for the previous eighteen years, to establish a monastic settlement in the mountainous area of the Wadi Natrun. The enormous popularity of this movement is indicated by the fact that within a few years the settlement had expanded to five thousand monks, each living in his own cell. Amoun's wife established a convent for women.[165] Like Antony, Amoun was conspicuously faithful to Athanasius and was one of the "fathers" with whom the latter corresponded. His monasteries also accepted an element of clerical and episcopal control. The monks would assemble for services on Saturdays and Sundays and they would be attended by eight priests under the authority of the bishop of Hermopolis. Even so there was no set form of discipline, except that it was severe. Work was certainly part of the monk's vocation, but each wrestled with the powers of evil as he thought best. A novice would learn ascetic practices from a "master." It was in these monasteries that the fantastic feats of asceticism took place, to be recorded with piety and awe by Palladius (367–c. 430), who spent eleven years in Egypt (c. 387–98). We hear, for instance, of Macarius, a townsman from Alexandria, who attempted to stay awake for twenty consecutive days, restricted his diet to cabbage leaves, and strove to stand upright throughout the whole of Lent; or Pachon who sought in vain to be eaten by the hyenas and other wild animals who shared his cave, in order to banish his bodily passions.[166]

In Upper Egypt meanwhile, monasticism was taking an entirely different form. Pachom (or Pachomius, c. 290–346), after his conversion to Christianity (c. 314), tried and failed to find peace in a solitary life under a master. He believed rather that people were made to live in society, and far from throwing up the ascetic's calling in despair, he was determined to make it a community activity. In c. 323 he moved to Tabennisi, south of Lycopolis on the east bank of the Nile. There he dreamed that he had been commanded by the Lord to "Stay here and build a monastery and many will come to you in order to become monks." He obeyed and began to gather around himself monks to form his first community.[167] He organized it along the quasi-military lines he had learned as a soldier in Licinius's army. His monks would associate in prayer and in work, which was to be useful and not merely as a penance. Jerome, who was well informed about the Pachomian houses, described how "Brethren of the same trades are

576

lodged together in one house under one superior. For example, weavers are together; mat-makers are reckoned as one household—each trade is under the several rule of its own superior. And, week by week, an account of their work is rendered to the abbot [*Patrem*] of the monastery.''[168] Excesses of fasting were discouraged. Everyone had one meal a day, though this might be postponed until evening for the particularly zealous. Prayers were to be said twelve times a day and the same number of prayers to be said each night. The Eucharist was administered by clergy twice a week. Pachomius himself, after resisting Athanasius's first attempt to persuade him to receive priest's orders, eventually it seems, accepted.

Discipline was strict. Each monk would be clothed in uniform dress—a brown habit with a hood, a sleeveless tunic, a mantle of goatskin, a girdle—and would have a stick. He would be under a superior who supervised his trade, who in turn took his instructions from the father of the monastery, who himself was subject to the supreme authority of Pachomius himself, and after his death (in May 346), that of his successor, Theodore.[169] Pachomius's movement, like Antony's, was enormously successful. When he died, there were already nine monasteries housing several hundred monks, and two nunneries.[170] Each Easter and on 13 August ("Founders' Day"?), there would be a general assembly of the monks at the original house at Tabennisi. In Jerome's day (c. 390), nearly fifty thousand monks would congregate to celebrate Easter.[171] Pachomius also was entirely loyal to Athanasius, and it was among his monasteries that the latter found refuge after his flight from Alexandria in 356.

Antony and Pachomius between them outbid the Meletians for the support of the Egyptian peasants (and, we may suspect, the Manichee missionaries also). They shared with Athanasius himself the credit for uniting Alexandrian and Egyptian Christianity under the leadership of the patriarch of Alexandria. Coptic and Alexandrian worked together.[172] This was a rare, if not a unique, partnership in the ancient world between the civilization of the conquerors, the Alexandrians, and a subject people. More remarkable, it accompanied a resurgence of the cultural identity of the latter. Coptic was the language of the great majority of the monks, as Christianity was their religion. Greek-speakers were few and far between. By the mid–fourth century Coptic had become a vehicle of composition as well as of translation, and more than that, it was the language of the monks' rivals, the Gnostics and the Manichees. The Nag Hammadi documents, copied c. 360–70, were written in the finest Coptic hand for a "Sethite" (Valentinian?) congregation who could read them.[173] While the new Coptic Christian era began with the Era of the Martyrs (that is, the accession of Diocletian in 284), hostility toward Greek-speaking landowners was reserved for pagans. The works of Clement and Origen, as forerunners of the monastic movement, were to be found in many an anchorite's library.[174] The diplomatic skills of the emperor, his advisers, and the Alexandrian episcopate are never shown to better advantage than in their dealings with the Egyptian monks.

SYRIAN AND MESOPOTAMIAN MONASTICISM

We are less well informed about the progress of Syrian and Mesopotamian monasticism, to a large extent an independent growth. One important piece of evidence is preserved in Eusebius's account of Bishop Narcissus of Jerusalem who "spent many years secretly in deserts and obscure parts of the country," c. 220.[175] He could hardly have been alone in this. Sozomen retains a tradition that Aones, a Syrian, introduced anchoritism into Syria in the same way as Antony had introduced it into Egypt.[176] We gain the impression, however, that Syrian monasticism was, if anything, even more exacting and individualistic than its Egyptian counterpart. Sozomen also refers to a certain Julian near Edessa, who was so rigid in his austerities that "he was said to live as if he were incorporeal, for he seemed to be freed from the flesh and to possess nothing but skin and bone."[177] He had many imitators. There were Boskoi monks,[178] those who grazed grass like animals, or burdened themselves with iron collars and heavy chains. On the fringes of orthodoxy, too, was growing up a great variety of ascetic cults—Audians (rigorists), Messalians (men of prayer), and Encratites of various types. Others, however, combined their asceticism with hard productive labor, people like Serenus who could claim, "All my life I have been sowing, reaping and making baskets."[179] Simeon Stylites, on the other hand, explained his leg chain by affirming that it kept him from wandering and his mind fixed undeviatingly on heaven.[180] True to the Greek tradition of allegorical interpretation, Meletius of Antioch considered that the iron was superfluous and might be taken symbolically.[181]

As in Egypt, Syrian monasticism grew in popularity through the reign of Constantius II. Like its neighbor, it also expressed an emergent non-Hellenic culture, not explicitly anti-Hellenic, but nonetheless signaling the end of the long Greek predominance in the religion and cultural life of Syria and Mesopotamia. The Syrian monks represented also a spirit of reform and a readiness to rebuke the rich on the basis of apt scriptural text.[182] Their work was accompanied by another sign of the times, namely the Syrian-Christian poetry of Ephraem Syrus (d. 373). Ephraem was a native of Nisibis and devoted to his native city. He was an ascetic, "a Son of the Covenant," and a teacher of some of the celebrated Syrian ascetics of the mid–fourth century.[183] But his greatest achievement lay in his verses—partly religious, partly patriotic—singing of the valiant defense of Nisibis against the Persians, lamenting losses and celebrating victories. His Christianity, deeply rooted in the Jewish-Christian tradition that had produced the *Gospel of Thomas*, was expressed in symbols and in the language of mysticism.[184] From this time on, the native-speaking Syrians of the north and east of the province and eastward in Mesopotamia possessed an enhanced identity through a Christianity distinct from that of the Greek cities of Syria.

The monks in Egypt and Syria represent the most important single change in society in the reign of Constantius II. Theirs was an entirely new approach to religion and a new way of life. Pachomius's monasteries were in themselves a new form of village community. Christianity had now a rural as well as an urban base and interpretation. The Byzantine world was never again to be without its "holy men," either exercising miraculous powers individually as in Syria during the fifth and sixth centuries, or living in great colonies such as grew out of the Pachomian settlements. The West was to be less fortunate. There were false starts, such as that initiated by Priscillian in the 380s, and in the next century even Sozomen was to declare that though there were individuals in the West devoted to "philosophy" (monasticism), there were no monks as he knew them in the East.[185] He was mistaken, for the colonies at Lérins had been in existence for thirty years when he wrote, but a long time was to elapse before the age of Benedict and by that time much of Italy was ceasing to belong to the "Roman World."

BIBLIOGRAPHY

NOTE

There is no single study to guide the reader through this period of great importance in European history. P. R. L. Brown's *The World of Late Antiquity* (New York: Harcourt Brace Jovanovich; London: Thames & Hudson, 1971), chaps. 3–5, is an excellent introduction, vividly written and based on a wealth of knowledge. Those who would probe further would be well advised to start with Sozomen's brief account, in his *Ecclesiastical History*, of how the Constantinian revolution may have been carried out, and work their way through the evidence from there. The books and articles I have consulted are listed herein.

Monasticism, on the other hand, has attracted a wealth of modern literature. Hans Lietzmann's final chapter in his *The Era of the Church Fathers*, vol. 4 of *A History of the Early Church*, Eng. trans. B. L. Woolf (New York: World Publishing, Meridian Books, 1961; London: Lutterworth Press, 1962), remains preeminent, and there is also P. de Labriolle's "Les Débuts du Monachisme," chap. 1, pp. 299–348, of *De la paix constantinienne à la mort de Théodose*, ed. Labriolle, G. Bardy, and J. R. Palanque, in vol. 3 of Fliche and Martin, eds., *Histoire de l'église depuis les origines jusqu'à nos jours* (Paris: Bloud et Gay, 1936), a particularly valuable chronology and references.

For the Donatists the present writer's *Donatist Church* may prove useful.

SOURCES

a. On the Circumcellions

Optatus. *De Schismate Donatistarum.* Edited by Ziwsa. III.4.
Augustine *Letters* 35, 88, 105, 108, 111, and 185, and in his anti-Donatist writings
  especially: *Contra epistolam Parmeniani* (*Against the Epistle of Parmenianus*)
  I.10.16, *Contra Gaudentium Donatistarum episcopum* (*Against Gaudentius, Bishop of the Donatists*) I.28.32, and *Enarrationes in Psalmos* 10 and 132. *Letter*

579

185 (to Count Boniface) is translated in *The Anti-Donatist Writings of St. Augustine,* by Rev. Marcus Dods, Edinburgh: T. & T. Clark, 1872.
Tyconius, *Tyconius-Studien,* ed. T. Hahn, Leipzig, 1900, p. 68.
Codex Theodosianus XVI.5.52 (30 January 412).

b. On Early Monasticism

Apophthegmata Patrum, PG 65; Latin text *PL* 73; Eng. trans. Owen Chadwick in *Western Asceticism,* LCC XII, Philadelphia: Westminster Press; London: SCM Press, 1958.
Palladius, *Historia Lausiaca;* C. Butler, ed., *The Lausiac History of Palladius,* 2 vols., Cambridge Texts and Studies vol. 6, nos. 1 & 2, Cambridge: Cambridge University Press, 1898–1904; see also *Lausiac History,* Eng. trans. W. K. Lowther Clarke, Translations of Christian Literature, series 1: Greek Texts. New York: Macmillan Co.; London: SPCK, 1918.
John Cassian, *Collationes Patrum (The Conferences), PL* 49; Eng. trans. NPNF, *Cassian.*
Athanasius, *Vita Antonii (Life of Antony), PG* 26.838–976; Eng. trans. NPNF, *Athanasius.*
Sozomen *Ecclesiastical History* I.13 and III.14.
Socrates *Ecclesiastical History* I.11 and 13 and IV.23.

c. On Manicheism

Allberry, C. R. C. *A Manichaean Psalm Book (Manichean Manuscripts in the Chester Beatty Collection).* Part II. Stuttgart 1938.
Adam, Alfred. *Texte zum Manichäismus,* KIT 175 (Berlin: Walter de Gruyter, 1954). Chap. 4.

SECONDARY WORKS

Amand de Mendieta, D. "La virginité chez Eusèbe d'Emèse et l'ascéticisme familial dans la première moitié du ive siècle." *RHE* 50.4 (1955): 777–820.
Berthier, A., Martin, M., and Logeart, F. *Les vestiges du christianisme antique dans la Numidie centrale.* Algiers: Gouvernement Général de l'Algérie, Direction des Antiquités, 1942.
Brisson, J. P. *Autonomisme et Christianisme dans l'Afrique romaine de Septime Sévère à l'invasion vandale.* Paris: Boccard, 1958. Chap. 4, "L'Impatience populaire."
Brown, P. R. L. "The Rise and Function of the Holy Man in Late Antiquity." *JRS* 61 (1971): 80–101.
Brusin, G., and Zovatto, P. L. *Monumenti paleo-cristiani di Aquileia e di Grado.* Udine, 1957.
Dagens, C. "Autour du Pape Libère, l'iconographie de Suzanne et les martyrs romains sur l'arcosolium de Celerina." *Mélanges* 78.2 (1966): 327–81.
Diesner, H. J. "Methodisches und sachliches zum Circumcellionentum." In *Kirche und Staat im spätromischen Reich,* pp. 33–77. Berlin, 1963.
Frend, W. H. C. "Circumcellions and Monks." *JTS* n.s. 20 (October 1969): 542–49.
———. "The Revival of Berber Art." *Antiquity* 15 (1942): 342–52.

Frere, S. S. "The Silchester Church: The Excavation by Sir Ian Richmond in 1961." *Archaeologia* 105 (1975): 277–302.

Grant, R. M. *Early Christianity and Society*. New York: Harper & Row, 1977.

Heussi, K. *Der Ursprung des Mönchtums*. Tübingen: J. C. B. Mohr (Paul Siebeck), 1934.

Judge, E. A. "The Earliest Use of Monachos for 'Monk' (P. Coll. Youtie 77) and the Origins of Monasticism." *JAC* 20 (1977): 72–89.

Lassus, J. "Edifices du culte autour de la basilique." *ACIAC* 1962 (Rome, 1965): 581–610.

Lepelley, C. "Les limites de la christianisation de l'état romain sous Constantin et ses successeurs." In *Christianisme et pouvoirs politiques*, pp. 23–41. Etudes d'Histoire religieuse. Lille: Editions universitaires, 1973.

Leschi, L. "A propos des épitaphes chrétiennes du Djebel Nif en Nisr." *Revue Africaine* 84 (1940): 30–35.

Liebeschuetz, W. "Epigraphic Evidence on the Christianisation of Syria." *Akten des XI internat. Limes Congresses*, pp. 485–505. Budapest: Hungarian Academy of Sciences, 1978.

MacMullen, R. "Social History in Astrology." *Ancient Society* 2 (1971): 105–16.

Marec, E. *Monuments chrétiens d'Hippone*. Paris: Ministère de l'Algèrie, Sous-direction des Beaux Arts, 1958.

Markus, R. A. "Paganism, Christianity and the Latin Classics in the Fourth Century." In *Latin Literature of the Fourth Century*, J. W. Binns, pp. 1–21. Boston and London: Routledge & Kegan Paul, 1974.

Marrou, H. I. "Culture, civilisation, décadence." In *Christiana Tempora*, pp. 3–30. Collection de l'Ecole française de Rome 35. Rome, 1978.

Mazzarino, S. *The End of the Ancient World*. Eng. trans. G. Holmes. London: Faber & Faber, 1966.

Meates, E. W. *Lullingstone Roman Villa*. London: William Heinemann, 1955.

Murray, R. *Symbols of Church and Kingdom*. New York and Cambridge: Cambridge University Press, 1975.

Painter, K. S. *The Water Newton Early Christian Silver*. London: British Museum, 1977.

Poirier, M. "Christus pauper factus est chez S. Ambroise." *RSLR* 15 (1979): 250–57.

Rousselle, A. "Du sanctuaire au thaumaturge, la guérison en Gaule au ive siecle." *Annales: Économies, Sociétés, Civilisations* 6 (1976): 1085–1107.

Simon, M. "Un document du syncrétisme religieux dans l'Afrique romaine." *CRAIBL* (1978): 501–25.

Tengström, E. *Donatisten und Katholiken: Soziale, wirtschaftliche und politische Aspekte einer nordafrikanischen Kirchenspaltung*. Göteborg: Acta Universitatis Gothoburgensis, 1964.

Toynbee, J. M. C. "A New Roman Mosaic Pavement Found in Dorset." *JRS* 54 (1964): 7–14.

Viner, J. *Religious Thought and Economic Society: Four Chapters of an Unfinished Work*. Edited by J. Melitz and D. Winch, chap. 1. Durham, N.C.: Duke University Press, 1978.

Vööbus, A. *A History of Asceticism in the Syrian Orient*. CSCO Subsidia 14 and 17. Louvain, 1958, 1960.

Zulueta, E. de. "De Patrociniis Vicorum, a Commentary on Codex Theodosianus, XI.24.1–6 (360–415)." In *Oxford Studies in Social and Legal History,* ed. P. Vinogradoff. Oxford, 1909.

Symposium: *Transformation et conflits au ive siècle ap. J. C.* (Colloque organisé par la Fédération internationale des Etudes Classique, Bordeaux 7–12 septembre 1970). Bonn: Rudolf Habelt, 1978.

NOTES

1. Sozomen *Ecclesiastical History* II.5.5, ed. J. Bidez and G. C. Hansen, GCS 50 (Berlin: Akademie-Verlag, 1960), p. 56. Compare Eusebius *Constantine* III.54–56. Jerome *Chronicle* year 331 attributes an edict to Constantine ordering the destruction of temples. Repeated by Theophanes, *Theophanis Chronographia,* ed. C. de Boor, 2 vols. (Leipzig, 1883, 1885; reprint ed., Hildesheim, 1963), p. 28, who makes the point that "their revenues were given to the churches of God." See also Harry Turtledove, Eng. trans., *The Chronicle of Theophanes: An English Translation of Anni Mundi 6095–6305 (A.D. 602–813),* (Philadelphia: University of Pennsylvania Press, 1982).

2. Sozomen *Ecclesiastical History* II.5.6.

3. Ambrose *Letter* XVII.

4. *CIL* VI.102, recording how Vettius Agorius Praetextatus, prefect of the city, restored and rededicated the "portus deorum consentium" in the Forum and demolished private buildings erected against the walls of temples. See G. Fowden, "Bishops and Temples in the Eastern Roman Empire A.D. 320–435," *JTS* n.s. 29 (April 1978): 53–78, esp. pp. 62–63.

5. Ammianus Marcellinus, XVI.10.17, ed. and Eng. trans. J. C. Rolfe, 3 vols., LCL (Cambridge, Mass.: Harvard University Press; London: William Heinemann, 1935–40).

6. See Brown, *Late Antiquity,* pp. 34ff.

7. See Lepelley, "Les limites de la christianisation," pp. 25–41.

8. Ambrosiaster (c. 380), "Here in the city of Rome, which is called 'most holy,' women are permitted to dismiss their husbands," *Quaestiones Veteris et Novi Testamenti* CXIV.16, ed. A. Souter, CSEL 50 (Vienna, 1908), p. 323. See also Mazzarino's essay, "Marriage in Late Roman Society," in *End of Ancient World,* pp. 120–36, and Jerome's protest that this was an issue on which the laws of Papinian said one thing, the laws of Paul another (*Letter* 77.2).

9. Ammianus XXIX.3.9. The bears were called "Goldflake" and "Innocence."

10. *Repertorium der christlich-antiken Sarkophage* 1 (*Rom u. Ostia*), ed. F. W. Deichmann/G. Bovini/H. Brandenburg (Wiesbaden: Deutsch. archeolog. Institut, 1967), Nr. 680. For Bassus's career, see A. H. M. Jones et al., *The Prosopography of the Later Roman Empire,* vol. 1, A.D. 260–395 (New York and Cambridge: Cambridge University Press, 1971), Bassus 15; and for an important short study on this and other fourth-century Christian sarcophagi from Rome, see W. Wischmeyer, *Die Tafeldeckel der christlichen Sarkophage konstantinischen Zeit in Rom, RQ* Supp. 40 (Freiburg: Herder, 1982), pp. 126, 163–77.

11. See J. W. Salomonson, "Iconographie chrétienne et tradition artisanale," paper delivered at Warsaw, *CIHEC* Colloquium, June 1978; forthcoming.

12. See the present author's "The Church of the Roman Empire 313–600," in *The Layman in Christian History*, ed. S. C. Neill and H.-R. Weber, pp. 57–87 (Philadelphia: Westminster Press; London: SCM Press, 1963).

13. Eusebius *Constantine* IV.2 and 3; and *Codex Theodosianus* I.16.7 of 331 (rage against rapacious officials); criticized c. 365–70 in *De Rebus Bellicis. A Roman Reformer and Inventor*, Eng. trans. and ed. E. A. Thompson (New York and London: Oxford University Press, 1952), II.1–5; and Ammianus XVI.8.12.

14. Ammianus XXVII.11.1 (ed. Rolfe, vol. 3, pp. 72–75); and Probus seems to have been a reasonably honest man! (ibid., 11.4). For his career and his Christianity, see Jones et al., *Prosopography*, vol. 1, pp. 736–40.

15. *De Rebus Bellicis* II (ed. Thompson, p. 94).

16. Firmicus Maternus *Matheseos libri VIII (Learning)* IV.14.2. See MacMullen, "Social History in Astrology," p. 115.

17. Thus, Flavius Philippus, praetorian prefect of the East, 344–45 (consul in 348), who owed his promotion to court eunuchs (Libanius *Oration* LXXII.11), though Constantius also felt great admiration for his abilities. See L. J. Swift and J. H. Oliver, "Constantius II on Flavius Philippus," *AJP* 83 (1962): 247–64. For other examples of promotions up the social scale to high official positions, see Libanius *Oration* XLII; and recorded by A. H. M. Jones, *Later Roman Empire*, p. 546, compare above, chap. 15 n. 51.

18. For the most friendly account of Aetius's rise from abject poverty to relative affluence, see Philostorgius *Ecclesiastical History* III.15 and compare with the hostile version of Gregory of Nyssa *Adversus Eunomium (Against Eunomius)* I.6 (*PG* 45.260C). He owed some of his success to his victory in a debate with the Alexandrian Manichee leader, Aphthonius.

19. Ammianus XXI.16.17. Also Aurelius Victor *Caesares* XL, "the good old days of Diocletian."

20. Augustine *Confessions* VI.10.16.

21. Ammianus XV.11.12.

22. Libanius, *Antiochikos = Oration* XI, ed. R. Foerster, 12 vols. (1909–27), vol. 1, p. 504. See A. J. Festugière, *Antioche païenne et chrétienne*, Bibliothèque des écoles françaises d'Athènes et de Rome 194 (Paris, 1959), pp. 23–37.

23. See below, p. 598.

24. *Peregrinatio Etheriae* XIX. See John Wilkinson, ed. and Eng. trans., *Egeria's Travels* (London: SPCK, 1971), pp. 115–16.

25. Ammianus XXII.9.4 (Nicomedia). Ibid., XXX.5.2 (Carnuntum, "now deserted and in ruins").

26. Thus the *Codex Theodosianus* on the Decurions in this period, XII.1.22 ("cum decuriones ad diversas militias confugiant"), 31, 37, 38, 42, and 45; XVI.2.19. See S. Dill, *Roman Society in the Last Century of the Western Empire*, new ed., rev. and enl. (New York: Macmillan Co., 1906), pp. 249–81.

27. For a convenient summary and discussion of the Album of Timgad, see B. H. Warmington, *The North African Provinces from Diocletian to the Vandal Conquest* (New York and Cambridge: Cambridge University Press, 1954), pp. 41–45, and for city elites indicated by phrases such as "dulcissimus concivis" (Augustine *Letter* 84.1), see P. R. L. Brown, *Augustine of Hippo: A Biography* (Berkeley and Los Angeles: University of California Press; London: Faber & Faber, 1967), p. 32.

28. Eusebius *Constantine* III.50.

29. Socrates *Ecclesiastical History* II.8. The church had been begun by Constantine in 327 (or 332). See Athanasius, *Apologia ad Constantium imperatorem (Defense Addressed to Constantius)* XV, *PG* 25.613B (great crowds on Feast Days), and similarly at Trier. For Bishop Fortunatianus's activity as a builder, see H. Leclercq, "Aquilée," *DACL* I.2, col. 2661. His church was described as a "magnificum templum." See N. Duval, P. A. Février, and J. Lassus, "Groupes épiscopaux de Syrie et d'Afrique du Nord," *Colloque d'Apamée de Syrie* (Brussels, 1972), pp. 215–51.

30. Lassus, "Edifices."

31. See Frend, *Donatist Church,* p. 305.

32. On Djemila, see Mme. Y. Allais's description in *Djemila* (Paris: Société d'Edition "Les Belles-Lettres," 1938); and P.A. Février, *Djemila* (Algiers: Ministère de l'Information et de la Culture, 1971). On Timgad, P. Monceaux, *Timgad chrétien* (Paris, 1911), p. 22. On the Donatist character of the "monastery," see E. Albertini, *CRAIBL* (1939): 100, and H. I. Marrou, "Sur une inscription concernant Optat de Timgad," *Christiana Tempora,* Collection de l'ecole française de Rome 35 (Rome: Palais Farnese, 1978), pp. 145–48.

33. See J. Lassus's introduction to Erwin Marec's *Monuments chrétiens d'Hippone,* pp. 6–7.

34. See above, p. 459.

35. Augustine *Letters* 126–27.

36. Augustine *Letter* XXXIV.6, "sermone impolitum."

37. See above, p. 408.

38. See the survey, culled mainly from Augustinian texts and inscriptions, of North African liturgical texts assembled by H. Leclercq, "Afrique" (liturgie postnicéenne de l') *DACL* I.1, pp. 620–38.

39. Optatus *De Schismate Donatistarum* VI.1.

40. See H. Leclercq, "Agape," *DACL* I, pp. 823–36 (African inscriptions).

41. *De civitate Dei (City of God)* II.28, "churches . . . where a seemly separation of the sexes is observed."

42. Augustine *Letter* LV.15, "Stantes oramus quod est signum resurrectionis."

43. A mosaic from Thabarka, also in the Bardo, shows the plan of a church excellently. The altar, on which candlesticks are set, is far down the nave. See Mohamed Yacoub, *Le Musée de Bardo* (Tunis: Ministère des affaires culturelles, 1970), p. 143 fig. 18. For the celebration of the Eucharist, see the survey of the evidence by Leclercq, "Africa," pp. 630–38.

44. As at Silchester, see Frere, "Silchester Church"; useful references. The *piscina* may have been used for some form of ritual ablution (p. 296, citing an example at Tyre quoted by Eusebius of Caesarea in *HE* X.4.39–40, c. 315); no one to pass within the gates of the church "with unhallowed and unwashen feet."

45. John Chrysostom, *Homily on the Gospel of St. John* XVIII.4, *PG* 59.120; cf. Jerome *Letter* LII.8; and Augustine *Tractatus in Joannis evangelium (Homilies on the Gospel of John)* XLV.13, *PL* 35.1725.

46. Egeria, *Peregrinatio Etheriae,* XXV.1, ed. P. Geyer, *CSEL* 39 (Leipzig: G. Freytag, 1898), p. 74.

47. *Peregrinatio Etheriae* XXXVI.5, trans. Wilkinson, *Egeria's Travels,* p. 136.

48. Athanasius *De Incarnatione* XLIX, in R. W. Thomson, ed., *Contra Gentes and De Incarnatione* (New York and London: Oxford University Press, 1971).

49. *Peregrinatio Etheriae* XLVII.3. The bishop of Jerusalem's attitude was "licet siriste noverit, tamen semper graece loquitur."

50. See Frend, "Revival of Berber Art."

51. H. I. Marrou's view, *History of Education in Antiquity,* Eng. trans. G. Lamb (New York and London: Sheed & Ward, 1956), p. 296.

52. *Ecclesiastical History* II.5.6–9 (ed. Bidez and Hansen, pp. 57–58).

53. See Lepelley, "Les limites de la christianisation," p. 35, and see below, p. 600.

54. *Tractatus super Psalmos* (*Homilies on the Psalms*) LXVII.20, ed. A. Zingerle, CSEL 22 (Vienna, 1891), p. 215.

55. See above, p. 505.

56. See J. M. Whittaker, "Coins and Christian Symbolism," *Spinks Numismatic Circular* 87 (January 1979): 3–4; and P. V. Hill, J. P. C. Kent, and R. A. G. Carson, *Late Roman Bronze Coinage,* A.D. 324–498 (London: Spink & Son, 1960), p. 41 and pl. III.19.

57. For Magnentius's religious outlook, see J. Ziegler, *Zur religiösen Haltung der Gegenkaiser in 4 Jhr n. Chr.* = Fas Hefte 4 (Frankfurt, 1970), p. 64. The coinage of Vetranio with the *labarum* and legend HOC SIGNO VICTOR ERIS is also of the highest interest in demonstrating the power of the Christian appeal at this time (A.D. 350).

58. *De incarnatione* (*Concerning the Incarnation*) XLIX.

59. See above, p. 313.

60. Augustine *Confessions* II.4.8; see Brown, *Augustine of Hippo,* pp. 30–31. Another example may be that of Basil of Caesarea's friend, Palladius, though Palladius may have been a catechumen when he married; Basil *Letter* 292; and see R. J. Deferrari's (ed. and Eng. trans.) note, Basil, *Letters,* 4 vols., LCL (Cambridge, Mass.: Harvard University Press; London: William Heinemann, 1926–34), vol. 4, pp. 206–7.

61. J. M. Rouquette, "Trois nouveaux sarcophages chrétiens de Trinquetaille (Arles)," *CRAIBL* (1974): 254–277, pl. 1 and pp. 257–63.

62. Stevenson, *Catacombs,* p. 142.

63. Theodoret *Ecclesiastical History* II.17; Felix was regarded as too favorable toward Arianism.

64. See Dagens's interesting study, "Autour du Pape Libère." We know of 199 inscriptions from Christian sarcophagi in Rome of the Constantian period; the largest single group, 9.5 percent, were those of senatorial class women. See Wischmeyer, "Sozialgeschichtliche Aspekte christlicher Sarkophaginschriften der konstantinischen Zeit aus Rom," *CIHEC* Colloquium, Warsaw, 1978, "Les Transformations dans la société chrétienne au IVe siècle," pp. 77–87.

65. Libanius, *Letter* MCDXI.1, ed. Foerster, vol. 11, p. 452, to Alexander.

66. He had deep affection for his mother and his special mention of her "chastity" *could* be a clue to her religion (as with the wife of Eustorgius, see n. 62 above):

> Morigerae uxoris, virtus cui contigit omnis,
> Fama pudicitiae lanificaeque manus
> Coniugiique fides et natos cura regendi
> Et gravitas comis laetaque serietas.
> [*Parentalia* 2, lines 3–6]

His aunt, too, he describes as possessing "the love of consecrated virginity" (*Parentalia* 6, line 8). For Ausonius's Christianity, which did not include certainty about life after death, see H. G. Evelyn-White, ed. and Eng. trans., *Ausonius*, 2 vols., LCL (Cambridge, Mass.: Harvard University Press; London: William Heinemann, 1919–21), vol. 1, pp. xii–xiv.

67. Ibid.

68. Jerome *Letter* VII.3.

69. *Late Antiquity*, pp. 32–33.

70. In Britain at the villa at Otford in Kent; see S. S. Frere, *Britannia: A History of Roman Britain* (London: Sphere Books, 1974), p. 314.

71. "Vergilium cecinisse loquar pia munera Christi," in *Cento Probae*, ed. C. Schenkl, CSEL 16, pp. 569–609 (Leipzig: G. Freytag, 1888), p. 570, line 23; and see also Markus, "Paganism, Christianity and Latin Classics," pp. 2–3.

72. Jerome *Commentary on Ezekiel* XL.5 (*PL* 25.375A); and he describes the darkness of the catacombs with an apt quotation from the *Aeneid*, Book III, "Horror ubique animos simul ipsa silentia terrent."

73. Augustine *Confessions* VIII.2.3–5.

74. See John Morris, "The Date of Saint Alban," *Hertfordshire Archaeology* 1 (1969): 1–8; also W. Levison, "St Alban and St Albans," *Antiquity* 15 (1941): 337–59.

75. There may have been others who refused the subsidy! See Sulpicius Severus, *Chronicorum* II.41, ed. C. Halm, CSEL 1 (Vienna, 1866), p. 94.

76. On the cemetery, see C. J. S. Green, "Interim Report on Excavations in the Roman Cemetery, Poundbury, Dorchester," *Proc. Dorset Nat. Hist. and Arch. Soc.* 91 (1969), pp. 123–28 (and forthcoming). On the temple, see R. E. M. Wheeler and T. V. Wheeler, *Maiden Castle, Dorset,* Soc. of Antiquaries Research Papers 12 (Oxford, 1943): 131–35. Built post–367 and repaired post–379.

77. Meates, *Lullingstone,* p. 143ff.; Meates dates the founding of the Christian rooms to c. 350 (p. 154).

78. K. S. Painter, "The Mildenhall Treasure: A Reconsideration," *British Museum Quarterly* 37 (1973): 154–80.

79. Toynbee, "New Roman Mosaic Pavement."

80. Described by K. S. Painter in "A Fourth Century Christian Silver Treasure Found at Water Newton," *RivAC* 51 (1975): 333–45; and in idem, *Water Newton Silver.*

81. Such as Thalassius, son of the prefect of the East, who turned a temple on his estate in Syria into a home for himself, Libanius *Letter* 1364.

82. *Ecclesiastical History* II.5.6.

83. *Oratio contra gentes (Speech Against the Heathen)* XXIX.

84. Cited from Stevenson, *Catacombs,* p. 115.

85. For Egypt, Athanasius *Incarnation* VIII.28. For North Africa, see *CIL* VIII.6700 = 19353, from Castellum Elephantum in Numidia, recalling the *dies thurificationis* imposed by Valerius Florus and the martyrs who died rather than submit.

86. *Ecclesiastical History* V.15.14, compare also III.14.28.

87. See Rouselle, "Du sanctuaire au Thaumaturge."

88. *Letter* CCX.

89. Ammianus XV.7.7–8; cf. XXX.5.11 (accusation against Faustinus).

90. Ibid., XIX.12.13–14.

91. Ibid., XVI.8.2. See P. R. L. Brown's study, "Sorcery, Demons and the Rise of Christianity," in *Religion and Society in the Age of Saint Augustine* (New York: Harper & Row, 1972), pp. 119–46.

92. *Confessions* VII.5.8 (Eng. trans. E. B. Pusey [New York: E. P. Dutton, 1926]).

93. Augustine *Psalmos* 88, *Sermo* III.4 (*PL* 37.1140). See my *Donatist Church*, p. 103 (references).

94. Athanasius *De Incarnatione* XXXI, trans. Thomson.

95. *De errore profanarum religionum* (*On the Error of Profane Religions*), ed. C. Halm, CSEL 2.16.4–5; Eng. trans. "The 'Manual of Intolerance' of Firmicus Maternus, c. 346–348," in *Creeds, Councils and Controversies*, ed. J. Stevenson (New York: Seabury Press; London: SPCK, 1966), pp. 3–4.

96. *Profane Religions* 28.6.

97. Recounted by Socrates *Ecclesiastical History* IV.23 (end).

98. Eusebius *Demonstratio evangelica* VI.18, *PG* 22.457C.

99. *Itinerarium a Burdigala—Jerusalem, PL* 8.783–94, at 790A. See E. D. Hunt, *Holy Land Pilgrimage in the Later Roman Empire* A.D. *312–460* (New York and London: Oxford University Press, 1982), chap. 3.

100. *HE* II.17. See above, p. 146, and also VII.32.30 concerning Bishop Achillas.

101. On Eusebius of Emesa's strange career, see Sozomen *Ecclesiastical History* III.6. On his theories of asceticism, see Amand de Mendieta, "La virginité chez Eusèbe."

102. Canon 9.

103. For Edessa, see Julian *Letter* XL. For Callinicum, see Ambrose *Letter* XL.16. Ambrose shows that the Valentinians also had their followers in the countryside (ibid.).

104. These documents have now been translated into English by a team directed by James M. Robinson (ed.), and published as *The Nag Hammadi Library* (New York: Harper & Row, 1978).

105. For the Lebaba inscription and the evidence for Marcionites in Syrian villages in the fourth and fifth centuries, see above, p. 448.

106. Athanasius's accusation in *Apologia pro fuga sua* (*In Defense of His Flight*) VI, repeated in *Historia Arianorum ad monachos* (*History of the Arians Addressed to the Monks*) LIX. For Sebastianus's career, see Jones, *Prosopography*, pp. 812–13.

107. See below, p. 661, for Manichees in North Africa.

108. *Psalm of Heracleides* 277. Cited from Allberry, *Manichaean Psalm Book*, p. 97, lines 30–34 (dating, c. 340); and see O. H. E. Burmester's review in *JTS* 40 (1939): 191–96.

109. Allberry, *Manichean Psalm Book*, p. 50, *Psalm* 243, lines 27–30.

110. Cited from T. Säve-Söderbergh, "Some Remarks on Coptic Manichaean Poetry," in *Coptic Studies in Honor of Walter Ewing Crum* (Boston: Byzantine Institute, 1950), pp. 159–73, esp. p. 160.

111. Sulpicius Severus, *Vita S. Martini* IX, ed. C. Halm, CSEL 1, pp. 109–37 (Vienna, 1866), p. 119.

112. See Jones, *Later Roman Empire*, p. 771; and another example, Potamius of Ossonoba (Lisbon) in Portugal (*Collectio Avellana* II.41, ed. O. Guenther, CSEL 35 [Leipzig: G. Freytag, 1895], p. 17).

113. *Sermon* 345.3. Compare *CIL*.VIII.25905 (Tipasa).

114. *Liber Pontificalis* XXXIV.29. See Jones, *Prosopography*, p. 383.

115. Thus Basil *In Divites* (*To the Wealthy*) VII, *PG* 31.297D–300A. See E. F. Bruck, *Kirchenväter und soziales Erbrecht: Wanderungen religiöser Ideen durch die Rechte der östlichen und westlichen Welt* (Berlin: Springer, 1956), pp. 6–21.

116. Basil, *Wealthy* VII, *PG* 31.300B.

117. *Codex Theodosianus* XVI.2.20. Compare Jerome *Letter* LII.6, in which he acknowledges grudgingly the need for such provisions.

118. See below, p. 604.

119. Ambrose *De officiis Ministrorum* (*On the Duties of the Clergy*) III.7.45–51 is a good example. Through an imaginary prefect of Rome he berates imaginary citizens for expelling poverty-stricken cultivators who had sought relief in the city in time of famine. Even animals were treated better!

120. *De Nabuthe* (*On Naboth*) I.1 (*PL* 14.731). Poverty, however, was not of necessity a blessed state. (*Expositio evangelii secundum Lucam [Exposition of the Gospel According to Luke]* II.41).

121. Canon 7.

122. Gregory of Nazianzus *Letter* 38 (cited from Deferrari, ed., *Basil*, vol. 2, pp. 228–29). Simplicia otherwise received little sympathy from the Cappadocians as they suspected her of heresy. See Basil *Letter* CXV, and Deferrari's note. For general legislation in the fourth century against the ordination of slaves, see *Codex Theodosianus* IX.45.3 (27 July 398).

123. Gregory of Nyssa *De opificio hominis* (*On the Making of Man*) II and III ("royal lodging," *PG* 44.132ff., and 16.184D on mutability as characteristic of the created order). More severe in *Homilies on Ecclesiastes* IV, *PG* 44.664.

124. Basil, *De Spiritu Sancto* (*On the Holy Spirit*) XX.51, *PG* 32.160–61.

125. Theodoret of Cyrrhus, *Sixth Discourse on Providence*, *PG* 83.644–65. Theodoret urged that human equality was impractical and would lead to a breakdown in the exchange of goods and services throughout society. See also Viner, *Religious Thought*, pp. 18–20.

126. Gregory of Nyssa *Homilies on Ecclesiastes* IV.1, *PG* 44.665.

127. *City of God* XIX.15. Slavery caused by sin, "but though not natural, it is, however, penal and is appointed by that law which enjoins the preservation of the natural order and forbids its disturbance." See also *Letter* CVIII.5.18.

128. Jerome *Commentary on Isaiah* XVI.58, *PL* 24.565.

129. Thus Crispina, martyred in December 304, is described by Augustine as "clarissima . . . nobilis genere" (*Psalmos* CXX.13). The Donatists do not refer to her wealth in their *Acta*.

130. Lactantius *Institutes* VI.20; and note also, Paulinus of Nola's hesitations concerning his adoption of a religious life after having filled the office of provincial governor.

131. Brusin and Zovatto, *Monumenti paleo-cristiani*; and see M. M. Roberti, "Considerazioni sulle aule Teodoriane de Aquileia," in ibid., pp. 209–44.

132. See Frere, *Britannia*, p. 270 for the general prosperity of Roman villas in Britain in the fourth century. In all probability the Fenland farms provided the

emperor Julian with the extra grain he needed for his campaign (Zosimus *Historia Nova* III.5). Sites such as the farm outside Godmanchester continued to be occupied into the fifth century (W. H. C. Frend, *Proceedings of Cambridge Antiq. Society* 68 [1978]: 5–17).

133. *BAC* (1936–37), Séance de la Commission de l'Afrique du Nord, pp. 197–201.

134. Ibid. (1934–35), p. 323.

135. *Expositio totius mundi et rerum*, ed. J. Rougé, SC 124 (Paris, 1966), p. 61, "provinciae Africae dives in omnibus. . . ." See also Frend, *Donatist Church*, pp. 52–56.

136. For instance, Optatus, *De Schismate Donatistarum* V.7 describing a worker in a vineyard, "curvato dorso et desudatis lateribus sinus terrae faciat"— hard effort for little reward.

137. Claudian *In Rufinum* (*Against Rufinus*) I.190; "metuenda colonis fertilitas" (though of general rather than specific North African application).

138. Sudden disasters rather than taxation caused peasant freeholders to abandon their land. For Egyptian examples, see Jones, *Later Roman Empire*, pp. 774–75; and for North Africa, Frend, *Donatist Church*, pp. 68–72.

139. For the Christianization of the Numidian countryside, see A. Berthier et al., *Les vestiges du christianisme*, pp. 77, 206ff. For the Donatist preponderance, see *Collatio Carthaginensis* 1.165, ed. S. Lancel, *Actes de la conférence de Carthage en 411* II.810, SC 195 (Paris, 1972); Optatus, *De Schismate Donatistarum* III.4; Augustine, *Letter* CXXIX.6; and *Ad Catholicos Epistola de Unitate Ecclesiae* 19.51, "Numidia ubi praepolletis" (addressing Donatists).

140. See below, p. 723.

141. Optatus *De Schismate Donatistarum* III.4; see my *Donatist Church*, pp. 171–75; and "Circumcellions and Monks."

142. Optatus, *De Schismate Donatistarum* III.4.

143. Ibid. Translated in Stevenson, *Creeds, Councils and Controversies*, p. 202.

144. Tyconius (in Beatus of Libana), cited from *Tyconius-Studien*, ed. Hahn, p. 68. Compare Augustine's statement, "ad eorum sepulcra [Circumcellion martyrs] ebriosi greges vagorum et vagarum . . ." (*Ad Catholicos Epistola* XIX.50).

145. Berthier et al., *Les vestiges du christianisme*, pp. 139, 147.

146. *Historia Nova*, ed. L. Mendelssohn (Leipzig, 1887; reprint ed., Hildersheim, 1963), IV.16.

147. Thus Augustine *Letter* 87.10 and *Parmenianus* I.10.16 (Donatists ± "Firmiani"); and compare Ammianus XXIX.5.15 (given the evidence of Augustine, the clergy employed by Firmus in peace parleys were likely to be Donatist).

148. Anonymous, *Passio Benedicti Martyris Marculi* (c. 360), PL 8.761A.

149. Optatus, *De Schismate Donatistarum* III.3 (pp. 79, 80 on Constans); Augustine *Contra litteras Petiliani* (*Answers to Letters of Petilian*) II.39.94, "Macarius . . . latine Beatus est, Ita plane de parte Macarii sumus."

150. Theodoret, *Haereticarum fabularum compendium* (*Compendium of Heretical Fables*) V.6, PG 83.423.

151. Leschi, "Des épitaphes chrétiennes." Optatus (*De Schismate Donatistarum* III.4, p. 83) and Augustine *Petilian* II.92.204, and *Against Gaudentius* I.28.32 confirm this type of Circumcellion suicide.

152. The best account of monasticism and its background is in Lietzmann, *Era of*

Fathers, vol. 4 of *History of Early Church*, practically the last thing Lietzmann wrote. Also, Labriolle's (very full) account, "Les Débuts du Monachisme"; and Heussi, *Der Ursprung des Mönchtums*.

153. Athanasius, *Life of Antony* XLIV, *PG* 26.908.

154. For Egypt, see the classic discussion of the development of patronage over the villages in the fourth and early fifth centuries by Zulueta, "De Patrociniis Vicorum," 1.2. For small proprietors, see Jones, *Later Roman Empire*, p. 778.

155. See Liebeschuetz, "Epigraphic Evidence"; and G. Tchalenko, "La Syrie du Nord; étude économique," *Actes du VI Congrès Internat. des études byzantines* (Paris, 1950), pp. 389–97.

156. Zulueta, "De Patrociniis Vicorum," p. 24. The patron became de facto possessor of his client's lands, whatever the formal agreement between them may have been.

157. Compare Libanius, *Oration* L.36 (Foerster, vol. 3, p. 487) and Theodoret *Letters* XLII, XLIII.

158. *Homily on Matthew* LXII.3, *PG* 58.591.

159. Athanasius *Life of Antony* LXXXI.

160. Sozomen *Ecclesiastical History* I.13.9 (petitions); and Rufinus, *Ecclesiastical History* I.8 (Constantine) "wrote to Antony as to one of the prophets."

161. This is demonstrated by Brown in "Rise and Function of Holy Man."

162. Thus Athanasius, *Doctrina ad monachos, PG* 28, pp. 1421–27, esp. pp. 1424B and C, and in the seventh century, the romance of Barlaam and Joasaph XII.103 (Loeb Library).

163. *Apophthegmata Patrum:* de abbate Sisoe, 48, *PG* 65.405.

164. Ibid., 25, *PG* 65.400C and D.

165. *Lausiac History*, ed. Butler, VIII; Socrates *Ecclesiastical History* IV.23; on dating, see L. Duchesne, *The Early History of the Christian Church: From Its Foundation to the End of the Third Century*, 3 vols. (London: Longmans, Green & Co., 1909–24), vol. 2, p. 391.

166. *Lausiac History* XVIII.3 (Macarius); and ibid., XXIII.3 (Pachon).

167. See Labriolle, "Les Débuts du Monachisme," pp. 338–39.

168. Jerome, *Regulae S. Pachomii translatio Latina* praefatio VI, *PL* 23.67B.

169. Sozomen *Ecclesiastical History* III.14, for a full and interesting account of life in a Pachomian monastery, and see also *Lausiac History* XXXII.

170. See Labriolle, "Les Débuts du Monachisme," p. 339; "La congrégation pakhomienne comprit donc au total, neuf couvents d'hommes et deux de femmes."

171. Jerome, *Regulae Pachomii* VII, *PL* 23.68.

172. An example of this harmony between the two peoples is given by Sozomen (*Ecclesiastical History* III.14.1) in his tale of the two monks named Macarius, the one a Coptic and the other an Alexandrian.

173. On dating, see Robinson, ed., *Nag Hammadi Library*, pp. 15–16.

174. *Lausiac History* LX.

175. Eusebius *HE* VI.9.6.

176. Sozomen *Ecclesiastical History* VI.33.

177. Ibid., III.14.

178. On the Boskoi, see Vööbus, *History of Asceticism*, vol. 1, p. 319, and for the independent origin of Syrian monasticism see ibid., p. 142ff.

179. *Apophthegmata Patrum:* de abbate Sereno II, *PG* 65.417.

180. Theodoret *Historia religiosa seu ascetica vivendi ratio* (*History of the Monks*) XXVI (*PG* 82.1472B).
181. Ibid.
182. Sozomen *Ecclesiastical History* III.16.13.
183. Ibid., III.16.
184. See Murray, *Symbols of Church and Kingdom*, pp. 29–32 (life of Ephraem), and 337–40 (sources and beliefs).
185. Sozomen *Ecclesiastical History* III.14.38.

17

Hero of a Lost Cause:
The Emperor Julian 360–63

THE EARLY YEARS

The world has always warmed to its fallen heroes. Hector rather than Achilles, Robert E. Lee and not Ulysses S. Grant stir the imagination of posterity, however lost or wrongheaded the causes they championed. They fill the Valhalla of our fantasies. The emperor Julian is in a similar class. The wonder of historian and artist is still aroused by the late-Roman prince, nephew of Constantine, who lived his early years in constant peril of sharing his father's fate, his youth in almost total isolation, and his early manhood as a wandering and dreaming student. Yet he almost overnight turned into a born leader, and an administrator who bent every effort during a reign of twenty months in a hopeless effort to restore the old religion. His death in battle at the age of thirty-two in a grandiose scheme to conquer the Persian Empire and emulate Alexander the Great seems only to add stature to what objectively was a wasteful and futile endeavor.

Until he became emperor, Julian's life was a commentary on the government of his cousin Constantius II. He was born in Constantinople in 331 (or early 332), the son of Julius Constantius, Constantine's half brother, and Basilina, whose father Julius Julianus had been virtually head of government under Licinius. His mother died a few months after his birth, but six years later, on 9 September 337, another even worse tragedy struck. His father and elder brother were murdered along with Constantine's other half brother Delmatius and his sons. Julian's half brother Gallus was spared because he was believed to be dying, and Julian himself because he was a child. Constantius was the only one of the sons of Constantine in the capital at the time, and it is difficult not to follow Ammianus Marcellinus and Julian himself and convict him at least of connivance in the massacre.[1]

Julian was sent away from the capital to the former seat of government, Nicomedia, and made a ward of Bishop Eusebius. In 338/39 that ambitious prelate gained his prize, the see of Constantinople, and Julian was entrusted to the care of Mardonius, a eunuch, perhaps a Gothic slave, and a nominal Christian, but one who had cultivated a love of Homer and the Greek classics. He was a brilliant though severe teacher and imprinted his puritan virtues on his pupil's mind. Years later, Julian remembered how he persuaded him to read Homeric descriptions of horse races, dances, and lyre playing rather than participate himself.[2] His existence, however, was lonely. As he wrote in anger to the Antiochenes (at the end of 362), "No doubt in your view, a soul's true beauty is to be found in a pleasure-loving life; but my teacher taught me to lower my gaze towards the ground as I went to school"[3]—a habit of self-deprecation which was to have its consequences later on.

Julian was not allowed to stay in Nicomedia. In 342 Constans was threatening Constantius with war over Athanasius. Perhaps for dynastic reasons, fearing the formation of a party around the princes in favor of Constans, the emperor ordered their removal to an imperial estate in the heart of Anatolia. The Macellum, north of Mt. Argaeus in Cappadocia, was about as isolated as it could be, consistent with reasonable comfort and, above all, security. Here, in what may have been a hunting lodge, Julian and Gallus experienced six years of "glittering servitude"[4] under the eye of royal eunuchs. Their education was given a more Christian turn. They became readers and found themselves dedicating churches to the martyrs.[5] Their tutor was Bishop George, a man of humble background and tactless manner,[6] later to be the ill-fated supplanter of Athanasius (356–61), but now in his prime, an Origenist cleric whose richly endowed library contained both Christian works and Neo-Platonist commentaries on Plato and Aristotle. He represented fully the new generation of educated Christians in the East, men who followed Origen and accepted Christianity as the climax of traditional philosophic studies, moving beyond Neo-Platonism toward a rational understanding of God and his universe.

Julian might have taken the same road, combining his love for philosophy with a passive adherence to victorious Christianity. But emotion began to play its part. He came to understand how his father and brother met their ends, and he formed a deep and lasting hatred for his cousin and all he stood for. His uncle, Constantine, he despised also, while Helena he regarded not as a saint, but as a "wicked stepmother."[7]

He was now a serious student. As he says of himself, "Some men have a passion for horses; others for birds, others, again, for wild beasts; but I, from childhood, have been penetrated by a passionate longing to acquire books."[8] When Bishop George was lynched on 24 December 361, Julian gave special instructions to the prefect of Egypt that his library should be safeguarded.

In 348/49 the long exile ended. Again, the reason is uncertain. Apart from the war on the eastern frontier, the empire enjoyed peace and security. Perhaps Constantius felt safe enough to bring the princes back to Constantinople. There Julian studied rhetoric with the philosophers, Nicocles and Hecebolius, one a pagan and the other not too firm a Christian, while Gallus remained at court. Events were to suggest, however, that had Gallus been a different man, the emperor's action would have been prudent. The years 350–51 were the crisis years of his reign. His brother had fallen to Magnentius. Vetranio was attempting to seize the Balkan provinces, and worst of all from a dynastic point of view, his kinsman Nepotian was established in Rome, with memories of the massacre of 337. Constantius acted as best he could. Following his victory at Mursa he sent for Gallus, and at his headquarters at Sirmium robed him with the insignia of Caesar. The two emperors publicly swore loyalty to each other, and Gallus, married to Constantius's sister Constantina, was dispatched to Antioch to govern the eastern provinces of the empire, while Constantius moved west to finish off Magnentius.

Unhappily, he had made a wretched choice. Unlike Julian, Gallus had "gone savage" in his enforced stay at the Macellum. He was far from being the saintly Abel of Gregory of Nazianzus's imagination.[9] Ill-health and brooding had done their work. He was quite unfit for administrative responsibility, and his wife made him worse. Ammianus, perhaps with prejudice, describes her as "a Fury in human shape, continually inflaming her husband's rage, no less thirsty for human blood than he" (XIV.1.2). Fortunately, there was a lull in Sapor's campaign against the Roman defenses in the east. In three years, however, Gallus had made himself intolerable. Constantius summoned him to Milan, and on the way had him stripped of his imperial insignia and executed (November 354). The imperial villa near Pola, already the scene of Crispus's judicial murder in 326, witnessed this execution as well.

The emperor was justified. Ammianus was a native of Antioch and his detailed description of Gallus's misrule cannot be gainsaid.[10] The Caesar had proved himself to be a bloodthirsty tyrant, but the effect on Julian of this new judicial murder of a close relative was lasting. Through the years 349–54 he remained on the sidelines. He was approaching manhood, and was showing what, given opportunity, he might become. Constantius feared a possible rival, "untoward consequences for himself," Libanius writes,[11] and so Julian was moved to Nicomedia and further studies. Thanks to the academic rivalries among his tutors he was able only to hear the lectures of Libanius indirectly, but at last he was free to move about in the provinces of western Asia as he would. While Gallus was Caesar, he traveled to Pergamum and then to Ephesus where he stayed. There he came under the lasting influence of two of the finest representatives of the late flowering of Neo-Platonism—Maximus of Ephesus and Priscus, both of whom were to accompany him on his fateful Persian campaign. Meantime in 354 Julian himself was summoned to Milan, but en route he was able to disembark near Troy. There he met the bishop Pegasius, another classicist at heart but who had seen where a career was to be made. Julian visited the famous sites and shrines and noted how this allegedly Christian bishop had preserved so reverently the sacred fire that burned still on the altar of Hector's shrine and the temple of Athena in perfect condition. He knew he had an ally.

By 351 Julian had become a convert to a mystical form of Neo-Platonism. He describes his convictions in his *Hymn to King Helios* (dedicated to Sallust) as well as in his tirade against the people of Antioch (*The Beard Hater*), and in some of his letters. He believed in a single unknowable Supreme Being, who emanated a creator-power which he identified with the Sun, "pure and undefiled and immaterial substance," midway between the Supreme Being and the created world.[12] He was the giver of life, creator of the visible universe, and lord of the beyond whose nature was only intelligible to the believer in rare moments of mystical contemplation. He reflected the divine harmony of the universe, giving individual existence to everything that is created.[13] Beneath him were ranged the various national deities—Athena for the Greeks, Attis for the Phrygians, and Jehovah for the Jews—who determined the natural characteristics of the races over whom they presided. The traditional pagan myths could be interpreted as allegories of the single great drama of creation.

Julian was saying that the Divine Word was not to be identified with Christ but with the power and glory of King Helios, the Sun. In a sense, therefore, Julian was retracing the steps taken by Constantine: *Soli invicto comiti* ("To the unconquered sun [my] companion") of his uncle's earlier years would have expressed Julian's beliefs, except that Julian also regarded Mithras as his guardian deity and source of inspiration.[14] Apart from this, he clothed his ideas in the theological language of the day, using the term *ousia* to describe the Sun's substance, which Christians used of the Christ-Word. On the other hand, he despised Christians and Christianity. Christians were superstitious atheists, he told Photinus, the exbishop of Sirmium.[15] "For these two things," he wrote elsewhere, "are the quintessence of their [Christian] theology, to hiss at demons and make the sign of the cross on their foreheads."[16] Greeks who had become Christians had not only chosen a culture inferior to their own, which lacked the moral virtue of Hellenism, but a religion that combined the worst features of Hellenism and Judaism in the worship of a pathetic failed revolutionary.[17] Their religion was based on a fabrication, a fiction concocted by evil men.[18] Monasticism, especially its exaggerated forms of asceticism, he disliked as contrary to the nature of humans, which was to be a social and civilized being (*zóon politikon*).[19] Christian social teaching, however, he admired, and sought to inspire the reformed pagan priesthood with the same ideals.

His was a romantic attachment to all things Greek—philosophy, religion, and way of life. He believed that the gods of Hellas—Zeus, Helios, Athene, and Hermes—were his benefactors, friends, and saviors. "For everywhere we shall be with thee," he has them say.[20] He longed to set right the ills of the world through their help. Of these years Libanius later wrote, "You wept at the ruin of our temples . . . and allowed those about you to observe in your present pain the aid to come. With the revival of such hopes, all the elite of intellect on continent and island aligned itself with you in goodwill, and united in preparing the throne for you, not by force of arms but by hidden prayer and secret sacrifice."[21] Words such as these illustrate the complete dominance Christianity had gained by 350 and the despair felt by the leading representatives of the old religion. There is nothing to show, however, that Julian himself aimed at removing his cousin, but the depth of his love for Hellenism is evident.

It was well, however, that he kept his ideas to a close circle of friends. While at Constantius's court at Milan in 354/55, his life was in danger. Julian was accused of leaving the Macellum without permission and consorting with, if not conspiring with, the luckless Gallus, but he found a friend in Constantius's wife, Eusebia. After another short period of enforced residence at Comum (Como) north of Milan, he was allowed to visit Athens.[22] The months he spent there (Spring–October 355) were probably among the happiest in his life. He found Priscus there also. He was secretly initiated into the Eleusinian mysteries, and above all he met quick-witted students of his own age, both pagan and Christian, on whom to test his ideas. Athens was the alma mater of the Cappadocian fathers—Basil of Caesarea, his brother Gregory of Nyssa, and friend Gregory of Nazianzus. As in modern times, friendships and antipathies formed at university tend to be lasting and Athens served the Cappadocians well throughout their lives. Julian knew and respected Basil,[23] but the instinctive barrier was already too strong for friendship. Gregory of Nazianzus remembered him with a mixture of admiration and distaste. He wrote in his rotund oratorical style:

> There seemed to me to be no evidence of sound character in his unsteady neck, his twitching and hunched shoulders, his wandering eye and wayward glance, his uncertain and swaying walk, his proud haughty nose, his uncontrolled and very loud laugh, his head jerked up and down for no reason and his halting, gasping speech.[24]

There could be some truth in this, granting the strain Julian was under—his half brother dead and himself suspected of disloyalty—with men like Paul the Chain as likely investigators of his conduct and ideas. He could not be left in peace for long. During 354 a disastrous situation had developed in Gaul. The civil war between Magnentius and Constantius had given the Germanic peoples their chance. In turn, Magnentius's brother Decentius, and Constantius's commander Silvanus, himself a semibarbarian, had failed to repulse them. When Silvanus himself fell tragically to the suspicions of Constantius, the frontier defenses collapsed. Colonia (Köln) and Moguntiacum (Mainz) fell, and the barbarian armies moved in a flood tide halfway across Gaul. Desperately, Constantius looked for help. Julian was summoned posthaste from Athens. On 6 November 355, his cousin invested him with the insignia and title of Caesar at Milan. Julian accepted with a few halting words of Latin—perhaps nearly all he knew! The new relationship was sealed by Julian's marriage to Helena, Constantius's sister. Then on 1 December as winter was closing in he was off to the scene of operations. His opportunity had come.

THE SUCCESSFUL GENERAL

Constantius was obviously of two minds whether to trust him or not. Julian himself, of course, felt that the resentments he harbored against his cousin were mutual. Libanius states that he "had authority for nothing save to wear the uniform."[25] Yet from June 356, when Julian set out on his first campaign against the invading tribes, this is not true. Constantius, perhaps with greater perception than he is credited, had decided to support his cousin fully. Julian had been declared consul for the year 356, and the emperor kept the Alamanni busy in the south, while Julian advanced from Autun to the Rhine and then northwards to recapture Cologne (September 356). The cooperation between the two commanders had proved itself, and Constantius had let his cousin play the leading and decisive part.

The following year proved crucial for Julian. From May onward Constantius was held at Sirmium by theological debate. Julian's study of Julius Caesar's *Commentaries* had been well spent. He caught the Alamanni returning to their own territories after a victorious raid as far as Lyons. Near Strasbourg he ambushed their army of thirty thousand men, drove it into the marshes and into the Rhine, and decimated it, capturing their king, Chnodomar, and killing six thousand of his troops. It was a decisive battle, ensuring relative peace for Gaul for nearly fifty years. In 358 the Franks and their allies were cleared from the area around the mouth of the Rhine, enabling a corn-fleet of no less than four hundred vessels from Britain to supply his troops in the reconquered territories. In 359 these gains were consolidated. The Rhine frontier had been restored.

Julian's successes coincided with threats from Persia. Sapor renewed the war in 359, and despite the heroic efforts of the garrison the great fortress of Amida, blocking a Persian advance into Armenia, fell on 5 October 359. Justifiably, Constantius turned to Julian for reinforcements. There were Gallic legionaries serving in his armies. Why should not more be sent? The troops concerned felt differently. Parts of Gaul had been devastated by the Germanic invasions. They had fought victoriously for their homes. Why should they now march two thousand miles to a distant torrid clime without their commander? "There was great excitement among the civilians and troops," Julian wrote.[26] In February 360, the troops at his headquarters at Lutetia (Paris) mutinied. Against his will, Julian was hoist Germanic fashion on a shield and proclaimed Augustus.

There is no reason to believe otherwise. Had he refused he risked being cut down by the angry troops. Now neither he nor Constantius wished to push matters to extremes. Constantius was involved in a long holding operation to protect Armenia against the Persians throughout 360, and he sent an officer to Gaul to persuade Julian not to aspire higher than to be Caesar. In November some of Julian's coins, struck to commemorate his five years of imperial service (*quinquennalia*), show him and Constantius as joint Augusti.[27] About this time he wrote to his cousin describing what had happened at Paris and offering to accept him as his senior, retaining the right of making the highest administrative appointments (praetorian prefect) throughout the empire.[28]

By January 361, however, he seems to have decided to accept the revolution. He moved his headquarters to Vienne, and there attended the celebration of the Epiphany on 6 January, the last Christian service in which he ever participated.[29] Not until July, after suspicion that Constantius might be stirring up Germanic peoples against him, did Julian begin his march east. He moved through the southern Black Forest, along the Danube to Sirmium, arriving there in October. Resistance to him began to crumble. Important officials, such as the historian and provincial governor Sextus Aurelius Victor, joined him.[30] Moving to Naissus (Nish) near his uncle's family estate, he abandoned whatever shred of loyalty he had felt for Constantius. In letters to the Athenians, Rome, Corinth, and some other (conservative) great city councils he attacked his cousin in biting terms. The *Letter to the Athenians* is practically an autobiography defending his conduct, and finally committing his cause "to the gods."

He threw off his disguise. To Maximus of Ephesus, he wrote, "I worship the gods openly, and the whole mass of the troops who are returning with me worship the gods."[31] His famous beard first made its appearance in Illyricum. Here was a pagan philosopher at the head of a victorious army on his way to confront the Christian emperor, who also led battle-hardened legionaries.

The decisive meeting never took place. Constantius, reluctantly turning from the Persian frontier, had reached Cilicia by the last week of October. There he was struck down, probably with malaria, and on 3 November 361 he died at Mopsucrenae at the age of forty-four after designating Julian as his successor. The new emperor entered Constantinople unopposed on 11 December.

The Pagan Emperor

One revolution had been successful, but what of the second? The attempt to restore the cult of the immortal gods as the religion of the empire was foredoomed to failure. In 360, surviving paganism may be likened to a number of sand castles—some big, some small—but all facing erosion and destruction by the advancing tide. The most imposing of these was the Roman Senate—"the Romans of Rome." Even if their womenfolk were opting for Christianity, the rule of the paterfamilias stood, and the male lines would remain staunch for the cults and Rome's tradition for another generation. Next in importance, with pride in their past and contempt for the upstart Christian religion and its outlandish cult of saints and martyrs,[32] were members of the old urban aristocracies, the holders of ceremonial priesthoods and civic offices. For three centuries these had represented the traditions of Rome in the provinces and would welcome Julian as "liberator." Some cities, such as Arethusa and Emesa with important shrines, were pagan, but others such as Bostra and Neocaesarea already had Christian majorities. Then there were sections of the rural population, both isolated pagan enclaves in Egypt and western Asia Minor, and whole populations solidly devoted to their traditional cults throughout most of the

Celtic lands extending from Illyricum to Britain. Had Julian's ambitions been centered in the West, history might have been different, for even around Rome Constans had found he could not close temples that for generations had provided the focus for traditional sports and festivities.[33] But the broad middle areas of population both in East and West had been lost. The most active, articulate, and influential sections of the provincials were now Christian. Little if any common ground existed to bind together the beliefs of the Senate, city councilors, and Celtic peasants in a common religious allegiance. Julian's efforts to establish a pagan "church" with its hierarchy and organization could hardly have succeeded.

Julian had laid his plans well and he brought tremendous energy to his task. His wife and infant son had died. At thirty he saw himself dedicated to a lifelong mission. While still at Naissus (Nish), he had begun to gather supporters around him. At this stage, he aimed at eminent pagan intellectuals; later at Constantinople he extended the same warm welcome to dissenting Christians—such as the "godless deacon" Aetius who, despite his unconventional opinions, had been one of the few stabilizing influences in his luckless half brother's career—and others whom he admired, such as Basil of Caesarea.[34] His "ministry," modeled on Plato's guardians, would include all "honest and reasonable men, intelligent and entirely capable," even if Christians.[35]

Within days of his arrival in the capital, Constantius's court was being purged. The multifarious crew of cooks, eunuchs, barbers, and petty functionaries was sent packing. The archoffender, the "execrable eunuch," Eusebius, the grand chamberlain, Paul the Chain, and other notables of the Constantian era were tried before a military tribunal at Chalcedon and executed. Others were exiled—Britain being among the places chosen for the discredited. The senate house rather than the imperial palace became the seat of government. In the first five months of 362, a stream of reforming edicts and rescripts issued from the capital. The ultimate aim was the restoration of the pagan empire, but not on the model of the Tetrarchy. Society and government were to be more open; three generations of siege conditions imposed by the bureaucracy were to be lifted.

Julian's first step was to dismantle Constantius's system of interlocking church-state government. By a decree of 9 February, all clerics exiled under Constantius were permitted to return to their own countries, including Athanasius to Alexandria and the Donatists to North Africa.[36] It was a cunning blow aimed at the former orthodoxies, semi-Arian and Catholic. Ammianus may have judged Julian's motives correctly. "On this he took a firm stand, to the end that, as this freedom increased their dissension, he might afterwards have no fear of a united populace, knowing as he did from experience that no wild beasts are such enemies to mankind as are most Christians in their deadly hatred of one another" (XXII.5.4).

Next month it was the turn of church's privileges. On 13 March, Julian proclaimed that no one could henceforth claim exemption from service as a city councilor on the grounds that he was a Christian.[37] Clergy also lost their share of taxes in kind (*annona*), exemption from municipal levies, and their privileged use of public transport. Their leaders were no longer to be civic functionaries. Power was handed back to the traditional representatives of the cities and their gods.

With similar ends in view, Bishop Eleusis of Cyzicus was told to rebuild at his own expense a Novatian church which his predecessor had destroyed (Socrates *Ecclesiastical History* III.11), while the Arians of Edessa were reminded that poverty was a Christian virtue and that they must "sell all that they had" as a penalty for attacking the Valentinians in the city (Julian *Letter* XL). Virgins and widows had to begin repaying the subsidies they had received out of taxation to the detriment of the remainder of the community (Sozomen *Ecclesiastical History* V.5.2).

Economic reforms proceeded at the same breathless pace. While in Gaul Julian had seen the effects on morale and prosperity of reducing taxes and canceling debts. He applied the same policies to the empire as a whole. To aid the cities ("to make possible the recovery of all the cities"), an edict of 15 March 362 ordered the restoration of land administered by the central authorities (*possessiones publicae*) to the cities so as to increase their resources from which they paid taxes.[38] He restored the monetary tax (the *aurum coronarium*) to what it had originally been—a free offering of congratulation by the cities to the emperor on set anniversaries of his reign.[39] In the same month, he announced that no changes in taxation were to be made without being referred to him personally.[40] In July on arrival in Antioch, he ordered circuit judges (*judices pedanei*) to be appointed to try minor cases in rural areas and hence cut down legal delays and fees.[41] The rural populations were aided also by strict control of the posting service, and all tax collectors were reminded that after five years' work they could be challenged to answer complaints of fraud.[42] Julian told the Thracians, in response to his edict on taxes, that they aimed at helping his subjects and not at amassing wealth from them.[43] The new spirit of government was shown by the very fact he was prepared to listen to far-fetched claims by Alexandrians for the repayment of seventy years of alleged overtaxation![44]

The effect of all this was electric. Inscriptions show how city councils of some distant Numidian towns hailed Julian as "liberator" and "restorer of religion."[45] In the upper valley of the Jordan an inscription dated (probably) to the spring of 363 and probably set up by the provincial council of Phoenicia (*koinon*) praised the emperor as "liberator of the Roman world, restorer of temples, re-creator of the common weal and destroyer of the barbarians."[46] Gregory of Nazianzus had to admit that the common people welcomed Julian's reforms.[47] In some cities—Heliopolis, Ascalon, Gaza, and above all, Arethusa—mobs set upon the Christians.[48]

The heart of the matter was the religious revolution. Almost at once,

Julian was warned of the passions religious changes would arouse. On 24 December 361, within a fortnight of his arrival at Constantinople, Bishop George, Athanasius's supplanter at Alexandria, was lynched by the mob, and high officials in the city suffered a similar fate.[49] It was a riot of a ferocity comparable to that which was to destroy Proterius in the same city in 457. While on this occasion pagans may have joined in, the fanatical loyalty of the Alexandrians to their bishop had already assumed a political coloring. Julian was appalled, but simply wrote to the Alexandrians reminding them that such conduct was unbecoming to Hellenes,[50] and telling the prefect of Egypt at least to secure George's imposing library and save it from destruction.[51] In North Africa, terrible things happened as the Donatists swept in like a forest fire. In a few weeks in the first half of 362, the Catholic ascendancy, built up over the previous fourteen years, had almost ceased to exist: churches were reconsecrated, eucharistic elements were heated up like a mulled punch and thrown to the dogs, Catholic nuns (*sanctimoniales*) were humiliated and rebaptized. Reports of scenes such as these hardly reached Constantinople, but they ensured that Donatism would be the majority religion of North Africa for another generation.[52] In sees up and down the East, rival bishops, casualties of Constantius's almost annual change of mind, confronted one another.

While the Christians were destroying each other, the emperor set about restoring paganism. It was not enough merely to reopen disused temples, restore their lands, and remove the *labarum* from the imperial standards. Julian realized how economic stress had been among the main causes of the gods' losing credit with the mass of the people. He indicates to an unnamed priest later in the year how social misery and selfish inequalities between rich and poor had caused apostasy from the gods. "Now the crowd when they see such men [rich who disregard the poor] blame the gods. However it is not the gods who are to blame for their poverty, but rather the insatiate greed of us men of property becomes the cause of this false conception of the gods among men, and besides of unjust blame of the gods."[53] The remedy was the establishment of a pagan priesthood of high moral standing, properly organized under provincial high priests with authority over lesser priests in cities and the countryside, including responsibility for their learning and ethical standards.[54] Apart from "reverence for the gods" and avoidance of Epicurean literature and immoral shows, the emperor insisted that "fairness," and indeed a social conscience, should form an essential part of a priest's qualification. Zeus was the god of servants and strangers and this aspect of his worship must never be neglected.[55] Julian, perhaps alone of Roman emperors in the third and fourth centuries, grasped how gross inequalities in society had led to a sense of social injustice and the rejection of long-established traditions by provincials in many parts of the empire. These injustices must be remedied if paganism was to survive against Christianity. Otherwise apathy would be followed by abandonment.

The results of centuries of neglect, however, could not be undone in a few months.

THE FAILED REVOLUTION

This is what Julian failed to understand. Christianity had taken far too firm a root to be dislodged, and as Gregory pointed out (*Oration* IV.74), to try to do so was nothing less than to destroy the Roman Empire and endanger the commonweal worse than the efforts of the enemy. By the beginning of May 362, Julian's mind was already turning to his second great ideal, emulation of Alexander the Great, by the conquest of Persia. In fact, as he set out on his ill-fated expedition the following year, he may have lowered his sights considerably. In the single campaign he planned, he seems to have hoped to reconquer Trajan's provinces of Mesopotamia together with the Persian capital, Ctesiphon, perhaps with wider horizons later on. Meantime, there were the Christians nearer home.

Julian had been determined not to add to the roll of martyrs. Christians were to be left alone but pagans were to be preferred in official appointments. He left Constantinople on 12 May 362. As he crossed Asia Minor en route to Antioch where his headquarters were to be, the enormity of his task became evident. There, paganism was in a hopeless condition. Even the families of priests were among converts to Christianity.[56] He wrote to Arsacius, the high priest of Galatia: "The Hellenic religion does not prosper as I desire." He stressed again how social neglect had aided the Christian triumph: "Why do we not observe that it is their benevolence to strangers, their care for the graves of the dead and the pretended holiness of their lives that have done most to increase atheism [Christianity]?" This must be overtrumped. Beggars must be cared for, and hospices for the poor and rich set up in the cities. Meantime, thirty thousand pecks (*modii*) of corn and sixty thousand pints (*sextarii*) of wine were to be set aside for distribution to the needy in Galatia. "For from Zeus come all strangers and beggars. And a gift, though small, is precious. Then let us not, by allowing others to outdo us in good works, disgrace by such remissness, or rather, utterly abandon, reverence due to the gods."[57]

The experience may have directed him to more drastic measures against the Christians. On 17 June he issued his notorious edict aimed at preventing Christians from teaching the classics (and perhaps their children from learning them). Logically he was right. The Christians could not have it both ways. For Julian it was a disgrace for them to instruct in a tradition they had deliberately rejected. But even his friends saw the situation otherwise.[58] As Ammianus wrote, "But this one thing was inhumane, and ought to be buried in eternal silence, namely, that he forbade teachers of rhetoric and literature to practise their profession, if they were followers of the Christian religion."[59] The classics, however, were one of the few trump cards Julian possessed. If he could confine Christian education to the relatively illiterate language of the Bible, he might eventually hope to detach educated provincials from it. The Christians themselves saw the danger, for in an incredibly short time two erudite Syrians, Apollinaris's father and son, had turned practically the whole Bible into Greek verse![60] Of these men of genius we shall hear more. They served notice that Julian would have to act fast and decisively if he were to succeed.

By the middle of 362 the Christians were beginning to recover from the immediate shock of the emperor's measures. As usual, Athanasius was at the center of the resistance. Within a short time of his return to Alexandria on 21 February 362, he gathered together a council of twenty-one bishops. These included representatives of the *homoiousion* and *homoousion* parties, his erstwhile opponents as well as his supporters. This council was probably his greatest triumph, for faced with the threat of the complete reversal of their situation, the Christian leaders were prepared to look at their differences again.[61] What was their real meaning underlying the difference of language? Athanasius, as we have seen, was not a man for verbal formulas. "Like in all respects" must imply "of the same substance," and this time his argument prevailed. After thirty-six years of argument the *homoousion* formula of Nicaea was accepted, with the explicit proviso that no Sabellianism was implied, and the Origenist distinction of the "individualities" or "manifestations" (*hypostaseis*) of the Persons of the Trinity was to be acknowledged. The Holy Spirit was recognized as coequal with the Father and the Son (for how else was the baptismal formula of the church to be understood?). In addition, the council discussed the emerging problem at Antioch of how, if Christ was of "one substance with the Father," he could also be of "one substance with us."[62] Athanasius knew when to leave matters open. It was sufficient triumph that the full participation of Christ in the divine nature had been acknowledged. The former *homoiousians* became the "New Nicenes."

Athanasius was the one cleric Julian feared, and when in the summer of 362, Julian heard that he had baptized some highly born pagan ladies of Alexandria, his anger knew no bounds. He threatened the prefect of Egypt with a heavy fine if he did not rid Alexandria of him by 1 December, and in an impassioned postscript ended with the words, "let him be persecuted."[63] Athanasius went (23 October), passing perhaps an instinctive judgment that Julian's reaction was "a little cloud that would soon pass."[64]

Events were already proving him right. In July Christians in Arabia, Egypt's neighbor, were raising their heads again and had rioted against the pagans in the capital city of Bostra. Julian had reached Antioch about 28 July. His letter to the citizens of Bostra, dated 1 August, while not threatening persecution, suggests a lessening of the confidence he had felt six months before as well as unconcealed hostility to Christianity. Even so, he concluded:

Wherefore, again and often I admonish those who are zealous for the true religion not to injure the communities of the Galileans or attack or insult them. Nay, we ought to pity rather than hate men who in matters of the greatest importance are in such evil case. (For in very truth the greatest of all blessings is reverence for the gods, as, on the other hand, irreverence is the greatest of all evils. It follows that those who have turned aside from the gods to corpses and relics pay this as their penalty.) Since we suffer in sympathy with those who are afflicted by disease, but rejoice with those who are being released and set free by the aid of the gods.[65]

Meantime, he faced trouble in Antioch.[66] First, the presence of his army and administrative staff caused a crisis in the city's food supplies. Prices of foodstuffs rocketed. Julian blamed "the black market" and tried to smother it by importing more supplies, but these merely enabled crafty traders to corner the market and enrich themselves by selling to the unfortunate peasants at high prices.[67] Then once more he was disappointed at the religious situation. In the previous generation pleasure-loving paganism had been replaced by pleasure-loving Christianity. No sacrifices sponsored by the guilds or tribes (quarters) of the city greeted the emperor's entry.[68] The celebrated grove and temple of Daphne[69] had been abandoned by its priests and wrecked by the Christians. It had been overshadowed by the shrine dedicated to St. Babylas, the bishop martyred under Decius, whose cult Julian's own half brother Gallus had favored so ostentatiously.[70] "But when I entered the shrine," Julian wrote, "I found there no incense, not so much as a cake, not a single beast for sacrifice." All the old, discouraged priest could produce in the emperor's honor was a goose taken from his own back garden.[71] Soon Julian became engaged in an unseemly wrangle with the citizens of Antioch. "For he was ridiculed as a Cercops [ape]," Ammianus recorded, "as a dwarf, spreading his narrow shoulders and displaying a billy-goat's beard, taking mighty strides" like some Homeric character. His constant sacrifices to the gods earned him the title of "slaughterer."[72] He ought to make a rope out of his beard![73]

Nor did Julian's reply to his assailants do him any good. His *Beard Hater* is a bitter, satirical work, containing some truths about the Antiochenes, but lowering his own dignity. Constantius may have been too distant, but no one wanted to hear about lice scampering about in their emperor's beard. Relations were further soured by the destruction of the temple of Daphne by fire, which Julian blamed on the Christians. In the fifth century Sozomen believed that Christians were arrested and tortured as a result.[74]

Julian's final anti-Christian gesture also miscarried. The emperor felt some admiration for the Jews as a genuinely traditional cult, and undertook to restore the Temple at Jerusalem. His aim may have been even more ambitious—to strike at the heart of Constantinian Jerusalem, to upstage the Holy Places by a new, rebuilt "sacred city of Jerusalem."[75] Unfortunately workers struck hidden gaseous deposits when they began to lay the new foundations. Explosions and fire greeted their efforts, and the attempt was abandoned in confusion.[76]

The Persian Dream

Through the winter of 362/63 plans were laid for the Persian campaign. Apart from Julian himself, few believed in the possibility of success. The last attempt to conquer Mesopotamia, that of Carus in 282, had failed. Subsequent wars had been fought for frontier forts. The restoration of the Roman position on the Tigris—the only military objective worth achieving to preserve Roman influence in Armenia—might once have been feasible, but no more. Julian's plan, however, involved a vast pincer movement, one claw being an advance down the Euphrates Valley with the bulk of his army, with the aim of capturing Ctesiphon, while his cousin Procopius with a smaller force moved south from Armenia. The junction would secure Mesopotamia for the empire, safeguard Roman interests in Armenia, and prepare the way for further conquests. It was William Howe and John Burgoyne anticipated by fourteen hundred years, and the Roman army met its Saratoga with the death of its commander.

Despite warnings and dire omens Julian left Antioch on 5 March 363.[77] The first stages of his campaign were extraordinarily successful. Fort after fort surrendered to him. If defied at Ctesiphon itself, he conquered almost all Mesopotamia within three months, thus equaling Trajan's feat against a far abler opponent who had won the two previous campaigns against the Romans. (Ammianus notes carefully the traces of Trajan's conquest which Julian found.) But Ctesiphon held out. Julian's army was now on the east bank of the Tigris and, in what can only be described as either an act of folly or the result of deception by a Persian agent, the emperor ordered his supply fleet to be burned. Thus on his move north to meet Procopius, he had to fend off Sapor's counterattack with the river at his back. Ephraem Syrus's comment is apt: "And he—Julian—commanded the ships of victory to be burnt and his idols and demons were confounded by a trick."[78] On 16 June the Persian counterattacks began in earnest and after ten days' heavy but not unsuccessful fighting, Julian was struck down by a spear thrust, "no one knows whence" says Ammianus (it was probably from an Arab auxiliary on the Persian side).[79] He died around midnight on 26 June surrounded by his philosopher friends. Next day, after Julian's friend Salutius had refused the purple, the troops elected a brawny Christian officer named Jovian as his successor. He extricated what was left of Julian's army after signing away Nisibis, Singar, and the five trans-Tigris provinces Galerius had taken in 298, and with these, Rome's influence in Armenia.[80]

The Aftermath

Thus ended one of the most astonishing careers in the ancient world. It is not easy to place Julian in the context of the post-Constantinian era and see him "effortlessly integrated within his age."[81] His contemporaries found it beyond their powers. With his cousin Constantius he shared an intensity of religious conviction, and, brought down to fundamentals, the worship of God through creative power of his Word would hardly seem to differ greatly from worship of God through the visible creative power of King Helios. The life and ministry of Jesus Christ played little part in Constantius's ecclesiastical councils. Julian showed how brittle that faith could be once the New Testament ceased to be regarded with the eye of faith. At his court, the Neo-Platonist philosophers also were figures of their day, resuming an influence momentarily held by their forebears at Constantine's court, and resembling in their authority the tightknit circle of Constantius's court bishops. In this respect, Priscus and Salutius might have found common ground with Valens and Ursacius. In no way also did Julian consider himself the successor to the Tetrarchy in his religious policy. The imperial diadem reflected the scion of the Constantinian house, although a rebel to its ideals. The image on the coins—even with the beard—fits neatly into the series Constantius–Valentinian I. But there one would pause. The febrile, backward-looking romantic who combined a student's love of the Greek classics with the instincts of a pamphleteer, and yet aspired to emulate Marcus Aurelius as a philosopher-ruler, was a phenomenon. To seek further to "relate him to the many cross-currents of the fourth century"[82] may prove labor in vain.

Few men have tried to crowd so much into so short a time. Dismantlement of the Constantian bureaucracy, restoration of paganism, reduction of Christianity to the status of a scarcely tolerated faith, institution of far-reaching social and economic reforms, and finally, conquest of the Persian Empire, all found their place in the emperor's twenty months' rule. When one asks what was left at the end, the answer is, more than Julian's detractors would concede. Julian had brought into the open what many of his educated contemporaries feared. Could one be a "Hellene," a lover of the classics, and a Christian at the same time? Also, some of the self-confidence of the Christian leadership in the East was destroyed. Would there be, perhaps, another Julian, another pagan emperor? Julian's memory aroused fear as well as respect in Gregory of Nazianzus and John Chrysostom. Seventy years after Julian's death Cyril of Alexandria thought it worth his time to refute the "Apostate's" tract *Against the Galileans*.

Yet for all this, the attempted pagan revival failed. Even some pagans greeted the news of Julian's death with relief. Few could really accept that "the safety of the state" depended on a sacrificial bull, as portrayed on Julian's large bronze coins.[83] The Antiochenes and Alexandrians were bored by the esoteric King Helios. They preferred the Galilean Redeemer who, sharing the essence of the Godhead, would save them from sin and death. The church, however, did not recover the position it had acquired under Constantius for another twenty years. In that time, paganism in the Celtic lands enjoyed a final era of prosperity, and in Britain, symbolized by the Lydney temple (built c. 364),[84] this was to have a lasting effect on the history of its people. In North Africa, Donatism remained the religion of the majority until the end of the century, also with far-reaching results. At Antioch, the free-for-all granted by Julian to dissenting Christians resulted in the imposition of Paulinus as an intrusive Nicene bishop favored by the West and Athanasius against the "New Nicene" Meletius, to add to other bones of contention between Eastern and Western Christendom. The "pale Galilean" had triumphed but Julian and the pagan gods had also exacted their price.

BIBLIOGRAPHY

NOTE

The story of Julian's reign is told by Ammianus Marcellinus XX–XXV (ed. and Eng. trans. J. C. Rolfe, 3 vols., LCL [Cambridge, Mass.: Harvard University Press; London: William Heinemann, 1935–40]). Julian's works have been translated into English, with a useful introduction by Dr. W. C. Wright (3 vols., LCL). Also J. Bidez, *L'Empereur Julien, Epistulae, Leges. Poemata, Fragmenta varia* (Paris: Collection Budé, 1922). Other important sources are *Orations* IV and V of Gregory of Nazianzus, *PG* 35; Julian's contemporary, Libanius, *Orations*, XIII and XVIII, ed. and Eng. trans. A. F. Norman (2 vols., LCL [Cambridge, Mass.: Harvard University Press; London: William Heinemann, 1969]), especially the funeral speech; Eutropius's *History,* and Ephraem Syrus's anti-Julianic works, ed. E. Beck, CSCO, 174–75, Scriptores Syri 78–79 (1957). The lost *History* of Eunapius of Sardis provided much of the material used by Ammianus and by the fifth-century Byzantine historian, Zosimus, in Book III of his *Historia Nova,* (fragments have been edited by C. Muller, *Fragmenta Historicorum Graecorum* IV [Paris, 1851]). Sozomen, *Ecclesiastical History,* Book V, gives a Christian view of Julian based, however, on good sources, including family recollections.

The most useful secondary study is G. W. Bowersock's *Julian the Apostate* (Cambridge, Mass.: Harvard University Press, 1978), a careful and thoroughly documented survey, though lacking a concluding chapter summing up the results of Julian's meteoric career. Robert Browning's *The Emperor Julian* (Berkeley and Los Angeles: University of California Press, 1976) is a fast-moving narrative, but less satisfactory in its treatment of the chronology of Julian's life and his policy towards the Christians. Older scholarship is represented by J. Bidez, *La Vie de l'empereur Julien* (Paris, 1930), and chapters in C. N. Cochrane, *Christianity and Classical Culture: A Study of Thought and Action from Augustus to Augustine* (New York and London: Oxford University Press, 1940); T. R. Glover, *Life and Letters in the Fourth Century* (reprint ed., New York: G. E. Stechert, 1925), chap. 3; P. de Labriolle, *La réaction païenne: Étude sur la polémique antichrétienne du Ier au VIe siècle* (2d ed., Paris: L'Artisan du livre, 1950), pp. 369–429, should also be consulted. The best treatment of Julian's personal religion and his understanding of "Hellenism" is that of P. Athanassiadi-Fowden, *Julian and Hellenism: An Intellectual Biography* (New York and London: Oxford University Press, 1981).

SOURCES

Cyril of Alexandria, *Contra Julianum* (refuting Julian's *Contra Galilaeos*), *PG* 76.489–1058.
Eunapius. *Vitae Philosophorum* (with Philostratus). Edited by W. C. Wright. LCL. 1921.

SECONDARY WORKS

Baynes, N. H. "The Death of Julian the Apostate in Christian Legend." *JRS* 27 (1937): 22–29.
Blockley, R. C. "Constantius Gallus and Julian as Caesars of Constantius II." *Latomus* 21 (1972): 433–68.
Festugière, A. J. *Antioche païenne et chrétienne.* Bibliothéque des écoles françaises d'Athènes et de Rome 194. Paris, 1959, esp. chap. 2.
Kent, J. P. C. "An Introduction to the Coinage of Julian the Apostate." *Numismatic Chronicle* 65, Ser. 19 (1959): 109–17.
Malley, W. J. *Hellenism and Christianity.* Analecta Gregoriana 210. Rome: Università Gregoriana, 1978.
Negev, A. "The Inscription of the Emperor Julian at Maʿayan Barukh." *IEJ* 19 (1969): 170–73.
Straub, J. "Die Himmelfahrt des Iulianus Apostata" from symposium, *Julian Apostata*, pp. 528–50. Darmstadt: Wissenschaftliche Buchgesellschaft, 1978.
Warmington, B. H. *The North African Provinces from Diocletian to the Vandal Conquest*, pp. 35–36. New York and Cambridge: Cambridge University Press, 1954.
Wirth, G. "Julians Perserkrieg: Kriterien einer Katastrophe," from symposium, *Julian Apostata*, pp. 455–507.

NOTES

1. Ammianus XXI.16.8, ed. Rolfe; Julian, *Letter to the Senate and People of Athens,* Eng. trans. and ed. Wright, vol. 2, LCL (1913), 270C–271B.
2. Julian *Misopogon (The Beard Hater)* 351D.
3. Ibid., 351A; also *Letter to Athens* 274D.
4. Julian *Letter to Athens* 271C: "We were watched as though we were in some Persian garrison." I have accepted Bowersock's chronology here, *Julian*, p. 25.
5. Gregory, *Oration* IV.23, *PG* 35.552A and Sozomen V.2.12–14.
6. For George's alleged birth in a fullery at Epiphaneia in Cilicia, see Ammianus XXII.11.4. In any event, he would seem to be an apt representative of "careers open to the talents" in the Constantian church and the social mobility for a fortunate few that resulted from its predominance.
7. Libanius, *Oration* XIV.30 (ed. Norman).
8. *Letter* XXIII (ed. Wright). George lent him books to copy.
9. Gregory *Oration* IV.25.
10. Ammianus XIV.7.
11. Libanius *Oration* XVIII.13.
12. Julian, *Hymn to King Helios* 140B (ed. and Eng. trans. Wright, LCL, vol. 1 [1913], p. 378).
13. Ibid., 140A.

14. See Athanassiadi-Fowden, *Julian and Hellenism*, pp. 38–41.

15. To Photinus, *Letter* LV. As with Basil of Caesarea, Julian did not agree with Photinus but was prepared to argue with him.

16. To a Priest, *Letter* XIX (ed. and Eng. trans. Wright, LCL, vol. 3 [Cambridge, Mass.: Harvard University Press; London: William Heinemann, 1923], p. 52).

17. The argument in Julian's *Contra Galilaeos* (*Against the Galileans*), refuted by Cyril of Alexandria, *Contra Julianum, PG* 76. See Malley, *Hellenism and Christianity,* esp. chap. 1, and *Letters,* vol. 3, ed. Wright, p. 320.

18. *Contra Julianum, PG* 76.560C.

19. *Letters* 89b, 288b (ed. Bidez).

20. To the Cynic *Heracleios,* 233D.

21. Libanius *Oration* XIII.13–14.

22. Ammianus XV.27–8.

23. Julian's *Letter* XXV (ed. Wright) to "Basil," who must surely be Basil of Caesarea. Julian writes as to a contemporary whom he admires, while disagreeing with him.

24. Gregory *Oration* V.23, cited in Browning, *Emperor Julian* (slightly altered by myself), p. 65.

25. Libanius *Oration* XVIII.42. See Bowersock, *Julian,* p. 35. Julian's Gallic campaigns are described excellently by Browning, *Emperor Julian,* chap. 5.

26. Julian *Letter to Athens* 283B. Compare Ammianus XX.4.4, for Julian's view that he must keep his promise to his Germanic recruits that they would not have to serve beyond the Alps.

27. See Kent, "Coinage of Julian," p. 111.

28. Ammianus XX.8.14. Promotion of officials in the West other than praetorian prefects was to be Julian's responsibility.

29. Ammianus XXI.2.5.

30. See Bowersock, *Julian,* p. 59.

31. *Letter* VIII (ed. Wright = *Letter* XXVI, in Bidez, ed., *L'Empereur Julien*).

32. Typical, a generation later, was Augustine's old teacher, Maximus of Madaura, see Augustine *Letter* XVI and Maximus's comments on the martyr Namphamo.

33. *Codex Theodosianus* XVI.10.3, rescript addressed to Cattulinus, Praefectus Urbi.

34. *Letter* XV, Julian calls him "bishop," and reminds him of old acquaintanceship. For his meetings with Julian at his brother's prompting, 352–53, see Philostorgius *Ecclesiastical History* III.15.

35. *Letter* XXVI. See Browning, *Emperor Julian,* pp. 125–31 on Julian's appointments.

36. Julian refers to his measure in his letter to Aetius. Athanasius entered Alexandria on 21 February 362. The exiled Donatists petitioned Julian to be allowed to return home (Augustine *Contra litteras Petiliani [Answers to Letters of Petilian]* II.97.224 and *Letter* CV.2.9).

37. *Codex Theodosianus* XII.1.50. See Sozomen *Ecclesiastical History* V.5.2 (ed. J. Bidez and G. C. Hansen, GCS 50 [Berlin: Akademie-Verlag, 1960], p. 199); and Theodoret *Ecclesiastical History* III.6.5.

38. *Codex Theodosianus* X.3.1. See Bowersock, *Julian,* pp. 74, 78. Ammianus thought that in some ways he went too far in his efforts to relieve the *curiales;* see

XXII.9.12 (the *curiales* themselves were becoming tyrannical; and for Julian's attempt to stop abuses, see *Codex Theodosianus* XII.1.54).

39. *Codex Theodosianus* XII.13.1, 29 April 362. See Ammianus XXV.4.15.

40. *Codex Theodosianus* XI.16.10.

41. Ibid., I.16.8; and see *CIL* III.459 (Amorgos), and 14198 (Lesbos).

42. *Codex Theodosianus* VIII.1.6.7.

43. *Letter* XXVII.

44. Ammianus XXII.6.2.

45. Nine Numidian inscriptions, mainly set up by city councils, celebrate Julian. Some explicitly honor the restoration of paganism. Timgad was one, *CIL* VIII.2387. Another was at an unidentified *municipium* on the site of Mr'keb Tahla, *CIL* VIII.18684. See Warmington, *North African Provinces*, pp. 35–36.

46. Commented on by Bowersock, *Julian*, pp. 123–24, following a report by Negev, "Inscription of Julian."

47. Gregory *Oration* IV.75.

48. Ibid., 86–91; Sozomen *Ecclesiastical History* V.10.6, and Theodoret *Ecclesiastical History* III.7 (other examples). The luckless Mark of Arethusa nearly came literally to a sticky end.

49. Ammianus XXII.11.8–11; Julian had been proclaimed emperor in Alexandria on 30 November (*Historia acephala* VIII).

50. Julian *Letter* XXI. He grants even that George may have deserved what he got! (380A). He considered George had abused his powers to remove pagan officials (*Letter* XVII to Zeno); and George was said to have asked concerning the Temple of the Genius (of Alexandria): "How long shall this sepulchre stand?" thus showing his contempt for Alexandria itself—see Ammianus XXII.11.7.

51. *Letter* XXIII.

52. Optatus, *De Schismate Donatistarum* II.17: "Venistis [the Donatists] rabidi, venistis irati, membra laniantes ecclesiae, subtiles in seductionibus, in caedibus immanes." Also II.18–21 and VI.1–8; see Frend, *Donatist Church*, pp. 188–89.

53. Fragment of a Letter to a Priest 290A.

54. To Theodorus, *Letter* XX.453A.

55. Ibid., and Letter to a Priest 291A–305.

56. Sozomen *Ecclesiastical History* V.16.

57. *Letter* XXII.

58. In fact, in *Codex Theodosianus* XIII.3.5 (17 June 362), the Christians are not mentioned, only the morals of intending teachers (as in a similar order by Jovian, *Codex Theososianus* XIII.3.6 of 11 January 364); but while the local *curia* had the right of appointment, Julian reserved to himself a final say in licensing applicants. His views about the need for "minds having understanding and true opinions about things good and evil, honourable and base," would be expected to militate against Christian appointments—see *Letter* XXXVI, perhaps the text of a second and more specific rescript, after 17 June 362. Other texts, see Bidez, *L'Empereur Julien*, pp. 69–75.

59. Ammianus XXII.10.7, and cf. XXV.4.20, "inhumane, that ought to be overwhelmed by eternal silence." Julian's own views are expressed in his *Letter* XLII.

60. Socrates *Ecclesiastical History* III.16.1ff.

61. Sozomen *Ecclesiastical History* V.18.3. Julian wished to prevent the Christians from acquiring dialectic skills.

62. For this council, see Kelly, *Early Christian Doctrines*, pp. 253–55; and Kidd, *History of Church*, vol. 2, pp. 208–15.

63. Julian to Ecdicius, *Letter* XLVI: "Infamous man! He has had the audacity to baptize Greek women of rank during my reign. Let him be driven forth."

64. Socrates *Ecclesiastical History* III.14; and Sozomen *Ecclesiastical History* V.15.

65. Julian, *Letter* XLI.438B (Eng. trans. by J. Stevenson in *Creeds, Councils and Controversies* [New York: Seabury Press; London: SPCK, 1966], p. 75). In general, Christians, Sozomen says, were harassed rather than persecuted by Julian; his grandfather and many relatives had to leave their village (*Ecclesiastical History* V.15.14). Gregory, *Oration* IV.83, gives a similar picture of vexatious accusations and mob violence.

66. Note the excellent account of Julian's relations with the Antiochenes in Festugière, *Antioche*, chap. 2.

67. Sozomen *Ecclesiastical History* V.19.1.

68. *Beard Hater* 362C.

69. Ibid., 346B.

70. Sozomen *Ecclesiastical History* V.19.12–14.

71. *Beard Hater* 362B.

72. Ammianus XXII.14.3.

73. *Beard Hater* 338D.

74. Sozomen *Ecclesiastical History* V.20.

75. Suggested in *Letter* LI. See E. D. Hunt, *Holy Land Pilgrimage in the Later Roman Empire A.D. 312–460* (New York and London: Oxford University Press, 1982), pp. 156–57.

76. Sozomen *Ecclesiastical History* V.22; Socrates *Ecclesiastical History* III.20.

77. See Browning's description of the Persian Campaign, *Emperor Julian*, chap. 10, and Wirth, "Julians Perserkrieg."

78. Ephraem Syrus, *Hymn against Julian*, ed. Beck, CSCO 174–75, 3.15.

79. Ammianus XXV.3.6. Bowersock's reasoning in favor of a Saracen auxiliary being responsible seems to me to be correct, *Julian*, pp. 117–18. For the subsequent legend of Julian's death at the hands of a Christian and finally, by the martyr Mercurius, see Baynes, "Death of Julian."

80. Ammianus XXV.7.9–13, "a shameful treaty." The worst feature was the betrayal of King Arsaces of Armenia.

81. See Polymnia Athanassiadi-Fowden, review of Bowersock, *Julian*, in *JTS* n.s. 30 (April 1979): 331–35, esp. p. 335.

82. Ibid.

83. These were ridiculed by the Antiochenes according to Sozomen *Ecclesiastical History* V.19. Julian "upset the world in the same way as his priests when offering sacrifice threw down the victims!" But Julian had some successes: see Gregory, *Oration* IV.81, *PG* 35.608B.

84. See R. E. M. Wheeler and T. V. Wheeler, *Lydney Park*, Society of Antiquaries Research Papers 9 (1932): 62–63.

18

New Perspectives in West and East 363–99

Julian's death was announced in Alexandria by the prefect of Egypt on 19 August 363. The "little cloud" had passed. For many Christians it was as though it had not been. On 16 September Christianity was once more proclaimed as the religion of the empire. Athanasius was already home. He wasted no time before writing an address to the emperor Jovian stressing that *homoousios* was now the creed of Christendom. On 27 September he met the new emperor at Hierapolis in Mesopotamia and, unlike his semi-Arian rivals, he was received with every mark of respect. Athanasius rode with Jovian into Antioch in triumph.[1] He now reverted to what he had always been instinctively—a loyal supporter of the empire and its rulers.

Almost at once other more lasting clouds were gathering. On 5 October a council of twenty-five bishops had assembled at Antioch under the presidency of Bishop Meletius. They acknowledged the Creed of Nicaea and reluctantly the *homoousios,* with the important gloss, "the Son is born of the substance of the Father, and in respect of substance is like him." This was more or less what had been agreed at Alexandria in 362, but the term *ousia* in any form still worried them.[2] Athanasius, however (if Basil of Caesarea is to be believed), came to Antioch with the firm intention of communicating with Meletius and thus sealing the union between "Old" and "New" Nicenes. Meletius for some reason delayed, and Athanasius then took the fateful step of acknowledging as rightful bishop his old friend, the Western-supported Paulinus. The Antiochene schism had deepened, and yet another cause of friction created between the Eastern and Western churches.[3]

This frustrating and time-consuming dispute was a reminder of the tensions left behind by the continuous twists of religious policy in the previous ten years. Though there was much talk of restoring peace, no love was lost between "Old" and "New" Nicenes. Moreover, wherever Lucifer of Cagliari turned up he found scope for causing schism and disorder. "Nicaea or nothing" could be a popular cause. Naples and Rome itself as well as Antioch were to be the scenes of conflict. These dissensions form an inescapable background to other significant events taking place in a period crowded with incident. With the emperor Theodosius I (379–95) emerges a concept of state-catholicism to which all subjects of the empire must adhere. The resulting patterns of church-state relations in East and West were to endure for centuries to come. The papacy under Damasus (366–84) and Siricius (384–99) at last bade for unrivaled authority in the West and recognition of its status in the East. There an uneasy equilibrium was emerging— between the bishop of the empire's capital and his colleagues in the ancient sees of Christendom. The problems of precedence between Constantinople, Alexandria, and Antioch were, however, made more difficult by the rise of a new doctrinal controversy as the implications of the acceptance of Nicaea's "of one substance with the Father" were grasped. How then was Christ's humanity to be understood?[4] Each of the three major sees in the

East had their own views. Finally, in East and West the church produced great men: Ambrose, Jerome, Basil of Caesarea, the Gregories of Cappadocia, and Apollinaris of Laodicea. These dominated the scene in a world where rival Christianities had become the stuff of popular politics.

Jovian's reign was short. He died at Dadastana on the borders of Galatia and Bithynia on 16/17 February 364 through accidental asphyxiation from the fumes of a charcoal brazier left burning at night. After an interregnum of ten days his successor was another Christian soldier, Valentinian I (364–75), who had once defied Julian when the latter was sacrificing to the gods, and had been ordered into retirement. At the end of March, he appointed his younger brother Valens (364–78) as emperor in the East. At Nish, on 1 June the military staffs were divided between them.[5] The pattern of two rulers, in East and West respectively, had become established.

THE WEST

Valentinian I

Valentinian was ideally suited to a situation that favored the gradual triumph of Nicene orthodoxy. He remained first and foremost a soldier who saw the effective defense of the Rhine frontier as his major task. Throughout his reign, pressures were building up from the Yorkshire coast to the mouth of the Danube as Germanic peoples sought new lands in the west. To Ammianus, the great disaster at Adrianople on 9 August 378, when Valens lost his life and his army in battle against the Goths, marked a climax in a long catalog of campaigns, in which ultimate advantage lay with the invaders. In such circumstances, the church could only be allowed to establish its own equilibrium. A Nicene by personal convictions, Valentinian "remained neutral in religious differences neither troubling anyone on that ground nor ordering him to reverence this or that. He did not bend the necks of his subjects to his own belief by threatening edicts, but left such matters undisturbed as he found them."[6] Ammianus may have been instinctively contrasting Valentinian's tolerant regime with Theodosius's imposition of catholicism, but his verdict was true enough. Except for the Manichees,[7] all other forms of Christianity and paganism were left unmolested. Bishops were bishops whether they adhered to Nicaea or Ariminum. Moreover, the church did not regain all its lost privileges. City councilors who became ordained must transfer their property to a relative who would undertake their duties, or direct to their municipality.[8] They could not keep their estates nor transfer them to the church. All immunities must be justified by reference to their advantage to the state.

This harsh irascible man would not be prepared to condone clerical disorder, as Pope Damasus (366–84) was to find at his cost. Equally, Valentinian would not interfere in purely ecclesiastical matters. "I am a layman," he told a group of *homoean* churchmen, "and should not interfere in these things [definition of the faith]. Let the priests whose concern these matters are, assemble as they please.''[9] The Nicene party in the West took full advantage of their freedom. Councils in Gaul (Lutetia/Paris) as early as 360, Rome in 369 and 372, and in Sicily in c. 365, condemned the Creed of Ariminum and its upholders. Gradually these were replaced by Nicenes. Not until November 373, however, was the climax reached when Auxentius, bishop of Milan, one of the architects of the Creed of Ariminum, died. The succession in the city where the emperor had his headquarters was crucial for both parties.

Ambrose of Milan

The story about how, among the milling crowd in the cathedral of Milan, a child suddenly called out "Ambrose bishop," has passed into the folklore of the early church.[10] Why the governor (*consularis*) of Aemilia-Liguria was so providentially on the scene can only be guessed. To keep the peace, certainly, but Ambrose was also a strong Nicene by upbringing and had theological leanings. He may have already established links with the Nicene party in the city. The cry was taken up. Ambrose was acclaimed bishop. Regardless of precedent and canons (including Nicaea, canon 9) he was baptized, hastened through the various ecclesiastical grades in eight days, and consecrated bishop on 7 December 373.[11]

He was then about thirty-four years old, a kinsman of the great pagan champion, Quintus Aurelius Symmachus, but born into the increasingly large minority of Christian members of the Roman aristocracy. His father had been praetorian prefect of the Gauls (c. 340), but had died soon after, leaving Ambrose to be brought up by his mother and sister. Theirs was a strongly religious household, accepting asceticism as the highest Christian calling. As we have seen, Ambrose's sister Marcellina received the veil from Pope Liberius in January 353.[12] The household, therefore, was among the earliest of those patrician palaces devoted to Christian piety and learning where Jerome and Pelagius taught a generation later. Ambrose's education included a study of Aristotle—to which he did not take kindly—and more important for his contribution to Western Christian thought, a knowledge of Greek. In due course, he followed his father into the imperial administration and it was as governor of Aemilia-Liguria in which Milan stood that he found himself in the city's cathedral on that fateful day in late November 373.[13]

He was to be bishop for nearly twenty-four years, until his death on 4 April 397. By then he had guided Western Christianity toward many of the characteristic ideas and practices that endured through the Middle Ages. He established asceticism as an accepted Christian way of life under episcopal control. He asserted the rights of the church over the state. He extinguished the remains of Arianism in the West, and ended any hopes of a pagan revival among the Roman aristocracy. Though not a scholar on a

618

par with Jerome or Augustine, he gave significant impetus to the application of Christian-Platonic exegesis to Scripture in the West—before it was
too late. He molded the Western Christian liturgy and hymnody in the
direction of congregational life. He was a busy, intolerant, and interfering
man, but there was also a touch of political savvy and, on one occasion,
even genius in his actions. Like Athanasius a generation before, he could
not afford to be a moderate. Schism, whether Luciferian or Arian-inspired,
or simply factious, threatened him even in Milan, however unassailable his
position appeared to be.[14]

We are concerned here with the relationship he helped to forge between
church and state in the West. This grew out of his conflict with Arianism. In
the first two years of his episcopate, while Valentinian I reigned, Ambrose
confined himself to episcopal duties. These included the advancement of
the growing cult of relics and the encouragement of conventual life. Already with the foundations of Bononia (Bologna) and Verona, one can
perceive the beginnings of medieval Christian piety in the West.[15] On 17
November 375, however, the emperor died of an apoplectic fit, riled by the
defiance of Germanic envoys at his headquarters on the Danube. It was
another three years before Ambrose could exert his influence. The new
emperor in the West was Valentinian's son Gratian, a youth of sixteen who
had been associated with his father as emperor since 367. But Valentinian
had married twice, and the troops at Sirmium had acclaimed his five-year-
old son Valentinian, by his second wife Justina, as emperor. After negotiations Gratian became emperor of the Gallic, Italian, and North African
provinces, leaving his half brother as emperor in the Balkans under the care
of his mother, an intelligent Sicilian lady with strong semi-Arian (*homoean*)
convictions. These were admirably adapted to the Balkan provinces.
There, in contrast to the West in general, the *homoean* creed had become
something of a "national" Christianity—with important subsequent effects
on the religion of the Goths.[16]

In the summer of 378 the situation developed dramatically in Ambrose's
favor. The Gothic tribes, pressed ever westward by the movement of the
nomadic Huns from the great plains of southern Russia, sought new lands
in Roman territory south of the Danube. For more than a century there had
been contacts between Goths and Romans, and thanks to the Gothic bishop
Ulphilas, many of the Goths had become *homoean* Christians and the Bible
had been translated into Gothic. The overtures of the Gothic kings were
well received at first. Lands were allotted to them in the Balkans and the
movement of the people across the Danube into Moesia (roughly modern
Bulgaria) was organized during 376. As in any similar situation, however,
difficulties soon arose. The Goths found themselves being fleeced by dishonest officials. When their complaints went unheard they took up arms.
The emperor Valens advanced to meet them, but this time the Romans paid
the penalty for disorganization and corruption. Their army was utterly

defeated near Adrianople on 9 August 378. The emperor himself fell, and the entire government of the empire devolved on a ruler hardly out of his tutor's hands.

In this crisis, Gratian showed tact and judgment beyond his years. His choice for emperor in the East was a Spaniard named Theodosius, about thirty years old. A major obstacle was that Theodosius's father, an outstanding general of the same name, having put down the revolt of Firmus in North Africa (372–75), had been executed on a trumped-up charge of treason at Carthage in 376. Yet one way or the other the son was persuaded to respond to the challenge of the times, and in January 379 he was invested as emperor. Up to this point, the main influence in Gratian's life had been the poet Ausonius who, as we have seen,[17] was a classicist first, and a Christian only second. Gratian had continued his father's policy of toleration for all that could be included within the mainstream of Christianity according to Nicaea and Ariminum. Inevitably, the Manicheans were excluded, and so too were the Eunomians and Photinians, perhaps representing to the emperor extremes of Arian and Sabellian belief.[18] Curiously, a halfhearted effort was made in 377 to put the Donatists out of the pale of imperial recognition.[19] A more decisive edict (*Codex Theodosianus* XVI.5.4) was, however, issued on meetings of heretics in April 378. The young emperor had begun to show rather more strongly orthodox leanings than his father and uncle. In the summer of 379 he decided to move to Milan where he met Ambrose.

The bishop of Milan established his influence over the young emperor immediately. Less than a year before, he had seen the hand of God strike down the pro-Arian Valens. The "Arian provinces," he asserted in a sermon in the autumn of 378, were being devastated, while those under Gratian's protection were safe and sound.[20] The flattery was apt. The ground was well prepared. A general antiheretical law—the first of many—was the result (3 August 379), and in January 380 Gratian asked Ambrose to instruct him fully in the Catholic faith.[21]

Secure in the emperor's favor, Ambrose turned his attention to the Balkans. Here Justina's support for the *homoean* interpretation of Christianity was not simply because it was "a manageable and accommodating form of state religion,"[22] but that it had become the religion of the majority of Christians in the immensely important Balkan territories of the empire. Parallel to the Catholic ascetic movement furthered by Ambrose, there were *homoean* women ascetics (*sanctimoniales*) who also held their creed with passionate conviction.[23] In the autumn of 380 Germinius, bishop of Sirmium, died.[24] As at Milan seven years before, the episcopal succession in this capital city was vital for the future of the Nicenes and their opponents in the area. Ambrose was again in the thick of things. His biographer Paulinus describes the scene in the cathedral of Sirmium. This time the demonstration led by *sanctimoniales* was directed against him, but Ambrose was able to get the Catholic candidate, Anemius, consecrated. The opposition, however, had impressed Gratian with its strength and he decided to convene a general council in Illyricum the following year.

Ambrose had intervened successfully far outside the bounds of his own diocese and in defiance of the known inclinations of Justina's court. He was well able to steer the proposed council in the way he wanted. Gratian apparently had promised the Illyrian bishops a council at which they should sit down with the Eastern and Western bishops and see whether agreement could be reached.[25]

This was not what Ambrose wanted. He aimed at bringing prominent Illyrian bishops to trial for heresy before their fellow bishops and thus strike a decisive blow at Arian Christianity in the West. Two bishops, Palladius of Ratiaria (a garrison town in Dacia) and Secundianus of Singidunum (Belgrade), were particularly objectionable to him. He brought pressure on Gratian. The two clerics were "rotten with perfidy." Why bring bishops from great distances to pass judgment on them?[26] he asked, bishops "whose only commendation was their grey hairs."[27] Gratian conceded. The council that began to assemble at Aquileia around Easter 381 was a council of Ambrose's friends from Italy and Illyricum. The wretched Palladius, the more outspoken of the two accused, realized he was trapped. After frequent intense cross-examinations by Ambrose regarding his attitude to Arius's letter to Bishop Alexander, he was prepared to admit that Christ was "true Son of God" and "was the Power of our God."[28] He denied he was an Arian. Surrounded by orchestrated murmuring of "Anathema to Palladius," he and Secundianus were at a hopeless disadvantage in the debates. Both were pronounced deposed from the priesthood. In view of the meeting of the Second Ecumenical Council at Constantinople almost at the same time and the condemnation of all forms of Arianism there, they could have expected little else. At Aquileia, however, Ambrose triumphed, not least because he had been able to organize proceedings without the lay arbitrators requested by Palladius. His reply, "Bishops ought to judge laymen and not laymen bishops," foreshadowed his stance in later conflicts with the emperor.[29]

Next year, the efforts of the pagan Roman aristocracy to have the Altar of Victory restored in the senate house received similar treatment from Ambrose (see below, pp. 702–3). The harmony between bishop and emperor seemed complete. Ambrose had achieved a position in the counsels of the state that not even Hosius or Eusebius of Caesarea could have claimed. Had Gratian enjoyed a normal span of life, the history of the church in the West could well have followed an entirely different course from what it did. In any event, the young emperor fell victim to a military revolution and was murdered at Lyons on 25 August 383 at the age of twenty-five. His supplanter was Magnus Maximus, the general commanding the troops on Hadrian's Wall, in religion a fierce, unbending Nicene Christian.

These events brought the empress Justina and her court from Sirmium to Milan. Her immediate objective was to save the throne for her son and fend off an invasion of Italy by Magnus Maximus. For this, Ambrose's aid was essential, and before long he was on his way to Trier. There he was successful. Magnus Maximus evidently agreed to stay his hand and Ambrose returned to Milan even more powerful than before.

This diplomatic success was to play an essential part in the succeeding dramatic events involving Ambrose and Justina's court. This latter was largely Arian-minded. Despite the decisions of Aquileia and the Second Ecumenical Council, Justina still accepted the decisions of the councils of Ariminum and Constantinople (360), while her court was open to brilliant young men of doubtful religious allegiance, such as Augustine of Thagaste in Numidia. At first relations with Ambrose were reasonably cordial. The court was inclined to support him in his final encounter with the pagan aristocracy over the Altar of Victory in 384. By Lent the following year, however, underlying tensions had finally surfaced. To the adherents of the late bishop Auxentius were now added Arian (*homoean*) officials from Pannonia and Gothic troops. Ambrose narrates the events as they now happened in a dramatic letter to his sister. Through her praetorian prefect of Italy, Justina asked for the Portian basilica situated outside the walls of Milan as a place for *homoean* worship. Ambrose, supported by his congregation, refused point blank. "A bishop cannot give up a temple of God," he told the prefect.[30] On the Wednesday before Easter, 9 April 385, a confrontation took place between the bishop and high officials of the court and Gothic soldiers in the "New Basilica," which was within the city walls. There was an uproar as Ambrose started to preach on Job's temptations. The latter's worst troubles, he affirmed, came from his wife. Ambrose's misogynism rose to the surface. "Each man is persecuted by some woman or other in proportion; as my merits are far less, the trials are heavier."[31] Examples of Eve and Jezebel came readily to his mind. He recounted his defiance of Justina and her court.

> At last the command was given: Surrender the Basilica. My reply was, it is not lawful for me to surrender it, nor advantageous for you, O Emperor, to receive it. By no right can you violate the house of a private person, and do you think that the House of God may be taken away? It is asserted that everything is lawful for the Emperor, that all things are his. My answer is: Do not, O Emperor, lay on yourself the burden of such a thought as that you have any imperial power over those things which belong to God. Exalt not yourself, but if you desire to reign long, submit yourself to God. It is written: "The things which are God's to God, those which are Caesar's to Caesar." The palaces belong to the Emperor, the churches to the Bishop.[32]

It was a dramatic moment in church-state relations in the West, and the court gave way.

Justina, however, was not yet defeated. In January 386 the right of assembly was formally reaffirmed in favor of believers in the creeds of Ariminum and Constantinople as decreed in the times of "Constantius of sacred memory."[33] The court, too, had been strengthened by the arrival of Bishop Auxentius, Ulphilas's biographer, who could expound and defend the *homoean* faith and provide an intellectual challenge to the Catholics. Ambrose defied the edict. "This bloody law," he called it[34]—though without much reason. He refused to hand over a basilica for Auxentius's use and also refused to leave Milan. The emperor, he declared, was within the church and not above it.[35] He himself remained within the precincts of his basilica, and once more the court capitulated. Now heaven itself came to his aid. Hoping to discover relics with which to furnish a new, magnificent church he was building, Ambrose ordered digging near the supposed tomb of the martyrs in the Church of Saints Felix and Nabor. On 16 June there emerged two large skeletons whose bones were covered with red ocher.[36] Ambrose had probably chanced on paleolithic burials,[37] but for his excited congregation these were the bones of the soldier-martyrs, Protasius and Gervasius, martyred in the Great Persecution and still marked by the blood of their wounds! A blind man was healed, and Milan "barren of martyrs hitherto," now had famous patrons and protectors.[38] Justina was finally discomfited.

There was little more she could do. The threat from Magnus Maximus came closer. She had to depend on Ambrose for another mission to the usurper (spring 387). This time it was in vain. Italy was invaded. Justina and her son fled to Thessalonica and appealed to Theodosius for help. The latter put loyalty to the House of Valentinian before any religious affinity he felt towards Magnus Maximus. In a swift campaign, the usurper was defeated and met his end at Aquileia on 28 July 388.

Why had Ambrose succeeded? Justina's dependence on him for protection against Magnus Maximus is one reason. His wealth of contacts among senators, including his former patron Petronius Probus, is another. More important, Ambrose represented the traditional Western view of relations between the Christian church and the empire. A generation before, Hosius and Liberius, to say nothing of Donatus, had preached the same message. Ambrose translated their statements of principle into a basis for action. In this, too, he spoke for the people. While many merely groaned and lamented, youths tore down the imperial hangings put up to indicate that the Portian basilica belonged to the state.[39] No action was taken against them though technically this was an act of treason. Ambrose showed in everything he did that he, as bishop, was undisputed master of Milan.

Theodosius remained in Italy for three years. Justina had died (c. 389) and Valentinian II was dispatched to Trier, nominally to rule the Gallic provinces, but the control of affairs passed to Theodosius and his dynasty. In 383 he had declared his elder son (Arcadius) Augustus. In a few months his powerful personality, too, clashed with Ambrose. At Callinicum, a fortress town on the Euphrates frontier, a Catholic mob with monks had rioted and destroyed a Jewish synagogue and a Valentinian chapel.[40] Theodosius ordered the bishop to repair both and to punish those guilty of riot. Ambrose intervened. In another of his long letters to Marcellina he described how he preached before the emperor. A dull rambling start on the story of David and Nathan suddenly took flight. Nathan had been right to expostulate with David, "that pious and gentle man." So he Ambrose might criticize Theodosius. Jews and pagans had been guilty of similar acts in Julian's reign, yet they had been left unpunished. Why should heresy and infidelity be favored now? Ecclesiastical penalties were hinted at. "Let me offer [the Eucharist] with a clear conscience, and set my mind at ease," he told Theodosius. Objections against the monks from a lesser mortal (albeit the *magister militum* Timasius) were brushed aside.[41] The bishop dealt with the emperor alone, and again he won.

The church's secular pretensions had been pushed to the limit. The claim was now for indirect control over state affairs, the right to veto any measure that appeared to affect the interests of orthodoxy. Religion came before public order. A year and a half later, however, Ambrose's severity and lack of compromise was to justify itself. In the summer of 390 the inhabitants of Thessalonica were guilty of seditious rioting resulting in the murder of one of Theodosius's senior officers. Some punishment was called for. With a refinement of premeditated barbarism, however, the emperor had the citizens invited to the amphitheater ostensibly for a special show. When all were seated, soldiers moved in and massacred them. In three hours, some seven thousand men, women, and children were done to death.[42]

This terrible deed would have been shocking in any context. News of Theodosius's intentions had leaked out. Ambrose, however, had been assured that they would not be carried out. In fact Theodosius relented too late. In mid-September, Ambrose sent him a personal and secret letter that has been rightly applauded as a masterpiece of firmness and tact. Three paragraphs may be quoted:

> I have written this, not in order to confound you, but that the examples of these kings may stir you up to put away this sin from your kingdom, for you will do it away by humbling your soul before God. You are a man, and temptation has come upon you; conquer it. Sin is not done away but by tears and penitence. Neither angel can do it, nor archangel. The Lord himself, who alone can say "I am with you" if we have sinned, does not forgive any but those who repent.
>
> I urge, I beg, I exhort, I warn, for it is a grief to me, that you who were an example of unusual piety, who were conspicuous for clemency, who would not suffer single offenders to be put in peril, should not mourn that so many have perished. Though you have waged battle most successfully, though in other matters, too, you are worthy of praise, yet piety was ever the crown of your actions. The devil envied that which was your most excellent possession. Conquer him whilst you still possess that wherewith you may conquer. Do not add another sin to your sin by a course of action which has injured many.
>
> I, indeed, though a debtor to your kindness in all other things, for which I

cannot be ungrateful, that kindness which has surpassed that of many emperors, and has been equalled by one only; I, I say, have no cause for a charge of contumacy against you, but have cause for fear; I dare not offer the sacrifice if you intend to be present. Is that which is not allowed after shedding the blood of one innocent person, allowed after shedding the blood of many? I do not think so.[43]

Theodosius's excuses and spurious comparisons between himself and King David as an adulterer and murderer, yet reinstated in divine favor, were dismissed. Excommunication until public penance had been performed was required by Ambrose and accepted by the emperor. The first milestone on the road to Canossa had been set up on that day. The heinous character of Theodosius's crime justified Ambrose's action. A vital principle of Western society had also been established. A Christian moral order stood above the will of the ruler or any reason of state. No arbitrary destruction of human life could pass without challenge by the church. In the last resort a ruler's misgovernment could bring about his excommunication and deposition.

Ambrose had proved his mettle as a statesman and gained his place in history. Was his, however, the only way of bringing the church's influence to bear on the emperor? Events three years earlier might point to different conclusions. In January 387 social and economic discontent had overflowed in Antioch, when a special demand for money was made to "celebrate" Theodosius's tenth and his son Arcadius's fifth anniversaries as rulers.[44] The imperial images were thrown down or defaced. This was an act of rebellion, a formal renunciation of allegiance to the reigning emperors. Terrified, the citizens of Antioch recoiled at what they had done. Everyone was evidently aware of Theodosius's uncertain temper. The sword, beasts, or the stake awaited guilty and innocent alike. Rumors spread of indiscriminate massacres being prepared. The churches became crowded. The presbyter John established his reputation as "the Golden-tongued" (*Chrysostomos*) by his Lenten sermons cajoling, comforting, exhorting, vividly imagining the conduct of the imminent proceedings against the city leaders, and discreetly reminding his hearers of the latent authority of the church even over the emperor himself.[45] This, however, was never to be tested. Eastern Christianity produced its trump card, its holy men. One of these, Macedonius, "the Barley Eater"—"a man totally ignorant of all learning" and clad in sheepskin—achieved what no other power could do. The avenging commissioners were told to inform the emperor, "You are an emperor, but you are also a mortal man. . . . Do not command God's image to be destroyed. Why all this stir about images of bronze?"[46] The medicine worked, reinforced by the tears of Flavian,[47] bishop of Antioch, and when blame was providentially placed on a demon of monstrous appearance, whom bystanders had actually "seen" in female form (as always!) goading on the riotous mobs, punishment was remitted.[48]

Here were two different styles of relationship. The West turned each issue into a trial of strength. Which sword is the sharper, the church's or the empire's? Statement of principles, enforcement of penance, excommunication, and ultimately deposition were the weapons in the church's armory. But for all this, the dead of Thessalonica could not be revived nor the panoply of sanction brought to bear before the crime was committed. In the East, the church's position seemed almost hopeless. The overwhelming power of the emperor was acknowledged,[49] but because of that, he was more open to human appeal; weeping and pleading became weapons more effective than the iron legalism of the Western episcopate. "Remember that you are a mortal man," were words addressed to one who could afford to condescend, for his ultimate authority was not open to challenge.

Ambrose's last six years were productive; he concentrated on upholding the prestige and position of asceticism in the church. With the East he tangled unsuccessfully over the generation-long schism in Antioch. Bishop Flavian, Meletius's successor, had the confidence of emperor and people alike. Ambrose was more at home condemning Bonosus, an Illyrian who doubted the perpetual virginity of the Virgin Mary, and Jovinian who taught that all baptized persons whether devoted to marriage or celibacy could be equally pleasing to God. He survived Eugenius's challenge to Theodosius, the final pagan effort at revival (392–94), and the death of Theodosius himself on 17 January 395. Ambrose died two years later, on 4 April 397.[50] His successor was an aged presbyter, Simplicianus, who twelve years before had been Augustine's catechist.

The choice was not without importance. While he lived, Ambrose was incomparably the most influential cleric in the West. He, not the pope, had contributed most to the overthrow of Arianism and paganism, and had assured the superiority of church over state that was to be the hallmark of the European Middle Ages. Once he had gone, however, Milan reverted to its former position as an important and influential see, but lacking the tradition, let alone apostolic claims that could render it a rival to Rome. Simplicianus symbolized Milan's reversion to its true status.

Damasus and Siricius

For Rome, the period of Milan's supremacy coincided with the steady and irreversible growth of its own authority in the West. The period started unpropitiously. Pope Liberius died, his past failings forgiven, on 24 September 366. His rival, Felix, had preceded him on 22 December 365; but legacy of the schism was bitter. Liberius had done his best to heal the wounds and the majority of the Roman community accepted Damasus, a deacon and one-time supporter of Felix, as bishop (1 October), but in the meantime, diehards who felt Liberius had forgiven too easily had consecrated another deacon, Ursinus, as soon as Liberius's death had become known. Riots followed,[51] culminating on 26 October in a horrible massacre of Ursinus's supporters in Liberius's church on the Esquiline Hill, in which 137 people were said to have perished.[52] The affair shocked contemporaries and brought the luxury and corruption of the Roman see into the open. Ammianus wrote:

> Bearing in mind the ostentation in city life, I do not deny that those who are desirous of such a thing ought to struggle with the exercise of all their strength to gain what they seek; for when they attain it, they will be so free from care that they are enriched from the offerings of matrons, ride seated in carriages, wearing clothing chosen with care, and serve banquets so lavish that their entertainments outdo the tables of kings.
>
> These men might be truly happy, if they would disregard the greatness of the city behind which they hide their faults, and live after the manner of some provincial bishops, whose moderation in food and drink, plain apparel also, and gaze fixed upon the earth, commend them to the Eternal Deity and to his true servants as pure and reverent men. But this will be a sufficient digression; let me now return to the course of events.[53]

His words were echoed moreover by Ursinian or Luciferian opponents of Damasus, whose account of the see of Rome at this period has survived, prejudiced certainly, but probably not inaccurate. The "royal" pretensions of Damasus were notorious and so, too, his churches "gleaming with gold" and "ornamented with precious marbles."[54] The importance of this evidence is that it shows how trends noticeable from the 250s onward had continued—the major role played by Roman *matronae* in the affairs of the bishopric, its wealth, and the ability of its bishops to aspire to a standard of affluence and power on a par with that of noble houses in the city. No pagan cult, whether endowed from imperial funds or not, could rival the wealth of the papacy at this time. Under Damasus pagan Rome became Rome of the apostles and martyrs.

Valentinian also disliked the ways of Damasus and his clergy. While sending Ursinus to exile (November 367), the part played by Damasus in fomenting disorder was not forgotten. The charge of inciting murder hung over his head for the next twelve years.[55] He achieved also an unenviable repute for soliciting bequests from rich *matronae*. An edict preventing clergy, monks, and "ex-clergy" visiting the homes of widows and young wards for such purposes seems to have been aimed principally at the Roman clergy,[56] among whom Damasus "the ear-tickler" was a notorious offender.[57]

In 378, however, the emperor was Gratian who was more favorable to Damasus. The latter was cleared finally of the various charges against him. A medley of nagging rivals and nuisances—which included the Donatist bishop of Rome (Claudian), the bishop of Parma, and Isaac, a Jew who moved readily between Christianity and Judaism and had instigated a charge of murder against Damasus in 371—were exiled.[58] A Roman council held in the autumn of 378 then petitioned the emperor that accused bishops, if they suspected the impartiality of their metropolitan, might take their case to be heard by the pope, or by a synod of at least fifteen neighboring bishops. Metropolitans could be judged by the pope or "by such judges as he might appoint." In addition, the pope should be exempt from trial by a secular court but be entitled to plead before the emperor's court. Gratian granted the first two requests, but "lost" the last amid a haze of honorific verbiage concerning the emperors' natural sense of justice.[59] The grant of the right to hear appeals by bishops over the heads of their metropolitan obviously increased papal authority in the West by making the pope superior to all metropolitans in the West.

Papal status was further enhanced in Damasus's last years. In 380 he installed Acholius as bishop of Thessalonica and made him papal vicar, that is, his personal deputy for the Illyrian provinces, a significant move designed to stake a claim in an area of interest to the increasing power of the church of Constantinople. In 382 another Roman council, called to define that church's attitude to the Council of Constantinople the previous year, laid down as a principle the primacy of the Roman church over all other churches by virtue of the pope's Petrine authority and not by virtue of conciliar decisions[60]—a challenge not only to the claims of Constantinople, but to the whole edifice of church-state relations as understood in the East. The next year Damasus made another momentous decision, selecting his friend, the presbyter Jerome, as his secretary. He gave him the task of compiling a new Latin translation of the Bible, made directly from the Hebrew for the Old Testament (and the Greek for the New), to supersede the older and discordant versions of Scripture in use in various parts of Christendom.[61] The publication of the Vulgate was another centralizing measure, reinforcing Rome's claims to be the authoritative center for biblical interpretation as the Septuagint had done in its day for Alexandrian Jewry. In later centuries the Vulgate was to become one of the pillars of the Roman primacy.

Damasus died on 11 December 384. His successor Siricius had few intellectual pretensions and did not conceal his dislike for the new breed of ascetic intellectuals in the West,[62] but he was a tough administrator and during his fifteen years as bishop he built on the foundations laid by Damasus to increase the authority of his see. With him begins the era of direct intervention by Rome in the day-to-day working of the Western churches. He addressed bishops in Gaul and Spain in the same tone as he used toward his own suffragan bishops. He did not confine himself to hearing appeals. His letters, written in the style of the imperial chancery, instruct and even threaten if the instructions are not obeyed. To Himerius, bishop of Tarragona, who had already submitted a series of requests for advice to Damasus, he wrote in 385, "How deeply smitten are we with grief when we are forced to bewail the misdeeds of all who share our status. . . . We bear the burdens of all who are heavy laden; nay more the blessed apostle Peter bears them in us, he who as we hope protects and guards us as sole heirs of his office."[63] A few years later, a letter to his suffragans reads in the same vein, "As we meditate in fear on the judgement of God . . . we dare not keep silent when a scandal arises. Necessity itself compels us to speak, for the Prophet says, 'Lift up your voice like a trumpet' [Isa. 58:1]."[64] He warned the Gallic clergy, "Let the offenders put the matter right in synod, and remove those on whom [clerical] status has been unwittingly conferred. Else, let us be informed of their names so that we may know from whom we must withdraw communion." This was the language of government. When the barbarians destroyed the Western empire, its people would not be left without a center of authority.

Between 378 and 398 one senses a major change in the manner in which papal authority was asserted. The pope now spoke as the mouthpiece of the apostle Peter, as *the* Apostolic See, superior to all others and even to church councils. The churches in Gaul and Spain, but not North Africa, were prepared to accept the situation. But as these claims were being made, and perhaps even provoking them, the Second Ecumenical Council in 381 had conferred on Constantinople equal status to Rome "save in honour," "because Constantinople is New Rome."[65] Apostolic foundation versus civic eminence;[66] the seeds had been sown for controversy between Rome and Constantinople that would stretch down to our own day.

THE EAST

Theodosius's summons of the Council of Constantinople in May 381 marked the climax of events extending back over the previous eighteen years. In this period the stage is dominated by the Cappadocian fathers and their foil and former friend, Apollinaris of Laodicea. In the background, the dispute with the West over the position of Meletius of Antioch was never silent, inhibiting agreement between Athanasius and his would-be colleagues in the East and delaying the final victory of the Creed of Nicaea over its rivals. The policy of the new emperor, Valens (364–78), also favored the creeds of Ariminum and Constantinople. Why should doctrines accepted by as many as five hundred bishops only four years before his accession be regarded as heretical?[67] With the support of successive bishops of Constantinople, Eudoxius (d. 370), by whom he was baptized in 367, and Demophilus (370–80), he attempted to enforce the creed of Ariminum/Seleucia/Constantinople on the Eastern episcopate as a whole. Nicaea had no standing. Even Athanasius was removed from Alexandria briefly (365–66), while Meletius of Antioch spent many years in exile, only returning to his see finally in 378. Basil of Caesarea and his friends were harassed by administrative actions designed to weaken their position while their opponents were favored.[68] Monks, too, received short shrift from this pragmatic emperor.[69] In Egypt they could be searched out and recalled to civic duties.

The Cappadocian Fathers

Basil the Great's importance in the history of the Greek-speaking churches cannot be overestimated. From Nubia to the Balkans, wherever Byzantine Christianity took root, he and his brother Gregory of Nyssa, and their friend Gregory of Nazianzus, appear on frescoes or mosaics—looking down on countless congregations as venerable exemplars of orthodox doctrine and the ascetic way of life. Eastern monasticism, a Trinitarian orthodoxy that combined piety and intellectual rigor, with a sense of zestful movement in theology, laid the foundations of what became Byzantine Christianity—all due in part to these three extraordinarily gifted and dynamic men.[70] The blend of classical learning and dogmatic Christianity characteristic of Eastern orthodoxy then as now also evolved because of them.

Basil (c. 330–79) we have met at Athens in 355 as a contemporary of Julian whose respect he retained.[71] He was always a convinced Christian, however, coming from one of those ruling Cappadocian families who had adopted Christianity in the late third century and continued to dominate their society. One grandmother, Macrina, had been a friend and convert of Gregory the Wonderworker, a grandfather had been martyred during the Great Persecution, but Basil's education included a thorough grounding in the pagan classics. He attended Libanius's lectures in Constantinople in 347, he spent nearly five years at Athens University, and he numbered among his friends in Caesarea the pagan philosophers Eustathius, disciple of Iamblichus and friend of the emperor Julian, and Maximus.

On his return from Athens to his native Caesarea in 356, he embarked on a lawyer's career with great verve but then, influenced by his sister Macrina, he turned to a more intensive dedication to Christianity. Austere and ambitious, he decided to seek spiritual ascent from philosophy toward the true Christian philosophy of asceticism. His visit in 357 to the monastic centers of Mesopotamia, Palestine, Syria, and Nitria, southwest of Alexandria, resembled a grand tour from which he retained lasting impressions. "I admired," he wrote, "their [the monks'] continence of living and their endurance in toil. I was amazed at their persistency in prayer and their triumphing over sleep. . . . They showed in very deed what it is to have one's sojourn for a while in this life and to have one's citizenship and home in heaven. I prayed that I might imitate them" (*Letter* 223.2).[72] Basil did so in his own way. The solitude to which he retired on his return was on a family estate situated in magnificent country overlooking the River Iris in Pontus. His call to Gregory of Nazianzus to join him reads like an invitation to a rather special type of camping holiday, far removed from the strains and struggles of the Egyptian monks.[73] Already in 359 Basil was in deacon's orders and a close associate of Bishop Basil of Ancyra. He was destined for an ecclesiastical career in which he would draw to the full on the experiences of earlier years. Thus, the monasticism with which he was to be associated seems to owe as much to urban ascetic households and to the monastic staffs attached to some bishoprics in the East, as it does to the Egyptian or Mesopotamian anchorites. According to his friend Gregory of Nazianzus, Basil aimed at taking the best from both systems, "so that the contemplative life might not be cut off from society, nor the active life be uninfluenced by contemplation."[74] In fact, however, the ideal of the hermit was replaced by that of the Christian-Platonist spiritual brotherhood.

Familial-like ties and service to one another dominate Basil's *Rules* and treatises on the monastic life.[75] Human beings were social and not solitary beings. The fundamental aim of any who sought perfection must therefore be the common life. Basil's monasteries were small, restricted to between thirty and forty members, directed by a superior. There was common dress and common property, but no excesses in fasting or other forms of asceticism were allowed. Emphasis lay equally on work and prayer. Prayer was said in six services during the day and two during the night. The ever-varying cycle of devotion was aimed at overcoming sloth and destroying evil thoughts and desires. The Eucharist was celebrated four times a week and the monasteries were under episcopal control. Thus far, one can detect the influence of Pachomian communities which Basil had visited, but Basil introduced a new dimension in monastic life for which he may claim originality. He established monasteries in cities as well as in the countryside—confirmation that religious life did not imply flight from the world but the overthrow of evil within it. To this end, the monk worked with his hands. He lived in his Bible, as did Basil himself. He staffed schools, orphanages, and hospitals.[76] If suited, he had scope for study as well as work. Basil's monasticism was a way of Christian life in which the monk was dedicated to the service of his fellows as well as to personal salvation. It came as near as any movement within the early church to a Christianity that aimed at changing society and transforming organized religion into a social as well as an individual creed.

Basil had other issues on his mind. Though strongly anti-Subordinationist and a critic even of the ideas of Dionysius of Alexandria, at heart he accepted the Origenist/Eusebian definition of the relation of Father to Son within the Godhead. In his *Letter* IX (c. 361) to Maximus the philosopher, who himself was interested in the views of Dionysius, Basil says, "If I may speak my own opinion, I accept the phrase 'like in substance' provided the qualification 'invariably' is added to it, on the grounds that it comes to the same thing as 'identity of substance,' according be it understood to the sound conception of the term."[77] He never wavered from this. He accepted *homoousios* after 362 as the term sanctified by Nicaea. He acknowledged the coequality of the Three Persons in the Trinity, on the grounds that baptism was in the name of all Three, and that if the Holy Spirit was "the finger of God," and demons were cast out by him, then he must also be

631

God. Being "third in dignity" did not imply he was third in nature, a "creature" created by the Son.[78]

These views matured but did not alter through Basil's career, first as presbyter from 362 and then from 370 as metropolitan of Caesarea. He remained as much an opponent of Sabellianism as any of his *homoiousion* colleagues. For him Sabellians were Jews and that was enough to damn them. As he explains to intellectuals (*Logiototatoi*) in Neocaesarea in 375, "it must be clearly understood, that anyone who does not acknowledge the community of essence falls into polytheism; so he who does not grant the individuality of the persons is carried off into Judaism."[79] It was not sufficient just to confess "three Persons." One had to try to express in human language the reality of Father, Son, and Holy Spirit sharing the common essence (*ousia*) of the Godhead yet retaining each their identifying quality or *hypostasis*. God was Father, the Son "was begotten," the Holy Spirit "proceeded," but together they equally composed the Godhead.[80]

Basil's Trinitarian thought was linked to his ideal as a Christian philosopher. He believed, as Origen had done, that humanity's spiritual aim was to raise the soul stage by stage toward God. Blessedness was the soul's rest in God. Evil was represented not so much by demonic powers as by a simple lack of goodness. To this essentially Platonic thought Basil added biblical imagery. Human beings "made in the image of God" had the means of increasing the intensity of that image through accepting the saving work of Christ. But if Christ was "unlike" God or was part of creation, his image would not be a true reflection of God. Hence, however expressed, the unity between Christ and God must be unequivocally acknowledged.

This theology, worked out by Basil and his friends, was eventually to triumph at the Council of Constantinople in 381. Before that was reached, however, Basil had been caught up in two other issues, one doctrinal and the other disciplinary and administrative; eventually they proved too much for him. The administrative problem concerned the church of Antioch, and as such, it involved personalities as well as principles. Athanasius and Meletius had failed to agree, as we have seen,[81] when they might have done during Jovian's short reign. They never got on good terms. This meant that the admirably Nicene but otherwise unacceptable Paulinus continued to be supported by Athanasius and the West, while Meletius was acknowledged by Basil, his Eastern colleagues, and the majority of the Antiochene Christians. Throughout the whole of his eight years as bishop, Basil was engaged in a complicated but futile effort, first to reconcile Meletius and Athanasius, and then on the latter's death (2 May 373), to secure Meletius's acceptance by Pope Damasus and Peter, Athanasius's successor. There was never any real chance of success. Difference of language, difference of theological terminology, and above all, different approaches to questions of ecclesiastical order and discipline drove the parties steadily further apart, and Basil made the task even harder by attempting to persuade the West to condemn Marcellus of Ancyra as well (that is, to agree to his anti-Sabellian interpretation of the *homoousion*). As a final straw, Jerome, then practicing Monasticism in the desert of Chalcis in northern Syria, kept Damasus posted with highly colored and inaccurate descriptions of the situation in Antioch. He summed up the situation with outright condemnation of Meletius: "I reject Meletius," he declared.[82] So did Damasus.

The problem was not merely personal. On analysis, the agreement between Basil and Athanasius on the *homoousion* was verbal only. Basil, we have seen, started from the *homoiousion* position as a disciple of Basil of Ancyra, and his acceptance of *homoousion* was a development of the theology of his former mentor.[83] Intellectually, Athanasius was a Platonist like Basil,[84] but he was also a populist, as much in sympathy with the ideas of Coptic monks as he was with those of his fellow Alexandrians. He tended, like the monks, to see salvation in terms of salvation from death and destruction by demonic powers, and as his *Life of Antony* shows, these were stark realities to him. The abyss and the river of fire that the soul must cross were as vivid in Egyptian Christian conscience[85] as similar terrors had been to the beholders of the *Book of the Dead* in the tombs of a former age. Heaven, therefore, could be gained only by a soul infused with the power of Christ, and that of necessity must be divine power. Nothing less than God could save. These ideas agreed with the Western understanding of the atonement, but had little in common with the Christian Platonism of Basil and his Eastern colleagues. Support for rival candidates for the throne of Antioch could hardly have been avoided.

Not surprisingly then, though the letters written by Basil to Athanasius and Damasus are courteous enough, they show increasing disillusionment.[86] After Athanasius's death, there was no one on whom Basil could rely for mediation. By 375 he was finding the pope "stuck-up and haughty, seated somehow up above and on that account unable to hear those on the ground who were telling him the truth."[87] Some eighteen months later he wrote to his friend, Eusebius of Samosata, at a loss to know what any new embassy to Rome could achieve. There came to mind the saying of Diomedes about Achilles, "You ought not to entreat him, because they say, the man is arrogant."[88] The emperor Anastasius was to say the same of Pope Hormisdas in 517.[89] Basil was not humble himself, and Damasus was conscious of his apostolic rights, but if disputes involving personalities could not be settled between Eastern and Western representatives, what chance would there be in matters of more fundamental importance?

During 376, Basil tried one more embassy. This time he got some satisfaction. He had mentioned Apollinaris of Laodicea as one of those whose views Damasus should condemn. The pope obliged. At a synod perhaps in 377, Apollinaris was excommunicated.[90] For Basil, however, it was too late. There was no peace at Antioch. "I seem for my sins to prosper in nothing," he wrote in despair.[91] Never in good health, continuously harassed by a variety of petty difficulties, he was now utterly worn out with the futility of the negotiations. He died on 1 January 379, not yet fifty.

Apollinaris of Laodicea

The question of Apollinaris and his christological views had become more serious during the 370s. Apollinaris himself was a dedicated Nicene, a longstanding friend of Athanasius, a correspondent of Basil, and in many ways qualified to bring the two men together. In an exchange of letters dating between 359 and 362 which would seem to be genuine, Apollinaris is shown to be exercising some influence on Basil's final acceptance of the *homoousion*.[92] Despite his championship of the cause of Christian intellectuals against Julian's ban on their teaching the classics, he was not consecrated bishop of Laodicea in Syria, but found himself, like Paulinus, the leader of a small, uncompromisingly Nicene community in the city. The problem which Apollinaris took up was the direct result of the Arian controversy. Already at the Alexandrian Council of 362 there had been discussion of how Christ himself was to be acknowledged. If he was "very God," how could he be "true man"? Athanasius had sidestepped the issue, contenting himself with agreeing with those Antiochenes at the council who rejected the notion that the soul of Christ, being understood as forming part of the divine Word, could have entered Christ in the same way as a soul had entered the bodies of the prophets.[93]

Apollinaris was less conciliatory. Returning to Syria he began to attack his opponents. "I am astonished to find people," he wrote, "confessing the Lord as God incarnate, and yet falling into the separation wickedly introduced by those who imitate Paul [of Samosata]. For they slavishly imitate Paul of Samosata, differentiating between him from Heaven whom they declare to be God, and the man derived from the earth."[94] So far, Apollinaris was in good company, for fear of the doctrines of Paul of Samosata had been shared by both the Eusebians and Athanasians in their attempts to interpret the mystery of the Godhead. Apollinaris's solution was, however, far more radical than either. Human nature was by definition depraved. Thus, God could not be conjoined with man, even perfect man, for that would entail two Sons, one by nature God, and the other God by adoption.[95] Instead he argued, like the presbyter Malchion a century before, "Rather the flesh [of Christ] united itself with the heavenly governing principle [that is, the Word] and was fused with it. . . . So, out of the moved and the mover was composed a single living entity—not two but one, composed of two complete self-moving principles."[96]

Apollinaris therefore rejected the existence of a human mind in Christ. If one accepted its existence, then one had to accept also the possibility of Christ's free will and ability to sin. The mind (*nous*) of Christ must be changeless, not "a prey to filthy thoughts, but existing as a divine mind, immutable and heavenly."[97] Humanity was saved by the incarnation (*sarkosis*) of the Word,[98] but could not be saved by a Being who even in the remotest degree could be liable to human weaknesses and failings. No mortal could create life. Christ was "in the form" of a servant only (Phil. 2:7) but by his own voluntary self-emptying accepted the conditions of human life and became incarnate through the Virgin.[99] The Virgin in truth was "the Bearer of God" (*Theotokos*).[100] Orthodoxy could be summed up in the formula, "one incarnate nature of the Word, to be worshipped with his flesh in one worship."[101]

This was a brilliant and logical system destined to exercise an enormous influence among East Roman Christians. Apollinaris preached with verve, proclaiming "the renewal of the temple afresh," and his ideas included much of what Origen and Athanasius had believed. These ideas demonstrated to the believer the possibility of sharing in the divine through participation in the divine elements of the Eucharist, appealed to the religious sense of a great number of Eastern Christians and yet they could not be accepted as the creed of Christendom. To assert belief in a Christ who lacked an essential part of human nature, namely the human mind, destroyed community between Savior and saved.[102] "Valentinian Gnosticism" was not too strong a criticism. Basil was quick to point out that if Apollinaris's doctrines were correct there was no need for the holy Virgin, "if the God-bearing flesh was not assumed from the material from which Adam was molded."[103] He regarded Apollinaris as a Sabellian and an innovator,[104] but not as a personal opponent. Basil's repudiation of his views was enough to have them condemned at the Council of Constantinople in 381.

Theodosius and the Council of Constantinople

By 381, Apollinaris had been in schism for six years and Basil dead for two and a half. Valens had fallen in battle against the Goths and a new emperor from the West was ruling in Constantinople. In some ways, Theodosius I (379–95) recalls Constantine. He arrived in New Rome, a soldier and Westerner, determined apparently to uphold the rectitude of Western doctrinal standpoints. In a relatively short time, however, the Eastern Christian leaders had restored their influence. The assertion of Western authority was forgotten. Nothing was to change in the pattern of East-West ecclesiastical relations from the point of view at Constantinople.

Theodosius spent much of the year 379 on or within reach of the Danube frontier attempting to restore the situation resulting from the catastrophe to Roman arms at Adrianople. On 17 November his victories were being proclaimed in the capital. Meantime steps were being taken by Basil's friends for a new ecumenical council to reestablish the Creed of Nicaea and condemn Arianism and Apollinarianism, and if possible, to pave the way for reconciliation with the West. In the autumn of 379 Meletius presided over a council of 153 bishops at Antioch. It accepted the oneness of the

Trinity and the full deity of the Holy Spirit, and rejected the teaching of Apollinaris on the one hand, and the various Arianizing groups that denied the deity of Spirit on the other.[105] At the same time the situation in the capital itself was being transformed. For forty years Constantinople had been a pro-Arian city. Successive bishops, Macedonius, Eudoxius, and now Demophilus occupied the Church of the Twelve Apostles. These were moderate and sensible individuals, but like their imperial masters, had accepted the *homoean* standpoint of the Creed of Ariminum. Now Valens was dead, and the Nicene minority began to take heart. They sent a delegation to Cappadocia to invite Gregory of Nazianzus to come to Constantinople. Gregory was bishop of Sasima, a wretched one-horse town near the Armenian frontier. He responded gladly. In a short time he galvanized the Nicenes from his Church of the Resurrection (*Anastasia;* see Sozomen *Ecclesiastical History* VII.5.3). But there was an unexpected hitch. Peter of Alexandria (373–80) wanted to control Constantinople himself, perhaps with wider ambitions to establish Alexandria as unchallengeably the most important see in the East. He sent in his own candidate, an outrageous but plausible philosophical quack named Maximus the Cynic.[106] Damasus of Rome rejected him, but Ambrose and the Council of Aquileia were taken in. So, for the moment, was Gregory.

The formal objection to Gregory was that he was already bishop of Sasima, and hence debarred by canon 15 of Nicaea from becoming bishop of Constantinople. No translations from one see to another were permitted. In the East, however, the canon was seldom observed. The confused situation had the city in a ferment, and the observation made by Gregory of Nyssa in a doctrinal sermon shows just how Christianity and its varying interpretations had now gripped the population. "If in this city," he claimed, "if you ask anyone for change, he will discuss with you whether the Son is begotten or unbegotten. If you ask about the quality of bread, you will receive the answer, that 'the Father is greater, the Son is less.' If you suggest that you require a bath, you will be told that 'there was nothing before the Son was created.' "[107] This was no isolated instance of hairsplitting. Nothing demonstrates the complete victory of Christianity so clearly as this intense interest in doctrinal niceties, nor the relevance of these as a barometer of popular feeling.

Such was the situation that confronted Theodosius. The new emperor, however, knew nothing of the East. The edict that he issued to "the inhabitants of Constantinople," but addressed in fact to "all the inhabitants of the empire" from his headquarters at Thessalonica on 28 February was strongly Western in outlook. All were ordered to follow "the form of religion handed down by the apostle Peter to the Romans, and now followed by Bishop Damasus and Peter of Alexandria" described as "a man of apostolic sanctity." All other teaching, described as "heretical poison," must be abandoned.[108] This was the first step toward enforcing a universal

Catholic faith over the whole empire. During the next months, however, Theodosius's ideas as to what Catholicism was would modify in favor of the views of his Eastern subjects.

In the late summer he fell ill, and fearing death approaching, allowed Acholius, the pro-Western bishop of the city, to baptize him. That act, however, marked the climax of Western influence on him. He entered his capital on 24 November. Next day he summoned Demophilus into his presence, and offered him the choice between accepting Nicaea or deposition. To his honor, Demophilus chose the latter. The Arians and their allies could only celebrate their Eucharist outside the walls. Gregory of Nazianus was called upon by Theodosius and was placed on the throne of the Church of the Twelve Apostles; but he was still bishop "in" Constantinople, not yet "of" that city. On 10 January 381 Theodosius issued a new edict proclaiming once more the sole orthodoxy of the Nicene faith, forbidding heretics the right of assembly, but omitting any reference to Damasus and Peter (or his successor Timothy, 380–85) as orthodox leaders. The "undivided substance" spoken of in the Creed of Nicaea was rendered correctly by the Greek term *ousia*.[109] One may perhaps see the influence of Gregory of Nazianzus in the change.

This ecclesiastical revolution was established "without tumult or bloodshed in all the provinces of the east." Thus wrote Theodoret of Cyrrhus some seventy years after the event.[110] To crown this achievement, perhaps at the formal request also of the aged bishop Ulphilas of the Goths,[111] Theodosius summoned an ecumenical council to meet in the capital in May 381. It was to confirm the decisions of Nicaea and find a new bishop for Constantinople. One hundred and fifty bishops, nearly all from Asia Minor and Syria, assembled and chose Meletius of Antioch to preside—significant of the change of heart at court, since Meletius was the man who remained obnoxious to the West and suspect in Alexandria. The condemnation of all forms of Arianism and Apollinarianism was accomplished without great trouble, though a considerable effort was made to win the support of those still uncertain how the relationship of the Spirit within the Trinity was to be defined (the "Macedonians").[112] Canon 1 of the council anathematized the catalog of offending opinions. The Niceno-Constantinopolitan Creed must have been agreed at the time also. This made slight but important changes in the christological section of the Creed of Nicaea. The fuller explanation of *homoousios,* "that is, from the substance of the Father," was omitted (not unwelcome to the "New Nicenes"), as well as "God from God," and "things in heaven and things on earth" (that is, the Son's creative work) were also left out, while some phrases, either scriptural or previously accepted *homoiousian* usage, such as "before all the ages" after "begotten of the Father," were inserted. It was a Cappadocian rather than an Athanasian statement. As Adolf von Harnack has pointed out,[113] from that time on the community of substance in the sense of equality or likeness rather than that of unity was the orthodox doctrine of the East. Significant too of the fifty years of doctrinal debate was the new paragraph devoted to the Spirit. While not stating explicitly that the Spirit was of the same substance as the Father and Son, it elaborated his role (which Nicaea did not do), "Lord and giver of life," "who spoke through the prophets," in the beautiful and sonorous tones that survive translation.[114]

The personal and disciplinary problems were, as might be expected, more difficult to solve. Meletius died at the end of May. There had been an agreement between him and Paulinus, his rival at Antioch, that whoever died first should be succeeded by the survivor. Paulinus therefore should have been recognized by the council. By now, however, anti-Western opinion was hardening in the East: The "younger bishops," Gregory of Nazianzus claimed, "chattered like daws and were as angry as a swarm of wasps"[115] at this possibility. The West and the Egyptians had become hated; the council elected Flavian, a man of similar views to Meletius as Meletius's successor, and the schism over Antioch was to be prolonged for another seventeen years. More difficult even than this was the problem of who was to be the first Nicene bishop of Constantinople for forty years. No one wanted Maximus the Cynic, and after hesitation, Gregory agreed to accept the see and replaced Meletius as chairman of the council. He hoped to continue Basil's efforts to heal the growing breaches between East and West, and had favored the acceptance of Paulinus at Antioch. The election of Flavian was a snub and in addition Gregory disliked the court ceremonial in which he was expected to take his part. At heart he was as touchy and arrogant as Basil had been, but he was also an orator who loved the great occasion, the chance of a splendid denunciation of the apostate Julian, a funeral oration in memory of Basil, and now a speech announcing his own resignation. He had much on his mind, and he spoke directly. The Eastern bishops were narrow-minded, and he himself was the wrong man to rival the highest in the land with outward display "and hiccough over the altars after an appetizing meal." "I did not know we ought to ride on fine horses and drive magnificent carriages, and be preceded by a procession and be surrounded by applause, and have everyone make way for us as if we were wild beasts, and open out a passage so that our approach might be seen from afar."[116]

This could have been true. Sasima was a long way from Constantinople, but even it had attractions. Christianity in both Old and New Rome had become the religion of the masses, and the bishops were expected to enshrine the material aspirations of their people. Their wealth, arrogance, and display were not taken amiss. In a crude but effective way it represented the triumph of Christianity over the traditional authorities in the state. Gregory was ill-suited for this role. He resigned after only a month (June 381). His enemies' victory was short-lived. Even the arrival of Acholius, "like a breath of the rough wind of the West"[117] changed nothing. Determined that the see of Constantinople should not become the object of outside interference, particularly from Egypt, canon 2 forbade "bishops outside a diocese to enter on churches beyond their borders," and canon 4 formally voided all "episcopal" acts carried out by Maximus the Cynic. Then, almost as an afterthought, in an appendix to canon 2 it was asserted, "However [*mentoi*] the Bishop of Constantinople shall have the primacy of honour after the Bishop of Rome, for Constantinople is New Rome" (canon 3).

For the government at Constantinople the reasoning was impeccable. Rome was one, whether on the Tiber or the Bosporus, and its bishops were therefore coequal, but Rome as the older city could claim precedence. This was not how the apostolic sees of Rome and Alexandria viewed matters. Being capital of the empire was no substitute for apostolic foundation. Both were bitterly aggrieved. The alliance between them was cemented anew so as to become a decisive factor in the relations between the great sees throughout the next seventy years.

The drama was to unfold slowly. Accepting Gregory's resignation, the emperor chose an elderly senator, Nectarius, as bishop.[118] It was an admirable choice. The new bishop knew the court and had no ecclesiastical past. During his sixteen years' rule he did very little, but "did it very well." Moderate and diplomatic, an unbaptized layman until his appointment, he was an ideal government man. In this too, he showed the difference between Eastern and Western thinking. There was no pantomime of pushing him through the subordinate grades such as Ambrose had experienced. Under no conceivable interpretation of events had he gone through "all the ecclesiastical orders," like popes Cornelius or Siricius, but his was to form part of the tradition of the capital. There were to be twelve more ex-lay archbishops of Constantinople, including the patriarch Photius.[119] Under Nectarius, the occasional gatherings of bishops who had business at court became regularized into the home synod to which appeals might be addressed and where conflicts throughout the East might be settled. Gradually, without anyone fully realizing what was happening, Constantinople began to make good its claim to precedence over the other Eastern sees. Discontented Egyptian clergy could turn their gaze toward the capital if their master in Alexandria displeased them.

THEODOSIUS'S STATE-CHURCH

The main issues, however, remained doctrinal. Theodosius continued his efforts to suppress every form of deviation, as well as paganism. The "legislative juggernaut" rolled on.[120] In 383, the "Macedonians" and Apollinarians were added to the growing catalog of heresies.[121] A ferocious law was promulgated against the Manicheans. Inquisitors were appointed and informers encouraged to denounce people suspected of unorthodoxy.[122] In March 388, Apollinarians were again singled out for ill-treatment. Their bishops were to be deprived of titles and of any access to the emperor, penalties suggested by Gregory of Nazianzus to Nectarius and perhaps passed on by him[123] to Theodosius. Eunomians (Arians) were vituperated in a law of 389 in which they were described as "eunuchs."[124] Then it was the pagans' turn to suffer. After years of harassment in the East by high officials drawn from Theodosius's immediate circle, in February 391 the celebration of pagan sacrifices and other pagan rites was forbidden.[125] Finally, this decade of repression reached its climax in a law of June 392 ordering that heretical clergy be fined ten pounds of gold and that their places of worship be confiscated.[126] Landowners, imperial bailiffs, and tenants alike were liable to be punished if forbidden practices took place on lands for which they were responsible. Thus, during the fourth century, the wheel had turned the full circle. From being persecuted, the Christians were now the persecutors. The Theodosian state, however, proved more successful in securing religious uniformity than Diocletian's. Precedents were being set in dealings with heretics which Christian monarchs were to follow for many centuries to come. With Ambrose, Theodosius shares both the credit and discredit of founding the medieval church-state.

The Theodosian age, however, was not only one of repression. The argument with the Arians and Apollinarians continued and the resulting theological reasoning served orthodoxy well. Gregory of Nazianzus stressed the essential unity of the three divine individualities (*hypostases*). "The Godhead is worshipped in the Trinity and the Trinity is gathered into unity. It is worshipped as a whole, and has royal power sharing a single throne and a single glory. . . ."[127] His friend, Basil's surviving brother, Gregory of Nyssa (d. circa 394/95), attempted to penetrate even deeper into the mystery of the inner unity and cooperation of the persons of the Trinity. Theology owes to him the concept of "coinherence," by which, while the Trinity was acknowledged as one in essence and unchanging in its nature, all three persons shared in its names, such as "God," "Saviour," "Holy" or "Just," and "Judge." The only difference related to cause and to being caused—Son and Holy Spirit being caused by the Father, whose divinity, however, they shared. The Godhead was one, even though various names might be used to describe the divine attributes,[128] or "modes of existence." The combination of the mystical with the intellectual, intuition with reason, was to remain the greatest contribution of the Cappadocians to early Christianity.

Arianism was fading. With the all-important exception of the Gothic Christians, it was dwindling to the level of a sect, though active among the artisans of the capital and respected there. The real issue after the Council of Constantinople was Apollinarianism, and the emergence of parallel but eventually incompatible theologies aimed at combating it. Apollinaris lived on into the 390s. What he had the boldness to declare corresponded in many important ways with what many Eastern Christians in their hearts believed. Somehow, God was involved through Christ in human suffering. The Word of God died and rose again. The Savior must be wholly divine in order to save sinful humanity. Many of Apollinaris's views were already foreshadowed by Athanasius, to whom the human soul of Jesus was wholly passive and the Word was the energizing force in his life. It is not perhaps surprising that an extract from one of Athanasius's works was reproduced almost word for word by Apollinaris. More serious for the orthodox was the appearance of a series of Apollinarian tracts, written perhaps by Apollinaris's disciples, which were based on leading authorities of the past, on Gregory the Wonderworker, Pope Julius, and Athanasius. These works were extremely well written. The compiler of "Julius's" letter to Prosdocius has imitated the pope's somewhat protesting, indignant style perfectly, while the attack ostensibly on Paul of Samosata could have fitted the atmosphere of the mid–fourth century. These documents were accepted without question. They influenced the ideas of Cyril of Alexandria and the fathers at Ephesus in 431. They served as the basis for Eutyches' vindication by Dioscorus of Alexandria in the great crisis of 449–51.[129] Before their exposure by Syrian monks in Anastasius's reign,[130] the Apollinarian forgeries proved to be among the most influential theological documents of the patristic era.

Certainly, the Cappadocians found themselves in difficulties. Gregory of Nazianzus could assert that Christ must possess the fullness of human nature in order to redeem it,[131] but even so he had to admit the domination of the divine over the human mind in Christ. Nor was Gregory of Nyssa's classic description of the littleness of Christ's humanity in contact with the majesty of the divine, as "though a drop of vinegar mingled in the deep was transferred to the substance of the sea."[132] Not only was this perilously close to the Arian view of the humanity of Christ, but it suggested a hybrid produced by the mingling of the human and divine natures in Christ. Was not Apollinaris's assertion, that the humanity of Christ was entirely absorbed into the divinity to make one nature of the incarnate Being, more acceptable?

The School of Antioch

If the Cappadocians laid the foundations for the Christology of the fifth-century patriarchs of Constantinople, the real challenge to Apollinaris was coming from a different quarter. For three-quarters of a century Antioch had been a cockpit where Nicenes and semi-Arians had struggled for ascendancy. In the last two decades of the fourth century, however, new concepts reaching back to the more truly Syrian tradition of Eustathius and even Paul of Samosata were emerging. Two Cilician bishops, Diodore, bishop of Tarsus (*flor.* c. 375–90) and his disciple, Theodore, bishop of Mopsuestia (d. 428), maintained forcefully the reality of the two natures in Christ. Jesus was a man and was part of the created order. God was by definition Creator, and the gulf between the two was inseparable. Applied to Christ, this entailed a complete human nature conjoined to a divine nature. "Jesus grew in age and in wisdom"; this cannot be said of the Word of God, because he is born perfect God of the perfect Father. So argued Diodore. "Growing in wisdom" itself implied that God only gradually bestowed all wisdom on him. The Gospels showed that Christ was David's son as man and David's Lord as the Word. There was union between the two natures brought about by the harmony of the human with the divine will, a harmony so complete as to form a single personality (one *prosopon*), but nonetheless a union of two distinct natures, not the absorption of the human by the divine.[133] Interestingly, Diodore had been a friend of Basil and the latter had preferred his theology to that of Apollinaris.[134]

By the death of Theodosius I at Milan on 17 January 395, rival christologies as well as rival ecclesiastical claims were beginning to confront each other. Already some prominent Western Christians were beginning to think of Christendom as divided into three distinct groupings of "Antioch," "Alexandria," and the "Apostolic See."[135] Except for the notable exception of Constantinople they were not far from the truth. Alexandria, despite the outspokenly Two-Nature theology of Didymus the Blind (d. 398), was tending toward an Apollinarian-based system; Antioch, on the contrary, toward a biblically based Two-Nature system. Constantinople was uneasily perched between the two, but inclining toward alliance with Antioch. Its next bishop was to be John Chrysostom, the famous presbyter of Antioch. So long as these great sees were governed by men of peace, the danger of an explosion remained latent. But what would happen when Nectarius passed from the scene, and when Alexandria was governed by a prelate who combined theological perception with unshakable determination to assert the rights of his see?

BIBLIOGRAPHY

NOTE

For the involved period between 363 and 381 covering the decline of Arianism and the victory of orthodoxy in East and West, only sketched here, see the two chapters, "Le déclin de l'Arianisme," by G. Bardy, and "La Victoire de l'Orthodoxie," by G. Bardy and J. R. Palanque, pp. 237–98, in *De la Paix constantinienne à la Mort de Theodose*, ed. P. de Labriolle, Bardy, and Palanque, vol. 3 of *Histoire de l'église*, ed. Fliche and Martin, and M. Meslin, *Les Ariens d'Occident 335–430*, Patristica Sorbonensia VIII (Paris, 1967).

For Ambrose of Milan, F. Homes Dudden's two-volume study, *The Life and Times of St. Ambrose* (New York and London: Oxford University Press, 1935), though full rather than inspired, has not been superseded.

For the papacy in this period, T. G. Jalland's pages in *The Church and the Papacy: A Historical Study* (New York: Morehouse-Gorham; London: SPCK, 1944), pp. 236–72, are well informed and well documented, a good introduction to the subject. The policy of the Theodosian autocracy is well told by N. Q. King's *The Emperor Theodosius and the Establishment of Christianity* (Philadelphia: Westminster Press; London: SCM Press, 1961).

For the Cappadocian fathers, E. Amand de Mendieta's *L'Ascèse monastique de Saint Basile* (Maredsous, 1949) is informative, but the reader is well advised to consult the three essays in Hans von Campenhausen's *The Fathers of the Greek Church*, Eng. trans. L. A. Garrard (London: A. & C. Black, 1963).

Canon G. C. Prestige's posthumous *St. Basil the Great and Apollinaris of Laodicea*, ed. H. Chadwick (London: SPCK, 1956) is a fine piece of scholarship throwing light on a significant but obscure incident in Basil's career.

Basil's *Letters* are translated by Roy J. Deferrari for the Loeb Classical Library and are indispensable for understanding this period. Finally, for the beginnings of the Apollinarian controversy, see C. E. Raven, *Apollinarianism: An Essay on the Christology of the Early Church* (New York: Macmillan Co., 1923)—still a fundamental study.

SOURCES

Ambrose of Milan, *Opera, PL* 14–17; Eng. trans. of *Letters* by H. Walford in the Oxford Library of the Fathers (1881); and selected treatises in H. de Romestin, ed. and Eng. trans., *Selected Works and Letters*, NPNF, vol. X (1896). See also Homes Dudden's essay on "The Writings of Ambrose," chap. 22 (pp. 678–710) of *St. Ambrose*.

Apollinarius of Laodicea. Extant texts in *Apollinaris von Laodicea und seine Schule: Texte und Untersuchungen*. Edited by H. Lietzmann, Tübingen: J. C. B. Mohr (Paul Siebeck), 1904; reprint ed., New York and Hildesheim: G. Olms, 1970.

Basil of Caesarea, *Letters*, ed. and Eng. trans. R. J. Deferrari, 4 vols., LCL (Cambridge, Mass.: Harvard University Press; London: William Heinemann, 1926–34); translation also of *Letters*, the *De Spiritu Sancto*, and the *Hexaemeron*, Eng. trans. and ed. Blomfield Jackson, NPNF, vol. 8 (1895); *Ad Iuvenes*, in N. G. Wilson, ed., *Saint Basil on Greek Literature*, text with notes, London: Gerald Duckworth & Co., 1975.

John Chrysostom. *Homiliae XXI de Statuis ad populam Antiochenum habitae. PG* 49.15–222.

Gregory of Nazianzus, *Opera, PG* 35–38; see also Eng. trans. of Theological Orations and some letters in *The Christology of the Later Fathers*, ed. E. R. Hardy and C. C. Richardson, pp. 111–232, LCC III, Philadelphia: Westminster Press; London: SCM Press, 1954; Funeral Orations trans. by L. C. McCauley, Washington, D.C.: Catholic University Press, 1953; reprinted, 1968.

Gregory of Nyssa, *Opera, PG* 44–46; Eng. trans. of some works in *Christology of Later Fathers*, ed. Hardy and Richardson, pp. 233–326; and Ascetical Works trans. by V. W. Callahan, in The Fathers of the Church, vol. 58, Washington, D.C.: Catholic University of America Press, 1966.

Paulinus of Milan. *Vita S. Ambrosii. PL* 14.27–46.

Preces Luciferianorum Marcellini et Faustini ad imperatores (*Libellus precum*). In *Collectio Avellana*, ed. O. Guenther. CSEL 35.1. Leipzig: G. Freytag, 1895.

Socrates *Ecclesiastical History* IV and V.

Sozomen *Ecclesiastical History* VI and VII.

Theodoret *Ecclesiastical History* V.
Zosimus *Historia Nova* IV.
For Theodosius's legislation, see *Codex Theodosianus* XVI, especially 5.5–24 and 10.7–12.

SECONDARY WORKS

Baynes, N. H. "Alexandria and Constantinople: A Study in Ecclesiastical Diplomacy." In *Byzantine Studies, and Other Essays*, pp. 97–115. New York: John De Graff; London: University of London, Athlone Press, 1955.

Browning, R. "The Riot of 387 in Antioch." *JRS* 42 (1952): 13–20.

Campenhausen, H. von. *Ambrosius von Mailand als Kirchenpolitiker.* Berlin and Leipzig, 1929.

Clarke, W. K. Lowther. *St. Basil the Great: A Study in Monasticism.* New York: Macmillan Co., 1913.

Duval, Y. M. "L'éloge de Théodose dans la 'Cité de Dieu' V, 26, 1. Sa place, son sens et ses sources." *Recherches Augustiniennes* 4 (1966): 135–79.

Ehrhardt, Arnold. "The First Two Years of the Emperor Theodosius I." *JEH* 15 (April 1964): 1–17.

Festugière, A. J. *Antioche païenne et chrétienne.* Bibliothéque des écoles français d'Athènes et de Rome 194. Paris, 1959.

Gaudemet, J. *L'Église dans l'empire Romain (IVe–Ve siècles).* Histoire du droit et des institutions de l'Église en Occident, ed. G. LeBras, vol. 3. Paris: Sirey, 1958.

Gottlieb, G. "Ambrosius von Mailand und Kaiser Gratian." *Hypomnenata* 40. Göttingen: Vandenhoeck & Ruprecht, 1973.

Green, M. R. "The Supporters of the Antipope Ursinus." *JTS* n.s. 22 (October 1971): 531–38.

Greenslade, S. L. *Church and State from Constantine to Theodosius.* Toronto: Ryerson Press; London: SCM Press, 1954.

Greer, R. A. "The Antiochene Christology of Diodore of Tarsus." *JTS* n.s. 17 (October 1966): 327–41.

Kidd, B. J. *The Roman Primacy to A.D. 461.* New York: Macmillan Co.; London: SPCK, 1936. Chap. 6.

Palanque, J. R. *Saint Ambroise et l'empire romain.* Paris, 1933.

Ritter, A. M. *Das Konzil von Konstantinopel und sein Symbol: Studien zur Geschichte und Theologie des II Oekumenische Konzils.* Forschungen zur Kirchen- und Dogmengeschichte, 15. Göttingen, 1965.

Rousseau, Phillip. *Ascetics, Authority and the Church in the Age of Jerome and Cassian.* New York and London: Oxford University Press, 1978.

Ruether, R. R. *Gregory of Nazianzus: Rhetorician and Philosopher.* New York and London: Oxford University Press, 1969.

Simonetti, M. "L'arianesimo di Ulfilas." *Romanobarbarica* I (1976): 297–323.

Taylor, Justin. "St. Basil the Great and Pope St. Damasus I." *Downside Review* 91 (July–October 1973): 186–203, 262–74.

Wiles, M. "The Nature of the Early Debate About Christ's Human Soul." *JEH* 16 (October 1965): 139–51.

——. "Ὁμοούσιος ἡμῖν." *JTS* n.s. 16 (October 1965): 454–61.

Wolfson, H. A. "Philosophical Implications of Arianism and Apollinarianism." *Dumbarton Oaks Papers* 12 (1958): 3–28.

NOTES

1. For the dating of these events, see O. Seeck, *Regesten der Kaiser und Päpste* (Stuttgart, 1919, reprinted, 1964), p. 213.

2. Socrates *Ecclesiastical History* III.25; Sozomen *Ecclesiastical History* VI.4.

3. That the fault was Meletius's is suggested by Basil, writing to Meletius early in 372 (*Letter* 89.2). Basil reminded his correspondent that it was impossible to win Athanasius's good will over the schism at Antioch "unless he receives his communion in some way from you also, who once deferred giving it." Athanasius had "been sent away without communion." Compare also *Letter* 258.3 where Basil reiterates that Athanasius "especially desired" communion to be established between him and Meletius but was thwarted. On the Antiochene schism, see F. Cavallera, *Le Schisme d'Antioche (ive–ve siècle)* (Paris, 1905).

4. See Wiles's short and valuable study, "Ὁμοούσιος ἡμῖν."

5. Ammianus XXVI.5.1.

6. Ibid., XXX.9.5.

7. *Codex Theodosianus* XVI.5.3.

8. Ibid., XII.1.59, 12 September 364.

9. The Council of Lampsacus (see Sozomen *Ecclesiastical History* VI.7.2–5) in the autumn of 364 agreed eventually on the *homoiousian* formula and accepted the creed agreed at Seleucia four years before.

10. Paulinus *Vita S. Ambrosii* (*Life of St. Ambrose*) VI; Rufinus *Ecclesiastical History* II.11; and for the fifth-century versions of the incident, see Socrates *Ecclesiastical History* IV.30; Sozomen *Ecclesiastical History* VI.24; and Theodoret *Ecclesiastical History* IV.6.7.

11. For the canonical aspects of Ambrose's elevation, see Dudden, *St. Ambrose*, vol. I, pp. 70–74. Jerome, *Chronicle*, gives 374 as the date. I prefer (with Stevenson, *Creeds, Councils and Controversies*, p. 126) 373. Time was needed for Ambrose's first phase of reform in his diocese. See Palanque, *St. Ambroise*, pp. 484–85.

12. *De virginitate* III.1, *PL* 16.231. See above, p. 562.

13. He and his brother began their careers as advocates in the court of the Italian prefecture at Sirmium. It was thanks to the patronage of the immensely wealthy but not particularly estimable senator Petronius Probus that Ambrose was promoted governor (Dudden, *St. Ambrose*, pp. 58–62).

14. Ambrose *Letter* XI. See Green's interesting work, "Supporters of Ursinus."

15. That at Bologna (Bononia) had already been founded by Eusebius, bishop of Vercelli, whom Ambrose admired greatly; see Ambrose, *De virginitate* XX.129, *PL* 16.314C. For Verona, see *Letter* V.19.

16. See Meslin, *Les Ariens d'Occident*, chap. 2; Constantius's advisers Valens and Ursacius among others had survived to a ripe old age, dying in possession of their sees between 371 and 378.

17. See above, p. 562.

18. *Codex Theodosianus* XVI.5.5, 18 August 378.

19. Ibid., XVI.6.2, 17 October 377, aimed at stamping out Donatism on landed estates, perhaps on political grounds because of Donatist support for Firmus. The vicarius of Africa at the time was Nicomachus Flavianus, an ardent pagan, so its enforcement was unlikely to have been severe.

20. Ambrose *De fide ad Gratianum* (*To Gratian, On the Christian Faith*) II.16.
21. *Codex Theodosianus* XVI.5.5. See Gottlieb, *Ambrosius und Gratian*, pp. 62–63, for the view that this law was directed against the Donatists.
22. Dudden's view, *St. Ambrose*, vol. 1, p. 188.
23. Paulinus *Life of Ambrose* XI.
24. Germinius had been bishop since 351; on his career see Meslin, *Les Ariens d'Occident*, pp. 67–71.
25. Palladius in *Gesta Concilii Aquileiensis* VI (*PL* 16.957), and Mansi, *Sacrorum Conciliorum*, pp. 602ff.
26. Ambrose *Letter* X.3, *PL* 16.981A.
27. *Letter* X.2, *PL* 16.980C–D.
28. *Gesta Concilii Aquileiensis* 19 and 31 (*PL* 16.961 and 963).
29. Ibid., 51 (*PL* 16.972A): "Sacerdotes de laicis judicare debent, non laici de sacerdotibus." The condemnation of Palladius and Secundianus at the plenary session of the council took place on 3 September 381 (Meslin, *Les Ariens d'Occident*, pp. 89–90).
30. Ambrose *Letter* XX.2. For the events see Dudden, *St. Ambrose*, chap. 11. The aim of the government throughout seems to have been to obtain the Portian basilica.
31. *Letter* XX.18.
32. Ibid., 19 (Eng. trans. NPNF).
33. *Codex Theodosianus* XVI.1.4.
34. *Sermo contra Auxentium de basilicis tradendis* (*Sermon Against Auxentium Concerning the Handing Over of the Churches*) XXIV.
35. Ibid., XXXVI.
36. Ambrose *Letter* XXII.2 and 12; and Paulinus *Life of Ambrose* XIV.
37. I follow J. B. S. Haldane's view "God-makers," in *Science and Human Life: The Inequality of Man and Other Essays* (London: Chatto & Windus, 1934), pp. 174–76; and see also the note by Meslin, *Les Ariens d'Occident*, p. 54 n. 137, on the various theories relating to these bones.
38. "Sterilis martyribus ecclesia mediolanensis," *Letter* XXII.7.
39. Ibid., XX.20.
40. Ibid., XL.6 and 16.
41. Ibid., XLI, esp. 26–28.
42. Sozomen *Ecclesiastical History* VII.25; Theodoret, *Ecclesiastical History* V.17; Paulinus *Life of Ambrose* XVII; Rufinus *Ecclesiastical History* II.18; and see Dudden *St. Ambrose*, pp. 381ff.
43. *Letter* LI. Eng. trans. in Stevenson, *Creeds, Councils and Controversies*, p. 141.
44. Libanius *Oration* XXII.4; compare also Sozomen *Ecclesiastical History* VII.23. See Browning, "Riot of 387."
45. John Chrysostom *Homiliae 21 de statuis* (*Twenty-One Homilies on the Statues*) III.2.
46. Theodoret *Ecclesiastical History* V.19.
47. John Chrysostom *On Statues* XVII stresses how the appeal to the hermits was zealously fostered by the bishops of the neighboring towns.
48. Sozomen *Ecclesiastical History* VII.23.4. Also stresses Flavian as mediator.
49. John Chrysostom *On Statues* II.2.

50. For Ambrose's final years and controversies, see Dudden, *St. Ambrose*, chap. 17.

51. On Damasus's dubious past and violence towards his opponents, see *Preces Luciferianorum, Letter* I (= *Collectio Avellana*, pp. 2–3).

52. Ammianus XXVII.3.12. See also *Collectio Avellana, Letter* I.7, on the same incidents from the Ursinian point of view.

53. Ammianus XXVII.3.14, 15, Eng. trans. Rolfe in LCL, vol. 3, p. 21.

54. *Preces Luciferianorum* (written in 383 or 384) 70–87 Damasus "auctoritate regali. . . ." For the ostentatious wealth of his see, see ibid., 121, p. 43.

55. The cry was "a sede Petri homicidas foras," *Collectio Avellana* I.9 (p. 4).

56. *Codex Theodosianus* XVI.2.20, 30 July 370. It was read in the Roman churches on the same day.

57. *Collectio Avellana* I.10 (p. 4), "matronarum auriscalpius." For a reconstruction of the conflict of 366–67 see Green, "Supporters of Ursinus."

58. *Collectio Avellana* XIII, Edict *De rebaptizatoribus*, addressed by Gratian and Valentinian II to the prefect of Rome, Aquilinus. Text also in *PL* 13.583–88.

59. For its significance, see Jalland, *Church and Papacy*, pp. 243–47.

60. See Jalland, *Church and Papacy*, pp. 253–57.

61. See J. N. D. Kelly, *Jerome: His Life, Writings, and Controversies* (New York: Harper & Row, 1976; London: Gerald Duckworth & Co., 1975), pp. 86–89.

62. Such as Paulinus of Nola. See below, p. 715.

63. Siricius *Letter* I.

64. Ibid., VI.

65. Canon 3 of the Council of Constantinople.

66. For this point of view, angrily expressed by Pope Leo after the Council of Chalcedon, see Leo *Letter* CVI.5.

67. For the figure, see Basil, *Letter* 244, ed. and Eng. trans. Deferrari, vol. 3, p. 463, referring to the number assembled at Constantinople in 360.

68. Note the example quoted by Basil as late as 376. The vicarius of Pontus summoned a council at Ancyra, ordered the bishops of Pontus and Galatia to attend, and then proceeded to exile some of the prominent Nicenes among them, and to force outspoken laymen to accept costly duties in the state service; Basil *Letter* 237.2.

69. *Codex Theodosianus* XII.1.63; and see also Sozomen *Ecclesiastical History* VI.40.1.

70. See the accounts of the careers of the Cappadocian fathers by von Campenhausen, *Fathers of Greek Church*, chaps. 7, 8, and 9, and for Basil in particular, see "Basilius," *DCB* 1: 282–97.

71. Above, pp. 575–77.

72. Written in c. 375 against Eustathius, bishop of Sebaste, a friend of earlier years, but one whose acceptance of *homoiousios* moved him towards Ariminum rather than Nicaea. Eustathius had introduced monasticism into Asia Minor.

73. *Letter* XIV. "Why need I mention the aromas from the land or the breezes from the river. Someone else might well marvel at the multitude of flowers or of song-birds. . . ."

74. Gregory of Nazianzus, *Oration* XLIII (Panegyric in Honor of Basil), 62 (*PG* 36, col. 577B).

75. See Clarke, *Basil the Great,* and Amand de Mendieta, *L'Ascèse monastique de Saint Basile.*

76. For Basil's hospital at Caesarea, see Gregory of Nazianzus, *Oration* XLIII.63, Eng. trans. Stevenson, in *Creeds, Councils and Controversies,* pp. 106– 7, and compare Sozomen *Ecclesiastical History* VI.34.9.

77. *Letter* IX (ed. Deferrari, vol. 1, p. 97).

78. *Letter* VIII.

79. *Letter* CCX (ed. Deferrari, vol. 3, p. 211).

80. Ibid., and compare *Letter* 236.6.

81. See above, p. 616.

82. Jerome *Letter* XV.2, "Non novi Vitalem, Meletium respuo, ignoro Paulinum." Unluckily, the forceful rejection of Meletius was decisive.

83. See A. von Harnack, *A History of Dogma,* Eng. trans. N. Buchanan, 7 vols. in 4 vols. (New York: Dover Publications, 1961), vol. 4, p. 84 n. 3.

84. See E. P. Meijering, *Orthodoxy and Platonism in Athanasius: Synthesis or Antithesis?* (Leiden: E. J. Brill, 1968), chap. 2.

85. For the "accusers of Amenti," and the "river of fire," see the Coptic "Assumption of the Virgin," in *Apocryphal New Testament,* Eng. trans. James, pp. 194–227, esp. p. 195.

86. See *Letters* 66, 69, 80, 90, 92, 239, and 242.

87. *Letter* CCXV to the presbyter Dorotheus. It was no use sending an emissary "who has a character foreign to servile flattery" to Rome.

88. *Letter* 239 to Eusebius of Samosata (ed. Deferrari, vol. 3, p. 419). See Taylor, "Basil and Damasus," p. 268, and for the chronology of the four missions dispatched by Basil to Rome, see Kidd, *History of Church,* vol. 2, pp. 261–65.

89. Anastasius to Hormisdas, *Collectio Avellana* (ed. Guenther), no. 138, p. 585. See below, p. 812.

90. Damasus, *Letter* II (*PL* 13.352–53).

91. *Letter* 266.2; Damasus still regarded Meletius as an "Ariomaniac."

92. Basil *Letters* 361–64. See Prestige's excellent short study on the authenticity of this correspondence, *Basil and Apollinaris,* pp. 1–37.

93. *Tomus ad Antiochenos* (*Synodal Letter to the People of Antioch*) VII, "and so dwell in a holy man at the consummation of the ages."

94. Apollinaris *Letter to Dionysius* I.1 (Lietzmann, pp. 256–57). The texts of Apollinaris are published by Lietzmann, *Apollinaris und seine Schule;* and see Kelly, *Early Christian Doctrines,* pp. 288–95; and von Harnack, *History of Dogma,* vol. 4, pp. 149ff. Some texts are given in Stevenson, *Creeds, Councils and Controversies,* pp. 95–96.

95. Apollinaris, Fragment 81 (ed. Lietzmann, p. 224); Stevenson, *Creeds, Councils and Controversies,* p. 95.

96. Apollinaris, Fragment 107 (ed. Lietzmann, p. 232).

97. Letter to the bishops of Diocaesarea II (ed. Lietzmann, p. 256). Dated c. 375.

98. Fragment 85: "The flesh must also be adored, since it formed an inseparable part of the *one* substance."

99. Against Diodore (Fragment 124, ed. Lietzmann, p. 237).

100. A point which he shares with his opponents such as Gregory of Nazianzus (cf. Gregory, *Letter* CI = *PG* 37.177C).

101. Letter to the emperor Jovian (ed. Lietzmann, p. 250; Stevenson, *Creeds,*

Councils and Controversies, p. 96); and see Frend, *The Rise of the Monophysite Movement: Chapters in the History of the Church in the 5th and 6th Centuries* (New York and Cambridge: Cambridge University Press, 1972; 2d ed., 1979), pp. 116–17; and Raven, *Apollinarianism,* pp. 202–3.

102. Thus Epiphanius *Medicine Box* 77.24, criticizing the views of Vitalis,'the Apollinarian bishop of Antioch.

103. Basil *Letter* 262 (ed. Deferrari, vol. 4, p. 86).

104. "Are not his sermons about God full of impious teachings, the old impiety of the empty-minded Sabellius being now revived by him in his books," *Letter* CCLXV.4; and compare also *Letter* CCLXI.

105. See Bardy and Palanque, "La Victoire de l'Orthodoxie," p. 283.

106. For Maximus's career and Peter's objectives in sponsoring his claims, see "Maximus" (11) in *DCB.*

107. Gregory of Nyssa, *De deitate Filii et Spiritus sancti* in *PG* 46.554–76, esp. 557.

108. *Codex Theodosianus* XVI.1.2, "cunctos populos." See King, *Emperor Theodosius,* pp. 28ff.

109. *Codex Theodosianus* XVI.5.6.

110. Theodoret *Ecclesiastical History* V.2.2. Kidd, *History of Church,* vol. 2, p. 281. Antioch was the exception due to factions in the city.

111. See Kidd, *History of Church,* vol. 2, p. 282.

112. Sozomen *Ecclesiastical History* VII.2; Socrates *Ecclesiastical History* V.4. Named after Macedonius, bishop of Constantinople. Regarding the relationship between the Father and Son, they were *homoiousians.*

113. Von Harnack, *History of Dogma,* p. 97.

114. See Kelly, *Early Christian Creeds,* chap. 10 for details; and see J. F. Bethune-Baker, *The Meaning of the Homoousios in the "Constantinopolitan" Creed* (Cambridge: Cambridge University Press, 1901), pp. 1–30.

115. Gregory of Nazianzus *Carmen de se ipso,* lines 1680–81. Maximus the Cynic was suspected of Apollinarianism; see Theodoret *Ecclesiastical History* V.8.

116. Gregory, *Oration* XLII.24 (trans. Stevenson, *Creeds, Councils and Controversies*).

117. Gregory, *Carmen de se ipso* XI, line 1802 (*PG* 37, col. 1155).

118. Nectarius may be the recipient of a letter from Basil (*Letter* V), condoling with him on the loss of his son in 358. At the time of his consecration he held the office of praetor (Socrates *Ecclesiastical History* V.8).

119. I owe this information to Professor D. M. Nicol of London University.

120. The thought is King's: "The juggernaut of Theodosian policy went grinding on its way," *Emperor Theodosius,* p. 54.

121. *Codex Theodosianus* XVI.5.11 and 12; following Theodosius's ingenious idea of convening a pan-heretical council! (Socrates *Ecclesiastical History* V.10; Sozomen *Ecclesiastical History* VII.12; and also Gregory of Nazianzus *Letter* 173, *PG* 37.28). The only deviationists whom Theodosius appears to have had any time for were the Luciferians who abominated Damasus; see *Preces Luciferianorum.*

122. *Codex Theodosianus* XVI.5.9. See King, *Emperor Theodosius,* chap. 3.

123. *Codex Theodosianus* XVI.5.14.

124. Ibid., 5.17.

125. Ibid., 10.10 (24 February 391, to Albinus the praetorian prefect). Previously

in 384, Theodosius had appointed a fellow Spaniard, Maternus Cynegius as prefect of the East, who was notable for his zeal against paganism. His wife was even more zealous than he, and persuaded him to destroy a temple in Osrhoene without the emperor's permission (Libanius *Oration* XXX.46); and for his career, see A. H. M. Jones et al., *The Prosopography of the Later Roman Empire*, 3 vols. (New York and Cambridge: Cambridge University Press, 1971), vol. 1: A.D. *260–395,* pp. 235–36.

126. *Codex Theodosianus* XVI.5.21.

127. Gregory of Nazianzus *Oration* VI.22; compare *Letter* 243.

128. Gregory of Nyssa, *Quod non sint tres dii* (*PG* 45.132–36); see Stevenson, *Creeds, Councils and Controversies,* pp. 113–14; and G. L. Prestige, *God in Patristic Thought,* 2d ed. (London: SPCK, 1952) p. 268.

129. See below, p. 768. Were Julius's letters really forgeries? I have raised the question, "Eastern Attitudes to Rome in the Acacian Schism," in *The Orthodox Churches and the West,* ed. D. Baker, Studies in Church History, vol. 13 (Oxford: Basil Blackwell & Mott, 1976), pp. 78–79. Who in the late 4th–5th centuries would think up the name Prosdocius as that of a prominent Roman Christian?

130. Evagrius *Ecclesiastical History* III.31. Letter of the Syrian monks to Alcison, bishop of Nicopolis in Epirus, c. 516.

131. *Oration* XXX.21 (*PG* 36.132), and compare his letters to Cledonius (*Letters* CI and CII). See Raven's criticisms, *Apollinarianism,* pp. 253ff.

132. Gregory of Nyssa, *Contra Eunomium* V.5 (*PG* 45.708); and see von Harnack, *History of Dogma,* pp. 86–87.

133. See Raven's discussion, *Apollinarianism,* p. 273ff., and Greer, "Antiochene Christology of Diodore."

134. Basil *Letter* 244.

135. Thus, Jerome answering Vigilantius (c. 405) on the subject of clerical marriage: "Quid facient Orientis ecclesiae? Quid Aegypti, et Sedis Apostolicae?" None of these allowed married clergy. *Contra Vigilantium* II (*PL* 23.356A).

19

The North African Dimension 370–430

In the last chapter we hardly mentioned the church in North Africa. It was at Milan in August 386 that Augustine's dramatic conversion to orthodox Catholicism took place and it was Bishop Ambrose who baptized him and his friend, Alypius of Thagaste, at Easter of the following year. It was to Italy, too, that other young and ambitious Numidians had sailed to seek their fortune. When Augustine decided to return to his home country, having nearly achieved his ambition to be a great public speaker and politician, he seemed to be throwing his career to the winds. Africa was wasted on its inhabitants, other Westerners were wont to say.[1]

The influence of the North African church had declined dramatically since Cyprian's day. Cyprian had ranged across the spectrum of ecclesiastical politics accepting appeals from distant Spanish congregations, giving his Roman colleague authoritative if unasked advice, and sending his emissaries as far afield as Cappadocia. In the Great Persecution, too, the North African martyrs were compared by Eusebius to those in Egypt for their numbers and fortitude.[2] Then came the outbreak of the Donatist controversy and the conversion of Constantine. In a curious way, the Council of Arles in 314 marked a watershed in the relations between the North Africans and the remainder of Western Christianity. The Gallic and other bishops were shocked at what they considered to be the intemperate attitude of Caecilian's accusers.[3] More important, they showed—by condemning Christian soldiers who rejected the military career in times of (Christian?) peace, and by decreeing that those who had been baptized by heretics in the name of the Trinity need not be rebaptized on entering the church— that they were turning their backs on North African attitudes.[4] They were now living, they may have reasoned, in "Christian times." Relationships with Constantine's empire must be placed on a new and friendlier footing, and Cyprian's puritanical concept of the church was no longer appropriate.

Caecilian survived to be present at Nicaea—one of the tiny band of Western clergy there—but he and his ideas were repudiated by the vast majority of African Christians. For a brief moment at the Council of Ariminum in 359, the Catholic bishop of Carthage, Restitutus, took the center of the stage as president of that ill-fated assembly, but with the return of the Donatists to power under Julian, contact between North African Christians and the rising churches on the northern shores of the Mediterranean declined once more. Each went their separate way. In the West generally, despite an underlying puritan tradition, Christianity was tending to absorb pagan cultures, to synthesize biblical teaching with classical education, Christian with pagan art, and to accommodate the church's law to the ways of existing society. Christ himself was portrayed even on the way to the cross as a teacher, scroll in hand, guiding humankind toward better things, rather than as a judge or victim.[5] In North Africa, Christianity, both Donatist and Catholic, continued the tradition of protest. Views tended to be formulated in terms of contrast with pagan society. No secular allusions were allowed to appear in Donatist theological tracts.[6] Christianity was regarded as a "law" distinct from secular law.[7] Augustine could take the concept of Two Cities as a commonplace among his hearers.[8] Judgment was an all-important influence on him as on his Donatist opponents, and predestination to salvation was familiar to Donatist popular writers two generations before the Pelagian controversy.[9] Sudden conversion through the power of the Spirit was the experience of the Donatist, Petilian of Constantine,[10] as well as of Augustine. Asceticism even, where not connected with the Circumcellions or the Manichees, sometimes took forms more reminiscent of the rule of the covenanters of Qumran than the conventual houses evolving under Ambrose's care in Italy.[11] Much of the harsh edge of North African Christianity was reflected in the concept of baptism and the huge baptisteries (pp. 518–19) that, all over Christian North Africa, symbolized the convert's complete renunciation of the world, its politics, its philosophies, and its literature.

Only in periods of crisis, such as the latter years of Constantius's reign, did the outlook of the North Africans coincide with that of the remainder of the Western Christians. Then the denial to the emperor of any distinctive role in the church would have united them, but even so, only Hilary of Poitiers in his final blast against Constantius in 361, and Lucifer of Cagliari would have found the views of the Donatist majority in North Africa congenial. Their arguments, however, lacked the doctrinal rigor that inspired Donatist protest.

The reemergence of North Africa as the driving force in Western Christianity in the early fifth century was, therefore, remarkable. It was also unwelcome. Challenged to vindicate their defense of Pelagius, the southern Italian bishops rose in their wrath against the pretensions of the "Punic sophist." A lifetime spent in wrestling with conscience and battling against inflexible opponents, however, enabled Augustine, with the support of a superb conciliar organization, to prevail. His ideas, and with them much of traditional North African theology, were forced upon a confused West. The disasters of the first years of the fifth century, culminating in the capture of Rome by Alaric on 24 August 410, had increased the acceptability of judgment and its associated theological concepts. Disasters interpreted as the "penalty of Roman guilt" came easily to the minds of the victims.[12] Augustine, albeit reluctantly, became the man of the hour.

THE DONATISTS

We trace the story as seen from North Africa. As Jerome stated in c. 392, the religion of Donatus "gained practically all Africa."[13] Though Donatus himself had misjudged the emperor Constans in 346/47 and, unlike Athanasius, ended his days in exile, his movement was not defeated. The Catholic ascendancy of 347–62 ended abruptly and terribly. For thirty years after the dramatic "return of the exiles," Donatus's successor, a non–North

African, Parmenian (362–91/92), ruled his church with assurance and vigor. No emperor, not even Theodosius, could shake him. Catholicism was reduced to a quiescent though inwardly protesting minority.

Donatism was a mass movement. It had been formed from a coalition of Carthaginian dissenters angry at the promotion of a tactless archdeacon to be primate of African Christianity, and the far more potent and uncompromising Numidian episcopate. The alliance had been cemented by the memory of the Abitinian and other confessors and by an immovable allegiance to the theology of Cyprian. It had found in Donatus of Casae Nigrae a leader of conviction, tactical skill, and ruthless dedication to the task of making this theology the religion of North Africa.

The ideas of Donatus and his followers were simple.[14] As God was one, so was his church, and its hallmark was purity. The integrity of the church lay in the integrity of its members, sealed by baptism and working in concord with the bishops. They witnessed to the faith by penance and suffering, and aspired finally to a martyr's death. There was no salvation outside this body of the elect. Other considerations—such as worldwide extent, imperial favor, even communion with apostolic sees (so long as communion with the see of Peter as the source of episcopacy was maintained)[15]—were irrelevant. "What we look for," said Petilian, the Donatist bishop of Constantine in c. 400, "is the conscience of the giver [of baptism] giving in holiness to cleanse that of the recipient. For he who knowingly receives faith from the faithless receives not faith but guilt."[16] Bishops at Cyprian's seventh council on 1 September 256 had said neither more nor less. They would have recognized the Donatists as their true successors and the supporters of Caecilian, the Catholics, as schismatics who needed to be baptized anew if they wished to join the true church, that body reformed and purified by Donatus.[17]

The church represented the elect on earth awaiting their call, like the African Christians of Tertullian's day, to heavenly refreshment. The word "Catholic" referred to what was whole. In images often used by Cyprian, Parmenian would describe the church as "a garden locked, a fountain sealed" (Song of Solomon 4:12) or as the ark caulked with pitch in order to prevent leaks in or out of it.[18] The Spirit moved the church and its councils. The word of the Spirit was in the Bible. A Christian was one who, like the martyr-bishop Marculus, had the Bible ever on his lips and martyrdom in his heart.[19] Or, as the writer of the *Acts of Saturninus* proclaimed, "In our Church, the virtues of the people are multiplied by the presence of the Spirit. The joy of the Spirit is to conquer in the martyrs and triumph in the confessors."[20] The doctrine of the Spirit was primary in Donatism as it had been in the church of Tertullian's day. The Donatists did not accept that any essential change had taken place in the situation of Christians in the empire through the conversion of Constantine. They must oppose "the world" (*saeculum*) in all its aspects. Though there might be long deceptive periods of peace and emperors might sometimes be willing, and even desire, to favor the church, earthly rulers and their representatives were cast in the role of persecutors. It was the emperor now, later it was to be the Vandal king.

Like the Jewish compiler of the Maccabean literature before them, the Donatists believed that from the time of Abel onward the unrelenting war against the righteous had continued and would continue. The long, terrible requisitory included by Petilian of Constantine in his pastoral letter to his clergy (c. 400-401) sums up Donatist thought:

> But what have you to do with the kings of this world in whom Christianity has never found anything save envy towards her? And to teach you shortly the truths of what I say: A king persecuted the brethren of the Maccabees. A king also condemned the three children to the sanctifying flames, being ignorant of what he did, seeing that he was fighting against God. And the Lord Jesus Christ was slain by a king's most wicked judge. . . . Nor indeed does the hand of the butcher glow save at the instigation of your [the Catholics] tongue.[21]

There was no place for "Christian times" in the Donatist philosophy.

The call was not to armed revolution, however, but to a readiness and an expectation of martyrdom. At the conference (or rather, confrontation) with the Catholics in May/June 411 at Carthage, the Donatist profession of faith opens, "Januarius and other bishops of the Catholic truth, that suffers persecution, but does not persecute."[22] Persecution by the authorities, abetted by false Christians (the Catholics) was to be the lot of the faithful. Donatus taught as Tertullian had taught, that it was the divine means of separating the just from the unjust on earth. Suffering was the way of salvation.

Given these assumptions, the question debated between Donatists and Catholics—"Where is the Church?"—could be answered quite simply. It was in Africa ("in the south" as indicated in the Song of Solomon 1:6, African version), in the community of Donatus.[23] Separation from Caecilian and his followers had been right. "Blessed is the man who walks not in the counsel of the wicked" (Ps. 1:1), quoted Petilian.[24] Augustine was to find himself confronted by clergy and people alike, by earnest groups that discussed passages of the Bible, convinced that he and his party were the "sons of traditors."[25]

Alongside the articulate, town-based leadership composed of able and self-confident lawyers like Petilian of Constantine and Emeritus of Caesarea, the Donatist church could count on the profound loyalty of the mass of the Numidian provincials. All authorities agree that the movement had originated among them and continued to dominate through the fourth and early fifth centuries.[26] For the Berber peoples of the Numidian high plains, Donatism was an expression of hope for relief from earthly toil and deep-felt protest against the injustices of the existing social and economic order.

A visitor to the area between the coastal Atlas and the Aurès mountains would have found uniformity in the life as well as the religion of the people. Towns were comparatively few and the majority of these had developed either as garrisons or as settlements of veterans. In the multitude of villages scattered over the whole area the ubiquitous olive press and grain silo would be associated with small, roughly built, whitewashed buildings, the scene of passionate devotion to the cult of martyrs.[27] These churches, sometimes recorded as built by local tribesmen,[28] were basilican in design with three naves, beaten earth floors, wattle and stone walls, and sloping tiled roofs. In front of the apse at the east end was a square enclosure where the altar was placed, and beneath the altar was a small stone trough in which would be placed cooking pots tightly sealed with plaster and containing relics of a martyr. The relics themselves sometimes had little to do with martyrs, consisting of bits of lead fragments, of ostrich eggshell, or bird bones; but no matter, reliquaries containing such objects were dedicated and re-dedicated, emphasizing the popular nature of the cult.[29]

Inscriptions, too, found in these churches commemorated martyrs and martyrdom. "Crown of martyrs" (*corona marturorum*), or "table of martyrs" (*mensa marturorum*), or the simple statement that "the just shall enter" (*iusti introient*), and even the Donatist watchword, "praise be to God" (*Deo laudes*), have all come to light.[30] Sometimes, as already noted, the annexes contained silos and storage jars, food perhaps for the roving bands of Circumcellions.[31] These Numidian chapels represented the heart of Donatism, each probably dedicated to some particular group of martyrs around whom religious life would revolve. In the end the believer would claim burial within the hallowed walls of the building. And in Timgad and Bagai were the great churches to which Donatists looked for inspiration. Nothing like the dedicated sectarianism of rural Donatist Christianity in Numidia existed anywhere else in the Greco-Roman world.

Ostensibly, the church over which Parmenian presided for thirty years was an imposing edifice representing popular victory over paganism and its Catholic allies. Despite dislike and misgivings, the Donatist leadership could find affinity with their fanatical brethren in the countryside. In moments of emergency, differences of social background and even language became less important than community of religious ideal. Augustine tells how his rival Macrobius, who spoke only Latin, put himself at the head of a Circumcellion band and entered Hippo in triumph in 410.[32] Donatist Africa united around its bishops and, faithful to the memory of Cyprian and Donatus, was on the way toward becoming as distinctive a Christian society as the Egypt of Athanasius and his successors.

The same visitor, however, might have detected flaws which were to become more obvious with time. Through its success, Donatism had become the African Christian "establishment." People were brought up in it, accepted it, but lacked the fire of conviction that had kindled the original

656

movement against Caecilian.[33] In the 390s its lawyers could win cases for repossession of churches and property against the Maximianists (schismatics in their own camp) by claiming that theirs was the true church in Africa. There was, however, an almost laughable unreality in their boasts that "nearly the whole world" revered the reforming work of Donatus.[34] There were just enough North Africans traveling abroad to return to their native country with doubts on that score. So long as African Catholicism survived it could spell danger to the Donatists. There were tendencies toward schism also. These resulted either from crises, such as the revolt of Firmus (372–75) that produced the Rogatists around Cartenna in Mauretania Caesariensis, or, one suspects, through groups asserting a superior holiness to their more staid fellow Donatists. Such movements might indicate more intense religious activity, but could weaken collective effort when confronted by a reinvigorated Catholicism at the end of the century.[35] Then, as Parmenian found, it was not enough to define the church as the bride with adornments, based on a reading of the Song of Solomon 1, and fit these to Donatism, when well-documented historical facts about the origins of the schism could be quoted in rebuttal. The evidence which Optatus of Milevis quoted at the Donatist bishop of Carthage, in c. 365, survived to be used with greater effect by an abler exponent of Catholicism when the time came. The real weakness, however, lay in the isolation of Donatism. The uncompromising assertion of traditional African theological truth and denunciations of Caecilian were unattractive to men like Augustine who loved their Latin classics and had experienced Catholicism overseas. He had no use for "assemblies of the just" (*conventicula justorum*).[36] Donatist Christianity never seems to have presented itself as a possible resting place to him at any stage of his career. The Donatists are not even mentioned in the *Confessions*. Others also who were loyal to the Donatist tradition had doubts. Could it really be claimed amid the overwhelming Christian victory over paganism that no true Christians existed beyond the shores of North Africa? Were all associated in Caecilian's guilt?

Tyconius

In the 380s a layman from proconsular Africa meditated on this problem while preparing a series of "keys" by which he believed all puzzles of scriptural interpretation could be unlocked. Tyconius's *Rules* of exegesis were to affect profoundly future Western interpretation of Scripture. In the eighth century Bede and the Spaniard Beatus of Libana were both indebted to him.[37] Tyconius was another educated Donatist whose work demonstrated once again the persistence of lay influence in his church's theology. As he worked through Scripture, however, intent on showing how every passage referred in some way to Christ and his church, he came on a paradox. Granted that every word in Scripture referred in some way or other to Christ and his church, how could one reconcile total separation from the sons of *traditores* with the statement that the church was described in the Song of Solomon as "dark, but comely" or that the seed of Abraham was "royal and servile" (cf. Genesis 16). The church on earth must contain sinners as well as saints, and whether one belonged to the one or the other depended surely, not on accidents of geography, but on the will of each individual. The two societies (or "cities" as Augustine would define them) were composed of individuals each guided by will, the one society destined to salvation, the other to damnation.[38] Tyconius was arguing from within the Donatist tradition. The "false Christianity," the church of Judas, was represented by the North African Catholics. That he placed his "societies" on a universal basis, however, took him beyond the African bounds of Donatist thought. He was not convinced by conventional arguments as to the need for separation from Gauls and Spaniards as associates in Caecilian's crimes or that the "field" (cf. Matt. 13:24) was "Africa" and not "the world,"[39] and he was excommunicated. This happened c. 385. He did not join the African Catholics but he was too important a thinker to drop out of memory. One of those who studied his ideas was Augustine of Hippo.[40]

Maximian

For all its show of unity, the Donatist coalition was fragile. When at last Parmenian died (391/92) the choice of his successor was unfortunate. Primian (*flor.* 392–411) was a ruthless, power-seeking ecclesiastic who relied on the Carthaginian mob and the Numidians to enforce his views. Soon, he was opposed by a group of clergy in Carthage led by a deacon named Maximian who was a descendant of Donatus himself. He represented a moderate standpoint within the church, and was supported by about 100 bishops from proconsular Africa and Byzacena. In 393 the opposition held a solemn council at Cebarsussa in Byzacena at which Primian was excommunicated (24 June), and the Donatist church was seriously divided. The Numidians and their allies reacted swiftly. Led by the formidable bishop Optatus of Thamugadi (Timgad) a council of 310 bishops assembled at Bagai on 24 April 394. There Primian's opponents were denounced like the schismatics of old, Dathan, Korah, and Abiram. Their "mouths were filled with bitterness and cursing."[41] They were consigned to outer darkness. Primian was vindicated. Indeed, the Maximianist movement collapsed fairly quickly. Some of its leaders were restored to communion. Others, including Maximian himself, passed into obscurity. The law in the shape of proconsular decisions was on the side of Primian, or was happy to leave "disputes between bishops" for the church to decide and to give homely advice to the Maximianists. But the fact that the Donatists were willing to forgive those who were guilty of schism and yet were unprepared to reunite with the Catholics did not pass unnoticed. The Catholics had elected Aurelius, a first-rate organizer and tactician,[42] as bishop of Carthage (391–427).

Aurelius wasted no time in encouraging a friend, returned from Italy to his native Thagaste three years before in order to establish himself in a monastic life, to take up active service in the church.[43] Augustine accepted ordination as presbyter in Hippo, a coastal town in Numidia, in 391.

AUGUSTINE

Up to that point even, he had had a remarkable career. He was born at Thagaste (Souk-Ahras) in the northern part of Numidia on 13 November 354. For once the date is important, for it falls in the middle of the Catholic ascendancy of 347–62. Thagaste, having previously been entirely Donatist, accepted the change of allegiance (an interesting example in the West of religious conformity to the emperor's order), and was one of the few Numidian towns that did not return to the Donatist camp in 362. His father, Patricius, was a city councilor, a medium landed proprietor of Thagaste, and a pagan, while his mother, Monica, was a Christian. Augustine was brought up a Christian, and Monica's moral influence was a decisive force in his life. Years later, he was to think of the church itself as a "strong woman"—who must be obeyed, like his mother.[44] Augustine failed to understand Patricius. He was not a "believer" like the rest of the family.[45] He remembered his father merely as ill-tempered. The gulf between the world into which Patricius had been born (c. 320) and Augustine's was already too great to bridge. Patricius's influence, however, should not be underestimated. He insisted on Augustine's classical education and no doubt inspired him with his early ambition for a public career. From him, too, Augustine drew his Roman and African patriotism that took him to the threshold of the heights of the imperial service, and is shown in his passionate defense of "Africanism" in a debate with his old tutor, Maximus of Madaura.[46]

The *Confessions* (written c. 397), whence many details of Augustine's life must be taken, was not an attempt at autobiography. The thirteen books combine an account of his conversion with a long prayer to God outlining his spiritual journey through the six ages of human life, from infancy to old age (at the age of forty-three!), when the soul, penitent but still convalescent, might aspire to contemplate the heavenly Jerusalem.[47] As a boy, Augustine was not particularly brilliant. He was, however, strongly imaginative and had a vivid and retentive memory. He wept for Dido as he read of her fate in the *Aeneid*,[48] but Homer and Greek left him cold. With romanticism went a jealous nature. A bad loser as a boy, he was to grow up passionately wanting to succeed at whatever he undertook.[49] In a secular career, this would not necessarily be a bad quality, but as a bishop and theologian concerned with the establishment of truth against error in an age increasingly dominated by theology, the failing was disastrous.

From Thagaste, Augustine moved, with his father's aid and blessing, to the higher school at Madaura on the northern edge of the Numidian high plains (368–70), where he found teachers who were still proud of their Latin and pagan heritage.[50] A year or so there was followed by a miserable period at home, and then in 371 his chance came—the opportunity to study at Carthage. Later, he was to paint his years as a student in the blackest colors—his activities with rowdies (*eversores* = "overthrowers"), his taking a mistress, the discovery of the theater and its scenes of passion, and above all his conversion to Manicheism.[51] But this is not how contemporaries saw him. Students at Carthage may have lacked a Julian or Basil of Caesarea in their midst, but they included some shrewd and thoughtful characters who were destined to represent radically opposed views in the community. Augustine's contemporaries numbered among them Vincentius, future Rogatist bishop of Cartenna; Fortunatus, the Manichean presbyter in Hippo; Cornelius, another Manichee intellectual; as well as Augustine's close friend Alypius, a fellow citizen of Thagaste; Honoratus, a pagan and subsequent convert (and lifelong adherent) to Manicheism; and Nebridius, the profoundly sensitive son of a wealthy Carthaginian family who during his short life followed Augustine through Manicheism to Platonist Christianity. It was a lively intellectual society that remembered Augustine for his qualities. Years later (in 408), Vincentius, already a "serious Christian," would remind him that he had "known him as a man devoted to peace and honest conduct, even when still far from the Christian faith."[52] His mind was set on the great things that elevated the soul toward heaven, a Manichean who had known him in Rome stated.[53] This is obviously near the truth, for at Carthage Augustine experienced two conversions, first (c. 372) toward the undivided pursuit of wisdom through philosophy, and second (in 373) as a means to that end, to the Manichean interpretation of Christianity.

Cicero's *Hortensius* spelled liberation from the restrictive influence of home. Patricius had died (c. 371) baptized as a Christian, and Monica's dominance in the life of the family was unchallenged. Unfortunately, few fragments of the *Hortensius* survive, but from these it would seem that Cicero stated the principle that all men sought to be happy (*beati*) and that the road thither lay through the soul, which was eternal and divine, exercising its true natural activity in its reasoning power pursued through a quest for knowledge. Thus humankind would avoid vices and errors and the return of the soul to heaven would be made easier. Wealth and possessions counted as nothing when compared with wisdom.[54]

This is what Augustine was waiting to hear, particularly the virtue of the quest itself. Early ambitions to be an advocate were thrown aside. "I was left with an unbelievable fire in my heart, desiring the deathless qualities of Wisdom, and I began to rise up and return to thee. . . . I was on fire to fly away from earthly things to thee."[55] Vincentius was right. Augustine at Carthage was already an idealist seeking after God and the perfect way of life. The supreme aim of happiness remained in his mind to the very end through all the vicissitudes of his career. At Cassiciacum in 386/87 after his final return to Catholicism, the definition of happiness and the question, Did happiness consist in finding the truth or in searching for it? were among the dominant themes of his philosophical discussion with his friends.[56] Later in *On the Trinity* and in the anti-Pelagian *Against Julian* he still draws inspiration from the *Hortensius*.[57] Though Augustine was now a Ciceronian, he was, however, still a "believer." He turned to the Bible in his quest for wisdom. He failed to find it among the anthropomorphic crudities of the Old Testament.[58] With ever-growing enthusiasm he turned toward Manicheism.

The choice was not surprising. If Donatism suited the majority of Christians in North Africa, its insular and rigorist traditions had always been opposed by those who either sought (like Augustine) a synthesis between philosophy and Christianity, and those who were prepared to go further— to reject the Old Testament as the Word of God and accept a mystical dualistic interpretation of Christianity.[59] The Gnostics and Marcionites of the second and third centuries had largely been absorbed by the Manichees. In the seventy-five years since Diocletian's rescript (31 March 297) banning them,[60] they had flourished in North Africa. Their following included civil servants, merchants, lawyers, and not a few Catholic clergy. They seem to have been organized in small groups or cells not only in some of the larger towns across North Africa, but also in the countryside, such as in the great olive-growing area south of Theveste.[61] They were few, as Augustine used to emphasize, but dedicated and influential.[62] They attracted would-be intellectuals such as Faustus of Milevis to whom they seemed to offer the only real advance from paganism, against the alternatives of a Jewish-Christian Catholicism and the martyr-theology of Donatism, which he regarded as no better than paganism itself.[63]

The North African Manichees insisted that Christianity properly understood was a religion that combined reason and revelation in a truly spiritual worship. "God needed no altar," Faustus believed, "other than a mind imbued with good arts and education" and rational being.[64] Therefore neither he nor his friends rejected classical literature in favor of the Bible alone, like their Donatist and some Catholic contemporaries. As the Gnostics before them, they claimed to possess the keys to personal salvation and knowledge of the secrets of the physical universe. "All mysteries of the beginning, the middle and the end . . . of the making of the world, the reason for the day and the night and the course of the sun and moon" would be made known to the believer.[65] The reason "must be found how and why souls have come into this world,"[66] the Manichean Fortunatus told Augustine during their public debate at Hippo on 27 August 392. While accepting a theology based on a strict and logical dualism between Light and Darkness and Good and Evil, the North African Manichees insisted on their devotion to the Savior Christ and to his interpreter, Paul.[67] They

661

denied, however, the value of cardinal teaching held by their African Christian opponents (and Paul) of the necessity of baptism, and the resurrection of the body.[68] For them, as for the Gnostics, Christ was the bringer of wisdom and illumination from the realm of Light, a Light-Being, the Savior whose suffering on the cross was reenacted in suffering throughout all creation.[69] The object of existence was to distill the light particles imprisoned in creation and return them to the realm of Light. Thus they would bring about its restoration as it had been originally before its disruption by the powers of Darkness.[70]

The true Manichee, the elect, imitated his Savior in a life devoted to asceticism and austerity. He observed the three Seals: of the Mouth (no blasphemy, observance of strict dietary rules), of the Hands (no productive work), and of the Body (chastity).[71] He must in no way seek to prolong the existence of the created order. He was a vegetarian, restricted in his diet to "light bearing" items which he could deliver from their "prison."[72] He was one on whom God's grace rested.[73] He was served by a disciple, a "Hearer." These were Manichees of "the second grade" who might live in the world, marry, and engage in normal occupations,[74] but must also be examples of chastity and intellectual inquiry. They must fast regularly on the Lord's Day.[75] Above all, they must serve as active missionaries of the revelation of Mani. Such was the faith—"the terrible heresy" (*pestilentissima haeresis*)[76]—that gained Augustine's allegiance in 373 and from whose influence he never entirely freed himself.

Even now at the age of nineteen Augustine was obsessed with the problem of evil, not least in the form of his own sexuality. The Manichee questioning attracted him, "Whence are the sins, and whence is evil in general? If from man, whence is man, and if from an angel, whence is the angel?"[77] The dualistic answer that also removed direct blame from himself seemed obvious. When he returned to Thagaste in 375, it was as a Manichee "Hearer," a zealous missionary for his faith, ready like his Coptic Manichee contemporaries to despise the religion of his parents,[78] not least the Jewish biblical elements of Monica's faith.[79]

His nine years as a Manichee (373–82) coincided with the formative period of his life. Their effect on his thought and emotions was enormous. Down to 397, that is, until he was forty-three, Manicheism was his overriding preoccupation. In the ten years following his reconversion to Catholicism, anti-Manichean tracts poured from his pen; the longest of all his controversial works, the thirty-three books of the *Reply to Faustus the Manichean* (written c. 400), was devoted to the same end. Yet the legacy in his theology is not easy to define. First, however, he retained a lasting sense of personal worthlessness. No meritorious action could come without grace. In this the Christian elect would differ little from the Manichee "elect." Their "image" as the Coptic Manichee would have said, had been chosen out[80]—predestined to grace and salvation. The rest of humanity, the "unredeemed mass" (Augustine retained the Manichean term), was destined for possession by the Devil and eternal fire. Allied to a profound sense of guilt was his preoccupation with chastity and the association of wickedness with sex. Both he and Alypius long admired the Manichees for their continence.[81] The famous plea, "Lord, give me continence and chastity but not now," belongs to Augustine's Manichee period.[82] Third, and more positively, his years as a Manichee may have heightened his sense of the communion of the saved as a worldwide mystical body of the elect that knew no political or cultural frontiers, the earthly counterpart of the Christ who pervaded the universe.

Eventually, Augustine simply moved beyond Manicheism. Some aspects of Manichean mythology he found ridiculous. How would God be more present in dates or honey than in a pig's body? Or how could a Christian worship the sun as God or part of God, and the moon also?[83] He became frustrated. He could not "advance" (*proficere*) in the Manichean faith.[84] In fact, in order to penetrate deeper into the "science" of Manicheism he would have had to have become an "elect," which his career (and his mistress) would not allow him to do. A discussion with Faustus of Milevis, the leading North African Manichee, was a disappointment,[85] for Faustus was a self-taught man who found Manichean dualism a reasonable answer to the problem of good and evil in the world, and Manicheism itself a much-needed release from the small-town paganism in which he had been raised. He was glad of Augustine's help to improve his knowledge of the classics. This, however, was not what Augustine wanted. He had hoped for a "demonstration of the truth" (*exhibitio veritatis*) of Manicheism to convince him beyond doubt, and all he received were more ambiguities and fables.[86] From now on he began to look for new horizons, spiritual as well as material. He had returned to Carthage. In c. 377 he had won a prize for declaiming a set piece of verse there, and with it the acquaintanceship of the experienced and level-headed proconsul Vindicianus.[87] By 380 his eyes were already on Rome, for he dedicated his first book (unhappily lost) on aesthetics (*On the Beautiful and the Fitting*) to a Roman orator named Hierius, who like him aspired to be a philosopher as well as a public speaker.[88] It may have been time, too, to have second thoughts about adhesion to a secret and persecuted sect. Italy beckoned.

In 382 he emigrated to Rome, leaving his mother to her tearful vigil in the church of St. Cyprian at Carthage.[89] He could not forget her, however, nor she him. Rome, too, was a disappointment; his students did not pay their fees, but he still remained attached to the Manichees, making friends among the Manichean community and contact with a Manichean monastery. There, however, he was further disillusioned by the unimaginatively harsh regime coupled with the licentious conduct, hypocrisy, and intrigue among the elect who were the inmates.[90] He must find another orbit.

This proved to be Milan and Neo-Platonism. In Rome, Augustine had

had one stroke of luck. He had attracted the notice of Quintus Aurelius Symmachus, the pagan champion and prefect of the city, and through his influence and that of his Manichean friends found himself appointed in the autumn of 384 as professor of rhetoric and public orator at the court of Valentinian II.[91] What better way to get at Ambrose than through this brilliant young African philosopher, open in his views but with decidedly anti-Catholic leanings and links even with the Manichees? So his backers may have reasoned, but for Augustine it was a triumph. With the exception of Aurelius Victor a generation before, no provincial North African had received such advancement. His fellow countrymen were not popular in official circles. Thick, buzzing accents apart,[92] they were regarded as querulous and legalistic, and those who came to Italy on business, such as Romanianus, Augustine's friend and patron in Thagaste, as ostentatiously rich.

Augustine had overcome these obstacles, and could look forward to a brilliant official career based on his success in the intellectually alert court of Justina and her son at Milan. His statement, "And I came to Milan . . . to Ambrose the bishop" (*Confessions* V.13.23), is altogether too simple a description of his stay. The years 384–87 were to be decisive in his life, but even to the moment of his baptism at Easter 387, they were full of drama, uncertainty, and questioning. The outcome, however, was to have its effects far beyond the Roman Empire in the West.[93]

Augustine encountered Ambrose early on. He could hardly have avoided doing so in his official position. He enrolled in the register of catechumens in the cathedral, that is, he made himself respectable, and he listened to Ambrose's sermons as one orator might listen to another. But his bent was still toward philosophy and success, with only so much Christian varnish as was necessary for his position (and reputation). Yet all the time he wanted to arrive at certainty. As it had many years before in Carthage, chance may have played its part in his next step. He came upon "a few books of the Platonists," he told readers of the *Confessions* with studied vagueness.[94] These were probably Plotinus's *On Beauty* and Porphyry's *On the Return (of the Soul)*, which he quotes in the *City of God*.[95] They fitted his mood. Christ, Porphyry had written, was a "man of excellent wisdom," and worthy in every way of honor but his disciples were not.[96] Augustine would have agreed. The literalism of Monica's religion still annoyed him. But more important was the positive reassurance he received that his break with the Manichees was justified. Platonism answered the problem with which he had been wrestling for thirteen years by teaching that evil—if it is to exist at all—must be placed within the realm of nonbeing.[97] Augustine began to listen to Ambrose's sermons with more attention, for Ambrose was using these ideas in an allegorical interpretation of Scripture derived from Origen, which sought to harmonize the Bible with reason in a Platonist sense.[98] This was something entirely new to Augustine and more immediately satisfying even than the intricate typology worked out by Tyconius and his colleagues in North Africa.

Augustine's interest might have gone no further, however, had not his personal problems begun once more to exert a tyrannical influence over his life. A great career demanded a splendid marriage. His "second-class marriage" (Peter Brown's phrase),[99] resulting even in his intelligent son Adeodatus, would not do. He was putting down roots in northern Italy. The patronage of brilliant and hugely wealthy individuals such as Symmachus and Manlius Theodorus was pointing the way to his future career. He would be completely at home in his friend Verecundus's villa at Cassiciacum (Cassiago) near Lake Como, whither he would retire with his friends in September 386 after his conversion. There, or at Justina's court, was where his heart was set. But now he had to be rid of his faithful mistress, and she was sent back to North Africa, vowing that she would know no other man.[100] Now, however, he must wait two years for his Italian heiress, and for a man of Augustine's age and temperament this was too much to ask. To this writer, this was to prove to be one of the decisive factors in Augustine's life. A successful, even if not a particularly happy match, coupled with splendid prospects, wealth, literary patronage, and estates, would have settled him.[101] His intellect was held by Platonism. He would have accommodated this with formal membership of the church as others were doing. The arrival of his mother in Milan had made little apparent difference. In the *Confessions* he notes that she abandoned, on Ambrose's prompting, the African usage of bringing offerings to the cathedral on the anniversary of martyrs.[102] This was not his religion. The prospect, however, of two years' enforced bachelor existence was a crushing blow. It was at this level of his being that Monica became important to him once more.

The opposite side of his character that had moved him as a Manichee toward "the renunciation of this world's joys" (*Confessions* VIII.2.17) began to reassert itself. Monica's influence now urged him in the same direction. An attempt (385–86) to establish a philosophical community with some close friends broke down—the wives objected.[103] Cumulative pressures began to mount. By the summer of 386 he was moving strongly in the direction of an ascetic Catholic Christianity. As in Rome three years before, the strains affected his health. Like a homing bird he went to Milan's cathedral.

But not to Ambrose. It was from Simplicianus, a presbyter already elderly though destined to outlive his bishop, that he sought help. As he says in the *Confessions*, Platonism was not sufficient. He found "no tears of confession," no surrender to God, no humility, no personal redeemer, and no call to imitate Christ.[104] Augustine's need had always been Christ, but an understanding of Christ that he could accept as a reasonable and reasoning being. Simplicianus was no Faustus of Milevis. There was no second let-down. He told him of the conversion of the Neo-Platonist philosopher Victorinus in Rome a generation before. Victorinus had insisted on making a public declaration of his faith. Augustine took the point.[105] Imitation of Christ required renunciation of pride; this he accepted, but what of his desire? He could not bring himself to submit. To use his words ten years later, "On all sides thou didst show me that thy words are true, and I convicted by the truth had nothing at all to reply, but the drawling and drowsy words: 'Presently, presently, leave me alone a little while.' "[106] Decision was near. The final straw was hearing the story of the conversion of two young officials on their way to Trier, the Western capital, on reading Athanasius's(?) *Life of St. Antony*.[107] Idealism and philosophy could be united in accepting the call to an ascetic Christianity. That was enough. A final moment of indecision, and then the words of a child playing in a Milanese garden, repeating the jingle, "Take and read; take and read." Augustine did. A Bible was at hand. His eyes fell on Rom. 13:13–14, "Not in reveling and drunkenness, not in debauchery and licentiousness, not in quarreling and jealousy. But put on the Lord Jesus Christ, and make no provision for the flesh, to gratify its desires." It was August 386.[108] He had made up his mind.

Calm followed the crisis. Augustine resigned his appointments as professor and public orator, and retired with his mother, brother, son, and friends to Cassiciacum. There in "cultured retirement" (*otium liberale*) they discussed philosophic problems, largely those raised by Manicheism, such as free will and its vindication, the falsity of the dualistic explanation of reality and humanity's responsibility for sin. Critics have shown that these dialogues could easily pass for philosophical debates in an intellectual climate where Platonism, not necessarily Catholic Christianity, predominated.[109] Only Monica's interventions, uncompromising and always insisting on the moral implication of what was being said, show the Christian character of the discussions. But Monica was all-important. She had not brought up Augustine as a Christian for nothing.[110] Easter 387 saw Augustine and Alypius baptized at Milan. Augustine determined to return to his native Numidia. At Ostia in October the same year, his mother died. In the intervening six months Augustine formed the image (Church = Catholic Orthodoxy = Monica) that remained with him throughout his life.

Augustine had found rest in an ascetic form of Catholic Christianity reflected in the teaching of Ambrose and his colleagues in northern Italy, but virtually unknown in Africa. The monastic-type settlement Augustine established at Thagaste with his mainly ex-Manichean friends in 388, though in Catholic territory, made no particular impact on the religious life of Numidia as a whole. Nor does it seem that Augustine intended it to do so. "I desire to know God and my own soul," he had written in his *Soliloquies* in 386/87; "Nothing else; nothing whatever."[111] This goal remained, with the addition of reconverting to his interpretation of Catholicism the numerous friends and acquaintances he had converted to Manicheism. His letters (*Letters* I–X) to Nebridius (388–90) breathe a Platonic Christianity concerned with dreams and their meaning and with scant reference to practical affairs. They are dateable only because Nebridius is known to have died c. 390. "Heresies and schisms" are mentioned only briefly in 390.[112] Augustine had no intention of entering the debate, "Where is the Church?" He had made up his own mind and wished only to be left in peace. But this could not last. Catholics in Numidia needed leaders and the monastery at Thagaste contained just such able individuals, even if they were former Manichees. The experiment began to break down. It may not have been wholly accidental that Bishop Valerius faced Augustine with a demand that he should accept ordination when he was visiting Hippo Regius on business connected with the monastery.[113] At the age of thirty-six a new era of his life had started.

The teacher had now to become the man of affairs. Still, the Manichees who were well established in Hippo remained his chief preoccupation. Donatists joined with Catholics in urging the new presbyter to challenge the Manichean presbyter Fortunatus, whom Augustine had once known as a friend.[114] The two were well matched, and the debate between them in the baths of Sossius on 27 and 28 August 392 was tense. For two days a vast audience followed every move in the contest.[115] In the West as well as the East, rival interpretations of Christianity aroused deep emotions as did nothing else. Augustine triumphed, Fortunatus conceded defeat and left Hippo. The debate showed that the weaknesses of Manicheism could be exposed convincingly. A case could be made for Catholic Christianity.

Next year another event took place, significant for the future of African Catholicism and Augustine's career. The new bishop of Carthage, Aurelius, was known as a zealous reformer and wasted no time in getting his church moving.[116] On 8 October 393 he held a plenary episcopal council at Hippo and invited Augustine, though only a presbyter, to preach the opening sermon. The partnership between a superb organizer and an intellectual leader had opened. It was to last until Aurelius's death in 427, and contributed in no small measure to the dominance that North Africa was to achieve in the councils of Western Catholicism.

The thirty-nine canons that were agreed upon were wide-ranging if miscellaneous.[117] Nothing but authorized Scripture and the acts of martyrs on their anniversaries should be read in church (canons 5 and 36). Clerics must not visit widows or virgins without the express authorization of the bishop (canon 24). No member of a household should be ordained without the entire household being Catholic Christians (canon 17). Clergy must not act as bailiffs of private estates (canon 15). Bishops must not journey overseas (to appeal against sentences?) without the provincial primate's permission (canon 27). Annual meetings were hinted at (canon 7a). The last was the most important decision, but important or trivial as these canons were, they showed that African Catholicism after touching a low point in the 380s was becoming once more highly organized and articulate. If the Donatists were to falter, it would readily step into their shoes.

At the time this seemed unlikely. The damage caused by the Maximianist schism was controlled and the years 390–98 saw Donatism as strong as ever. No African council ever equaled "the universal council" of Bagai in April 394 for numbers and fervor. Primian and Optatus of Thamugadi were unrivaled popular religious leaders. For Augustine the decade was frustrating. His early attempts, first to ridicule the Donatists, and then to draw local Donatist leaders into a debate failed. He admitted he "was not yet experienced" in Donatist teaching.[118] His election in 395 as coadjutor to the aging and ineffective Valerius, Catholic bishop of Hippo, and then, on the latter's death in 396, as bishop hardly helped him, as he was suspected of undercover Manicheism by Catholics and Donatists alike.[119] He was glad of his residual contacts in Milan instanced by Bishop Simplicianus's string of questions on details of scriptural interpretation, and of his more worldly wise friend Alypius, now bishop of Thagaste, for his literary introduction to the renowned Paulinus of Nola. It may have been at the latter's insistence that he sat down during 396/97 to write of his conversion experience in the *Confessions*.[120] For all the depth of their meditation and ruthless baring of soul and motive, they indicate a mood of depression. Book X finds Augustine "converted" but also still "convalescent," rather than assured and exalted (like Cyprian).[121] At the age of forty-three he saw himself with little to look forward to except death's release.

Augustine and the Donatists 397–412

The politician in him, however, revived. He could not repress his love of controversy, and the Donatists provided a ready quarry. In 397 he wrote his first serious work against them (*Against the Heretic Donatus*), now lost. He also made the effort to travel to Thubursicum Bure, at the extreme east of Numidia, to discuss Donatism with groups of Donatist laity.[122] By this time, North Africa was gripped by political crisis. The revolt of the military commander (*comes*) Gildo in 397 was not part of a nationalist movement but it was a political act of defiance against the emperor Honorius, by a great native feudatory who combined vast landed estates with a military command.[123] If it had been successful, the North African provinces might have seceded from the empire of the West and a native kingdom under Gildo could have emerged (nominally under the suzerainty of the East). The rebel was supported by at least some of the Donatist leaders, particularly by the all-powerful Optatus of Thamugadi. The latter, aided by Circumcellion bands, may have had ideas of land reform beyond mere terrorism and dispossession of opponents.[124] But the revolt failed ignominiously. Gildo was defeated by his brother Mascezel, who had remained loyal to Rome (late April 398), and was executed. The Donatists found themselves, through Optatus, suspected of disloyalty as well as being arraigned as heretics.[125]

For the first time in fifty years the Catholics were able to take advantage of the situation. In 397 Aurelius had convoked another African council, and henceforth the yearly gatherings of bishops at Carthage became a symbol of African Catholic power. His leadership was unquestioned and he added a sense of purpose and decisiveness that his predecessors lacked.[126] Augustine also was prepared. Many of his friends from Manichee days were now in strategic positions as Catholic bishops in Numidia. They could be guaranteed to support him. In the next dozen years (399–412), Augustine was to carry on a relentless offensive against his Donatist opponents, designed to force them to accept ground of his choosing, namely the grand debate in which the winner took all and the loser would be condemned to the penalties that the imperial government had promulgated against heretics.

The details of the campaign have often been recorded and need not be retold here.[127] Important for the future of Western Christendom are the arguments deployed by Augustine and his conception of the use of the coercive power of the state in support of the Catholic cause. First, Augustine asserted the Catholic claim to universality against the Donatist claim of integrity. If the church were not to be worldwide in extent, how could God's promises to Abraham be fulfilled? "By your descendants shall all the nations of the earth bless themselves" (Gen. 22:18); "You shall be the father of a multitude of nations" (Gen. 17:4). How could this be, if the church were confined to Africa? It must therefore be "diffused throughout the whole world" (*toto orbe diffusa*).[128] There must also be communion with the apostolic sees (not only Rome), if the church were to be the church of Christ. What wrong had Ephesus or other churches founded by the apostles done the Donatists, he asks the Donatist bishop of Caesarea, to deserve excommunication?[129] Second, given its extent and varied character—the net cast into the sea, bringing up every kind of fish (cf. John 21:6)—the church on the earth must be a "mixed body" containing "clean" and "unclean" who would not be separated until judgment. The Lord's "field" was the world, not Africa, and the harvest was the end of the world, not "the time of Donatus."[130] The church on earth was only a distorted mirror of the City of God. Unity among its members through common participation in the Sacraments was essential, however. Schism, on the other hand, denoted lack of charity and was the worst of sins; Cyprian's arguments were therefore turned cleverly against the Donatists,[131] and what was worse, historical facts demonstrated the lack of justification for their schism.

The church, therefore, was the true people of God, worldwide in extent, bound together by the sacraments whose head and root was not the individual minister but Christ himself. Their priority was therefore guaranteed, by whomsoever administered.[132] Irregular administration by someone outside the church would not benefit the recipient, but did not compromise their divine character[133] (a piece of casuistry because a sacrament originating from Christ that failed to benefit its recipient is not possible). Augustine's aim, however, was to brand his opponents' insistence on the rebaptism of their converts as heretical, and hence to make them liable to the Theòdosian laws against heresy.

Securus iudicat orbis terrarum ("Untroubled, the world judges," *Against the Epistle of Parmenianus* III.4.24). There was no scope for minority opinions. The church was the "true mother of all Christians"[134] with disciplinary powers to correct the recalcitrant and seek out the wayward. In vain the Donatist grammarian Cresconius urged (c. 406) that truth often originated in minorities, and these therefore should be respected.[135] Augustine was slowly moving toward his second contribution to Western Christian thought, a new concept of church-state relations which if founded on Scripture also approximated that of the Theodosian church-state. For him, too, deviation from orthodoxy would become an offense punishable by the state.

Persecution of Christians by Christians was the final step in a long development extending back to the time when Constantine had denied heretics the privileges he granted to orthodox clergy. In 345 the bishop of Constantinople, Macedonius, had persuaded Constantius to use troops to suppress the Novatianists in Paphlagonia,[136] and, as we have seen, during their short period of ascendancy in 358 the *homoiousians* (followers of Basil of Ancyra) had had their *anomoean* opponents expelled from their clerical charges and exiled.[137] But such acts were reprobated and when Priscillian was executed in 385 at the orders of the usurper Magnus Maximus, nominally for sorcery but in reality as a heretic, there was an outcry from Martin of Tours, Ambrose of Milan, and Pope Siricius himself.[138] What Augustine was to do in his letters and discussions between 399 and 412 was to justify the state's intervention in the religious lives of its subjects so that persecution became accepted as part of its role.

In the background was his belief, going back to Irenaeus and perhaps even into Judaism, that the state had originated as the result of Adam's fall.[139] It had been established by God as the means of exercising discipline on earth and to restrain sinful humanity. In consequence, the state had the civil duty of repressing crime and vice. Since Constantine's conversion it had acquired the further duty of securing liberty for the church to pursue its work of salvation and of protecting it against its enemies, which included heretics and schismatics.[140] It was idle for the Donatists to claim that the Christian church was and would always be in opposition to the state. Just as in Old Testament times Nebuchadnezzar had repented his persecuting ways and finished by showing favor to Daniel (Augustine *Petilian* II.92.204), so now in "Christian times." Constantine and Theodosius had shown themselves model rulers, governing by wise and salutary laws and sustaining the church. Times had changed. Indeed, quite suddenly the two-swords concept of church-state relations was transformed from a theory founded on a forced interpretation of disciples' words to Jesus (Luke 22:38), to the basis of action between divinely appointed partners exercising spiritual and temporal authority over humankind.

Augustine himself never doubted the right of the Catholics to invoke the aid of the authorities against heretics and schismatics. He believed he would be called to account at judgment if he had failed to do all in his power to seek out and correct "erring brethren."[141] There was an underlying fear, too, of the more immediate consequences of heresy, namely of social revolution involving the uprising of the country populations, inspired by Donatist ideals, against their urban, landowning masters. "Rural audacity contrary to apostolic discipline" (for example, *Letter* CVIII.6.18) came quickly to the mind of one to whom relations between individuals and classes of society were fixed by divine ordinance for all time, and whose belief in Roman Africa never wavered.

As early as 396 Augustine appealed to the magistrates of Hippo to take note of the illegal activities of his Donatist rival.[142] After the failure of Gildo's revolt he felt on firmer ground. In his *Parmenianus* (c. 399), he identified the Donatists as heretics (not merely "schismatics") who could be subjected to imperial legislation in exactly the same way as other criminals and misbelievers, including poisoners and pagans.[143] When in 400–401 Petilian, Donatist bishop of Constantine, claimed freedom of conscience for all Christians in the tradition of the Constantinian church, Augustine told him it was his duty as a Catholic bishop to admonish *all* Christians: "Whoever was not found within the Church was not asked the reason, but was to be corrected and converted, or if admonished [*correptus*], he had no reason for complaint."[144] The final stage, the actual invocation of repressive measures against his opponents, was accepted by Augustine reluctantly, partly out of horror at the treatment by the Donatists of the Catholic bishop of Bagai in 404, and partly because it worked! As he wrote to Vincentius, the schismatic Donatist ("Rogatist") bishop of Cartenna:

> For originally my opinion was, that no one should be coerced into the unity of Christ, that we must act only words, fight only by arguments, and prevail by force of reason, lest we should have those whom we knew to be avowed heretics feigning themselves to be Catholics. But this opinion of mine was overcome not by the words of those who controverted it, but by the conclusive instances to which they could point. For in the first place, there was set over against my opinion my own town, which although it was once wholly on the side of Donatus was brought over to the Catholic unity by the fear of the imperial edicts. . . . There were so many others which were mentioned to me by name, that from the facts themselves, I was made to own that to this matter the word of Scripture might be understood as applying, "Give opportunity to a wise man and he will become wiser."[145]

671

In this letter Augustine used the text from Luke (14:23) "compel people to come in" to justify persecution.[146] Seldom have Gospel words been given so unexpected a meaning. Persecution, as the pagan town councilor Nectarius of Calama described to Augustine, was terrible enough for its sufferers.[147] Given scriptural support in the mouth of Augustine it became one of the grimmer legacies of the African Catholics to Western Christendom.

Augustine's campaign, conducted skillfully through the years 399–412, achieved a fair measure of success. In 405 he finally persuaded Honorius's government at Ravenna to proclaim unity and outlaw Donatism.[148] These measures on their own had relatively little effect.[149] Some of the wealthier Donatists converted to Catholicism, but this was balanced by conversions to Donatism and a massive upsurge of Circumcellion activity. At last, however, in May 411 Augustine succeeded in having the two sides brought together in a conference at Carthage presided over by his friend, the imperial tribune and notary Marcellinus. The tally of episcopal signatures attended by members of the conference in the presence of Marcellinus showed both churches of approximately equal strength: 284 representatives each.[150] After three sessions of intense and often bitter debate (Petilian of Constantine alone spoke 150 times for the Donatists!), the imperial commissioner declared that the Catholics had made good their claim to be the true church of North Africa. The Donatists were convicted of "falsehood." On 30 January 412, an imperial edict banned the Donatist church, confiscated its property, and imposed heavy fines on those who refused to join the Catholic church. The death penalty, however, was avoided. There were to be no more Donatist martyrs.[151]

Donatism was driven underground. Its churches were taken over, its leaders became fugitives. Some Donatist congregations submitted. Between 412 and 421 Donatism recurs from time to time in Augustine's letters and sermons. He was a harsh victor. These adversaries, unlike the Manichees, he never understood. The Circumcellions he abominated. The long, grim letter he wrote in 417 to brief Count Boniface the military commander about Donatism justifies repressive tactics to the full.[152] Times had changed since the apostles. Everything was in due season; the wedding guests could be compelled to come in. We leave him in 421 writing to another imperial commissioner, Dulcitius, who had the task of trying to persuade the Donatist bishop of Thamugadi to give up his church, that it was better that the bishop and his associates should perish in their own flames than that all Donatists should burn in the flames of Hell for their sacrilegious error.[153] The questing, sensitive youth had become the father of the inquisition.

In other even more significant directions Augustine's theology had become hard in its rigorous logic. Donatism had interrupted other works on the first chapters of Genesis intended as a final answer to the Manichees, and a great study on the *Trinity* that provided the West with its own understanding of the mystery of the three persons akin to, yet independent of, the Platonism of Eastern Trinitarian thought. At no time, however, were the problems of free will and grace far from his thoughts. In the *Confessions* he is deeply introspective and proclaims his utter dependence on God's grace for every step he had made toward salvation.[154] Sin was not a matter even of wanton acts, like his theft of pears, but a symptom of the desperate condition of humanity itself. Adam had indeed sinned by act of will (not by nature), that is, disobedience to God's command, but no progress toward righteousness was possible unassisted by God's grace. In his answers to Simplicianus's questions in 397, Augustine admitted "without grace it is impossible to resist concupiscence." Years later, writing the *Revisions* (*Retractationes*) in c. 426, he recorded how at the time he had pondered over the problems of free will and grace and that grace had prevailed.[155] Human beings indeed were a "sinful mass" (*massa peccati*). Only a limited number would be saved. These fortunate were already predestined from the beginning of time.[156] Thus, thirteen years before Pelagius set foot in Africa, Augustine had already reached his main conclusions. His most lasting legacy to Western Christendom was not the product merely of the Pelagian controversy. It arose out of the core of the North African theological tradition, accentuated by his meditations on the meaning of his own experiences.

The long-drawn-out and increasingly bitter controversy with the Donatists closed Augustine's mind. Before he had joined battle seriously in 395, he had ruminated over the "license" involved in the rowdy celebration of the "joys of the martyrs" at Hippo.[157] Ten years later, he knew that liberty in practice meant "liberty to err." The text from *Hortensius*, "Oh, wretched man! who was at liberty to sin" (*O miserum cui peccare licebat*) was evidently remembered.[158] What fate was worse for the soul than "liberty of perdition"?[159] Moreover, Who, he asks, shall divert the foreordained course of God? The survival of Catholic Christianity was guaranteed. What right had the Donatists to claim to be the only Christians?[160] Connections were forming in his mind between the necessity of grace and the justification of coercion against those who would attempt to resist what had been predestined by God. Pelagius forced Augustine to apply his conclusions not only to Africa but to the human race itself.

PELAGIUS AND PELAGIANISM

Pelagius, whether or not he was born the son of a Roman civil servant in Britain c. 360, had been in Rome a long time,[161] and but for the city's fall to Alaric on 24 August 410, nothing much might have been heard of him. Yet for some thirty years he had been the chaplain to the illustrious Roman senatorial house of the Anicii, a friend, like Augustine himself, of Paulinus of Nola, and through him on good terms with the southern Italian bishops. At this time his adversary, not on doctrinal but personal grounds, had been Jerome, with whom he seems to have quarreled during the latter's stay in

Rome 382/85.[162] Nothing demonstrates more clearly than Pelagius's early career and immunity from doctrinal accusations, the relative isolation in which what became the rival theological traditions of the West had been developing.

Pelagius's ideas may be gleaned from his *Expositions of the Pauline Letters*, and his surviving letters, written to the Roman *matronae* Livania and Celantia and the noble virgin of the house of the Anicii, Demetrias.[163] They were unequivocal and direct. The whole gospel was to be obeyed: "For we ought not choose just some of the commandments of good at our own inclination, but to fulfill them all as a whole," he wrote to Demetrias (c. 414).[164] This was possible if one made the effort. God did not command the impossible; rather "You, therefore, must be perfect, as your heavenly Father perfect" (Matt. 5:48) meant what it said. "No one," he says to Demetrias, "knows better the measure of our strength; and no one has a better understanding of what is within our power than he who endowed us with the very resources of our power"; God's righteousness prevented him commanding the impossible from individuals.[165] In practice, Pelagius urged that moral reform was necessary to change society. The abuses of wealth and official corruption were intolerable. Public executions were iniquitous. The rich could not enter heaven unless they renounced their wealth.[166] Everyone was a "monk," but that involved battling to remedy the ills of the world, not forsaking it.

Whether regarded from a theological or moral point of view Pelagius's outlook was the opposite of Augustine's. For him every person's sin was one's own. Adam's fault lay in his example—he did not infect the human race, but he did lead it astray. Pelagius's disciple Julian of Eclanum summed up (c. 420) what many educated Western Christians outside Africa were thinking. There was no "great sin" (as Augustine supposed) behind the misery of the human condition. "It is improbable. It is untrue. It makes it seem as though the Devil was the maker of man. It vitiates and betrays the freedom of will . . . by saying that men are incapable of virtue, that in the womb of their mothers they are filled with bygone sins."[167] The trouble was habit and not nature. Human beings, however, were not bereft of aids. They had the word of God in the two Testaments and the exhortations of Paul; the power of grace too was a constant aid, not indeed as "grace and favour" through the patronage of saints and martyrs available to the gross sinner at judgment, but as aid and enlightenment, an "assistance" (*adjutorium*) to endeavor, the sign of the outflowing of God's eternal mercy— ideas nearer the original sense of the term than Augustine's concept.[168]

Pelagius's was a heroic ideal, and one which few would achieve. He had, however, based his views on the writings of acknowledged orthodox writers of East and West, on Lactantius, Hilary, Ambrose, John Chrysostom, and even Jerome, and Augustine's *De libero arbitrio (On Free Will)*.[169] He was strongly anti-Manichean at a time when the Manichees were numerous

674

in Rome. In circumstances other than those of the first decade of the fifth century his teaching might have provided a basis for a Christian ethic which would have set the seal on the conversion of the empire. Medieval Europe might possibly have been built on different and more optimistic foundations. As it was, for some of those who lived beyond the grasp of the armies of Radagaisus and Alaric, Pelagius's message came as a call to conversion and action. "When I lived at home," wrote a man who had fallen under the influence of a lady who led a group of Pelagians in Sicily, "I thought I was a worshipper of God. Now for the first time I have begun to know how I can be a true Christian."[170] Groups of Christians devoted to Pelagius's views formed rapidly from one end of the empire to the other, in Sicily, Rhodes, Gaul, North Africa, and above all in Britain. There, perhaps (it must remain "perhaps"), the revolution of 410 in which "the British cities" declared their independence of Honorius's government may have owed something to Pelagianism.[171]

For a generation Pelagius and Augustine had been preaching differing concepts of humanity's relation to God, and but for the disaster of Alaric's invasion, Italian and North African theologies of grace might have continued to evolve in relative independence. Most Italian bishops would probably have agreed with the general tenor of Pelagius's views. Maximus of Turin, for instance, saw grace as the reward of faith and good conduct. There would be grades hereafter corresponding to grades of faith (*Sermon* LXXX). Almsgiving was a means of acquiring grace (*Sermon* XVIII) as was the practice of asceticism (*Sermon* LXVI). That is to say, it was a power bestowed by God, but in response to meritorious acts by the individual. For him as for Paulinus of Nola imitation of Christ did lie within the individual's power with grace assisting. The North African concept of prevenient grace would have sounded as questionable to Maximus as it did to Pelagius. Pelagius knew of the *Confessions* as they were circulated in Rome, and had thought their author a rather slack and fatalistic Christian. "Give what thou commandest and command what thou wilt" (*Confessions* X.33), suggested futility of human effort at reform. But he had a high regard for some of Augustine's other works, and when they were in brief contact on Pelagius's arrival in Africa as a refugee, Augustine formed a good opinion of him. He regarded him as a "holy man" who had made no small progress in the Christian life.[172]

The trouble arose from statements made by Celestius, Pelagius's disciple. He had also escaped from Rome and in 411 arrived in Carthage where he applied to Bishop Aurelius for ordination.[173] Before he got very far, however, he found himself charged with heresy. Evidently, he had set out Pelagius's principles without compromise. Adam was made mortal and would have died anyhow. Eve's sin hurt Eve but not the human race. Infants were born in exactly the same state as Adam had been before he sinned. Since it was not through Eve that sin and death entered the world,

675

it was not through the resurrection and the reversal of Eve's sin that the human race attained eternal life. Law and gospel were of equal value in guiding humankind toward salvation, and there were sinless beings before Christ. Finally the rich, even if baptized, could not be saved unless they gave their goods to the poor. Ordination was refused and Celestius was excommunicated.[174]

Unwittingly, Celestius had struck a blow at the foundations of North African theology. Nor was this merely a matter of traditional habit of thought. Even as he engaged in controversy with the Donatists, Augustine had written, "What is it that David says, except that he was conceived in iniquity unless because he derived his iniquity from Adam?"[175] If the Donatists were to be "taught by inconveniences," it was because humanity itself must be treated like an invalid, that is, with authority.[176] However, not until the tribune Marcellinus wrote to him for advice concerning the new Pelagian views did Augustine set out his own. In reply he wrote (in 412/13) the classic *On the Spirit and the Letter* in which he pointed out that the "letter that killeth" was the Mosaic Law, that prescribed what one should do but denied one the strength to do it, and the "Spirit that giveth life," the Holy Spirit, through whom the human will was lifted up and enabled to love and to obey the law of God. No fruit was good that did not grow from the root of love.[177]

Augustine had written a profound work on the soul's relation to God. He had made a contribution to the problem of free will and grace without forcing the Western churches to an irrevocable choice between two incompatible ideas. But by 415, however, he was becoming alarmed at the implications of Pelagius's teaching as he understood it. In the "cause of grace" (*causa gratiae*) he identified his own experiences with the teaching of the church. He forgot others had come to their faith along different paths. His worst enemy was his pursuit of controversy to the bitter end, and his inability to concede the least right to an opponent. He wrote *On Nature and Grace* in response to Pelagius's work *On Nature,* and entered the controversy with zest.[178]

Even so, the dispute might have died down—or at least been confined to the meaning of infant baptism[179]—had it not become part of another controversy involving that least peaceable of Augustine's contemporaries, Jerome. Pelagius had moved from Africa eastward to Palestine. There his ideas were warmly received. That individuals through a right exercise of free will climbed step by step toward true spirituality was a truism. Of course, grace was an aid,[180] but not the sole divine means of setting an individual among an elite of the saved.

Unfortunately, at this point Pelagius injected a new element into the cauldron of personal rancors and theological disputes that centered on Jerome. The current controversy had nothing to do with infant baptism but concerned humanity's ability to achieve a perfect state. Jerome was already at odds with Palestinian monks on this question. He saw Pelagius's teaching as confirming their claims that by following the true philosophy of the ascetic life individuals could attain a state of "lack of passion" (*apatheia*). No one had ever lived without sin, he retorted.[181] The Pelagians were making too much of the word "grace." Theirs was a Stoic or Pythagorean Christianity, he asserted, perhaps nearer the mark than he imagined.

In 415 he too received reinforcements by the arrival of a Spanish presbyter, Paulus Orosius, from Galicia in northwestern Spain. Spain had also been invaded by Germanic barbarians, and Africa was a haven for refugees from there as well as from Italy. Orosius visited Augustine, originally to consult him about Priscillianism which had taken a firm root in his province; but Augustine found him interesting and sent him off to Palestine with letters to Jerome discussing the origin of the soul and the question of equality of sins.[182] The latter was no longer an academic issue, where what could be interpreted by opponents as the Christianized Stoicism of Pelagius and his followers was coming increasingly into the forefront of debate.

The Palestinian bishops were becoming fed up with Jerome and were not impressed by Orosius. A council held at Diospolis (Lydda), on 20 December 415 under Eulogius of Caesarea and including John of Jerusalem, found Pelagius at his best. "Have you said that all men are guided by their will?" he was asked. "Yes, I said so because our will is free. God assists us when we choose the good, and the man who sins is blameworthy because he has free-will."[183] This key statement was accepted readily, and Pelagius had little difficulty in disposing of other charges, especially when he accepted the need of grace, as well as individual effort, in every act to attain sinlessness, and by implication rejected Origen's universalism. The church, he affirmed, must be "without spot or wrinkle," as the Lord had made it in baptism. In fact, at this council Pelagius had come as near as any Western theologian to bridging the gap between Eastern and Western views of humanity, and had also set out a high ideal of the nature of the church and its relation to its individual members. He was acquitted, but soon after Jerome's cell was attacked and ransacked, whether by Pelagius's supporters or not. The attack on this socially distinguished Latin colony, which included members of the Roman aristocracy, could not be forgiven in the West.

Nor could Pelagius's acquittal be accepted in Africa, and at this point the superb conciliar organization of the North African Catholics proved decisive. No sooner had Orosius returned to Africa (summer 416), bringing with him the ill tidings from Jerome as well as relics of St. Stephen, than a council was assembled at Carthage. The decision was to ask Pope Innocent (401–17) to anathematize Pelagius and Celestius. Almost simultaneously a Numidian council held at Milevis, at which Augustine was present, added doctrinal weight to a similar request. Pelagius was robbing adults of prayer, and infants of baptism. If he was right, what need was there for God?[184]

The case was well presented, but why did it carry conviction? Augustine's proof-text, the mistranslation of Rom. 5:12 ("in whom" instead of "on account of whom") designed to demonstrate that Adam's sin had been literally transmitted to the human race, had been expounded years ago by the Roman lay theologian known to history as Ambrosiaster.[185] Pelagius's position was also strong. In the East, Jerusalem and Ephesus were sympathetic toward him, and as is known from Augustine's letters to Atticus of Constantinople and Cyril of Alexandria (in the Divjak collection), his opponent was finding it difficult to convince those powerful bishops that he was indeed a heretic.[186] In the West, he had support not only among the southern Italian episcopate, but in Rome where the influential deacon Sixtus (probably later Pope Sixtus III, 432–40) was his friend. More significant were the links he retained with members of the Roman aristrocracy and, above all, with Paulinus of Nola who could demonstrate from his own career that there had been a gradual evolution toward a life dedicated to Christian service with grace manifestly "assisting."[187] But once again the historian must point to the personal factors that sometimes win the decision in finely balanced situations. Paulinus was not a fighter. Elegant constructions at Nola in honor of St. Felix, long-winded, soul-searching correspondence with friends, and the pleasure of periodic visits to members of Roman society filled his life. He had a genius for friendship and mediation between people, but he lacked both will and strength to withstand Augustine.[188]

In January 417 Pope Innocent accepted the North African case. There was need for grace because humanity depended upon God (Pelagius would have agreed!). Pelagius and Celestius had denied this and were therefore excommunicated. On 23 September Augustine preached one of his most famous sermons (*Sermon* CXXXI) in Carthage. "In this matter [Pelagianism] the decision of two councils have been sent to the apostolic see. Letters have come thence as well. The case is finished. [*Causa est finita*]. Would that the error were finished also!" He had used the same phrase against the Donatists at Hippo a quarter of a century before. For Augustine, all surrender must be unconditional surrender.[189]

It was not quite the case. Innocent had died on 12 March 417. His successor Zosimus was of Greek origin, out of sympathy with North Africa, but prone to make wrong decisions that undermined his credit. Pelagius remained in the East, the date and place of his death are unknown; but Celestius, ordained presbyter at Ephesus, returned to face his accusers. Once again he nearly succeeded. At an examination in the basilica of San Clemente presided over by Zosimus himself just as Augustine was about to speak (September 417), Celestius established that his "faith was completely satisfactory," as Zosimus had informed Aurelius of Carthage. The news arrived early in November. The wheel had one more turn to make. Through the winter Rome was given over to furious debate which spilled over into violence. The emperor Honorius, terrified lest disorder should become revolution, condemned the Pelagians and ordered their supporters out of the city (30 April 418). On 1 May, the North Africans made their final effort. A great council of 214 bishops was held at Carthage. Again Pelagius and his teaching were condemned and this time Zosimus capitulated. An *Epistola tractoria* (*Epistolary Sermon*, a judicial letter) confirmed the decisions of the Council of Carthage of 416 and Pope Innocent's decision. Compliance was demanded of the Italian's episcopate (summer 418). To their credit, 18 southern Italian bishops, including Julian of Eclanum, preferred to resign.[190]

Augustine had won. It would be pleasant to pass over the long aftermath, but it was during the dozen years of controversy with Julian of Eclanum that Augustinianism was defined and refined to influence Western European theology and ethics to our own day. Julian was the man to get the worst out of Augustine. An Aristotelian, shrewd and resourceful, completely convinced that he was defending a civilized tradition of Christian theology against its destruction by "the Carthaginian orator," he drove an exasperated and aging Augustine into increasingly extreme statements. Adam's sin became exaggerated beyond recognition and irrevocably associated with sex. This was the "deep sin" that vitiated all humankind. "The common decency by which we cover our genitals"[191] was grist to Augustine's mill. Adam and Eve's instinctive conduct when they had disobeyed God by eating the forbidden fruit, was to be "ashamed" and "cover their genitals with fig-leaves." That was it.

The nine years he had been a Manichee were reasserting themselves. A Latin Manichean commentary on Paul had stated that the evil of concupiscence was natural and permanent and was the origin of evil itself.[192] It had also defended infant baptism, contrasting it with the "shame" of intercourse. If human nature was still "good," whence came the vice that "darkened and weakened it?"[193] This was one of the questions the Manicheans were asking. If God was good and all powerful, how could the mass of humanity be predestined to suffer punishment? That the incarnation had removed the gulf between God and people was of small comfort when only a few of the predestined elect would benefit. If Augustine surveyed the human race as a whole and found a common factor in its sin, Julian could point to the justice and equity of God ("He judges the world with righteousness, he judges the peoples with equity" [Ps. 9:8]), who had not spared his son in order to redeem humanity.[194] God did not impose collective punishment, including even tiny babies in its net, for the sin of one person. But, replied Augustine, the justice of God was not the justice of humankind. God did allow the human race to be visited by his wrath.[195] Disease, demons, catastrophes against which people were helpless were all around us. Thus had argued the Manichees also. As Julian told him, "just as an Ethiopian could not change his skin or a leopard change his spots, nor could he,

Augustine, change his Manichaeism."[196] Had Augustine remained a Manichee, one of his former acquaintances in the sect told him, he would have been another Paul.[197] As it was, had not Manicheism exacted its price from the leader it had lost?

Appeals to Rome

The arrival of the Vandals before the walls of Hippo together with malaria mercifully put an end to the debate on 28 August 430. The final legacy of the North African church to the West was more constructive. In his sermon at Carthage recounting the condemnation of the Pelagians, Augustine had indicated the role of the church of Rome in the affair. It was not to judge anew, but to confirm and lend its weight to the sentence already agreed by the two African councils. In the crisis months of 417–18 Aurelius and his colleagues told Pope Zosimus that they had ordained that the sentence passed by "the venerable Bishop Innocent" should stand (1 May 418).[198] The collectivity of bishops therefore was the judge as it had been in Cyprian's day. Nearly twenty years before, at the end of a long debate with the Donatists on the validity of the ideas of baptism held by Cyprian and his contemporaries, Augustine had said that for matters of local import a provincial council would determine, and for more important affairs a general council must decide.[199] Conciliar government was accepted as sovereign by both Donatists and Catholics. Yet both would also have agreed with Pope Innocent that "the very episcopate" (though not the "very authority of this name") emerged from the apostolic see.[200] Where did the division of authority lie? Did the Roman church have the right of intervention in the internal affairs of other churches? Did a bishop receive his authority through the pope?

Fortunately for the North Africans (and for the future perhaps) both cases where the appellate jurisdiction of the papacy was tested were thoroughly discreditable to the appellants.[201] Thanks, however, to the discovery by Johannes Divjak of the thirty-one new Augustinian letters and memoranda, some entirely new light has been thrown on the case of Bishop Antoninus of Fussala, outlined in *Letter* CCIX. The long and detailed account that Augustine wrote to the Roman *matrona* Fabiola the Younger in 423/23 (Divjak, ed., *Letter* XX) shows first and foremost the immensity of the personal disaster which he suffered by his hasty consecration (in c. 416) of an untried lector, Antoninus, as bishop of Fussala, the former Donatist congregation at the native township (*oppidum*) of Fussala in his diocese. Antoninus had been brought up in Augustine's monastery at Hippo, but was far below the canonical age for promotion to the presbyterate, let alone the episcopate.[202] His sole commendation was that he was a Punic-speaker and Augustine was determined to consolidate the Catholic hold on what had once been Donatist territory.[203] The appointment, however, was a disaster. Antoninus instituted a reign of extortion and terror, and after some five years of suffering, the community appealed to Augustine,[204] At a judicial council held at Hippo Antoninus was condemned. He was to be removed from Fussala but would be allowed to retain the title of bishop,[205] provided he made restitution for his robberies and the fraud perpetrated against his congregation. This he did, but just as the new bishop was about to be consecrated, Antoninus appealed not merely to a plenary Numidian council but to Pope Boniface (418–22), declaring that either he ought to sit on his episcopal throne or not be bishop at all.[206] Augustine's letter to Fabiola, who evidently had some sympathy for Antoninus, illustrates the cumbersome system of appeals which now came into play. Pope Boniface sent an episcopal commission to North Africa to make an on-the-spot inquiry as to whether or not Antoninus had any justification for his appeal,[207] but Boniface died before the investigation had begun (September 422). After one hearing the papal commission faded into the background and the proceedings devolved on the Catholic primate of Numidia.[208] Antoninus, however, refused to accept a compromise whereby he would give up Fussala but retain jurisdiction over some villages which were prepared to have him. To the anger of his Numidian colleagues, he again appealed to Rome—this time to Pope Celestine (422–32) to whom Augustine outlined the case against Antoninus in *Letter* CCIX.[209] As no more is heard of Antoninus it may be assumed that his appeal failed and Fabiola withdrew her support from him. The shock, however, to Augustine's anti-Donatist strategy and to his own credibility was lasting.[210] His old age was not destined to be serene.

Letter CCIX and Divjak, ed., *Letter* XX show that appeals to Rome on disciplinary matters affecting bishops were not uncommon,[211] but that the role of the papacy was usually confined to upholding the decisions of North African disciplinary tribunals. In case of conflict, however, North Africans were prepared to invoke conciliar canons, not least those of Nicaea which, in common with their Eastern colleagues, they regarded as having sovereign authority.[212] In the background was always the imperial court. The importance of conciliar authority becomes clear from the case that was running concurrently with that of Antoninus.

The North Africans had won by tact and persuasion and latent strength. The second case, however, was more serious. It concerned a priest named Apiarius from Sicca Veneria (Le Kef in western Tunisia). He had committed serious offenses and had been deposed and excommunicated by his bishop, Urbanus, who was also a friend of Augustine.[213] Like Antoninus, he took his case to Rome where Zosimus was pope. Whether out of spite or because he was genuinely misinformed, Zosimus took up his case and threatened his bishop with excommunication. Once again, however, the North African conciliar system proved too strong even for the papacy. While Zosimus was sending legates to investigate the matter and report— the first recorded time a pope had acted in this way toward a Western episcopate—Aurelius assembled his council. On 1 May 418, at the same time as it condemned Pelagius finally, the council forbade "presbyters, deacons and inferior clergy" to appeal overseas.[214] The channel for redress lay through their bishops and thence to African councils or to the provincial primates. When they arrived and threatened Urbanus with excommunication if he failed to cancel his proceedings against Africans, the legates found the North Africans prepared. To make matters worse, they tried to support their case—that lower clergy might appeal to Rome—with allegedly Nicene canons. These were in fact from the Council of Sardica and were far less authoritative.

At a plenary council of the African church on 25 May 419, the legates, now acting for Pope Boniface, at first persisted in their belief that they were basing the appellate rights of the papacy on Nicaea. Inevitably, their mistake was demonstrated.[215]

The North African bishops, however, did not press home their advantage. A compromise was reached by which Apiarius was allowed a second chance at Tabarca on the Tunisian coast. All went well for a year or two, when once again he offended and was excommunicated. Again he appealed to Rome, this time to Pope Celestine, and Celestine not only restored him but had him accompanied back to Africa by a legate—Faustinus whom the North Africans had previously found arrogant and overbearing. This time no punches were pulled. Apiarius confessed a catalog of misdeeds. Faustinus returned to Rome discomfited and this time the bishops followed him up with a letter (*Optaremus*) barbed with polite rebuke: "We earnestly implore you in the future not to admit readily for a hearing persons coming hence, nor choose to receive to your communion those who have been excommunicated by us, because your Reverence will readily perceive that this has been prescribed by the Nicene Council."[216] And much more. The African bishops knew their rights. Respect and communion the papacy would receive, but not right of unsolicited and indiscriminate intervention in the internal affairs of the North African church.

Catastrophe

It was the last time for many years that this or any other church in the West was to demonstrate its independence in such a fashion. It was now 426. The prosperity of North Africa, its churches, and people was drawing to a close. Augustine and Aurelius were aging. In that year Augustine would be consecrating a coadjutor as thirty years before Valerius had consecrated him. Disaster, when it fell, came first from African peoples, who or what we do not know. They were destructive barbarians.[217] Despite warning signs,[218] the African churches had spent too much time and energy on their quarrels, too little on missionary work among the peoples on their borders. These borders were now being overrun, the clergy killed, churches burned down, and congregations dispersed.

Then a new enemy struck. In the spring of 429 Gaiseric, the king of the Vandals, conveyed some eighty thousand of his people and their allies from southern Spain and landed in western Mauretania. By the next year they had advanced through the Mauretanias and Numidia, and were besieging Hippo. Augustine did not despair, "I am a long-winded old man, and ill-health has made me anxious. . . . I will not desert you."[219] Brave words, but the city was a prey to panic and disorder. We leave the final scene in Augustine's life for his biographer Possidius to describe (c. 435): "The man of God saw whole cities sacked, villas razed, their owners scattered as refugees, the churches deprived of their bishops and clergy, and the holy virgins dishonoured and dispersed, some tortured to death some killed outright. . . ."[220] It is a description reminiscent of Gildas's "folk memories" of the end of Roman Britain. The downfall of Catholic Africa was spectacular, though it proved only temporary. Similar scenes were being repeated in other Western provinces of the empire. Had the Christians themselves contributed to the catastrophe?

BIBLIOGRAPHY

NOTE

The literature on the North African church in Augustine's time and on Augustine himself is justly huge and includes some excellent books. Of these I regard Peter Brown's *Augustine of Hippo: A Biography* (Berkeley and Los Angeles: University of California Press; London: Faber & Faber, 1967), with its erudition and sensitive handling of Augustine, as the best, and it contains a full bibliography to 1965.

On the *Confessions*, see P. Courcelle, *Recherches sur les Confessions de St. Augustin* (Paris: Boccard, 1950); and, for Augustine's crucial period at Milan, Courcelle's "Du manichéisme au néo-platonisme," chap. I (pp. 17–26) of *Les 'Confessions' de Saint Augustin dans la tradition littéraire. Antécédents et postérité* (Paris: Études Augustiniennes, 1963). For Manicheism in Augustine's life, F. Décret's doctoral thesis provides a very full and convincing account of the abiding influence of the Manichean period in Augustine's later life: F. Decrét, *L'Afrique manichéenne (ive–ve siècles). Étude historique et doctrinale* (Paris: Études Augustiniennes, 1978).

For Neo-Platonist influences, Prosper Alfaric's *L'Evolution intellectuelle de S. Augustin* (Paris: Nourry, 1918) still holds the field.

Augustine's controversies are dealt with ably by G. Bonner, *St. Augustine of Hippo: Life and Controversies* (Philadelphia: Westminster Press, 1964; London: SCM Press, 1963).

For the Donatists see P. Monceaux, *Histoire littéraire de l'Afrique*, vol. 4; the present author's *Donatist Church*; and E. Tengström, *Donatisten und Katholiken: Soziale, wirtschaftliche und politische Aspekte einer nordafrikanischen Kirchenspaltung* (Göteborg: Acta Universitatis Gothoburgensis, 1964).

Pelagianism is the subject of John Ferguson's *Pelagius: An Historical and Theological Study* (Chester Springs, Pa.: Dufour Editions; Cambridge: W. Heffer & Sons, 1957); R. F. Evans, *Pelagius: Inquiries and Reappraisals* (New York:

Seabury Press; London: A. & C. Black, 1968); and above all, G. de Plinval, *Pélage: Ses écrits, sa vie et sa réforme* (Lausanne, 1943); and also Peter Brown's two essays on Pelagius's circle, "Pelagius and His Supporters: Aims and Environment" (*JTS* n.s. 19 [April 1968]: 93–114), and "Patrons of Pelagius: The Roman Aristocracy Between East and West" (*JTS* 21 [April 1970]: 56–72), republished in his *Religion and Society in the Age of Saint Augustine* (New York: Harper & Row, 1972), pp. 183–207 and 208–26.

For a succinct account of the attempts by Popes Innocent I and Boniface I to assert their jurisdictional authority in North Africa, see B. J. Kidd, *The Roman Primacy to A.D. 461* (New York: Macmillan Co.; London: SPCK, 1936).

In general, note also the essays of varying length, subject, and quality in the three volumes of *Augustinus Magister* (Paris: Congrès international augustinien, 1954–55).

On the Divjak Augustinian documents, see C. Lepelley, ed., *Les Lettres de Saint Augustin découvertes par Johannes Divjak* (*Communications presentées au Colloque des 20 et 21 septembre 1982*) (Paris: Études Augustiniennes, 1983).

SOURCES

A full list of the works of Augustine together with English translations will be found throughout Brown's *Augustine of Hippo*. Donatist works are listed in my *Donatist Church*, pp. 337–38. Maps relating to Donatism will also be found in that work.

African Church Councils, in E. Munier, *Concilia Africae*, CCSL 149, A.345–A.525 (1973).

Pelagius's works, see *Expositions of Thirteen Epistles of St. Paul*, Contributions to Biblical and Patristic Literature, Texts and Studies, vol. 9, nos. 1 and 2, New York: Macmillan Co.; Cambridge: At the University Press, 1922–26; and the discussion regarding the authentic and inauthentic Pelagian writings in Altaner, *Patrology*, pp. 439–41.

Possidius, *Vita Sancti Augustini*, PL 32.33–64; and ed. and Eng. trans. H. T. Weiskotten, Princeton, N.J.: Princeton University Press, 1919.

SECONDARY WORKS

Adam, A. "Das Fortwirken des Manichäismus bei Augustinus." *ZKG* 69 (1958): 1–25.

Andresen, C. *Bibliographia Augustiniana*. Darmstadt: Wissenschaftliche Buchgesellschaft, 1962. A complete Augustinian bibliography arranged in topics to 1961.

Armstrong, A. H. "Salvation, Plotinian and Christian." *Downside Review* 75 (1957): 126–39.

Bardy, G. *S. Augustin: L'homme et l'oeuvre*. Paris: Descleé de Brouwer, 1948.

Berthier, A., Martin, M., and Logeart, F. *Les vestiges du christianisme antique dans la Numidie centrale*. Algiers: Gouvernement Général de l'Algérie, Direction des Antiquités, 1942.

Brisson, J. P. *Autonomisme et Christianisme*.

Brown, P. R. L. "Religious Coercion in the Later Roman Empire: The Case of North Africa." *History* 48 (1963): 283–305.

Burnaby, J. *Amor Dei: A Study of the Religion of St. Augustine*. Toronto: Musson Book Co.; London: Hodder & Stoughton, 1938.

———. "The *Retractationes* of Saint Augustine: Self-criticism or Apologia?" *Augustinus Magister* 1 (1954): 85–92.

Crespin, R. *Ministère et Sainteté: Pastorale du clergé et solution de la crise donatiste dans la vie et la doctrine de Saint Augustin.* Paris: Études Augustiniennes, 1965.

Diesner, H. J. "Die Circumcellionen von Hippo Regius." In *Kirche und Staat im spätrömischen Reich*, pp. 78–90. Berlin, 1963.

———. "Die Lage der nordafrikanischen Bevölkerung im Zeitpunkt der Vandeleninvasion." *Historia* 11 (1962): 97–111.

Frend, W. H. C. "Circumcellions and Monks." *JTS* n.s. 20 (October 1969): 542–49.

———. "Fussala: Augustine's Crisis of Credibility (*Ep.* 20)." In *Les Lettres d'Augustin découvertes par Divjak*, ed. Lepelley, pp. 251–65.

———. "The Gnostic-Manichaean Tradition in Roman North Africa." *JEH* 4 (1953): 13–26.

———. "The Organisation of the Donatist and Catholic Churches in the North African Countryside." In *Settimani de studio del Centro italiano di Studi sull' alto medioevo*, vol. 28, pp. 601–37. Spoleto, 1982.

———. "The Revival of Berber Art." *Antiquity* 15 (1942): 342–52.

Hagendahl, H. *Augustine and the Latin Classics.* 2 vols. Studia Graeca et Latina Gotheburgensia 20. Göteborg: Acta Universitatis Gothoburgensis, 1967.

Leschi, Louis. "Basilique et cimitière donatistes de Numidie (Ain Ghorab)." *Revue Africaine* 78 (1936): 27–46.

Liebeschütz, W. "Did the Pelagian Movement Have Social Aims?" *Historia* 12 (1963): 227–41.

Lo Bue, F. *The Turin Fragments of Tyconius' Commentary on Revelation.* Contributions to Biblical and Patristic Literature. Texts and Studies n.s. 7. Cambridge: Cambridge University Press, 1963.

Mandouze, A. "Encore le Donatisme! A quoi l'Afrique?" *L'Antiquité classique* 29 (1960): 61–107. Discussion of J. P. Brisson's work.

Markus, R. A. *Saeculum: History and Society in the Theology of St. Augustine.* New York and Cambridge: Cambridge University Press, 1970.

Marrou, H. I. "La basilique chrétienne d'Hippone d'après le résultat des dernières fouilles." *Revue des études augustiniennes* 6 (1960): 109–54.

———. *Saint Augustin et la fin de la culture antique.* 4th ed. Paris: Boccard, 1958.

Marschall, W. *Karthago und Rom.* Päpste und Papstum, vol. 1. Stuttgart: Hiersemann, 1971.

Menasce, P. J. "Augustin manichéen." In *Freundesgabe für Ernst Robert Curtius*, pp. 79–93. Bern, 1956.

Monceaux, P. "Le manichéen Fauste de Milev: Restitution de ses 'capitula.'" In *Mémoires de l'Académie des Inscriptions et Belles Lettres.* Paris, 1924.

Moreau, M. *Le Dossier Marcellinus dans la Correspondance de saint Augustin.* Paris: Études Augustiniennes, 1973.

Morris, J. "Pelagian Literature." *JTS* n.s. 16 (April 1965): 26–60.

Myres, J. N. L. "Pelagius and the End of Roman Rule in Britain." *JRS* 50 (1960): 21–36.

O'Meara, J. J. *The Young Augustine: The Growth of St. Augustine's Mind up to His Conversion.* New York and London: Longmans, Green & Co., 1954.

Pincherle, A. "Da Ticonio a Sant' Agostino." *Ricerche Religiose* 1 (1925): 443–66.
Pizzolato, L. F. *Le "Confessioni" di Sant' Agostino: da biographia a "confessio."* Milan: Societa editrice vita e pensiero, 1968.
Simon, M. "Punique ou berbère? Note sur la situation linguistique dans l'Afrique romaine." In *Annuaire de l'Institut de Philologie et d'Histoire Orientales et Slaves* 13 (Mélanges Isidore Lévy), pp. 613–29. Brussels, 1955.
Souter, A. "The Character and History of Pelagius' Commentary on the Epistles of St. Paul." *Proceedings British Academy* 7 (1915–16): 261–96.
de Veer, A. C. "L'exploitation du schisme maximianiste par S. Augustin dans sa lutte contre le Donatisme." *Recherches augustiniennes* 3 (1965): 219–37.
Williams, N. P. *Ideas of the Fall and of Original Sin: A Historical and Critical Study.* New York and London: Longmans, Green & Co., 1927.

NOTES

1. *Exposito totius mundi et rerum*, ed. J. Rougé, SC 124 (Paris, 1966), p. 61: "Ipsa autem regio Africae est valde maxima et bona et dives; homines autem habens non dignos patriae."

2. Eusebius *HE* VIII.6.10.

3. "Effrenatae mentis homines," Synodical letter to Pope Sylvester in Optatus, *De Schismate Donatistarum*, App. IV, p. 207. See above, p. 491.

4. Canons 3 and 8. Compare also canon 13 by which only clergy proved from the public records to have been "traditores" should be removed from office, and even then their ordinations should stand.

5. See Vieillard-Troieskouroff, "Le sarcophage de S. Nicaise," *Mélanges H. I. Marrou* (Paris: CNRS, forthcoming).

6. Cresconius, cited in Augustine, *Contra Cresconium Grammaticum (Against Cresconius the Grammarian)* III.78.89, *PL* 43.445–595, esp. p. 544.

7. "Sacerdotalis legis sacrae (christianae)," on an inscription dated to 361 from Koudiat Adjala in Mauretania Sitifensis. See P. A. Février, "Inscriptions funéraires de Mauretanie," *MEFR* 76 (1964): 158; and compare *Acta Saturnini* IV, *PL* 8.692.

8. Augustine, *Enarrationes in Psalmos* 136.1, *PL* 37.2, col. 1761. Christians were "citizens of Jerusalem," a fact which "everyone brought up in the traditions of the holy church should know." In this sermon "ad Plebem" Augustine gives an excellent summary of his ideas on the Two Cities.

9. Thus *Passio Benedicti Martyris Marculi* 1, *PL* 8.760; and also a fourth-century sarcophagus from Timgad, "Simpliciis Karissimis Filiis Praelectis ad vitam aeternam Evanthii" (published by M. Christofle, *Rapport sur les Travaux de Fouilles et Consolidations effectuées par le Service des Monuments historiques de l'Algérie* (Algiers, 1938), p. 452.

10. For Petilian's sudden and perhaps forced conversion, see Augustine *Sermo ad Caesariensis ecclesiae Plebem* VIII; and *Petilian* II.104.239.

11. The Abelonii ("sons of Abel") Augustine mentions as a community vowed to continence; like the Covenanters of Qumran, they would adopt children from neighboring villages to bring up in the sect (*De haeresibus* 87, *PL* 42.47). They were a rural, Punic-speaking community.

12. Paulus Orosius *Historiae adversus paganos* (*Histories Against the Pagans*) VII.28.6, "Poenaliter accidisse." See S. Mazzarino, *The End of the Ancient World*, Eng. trans. G. Holmes (London: Faber & Faber, 1966), chap. 4.

13. *Illustrious Men* XCIII.

14. The best account is that by Brisson, *Autonomisme et christianisme*, chap. 2.

15. Victor of Garba was sent to Rome (c. 314) to maintain "the true succession" in the see of Peter in place of the *traditor* Pope Miltiades; see Optatus *De Schismate Donatistarum*, II.4; and for the Donatist accusation against Miltiades, see Augustine, *Ad Donatistas post Collationem* XIII.17.

16. Petilian, cited by Augustine *Petilian* II.2–5. The additions of "in sanctity" and "knowingly" were clarifications by Petilian (or perhaps, as Petilian claimed, had been suppressed by Augustine!); see ibid., III.20.23 and 23.27.

17. On Donatus as a "reformer," see Cresconius cited by Augustine in *Against Cresconius* III.56–62.

18. Parmenian, cited by Optatus *De Schismate Donatistarum* I.10 and II.10.

19. *Passio Marculi* I, PL 8.762.

20. *Acta Saturnini* XX, PL 8.703.

21. *Petilian* II.92.202. See Frend, "The Roman Empire in the Eyes of the Western Schismatics During the 4th Century," *Miscellanea Historiae Ecclesiasticae* (Louvain, 1961), pp. 16–17 (reprinted in *Religion Popular and Unpopular* [London: Variorum Books, 1976], chap. 10).

22. *Gesta Collationis Carthaginiensis* III.258, ed. S. Lancel, SC 224, 4 vols., vol. 3, p. 1195. Compare Petilian in *Petilian* II.103.236.

23. Augustine(?) *Ad Catholicos Epistola de Unitate Ecclesiae* XI.2: "Inter nos et Donatistas quaestio est, ubi sit corpus, ubi sit ecclesia." The Donatist answer is quoted by Augustine *Sermon* XLVI.35.

24. Petilian, cited by Augustine *Petilian* II.46.107.

25. For example, *Letters* XLIII and XLIV, for a Donatist group at Thubursicum Bure (Teboursouk in western Tunisia), and in Hippo, *Retractationes* (*Revisions*) II.19 (Centurius).

26. Optatus *De Schismate Donatistarum* III.4; Augustine *Letters* LVIII.1 and CXXIX.6; *Ad Catholicos Epistola* XIX.51; and Petilian at the Conference of Carthage, *Gesta Collationis Carthaginiensis* I.165, ed. Lancel, vol. 2, p. 810. See also Monceaux, *Histoire littéraire de l'Afrique*, vol. 4, p. 52; and Frend, *Donatist Church*, pp. 49–53.

27. See Berthier et al., *Les vestiges du christianisme*, 2e partie "Les Vestiges."

28. See *Année épigraphique* (1894), 25 and 28. For local masons see Berthier et al., *Les vestiges du christianisme*, p. 67, "oc officina . . ."; and also pp. 93, 98, and 111.

29. Berthier et al., *Les vestiges du christianisme*, p. 191 (also, own observations 1938 and 1939). Also, for a typical Donatist church and village in Numidia, see Leschi, "Basilique et cimitière."

30. Berthier et al., *Les vestiges du christianisme*, pp. 45, 46, 77, 118, 126–29, 141, 146–47. Compare Monceaux, *Histoire littéraire de l'Afrique*, vol. 4, chap. 4.

31. See above, p. 573.

32. Augustine *Letter* 108.5.14, and compare also *Letter* 139.2—Macrobius leads Circumcellions in the countryside around Hippo and reopens Donatist churches closed after the conference of 411.

33. Augustine *Psalmos* LIV.20, quoting a reply to his claim that the Donatists were "perishing in heresy and schism," "What has that to do with me? As I have lived yesterday, so I shall live today; what my parents were, so I intend to be"; see Possidius *Vita Augustini* (*Life of Augustine*) VI and IX on the quiescent and tolerant attitudes of the Donatists in Hippo when Augustine first arrived.

34. *Against Cresconius* III.56.62.

35. For Donatist schismatics such as the Rogatists, see Augustine *Letters* 87.2 and 93.1; for the Trigarists, see *CIL* VIII.8650, and Monceaux, *Histoire littéraire de l'Afrique*, vol. 4, pp. 128–31.

36. *Contra epistolam Parmeniani* (*Against the Epistle of Parmenianus*)III.5.27.

37. See *The Rules of Tyconius*, ed. F. C. Burkitt, Cambridge Texts and Studies 3.1 (Cambridge: At the University Press, 1894), pp. xviii–xxiv, and T. Hahn, ed., *Tyconius-Studien* (Leipzig, 1900).

38. See the *Donatist Church*, pp. 316–17, and Bonner, *Augustine of Hippo*, pp. 244–46.

39. Parmenian, quoted by Augustine *Parmenianus* I.2.2 and I.14.21.

40. For instance, in the *De doctrina christiana* (*On Christian Doctrine*) III.30–37, and explicitly in *Letter* XLI.2 to Aurelius.

41. The council's sentence is quoted by Augustine in *Against Cresconius* IV.4.5. Also, *Gesta cum Emerito* X.11, and the whole is pieced together in *PL* 11.1189–91.

42. *Against Cresconius* IV.3.3. Primian's claims were heard by "the *legatus* of Carthage and four if not more proconsuls." None raised the question whether the Donatists were not themselves heretical. On 22 December 396 the proconsul Seranus told the Maximianists in the tradition of the Western emperors before Theodosius: "Lis episcoporum secundum legem ab episcopis audienda est; episcopi judicaverunt. Quare non, aut sub satisfactione ad chorum reverteris vetustatis, aut ut habes scriptum, terga persecutoribus prodis." A scriptural touch by the authorities, who show that they respected the Donatist community as that sanctioned by tradition ("vetustas"). The strength of the Donatist position before Gildo's revolt could not be illustrated better.

43. See Augustine *Letter* XXII. It looks as though Augustine even as presbyter was holding to the ideal of "withdrawal from this world's cares," and that the link with Aurelius had been forged by Alypius.

44. Augustine *Sermon* 37.2 (I owe this reference to Brown, *Augustine of Hippo*, to which I am much indebted throughout the remainder of this chapter.) For a less complimentary view of Monica's hereditary influence as that of a *meribibula* (a "drunk"), see Julian of Eclanum, cited in Augustine, *Contra Julianum opus imperfectum* (*Incomplete Work Against Julian*) I.68, ed. M. Zelzer, CSEL, 85.1 (Vienna, 1974), p. 73. Julian was arguing that Augustine had a guilt complex, and that there was no stain involved in honorable married life.

45. *Confessions* I.10.17.

46. Augustine *Letter* XVII, written c. 389, and note his attack on Manicheism as "Persian," *De haeresibus* (*On Heresies*) XLVI and *Contra Faustum Manichaeum* (*Reply to Faustus the Manichean*) XIII.2.

47. On the idea of the schematic "ages of man" determining Augustine's division of the books of *Confessions*, see Pizzolato, *Le "Confessioni" de Sant' Agostino*.

48. *Confessions* I.17.27 and cf. I.13.20. For Augustine's abiding admiration of Virgil, see *City of God* I.3, "this great poet."

49. *Confessions* I.9.15 and cf. VI.6.9, "I panted after honours, gains, marriage. . . ."

50. *Letter* XVI.2; and for strong pagan survivals in Hippo(?) itself, see *Sermon* XXIV.6.

51. *Confessions* III.3.6.

52. Cited by Augustine *Letter* XCIII.13.51 to the same Vincentius, a striking reminiscence from one who had not seen him for some thirty-five years.

53. Secundinus, *Epistola ad Augustinum* III, *PL* 42.575.

54. Augustine *De Trinitate* (*On the Trinity*) XIV.19.26 = Cicero *Hortensius*. Cited from Hagendahl, *Augustine and Latin Classics*, vol. 1, p. 88. The key question from the *Hortensius* is preserved in *De beata vita* X: "Ecce autem," ait [Cicero] "non philosophi quidem, sed prompti tamen disputandum omnes aiunt esse beatos, qui vivant ut ipsi velint" (as Augustine was doing at Cassiciacum), *PL* 32.964.

55. *Confessions* III.4.7.

56. *Contra Academicos* (*Against the Academics*) I.2.6 (searching for truth) and compare ibid., I.2.5. Note also how Licentius, though nominally a Christian, could state to Augustine that "our forebears" (that is, pagans) were both wise and happy while searching for truth and yet not be rebuked.

57. See Hagendahl's list of quotations from the *Hortensius* in *Augustine and Latin Classics*, pp. 81–83.

58. *Confessions* III.5.9.

59. See the discussion of these permanent tendencies in North African Christianity in my "Gnostic-Manichaean Tradition."

60. I have accepted the date proposed by William Seston, "De l'authenticité et de la date de l'Edit de Dioclétien contre les Manichéens," *Mélanges de philologie et d'histoire ancienne offerts à Alfred Ernout* (Paris, 1940), pp. 345–54. For 31 March 302, see Décret, *L'Afrique manichéenne*, vol. 1, pp. 162–65, and note in vol. 2, pp. 112–13.

61. On secret Manichees, see Augustine *Letter* LXIV.3; for the Manichee cells in North Africa in Augustine's time, see Décret, *L'Afrique manichéenne*, pp. 178ff. For the remarkable papyrus found sixty miles southwest of Theveste (Tébessa), see P. Alfaric, "Un manuscript manichéen," *Rev. de l'Histoire et de Littérature religieuses*, nouv. sér. 6 (1920): 62–98. "Hearers" were required to serve the "Elect."

62. Augustine *Reply to Faustus* XX.23, and cf. ibid., XIII.5. Yet, "quam plurimos" (Manicheans) in Hippo? See Possidius *Life of Augustine* VI.1.

63. Faustus in *Reply to Faustus* XIII.1, "Nos natura gentiles sumus. . . ." See Décret, *L'Afrique manichéenne*, p. 187. Interestingly, Faustus claims (*Reply to Faustus* XIII.1) that the Sibylline oracles, Hermetic works, and Orphic writings could aid the pagan to accept Christianity (Manicheism). Did Lactantius think the same way, only in the direction of Catholicism?

64. Faustus, in Augustine *Reply to Faustus* XX.3, "sim modo sim dignus, rationabile Dei templum puto: . . . aram, mentem bonis artibus et disciplinis imbutam."

65. Augustine, *Contra Felicem* I.9, *PL* 42.525.

66. Augustine *Acta seu disputatio contra Fortunatum Manichaeum* (*Against Fortunatus the Manichean*) I.6.

67. For Paulinism, see the Manichean manuscript cited above (n. 61), and my "Gnostic-Manichaean Tradition," p. 22.

68. Augustine, *Contra duas epistolas Pelagianorum* (*Against Two Letters of the Pelagians*) IV.4.5 (*PL* 44.613), "baptismum . . . quod Manichaei dicunt in omni aetate superfluum," and cf. *De haeresibus* XLVI (*PL* 42.38); but see, for a contrary view, Faustus in *Reply to Faustus* XXIV.1 (n. 193 below). Against the resurrection of the body see Euodius in *De Fide contra Manichaeos* XL, *PL* 42.1151.

69. Faustus, cited by Augustine *Reply to Faustus* XX.2, "Christ hanging from every tree," symbolizing the suffering of the world and indeed of God himself.

70. For the basic Manichean credo, see above, p. 316.

71. Augustine *De moribus Manichaeorum* (*On the Morals of the Manicheans*) XIX.67 and cf. XIII.30, "Electus enim vester tribus signaculis praedicatus." See Décret, *L'Afrique manichéenne*, vol. 1, pp. 25–30, and vol. 2, pp. 34–36 (references).

72. Augustine *Morals of Manicheans* XV.37.

73. Thus in 392, Fortunatus (not Augustine) quotes the whole of Eph. 2:1–17 to support his argument that grace was wholly necessary for salvation (*Against Fortunatus* I.16).

74. *Morals of Manicheans* XVIII.65.

75. Which they would have claimed was more "Christian" than fasting on the Sabbath as the Roman Christians did (Augustine *Letter* XXXVI.12.27)

76. *Against Cresconius* IV.64.79 (that is, Augustine's view c. 406); and fifteen years later, *Contra Julianum* I.9.43, *PL* 44.671.

77. *De duabus animabus contra Manichaeos*, VIII.10, *PL* 42.101; and compare *Against Fortunatus* I.19. For the influence of his search for understanding of the problem of evil in his conversion to Manicheism, see *De libero arbitrio* (*On Free Will*) I.2.4: "*Augustinus:* Eam quaestionem moves, quae me admodum adulescentem vehementer exercuit et fatigatum in haereticos impulit atque dejecit."

78. *Confessions* III.11.19, and for rejection of parents' views, see Coptic Mani *Psalm* CCLIX, lines 29–32, in *A Manichaean Psalm Book* (*Manichaean Manuscripts in the Chester Beatty Collection*), ed. C. R. C. Allberry (Stuttgart, 1938), p. 87 and Faustus's claim in Augustine, *Reply to Faustus* V.1.

79. For Manichean contempt for the Old Testament and their effective propaganda against it, see Augustine, *De utilitate credendi* II.4, *De Genesi contra Manichaeos* I.1.2, *Reply to Faustus* I–X; Secundinus *Epistola ad Augustinum* III.

80. Thus, a Manichean psalm, cited by H. J. Polotsky and H. Ibscher, *Manichaeische Handschriften* (Stuttgart, 1934), p. 3, line 25.

81. *Confessions* VI.7.12; and compare *Morals of Manicheans* XV.36, "chastity, prayers and psalms" of the Manichees.

82. *Confessions* VIII.7.17, "adolescens."

83. *Morals of Manicheans* XVI.42 and for sun- and moon-worship, ibid., 41–42, and *De haeresibus* XLVI, *PL* 42.38.

84. *Confessions* V.7.13.

85. Ibid., 6.10.

86. Augustine's bitter disappointment comes out in *De utilitate credendi* VI.13 "falsa pollicitatione rationis"; and *Contra epistolam Manichaei quam vocant Fun-*

damenti (*Against the Epistle of Manicheus Called Fundamental*) XI.12, "pollicitatio est, nondum exhibitio veritatis"; as well as *Confessions* V.3. See Décret, *L'Afrique manichéenne*, vol. 1, pp. 244–49.

87. Vindicianus influenced him strongly against accepting the claims of astrology. See *Confessions* VII.6.8–9.

88. Ibid., IV.14.21.

89. Ibid., V.8.15. For the probable site, see L. Ennabli, "La basilique dite de Ste. Monique à Carthage," *Collection de l'Ecole française à Rome* 25 (Tunis and Paris, 1975), pp. 14–16.

90. *Morals of Manicheans* XX.74, and for similar ill behavior among the Manichees at Carthage, ibid., XIX.68–72.

91. See Brown, *Augustine of Hippo*, pp. 70–72.

92. The substitution of "z" for "di" in *zaconus* = *diaconus* or the thick vowels as "Botrus" = "Petrus" (Optatus *De Schismate Donatistarum* I.18). For the unpopularity of the Africans, see Brown, *Augustine of Hippo*, p. 23.

93. See Courcelle, *Les 'Confessions' de Saint Augustin*, chap. 1.

94. *Confessions* VII.9.13, and also studied distaste for the donor, "a certain man puffed up with conceit." A different account is given eight years previously in *Against Academics* II.2.5 when Augustine tells Romanianus how "suddenly some substantial books appeared . . . and sprinkled on this little flame a few drops of precious ointment." These turned him once more to philosophy. So much for episcopal reminiscences ten years after the event!

95. See O'Meara, *Young Augustine*, p. 136.

96. See above, p. 442.

97. See Brown, *Augustine of Hippo*, pp. 94–99; and O'Meara, *Young Augustine*, pp. 143–55, for Plotinus's influence on Augustine.

98. See Courcelle, *Recherches sur les Confessions de St. Augustin*, pp. 97ff.

99. Brown, *Augustine of Hippo*, p. 62, and compare ibid., p. 89.

100. *Confessions* VI.15.25.

101. Compare, for instance, *De utilitate credendi ad Honoratum* (*On the Value of Belief, Addressed to Honoratus*) III on Augustine's ambitions at this time (*PL* 42.67), "De pulchritudine uxoris, de pompa divitiarum, de inanitate honorum. . . ."

102. *Confessions* VI.2.2.

103. Ibid., 14.24. Alypius exerted a strong influence on Augustine to dissuade him from marrying, ibid., 12.21.

104. Ibid., VII.9.13–15.

105. Ibid., VIII.2.

106. Ibid., 6.12.

107. Ibid., 6.15. Augustine does not specify the author of the *Life of Antony*.

108. See Brown's superb account, *Augustine of Hippo*, pp. 115–27.

109. Thus, Alfaric, *L'Evolution intellectuelle*, pp. 400–409. For an exhaustive analysis of Augustine's Cassiciacum dialogues, see Marrou, *Saint Augustin*, esp. pp. 161–86.

110. See, for instance, *De beata vita* II.16.

111. *Soliloquies* I.2.7, *PL* 32.872.

112. *Letter* XX.3 to Antoninus in 390 referring to "every form of schism" contrasted with "the Catholic Church."

113. In fact, to recruit Evodius to the monastery. See Augustine *Sermon* CCCLV.2 (though preached nearly forty years later). For Augustine's monastery at Thagaste, see Brown, *Augustine of Hippo*, chap. 13.

114. Possidius *Life of Augustine* VI.1. Note Augustine's opening statement in the debate, "I now think as error what I had previously thought to be the truth. Whether I am right in my opinions I wish to hear from you," (*Against Fortunatus* I.1, *PL* 42.113), evidence, perhaps for a continued underlying attraction of the Manichean system on him five years after his baptism.

115. Thus the hubbub that ended the first day's debate, see *Against Fortunatus* I.19, col. 121: The audience roared protest at Fortunatus's assertion of the Docetic nature of Christ.

116. See Augustine *Letter* XXII.2; great hopes were being set in 392 on Aurelius's reforming zeal.

117. See Munier, *Concilia Africae* A.345–A.525, pp. 20–46 (with notes and critical apparatus). Eleven councils were held between 393 and 407 when even the patient African bishops decided on no more until really necessary.

118. "Nondum expertus," *Revisions* I.21, concerning the Donatist teaching regarding baptism.

119. Petilian's evidence quoted by Augustine *Petilian* III.16.19; and see Courcelle, *Recherches sur les Confessions de St. Augustin*, pp. 238–45, and W. H. C. Frend, "Manichaeism in the Struggle Between S. Augustine and Petilian of Constantine," *Augustinus Magister* 1 (1954): 859–66.

120. Courcelle's view, *Les 'Confessions' de Saint Augustin*, pp. 559ff.

121. The "convalescent" element in Augustine's thought at this time is brought out in *Confessions* X.4.6, "This is the fruit of my confessions of what I am, not what I have been," and "Too late I loved thee, o thou beauty of ancient days, yet ever new. Too late I loved thee" (ibid., 27.38). "Thou art the physician, I the sick. Thou merciful, I miserable." (ibid., 28.39).

122. *Letters* XLIII and XLIV.

123. His estates were so vast that after his execution they had to be administered by a separate office (*Notitia Dignitatum*, ed. O. Seeck [Berlin, 1876] occid. XII.5); and see *Codex Theodosianus* VII.8.7 and IX.42.16.

124. For the social revolutionary ideas of Bishop Optatus, see my *Donatist Church*, p. 222, and for a different view, Tengström, *Donatisten und Katholiken*, pp. 74–78.

125. See Augustine *Petilian* II.83.184, and *Parmenianus* II.2.4. Tengström, *Donatisten und Katholiken*, pp. 84–90, correctly points out that the Donatists were not dubbed "Gildoniani" (as they had been "Firmiani," twenty-five years before), but there was no doubt about Optatus's association with the rebel. Sometimes modern classical scholars expect a superhuman degree of precision from their source.

126. Conc. Carthage III (28 August 397), Collectio Hispana Canon 45: "Aurelius episcopus dixit: . . . Ego enim cunctarum ecclesiarum dignatione Dei, ut scitis, sollicitudinem sustineo" (Munier, *Concilia Africae*, p. 339). And note his decisive utterances based on a mixture of tradition and equity throughout these assemblies.

127. See my *Donatist Church*, chaps. 14 and 15; Bonner, *Augustine of Hippo*, chap. 7; and Brown, *Augustine of Hippo*, chaps. 19 and 20.

128. *Letter* XLIII.1; and see also Augustine's argument in *Parmenianus* I.1.1; and *Ad Catholicos Epistola* VIII.22 and XXV.75, *Letter* 87.10.

129. *Letter* 87.5 (ed. Al. Goldbacher, CSEL 34.2 [Leipzig: G. Freytag, 1898], pp. 401–3), and compare *Letter* 43.9.25. For Peter, "bearing in a figure the whole church," *Letter* 53.2.

130. *Petilian* III.2.3, "Ager enim est mundus non Africa, messis finis saeculi non tempus Donati"; also *Ad Catholicos Epistola* XIII.34.

131. *Against Cresconius* II.6.9, III.19.25; and *De baptismo* (*On Baptism*) VI.1–6.

132. For an extreme statement of this view, see *Tractatus V in Joannis evangelium* XVIII, *PL* 35.1423: "Et [baptisma] quod dabatur a Paulo et quod dabatur a Petro, Christi est; et si datura est a Juda Christi est"; compare *On Baptism* VII.53.101–2. Bishops in Cyprian's time would have regarded such a view as making the church a "bride of Judas" (*Sententiae episcoporum de haereticis baptizandis* [*Opinions of the Bishops Concerning the Baptizing of Heretics*] LXI, ed. W. Hartel, CSEL 3.1, pp. 435–61 [Vienna, 1868], p. 455: "Qui haereticis ecclesiae baptismum concedit et prodit, quid aliud quam sponsae Christi Iudas exstitit?")

133. *Letter* LXI.2: "nihil tamen proderant quando caritas non erat"; and compare *Letter* XLIX.3.

134. *De vera religione* (*Of True Religion*) IV.6.

135. Cresconius in *Against Cresconius* III.66.75 "In paucis, inquis [Cresconius], frequenter est veritas, errare multorum est"; cf. ibid., IV.53.63.

136. Sozomen *Ecclesiastical History* IV.21.1.

137. Above, p. 540.

138. Sulpicius Severus *Chronicle of the World* II.51; and *Dialogi* (*Dialogues*) III.11.13, *Collectio Avellana* XL, and Ambrose *Letter* XXIV.5. See H. Chadwick, *Priscillian of Avila: The Occult and the Charismatic in the Early Church* (New York and London: Oxford University Press, 1976), pp. 146–48. See below, p. 713.

139. Thus Irenaeus *Heresies* V.24.2. See A. A. T. Ehrhardt, *Politische Metaphysik von Solon bis Augustin* (Tübingen: J. C. B. Mohr [Paul Siebeck], 1959–69), vol. 2., p. 113.

140. *City of God* XIX.23; but the ideas are foreshadowed in Augustine's answer to Petilian's attack on the secular monarchy and its officials in *Petilian* II.92.203; and see also *Letter* CV.2.9 and 3.11 ("hoc iubent imperatores quod iubet et christus," that is, unity).

141. *Letter* XLIII.2: "erit igitur mihi ad defensionem testis haec epistola in iudicio Dei. . . ."

142. *Letters* XXXIV and XXXV.

143. *Parmenianus* I.10.16 and 12.19.

144. *Petilian* II.85.189; and see for a similar statement concerning individuals being brought within the communion of Christ's church by the authority of kings, *Psalmos* LXXI.13.

145. *Letter* XCIII.5.17. Eng. trans. in *Works*, ed. Marcus Dods, 15 vols. (Edinburgh: T. & T. Clark, 1872–1934), vol. 6, pp. 409–10.

146. *Letter* XCIII.2.5. See Frend, *Donatist Church*, pp. 238–41; and Brown, "Religious Coercion."

147. *Letter* CIII.4 (written c. 408).

148. *Codex Theodosianus* XVI.5.37 and 38.

149. Evidence for the decline of Donatism at this period has been assembled by Lancel, *Gesta Collationis Carthaginiensis*, vol. 1, pp. 123–30.

150. Lancel, *Gesta Collationis Carthaginiensis*, vol. 1 provides an excellent historical guide to the background of the proceedings.

151. *Codex Theodosianus* XVI.5.52. For the determination not to create martyrs out of the edict's enforcement, see Augustine *Letter* 134.2–4.

152. *Letter* 185.

153. Ibid., 204.4. Bishop Gaudentius threatened to burn down his cathedral rather than surrender it. *Letter* 173.1 is an example of a similar argument with a Donatist presbyter who had thrown himself down a well.

154. Thus *Confessions* IV.1.1, "What am I to myself without thee, but a guide to my own downfall?" (Eng. trans. E. B. Pusey [New York: E. P. Dutton, 1926]).

155. *Revisions* II.1, "laboratum est quidem pro libero arbitrio voluntatis humanae: sed vicit Dei gratia."

156. An important passage in *On Baptism* IV.3.4 (written c. 398).

157. *Letter* XXIX.2ff.; compare ibid., XXII to Aurelius.

158. In *City of God* V.26. See Hagendahl, *Augustine and the Latin Classics*, p. 94.

159. *Letter* CV.16, "in mare perniciosae libertatis exeamus."

160. *Psalmos* XXXII.14; and compare *Parmenianus* I.4.6.

161. See Plinval, *Pélage*, pp. 57–63. Augustine, *Letter* 186.1, knew him as "Brittonem."

162. Augustine *Contra Julianum* (*Against Julian*) II.36, cited by Plinval, *Pélage*, pp. 52–55.

163. For Pelagius's writings, see Plinval, *Pélage*, chap. 1; *Expositions of Epistles of Paul;* and Morris, "Pelagian Literature."

164. Jerome, *Pelagii ad Demetriadem* XVI, *PL* 30.31.

165. Ibid. Stevenson's translation, *Creeds, Councils and Controversies*, p. 219.

166. *De Divitiis* VIII.2.3. Cited from Morris, "Pelagian Literature," p. 47.

167. Augustine *Incomplete Work Against Julian* III.67 and 70. I have used Brown's trans., see *Augustine of Hippo*, p. 387.

168. On grace = "grace and favour," see Myres's splendidly ingenious article, "Pelagius and End of Roman Rule," with the dialogue between the orthodox but sinning Christians and the Judge at the day of judgment (p. 28). Against the view that Pelagianism had far-reaching social aims, see Liebeschütz, "Did the Pelagian Movement Have Social Aims?"

169. Augustine *De natura et gratia* (*On Nature and Grace*) LXXI–LXXX. See Evans, *Pelagius*, p. 85.

170. *Letter Honorificentiae tuae* I, cited from Brown, *Augustine of Hippo*, p. 347.

171. Zosimus *Historia Nova* VI.5: Britons "living on their own, without obeying Rome's laws"; and see Myres, "Pelagius and End of Roman Rule," pp. 31ff.

172. Augustine *De peccatorum meritis et remissione* (*On the Merits and Remission of Sins*) III.1; and the tone of his *Letter* CXLVI to Pelagius.

173. Augustine *Letter* CLV.3.22.

174. *De peccato originali* (*On Original Sin*) III–IV.3. Celestius was accused of heresy by Paulinus, Ambrose's deacon and biographer, who was in Carthage at the

time on business concerned with the administration of property belonging to his see.

175. *Psalmos* L.10.

176. The theme of *Psalmos* L.6–11.

177. *De spiritu et littera* (*On the Spirit and the Letter*) XXVI, and compare XXXI and XXXII (necessity of grace for righteousness). See Burnaby, *Amor Dei*, pp. 233–34.

178. For the precise moment when Augustine begins to attack Pelagius himself, see Evans, *Pelagius*, pp. 70–71.

179. On 27 June 413 Augustine asserted in a sermon preached in Carthage (*Sermon* 294) that infants must be baptized as soon as possible after birth to free them "from the infection of the ancient death drawn from their first birth." And against murmurings in the congregation he appealed to Cyprian's teaching (*Letter* LXIV.5) in support.

180. Thus Eusebius *HE* III.37.3: "Apostolic missionaries were helped by the grace [*chariti*] and co-operation of God."

181. Jerome *Dialogi contra Pelagianos* (*Dialogues Against the Pelagians*) I.16; and compare I.21–22, and his letter to Ctesiphon, *Letter* 133. For the repercussions of Pelagius's arrival in Palestine on Jerome's controversies, see Evans, *Pelagius*, chaps. 2 and 3.

182. Jerome *Letters* 131 and 132; Augustine *Letters* 166 and 167.

183. Augustine *De gestis Pelagii* (*On the Proceedings of Pelagius*) V, and compare LIV–LV (Pelagius on the possibility of sinlessness).

184. Augustine *Letter* 177 to Pope Innocent. At the end of *Proceedings of Pelagius* (chap. 66) Augustine demanded immediate sanctions against Pelagius. He believed Pelagius responsible for the attack on Jerome's establishment. Pope Innocent also wrote to Bishop John of Jerusalem protesting against "Plunder, slaughter, fire" being perpetrated in his diocese! (*Letter* XXXV).

185. Ambrosiaster *Exposition of Romans* V.12. The text is given in Stevenson, *Creeds, Councils and Controversies*, p. 216. Augustine himself persisted to the end in asserting that "in Adam all die"; see *Incomplete Work Against Julian* II.174.

186. *Letters* IV and VI, ed. J. Divjak, CSEL 88 (Vienna, 1981).

187. Thus, Augustine to Paulinus, *Letter* 184.34, citing Paulinus's views. For Pelagius's aristocratic connections, see the two articles by Brown, "Patrons of Pelagius" and "Pelagius and Supporters."

188. See my "The Two Worlds of Paulinus of Nola," in J. W. Binns, *Latin Literature of the Fourth Century* (Boston and London: Routledge & Kegan Paul, 1974), chap. 4, pp. 114–15.

189. *Psalmus contra partem Donati* (*Psalm Against the Donatist Sect*), line 37, *PL* 43.25, "Olim iam causa finita est."

190. See Brown, "Pelagius and Supporters," pp. 98–99, "Alaric therefore unwittingly sealed the fate of the Pelagian movement." The text of Honorius's rescript is in *PL* 48.379–86, and Mansi, *Sacrorum Conciliorum*, IV, pp. 444ff.

191. *Sermon* CLI.5 and compare *Merits and Remission* I.57 (Virgin birth was necessary to Christ's perfect innocence). See Brown, *Augustine of Hippo*, p. 388.

192. *Ep. ad Menoch* (a Persian princess), cited by Julian in *Incomplete Work Against Julian* III.166ff.; "Videsne concupiscentiam mali esse originem" (ibid.,

III.187); and compare Augustine *De nuptiis et concupiscentia* (*On Marriage and Concupiscence*) I.27, "Hoc est malum peccati in quo nascitur omnis homo."

193. See also Faustus cited by Augustine *Reply to Faustus* XXIV.1. Human birth was "a genitoribus turpiter et per libidinem sati" and hence "etiam omnis religio et maxime christiana ad sacramentum rudes infantes appellat." This clear statement of the need of infant baptism (or at least some form of *sacramentum*) would seem to contradict other Manichean views that "baptism was unnecessary" (see above n. 68). Baptism, however, need not have been by water.

194. Julian, cited by Augustine *Incomplete Work Against Julian* I.48 (ed. Zelzer, p. 38).

195. *Against Julian* V.3.8; and compare *City of God* XXI.24.78, "For this life for mortals is the wrath of God." Those who quote Ps. 31:19, "How abundant is thy goodness," were "perversely compassionate."

196. *Against Julian* IV.42. See Plinval, *Pélage*, p. 363, and E. Buonaiuti's essay, "Manichaeism and Augustine's Idea of 'Massa Perditionis,' " *HTR* 20 (1927): 117–27.

197. Thus, Secundinus in his letter to Augustine, V, "temporibus nostris renova Paulum . . ." (*Epistola ad Augustinum, PL* 42.576).

198. The text is cited by Prosper *Liber contra collatorem* (*Against Cassian the Lecturer*) V.320, quoting from the covering letter of the council of 1 May 418, but Prosper considers the Africans wrong to have criticized Pope Zosimus. Augustine, *Contra duas epistolas Pelagianorum* II.4.5–6 (ed. C. Urba and J. Zycha, CSEL 60, pp. 423–570 [Vienna: G. Freytag, 1913], pp. 465–66), believes the pope to have been mistaken because of his relative ignorance of Pelagianism.

199. *On Baptism* VII.101.

200. Thus Innocent, *Letter* II.1, *PL* 20.468.

201. On these cases, see Kidd, *Roman Primacy*, pp. 96–105; T. G. Jalland, *The Church and the Papacy: A Historical Study* (New York: Morehouse-Gorham; London: SPCK, 1944), pp. 288–91; and C. Munier, "La Question des offerts à Rome d'après la *Lettre* 20* d'Augustin," in Lepelley, ed., *Les Lettres d'Augustin découvertes par Divjak*, pp. 287–99.

202. Pope Siricius had laid down in 385 minimum ages of forty for ordination as presbyter and fifty as bishop (to Bishop Himerius of Tarragona, *Letter* I, paras. 13 and 14, *PL* 13.1142–43). In North Africa, the minimum age seems to have been twenty-five for clerical ordination. Antoninus was "non multo amplius quam viginiti aetatis annos" (Divjak, ed., *Letter* XX.4.1).

203. *Letter* XX.3.3.

204. Ibid., 6.

205. Ibid., 8.1.

206. *Letter* CCIX.7, "aut in mea cathedra sedere debui aut episcopus esse non debui."

207. *Letter* XX.12.1. The legates were instructed to ascertain, "utrum ordinem rerum fideliter indicasset" (Antoninus).

208. Ibid., 17. The legates appear to take no part in the proceedings after the hearing at the village of Thegulata.

209. Ibid., 25.3.

210. Augustine offered Celestine his resignation as bishop and his tone to Fa-

biola is pathetic and pleading. The people of Fussala had come to "hate Catholicism" and himself (ibid., 26.1).

211. *Letter* CCIX.7–8.

212. See *Letter* XXII.5.4 (ed. Divjak, p. 115).

213. Ibid., 229.1, and Divjak, ed., *Letter* XX.2. Urbanus had previously been prior (*praepositus*) of Augustine's monastery at Hippo.

214. Canon 17.

215. For the events, see L. Duchesne, *The Early History of the Christian Church: From Its Foundation to the End of the Third Century*, 3 vols. (London: Longmans, Green & Co., 1909–24), vol. 3, pp. 169–72, 176–80.

216. Celestine, *Letter* II, *PL* 50.422–27. For the canons of the Council of Carthage of 419 and the *canones in causa Apiarii* produced by the North Africans, see Munier, *Concilia Africae*, pp. 79ff.

217. Augustine *Letter* CCXX.7.

218. Ibid., CXI.6–7, "barbarian raids" in Mauretania c. 410.

219. *Sermon* CCCLV.7.

220. Possidius *Life of Augustine* 28.

20

Christianity and Barbarism: The West 380–450

The fall of Hippo to the Vandals and the death of Augustine in August 430 mark the end of an era in Western Christianity. During the previous twenty years African Catholicism had taken over the leadership of the West. Augustine's contribution toward the Western church's teaching on the sacraments, on grace, and on the relations between church and state was decisive, and would survive all upheavals even to the beginning of the present century. Outwardly too the North African church was prosperous. Since the 380s paganism had been in retreat, its temples unfrequented, many of its one-time adherents ready to conform to Christianity. Now, Donatism and Pelagianism had been struck down and Catholicism had emerged as the sole visible heir to the triumphant North African theological tradition. The wealth of that heritage was reflected by a veritable explosion of church building. Augustine mentions five large churches in Carthage, in four of which he had preached,[1] and it is hard to believe that the Damous el Karita, outside the north wall of the city, was not at its maximum extent with its forest of columns dividing the naves and magnificent semicircular courtyard on the one side, and developing monastery on the other.[2] And in this Carthage did not stand alone. In Hippo Diarrhytus (Bizerta) Bishop Florentius built a new church to house an ex-Donatist congregation and called it after himself "Florentia."[3] The church, too, for all its petty quarrels, corruption, and inefficiency revealed in the disciplinary decrees of the councils between 393 and 425, was not obviously set for decline. Only when one reads that congregations had sometimes to be addressed through an interpreter does one realize the extent of the gap that divided the great majority of the clergy from part of their flocks.[4] The suddenness of the disaster in 429 that overtook Catholic Christianity, ostensibly in its prime, suggests, however, that popular support may have been lacking in a way which would hardly have been possible in the East.

The mood, too, of the Western Christian leaders had been changing from the more serene and optimistic attitude of the Theodosian era. Events of the previous twenty years had shown *Roma aeterna* to be a myth. The disaster of the fall of Rome to Alaric in 410 reverberated around the Christian world. Jerome's anguish may have been tinged with self-pity, but from his cell at Bethlehem he wrote of it as a catastrophe for the world itself.[5] The capital of the Roman Empire had been engulfed in one great fire.[6] Happy were those who were no longer alive. A child growing up in those years would experience tears and sorrow rather than joy and laughter.[7] Only Augustine, also writing from a distance but reinforced by firmly held theological assumptions, could watch the tragedy dispassionately. In 411 he took up the challenge made by pagans to the Christians: "When we used to sacrifice to our gods, Rome was flourishing. Now our sacrifices are forbidden, and see what is happening to Rome everywhere."[8] In the *City of God*, started in 411 in the white heat of controversy but ended in a more reflective mood fifteen years later, Augustine argued that it was useless for pagans to blame disasters on neglect of the old gods. These had not helped Rome before. They would not do so now. The life of empires as of individuals lay in the hands of God. Things that he had made would pass away; how much sooner that which Romulus had founded.[9] All people so long as they were mortal were miserable. The individual should fix his or her gaze only on salvation. Pagan Rome, the type of the earth-bound (*civitas terrena*), was doomed to disappearance. The barbarians were merely the instruments of providence. His was not a message to inspire resistance to the last.

There is something to be said for Edward Gibbon's cynical judgment that the Roman Empire in the West succumbed on account of "Christianity and barbarism."[10] Of the barbarians there can be no doubt. The end came suddenly. In the first years of the fifth century Paulinus of Nola was writing to friends in Gaul who give no hint of the disaster that was about to befall their province. On the last night of 406, however, the Vandals, Alans, and Suebi crossed the frozen Rhine to invade Gaul in force. The westward movement of entire peoples changed the course of history. The Roman Empire was "assassinated," to accept A. Piganiol's judgment.[11] But if one looks below the surface of the military events one may also detect some subtler changes of opinion that undermined the provincials' will to resist. These changes deprived the empire in the West of the popular support that had sustained it through the almost equally grave crisis of the mid–third century. Added to the feebleness of Honorius's government, protected by marshes that made Ravenna almost inaccessible, was a breakdown of will among the natural leaders of the community. Estrangement (*alienatio*), turning one's back on the business of the world in order to assure one's own salvation without distraction, was the logic of the Western creed. Accepted as the Christian ideal for the times, it contributed to the fall of the empire that Christianity had conquered only a short while before.

THE END OF THE PAGAN IDEAL

How and why did this happen? The first factor is the decline, and finally the end, of *Roma aeterna* as a political ideal, whether interpreted by the pagan aristocracy of Rome or by their Christian successors. After c. 395 it had become replaced by the notion that the world and with it Rome had grown old (*senectus mundi*) and was destined soon to perish. The outlook that Cyprian had voiced with mournful emphasis in his debate with the pagan Demetrianus was accepted almost as a truism by the generation of Augustine and Orosius. With its acceptance went a collapse, despite Claudian and Prudentius, of that sense of Roman superiority over all other peoples that had sustained the spirit of Rome in earlier crises. Such pride in tradition dissolved before the critique of "love of rulership" (*amor dominandi*) leveled by Augustine against the pagan Roman past in the first books of the *City of God*. Its revival under Justinian was a costly anachronism.

In the last quarter of the fourth century, however, there was still a place for traditional pagan aristocratic leadership. In this period pagan Rome produced its final defenders whose ideals still inspire respect today. Quintus Aurelius Symmachus (d. circa 402), briefly Augustine's patron, and his friend Vettius Agorius Praetextatus (d. 384), and Virius Nicomachus Flavianus (d. 394) were typical of the pagan aristocracy of Rome. They came from families of ancient lineage and great wealth. They were used to holding consulships and provincial governorships but they were also men of letters, immersed in the minutiae of grammar and poetic allusions in ancient texts. They were proud of their own and their city's tradition. These were the men who tried to stem the advance of Christianity, and failed, just as Justina and her court at Milan failed against the uncompromising Catholicism of Ambrose and the emperor Theodosius.

While Valentinian I reigned, however, those days seemed far off. A panegyric addressed by Symmachus (in January 370) to that emperor and his son Gratian still breathed the spirit of the past. Rome had defeated the barbarians. Noble families were still responsible for the different cults of the city of Rome. Priests (*flamines*) and women of honorable estate (*matronae castae*) maintained the official, that is, pagan, religion. "The gods" were the emperors' helpers.[12] A dozen years later much had changed. Gratian was emperor, and under Ambrose's influence he had declined the traditional title of *Pontifex Maximus*. In 382, as though to emphasize that the breach with the past was complete, Gratian withdrew funds from pagan ancestral rites, canceled grants and immunities to the Vestals, and removed the statue and altar of Victory from the Senate building. Constantius II had done this in 357, but he had not touched the priesthood. Gratian's acts, combined with the withdrawal of financial support, threatened the pagan traditions of Rome more seriously.[13] The pagan members of the Senate protested and petitioned for these measures to be reversed, but they were thwarted.

Symmachus Versus Ambrose

"The holy Damasus, bishop of the Roman Church, chosen by God," wrote Ambrose to Valentinian II, "sent me a statement which Christian senators beyond counting had given him, to the effect that they had directed that no such thing would be done."[14] The pagan petition was thrown out. Then, in August 383, Gratian was murdered and the more liberal regime of Justina and Valentinian II was established in Milan. Symmachus became prefect of Rome in 384, a position which gave him access to the emperor on a variety of administrative problems. Among these he was able as ex officio priest of the public religion to include the altar of Victory.

The ensuing debate, which opened with a well-organized paper by Symmachus (Symmachus *Relatio* 3), is one of the great moments in the conflict between Christianity and paganism in the fourth century.[15] The latter was now irrevocably on the defensive.[16] Symmachus pleads for the status quo. "There was no conflict of interest," he urged, "for all were concerned in the glory of the age and the maintenance of ancestral usage." Different nations had different faiths. The best was what helped the state most, so experience might prescribe where reason wavered. Rome personified asked leave "to live in its own way." "The great secret can hardly be reached by one faith and it is only fair to suppose that whatever men worship is one after all" (*Relatio* III.9–10). Moreover, to swear an oath in the presence of the goddess was greatly effective in preventing perjury.[17] Except for this last and not unimportant point, the pagans had not shifted their ground during the whole of the long controversy with the Christians. The arguments could have been used by Cicero, or by Caecilius in Minucius Felix's *Octavius*. Religion, pagan as well as Christian, had moved toward accepting a universal monotheism.[18] The debate was whether the "gods of Rome" (and other nations) or Jesus of Nazareth were the savior of humankind.

Ambrose answered. He wrote two letters to Valentinian, one before and one after he had received the Senate's appeal. He had an advantage of not being confined to a script, however eloquent. If necessary, he could speak directly to the emperor and his council, and he could (and did) threaten episcopal sanctions.[19] He urged the young emperor not to be misled by bad advisers; pagans had persecuted the church as late as Julian's reign; tradition and custom were not typical of the natural world. There must always be scope for change and improvement and, in this case, change from pagan error to Christian truth. Surely "are not the baths, the colonnades, the streets filled with images enough for him?"[20] he retorted. Ambrose was using traditional arguments employed by Christian apologists from the time of Clement of Alexandria, but they had gained relevance. He wrote confidently. Paganism was archaic even if well presented. The gold of wisdom was to be found in Scripture (*Letter* XVIII.2). Valentinian's court was not pro-pagan even if it was anti-Nicene. Symmachus's petition was dismissed. The altar of Victory was not restored.[21]

The debate, however, did not maintain its lofty tone throughout. The pagans were also concerned about the financial effect of the emperor's measures, and nearly half of Symmachus's speech was devoted to the "scandal" of terminating state subsidies to the Virgins and the sacrificial cult. Ambrose was quick to seize on the opening. Pagans worried about cash (*illos dispendium movet*).[22] Christianity had thrived on persecution. There was justice in this argument. Constantius II's simple removal of the altar and statue of Victory had not aroused protest. The difference between the two sides had been demonstrated once more. Western Christianity would always retain a sense of protest against idolatry and a glorification of its heroic past. Paganism had its deeply felt and deeply rooted tradition, a belief in the protecting power of the immortal gods and the concert of lesser deities and guardian spirits. Its representatives, however, were not confessors for their faith by training or inclination.

Rome Becomes Christian

In the next decade the advantage passed decisively to the Christians. The pagan leaders in Rome recognized Theodosius as their adversary, and some, including apparently Symmachus himself, were prepared to treat with the usurper Magnus Maximus on his arrival in Italy in 387 (thus, Socrates *Ecclesiastical History* V.14). This was disastrous, for the astute mixture of clemency and pressure that Theodosius was able to exert when he visited Rome in June 389 swayed many doubters to the Christian cause.[23] Never again could the pagans among the "Romans of Rome" claim to speak for a majority. In addition, steady social pressures began to tell. The price of retaining honors, wealth, and privilege was seen more and more to depend on accepting Christianity. There must have been others like the old prefect of the city, Publilius Caeionius Caecina Albinus, whom Jerome describes as a priest (*Pontifex*) surrounded by Christian kinsfolk, with the apt comment, "I think that even Jupiter himself, if he had had such kinsfolk could have believed in Christ" (*"Ego puto etiam ipsum Jovem, si habuisset talem cognationem potuisse in Christum credere"*).[24] After three generations of opposition to their husbands' religion the Roman *matronae* had their way.

When Valentinian II was murdered in May 392, the usurpation by Eugenius (392–94) produced one final pagan reaction.[25] The statue (but probably not the altar) of Victory was restored and payments were made to senators to hand over to pagan priests. (Funds were also allotted to Italian bishops.) At Ostia a shrine to Hercules was ceremonially restored by a senior official. Once more, however, Theodosius triumphed. The god of battles was once more on the Christian side (September 394). This time Theodosius told the Senate that the funds provided for sacrifices had become a burden on the state and the money was needed for military requirements.[26] That was that. Nicomachus Flavianus committed suicide. The old religion went underground. Its dwindling adherents protested bitingly after the fall of Rome and then relapsed into silence. The revolution begun by Constantine was completed when, on 7 December 416, pagans were barred from entry into imperial service (*Codex Theodosianus* XVI.10.21). In the next generation members of the Roman aristocracy were to become the founders and benefactors of churches in the city and as devoted to the cause of papacy as their forebears had been to the pagan empire.[27] In so doing, their families and their influence were destined to survive through the crises of the end of the empire in the West and of Justinian's *Reconquista* into the European Middle Ages.

Thenceforth, with the single exception of the Gallic nobleman Rutilius Namatianus (*flor.* 415–17), glorification of Rome was taken up by Christians, such as Claudian or Prudentius. In the four months remaining to him after his overthrow of Eugenius in September 394, Theodosius made some momentous decisions. The empire was formally divided. His elder son, Arcadius, age seventeen, was to rule the East; his younger, Honorius, age ten, the West. Both were weak. Stilicho, a half-barbarian Vandal general of great astuteness and capacity, was appointed Honorius's guardian. His claim that on his deathbed Theodosius had entrusted Arcadius to his care also was resisted vigorously by the rulers of the East.[28] On Theodosius's death, 17 January 395, something like a frontier divided the two halves of the empire. The bone of contention was the prefecture of Illyricum, covering Dalmatia and the western Balkan provinces. The intrigues between the two courts allowed first Alaric, the Visigothic leader, to plunder the Balkans at will in 397, and then the Kabyle chief Gildo to try to play off one emperor against the other (397–98) while he established his rule in Africa. In this period, the empire's defenses still held. The fear was of a takeover of the empire by semibarbarian leaders, whether Stilicho or Alaric, or in the East by Gainas. Roman patriotism found its last exponents.

CLAUDIAN

Claudius Claudianus (c. 350–c. 405) was an unlikely champion of tradition. He was an Egyptian Greek who sought his fortune in Rome and stayed the course there better than Augustine. A minor poet in his own country, he turned himself into a Latinist, and even before Theodosius died was celebrating the consulate of two illustrious Roman nobles of the family of the Anicii. Instantly successful, he hitched his wagon to Stilicho's star to become the Kipling of his day. For the next ten years a steady stream of patriotic verse issued from his pen. "No difficulties delayed our victorious arms," he wrote in 398 concerning the defeat of Gildo, "news of victory outstripped the news of the war that occasioned it. What God wrought this for us [surely the "Christian God," if Claudian had been thinking what he was saying!] . . . ? Winter brought us news of the enemy, spring destroyed him."[29] Claudian does not mention the part played by Gildo's brother, Mascezel, in the successful outcome. This was a victory for Honorius and for Roman arms.

Of Rome itself Claudian wrote in the short space between Theodosius's victory over Eugenius and his death, "Goddess and friend, mother of laws, thou whose empire is coterminous with heaven, thou that art called the consort of the Thunderer, say what has caused thy coming."[30] Roman tradition and Roman mythology breathe from every line he wrote, and he displayed Roman patriotism at its most chauvinistic. No abuse was too gross for Rufinus and Eutropius, Arcadius's guardians. As Honorius celebrated his fourth consulship in 398, his optimism for Rome's future was unrestrained. Addressing the wretched Honorius, he wrote: "Prosperity awaits our empire; thy name is earnest for the fulfilment of our hopes. The past guarantees the future; each time that thy sire made thee chief magistrate of the year, the laurels of victory crowned his arms."[31]

So long as Stilicho stood in the place of Theodosius, there was a chance that these hopes might be fulfilled. The first few years of the fifth century brought a fleeting impression of stability. Alaric was checked at Pollentia and later at Verona in 402. The mixed horde of barbarians led by Radagaisus was surrounded and destroyed at Fiesole in August 405. Even the Picts and Scots felt Stilicho's determination to hold the frontiers.[32] Alaric would suffer Hannibal's fate, Claudian proclaimed.[33] He was not alone in realizing that only Stilicho could heal the scars caused by the Visigothic wars. But just when his skill as a commander was needed in the crisis of 407–8, when the Rhine barriers fell and yet another British usurper led his troops into Gaul, Stilicho was assassinated (August 408). The road to Rome was open to Alaric and there were traitors within the gates. In these years, Christians in the West turned their backs on hopes founded on the past, to the "certainties" that Augustine had sought and won for himself in dedicated service to the Christian truth.[34]

PRUDENTIUS

Before this transition was completed, Rome inspired one last paean of patriotic verse from a Christian more convinced of his faith than Claudian. Prudentius (Prudentius Aurelius Clemens), like Theodosius, was a Spaniard, born in c. 348.[35] He entered the imperial service, was twice a magistrate of important cities (or provincial governor), proud to be an administrator of Roman laws and of his senatorial rank, and reaching the climax of his career in 405 through being honored perhaps as an "immediate counsellor" (*proximus*) of Honorius. He died probably not long after, for his poems mention neither Stilicho's murder nor the fall of Rome. Like Claudian, he appears to have crammed the whole of his poetic achievement into a few years around the turn of the fifth century.

With Paulinus of Nola, Prudentius shares the title of the first Latin Christian poet. Others before him, such as his compatriot Juvencus (c. 346) and Pope Damasus, had written Christian verses. Ambrose had composed hymns to be sung antiphonally by the congregation arranged on each side of the nave of the church, but Paulinus and Prudentius were the first to write lines that would be read as poetry by Christians reared in the classical tradition of Virgil and Horace.

Prudentius stresses his Christianity. He could also be generous to the defeated foe. Julian, in particular, he admired in verse:

> Yet one was left, her princes' ranks among
> As I remember well, when I was young,
> A captain brave, an author wise of laws
> In speech, in action, worthy of applause,
> Who loved his country well, but could not have
> The worship of the One True God above.[36]

His pride in Rome's achievement never dwindled. Rome was always "queen," and "golden," "splendid head of the world," "mistress of empire." Like Claudian, he hated and despised the barbarians; the difference between them (and pagans) and Romans was like that between four-footed animals and human beings![37] Augustus, the empire's founder, was "father of his country," "governor of the people and the Senate, leader of armies, and at the same time dictator, upright censor and judge of morals, protector of goods, avenger of crimes, dispenser of honours."[38] Yet writing in c. 403 in his great poem in answer to Symmachus's apologia for paganism twenty years before, Prudentius turns this praise into argument in favor of Christianity. The emperors had indeed gained victories while invoking the aid of spurious gods, but in reality it was Christ who gave them the victory. And had not Constantine (and Stilicho) gained triumphs under the sign of the labarum?[39] Christian Rome was the legitimate successor of pagan Rome. Like Ambrose, Prudentius saw the victory of Christianity, the religion of the future, as a sign of progress. Progress was surely the distinguishing mark between humans and the beasts. God had made Rome for his own ends to unify the race of humankind and so prepare the way for Christ. Now Christ had triumphed. Rome was no longer old and feeble as Symmachus had claimed. Free from the danger of the Goths, Rome was ready to extend its sway to the heavens themselves.[40]

Of the two themes, imperial and Christian, the Christian dominates Prudentius. For all his debt to Virgil his personal outlook was far removed from that of pagan Rome. His long poetic allegory, the *Fight for the Soul* (*Psychomachia*)—a sort of Holy War—is partly a study of the psychology of the human soul (resembling in this respect Augustine's *Confessions*), partly a latent criticism of Roman society. Seven virtues combat seven vices. Pride is shown as ruthless arrogance; luxury is described in terms of languid, supercilious decadence, terms in which Ammianus had described the rich senatorial aristocracy at Rome. Avarice is vividly portrayed as soldiers killing their comrades to steal their armor.[41] There is the final note of Christian idealism in his outright condemnation of gladiatorial combat, and prayer to the emperor to end this blot on Rome's repute.[42]

There were more honorable ways of dying. Rightly, Prudentius is remembered for his sketches of martyrdoms in the *Peristephanon* (*On the Crowns of Victory*). The victims of the third-century persecutions had long passed into folk-memory. Prudentius's verses would keep that memory fresh. Legend was replacing fact. Pagan magistrates are portrayed in stereotype—cruel and stupid foils to the idealistic heroism of youthful confessors. Tortures take on the bizarre quality one finds much later in Byzantine *Acts of the Martyrs;* the bravery, defiance, and powers of endurance of the confessor are unbounded. Romanus damns paganism long after his tongue has been torn out.[43] Quirinius addresses the pagan crowd while floating down the river into which he has been hurled.[44] Eulalia kicks over a sacrificial meal and spits at her persecutors.[45]

707

Many of the martyrs were Spaniards as was Prudentius himself. Provincial pride even in the city of Saragossa "rich in piety"[46] was rivaling his Roman pride. It was a new type of patriotism inspired by the ideals of local martyrs who died defying the representatives of pagan Rome. Here Prudentius and Paulus Orosius were speaking with one voice. In the West, Christian successor-states based on geographical divisions were beginning to take shape even before the appearance of the Germanic barbarians. Not surprisingly, both authors were read and reread during the Middle Ages.

Pockets of Resistance

The end of paganism in Rome itself was accompanied by its decline elsewhere in the West. The basic transformation of society from "generally pagan" to "generally Christian" was neither complete nor systematic. Even in North Africa, Augustine mentions two cities, Sufes and Calama, where anti-Christian riots took place (c. 400) with the acquiescence of the city councils.[47] At Calama there had been a Christian bishop since the late third century.[48] At Hippo there was a substantial pagan minority, though by now the city itself was dominated by the outward symbols of Christianity,[49] and Augustine points to the decline of the pagan population there.[50]

In the last quarter of the fourth century there were energetic bishops in the West who began to spread Christianity beyond the walls of the major cities into areas hardly touched by evangelism. In two such areas, northern Italy and northern Gaul, the progress of Christianity can be documented. In northern Italy, Ambrose was personally responsible for creating new bishoprics and appointing trustful clergy to them. Imola at the beginning of his episcopate, Vercelli and Novara near the end of his life, were communities which benefited from his zeal.[51] In one area in the valley of the Adige, however, the attempt to challenge a pagan stronghold ended tragically. Following perhaps the Ambrosian missionary pattern, Bishop Vigilius of Trent dispatched a team of three ascetics—Sissinius, Martyrius, and Alexander—into the remote Val di Non, north of his episcopal town, to establish a mission.[52] Their preaching, however, aroused the fury of the inhabitants and on 29 May 397 their mission building was burned and all three were lynched. Eventually there was a happier ending. Churches were built, and a cult of martyrs established.[53] Even the now-repentant murderers were treated leniently. Nonetheless, Christians were still defensive in their outlook. In another generation, however, Christianity was beginning to leave evidence of progress in the less-accessible areas of the Tirol, in churches such as at Imst and Martinsbühel, just before the province of Rhaetia became a prey to invading barbarians.[54]

In northern Gaul, the destruction of paganism preoccupied Martin of Tours, whose combination of episcopal office and an ascetic vocation foreshadowed new and far-reaching developments in the Western Church. Martin (c. 330–97) was a Pannonian by birth who had served in the army of

Constantius II (or Julian), perhaps in a medical as well as a fighting capacity. He became a Christian, converted his mother (but apparently not his father), and on leaving the army in c. 360 he joined Hilary of Poitiers and founded a hermitage at Ligugé.[55] He attracted numerous disciples—a sort of collective solitude—but his advancement to the nearby bishopric of Tours (c. 370) as the town's second bishop was not taken well by the Gallic bishops who objected to his dirty appearance and unconventional dress![56]

Apart from a minimum of episcopal administration Martin devoted the next fifteen years to a concentrated mission among the peasant populations in the Loire and Seine valleys, where the deities of Romano-Celtic paganism still held sway. "Few if any had heard the name of Christ there," wrote Martin's biographer, Sulpicius Severus, c. 390.[57] His methods were simple. Where miraculous cures failed to convince the villagers that his God was all-powerful, Martin employed direct action. At Levroux in Normandy he destroyed a large shrine despite the protests of the worshipers. In the territory of the Aedui he brushed aside the threat that he would himself be sacrificed if he interfered with traditional worship.[58] To consolidate the position he left behind him a rudimentary parish system so that the church would effectively supersede the temple as the center of worship in the district. He had considerable success. The coin series from the Romano-Gallic temples tends to cease with Gratian (d. 383), Magnus Maximus (383–88), and Valentinian II (375–92), despite the outpouring of the Gallic mints of vast numbers of small copper coins (4 AE) in the early part of the reigns of Arcadius and Honorius, that is, c. 400.[59]

Martin's influence may have extended to Britain. It is difficult to dissociate the Candida Casa at Whithorn in Wigtownshire from him, when the historian Bede states that Ninian was his disciple and named the church "after the holy Martin" in c. 397.[60] Romano-British paganism, so vigorous down to the end of the reign of Valens (378) and represented by the Lydney temple and its cult buildings (post-364), was showing signs of decline. Coin series on temple sites, such as at Woodeaton (Oxon), are rare after 378.[61] Ninian's mission north of the Wall, extending outwards from an already-established Christian community, and combining episcopacy with asceticism would be expected at this period.

By the end of the fourth century all the western provinces, including Britain, were witnessing the development of an authentically Christian civilization in which mission, theological learning, dogmatic discussion, church building, and the cult of saints and martyrs with their relics and legends all had a place. Pagan traditions were beginning to take on the role that they were to retain for centuries to come—that of carnival gods or extra aides in time of peril.[62] "Uncounted multitudes," wrote Himerius of Tarragona in 385, "were receiving the mystery of baptism."[63] Increasingly, the fourth to early fifth century basilica was coming to dominate peaceful landscapes. Churches were springing up everywhere. In western Sardinia even, two basilicas apparently of this date, one in an earlier Christian cemetery, have been found near Cornus.[64] Once-pagan villas, such as Lullingstone (Kent), now had a suite of rooms set aside for Christian worship.[65] In Gaul, Sulpicius Severus described the churches he built for his tenants on his estate of Primulacium.[66] In southern Italy, celebrations of the feast of Felix of Nola superseded rites in honor of the pagan deities who once protected the crops and commerce of the people of Nola. The stories of miracles aiding the peasant worshipers of Felix, told by Paulinus, illustrate how on the very eve of the barbarian irruption, Christianity was responding to popular beliefs.[67] Traffic in relics was increasing whether "prestige objects" such as those of St. Stephen which Paulus Orosius brought back with him from Palestine for Augustine in 416,[68] or more ordinary remains of saints, such as those of St. Alban in his shrine on the hill outside Verulamium.[69] This trade was already becoming an abuse, but it was a sign of the times. Pilgrimages to these centers of devotion and the veneration of relics connected with them were symptoms of a growing ascetic and otherworldly interpretation of Christianity in the West. Clergy and their congregations alike were affected by the new spirit. Even busy administrators and missionaries such as Victricius of Rouen (d. circa 405), a bishop trusted on both sides of the channel, and Chromatius of Aquileia (d. circa 407)—the friend of Ambrose, Rufinus and Jerome—equated Christianity with asceticism.

The popularization of Christian asceticism to the detriment of the practical values implicit in the faith helps to explain why Western Christianity was not destined to reap the full harvest of its victory. As the barbarian armies gathered on the frontiers, a new climate of opinion was establishing itself in which the ascetic virtues were associated not only with personal devotion but with hostility toward public service. This, indeed, was a tragedy; since the time of Gratian, if not since Constantine's day, members of the senatorial aristocracy had been increasingly entrusted with the task of ruling the empire.[70] At a crucial moment in the last quarter of the fourth century, too many members of the lettered classes forsook their traditional role as leaders in favor of an uninterrupted quest for personal salvation. *Roma aeterna* could not survive *alienatio* (alienation—the rejection of the world).

Alienation

Prudentius represents the bridge between the two outlooks. A dedicated Christian, he shared Claudian's optimism for the future, perhaps the last Western Christian poet to do so for centuries to come. His robust faith in the empire just outweighed his self-doubt and romantic attachment to the ideals of the Christian ascetic. Some of his fellow citizens were already following the latter exclusively. In Spain Melania the Elder and Priscillian both renounced the world in c. 375. Their examples were to be followed by other Westerners such as Jerome, Paulinus of Nola, Augustine, and Honoratus of Lérins, to name a few. Personal tragedies, unfortunate sexual experiences, or deep fear of judgment may have influenced their decisions, but other factors are necessary to transform individual actions into a historical trend. No one can yet say precisely why it arose at this particular time.[71] One can only point to some of the psychological, theological, and material factors which contributed to its emergence. We have already discussed the popularity of Manicheism in North Africa, and of Augustine's conversion from Manichean to Catholic asceticism. In Spain, the steady intensification of the cult of relics and martyrs in the latter part of the fourth century heralded the advance of the ascetic ideal.[72] Some members of the aristocracy may have felt guilty about the huge disparity between their own wealth (measured in thousands of pounds of gold a year) and that of the great majority of the population. This guilt, combined with consciousness of approaching judgment, may have contributed to the growth of asceticism. One may detect this attitude in Jerome's advice, "He who would renounce the world should not sell to advantage the goods he has despised to the point of putting them up for sale. If you have your possessions at your complete disposition, sell them, and if not, throw them away" (*Letter* LVIII.2). Such advice would have ruinous economic and social consequences for the mass of the provincials not afflicted with wealth.

Meantime, the ascetic movement extended through a spectrum of religious experience from the near-Manicheism of Priscillian and his friends to the regulated monasticism of John Cassian. All, however, represented aspects of the flight of the Western elite from the world they might have helped to govern.

PRISCILLIAN

Priscillian's career ended in tragedy in 385.[73] A member of the provincial aristocracy perhaps from the southeastern corner of the province of Gallaecia (Galicia), a man of intellect and inquiring mind according to his contemporaries,[74] he was apparently converted (c. 375) to a Christianity that required the strictest asceticism. The precise nature of his beliefs remain unclear. He denied being a Manichee and denounced heresies vigorously. His most recent critic speaks of him "leading an evangelical ascetic movement in the Spanish churches which encouraged charismatic prophecy among both men and women, with the study of heretical apocrypha."[75] One can perhaps go a little further, for other traits in his religion, such as his mysticism, love of the occult, insistence on secrecy, and Docetic Christology point towards Gnosticism. From Jerome's references (in *Illustrious Men* and elsewhere) to Mark of Memphis as an influence on Priscillian,[76] it might be assumed that Priscillian represented a revival of Marcosian Gnosticism that had continued to exist as a Christian underground in southern Gaul and Spain. Gnosticism rather than Manicheism

711

seems to have lain at the heart of his religion, but whatever its origins his asceticism led him to the view that the world was satanic, that acceptance of baptism involved "a total abandonment of the foul darkness of secular activities"[77] and that study of the Scriptures was the means of understanding the depth of Satan.[78] Before long his enthusiasm had brought together like-minded men and women particularly among the local nobility and including two bishops, Instantius and Salvianus. By 380 the churches in Spain were riven with controversy. Priscillian found himself opposed by two metropolitans, Idacius (Hydatius) of Mérida and Hyginus of Córdoba. The latter, however, actually came to sympathize with him and he was supported also by the metropolitan of Galicia, an indication of the currents at work in Spanish Christianity in this period.

In October 380, a council was held at Saragossa, attended not only by Spanish bishops but by two bishops from Aquitaine, an interesting example of the close ecclesiastical and cultural contacts that existed on either side of the Pyrenees.[79] Some Priscillianist propositions were condemned but not Priscillian himself. Unfortunately, the task of carrying out the will of the council was entrusted to one of his enemies, Ithacius, bishop of Ossonoba (Lisbon?), a man described by Sulpicius Severus as a "loud and brazen individual given over to luxury and coarse living."[80] At first Priscillian rode out the storm. In 381 he was consecrated bishop of Avila in the extreme southeastern corner of the ecclesiastical province of Galicia. His enemies, however, appealed to Gratian's government, charging Priscillian with Manicheism. He left Spain for Bordeaux. Here, too, his mysticism and ascetic piety won immediate support, especially from aristocratic women. One of these, Euchrotia, was the wife of a well-known pagan teacher of rhetoric in Bordeaux and she and her daughter joined Priscillian.[81] The latter's devotions now became as controversial as his views. To pray naked might be taken as a strict imitation of Adam and Eve, but it also inflamed opposition, particularly that of Delphinus, the bishop of Bordeaux who had signed the canons of Saragossa. Nor did Priscillian have better luck with Ambrose in Milan whose aid he sought (winter 381–82), nor indeed with Damasus in Rome.

The matter might have ended in stalemate, however, but for political events. In the summer of 383, Gratian was overthrown by the usurper Magnus Maximus and murdered at Lyons (25 August 383). Maximus was a strongly orthodox Nicene and ready to demonstrate the fact on all occasions in order to secure the loyalty of the Gallic and Spanish bishops. In 384 the case against Priscillian was reopened, this time at Bordeaux. The charge seems to have been Manicheism, as before. Priscillian, for reasons not entirely clear, appealed from the decision of the council to the emperor, a disastrous move. He and some of his following were arraigned not for Manicheism but on even more serious charges of sorcery. In 385 Magnus Maximus entrusted the case to his praetorian prefect Evodius, and the latter found them guilty.[82] Despite appeals by Ambrose of Milan and Martin of Tours, Priscillian, the Aquitanian widow Euchrotia, four clergy, and a poet named Latronianus were executed. Priscillian's friend Instantius was banished to the salubrious if lonely Scilly Isles.

Condemnation on a charge of magic almost automatically carried the death penalty. Magnus Maximus felt sure enough of his ground to send the minutes of the trial to Pope Siricius. The latter protested but did not accuse him of executing a bishop. Other Western Christians recoiled in horror. For the first time, a Christian had been condemned to death on what appeared to be a religious issue.[83] Thirty years after his death Priscillian's ideas and writings were revered among influential lay and clerical circles in Tarragona.[84] The fallen bishop of aristocratic lineage became a popular saint. Punishment of some of his adversaries failed to still discontent. In Galicia, Priscillianism rapidly developed into something like a secret society among the people, outlasting the barbarian conquest of the province to continue to embarrass the Catholic bishops as late as the last years of the sixth century.[85] Its aims remain unclear; perhaps, in a vague way, it was an assertion of provincial identity, perhaps a protest against the wealth of the church in the richer provinces of the Spanish peninsula. The answer has yet to be found. The suggestion that the shrine of St. James of Compostella once honored Priscillian remains an attractive speculation.[86]

PAULINUS

Priscillianism originated as an aristocratic movement and its early adherents on both sides of the Pyrenees came from that level of society. If it ended in disaster it also pointed the way to others who were prepared to forsake a secular career and its responsibilities to dedicate themselves to a religious ideal. One of those who nearly found himself caught up in the anti-Priscillianist inquisitions was another provincial aristocrat with great estates in Spain and southern Gaul, Meropius Pontius Anicius Paulinus (c. 355-431). Paulinus provides a classic example of alienation and tells the historian much about his spiritual career and his motives. He grew up as a member of the new Christian Gallic nobility. His family estates near Narbonne, Bordeaux, and Fundi in Campania were described as "kingdoms." His father was a senator, and he himself after training as a lawyer and public speaker at Bordeaux was appointed supernumerary consul (*consul suffectus*) in 378 and provincial governor of Campania in 381. At this time he was strongly influenced by the poet Ausonius, and his loves were the history and poetry of classical Rome.[87]

How Paulinus came to change his outlook completely, to throw up his career, and spend the thirty-six years from 395 until his death in 431 as the faithful guardian of the shrine of the martyr St. Felix of Nola, can be followed in detail from his writings. In 383 he returned to Gaul, perhaps as a result of Magnus Maximus's usurpation rather than from religious motives. His early surviving poetry breathes the leisured life of the country-side and pride in Roman history. He was bound to Ausonius by strong ties of friendship. Then he married Therasia, a Spanish heiress with estates around Saragossa, resolutely Christian and related to Melania the Elder. Events began to draw Paulinus toward a more intense commitment to Christianity. He became a friend of Martin of Tours, now at the height of his fame. His brother was murdered and he was suspected of being impli-cated. Priscillianism and Magnus Maximus's usurpation had evidently re-sulted in deadly feuds among the intellectuals in Bordeaux. No prominent person was safe from attack. The public assessor had already visited Paulinus's home to view his possessions before auctioning them, but at the last moment the charges were dropped. Fear of facing the "Lord our Judge," however, began to oppress him. In 389 he was baptized, signifying his resolve not to resume an administrative career.[88] In a few months he had left Aquitaine for good, to settle on his wife's estates. As he wrote in this period,

> Happy is he who has separated his life far from the crowds of the ungodly, and has remained not in the way of sinners, nor has sat in the seat of pestilence, but has fixed his whole mind on the law of God and desires [to keep] His commands each day and night of his life, and ennobles his mind with chaste injunctions.

The meter and some of the ideas were from Horace, but the message was that of the psalmist.[89]

The death of an infant son was a further blow. Ties with Ausonius were gradually relaxed. Therasia became the principal influence in his life. Con-tact was made with Jerome far off in Palestine, and in 394 Jerome sent him his *Against Jovinian* with its exuberant defense of asceticism as the sole means of approach to God. Paulinus's mind was made up. He avoided the embarrassing consequences of forcible ordination at Barcelona at Christ-mas 394, and with Therasia made his way overland to Nola. The shrine and its saint, a reputed martyr in the time of Decius, had aroused his wonder in boyhood. Now he returned to serve him for the rest of his days.[90]

Paulinus's motives had been escapist. In his early letters from Nola to his friend Sulpicius Severus and also in his final surviving letter (dated 421), he states that he was a "refugee from the hubbub of this world."[91] To Auso-nius he had written before he left Spain how he "loved to repose void of empty cares and shun the din of public life, the bustle of affairs and all concerns hostile to the gifts of heaven."[92] And he encouraged his friends to follow his example: Licentius, Romanianus's son, Victricius of Rouen an exsoldier, Aper a high official, and Amanda his wife.[93] His approach to life was purely individual, a revival if not an actual continuance of the pre-Constantinian ethic of the West. Like Augustine, whose friendship he val-ued, he was concerned with his inner self and its salvation. His ideal was (as was Augustine's until 396-97) "cultured retirement" (*otium liberale*) inspired by dedication to Christianity and looking for its model in a bygone heroic Christian age.

At Nola he led an abstemious, but not severe life. He retained sufficient estates to secure his supply of vintage wine. He ate reasonably well.[94] His library was well stocked. There were servants to take his letters as far afield as Bethlehem, Gaul, or North Africa—another sign of the continued security of Mediterranean communications as late as A.D. 400. In the summer he would visit senatorial friends in Rome and come the winter he would write a poem in honor of Felix, which he would recite to admiring peasants each 14 January.[95] Under Paulinus's guidance Felix's *memoria* was transformed into a magnificent church. Typically, the pious founder quarreled with a peasant who refused to surrender his hut to the equivalent of compulsory purchase. Fire from heaven was invoked to remove this obstacle.[96] The local worthies at Nola also objected to the prodigal use of precious water in the courtyard fountains.[97] Neither Felix nor Paulinus were unmixed blessings to the community, though the place of pilgrimage that developed must have provided some compensation. Though he became bishop of Nola c. 408, episcopal duties did not weigh heavily on Paulinus. Nor did the news from the north. Neither Alaric nor Radagaisus figure in his correspondence, though his *Carmen* XXI rejoices in the defeat of the Goths thanks to the intervention of the saints and martyrs.[98] Tertullian's "nothing is more foreign to us than the state"[99] was reflected faithfully in Paulinus of Nola, in times when the empire needed all its inherited skills of administration in order to survive. He died in 431 without ever returning to his native land.

JEROME

Jerome (c. 347-420) provides a third example of renunciation of the world in favor of service to Christ—the stark either/or of Western Christianity. He was never an official like Paulinus. His life, however, shows him a prey to contradictions divided between deeply patriotic and even soldierly instincts and the demands of the ascetic ideal. The tension proved too great and resulted in the incredible spite and ill-humor that alienated contemporaries and obscured his own critical genius. A quasi exile from Rome, hounded by public opinion in 385 until his death on 20 September 420, he lived in a well-appointed cell near Bethlehem attended by aristocratic ladies, but even at this distance from the capital his effect on the religious outlook of the Roman aristocracy was profound. No one, not even Augustine, drew so clear a distinction between the classical past and the Christian present, the more impressive because of his genuine admiration for the virtues of pagan Rome.[100] This teaching, combined with his commentaries on Scripture and the Vulgate, were his lasting legacy to the formation of the early Middle Ages in the West.

We have already seen Jerome in Rome in his early years, wrestling even then with his love of Cicero and veneration for the tombs of martyrs.[101] It was not disappointment nor personal tragedy that turned him toward asceticism, but the obvious unworthiness of the church in his native Dalmatia. His choice was made in 369 when he was baptized. As he says in the life of the monk Malchus, "The Church after it had arrived at [the existence of] Christian princes became greater in power [as measured] by its wealth, but less in virtue."[102] His bishop, graphically described as "an ailing pilot of a sinking ship," disgusted him,[103] as did his fellow townspeople—Christians who thought only of their bellies! He migrated to Aquileia (c. 374) where he found a more hospitable climate for his views. With some like-minded and articulate contemporaries he established a community in which secular ambitions were renounced and apostolic simplicities embraced. One lived a life of detachment, abstinence, and the contemplation of divine truths.

In the West, however, despite Athanasius's example, and despite Martin of Tours, such ascetic communities were hardly understood and were not popular. There is an interesting passage in a work entitled *The Discussions Between Zacchaeus and Apollonius* recording a supposed dialogue between a Christian and a pagan in Rome (c. 360). The pagan asks, "Tell me, what is that community or sect of monks and why are they the object of hatred even among Christians?"[104] The Christian had to reply that there were misfits among monks as in any other calling; but the prejudice survived. There was also the suspicion that ascetics were in reality Manichees. In Rome in the 380s the populace would abuse a Christian woman who was pale through fasting, as "a miserable Manichaean nun."[105] Pilgrimages to the East, however, were beginning to make the monastic life more acceptable. Melania the Elder visited Antony's hermitage at Pispir on the east side of the Nile c. 375 and Rufinus, Jerome's friend in Aquileia and later his adversary, spent some time in the monastic settlements of Scetis and Nitria. Jerome's zeal as well as his controversial personality gave a powerful impetus toward transforming asceticism from an eccentric way of life by individuals into the representative Christian movement among the Roman and Romanized aristocracy of the West.

In 375 Jerome's group broke up. There may have been some sort of scandal, not the last in Jerome's life. Jerome himself went east (together with his library) to experience, he hoped, the exacting conditions of solitary asceticism. It was at this stage that the conflict within him between his love for the classics and what he believed to be the demands of Christianity reached a climax. "After many nights in vigil," he records, "after floods of tears called from my inmost heart in recollection of my past sins, I would once more take up Plautus." There followed the dream with its famous assertion from Christ as Judge, "You lie, you are a Ciceronian, not a Christian for where your treasure is, there is your heart."[106] This episode throws light on Jerome's outlook and that of some of his contemporaries.

First, incompatibility between Christianity and the empire's pagan past is extended to the latter's cultural heritage. Far from the classics providing a sound preliminary for understanding the divine truths, as Basil of Caesarea was advising his nephews at this time,[107] the classics were to be rejected and cast aside. Awesome penalties would be inflicted, Jerome feared, if he "should ever again read the works of the Gentiles." Second, one sees, as in Paulinus's career, the profound influence of judgment on the actions of the Western Christians. The tortures applied to the accused in the imperial courts of the day would be as nothing to those ordered by Christ himself. In the West "fear of the Lord" tended to mean what it said.[108]

Jerome was disappointed with the desert of Chalcis. It was overcrowded with quarrelsome ascetics. He regarded these as hypocrites in filthy robes, with long lank manes for hair, hauling about heavy chains, but arrogant to a degree. "From the depths of our caverns we damn the world," he portrays them as declaiming.[109] They debated episcopal decisions and denounced him as a Sabellian. Jerome replied in kind. He was aggressively Latin in his views, a "Roman Christian" he called himself,[110] and eventually allowed himself to be ordained in Antioch by the influential but rigorously Nicene Evagrius, the leader of a small splinter group of pro-Western Antiochenes, favored by Pope Damasus. The Syrian monks were happy to see him go in 377. In his travels (practically undocumented) during the next five years he visited Constantinople and at some stage learned Hebrew as well as Greek.

At Rome, the years 382 to 385 were his most productive. For once his loyalty was rewarded. Damasus appointed him his secretary and consulted him on how to refute the Apollinarians. Finally, he commissioned him to compile a revised Latin version of the Psalms and the New Testament. Had he been content with this Jerome would have flourished in Rome. Instead, he launched himself into the complexities of aristocratic Roman society. He became the spiritual adviser to the Christian noble house of the Aemilii which included Paula (d. 404) and her daughters, Eustochium and Blesilla. The women took to asceticism under Jerome's direction. Jerome described Paula as mourning and fasting, squalid with dirt, her eyes dim with weeping, praying for divine mercy all night. "The psalms were her songs, the Gospel her whole speech."[111] With her daughters she became learned in Greek and Hebrew. The trouble was that Roman society expected more from their young women than intense religious virtues.

Jerome was encouraged by a resounding triumph in 383/84 over the lay theologian Helvidius who taught that Mary enjoyed a normal family life after Jesus' birth (and hence marriage was as high a state as celibacy).[112] It was a danger signal, for whether wittingly or not Helvidius had attacked the key pro-celibate argument, namely that Mary was perpetually virgin. Jerome had risen to the occasion. He multiplied his exhortations toward asceticism and the exclusive reading of Scripture. His confidence was unbounded and so was his presumption. "Nowadays," he wrote, "we see even bishops abandoning the Gospels to read comedies, hum the erotic words of pastoral poems, and stick fast to Virgil, thus voluntarily making themselves guilty of what schoolboys do under compulsion."[113] This might pass from the man chosen by Damasus to provide a new translation of Scripture. What was not forgiven were the results of his teaching on Blesilla. She was not one to listen with equanimity to teaching that all sexual activity was defiling. She collapsed with a nervous breakdown brought about by intensive fasting. Soon she was dead, and Paula fainted at her funeral. The unusual show of emotion aroused the populace. Indignation knew no bounds. Jerome was hounded as "leader of the detestable tribe of monks." Charges of a disgraceful character were leveled against him, and readily believed.[114] Early in 385 he took ship to Palestine accompanied by Paula and Eustochium, never to return to Rome. The affair was not forgotten. Yet it may even have helped to assure Jerome of a ready audience for his diatribes against opponents of asceticism. He retained some friends in Rome; in 393 Pammachius, a friend of Paulinus, sent him a copy of Jovinian's tract,[115] and there were others, such as Oceanus and Ctesiphon, to whom he continued to write.

Jovinian was a one-time monk and had gone about barefoot and dirty, clad in a filthy black tunic, and living on a diet of bread and water. Not surprisingly perhaps, he had become disillusioned, and began not only to lead a very normal life but wrote a defense of his changed attitude founded on Scripture. He based himself on the sovereign value of baptism. All baptized persons, whether celibate, married, or widowed, enjoyed the same status as Christians. If they sinned they could repent. All would be treated equally at judgment. Jovinian's arguments preceded or perhaps accompanied Pelagius's, for it will be recalled Pelagius also argued on the basis of the unity of all baptized persons—arguments that struck a chord in Italy and Rome where baptism was itself taken as an act of deep commitment to the faith.[116] In arguing thus, Jovinian turned on their heads the arguments that had led Priscillian and Jerome to asceticism.

His tract appeared when Eugenius was firmly in control at Rome (392–94). It reflected, therefore, something of the mood of the new pagan-Arian alliance. Hence, Jerome's impassioned vindication of asceticism had political as well as religious and intellectual impact. Abuse, subtle argument, and sheer perversity restored the ascetic virtues to their pride of place, "Eating meat, drinking wine, having a well-filled belly—there you have the seedbed of lust."[117] If Jovinian was right, why should we not all sin to our heart's content, confident that on repentance all would be restored to apostolic status?

Jerome's *Against Jovinian* probably did more to establish asceticism as the norm of Christian life in the West than anything else he wrote. The work *Against Vigilantius,* written in a single session of white-hot energy in c. 406, reinforced the link between the veneration (if not worship) of the relics of martyrs and prayers to saints and martyrs with the ascetic interpretation of Christianity. No one could object now to the all-night vigils, the candles, the alleluias about which Vigilantius complained without impugning the authority of Jerome.[118]

Jerome, for all his ill-humor and contempt for the opinions of his opponents, had popular opinion on his side. The practices which annoyed Vigilantius were becoming part and parcel of the religious life of Western Christians. Cult as much as belief aided the survival of Catholicism through the long crisis of the establishment of the Arian barbarian kingdoms. The controversies and the great debate between Augustine and Pelagius, however, show why Christian Stoicism did not prevail as the religion of the West, as Platonist Christianity prevailed in the East. They indicate, too, how it was that in the crisis of the empire's fortunes the Christianized aristocracy in the West turned away from duty to world-renouncing ideals.

HONORATUS

The last chapter in this saga is the most constructive. Medieval Western monasticism can trace its origins back to the settlements that began to take shape on the rocky islands off the Provençal coast, c. 410, and in particular at Lérins opposite Cannes. Honoratus (c. 365–430) who founded the monastery at Lérins (c. 410) was also a Gallic aristocrat whose family had held consular honors, and who, like other aristocratic idealists of the day, had rejected worldly prospects at an early age, with his father's reluctant understanding. After years of travel, he chose the rocky island of Lérins as the site of his monastic settlement and was joined immediately by like-minded individuals.[119] It was a religious escape, attracting idealists from all over the West,[120] and Honoratus's relative and biographer, Hilary of Arles, while describing in 430 the religious motives behind the influx of recruits, makes no mention of political events.

Lérins, however, was not destined to remain merely a refuge like its contemporary settlement on Capri. Honoratus eventually turned his latent administrative skills to the regular service of the church and became bishop of Arles for three years between 427 and 430. This was an early sign of a new, responsible vocation which was to benefit the church greatly in the next centuries. Meantime, Honoratus's example as a leader had inspired the neighboring bishops to found monasteries themselves. In 417 Castor, bishop of Apt, ninety miles north of Marseilles, established a community at Apt. Under episcopal control questions soon arose concerning the aims of the monastic community and by what methods these could be achieved.[121] It was at this stage that one of the most remarkable men of his time arrived from Rome, perhaps as a refugee.

JOHN CASSIAN

John Cassian (c. 365–433) was probably a native of Dobrudja at the eastern end of Rome's Danube frontier.[122] He was drawn to monasticism, and not later than 392 sought admission to a monastery near the cave of the Nativity at Bethlehem. Later he was allowed by his community to visit Egypt and the deep impression the Egyptian monks made on him is reflected by the twenty-four *Conferences* he remembered and published when he came to Gaul years later. He moved to Constantinople (399) and Rome, before arriving in southern Gaul c. 414, where he was ordained presbyter. He was to leave his mark permanently on his adopted country.

Much as he admired the Egyptian solitaries, he saw that their ideal was only for the perfect. "It is perfect men who ought to go out into the desert," he wrote.[123] The novice must begin with the community life like that of the Pachomian community. When in c. 420 Bishop Castor asked him for advice on the Eastern or Egyptian rules for his own monks, Cassian was ready with his reply. He was a realist. He had seen the faults of the Egyptian monks and he knew that what might suit conditions in Egypt would not suit conditions in Gaul. The *Institutes* that he compiled (c. 426), and the *Conferences* with the Egyptian monks he set down (c. 429) were designed as a rule for beginners, precept being buttressed by examples drawn from the great masters of the ascetic life. The community that the novice entered was a temple of God, consecrated to his service, and he must bear himself worthily. In fact, this meant common worship in the five daily offices of Dawn (later Laudes), Terce, Sext, None, and Vespers, to which was added a long vigil on Saturday from Vespers until the cockcrow.[124]

Between these services the monk must work, for work cured natural weariness with routine. There was greater emphasis on copying manuscripts rather than agricultural work, for Cassian wanted his monks to spend as much time as possible in their cells. The Gallic monk lived quietly in his community. Daily life was austere, but not to excess. Three to four hours' sleep was advised, and the diet consisted mainly of bread and cooked vegetables. Outside, in woods and on islands, some might practice the higher vocation of the anchorite. Meantime, the monk's duty was to defeat the eight capital sins and to take the first halting steps up the ladder of ascent toward an apprehension of God through prayer.[125]

As Owen Chadwick says, Cassian bequeathed to Latin Christianity "the map of a pilgrim's progress,"[126] but so far as society was concerned it still tended to be a negative ideal. There was no encouragement to bring wasteland into cultivation, no attempt to absorb the values of pagan learning into Christianity, and little motivation to serve one's fellows as Basil's monks were doing. Cassian's monks still deserved the gibe by Rutilius Namatianus against their fellows on Capri: "They dread the gifts of Fortune while her ills they fear. Who to shirk pain would choose a life of pain?"[127] Yet the tide had turned. *Conversio*, a positive turning to God, was replacing *alienatio*, the negative rejection of the world, as the Christian ideal. With Cassian and Honoratus one can begin to see the emergence of ordered monasteries in Gaul.[128] It would, however, take another century and the genius of Benedict before alienation was combined effectively with service in monastic life.

Cassian's work had come too late to alter the attitudes of many Christian leaders toward the empire. There is little doubt that alienation had sapped the spirit of resistance to the Germanic barbarians. Collective reaction among Christians in the line of the invading armies varied from panic and despair to indifference and fatalistic acquiescence in events. Popular resistance was minimal. The first half of the fifth century failed to produce local aristocratic leaders such as Sidonius Apollinaris, the hero of Clermont in the 470s. In Aquileia, Bishop Chromatius continued (c. 401) to preach against the Jews in his diocese as though these were a worse menace than the Visigoths.[129] In Turin (c. 401) Bishop Maximus scorned the efforts of the magistrates to restore the dilapidated defenses of the city. Their thoughts, he told them, should be fixed on the approaching judgment. They should be thinking of saving their souls rather than preserving their lives.[130] When commanders less able than Theodosius I relied for victory on the protection of saints and martyrs[131] instead of on their own tactical sense and the courage and resource of their armies, the fall of the empire in the West could not be long delayed.

THE CHURCH AND THE INTERNAL CRISIS OF THE EMPIRE

Cassian's monasteries were established during the long interlude that separated the first stormy appearance of the Visigoths in southern Gaul in 413 and their final conquest of the territory around 473. Whatever the political and military situation, however, the Gallic aristocrats who had abandoned public service for the ascetic life showed little awareness of it. Paulinus, writing to Sulpicius Severus in Aquitaine c. 395, scorned the society he was quitting: "Let them enjoy their pleasure, high offices and wealth, if indeed they are theirs. For they prefer those on earth where our life ends to those in heaven where it abides."[132] Spain and southern Italy he described in terms of peace and prosperity. Nothing disturbed the joys of early spring as he declaimed his yearly poem in honor of Felix's birthday (*natalicia*) at Nola. A farmer's loss of cattle or a fat pig returning to the saint's shrine after being abandoned by its owner seemed the worst of rural tragedies.[133]

In the few years around 410 this would be changed as Nola itself experienced the passage of Alaric's army pushing south from Rome, aiming perhaps to settle in North Africa. Alaric, however, died in Calabria in 411, his vision unfulfilled. North Africa itself enjoyed another twenty years of prosperity to end, as we have seen, with dramatic suddenness before a combination of an uprising of African tribes within the Roman frontier and the invasion of the Vandals under Gaiseric in 429.

The combination is important. Military "assassination" might never have happened had it not been supported by the uprising of important groups of rural and nomadic peoples who had little share in the relative

721

prosperity of the times.[134] In the first decades of the fifth century barbarism was not merely that of the Germanic invaders. Large sections of the native populations in the West were scarcely touched by Romanization.[135] Some of those who were had become embittered at their lot and were ready to join the invaders. The Catholic bishops, prisoners of their own status in Roman society, failed to find remedies even when they recognized the need. The economic and social effects of alienation aggravated matters further.

It is difficult to generalize from one part of the empire to another, but it would seem that towns, whether in North Africa or in distant Britain, were becoming less important as centers of trade and local life than places where a few rich and powerful families would maintain luxurious townhouses and collect their rents. The fourth-century villa in Colliton Park, within the walls of Roman Dorchester, may have been one such.[136] North Africa provides other examples, such as the "House of Birds" or "House of the Donkey" in Djemila, named after the designs of their fine mosaics.[137] At Hippo, Augustine's neighbor was Julianus, a rich senator,[138] and he and similar wealthy families provided the environment in which Augustine lived and worked. Outside the towns too, the economy seems in many areas to have been dominated increasingly by the large villas and their associated estates. Examples of large fourth-century British villas, such as Chedworth, Bignor, or North Leigh, come readily to mind. In proconsular Africa, the magnificent mosaics, especially those in the Bardo Museum at Tunis, show self-contained manorial communities developing in the fourth century, where the owners lived lives of elegant leisure, the men hunting, the women seated at ease fanning themselves and petting animals.[139] In Numidia too, Hippo for instance was surrounded by prosperous farms, some owned by absentee senatorial landowners, while others were retained in the hands of members of the old city aristocracy and by some small proprietors. Augustine's congregation was composed of city and country dwellers, with the latter coming into the city to listen to him. Whatever their origin, his congregation included a large number of the people who knew about "large and elegant domains" and "ivory beds," and would appreciate allegories drawn from the life of an owner of a wealthy estate.[140] Augustine had no criticism of that society itself. Each should be content with their lot and the rich should give thanks to Jesus Christ who had consolidated their domains.[141]

By now Catholic Christianity was a major landowner. Augustine, as we have seen, found himself administering considerable estates on behalf of the church at Hippo, and he lamented the fact.[142] On ordination, clergy were expected to hand over their property to the church in which they were to serve, and there was a regular flow of bequests from members of the congregation.[143] Already church estates were extensive enough to require specialized clerical administrators to look after them,[144] and it was admitted they had become a source of envy.[145] There was little to be done, for the church depended on the good will of its fellow landowners to enforce antiheretical legislation on the rural population, especially in Donatist Numidia.[146]

The situation in c. 400 was not, however, intolerable. One neglects too often to take into account custom and security as stabilizing forces helping people to bear conditions that might seem oppressive and exploitative. Where a town such as Thagaste was blessed with a patron (*patronus*) like Romanianus, immensely wealthy but openhanded, approachable, and just, discontent would be muted.[147] Where there were landowners who charged double rents[148] and employed extortionate bailiffs, ideas of rebellion simmered. On the eve of the barbarian invasions, there were too many of the latter in the West. Examples may be quoted for both North Africa and Gaul. Two decrees (*Novellae*), addressed by the emperor Valentinian III to the North Africans in 443, describe the remaining Roman territory as characterized by "the bankruptcy of all fortunes," where the rich were oppressing the poor and the cruelty of the creditors outmatched that of the barbarians. Debt and crushing interest rates were among the chief causes of the trouble.[149] The strictures were the same as the complaints of the Circumcellions both in the 340s and in Augustine's day. In southern Gaul in c. 439, Salvian, the presbyter of Marseilles, a stern moralist who retained a lingering respect for the virtues of the Roman republic, wrote of the rapacity, and desperation, of the city authorities, obliged to use any and every method to get the taxes in. Those afflicted were sometimes "driven by bitter woe to pray for the arrival of the enemy" (that is, the barbarians).[150] Loyalty to the empire was being undermined irreparably.

This is what happened. Peasant revolts in Brittany, the Loire Valley, and in the Ebro Valley between 415 and 441 coincided with the steady extension of the power of the Germanic invaders.[151] In North Africa, Augustine painted a grim picture of Circumcellion activity in a letter to Count Boniface in c. 417:

> Who dared to exact payment of a debt from one who had consumed his stores, or from any debtor whatever, that sought their assistance or protection? Under the threat of beating, and burning, and immediate death, all documents compromising the worst of slaves were destroyed, that they might depart in freedom. . . . Anyone who had shown a contempt for their hard words were compelled by harder blows to do what they desired.[152]

Masses of ink have been expended on the Circumcellions,[153] but few would deny that they represented a revolutionary peasant movement inspired by apocalyptic ideas, the revival of whose activities in the late fourth century coincided with deepening contrasts between the fortunes of rich and poor in North Africa.

Confronted with the combination of barbarian invasion and social discontent the Catholic clergy could only exhort their hearers to behave more justly. "Listen you rich," Augustine warned in 429, in an address of rare insight, "who have money, yet burn with greed, while the poor look on and murmur, groaning, praising and envying, aspiring to be your equals, yet rueing their inferiority, and amidst their praises of the rich they often say 'They are the only ones. They alone live.' "[154] And he pointed to the result (*Sermon* 345.3), of slaves suddenly turning on their masters and betraying them to the enemy for money.

Augustine himself could only warn. The earthly condition presupposed sin, which would cease only with the triumph of the city of God. In the meantime social conditions were fixed by divine dispensation and could not be changed. Christ did not command slaves to be turned into free men, he reminded his hearers. Powers were "ordained by God" and must be obeyed.[155] "Peasant audacity" stirred up riot against landlords. The "worst of slaves" joined the Circumcellions.[156] Augustine's disciple, Paulus Orosius, had similar views. The Bagaudae he had perhaps experienced in Spain were "a peasant band," stirring a pernicious tumult.[157] In southern Gaul, Salvian lamented that the clergy there "were either silent in the face of these abuses [extortions by tax collectors] or, if they did utter, their words were no more effective than silence."[158]

Thus a disastrous situation prevailed in the West. Paradoxically members of the senatorial aristocracy only made matters worse by their sale of land as proof of their dedication to Christ. Apart from debt and extortion the worst moment for many cultivators came with a change of owner. The new proprietor might have gained his holding with an eye to exploiting it more efficiently than his predecessor or to spite a rival. In any event he lacked the rapport with his new tenants that could only come with time. Claudian paints a horrific picture—in terms intelligible to his Western audience—of the Eastern prefect, Flavius Rufinus's activities, "drawing them [the husbandmen] from their homes and expelling them from the lands of their fathers," "forcing whole peoples into slavery."[159] This was where the desire of some Christian aristocrats to rid themselves overnight of their possessions could be disastrous. Paulinus, Pinianus, and Melania were very rich. Melania had estates in Spain, Italy, Sicily, North Africa, and Britain. Paula owned most of the town of Nicopolis in Illyricum.[160] Suddenly to unload such territories onto the market was to provide a field day for speculators and exploiters. In c. 389 Ausonius made the point to Paulinus: "A hundred new masters" would take over his former great estates.[161] The inhabitants would no longer be protected from greedy bailiffs or from the vagaries of the harvest. Prudentius added his own warning put into the mouth of an imaginary pagan objector to the ascetic way of life: "One sells ancestral lands to disgraceful speculators. The heir tricked of his succession laments. One looks on it as the very climax of piety to deprive one's children. Public utility, the finances of the emperor and the state require that money should be devoted to payment of taxes and thus towards aiding our emperor."[162] Others less articulate shared his doubts. Vigilantius, who took to Jerome some of the proceeds of the sale of Paulinus's estates, saw no reason why this money should subsidize aristocratic monks in the East when it was needed for the far more necessary work in society to be done by churches in the West.[163] The wealthy individual's ascetic vocation could not be harmonized with the close-knit relationship between patron and client, owner and cultivator that held together late Roman society. To desert one's responsibilities for whatever reason merely placed new burdens on the shoulders of one's erstwhile dependents. In the first half of the fifth century many an aggrieved peasant went to the Bagaudae or Circumcellions for help rather than to the church.

A final factor in the crisis that confronted Western Catholicism in this period was the existence of unassimilated pagan tribes within the Roman provincial frontiers in North Africa, Spain, and the British provinces. The internal, fortified border posts (*limes*) designed to police the Kabyle and the Aurès Mountains in North Africa, Cantabria in northern Spain, and Snowdonia in North Wales do not seem to have attracted many missionaries. In c. 400 a rather perplexed correspondent of Augustine asks whether the oaths sworn by the pagan Arzuges (living near the Tripolitanian *limes*) were to be accepted.[164] Augustine himself realized the danger posed by the "innumerable barbarian peoples" living beyond and within the African *limes* who were still pagan.[165] He had replied to the same correspondent (*Letter* XLVII.2) pointing out how "not only along the frontiers, but throughout all the provinces [of Africa] we owe our peace to the sworn oaths of barbarians." The situation was perpetually menacing but the hint was not taken. Perhaps the Christians feared and hated the barbarians for their raids too much to think of saving them from hell.[166] In none of the voluminous works of Augustine nor in Optatus of Milevis is there any suggestion of a missionary policy aimed at converting the barbarians to Christianity. In northern Spain the same may also be true. While there had been a bishopric at the garrison town of Legio (Leon) since 250, Cantabria remained largely pagan a century and a half later. Further east, Paulinus of Nola described the Basques as "barbarians," "heathens," and "bandits."[167] At this stage in his career the hostility of a provincial aristocrat outweighed the Christian's sense of mission. When the storm broke as successive waves of Germanic barbarians swept through the western provinces of the empire and on into North Africa, Catholicism would not avoid sharing the disaster that befell the Roman administration and the landed aristocracy. In many parts "nobles and priests" found themselves singled out for barbarian spoil and popular vengeance.[168]

Adaptation

The church, however, was destined to survive, and we may end this chapter by considering briefly three different tendencies—intellectual, practical, and institutional—that contributed to that result. The intellectual is represented by Paulus Orosius and his attitude toward the empire, the barbarians, and the provinces. Orosius shared the same general outlook as Augustine but was more optimistic than his master. He possessed a greater sense of history and perception of current events while lacking Augustine's majestic concept of the force of human will or love in directing man's affairs. Faithfully, Orosius pursued the task prescribed for him by Augustine in 416,

> to set down from all sources, gleaned from histories and chronicles down to the present day, whatever disasters resulted from wars or catastrophes, from plagues and famines or horrible experiences, from earthquakes, or untoward occurrences from flood or fiery eruptions, and the dire effects of thunderbolts and hailstones, or miseries engendered from parricides and crises in the last centuries.[169]

His *History Against the Pagans* was to be a catalog of woe, showing first, that events of the recent past such as Rome's fall were not as terrible as pagans had sought to make out, and second, that in humanity's fallen condition disasters were only to be expected. At the end of this early demonstration of the providential concept of history, as schematically applied as its Marxist successor, Orosius strikes a different note. In contrast to Augustine, he regarded the empire founded by Augustus as the providentially established vehicle of Christianity, and hence, with the progressive spread of the faith, the state of human affairs must also have improved.[170] Thus, even the challenge of the Goths to Rome should be viewed positively. In his native Spain too, he had seen the Germanic invaders turn rapidly from blind pillage to relatively peaceful occupation of the land, and he had observed that to some their rule appeared less onerous than Roman administration.[171]

He had found also that the Goths had no real hatred of Rome. Galla Placidia had married the Gothic prince Ataulf. Was it not possible for a Romano-Gothic commonwealth to come into existence inspired by Christian virtues, the successor to the old pagan empire that had been destroyed?[172] *Romania*, meaning the sense of fatherland, peace, religion, and law, would survive the city of Rome. Even the heresy of the Goths was not their own fault. It was due to the emperor Valens's wicked deception in sending them Arian missionaries, and Valens had perished miserably.[173] Much of this proved to be wishful thinking, the product of temporary developments which were soon consigned to oblivion, but Orosius had sown a seed and for a century and a half Romano-Gothic union would play its part in the thinking of the Western Christian leaders. The Goths, however, were more strongly Arian than Orosius imagined. They had accepted the leadership of Ulphilas, whose Gothic Bible had allowed Arian (*homoian*) Christianity to become the expression of Gothic sense of tribal or even national identity, and they were to prove to be militant bearers of their creed among the other Germanic peoples. Orosius, however, shows that the idea of harmony between Rome and her invaders did not seem impossible to a Christian provincial who also felt pride in his people's former resistance to Rome.[174] Even at this time of disaster some Western Catholics were contemplating the future conversion and absorption of their Gothic conquerors.

Mission

Mission to the barbarians had been in the minds of some of the more far-sighted Catholic leaders in the generation before the great invasions. Conversion of the Germanic rulers and their peoples was seen as an insurance, as the best means of bringing them into the Roman orbit and rendering them less dangerous. As usual, Ambrose of Milan was among those who read the signs of the times most clearly. Probably around 395 he wrote to Queen Fritigil of the Marcomanni who had been converted to Christianity. The queen had sent gifts for the church and had requested Ambrose to instruct her in the faith. Ambrose replied, according to Paulinus his biographer, in the form of a catechism and "in the same letter urged her to persuade her husband to remain at peace with the Romans." In this she succeeded, for her husband "put himself and his people under the protection of the Romans, while she also came to Milan."[175] This shrewd piece of late Roman diplomacy was not isolated. About the same time, Paulinus of Nola praised his friend Victricius, bishop of Rouen, for "having rendered the Channel coast safe by spreading Christianity among the still pagan Nervii," and similarly the Morini further east, picturesquely described as "dwelling at the edge of the world battered by a deafening ocean."[176] Again, in a poem addressed to Nicetas, bishop of Remesiana in Illyricum, Paulinus praised his friend for having preached successfully to the Bessi settled around Nish (Naissus). These people had apparently lain outside the area of urban episcopal interest until then. Now, Nicetas could boast that the Bessi, "harsher than their winter snow were led like sheep into the hall of peace."[177] Barbarism and aggression could be changed for the better by conversion to Catholic Christianity.

Development of the Papacy

A century would pass before attempts to convert the barbarians to Catholicism would show any lasting success. Meantime, however, the hub of the wheel, the institution of the papacy, survived. It had not fallen with pagan Rome, and through the first decades of the fifth century, despite the aberrations of Pope Zosimus's pontificate, it gradually extended its authority over the surviving churches in the West. Innocent I (401–17), Boniface I (418–22), Celestine (422–32), and Sixtus III (432–40) were all able men, representative of the new type of administrator who was taking service with the church instead of the empire. Through them the papacy was able to fill the vacuum left in the West by the progressive weakness of the imperial power. Though control over Thessalonica and with it a bridgehead in Greek-speaking Christendom was disputed by Constantinople, events in the West moved in the papacy's favor. Augustine, while joining his colleagues in denying the papacy's right to encroach on the traditional prerogatives of the North African church, accepted the pope as "President of the Western Church."[178] In any event, when Carthage fell to Gaiseric in 439 the papacy had no more to fear from that quarter. Six years later, in 445, almost as a final gesture to the West, Valentinian III (425–55) ordered that,

> inasmuch then as the primacy of the Apostolic see is assured by the merit of St. Peter, prince of the episcopal order, by the rank of the city of Rome, and also by the authority of a sacred synod, lest presumption endeavour to attempt any unauthorized act contrary to the authority of that see, then at length will the peace of the Churches be everywhere maintained, if the whole body acknowledges its ruler.[179]

The bishops of Gaul or any other province were forbidden to do aught without the pope's authority which in turn "shall be the law of all."

It was no empty gesture, for the papal throne was occupied by the first and perhaps the ablest of a long line of medieval popes, Leo I (440–61). Already Hilary of Arles (bishop, 429–49), whose councils at Orange in 441 and Vaison in 442 had done much to hold the church in southern Gaul together, had felt the pope's displeasure. Leo had no doubt that he spoke in Peter's name, "persevering in the strength of the Rock, has not abandoned the helm of the Church which he undertook to control."[180] The measured cadence of his style, his love of antithesis and parallelism, of biblical citation and liturgical reminiscence that combined in a concise message or instruction, remain unmistakable to this day. During his pontificate the whole Latin church was centered around the see of Rome.

The extent, however, both of Leo's power and the church over which he presided should not be exaggerated. By 450 Britain had been lost irretrievably, North Africa had fallen to the Arian Vandals, and there were Arian rulers administering much of Gaul and Spain. On the Rhineland where the barbarians had settled, Christianity was in retreat and Christian cemeteries had fallen out of use.[181] Further north, in what is now Belgium, the Franks were pagan. And what of Attila's Huns who in 450 were casting their eye on the fertile lands of Gaul? At that moment few would have rated the survival of Western Catholicism highly.

Appalling catastrophe had befallen the West. "All Gaul burnt like a torch," was the despairing comment of one contemporary.[182] Even the price of survival was heavy. It would take centuries before Western Europe reached the level of prosperity attained in the last quarter of the fourth century. Something, too, of the Christian-classical society represented by

728

Jerome, Prudentius, Paulinus, and Augustine had passed away. No longer would leading Christians have either the time or the education to pen the enormously long letters that are the feature of Jerome's and Paulinus's correspondence. Events involved also the collapse of the lay theological tradition to which Christian thinkers such as Ambrosiaster, Tyconius, and even the humble Donatist grammarian, Cresconius, had contributed. It was now a question of what, if anything, could be salvaged of past educational tradition. For educated women such as Paula and Eustochium the fifth century represents the end of an age. Though moralists will always exaggerate, decline in every aspect of material and moral life is obvious. It is not merely that Roman villas were abandoned and cities lost their populations. There is clearly a difference of quality and fiber between the pagan Roman aristocrats and their provincial imitators at the end of the fourth century, proclaiming the virtues of thrift and patriotism, and the debauched and demoralized provincials whom Salvian describes as typical of the Roman world while the Vandals approached Carthage.[183] Some time around the fall of Rome the long Indian summer of the Western Christian and classical world moved into the winter of the Dark Ages. Victory had gone to the Germanic invaders and to Augustinian theology. To this extent Gibbon's judgment was correct.

BIBLIOGRAPHY

NOTE

A detailed study of the contribution of Christianity, particularly in its ascetic forms, to the collapse of the Roman Empire in the West has yet to be written. See, however, the suggestive essay by A. Momigliano, "Christianity and the Decline of the Roman Empire," in *Conflict Between Paganism and Christianity*. Useful works on specific themes include the following: John Matthews, *Western Aristocracies and Imperial Court, A.D. 364–425* (New York: Oxford University Press; Oxford: At the Clarendon Press, 1975), which contains a first-rate critical account of the transition of the upper classes in Rome and the Western provinces from paganism to Christianity in the last quarter of the fourth century. H. Chadwick, *Priscillian of Avila: The Occult and the Charismatic in the Early Church* (New York and London: Oxford University Press, 1976), which lacks, however, adequate perception of either the religious or social and political background to Priscillian's movement. J. N. D. Kelly, *Jerome: His Life, Writings, and Controversies* (New York: Harper & Row, 1976; London: Gerald Duckworth & Co., 1975), is a fine study, but to my mind persistently makes Jerome too old a man for the active and controversial life he led. R. A. Markus, *Saeculum: History and Society in the Theology of St. Augustine* (New York and Cambridge: Cambridge University Press, 1970), is an excellent study of the political thought of Augustine and Paulus Orosius and is essential for understanding the prevalent political outlook of Christian leaders in the first decades of the fifth century. The classic works by T. R. Glover, *Life and Letters in the Fourth Century* (reprint ed., New York: G. E. Stechert, 1925), and Samuel Dill, *Roman Society in the Last Century of the Western Empire* (new ed., rev. and enl., New York: Macmillan Co., 1906), retain their value concerning both the history and literature of the time, while Edward Gibbon's chaps. 30 and 31 of *The Decline and Fall of the Roman Empire* should never be neglected.

SOURCES

Augustine, *De Civitate Dei*, ed. E. Hoffmann, CSEL 40, parts 1 & 2, Leipzig: G. Freytag, 1899–1900; *The City of God*, Eng. trans. P. Schaff, 2 vols., NPNF, Edinburgh: T. & T. Clark, 1871; and Books I–III, vol. 1, Eng. trans. and ed. G. E. McCracken, LCL, Cambridge, Mass.: Harvard University Press; London: William Heinemann, 1957.

———. *Enarrationes in Psalmos*. *PL* 36 and 37.

———. *Sermones*. *PL* 38 and 39.

Ausonius, *Opera*, ed. C. Schenkl, *MGH* (A.A.) V.2, Berlin 1883; Eng. trans. and ed. H. G. Evelyn-White, 2 vols., LCL, Cambridge, Mass.: Harvard University Press; London: William Heinemann, 1919–21.

John Cassian, *Opera*, ed. M. Petschenig, CSEL 13 (*Collationes*), Vienna, 1886, and 17 (Prolegomena, study of mss., *De Institutis coenobiorum* and *De Incarnatione domini contra Nestorium*), Vienna, 1888. No complete Eng. trans., but E. C. S. Gibson's trans. in NPNF, Oxford, 1894, includes all but *Institute* VI and *Conferences* XII and XXII. Fr. trans. and ed. of the *Conferences*, by E. Pichery, SC 42, 54, 64, 2 vols., 2d ed. Paris, 1966, and vol. 3, 1971; and *Institutes*, J. C. Guy, SC 109, Paris, 1965.

Claudian, *Opera*, ed. T. H. Birt, *MGH* (A.A.) X, Berlin, 1892; Eng. trans. and ed. M. Platnauer, 2 vols., LCL, Cambridge, Mass.: Harvard University Press; London: William Heinemann, 1922.

Hilary of Arles. *Vita S. Honorati*. Edited and Fr. trans. M. D. Valentin. SC 235. Paris, 1977.

Jerome (Hieronymus), *Opera*, CCSL 72, 73/73A, 74, 75/75A, 78, Turnhout 1958–64; *Select Letters*, Eng. trans. and ed. F. A. Wright, LCL, Cambridge, Mass.: Harvard University Press; London: William Heinemann, 1933; and *Letters* together with other works including *Adversus Jovinianum* and *Adversus Vigilantium*, Eng. trans. and ed. W. H. Fremantle, NPNF, Oxford, 1893.

Paulus Orosius, *Historiarum libri VII adversus paganos*, ed. C. Zangemeister, CSEL 5, pp. 1–564, Vienna, 1882; *Seven Books of History Against the Pagans: The Apology of Paulus Orosius*, ed. and Eng. trans. I. W. Raymond, New York: Columbia University Press; London: Oxford University Press, 1936.

Paulinus of Nola, *Epistolae et Carmina*, ed. W. Hartel, CSEL 29 and 30, Leipzig: G. Freytag, 1894; Eng. trans. P. G. Walsh, *The Letters of St. Paulinus of Nola*, ACW 35 and 36, Westminister, Md.: Newman Press, 1966–67; *The Poems of St. Paulinus of Nola*, ACW 40, 1975.

Priscillian, *Canons* and *Tractates* contained in the *Würzburg Tract* II, ed. G. Schepss, CSEL 18, Vienna: F. Tempsky, 1899.

Prudentius, *Carmina*, ed. J. Bergman, CSEL 61, Vienna–Leipzig, 1926, and *Opera*, ed. M. P. Cunningham, CCSL 126, Turnhout, 1966, good bibliography; Eng. trans. F. St. J. Thackeray, *Translations from Prudentius*, London, 1890; and Eng. trans. and ed. H. J. Thomson, 2 vols., LCL, Cambridge, Mass.: Harvard University Press; London: William Heinemann, 1949, 1953.

Rutilius Namatianus. *De Reditu Suo*. Edited by C. H. Keene. Eng. trans. G. F. Savage-Armstrong. London: G. Bell & Sons, 1907.

Salvian of Marseilles, *De Gubernatione Dei*, ed. F. Pauly, CSEL 8, pp. 1–200, Vienna, 1883; *On the Government of God*, Eng. trans. E. M. Sanford, New York: Columbia University Press; London: Oxford University Press, 1930.

Sulpicius Severus, *Vita S. Martini* and *Chronicorum*, ed. C. Halm, CSEL 1, Vienna, 1866; *Vita S. Martini*, ed. and Fr. trans. J. Fontaine, SC 133–35, Paris, 1967–69.

Symmachus, *Opera*, ed. O. Seeck, *MGH* (A.A.), VI.1, Berlin, 1883, reprinted 1961; *Relations*, Eng. trans. by R. H. Barrow (ed.) in *Prefect and Emperor: The Relationes of Symmachus* A.D. 384, New York and London: Oxford University Press, 1973.

Zosimus, *Historia Nova* (bk. V), ed. L. Mendelssohn, Leipzig, 1887, reprinted Hildesheim, 1963; *Historia Nova: The Decline of Rome*, Eng. trans. J. J. Buchanan and H. T. Davis, San Antonio: Trinity University Press, 1967.

SECONDARY WORKS

Baynes, N. H. "The Political Ideas of St. Augustine's *De Civitate Dei*." In *Byzantine Studies, and Other Essays*, pp. 288–306. New York: John De Graff; London: University of London, Athlone Press, 1955.

Binns, J. W., ed. *Latin Literature of the Fourth Century*. Boston and London: Routledge & Kegan Paul, 1974.

Blasquez, J. M. "The Rejection and Assimilation of Roman Culture in Hispania During the Fourth and Fifth Centuries." Eng. trans. by D. A. Collins of paper presented in the *6th Congress of Classical Studies*, Held in Madrid, 1974, pp. 217–42. Bucharest and Paris, 1976.

Brown, P. R. L. "Christianity and Local Culture in Roman North Africa." *JRS* 58 (1968): 85–95.

Cameron, A. "Claudian." In *Latin Literature*, ed. Binns, pp. 134–59.

———. "Gratian's Repudiation of the Pontifical Robe." *JRS* 58 (1968): 96–99.

Chadwick, N. K. *Poetry and Letters in Early Christian Gaul*. Philadelphia: Albert Saifer; London: Bowes & Bowes, 1955.

Chaffin, C. E. "The Martyrs of the Val di Non." *SP* 10 = TU 107, pp. 263–69. Berlin, 1970.

Diesner, H. J. "Augustinus und die Barbaren der Völkerwanderung." *Revue des Études augustiniennes* 23 (1977): 83–91.

———. *Studien zur Gesellschaftslehre und sozialen Haltung Augustins*. Halle, Saale: M. Niemeyer, 1954.

Edden, Valerie. "Prudentius." In *Latin Literature*, ed. Binns, pp. 160–82.

Février, P. A. "Le développement urbain en Afrique du Nord." *Cahiers archéologiques* 14 (1964): 1–47.

Fontaine, J. "Société et Culture chrétienne sur l'aire circumpyrénéenne au siècle de Théodose." *Bulletin de Littérature ecclésiastique* (Toulouse) 4 (1974): 241–82.

Frend, W. H. C. "The Early Christian Church in Carthage." *Excavations at Carthage 1976, Conducted by the University of Michigan*, vol. III, ed. J. Humphrey, pp. 21–40, Published for ASOR, Ann Arbor, 1977.

———. "The Two Worlds of Paulinus of Nola." In *Latin Literature*, ed. Binns, chap. 4, pp. 100–133.

Girardet, K. "Trier 385: Der Prozess gegen die Priszillianer." *Chiron*, vol. 4, pp. 577–608. Munich: Verlag C. H. Beck, 1977.

Goetz, H. W. *Die Geschichtstheologie des Orosius*. Impulse der Forschung. Darmstadt: Wissenschaftliche Buchgesellschaft, 1980.

Green, R. P. H. "The Poetry of Paulinus of Nola, a Study of His Latinity." Collection Latomus, vol. 120. Brussels, 1971.

Guy, J. C. *Jean Cassien. Vie et doctrine spirituelle*. Paris, 1961.

Jones, A. H. M. *The Decline of the Ancient World*. New York: Holt, Rinehart & Winston; London: Longmans, Green & Co., 1966.

Lienhard, J. T. *Paulinus of Nola and Early Western Monasticism*. Theophaneia 28. Cologne: Hanstein, 1977. Good bibliography.

Marec, E. "Deux mosäiques d'Hippone." *Libyca* 1 (1953): 95–108.

Matthews, J. F. *Western Aristocracies*. See also the notable review article by P. Wormald, "The Decline of the Western Empire and the Survival of Its Aristocracy," *JRS* 66 (1976): 217–26.

Mazzarino, Santo. *End of Ancient World*. Esp. chap. 4, "The Judgments of God as an Historical Category," pp. 58–76.

Painter, K. S. "Villas and Christianity in Roman Britain." *British Museum Quarterly* 35 (1971): 156–71.

Palanque, J. R. "L'expansion chrétienne." Chap. 5 of vol. 3, *De la paix constantinienne*, ed. Labriolle, Bardy, and Palanque, of *Histoire de l'église*, ed. Fliche and Martin.

Paschoud, F. *Roma Aeterna*. Institut Suisse de Rome, 1967.

Pricoco, Salvatore. *L'Isola dei Santi; il cenobio di Lerino e le origini del monachesimo gallico*. Urbino: Instituto di Filologia classica, Università di Urbino, 1978.

Rousselle, A. "Du sanctuaire au thaumaturge, la guérison en Gaule au ive siècle." *Annales: Économies, Sociétés, Civilisations* 6 (1976): 1085–1107.

Ruggini, L. C. "Apoteosi e politica senatoria nel ive s.d.c: il dittico dei Symmachi al British Museum." *Rivista storica Italiana* 89, 3–4 (1977): 425–89.

———. "Il vescovo Cromazio en gli Ebrei di Aquileia." *Antichità Altoadriatiche* 12 (1977): 353–81.

Straub, J. "Christliche Geschichtsapologetik in der Krisis des römischen Reiches." *Historia* 1 (1950): 52–81.

Thompson, E. A. "Peasant Revolts in Later Roman Gaul and Spain." *Past and Present* 2 (1952). In *Studies in Ancient Society*, ed. M. I. Finley, chap. 14. Boston and London: Routledge & Kegan Paul, 1974.

Torti, G. "Patriae sua Gloria Christus: aspette della romanità cristiana di Prudenzio." *Instituto Lombardo—Accademia di Scienze et Lettere* 104 (1970): 337–68.

Varady, L. "Stilicho proditor arcani imperii," *Acta antiqua Academiae scientarum Hungaricae* 16, 1–4 (Budapest, 1968): 413–32.

Wheeler, R. E. M., and Wheeler, T. V., *Lydney Park*. Society of Antiquaries Research Papers 9. London: Oxford University Press, 1932.

NOTES

1. The Basilica Sancti Petri (III Region, *Sermon* 15); Basilica Gratiani (*Sermon* 156); Basilica Honoriana (*Sermon* 163); Basilica perpetua Restituta (*Sermons* 19, 29, 40, 112, and 277); and Basilica Novarum (*Breviculus collationis cum Donatistis* [*Summary of the Conference with the Donatists*] III.13.25). Carthage was probably

divided by this time into seven archidiaconal regions each with its church. See my "Early Church in Carthage."

2. Frend, "Early Church in Carthage," pp. 26–27. Its maximum dimensions were 65 × 45 meters.

3. Augustine, *Sermon* 359.9 (*PL* 39.1597), "basilica Florentia." The basilica of Cresonius at Cuicul could be of the same period, but see Février, "Le développement urbain," p. 18.

4. Augustine *Letters* LXVI.2 and CVIII.14 (Donatist use of an interpreter). Augustine himself always attempted to bridge the gap in his sermons, to enable all to understand them. See Brown, "Christianity and Local Culture," pp. 91–95.

5. Jerome *Commentary on Ezekiel* I, praefatio 3, "in una urbe totus mundus interiit," and cf. *Letters* 123.16 and 127.12.

6. See Jerome, *Letter* 128.4, *PL* 22.1099.

7. Jerome, *Letter* 128.4 and 5 (Jerome is writing about the education of Pacatula). See Dill, *Roman Society*, pp. 306–7.

8. Augustine *Sermon* 296.6 and *Letter* 138.10 ("our religion is accused as an enemy to the Republic"); and compare also the view of the pagan Volusianus in Augustine, *Letter* 136.2, "per christianos principes christianam religionem maxima ex parte servantes tanta . . . reipublica mala evenisse"; See Baynes's masterly, "Political Ideas," in *Byzantine Studies*, or *Historical Assoc. Pamphlet* 104 (London, 1936).

9. The quotation is from Augustine, *Sermon* CV.7.10 (*PL* 38, col. 623), preached in 410. Compare Augustine, *City of God* I.34 and IV.5, for the same sentiment.

10. Gibbon, *Decline and Fall*, chaps. 28–30; and see Momigliano, "Christianity and Decline of Roman Empire."

11. A. Piganiol, *L'Empire chrétien*, p. 422 (= *Histoire Générale*, IV.2 = *Histoire romaine*, ed. G. Glotz [Paris: Presses universitaires de France, 1947]).

12. Symmachus, *Oratio* 2.31–32, ed. Seeck, pp. 329–30. Note the optimism, even if wholly fallacious, of the orator's charge, "dicam senatui plebique Romanae: fasces in provincias novas mittite: trans Rhenum judices praeparate"—civil government for new trans-Rhenine provinces!

13. See Cameron, "Gratian's Repudiation."

14. Ambrose *Letter* XVII.10.

15. For the pagan case, see Symmachus, *Relatio* 3, ed. Seeck, pp. 280–83, and Barrow, ed., *Prefect and Emperor*, pp. 32–47. For Ambrose's reply, see *Letters* XVII and XVIII. See Glover, *Life and Letters,* pp. 153–56; Matthews, *Western Aristocracies*, pp. 205–10; and Paschoud, *Roma Aeterna*, pp. 75–79.

16. See Matthews, *Western Aristocracies*, chap. 4, especially concerning the "zealous evangelism" of some members of the Spanish aristocracy, not least those in Theodosius's entourage.

17. *Relatio* III.5.

18. Thus Volusianus cited by Augustine *Letter* 234.2; and *Letter* 16 (end), Maximus of Madaura to Augustine.

19. *Letter* XVII.13. "Licebit tibi ad ecclesiam convenire: sed illic non invenies sacerdotem aut invenies resistentem."

20. *Letter* XVIII.31.

21. What happened to the statue of Victory is less clear. It was restored under Eugenius, and Claudian, *Ôn Stilicho's Consulship* III, 202–4 and 212–13, and *Pan-*

egyric on the Sixth Consulship of Honorius, 597–98, suggest that it was still "in her temple" (the Senate house?) in 404.

22. I follow Baynes in thinking that while finance was important, tradition was even more so in the eyes of these aristocrats. See Baynes's review of J. A. McGeachy, "Quintus Aurelius Symmachus and the Senatorial Aristocracy of the West" (Ph.D. diss., University of Chicago, 1942), in *JRS* 36 (1946): 173–77, and in *Byzantine Studies*, pp. 361–66.

23. Theodosius was in Rome 13 June–30 August 389 (O. Seeck, *Regesten der Kaiser und Päpste* [Stuttgart, 1919; reprinted, 1964], pp. 275–79). For the collapse of the pagan majority in the Senate and numerous (six hundred!) conversions to Christianity among the senators and their families, see Prudentius *Contra Symmachum (Against Symmachus)* I.544–67.

24. Jerome *Letter* CVII.1. See P. R. L. Brown, "Aspects of the Christianisation of the Roman Aristocracy," *JRS* 51 (1961): 1–11, and in *Religion and Society*, pp. 161–83. Temples lay ruined; crowds thronged the tombs of the martyrs.

25. Eugenius was secretary to Arbogast, the Frankish praetorian prefect suspected of murdering Valentinian II. A Christian himself, he saw that if he was to survive against Theodosius he must base his authority on that of the Senate and Rome. For his alleged restoration of the altar and subsidies for the Vestals(?), see Paulinus *Life of Ambrose* XXVI, and for the temple at Ostia, see Paschoud, *Roma Aeterna*, p. 85, citing a "recently discovered inscription." Interestingly, Eugenius's forces fought Theodosius in 394 allegedly (Theodoret *Ecclesiastical History* V.25) under the banner of Hercules, a reminiscence perhaps of the god who had protected the Western members of the Tetrarchy a century before. Also, Rufinus *Ecclesiastical History* II.33 (Eugenius represented "paganism").

26. According to Zosimus *Historia Nova* IV.59.3; that this may be simply an echo of pagan senatorial propaganda is suggested by Paschoud, *Roma Aeterna*, pp. 83–85. But see *Codex Theodosianus* XVI.10.19 of 15 November 407 (or 408) which orders that supplies in kind (*annona*) belonging to the temples should henceforth be diverted for the benefit of the soldiers. Images should be smashed and temples put to public use. For the final flicker of the old religion in 408/9, see J. F. Matthews, "The Historical Setting of the 'Carmen contra Paganos,'" *Historia* 19 (1970): 464–79.

27. See Brown, "Aspects of Christianisation," in *JRS*, pp. 10–11.

28. Claudian, *Panegyric on the Third Consulship of Honorius*, line 153, "geminos dextra tu protege fratres." See Cameron, "Claudian," pp. 137–38. T. R. Glover's "Claudian," chap. 10 of *Life and Letters*, remains a valuable appreciation of Claudian.

29. *De Bello Gildonico (War Against Gildo)*, lines 14–16.

30. *Panegyric on Probinus and Olybrius*, lines 126–29.

31. *Panegyric on the Fourth Consulship of Honorius*, lines 619–22, ed. Platnauer.

32. For texts relating to Stilicho's victories over the Picts and Scots 396–400, see M. Miller, "Stilicho's Pictish War," *Britannia* 6 (1975): 141–46.

33. *On Stilicho's Consulship* II, line 204.

34. For instance, Augustine *De vera religione (Of True Religion)* IV.7 (*curiositas* as the parting of the ways between pagan and Christian Platonism). See P. R. L. Brown, *Augustine of Hippo: A Biography* (Berkeley and Los Angeles: University of California Press; London: Faber & Faber, 1967), pp. 134–35.

35. T. R. Glover's "Prudentius," chap. 11 of *Life and Letters*, remains the classic; and see also Paschoud, *Roma Aeterna*, pp. 222–33.

36. *Apotheosis*, lines 449–54, Eng. trans. Sir George Young, in Thackeray, trans., *Translations from Prudentius*.

37. Prudentius *Against Symmachus* II.816–19.

38. Ibid., I.31ff.

39. Ibid., I.461–69. Compare II.619–22.

40. Ibid., I.585–90, and note his hope put into the mouth of St. Laurence, that Christian Rome might be the supreme city in a Christian empire (*Peristephanon* [*On the Crowns of Victory*] II.413–84).

41. *Psychomachia* (*Fight for the Soul*) 470–79.

42. *Against Symmachus* II.1121–32, and for those more effective protests by the monk Telemachus, Theodoret *Ecclesiastical History* V.26.

43. *Crowns of Victory* X.926–60.

44. Ibid., VII.56ff.

45. Ibid., III.126ff. See Edden, "Prudentius."

46. *Crowns of Victory* I.4–6.

47. Augustine *Letter* L (Sufes), sixty Christians were killed; and *Letters* XC and XCI (Calama), "A crowd of dancers actually passed along the same street in front of the church doors. . . ." When the clergy protested they were stoned (XCI.8).

48. Optatus *De Schismate Donatistarum* I.13 (Calama a bishopric in 303).

49. Thus, Augustine *Sermon* CXCVI.4; and see Marec, "Deux mosäiques," and *Monuments chrétiens d'Hippone* (Paris: Ministère de l'Algérie, Sous-direction des Beaux Arts, 1958).

50. *Sermon* CCCII.19. Even so, many of the traditional ruling classes in the Numidian towns remained pagan and skeptical of the compatibility between culture and Christianity (Augustine *Psalmos* XXXIX.26).

51. Ambrose *Letter* II. See Palanque, "L'expansion chrétienne," pp. 473–76, and idem, *Saint Ambroise et l'empire romain* (Paris, 1933), pp. 314–17.

52. Vigilius, *Letter* I, *PL* 13.550, to Simplicianus of Milan. See Chaffin, "Martyrs of Val di Non," comparing Vigilius's account with that of Maximus of Turin.

53. Chaffin, "Martyrs of Val di Non," p. 266.

54. See A. Wotschinzky, "Archäologische Zeugnisse aus den ersten christlichen Jahrhunderten in Tirol," *Tiroler Heimatblatt* 1/3 (1965): 23–26.

55. On Martin's early career and possible acquisition of medical skills, see A. Rousselle, "Du sanctuaire au thaumaturge," pp. 1095–1100. Mlle. Rousselle places Martin's first contact with Hilary as early as 356.

56. Sulpicius Severus, *Vita S. Martini* X.3 (ed. Halm). Martin was, however, supported by the people of Tours and neighboring towns.

57. *Vita S. Martini* (*Life of St. Martin*) XIII.9.

58. Ibid., XIII.1–8.

59. See L. de Vesly, *Les Fana ou les petits temples gallo-romains de la région normande* (Paris, 1909), pp. 78 and 113; also Matthews, *Western Aristocracies*, pp. 156–59 (interesting details). For the establishment of parishes, see C. Jullien, *Histoire de la Gaule*, VII, 270.

60. Bede *Ecclesiastical History* III.4 (I find it difficult to credit the Frankish cult of Martin, which flourished in the sixth century, with the association of Ninian with Martin. In southeastern Britain this would be possible, but hardly north of the Wall). For discussion of the evidence for Carlisle being a bishopric and Ninian's

consecration and dispatch thence to an existent Christian community, see C. Thomas, *The Early Christian Archaeology of North Britain* (New York and London: Oxford University Press, 1971), pp. 13–22.

61. See Painter, "Villas and Christianity," and for Woodeaton, R. G. Goodchild and J. Kirk, "The Romano-Celtic Temple at Woodeaton," *Oxoniensia* 19 (1954): 36; and for Lydney, see Wheeler and Wheeler, *Lydney Park*, pp. 30–33, though unstratified coins on the site include seventeen of Arcadius (383–408).

62. Such as the continued celebration of New Year's Day in Barcelona with processions in animal masks, or the instance given by Gregory of Tours (c. 586) of the experience of St. Nicetius. When a storm threatened to overwhelm a boat he was on, the passengers immediately began to invoke Jupiter, Mercury, and Juno! (*De Sancto Nicetio*, MGH SS. Rer. Meroving. I, p. 732).

63. Siricius *Letter* I.3, *PL* 13.1131, to Himerius citing Himerius's claim. Our knowledge of rural Christianity in Spain would seem to start with the Council of Saragossa in 380.

64. The discovery of two "early Christian churches" was reported in the Sardinian press of 28 August 1978. Excavations were still proceeding.

65. G. W. Meates, *Lullingstone Roman Villa* (London: William Heinemann, 1955), chaps. 12–14. Mérida in southeastern Spain provides another example.

66. Paulinus of Nola *Letter* XXXII: two basilicas and a baptistery built in the village c. 402.

67. Paulinus, especially *Carmina* XVIII and XIX, trans. Walsh, ACW 35 and 36.

68. *City of God* XXII.8.

69. Bede *Ecclesiastical History* I.7.

70. See Wormald, "Decline of Western Empire," p. 220, reviewing Matthews's *Western Aristocracies*.

71. Ambrose, c. 385, for instance, regards the duty of "the perfect soul" not as "flight from the earth, but remaining on earth and clinging to justice and sobriety," *De Isaac* 3.6 (CSEL 32.645 [Leipzig: G. Freytag, 1896]) but he also encouraged Christian women to the ascetic vocation. For a study of the problem, see R. A. Markus, "*Alienatio:* Philosophy and Eschatology in the Development of the Augustinian Idea," *SP* 9 = TU 94 (Berlin, 1966): 431–50.

72. See for instance, Paulinus, *Carmen* XXXI, lines 601ff., and compare Prudentius *Crowns of Victory* III, lines 196–215.

73. See H. Chadwick, *Priscillian of Avila*, as the best study of Priscillian; it is, however, weak on the historical origins and environment of the movement.

74. Sulpicius Severus *Chronicle of the World* II.46.

75. H. Chadwick, *Priscillian of Avila*, p. vii.

76. *Illustrious Men*, 121, and for Marcus as an "Egyptian," see *Commentary on Isaiah* XVII.64 (*PL* 24.647). Also Sulpicius Severus *Chronicle* II.46. See also H. Chadwick's discussion, *Priscillian of Avila*, pp. 21–22.

77. Priscillian(?), *Würzburg Tract* II, ed. Schepss, p. 34.

78. Ibid., I, p. 28, line 26. See H. Chadwick, *Priscillian of Avila*, p. 8.

79. See Fontaine, "Société et Culture chrétienne."

80. Sulpicius Severus, *Chronicorum* II.50.2 (ed. Halm, p. 103).

81. Ibid., II.48.3.

82. Sulpicius Severus *Chronicle* II.50.8, and compare H. Chadwick, *Priscillian of Avila*, p. 143: "The primary charge on which the prefect Euodius found Priscil-

lian guilty was that of sorcery." Also, A. Rousselle, "Quelques aspects de l'affaire priscillianiste," *Rev. des Etudes anciennes* 83 (1981): 85–96.

83. On Maximus's justification and the reactions to the case, see Girardet, "Trier 385," pp. 594–95, on Maximus's correspondence with Siricius (= *Collectio Avellana* 40).

84. See Augustine, *Letter* XX (ed. Divjak).

85. See H. Chadwick, *Priscillian of Avila*, pp. 166ff.

86. Ibid., pp. 232–33.

87. See my "Two Worlds of Paulinus."

88. Ibid., pp. 106–7. A group of six poems (*Carmina* IV–IX) shows Paulinus to be profoundly Christian in outlook but still enjoying the pleasures of the countryside on his wife's estates. For the papal view that administrative responsibility was incompatible with Christian commitment, see Siricius *Letters* V.2 and VI.1, and Innocent *Letters* II.2 (to Victricius of Rouen), and VI.11.

89. *Carmen* VII, lines 1–6.

90. *Carmen* XVI, Felix's miraculous escape from his pursuers (lines 155–92).

91. *Letter* V.4 and compare *Letter* LI.2, "ab istius mundi strepitu profugam."

92. *Carmen* X, lines 165–68 = Ausonius *Letter* XXXI. Compare Paulinus *Letter* XXV to Crispinianus for the same view.

93. Thus, *Letter* XVIII.7 to Victricius, and *Letter* VIII.3 to Licentius, and *Letter* XXXIX (Aper and Amanda).

94. His regime is well described by N. K. Chadwick, *Poetry and Letters*, pp. 72–73.

95. Thirty-three surviving poems, including thirteen written for the saint's *natalicia* between 395–407, commemorate Felix.

96. *Carmen* 28.61ff., Frend, "Two Worlds of Paulinus," pp. 121–22. Paulinus stresses the amenity aspect of his action!

97. *Carmen* XXI.758ff. Paulinus tells the townsfolk of Nola to set about repairing a long-abandoned aqueduct!

98. *Carmen* XXI.25–36; and compare *Carmen* XXVI.425–27, where the aid of Felix is invoked to keep the war "far from our territories."

99. *Apology* 38.3. See above, pp. 419, 435 n. 171.

100. Thus *Letter* LX.51: "Quid memorem Romanos duces quorum virtutes quasi quibusdam stellis latinae micant historiae."

101. Above, p. 563.

102. *Vita Malchi monachi captivi* I, *PL* 23.55.

103. *Letter* VII.5. See Kelly, *Jerome*, p. 31. I think Kelly, by accepting 331 as the date of Jerome's birth, consistently makes him too old a man—and thus not truly credible.

104. Zacchaeus, *The Discussions Between Zacchaeus and Apollonius* III.3, *PL* 20.1151.

105. Jerome, *Letter* XXII.13 and 38.

106. Ibid., XXII.30.

107. See below, p. 747.

108. Note Jerome's self-revealing remark: "Now in my fear of hell I had consigned myself to this prison . . ." (*Letter* XXII.7).

109. Ibid., XVII.2, "de cavernis cellularum damnamus orbem."

110. Ibid., XV.3. See Kelly, *Jerome*, chap. 6.

111. *Letter* CVIII.26 (*PL* 22, col. 902).
112. Jerome, *De perpetua virginitate B. Mariae, adversus Helvidium* 5, *PL* 23.197, and compare *Letter* XXII.38 (ed. Wright, p. 146). See Kelly, *Jerome*, pp. 104–6.
113. *Letter* XXI.13 (*PL* 22, col. 386).
114. Ibid., XLV.2–4.
115. See Kelly, *Jerome*, pp. 180–87, on Jovinian's views.
116. See above, p. 716.
117. *Adversus Jovinianum* (*Against Jovinian*) II.7 (*PL* 23, col. 310).
118. See Kelly, *Jerome*, pp. 288–90.
119. See Hilary of Arles, *Vita S. Honorati*, ed. Valentin, introduction, pp. 20ff.
120. *Vita S. Honorati* (*Life of St. Honoratus*) XVII.3, "Omnes undique ad illum (Honoratum) certatim confluebant."
121. Regarding Castor, see O. Chadwick, *John Cassian* (2d ed., New York and Cambridge: Cambridge University Press, 1968), pp. 37ff.
122. For Cassian's career, see O. Chadwick, *John Cassian*, pp. 9ff.
123. Cassian *Institutes* VIII.16–19; and compare *Conferences* XXIV.8.3. See O. Chadwick, *John Cassian*, pp. 53.
124. See O. Chadwick, *John Cassian*, p. 77. Jerome shows that virgins were in the habit of praying during the night as well as at dawn (*Letter* XXII.37). The fixed hours of prayer were "common knowledge." For the origins of Laudes and Prime, see remarks by J. Brou in *JTS* 48 (1947): 240–41.
125. See O. Chadwick, *John Cassian*, chap. 3, on "The Journey of the Soul."
126. O. Chadwick, *John Cassian*, 162.
127. *De Reditu Suo*, ed. Keene, I, lines 443–44.
128. See C. Courtois, "L'evolution du monachisme en Gaule," in *Il Monachismo nell' alt medievo e la formazione della civilta occidentale* (Spoleto: Centro Italiano di Studi sull' alto medioevo IV, 1957), pp. 42–73.
129. See Ruggini, "Il vescovo Cromazio." Alaric had penetrated northeastern Italy in the autumn of 401.
130. *Sermo* 85.2, ed. A. Mutzenbacher, CCSL 23 (Brepols, 1962), p. 348.
131. Theodosius besought the aid of John the Baptist in his campaigns against Eugenius (Sozomen *Ecclesiastical History* VII.24), and consulted an Egyptian hermit before attacking Magnus Maximus (Augustine *City of God* V.26). Others less skillful were more superstitious. Note Claudian's well-known epigram addressed to the *Dux* Jacobus (cited from Glover, *Life and Letters*, p. 241):

> So the saints from the Alps the invaders repel,
> So Susanna the chaste lend her forces as well,
> So Thomas be with you instead of a shield,
> So Bartholomew go as your squire to the field,
> So whoever shall win the chill Danube to fight,
> Like the horses of Pharoah be lost to your sight.
>
> ....
>
> So your hand ne'er be stained by the blood of a foe,
> Those verses, Duke Jacob, I pray you let go.

132. Paulinus *Letter* V.
133. Paulinus *Carmen* XX.388ff. (straying cow); and XIX.375ff. (fat pig).

134. The point is well made by H. J. Diesner, *Der Untergang der römischen Herrschaft in Nordafrika* (Weimar: Böhlan, 1964), pp. 94ff.

135. One opinion may be quoted, that of H. G. Pflaum, regarding the inscriptions from Castellum Celtianum in the territory of the Numidian capital Cirta, "La romanisation des districts ruraux de la confédération cirtéene n'a jamais été profonde et malgré leur onomastique en apparence si romaine les habitants de *Castellum Celtianum* sont restés Berbères comme avant. . . ." H. G. Pflaum, "Castellum Celtianum," *Carnuntina* (Graz and Cologne, 1956), pp. 126–45, esp. p. 145.

136. C. D. Drew and K. C. C. Selby, "Colliton Park Excavations I," *Proceedings of the Dorset Natural History and Archaeological Society* 59 (1937): 5–14 (a fine large house that eventually degenerated into a squatter's slum c. 390).

137. Y. Allais, *Djemila* (Paris: Société d'Edition "Les Belles-Lettres," 1938), p. 45 and plates.

138. Augustine *Letters* XCII and XCIX. See Marec, "Deux mosäiques," and Février, "Le développement urbain," p. 23.

139. Illustrated in Susan Raven, *Rome in Africa* (New York: M. Evans & Co., 1969), pp. 128, 129.

140. Augustine, *Psalmos* 33.14, *PL* 36.316, "lectis eburneis"; and compare *Sermon* XVI.2 and LI.4.5, and *Psalmos* 48.8.

141. *Psalmos* CXXIV.7, *PL* 37.1653: "Quantum debent divites Christo, qui illis composuit domum."

142. *Tractatus in Joannis evangelium* (*Homily on the Gospel of John*) VI.25, and see above, p. 558.

143. Canon 49 of Council of 397, Mansi, *Sacrorum Conciliorum* III.892, and E. Munier, *Concilia Africae*, CCSL 149 (1973), p. 341. For the scenes at Hippo when Augustine's congregation thought that Pinianus, one of the richest landowners in the empire, would become a presbyter there, see Augustine *Letters* CXXIV, CXXV, CXXVI.

144. Augustine claimed, *Letter* CXXVI, 8 and 9, that the oversight of such administration was nothing but a burden to him.

145. Possidius *Vita Augustini* (*Life of Augustine*) XXIII.

146. Note Augustine's early efforts to win the support of local landowners, *Letters* 33, 34, 35, and 58; and after 405, see *Letters* 89, 112, 139. See. P. R. L. Brown, "Religious Coercion in the Later Roman Empire, the Case of North Africa," in *Religion and Society*, pp. 301–31.

147. On Romanianus, see Augustine *Contra Academicos* (*Against the Academics*) II.2.3.

148. Augustine *Letters* 247 and 251.

149. *Novellae* XII and XIII; *Novel* XII is dated 19 October 443; and *Novel* XIII, 21 June 445. For the crushing character of debt in North Africa at this time, see *Novel* XII.1, Mommsen and Meyer, p. 94.

150. Salvian, *Government of God* VII.16, ed. Sanford, p. 211, referring to Africa; and see IV.4 and 5 for a similar situation in southern Gaul.

151. See Thompson, "Peasant Revolts."

152. *Letter* 185.4.15; Augustine, *Works*, ed. and Eng. trans. Marcus Dods, 15 vols. (Edinburgh: T. & T. Clark, 1872–1934), vol. 3, pp. 491–92. See Frend, *Donatist Church*, pp. 73–74.

153. See bibliography relating to chapter 19, p. 685.

154. *Sermon* 345.1, *PL* 39, col. 1517. "Isti soli vivunt," and compare *Psalmos* 32.17, 38.8, and 39.7.

155. *Enarrationes in Psalmos* CXXIV.7, *PL* 37.1653–54.

156. *Letter* CVIII.18 (ed. Al. Goldbacher, CSEL 34.2 [Leipzig: G. Freytag, 1898], p. 632.

157. Orosius, *Against Pagans* VII.25 (ed. Zangemeister, p. 488).

158. *De Gubernatione Dei* (*On the Government of God*) V.5.20.

159. Claudian *In Rufinum* (*Against Rufinus*) lines 189–95. Rufinus himself was a Westerner, a "Celt."

160. Jerome, *Preface to the Commentary on Titus* (*PL* 26, col. 590).

161. Ausonius *Letter* XXVII.115–16, Ausonius weeping for "a realm rent in pieces between a hundred owners."

162. *Crowns of Victory*, Hymn II, 73–92.

163. Jerome *Contra Vigilantium* (*Against Vigilantius*) XIII and XIV.

164. Augustine *Letter* XLVI.1 (ed. Goldbacher, p. 123).

165. *Letter* CCXXV and cf. *Letter* CXCIX.

166. See Blasquez, "Rejection and Assimilation of Roman Culture in Hispania."

167. In Ausonius *Letter* XXXI.214–15, and 219–20, "gens barbara ritus."

168. Thus, Victor Vitensis, *Historia persecutionis africanae provinciae,* ed. M. Petschenig, CSEL 7, I.7, and see my comments in "The Divjak Letters: New Light on St. Augustine's Problems, 416–428," *JEH* 34.4 (1983).

169. *Against Pagans,* ed. Zangemeister, praef. 10.

170. *Against Pagans* VI.22.

171. Ibid., VII.41.7.

172. Ibid., 43.5–6.

173. Ibid., 33.19. For Spanish resistance to Rome, see V.4.

174. And also Gallic resistance to Rome; see ibid., VI.12.7, excusing lack of Gallic resistance to the Visigoths. The Romans had beaten the Gauls so badly!

175. Paulinus of Milan *Vita S. Ambrosii* (*Life of St. Ambrose*) XXXVI.

176. Paulinus of Nola *Letter* XVIII.4.

177. Paulinus of Nola *Carmen* XVII.206–8.

178. *Contra Julianum* I.13, *PL* 44.648.

179. *Constitutio Valentiniani* I.3 = Leo *Letter* XI, see "Valentinian III on the Roman Primacy and on Hilary of Arles, 445," in *Creeds, Councils and Controversies,* ed. Stevenson, pp. 303–4. Note that "the rank of the city" is added to "Apostolic authority" by Valentinian as a justification for the pope's status.

180. *Sermon* III.3 (Stevenson, *Creeds, Councils and Controversies,* p. 305).

181. See H. Eider, "Ausgrabungen im spätantiken Trier," in *Neue Ausgrabungen in Deutschland,* ed. W. Kramer (Berlin, 1965), pp. 359–63 (I owe this reference to Mr. Christopher Green).

182. Orientius *Commonitorium* (ed. R. Ellis, CSEL 16, p. 234) II.184, "Uno fumavit Gallia tota rogo."

183. His description (*Government of God* VII.14) of the whole territory of Africa as "one house of vice," and similarly, 15.

21

The Road
to Chalcedon
398–451

The division of the empire between the sons of Theodosius proved to be religious as well as political. In the previous twenty years, though relations were soured by the continuance of the Antiochene schism, and despite differences of language and conflicting views of authority, the churches in East and West had seemed to be moving toward better mutual understanding. Basil's embassies to Rome during the 370s are evidence for a desire on the part of Eastern church leaders to find common ground with the West. Basil's homilies on poverty and monasticism were received enthusiastically by Ambrose, and the latter's introduction of allegorical interpretation of Scripture into his sermons also indicated his implicit admiration for Eastern theology. Origen's works were becoming increasingly well known and were being translated by Rufinus, alternately friend and enemy of Jerome. For Jerome himself, Origen (c. 384) was "a teacher second only to Paul." "No one," he declaimed, "had laboured more [than Origen] with incomparable eloquence and knowledge . . . which, when once he had opened his lips, made others seem dumb."[1] His reward had been jealousy and unjust condemnation by Bishop Demetrius backed by Rome. Jerome had also translated Eusebius's *Chronicle* and brought it up to date; while in Africa, Alypius of Thagaste asked Paulinus of Nola to find him a copy.[2] Bridges were being built, and despite all that was to happen in the first decade of the new century, Egyptian monasticism as interpreted by John Cassian was to remain a lasting legacy from Eastern Christendom to the West.

Unfortunately, the rapprochement was not to last. By 395 discussion of Origen's many-sided views had become confused with Jerome's personal quarrels and with squabbles among Egyptian monks. Jerome must take opposite sides over Origen's orthodoxy to that of his adversary John, bishop of Jerusalem. Added to this, in 394 Jerome found an ally in Epiphanius of Salamis (367–404), a Jewish farmer turned Christian and thence to become the greatest heresy-hunter of the patristic age. Jerome's admiration for Origen soured. He declared his doctrines were "poisonous." "No, he had never been an Origenist."[3] Once again, at a crucial moment events conspired to prevent a cross-fertilization between Eastern and Western theologies. More powerful factors driving East and West further apart reasserted themselves. "The Greek classics, I abominated. Not one word did I understand."[4] If Augustine felt this way about the East, its literature, and its language, would lesser men, even Paulinus of Nola, think otherwise?

Western attitudes, however, hardly worried the East. Though in 410 the government of Theodosius II (408–50) sent troops to reinforce the garrison of Ravenna against a possible attack by Alaric,[5] sympathies between the two halves of the empire tended to be lukewarm. There were manifestations of good will as in 437 when the Western emperor, Valentinian III (425–55) came to Constantinople to marry Licinia Eudoxia, daughter of

Theodosius II. There were periods of strain that marked the long-drawn-out quarrel over the control of the see of Thessalonica (400–425), and in 449–50, after Pope Leo's legates were brutally affronted by Archbishop Dioscorus at the Second Council of Ephesus (the so-called Latrocinium or Robber Council). Such incidents, however, could have been included' among otherwise normal relations between two independent states served by their own churches. Apart from Gaiseric's capture of Rome in 455, when the seizure of Licinia Eudoxia and her daughter flouted the dignity of the imperial court, the disasters befalling the West caused hardly a ripple.[6] At Constantinople increasingly complex questions of theology, combined with ecclesiastical and urban rivalries, occupied the emperor and his advisers. The climax of the patristic age concerned the interlocking problem of doctrine and authority involving the great sees of Christendom. Among these, Rome still spoke with the power associated with the see of Peter, but from a position increasingly removed from the center of events.

THE SURVIVAL OF THE EAST ROMAN PROVINCES

In 395 few would have foretold that while the Western provinces of the empire would be the scene of irreversible changes, those in the East would be entering on a long period of relative stability and well-being. Ostensibly, the East shared the same perils as the West, and in addition lacked the shrewd and steadfast, if also ambitious, leadership of Stilicho. Arcadius's chief minister, Flavius Rufinus, was cruel and venal. His displacement even by the eunuch Eutropius in 398 was hardly regretted. In Constantinople itself, there were the same feuds between the Roman "nationalists" and the barbarian soldiers and their leaders in imperial service, as existed in the West, and hatred of the barbarians was fanned by the orthodox Christian leadership. The Gothic commanders Gainas and Tribigild found their bid to imitate Stilicho (399–401) ruthlessly suppressed with the aid of the populace of the capital.[7] Politically these events marked a turning point in the fortunes of the Eastern provinces. In the last resort the people showed that they would not be dominated by Arian Gothic generals. While the combination of enemies threatening the existence of the empire was every whit as dangerous as that in the West, the situation held. Huns, Persians, Berbers in Cyrenaica, and Blemmyes in southern Egypt wrought havoc but failed to win decisive successes. The Long Wall across the isthmus on which Constantinople stood—completed in 413 by the prefect Anthemius—protected the capital itself.[8] Subsidies, themselves evidence for the relative prosperity of the East, bought off the Huns at strategic moments, but in the last resort it was the will of the Eastern provincials that assured their survival. Their morale outweighed even the military inefficiency of their leaders.

In the fifth century, therefore, the Eastern empire survived because, in contrast to the West, the great majority of its people wished it to do so. The tradition of valiant and spontaneous resistance to the barbarians born of a sense of innate superiority, such as the Athenians under Dexippus (c. 260s) showed against the Heruli, was continued in the Christian empire.[9] Far from being crushed by the onset of the Visigothic invasions in 378, the citizens of Constantinople clamored for arms to defend their city against the enemy.[10] In the 440s, their example was followed by the Balkan peoples who harassed the invading Huns unmercifully and defended their cities against them.[11] Individual acts of treachery there were, but those, though described dispassionately by Byzantine historians, were nonetheless condemned. Few preferred barbarian to Byzantine rule. Synesius, bishop of Cyrene (c. 410), saw destructive barbarian invasions in his province as a serious disturbance in an otherwise relatively carefree existence. Though in c. 412 "everything appeared to be balanced on a razor's edge"[12] he had no doubt that with God's help disaster would be averted. Peace was the normal condition of affairs even in the first decade of the fifth century.[13]

The other condition of normality was orthodox Christianity. The church was now an established profession; some of the major sees employed hundreds of staff. At Edessa in the 440s there were more than two hundred clergy. At Alexandria, Cyril could call on six hundred *parabalani* (technically, hospital attendants) for strong-arm assistance against his opponents, and there were revenues to match.[14] At the same time, the Theodosian dictatorship that aimed at establishing the Catholic church-state to the exclusion of paganism and heresy had not been unpopular. For some Christians in both town and countryside, the emperor's antipagan measures provided a pretext to pay off old scores against the former pagan ruling classes. Few acts better consolidated the power of Archbishop Theophilus in Alexandria and the alliance of his see with the monks than the destruction of the Serapeum in Alexandria in 391.[15] The hegemony of the pagan intellectual aristocracy in the city was ended, a fact brutally emphasized by the unpunished murder in 415 of Hypatia, the Neo-Platonist philosopher. The "city of the orthodox" would never shrink from violence to further its cause.

In Phoenicia and Syria also, the last two decades of the fourth century witnessed forceful action by monks overthrowing pagan shrines and seizing temple lands for themselves on the grounds that the land was "sacred"— and hence belonged to the church.[16] John Chrysostom also used the Syrian monks to combat paganism in the 380s, while the bishop of Apamea employed gladiators for the same purpose. He found martyrdom (Sozomen *Ecclesiastical History* VII.15) but his cause was well on its way to victory. Soon after the end of the century even Gaza, a pagan stronghold, finally submitted to Christianity. It fell to a campaign involving successive miracles combined with an imperial order to close all the city's shrines and a fortunate collapse of the temple of Aphrodite.[17] In July 399 the government of Arcadius administered a *coup de grace* in issuing a short but unambiguous order that, without exception but without tumult, rural temples should be destroyed.[18] Henceforth in the East, "Roman" was to be identified with "orthodox Christian." Religion and patriotism were welded into an unbreakable alliance that was to last as long as Byzantium, indeed as long as "Holy Russia" lasted.[19]

What constituted "orthodox Christianity"? This was the question that dominated East Roman politics and theology in the first half of the fifth century and beyond. Serenity in the face of the external enemy could be maintained. Solidarity between provincials in the various disparate provinces of the empire could be achieved. Continuity with the past was accepted as part of the empire's heritage, but this consensus eluded the efforts of successive emperors. Even so, despite the strains to which it was subjected in the great religious crises of the period, the empire did not collapse amid an upsurge of separatist religious and social movements as did its counterpart in the West.

Solidarity rested on two bases. First, there was a loyalty to the person and mystique of the emperor, the visible symbol of the Christian state. Second, the monks and holy men formed the essential link that bound all classes together, despite every type of social tension and injustice, in a realm believed somehow to be a dim reflection of the divine polity. In touch with the unseen world they exactly fitted this belief.

The East never accepted the Two Cities theory of human society nor its corollary, the Two Swords theory of the relations between church and state. At all levels, Byzantine society consolidated around the person of the emperor. The Cappadocians, for instance, while strongly critical of the emperor Valens's Arianizing policy, had no doubt that the emperors had been entrusted by God with sovereignty over the world, and like stars, filled the world with the light of peace and piety.[20] In moments of enthusiasm, Theodosius II or Marcian would be hailed by Eastern bishops as "priest" as well as ruler.[21] Though all were made aware through the bronze coinage that the safety of the state depended on the military prowess of its leader fighting under the symbol of Christ, the emperor was revered for other qualities. To the remaining pagans and Christians alike he was "the true philosopher" representing in himself the traditional qualities of the ruler—prudence, justice, and mercy as well as temperance and courage. Sozomen, a lay historian, addressing his *Ecclesiastical History* to Theodosius II, wrote:

> You are therefore humane and gentle, both to your neighbours and to all mankind, imitating your Protector the Heavenly Emperor, since he loves to send rain on the just and the unjust and furnishes other things ungrudgingly.[22]

And again:

> But you, O most powerful [emperor], gathering in all the virtues, you have excelled everyone in piety, love of humanity [*philanthropia*] courage, temper-

ance and greatness of mind [*megalopsychia*] proper to the imperial dignity. Eternity will boast of your government because it is less tainted with blood or murder than all the reigns of your predecessors.[23]

Arcadius was feeble by ordinary standards, but he was remembered with affection as a founder of monasteries and orphanages.[24] Theodosius II was dominated by his more forceful sister, Pulcheria, and swayed by a succession of court chamberlains, of whom the eunuch Chrysaphius (d. 450) was the most notorious; but he also had diplomatic skill and a feel for public opinion. He survived the crises of the first half of the fifth century only to die by falling from his horse after a reign of forty-two years. Behind that success may have been his sympathies for the nonaristocratic classes in his empire—the craftsworkers and merchants—and above all his understanding of the monks. Whereas the Western ecclesiastics would dissuade the able from accepting administrative responsibilities for fear of contaminating themselves with bloodshed,[25] the Easterners praised Theodosius (and his council) for having softened the effects of government by his wise and temperate administration. In this Christ-oriented society the emperor was God's vice-gerent and "imitator of the Heavenly Emperor,"[26] leading his subjects to both material and spiritual salvation. In return, he could expect loyalty from them, and he received it. One example, when in April 449, at the climax of the christological controversies, when the East was riven with discord over the alleged survival of Nestorian teaching among some of the leading Syrian bishops, the imperial commissioner Thomas Chareas visited Edessa, he was met with astonishing demonstrations of support for the emperor: "Long live the Roman Empire," "Multiply the victories of Theodosius," "One God, Victory to the Romans." Though the shouts were also directed against Ibas, the bishop of Edessa who was suspected of Nestorianism, the loyalty was unmistakable, and Edessa itself had once been a Parthian stronghold. The stress on "One God" indicated that what was to become the Monophysite cause would also be loyal. "One God" and "One Empire" ran together in the minds of Eastern Christians.[27] And "one faith," if this could be defined.

Eastern monasticism was also a consolidating force that turned popular feeling toward the emperor. Without the monks, loyalty would have been difficult if not impossible to sustain in the face of the gross abuse in taxation, oppression by patrons, moneylenders, and soldiers, and threats from brigands and external enemies that the Eastern provincials suffered. At the beginning of the fifth century, however, the monks were a major factor in the life of the Eastern provinces both in town and countryside alike, including the capital.[28] One must be wary of statistics, but Rufinus's estimate of ten thousand monks in the monasteries and twenty thousand virgins in and around Oxyrhynchus c. 390,[29] and Jerome's claim that "nearly fifty thousand monks" took part in the annual convention of Pachomian monasteries, indicate that they were very numerous.[30] In Oxyrhynchus monks occupied abandoned temples and public buildings—another symptom of the change that had come over society with the "triumph of Christianity." They had simply taken over the city. In Syria and Palestine colonies of monks were also growing up. In Palestine they were associated increasingly with holy places along the pilgrim routes.[31] In Constantinople the 380s saw the foundation of the first of the great monasteries that in the next century were to exercise such influence on the religious life of the city.[32]

Apart from concern with their own individual salvation the monks filled the role of divinely inspired tribunes of the people. As holy men in direct contact with unseen angelic powers they could administer justice whose honesty seemed to be guaranteed by God himself. Simeon Stylites (d. 459) and his contemporaries arbitrated in disputes between villages, rebuked extortionate landowners, proved wills, and above all, forwarded petitions to the emperor.[33] Thus, a villager who had a grievance would be able to bypass the ordinary processes of law, which might be venal and expensive as well as dilatory, and through a holy man place his or her trouble before the emperor himself. This facility provided the East with a safety valve which the West did not possess. Coupled with their hatred of the idolatrous heathen invader, whether Persian or Blemmye, the monk for all his disdain for the world he had left was loyal to the empire. He was ready even to guard the defenses of the frontier fortresses in emergencies.

Hostile to paganism in all its manifestations though they were, the monks or their more articulate representatives regarded themselves as "true philosophers."[34] This was readily conceded to them. They had reached the heights of humanity's endeavor in the long ascent toward imitation of the divine. The attainment of the "citizenship of Jerusalem" was a positive aim contrasting with the more negative "avoidance of sin" that motivated much of the Western ascetic's withdrawal from the world. The title of "philosopher" indicates, too, a continuity with the past; links, whether conscious or not, with the aims of the Neo-Platonists. Compare, too, the outlook of Basil of Caesarea toward pagan literature with that of his Western contemporary Jerome. Jerome felt guilty every time he thought of Cicero and censured clergy for reading anything but the Scriptures. Basil's *Address to Young Men* (c. 370), addressed to his nephews, rejected the idea that Christian education should be confined to Christian writings, or that pagan works should always be avoided.[35] Every author who benefited the character should be read. Pagan and Christian philosophy had their points of contact and the pagan should be studied by the young as a mirror through which they could appreciate the true philosophy of Christianity.[36] Basil was following in the footsteps of Clement and Origen, but also laying the foundation for Byzantine education for centuries to come.

A generation later, Synesius (c. 370–413) lived out the same experience. He was a Platonist, a member of the local aristocracy settled around the old

Greek city of Cyrene in Cyrenaica. In 399 he represented his city on an embassy to Constantinople to protest against extortionate taxes. He exhorted the "dull, and heavy-eyed, and bovine" Arcadius to live for the people's good, rid himself of pomp and circumstance, and listen to others besides courtiers. "Let none but the Romans serve in the army. Turn out the Goths and make them slaves."[37] This was not mere chauvinistic bombast. Back in Cyrenaica, Synesius inspired the defense of Cyrene against the Berbers, despite his brother's plea that defense should be left to soldiers. When peace returned, he divided his time, he said, between work and prayer. His inspiration was the philosophy of Hypatia, the Alexandrian genius of Neo-Platonism until she was foully murdered by a Christian mob in 415.[38] Synesius had been dead for two years by then, having meantime become a Christian and bishop of Ptolemais on the Cyrenaican coast in 409. How he made the transition is not certain. Partly, it may have been due to his Alexandrian Christian wife, partly to experiences in Constantinople and in particular his impression of John Chrysostom, but mainly, to follow T. R. Glover, to his sense of solidarity with the provincials he found himself leading and representing.[39] He was acclaimed bishop of Ptolemais by the inhabitants. In a letter to his brother he makes it clear that he was not changing his views for the sake of the position:

> For my part, I can never persuade myself that the soul is of more recent origin than the body. Never would I admit that the world and the parts that make it up must perish. The resurrection, which is an object of common belief, is nothing for me but something sacred and ineffable, and I am far from sharing the views of the common crowd about it.
>
> If I am called to the episcopate I declare before God and man that I refuse to preach dogmas in which I do not believe.[40]

Thus he had insisted to Theophilus, archbishop of Alexandria (d. 412), and to his lasting credit this otherwise unpleasant ecclesiastic had accepted him. The Neo-Platonist philosopher had moved almost imperceptibly into the role of Christian bishop and leader of his community.

Eastern Christianity was associated with continuity, in the awe attached to the imperial majesty, in artistic expression,[41] in literature, philosophy, and political theory, as well as with many of the religious ideals of the past. All this contributed to the strength of the Eastern provinces of the empire in face of mounting external threat in the first half of the fifth century.

Consensus, on the other hand, could not be won. At no time during the christological controversies, however, did the emperor lose control of the situation. Theodosius II believed that the welfare of the empire depended on its orthodox belief and worship. It was his duty to see that these were observed by all. He and his successor Marcian summoned the great ecclesiastical councils and they or their chief officers presided over them. After Ephesus I, Theodosius threatened the feuding archbishops of Alexandria and Antioch with punishment if they failed to compose their differences; and the Formula of Reunion (433) resulted. At Chalcedon in 451, Marcian's officials told the bishops that a place must be found for the *Tome* of Leo in the proposed Definition of Faith and when it was finally drafted Marcian himself pronounced it.[42] For all the controversies that embittered relations between the great sees, their incumbents were outspokenly loyal to the person of the emperor. Nothing threatened the stability of the empire itself or its monarchy. Provincial separatism was far from the mind even of Dioscorus.

The stories of John Chrysostom and Theophilus of Alexandria, of Cyril and Nestorius, of Flavian of Constantinople and the archimandrite Eutyches, of Dioscorus, and Leo have passed into legend. Here we content ourselves with such details as bear on our main themes. The tragic episcopate of John Chrysostom (398–404) opens the struggle for supremacy in the East waged between Constantinople and Alexandria, foreshadowing the ultimate division between Chalcedonian and Monophysite in Eastern Christendom.

JOHN CHRYSOSTOM AT CONSTANTINOPLE 398–404

John we have seen as the presbyter at Antioch who calmed the congregations during the terrible days of 387 when the fate of the city itself hung in the balance.[43] Born c. 347, the son of a military commander, he was brought up a Christian by his mother but carried the self-assurance of his status throughout his life. He despised the Goths, even the Catholics among them.[44] He was harsh toward heretics and Jews. His denunciation of the latter as "deicides" forms one of the links in the ugly chain of early Christian anti-Semitism.[45] At the same time, he shares with the emperor Julian the distinction of being one of the few prominent men in the fourth century who understood something of the plight of the majority of the provincials who lived on the land. He sympathized with their sufferings though his remedies went no further than to prick the consciences of the rich to provide ever more alms for relief.

One example of his analysis, given in the twelfth *Homily on Timothy,* may be quoted.[46] John begins with a dialogue between himself and some more or less imaginary wealthy man. The latter quotes Abraham and Job as Old Testament examples of how righteousness could be combined with riches. John replies, "Yes, but their wealth was God-given. It came from natural increase and not injustice." As R. M. Grant points out, John's was a rural not an urban ideal. Like his contemporary Libanius, he brought the case of the peasants to the notice of the emperor, and unlike Libanius he had the means of working upon influential Christian congregations as well. He turns to the rich man. "Tell me, where did your wealth come from? From whom?" "My grandfather and my father," was the reply. "Would you be able to go back in your family," retorts John, "and show that the acquisition was just? No, you could not. The beginning, the source must be someone's injustice. From the beginning did God make one rich and another poor? Did he guide one and show him many treasures of gold, but deprive the other of the search? No, he provided the same earth for all. Since it was common property, how is it that you have so many acres, while your neighbor has not a spoonful of earth?''

Christian political theory, looking back to an original community of goods, was pushed no further, and no more than his contemporaries did John assail either property rights in themselves or slavery.[47] He was an idealist hoping for greatly increased charitable funds to be placed in the church's hands and for these to be used to even out excessive differences between the rich and poor, but with all that he remained haughty and condescending toward the latter. His *Homily on 1 Timothy* was preached probably shortly after his arrival in the capital, and it was his twelfth on this book. He was far too talkative. "Too great a latitude of speech,"[48] commented the not-unsympathetic historian Socrates a generation later. The eighteen volumes of his tracts and discourses published in Migne's *Patrologia Latino-Graeca* speak for themselves. There were Saturday and Sunday homilies and additional sermons on saints' days and during Lent. He was always preaching and exhorting and his assertiveness and quick fire of rhetorical questions could hardly have won him friends. Added to this he was tactless toward colleagues. Visiting bishops were not entertained as they thought they ought to be. One muttered, "I will cook a dish for him," as he left in disgust.[49] Too much promotion was given to monks. The court came to reject his denunciations of frivolity and luxury, and were annoyed at allusions to "Jezebel" (the empress Eudoxia) and other biblical miscreants.[50] Perhaps the empress had connived at the murder of the eunuch Eutropius in 399 from whom she had benefited. John could have been more careful.

The archbishop's difficulties, however, arose from a different quarter. Constantinople had aroused jealousy at its sudden rise to secular and ecclesiastical preeminence. Intellectuals from Asia Minor still regarded it as "too Latin."[51] During Nectarius's rule, however, it had gradually extended its influence over the metropolitans of the province of Thrace and those of Asia Minor. Through the emergence of a standing council of bishops in the capital—the Home Synod—it was becoming a magnet for appeals from other sees. The first recorded meeting of the Home Synod in May 400 was concerned with "seven articles of grievance" against Antoninus, bishop of Ephesus. John was particularly angered at a charge of massive corruption leveled against the latter, and determined to investigate on the spot. By the time he reached Ephesus, however, Antoninus had died, and John, holding a council of seventy bishops from the provinces of Asia, Lydia, and Caria, consecrated a new bishop in his stead, and then deposed six bishops for simony.[52] Before returning to the capital he carried out a mission against

Novatianists and Quartodecimans in Phrygia. All this may have been done with the best of motives, but John was establishing a precedent for intervening in the provinces of Asia and consecrating the chief bishop of the area, whose claim to archiepiscopal status was as good as, or (in terms of apostolic foundation) better than his own. The enmity of the see of Ephesus throughout the fifth century was to cost the archbishops of Constantinople dear.

Toward the end of 401 came the affair that was to embroil John with Archbishop Theophilus of Alexandria. A number of monks from Nitria arrived in the capital, complaining that they had been persecuted as Origenists by Theophilus. Immediately, issues of precedence and jurisdiction arose, and associated with these was a question of doctrine. John was at a disadvantage, for both Pope Anastasius (399–401) and Jerome had condemned Origenism.[53] The "Tall Brothers," however, impressed the imperial court. It was agreed that their complaints should be heard by the praetorian prefects (another example of lay jurisdiction over church affairs in the East), while Theophilus himself was to be summoned to explain his conduct before John. It is difficult not to sympathize with Theophilus's exasperation, first torn one way or another by rival arguments for or against Origen's teaching, and now ordered to the capital to defend his actions against insubordinate Egyptian monks. Meantime, however, John's position strengthened through the failure in 402 of Epiphanius of Salamis, who appeared in the capital, to press charges of Origenism on him. When Theophilus arrived at last in June 403, he still could not be sure of vindicating himself.

By this time, however, John's enemies were out to bring him down. Theophilus established himself on the Asiatic side of the Bosporus in what was technically Bithynia and therefore outside John's immediate jurisdiction. He came, said John's biographer, with a train of Egyptian bishops and strong-arm monks and with bribes—"like a beetle laden with dung."[54] He found an ally in the metropolitan Paul, exarch of Heraclea, whose see had been superior to Constantinople while the latter was still Byzantium and was jealous of its rise to eminence. So in a villa known as the Oak, belonging to the former prefect Rufinus, a synod of thirty-six bishops, presided over by Paul but led on by Theophilus, condemned John on a number of disciplinary charges ranging from maladministration and stinginess to off-the-cuff utterances about individual clerics (July 403). In this case, the people of the capital had their say. They rallied to John. Another synod of sixty bishops quashed the findings of the Synod of the Oak[55] and Theophilus retired uncondemned himself, but unable to fulfill his boast to "depose John."

"My church remained faithful to me," John pronounced to an excited people on his return to Constantinople. "What was done to Abraham has now been done to me. There was the Egyptian then, there is the Egyptian now. Then he had his servant, now he has his protector. Pharaoh has desired to take [the church] from me, as he of old had taken Sara. But once more Sara has remained pure: the adulterers are put to confusion."[56] Two months later (October 403) he was in trouble again. A statue of the empress was inaugurated outside the church of St. Sophia amid boisterous scenes. Once more the "Golden Tongue" wagged. Once more John denounced Eudoxia in biblical terms. It was as Herodias this time. This breach was irreparable and finally, on 9 June 404, Arcadius signed an order banishing John. He died in exile in September 407.

John's failure tells us something about the structure of the church in the East Roman provinces. There was no single ecclesiastical center of authority. The major sees were expected to work together in harmony. When that broke down, recourse had to be made to a council, whose decision could be quashed by another at which more bishops were present. (Thus, canon 12 of the Council of Antioch in 341.) Eventually, if there was no consensus, the emperor had to decide where right lay. John's position was in no way parallel to Ambrose's at Milan. He might protest the theoretical superiority of the priestly over the imperial office,[57] but in practice he had no option but to obey the emperor's command. His popularity, his saintly character, and the support of the see of Antioch made no difference. There was no threat of uprising on his behalf such as Valentinian II and Justina had encountered when Ambrose was ordered into exile. Nothing shows more clearly the differences between Eastern and Western attitudes toward the empire than the contrasting fates of Ambrose and John Chrysostom.

In 406 Arcadius appointed Atticus, an opponent of John, as archbishop.[58] The peace which lasted throughout his twenty years' episcopate is important. Theophilus died in 412, to be succeeded by his nephew, Cyril (412–44), but neither made any further attempt to embarrass the church in the capital. Atticus went out of his way to conciliate Cyril.[59] The Alexandrians accepted the principle of consensus in ecclesiastical affairs like other Eastern bishops. The great conflict between Cyril and Nestorius, though concerned with profound doctrinal differences, was also set off by the tactless utterances of the archbishop of the capital and his apparent rejection of teaching which Cyril of Alexandria had been affirming as self-evident for years.

NESTORIUS AND CYRIL 428–31

Atticus's death in 426 was followed by two years of uncertainty. His successor Sisinnius died after little more than a year in office. Subsequent disputes in the church at Constantinople were cut short by Theodosius II's appointment of Nestorius, another presbyter from Antioch, as archbishop on 10 April 428.

Nestorius was a disciple of Theodore of Mopsuestia (d. 428) and this time the Antiochene background was crucial. We have seen[60] how by the end of the fourth century discussions regarding the person of Christ, arising out of the Arian controversy, had been moving along two divergent paths. Apollinaris and his many able and articulate supporters maintained that Christ must have been free from even the possibility of taint from matter if he were to redeem humanity. "If the nature of the blood of the crucified only Son had been the same nature as the blood of the sons of Adam, how could it have expiated the sins of the sons of Adam?"[61] Barsumas, the powerful Syrian monk (*flor.* 440–50), spoke for many in the East. On the other hand, the exact opposite could be argued, as it had been both by the Cappadocian fathers and the rising school of Antioch. Christ, as second Adam, must possess the fullness of human nature in order to redeem it. The argument went back as far as Irenaeus. Christ's humanity, including his will, must be as real as his divinity. There was one person—the Antiochenes used the term *prosopon,* indicating the outward appearance of an individual—but two natures, each nature being complete and personal. Thus argued Theodore of Mopsuestia, but he qualified the duality, "when we are thinking of their union, then there is in Christ but one person and one Son."[62]

Cyril had been archbishop of Alexandria for sixteen years, since 412, when Nestorius was appointed to Constantinople. Much can be said against him. Complicity in Hypatia's murder, meanness toward the memory of John Chrysostom, outrageous treatment of Nestorius at the Council of Ephesus, all this is true, and he was as unscrupulous as his uncle had been in his use of bribes to gain his ends. His Antiochene opponents had some justification in wishing that a heavy stone would be placed over his grave to prevent any return of his spirit to earth![63] But with all that, he had a theological sensitivity far beyond that of his opponents. He knew how to express the deep christological beliefs of the majority of Greek-speaking Christians. At the height of Cyril's conflict with Nestorius in 431, his doctrines won fervent popular support in Ephesus as well as in Alexandria.[64] In the next century they inspired martyrs. With Origen and the Cappadocians, Cyril shares the distinction of molding a whole tradition of Greek Christianity whether Orthodox or Monophysite. In his native Egypt, Coptics and Alexandrians alike looked back to him as the true champion of orthodoxy.

Cyril was a dedicated follower of Athanasius. As he himself said, "we follow in all respects the opinions of the holy fathers, but especially those of our blessed and all-renowned father, Athanasius."[65] Indeed, part of the ambivalence of his theology may be due to his unwitting acceptance of some Apollinarian forgeries, notably the *Letter to the Emperor Jovian,* as genuine because they had been put under the name of Athanasius. Like Athanasius, he believed in the full humanity of Christ, within the limitations imposed on that belief by the Word-Flesh (*logos-sarx*) theology.[66] The "flesh" assumed by the Word was man with a soul and a mind. The Word, however, always remained constant. The "nature," therefore, of Christ was always God. "Man" was regarded as representative of humanity, the second Adam, not a particular perfect individual, even the man Jesus of Nazareth. What happened at the incarnation was that, while continuing eternally as God, the Word took on "the form of a servant" (Phil. 2:7) by assuming a body "making the flesh his own by way of dispensation."[67] The single nature of the Word was now "the Word [become] flesh" (John 1:14), but in taking flesh, the Word "remained as he was before."[68] Hence, not surprisingly, Cyril could adopt as his own the Apollinarian formula of "one nature, and that incarnate of the Divine Word."

For him, Christ was in every way "one and unique." In attempting to reconcile this view with the New Testament narrative of Jesus' upbringing, ministry, suffering, and death, Cyril asserted that Christ "voluntarily" came under the law according to the condition of human nature and submitted himself to suffering and death. This self-emptying (*kenosis*) of the Godhead played an essential part in his teaching, and enabled him to assert the fullness of Christ's humanity without accepting that Christ possessed a human nature distinct from the divine.[69]

The Antiochenes disagreed.[70] Like their predecessors, whether heretical or orthodox, Diodore of Tarsus and Theodore of Mopsuestia distinguished in Christ the Son of God from the son of David. The latter was inhabited by the former. The body was the temple (cf. John 2:21) for the Word. Just as man though created "in the image of God" was and would remain part of the created order, so the human nature of Christ remained human. It could be joined to the divine but never fused with it to make "one nature" in the sense affirmed by Cyril. "There is a great difference" argued Theodore, "between us and God: and we ought not to overlook this difference when we are thinking of the divine nature [of Christ] and the works done by him."[71] To redeem humanity the Word assumed a man (not "man" or "humanity" as claimed by Cyril), "perfect man of the seed of Abraham and David." "The name [Jesus Christ] is that of the man whom God put on."[72] On the cross he suffered by will and not by necessity. He saved, through his example, the "great pioneer" (Heb. 12:2) and overthrower of death, as Nestorius was to claim.[73] The difference in understanding the nature of Christ as second Adam was the crucial stumbling block in the way of agreement between the two Christologies.

The possibility of crisis had been recognized at least in Alexandria in the decade before Nestorius arrived in Constantinople. Since 421 Cyril had been denouncing Antiochene theology and defining his own position based on what he believed Athanasius had taught.[74] He soon appreciated the danger of Theodore's disciple becoming the new archbishop in the capital. Like John Chrysostom before him, Nestorius was loquacious and tactless, but also limited as a theologian, and to this extent responsible for his own downfall. As the contemporary historian Socrates described him, he was "disgracefully illiterate," and causing needless alarm by his "extreme ignorance."[75] In fact, he was primarily a pastor and preacher, and neither

754

knew nor probably cared about any school of theology except the Antiochene. These qualities brought him trouble within days of his arrival. "Give me, O emperor, the earth purged of heretics, and I will give you heaven as a recompense. Assist me in destroying heretics and I will assist you in vanquishing the Persians."[76] Fine words, until the ordinary people realized it was the Arians he meant to destroy. These, despite the condemnation of their views in 381, had continued to be respected citizens, and when he fired their chapel and the flames spread to other buildings, objections were not slow in coming. Nestorius "the fire-raiser" had made a bad start in his primatial city.[77]

Worse was to follow. The Virgin Mary had not figured largely in fourth-century Christian art, but birth narratives exalting her, such as the *Protevangelium of James*, a Gnostic composition, had won their place in popular Christian belief. For the masses in Constantinople as in Alexandria she was "God-bearer" (*Theotokos*), and was beginning to assume her place among the hierarchy of heavenly protectors of their cities that would be hers before many years were passed. In addition, as Socrates pointed out, Mary had been called *Theotokos* by both Origen and Eusebius of Caesarea, and no one had objected.[78] For Nestorius, however, the term *Theotokos* was pagan and blasphemous. As his chaplain (*syncellus*) told a congregation in the capital on 22 November 428, the Virgin gave birth to the man Jesus, not to the divine Word.[79] The most Nestorius would concede was that she was Christ-bearer (*Christotokos*). He considered that in any event the term conflicted with the text of Heb. 7:3 (Melchizedek "without father or mother or genealogy"). His congregation was scandalized and protested. Controversy started, and by the spring of 429 news of Nestorius's preaching had reached Cyril in Alexandria.

Cyril's first letter to Nestorius (June 429) was complaining and unconciliatory, but all he asked was for Nestorius to "acknowledge the one word *Theotokos.*"[80] At this stage he was being obliged to prove the scriptural warrant for the term to his own monks.[81] No doubt he recoiled from a breach with Nestorius. The latter did not budge, however, but during 429 rendered his position more exposed by his generous hospitality to Pelagian exiles, including Julian of Eclanum. This could not fail to embroil him with Pope Celestine.

It was not until February 430 that Cyril wrote again. Once more, as in John Chrysostom's time, the pretext was disciplinary. The previous year monks appealed to Constantinople against his tyrannical conduct, and Cyril scented danger. As his predecessors had been, he was sensitive about his position at court. Alexandrians had complained to Nestorius about him without justification, he said. This peg, however, enabled him to elaborate his Christology in masterly style.[82] Basing himself on the words of the Creed of Nicaea, he asks Nestorius to consider what was meant when it was confessed that God "was incarnate and was made man."

755

For [he goes on] we do not affirm that the nature of the Word underwent a change and became flesh, or that it was transformed into a complete human being consisting of soul and body; but rather this, that the Word, having in an ineffable and inconceivable manner essentially (καθ᾽ ὑπόστασιν) [*kath' hypostasin*] united to himself flesh animated with living soul, became man and was called Son of Man, yet not of mere will or favour, nor again by the simple assumption to himself of a human person, and that while the natures which were brought together into this true unity were diverse there was of both one Christ and Son: not as though the diverseness of the natures were done away by this union, but rather Godhead and Manhood completed for us the one Lord and Christ and Son by their unutterable and unspeakable concurrence into unity.[83]

The challenge to the structure of Antiochene Christology was clear, as well as the Apollinarian-type phraseology. Cyril denied that the one Son preached by Nestorius implied the transformation of the Word into a perfect man, Jesus Christ. Jesus and the Word were not joined together as two entities forming a union. This was to suggest the existence of "two sons." The Word becoming flesh showed that he took his flesh from the Virgin, and the Virgin was therefore rightly called *Theotokos*.

Cyril sent his letter to Celestine with a Latin translation. Celestine, irked by Nestorius's reception of the Pelagians, and annoyed still further when he received a letter from Nestorius addressed to him as "fellow-minister," with no honorific titles, took Cyril's side. In this he was also following advice given to him by his agents in the capital. On 11 August 430 he wrote to Cyril, delegating him to represent himself in proceedings against Nestorius. "Tell him that he will not be able to retain our communion if he continues in his way of error, opposing apostolic teaching."[84] He also wrote to Nestorius ordering him to retract his teaching publicly within ten days or be excommunicated.[85]

Cyril was in no such hurry, and it was he and not Celestine who called the tune. Through the early autumn he sought allies in Juvenal of Jerusalem (422–58) who now takes his bow on the stage of ecclesiastical politics, and John of Antioch (428–41) who was aghast at Cyril's report of Nestorius's teaching. He wrote to Nestorius, "Ten days! A single day, or a few hours is enough." There was ample precedent for the term *Theotokos*,[86] but he had not seen Cyril's second letter and evidently believed Nestorius was being obstinate; he did not realize the wider implications of Cyril's move and he saw no threat to himself or his see, and he thought Cyril was right about *Theotokos*. Cyril was now in the strongest position he ever achieved. Had he been a moderate individual, he could have vindicated the term *Theotokos* and increased the authority of his see as the guarantor of orthodoxy in the East without a crisis. In November he was still holding back. In that month, armed with the authority of his own episcopal council at Alexandria, he made a last appeal to Nestorius. In many ways the third letter to

Nestorius is the most revealing of Cyril's writings.[87] Gone was the bluster of previous letters. Cyril wrote from his heart. From the words of the Creed of Nicaea which he quoted in full, he deduced that the only-begotten Word of God, true God of true God, "of his condescension emptied himself, and became incarnate and was made man," being truly born of the Virgin assumed flesh from her.[88] This did not involve abandonment of the Godhead nor the change of flesh into Godhead (that is, Apollinarianism). Instead, we confess "the essential [*kath' hypostasin*] union of Word with the flesh, we worship one Son and Lord, Jesus Christ, neither sundering man and God. . . ." "Unity of dignity," or authority, or honor, or conjunction (*synapheia* = συνάφεια) all involved the juxtaposition of different natures and were inadequate to express that union.[89]

Then Cyril moved to the core of his personal religion, the Eucharist.[90] Christ "being as God life-giving by nature, when he became one with his own flesh he made that flesh life-giving." He goes on, "through the bloodless sacrifice of the Eucharist we are being made the partakers of the holy flesh and precious blood of Christ, the Saviour of us all."[91] Hence, as he had always maintained, only the most fundamental union between Godhead and manhood could endow human flesh with the divine power so as to guarantee its invincibility against the powers of death. Humanity's salvation, to become divine, required a Savior whose total divinity could not be in doubt. "To one Person, therefore," Cyril concluded, "must be attributed all the expressions used in the Gospels, the one incarnate individuality [*hypostasis*] of the Word, for the Lord Jesus Christ is one according to the Scriptures."[92]

Cyril should have stopped there. The remaining passage about Christ's high priesthood and the role of the Spirit added little to the force of his argument. It is more than doubtful whether John of Antioch would have accepted so thorough a critique of Antiochene terminology, and especially the assertion of the "one incarnate hypostasis of the Word" which was Apollinarian in origin. The Twelve Propositions (*Anathemas*) which Cyril appended to his letter, however, and to which he demanded Nestorius's assent were deliberately provocative.[93] They pushed Alexandrian theology into Apollinarianism and, in so doing, deprived Cyril of his claim to speak for Christendom itself against Nestorius. In these *Anathemas* Cyril showed himself as much an extremist as his opponent. Was it really a matter of anathema (*Anathema IV*) "if anyone distributes to Two Persons [*prosopa*] or Subsistencies [*hypostaseis*] the expressions used in the Gospels and Epistles . . . attributing some to a man conceived of separately apart from the Word, which is of God, and attributing others as befitting god, exclusively to the Word"? Stripped of the caricature, this was precisely how Western theologians, notably Ambrose, had interpreted the gospels in their efforts to refute Arianism. It was to form the basis for Pope Leo's argument in the *Tome* in favor of the acknowledgment of Christ "in two

757

natures." In addition to insisting (*Anathema* XII) on the confession that "the Word of God suffered in the flesh and was crucified in the flesh," though corresponding to what the majority of Eastern Christians believed, it tended to reduce Christ to an abstraction and to deprive the New Testament account of his life and teaching of any historical meaning. Such could not be the creed of Christendom.[94]

The Antiochenes were at last aroused to the danger to their own Christology and belatedly rallied to Nestorius. In a very short time Nestorius and Theodoret of Cyrrhus had composed twelve *Counter-Anathemas*.[95] The human nature of Christ did involve a distinct human personality; Jesus Christ was "a man," not merely representative man, though inseparably connected with the Word. The "hypostatic union," however, was denied. Though the language of the antagonists often approached each other and Theodoret was prepared to accept the term *Theotokos* as orthodox, their basic ideas remained poles apart. And now, confronted with the threat of schism involving Constantinople and Antioch on the one hand, and Rome and Alexandria on the other, Theodosius intervened. Already on 19 November he convened a general council to meet at Ephesus by Pentecost 431.[96] It was to be presided over by Count Candidian, commander of the imperial bodyguard, who would represent the emperor himself. His task was to maintain order and see that justice was done, but not to intervene in doctrinal debates.

Council of Ephesus I

If the opposing sides seem to have been evenly matched, a closer look would reveal that nearly all the advantages lay with Cyril. For two centuries the see of Alexandria had been indisputably the focus and leader of Christianity in the Nile Valley and in Cyrenaica. Opposition from the Cyrenaicans, strong and articulate in the late third century, had faded after the Council of Nicaea. To his contemporaries, the archbishop of Alexandria had stepped into the position once held by the Pharaohs. There was reality in this assessment. Cyril disposed not only power but formidable wealth drawn from tithes and a monopoly of the linen trade, once the prerogative of the priests of Serapis who wore linen vestments. He could count on the loyalty of his suffragans, armies of monks, and the lay brethren (*parabalani*)—now recruited to a strength of up to six hundred. Whatever their violence, monks were surrounded by the mystique derived from Antony and Pachomius. The trump card of papal support could be played in the last resort. With that in hand, Cyril could not have been in danger.

Antioch, in contrast, formed no such center of unity. In theory, with 127 bishops and 11 metropolitans the "mother see of the East" was far more powerful than Alexandria. In fact, this was far from true. The regional differences between the territories that made up John's area of jurisdiction

THE ROAD TO CHALCEDON 398–451

were as real now as they had been in the past. Theologically, its bishops had vacillated in the fourth century between Eustathius whose views were recognizably akin to those of Paul of Samosata, through the Origenism of Leontius (344–57) and Eudoxius (357–60), to the New Nicene position of Meletius, and then finally to the ultimately pro-Nestorian sympathies of John. But John could not rely on the unanimous support of his bishops. Succensus of Diocaesarea in Isauria and Acacius of Melitene were openly Cyrillians, and would be joined later by the important bishop Rabbula of Edessa. Antioch's vast expanse of territory proved a disadvantage. At the time of Ephesus its jurisdiction coincided with that of the Diocese of the East (see map E), but this involved its archbishops attempting to assert their authority over churches in five separate areas with little community of identity or even language. The predominantly Greek cities of Isauria, Cilicia, and Syria formed the intellectual heart of the archdiocese, but there was no unity of outlook. Apollinarius himself had been bishop of Laodicea on the Syrian coast. He and his contemporary Diodore of Tarsus had represented different theological worlds. To the east lay Osrhoene with Edessa and Mesopotamia, and across the Persian frontier there were Christians whose language and culture was Aramaic but who still looked to the "West," that is, Antioch, for leadership. These Eastern churches were tending to favor Nestorius. To the south, however, lay Phoenicia and Palestine, already under the rising authority of the church of Jerusalem with its Holy Places and its monasteries. These latter in particular were inclined to support Alexandrian Christology. Cyprus was self-consciously independent.

Even without Cyril this conglomeration was in danger of falling apart. There is no need, however, to regard the Persian synod of 424, presided over by the Catholicos Mar Dadiso, as a parting in anger between Antioch and the Persian Christians. The decision not to allow complaints against the Catholicos to be taken to "the western patriarch" probably did no more than reflect the fact that the church in Persia valued its "millet" status vis-à-vis the Persian monarchy and wanted to be seen to be independent of Roman influence and governed by its own supreme head, the "Catholicus of all Eastern Christendom."[97] The same council thanked the "West" warmly for its previous help. Less friendly were Antioch's relations with Cyprus and Jerusalem. Cyprus was claiming a separate status. It resented the authority of Antioch, even if that had been supported by Pope Innocent.[98] At Ephesus, Evagrius, a Cypriot bishop, would denounce John of Antioch as one who wished "to subjugate our island and secure the prerogative of ordaining our bishops contrary to canon and custom."[99] Religious particularism was not confined to the West and Cyprus could be expected to support Cyril. Even more so, Jerusalem. Since 422 its bishop had been Juvenal, and whatever he may have thought about the rights and wrongs of

Cyril's Christology he was determined to secure archiepiscopal status for Jerusalem.[100] That put him firmly in Cyril's camp against his nominal superior at Antioch.

Constantinople had similar difficulties. We have seen how in 403 both Heraclea and Ephesus threw in their lot with Theophilus against John Chrysostom.[101] In 431, Memnon of Ephesus was determined to challenge Nestorius's control over ordinations in the provinces of Asia Minor, and at the council he and his forty suffragans were among Cyril's firmest supporters.

Even so, the christological issue was all-important, but here too Cyril spoke for the majority. His support included much of the populace in Constantinople, as well as educated laymen, such as Eusebius the lawyer from Dorylaeum, who denounced Nestorius as a heretic who held similar views to Paul of Samosata. Nestorius's downfall therefore was not due primarily to the support Cyril received from his Egyptian bishops and monks or even from Juvenal of Jerusalem, nor from sundry malcontents, but the alienation of a great majority of bishops from Asia Minor, brought up in the same Platonic/Christian tradition of the Cappadocian fathers, led by Memnon of Ephesus. These swayed the decision in Cyril's favor and thereby temporarily raised the see of Alexandria to a position of preeminence in Christendom.

Whatever may have been the emperor's plans, on 22 June Cyril was able to assemble, preside over, and control a council of two hundred bishops drawn mainly from Asia Minor. Nestorius had no possible chance. On the crucial question of whether his or Cyril's teaching accorded with that of the Council of Nicaea, Cyril had the advantage. A letter received from Nestorius was considered not to do so. By the evening he had been condemned as "the new Judas," declared deposed on account of his impious sermons and disobedience to the canons, and deprived of all priestly status.[102] Cyril himself had run the proceedings from start to finish and reduced Count Candidian to a cipher.[103] There were torchlight processions and dancing in the streets of Ephesus that night, as Cyril wrote an account of events to his congregation at Alexandria, and told how the *Theotokos* had been vindicated and villains such as Nestorius had been brought low[104]—and so, if he had paused to consider, had been the authority of the emperor.

The rest was a slow anticlimax. John of Antioch arrived four days later and immediately held a rival assembly of forty-three bishops in his lodgings with Count Candidian in attendance. It declared Memnon and Cyril deposed unless and until they repudiated the twelve *Anathemas*. On 10 July the papal legates landed at Ephesus to add their weight to Cyril's cause. The initiative now lay with Cyril's partisans, and these had no intention of allowing the legates to take it from them. Pleasure was expressed that Celestine was "one with the synod" and "a guardian of orthodoxy";[105]

little notice was taken of them or their pronouncement that "Peter lived in his successors and exercised judgement in them."[106] Nonetheless it swung the advantage once more to Cyril, and John of Antioch and his supporters were excommunicated.

The last word, however, rested with the emperor. His eventual solution would probably have come about without Cyril's massive bribes at the imperial court.[107] Nestorius was replaced by Maximian, a prelate far more favorable to Cyril, the latter's twelve *Anathemas* were not accepted, and steps were taken to bridge the gulf between him and his colleague at Antioch. From now on these archbishops of the four great sees—Rome, Constantinople, Alexandria, Antioch—would be known as patriarchs, a status denied for the time being, however, to Juvenal. Cyprus achieved its autocephalous status (canon 8). As a final though almost accidental act before the council broke up, it was decreed that "no one should present or compose or frame a creed different from that of Nicaea."[108] This was the touchstone of orthodoxy, literally spoken by the Holy Spirit, thus declared the bishops.

THE FORMULA OF REUNION 433

Ephesus expressed "the belief of the whole world,"[109] so the majority of the bishops proclaimed. Though it had been Cyril's council, the next years showed how thoroughly Theodosius understood and controlled the religious situation in the East. Despite great bitterness between the Antiochene and Alexandrian bishops, the court maneuvered steadily toward a position whereby Antioch would accept Nestorius's deposition and the orthodoxy of the term *Theotokos*, while Alexandria would drop the twelve *Anathemas* and agree to a common formula of faith. A timely threat that John and Cyril would both be kept under surveillance at Nicomedia speeded up negotiations. By April 433 John's emissary Paul, bishop of Emesa, was able to report success, and Cyril's relieved and even exultant "Let the heavens rejoice" (*Laetentur caeli*) spelled out the terms of agreement.[110] The Creed of Nicaea was indeed a sufficient statement of faith, but a supplementary declaration might be in order so as to "bar the way against those who wish to attack us." (Cyril never believed well of anybody!) Thus it was affirmed that Jesus Christ,

> the only-begotten Son of God, perfect God and perfect Man, consisting of a rational soul and a body begotten of the Father before the ages as touching his Godhead, the same, in the last days, for us and for our salvation, born of the Virgin Mary as touching his Manhood; . . . For out of two natures a union has been made. For this cause we confess one Christ, one Son, one Lord.
>
> In accordance with this sense of the unconfused union, we confess the holy Virgin to be *Theotokos*, because God the Word became incarnate and was made man, and from the very conception united to himself the temple taken from her. And as to the expressions concerning the Lord in the Gospels and

Epistles, we are aware that theologians understand some as common as relating to one Person, and others they distinguish, as relating to two natures, explaining those that befit the divine nature according to the Godhead of Christ, and those of a humbler sort according to his Manhood.[111]

Cyril had every right to quote Eph. 2:14 (the dividing wall of hostility has broken down),[112] for the Formula of Reunion was a very considerable achievement. For two centuries, Antiochene and Alexandrian Christologies had been developing, when not in isolation, amid mutual suspicion. The results, we have seen, were two different understandings of the Person of Christ, whose representatives regarded each other with horror and loathing; "hatchers of serpents' eggs" had been the last Antiochene comment on Cyril and his supporters.[113] But on deep consideration by both parties, urged on by the court, just sufficient ground for agreement emerged. If Christ indeed was One, and yet composed of "rational soul and body," he must be "out of two natures," for the "rationality" of the soul and body in itself involved "recognition of its own subsistence and nature." Cyril was prepared to acknowledge that in the act of mystic contemplation (*theoria*) the natures might be distinguished,[114] yet at the same time, the union remained unconfused and the Son was always one and the same. And, while the Antiochenes as a whole were now prepared to accept *Theotokos* as an orthodox term rather more generously than had Theodoret three years before, they gained their point by stressing the scriptural warrant for acknowledging the two natures of Christ and distinguishing between them.

The Formula of Reunion was to form the basis for the Chalcedonian Definition eighteen years later. Both patriarchs had gone as far as could possibly be expected in order to find a settlement. They had succeeded without noticeable Western help. Sixtus III's comment to John of Antioch, "You have learnt by the outcome of this affair what it means to be like-minded with us," came from the sidelines.[115] Not surprisingly, both John and Cyril were attacked violently by many of their supporters. Yet the agreement stood. In 439 the historian Socrates closed his *Ecclesiastical History* with a remarkable statement:

> In such a flourishing condition were the affairs of the Church at this time. But here we shall close our history, praying that the Churches everywhere with the cities and the nations may live in peace: for so long as peace continues, those who desire to write histories will find no materials for their purpose.[116]

Peace and prosperity reigned in Theodosius's dominions. It was the year in which Carthage fell to the Vandals and the Visigoths tightened significantly their control of southern Gaul.

THE INTERLUDE 433–46

For more than a decade there was relative peace. Huns might threaten in the Balkans, but the city of Constantinople was a pleasant place for its residents. Lovers of sedition had chosen to be quiet. Nestorius, far away in exile, had been forgotten. Cyril failed to gain any further advantages at Antioch's expense. Other combatants of Ephesus were leaving the scene. John of Antioch died in 441. To audible sighs of relief, Cyril died in 444; Pope Sixtus gave way to Leo in 440, and Proclus who had succeeded Maximian in 434 himself died in 446.

Apart from maintaining harmony with his fellow patriarchs, one momentous achievement may be credited to Proclus. Since Jovian's disastrous treaty with Persia in 363, the Armenians had battled hard to maintain a semblance of independence. Persian Christianity, with which they maintained strong links, favored Antioch. The leaders of the Armenian church, such as Mesrob (d. 440) one of the initiators of an Armenian-Christian script, followed Antioch's lead, and Mesrob admired Theodore of Mopsuestia profoundly.[117] Then, just as Antiochene theology seemed to be gaining complete dominance, Nestorius was deposed and the Antiochene position became vulnerable. Cyril's supporters in Syria redoubled their efforts to wean the Armenians from "the Jewish heresy." In 436 the Armenians decided to approach Constantinople. Proclus found himself in the position of arbitrator, and his *Tome to the Armenians*, dispatched in 437, became one of the foundation statements of belief for the Armenian church from that time on. Proclus had opposed Nestorius's theology during the latter's episcopate. He was a Cyrillist by conviction and he wrote a straightforward summary of Cyril's Christology. Christ as Word of God became true man without passing through human experience (*apatheia*), taking on himself the form of a servant but remaining as he was, without addition or change. The Word was not united "with a perfect man" but "became flesh by having descended into the nature itself" and underwent human experiences voluntarily. "We confess the incarnation of the divine Word, one of the Trinity," affirmed Proclus. Union was not the union of opposites, and as the Word took on flesh to repay the debt of humanity's sin, so the Word incarnate suffered on the cross. While Theodore was not denounced by name, his main writings were, and the Armenians themselves took the hint. Ephesus and Cyril's teaching they accepted as orthodox, with all the consequences for their future relations with Constantinople after Chalcedon.[118]

Proclus's rule may be compared with that of Atticus, a long lull between successive conflicts with Alexandria. This time the consequences would not be healed so readily. The personal blame for the great crises that convulsed Christendom between 447 and 451 must, however, fall on Cyril's successor Dioscorus (444-51; d. 454). His adversary Flavian (446-49) was a discreet and moderate individual, far from a supporter of Nestorian theology. Dioscorus himself is an enigma. He has gone down in history as a man of violence and one of the great villains of the patristic age. This is not, however, how he appeared at first to his contemporaries. His future adversary on the Antiochene side, Theodoret, bishop of Cyrrhus (d. 458), congratulated him on his universal reputation for modesty and reason.[119] Domnus of Antioch (441–49), John's nephew but weak successor, believed that he had an ally and that there would be harmony between the two sees;[120] and from Rome Pope Leo wrote a kindly and patronizing letter instructing Dioscorus on the proper procedure for ordaining clergy, and that if at the time of the great festivals the churches in Alexandria were too full, he should not hesitate to celebrate the liturgy twice on the same day.[121]

How were such errors of judgment possible? The clue may be found in a letter from a certain presbyter Alypius to Cyril a long time before: "Through his valiant struggles Athanasius had exalted the holy see of St. Mark the Evangelist to the highest degree, and Cyril was following in his footsteps."[122] This was Dioscorus's ambition. None would rival the see of Alexandria. Unfortunately, as Zacharias Rhetor (c. 490) pointed out, he lacked Cyril's intelligence,[123] and to make matters worse he quarreled with Cyril's relatives who held posts of influence in his archiepiscopal see. "He turned the see of St. Mark upside down," it was said.[124] To further his ambitions he gave full rein to his latent aggression in frenzied efforts to stamp out the embers of Nestorianism wherever they might be found.

DIOSCORUS AND EUTYCHES

It was now twenty years later. Many of the chief actors of the Nestorian crisis had passed away. Others, however, remained, their encrusted intransigencies sharpened by a sense of personal grievance or need for self-justification. Details of the great crises that began with a new phase in the continuing controversy between Alexandria and Antioch, and then spread to involve Constantinople and finally Rome, have often been told.[125] Only an outline is offered here. As in their previous encounter, the Alexandrians had a good deal of support in the patriarchate of Antioch itself and from influential Syrian monks, though the most influential of all, Simeon Stylites (d. 459), was loyal to Domnus. In addition, Dioscorus could rely on Juvenal, not at all abashed by his failure while Cyril was alive to achieve patriarchal dignity. His aim was ultimately to replace Antioch by Jerusalem as the most important see in the Roman East, and he saw his chance of moving toward that end.[126] Most important of all for Dioscorus's success was his foothold in the capital through the active sympathy of Eutyches, an aged but vain and crafty archimandrite ruling a monastery of three hundred monks, and influential at the imperial court. He could also take the benevolent neutrality of Rome for granted, for had not the pope attributed Nestorius's downfall to his own authority combined with Cyril's perseverance?[127]

On the other hand, despite Domnus's weakness, the Antiochene cause was not lacking in defenders. Of these, the ablest was Theodoret, bishop of Cyrrhus, north of Antioch, who combined missionary zeal directed against surviving Marcionite and Arian villages in his diocese[128] with the growing conviction that Alexandrian Christology was Apollinarian. He was on excellent terms with many leading monks, had a feel for the political situation which made him a correspondent with high officials in the capital, and was the possessor of a historian's sense of perspective. He had already provided much of the intellectual defense of Nestorius's position just before the Council of Ephesus. He was ready to do battle again.

In 446 Dioscorus began to move against alleged remnants of Nestorianism in the patriarchate of Antioch,[129] disregarding the second canon of the Council of Constantinople of 381 that forbade the intervention of bishops in the affairs of other sees. In response, Theodoret wrote a satirical dialogue called *Eranistes*, or *The Beggar*, against the Alexandrians in which the orthodox speaker stressed the reality of the human nature of Christ distinct from his divinity. He accused a Cyrillist opponent of confusing his natures and therefore making God himself liable to change and suffering, though he conceded that he who suffered as man was also the selfsame one who was God the Word.[130]

Unfortunately, there were also hostages to fortune. In Ibas, bishop of Edessa (435–58), Antiochenes possessed a hard-hitting but indiscreet controversialist. Had he really said that "Hell was only a threat," and that the "Jews crucified a man"?[131] Enough people believed this to pin a charge of blasphemy on him. Then there was a disciplinary problem. Domnus had consecrated the former count Irenaeus as bishop of the city of Tyre. Irenaeus had been feared and hated by Cyril. It was discovered that he had been twice married, and this could be urged against him to secure his deposition and discredit Domnus. For his part the emperor Theodosius feared that Nestorianism was the work of demons set on undermining the stability of the empire. During 448, under the influence of his grand chamberlain, Chrysaphius, he proscribed the writings of Nestorius along with those of Porphyry,[132] deposed Irenaeus, and left no doubt that he favored Dioscorus against all comers.[133]

One of these was his own patriarch Flavian (446–49). So far as can be ascertained, Flavian's ideas followed those of the Cappadocian fathers. He was a Word-Flesh theologian, an anti-Apollinarian who asserted the reality of the two natures of Christ as set out in the Formula of Reunion. He found the ideas of archimandrite Eutyches puzzling but disturbing. Eutyches seemed to be preaching with some vehemence that the Word himself had been made flesh (not merely "assumed flesh") and hence that the "flesh" of Christ could not be derived from Mary, but from some other, heavenly source. Christ's humanity was not therefore humanity in the normal sense of the term, and hence he was not "consubstantial with us."[134] On 22 November 448, after delays and prevarication, Eutyches was condemned by the Home Synod convoked by Flavian and presided over by Count Florentius representing the emperor. Eighteen archimandrites and thirty-one bishops were present. His accuser was the same Eusebius of Dorylaeum, now bishop of that city, who had accused Nestorius twenty years before.[135] The Word-Flesh theology as understood in the capital and in much of Asia Minor found itself placed awkwardly between the Word-Man theologies of Antioch and the out-and-out Cyrillists of Alexandria.

Despite their apparent success in the capital, Dioscorus's opponents were undone by their disunity. Eutyches did not accept the sentence of deposition and appealed to the councils of Rome, Jerusalem, Alexandria, and also sent a copy of his appeal to the bishops of Thessalonica and Ravenna[136]—the last-named as the imperial headquarters in the West, which he no doubt thought had acquired a status similar to Constantinople. The immediate effect of his appeals was to bring Pope Leo into the controversy, and the pope's first reaction was difficulty in understanding just why Eutyches was being blamed,[137] and even more important, why Flavian had not reported the case to him earlier. Flavian found himself ignored by Leo in the weeks when the latter's aid would have been crucial.

Council of Ephesus II

Matters now moved steadily toward their climax. Once again, the part played by the emperor was decisive. Theodosius, angered by what he regarded as an unseemly squabble between Flavian and the archimandrite, began to lose confidence in Flavian. He put the blame for the trouble squarely on his shoulders. If he needed any further confirmation of the strongly anti-Nestorian sentiment of his subjects he received it from alarming reports of disorders in Edessa against Bishop Ibas. His commissioner, Count Thomas Chareas, who visited the city on 12 April 449, found himself overwhelmed by loyal demonstrations in favor of the emperor and the empire coupled with hostility toward the bishop who was accused of Nestorian blasphemy and peculation.[138] Meantime, even though the Home Synod in the capital had not yet reviewed the sentence on Eutyches, Theodosius ordered a representative council with judicial powers to meet at Ephesus on 1 August 449 to decide between Flavian and Eutyches. All patriarchs were to be represented, along with Juvenal of Jerusalem and ten bishops from each metropolitan diocese. The presidency was given to Dioscorus, with the counts Eulogius and Helpidius on hand to maintain order. Dioscorus's instructions were "to settle the controversies that had suddenly arisen" and "to root out error with zeal."[139] The latter fitted his ideal perfectly. All was going his way. By 21 July Ibas had been deposed and replaced.[140] Theodoret of Cyrrhus was banned from participating at Ephesus at the emperor's instruction. The council was to be Dioscorus's, as its predecessor had been Cyril's.

Pope Leo received his summons to Ephesus on 13 May. Still he procrastinated. Not until one month later—13 June—did he send his reply to Flavian's letter that he accepted the invitation to be present. The *Tome* of

Leo, whatever its intention, arrived too late to help Flavian. Had he written at once, his words might have had some effect. At least they would have demonstrated to Theodosius and his advisers that the patriarch of the West was far from agreeing with Dioscorus and his friends. As it stands, the *Tome* is a splendid piece of ecclesiastical prose, with the sonorous rhythms and balanced cadences that one recognizes in Leo's letters and sermons.[141] In content, it was a summary of established Western Christology, owing much seemingly to Ambrose's writings against the Arians. Eutyches was mistaken, Leo declared. He had not read the Scriptures. Christ had received "the reality of the body" from "body of the Virgin"—"that is, in that flesh which he took from humanity and which he quickened with the spirit of a rational life." He continued: "the distinctive character of each nature and substance remaining therefore unimpaired and coming together into one Person, humility was assumed by majesty, weakness by power, mortality by eternity." The explicit recognition of the two natures, human and divine, in Christ was combined with the idea of their interchange (that is, *communicatio idiomatum*) important for the Western concept of the atonement. To prove the truth of this interchange the *Tome* enumerated aspects of Christ's life which demonstrated the reality and distinction of each nature:

> For just as God is not changed by the comparison exhibited, so the manhood is not absorbed by the dignity bestowed. . . . As therefore, to pass over many examples, it does not belong to the same nature to weep for a dead friend with emotions of pity and to recall the same friend from the dead with a word of power.[142]

It was a brave attempt to find an answer based on Scripture to the paradoxes of existing Christology, which did not flout the accepted religious philosophy of the day. The *Tome* could be reconciled with the Formula of Reunion, but not with Cyril's twelve *Anathemas*. Even at Chalcedon, where the tide was flowing strongly against Dioscorus, these statements and the thought behind them were challenged. From his exile far away in an Egyptian oasis, the aged Nestorius welcomed the *Tome* as "an orthodox and irreproachable confession of faith."[143]

Even so, Leo could not conclude the *Tome* without rebuking Flavian once more, this time for theological obtuseness.[144] It was no way to encourage an ally in critical danger. It was now August. On the eighth, the council of about 135 bishops together with the monk Barsumas met in the church of the *Theotokos* at Ephesus. The papal legates, Bishop Julius of Puteoli and the deacon Hilarus, Leo's successor, were there; so too were Domnus of Antioch, Juvenal of Jerusalem, and Flavian. An observer would have noted that Flavian had been placed fifth in order of precedence, below Juvenal. The whole scene was dominated by Dioscorus seated on a throne high above the assembled bishops. Already he was being hailed as "a supreme guardian of the faith."[145] Had he played his hand coolly he could have gained his see's greatest triumph. Alexandria, "city of the orthodox," would have assumed the leadership of the Eastern Christian world.

In the event, his violent nature got the better of him. He opened the session properly enough by having the imperial letters of summons read. These were strongly critical of any Two-Natures Christology, but then, without refusing to read Leo's *Tome*, Dioscorus moved straight to the conflict between Eutyches and Flavian.[146] In a sense, it was a logical decision for this was the council's business outlined in the emperor's instructions, whereas Leo's *Tome* was merely a letter to Flavian. Eutyches had an unexpectedly strong case. The previous Council of Ephesus, as well as the contemporary writer Marius Mercator, had accepted as authentic letters purporting to have been written by Pope Julius to a certain bishop Dionysius and to Prosdocius, the one condemning the extreme Two-Nature Christology of Paul of Samosata and the other upholding the sacred status of the Virgin Mary.[147] Eutyches followed up this documentation with a confession of faith in which he admitted that the incarnate Christ was made from the flesh of the Virgin and for our salvation was made man. The council was entranced. "Two natures before the union, one afterwards. Is this not what we all believe?" asked Dioscorus. At once the mood of the assembled bishops changed. Anger exploded against Eutyches' accusers. "Eusebius, to the flames. Burn him alive. Cut in pieces the man who divides Christ." "Anathema to him who says two natures after the incarnation."[148] It was good that Leo's *Tome* was not read, for in that atmosphere its author and his representatives would have been excommunicated then and there.

Eutyches was declared orthodox and restored. Then Dioscorus, abetted by Juvenal, showed his hand. Extracts from the proceedings of the sixth session of Ephesus were read out; these forbade anyone on pain of deposition to teach any belief other than that of the Creed of Nicaea. All, including papal legates, agreed. But, claimed Dioscorus, Eusebius and Flavian with their formulas regarding the Two Natures had infringed this canon; and moreover, they had caused disturbance and scandal among the holy churches and orthodox laity. They merited deposition. Even the assembly was dumbfounded. "I disclaim you," retorted Flavian. *"Contradicitur,"* shouted the deacon Hilarus, before disappearing to the comparative safety of the sanctuary. It would not have mattered what he had shouted, for in this Greek-speaking assembly no one heeded an ejaculation in Latin.[149] Dioscorus had planned well. Blank forms had been prepared for the bishops to sign, and amid the vociferations of the monks and soldiers brandishing manacles a unanimous decision was forthcoming. Flavian was hustled and assaulted, and as a result of his injuries, died in exile, perhaps in February 450.[150]

At a second session of the council on 22 August, Dioscorus completed his triumph by having Domnus of Antioch deposed as a protector of the heretics Theodoret and Ibas, even though he had agreed to their deposition. He was declared "worse than Ibas"; his pusillanimity had availed him nothing.[151] The council ended by declaring the twelve *Anathemas* canonical,[152] while Juvenal at last received patriarchal status for his see, with a handsome endowment of six relatively small provinces at the expense of Antioch.[153] In November Anatolius, Dioscorus's delegate (*apocrisiarius*) at Constantinople, was consecrated patriarch in Flavian's stead.

Without the violence and double-dealing, the findings of the council might have stood. No one questioned Dioscorus's orthodoxy, and two years later at Chalcedon he was condemned for disciplinary offenses, not for heresy. The meeting of "this great and holy synod," as it was called by its participants,[154] had been in fact a fully representative assembly of bishops from Theodosius II's dominions. Its findings were held "to agree with Nicaea."[155] They agreed too with public opinion in the East. The emperor himself was satisfied. He accepted Flavian's deposition and reassured his anguished relations in the West that everything had happened in the best possible way.[156] On the other hand the influence of Pulcheria, Leo's ally at Constantinople, if considerable, was still limited. Though the papacy became the focus of appeal by Flavian, Theodoret, and Eusebius, it is an open question whether Leo's negotiations with Patriarch Anatolius and the emperor's sister Pulcheria would have succeeded had not Theodosius died unexpectedly, thrown from his horse while hunting on 28 July 450.

There was a complete revolution. Pulcheria took over the government, and chose as her consort Marcian, an able soldier who had served in the West. The grand chamberlain Chrysaphius was executed,[157] and Eutyches was again exiled. In October Flavian's body was brought to rest in Constantinople and his name restored to the diptychs (that is, to be recorded at the Eucharist among those to be remembered with honor). Pulcheria and Marcian protested their loyalty to the pope. Through the winter and spring of 450–51 negotiations went on to arrive at some agreement between Rome and Constantinople. Anatolius's position was relatively strong. He had crowned Marcian emperor, and Ephesus II had been accepted throughout the East.[158] However, the *Tome* of Leo had escaped condemnation, and Anatolius was prepared to agree with Leo that orthodoxy could be based on Cyril's second letter to Nestorius. The crux as always was the relationship between the two sees. Anatolius wanted Leo to accept canon 3 of the Council of Constantinople in 381 with its statement of the prerogatives of his own see. Leo wavered. In April Eusebius of Dorylaeum was to claim at Chalcedon that he was ready to accept.[159] It would have been a momentous decision, for it would have removed the major cause of dissension, and finally of schism, between Old and New Rome. Was it not possible to harmonize the apostolic claims of Old Rome with the secular claims of New Rome? Had not, after all, the former drawn Peter and Paul to itself on account of its secular status as capital of the empire? Such possible lines of rapprochement, however, led nowhere. On 23 May 451, Marcian summoned an ecumenical council to meet at Nicaea on 1 September, "to end disputations and settle the true faith more clearly and for all time."[160] Leo's instructions to his representatives issued in June contained no concession to the ecclesiastical claims of the capital; indeed, if raised, these were to be resisted.

CHALCEDON 451

The opening of this great council was delayed until October and then shifted to Chalcedon. Some 520 bishops from all over the East from Egypt to Illyricum assembled, the West being represented by the papal legates led by Paschasinus, bishop of Lilybaeum.[161] Once again the pivotal position of the emperor was to be demonstrated, and also the theological traditions represented by the great sees regardless of their incumbents. In fifteen sessions extending from 8 October to 10 November, not only was what became known as the Chalcedonian Definition hammered out, but a number of other important dissensions were adjudicated. Canons were agreed upon, and finally with the twenty-eighth canon the status of Constantinople was unequivocally established.

Dioscorus, unabashed and defiant to the end, arrived with seventeen Egyptian bishops and promptly excommunicated Leo. This proved to be the last straw. Apart from him, the bishops assembled in a chastened mood. They needed a scapegoat for the proceedings of Ephesus II and the death of Flavian, by now "the martyr Flavian." Dioscorus obliged. He found himself in the unwonted position of being the accused. As the proceedings of Ephesus II were read out, the bishops became more hostile. Juvenal, probably by prior agreement with Anatolius, deserted him—thus safeguarding his newly established patriarchate—and so did four of his own bishops.[162] Even so he defended himself valiantly: "I can prove from Athanasius, Gregory and Cyril that after the union we ought to speak of only one incarnate nature of the Word. I will be rejected together with the Fathers, but I am defending the doctrine of the Fathers and yield on no point."[163] Emotion, however, was taking over at Chalcedon as it had at Ephesus only two years before. The assembled bishops wanted to be rid of Dioscorus. They aimed at unity between the major sees and were prepared even to tolerate Juvenal for this purpose. So it was, "Cyril and Leo taught alike,"[164] "Flavian's doctrine accorded with Cyril's,"[165] whether or not it did. Cyril indeed presided in absentia. His teaching was orthodox. All else, including Leo's *Tome*, had to stand the test of agreement with him. One compromise was made, however, whose effects were to be far-reaching. When it came to preparing the Definition, the first draft presented at the fifth session of the council on 22 October seems to have affirmed that Christ was "of two natures." This was acclaimed until the imperial commissioners who were presiding reminded the bishops that Leo's *Tome* had been accepted as orthodox. This included the statement that "the two natures are united without change, without division and without confusion in Christ."[166] Another three days passed in committee work and lobbying.[167] The final draft was read to the council by Marcian himself on 25 October. It was again hailed with enthusiasm. Marcian and Pulcheria were "torches of the orthodox faith," Marcian "the new Constantine," Pulcheria "the new Helena."[168] The Definition approved the recognition of Christ "in two natures, unconfusedly, unchangeably, indivisibly, inseparably,"[169] and retained the *communicatio idiomatum* of the *Tome*, "the difference of the Natures being in no way removed because of the Union, but rather, the properties of each nature being preserved and concurring into one Person and one Substance. . . ." The attempt at balance and compromise was patent, the first two of the qualifying adverbs seeking to exclude Eutychianism, and the second two Nestorianism. But the definition, "in two natures" leaned toward Antioch and the West. How far would it be acceptable to the Eastern Christians who had welcomed the decisions of Ephesus I and II with such rapture?

The Chalcedonian Definition read:

Wherefore, following the holy Fathers, we all with one voice confess our Lord Jesus Christ one and the same Son, the same perfect in Godhead, the same perfect in manhood, truly God and truly man, the same consisting of a reasonable soul and a body, of one substance with the Father as touching the Godhead, the same of one substance with us as touching the manhood, like us in all things apart from sin; begotten of the Father before the ages as touching the Godhead, the same in the last days, for us and for our salvation, born from the Virgin Mary, the *Theotokos*, as touching the manhood, one and the same Christ, Son, Lord, Only-begotten, to be acknowledged in two natures, without confusion, without change, without division, without separation; the distinction of natures being in no way abolished because of the union but rather the characteristic property of each nature being preserved and concurring into one Person and one subsistence [*hypostasis*] not as if Christ were parted or divided into two persons, but one and the same Son and Only-begotten God, Word, Lord, Jesus Christ; and our Lord Jesus Christ instructed us, and the Creed of the Fathers was handed down to us.[170]

The parentage of the Formula of Reunion is obvious, but some of Cyril's emphasis on the Oneness of Christ was preserved in the reiteration of "same," "self-same," and *Theotokos* was guaranteed its status in the language of orthodoxy; but one must also note the presence of some strongly pro-Antiochene officers of state among the imperial judges. Such a one was Anatolius, pretorian prefect and correspondent of Theodoret. Their views carried more weight than perhaps the *Acta* showed. The assembly was in no position to resist. Four hundred fifty-two bishops eventually signed the Definition. The misgivings of some of them, however, were to be only too well justified.

The final hurdle came at the very end of the proceedings. Theodoret and Ibas had been rehabilitated somewhat reluctantly, Theodoret having agreed formally to Nestorius's deposition.[171] Domnus, however, was not restored. He was given an indemnity instead. A quarrel between rival claimants for the see of Ephesus was settled,[172] when at last the bishops considered how Constantinople could be protected against yet another attack from the Alexandrian patriarch. The prohibition on the intervention of one major see in the affairs of another had proved to be insufficient and there was the half century of grumbling dispute about the rights of Constantinople over the see of Ephesus. The latest clash had taken up two entire sessions of the council's time. Now, at the fifteenth session, after many metropolitans in the Asian provinces declared that they had been consecrated by the patriarch of the capital, and disclaimed any coercion in this matter, the lay commissioners gave their verdict that canon 3 of the Council of Constantinople should stand.

> For [canon 28 of Chalcedon read] the Fathers properly gave the primacy to the Throne of the elder Rome because that was the imperial city; and the 150 most religious bishops, being moved by the same intention gave equal privileges to the most holy Throne of New Rome, judging rightly, that the city which was honoured with the sovereignty and senate which enjoyed equal privileges with the elder and Royal Rome should also be magnified like her in ecclesiastical matters, being the second after her."[173]

Therefore, the metropolitans of Thrace, Pontus, and Asia as well as "bishops of the aforesaid dioceses that are among the barbarians shall be ordained by the above-mentioned most holy Throne of the city of Constantinople." Also, bishops working among northern barbarians would depend on the capital just as the bishops in Axum depended on Alexandria. One hundred eighty-three of these assembled bishops signed the canon, but the Roman legates left in indignation.

It was not, however, an unreasonable decision. The de facto seniority of Constantinople among the Eastern bishoprics had long been acknowledged. Indeed, one of the issues that had led to Chalcedon had been the frustration felt by the Alexandrian patriarch at this situation. Moreover, in less-than-guarded moments the papal delegation had acknowledged Constantinople's precedence over the other Eastern patriarchs. The council also had settled other issues of ecclesiastical order. The boundaries of Antioch and Jerusalem had been established. Why, therefore, should not the vastly more important issue of the authority of the see of Constantinople be decided? Henceforth, Christendom was to be divided into five patriarchates, whose bishops were supreme within the boundaries of their jurisdictions, and on whose harmony the peace of the church would rest.

Rome's opposition to granting Constantinople the status agreed to at the Second Ecumenical Council in 381 served notice that harmony would be difficult to achieve.

Chalcedon certainly marks the end of an era. A century after its triumph during the reign of Constantius II the church had become the most powerful single factor in the lives of the peoples of the empire. The Virgin and the saints had replaced the gods as patrons of cities. The bishops were equated in precedence and often in salary with a provincial governor.[174] The clerical career was as formalized as that of the civil services. In both East and West episcopal sees coincided with civil territories. The wealth of some of the greater bishoprics was massive and had been used by Alexandria in the crises of 431 as a weapon to sway the imperial court to Cyril's viewpoint. At Chalcedon, the two defeated candidates for the see of Ephesus were each mollified by the almost princely pension of two hundred gold solidi a year from the funds of that church.[175] The century had seen fundamental shifts in the structure of society to the church's advantage.

To material power had been added the immense authority accorded to the church's teaching. The stability of the empire was believed to rest on its orthodoxy, and hence the desperate efforts to find some way of bridging the gulf between the rival Word-Flesh and Word-Man theologies represented by Alexandria and Antioch respectively. Chalcedon succeeded as nearly as humanly possible, but as a compromise it failed to satisfy the more dedicated believers on either side. For Rome, Chalcedon was an unalterable Definition of Faith; for the majority in the East, it represented a compromise acceptable to the emperor, but one which went near to vindicating Nestorius. Moreover, it was to be remembered as the symbol of Juvenal's treachery to Dioscorus, and a demonstration of how powerful but corrupt clerics, such as Basil of Seleucia, could deny with impunity what they had accepted only two years before. The Egyptian bishops knew what awaited them at home if they signed the Definition: "We shall be killed if we subscribe to Leo's epistle. Every district in Egypt will rise against us. We would rather die at the hands of the emperor and at your [the council's] hand than at home."[176] They spoke truly, as the lynching of the unfortunate Proterius in 457 showed. In the sphere of metaphysics as in that of ecclesiastical precedence no consensus could be won.

BIBLIOGRAPHY

NOTE

The climax of the patristic period, with its rich and varied documentation, has been recorded by the great scholars of the past. The student can follow much of the detail in L. Duchesne, *Early History of Church*, vol. 3. R. V. Sellers, *The Council of*

Chalcedon: A Historical and Doctrinal Study (London: SPCK, 1953), is also indispensable; as are the essays in H. Grillmeier and H. Bacht, eds., *Das Konzil von Chalkedon: Geschichte und Gegenwart*, 3 vols. (Würzburg: Echter-Verlag, 1953). The original sources have been studied and published by Eduard Schwartz in his monumental *Acta Conciliorum Oecumenicorum (ACO)*, (Berlin, 1914–40).

For a good characterization of Juvenal of Jerusalem, and a sketch of the events in Palestine 422–53, see E. Honigmann, "Juvenal of Jerusalem," *Dumbarton Oaks Papers* 5 (Cambridge, Mass., 1950), pp. 209–79. Nestorius has his admirers in J. F. Bethune-Baker, *Nestorius and His Teaching: A Fresh Examination of the Evidence* (New York: Macmillan Co., 1908); and Friedrich Loofs, *Nestorius and His Place in the History of Christian Doctrine* (New York: Macmillan Co., 1914). Cyril awaits a full appreciation of the light and shade in his character.

For the relations between the East and West Roman Empires in this period, see in particular W. E. Kaegi, *Byzantium and the Decline of Rome* (Princeton, N.J.: Princeton University Press, 1968); and for Byzantine civilization in this period, see the essays by N. H. Baynes published in his *Byzantine Studies*.

SOURCES

Acta Conciliorum Oecumenicorum. Ephesus I, 5 parts (1922–30), and Chalcedon II, 6 parts (1932–38).

Basil of Caesarea. *Ad Iuvenes.* In *Saint Basil on Greek Literature*, ed. N. G. Wilson. London: Gerald Duckworth & Co., 1975.

Pope Celestine. *Epistolae. PL* 50.417–558.

John Chrysostom, *Homiliae* (cited in text), *Opera Omnia quae exstant, PG* 54, 62, 63. No complete Eng. trans. exists, but the principal works are trans. in NPNF. French trans. and introduction to specific works are to be found in SC 13, 28, 50, 79, 117, 125, 138, 188, 272, 277, 300.

_____. *Orationes VIII adversus Judaeos. PG* 48.843–944.

Cyril of Alexandria, *Opera, PG* 72–77; Eng. trans. in NPNF; and see also T. H. Bindley and F. W. Green, eds., *The Oecumenical Documents of the Faith: The Creed of Nicaea, Three Epistles of Cyril, the Tome of Leo, the Chalcedonian Definition*, 4th ed., rev., New York: British Book Centre; London; Methuen & Co., 1950, for texts, notes, and translations of Cyril's second and third letters to Nestorius and his letter to John of Antioch. Also G. M. de Durand, Fr. trans. of Cyril's works in SC 97, 231, 237, and 246.

Pope Leo, *Epistolae, PL* 54.551–1254. For Eng. trans. of the *Tome*, see Bindley and Green, *Oecumenical Documents*, pp. 224–31.

Mark the Deacon, *Vita Porphyrii Gazensis*, ed. H. Grégoire and M. Kugener, Paris, 1930; and *The Life of Porphyry of Gaza*, Eng. trans. and ed. G. F. Hill, New York: Oxford University Press, 1913.

Nestorius, *Liber Heraclidis*, ed. and Fr. trans. F. Nau, Paris, 1910; and *Nestorius, Bazaar of Heracleides*, Eng. trans. and ed. G. R. Driver and L. Hodgson, New York: Oxford University Press, 1926.

Palladius, *De Vita S. Joannis Chrysostomi ex Dialogo historico Palladii Helenopoleos episcopi, PG* 47.5–82; Eng. trans. and ed. P. R. Coleman-Norton, New York: Macmillan Co.; Cambridge: Cambridge University Press, 1928.

Priscus of Panium, *Fragmenta* = Frag. Hist. Graec., ed. C. Muller, Paris, 1857, IV.71–110.

Prosper Tiro. *Chronicon. PL* 51.536–606.

Rufinus. *Historia monachorum. PL* 21.387–461.

Pope Sixtus. *Epistolae. PL* 50.581–613.

Socrates, *Ecclesiastical History*, Books V–VII, *PG* 67.29–872; Eng. trans. in NPNF.

Sozomen, *Ecclesiastical History*, Books VII–X, ed. Bidez and Hansen, GCS 50; Eng. trans. in NPNF.

Synesius, *Epistolae, PG* 66.1322–1561; *Letters*, Eng. trans. and ed. A. Fitzgerald, New York and London: Oxford University Press, 1926.

———. *Oratio de Regno. PG* 66.1054–1110.

Theodore of Mopsuestia. *In Epistolas beati Pauli Commentarii*. Edited by H. B. Swete. 2 vols. Cambridge, 1880–82.

———. *On the Nicene Creed*. Eng. trans. and ed. A. Mingana. Woodbrooke Studies 10. *BJRL* 16 (1932): 200–318.

Theodoret of Cyrrhus. *Ecclesiastical History*. Edited by L. Parmentier and F. Scheidweiler. GCS 44. Leipzig: Hinrichs, 1954.

———, *Epistolae, PG* 83.1171–1492; and ed. Y. Azéma, SC 40, 98, and 111.

SECONDARY WORKS

Baynes, N. H. "The Thought-World of East Rome." In *Byzantine Studies*, pp. 24–46.

Camelot, T. "De Nestorius à Eutyches: l'opposition de deux christologies." In *Das Konzil von Chalkedon*, ed. Grillmeier and Bacht, vol. 1, pp. 213–42.

Chadwick, H. "Eucharist and Christology in the Nestorian Controversy." *JTS* n.s. 2 (October 1951): 145–64.

———. "The Exile and Death of Flavian of Constantinople: A Prologue to the Council of Chalcedon." *JTS* n.s. 6 (April 1955): 17–34.

Coster, E. H. "Synesius. A *curialis* of the Time of Arcadius." *Byzantion* 15 (1940–41): 10–38.

Draguet, R. "Le christologie d'Eutyches après les Actes du Synode de Flavien, 448." *Byzantion* 6 (1931): 441–57.

Dvornik, F., *Byzance et la primauté romain*, Paris, 1964; E. A. Quain, Eng. trans., *Byzantium and the Roman Primacy*, Bronx, N.Y.: Fordham University Press, 1966; reprinted 1979.

Frend, W. H. C. "The Monks and the Survival of the East Roman Empire in the Fifth Century." *Past and Present* 54 (1972): 3–24.

Grant, R. M. *Early Christianity and Society*. New York: Harper & Row, 1977.

Grillmeier, A. *Christ in Christian Tradition: From the Apostolic Age to Chalcedon (451)*. Eng. trans. J. S. Bowden. New York: Sheed & Ward; Oxford: A. R. Mowbray, 1965.

Jalland, T. G. *The Life and Times of St. Leo the Great*. New York: Macmillan Co., London: SPCK, 1941.

Nicol, A. D. "The Byzantine Church and Hellenic Learning." In Studies in Church History, vol. 5, pp. 23–57. Oxford: Basil Blackwell & Mott, 1969.

Oost, S. I. *Galla Placidia Augusta: A Biographical Essay*. Chicago: University of Chicago Press, 1968.

Raven, C. E. *Apollinarianism: An Essay on the Christology of the Early Church*. New York: Macmillan Co., 1923.

Sarkissian, K. *The Council of Chalcedon and the Armenian Church*. London: SPCK, 1965.

Simon, M. "Le polémique anti-juive de saint Jean Chrysostom et le mouvement judäisant d'Antioche." In *Recherches d'histoire*, pp. 140–53.

Thompson, E. A. "The Foreign Policies of Theodosius II and Marcian." *Hermathena* 76 (1950): 58–75.

_____. *The History of Attila and the Huns*. New York and London: Oxford University Press, 1948.

NOTES

1. Jerome *Letter* XXXII.4. Rufinus also translated Gregory of Nazianzus's *Nine Orations*, c. 399 (ed. A. Engelbrecht, CSEL 46.1 [Vienna, 1910]).

2. Paulinus, *Letter* III.3 (ed. W. Hartel, CSEL 29 [Leipzig: G. Freytag, 1894], p. 15), he had found one copy in Rome in a relative's library.

3. Jerome, *Letter* 84.3, *PL* 22.746. See Kidd, *History of Church*, vol. 2, pp. 434–35.

4. Augustine *Confessions* I.14.23; compare I.13.20.

5. Sozomen *Ecclesiastical History* IX.8.6; and Zosimus *Historia Nova* VI.8.2; also Procopius *De bello vandalico (The Vandal War)* I.2.36. See Kaegi, *Byzantium*, p. 17.

6. Thus, Kaegi, *Byzantium*, pp. 51–54, on the Eastern disengagement from the West during the fifth century. In the Eastern provinces, even so alert a politician as Synesius of Cyrene makes no reference to Alaric's capture of Rome.

7. Zosimus *Historia Nova* V.19. Gainas was driven out of the capital on 12 July 400 in an outburst of popular fury. For the dating, see O. Seeck, *Regesten der Kaiser und Päpste* (Stuttgart, 1919; reprinted 1964), p. 301.

8. *Codex Theodosianus* XV.1.5.1 (4 April 413); and Socrates, *Ecclesiastical History* VII.1.

9. See Fergus Millar, "P. Herennius Dexippus: The Greek World and the Third-Century Invasions," *JRS* 59 (1969): 12–29.

10. Socrates *Ecclesiastical History* IV.38. Their boldness cost the empire dear, for the emperor Valens thereupon went out to meet the invaders and lost his army and his life at Adrianople on 9 August 378.

11. Priscus (ed. Muller), frag. 5, p. 75; and also the defense of Theodosiopolis against the Persians by Bishop Eunomius, related by Theodoret *Ecclesiastical History* V.37.7.

12. Synesius, *De Regno*, in *Essays and Hymns: Including the Address to the Emperor Arcadius and the Political Speeches*, Eng. trans. and ed. Fitzgerald (New York and London: Oxford University Press, 1930), p. 18.

13. Thus, John Chrysostom, *Homilia in Isaiah* II, *PG* 56.33, dilates upon "those vast spaces the sun shines upon," extending from the Tigris to Britain, which were enjoying peace. "Of wars we hear only rumours." This, in the year 400! For the general feeling of prosperity among the Eastern cities c. 438, see Socrates *Ecclesiastical History* VII.48. It was on this note that he ended his *Ecclesiastical History*.

14. For Edessa, see Schwartz, *ACO* II.1.386, and the details provided by Jones, *Later Roman Empire*, p. 911.

15. Socrates *Ecclesiastical History* V.16; Sozomen *Ecclesiastical History*

VII.15; Rufinus *Ecclesiastical History* II.23; and Theodoret *Ecclesiastical History* V.22.

16. See Libanius's vivid account of the misdeeds by "men in black with the appetites of elephants" destroying country temples, *Pro Templis, Oratio* XXX.8 (in *Libanii Opera,* ed. R. Foerster [Leipzig: Teubner, 1926], p. 91), and compare Theodoret *Ecclesiastical History* V.29, and John Chrysostom *Letter* CXXVI.

17. The account of the gradual erosion of the pagan position in Gaza from 395 onward is given by Mark the Deacon, *Prophyry of Gaza,* ed. Hill. For pagan survival in some of the larger cities of Arabia, Phoenicia, and Syria, see Sozomen *Ecclesiastical History* VII.15.11. Also, Downey, *Gaza* (Univ. of Okla. Press, 1963).

18. *Codex Theodosianus* XVI.10.16.

19. For "Holy Russia," note the Muscovite prejudice against Marshal Barclay de Tolly in the war of 1812 because he was a Baltic Protestant.

20. Gregory of Nazianzus *Oration* XXXVI (end of 380), and Gregory of Nyssa, *De deitate Filii et Spiritus sancti, PG* 46.557D–560A.

21. For example, Ephesus II in 449. "Multos annos imperatori . . . fidei custodibus multos annos, multos annos pontifici imperatori" (Latin translation, see Schwartz, *ACO* II.3, p. 121); and similarly at Chalcedon in 451 (ibid., II.1.2, Nr. 20, p. 157). See W. Ullmann, "Über die rechtliche Bedeutung der spätrömischen Kaisertitulatur für das Papsttum," *Ex Aequo et Bono,* Festsch. W. M. Plöchl (Innsbruck, 1977), pp. 23–45, esp. p. 31.

22. Sozomen *Ecclesiastical History* Praefatio 9. Compare Theodoret *Ecclesiastical History* V.36.5; and contrast the military tradition of the early empire "ducis boni imperatoriam virtutem esse," Tacitus *Agricola* XXXIX.

23. *Ecclesiastical History* Praefatio XV; and see Kaegi, *Byzantium,* pp. 199–204 (references).

24. Socrates *Ecclesiastical History* VI.23; and compare the Monophysite view echoed in Michael the Syrian, *Chronicon,* ed. J. B. Chabot, 3 vols. (Paris, 1899–1911), VIII.1.

25. Above, p. 420.

26. See on this theme N. H. Baynes, "Eusebius and the Christian Empire," in *Byzantine Studies,* pp. 168–72.

27. For the text of Chareas's reports, see J. Flemming, "Akten der ephesinischen Synode von 449," *AGG* n.s. 15 (1917): 1–159, esp. pp. 15–55.

28. See P. R. L. Brown's informative survey, "The Rise and Function of the Holy Man in Late Antiquity," *JRS* 61 (1971): 80–101; and my "Monks and Survival of East Roman Empire."

29. Rufinus, *Historia monachorum* V, *PL* 21.408–9. See H. Lietzmann, *Geschichte der alten Kirche,* 4 vols. (Berlin: Walter de Gruyter, 1932), vol. 4, p. 139.

30. Jerome, *Regulae S. Pachomii translatio Latina,* Praefatio 7 (*PL* 23.68). Shenoute's White Monastery had a population of twenty-two hundred monks with eighteen hundred nuns in a dependent convent; see J. Leipoldt, "Schenute von Atripe," TU (1904): 93.

31. For the frequent coming and going of aristocratic pilgrims from the west to the Holy Land in the reign of Theodosius and his successors, see E. D. Hunt, *Holy Land Pilgrimages in the Later Roman Empire, A.D. 312–460* (New York and London: Oxford University Press, 1982), chap. 7.

32. The first monastery in the capital would seem to have been that of Isaac, son of Faustus, at Psamathia outside the city in 383. For the comparative lateness of monasticism in Constantinople, see J. Pargoire, "Les débuts du monachisme à Constantinople," *Revue de Questions Historiques* n.s. 21 (1899): 67–143.

33. Theodoret *Historia religiosa* XXVI, *PG* 82.1484. Also, Brown, "Rise and Function of Holy Man," pp. 87–88.

34. Sozomen *Ecclesiastical History* II.14; III.14.28; and VI.28.1. See F. Dölger, "Zur Bedeutung von φιλόσοφος und φιλοσοφία in byzantinischen Zeit," *Byzanz und die europäische Staatenwelt* (Ettal, 1953), pp. 197–208, indicates also that true philosophy involved turning the mind exclusively towards God.

35. As advised by Jerome *Letter* XV.2 and XXII.29–30.

36. Basil, *Ad Iuvenes*, ed. Wilson, paras. 6ff.; and see Nicol, "Byzantine Church," p. 25.

37. Synesius, *De Regno* XIV, *PG* 66; and in *Essays and Hymns*, ed. Fitzgerald, pp. 134–35; and see Coster, "Synesius."

38. Synesius *Letter* CV, Eng. trans. also by Stevenson in *Creeds, Councils and Controversies*, pp. 264–67. For Hypatia's murder, see Socrates *Ecclesiastical History* VII.15. It would seem that Cyril of Alexandria at least turned a blind eye to what happened.

39. T. R. Glover, *Life and Letters in the Fourth Century* (reprint ed., New York: G. E. Stechert, 1925), pp. 337, 347–48.

40. Synesius *Letter* CV, Eng. trans. Stevenson, *Creeds, Councils and Controversies*, p. 266, slightly altered.

41. For example, the polychrome roundels, interlaces, and peltae that are the feature of the borders of mosaics in houses or churches from the fourth to the sixth centuries.

42. See Schwartz, *ACO* II.1.2, 125, 141–55; and my *The Rise of the Monophysite Movement: Chapters in the History of the Church in the 5th and 6th Centuries* (New York and Cambridge: Cambridge University Press, 1972; 2d ed., 1979), pp. 3–4.

43. See above, p. 625.

44. John Chrysostom, *VIII homilia, habita postquam presbyter Gothus*, I, *PG* 63.502. He described the Catholic Goths as "the most barbarous of all men," who should "regard it as a privilege to stand along with the sheep of the church in a common pasture and in one fold and at one table set before all alike." See also Theodoret *Ecclesiastical History* V.32.2 on his contempt for Gainas and encouragement to the populace of the capital to defy him.

45. See the series of sermons directed against the Jews of Antioch, *Adversus Judaeos, PG* 48.844ff., discussed by Simon, "Le polémique anti-juive de Chrysostome."

46. John Chrysostom, *I Timothy Homilia XII.4, PG* 62.562–64. See Grant, *Early Christianity*, pp. 114–16, to whom I owe the reference to this passage and the translation.

47. See John Chrysostom, *De Anna Sermo V.3, PG* 54.673 (defense of property); and *Philemon Homilia III.2, PG* 62.718 (slavery). See Grant, *Early Christianity*, pp. 93–95.

48. Socrates *Ecclesiastical History* VI.21.2.

49. Palladius, *Vita Johannis Chrysostomi* VI, *PG* 47.21.

50. For a catalog of Chrysostom's denunciations, see Kidd, *History of Church*, vol. 2, pp. 418–20.

51. Thus, Eunapius the Sophist complained that the inhabitants could not even pronounce his name properly, *Vitae Sophistarum* (ed. W. C. Wright [with Philostratus], LCL [Cambridge, Mass.: Harvard University Press; London: William Heinemann, 1921] VI.2.8. Constantinople as an exploiting and predatory city, see Libanius (ed. Foerster) I.76 and 279.

52. Socrates *Ecclesiastical History* VI.11.10; Sozomen *Ecclesiastical History* VIII.6.2; Palladius *Dialogue de vita S. Joannis Chrysostomi* (*Dialogue on the Life of St. John Chrysostom*) XV.

53. See Kidd, *History of Church*, vol. 2, pp. 437–44, and Duchesne, *Early History of Church*, vol. 2, chap. 3, for the details of this involved story.

54. Palladius *Life of John Chrysostom* VIII and IX, regarding Theophilus's quarrelsome nature. Edward Gibbon's comment is apt: Theophilus was "a bold, bad man, whose hands were alternately polluted with gold and with blood" (*The Decline and Fall of the Roman Empire*, chap. 28 = vol. 3, p. 200 in the Bury ed.).

55. Sozomen *Ecclesiastical History* VIII.19.8.

56. *Sermo 2 Post reditum, PG* 52.443.

57. *Homiliae 21 de statuis* (*Twenty-One Homilies on the Statues*) III.2. See above, p. 626.

58. In the interim, Arsacius, brother of Archbishop Nectarius, occupied the throne 28 June 404 to 11 November 405. He was "a man with less power of speech than a fish and of action than a frog!" Palladius *Life of John Chrysostom* XI.

59. His tact and lack of distinction (Socrates *Ecclesiastical History* VII.2) gain in significance in view of what was to happen in Nestorius's time.

60. See above, pp. 640–42.

61. Barsumas; told in the eighty-first miracle in the canon, *Life of Barsaumas* (d. 459), written c. 550–650 and cited from E. Honigmann, *Le Couvent de Barsauma et le patriarcat jacobite d'Antioche et de Syrie*. CSCO Subsidia 7 (Louvain, 1954), p. 15. For Barsumas's influence on the crisis of 447–51, see my *Rise of Monophysite Movement*, p. 91. He was purely Syriac-speaking.

62. Theodore, *De Incarnatione*, ed. H. B. Swete, vol. 2, p. 299.

63. Theodoret of Cyrrhus, *Letter CLXXX*; though the addressee, John of Antioch, is obviously wrong as John had died in 441, the letter was quoted against the memory of Theodoret at the Fifth General Council (Mansi, *Sacrorum Conciliorum*, vol. 9, p. 295), and would seem to be genuine.

64. Cyril *Letter XXIV, PG* 77.137, written just after the council's decision to condemn Nestorius; and see Theodoret *Letter CLII*, for the Antiochene view of Cyril's success.

65. *Letter XXXIX* (*PG* 77.180).

66. For an account of Cyril's theology, see Grillmeier, *Christ in Christian Tradition*, pp. 400ff.; A. von Harnack, *A History of Dogma*, Eng. trans. N. Buchanan (7 vols. in 4 vols., New York: Dover Publications, 1961), vol. 4, pp. 174–78; and Chadwick's important article, "Eucharist and Christology."

67. Cyril, *Letter* I (to the Monks), particularly *PG* 77.24 and 25.

68. Cyril, *Letter* IV (second letter to Nestorius), *PG* 77.48D.

69. Thus *Letter XXXI, PG* 77.151D; and compare also *Letter XL, PG* 77.193C.

70. For the Antiochene Christology, see R. A. Norris, *Manhood and Christ: A*

Study in the Christology of Theodore of Mopsuestia (New York and London: Oxford University Press, 1963); J. Tixeront, *Histoire des Dogmes*, 3 vols. (Paris: J. Gabalda, 1924–28), vol. 3, pp. 17ff.; and Raven, *Apollinarianism*, pp. 280ff.

71. Theodore, *On the Nicene Creed*, ed. Mingana, chap. 2, *BJRL*, p. 232.

72. Theodore, *Expositio Symboli*, ed. Swete, vol. 2, p. 328. ‚Compare F. W. Norris and B. Drewery, "Antiochien," *TRE*, vol. 3, pp. 99–113, for the Antiochene emphasis on sound text and historical and literal exegesis.

73. See Bethune-Baker, *Nestorius and Teaching*, pp. 109ff.; and Chadwick, "Eucharist and Christology," p. 160.

74. For the consistency of Cyril's Christology before 428, see Chadwick, "Eucharist and Christology," pp. 150–52, citing relevant literature (p. 151 n. 4).

75. Socrates *Ecclesiastical History* VII.32.10—fair-minded and well read as usual.

76. Ibid., 29.6.

77. Ibid., 29.7–9.

78. Ibid., 32.14–18. Origen apparently uses the term in *Commentary on Romans* I.1.5, cited by Socrates, *Ecclesiastical History* VII.32.17, but Eusebius's *Constantine* III.43.2 shows its use was fairly common in the early fourth century. In the West, Tertullian described the Virgin as "mater Dei" in *De patientia (Concerning Patience)* III and Ambrose similarly, in *Hexaemeron* V.65, *PL* 14.248A.

79. Socrates *Ecclesiastical History* VII.32.2. Compare, for the underlying consistency of the Antiochene view, *Acta Archelai*, ed. C. H. Beeson, GCS 16 (Leipzig: Hinrichs, 1906), 58.11 and 60.3.

80. Cyril *Letter II*, *PG* 77.41C.

81. Cyril *Letter I*—a long letter, singularly weak in scriptural justification for *Theotokos*, but effective in arguing that if Christ was not by nature God, and hence the Virgin the "God-bearer," how could he overthrow death and claim to be the object of Christian worship? *Theotokos* was the logical consequence of the Creed of Nicaea and Athanasius's theology. This was enough to win the monks' support.

82. Cyril *Letter IV*, *PG* 77.44–50; and Schwartz, *ACO* I.1.1, 25–28.

83. Cyril, *Letter IV*. Eng. trans. in Stevenson, *Creeds, Councils and Controversies*, p. 277, slightly altered.

84. Celestine *Letter XI.4*, *PL* 50.464.

85. Celestine *Letter XIII.11*, *PL* 50.484.

86. John of Antioch to Nestorius, Mansi, *Sacrorum Conciliorum*, vol. 4, pp. 1061–68, esp. 1064A; Schwartz, *ACO* I.1.1, pp. 93–96, esp. p. 94.

87. *Letter XVII*, *PG* 77.105–22 = *ACO* I.1.1.33–42.

88. *Letter XVII.3*.

89. Ibid., XVII.5. I prefer "essential union" to Stevenson's "personal union," which does not quite get Cyril's meaning (Stevenson, *Creeds, Councils and Controversies*, pp. 281–82).

90. The point made by Chadwick, "Eucharist and Christology," p. 153.

91. Cyril *Letter XVII.7*.

92. Ibid., 8.

93. Thus Kelly, *Early Christian Doctrines*, p. 324.

94. See my summary in the *Rise of Monophysite Movement*, p. 125.

95. See the analysis of Nestorius and Theodoret's *Counter-Anathemas* in

Bindley and Green, *Oecumenical Documents*, pp. 124–37, and Kidd, *History of Church*, vol. 3, p. 231.

96. For the dating, see Seeck, *Regesten*, p. 357.

97. See the translated text given in Stevenson, *Creeds, Councils and Controversies*, pp. 259–60. The church in Persia had been persecuted under Bahram's predecessor, Yazdegerd.

98. Innocent *Letter* XXIV.3, *PL* 20.549A.

99. Mansi, *Sacrorum Conciliorum*, vol. 4, pp. 1468C–E; also Schwartz, *ACO* I.1.7, p. 121 line 21.

100. On the development of Juvenal's aims at this period, see Honigmann, "Juvenal of Jerusalem," 212–33.

101. Above, p. 751.

102. Schwartz, *ACO* I.1.2, p. 54.

103. Nestorius commented years later: "Cyril presided; Cyril was accuser; Cyril was judge; Cyril was bishop of Rome; Cyril was everything," *Liber Heraclidus*, ed. Nau, p. 117.

104. Cyril *Letter* XXIV; and similarly Theodoret *Letter* CLII; also Nestorius, *Liber Heraclidus*, ed. Nau, p. 119, referring to "idlers and peasants" stirred up against him by Memnon.

105. *ACO* I.1.3, p. 57.

106. Ibid., I.1.3, p. 10 = Mansi, *Sacrorum Conciliorum*, vol. 4, p. 1296. See E. Caspar, *Geschichte des Papstums von den Anfängen bis zur Höhe der Weltherrschaft*, 2 vols. (Tübingen, 1930–33), I, p. 409.

107. For the extent of Cyril's bribes at Theodosius's court, see Bury's note, *History of the Later Roman Empire: From the Death of Theodosius I to the Death of Justinian*, 2 vols. (New York: Dover Publications; London: Constable & Co., 1958), vol. 1, p. 354 n. 2.

108. Agreed at the final session of the council on 22 July 431, and listed as canon 7, but in fact a decision (ὅρος) rather than a canon; see Schwartz, *ACO* II.1.1, p. 91, para. 159, and Stevenson, *Creeds, Councils and Controversies*, p. 296.

109. Thus the synodical letter sent by the Cyrillist majority to the emperors, Mansi, *Sacrorum Conciliorum*, vol. 4, pp. 1421–25. For a less enthusiastic comment, see Duchesne, *Early History of Church*, vol. 3, pp. 257–58.

110. Cyril *Letter* XXXIX; English text in Stevenson, *Creeds, Councils and Controversies*, pp. 290–94.

111. *Letter* XXXIX. Eng. trans. in Stevenson, *Creeds, Councils and Controversies*, p. 291.

112. Cyril *Letter* XXXIX.1. See Kelly, *Early Christian Doctrines*, pp. 328–30.

113. Theodoret in a sermon after the Council of Ephesus, see Mansi, *Sacrorum Conciliorum*, vol. 4, p. 1409B.

114. For discussion of this term whose use goes back to the Orphic mysteries, see R. C. Chesnut, *Three Monophysite Christologies: Severus of Antioch, Philoxenus of Mabbug, and Jacob of Sarug* (New York and London: Oxford University Press, 1976), pp. 37–44. It always has the sense of inward contemplation, the first steps toward advance to the knowledge of God. To suggest with L. R. Wickham (in his review of my *Rise of Monophysite Movement* in *JTS* n.s. 24 [1973]: 591–99, esp. p. 596) that it denotes "in theory" is surely misleading ("the distinction of natures

θεωρίᾳ for Cyril means, near enough, 'theoretically' ''), and a surprising statement to find in the *JTS*.

115. Sixtus, *Letter* VI.5, *PL* 50.609A.

116. *Ecclesiastical History* VII.48; see also above, n. 13.

117. See Sarkissian, *Council of Chalcedon*, pp. 93–97.

118. For the *Tome of Proclus* see Mansi, *Sacrorum Conciliorum*, vol. 5, pp. 421–38, analyzed in Kidd, *History of Church*, vol. 3, pp. 273–74, and put in its context by Sarkissian, *Council of Chalcedon*, pp. 111–25, who shows that while in the Greek text Theodore was spared, this was not the case in the Armenian text of the *Tome* (p. 124).

119. Theodoret *Letter* LX.

120. Domnus to Flavian, among Theodoret's letters, *Letter* 86: "I thought I should find an ally and fellow-worker in the most godly bishop of Alexandria, the lord Dioscorus."

121. Leo *Letter* IX.

122. The presbyter Alypius to Cyril = Cyril *Letter* XXIX, *PG* 77.148B.

123. Zacharias Rhetor, *Ecclesiastical History* III.1, ed. E. W. Brooks, CSCO Script. Syri III.5 and 6 (Paris and Louvain, 1919–24). Dioscorus was a "vir pacabilis et ἀγωνιστής," though he did not possess the ability and forthrightness (παρρησία) of Cyril" (Brooks's Latin trans. of the Syriac = CSCO III.5, p. 101). These are all curious judgments in view of Dioscorus's recorded behavior at Ephesus II and Chalcedon.

124. Domnus to Theodoret = Theodoret *Letter* 86.

125. See Duchesne, *Early History of Church*, vol. 3, pp. 271–315; Kidd, *History of Church*, vol. 3, pp. 277–339; Sellers, *Council of Chalcedon*, chap. 2; and briefly in my *Rise of Monophysite Movement*, chap. 1.

126. See Honigmann, "Juvenal of Jerusalem," pp. 231–33.

127. Prosper Tiro, *Chronicon* ad ann. 428, echoing pro-papal opinion "Cui impietati [Nestorius] praecipua Cyrilli Alexandrini episcopi industria, et papae Caelestini repugnant auctoritas" (*PL* 51.594 = Mommsen, ed., *MGH* AA. 9, Chron. Minora I, p. 472).

128. Theodoret *Letters* LXXXI, CIV, and CXIII (*PG* 83.1259, 1261, 1298, 1316): "a thousand converts from eight Marcionite villages." See above, p. 448.

129. Theodoret's complaints, *Letter* 110, and attacks on his own orthodoxy, *Letter* 83. See my *Rise of Monophysite Movement*, pp. 28–29.

130. *Eranistes* I, *PG* 83.37A; and see Kidd, *History of Church*, vol. 3, pp. 287–88. That Leo and Theodoret thought alike seems clear, but the division between both and Cyril was more than "verbal."

131. Ibas was tried before the tribune and notary, Damascius, at Tyre in February 449 but was acquitted (Schwartz, *ACO* II.3, p. 17).

132. *Codex Justinianus* I.1.3.

133. September 447. His successor Photius was consecrated without reference to Domnus on 9 September; see Seeck, *Regesten*, p. 379.

134. See Draguet's discussion in "Le christologie d'Eutyches"; and Camelot, "De Nestorius à Eutyches."

135. Schwartz, *ACO* II.1.2, p. 104. See my exculpation of Florentius on the charge of double-dealing, *Rise of Monophysite Movement*, p. 32 n. 2.

136. *ACO* II.3.1, p. 6.

137. Leo *Letter* XXXIV.1, "Diu apud nos incertum fuit, quid in ipso [Eutyche] catholicis displiceret." He regarded Eutyches as a fool rather than a heretic: "imperite atque impudenter errare detectus est," *Letter* XXIX.

138. The texts of Chareas's reports are published among the *Acta* of the Second Council of Ephesus ("the Robber Council") by Flemming, in "Akten der ephesinischen Synode," pp. 15–55.

139. Flemming, "Akten der ephesinischen Synode," pp. 3–5.

140. For the dating, see Seeck, *Regesten*, p. 383, citing *Edessene Chronicle*, p. 7 para. 64 (ed. I. Guidi, CSCO Script. Syri III.41 [Paris, 1903], 1–11).

141. For the text and a useful commentary, see Bindley and Green, *Oecumenical Documents*, pp. 159ff. For Leo's relations with Flavian prior to the Council, see Caspar, *Geschichte des Papstums*, vol. 1, p. 483; and Frend, *Rise of Monophysite Movement*, p. 38.

142. *Tome*, para. 4, Eng. trans. Stevenson, *Creeds, Councils and Controversies*, pp. 318–19.

143. Nestorius, *Liber Heraclidus*, ed. Nau, p. 298.

144. Flavian was told he had not been severe enough on Eutyches' absurd statements about "one nature after the union" (Leo *Tome* VI). Leo had no idea of the way in which the theological outlook of the East had been developing.

145. Michael the Syrian, *Chronicon*, ed. Chabot, VIII.7; and for the contemporary Western view of his ambitions towards the primacy of Christendom, see Prosper Tiro, *Chronicle* ad ann. 449: "In quo concilio Dioscorus Alexandrinus episcopus primatum sibi vindicans. . . . ."

146. Dioscorus did not rule out Leo's *Tome* on principle, but he accepted Juvenal's view that other business took precedence. See my note in *Rise of Monophysite Movement*, p. 40 n. 4.

147. The texts of these letters are in *PL* 8.929–35 and 937–38 and for Prosdocius's 953–61. For the acceptance of the authenticity of *Epistola ad Prosdocium* at Ephesus, by Marius Mercator, and by the African bishop Facundus in the sixth century, see the texts quoted in Migne, *PL* 8.961. These particular forgeries(?) had a far-reaching effect in the subsequent debate over Chalcedon.

148. Recorded in the *Acta* of the council read at Chalcedon, *ACO* II.1.1, p. 140, para. 491.

149. The Latin was transcribed in the *Acta* as the quaint-looking κοντραδικιτουρ with the explanation, ὅ ἐστιν, ἀντιλέγεται (*ACO* II.1.1, p. 191, para. 964). For the deacon Hilary's account of the event written to Theodosius's sister Pulcheria, see in Leo *Letter* XLVI.

150. See Chadwick's survey of the evidence, "Exile and Death of Flavian."

151. *Acta* of this session in Flemming, "Akten der ephesinischen Synode," p. 119.

152. Ibid., p. 147.

153. Mansi, *Sacrorum Conciliorum*, vol. 6, col. 909. See Honigmann, "Juvenal of Jerusalem," p. 238. The provinces were the Palestinian provinces, Arabia and Phoenicia I and II.

154. Flemming, "Akten der ephesinischen Synode," p. 145.

155. Ibid.

156. Theodosius's letters are included in Leo's correspondence as *Letters* LXII–LXIV, and in Schwartz, *ACO* II.3.1, pp. 15–17.

157. As much, however, as a result of a change of foreign policy (more vigorous attitude towards Attila) as religious policy; see Thompson, *Attila and Huns*, pp. 33, 189.

158. See P. Charanis, "Coronation and Its Constitutional Significance in the Later Roman Empire," *Byzantion* 15 (1940–41), pp. 49–66, esp. p. 53; and Frend, *Rise of Monophysite Movement*, p. 46.

159. An embassy to Leo had arrived in Rome in April 451. Eusebius of Dorylaeum, though a refugee in the city, was present and affirmed that he took part in the negotiations: "sponte subscripsi, quoniam et hanc regulam [canon 3] sanctissimo papae in urbe Roma relegi, praesentibus clericis Constantinopolitanis eamque suscepit [Leo]." See Chadwick, "Eucharist and Christology," pp. 27–28.

160. Text in Mansi, *Sacrorum Conciliorum*, vol. 6, p. 552.

161. For the numbers, see Leo *Letter* 98 (letter of the bishops of the council to Leo). For a succinct account of the proceedings, see Sellers, *Council of Chalcedon*, pp. 103–27.

162. *ACO* II.1.1, p. 115 (para. 282). See Honigmann, "Juvenal of Jerusalem," pp. 242–43.

163. *ACO* II.1.1, p. 117, para. 299.

164. Ibid., II.1.2, p. 81, para 23; and compare ibid., p. 124, para. 20; popes from Celestine to Leo had believed as Cyril believed.

165. Ibid., II.1.1, p. 115, para. 277.

166. Ibid., II.1.2, p. 123, paras. 7 and 8; and pp. 124–25. Sellers, *Council of Chalcedon*, pp. 116–21; and my comments in *Rise of Monophysite Movement*, p. 3 n. 4.

167. For Juvenal's place on the drafting committee and his negotiations with Maximus of Antioch on behalf of his own position, see Honigmann, "Juvenal of Jerusalem," p. 245. At the session of 23 October he agreed to surrender to Antioch the three non-Palestinian provinces he had gained the year before.

168. *ACO* II.1.2, p. 140, para. 5, and p. 155, para. 11.

169. See von Harnack, *History of Dogma*, vol. 4, p. 222, "four bald negative terms."

170. Eng. trans. Stevenson, *Creeds, Councils and Controversies*, p. 337. See Sellers, *Council of Chalcedon*, pp. 120–25, and Kelly, *Early Christian Doctrines*, pp. 338–42.

171. Ninth and tenth sessions, *ACO* II.1.3, 7–14; Theodoret's anathema of Nestorius, p. 9, para. 13. He also agreed with Leo's *Tome* (ibid.).

172. Twelfth and thirteenth sessions = *ACO* II.1.3, pp. 42–53.

173. Canon 28 did not deny the *presbeia* of Old Rome, but would not grant a *pronomia*, involving jurisdictional rights such as Constantinople was asserting over Ephesus. It also made no reference to the apostolic and Petrine character of Rome. Earlier in the proceedings, Paschasinus had stated that he regarded Anatolius as "the first" in seniority after himself, to which the bishop of Cyzicus replied immediately: "Yes, you know the canons" (that is, canon 3 of the Council of Constantinople). (Twelfth session on 20 October, *ACO* II.1.3, pp. 52–53). It looks as though divided counsels and/or confusion reigned in the ranks of the papal delegation throughout. See Dvornik, *Byzance*, pp. 45–46.

174. See Jones, *Later Roman Empire*, pp. 906, 1378 (refs. to comparative figures).

175. Acts of the thirteenth session = *ACO* II.1.3, p. 58, para. 26; by way of "subsistence and consolation." They would be living well! See Jones, *Later Roman Empire*, p. 906.

176. Mansi, *Sacrorum Conciliorum*, vol. 7, cols. 58–60 = *ACO* II.1.2, p. 113, paras. 54–58.

THE PARTING OF
THE WAYS

PART 4

The Catholic Recovery in the West
451–536

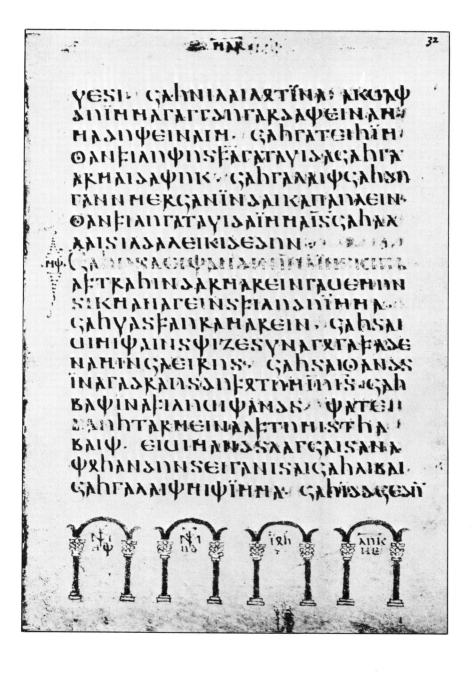

The crisis that shook the churches in 449–51 had ended in a series of compromises. At Chalcedon, Cyril had been hailed as the master theologian against whose teaching orthodoxy must be measured, but the twelve *Anathemas* had been passed over in silence and the Definition of Faith contained more that harmonized with the Christology of Antioch and the West than with that of Alexandria and even of Constantinople. The explosion of rage that greeted the news of the decisions of the council, especially in Alexandria and Jerusalem, showed that whatever the leaders might have concluded in the emperor's presence, the monks and the populace were not deceived. "Nestorius has been vindicated"; Leo's *Tome* "was Jewish." Juvenal of Jerusalem was "a traitor."[1] Out of this groundswell of anger and the deep conscientious doubts of the "hesitants" (*Diakrinomenoi*), the Monophysite movement was gradually to take shape.

Just as serious, however, was the rift that had opened between Rome and the majority of the Eastern bishops at the last session of the council. The questions of authority and precedence between Old and New Rome raised by the twenty-eighth canon were never to be settled. That the Acacian Schism (484–519) did not become permanent was due partly to the disproportionate influence wielded in the capital by the residual Latin-speaking provinces even after the end of the Western empire in 476, and partly because most Western Catholics still looked to the emperor as their ultimate protector against their Germanic Arian masters. The positions taken up by Rome and Constantinople then and at Chalcedon, however, were not to be reversed. Politics rather than religion postponed the final schism until 1054. Now we turn to the evolution of events in the eighty years following Chalcedon—mainly through Western eyes.

Pope Leo would not accept the twenty-eighth canon. In vain the bishops at Chalcedon wrote to him praising the part played by the *Tome* in winning agreement. "And we were all delighted, as at an imperial banquet, revelling in the spiritual food which Christ supplied to his invited guests through your letter." The legates had dissented only to leave the honor of accepting the council's decrees to Leo himself as his own work![2] The pope was not deceived. For him, Constantinople was a simple metropolitan see and the canon of the Second Ecumenical Council exalting it to equality with that of Peter was of no account.[3] On 7 February 452, Marcian sought to end the controversy by proclaiming the orthodoxy of the council's decrees. "From the different provinces the most religious bishops came to Chalcedon in accordance with our commands, and have taught by clear definition. Therefore let profane wrangling cease." All were bound to accept the decisions of the sacred council.[4]

Leo stood his ground. On 22 May 452, he annulled canon 28 in the strongest terms, as "against reverence for the canons of the Fathers, against the statutes of the Holy Ghost, and against the examples of antiquity."[5] No vote would prove the contrary. He spoke his mind in letters to

Marcian, Pulcheria, and Anatolius. These letters included a blistering attack on Patriarch Anatolius himself. The basic disagreement between papal and conciliar authority was clear.

Rome, however, lacked the means of success. The events of Ephesus II had ended the century-old alliance with Alexandria, the Rome-Alexandria axis around which Theodosius I had built Catholic orthodoxy. On Maundy Thursday 457 all hopes of restoring the past ended with the lynching of Proterius, the Chalcedonian choice as Dioscorus's successor to the patriarchate of Alexandria. From now on, Chalcedon was a minority cause in Egypt. The see of Mark could no longer be relied upon to support the see of Peter.

From Leo's point of view the situation in Italy and the former Western provinces of the empire was almost as disastrous. In 452 Attila had threatened Rome. In 455 the city was sacked by Gaiseric the Vandal. The barbarian successor-states were either Arian as the Visigoths and Vandals, or pagan as the Franks and Anglo-Saxons. Yet the position was held. Leo himself shows an extraordinary serenity in this situation. His carefully drafted budgets of letters to the Eastern court show his prime determination to assert his authority there, come what might elsewhere. In 457 he was more concerned about the dreadful events in Alexandria than the apparent disintegration of Catholicism in North Africa and other parts of the West.

He was justified in the long term. Over three generations, Catholicism gradually regained a dominant position in the West, except in Britain and, until 587, in Visigothic Spain. The key factors in its success were, first, that the mass of the provincials of the conquered territories retained their Catholicism, or at least their non-Arian Christianity. Second, Catholic episcopal and parochial organization survived. In Gaul in particular, episcopal councils and the tradition of Western ecclesiastical polity continued. In the Visigothic dominions ten Catholic councils were held between 419 and 540.[6] More important was the staffing of the Gallic episcopate with a succession of clerics of great ability, drawn from the former provincial aristocracy and often schooled at Lérins, who could impose their will on their conquerors. Lérins itself emerged as one of the foundations on which eventual Catholic victory was based. These episcopal aristocrats also enhanced the already considerable economic power of the church in Gaul. In addition, there as well as in Italy and North Africa, the attraction of the higher civilization represented by the bishops and the still-Romanized provincials gradually undermined the position of the Arian church among the barbarians themselves.[7] Latin language and Latin religion both finally prevailed. Moreover, Catholicism in Gaul received great encouragement from Clovis's conversion, whose Franks were more than a match for the Visigoths, Burgundians, and the Alamanni. Finally, amidst all the confusion and demoralization of the times, Rome and the papacy retained their aura.

The loyalty of the Gallic episcopate was never in doubt. Elsewhere in the West, an exiled African bishop, Fulgentius of Ruspe, proclaimed with his African Catholic colleagues (c. 520), "the Roman Church, which is the summit of the world, holds and teaches, and with it the whole Christian world [the words of Peter and Paul]."[8] The bishops may have merely wished to impress the deacon, Paul, from Constantinople but they also expressed a sense of Rome-based unity prevalent among the Catholic episcopate in Arian-dominated surroundings.

From a low point in c. 450, marked perhaps by Severinus's experiences of the impoverishment, cynicism, and despair among the Christians he found in Noricum,[9] Catholicism progressed toward recovery. By 536 it had been restored to preeminence in Gaul and North Africa. Belisarius had set foot in Italy and would capture Rome itself on 9 December 536. The once-powerful Arian Ostrogothic monarchy was not destined to survive. In 529, another ascetic-minded aristocrat, Benedict of Nursia (c. 480–547), began to establish a form of monasticism finely adapted to the needs of the people, and eventually ensured that there was no relapse into paganism or Germanic Arianism.

BRITAIN

We start, however, with the exception to the rule, Britain. Available evidence suggests that at the end of the fourth century the church in Britain resembled in every way the other churches in the West. Its organization was episcopal, perhaps based on the twenty-eight city-states (*civitates*) of Britain. We hear of bishops, priests, and deacons, and even lay elders (*seniores*).[10] To judge from the wall paintings from the house-church at Lullingstone, neither church buildings, nor worship, nor art differed from those on the Continent.[11] For the baptismal liturgy, the hexagonal font identified in the fort at Richborough has parallels in churches on the Rhineland.[12] Of the faithful themselves, Christianity in early fifth-century Britain as elsewhere had its solid, worldly members, like St. Patrick himself in his early years.[13] It was also intellectually alert. Pelagianism, not paganism, was the threat which Germanus of Auxerre encountered among the British leaders when he arrived in 429,[14] and on the ridge a mile east of Verulamium where he met them, the shrine of St. Alban was already a center of pilgrimage.[15]

Britain, however, lacked its Martin of Tours. After decades of field work, no positive evidence exists for the spread of Christianity among the rural populations. Temples may have been decaying, but they do not seem to have been replaced by chapels. There is no evidence for a parish system.[16] Germanus had to baptize his rustic troops before he joined battle against the Picts in 429.[17]

This is where Britain differed from the Continent. We know of nothing to compare with Victricius of Rouen's description of the well-organized and enthusiastic Christianity of his episcopal see c. 395,[18] and lack of support in the countryside would have meant fewer church estates, less rent, and fewer endowments. The British church's poverty asserted at the Council of Ariminum in 359 may not have been voluntary. In the fifth century British Christianity produced some distinguished writers, such as Fastidius (*flor.* c. 450) who traveled to Gaul and wrote long letters on *The Christian Life* and *On Preserving Widowhood*,[19] reflecting therefore a similar interest in ascetic Christianity on both sides of the Channel; but such men were few. Christianity had taken root too late and had failed to destroy Romano-Celtic paganism as Martin had succeeded in doing in northern Gaul. In the fifth century, Christian basilicas and the house-churches of wealthy villa-owners perished together with the spoken Latin language.[20] The monastic settlements that begin to appear in the West c. 480, such as at Tintagel, represent a new form of Christianity derived from the Mediterranean, perhaps via southern Gaul, that owed little if anything to its episcopally organized predecessor.[21] The years 450–80 are indeed blank regarding Christianity even in sub-Roman Britain.[22]

In the Anglo-Saxon-occupied areas, even in Kent, Christianity had left memories and ruins rather than congregations. The church dedicated to St. Martin outside Canterbury, "built of old while the Romans yet inhabited Britain," the historian Bede says,[23] seems to have been restored as a special favor by King Ethelbert for his Christian Frankish queen, Bertha. For the rest, Augustine and his fellow missionaries had to start their evangelization of Anglo-Saxon England practically from scratch.

St. Patrick

Before its disappearance, however, Romano-British Christianity left a final legacy to the West. Patrick's Christian background and his capture by the Scots (Irish) in c. 405 are well known.[24] Before his mission, beginning c. 432, there were Christians in Ireland, for in c. 430 Pope Celestine consecrated Bishop Palladius as the first bishop "to the Irish believing in Christ." His object was to minister to their spiritual needs and free them from Pelagianism.[25] Patrick's aim was different. Pelagianism is not mentioned in his writings. His eye was on the conversion of the Irish and the organization of the church among his former captors. As a prisoner he had been employed as a shepherd, somewhere in the west perhaps near Killala, County Mayo. To quote his words, "and daily I often used to pray—love of God and fear of him increased more and more, and my faith grew, and my spirit was moved, so that in one day [I would say] as many as a hundred prayers, and at night nearly as many, when I used to stay even in the woods and on the mountain."[26] After six years he escaped, and eventually reached Gaul on a ship carrying a cargo of Irish wolfhounds. He was able to return to Britain which in c. 411 he found peaceful enough to dissuade him from going back to Ireland. Then he received his call to evangelize, a dream in which he saw himself summoned by his former captors through a Christian(?) named Victorius to return to Ireland. He obeyed. First, he sailed for Gaul, may have been ordained deacon and presbyter by Amator (d. 418), Germanus's predecessor as bishop of Auxerre, and after training there (or at Lérins) returned to Britain. There, he was consecrated bishop in c. 432, in face, however, of opposition which he remembered and resented throughout his life.[27] Why did he fall out with the British church?[28] There may have been nothing more than suspicion of a crime, such as had dogged Paulinus of Nola in Aquitaine. It is not known. The effect, however, was to make Patrick a permanent exile from his native land, and by preference a dweller "among barbarians" (*Letter to Coroticus* I).

Patrick shared much of the outlook of his Gallic contemporaries—"Christian" = "Roman" (*Letter to Coroticus* II). In part, Patrick's idealism was aimed at bringing civilization to the barbarians who captured, maimed, and destroyed under the influence of their heathen gods. He also returned to an existing Christian community, but this was only the beginning. He was not an ecclesiastical diplomat but an enthusiast, and seemingly less concerned than other Western missionaries with negative avoidance of judgment than in spreading the faith. Judgment was preached, but it was balanced by emphasis on the love of God and the expiatory work of Christ, the presence of the Spirit within the believer and a faith founded on Scripture.[29] By the end of his life (c. 460) he had preached, baptized, and organized through much of Ulster and Connaught. "Thousands" were baptized,[30] and though the career of Columba a century later shows how strong was the influence of paganism in many aspects of Irish daily life and belief, the power of the Druids was to a great extent destroyed. The foundations of a Christian church throughout Ireland had been laid.

Patrick's method of evangelization was to work through the chiefs and their families and to build up local churches with their support.[31] His organization was episcopal. He stressed his own status as a bishop[32] and fixed his see at Armagh, near the royal center of the kings of Ulster. His encouragement of virginity, the order of widows, and the building of convents and monasteries was no more than one would expect from a high-born (*nobilis, Letter to Coroticus* X) cleric trained in the Gallic monastic tradition. One suspects the same source as intensifying his aristocratic bias, as when he describes his successes in converting the families of the nobility.[33] Patrick's church in Ireland was designed to be organized no differently from those he knew in Britain and on the Continent.

The movement toward a strongly individualistic monastic Christianity in Ireland belongs to the sixth century as it does in the rest of Celtic Britain. Its progress may be associated with the consolidation of the Anglo-Saxon kingdoms that cut southeastern Britain off from the remainder of Western Europe after c. 470, and the consequent return of the Atlantic trade route to the Mediterranean (direct, or overland via southern Gaul) to importance.

Byzantine-type monasteries and art forms penetrated along the same routes that brought Mediterranean wine and pottery to western Britain and Ireland.[34] In its acceptance of what it believed to be the ancient Alexandrian calculation of Easter,[35] the broad Byzantine-type tonsure, and important elements in its art, the Celtic church appears to owe much to Byzantium. This affiliation rather than remoteness from Rome lay behind the misunderstandings and conflict with Augustine and his missionaries.[36]

NORTH AFRICA UNDER THE VANDALS

In contrast to sub-Roman Britain, the history of North Africa under the Vandals (430–534) is relatively well documented. It provides a classic example of the submergence of Catholic Christianity in this period followed by its recovery and ultimate triumph.

Gaiseric

In c. 490, half a century after the fall of Carthage to Gaiseric (19 October 439), Victor of Vita looked back on the preceding era as one of unrelieved gloom following an age of great prosperity for Catholicism. The Vandals, he records, raged in particular against "the churches and basilicas of the saints and against the cemeteries and monasteries."[37] Bishops and priests were slain "without compunction and their wealth seized." Indeed, Catholicism and the nobility are associated in Victor's mind as the twin objects of Vandal persecution,[38] an indication perhaps of the real gainers from the proscription of the Donatists after 412. Writers a generation earlier than Victor betray a similar outlook. Possidius (c. 435), Augustine's biographer, saw the arrival of the Vandals as an unmitigated disaster, responsible for the destruction of "innumerable churches" and the burning of Hippo itself.[39] He speaks of the sacking of cities and estates, of the murder, torture, and enslavement of the inhabitants and of their refuge in caves and woods. Another, anonymous, contemporary adds to the tale the collapse of faith and the despair of the Catholic Christian population.[40]

Rome and Roman civilization found an enemy of uncommon rancor. Gaiseric had led his people into North Africa, in order to gain a kingdom of their own, undisturbed by rival Germanic groups and untrammeled by the constraints of federate status accepted by the Visigoths and Burgundians. He was determined that that kingdom should be self-sufficient.[41] The capture of Hippo and the defeat of the Roman forces under Aspar in 431–32 marked his first step. In 435 Gaiseric accepted a treaty that gave him most of Numidia. Four years later (19 October 439), however, he seized Carthage in a surprise coup. Thenceforth, he could deal with the emperors in Ravenna and Constantinople as an equal. The treaty of 442 gave him what he wanted—Carthage, proconsular Africa, and Numidia east of Cirta—the most fertile and strategically best-placed parts of North Africa. The remainder Valentinian could keep. The marriage alliance Gaiseric played at contracting through Valentinian's daughter, Eudocia, from 445/46 enabled him to consolidate his power without imperial interference. Then in June 455, within a few months of Valentinian's murder, Gaiseric posed as his avenger by sacking Rome, which had conveniently fallen into the hands of his supplanter.[42] Apart from immense loot, he gained the bonus of capturing Valentinian's wife and two daughters. Eudocia was now married off to his son Huneric, her sister and mother used as pawns in long-drawn-out negotiations with the East Roman empire. Nothing could shake him. The fleet he created and his occupation of parts of Sicily and Sardinia threatened Roman commerce in the western Mediterranean, and gave an even-greater impression of its destructive power to contemporary observers.[43] He frustrated the efforts of Majorian, the last Western emperor of any standing and ability (457–61), to remove him, and defeated the far more ambitious expedition by the emperor Leo in 468. He extended Vandal rule to the coast towns of Mauretania. He used the Berbers of the interior as his allies and he cared not one jot for Catholicism, the empire, and their supporters in North Africa.

Such was the man whose rule Victor of Vita experienced. Catholicism was too strong to be proscribed, but it could be rendered harmless to the Vandal community. Thus in Carthage itself the churches within the walls of the city, including the Basilica Restituta, the Catholic cathedral, were taken over for Arian worship,[44] or allowed, as was at least one of the larger churches near the port, to fall into decay.[45] Most of the churches outside the walls were left to the Catholics, with the exception of the two dedicated to Cyprian's memory.[46] Worship was allowed, but any symbols of past glory that could be dangerous to the regime were suppressed. Similarly, for long intervals between 439 and 454 and between 457 and 480, the Catholics were denied the presence of a bishop of Carthage, while in territory settled by the Vandals, especially in proconsular Africa, their clergy were prevented from serving their congregations. The Donatists also fared badly. Outside the Roman-held province of Mauretania we hear little of them. They also regarded Gaiseric as a persecutor and forerunner of antichrist, but after the final edition of the *Liber Genealogus* in which this description occurs (in 463) they fade from history until the time of Pope Gregory the Great.[47]

Huneric

Gaiseric at last ended his days in January 477. His son and successor, Huneric (477–84), inherited his father's hostility to the Catholics and his deviousness. Having allowed the restoration of a Catholic bishop of Carthage under pressure from the emperor Zeno in 480/81 he seems to have decided to bring matters to a head with the African Catholics once and for all. He was determined that no *homoousion* service should be held within the *sortes Vandalorum* (that is, the territories settled by the Vandals).[48]

The precedent of the imperial measures against the Donatists came to mind. He would summon a conference in which the case for Catholicism and Arianism would be argued out and he would reward the winner. The decision was promulgated on 20 May 483. The conference was to meet on 1 February 484. A list of bishops preserved in one manuscript of Victor's *History of the Persecution of the African Province* gives 466 names, a great proportion of these from Mauretanian sees outside effective Vandal control. It has been argued that many of the 120 Mauretanian bishoprics listed occur only here and are fictitious or the result of duplications by the Carthaginian scribes.[49] This is possible, but even without the Mauretanians, the Catholics mustered at least 300 bishops at Carthage from all over Vandal Africa and the Vandal-held Mediterranean islands. Not surprisingly, the conference itself was a fiasco. The Catholics objected to the preeminent role accorded to the Arian archbishop Cyrila, and his claim to be patriarch of Carthage.[50] On 25 February 484 Huneric closed the sessions and ordered the Catholic bishops to convert to Arianism by 1 June 484. Those who refused were condemned to exile, scourging, and even death. Their churches were taken over by the Arians. Huneric grimly applied the financial penalties once exacted by the Catholics against recalcitrant Donatists.[51]

Huneric died on 22 December 484. His two successors, Gunthamund (484–96) and Thrasamund (496–523), dropped the violence but maintained the pressure. Thrasamund was the most attractive of the Vandal rulers, enjoyed religious debates, and would invite the acknowledged Catholic champion Fulgentius, Bishop of Ruspe (c. 462–527), to write a reply to an Arian tract "within the hour."[52]

After c. 460, however, the Arian position was never as strong as it looked. There were too few Vandals. In their highly organized state their rulers had to rely on Latin-speaking administrators. Though some of these seem to have been willing to conform to Arianism, many refused.[53] Beyond the immediate Vandal settlements in proconsular Africa, the impact of the Vandals on the landowners who lived on their great estates in Byzacena, or on the cultivators further south beyond Theveste, was minimal. The *Tablettes Albertini*, deeds of sale dated to September 493 relating to an estate in that area, show that the system of land tenure under the *Lex Mancia* still governed conditions of service on large holdings. There was a considerable class of free peasants whose conditions seem if anything to have been slightly better than under the later empire. The fifteen different hands which appear on the *Tablettes* show that some of the peasants were literate and knew how to write simple legal documents in lower-case cursive that can be read today. Latin, though somewhat debased, was obviously in normal use. Their leaders were a presbyter and *magistri*. Except for the name of King Gunthamund there was no trace of the Vandal occupation.[54] Thrasamund's reign saw the poets Luxorius, Flavius, Felix, and

Dracontius flourish, praising in Latin panegyrics the king's achievements. The Vandal proprietor enjoyed the same type of house, farming, and pleasures as his Afro-Latin neighbor. Arianism with its Gothic Bible and Germanic liturgy[55] was becoming progressively a relic of a more heroic past.

Despite their pretensions to the title of patriarch the Vandal bishops of Carthage made little mark as administrators or intellectual leaders. On the other hand, even at the nadir of its fortunes in c. 480, the Catholics in Carthage counted "more than five hundred clergy" on their staff, and in proconsular Africa itself could muster forty-four out of fifty-four listed bishops for the conference of 484.[56] Its organization had survived the worst that Gaiseric and Huneric could do.

Fulgentius of Ruspe

Gradually the Catholics regained intellectual ascendancy. In the first decades of the sixth century, they produced one leader of the quality of Remigius of Rheims or Avitus of Vienne, who served their cause so effectively in Gaul. Fulgentius of Ruspe was born into the Afro-Latin aristocracy.[57] His grandfather Gordianus had fled to Italy on the fall of Carthage in 439, glad to save his life while his estates in or near the city were handed over to the Arian clergy. Shortly before 460, however, it seems that Gaiseric restored the family to their extensive estates in Byzacena (near Thelepte). Fulgentius grew up amid secure and prosperous surroundings in a family that included both slaves and clients among its responsibilities. His father died young. He was brought up, like so many Christian religious leaders of the time, by a strongly Catholic mother, but his education included the classics as well as Scripture. By 480 when he was seventeen or eighteen he was already in charge of the family estates.[58] He was evidently willing to accept the Vandals de facto, for shortly thereafter he entered their service and had become a superintendent (*procurator*) of the public lands in Byzacena with a large staff of officials under him. The job could involve the holder in financial loss, and this, coupled with the burden of responsibility, was among the reasons prompting him to resign and seek a monastic career. His biographer, the deacon Ferrandus, indicates a flourishing monastic life at the time. Fulgentius was not particularly welcome, and his novitiate was long, lasting from c. 483 to c. 490. The life was not rigorous by Egyptian or Gallic standards, however, and later Fulgentius would select areas "where orchards promised good returns,"[59] for the site of monasteries. It was not a call to the desert.

Despite a breakdown in health, Fulgentius persevered. He transferred his property to his mother and brother and planned to visit the monasteries of Egypt. The plan, however, miscarried. The year 497/98 saw raids by Berber groups on the prosperous areas of Byzacena, a harbinger of things to come.[60] Fulgentius and some companions sought the comparative safety of proconsular Africa, but on land settled by the Vandals they were suspect. Thrasamund's policy was to watch the movements of prominent Catholics, to prevent Catholic propaganda, and to attract where possible converts from the Afro-Latin population, holding in reserve the weapon of relegation to Sardinia for recalcitrants. In the countryside, however, most of the population seems to have been on the Catholic side, and Fulgentius lacked for nothing on his trek into the western part of the proconsular province.[61]

In 502, after a visit to Sicily and Rome, he was suddenly and almost clandestinely consecrated bishop of Ruspe on the Byzacenian coast, and just as promptly the blow descended. He was exiled with other Catholic clergy to Cagliari; there he remained thirteen years, but not idly. He developed into a forceful controversialist; anti-Arian, anti-Pelagian, and even anti-Donatist writings flowed from his pen, after the manner but not after the ability of Augustine.[62] Thrasamund was impressed, recalling him in c. 515 with the object apparently of debating with him. The king was one of the few theologically minded rulers among the Germanic kings; but little of value emerged. Fulgentius reproduced traditional Western arguments, relying on the maintenance of the strict distinction between Father and Son to claim that the divine nature of Christ must ipso facto share fully in the nature of God, and similarly the Spirit.[63] The argument tended to be circular, but serves as a reminder how important it was for the Catholic theologians of North Africa to uphold the Two Natures Christology against all comers. It helps to explain their strong opposition to the condemnation of the Three Chapters and hence the Antiochene theological tradition at the Council of Constantinople in 553.

By 517, Thrasamund had had enough, and Fulgentius was back in Sardinia. So long as Thrasamund ruled, the Vandal position was tenable, reinforced as it had been since c. 500 by his marriage with Amalafrida, sister of Theodoric the Ostrogoth. In Constantinople the emperor Anastasius, at issue with the papacy, gave little encouragement to the African refugees in the capital. In 518, however, this prop was knocked away. The ending of the Acacian Schism boded ill for the Germanic kingdoms in Italy and Africa. The politics of Catholic orthodoxy moved steadily in the direction of their suppression.

In 523 Thrasamund's death raised Catholic hopes further. His successor Hilderich (523–30), middle-aged son of Huneric and Eudocia, was pro-Byzantine and followed his mother's religious views. Amalafrida was banished from court and met her end c. 526.[64] Freedom was restored to the Catholics, and exiles, including Fulgentius, returned. In 523 councils were held in Byzacena at Sufes and Iunca, the latter an important monastic center. Two years later (5–6 February 525) Bonifatius, bishop of Carthage, assembled a council of sixty-one bishops.[65] It was a curiously low-key affair. The "recent restoration of liberty" was hailed, but Bonifatius introduced few far-reaching plans for reorganizing a church harassed by persecutions in the previous ninety years. Time was taken up principally with the rivalries of bishops and monastic leaders in Byzacena. In itself this might indicate the latent strength of Catholicism in Vandal Africa, for the church in Byzacena lacked nothing in quarrelsome vigor. Also one has the impression that, outside Carthage, the scattered Vandal population was blending with the Afro-Latins to the latter's advantage. Churches at Ammaedara and Mactaris have produced sixth-century inscriptions commemorating dignitaries and their families with Germanic names. While these could be Goths, or the churches could have been in Arian use for a time, the association of these with other Latin inscriptions also suggests that the dedicants may have become absorbed into the Catholic community, which had retained its wealth and influence in Byzacena.[66] In Carthage itself, the Vandals celebrated the feast of Cyprian on 13 September,[67] and Victor indicates that in Huneric's reign even more Vandals in court circles were in the habit of attending Catholic services.[68]

By now, however, the days of the Arian Vandals were numbered. Control of the outlying areas of Gaiseric's kingdom was passing to the Moors. New, more powerful enemies were threatening from the southeast. The confederation of nomadic tribes, the Louata, was pressing westward from Cyrenaica and by 520 had reached the Vandal frontier in Tripolitania.[69] The Vandal cavalry was no match for the camel-mounted nomads, and by 530 much of southern Byzacena was controlled by the latter. It mattered little that Hilderich was deposed and that a final national reaction set in under his supplanter Gelimer (530–34). Gelimer was sufficiently hostile to the Catholics to arouse the anger of the exiles in Constantinople. Their pressure succeeded, for the empire was ruled by Justinian who aimed at reconquering the West. In the summer of 533 a great fleet, blessed by the patriarch and commanded by Justinian's general Belisarius, sailed for Carthage. By 13 September, the city had fallen. Vandal counterattacks were warded off and Gelimer became a helpless fugitive in Numidia. His kingdom was ended in 534. On 1 August 535, Catholicism was restored in all its former authority and privileges.[70] It was just short of a century since Possidius had ended his *Life of Augustine* with a tale of woe worthy of Gildas's *The Ruin of Britain*.

GAUL

The fate of Arianism in North Africa demonstrated that the Germanic invaders, however determined their rulers, could not impose their religion on the mass of the Catholic provincials, providing the church's organization survived. In Gaul also, when a similar situation arose in the south and east of the country, the Catholic episcopate triumphed. For a long time there were other possibilities until the decisive event took place sometime about 500—the conversion of the Frankish king Clovis to Catholicism.

Historical "might-have-beens" have their interest. In contrast to the

Vandals, the Visigoths did not consider themselves enemies of the Roman empire. Their leaders wanted land for their people and on the whole were satisfied with their federate status and settlement in Aquitaine offered to them by the Roman authorities in 418.[71] As federates and allies they were entitled to one-third of the rents and dues of the lands they occupied. They seem to have settled in farming communities[72] and at the same time fought insurgent Armoricans and Bagaudae. The wars that led to the gradual extension of Visigoth territory eastward into Narbonne and southeastward toward Tarragona were piecemeal and usually provoked by quarrels with local Roman authorities. Threatened by Attila, Visigoths and Romans fought side by side under Aetius, and Theodoric I, the Visigoth king, was killed in the great battle of the Catalaunian Plains (Châlons) in 451. Four years later, the Gallic nobleman Avitus, father-in-law of Sidonius Apollinaris, was proclaimed emperor by the Gallo-Romans and Visigoths jointly. The union of peoples and cultures seemed imminent.

Sidonius Apollinaris

The letters of Sidonius Apollinaris (c. 431–80) give a glimpse, from the point of view of a member of the Gallo-Roman nobility, of some of the realities of the situation and psychological barriers in the way of union between the two peoples. In Sidonius's early manhood the Visigoths controlled much of the vast territory extending from the Loire to southern Spain, though parts of central and southeastern Gaul were still under Roman rule. The newcomers, however, had shown themselves willing to work with the Gallo-Romans. The social status quo was not disturbed. While the Bagaudae and their sympathizers had sought their rule rather than the Roman,[73] the Visigoths did not reciprocate. Once in control, they showed little sympathy for the peasants. In 454 they inflicted a crushing defeat on the Bagaudae in the province of Tarragona. Brigandage, Sidonius's correspondence suggests, was a hazard but not endemic. Roads were not always secure,[74] but his villa on his wife's estates at Avitacum (near Lyons?) was unfortified. Life continued as it had done in the past, with hunting, lavish banquets, and polite correspondence with neighbors.[75]

Sidonius's father had been praetorian prefect of the Gauls, a Catholic like himself and a patriot. Sidonius wrote to his brother-in-law in patriotic style that "the country that gave us birth has the right to hold the highest place in our affection."[76] It was in this spirit of civic duty, rather than worldly renunciation assumed by so many of his contemporaries, that he accepted the bishopric of Clermont in 469. The year before he had been prefect of Rome.

Sidonius was not altogether deceiving himself. Thanks largely to the diplomacy and military genius of Aetius (murdered 454), in the 450s and 460s southern Gaul experienced a final glow of Gallic Christian civilization, the blending of the Roman classics with the fathers of the church. Sidonius's letters move effortlessly between biblical and classical quotations, appeals to courage in defense of *Romanitas*, and reliance on prayer and the relics of martyrs.

Sidonius's friend Faustus, bishop of Riez (c. 430–c. 495), was the outstanding Gallic intellectual of the age, who sought to find a *via media* between predestination as affirmed by Augustine's and Pelagius's views.[77] While accepting Augustine's teaching regarding original sin, he insisted on the necessity of human effort in response to divine grace, and like Julian of Eclanum before him, he believed that Augustine's views were a relic of Manicheism. Like many other Gallic bishops of the day, he was a product of Lérins. The monastic settlement was still flourishing in the early part of his adult life, and while there, Faustus attempted to guide the monks from negative exertions aimed at ever-greater asceticism to a more deeply contemplative yet also more practical sense of their vocation. In the growing disorganization of existence due to the Gothic invasion he attempted to establish hostels for wayfarers and hospitals for the sick and poor. His work was another influence in the formation of the monastic ideal of medieval Europe.[78]

Another of Sidonius's contemporaries was Gennadius (d. 496), a scholar and presbyter of Marseilles. He also was a "semi-Pelagian," one of the few Westerners familiar with Greek, who left to the West a final continuation of Jerome's *Illustrious Men* to his own day, and for whom Faustus was a "man very devoted to Scripture," and an outstanding teacher.[79]

By this time, there was little scope for scholarship in theology. Ever since the Suebic general Ricimer, who controlled Italy, had defeated Avitus (October 456) the Romano-Gothic alliance had come under strain. Some nobles were prepared to throw in their lot with the Goths and were prepared to see a Gaul divided between Goth and Burgundian.[80] The majority felt otherwise (Sidonius *Letter* II.1.4). Sidonius himself despised the "seven-foot" Burgundians who occupied his house in c. 461 as "repulsive and stinking" nuisances who prevented him from composing his verses (*Carmen* XII). When Euric succeeded Theodoric II as king in 466, however, he cut progressively the ties that had bound Goth and Roman. A ragbag army of Bretons, Gauls, and Romans was defeated in 469. Auvergne was invaded. Soon Sidonius's see of Clermont was the only major city in the province holding out. The Visigoths pushed forward to the Loire and the Rhone (Sidonius *Letter* III.1.5). From Italy, the emperor Nepos (475–76) authorized four Gallic bishops to enter into negotiations with the conquerors. Clermont was surrendered and by 481 all Provence and Auvergne passed to Euric's control.

For the time being the Catholics continued to enjoy religious freedom. At Bourges, the provincial capital, Sidonius writes that people had time to divide into frivolous factions disputing over the vacant see. Needless to say, he found a suitable candidate himself.[81] He also read the signs of the times. The church was "in a tottering condition." Diocese and parish lay waste without minister. Bishops had died and not been replaced.[82] Leading anti-Arians, such as Faustus of Riez, soon would find themselves exiled from their sees.

Germanic Arianism was reaching the height of its influence in Gaul. In 456 the Burgundians, moving toward Lyons from the lands assigned to them near Lake Geneva, had allied themselves with the Visigoths and exchanged Catholicism for Arianism. About the same time in northwestern Spain, the Suebi who had vacillated between paganism and Catholicism accepted the teaching of Ajax—one of the few Gothic (or pro-Gothic) missionaries whose work has come down to us—and also became Arians.[83] Euric himself was a convinced Arian. He did not conceal his resentment at the arrogant Gallo-Roman nobility, who in turn regarded his people as "skin-clad barbarians."[84] Under his rule, Gallo-Roman and Catholic became estranged from their Visigothic conquerors. The "noble savage" concept, prominent under Salvian, was dropped. The Catholic episcopate began to seek new allies in Euric's rivals.

These rivals were the Franks who had extended their rule westward from the Rhine and modern Belgium toward Paris. In the 470s they had also played second-string to the Visigoths. Childeric (d. 481), one of the kings of the Salian Franks, had married a Visigothic princess, and Lantechildis, one of their daughters, was an Arian; another daughter had married the Visigoth king Theodoric II; their son Clovis remained pagan. For many Catholic leaders of the time, paganism was less of a threat than heresy. It is noticeable that Victor of Vita is more charitable in his judgments of the pagan Moors than of the Arian Vandals.[85] One straw in the wind had been Bishop Lupus of Troyes's attachment to Attila's forces during the 430s. If Attila had triumphed, the possibility of his conversion to Catholicism and gradual civilization of his Huns and their allies might have been expected.[86] Remigius, bishop of Rheims, may have entertained similar hopes concerning Clovis.

Clovis

The Franks were warriors, second only to the archpirates the Saxons, a people to be feared. Sidonius describes them as barbarians, "grey-eyed, shaven faced with yellow hair."[87] For two centuries they had fought the Romans on the Rhine frontier. Their kings had been thrown to the beasts in the amphitheater of Cologne by Constantine.[88] Only exceptionally had Franks allowed themselves to become Romanized. In the mid–fifth century they formed a loose confederation under their own kings, all of whom, according to Gregory of Tours (c. 580), belonged to the same ruling family.[89] On Childeric's death in 481 Clovis succeeded him at the age of about fifteen. He was at that time king only of the Salians settled around Tournai, but in the next ten years he brought the various Frankish tribes under his sovereignty, pushed westward and destroyed the last remnants of Roman rule in the valley of the Loire. It was after this event in 486 that Remigius of Rheims wrote to him offering his allegiance and urging him to work always in accord with the bishops for the great benefit of his country.[90] Remigius became one of his counselors. His decisive step, however, was his marriage in 493 with Clotilde, a Catholic niece of the Burgundian king Gundobad. Clotilde harbored no happy memories of life in the Arian court, and from the outset added her influence to that of Remigius to convert Clovis to Catholicism.[91] Clovis allowed his sons by Clotilde to be baptized, but his heir, a son named Theodoric from a previous legal liaison, like him remained pagan.[92]

In the 490s Clovis aimed to extend his realm up the Rhine Valley at the expense of the Alamanni and also south of the Loire into Visigoth territory. The latter attempt failed after initial successes, and the Alamanni also resisted strongly. Clovis is then said to have vowed to Clotilde that he would become a Christian if he succeeded in defeating the Alamanni. Like Constantine, his prayer was answered. Victory was his and he became a catechumen. His final decision was made after experience of the cult of St. Martin which from now on became a symbol of Frankish influence.[93] Probably on Christmas Day 499, he was baptized, along with his son Theodoric, by Remigius at Rheims. A considerable number of his army (the sources say three thousand) joined him in the first mass baptism of the Germanic peoples into Catholic Christianity.[94]

By no means all the Franks followed Clovis's example.[95] The effect was greater among the Gallo-Romans. The bishops now had an ally. Powerful figures, such as Caesarius of Arles (bishop, 503–42) remained nominally loyal to the Visigoths but their hearts were with Clovis. This, however, was not always the case with the influential laity. Sidonius's own son fought heroically for the Visigoths against the Franks at Vouillé in 507, and the inhabitants of Rodez threw their bishop out when they suspected him of collaboration with the Franks. Euric's successor, Alaric II (484–507), was an administrator rather than a warrior. Aided by Gallo-Roman lawyer, Leo of Narbonne, he published (in February 506) a codex of "laws of the Visigoths and Romans" in hopes of removing one major source of grievance among the ex-Roman provincials, and of taking his kingdom a long step forward toward the fusion of the two peoples.[96] In the same spirit of openhandedness and tolerance he followed the codex with the grant of permission to the Catholic bishops in his domains to hold a council at Agde (September 506) to regulate the discipline of Catholic Christianity within the Visigoth state.[97] He was too late. Arianism was now the enemy. Next year, Clovis struck and Alaric lost his life at the battle of Vouillé in Poitou. Nearly all Visigothic Gaul fell to Clovis. In the following years only the intervention of the Ostrogothic kingdom in Italy saved the southeastern strip of Gaul, Septimania, and temporarily preserved a link on the eastern border with Italy for it.

In July 511 a council at Orléans worked out the details of the alliance between Catholic Christianity and the Frankish kingdom. The emperor Anastasius added his approbation by making Clovis honorary consul. When Clovis died on 27 November of the same year, Frankish Gaul was Catholic Christian and by far the strongest power west of the Alps. The seal was set on the new order by the re-creation of the papal vicariate of Arles in favor of Caesarius, though the Visigoths clung to the city and surroundings for another twenty years.

The end of Arianism in the Burgundian kingdom, centered now on Lyons, followed almost as a matter of course. Here, the part of Remigius was played by Avitus, bishop of Vienne (d. 518). Avitus was a member of the Gallo-Roman nobility, a writer and poet as well as a bishop, but unlike Sidonius Apollinaris, also a man with a missionary instinct. The Burgundian king Gundobad read the signs. He allowed the bishops in his kingdom to proselytize, and their converts included his son Sigismund.[98] Avitus does not seem to have been content with this, for after the battle of Vouillé he entered into correspondence with Clovis, which can only be said to be treasonable.[99] Gundobad died in 516. Next year, a council of twenty-four bishops at Epaon signified the transfer of allegiance to Catholicism. The conversion, however, prolonged the life of the Burgundian kingdom for a few years only. It was potentially too wealthy and too well placed to be allowed to survive and too weak to bar the Franks from moving into Italy. In 534 Sigismund perished in battle and the Burgundian realm was annexed by the Franks. The Ostrogoths also suffered. In the war of 532–34 Arles fell to Childebert. Caesarius rejoiced in the change to a Catholic ruler.

The Gallo-Roman episcopate had its way. Despite tactical turns neither episcopacy nor aristocracy had ever accepted the Visigoths. Pride of birth and religion had prevailed. Whether the Frankish victory was in the interest of the future civilization of the West is another matter. Merovingian Gaul became a scene of perpetual internecine strife among members of the Frankish royal house with resultant decay in standards of civilization. When every allowance has been made for the civilizing work of the Catholic clergy, and later of the Benedictine monks, it remains an open question whether a Romano-Visigothic commonwealth welcomed by Paulus Orosius, and accepted by many influential Gallo-Romans until the reign of Euric, would not have served the interests of Western Europe better than the Catholic alliance with the Franks.[100] The European Dark Ages begin with Clovis.

ITALY

The Ostrogoths failed to save their fellow Goths from defeat and the Burgundians from absorption by the Franks. In 534 they were themselves in danger from Justinian's Western policies. In the eight years since Theodoric's death the fortunes of the Ostrogothic kingdom had changed disastrously. Like that of the Vandals, its existence had depended on the genius of a single man and when Theodoric passed from the scene in August 526 he left no adequate successors.

Theodoric the Ostrogoth

In the autumn of 476 Romulus Augustulus, the last Roman emperor in the West, had been deposed by his Germanic master, the Rugian Odoacer.[101] The latter proclaimed himself king and returned the imperial insignia to the emperor Zeno at Constantinople.[102] Zeno granted him the rank of "patrician" (*patricius*) and accepted him de facto as ruler of Italy. The Roman Senate resumed some of its powers, including that of striking bronze coinage.[103] The Colosseum was restored to use. So far as is known, church and society remained as they had been. Odoacer was too concerned with his own security to interfere and he was forced to lean on the Roman aristocracy for administrative support. From 488 onward he was engaged in a struggle with the Ostrogoths who, led by their young king Theodoric, were being encouraged by the Byzantines to seek homes in Italy. In 493 after a siege lasting two and a half years Ravenna fell. Odoacer was executed, Theodoric established an Ostrogothic kingdom on Italian soil, and the East Roman Balkan provinces were freed from any threat from him.

Theodoric had been brought up in Constantinople and like most other Gothic leaders was basically well disposed toward Rome and her civilization. The ex-Roman official classes accepted his rule as at least being preferable to that of Odoacer. The settlement of the Ostrogothic people on Italian soil, mainly in the Po Valley, was carried out with the minimum of disturbance. In particular, Theodoric heeded the advice of Epiphanius, bishop of Ticinum (Pavia) that a "good ruler took care of the prosperity of the landowners"[104] and he also took over many of Odoacer's senior administrators. One of them, Liberius, served him so well that it was said with some exaggeration that he settled countless Goths without the Romans so much as noticing.[105] Senate, aristocracy, and the papacy were to be treated with respect by the new rulers.

Theodoric's mother Ereriliva was a Catholic, and he personally favored toleration. As he said himself to the Jews of Genoa, "We cannot order one religion, for no one can be compelled to believe against his will."[106] Like the earlier Visigothic kings, his aim was harmony leading eventually to fusion between the Goths and Romans. As the Ravenna chronicler stated, "Thus he governed both peoples, the Goths and the Romans as one, and while he himself was of the Arian sect, he attempted nothing against the catholic religion."[107] The Senate he addressed flatteringly as "vanquisher of the world, champion and renewer of liberty,"[108] while styling himself simply "Theodoric, king."

Theodoric came nearer to achieving a permanently viable relationship between the Goths and Romans than any of the Germanic rulers. He admired Roman statecraft (*civilitas*), did his best to preserve it, and strove to inculcate it among the Goths. Clash of interests was avoided so far as possible since the Goths formed the army while the Romans filled most appointments in the civil administration.[109] The offices and titles of imperial administration were retained. Justice was to be impartial as between Goth and Roman. Theodoric's capital, Ravenna, resembled Constantinople. The king's palace with its curtains and hangings, depicted in the basilica of San Apollinare Nuovo, and nearby the splendid baptistery and mosaic representing Christ's baptism, could have been imperial buildings in Constantinople.[110] At Rome the Senate applauded the king and even a council assembled in March 499 by Pope Symmachus shouted, "Christ hear us. Long live Theodoric." At the height of the Laurentian Schism, the king's arbitration had been sought and his award to Symmachus accepted.[111]

Other factors were working in the same direction. For a generation now, the Roman nobility, whether in Gaul or Italy, had felt a loosening of ties with Constantinople. Arvandus, the prefect of Gaul (c. 470), had regarded the emperor Anthemius (467–72) as "a Greek emperor" with little call on his loyalty.[112] Similar sentiments were intensified in Theodoric's Italian kingdom. Many senators, notably Cassiodorus (c. 490–584) who had been brought up after the ending of the Roman Empire in the West, came to believe in an independent Italy under Gothic rule, and also looked upon the East Roman Empire as foreign and "Greek."[113] Cassiodorus himself was to serve the Ostrogothic monarchy long and loyally, successively as quaestor, master of offices (*Magister officiorum*), and then from 533 to 540 as praetorian prefect. Concerning the time of his consulship in 514 he wrote, "It was to the credit of the Gothic rulers that the longed for concord returned to the reunited clergy and people of the Roman Church."[114] If some senators still linked Anastasius and Theodoric as joint *domini*, it was obvious to most that Italy had ceased to all intents and purposes to be part of the empire.[115] To Boethius, Anastasius was "emperor of the east" with the implication that his writ did not run in the West.[116] In contrast to the Gallic episcopate, the views of the Italian clergy from the pope downward were similarly inclined. Ennodius, the Gallic noble who became bishop of Ticinum (Pavia) in 513 (d. 521), was outstandingly loyal to Theodoric,[117] though he had personal reservations and he rejected any assumption of Roman dress and manners by the Goths.[118] The popes themselves showed no disposition to change temporal sovereigns until after the long dispute with Constantinople ended in 519—but then they did. The foundations on which Theodoric and his advisers built were always brittle.

THE ACACIAN SCHISM AND ITS AFTERMATH

Through most of Theodoric's reign the papacy's main problem concerned its relations with Constantinople. After Leo's death in 461, there is no trace of correspondence between pope and emperor for another fifteen years. Then the extinction of the Western Roman Empire and the concentration of imperial authority at Constantinople resulted in the return of more active communications. As in the past, disagreements were both doctrinal and disciplinary, and once again the latter provided the motive force of the mutual exacerbation which led to the Acacian Schism (484–519) and subsequent tensions.

The years that followed the Council of Chalcedon had seen the formation of a considerable body of opinion—particularly among the monks in Egypt, but also in Syria and Palestine—violently opposed to the Two Natures formula. At Constantinople, however, the patriarch Gennadius (458–71) had tended if anything to emphasize that aspect of the Chalcedonian Definition. On his death in 471 the new patriarch Acacius (471–89) was more flexible and more politically astute. Ideas in Constantinople moved closer to those prevailing in Alexandria, where the majority supported the exiled anti-Chalcedonian patriarch, Timothy Aelurus (d. 477), against his rival loyal to Chalcedon, also called Timothy (Salafaciolus or "Wobble Cap"). A crisis came to a head early in 475. The emperor Zeno (474–91) was unpopular and a palace revolution forced him to flee his capital and leave power in the hands of a usurper, Basiliscus (475–76). The latter saw his main chance of survival in placating the anti-Chalcedonian party throughout the East. Timothy Aelurus was allowed back to Alexandria, another anti-Chalcedonian, Peter the Fuller, was established as patriarch of Antioch, and a council was held at Ephesus that formally denounced Chalcedon, its Definition, and its canons, and granted patriarchal dignity to Ephesus itself.[119] At this point, the patriarch Acacius objected. Nothing could be accepted that threatened the legal standing of the patriarchate of Constantinople. The populace of the capital, spurred on by Daniel Stylite, rallied to his support. Basiliscus was forced first to recall his edict invalidating Chalcedon, and then in August 476 to give way to Zeno. Within a few months, the latter was sole ruler of what remained of the Roman world. Constantinople was declared, in a subsequent edict (17 December 476), "mother of our Piety and of all Christians of the orthodox religion."[120] Chalcedon was not renounced.

Acacius, however, had invoked the help of Rome in his struggle for survival. Though Timothy Aelurus died on 31 July 477, the opposition in Alexandria consecrated another presbyter from the time of Cyril and Dioscorus. This individual, Peter Mongo (Greek *Moggos*, "the hoarse one"), however, had much against him, and Acacius wrote to Pope Simplicius (468–83) in the autumn of 477 denouncing him in scathing terms as "a friend of darkness." He should not be recognized by Rome.[121] He could have saved himself much trouble, for Rome had never recognized anyone but Timothy "Wobble Cap" as patriarch of Alexandria.

In the next years, Acacius was forced to walk a tightrope, maintaining his links with Rome and Alexandria, but coming gradually to the conclusion that the latter was the more immediately important. The deteriorating situation in Antioch first confronted him with the necessity of having to choose.

It will be remembered that during the fourth and early fifth centuries the doctrinal attitude of "the mother Church of the East" had oscillated between the semi-Arian and Apollinarian outlook of the strong Hellenistic Christian minority and the more Syrian, biblical tradition represented by Eustathius and the Antiochene School of Diodore, Theodore, John of Antioch, and Nestorius.[122] The thirty years following Chalcedon saw a gradual but irreversible shift away from Nestorian-oriented Christianity. However near to orthodoxy Chalcedon had proved Nestorius to be, his had become a bad name. The death of Ibas of Edessa in 458 was a signal for a further decline of the biblical tradition of Syrian Christianity within the frontiers of the empire, and the final migration of the school of Edessa to Nisibis across the Persian frontier in 482 could be foreseen. The real hub of the Nestorian movement among Eastern Christians was to be henceforth among the Christians in Persia. These developments left the field free for Chalcedonians and anti-Chalcedonians to battle for possession of Antioch itself. One bishop gave up in despair, his supplanter the anti-Chalcedonian Peter the Fuller was dismissed, while a third, Stephen, was murdered in 479. This deed outraged Pope Simplicius,[123] but Antioch needed a strong hand and not distant sympathy. In 481 Acacius consecrated a new pro-Chalcedonian patriarch Calendio in Constantinople, while assuring Simplicius that the election would be confirmed by a provincial synod at Antioch.[124] It never was. Neither Simplicius nor his successors forgot what they regarded as Acacius's duplicity.[125]

Meantime, Acacius had become convinced that common ground must be sought with the anti-Chalcedonians. He was supported in this by Martyrius, patriarch of Jerusalem (d. 486), and events in 482 gave him his opportunity. In February, Timothy "Wobble Cap" died. Political considerations militated against Zeno recognizing his chosen successor.[126] Acacius entered into relations with Peter Mongo and on 28 July 482, acting on his advice, Zeno dispatched a letter known to history as the *Henotikon* or instrument of unity to "the bishops, monks, and laymen of Alexandria, Egypt and Cyrenaica."[127] It aimed at reconciling Alexandria and Constantinople and healing the schism in the church in Egypt that had followed the deposition of Dioscorus by the Council of Chalcedon thirty years before. Zeno and Acacius were prepared therefore to concede practically every point of consequence to the anti-Chalcedonians, so long as Chalcedon itself was not rejected. Thus, the emperor assured the Egyptians that "both we and the churches everywhere neither have held nor hold nor shall hold, nor know persons who hold" a creed other than Nicaea, confirmed by Constantinople and Ephesus I. Nestorius and Eutyches were alike condemned, but Cyril's twelve *Anathemas* were to be received as canonical. It was to be confessed that Jesus Christ, "incarnate from the Holy Spirit and Mary the Virgin and *Theotokos*, is one and not two, for we say that both his miracles and his sufferings which he willingly underwent in the flesh are of one person." Anyone who thought anything else now or at any time, at Chalcedon or at any other synod was anathema.

The *Henotikon* made no reference to the papacy but it implied the rejection of Leo's *Tome*. It was not the immediate cause of the schism between Rome and Constantinople.[128] Simplicius lacked a representative in the capital, or, as Pope Celestine possessed in the Nestorian crisis, able and articulate friends who could keep him abreast of opinion there. He became increasingly suspicious of Acacius's actions, but had no clear picture of how matters were evolving. By July 482, the latter's apparent intention to enter into communion with Peter Mongo outraged him.[129] Simplicius regarded Acacius as a double-dealer. Worse, after his death in March 483, his successor Felix III (483–92) believed that Acacius had styled himself "head of the whole church."[130] When Acacius skillfully bamboozled a papal delegation to Constantinople into participating in a service in which the names of Dioscorus and Peter Mongo were among those to be commemorated, his anger knew no bounds. A Roman synod excommunicated Acacius on 28 July 484. A monk belonging to the monastery of the Sleepless Ones (named from their unceasing round of liturgy that occupied the entire twenty-four hours of each day) pinned the sentence to the patriarch's pallium as he was celebrating the Eucharist.

The schism lasted for thirty-five years. The *Henotikon* itself was not the real issue. Schism had arisen through mutual antipathies and disciplinary considerations. The rancor felt in Rome was hardly reciprocated in the East. When Acacius died in 489, his successors duly sent their letters of election to the pope and though the latter refused to acknowledge these,[131] there was no movement in the East to renounce communion with Rome. While anti-Chalcedonians might denounce the *Tome* of Leo, no hostility against the see of Rome itself can be read into the voluminous tracts and letters of the time.[132]

Such is the background to the important correspondence between the emperor Anastasius, who succeeded Zeno in 491, and Pope Gelasius (492–96). The emperor was anxious to heal the breach, but Gelasius offered no compromise. He himself may have been a North African by birth, but whatever his background his application of typical North African teaching relating to guilt by association made negotiations impossible. For the pope, the case was simple. Acacius, by communicating with Peter Mongo, was tarred with the same brush as Timothy Aelurus, Dioscorus, and Eutyches. He was a heretic and his successors must disavow him or be regarded as heretics themselves.[133] As for the position of the emperor in the church, Gelasius stressed the utter inferiority of imperial to papal power. Writing to Anastasius in 494 he states, "There are in fact two [powers], emperor Augustus, by which the world is sovereignly [*principaliter*] governed; the consecrated authority of the bishops and the royal power. Of these, the responsibility of the bishops is the more weighty, since even for the rulers of men they will have to give an account at the judgement seat of God."[134] His "most gracious son," Anastasius was reminded that he humbly bowed his head before the priests who dispensed the sacraments.

Much of this had been said before, even by the Pharisees to their Hasmonean masters, and it was implicit in Ambrose's attitude toward Valentinian II and Theodosius I, but Gelasius was applying the theory to a political situation concerning the working relations between pope and emperor. A generation before in the crisis years of 449–51, Pope Leo had been ambivalent in his utterances on this theme. Sometimes he would concede a priestly status to the emperor,[135] at others he pointed out the contrast between the worldly and heavenly affairs (*rerum secularum . . . rerum divinarum*).[136] But he never questioned the emperors' use of the title *inclitus pontifex* ("most excellent priest") nor their right to summon councils of the church and in general to supervise its external life. Theodosius II, Marcian, and Leo I are all addressed with deference. The emperor was the indispensable protector of the church.[137]

With Gelasius, however, the balance has changed. The emperor is accorded no priestly function. He is neither *pontifex* nor *sacerdos*. Human and divine functions in society are strictly separated, and human organizations must serve primarily the needs of the heavenly.[138] It was the emperor's role to learn from the clergy and especially from Peter what were heavenly matters, not for him to pass judgment on them.[139] Gelasius told Anastasius that as Catholic emperor he was "a son and not a leader of the Church."[140] That function belonged to the pope as Peter's heir. There was only one head to whom the rule over the whole congregation of the faithful had been committed. The emperor might wield secular power (*potestas*) but authority (*auctoritas*) belonged to the church. Thus the *Henotikon* was an inexcusable intrusion by the emperor into the ecclesiastical sphere,[141] and not, as Zeno might have argued, a public act within his competence as emperor designed to restore unity to the church. The contrast between the episcopate's obedience or at least acquiescence in the East to the *Henotikon* and Gelasius's uncompromising rejection of it and of Acacius, shows how fundamental was the gulf that now separated Eastern and Western attitudes toward the authority of the emperor in Christendom.

Underlying Gelasius's confident assertions was the growing antipathy in the West for Byzantium as such. Gelasius shared this. He treated the Byzantines with contempt and may even have planned to restore papal influence in the Latin-speaking provinces of the empire at the expense of the emperors and Constantinople. Writing to the bishops of Dalmatia and Dardania (that is, the Balkan provinces of the empire) in February 493, he referred to their eastern brethren as "Greeks among whom there is no doubt that heresies abound."[142] He contrasted "the Greeks" at Constantinople with the "Roman senate" and the "Roman Church."[143] What right, too, had a bishopric in the diocese of Heraclea (Thrace) to call itself "apostolic," he asked in another letter to the bishops of Dardania.[144] In his outlook and attitude he reflected the growth of a more national Italian sentiment in Rome that was becoming increasingly impatient of an overlordship, however shadowy, exercised by the rulers of Constantinople.

While Anastasius ruled, there was no hope of reconciling the papacy and Constantinople. Negotiations dragged on year after year. Gelasius was succeeded by Pope Anastasius II (496–98), followed by Symmachus (498–514), who in turn gave way to Hormisdas (514–23). Only with Anastasius II did the possibility of restoring the unity of Christendom appear through almost simultaneous negotiations between the papacy and Alexandria and Constantinople. Anastasius's death in November 498 ended these feelers, and the advent of Symmachus restored to influence the "national" anti-Byzantine faction among the Roman senators and clergy. The state of mutual anger and frustration which years of fruitless talk produced may be seen from the emperor Anastasius's final remark to Pope Hormisdas in July 517: "From henceforth we shall suppress in silence our requests thinking it absurd to show the courtesy of prayers to those who with arrogance in their mouth refuse even to be entreated. . . . You may insult and thwart me but you may not command me."[145] Hostility between pope and emperor contrasted with mutual acceptance of pope and Ostrogoth king.

These years saw the establishment of an apparently firm *modus vivendi* between the successive popes and the Ostrogothic kingdom. Geiasius was markedly more polite to Theodoric than he was to Anastasius, and so long as the Acacian Schism lasted, the Ostrogothic position remained secure. In July 518, however, a dramatic change took place in the political and religious situation in the empire. Anastasius died on the night of 8/9 July while a memorable thunderstorm broke over his capital. His successor was an elderly soldier from Illyricum named Justin, Latin-speaking and loyal to the papacy. Within a few months, on his initiative a papal delegation was on its way to Constantinople. At the same time, opinion all over the East, except in Egypt, was rallying to the formula: "Four Gospels, four Councils, five Patriarchs." The anti-Chalcedonians with their leader Severus, patriarch of Antioch, were everywhere discomfited. In September 518 Severus fled his see for the haven of Alexandria. When the papal legates arrived in Constantinople on 28 March 519, they were received in triumph.[146]

To all appearances this is what they achieved. Not only was Acacius solemnly condemned, but his successors and the two emperors, Zeno and Anastasius, shared in the anathema, a complete sweep of the papacy's opponents over the last thirty-five years. Combined with this, a statement was signed by the patriarch John (518–20) that Rome had always been apostolic and orthodox.[147] There was, however, some "small print" which did not escape observers in Constantinople. First, the initiative toward settlement had come from the emperor, and without this Pope Hormisdas would have been as helpless as Leo had been after Ephesus II. Second, the emperor had no intention of bringing about the reunion of the two Romes at the expense of his patriarch. Patriarch John (518–20) was the first to style himself openly "Ecumenical Patriarch,"[148] a title which was to become another bone of contention between Rome and Constantinople later in the century. Finally, the twenty-eighth canon of Chalcedon was not renounced, while the Second Ecumenical Council with its canons was tacitly accepted by the papacy. Moreover, as matters turned out, the anathemas against all but Acacius soon became dead letters. Only Acacius was sacrificed while the new dynasty served notice that it considered the Roman Empire as the sovereign power in the West as well as the East. The end of the Acacian Schism marked the first step in the Justinianic *Reconquista*.

THE DECLINE OF THE OSTROGOTHIC KINGDOM

This aspect of the papal rapprochement with Constantinople boded ill for Theodoric. As in North Africa, the ending of the schism changed the attitude of the Catholic episcopate toward the Eastern capital and affected that of some of the nobility and people. At the same time, not all was well with Theodoric's court. In 519, his son-in-law and heir presumptive, Eutharic, had died and the kingdom would devolve on his grandson, Athalaric, who was still a child. Worse, his external policy, based on alliances with other Arian/Germanic kingdoms, was beginning to disintegrate. Despite his intervention and tactical successes, the Burgundians were falling under Frankish domination. Hilderich in North Africa was openly abandoning both Arianism and Vandal independence of Constantinople. His imprisonment and eventual murder (in 526) of Theodoric's sister Amalafrida, wife of Thrasamund, was a declaration of hostility. No wonder a proimperial party reasserted itself among the Roman senators. Theodoric began to feel himself threatened and betrayed by members of a class he had trusted for so long.

The tragedy of Boethius was a sign of the times. Anicius Manlius Severinus Boethius, consul in 510, had been singled out for favor by Theodoric and in 522 was appointed master of offices (*Magister officiorum*) or head of the civil administration. A foolish and thoughtless attempt to play down the undoubted disloyalty of a senatorial colleague caused his arrest and imprisonment in 523.[149] He was condemned to death and Theodoric was determined to make him an example. While awaiting his end confined to the comparatively luxurious surroundings of a country estate, perhaps near Pavia, he wrote a work which secured his fame throughout the Middle Ages. The *Consolation of Philosophy* rivaled Orosius's *Histories Against the Pagans* in shaping the outlook of some early medieval rulers, notably King Alfred. This quintessence of Stoic and Christian moral

813

teaching that bade the reader think of Socrates as an example of heroic resignation in face of injustice,[150] preserved something of the classical tradition in the centuries that followed. Homer, Virgil, Horace, Lucan, and Tibullus among poets, Plato, Aristotle, Cicero, and Seneca among philosophers shared with the Bible and Augustine in shaping their author's thoughts. Similarly, Boethius's earlier translations of some of Aristotle's works ensured that current interpretations of Scripture and canon law would be tempered by the wisdom of the previous age. Boethius was executed in October 524. Next year, his son-in-law Symmachus suffered the same fate.

In the last year of Theodoric's life the threat from Constantinople increased. Justin and his nephew and coruler, Justinian, began to persecute their Arian subjects, mostly Goths. Theodoric reacted swiftly. He sent Pope John I (523–26) on an embassy to try to persuade the emperor to revoke these measures. The pope was partially successful in this strange role, but John showed how matters had changed since Anastasius's time by solemnly crowning Justin emperor while allowing the latter first to prostrate himself before him.[151] The pope's welcome back to Italian soil was predictable, but the shock of Theodoric's anger was too much for him and he died on 18 May. In the final weeks of his reign Theodoric is credited with ordering the surrender of Catholic churches to the Arians. True or not, many of his Catholic subjects wished him in hell when he passed from the scene on 30 August.[152]

The last phase of Gothic independence makes for distressing reading. The kingdom was left to Athalaric, then aged ten, with his mother Amalasuntha as regent. All around the borders of the kingdom its enemies triumphed while the Goths themselves were dividing into pro- and anti-imperial factions. Only serious internal preoccupations and the Persian War of 530–32 appeared to delay the intervention of Justinian—since 1 August 527 the sole emperor at Constantinople. Athalaric died in October 534. For a few months Amalasuntha ruled with Theodoric's nephew, Theodahad. Both were reputed pro-imperial, but not imperial enough to suit the Catholics. The language of Roman pride which Theodahad spoke in addressing the Roman Senate could not easily be reconciled with political independence from the center of empire in New Rome. As in Africa among the Vandals, some of the richer Goths had blended with the Romans,[153] without, however, inducing a spirit of either national or religious compromise among the latter. As a result the leadership of the kingdom had become divided and rootless. Men like Cassiodorus, Catholics but loyal to the Gothic connection, found ever-diminishing support for their aim of a Romano-Gothic state. At heart, too, many of the Gothic nobility had little use for the refinements of Roman education, and showed this by their demand that Athalaric should be educated in martial sports "in that excellence which is in keeping with the custom of the barbarians," and that his tutors who were teaching him otherwise, be dismissed.[154] In 535 another revolution resulted in Amalasuntha's deposition and death, and this provided Justinian with the pretext he needed to extend the *Reconquista* to Italy, with utterly disastrous consequences for the peninsula.

By this time, Catholicism was victorious everywhere in the West except in Spain where the Visigoths would retain their Arianism for another fifty years, and in Britain now divided between Celts and Anglo-Saxons. Elsewhere, the older Latin civilization represented by the aristocratic and often monastic-disciplined episcopate prevailed over the Germanic national churches. Success had fallen to superior organization and civilization backed by the passive support of the mass of the people. For good or ill, medieval Europe would be based on the papacy, and on the Catholic but barbarian monarchies the most powerful of which was that of the Franks. And in the background, thanks largely to Justinian, would be the imperial idea whose ghost was destined to survive until the Napoleonic era.

BIBLIOGRAPHY

NOTE

For this final phase of the history of Christianity in the ancient world, there is the excellent *The Birth of the Middle Ages, 395–814*, by H. St. L. B. Moss (New York and London: Oxford University Press, 1935), who seeks to bridge the ancient and medieval worlds in their political and religious development. Peter Brown's masterly *The World of Late Antiquity* (New York: Harcourt Brace Jovanovich; London: Thames & Hudson, 1971) treads a similar path with the benefit of more recent scholarship and with a greater emphasis on the art and religion of the period and on Rome's relations with Persia. The older work by S. Dill, *Roman Society in the Last Century of the Western Empire* (new ed., rev. and enl., New York: Macmillan Co., 1906), provides much valuable factual material on the relations religious and secular between the invading barbarians and the Roman provincials in the West. J. B. Bury, *History of the Later Roman Empire: From the Death of Theodosius I to the Death of Justinian*, 2 vols. (New York: Dover Publications; London: Constable & Co., 1958), vol. 1, provides the necessary chronological account of the period. On particular topics: for Dark Age Britain, see Leslie Alcock, *Arthur's Britain: History and Archaeology*, A.D. *367–634* (Baltimore and Harmondsworth, Eng.: Penguin Books, 1973); and for Patrick, R. P. C. Hanson, *St. Patrick: A British Missionary Bishop* (Nottingham, 1966), and *Saint Patrick: His Origins and Career* (New York and London: Oxford University Press, 1968), as well as L. Bieler's many erudite contributions to this field of study. On North Africa, Ch. Courtois's *Les Vandales et l'Afrique* (Paris: Arts et Métiers graphiques, 1955) is a fundamental study and apart from chap. 1, which is devoted to the prehistory of the Vandals, is instructive and readable despite its thesis proportions.

On the Visigoths and the age of Sidonius Apollinarius, C. E. Stevens, *Sidonius Apollinaris and His Age* (New York and London: Oxford University Press, 1933), remains the best single study, but students will also find O. M. Dalton's introduction to his translation of the *Letters* of Sidonius (2 vols., New York: Oxford University Press, 1915) valuable.

On the Ostrogothic kingdom, Wilhelm Ensslin's *Theoderich der Grosse* (Munich: Münchener Verlag, 1947) is the standard work, and see also J. J. O'Donnell, *Cassiodorus* (Berkeley and Los Angeles: University of California Press, 1979). For the Acacian Schism, Walter Ullmann's *The Growth of Papal Government in the Middle Ages: A Study in the Ideological Relation of Clerical to Lay Power* (New York: Barnes & Noble, 1956; London: Methuen & Co., 1955) sets this quarrel with Constantinople in its historical perspective. For its ending and the subsequent relations between the Old and New Romes, see A. A. Vasiliev, *Justin the First: An Introduction to the Epoch of Justinian the Great*, Dumbarton Oaks Studies 1 (Cambridge, Mass.: Harvard University Press; London: Oxford University Press, 1950).

SOURCES

Avitus of Vienne. *Opera.* Edited by R. Peiper. *MGH* AA VI.2. Berlin, 1883.
Boethius, *Philosophiae Consolationis,* ed. W. Weinberger, CSEL 67, Leipzig, 1934; *The Consolation of Philosophy,* Eng. trans. H. R. James, London: George Routledge, n.d.
――――. *The Theological Tractates* and *The Consolation of Philosophy.* Eng. trans. and ed. E. K. Rand, H. F. Stewart, and S. J. Tester. LCL. Cambridge, Mass.: Harvard University Press; London: William Heinemann, 1973.
Cassiodorus. *Chronica.* Edited by Th. Mommsen. *MGH* AA XI. *Chron. Minora* II, pp. 111–61. Berlin: 1894.
――――, *Variae,* ed. Th. Mommsen, *MGH* AA XII, Berlin, 1894; and ed. Å. J. Fridh and J. W. Halporn, CCSL 96 (1973), bibliography.
Ennodius, *Opera,* ed. F. Vogel, *MGH* AA VII; and ed. W. Hartel, CSEL 6, Vienna, 1882; *The Life of Saint Epiphanius,* ed. and Eng. trans. G. M. Cook, Washington, D.C.: Catholic University of America Press, 1942.
Eugippus, *Vita S. Severini,* ed. P. Knoell, CSEL 9.2, Vienna, 1886; and ed. and Germ. trans. F. Noll, Berlin, 1963.
Excerpta Valesiana, ed. and Eng. trans. J. C. Rolfe, in *Ammianus Marcellinus,* vol. 3, LCL, Cambridge, Mass.: Harvard University Press; London: William Heinemann, 1939, pp. 506–69; and ed. Th. Mommsen, *MGH* AA IX, *Chron. Minora* I, Pars prior, pp. 7–11, and Pars posterior, pp. 306ff.
Ferrandus. *Vita Sancti Fulgentii* (*Life of Fulgentius*). PL 65.117–50.
Fulgentius, *Opera,* CCSL 91, 91A; *PL* 65.117–963.
Gelasius, *Epistolae,* ed. E. Schwartz from the *Collectio Veronensis* in *ABAW* n.s. 10 (1934); and also in *Collectio Avellana,* ed. O. Guenther, CSEL 35.1, nos. 94–101 (pp. 357–468), Leipzig: G. Freytag, 1895. See also A. Thiel, *Epistolae Romanorum Pontificum genuinae,* vol. 1, Braunsberg, 1867.
Gildas, *De Excidio et Conquestu Britanniae,* ed. Th. Mommsen, *MGH* XIII. *Chron. Min.* III, pp. 3–85, Berlin, 1898; Eng. trans. M. Winterbottom, Chichester, Eng.: Phillimore & Co., 1978.
Hydatius. *Chronicon.* Edited by Th. Mommsen. *MGH* AA XI. *Chronica Minora* II, pp. 1–37. Berlin, 1894.
Leo. *Epistolae.* PL 54.551–1254.
Patrick (Patricius), *Confession et Lettre à Coroticus,* ed. R. P. C. Hanson and C. Blanc, SC 249, Paris, 1978; L. Bieler, *Libri epistolarum Sancti Patricii episcopi,*

THE CATHOLIC RECOVERY IN THE WEST 451–536

2 vols., Dublin, 1952; *Works*, Eng. trans. and ed. L. Bieler, ACW 17. Westminster, Md.: Newman Press; London: Longmans, Green & Co., 1953.

Prosper of Aquitaine, *Chronicon, PL* 51.536–606; and ed. Th. Mommsen, *MGH AA* IX, *Chron. Min.* I, pp. 343–485.

Remigius of Rheims. *Epistolae.* Edited by W. Gundlach. *MGH.* Epistolae III (*Ep. Austrasicae*, pp. 112–14). Berlin, 892.

Sidonius Apollinaris. *Epistolae. MGH AA* VIII. Edited by C. Luetjohn. Berlin, 1887.

Victor Vitensis. *Historia persecutionis africanae provinciae* (*History of the Persecution of the African Province*). Edited by M. Petschenig. CSEL 7, pp. 1–107. Vienna, 1881.

SECONDARY WORKS

Bardy, G. "Sous le régime de l'Hénotique: la politique religieuse d'Anastase." Chap. 2 of part 2 of *De la mort de Théodose à l'élection de Grégoire le Grand*, ed. P. de Labriole et al. Vol. 4 of Fliche and Martin, eds., *Histoire de l'Eglise*, pp. 299–320.

Bertolini, O. "Gothia e Romania." *Settimana di Studio* III, 1 *Goti in Occidente Problemi*, pp. 13–33. Spoleto: Centro Italiano di Studi sull'alto medioevo, 1956.

Bieler, L. "St. Patrick and the British Church." In *Christianity in Britain, 300–700*, ed. M. W. Barley and R. P. C. Hanson, pp. 123–30. Leicester: Leicester University Press, 1968.

Casey, P. J., ed. *The End of Roman Britain. BAR* (British Series, 71). Oxford, 1979.

Chadwick, H. *Boethius: The Consolations of Music, Logic, Theology, and Philosophy.* New York and London: Oxford University Press, 1981.

Chadwick, N. K., ed. *Studies in Early British History.* New York and Cambridge: Cambridge University Press, 1954.

Courtois, C., et al. *Les "Tablettes Albertini," actes privés de l'époque vandale.* Algiers and Paris: Arts et Métiers graphiques, 1952.

——. *Victor de Vita et son oeuvre.* Algiers: Gouvernement-générale de l'Algére, Service d'Antiquités, Imprimerie officielle, 1954.

Diesner, H. J. *Fulgentius von Ruspe als Theologe und Kirchenpolitiker.* Berlin: Evangelische Verlagsanstalt, 1966.

——. "Severinus und Eugippus." In *Kirche und Staat im spätrömischen Reich*, pp. 155–67. Berlin, 1963.

——. *Das Vandalenreich.* Leipzig: Köhler and Amelang, 1966.

——. *Die Volkerwanderung.* Leipzig, 1976.

Goffart, W. *Barbarians and Romans*, A.D. *418–584.* Princeton, N.J.: Princeton University Press, 1980.

Gordon, C. D. *The Age of Attila: Fifth Century Byzantium and the Barbarians.* Ann Arbor: University of Michigan Press, 1960.

Hughes, K. W. *The Church in Early Irish Society.* Ithaca, N.Y.: Cornell University Press, 1967; London: Methuen & Co., 1966.

Jones, A. H. M. "The Constitutional Position of Odoacer and Theoderic." *JRS* 52 (1962): 126–30.

Labriolle, P. de. "L'Eglise et les barbares." Chap. 5 of part 2 in *De la mort de Théodose*, ed. Labriolle et al., pp. 353–96.

Levison, W. "St. Alban and St. Albans." *Antiquity* 15 (1941): 337–59.

Löwe, H. "Theoderich der Grosse und Papst Johann I." *Historisches Jahrbuch* 72 (1953): 94ff.

Moorhead, John. "Boethius and Romans in Ostrogothic Service." *Historia* 27 (1978): 604–12.

Moss, J. R. "The Effects of the Policies of Aetius on the History of Western Europe." *Historia* 22 (1973): 711–31.

Nicol, D. M. "The Byzantine View of Western Europe." *Greek, Roman and Byzantine Studies* 8 (1967): 315–39.

Schäferdiek, K. "Germanenmission." *RAC* 10 (1977): 492–547.

Taylor, J. "The Early Papacy at Work: Gelasius I (492–96)." *JRH* (1977): 317–32.

Tessier, Georges. "La Conversion de Clovis et la christianisation des Francs." *Settimana di Studi* XIV, *La Conversione al cristianesimo nell'Europa dell'alto Medioevo*, pp. 149–89. Spoleto: Centro Italiano di Studi sull'alto medioevo, 1967.

Thomas, Charles. *Christianity in Roman Britain to A.D. 500.* Berkeley and Los Angeles: University of California Press, 1981.

———. *The Early Christian Archaeology of North Britain.* New York and London: Oxford University Press, 1971.

Thompson, E. A. "The Settlement of the Barbarians in Southern Gaul." *JRS* 46 (1956): 65–75.

Ullmann, W. "Der Grundsatz der Arbeitsteilung bei Gelasius I." *Historisches Jahrbuch* 97/98 (1978): 41–70.

———. "Leo I and the Theme of Papal Primacy." *JTS* n.s. 11 (April 1960): 25–51.

———. "Über die rechtliche Bedeutung der spätrömischen Kaisertitulatur für das Papsttum." *Ex Aequo et Bono*, Festsch. W. M. Plöchl (Innsbruck, 1977), pp. 23–43.

Wallace-Hadrill, J. M. *The Barbarian West, 400–1000.* 3d rev. ed. London: Hutchinson & Co., 1967.

———. "Gothia and Romania." *BJRL* 44 (1952): 213–37.

NOTES

1. See the popular outcries preserved by the Monophysite, John Rufus, *Plerophoria*, ed. F. Nau, *Patrologia Orientalis* 8.1 (Paris, 1912), esp. pp. 9, 17–19, 21, 38, 39, and 52.

2. Leo, *Letter* 98.4, *PL* 54.957C. Anatolius, in Leo *Letters* 101–5, made out that the legates lacked instructions concerning Leo's attitude toward Constantinople.

3. Thus *Letter* CVI.2.

4. The text is in E. Schwartz, *Acta Conciliorum Oecumenicorum* (Berlin, 1914–40), II.2.3, pp. 21–22. See A. Michel, "Der Kampf um das politische oder petrinische Prinzip der Kirchenführung," in *Das Konzil von Chalkedon: Geschichte und Gegenwart*, ed. H. Grillmeier and H. Bacht, 3 vols. (Wurzburg: Echter-Verlag, 1953), vol. 2, pp. 491–562.

5. Leo, *Letter* CIV.2, *PL* 54.993C; and compare *Letters* CV and CVI.

6. Thus, Labriolle in "L'Eglise et les barbares," p. 366, who mentions also the social work carried out by the bishops as a factor in Catholicism's survival.

7. Note the alleged respect even of the Rugi for Epiphanius, bishop of Ticinum in 493: "Qui sine grandi stupore credat dilexisse et timuisse Rugos episcopum et

catholicum et Romanum, qui parere regibus vix dignantur?" Ennodius, *Vita Epifani* 119, ed. F. Vogel, *MGH* AA VII (Berlin, 1885), p. 99.

8. Fulgentius *Letter* XVII.21, ed. J. Fraipont, CCSL 91A, pp. 447–629 (Turnholt, 1968), p. 580, and compare Victor of Vita, *History* II.43, "quae (ecclesia Romana) caput est omnium ecclesiarum."

9. Eugippus, *Vita S. Severini* I.2–3, ed. Knoell, and see Diesner, "Severinus und Eugippus," useful bibliography

10. Patrick, *Confession* XXVI, ed. Hanson and Blanc, p. 98, *"seniores,"* and chap. 1 ("presbyter" and "deacon").

11. G. W. Meates, *Lullingstone Roman Villa* (London: William Heinemann, 1955), pp. 126ff.; and compare J. M. C. Toynbee, *Art in Roman Britain* (New York and London: Phaidon Press, 1962), p. 196 (parallel to Lullingstone monogram with Roman catacomb examples); and also more generally in Toynbee's *Art in Britain Under the Romans* (New York and London: Oxford University Press, 1964), pp. 226–27.

12. See P. D. C. Brown, "The Church at Richborough," *Britannia* 2 (1971): 225–31, and pl. XXX.

13. *Confession* I; "We turned away from God and did not keep his commandments, and did not obey our clergy." See Bieler, "St. Patrick and British Church."

14. Prosper, *Chronicon* ad ann. 429, *PL* 51.594. On Germanus's possible military background (Count of the Saxon Shore?), see N. K. Chadwick, *Studies in Early British History*, pp. 227ff.

15. For the survival of the shrine of St. Alban into Anglo-Saxon times, see Bede, *Ecclesiastical History of the English People*, ed. Bertram Colgrave and R. A. B. Mynors (New York: Oxford University Press; Oxford: At the Clarendon Press, 1969), I.7; and see Levison, "St. Alban and St. Albans."

16. The evidence one way or the other remains difficult to handle. See Ph. Rahtz and Lorna Watts, "The End of Roman Temples in the West of Britain," in *End of Roman Britain*, ed. Casey, pp. 183–210, for suggestions of post-Roman survival of some Romano-British temples in southern and western Britain, such as the "Round Temple" at Maiden Castle.

17. Bede *Ecclesiastical History* I.20: "Madidus baptismate procedit exercitus." See my *"Ecclesia Britannica:* Prelude or Dead End?" *JEH* 30 (April 1979): 129–44, esp. p. 142.

18. Paulinus of Nola *Letter* XVIII.5: "Your deserving sanctity has transformed Rouen into the entire appearance of Jerusalem." He goes on to refer to "crowded churches and chaste monasteries" in the city, to "widows slaving night and day in holy tasks," and to "the chaste love" of married couples. All this is interesting for the ideal of Christian life even in a distant city in the West on the eve of the barbarian invasions.

19. Gennadius *Liber de Scriptoribus ecclesiasticis* LVI: "sana et Deo digna doctrina," *PL* 58.1091. See J. R. Morris, "Pelagian Literature," *JTS* n.s. 16 (April 1965): 26–60, esp. pp. 33–35.

20. See Alcock, *Arthur's Britain*, pp. 195–96. Though Gildas preserves folk-memory of the violent end of Roman Britain, villas and villages more often show signs of decay leading to abandonment rather than of destruction. See S. Sheppard Frere, *Britannia: A History of Roman Britain* (London: Sphere Books, 1974), pp. 373–76. The find at Water Newton, on the other hand, suggests hurried disposal of

church valuables, as does the discovery of the leaden font at Aston in Northants down a Roman well (M. W. C. Hassall and R. S. O. Tomlin, "Roman Britain in 1976," *Britannia* 8 [1977], II, pp. 426–49, esp. pp. 443–44 and pl. XXIX b).

21. Thus, Thomas, *Early Christian Archaeology*, pp. 25ff.

22. The case for continuity between Romano-British and sub-Roman Britain (that is, after A.D. 500) is also put by Thomas, *Christianity in Roman Britain,* chap. 10, "Christianity was not expunged by the arrival of a few thousand pagan Germans" (p. 347).

23. Bede *Ecclesiastical History* I.6. There is some rather shadowy evidence to date of the continuance of Christian tradition on a few late Roman sites. For instance, in Canterbury itself, three of the town's Roman cemeteries survived into medieval times (I owe this information to Mr. Nicholas Brooks), and the cult of "St. Sixtus" in Jutish Kent should not be forgotten. For Faversham, see Lord Eric Fletcher and Col. E. A. Meates's reports in *AJ* 49 (1969): 273–94, and 57 (1977): 67–72. Gloucester and Lincoln may provide other examples (see *Times* reports on 19 August and 23 July 1978, respectively). On the other hand, the church at Silchester was never restored, and representing the Jutes, Ethelbert himself seems to have been suspicious of Christianity as some sort of magic; see Bede *Ecclesiastical History* I.25.

24. See, for instance, the summary by Charles Thomas, "Saint Patrick and Fifth-Century Britain," in *End of Roman Britain*, ed. Casey, pp. 81–101. I prefer the traditional chronology reproduced in this chapter and justified by Hanson (*St. Patrick: Origins,* pp. 187–88), but note the alternative that puts Patrick's birth c. 415, his capture c. 430, consecration as bishop c. 450, and activity in Ireland 450–90 or 495, set out by Thomas.

25. For Palladius, see Prosper *Chronicle* ad ann. 431. He may have been the influential, aristocratic deacon who had persuaded Celestine to send Germanus to Britain; see N. K. Chadwick, *Poetry and Letters in Early Christian Gaul* (Philadelphia: Albert Saifer; London: Bowes & Bowes, 1955), p. 248.

26. Patrick *Confession* XVI.

27. Ibid., XXVI.

28. See Bieler, "St. Patrick and British Church"; also Hanson and Blanc, *Confession et Lettre à Coroticus,* pp. 36–37.

29. See Hanson and Blanc, *Confession et Lettre à Coroticus,* p. 50.

30. Patrick *Confession* L.

31. Ibid., XLI; and cf. LII: presents to the kings and reference to "their sons who accompany me."

32. *Letter* I.1.

33. *Confession* XLII.

34. For North African and other Mediterranean pottery in sub-Roman sites in western Britain, see Alcock, *Arthur's Britain,* pp. 201ff.

35. On the Easter question and the Celtic Church, see Ian Finlay's discussion, *Columba* (London: Gollancz, 1979), pp. 198–204, and Colman's reference to the influence of Anatolius (of Alexandria) in the Celtic computation of Easter, Bede *Ecclesiastical History* III.25. Also see over, p. 880.

36. Bede *Ecclesiastical History* II.2.

37. Victor, *History*, ed. Petschenig I.5, and compare I.4 and 9: "Praesertim in ecclesiis basilicisque sanctorum, coemeteriis monasteriisque sceleratius

saeviebant" (I.4). Houses of prayer were subjected to "more destruction than the cities and towns themselves."

38. Ibid., I.14, "ut episcopos atque laicos nobiles de suis ecclesiis vel sedibus nudos penitus aufugarent."

39. Possidius *Vita Sancti Augustini* 28, "aedificia ecclesiarum quamplurimis locis ignibus concremata . . ." (*PL* 32.58). see H. J. Diesner, "Augustinus und die Barbaren der Völkerwanderung," *Revue des Études augustiniennes* 23 (1977): 83–91, esp. p. 89.

40. Possidius *Vita Augustini* (*Life of Augustine*) 28, 6–8. Also Victor, *History* I.9, and Augustine, *De Tempore Barbarico tractatus unus*, *PL* 40.699–707.

41. Courtois's view, "Ce qu'ont poursuivi Geiseric et ses successeurs, c'est l'empire du blé," *Les Vandales*, p. 213. Valentinian III recognized Gaiseric accurately as "hostis imperii nostri" (*Novel* 9 of 24 June 440), referring to the rumored creation by Gaiseric of a fleet based on Carthage.

42. See Diesner, *Das Vandalenreich*; in addition, Valentinian's murderer, Petronius Maximus, had married Eudocia to his son Palladius!

43. Thus Sidonius *Carmen* II, 349–51; "Hinc Vandalus hostis/urget et in nostrum numerosa classe quotannis/militat excidium," c. 465.

44. Victor *History* I.15.

45. Own observations while working in 1976 for the University of Michigan "Save Carthage team" under Professor J. H. Humphrey on a fourth-century and Byzantine church site at Salammbo.

46. Victor *History* I.16.

47. For the dating of the *Liber Genealogus*, see Monceaux, *Histoire littéraire de l'Afrique*, vol. 4, p. 102.

48. Victor *History* III.4.

49. See Courtois, *Victor de Vita*, pp. 91–100. It would seem that the list of bishops was the official list kept in the archives of the church at Carthage, but except for proconsular Africa it probably did not represent the situation in 484.

50. Victor *History* II.18.54.

51. Compare the scale of fines given in Victor *History* III.3–14 and the *Codex Theodosianus* XVI.5.52 of 30 January 412, an interesting indication, perhaps, of the continued familiarity of Roman law in the Vandal domains. See also Courtois, *Les Vandales*, p. 296; and Diesner, *Das Vandalenreich*, pp. 80–81; and below, n. 54.

52. Fulgentius, *Ad Trasimundum* I.1, *PL* 65.224, "quod nuper mihi quoddam volumen, baiulo Felice, praeceperis destinari, iubens me ilico respondere." Compare Ferrandus *Life of Fulgentius* XXI.21.

53. For Gaiseric's pressure on court officials to convert to Arianism, see Victor, *History* I.45 (Felix), I.48 (Saturus); and Prosper, *Chronicon* ad ann. 437, *PL* 51.567. On the other hand, a few non-Germanic names appear among those of Vandal officials: for example, Elpidoforus = Victor *History* III.34–37; Antonius, a bishop, ibid., III.42; Nicasius, a Donatist convert to Arianism, III.71 and Iucundus, I.48.

54. Les "*Tablettes Albertini*," Courtois et al. p. 211. For the survival of Roman law indicated in the deeds, see Ch. Saumagne, chap. 3, "Le Droit," in ibid., esp. p. 175. For a good brief résumé of their importance, see Susan Raven, *Rome in Africa* (New York: M. Evans & Co., 1969), pp. 155–58 (illustrations).

55. Victor *History* II.18.55. As late as 483 Bishop Cyrila claimed, "Nescio Latine," though this was patently untrue.

56. Victor, *History* III.9.34 (ed. Petschenig, p. 89).
57. The date of his death is obscure. It is often given as 1 January 533: thus Altaner, *Patrology*, p. 489. His biographer was the Carthaginian deacon, Ferrandus (*flor.* 520–50). His life and thought have been summarized by G. Lapeyre, *S. Fulgence de Ruspe* (Paris, 1929); and Diesner, *Fulgentius*.
58. *Life of Fulgentius* I.4, *PL* 65.119.
59. *Life of Fulgentius* XXVI.
60. See Courtois, *Les Vandales*, p. 343.
61. *Life of Fulgentius* IX.17. Ferrandus describes the Arians as a "sect" and their presbyter Felix as "natione barbarus." The religious and national cleavage between Afro-Latins and Vandals seems to have remained complete in this area.
62. Ibid., XIV.28.
63. See Diesner's analysis, *Fulgentius*, pp. 38–39.
64. See Courtois, *Les Vandales*, p. 401, on Amalafrida's career and fate.
65. For the *Acta*, see Munier, *Concilia Africae*, pp. 255–82. See Courtois, *Les Vandales*, p. 305, for the distribution of the bishoprics represented.
66. See L. Poinssot and G. L. Feuille, "Inscriptions chrétiennes d'Ammaedara (Haidra)," *BAC* (1941–42): 19–26; N. Duval, "L'Eglise de l'Evêque Melleus à Haidra," *CRAIBL* (1968): 221–44, esp. pp. 228–44, and ibid. (1969): 409–36; and *Recherches archéologiques d'Haidra: Vol. 1, Les Inscriptions chrétiennes,* Collection de l'Ecole française de Rome 18 (Rome, 1975). For Mactaris, see *Année épigraphiques* 44 (1953): 179.
67. Procopius, *History of the Wars*, ed. and Eng. trans. B. H. Dewing, 5 vols., LCL (Cambridge, Mass.: Harvard University Press; London: William Heinemann, 1914–40), vol. 2, III.21.21–25.
68. Victor, *History* II.8 (ed. Petschenig, p. 27).
69. See Courtois, *Les Vandales*, pp. 343ff.
70. Justinian *Novel* 37.5 and 8 (see below, p. 833).
71. Prosper *Chronicon* ad ann. 419. See the illuminating article by Thompson on the mutually beneficial character of the Visigothic settlement in Aquitania for the Goths and Gallo-Roman landowners, "Settlement of Barbarians."
72. See Goffart, *Barbarians and Romans*, p. 28.
73. Salvian, *De Gubernatione Dei* V.22, ed. F. Pauly, CSEL 8, pp. 1–200 (Vienna, 1883): "Itaque passim vel ad Gothos vel ad Bacaudas vel ad alios ubique dominantes barbaros migrant . . ."—the situation seen from Marseilles c. 440. Also the oblique criticism of the Roman official Seronatus (see below, n. 80) that "his actions are filling the woods with dangerous fugitives from the estates" (Sidonius *Letter* II.1.3)—a resurgence of the Bagaudae in the 460s?
74. Sidonius, *Letter* IX.10.2, ed. Dalton, vol. 2, p. 123.
75. Sidonius *Letter* I.3, dated c. 461–67; Ibid., II.2.11 (arched hearths and "roaring fires"); and Dalton's introduction, pp. civff. and cx–cxii (games). Sidonius could be describing life on an Elizabethan manor!
76. Ibid., III.3.1 (ed. Dalton, vol. 1, p. 67).
77. See N. K. Chadwick, *Poetry and Letters*, pp. 198–204.
78. Ibid., p. 194.
79. Gennadius, *Scriptoribus* LXXXV, *PL* 58.1109; and concerning Gennadius himself, see N. K. Chadwick, *Poetry and Letters*, pp. 206–7.
80. Thus, Seronatus criticized as pro-Visigoth by Sidonius *Letter* V.13.3; *Letter*

VII.7.2: "infamous betrayer of imperial provinces to the barbarian"; and *Letter* II.1.1: "this Catiline of our day."

81. Sidonius *Letter* VII.5 and 8 (ed. Dalton, vol. 2, pp. 104, 113). Date: 470.

82. Ibid., VII.6, 7, and 8 (ed. Dalton, vol. 2, p. 108).

83. Hydatius, *Chronicon* 232, ed. Mommsen, pp. 34–35. Ajax is described as a "senior Arianus," a convert to Arianism, and "natione Galata." Another Arian Gothic missionary was Modhar who was active in southeastern Gaul (Sidonius *Letter* VII.6.2).

84. Sidonius *Letter* VII.14.10: "I avoid them [the barbarians] even when they bear a good name." Sidonius described Euric as an Arian: "the very name of Catholic so embitters his countenance and heart that one might take him for the chief priest of his Arian sect rather than for the monarch of his nation" (*Letter* VII.6.7.). His cool dislike of the "stinking Burgundians" who were billeted in his house c. 461 is shown in *Carmen* XII.

85. He has no good word for the Vandals ("barbara ferocitas," *History* III.63, etc.), but the Moors though brutal could occasionally be bribed into humanity (ibid., II.32). In Gaul, the Catholic clergy also looked more favorably on pagans who could be converted than on Arians who were in error.

86. I have followed N. K. Chadwick, *Poetry and Letters*, pp. 278–82. For Sidonius, Lupus was "foremost of our Gallic bishops" (*Letter* VII.13.1).

87. Sidonius *Carmen* VII.236; and compare *Letter* VIII.6.14 on the Saxons.

88. See above, p. 481.

89. Gregory of Tours, *Historia Francorum*, II.9, ed. W. Arndt and B. Krusch, *MGH* Script. rerum Meroving. (Hannover, 1885; 2d ed. [B. Krusch and W. Levison, eds.], 1951), p. 77; though he confesses his ignorance as to who these earlier Frankish kings were.

90. Remigius, *Ep. Austrasicae* 2, ed. Gundlach, 113: "Consiliarios tibi adhibere debes, qui famam tuam ornare." Clovis took the hint!

91. Gregory *Historia Francorum* (*History of the Franks*) II.28–29.

92. Stressed by Schäferdiek, "Germanenmission," pp. 535–56.

93. Gregory *History of Franks* II.30; and compare Avitus of Vienne *Letter* XLVI; and Nicetius of Trier, *Letter* ad Chlodoswind (*Ep. Austras.* VIII), ed. R. Peiper, in *MGH* Epist. III, 122.

94. *History of Franks* II.31, though the numbers may be symbolical rather than actual, cf. Acts 2:41.

95. Thus, Schäferdiek, "Germanenmission," pp. 537–38.

96. That the lack of a common code of law was felt as a grievance by the Gallo-Romans is shown by Sidonius *Letter* II.1.3, contrasting disparagingly "the laws of Theodoric" with the *Codex Theodosianus*.

97. For a résumé of the results of this council of thirty-four bishops under the presidency of Caesarius, see G. de Plinval, in *De la mort de Théodose*, p. 408.

98. Avitus, *Letters* VIII and XLV, ed. R. Peiper, *MGH* AA VI.2 (Berlin, 1883), pp. 40 and 74.

99. Implied in the conference which Gundobad held with the bishops after Clovis's conversion and when the Franks were threatening his kingdom. See Peiper, ed., pp. 161–64. He had also written previously to Clovis congratulating him on his conversion (Avitus *Letter* XLV, "Vestra fides nostra victoria est").

100. The point has been made long ago by Thomas Hodgkin, *Italy and Her*

Invaders (8 vols., New York: Oxford University Press, 1916), vol. 2, p. 392; and repeated by Dalton (ed.) in Sidonius, *Letters,* vol. 1, introduction, p. xxii.

101. On Odoacer's origins, see Eugippus, *Vita Severini* VII, ed. Knoell, p. 22.

102. See Jones, "Constitutional Position of Odoacer and Theodoric."

103. See Ph. Grierson, "The *Tablettes Albertini,* and the Vaiue of the Solidus in the Fifth and Sixth Centuries AD," *JRS* 49 (1959): 73–80, esp. p. 77.

104. "Boni imperatoris est possessoris opulentia." Ennodius, *Vita Epifani* 187, ed. Vogel, p. 107. An Italian example of the close association that existed now between the Catholic church and landed nobility.

105. Ennodius, *Letter* IX.23, ed. W. Hartel, CSEL 6, pp. 260–422 (Vienna, 1882), p. 245; and for Theodoric's favor to the senatorial landowning interest, see Ensslin, *Theoderich,* pp. 90–96.

106. Cassiodorus, *Variae* II.27, ed. Mommsen, p. 62.

107. *Excerpta Valesiana* XII.60, ed. Rolfe.

108. See Cassiodorus *Variae* VIII.10, 11; and IV.4.5, "cana libertas." For Theodoric's constitutional position, see Bury, *Later Roman Empire,* vol. 1, pp. 454–58.

109. For details of the division of ranks and authority between Goths and Romans, see Jones, "Constitutional Position of Odoacer and Theodoric," pp. 129–30.

110. Illustrated and described by Giuseppe Bovini, *Eglises de Ravenna/ Churches of Ravenna,* Fr. and Eng. trans. Q. T. S. (Novara: Instituto geografico de Agostini, 1960), pp. 76–112.

111. "Exaudi Christe: Theodorico vitam," *Dictum* XXX, *Acta Synhodorum habitorum Romae,* p. 405, lines 7–8 (Cassiodorus, *Variae,* ed. Mommsen). Compare also *Excerpta Valesiana* XII.65–66; see Ensslin, *Theoderich,* p. 110.

112. Sidonius *Letter* I.7.5. Sidonius regarded him as a traitor and his impeachment in 468 was one of the Roman Senate's last exercises of sovereignty in Gaul; see Dalton, ed., *Letters,* pp. xxx–xxxiii.

113. Cassidorus, *Variae,* ed. Mommsen, V.17.3: "Non habet quod nobis Graecus imputet aut Afer insultet."

114. *Chronica* ad ann. 514, ed. Mommsen, written perhaps at the request of Eutharic, Theodoric's son-in-law and heir apparent, c. 519. See O'Donnell, *Cassiodorus,* p. 42.

115. Jones, "Constitutional Position of Odoacer and Theodoric," p. 128.

116. Boethius, *In Categorias Aristotelis* III (*PL* 64.264A). See H. Chadwick, *Boethius,* chap. 1.

117. For a short but well-documented summary of the relations between the Goths and the Gallo-Romans and the Italian nobility, see Patrick Wormald, "The Decline of the Western Empire and the Survival of Its Aristocracy," *JRS* 66 (1976): 217–26, esp. pp. 222–23. Ennodius pronounced a panegyric honoring Theodoric.

118. See Ennodius, *Carmina* II.57, ed. W. Hartel, CSEL 6, pp. 507–608 (Vienna, 1882), p. 575: "Barbaricam faciem Romanos sumere cultus|Miror et inmodico distinctas corpore gentes"—as sharp a statement of "apartheid" between Goths and Romans as one could find.

119. For these events, see my *The Rise of the Monophysite Movement: Chapters in the History of the Church in the 5th and 6th Centuries* (New York and Cambridge: Cambridge University Press, 1972; 2d ed., 1979), pp. 166–74.

120. *Codex Justinianus* I.2.16.

121. Acacius to Pope Simplicius, *Collectio Veronensis* 4, *PS*, pp. 4–5, "filius noctis existens et operum dei lucentium alienus."

122. See above, p. 641.

123. Simplicius, *Letters* LXVI and LXVII in the *Collectio Avellana*, ed. Guenther, CSEL 35.1 pp. 147–50, dated 22 June 479. For Stephen of Antioch's murder, see Michael the Syrian, *Chronicon* IX.6 (ed. J. B. Chabot, 3 vols. [Paris, 1899–1911], vol. 2, p. 149).

124. *Collectio Avellana* LXVI and LXVII.

125. The case was remembered against Constantinople at the time of the final break in 1054!

126. John Talaia; for the events, see my *Rise of Monophysite Movement*, pp. 174–77.

127. The complete text of the *Henotikon* has been reconstructed by E. Schwartz in "Codex Vaticanus Graecus 1431, eine anti-chalkedonische Sammlung aus der Zeit Kaiser Zenos," *ABAW* Phil. Hist. Kl., Abt. 32.6 (1926), No. 75, ff. 52–54. Incomplete versions are to be found in Zacharias Rhetor, *Ecclesiastical History* V.8, ed. E. W. Brooks (CSCO Script. Syri III.5 and 6 [Paris and Louvain, 1919–24]); Evagrius *Ecclesiastical History* III.14; Nicephorus Callistus *Church History* XVI.12; and Liberatus of Carthage, *Breviarium causae Nestorianorum et Eutychianorum*, ed. E. Schwartz, XVII.113–17 (*ACO* II.5 [Berlin: Walter de Gruyter, 1936], pp. 98–141).

128. See Frend, "Eastern Attitudes to Rome in the Acacian Schism," in *The Orthodox Churches and the West*, ed. D. Baker, Studies in Church History, vol. 13 (Oxford: Basil Blackwell & Mott, 1976), pp. 69–81, esp. pp. 22–23.

129. Simplicius, *Letter* 68 in *Collectio Avellana*, ed. Guenther, pp. 151–54; and see also 69 (pp. 154–55), written on 6 November 482, complaining of Acacius's silence.

130. Felix III to Acacius, *PS*, p. 73: "Mihi crede, nescio quemadmodum te ecclesiae totius asseras esse principem."

131. See Bardy's chapter, "Le régime de l'Henotique."

132. See Frend, "Eastern Attitudes to Rome," pp. 76–77.

133. Gelasius, "Commonitorium Fausto magistro" = *Coll. Veronensis* 7, *PS*, p. 17): "In consortium damnatorum est damnatus Acacius"; and repeated in *Letter* XVIII to the bishops of Dardania = *Collectio Avellana* XCV.

134. Gelasius *Letter* XII, 2–3. Analyzed by Ullmann, *Growth of Papal Government*, pp. 18–20. For Gelasius, Constantinople also had no rights other than those of a metropolitan bishopric. He rejected, as Leo had, both canon 3 of the Council of Constantinople and the twenty-eighth canon of Chalcedon.

135. Thus, *Letter* XXIV to Theodosius II (18 February 449), "Litteris, quas ad me misistis, ostenditur ut vobis non solum regium, sed etiam sacerdotalem inesse animum gaudeamus," and compare Simplicius's statement on the same lines to Zeno in 479 (*Collectio Avellana* LXVI).

136. Leo *Letter* CIV, "alia tamen ratio est rerum saecularium alia divinarum," an argument which Gelasius pressed home. See Ullmann, "Leo I."

137. See Ullmann, "Über die rechtliche Bedeutung der spätrömischen Kaisertitulatur für das Papsttum," p. 31.

138. Well expressed by Ullmann in his study of Gelasius's policies, "Der Grundsatz der Arbeitsteilung," pp. 50–52.

139. Gelasius, *Letter* X.9, Thiel = *Collectio Veronensis*, *PS*, pp. 18–19, no. 7,

and compare *Letter* I.10, "quod ad religionem competit, discere ei convenit, non docere." See Ullmann, "Der Grundsatz der Arbeitsteilung," p. 56.

140. Gelasius, *Letter* I.10, "Quod si dixeris [Anastasius]: Sed imperator catholicus est, salva pace ipsius dixerimus: filius est non praesul ecclesiae" (*PS*, p. 35).

141. Gelasius, *Letter* I.10, "Non sibi vindicet alienum jus et ministerium quod alteri deputatum est." Examples from history showed how "royal power" could be subjected to penance. Thus, Gelasius *Letter* XVIII = *Collectio Avellana* XCV.60 (ed. Guenther, p. 390).

142. Gelasius *Letter* VII.2 = *Collectio Avellana* LXXIX (ed. Guenther, p. 220).

143. Gelasius, *Commonitorium Fausto magistro* (*Collectio Veronensis*, Schwartz, *PS*, p. 16, no. 7). See also Nicol, "Byzantine View," p. 318.

144. Gelasius *Letter* XVIII = *Collectio Avellana* XCV.21 (ed. Guenther, p. 376). His anger at Acacius and the see of Constantinople was unbounded.

145. Anastasius to Hormisdas = *Collectio Avellana* 138 (ed. Guenther, p. 565).

146. See the account of the events given by Vasiliev, *Justin the First*, pp. 136–60.

147. For the final negotiations, see Vasiliev, *Justin the First*, pp. 161ff. Important is the contemporary account of the deacon Dioscorus, an Alexandrian in papal service, *Collectio Avellana* 167.

148. Mansi, *Sacrorum Conciliorum*, vol. 8, p. 1038. (Patriarch John's style.)

149. The *Excerpta Valesiana* I.14, 86, considers the whole affair as evidence for Theodoric's "plotting evil against the Romans." See Ensslin's account, *Theoderich*, pp. 316–20, and H. Chadwick, *Boethius*, p. 53.

150. Boethius, *Consolation of Philosophy* I.3, ed. James: "In his lifetime too, Socrates, his [Plato's] master won with my [philosophy's] aid the victory of an unjust death." See also S. Gruber, *Kommentar zu Boethius de Consolatione Philosophiae* (New York and Berlin: Walter de Gruyter, 1978); and review by Henry Chadwick in *JTS* n.s. 30.2 (October 1979): 572–73.

151. "Iustinus Augustus, dans honorem Deo, humiliavit se pronus et adoravit beatissimum Iohannem papam," *Liber Pontificalis*, ed. Duchesne, p. 275.

152. *Excerpta Valesiana* XVI.95 credits Theodoric with a painful death, as divine punishment, befalling him on the very day "he rejoiced to attack the Catholic churches."

153. Ibid., XII.61: Theodoric's shrewd dictum, "Romanus miser imitatur Gothum, et utilis [wealthy] Gothus imitatur Romanum."

154. Procopius *History of the Wars* V.2.18 (I owe this reference to Mr. Patrick Wormald).

23

Justinian and the Byzantine Achievement 527–65

JUSTINIAN'S RENEWAL (*RENOVATIO*)

The age of Justinian is one of the great creative ages of European history. The emperor's influence extended over forty-seven years from September 518—when, as Count Justinian, he wrote to Pope Hormisdas telling him that he was expected in the capital to terminate the Acacian Schism "without any delay"[1]—until his death in November 565. By that time he had espoused an extreme form of Monophysitism as his personal religion. This raises questions, of course, about the true consistency of his religious policy during his long reign. In that central period, from 1 August 527, when he succeeded his uncle to become sole emperor, until about the time of the Fifth Ecumenical Council in 553, his achievement had been outstanding. The map of the Mediterranean had been changed. Large parts of the West had been restored to the emperor's direct rule. The concert of Old and New Rome had become once more a reality. Despite costly wars and still more costly building programs, the Byzantine currency was stable, and its gold solidi were sought eagerly far beyond the empire's frontiers as guarantors of value.[2] Byzantine merchants traded down the Red Sea and across the Indian Ocean to Ceylon, the emporium for the silk of China and the products of India. Aided by this wealth, a distinctive Byzantine civilization had come into being that embraced art, architecture, religion, and government. Christian missions followed the trade, not least to the Nubian kingdoms in the Nile Valley. The empire was served by the genius of generals such as Belisarius and Narses, architects of the inspiration of Anthemius of Tralles, lawyers as able as Tribonian, while its successes were told by the historians Procopius of Caesarea and Agathias. Justinian chose his men well, commented Procopius (*Buildings* I.1.26). This was not just a glittering court civilization. A provincial of moderate means and ambitions, such as John the Lydian, could make for himself a place in the imperial service, net a thousand solidi in a single year, and find time to write (c. 554) an extensive work on the administration of government in his time.[3]

In contrast, Western Christendom was on the verge of a long regression in social, economic, and political life that characterized the early Middle Ages. Britain was already an area known to Procopius only by legendary happenings[4] and so remote that it could be offered to the Ostrogoths![5] For Gaul, Gregory of Tours chronicled sadly the new era of Frankish triumph, characterized by perpetual and apparently aimless and destructive wars, by rape and murder, and by the slow eclipse of the remnants of the Gallo-Roman tradition.

All "renewals" in the later Roman Empire were conservative in aim. Justinian's *renovatio* was no exception. The emperor saw himself as the heir to Rome's greatness, extending back not merely to Augustus, but to the kings Romulus and Numa Pompilius and to Aeneas himself.[6] He modeled imperial administration on what he believed had been that of Julius Caesar,[7] and he believed, as had Livy, in a "Roman" superiority that was destined once more to subdue the Germanic peoples who had temporarily usurped Roman territory.[8] It was perhaps no accident that Justinian occupied the early years of his reign in supervising a vast work of reediting Roman law. Though an autocrat,[9] believing that law was the expression of his "divine will" he also regarded himself, as did the emperor in the past, as a magistrate and legislator. "The supreme protection of the common weal," he wrote in 529, "consists of two powers, that of the laws and that of arms. The blessed race of the Romans is superior over all other nations and has succeeded in conquering every people in the past, as it will succeed in subduing them, with the grace of God, in the future."[10] "All cities are bound to follow the usage of Rome, which is the capital of the world," he wrote to Tribonian in 530, "not it to follow other cities."[11] At the same time, all hope rested on "the Supreme Trinity's sole providence." Much of the spirit of the emperor's secular and religious program was summed up in those sentences.

Reorganization, restoration, and orthodox religion were inseparably associated. The first step, the reorganization of legal practice, was carried out mainly by his minister, Tribonian. This resulted by 534 in the emergence of a single code of law with constitutions extending back to the reign of Hadrian (117–38), and a handbook of law for students—the four books of the *Institutes*. It was the final flourish of the Latin heritage, for the *Novellae*, the legislation promulgated after 534, were usually in Greek. "We have drawn up this decree," admitted Justinian, "not in the national language [*patrios phōnē*], but in the spoken Greek, so that it may become known to all through ease of understanding."[12] For all the imperial emphasis on Rome and Latinity, the essentials of Justinian's world were Byzantine Greek. For many who experienced it, the restoration of the empire in the West, and especially in Italy, appeared like the imposition of an extortionate foreign rule.

Dominating Justinian's horizons, however, were questions of religion. This fact alone made his character impenetrable to traditional historians such as Procopius of Caesarea. To him, he was an "innovator and the greatest destroyer of established institutions,"[13] just as Julian had judged Constantine nearly two centuries before, and his attempts to enforce religious uniformity throughout the empire were written off not only as bigotry but as the product of a demonically inspired mind.[14] Justinian was a man of enormous energy, strength of purpose, and zeal, but also a man of paradoxes, a Latin who rejoiced in a common bond of Latinity with Pope Agapetus (535–56), yet a Byzantine theologian no less subtle and perceptive than his clerical advisers, and as his edicts show, as learned in Scripture and the fathers as he was in the history and institutions of Rome. In his heart he leaned toward Monophysitism, not merely the creed of Severus of

Antioch, but the Aphthartodocetism (the earthly body of Christ was in its nature thought to be incorruptible) of Julian of Halicarnassus; yet by policy and political judgment he was a Chalcedonian realizing that his Western policy depended on his unreserved adhesion to the "four Councils" and the "five patriarchates." Even so, until her death in June 548, he was under the spell of his Monophysite wife, Theodora, and her influence remained with him throughout his reign. He symbolized both the internal contradictions and the integration of the Byzantine world whose distinctive character he did so much to mold.

The priestly element in the emperor's office was not new. It had been accepted by the clergy of the East Roman provinces from Theodosius II onward.[15] Zeno's *Henotikon* was claimed by the emperor to promulgate the teachings of orthodoxy throughout the empire. Justinian pushed these ideas further toward their logical conclusion. He saw church *and* state as part of a single organism with himself as their earthly director. He held that the stability and indeed the survival of the empire and its people depended on their right belief, expressed in the right worship of God. "Hope in God," he wrote, "is our sole recourse for the existence of the monarchy. It is that which assures the safety of our rule and our empire. It is necessary that all our legislation flows from this principle, which is for it the beginning, middle and end" (*Novel* CIX, preface). The holy churches "sustain the empire"[16] and the emperor reckoned his concern for them as "no less valuable than life itself."[17] Hence, though he made a formal distinction between "priesthood and empire" as "the twin gifts of God" for the service of divine matters and human affairs respectively,[18] he considered as his duty both the regulation of major theological issues and the day-to-day running of the church. His legislation covered matters as diverse as the character necessary for an abbot, the proper upkeep of church property, gambling by clergy, and the use of biblical oaths in the courts.[19] He himself would enter into debate with Monophysite shipmasters from Alexandria (they refused to be drawn!).[20] Eventually he prepared the grand strategy that led to the Fifth General Council.

Already in 527 his aims were set. In the first three years of his reign, he showed his determination to base the empire's faith on the orthodox councils and the harmony of the five patriarchates, among whom that of Old Rome retained a primacy of honor with the right to be kept informed of all ecclesiastical decisions. For the rest, "all roads that lead to error were to be closed."[21] Right belief was a condition of admission to the service of the state and of the teaching professions, the right to inherit property and most of the common rights of citizenship.[22] Every conceivable effort would be made to conciliate the Monophysites, but in the last resort Chalcedon could not be abandoned. Even schism with the Monophysites was preferable. Other forms of religious dissent were dealt with less gently. Between 527 and 529, laws were promulgated successively against Nestorianism, Eutychianism, Apollinarianism, and against the Manicheans, the Samaritans, and all other heretics, including the resilient Montanists in Asia Minor.[23] Only the largely Arian Gothic soldiery (*foederati*) were exempted temporarily from the disabilities imposed on heretics.[24] Nor were the few remaining aristocratic pagan families spared, and in 529 the Academy of Athens, the last surviving center of pagan intellectual life, was closed.[25] This step, however, did not mean what it would have meant in the West—the denial of all pagan cultural values. Far from it! Homer, Plato, and Aristotle would retain their place in Byzantine education, and the latter two would, with Eusebius of Caesarea, significantly influence Byzantine political theory. Hellenism was absorbed into Eastern Christianity to provide a lasting foundation for the Byzantine church-state.[26]

The great design to extend the empire westward until it reached the bounds of Honorius's territories, however, nearly did not happen due to two unconnected events. The Persian War of 530–32 was another of those costly and indecisive encounters between the two empires, but the emperor had the wit to see that the balance between them lay with the great confederation of Arab tribes that dominated the no man's land separating them. The steady conversion of the southern group, the Ghassanids, not to Orthodoxy but to Monophysitism was a triumph, but also one that brought with it new and dangerous problems for the empire.

The Persian War ended in 532, a few months after the event which nearly cost Justinian his throne. The causes of the Nika riot that broke out in Constantinople on 13 January 532 are obscure.[27] However, discontent with the taxes levied by Justinian's praetorian prefect, John of Cappadocia, the unpopularity of the city administration, and a vague feeling that one of the nephews of Anastasius would be an improvement on Justinian combined to precipitate an attempt at revolution. On 13 January the Circus factions, the Blues and Greens, united in demanding pardon for two criminals, one a supporter of the Blues, the other of the Greens, who happened to have escaped the executioner through the intervention of Providence. From there, the affair escalated to demands for the resignation of Justinian's ministers, to, finally, on 18 January, outcries that the emperor himself should go. As Anastasius before him in 512 when faced with a riotous populace, Justinian was prepared to abdicate. His resolve, however, was strengthened by his empress, Theodora, the daughter of a fighter of wild beasts in the amphitheater (*bestiarius*) and of tougher caliber than he. ("I agree with an old saying that 'Empire is a fair winding-sheet.' ") The crisis was overcome. Henceforth, hers was the voice that counted in the empire's affairs, and her influence on its religion could hardly have been greater. A woman of the people, she shared the Monophysite inclinations of most of her contemporaries in the Byzantine world. As empress she could make those feelings explicit. As early as 523 she had intervened with her husband on behalf of the bishop of Amida who had been deposed for his Monophysite leanings. The sudden twists and turns of Justinian's policy that resulted, despite all, in the permanent survival of the Monophysite movement were due largely to her influence. Even through the hieratic conventions of Byzantine portraiture, the mosaic in the church of San Vitale at Ravenna portrays her as a woman of great charm, distinction, and purpose. At decisive moments, the full force of her ability would be placed wholly on the side of the Monophysites.[28]

Justinian recovered from the Nika riot, and his throne was never again threatened. By the summer of 533, he was ready to concentrate on the reconquest of the former western provinces of the empire. For him, these had "once been possessed by the ancient Romans to the limits of both oceans and had been lost by subsequent neglect."[29] Moreover, this policy, whatever its final results, was not unpopular with many of his subjects. Thus Cyril of Scythopolis (the biographer of the Palestinian monastic leader and orthodox champion St. Sabas [d. 532]) wrote in c. 554 that Sabas had predicted to Justinian, during a visit in 532, that God would restore the empire to the limits of Honorius's domains if the emperor "adhered to orthodox religion and destroyed Arianism along with other heresies."[30] Less expected are the almost equally positive evaluations of Justinian's western aims in John Lydus and, outside the pages of the *Secret History,* in Procopius.

THE REOCCUPATION OF NORTH AFRICA 533–34

The time, as we have seen in the last chapter, was propitious. The Ostrogoths were isolated and ineffective. The Vandal kingdom in Africa was tottering more from the advance of the Berber Nomads than overt Afro-Catholic disaffection with the renewed pro-Arian policies of Gelimer (usurper of Hilderich's throne). Justinian, however, seems to have taken only the latter into account, and even so he hesitated to strike. Memories of Leo I's disastrous expedition of 468 haunted him and his advisers. At length, however, the Afro-Catholics in the capital had their way[31] and in the summer of 533 a great armada commanded by Belisarius left for Vandal Africa, blessed by the patriarch of Constantinople. This time there was no mistake. Belisarius routed the Vandals at Ad Decimum on 13 September 533. Carthage was occupied the next day. Vandal counterattacks were defeated, and by the middle of the following year the Vandal kingdom was no more. Victory had been gained at a trifling cost.

Justinian's measures in North Africa illustrate his aims had he been able to move rapidly into Italy, Spain, and Gaul. The century of Vandal rule was treated as though it had never been. The kingdom was extinguished and many of the surviving Vandals transported east, resettled, and enrolled in five cavalry squadrons for service against the Persians. On 13 April 534, edicts (*mandata*), addressed to the new praetorian prefect of Africa and to Belisarius, established a fresh imperial prefecture and civil administration based on Carthage.[32] The religious cast of the emperor's mind is indicated by his constant references to "the prayers of the Holy and Glorious, ever-Virgin and Theotokos Mary," and the assertion to Belisarius that, "in the name of Our Lord Jesus Christ, we advance always to all plans and to all actions." On 1 August 535, a further edict restored the Catholic church to all rights and privileges that it possessed before the Vandal invasion. No toleration whatsoever was to be granted to heretics or schismatics.[33]

In keeping with his backward-looking ideals, Justinian based the new Byzantine Christian West on the cities. No matter that under the Vandals many of these had declined to the point of extinction whereas the country-side had been relatively prosperous. All were to be restored. Leptis Magna, half buried beneath encroaching sands, was equipped with a vast new stone church and civil basilica.[34] Thick deposits of silt and rubble overlay the forums of Sufetula, Thuburbo Maius, and Dougga,[35] but these were rebuilt with new, splendid churches and public buildings. No effort was spared. Inscriptions record that Theveste and Zabi were rebuilt—from the ground up (a fundamentis)[36]—and similar measures were taken to breathe new life into Timgad and Bagai in southern Numidia.[37] The optimistic spirit in which much of the reconstruction was carried out is perhaps typified by the Byzantine officer who celebrated the restoration of a cistern near Mactaris with a line remembered from the Aeneid I.167-68, combined with thanks to the Creator.[38]

The main effort was, however, lavished on Carthage itself. Procopius, writing his Buildings (c. 560), claimed that Justinian "cared for Carthage,"[39] renaming it "Justiniana" and rebuilding the entire circuit of its walls that had been pulled down by the Vandals. He goes on,

> he dedicated shrines, one to the Theotokos, in the [governor's] palace, one outside this, to a local saint Prima. Furthermore, he built stoas [colonnades] on either side of what is called the Maritime Forum, and a public bath, a fine sight, which he named Theodorian after the empress. He also built a monastery on the shore inside the circuit wall, close to the harbour which they call Mandracium; by surrounding it with very strong defences, he made it impregnable.[40]

Procopius tells us much about the aims of Justinian's Reconquista. While civil administration and city buildings were restored, the restoration of Catholicism took precedence, and the church was to be brought into the closest relationship with the government. The specifically Byzantine character of the new order was emphasized by the church dedicated to the Theotokos on the Byrsa within the governor's residence, though in North Africa concessions were made to opinion in the form of continued dedication to local saints. Byzantine Carthage was full of churches. The Mandracium and at least four large basilicas and outbuildings were clustered in an area of about half a square kilometer inland from the port.[41] Outside the walls, the churches dedicated to Perpetua and Felicitas and to Cyprian were repaired on a lavish scale.[42] Next to the governor, the most important person in the city was the bishop. Reparatus (535–52) acted as the governor's deputy in his absence and in 544 appeared to be the natural mediator in the conflict between the governor and Areobindus, the rebel leader (*Dux*) of Numidia. To Procopius, "Reparatus the priest" was a name to conjure with,[43] and yet when he incurred the emperor's displeasure in the Three Chapters controversy he was dismissed at will. His subordinates, the archdeacons in charge of the seven districts (*regiones*) of Carthage, were also men of wealth and influence, and in Liberatus (d. 566), archdeacon of Region 6, produced an intellectual leader and historian of courage and ability.[44]

All over North Africa this pattern was repeated. The Afro-Catholics had hailed Belisarius's arrival with joy. Arianism seems to have vanished almost overnight. At Carthage, Arian priests preparing to celebrate the feast of Cyprian (14 September) fled precipitately on news of Belisarius's victory, and their places were immediately taken by Catholics.[45] More than one cleric was praised as a "presbyter of unity" in vivid mosaic.[46] Between 535 and 550 magnificent churches were built in the restored cities whose ruins in Sufetula, Haidra, Sicca Veneria, Thuburbo Maius, and Theveste, to mention only a few, still awake the tourist's wonder. In these towns, too, though municipal government was restored as in former days, the chief citizen was undoubtedly the bishop, as in Carthage. Justinian's policy was to make the bishops responsible for supervising public works, inspecting public accounts, inquiring into alleged exactions by officials, as well as for their traditional duties of administering bequests and charitable funds and securing the freedom of any who wished to forsake disreputable professions.[47] Behind the church stood the army, ably led by Justinian's general and civil commissioner (*patricius et magister militiaeque*), Solomon of Dara, who was responsible for initiating the system of massive protecting fortresses usually constructed from blocks once used to build pagan monuments. These and the churches remain to this day the most striking reminders of Byzantine Africa, the symbol of Justinian's *renovatio*.

North Africa with Sicily, occupied in 535, were the model territories of the *Reconquista*, but everywhere Justinian has left the same impressive monuments of his rule. The neighboring province of Cyrenaica has also produced fine Byzantine churches and official buildings.[48] In Syria, the frontier defenses (*limes*) of Chalcis were repaired, and the fine walls that for centuries guarded Aleppo and Chalcis were Byzantine.[49] Everywhere churches sprang up; no less than eight in the Transjordanian city of Gerasa (Jerash).[50] Fortress, church and fortified monastery, such as St. Catherine's in the Sinai Peninsula, were the hallmarks of Justinian's age.[51]

BYZANTINE ART AND ARCHITECTURE

Churches and Religion

The North African churches, though larger and more ornate than their fourth and fifth century predecessors, were still built on a basilican plan. Modifications, such as the addition of side chapels and an apse at the west end, were probably connected with the elaboration of Byzantine ritual.[52] In Constantinople since 529, however, a new form of Christian architecture was coming into being by which Byzantine civilization would always be known.

The great cathedral of Hagia Sophia was the result of the Nika riot which saw the demolition of its five-aisled predecessor. With tremendous energy Justinian set about the work of restoration. Anthemius of Tralles and his assistant Isidore of Miletus perhaps modeled their design on the Church of Saints Sergius and Bacchus near the imperial palace, finished only a year or so before. The novel feature of this church was its basic plan—that of a Greek cross supporting an octagonal dome on pillars, the latter replacing the apse as the focus of the worshiper's attention. The altar was directly under the dome. The latter represented the dome of heaven, ruled over by Christ and linked with his creation through the descending order of archangels, angels, evangelists to earthly rulers, and thence to the faithful themselves. An inscription in Latin around the base of the dome praised Justinian and Theodora. Hagia Sophia embodied the same religious and political concepts on a grander scale. The dome rose above the quadrilateral space between the arms of the cross to a height of 180 feet.[53] It was supported on huge columns and every space was decorated with mosaics or faced with marble. If the exterior was impressive enough, it was the interior that was designed to inspire the worshiper. The dome of heaven was traversed by a great cross set amidst the stars, and associated with Christ were the other holy and angelic beings who peopled heaven. The curtains of the great cathedral depicted the Virgin, the heavenly guardian of their monarchy, with Justinian and Theodora. The emperor himself was invested with religious symbolism.

The liturgy, the approach to the divine world, had now become the preserve of the clergy; many of the prayers at the altar in the Eucharist would be said mystically, almost inaudibly, while the congregation obeyed the command of the priest yet glimpsed the world beyond set above them in the great dome and its distant reflection in the earthly rule of the emperor. As Theodosius II before him, Justinian gauged the mood of his people. The unity between class and class, city and city, found its expression through the liturgy and the new churches in which it was recited. The triumphant achievement of Anthemius[54] was the visible expression of this unity in architecture.

835

Hagia Sophia was completed in five years, and was dedicated by the patriarch on St. Stephen's Day 537. When Ravenna fell to Belisarius in 540 and became the capital of Byzantine Italy, the same skill and energy were put into the completion of the Church of San Vitale, subsidized this time by a private citizen, the banker Julianus. The result was also a work of genius.[55] Once more, the representations of Justinian and of Theodora and their court made the worshiper aware how the monarchy was an extension of the hierarchy of heaven, which included their earthly rulers, their friends, and their military, civil, and ecclesiastical advisers. The spiritual was never entirely divorced from the material. Holiness was not, as it tended to be in the West, confined to the world beyond.

The mosaics at San Vitale and San Apollinare in Classe illustrate this. Though the iconographic representation of the imperial family had been a feature of the coinage since the time of Constantius II, its extension to mosaics was a major step in the history of European art. The genius of the artists in the Ravenna churches overcame the now-traditional conventions determining the cast of eye and even the length of the nose of the subject. Justinian, his empress, and their court emerge as individuals, the one serious and benign with grizzled hair and rubicund face, the other pale, intense, and distinguished.[56] At San Apollinare, the great apsidal mosaic symbolized the glory of the cross in the midst of the transfiguration, foreshadowing the greater glory of the coming Christ. As has been said, never has art seen so many changes in so short a time as during the first half of the sixth century.[57] The changes resulted from the new tide of religious feeling that was moving through the whole Byzantine world, guided by the unsparing zeal of the emperor himself.

Byzantine religion was truly interpreted by its representatives, the clergy and monks. Between them these provided a pattern of ascetic devotion. In this, the *Theotokos*, in contrast to the Roman West where the Virgin's cult hardly develops before the seventh century,[58] was preeminent. She was Ever-Virgin "queen of heaven,"[59] mediator between the spiritual and the material worlds, protector of cities, and guardian over the welfare of the empire. In Carthage this has been noted, but all over the Byzantine Empire one finds the same marks of devotion. The harvest of Byzantine inscriptions from Palestine shows that whereas in the fourth century churches would be dedicated usually to Christ, in the sixth the Virgin and the military saints, reputed heroes of the Great Persecution, now held pride of place.[60] Thus, fourteen inscriptions invoke "Holy Mary" (*Hagia Maria*), eleven more hail her as *Theotokos*; others add the attribution of "Immaculate" (*Akēratos*), "Most Blessed" (*Kecharitōmenē*), "Mistress" (*Despoina*), "Virgin" or "Ever-Virgin" (*Aei-Parthenos*). Of the military saints, Georgius, whose martyrdom is associated with the town of Diospolis (Lydda/Lod), was the subject of twenty-six known dedications, Sergius and Bacchus of twenty-one, Theodore "the general" of eight, Cosmas and

Damian of six. As in Nubia in the classic age of Christianity (800–1050), the military saints were regarded as servants of the archangel Michael who with the Virgin herself protected the rulers and their people from evil.[61] Many churches became centers of pilgrimage. One of the most famous was that of St. Sergius at Resapha on the Persian frontier, where emperor, Persian monarch, and Arab chieftain all paid their respects and contributed their gifts.[62] In Egypt, the holy water that welled up from the Shrine of St. Menas was known throughout the Byzantine world. Little wonder that the vocation of clergy and the calling of the monks were never so popular. In 535 the great church in the capital with four other churches were served by 525 clergy (60 priests, 100 deacons, 90 subdeacons, 110 lectors, 40 deaconesses, 25 cantors, and 100 doorkeepers).[63] In Antioch, Bishop Severus (512–18) found that people would donate large sums in order even to be allowed to wear the garb of priests—and then sometimes claim pay and distributions.[64]

Outside the ranks of the clergy were the monks. In the capital alone there were eighty-five monasteries for men at the beginning of Justin's reign and thirty-nine more across the water at Chalcedon.[65] No Byzantine city in East or West would have lacked them. From the great and often fiercely rival monastic houses in Constantinople to the anchorite's cave in Upper Egypt the holy man symbolized the religious outlook of the empire. Early medieval Western observers were baffled by the "over-production of the holy," as Peter Brown has described it.[66] And the power of the saints was correspondingly great. "Neither yet think that this power of the saints before whom these people come and groan is a void thing, lest it be roused against you and your home perish."[67] So wrote the Monophysite missionary and man of letters, John of Ephesus. This was accepted by holy man and provincial alike. In the previous century, Simeon Stylites and his disciple Daniel had wielded their authority in the counsels of Theodosius and Zeno, respectively. Daniel's influence had been cast decisively against the usurper Basiliscus in 476. He regarded the capital itself as a "second Jerusalem," while the inhabitants accepted him as their God-inspired adviser and protector.[68] In Justinian's reign, Sabas (d. 532), the venerable Chalcedonian leader of the Palestine monks, and Zooras, the Monophysite from Mesopotamia who acted as Theodora's confessor, effectively combined the roles of political advocate and guru—so appropriate for their time.

THE EMERGENCE OF THE MONOPHYSITE CHURCH 519–31

Sabas and Zooras, so similar in their religious outlook, represented the two sides of a divide which no stroke of diplomacy could heal. To some contemporaries, the Chalcedonian-Monophysite dispute could be narrowed down to a single letter "K" rather than "N"—*out of* two natures (*ek duo physeōn*) rather than *in* two natures (*en duo physesin*)—the devil's work, as the exasperated official and historian Evagrius of Antioch described it at the end of the century.[69] It provides a classic instance of how popular mythology and prejudice can find a point of disagreement which defies any formula. In Justinian's reign despite the emperor's theological acumen and the patent loyalty of the Monophysite leaders to Byzantium, the two systems moved steadily apart, and where there had once been only differences of opinion there were now rival churches.

The architect of the Monophysite system was Severus, patriarch of Antioch (512–18); he died twenty years later in exile in Egypt. He was already a familiar figure in the capital. He was a man of contrasts. A Greek of aristocratic birth from Pisidia, a theologian self-consciously in the tradition of the Cappadocian fathers, his theological legacy was to the Syrian Jacobites. In his lifetime, he was supported by the native Syrian but rejected by the majority of the Greek city dwellers in Syria. By nature a pedantic extremist, he nonetheless believed his theology traveled the "royal road" of good sense and moderation.[70] A monk, he was also an enormously busy man of affairs and administrator of his diocese. Profoundly loyal to the Byzantine state, he was the victim of persecution by one emperor and he profoundly distrusted his successor. Strongly opposed to the creation of a separate Monophysite hierarchy, he found himself obliged to consent to the establishment first of a presbyterate and then of a Monophysite episcopate. As exiled patriarch of Antioch he became the "ecumenical leader" of a rival church.[71]

Basing his theology on his understanding of Scripture and the fathers, above all of Cyril, he felt it was his duty to maintain the church pure in doctrine regardless of the consequences. "Accuracy" was his key word. He opposed the *Tome* of Leo because he regarded its statements concerning Christ as inconsistent and, where intelligible, Nestorian. How could Christ die "in two natures," he asks. Which nature did Leo think had been nailed to the cross? How was it credible for the incarnate Christ's two natures to quote Scripture against each other?[72] On the other hand, he was equally severe on those who attempted to deny the true humanity of Christ. He accepted the condemnation of Eutyches, and criticized Dioscorus as "contentious," "fighting unnecessarily about words."[73] He anchored his position to that of Cyril.[74] Like Cyril he used *physis* and *hypostasis* as synonyms to express the individuality of Christ. He would concede, as Cyril had, that "in the act of contemplation" (*theoria*) one could conceive the duality of the human and divine natures.[75] But *out of* these natures came the one incarnate nature of Christ, with one source of activity (*energeia*), the divine word. Thus, though Christ's works were varied and included the performance of miracles as well as ordinary human activities, they were the work of a single nature activated by a single energy. As J. Meyendorff pointed out,[76] Severus not only had an answer to the Chalcedonian position, but looked forward to the attempted compromise between that position and Monophysitism in the Monenergist movement (the notion of one [divine] activity in Christ) of Heraclius's time (610–41).

Inevitably, Severus's teaching, combined with its tactless enforcement and his personal rigidity, made him enemies. Antioch bore no comparison with Alexandria as a power base. Whereas John III Nikaiotes (from Nikiou in the Delta), the Alexandrian patriarch (505–17), could offer the emperor Anastasius two thousand pounds of gold if he would renounce Chalcedon,[77] Severus found Antioch practically bankrupt. It was "crippled with debt and strangled by creditors," he wrote.[78] Some of his suffragans were paid a beggarly one solidus a month.[79] Severus had not the means either to discipline the unruly or win over the waverers, and during his regime his patriarchate began to be fragmented. In the Syrian-speaking territories, such as the monasteries around Chalcis ad Belum (Quennesrin) he was immensely popular, heart and soul with the "God-loving people."[80] Isauria too was grudgingly loyal, but Nestorianism remained latent in Cilicia and parts of northern Syria, while in western Syria (Syria II) where the countryside was still dominated by the Greek cities, Severus's name was anathema. In 517 the bishops and monks of Syria II appealed to Pope Hormisdas against their patriarch's "daily attacks on the holy synod of Chalcedon" and on "our blessed father, Leo."[81] The revolution that followed Justin I's accession the next year was directed as much against Severus as against the policies of the dead emperor. Severus was forced to flee to Alexandria (September 518). His chief supporter, Philoxenus of Mabbug (Hieropolis), was arrested and ended his days in exile, while fifty-five bishops of the patriarchate of Antioch were deposed.

Severus's enemies, however, made themselves unpopular. Hormisdas tried to press his victory too far. Gradually a groundswell of opposition rose against the Western Definition of Faith. At first Severus kept in touch with his supporters through emissaries. From Alexandria a flood of instructions and orders flowed from his pen. Soon, however, his congregations, particularly monks who had been expelled from their monasteries, began to establish rudimentary communities, served by their own non-Chalcedonian clergy. These groups pressed the patriarch to have this priesthood placed on a permanent footing. Severus temporized, but when by 529 it became clear that no change for the better could be expected, a decision was inevitable.

The events that led to the establishment of a Monophysite hierarchy and the permanent division of the Byzantine world between Chalcedonian and Monophysite are told by John of Ephesus in the *Life* of his friend John of Tella:

> At the end of ten years of persecution [that is, 529/30], the faithful who remained in diverse places began to be concerned about ordinations and consulted the faithful bishops; but these latter feared to bring down on themselves

even fiercer flames of persecution, and they refused to make ordinations openly, although they had made some in secret. Then complaints from the faithful persecuted arose from all sides against the blessed bishops because of the great deficiency of clerics; and they wrote and besought the bishops to make ordinations for the faithful, for the matter was urgent.[82]

Severus still hesitated. He believed that "true ordination" was not a matter of diocese or parish but of belief. For him the proper administration of the "rational and bloodless sacrifice" to believers was the essential means of salvation, and most would have agreed. Eastern Christians believed that deprivation of the sacraments, or failure to receive them at the hands of a priest of proven orthodoxy, could damage the soul as it struggled toward salvation, and indeed, bring whole communities to ruin.[83] Severus insisted accordingly on "accurate belief" but had no intention of establishing a church on a territorial basis, such as had happened in the West during the Donatist Schism. It was a question simply of how the orthodox sacraments should be dispensed in the circumstances created by Justin's persecution and resulting exile of anti-Chalcedonian clergy loyal to Severus.

Severus's council at Alexandria decided that the faithful must be served by a truly orthodox hierarchy. The results of the decision were sensational. Again, to quote John of Ephesus, hundreds of people from all over the Byzantine East came to John of Tella for ordination. It was "like a river that had burst its bank." "Every day, fifty, a hundred and sometimes as many as two or three hundred men, came for ordination."[84] John of Tella himself claimed to have admitted no less than 840 monks from his own monastery to the diaconate in a single year (530?).[85]

The years 530/31 mark a turning point in the religious history of Byzantium. From now on, there were to be two churches and two hierarchies, one approved by the emperor, in accordance with Chalcedon, the other Monophysite.

Attempts at Reconciliation 531–36

Justinian was alert to the danger. Apart from Egypt, whose Monophysite patriarch Timothy IV (518–35) neither Justinian himself nor his uncle had dared to remove, the main thrust of the Monophysite movement was now east of Antioch. The legacy of Philoxenus of Mabbug and the restless activity of John of Tella combined to build up a solid following among the monks and populace of this sensitive strategic area. Security of Rome's eastern frontier depended, in the sixth century as in the fourth, on the will of the inhabitants. Justinian dared not risk alienating them. Isauria, too, ruled by its feudal chieftains, of whom the emperor Zeno was a prime example, was as strongly Monophysite as it had been pro-Cyril during the Nestorian controversy. Similarly Pamphylia. Moreover, pro- and anti-Monophysite factions divided many of the main towns of the other provinces of Asia Minor, including Ephesus.[86]

840

Yet for all this popular support, Severus was not secure. As with many highly articulate groups in exile quarrels had broken out among the Monophysites in Alexandria. Julian, bishop of Halicarnassus in Caria, the most influential voice among the Monophysites of western Asia Minor, put forward the view that the flesh of Christ was incorruptible (*aphthartos*) from the moment of conception, whereas Severus maintained, with greater attention to Scripture, that incorruption began with the resurrection. The standpoints were as old as the division between Cyril and Eutyches, and though Julian denied Eutychianism, this was the true basis of the controversy.[87] It was never to be healed and henceforth the Julianists would dog the Severans into every corner of the expanding Monophysite world.[88]

Justinian, however, was also ready for dialogue. Severus was too big to ignore; there was a strong Monophysite undertow among the poor of Constantinople that made itself felt during the Nika riots,[89] and he believed that with the formula of the Theopaschites (*Theopaschitai*) he had a possible means of healing the doctrinal breach. "One of the Trinity *suffered* in the flesh," had an impeccable Constantinopolitan background, having been used by the patriarch Proclus in his *Tome to the Armenians* in 437, and it embraced the beliefs contained in the Monophysite addition to the *Trisagion* (". . . who was crucified for us") without explicitly stating them. The formula also corresponded to Cyril's twelfth *Anathema*, insisting that "God the Word *suffered* in the flesh" and it emphasized the role of Mary as *Theotokos*. In the period immediately following the end of the Acacian Schism in 519, it had been canvassed by the Scythian monks in the capital (that is, monks probably from the Dobrudja area). Justinian had tried vainly to press the formula on Pope Hormisdas as the best means of restoring peace in the East.[90] A dozen years later, he took it up once more as a formula of reconciliation.

Through much of 532 and early 533 a series of discussions were held in the capital between Chalcedonian and Monophysite representatives; the results were inconclusive. The Chalcedonians gained the advantage in discussing the origins of the controversy, just as the African Catholics succeeded with the Donatists in 411, but they failed to answer the Monophysite contentions that the Two Natures doctrine was an innovation and that at Chalcedon Cyril's *Anathemas* had not been accepted, while on the contrary the Antiochene theologians had been vindicated.[91] Twenty years later when Justinian tried to meet the Monophysites by the formal condemnation of the Antiochenes at the Fifth General Council, it was too late. At this stage he tried to impose his own solution.

On 15 March 533, Justinian published an edict addressed to the people of the capital and twelve major cities of the empire.[92] The canonical status of the Four Councils was affirmed. The role of *Theotokos* was emphasized. So also was the Theopaschite formula. No mention was made of the *Tome* of Leo but the Nestorian concept of the Two Natures was condemned.

841

Pope John II (533–35) was informed first among the bishops, and his reply, accepting the edict as orthodox ("according to apostolic teaching"), was itself given the force of law by Justinian. The emperor might appear to have squared the circle, but a formula that seemed to meet nearly all the Monophysite requirements was rejected because Chalcedon was retained— not for the last time. Folk-mythology was replacing reason. Most of Severus's followers would have agreed with the citizens of Amida, the key fortress on the eastern frontier: "We will never accept the synod [Chalcedon] and the *Tome* [of Leo]."[93]

Trust was lacking. Persecuted for ten years, the Monophysite leaders, though profoundly loyal to the empire and the imperial office, needed more than a formula to satisfy them. Severus himself had not attended the conference, his view being that Justinian was not to be trusted.[94] In the winter of 534, however, he did accept an invitation to the capital to become involved in a bizarre yet crucial incident in the history of the Monophysite church in the following year.

First, on 7 February 535, Timothy IV of Alexandria died. Theodora acted at once, even anticipating Timothy's death and sending her chamberlain to Alexandria on 10 February to obtain an appropriate succession. The choice fell on the deacon Theodosius, a Monophysite and firm friend of Severus. Her plan, however, was nearly thwarted by Severus's Julianist opponents. The Alexandrians never took kindly even to benevolent imperial intervention in elections to their patriarchate, while the monks, as at the time of the *Henotikon*, favored genuine Monophysitism. For 103 days Theodosius battled with the Julianist candidate, the monk Gaianus. The latter had a fanatical following among the people and was regarded as a prophet. Theodosius's position was secured in May only through military intervention.[95] Next month, Theodora acted again, this time for even greater stakes. The patriarch of Constantinople, Epiphanius, died (10? June), and Theodora managed to win the succession for Anthimus, bishop of Trebizond, a cleric of a severely ascetic outlook, one of the Chalcedonian delegates at the conference with the Monophysites three years before. Anthimus, however, had been impressed by his opponents' arguments, had formed a close friendship with Severus, and now acquiesced in the latter's implacable hostility to Chalcedon. This soon became evident from the freedom allowed to avowed Monophysites, and is confirmed by the letter Anthimus later wrote to Severus proclaiming his acceptance of Cyril's *Anathemas*, Severus's anti-Chalcedonian interpretation of the *Henotikon*, the Theopaschite formula, and, foreshadowing future developments, the condemnation of the Antiochenes, Theodoret of Mopsuestia and Ibas of Edessa.[96] The "three patriarchs were now in communion, linked by mutual affection and faith," proclaimed Zacharias.[97] Justinian's Western policy was being undermined in his own capital, and every pro-Chalcedonian took fright, not least the aggressive ex-count Ephraim (526–44), who occupied Severus's former patriarchate of Antioch.

At Rome, Pope Agapetus (535–36) was far more alert to the dangers at Constantinople than Simplicius had been. By a fortunate coincidence King Theodahad of the Ostrogoths (Amalasuntha's supplanter, 535–36) sent him with an embassy to appeal to Justinian to suspend his invasion of Sicily and Dalmatia (winter 535/36). Once again as in Justin's reign, the mystique of Old Rome prevailed, and Agapetus was a wiser man than Hormisdas had been. On his arrival in Constantinople he did not condemn Anthimus as a heretic. Rather, he invoked the Nicene canon (canon 15) that forbade bishops to be transferred from one see to another.[98] Anthimus submitted. Liberatus of Carthage recounts that he handed over his pallium and allowed Theodora to provide him with a safe refuge.[99] Agapetus himself consecrated his successor, the Alexandrian-born Menas (13 March 536), another shrewd move of papal diplomacy. Though he died suddenly on 22 April, a lengthy and impressive Home Synod proceeded to condemn Anthimus and Severus as heretics (May–June 536). The pope had allowed the Eastern bishops to do his work for him.[100]

Justinian confirmed the council's findings on 10 June. The imperial edict banned Anthimus, Severus, Zooras, and their supporters from the capital and all the great cities of the empire, and ordered copies of Severus's writings to be burned.[101] Severus was accused of waging "an undeclared war" in setting the churches against each other, and of "uttering blasphemies as damnable as those of Arius and Apollinaris." On 6 August the condemned men were expelled from the capital.[102] Severus returned to Egypt to die on 8 February 538, an exile from his homeland, his patriarchal see, and even from Alexandria, but not before he had taken a vital step to protect Monophysite orthodoxy. At last, he authorized the consecration of bishops and not merely of lower clergy as he had done eight years before.[103]

Papacy and Patriarchate 536–40

The decision of the Home Synod ended the emperor's attempt to reunite Chalcedonian and Monophysite on the basis of mutual acceptance of the Theopaschite formula. Repressive measures against the Monophysites were renewed, especially in the patriarchate of Antioch. There, the Chalcedonian patriarch Ephraim was triumphant. Chalcedon was proclaimed without reservation in some cities and Severus's supporters were hunted down. John of Ephesus and Zacharias report how some were imprisoned and others burned alive.[104] Among the victims was John of Tella, the founder of the independent Monophysite presbyterate and one of Severus's closest collaborators. After lengthy and exasperating interrogation John was executed at the order of the patriarch Ephraim, early in 538. With him, the roll of Monophysite martyrs opens.[105]

Egypt, however, was to be the testing ground of the effectiveness of Justinian's rapprochement with the papacy. Personal friendship between the emperor and pope—remembered in medieval times[106]—as well as military events had eased its progress. On 31 December 535 Belisarius completed the reconquest of Sicily. Theodahad's final appeal for peace, brought to the capital by Pope Agapetus, was refused. In November 536 Naples fell to the Byzantines and on 9 December Belisarius entered Rome. The pope was the emperor's subject once more, but even before this the papacy had taken steps to ensure the continuity of its presence in the capital. The lesson of the Acacian Schism had perhaps been learned. The deacon Pelagius (later Pope Pelagius I, 555–61) became the first papal nuncio (apocrisiarius) at Constantinople. He was shrewd and vigorous and at once started to fulfill his immediate objective of restoring the traditional link between Rome and Alexandria, interrupted since the departure of the last Chalcedonian patriarch, John Talaia, in 482. First, Theodora's nominee, the patriarch Theodosius, had to be removed. At the beginning of 537 he was summoned to the capital, and when he refused to subscribe to the Chalcedonian Definition was declared deposed. After a year's exile at Derkos in Thrace his luck changed again. Thanks to Theodora, he found asylum in the palace of Hormisdas in the capital. From there he gradually built up the Monophysite church over which he achieved complete ascendancy until his death in 566. In the meantime, on Pelagius's recommendation Justinian replaced him in Alexandria with a Pachomian abbot named Paul. This man had quarreled with monks in his monastery at Canopus and was in the capital in order to persuade the emperor to bring them in line. He was consecrated patriarch by Menas and Pelagius, and sent back to Alexandria with a formidable combination of civil and ecclesiastical powers. Paul was thus the first of a long line of Chalcedonian patriarchs in Alexandria who combined ecclesiastical with civil and even military government, a reflection of the harshly authoritarian aspect of Justinian's religious policy, one deserving the label "Caesaro-Papism."[107]

In Egypt the situation was balanced on a knife edge. Though Paul himself proved a disastrous choice, a more reputable successor was found in the person of the Palestinian monk, Zoilus (540–51). Alexandria seemed to acquiesce in the new situation. The will of the emperor, it was said, was always obeyed there.[108] Two factors, however, preserved Egypt for Monophysitism: the considerable role which the monasteries were playing in the rural economy of Egypt, and the missionary success of Theodora's agents in Nobatia, the Nubian kingdom on the southern frontier of Egypt. In addition, a long-lived Monophysite episcopal succession in the Nile Valley just survived the crisis caused by the revival of the Chalcedonian episcopate.

By Justinian's time, the monasteries had become a dominating fact in the lives of the Egyptian peasants (fellahin).[109] Enormously wealthy through gifts and bequests, some monasteries, notably Shenoute's White Monastery, rivaled the great estates of the Egyptian-Byzantine nobility. The peasants were sharecroppers, leasing their seed and equipment from the central monastery stores and paying a perpetual rent. The *Book of the Patriarchs*[110] describes how in the patriarchate of Peter IV (567–69) there were some "600 flourishing monasteries" near Alexandria and "32 farms called Sakatina" where all the inhabitants "held the true path." Economic and religious interdependence of the peasants and the monasteries was a force preventing restored Chalcedonians from penetrating far beyond the walls of the larger towns. The monks determined the religion of Egypt, but the presence of a Chalcedonian minority supported by the emperor and "the rich men of the province" was a divisive factor that weakened the popular will to resist Persian and Arab invaders in the next century.[111]

The Monophysite Missions

The maintenance of the Monophysite grip on the Egyptian countryside resulted in a further triumph for Theodora and her friends. Christianity had been penetrating Nobatia from southern Egypt since the middle of the fifth century.[112] In 453, however, the imperial authorities had signed a treaty with the Nobatians which allowed the latter to make a yearly sacrifice to Isis on the island of Philae on the boundary between the empire and their kingdom. The presence of this temple was an affront to Justinian even though by 539 when the emperor decided to denounce it, Theodore, bishop of Philae (524–76), had built a church there as well.[113] Both emperor and empress were agreed that Nobatia must be converted to Christianity, but disagreed concerning the faith to be preached there. For Justinian, it was to be another political stroke like the conversion and baptism of Grod, king of the Huns in Crimea, in 528; for Theodora a victory for Monophysite orthodoxy. This time, however, Theodora won. The story is told by John of Ephesus[114] how she wrote to the military commander of the Thebaid bordering Nobatia, truthfully informing him that she and her husband would be sending a mission to Nobatia, but that the monk Julian—in fact, her representative—would be its leader. The commander was taken in. In 542 the caravan arrived, loaded with gifts including gold and baptismal robes, and was soon on its way to the Nobatian capital, Pachoras (Faras). The king and his court were converted, and when Justinian's mission eventually arrived the king informed its leader that the emperor's alliance he would accept, but not his "wicked faith."[115] To make success doubly sure, Theodore of Philae joined Julian at the royal court.[116] The conversion had a cultural as well as a religious side, for from now on the main cultural influence in Nobatia was to be Byzantine Greek. The court was modeled on that of Constantinople, and the liturgy was based on that of St. Mark.[117] Centuries after the Moslem conquest of Egypt the Nubian kingdom remained a bastion of Byzantine culture, language, and religion.

The conversion of Nobatia to Monophysitism was a triumph for Theodora. Though Justinian and his successor Justin II were able to secure its southern neighbor Makurrah for Chalcedon,[118] the Nile Valley was destined to be Monophysite. Far to the south, the position of Monophysitism in the kingdom of Ethiopia had been rendered impregnable by missionaries from Syria and Egypt at the turn of the sixth century. Justinian's mission under Nonnus[119] to Ethiopia, the Yemen, and further north in Arabia, had no permanent effect on the balance between Chalcedonian and Monophysite. In Ethiopia too, a strongly monastic Christianity developed, and the head of the Ethiopian church (the Abuna) would be receiving his consecration at the hands of the Monophysite patriarch of Alexandria.

There were also Monophysite missions among the Arab groups that moved from oasis to oasis down the Red Sea coast as far as Yemen. Here through the sixth century, Ethiopian influence barely held the allegiance of the Christians against rival Nestorians (supported by Persia), and the Jews.

Armenia

On the empire's northeastern flank, Armenia had become Monophysite, but through an entirely different set of circumstances.[120] One of the effects of the emperor Jovian's surrender of Nisibis to the Persians in 363 had been to make Persian influence supreme there. In Persia, Antiochene theology was dominant among the Christians; to the time of the Council of Ephesus I it was also strong in Armenia. The condemnation of Nestorius, however, brought about change. Gradually, the pro-Byzantine party reasserted itself and in 437 Proclus, patriarch of Constantinople, dispatched the *Tome* which went under his name to the Armenians. The orthodoxy of the Council of Ephesus was emphasized and the Two Natures Christology of the Antiochenes was denounced. This did not make the Armenians Monophysite, but at the time of Chalcedon the Christians were fighting for their religion and national identity against the Persians. Their final victory coincided almost exactly with the promulgation of the *Henotikon* in 482. In addition, influenced by the works of Timothy Aelurus, the Armenian church moved steadily into the Monophysite camp. Though it had not been represented at Chalcedon, the council and Leo's *Tome* were denounced as Nestorian at the Council of Dvin in 506/8.[121] Instead, the *Tome* of Proclus and the *Henotikon* of Zeno remained the touchstones of Armenian orthodoxy.

In councils also held at Dvin between 524 and 527 Chalcedon was again rejected. The reaction under Justin failed to influence the Armenians. In the reign of Justinian, Armenia found itself strongly on the side of the Monophysites. Even the moderate Monophysitism of Severus was discarded in favor of the views of his rival, Julian of Halicarnassus.[122]

These Monophysite border kingdoms were the offshoot states of Byzantium. Even though they might quarrel violently with their root, Constantinople, in one way or another all reflected the achievement of early Byzantine civilization. All derived their liturgies, Scriptures, and their basic religious outlook from Byzantium. Missionaries from the Byzantine Empire provided the incentive and possibly also the guidance for the states to adopt a script in which their liturgy and sacred writings could be set down and thus transmitted to the people. Political independence combined with autocephalous ecclesiastical status enabled the native language to flourish alongside of Greek as the language of worship and expression of national identity.

Armenia and Ethiopia both survived centuries of Islamic pressure largely because Monophysite Christianity was the national religion, and the people identified with its saints and its liturgy. The Nubian kingdoms were eventually (c. 1450) overwhelmed by Moslem nomads from the Sahara and the movement of Arab groups on their eastern borders.[123] In about A.D. 1000 the cathedral library of Q'asr Ibrim (Primis) in Nobatia seems to have contained about the same number of devotional works in Nubian as in Greek,[124] and even at that time Nubian Greek was still recognizably Byzantine Greek. For Nubia too, the wondrous frescoes from Faras depicting the religious life of the court of the kingdom of Nobatia over four centuries (800–1200), follow the patterns of Byzantine art through that period.[125] So long as they existed, the titles of the Nubian kings and their ministers were based upon Byzantine models.[126] Even after centuries of Islamic influence, the Eastern Christians beyond the shrinking frontiers of the Byzantine Empire still looked to Constantinople as their spiritual home, and debated whether or not Chalcedon and the emperor Marcian were responsible for all the ills that had befallen Constantine's empire.[127]

Jacob Baradaeus 542–78

The vigor of the Monophysite churches beyond the Byzantine frontiers was paralleled by a remarkable series of missions carried out all over the Byzantine Empire itself. In the thirty years between 540 and 570 these were to alter very considerably the religious map of the eastern Mediterranean. In c. 540–41 John of Hephaestus in Egypt had undertaken a missionary journey in Asia Minor and the Aegean Islands, ordaining clergy as he went.[128] The decisive advance associated with the name of Jacob Baradaeus, however, came about partly by chance. In 542 al-Hareth Ibn Jabala, the king of the Ghassanid Arabs who dominated the deserts between the Roman province of Arabia and the Persian frontier, sent an embassy to Theodora asking her to send "orthodox" (that is, Monophysite) bishops to his people. Theodora persuaded Theodosius to consecrate two monks as bishops. One, Theodore, nominally based at Bostra, the capital of the Roman province, was sent to the Arabs; the other, Jacob Baradaeus, an eastern Syrian from Tella, was consecrated metropolitan of Edessa. Jacob was given authority over the Monophysite communities throughout the Byzantine East, from the Egyptian border to Constantinople itself and the

Aegean Islands.[129] The aim, as in Severus's time, was to serve individual congregations, not to establish Monophysitism on a territorial basis as an eastern Donatism. Indeed, the restoration of Monophysitism in Ephesus, the scene of the emperor Theodosius II's councils of 431 and 449, seems to have been regarded as higher priority than work in Syria. John, a monk from Amida and future historian of Monophysitism, who had earned fame by carrying out an extraordinarily successful mission on behalf of Justinian in the 540s among the still-pagan countryfolk in the province of Asia,[130] became Jacob's representative in that city.

Jacob's wide-ranging mission, combined with his magnetic personality, fused the scattered Monophysite communities into a permanent church. Even so, the process was gradual. It would seem that only after the Fifth General Council in 553 did Jacob embark on a major program of establishing a rival hierarchy to the Chalcedonian one. Then, "swift as Azael," as Bar-Hebraeus described him,[131] and according to John of Ephesus, traveling sometimes thirty or forty miles a day and covering great areas of Syria, Isauria, Cappadocia, and even Armenia and the Aegean Islands, he set about ordaining clergy for the Monophysite congregations. He "caused the priesthood to flow like great rivers over the whole world of the Roman domains,"[132] it was said. His opponents "gnashed their molars at this mighty man in the Lord." Jacob's aim was not schism. Like his predecessors his object was the conversion of the empire itself to Monophysitism. He saw, however, that the provincials must be won over en masse whereas they had aspired to persuade the emperor to take the initiative in renouncing Chalcedon.

In vain Justinian's agents attempted to track Jacob down and arrest him. Not even Theodosius's doubts as to the wisdom of establishing so many bishoprics discouraged him. When he died in 578 he left behind twenty-seven metropolitans and, it was said, one hundred thousand Monophysite clergy.[133] His permanent legacy was the Syrian Monophysite church, known to posterity as the Jacobite church after its great missionary.

THE EMERGENCE OF NEO-CHALCEDONIANISM

All this time the initiative had lain with the Monophysites. Where accepted outside the capital, that is, in Palestine, western Syria, and the western Latin-speaking provinces of the empire, Chalcedon had tended to be regarded as the emperor's creed, a religious compromise, perhaps just acceptable as a basis of faith, but arousing no special fervor. Under the challenge of the Monophysites, the Chalcedonians began to rethink their position and assess whether in fact it did not contain deeper insights into ultimate reality than its rival. The process may be traced back into the reign of Anastasius, to that theological stormy petrel Nephalius who tried to show from Cyril's own works that the latter's Christology was truly compatible with Chalcedon. There followed the more profound work of John the Grammarian, between 514 and 518, who set his mind on interpreting Chalcedon, aiming at establishing common ground between Severus and his opponents. John pointed to the fact that in Christ the same nature could not at one and the same time be consubstantial with God and with man, and hence acknowledgment "*in* two natures" as defined at Chalcedon was correct. But this could also be interpreted as synonymous with Cyril's formula "one incarnate nature of the God-Word," for Christ's humanity never existed apart from his divinity. The two constituted a single hypostasis or nature.[134] The real advance lay in the acceptance of the preexistence of the Word's hypostasis to which Christ's humanity was united. John, however, was a layman and lived in Cilicia, so his influence on the counsels of the church in the capital was small. Justinian, however, grasped the value of these ideas when they were put forward. They seemed to do for Chalcedon what the Cappadocian fathers had done for Nicaea, namely make the Definition of Faith acceptable to the majority of educated Byzantines.

Leontius of Jerusalem (in accord with Meyendorff's identification) also saw that the heart of the problem was the true understanding of the hypostatic union between Father and Son.[135] Between 532 and 536 he attempted to meet this challenge. Like John the Grammarian, he affirmed that Christ's humanity possessed no true nature or hypostasis of its own, and existed only as part of a whole that was Christ—the incarnate Word. Their unity took place before the incarnation (Leontius opposed the Origenist view that Christ's manhood preexisted separately from the Word). At the incarnation the human nature became "enhypostasized" so as to permit its unity with the Word, which thus subsisted "*in* two natures" as set out in the Chalcedonian Definition. "The Word," to quote Leontius, "in the last times, having himself clothed with flesh his hypostasis and his nature, which existed before his human nature, and which, before all the worlds, were without human nature, hypostasized human nature into his own hypostasis."[136]

This was a key statement for it enabled Leontius to move to other aspects of the mystery of the incarnate Word, namely his consubstantiality with humankind. Like Severus, Leontius reached back through the fathers to the Bible for his solution. As Meyendorff points out,[137] he aimed at incorporating into Chalcedonian Christology the Pauline notion of the new Adam and the related concept of the church as the Body of Christ. Seen thus, Christ's nature was not that of an individual man, but "the hypostatic archetype of the whole of mankind" in which our nature, "made the body of the Word," was linked with Christ. Christ united "all mankind" not "one particular man, to the divinity." The term "flesh" designated human nature as a whole. Similarly, the ecclesiastical art and architecture of Byzantium reflected this projection—soon to become the hallmark of metaphysical theology—of holiness from the divine world to the human. Leontius belongs emphatically to the creative age of Justinian's reign and to the Palestinian monastic tradition that strove throughout the fifth and sixth centuries to find a *via media* between rival interpretations of Cyril's Christology. He replaced static concepts of Chalcedonian orthodoxy with a dynamic view of the Godhead and of the human relation to it. Platonic and biblical ideas were united in a theology that sought to demonstrate how humankind's true life was in God, and how through Christ the human and divine natures were no longer to be regarded as exclusive. The tragedy was that these ideas, which rejected Apollinarianism (the human nature of Christ absorbed by the Word) as well as the Antiochene insistence on the complete differentiation of human and divine, came too late to prevent the final break with the Monophysites. At the time of Zeno's *Henotikon*, Leontius's Christology might have provided the intellectual substance for unity throughout the East. As it was, its importance was to be confined to the Chalcedonian-minded populations.

Justinian, however, was won over to Leontius's views, but in the next seven years after the condemnation of the Severans in 536, the immediate effort at compromise took the form of a revival of Origenism.[138] One can perhaps detect an element of despair in this. If neither Chalcedon nor Severan Monophysitism gave acceptable accounts of salvation, what was left? Reversion to Origen's ideas, particularly his eschatology that asserted a mechanical universal salvation, proved to be an anachronism. Leontius of Byzantium's attempt to establish middle ground between Chalcedonianism and Monophysitism on the basis of Origen's Christology failed to convince.[139] Justinian's edict condemning Origen and the Palestinian Origenists in 543[140] was also a tragedy, for it spelled doom for the great majority of Origen's works, henceforth outlawed.

THE THREE CHAPTERS 544–54   •

All these debates concerning Monophysitism, Origenism, and Neo-Chalcedonianism were intelligible only in the religious environment of the East. The further Justinian pushed his conquest of the West, the less understanding of these ideas there was, and the less attainable theological agreement would be. Western Christology was unalterably Two Nature, and apart from this, doctrinal questions would once again become increasingly confused with issues of ecclesiastical precedence and discipline, as they had been at the time of the councils of Ephesus and Chalcedon. By 543 this was becoming clear. After the fall of Rome in 536 and Belisarius's successful defense of the city against Gothic counterattack which lasted most of 537, Belisarius, his wife Antonina, and—inevitably—Theodora maneuvered to place on the papal throne the weak but ambitious Vigilius (537–55).[141] At first, the latter attempted to please his patrons. In c. 538 he assured Theodora that, ''we do not confess two natures in Christ, but that Christ was from two natures, one Son, one Christ, one Lord.''[142] This was the

Monophysite position, but it could evidently be held by a Roman bishop. The information comes from the Western chroniclers, Victor of Tunnuna and Liberatus, and there is no particular reason to doubt it. Vigilius's folly soon caught up with him, however, and by September 540 he was writing to the emperor confessing a strictly Two Nature doctrine,[143] and three years later he joined ranks in the condemnation of the Origenists.

Origenism had been a movement of opinion rather than an incipient schism. In Theodore Ascidas, a one-time leader of the Origenist Palestinian monks and by 543 metropolitan of Caesarea in Cappadocia, the emperor acquired a new spiritual adviser. Gradually, we are told by Evagrius, he ousted the papal representative Pelagius from influence at court.[144] This was an important moment in the religious history of the reign, for Theodore's interests were purely Eastern. If Origenism itself was unacceptable as the foundation for unity throughout the East, might not a way be found by removing from Chalcedon those parts of the council's decisions most disliked by both the Origenists and Monophysites? Could the works of Theodore of Mopsuestia (d. 428),[145] Theodoret (against Cyril's twelve *Anathemas*), and the *Christological Letter* of Ibas of Edessa (to the Persian presbyter Maris, criticizing Cyril's activities and theology at the time of the first Council of Ephesus) be defended? These were the "Three Chapters"—all considered sympathetic to Nestorius—whose condemnation Theodore Ascidas now sought.

Theodore had brought together Justinian and his empress in a common purpose of reuniting the church throughout the empire on a basis not very different from Zeno's *Henotikon*. Cyril was once more exalted to the position of master-theologian; his twelve *Anathemas* were accepted by implication through the condemnation of Theodoret, and the Antiochene tradition of theology was finally rejected. Chalcedon though not renounced was emasculated. The plan ultimately miscarried, however, due to exactly the same causes that destroyed Zeno's *Henotikon*, in addition to the hurdle of Severus's condemnation in 536. The Antiochene contribution to Chalcedon had rendered its Definition acceptable to the West. The acknowledgment of Christ in Two Natures, perfect in manhood as well as in Godhead, was fundamental to Western theology. The Western interpretation of atonement and salvation depended on the unequivocal assertion of this truth. Whatever his own views, Pope Vigilius could not reconcile the faith of the Western churches with that now reflected in Neo-Chalcedonianism. Justinian, like his predecessors Zeno and Anastasius, found himself forced to choose willy-nilly between the views of the great majority of his Eastern subjects and the imperial idea that assumed the inclusion of Eastern and Western Greek and Latin churches within a single united Christendom. The *Reconquista* could not be reconciled with the condemnation of the Three Chapters.

Sometime between 543 and 546 Justinian published an edict condemning the Three Chapters and invited the Eastern and Western episcopate to subscribe.[146] The Eastern patriarchs were at first unwilling to sign. This measure had been among the demands of the Monophysites, notably Philoxenus of Mabbug's, since the beginning of the century. Why should it be conceded now? Was it not also a bad precedent to anathematize those who had died in the peace of the church? The Westerners were unanimous in their refusal.[147] In Italy, the war was now going badly for the Byzantines. The Goths had found a new skillful leader, Totila, and at the end of 545 he was again besieging Rome. Vigilius's resolve was strengthened, and when in March 547 he at length reached Constantinople to confer with the emperor, he seems to have been determined to reinforce Western objections with his own.

The details of the pope's subsequent vacillations need not be recounted here.[148] However, two points stand out: first, the quasi-unanimous opposition to the emperor's policy of the Western churches, led by the vigorous restored African Catholics,[149] and second, the scale of the emperor's acknowledged powers over recalcitrant ecclesiastics. At one time in 551, not only was Reparatus, archbishop of Carthage, deposed and exiled, but the patriarchs of Jerusalem and Alexandria shared his fate. Only Menas, patriarch of Constantinople, sincerely supported Justinian's policy and survived his displeasure.

One of Theodora's last acts, before the onset of the illness that took her life on 29 June 548, was to reconcile Vigilius and Menas. On Easter eve 548 Vigilius pronounced a formal judgment addressed to Menas in which he condemned Theodore of Mopsuestia and the other writings anathematized in Justinian's edict, while safeguarding carefully the authority of the Council of Chalcedon.[150] The pope's *Iudicatum* (*Verdict*) merely aroused anger. He found himself repudiated by his own theological adviser (the African, Facundus of Hermiane, who saw that the object of Theodore's condemnation was to weaken the authority of Chalcedon).[151] He was excommunicated by the North African church in 550,[152] and disowned by the Chalcedonian patriarchs of Jerusalem and Alexandria. In terror, he withdrew the *Verdict* but not before he had sworn to the emperor on the Gospels and the nails of the cross that he would do all in his power to have the Three Chapters condemned at a general council.

Before that met in the secretariat of Hagia Sophia on 5 May 553, the pope had excommunicated Menas and Theodore Ascidas, had been assaulted in the Church of Saints Peter and Paul by soldiers, and had demanded and received from the patriarch of the capital and his clergy a declaration accepting in reverential terms both the *Tome* of Leo and Chalcedon's Definition. In the end, however, Justinian had his council practically on his own terms. In 551, in sovereign contempt for the "rustics" who disagreed with him, he had published his *Confession of the True Faith*, addressed to "the whole fulness of the Catholic Church."[153] This anticipated his program for the council and marks the climax of imperial theology even in the Byzantine Empire. Justinian asserted the orthodoxy of the Theopaschite formula, but combined it with that of the Two Natures of Christ as understood by Leontius of Jerusalem. The nature could exist only within the hypostasis, and it was by the hypostasis of the divine Word that the humanity of Christ received its entire existence in the womb of the Virgi 1 *Theotokos*. Christ therefore was both God and man—Two Natures—in his composite hypostasis. A generation previously, Severus might have found this an arguable case. Now, so far as the Monophysites were concerned, it was hardly relevant, and the West either did not understand it or rejected it.

No bishops came to Constantinople from Spain, Dalmatia, or Illyricum; a few only from Africa; the remainder were from the Eastern dioceses.[154] Vigilius once more tried to compromise. He would condemn Theodore but not the letter of Ibas, or Theodoret (that is, he was prepared to see the reputation of Cyril tarnished as this would enhance the standing of Pope Leo). This was rejected. At the council itself the bishops turned intellectual somersaults in their efforts to uphold Chalcedon yet condemn the Three Chapters. Of the letter of Ibas in particular, they cried out: "It has nothing to do with the Council of Chalcedon. Long live the emperor. Long live the orthodox emperor."[155] The wretched Vigilius was imprisoned until 8 December 553 when he wrote to the patriarch of Constantinople, Eutychius (who had succeeded Menas in August 552), agreeing to condemn the Three Chapters. This he did formally in a document named the *Constitutum* (*Resolution*) on 23 February 554.[156] His acquiescence benefited him little, for he never saw Italy again; he died at Syracuse on his way home in June 555.

Not surprisingly, schisms broke out in the West as a result of the council's decision; that dividing Aquileia from Rome lasted in an acute form for forty years and did not finally abate until A.D. 700. Pope Pelagius I (555–61) could gain credibility only by basing his faith on that of Leo's *Tome* and Chalcedon's Definition and by refusing to accept the Fifth General Council as making an issue relating to the faith (*causa intra fidem*).[157] The council, however, was a triumph for Eastern theology and for the personal views of Justinian. Cyril of Alexandria had been proclaimed as "the almost absolute *regula fidei* in christological matters,"[158] and the seal of orthodoxy set on the dynamic concept of human salvation through human nature "enhypostatized into the Word." Apart from Rome itself, the West had been viewed as irrelevant in theological matters. It was now the Monophysites' turn to be berated as "conservative," fighting the battles of bygone ages. Had it not been for the emotions that the very words the *Tome* of Leo and Chalcedon's Definition aroused, the Fifth General Council might have provided the basis for a permanent settlement in the East. But, as had happened with Justinian's initiative twenty years before, it was too little too late.

THE FAILURE OF THE *RECONQUISTA* 555-65

"Let the Roman traveller follow the steps of Hercules over the blue western sea and rest on the sands of Spain, and he will still be within the borders of the wise emperor's sovereignty."[159] Thus Agathias maintained, whether sincerely or no, the fiction that the Byzantine reconquests were "Roman" and that Justinian's domain still bore some relation to the empire of the Antonines and Constantine. Ostensibly, the year of the Fifth General Council had brought Justinian's aims nearer fulfillment than ever before. Final victory over the Ostrogoths had been achieved by his general, Narses,[160] and a brilliant diplomatic coup had secured him almost one-third of Visigothic Spain.[158] In fact, the empire had become fatally overextended. Even before these successes, Procopius in his *Secret History* had already foreboded that Justinian's conquests in the West "had brought the empire to its knees"[162] and described Justinian and Theodora as demonic characters guilty of gross and terrible crimes.

The last fifteen years of Justinian's reign were years of growing disillusionment and disaster. In his single-minded determination to root out the Arianism of the Germanic kingdoms, and resume the former western territories of the empire as his by right, Justinian had overlooked the existence of more formidable enemies of civilization against whom these kingdoms acted as a buffer. North Africa, the Danube provinces, and Italy were to face similar situations. No sooner had the Vandals and Ostrogoths been removed than the Byzantines were confronted by new and more savage foes. In North Africa every sizable community needed protection, while successive lines of fortresses faced southward to defend the settled areas against the advance of Berber nomads across the broad plains of Byzacena and southern Numidia. Some of these forts, like that at Ammaedara, enclosed considerable areas. More often, they protected the old city forum only—hence the fine state of preservation of many of the North African temples and public buildings since these were simply incorporated in them and used as strongpoints (see p. 903T). The cost in men and resources must have been enormous. It is calculated that Theveste alone, where only the center of the town was enclosed, required the labor of eight hundred to eight hundred fifty men working for two whole years.[163]

The effort was repeated all over the Byzantine world. Procopius lists some six hundred fortresses built in Justinian's reign to protect the Balkan provinces.[164] Inland as well as frontier districts had to be defended. And across the Danube as though he had set his sights on the reconquest of Dacia, Justinian held on to great bridgehead bastions, such as at Sucedara in Romania. In Palestine, monks besought the emperor to build a *kastron* ("fort") from public funds to defend them against Saracen marauders.[165]

This request tells us much about the insecurity even of monastic life, the ever-mounting demand on the treasury for military works, and the increasing threat from barbarous groups. Among these, the real enemies of the

Byzantine Empire were the vast confederations of nomadic peoples threatening from north, east, and south. In the east the danger would be warded off through the conversion of most of the Ghassanid peoples to Monophysitism, but as events were to show, the respite was limited. In the south, however, Procopius and Corippus tell of ceaseless wars against the Berbers in North Africa. Though the Byzantines were more often successful than not, the impression is left that the nomads, with their camels, flocks, herds, and horrific pagan rites, were slowly gaining the upper hand. Three-quarters of a century before the arrival of the Arabs, "Forgotten Africa" was coming into its own.

In the Balkans, the Slavs (Sclaveni) were the new enemy. In 550, Procopius noted, "Illyricum and Thrace from the Ionian Sea to the suburbs of Byzantium were overrun almost every year since Justinian's succession to the throne by Huns, Sclaveni and Antae who dealt atrociously with the inhabitants. In every invasion I suppose that about two hundred thousand Roman subjects were killed or enslaved; the whole land became a sort of Scythian desert"[166]—an exaggeration if only because there is no other evidence for serious invasions by Slavs before 545, but indicative of the despair and devastation caused by these new enemies. By the end of the reign most of the adversaries that were destined to despoil and nearly destroy the empire were in the field. And all the time the taxes needed to bribe their chiefs, build the forts, and equip the armies to oppose them were becoming more oppressive. John Lydus, no enemy of the administration, described how "foreign invasion seemed less formidable to the tax-payers [in the east] than the arrival of agents of the fisc."[167] Yet by Justinian's death, the treasury was virtually exhausted and Italy, for whose reconquest so much had been expended, was ruined.

In most respects, therefore, the *Reconquista* was a costly failure. Zeno and Anastasius had a truer understanding of the needs of the empire than had Justinian. Yet the malignity of Procopius's *Secret History* is misplaced. The achievements of Justinian's reign were massive and would stand the empire in good stead in the crises of the next century. Roman law had been codified for all time, there was a far-flung trade in both luxuries and necessities, a magnificent artistic tradition, and an orthodoxy capable of exposition and defense by skilled and subtle-minded theologians. There would be henceforth a Byzantine civilization with which the emperor's subjects, whether clergy or laity, orthodox or Monophysite, could identify. The reconquered provinces, too, brought gains as well as losses. For a century North Africa would be among the main, if not the main, supplier of olive oil to the empire. The Arab conquerors would marvel at the wealth of the provincials from that source. North African exports of wine and pottery were reaching shores as far away as the British Isles.[168] The ports of southeastern Spain had been won cheaply and were thought to be worth retaining for seventy years (until 624).

In Italy, on the other hand, the restoration of direct imperial rule was to have profound and dire consequences. Totila had tried to rally Goths and Italians under a banner of Romano-Gothic self-identity fueled by anti-Greek sentiment. He failed. The history of Italy was to take a new and fateful turn. Until 1071, when the Normans expelled the Byzantines from Bari, there would continue to be a Byzantine presence in Italy. It is difficult not to argue that this strengthened significantly the hold exercised by the imperial idea in the West. Papacy and empire could never quite follow the separate paths that their ecclesiastical differences indicated so long as political ties between the two remained. Moreover, Christianity in the West could not become the domain of clergy alone while lay influence remained in the person of the emperor and his representatives. Nevertheless, Eastern and Western Christendom had become different and distinctive civilizations. The death of Justinian marked the failure of the last great effort to hold these in unity; and Italian soil was to be a cockpit for Byzantine, papal, and Lombard ambitions. The half century that followed Justinian's reign would witness a further definition of the boundaries that now divided the great cultural and religious traditions of the Mediterranean and of Europe beyond its shores.

BIBLIOGRAPHY

NOTE

To date, there is no full assessment in English of Justinian and his policies towards the political, religious, and economic problems of the Byzantine Empire. The period of the lives of Justinian and Theodora are covered by the fine narrative histories of Procopius (to the 550s) and Agathias (covering the years 552–68). These accounts, together with the magnificent artistic legacy of Justinian's reign, have inspired a number of fast-moving histories concentrating on the military and artistic achievement of the reign but less inclined to probe deeper in order to understand the nature of the religious conflicts and the evolution of social and economic life in the provinces of the empire. Of the narratives, Robert Browning, *Justinian and Theodora* (New York: Frederick A. Praeger; London: Weidenfeld & Nicolson, 1971) is a well-arranged and beautifully illustrated history of the period, lacking, however, full critical apparatus. Its final paragraph, opening "the Byzantine court was photogenic if nothing else" (p. 260), indicates the author's tendency to concentrate on the court life and society of the age. One should consult the second volume of J. B. Bury's *History of the Later Roman Empire: From the Death of Theodosius I to the Death of Justinian* (New York: Dover Publications; London: Constable & Co., 1958); "Justinian the Great and His Immediate Successors (518–610)," chapter 3 of vol. 1 of A. A. Vasiliev's *History of the Byzantine Empire* (2 vols., Madison: University of Wisconsin Press, 1958); and the essays by scholars in N. H. Baynes and H. St. L. B. Moss (eds.), *Byzantium: An Introduction to East Roman Civilization* (New York and London: Oxford University Press, 1961).

There are numerous studies, however, on specific themes. For Neo-Chalcedonianism and Monophysitism, the various essays collected in A. Grillmeier and H. Bacht, eds., *Das Konzil von Chalkedon: Geschichte und Gegenwart* (3 vols., Würzburg: Echter-Verlag, 1953), vol. 2, are a necessary foundation for further study. J. Meyendorff's chapters 3–6 in his *Christ in Eastern Christian Thought* (New York: St. Vladimir's Seminary Press, 1975) are essential for the understanding of the development of Neo-Chalcedonianism. Origenism is the main subject of D. B. Evans, *Leontius of Byzantium: An Origenist Christology*, Dumbarton Oaks Studies 13 (Washington, D.C.: Dumbarton Oaks, 1970). E. Schwartz, "Zur Kirchenpolitik Justinians," *SBAW* Phil. Hist. Abr. 16.2 (Munich, 1940, pp. 32–82, and reprinted in *Gesammelte Aufsätze* IV, pp. 276–328), is significant if heavy going. The present writer's *Rise of Monophysite Movement*, chap. 7, may also be found useful. For art, David Talbot Rice's *Art of the Byzantine Era* (London: Thames & Hudson, 1963) and *The Byzantines* (New York: Frederick A. Praeger; London: Thames & Hudson, 1962) are indispensable works; and for the politico-religious outlook of the times, see the studies contained in N. H. Baynes, *Byzantine Studies*.

For mission, see K. Sarkissian, *The Council of Chalcedon and the Armenian Church* (London: SPCK, 1965) on Armenia; and for Nubia there is K. Michalowski's splendid production, *Faras* (Warsaw: Wydawnictwo Artysczno-Graficzno, 1974).

Sources

Agathias, *Historiae,* Corpus Scriptorum Historiae Byzantinae, ed. B. G. Niebuhr, Bonn, 1828; *The Histories,* Eng. trans. and ed. J. D. Frendo, New York and Berlin: Walter de Gruyter, 1975; see also *PG* 88.1269–1596.

Cyril of Scythopolis, *Vitae Sanctae Sabae,* ed. E. Schwartz, TU 49.2, Leipzig, 1939; see also *PG* 114.

Documenta ad origines Monophysitarum illustrandas (*Document to Illustrate Monophysite Origins*). Edited by J. B. Chabot. CSCO Scriptores Syri II.37. Paris: Typographeo republicae, 1907–33.

Elias. *Vita Johannis episcopi Tellae.* Edited and Lat. trans. E. W. Brooks. CSCO Scriptores Syri I.2.25, pp. 21–60. Paris, 1907.

Evagrius, *Historia Ecclesiastica,* ed. J. Bidez and L. Parmentier, London, 1898; *PG* 86.2, cols. 2115–2886; Eng. trans. in *Theodoret and Evagrius,* Bohn's Ecclesiastical Library, pp. 251–467, London, 1854.

Facundus of Hermiane. *Liber contra Mocianum. PL* 67.853–67.

——. *Liber pro defensione trium capitulorum concilii Chalcedonensis. PL* 67.527–853.

John of Ephesus. *Historia Ecclesiastica.* Part 3. Edited and Latin trans. E. W. Brooks. CSCO Scriptores Syri III.3. Paris and Louvain, 1935–36.

——. *Lives of Eastern Saints.* Edited and Eng. trans. E. W. Brooks. *Patrologia Orientalis* 17–19. Paris, 1923–26.

John Lydus, *De magistratibus populi Romani,* Book 3, ed. R. Wuensch, Leipzig: Teubner, 1903; and ed. B. G. Niebuhr, Corpus Scriptorum Historiae Byzantinae, Bonn, 1837.

John Malalas. *Chronographia.* Edited by L. Dindorf, Corpus Scriptorum Historia Byzantinae. Bonn, 1831.

Justinian, *Novellae,* ed. C. E. Zacharias von Lingenthal, 2 vols., Leipzig: Teubner, 1881–84; and ed. R. Schoell and G. Kroll, Berlin: Weidmann, 1954; see *PG* 86.

Leontius of Byzantium. *Contra Nestorianos et Eutychianos* (*Against the Nestorians and Eutychians*). *PG* 86.1.1267–1398.

Leontius of Jerusalem. *Tractatus contra Nestorianos*. *PG* 86.1399–1768.

Liberatus (archdeacon of Carthage), *Breviarium causae Nestorianorum et Euty-chianorum*, ed. E. Schwartz, *ACO* II.5, pp. 98–141, Berlin: Walter de Gruyter, 1936; also, *PL* 68.969–1052.

Procopius of Caesarea, *Opera*, ed. and Eng. trans. by B. H. Dewing, 7 vols., LCL, Cambridge, Mass.: Harvard University Press; London: William Heinemann, 1914–40; also J. Haury and G. Wirth, *Procopii Caesariensis opera omnia*, 3 vols., revised, Leipzig: Teubner, 1963.

Severus of Antioch. *Cathedral Homilies*. Edited by M. Brière, R. Duval, F. Gaffin, and M. A. Kugener, *Patrologia Orientalis* 4.1; 8.2; 16.5; 20.2; 22.2; 23.1; 25.1 and 4; 26.3; 29.1; 35.1.

———. *Philalethes*. Edited by R. Hespel. CSCO Scriptores Syri 69. Louvain, 1952.

———. *The Sixth Book of the Select Letters of Severus Patriarch of Antioch in the Syriac Version of Athanasius of Nisibis*. Edited and Eng. trans. E. W. Brooks. 4 vols. (Syriac and English). London: Williams & Norgate, 1902–3.

Severus of Asmounein. *History of the Patriarchs*. Edited and Eng. trans. B. T. A. Evetts. *Patrologia Orientalis* 1 (Paris, 1907), and *Patrologia Orientalis* 5. (Paris, 1910).

Victor of Tunnuna. *Chronicle*. Edited by Th. Mommsen. *MGH* Chron. Min. II, pp. 184–206. Berlin, 1894.

Zacharias Rhetor, *Ecclesiastical History*, ed. E. W. Brooks, CSCO Scriptores Syri III.5 and 6, Paris and Louvain, 1919–24; Eng. trans. F. J. Hamilton and E. W. Brooks, *The Syriac Chronicle Known as that of Zachariah of Mitylene*, London: Methuen & Co., 1899.

SECONDARY WORKS

Alexander, P. J. "The Strength of Empire and Capital as Seen Through Byzantine Eyes." *Speculum* 37.2 (1962): 339–57.

Amann, E. "Les trois chapitres." *DTC* 15, cols. 1868–1924.

Armstrong, G. T. "Fifth and Sixth Century Buildings in the Holy Land." *The Greek Orthodox Theological Review* 14 (1969): 17–30.

Cameron, Alan. "The Last Days of the Academy at Athens." *Proceedings of the Cambridge Philological Society* 195 (1969): 7–29.

Cameron, Averil. "The Theotokos in Sixth Century Constantinople." *JTS* n.s. 29 (April 1978): 79–108.

Chestnut, R. C. *Three Monophysite Christologies: Severus of Antioch, Philoxenus of Mabbug, and Jacob of Sarug*. New York and London: Oxford University Press, 1976.

Dagron, G. A. "Aux origines de la civilisation Byzantine: Langue de culture et langue d'Etat." *Revue Historique* 241 (1969): 23–56.

Dinkler, E. *Das Apsisimosaik von S. Apollinaire in Classe*. Cologne and Opladen: Westdeutscher Verlag, 1964.

———, ed. *Kunst und Geschichte Nubiens in christlicher Zeit*. Recklinghausen: Bongers, 1970.

Downey, G. *Constantinople in the Age of Justinian*. Norman: University of Oklahoma Press, 1960.

Draguet, R. *Julien d'Halicarnasse et sa controverse avec Sévère d'Antioche sur l'incorruptibilité du Corps de Christ*. Louvain and Paris, 1924.

Duval, N. "Etudes d'architecture chrétienne nord-africaine." *MEFR(A)* 84 (1972): 1071–1172 (a basic study).

——. "L'Eglise de l'Evêque Melleus à Haidra." *CRAIBL* (1968): 221–44.

Frend, W. H. C. "Nubia as an Outpost of Byzantine Cultural Influence." *Byzantino Slavica* 28 (1968): 312–26.

Garrigue, P. "Une basilique byzantine à Junca en Byzacène." *Mélanges* 65 (1953): 173–96.

Geanakoplos, D. J. "Church Building and 'Caesaro-Papism,' A.D. 312–565." *Greek, Roman and Byzantine Studies* 7 (1966): 167–86.

Goodchild, R. G. "The Roman and Byzantine *Limes* in Cyrenaica." *JRS* 43 (1953): 65–76.

Honigmann, E. "La hiérarchie monophysite au temps de Jacques Baradée, 542–578." CSCO Subsidia 2, pp. 157–243. Louvain: Imprimerie orientaliste, 1951. (= part 2 of *Evêques et Evêchés monophysites d'Asie autéreur au VIe siècle*).

Hussey, J. M. *The Byzantine World*. New York: Harper Torchbooks, 1961.

Kaegi, W. E. "Arianism and the Byzantine Army in Africa." *Traditio* 21 (1965): 23–53.

Klauser, Th. "Die Hagia Sophia." *JAC* 13 (1970): 107–18 (discussion of the work and views of H. Kähler and Cyril Mango).

Marrou, H. I. "Autour de la bibliothèque du pape Agapit." In *Christiana Tempora*, pp. 167–212. Collection de l'Ecole française de Rome 35, 1978; or *Mélanges* 48 (1931).

Moeller, C. "Le chalcédonisme et le néo-chalcédonisme en Orient de 451 à la fin du VIe siècle." In *Das Konzil von Chalkedon*, ed. Grillmeier and Bacht, pp. 637–720.

Mouterde, R., and Poidebard, A. *Le limes de Chalcis; organisation de la steppe en haute Syrie romaine*. Délégation générale de la France au Levant, Bibliothéque archéologique et historique 28. Paris: Geuthner, 1945. Discussed by J. W. Crowfoot, *Antiquity* 20 (1946): 218–20.

Richard, M. "*De Sectis* et Léonce de Byzance." *RHE* 35 (1939): 695–723.

Rubin, B. "Prokopios von Kaisareia." *PW* 23.1, cols. 273–599. Extensive bibliography.

——. *Das Zeitalter Justinians*. Berlin: Walter de Gruyter, 1960.

Tafla, B. "The Establishment of the Ethiopian Church." *Tarikh* 2.1 (*Journal of the Historical Society of Nigeria*, New York: Humanities Press; London: Longmans, Green & Co., 1967): pp. 28–42.

Ullendorff, E. *Ethiopia and the Bible*. New York and London: Oxford University Press, 1968.

NOTES

1. *Letter* 147 in *Collectio Avellana*, ed. Guenther, CSEL 35, p. 593.

2. The story, for instance, of the encounter of the Roman merchant, Sopatros, with a Persian rival at the court of the king of Ceylon, told in Bury, *Later Roman Empire*, vol. 2, pp. 332–33.

3. *De magistratibus* III.27. John Lydus came to the capital in the reign of Anastasius and served the central administration for forty years. See the outline of

his career in E. Barker, ed. and Eng. trans., *Social and Political Thought in Byzantium: From Justinian I to the Last Palaeologus* (New York and London: Oxford University Press, 1957), pp. 76–80.

4. Procopius, *History of Wars,* VIII.20.47, ed. Dewing.

5. Ibid., VI.6.28.

6. *Novel* 47, ed. Schoell and Kroll = 66 in ed. Lingenthal. Schoell and Kroll's numbering is used throughout in preference to Lingenthal's which is based on his reconstruction of the chronological order of the *Novellae.*

7. For example, *Novel* XXX (Schoell and Kroll) publ. in 536, *De Proconsule Cappadociae,* preface, in which Justinian recalls how the city of Caesarea owed its name to Julius Caesar, from whom the monarchy took its origin.

8. Ibid., XXX.11 (the former territories "had been lost by neglect"), and Belisarius's alleged statement before the battle of Ad Decimum in September 533, "We are here in order to recover what is ours," Procopius *History of the Wars* III.19.5, and compare VI.6.32.

9. Agathias *Histories* V.14, "he showed himself an autocrat in name and action."

10. Preface, addressed to Menas, the praetorian prefect, of the *Codex Justinianus,* ordering its use throughout the empire 7 April 529.

11. Preface to the *Digest,* 15 December 530, cited from P. R. Coleman-Norton, comp., *Roman State and Christian Church: A Collection of Legal Documents to* A.D. *535,* 3 vols. (London: SPCK, 1966), vol. 3, p. 1087.

12. *Novel* XV.1 (end) = 7 (ed. Lingenthal, p. 80); and see Jones, *Later Roman Empire,* vol. 2, pp. 988–90, for the decline of Latin in the East Roman Empire. In *Novel* XXII.2 Latin is called "the ancient and national language." Also Dagron, "Aux origines de la civilisation Byzantine," pp. 44–46.

13. *Historia arcana (Secret History),* ed. Dewing, VI.21.

14. *Secret History* XVIII.29. For Procopius's views on religion, see *History of Wars* V.3.6, "insane folly to investigate the nature of God." To him, Jesus was "servant [*pais*] of God" (ibid., II.12.20–25).

15. Shown, for instance, in the replies by the East Roman bishops to the "plebiscite" by the emperor Leo I in 457/58, on whether Timothy Aelurus should be recognized as patriarch of Alexandria or not. For Agapetus of Rhodes, the emperor was "truly priest" as well as emperor (E. Schwartz, Codex Encyclicus, *Acta Conciliorum Oecumenicorum* [Berlin, 1914–40], vol. 2, 5, p. 44, no. 33).

16. *Codex Justinianus* I.3.42.

17. *Novel* LVII, epilogue.

18. *Novel* VI of 6 March 535 to the patriarch Epiphanius (preface).

19. *Codex Justinianus* I.3.46 (elections); I.2.24 (church property); I.4.34 (misconduct); II.5.2 (oaths).

20. Michael the Syrian, *Chronicon,* ed. J. B. Chabot, 3 vols. (Paris, 1899–1911), IX.23, vol. 2, p. 205. "We are used to wrestling with the sea, not becoming mixed up in theological arguments," they said.

21. Procopius *De aedificiis (Buildings)* I.1.

22. *Codex Justinianus* I.5.18, Coleman-Norton, *Roman State and Christian Church,* pp. 1008–11.

23. Thus, *Codex Justinianus* I.5.12, 13, 16 (Manicheans); 17 (Samaritans); and 18–21 (Montanists).

24. Ibid., I.5.12, Coleman-Norton, *Roman State and Christian Church*, p. 997. See Kaegi, "Arianism and Byzantine Army."

25. For the end of the Academy, see Alan Cameron, "Last Days of Academy." Some pagans, such as Tribonian (d. 542), remained in the emperor's service.

26. As instanced in the dialogue, *De Scientia politica*, analyzed by Barker, *Social and Political Thought*, pp. 63–75.

27. I have followed Bury, *Later Roman Empire*, vol. 2, pp. 39–48; see also P. Karlin-Hayter, "Les Akta ΔΙΑ ΚΑΛΑΠΟΔΙΟΝ," *Byzantion* 43 1973 (1974): 84–106.

28. John of Ephesus, *Lives of Eastern Saints*, L, ed. Brooks, pp. 153–54. She was "desirous of furthering everything that would assist the opponents of the synod of Chalcedon." For her general influence as Justinian's "partner in our counsels" (*Novel* VII, A.D. 535), see Bury, *Later Roman Empire*, pp. 27–35.

29. *Novel* XXX.11.

30. *Vita Sabae*, ed. Schwartz, chap. 72, pp. 175–76. For this and other favorable views of Justinian's Western policy, see W. E. Kaegi, *Byzantium and the Decline of Rome* (Princeton, N.J.: Princeton University Press, 1968), pp. 212–14.

31. For the activities of the Afro-Catholic "lobby" in Constantinople, see Procopius *History of Wars* III.10.19; and Zacharias Rhetor, *Ecclesiastical History*, ed. Brooks, IX.17. For discussion of these texts and the fall of the Vandal kingdom, see Kaegi, "Arianism and Byzantine Army," pp. 23–33. For the enrollment of the Vandals in Justinian's army, see Procopius *History of Wars* IV.14.15.

32. *Codex Justinianus* I.27.1, 2.

33. *Novel. de Africana ecclesia*, 37.5 and 8. However, no immediate steps were taken against Arian clergy. If they converted to Catholicism they would not be deposed.

34. Procopius, *On Buildings*, VI.4.1, ed. and Eng. trans. Dewing and G. Downey, vol. 7, LCL, p. 112.

35. Own observations in 1938–39. The North African cities were not the only ones to decline in the fifth century. At Porto Torre on the north coast of Sardinia, one and a half meters of rubble separated the Byzantine level from that of the Roman street in the area of the baths. These appear to have been converted into a church in Byzantine times.

36. *CIL* VIII.1863 (Theveste) and 8805 (Zabi) near the Chott el Hodna.

37. Procopius *History of Wars* IV.19.7 (Bagai), and 13.26 (Timgad).

38. Recorded in the field by E. Luret and Ch. Monchicourt, *Enquête sur les installations hydrauliques romaines en Tunisie*, ed. P. Gauckler (Tunis: Direction des antiquités et Beaux Arts, 1899), II.252.

39. *Buildings* VI.5.8, and *Novel* 37.

40. *Buildings* VI.5.11.

41. For the Dermech group, see Duval, "Etudes d'architecture," pp. 1081–92; and for the fine basilica in Regio VI (?), partially excavated by the Tunisians in 1971, and others nearby, see my "Early Church in Carthage," p. 25.

42. *CIL* VIII.25308 (Perpetua); all known major Christian sites in Carthage were reused in Byzantine times, and the finest inscriptions and most lavish mosaics belong to that period. For the church probably dedicated to Cyprian, see L. Ennabli, "Les Inscriptions funéraires chrétiennes de la basilique de Sainte-Monique à Carthage," *Collection de l'Ecole française à Rome*, No. 25 (1975).

43. Procopius *History of Wars* IV.26.17–23.

44. On Liberatus, see the *DCB* III, pp. 716–17, and on the Carthaginian arch-deaconries, see H. Leclercq, "Carthage," *DACL* II.2, col. 2271.

45. Procopius *History of Wars* III.21.19–25.

46. As at Kelibia (fine baptismal mosaic); and Ammaedara (the church of Bishop Melleus). See Duval, "L'Eglise de Melleus."

47. *Codex Justinianus* I.4.26, 24 June 530.

48. See R. G. Goodchild, "Boreum of Cyrenaica," *JRS* 41 (1951): 11–16, and idem, "Roman and Byzantine *Limes*."

49. See Crowfoot's review of Mouterde and Poidebard, *Le Limes de Chalcis.*

50. See C. H. Kraeling, ed., *Gerasa, City of the Decapolis* (New Haven, Conn.: American Schools of Oriental Research, 1938).

51. See Geanakoplos, "Church Building"; idem, "Church and State in the By-zantine Empire: A Reconsideration of the Problem of Caesaropapism," *CH* 34 (1965): 381–403; and Armstrong, "Fifth and Sixth Century Buildings"; and idem, "Imperial Church Building and Church-State Relations, A.D. 313–363," *CH* 36 (March 1967): 3–17, on Justinian's policy of demonstrating the empire's allegiance to orthodoxy through ever-increasing numbers of churches. The government even seems to have held stocks of columns and capitals which it distributed to those desiring to build orthodox churches!

52. See Garrigue, "Une basilique byzantine."

53. See Klauser, "Die Hagia Sophia" (discussion of work by H. Kähler and Cyril Mango); and Bury's short description, *Later Roman Empire*, pp. 48–54. Klauser stresses how cult and building were adapted to each other (pp. 115–16).

54. The work of Anthemius is praised by Agathias *Histories* V.8; he "designed wonderful work both in the city and many other places, which would suffice to win him everlasting glory in the memory of men so long as they stand and endure." Compare Procopius *Buildings* I.1.27, "the church has become a spectacle of mar-vellous beauty, overwhelming to those who see it, but to those who know it from hearsay, simply incredible."

55. The church had been begun at the end of Theodoric's reign but was finally completed and consecrated on 17 May 548 by Bishop Maximian. It cost twenty-six thousand solidi. See G. Bovini, *Ravenna,* Eng. trans. G. Ferrari (Faenza: Fratelli Lega, 1959), p. 7.

56. "Bella come un sogno d'oriente," words of Cesare Conti quoted by Bovini, *Ravenna,* p. 7. For San Apollinare, built c. 549–54, see Dinkler, *Das Apsismosaik,* pp. 77ff.

57. Rice, *Art of Byzantine Era*, p. 52.

58. See Th. Klauser, "Rom und der Kult der Gottesmutter Maria," *JAC* 15 (1972): 120–35. Rome had its Sancta Maria Maggiore, built in the pontificate of Sixtus III (432–40), but the conversion of the Pantheon by Pope Boniface IV into a church dedicated to the Virgin in the reign of Phocas (602–10) seems to have been a turning point in the expansion of the cult in the West.

59. Corippus *In laudem Justini* (*In Praise of Justin*) LIII. See Cameron, "Theotokos in Constantinople," p. 82.

60. Cataloged by I. Meimaris in his unpublished dissertation, "Saints, Martyrs and Church Officials in the Greek Inscriptions Pertaining to the Christian Church in Palestine" (Hebrew University of Jerusalem, 1978).

61. See my "The Cult of Military Saints in Christian Nubia," in *Theologia Crucis, Signum Crucis: Festschrift für Erich Dinkler zum 70. Geburtstag*, ed. C. Andresen and G. Klein, pp. 155–65 (Tübingen, 1979).

62. See M. J. Higgins, "Chosroes II's Votive Offerings at Sergiopolis," *Byzantine Zeitschrift* 48 (1955): 89–102.

63. Justinian *Novel* III.1, publ. in 535. See also Jones, *Later Roman Empire*, p. 911.

64. *Sixth Book of Select Letters*, ed. Brooks, 1.8 (p. 43).

65. See Schwartz, *ACO* III.260–62. Other figures, see Jones, *Later Roman Empire*, pp. 931 and 1388 n. 154.

66. Peter Brown, "Eastern and Western Christendom in Late Antiquity: A Parting of the Ways," in *The Orthodox Churches and the West*, ed. D. Baker, Studies in Church History 13 (Oxford: Basil Blackwell & Mott, 1976), pp. 1–24, esp. pp. 11, 21.

67. John of Ephesus, *Lives of Eastern Saints*, ed. Brooks, *Patrologia Orientalis* 17, p. 72.

68. *Vita Danielis Stylitae*, chaps. 45, 73ff., in *Three Byzantine Saints: Contemporary Biographies*, ed. and Eng. trans. E. A. S. Dawes and N. H. Baynes (Oxford: Basil Blackwell & Mott, 1948), pp. 7–71, esp. pp. 33, 53ff.

69. Evagrius, *Ecclesiastical History* II.5, *PG* 86.2.2516A (δύο is treated as indeclinable).

70. "Royal road," see Severus's opening sermon to the people of Antioch, 24 November 512 = *Homily* 83, ed. Brière, *Patrologia Orientalis* 20, pp. 405–6.

71. The term used by Jacob Baradaeus writing to the (Monophysite) patriarch Theodosius in 564, cited from *Monophysite Origins*, ed. Chabot, p. 63.

72. Severus, *Letter to Count Oecumenius*, ed. E. W. Brooks, *Patrologia Orientalis* 12.2 (Paris, 1919), pp. 180ff.; and *Liber contra Impium Grammaticum* III.1.5, ed. J. Lebon, CSCO Script. Syri IV.5 (Louvain, 1936), p. 49 of translation.

73. Severus, *Ad Nephalium*, ed. J. Lebon, CSCO Script. Syri IV.7 (Louvain, 1949), p. 9 of translation.

74. *Letter to Oecumenius*, p. 185, "For from Cyril's words as from a sacred anchor I do not depart."

75. For the importance of this term in Severus's theology, see Chesnut, *Three Monophysite Christologies*, pp. 37–44, and compare above, p. 763.

76. J. Meyendorff, *Christ in Eastern Thought*, p. 41.

77. Theodore Lector, *Historia Tripartita*, Epitome, ed. Hansen, GCS (Berlin, 1971), M 477, p. 136.

78. Severus, *Sixth Book of Select Letters*, ed. Brooks, 1.9, p. 44; and cf. 1.17, p. 64.

79. Ibid., 1.22, p. 78. See Frend, *Rise of Monophysite Movement*, pp. 223–25 for other examples.

80. Severus, *Cathedral Homilies* 56, *Patrologia Orientalis* 4.1, pp. 78–82.

81. *Collectio Avellana* 139, ed. Guenther. See Frend, *Rise of Monophysite Movement*, pp. 228–29.

82. John of Ephesus, *Lives of Eastern Saints*, ed. Brooks, *Patrologia Orientalis* 18, pp. 515–16, written c. 566.

83. Severus, *Sixth Book of Select Letters*, III.4, ed. Brooks, pp. 246–47. For the popular view of the damage that deprivation of sacraments would cause, note the

outcries of the Christians at Ephesus in 451: "Our children will perish and our city be ruined" without Sacraments (*ACO*, ed. Schwartz, II.1.2, p. 52); and in Severus's time, the shouts of the people of Antioch, "We want to baptize our children. We want to participate in the holy mysteries" (John of Beit-Aphthonia, *Vita Severi*, ed. M. A. Kugener, *Patrologia Orientalis* 2, p. 241).

84. John of Ephesus, *Lives of Eastern Saints*, ed. Brooks, *Patrologia Orientalis* 18, p. 519.

85. Ibid., p. 521.

86. See my *Rise of Monophysite Movement*, p. 249, and map 1, pp. 250–51.

87. The question whether Christ's flesh, inseparably united to the Word, was corruptible or not, had worried Cyril; see *Letter* XLV to Succensus and *Oratio de recta fide ad Theodosium Imp.* 21. For Julian's views, see Draguet, *Julien d'Halicarnasse* and R. Hespel, *Le Polémique anti-julianiste de Sévère d'Antioche*, CSCO 244 and 245, Script. Syri 104–5 (Louvain, 1964).

88. Particularly in Egypt, but also in Armenia, Ethiopia, and even in the Balkan provinces of the empire.

89. Frend, *Rise of Monophysite Movement*, p. 263.

90. *Collectio Avellana* 191, ed. Guenther; see Frend, *Rise of Monophysite Movement*, pp. 244–47.

91. Extant text of the debate (mainly the account given by Innocentius of Maronia, one of the Chalcedonian representatives) is preserved in Schwartz, *ACO* IV.2, pp. 169–84 = Mansi, *Sacrorum Conciliorum*, vol. 8, pp. 817–33.

92. *Codex Justinianus* I.1.8, reproduced with brief comments in Coleman-Norton, *Roman State and Christian Church*, pp. 1149–56.

93. Michael the Syrian, *Chronicon*, IX.26, ed. Chabot, vol. 2, p. 222.

94. John of Ephesus, *Life of Severus* (fragments), ed. Kugener, *Patrologia Orientalis* 2, 302–3; and in *Lives of Five Patriarchs* (ed. Brooks, *Patrologia Orientalis* 18, p. 687).

95. According to the sources used by Michael the Syrian, *Chronicon* (ed. Chabot II.193–94), six thousand perished in street battles. As in 451, 457, 482, and 516, the Alexandrian crowd showed their hostility towards their own notables and the imperial authorities.

96. The text, preserved by Zacharias, *Church History* IX.21, dates probably to after his deposition. His opponent the patriarch Ephraim of Antioch complained merely that his synodical letter, dispatched after his consecration, failed to condemn Eutyches strongly enough. See Schwartz, "Zur Kirchenpolitik Justinians," pp. 2, 32–81, esp. p. 45, and Frend, *Rise of Monophysite Movement*, p. 271.

97. *Church History* IX.19.

98. Ibid. Justinian, *Novel* XLII, recognizes the part played by Agapetus in removing Anthimus.

99. Liberatus *Breviarium* XX (ed. Schwartz).

100. The voluminous *Acts* of the council have been preserved in Mansi, *Sacrorum Conciliorum*, vol. 8, pp. 873–1176. Severus and Zooras were condemned on the demand of the monks of the capital.

101. *Novel* XLII.

102. Zacharias *Church History* IX.15. Also *The Letter of Severus to the Eastern Monks*, preserved in Michael, *Chronicon*, ed. Chabot, vol. 2, pp. 221–23.

103. John of Ephesus, *Lives of Five Patriarchs,* ed. Brooks, p. 687; and compare Elias, *Vita Johannis,* ed. Brooks, p. 39.

104. Zacharias *Church History* X.2; and John of Ephesus, *History of the Convents of Amida,* ed. Brooks, *Patrologia Orientalis* 18, p. 620. See also Michael the Syrian, *Chronicon* IX.8, ed. Chabot, vol. 2, p. 187.

105. Zacharias *Church History* X.1; Elias *Vita Johannis,* pp. 52ff.; and John of Ephesus, *Life of John of Tella,* ed. Brooks, *Patrologia Orientalis* 18, pp. 524–25.

106. Dante *Paradiso* VI.13ff.; cited from Bury, *Later Roman Empire,* p. 378 n. 2.

107. For the events, see L. Bréhier, "La politique religieuse de Justinien," in *Histoire de l'Eglise,* ed. Fliche and Martin, vol. 4, *De la mort de Théodose à l'élection de Grégoire le Grand,* pp. 437–66, esp. pp. 454–56.

108. Michael the Syrian, *Chronicon* IX.29, ed. Chabot, vol. 2, pp. 243–44.

109. E. R. Hardy, *Christian Egypt: Church and People; Christianity and Nationalism in the Patriarchate of Alexandria* (New York and London: Oxford University Press, 1952), pp. 166–69.

110. *History of the Patriarchs,* ed. Evetts, *Patrologia Orientalis* 1, part 1, p. 472.

111. For an estimate of the relative strengths of the Chalcedonian (Melchite) and Monophysite (Coptic) churches at the end of the sixth century, see Hardy, *Christian Egypt,* pp. 135ff.

112. See K. Michalowski, "Open Problems of Nubian Art and Culture in the Light of the Discoveries at Faras," in *Kunst und Geschichte Nubiens,* ed. Dinkler, pp. 11–20, esp. pp. 12–13.

113. Information from the Egyptian Antiquities Service, 1974, concerning their excavations on Philae; for the influence of the bishopric of Philae on the expansion of Christianity into Nubia, see S. Jakobielski, *Faras,* vol. 3, A History of the Bishopric of Pachoras (Warsaw: Panstwowe Wydawnichtwo Naukowe, 1972), pp. 20–22.

114. John of Ephesus, *Historia Ecclesiastica,* parts III–IV, 6–7, ed. Brooks.

115. Ibid., IV.7.

116. Traditionally, the king was Silko, who was a monotheist and may have been a Christian, and who has left a triumphant account of his campaigns against the Blemmyes on an inscription engraved on the wall of a temple of Talmis (Kalabscha) = *OGIS* 1, no. 201. However, the discovery at Q'asr Ibrim of a letter from the king of the Blemmyes to the king of the Nobades referring to Silko and datable on paleographic grounds to c. 440 shows that this identification is no longer possible. See T. C. Skeat, "A Letter from the King of the Blemmyes to the King of the Noubades," *JEA* 63 (1977): 159–70.

117. The writer's discoveries of liturgical manuscripts in the cathedral at Q'asr Ibrim in 1964 are being published for the Egypt Exploration Society (forthcoming 1984).

118. John of Ephesus *Church History* III.4.53; see Frend, *Rise of Monophysite Movement,* pp. 299–303.

119. See Bury, *Later Roman Empire,* vol. 2, p. 326.

120. See my sketch in *Rise of Monophysite Movement,* pp. 308–15, which I have drawn upon here; and also for greater detail, V. Inglisian, "Chalkedon und die

armenische Kirche" in *Das Konzil von Chalkedon,* ed. Grillmeier and Bacht, vol. 2, pp. 361–417.

121. See Sarkissian, *Council of Chalcedon,* pp. 207–13 and 194–95.

122. See Draguet, *Julien d'Halicarnasse,* p. 260.

123. See W. Y. Adams, "Post-Pharaonic Nubia in the Light of Archaeology. II," *JEA* 51 (1965): 160–78, esp. pp. 175–77, and idem, "Post-Pharaonic Nubia in the Light of Archaeology. III," *JEA* 52 (1966): 147–62, esp. p. 150.

124. See the preliminary report by the author and I. A. Muirhead, "Greek Manuscripts from the Cathedral of Q'asr Ibrim," *Le Muséon* 89, fasc. 1–2 (1976), pp. 43–49.

125. Published by Michalowski, *Faras.*

126. See Frend, "Nubia as Outpost," pp. 321–22.

127. Thus Michael the Syrian, *Chronicon* (compiled c. 1199), VIII.14: "The unity of the empire was broken by Marcian, at the same time as he divided the faith" (ed. Chabot, vol. 2, p. 122).

128. John of Ephesus, *Life of John Hephaestopolis,* ed. Brooks, *Patrologia Orientalis* 18, pp. 535–39.

129. John of Ephesus, *Life of James and Theodore,* ed. Brooks, *Patrologia Orientalis* 19, p. 154; and compare John's comment (*Patrologia Orientalis* 18, p. 693) that his "diocese extended from the imperial city to Alexandria."

130. John eventually had seventy thousand of the inhabitants baptized and built ninety-eight new churches and twelve monasteries for them. See John of Ephesus, *Historia Ecclesiastica,* III.3.37, ed. Brooks, p. 127; and *Patrologia Orientalis* 18, p. 168.

131. Bar-Hebraeus, *Ecclesiastical History,* ed. J. B. Abbeloos and T. J. Lamy, 3 vols. (Louvain, 1877), p. 215.

132. John of Ephesus, *Life of James Bar'adai,* ed. Brooks, *Patrologia Orientalis* 18, p. 696.

133. John of Ephesus, *Lives of James and Theodore,* ed. Brooks, pp. 156–58. See Honigmann, "La hiérarchie monophysite."

134. I have followed Meyendorff, *Christ in Eastern Thought,* pp. 72–73. See also Moeller, "Le chalcédonisme et le néo-chalcédonisme," pp. 670–76.

135. Meyendorff, *Christ in Eastern Thought,* pp. 73–74. For Leontius's namesake "of Byzantium," see Evans, *Leontius.*

136. Leontius, *Tractatus contra Nestorianos* V.28, *PG* 86.1748D; and compare VII.2, col. 1761B. See Meyendorff, *Christ in Eastern Thought,* p. 74.

137. Meyendorff, *Christ in Eastern Thought,* pp. 74–75.

138. On this movement, see Evans, *Leontius,* esp. pp. 153ff.

139. See Meyendorff, *Christ in Eastern Thought,* pp. 63–64.

140. *Edictum contra Origenem,* Schwartz, *ACO* III, p. 213, lines 15ff.

141. See Liberatus *Breviarum* XXII for a frank and adverse view of Vigilius.

142. The date is uncertain. The Western chronicler Victor of Tunnuna quotes one letter (sub ann. 542), and Liberatus a second (*Breviarum* XXII). I cannot think both writers contemporary with the events either fabricated them or mistook their authorship (see my note, *Rise of Monophysite Movement,* p. 276 n. 2).

143. *Collectio Avellana* XCII.

144. Evagrius *Ecclesiastical History* IV.38; and compare Liberatus, astringent as usual about Eastern theologians he disliked. In *Breviarum* XXIV, he writes of

Ascidas, "dilectus et principum, secta Acephalus [that is, a Monophysite], Origenis autem defensor acerrimus et Pelagio aemulus"—a telling one-sentence pen-portrait.

145. See Bréhier, "La Politique religieuse de Justinien," pp. 461–62, regarding the Three Chapters and a summary of Theodore of Mopsuestia's Christology.

146. The edict itself and its date of issue are lost. Fragments of the text are preserved by Facundus of Hermiane, *Contra Mocianum, PL* 67.859, 860; and see Schwartz, "Zur Kirchenpolitik Justinians," pp. 73–81. Facundus regarded the edict as "Monophysite."

147. See Bréhier, "La Politique religieuse de Justinien," p. 462.

148. Ibid., pp. 463–65.

149. See Aloys Grillmeier, "Vorbereitung des Mittelalters. Studien über das Verhältnis von Chalkedonismus und Neu-Chalkedonismus in der lateinischen Theologie von Boethius bis zu Gregor d. Gr.," in *Das Konzil von Chalkedon,* ed. Grillmeier and Bacht, vol. 2, pp. 791–839, esp. pp. 807–14.

150. *Epistola legatis Francorum, ab Italiae clericis directa, PL* 69.115; written c. 552, puts Vigilius's acts in as favorable light as possible; L. Duchesne, *L'Eglise au VIe siècle* (Paris: Boccard, 1925), pp. 189–90.

151. Facundus, *Contra Mocianum, PL* 67, col. 857.

152. For Reparatus's Council of Carthage, see Victor of Tunnuna, *Chronicle of the World,* sub ann. 549. It demanded that Vigilius should do penance before being restored to communion. Facundus himself, true to the Western tradition, considered that the emperor should execute the canons of the church, not fix or transgress them.

153. Text in Mansi, *Sacrorum Conciliorum,* vol. 9, pp. 537–82 and analysis in C. J. Hefele—H. Leclercq, *Histoire des conciles* (Paris, 1907), III.1, pp. 46–56.

154. On the Fifth General Council, see Hefele—Leclercq, *Histoire des conciles,* III.1, pp. 105–32; and Bréhier's "La Politique religieuse de Justinien," pp. 472–76.

155. Cited from Hefele—Leclercq, *Histoire des conciles,* III.1, pp. 118–20.

156. Text in Mansi, *Sacrorum Conciliorum,* IX, col. 457–88. For Vigilius's capitulation, see Bréhier, "La Politique religieuse de Justinien," pp. 476–77.

157. Grillmeier, "Vorbereitung des Mittelalters," pp. 827–28.

158. Meyendorff, *Christ in Eastern Thought,* p. 84.

159. Agathias, introduction to the *Greek Anthology* (IV.3, 82ff.), and see Bury's note, *Later Roman Empire,* vol. 2, p. 288 n. 1.

160. Both Busta Gallorum and Mons Lactarius were fought in 552; Narses defeated the Franco-Alamannic invasion of Italy, designed to aid the Ostrogoths, and the resistance of the latter was broken in the campaigns of 553 and 554. See Bury, *Later Roman Empire,* vol. 2, pp. 263ff.

161. For Justinian's acquisition of part of southern Spain, see ibid., pp. 286–88.

162. Procopius *Secret History* VII.1.

163. For the scale of these forts, which could be surveyed at the end of the nineteenth century before urbanization and intensive cultivation began to take their toll of North African sites, see Ch. Diehl, *L'Afrique byzantine* (Paris, 1896; reprinted, New York: Burt Franklin, n.d.), pp. 167–225. Theveste itself was a rectangular fort 350 × 305 yards, with three gates and corner towers (ibid., p. 220).

164. Procopius *Buildings* IV. For some details see Bury, *Later Roman Empire,* vol. 2, pp. 308–10. Also Evagrius *Ecclesiastical History* IV.18 (Africa).

165. Cyril of Scythopolis, *Vita Sabae* 72, ed. Schwartz, p. 175.

166. Procopius *Secret History* XVIII, XX.

167. John Lydus, *De magistratibus* III.70 (Bonn ed. p. 264); and compare Corippus *In Praise of Justin* II.260ff. The treasury exhausted by the end of Justinian's reign "unde tot exhaustus contraxit debita fiscus."

168. See C. A. R. Radford, "Imported Pottery Found at Tintagel, Cornwall," in *Dark-Age Britain: Studies Presented to E. T. Leeds,* ed. D. B. Harden, pp. 59–70 (London: Methuen & Co., 1955).

24

"And East Is East…"
565–604

"In almost every way we can see the parting ways mirrored in the career of Gregory the Great." Thus R. A. Markus speaks of the late sixth century.[1] In terms of religion and culture this was to prove the case. Scholars, in particular Professor Averil Cameron,[2] have shown how the reign of Justinian's nephew and successor, Justin II (565–78), marks a turning point in Byzantine religion and artistic life that reflected its growing separation from the West. The strictly orthodox emperor and his equally pious wife, Sophia, encouraged an atmosphere in which the veneration of icons expressed the popular devotion to the Virgin Mary and her acceptance as divine protectress of the capital and other cities of the empire. There was no distinction in this regard between court and commoner. Icons, moreover, were allied to imperial ceremonial, which emphasized the concept of the emperor as the living embodiment on earth of Christ in heaven, carrying out a fixed calendar of ceremonial in which he was associated at all times with the patriarch of Constantinople. Church and state were completely integrated. Religion now pervaded almost every aspect of life in the empire. Though some senatorial families still maintained a foot in both Rome and Constantinople, the two cities had come to represent distinct cultural traditions and interpretations of Christianity.

In other aspects of life, however, notably relating to economic conditions and commerce, the Mediterranean retained elements of unity.[3] Under Justinian, it had once again become a Byzantine sea; its ports were linked by trade; its commerce extended as far as India on the one hand, and Celtic Britain on the other. An emperor, Heraclius for example, could still be proclaimed in Carthage as well as in Constantinople. Olives and vines grew in the lands around its shores. Society, however, had undergone profound changes during the sixth century. Whether one looks at Visigothic Spain, Byzantine Africa and Italy, or at Egypt or Syria, one sees societies and economies dominated by vast and often ecclesiastically owned haciendas administered by a hierarchy of bailiffs (*conductores*), and worked by serfs who paid dues and performed services on estates they could not leave, but which provided them with their subsistence. Many once-populous cities inland had declined to the level of villages. Except for the absence of an oath of allegiance that bound the vassal to the lord, the Byzantine Empire of the late sixth century contained many characteristics of medieval feudalism. Yet the situation was accepted. There were no popular revolts and no recorded recurrence of the Bagaudae in the West. Compared with the alien societies that were threatening its borders, the Byzantine Empire seemed to its subjects a preferable as well as a God-ordained choice.

ROME AND CONSTANTINOPLE

These alien societies, however, were about to impose their own patterns. The Christian renewal (*renovatio*) which Justinian and his successor Justin II (565–78) intended to last forever was brought down within a generation by the new phase of massive tribal migrations (*Völkerwanderungen*) that had been gathering force from the 540s. This was marked by the onset of the Slavonic peoples into the Balkans, destroying the bridge of language, culture, and religion that had united Rome and Constantinople in the previous two centuries. In the quarter of the century between 550 and 575, the human flood seeped through the length and breadth of the Balkan provinces, sometimes destroying, sometimes settling on deserted land, leaving the towns as islands in a new, alien environment. By the reign of Tiberius II Constantinus (578–82) the Slavs were moving into Thessaly, and thence southward across the Isthmus of Corinth into Sparta. Much of Greece was depopulated. Survivors fled to the islands off the coast.[4]

The decline in standards of life, measured by any yardstick, was catastrophic. It was as though civilization itself had been stopped in its tracks. In the Balkans, there were splendid cities, such as Justiniana Prima founded by Justinian himself near his birthplace, dominated by churches and public buildings, and producing fine examples of Byzantine Christian art.[5] Soon they were abandoned,[6] to be replaced by villages and encampments whose Slavonic inhabitants were unfamiliar with so much as the potter's wheel. Life had regressed to the seminomadic state out of which it had evolved with the Roman conquest six centuries before. Elsewhere there were similar developments. In North Africa, the decline was less steep though more lasting. Byzantine inscriptions are rare after 580. Lower standards of well-being prevailed. The city of Carthage declined in size and population. The mosaics in private houses would be replaced by floors of beaten earth. The port itself showed signs of disuse.[7] The countryside would be sustained by its olive plantations for another century, but churches shared the decline of all types of building. The battle against the Berber groups was gradually being lost for both settled agriculture and Christianity. In the 570s Visigothic Spain was already receiving North African monks as refugees.[8] The arrival of the Arabs in 647 only accelerated existing trends. In other parts of the West, ruined cities and declining standards of literacy and literature marked the passing of Justinian's age.[9]

In Italy, the changes about to take place were destined to affect permanently the relations between Rome and Constantinople as well as the political and economic life of the peninsula. In the 540s and 550s Lombards had served in the Byzantine armies fighting the Goths. In 568, however, their king Alboin decided to try his fortune in Italy, where the Goths had failed, by establishing a permanent home for his people there. His invasion was strikingly successful. The Italians warned Justin II in 567 that their loyalty might be brittle. There was appalling poverty after twenty years of war, and, in addition, deep discontent particularly in the north over the condemnation of the Three Chapters. Both the papacy and the imperial government were despised for accepting the condemnation. To make matters worse, a horrible plague that crushed morale and hope for the future had made its appearance in 567. Great numbers of people died in terrible conditions.[10] When the Lombards struck they were not resisted effectively.Though Pavia held out for three years, Milan fell on 4 September 569. By 571 they had conquered the Po Valley; next year they moved south to seize Spoleto and Benevento.[11] In 573 they advanced on Rome, and Gregory, son of a noble family, was confronted as prefect of Rome with the crisis. It was surmounted, but Gregory turned his back on secular duties, and sold his family estates in Sicily to endow monasteries upon them. In so doing he showed once again that the ablest minds in the West were bent on finding a better outlet for their gifts in serving the permanent institution of the church rather than trying to bolster up a declining state.[12] The first onset by the Lombards was never turned back. The Byzantines were defeated in 575 and thereafter were hard put to save the Italian coastal cities and the land connection linking Rome and Ravenna. Slowly but surely the papacy would be forced to look for a new Western protector in place of the emperor, though the recognition of the fact—symbolized by Charlemagne's coronation by Pope Leo III in 800—was still more than two centuries away.

The parting of the ways was not merely to be between Rome and Constantinople, however. The second half of the sixth century witnessed a long step forward in the process of separating the four great traditions—Antioch, the Alexandrian tradition of Cyril, Byzantine orthodoxy, and the papacy—of early Christianity into self-contained geographical areas on which they imposed their identities. In that of *Antioch,* except for the brief appearance of Nestorian bishops in the wake of Khosrow II's invading Persian armies in the first decade of the seventh century, Nestorian influence would be located permanently beyond the eastern frontier of the empire. Within the limits imposed by Zoroastrianism as the established religion of the Sassanid dominions it enjoyed a relative prosperity. In 630 on the eve of the collapse of the Persian monarchy, there were ten metropolitanates and eighty-three bishops on Persian soil, and another eighteen further east—a considerable achievement in view of the lack of royal patronage.[13] About 550, the Nestorian Catholicos Mar Aba I of Ctesiphon consecrated a bishop of the Huns in Bactria on the eastern frontier of Persia with India.[14] The Syriac record tells of the request coming through an embassy by the Huns to the Persian monarch, who was amazed at the power of Jesus and that even the Christian Huns acknowledged the Catholicos as their head.[15] It was a pointer as to the future direction of Nestorianism. The main work of the Nestorian church henceforth was to be even further east than Bactria—in China which their missionaries reached by 635,[16] and in Central Asia where in the eighth and ninth centuries under the great patriarch Timotheos (*flor.* 780–823) they would challenge Islam for the conversion of the Turkish and Mongol groups.

Its rival even in Persia, the *Alexandrian tradition of Cyril,* was now represented primarily by the Monophysites. During the second half of the sixth century their missionary drive combined with the loyalty of the Egyptian and Syrian peasants to the monks, ensured that Monophysitism would predominate in the territory extending from northern Syria to the Euphrates frontier and thence south to Egypt and the Nile Valley. It would include the Nubian kingdoms and Armenia beyond the southern and eastern political frontiers of Byzantium, respectively.

On the other hand, by 600 *Byzantine orthodoxy* prevailed in Palestine, Asia Minor, and the remaining Greek-speaking European provinces of the empire. Its religious frontier with Rome became more marked through the loss of the Danube provinces to the Slavonic invaders and the erosion of the Byzantine position in Spain. Direct and often unsatisfactory contact with Rome was confined to the residual Byzantine-held areas in Italy and North Africa.

The papacy for its part had by now regained to the full its position of authority in the West. The conversion of the Visigoth king Recared in 587 and the Catholic baptism of the heir to the Lombard throne in December 603 foreshadowed the end of the Germanic-Arian phase in the religious history of the West, though another half century was to elapse before the conversion of the Lombards was assured. At the same time, the Roman mission to the Anglo-Saxons in 597 pointed to a new area for the expansion of papal influence in northwestern Europe. Nearer home Pope Gregory found his policies dominated by the military and administrative problems of Rome and Italy. A Western Europe that looked to Rome and was only marginally affected by events in the Byzantine world was beginning to emerge during his pontificate (590–604).

For the Byzantine emperors relations with Persia, leading to a long-sought agreement over respective zones of influence in Armenia in 591, took precedence over most Western issues. After the death of Justin II in 578, the empire was regarded as "Greek,"[17] though it was not until 629 in the reign of Heraclius that the title *basileus* (king), long used by the Christians to describe the emperor, became his official style in laws and on the coinage, and one of the last links with imperial Roman tradition and the Latin language was broken. Under Tiberius II and Maurice, there was no rupture with Rome but the western possessions of the empire were retained increasingly on a care and maintenance basis, backed by whatever gold and diplomacy could safeguard.[18]

CHALCEDONIANS AND MONOPHYSITES

For the Byzantine state the most pressing religious issue in the half century following the death of Justinian remained the Monophysites. The course of events was dominated by two incidents, not perhaps vital in themselves, but far-reaching in their results, namely the failure of the conference at Callinicum in 568 or 569, and the Al-Mundhir affair in 581.

The parallel between the situation in the first years of the reign of Justin II with that in the early part of that of his uncle is striking. Chalcedonians and Monophysites were both ready for yet one further effort at reconciliation. The venerable and respected leaders of the Monophysites, the patriarch Theodosius, John of Ephesus, and Jacob Baradaeus, were far from being religious separatists at heart, and when Theodosius died on 22 June 566, he was given the equivalent of a state funeral in the capital.[19] They saw their cause also weakened by schism such as had confronted Severus and his colleagues at the beginning of Justinian's reign. This time it was Tritheism, a neo-Arianism(?) arising from the strict differentiation by some Monophysite thinkers of the individualities of the persons of the Trinity, and the tendency to subordinate one to the other. Like Julianism a generation before, the Tritheists tried to spread their teaching throughout the empire.[20] There was another parallel: the empress Sophia at first tended to favor Monophysitism though less outspokenly than Theodora had done.[21] Finally, the papacy was weakened by the persistence of opposition to the decisions of the Fifth General Council and disinclined to intervene. What was different, however, and ultimately fatal to every attempt at reunion, was the temper of the rural population in northern and eastern Syria and on the Euphrates frontier, largely as the result of Jacob Baradaeus's missions. These wanted "out with Chalcedon"; otherwise no compromise would be acceptable.

Through 566 to 568 hopes for peace were high. In the capital, the patriarch John Scholasticus chaired meetings between rival groups of Monophysites, and having patched up a compromise between the Tritheists and the parent body, set about the harder task of finding a settlement between Chalcedonians and Monophysites.[22] The latter, unlike the Chalcedonians themselves, had not moved since the last conference thirty-five years before. They agreed, however, that if the formula "out of Two Natures, One," and Cyril's twelve *Anathemas* were accepted as canonical, and the condemnation of Severus of Antioch at the Home Synod in 536 was abrogated, peace might be restored. In return, they were prepared to accept the Chalcedonian patriarch of Antioch and drop their own nominee. Hopes were raised further by the arrival in the capital of the Catholicos of the Armenian church and his entry into communion with the patriarch John. He had come to ask for aid in the face of renewed Persian persecution of his church. As so often happened, what was worked out by leaders in the capital would fare ill when presented to the Monophysites in their own areas.

The emperor entrusted negotiations with the Syrian Monophysites to a member of the court, the patrician John, who arranged for a conference to be held in the monastery of Mar Zakai near the frontier fortress of Callinicum. The conference was a fiasco. At first all went well with John announcing the terms of the accord worked out in the capital. Then the monks took a hand. "Show us what you have written," they shouted. "If it is orthodox we will accept it. If not we will not accept it." "Orthodoxy" meant the outright denunciation of Pope Leo's *Tome* and Chalcedon's Definition of Faith, and as these had studiously been omitted from John's brief, the audience shouted its disapproval. The brief was seized from the patrician's hand and torn to shreds. Jacob Baradaeus himself was threatened with anathema by the monks. Without another word and without even waiting for his meal, John crossed the bridge into Persian territory to carry out another task of conciliation for the emperor, this time at the Persian court.[23]

It was another sixty years before there was a further, and final, chance of reconciliation on the morrow of the emperor Heraclius's victory over the Persians and the recovery of the True Cross in 630. In the interval whatever ambiguities existed between Chalcedonian and Monophysite areas in Syria and Egypt had disappeared. The Monophysite authorities on whom Michael the Syrian drew gave the impression of unanimous Monophysite support, impervious to any argument, in the countryside—all the way east from Antioch to the Euphrates frontier. In the reign of Maurice (582–602) while some of the towns remained Chalcedonian, the villages would refuse to accept a bishop who was not consecrated by the Monophysite patriarch.[24] When asked in the reign of Maurice's predecessor, Tiberius II (578–82), why they refused to give up the Monophysite *Trisagion,* Syrian women replied, "We are but women; we know nothing about controversy, but from the tradition of the Eastern Fathers we will not depart so long as we live."[25] In the Syrian as well as the Egyptian villages, the Monophysite monastery now dominated the scene, owning the land, hiring the laborers and building the churches. And, as even a casual survey of the ruins of the Christian villages indicate, these monasteries brought prosperity and security as well as a Christian civilization which was fast losing touch with the Hellenism of the emperor's church.[26]

Maurice

Conflict was bound to occur when the empire was ruled by a convinced and uncompromising Chalcedonian. Such an emperor was Maurice (582–602), but before he came to the throne he had been at the center of an incident which alienated a powerful Monophysite group and ultimately spelled disaster for the Byzantines. During the previous half century the Arab groups that formed the Ghassanid confederation dominating the desert area on the flank of the provinces of Palestine and Arabia had been converted to Monophysite Christianity. Since 542, there had been a Monophysite "Bishop of the Arabs" with his see at Bostra, the capital of the province of Arabia.

The alliance with Ghassanids was vital to the security of the empire, protecting it from incursions of desert peoples from Arabia and covering its southern flank in any war against Persia. In 580, Byzantium was at war with the Persians. It was not going well. The emperor Tiberius invited the Ghassanid king Al-Mundhir to make a state visit to the capital, and among other matters to concert a counterattack on the enemy's flank from Circesium, the most southerly Byzantine fort on the Euphrates. Maurice, then holding the rank of count (*comes*), was in command of the expedition, but when he arrived to move his army across the river into Persian territory he found the vital bridge destroyed. Had Al-Mundhir turned traitor? It is not known.[27] He may have hedged his bets with the Persians, for he had reason to suspect that the Byzantines would not be sorry to see him out of the way. Maurice, however, had no doubt. Al-Mundhir was arrested, tried, and exiled to Sicily. The insult to Arab pride was never forgotten. Al-Mundhir's heir declared he would never willingly look on the face of a Roman again.[28] He kept his word; from now on, the Arabs were among Byzantium's enemies, raiding Palestine and making common cause with the Persians, until the day of reckoning came in 634, when they formed the vanguard of the invading armies of the new religion of the prophet.

The Al-Mundhir affair was symptomatic of the relations which Maurice would have with the Monophysites when he became emperor in 582. He was a Chalcedonian and also an impatient, intolerant ruler. For the next twenty years the Monophysite population of Syria was harassed by niggling persecution. Such action undermined Maurice's diplomatic efforts to come to a permanent understanding with the Persians. On his death, murdered with his whole family in November 602, Khosrow took a chance on invading the empire on the pretext of avenging Maurice's death.[29] His armies were welcomed by the Monophysite populace who demonstrated that they might now prefer a second-class status under a foreign, pagan ruler who respected their faith to a Christian emperor who persecuted them. "The heresy of the emperor Maurice" was responsible for every ill, it was claimed.[30] Similar sentiments would be voiced with even greater force when the Arabs launched their invasion of the empire in 634. In this respect the Persian occupation foreshadowed the Arab conquest.

Monophysite Expansion

Meantime, Monophysite influence was extending eastward in the Persian Empire and to southern India, Arabia, and Nubia. In the last-mentioned, the reign of Justin II saw rival Chalcedonian and Monophysite missions at work. The Chalcedonians won over the Nubian middle kingdom of Makurrah and filled its ruler with the same hostility against the Monophysites as had inspired the Nobatians against Chalcedon a generation before.[31] The Monophysites, however, rose to the occasion. Shortly before he died in 566, the patriarch Theodosius consecrated the presbyter Longinus as bishop of the Nobatae. Two years passed before Longinus could leave the capital and then it was in disguise. "Aware that he was being watched and would not be permitted to leave, he disguised himself and put a wig on his head, for he was very bald."[32] So he set out for Nobatia, but his main work was to be in Alwah, the southernmost kingdom of Nubia. Intrepid and using a land route to avoid the kingdom of Makurrah, Longinus reached Alwah about 580 and once again achieved brilliant success. Rival Julianist missionaries based in Axum in Ethiopia were refuted and Alwah converted to Severan Monophysitism.[33] Sometime before the union of the northern and middle Nubian kingdoms under King Mercurius (c. 710), Makurrah also had ceased to be Chalcedonian.

The story of these individual Monophysite missionaries in the sixth century is an extraordinary one. Working in ones and twos they had been responsible for consolidating Christianity in Ethiopia and in parts of southern Arabia and had converted the Nubian kingdoms. Athanasius's dream of extending Alexandrian ecclesiastical power down the Nile had been realized. By 600, except for Makurrah, the stretch from the Delta to Lake Tana was Monophysite,[34] and formed part of a vast ecclesiastical "empire" separate from, even if akin to the Chalcedonian church. The essential kinship in belief and liturgy, however, should be stressed. Both sides of the Chalcedonian-Monophysite divide shared the same monastic-oriented religious outlook and celebrated practically the same liturgies. The observer would have found little to distinguish between a Chalcedonian and Monophysite saint. The Chalcedonians, the historian Evagrius (d. circa 595) and John Moschus (d. 619), have each assembled accounts of the marvels that reflect the religious life of the Byzantine East.[35] We hear of one saint in Coele-Syria who, at death, was buried in a tomb which was then used for two strangers who were buried on top of him. He caused an earth tremor to get their bodies placed in the right position—below his![36] Then there was Zoilus the reader, who renounced all family ties to practice the art of calligraphy in a rat-infested cell.[37] Ascetics such as he represented the ideals of rulers and ruled alike in the Byzantine world. Maurice, though a harsh anti-Monophysite, was also a venerator of saints and relics, a friend of Theodore of Sykeon, who owed his repute for sanctity to his ability to live in conditions of unbelievable squalor. Pilgrimages to distant shrines, like that of St. Sergius of Resapha, the traffic in relics of apostles and saints, the patronage of the holy and, above all, of the Virgin, such were the guarantees of peace and order in the Byzantine world accepted by Chalcedonian and Monophysite alike at the end of the sixth century. When the test came in 626 with the Avars and Persians at the walls of Constantinople, the citizens of both allegiances, unlike those of Rome in 410, rallied to the defense of their city sustained by their faith in the heavenly protectors of the capital of the Christian empire.[38]

THE CELTIC IRRUPTION

Meantime, on the western fringes of the civilized world a missionary movement was under way, strangely similar to those of the Monophysites in the

Nile Valley and Ethiopia. The precise nature of the links between the Celtic monk and his Byzantine counterpart remains obscure, but hermitages on the island of Loch Lorne or on the Skerries, or the larger collections of cells at Kells or Iona resemble nothing so much as either the anchorite shelters found in the Egyptian and Nubian deserts or settlements established by Antony and Amoun and their disciples. On these Celtic monastic sites, the small rectangular church was set amid a cluster of beehive huts and surrounded by a strong and even elaborate wall. There seem even to have been "family groups," for on Church Island off Valentia, skeletons of both men and women have been found buried in close proximity to the chapel.[39] In addition, one may point to the intense penitential discipline with its fasts and ordeals that characterized Celtic and, in particular, Irish monasticism. This again has no parallel in Western Europe but resembles the severities practiced by the Syrian and Egyptian monks. The art, too, of the Celtic church, while reviving and continuing pre-Roman traditions, seems to have assimilated something from the Byzantine East. The spirals and interlaces of Durrow find parallels as far afield in the Byzantine world as the seventh/eighth-century capitals from Q'asr Ibrim in Nubia.[40] In addition, the presence of the Greek cross and jeweled crosses carved on Celtic Christian inscriptions suggests a Byzantine rather than a Latin origin. It is difficult to account for certain contentious features of Celtic monastic Christianity, such as the conscious adherence to a supposedly Alexandrian method of calculating Easter[41] and the use of broad Byzantine-type tonsure. Bede suggested they were due to their remoteness from the Western centers of Christianity,[42] but influences originating in the eastern Mediterranean seem more likely.

Precise dating remains problematical. It would seem, however, that by the second quarter of the sixth century, the episcopal organization exemplified by Patrick's mission in Ireland was giving way both there and in Celtic Britain to a regime of monastic bishops based on clan affiliations rather than on territorial dioceses.[43] The monks had continued the tradition of the bardic schools. Both Gildas (*flor.* 540) and Columba (521–97) studied the Latin fathers and the Latin language at such schools. Though these enforced community life, their pupils were often zealous individuals prepared to travel great distances to spread the gospel and found monasteries. The mid–sixth century is the classic period for the travels of the Celtic saints, men such as Samson of Dol, whose influence was felt in Cornwall as well as Brittany. Samson's career (c. 490–560) marks, perhaps, the point of transition between the urban-episcopal and monastic-episcopal systems of church government among the Celtic peoples. Samson was a pupil of Illtyd "teacher of the Irish saints" at Llantwit; he was ordained deacon and presbyter by Bishop Dubricius (of Caerwent?), but he was inspired by the ideal of winning souls wherever the Spirit might lead him, rather than administering a fixed cure. His travels took him from South Wales to

Cornwall and thence to Brittany, to Paris, and back to Brittany where he died.[44] He typified "the few," to whom Gildas's clarion call—aimed at reforming gross abuses among the rulers, clergy, and even monks of his day—had been addressed (c. 540).[45] In Ireland also, the 540s and 550s saw the establishment of monasteries such as Clonard, Clonfert, and Clonmacnoise—bases for learning and the copying of manuscripts such as the masterpiece of Celtic art for all time, *The Book of Kells*.

Dispute over the right to copy a manuscript of the Psalms, the property of his old teacher Finnian, was a major factor in the chain of events that led to the exile of Columba, the prince of the royal house of Uí Néill, from Ulster to Iona in 563.[46] There, on the island that at that time probably formed part of Dal Riada, a dependency of the kingdom of Ulster, Columba established a monastic settlement.

Columba's aim was no doubt partly missionary. Some Picts on the island of Mull and on the mainland near Iona were converted. He never forgot, however, that he was a prince of the royal house of Ulster and much of his activity was designed to secure Dal Riada against Picts by means of alliances. These included an understanding with the most powerful ruler of the Picts, King Brude of Inverness, and more effectively through the selection of a capable king of Dal Riada in Aidan whom he himself crowned in 574.[47] Under his aggressive leadership, however, Iona became a powerful center of Celtic Christianity, extending its influence eastward and perhaps inducing others, such as Kentigern, to extend the tide of monasticism as far east as Glasgow and the islands on Loch Lomond (Inchallioch). When Columba died in 597 his monastery was the most important Christian center in Britain.

It was to continue to be so for another fifty years. When the mission of Augustine and his companions faltered after the death of Ethelbert of Kent in 616, it was to Iona that the Christian party in Northumbria looked. Oswald, an exiled member of the Northumbrian royal house, was baptized there; and on returning to his native country he became king and defeated the Welsh forces under Cadwallon in 635. He then summoned the Iona monk Aidan (d. 651) to his court. Aidan ignored the Roman ruins of York where Augustine's disciple, Paulinus, later the bishop of Rochester, had established himself in 627 and chose instead as his monastic center and bishopric the island of Lindisfarne just off the Northumbrian coast—a Northumbrian Iona. Thence he initiated the tours of preaching and baptizing which were continued by his disciples through Mercia, East Anglia, Essex, and among the West Saxons, that prepared the way for the final conversion of these kingdoms.[48] He was aided by the progress of the Northumbrian armies, now at the height of their power, but his own method was simply that of individual example. Bede, whose sympathies were wholeheartedly with Augustine and his followers, could say of Aidan, "he was a man who sought nothing of this world, and did not set his desire on anything in it." Everything he received from kings or rich people, he gave to the poor. He went through towns and villages on foot and not on horseback unless compelled by some major necessity. And those he encountered, whether rich or poor, he would invite to take the Christian sacrament if unbelievers, or if believers to devote themselves to alms and good works. He lived as he taught.[49]

That Celtic Christianity did not ultimately prevail in Britain was due to similar causes that proved fatal to Germanic Arianism. The dislike of a powerful section of the Northumbrian nobility for what they considered a provincial interpretation of the faith, and the aura of Rome and its superior organization proved decisive. In the 650s Rome was already a magnet drawing young nobles, such as Benedict Biscop to it. Wilfrid (634–709) too wanted to be a real bishop in the Roman style with his seat at York. King Oswy, king of the Northumbrians, married to a Kentish Catholic princess, wanted to celebrate Easter on one day and not two. At the Synod of Whitby in 664, both had their way.[50]

By this time, the vigor of the Celtic church had begun to wane. Outside the British Isles, however, the great age of the individualist monks moving from place to place on eternal "pilgrimage for the sake of Christ" continued through the first half of the seventh century.[51] The most famous of these was Columbanus (c. 550–615), like Columba an Irishman from Ulster. Leaving St. Comgall's monastery at Bangor in County Down with twelve companions in c. 585 he traveled to Gaul on what might be described as a pilgrimage through the Merovingian dominions. He settled in King Guntram's Burgundy and founded there (c. 590) the monasteries of Luxeuil, Anegray, and Fontaine, all chosen because of their isolation in desolate countryside.[52] His *Rule* fitted his choice of area. It was severe. Self-deprivation and humble obedience were all-important. The monk must eat what he was told to eat and do the work, often severe, set for him. He must live under the rule of one father and in the society of many. As in Amoun's monasteries two centuries before, the rod was ready to punish the slightest disobedience. After nearly twenty years, however, Columbanus roused the ire of Queen Brunhilde, now moving towards the ghastly end of her violent life. He escaped in 610, entered a new mission that took him from Brie, east of Paris, down the Moselle and then south, up the Rhine to Switzerland to found the abbey of Bregenz. Thence one of his followers, Gall, moved on to found the famous abbey that bears his name. Both were to be centers of mission. For Columbanus there was no rest. On he went, across the Alps into Lombard territory still nominally Arian, to establish yet another center of mission and learning at Bobbio in the Apennines. All the time he held fast to the rites of the Celtic church. Though no schismatic, in Gaul he defended the Celtic date of Easter at a synod in 602/3,[53] and criticized the "sunless ceremony" practiced once every fourteen years in Rome.[54] He told Pope Gregory, "a living saint might well correct the errors of a dead one."[55] It was a pity Colman of Iona lacked so ready an answer to Wilfrid at the Synod of Whitby in 664.

ST. BENEDICT AND MONASTICISM

Columbanus died in 615. In Merovingian Gaul his tradition was continued for another generation by Amandus, an Aquitanian noble (d. circa 675) and an individualist preacher and ascetic, who contributed to the re-Christianization of Flanders founding monasteries at Ghent and near Tournai; and later traveled across Germany as far afield as Carinthia to continue his mission there.[56] Columbanus's own disciples worked in a similar spirit. St. Gall completed the conversion of the Alamanni. Eustasius, his successor as abbot of Luxeuil, converted the heretical Varasci in the neighborhood of Besançon in c. 616, and went on to preach the gospel in Bavaria.[57] Famous monasteries were founded between 610 and 650 at Echternach, Malmédy, Stavelot, and Vimeu at the mouth of the Somme.[58] The pace was hot, but Columbanus's rule lacked the disciplined organization to match the individual drive toward perfection. The future lay with the better-structured, more institutionalized, and more humane monasticism represented by the *Rule of St. Benedict* which was now beginning to be known outside Italy.

St. Benedict (c. 480–c. 547) himself had died in the midst of the Gothic war at the monastery he had founded at Monte Cassino.[59] He represented in nearly every respect the opposite approach to Columbanus's. His was the final flowering of the Western aristocratic tradition of monasticism, but which combined estrangement from the world with clear ideas about how secular life was to be replaced by service to God. The arbitrary harshness of the Columban rule was replaced by a fixed relationship between abbot and monk. The spiritual life of each monk was regulated by prayer, manual work, and study throughout the day.[60]

Benedict was not the first in the field. He may have been preceded by an anonymous sixth-century Italian compiler of the *Regula Magistri* which he stripped of pedantries, shortened, and humanized so as to form the basis for his own *Rule*.[61] There were also other monastic leaders at the time who preferred the older tradition of personal renunciation of the world. Both Pope Gregory and Cassiodorus refer to the founding of monasteries on great estates c. 560.[62] Cassiodorus himself retired to Vivarium near Squillace in southern Italy on his return from Constantinople in c. 561 to live twenty-three years of retirement in one of the monasteries he founded on his property there. These monasteries combined a Basilian sense of social obligation with the anchorite's lonely search for communion with God. They provided for travelers and the poor on the one hand, while on the other ensuring a regime of silence and solitude for the monks. There was also an emphasis on the study of the Bible and the fathers.[63] There seems to have been no formal rule, but like Augustine's monastery at Thagaste, a congenial environment for a community of a few well-disciplined and scholarly individuals.

Benedict's ideas were quite different. Though he had received a good secular education, he had abandoned any thought of putting this to use when he assumed a solitary ascetic life, making his home in a cave not far from Subiaco. His move to Monte Cassino was forced on him by the hostility of a local presbyter in c. 520. By now, however, he had come to the conclusion that the solitary life was for the near-perfect; but for the ordinary seeker after God, disciplined existence in a community was essential. His *Rule* consisted of a prologue and seventy-three headings—a directory of the spiritual life and daily routines of a monastery. It followed Basil, Augustine, and above all, John Cassian, but running through it was an element of practical good sense and understanding of what could really be expected from the average postulant who became a monk. This, combined with the author's spiritual perception, impressed itself on men of his time, such as Pope Gregory, his admirer and biographer, and contributed to the survival of the *Rule of St. Benedict* to our own day.

The Benedictines would eventually be giving powerful aid to the survival of the Latin classical tradition; but that was not yet the case and far from Benedict's intention. His *Rule* prescribed some time for studying sacred texts but none for the liberal arts. Pope Gregory's description of him as "sagely ignorant and wisely uneducated" indicates the low opinion he had of classical literature.[64]

Benedict's "school" was exclusively dedicated to the service of God. Therefore, the monk's day was carefully regulated. There was no time for leisure. Such leisure (disparaged as *otiositas*), in fact, he regarded as the enemy of the soul.[65] The emphasis was on worship; and the recital of the seven canonical hours was the monk's primary duty. The hours varied according to season. In mid-March, for example, the average day would start at 2 A.M. when Vigils or the night office would be said. An hour's meditation or reading of Scripture would follow. Lauds would be said at first light and Prime at sunrise around 6 A.M. There would be more meditation and reading until the time for Terce at 9. Between 9:15 and 4 P.M. there would be work in the fields broken at Sext which was said at noon. After work there would be Vespers at 4:30, the single (meatless) meal of the day at 5, and Compline at 5:45. The monks then would retire for rest and rise early to begin the new round at 2 A.M. the next morning.[66] The Eucharist would be celebrated on Sundays and holy days. In the shorter days of winter the monks would have more rest, but in the summer less.

It was a severe but not impossible regime and, as has often been pointed out, on a material level it corresponded to the standard of life of an Italian peasant of the day, to which was added a considerable degree of security and a sense of ordered purpose. There was to be nothing harsh or severe (*nihil asperum, nihil grave*),[67] but a balance between prayer, reading, and manual work which could be and was developed as time went on. There was also a family spirit. Cassian had insisted on the links of friendship and voluntary submission to a superior as well as the acceptance of vows of chastity, poverty, and obedience as the bonds that kept his monks together. Benedict demanded vows of chaste conduct and obedience to the *Rule* from each novice (rule 58/17) but added a new requirement, namely "stability" (*stabilitas in congregatione*, rule 4/78). No Benedictine monk might leave his own house and move to another. He must live out his whole life with the family that had accepted him and share his worldly goods with them.[68] This proved to be among the real strengths of the movement. Though for the first generation after his death in c. 547, the Benedictine monks constituted a closed and inward-looking order, the monasteries began naturally both to carry out collective acts of charity and to produce the type of severely disciplined and not unlettered individual who could be called upon by the papacy for service in the mission field or the administration. In addition, the monastery provided the secure and unhurried existence which enabled a monk with scholarly gifts, such as the Venerable Bede (d. 732), to flourish. Almost by accident, the Benedictines came to preserve much of the heritage of the classical past.

Benedictine monasticism spread slowly. By the end of the sixth century it still seems to have been unknown outside Italy. For another three-quarters of a century it competed in Merovingian Gaul with the harder *Rule* of Columbanus. In this period communities were often governed by rules reflecting a mixture of Columbanus and Benedict. In Anglo-Saxon England Benedict was to prevail only after the Synod of Whitby. Six years later in 670 the synod of the Gallic church at Autun made the *Benedictine Rule* obligatory on all monasteries in Merovingian Gaul. Once accepted there was no looking back. The *Rule* gradually became the standard for western and northern Europe until the great monastic upsurge that followed the Hildebrandine reforms. Thus Benedict takes his place as one of the founders of the European Middle Ages.

POPE GREGORY I

In Italy the influence of Benedict had been accepted more readily, due largely to the dedication and farsightedness of Pope Gregory I (Gregory the Great, 590–604). Gregory had been prefect of Rome in 573 when, as already mentioned, he organized the city's defense against the advancing Lombards. Then he resigned his secular career, converted his Sicilian estates into monastic properties, and for a few years lived in his great house in Rome with some friends maintaining an ascetic community. Thus far, he imitated Cassiodorus. He could not, however, remain long in obscurity. He was ordained deacon by Pope Benedict I (575–79) and sent by his successor Pelagius II (579–90) as the papal delegate (*apocrisiarius*) in Constantinople. Here he lived like a foreign diplomat, apparently learning little or no Greek,[69] and acting as representative of Western Christian interests at the courts of Tiberius II and Maurice in a city where Latin was now scarcely understood.[70] His main contacts were with Western Christian leaders, especially with Leander of Seville, who succeeded in converting the Visigothic king and his kingdom to Catholicism in 587. Asceticism on the Benedictine model and sense of mission already held a high place among Gregory's ideals when he returned to Rome in 585. Four years later, the city was devastated by floods and the plague. Pelagius fell victim to the latter, dying on 15 January 590. For several months no new election could be made. Not until 3 September and after much persuasion was Gregory consecrated pope in St. Peter's. As a symbol of the links that bound the church in Gaul to the papacy, Gregory of Tours (d. 594), then a deacon, was present at the ceremony.

Gregory I has often been compared to Leo I as "the founder of the medieval papacy." In fact, the century and a half that divides the two pontificates had changed the political, economic, and ecclesiastical situations beyond recognition, and conditioned their respective actions accordingly. In Leo's day the empire in the West was still a reality, with its court at Ravenna. A great deal of the pope's time was devoted to diplomacy between the Eastern and Western courts, and to his relations with the emperor at Constantinople. The crisis of the Robber Council was followed by Chalcedon, and the threat of isolation from the Eastern patriarchates. After his dispute with Hilary of Arles in 445, Western affairs occupied Leo less despite the menace posed by the emergent Germanic-Arian kingdoms. With Gregory, the emphasis is reversed. Relations with Constantinople were fully maintained, not least with the infamous Phocas (602–10), and Gregory was personally a loyal supporter of the empire, but his attention was directed increasingly to affairs nearer home. Most of his letters are concerned with the problems of papal estates and Italian bishops, with the prospect of the conversion of the Lombards to Catholicism, the extirpation of paganism in Sardinia, the revival of Donatism in North Africa, and the mission to the Anglo-Saxons. There were some important exchanges with the emperor Maurice, but with the progressive collapse of civilized society in the Balkans, the papacy found itself less able to intervene effectively in the affairs of the Greek-speaking churches. Its effort was directed once more toward western and northwestern Europe. The mission to King Ethelbert of Kent in 597 began the process that led to the conversion of the Germanic peoples beyond the old frontiers of the empire, and through them to the Czechs and the Hungarians, and, finally, to the Poles and the Slavonic peoples on the Baltic.

The events of Gregory's pontificate have been told in detail elsewhere.[71] Here we outline briefly some aspects of his fourteen-year reign that led to the emergence of the pope as the central figure in the secular and ecclesiastical life of Italy and the West, and the implications of this development on the relations between the papacy and Constantinople. Scholars have rightly esteemed Gregory's gifts as a pastor and administrator.

First, throughout his pontificate Gregory found himself responsible for feeding and caring for an increasingly destitute population in Rome and maintaining the city's defense against the Lombards. Rome itself was in a sorry state, half empty and increasingly ruined, typical of the decline of urban life throughout the West. In a moment of despair as he was writing his *Homily on Ezekiel*, Gregory recorded how, "for us the mysteries of this prophecy are clearer than day. We see in this city the walls going to ruin, the houses falling down, the churches destroyed by the whirlwind, and the buildings crumbling from old age, because ruins collapse upon ruin."[72]

It was already Rome of the Middle Ages. There was now "no Senate or Roman people."[73] The old pride and the old traditions of the past had gone. The papacy was the sole survivor, the only authority to which the inhabitants could turn. The first letter preserved in Gregory's carefully kept *Register of Letters* is a request to the praetor of Sicily for more corn to be dispatched to the city.[74]

Like everything else in Gregory's life, charity itself was carefully organized. In Rome, a careful list was kept of those who were assisted, and the date and amount of the aid were duly noted. Frauds and humbugs were sharply discouraged, but in Gregory's palace, the Lateran, strangers were entertained and food cooked for the sick.

Second, like Gelasius before him, Gregory personally kept the affairs of the churches under his immediate control. His letters to suffragans, and in particular the extensive correspondence devoted to the Sicilian episcopate, show him intervening at every stage to attempt to secure the election of those whom he considered to be the right candidate—such as the abbot of one of his monasteries; and, when the election had taken place, to ensure that the successful candidate should live up to the exacting standards of his office.[75] Villages must be provided with clergy, pagans and Jews converted, episcopal towns sited in defensible positions. The easygoing, such as Leo of Catana, were as liable to find themselves summoned to Rome to explain themselves as were the arrogant, such as Gregory's luckless archdeacon (and possible rival for the papacy in 590) Laurentius, dismissed for arrogance (*superbia*) in September 591.[76] All were expected to toe the line without complaint.

Third, a great deal of effort was deployed in administering the papal estates. These had grown to vast proportions. There were fifteen patrimonies to be found in every province and former province in the West, but especially in southern Italy, Sicily, and North Africa. In Italy, if not in both Sicily and Africa, the papacy was by far the largest single landowner. Each patrimony was administered by a rector, the personal agent of the pope, and below him, looking after individual estates and farms, was a hierarchy of clerical administrators, guardians (*defensores*), agents (*actionarii*), and bailiffs (*conductores*). Under Gregory this mushroomed into a clerical civil service of huge proportions of whom the favored members were Roman subdeacons, such as the subdeacon Peter who was rector of the papal estates in Sicily.[77] As John the Deacon, Gregory's biographer, wrote, the pope "appointed industrious men of his own church as *rectores patrimonii*," in order to "safeguard church affairs and look after the poor."[78] Though only a subdeacon, Peter's authority was as far-reaching as that of most provincial authorities. His duties were set out in a series of detailed instructions issued by Gregory during 591. He was to settle property disputes and lawsuits, sell off unprofitable herds, reduce estate duties paid by converted Jews in order to encourage conversions. He was to prevent the exploitation of the peasants by the bailiffs, to manage church hostels, build a monastery, pay poor relief, use his influence with the bishop of Syracuse on behalf of two individuals, offer discreet bribes to imperial officials to secure their good will and execute the will of a deceased faithful Christian, and finally provide horses for the pope. This papal Figaro had a staff of four hundred *conductores* to do his bidding, and well he needed them.[79]

We hear less of his colleague in Africa, Hilarus,[80] but in western Numidia, Gregory's trusted agent was Bishop Columbus, probably of Nicivibus (N'gaous). Here, apart from administration, Columbus had to contend with what appears to have been a sudden and increasingly formidable revival of Donatism.[81] Why is not known. One may suspect rather than prove that this resurgence of a schismatic movement in its former homeland may have been connected with a depression of status in the colonate as a result of working on a papal patrimony. Would the traditional freedoms under the *Lex Mancia* still apply?

The overwhelming majority of the papal administrators would be clerics, with monks often in positions of authority. The residents in the Lateran palace lived a communal monastic existence and the executive agents of papal policy, the *defensores*, would be monks or deacons. Not even the financial officers were laymen. Whatever the cultural background derived from his upbringing as a Roman aristocrat, Gregory showed he had little use for the classical heritage of the West. In a notable exchange with Bishop Desiderius of Vienne, he put in its ultimate form the antithesis between ecclesiastical and pagan learning. "For the same mouth," he wrote, "cannot sing the praises of Jupiter and of Christ. Consider yourself, how offensive, how abominable a thing it is for a bishop to recite verses which are unfit to be recited by a religious layman."[82] Cassiodorus's ideal of a Christian humanism under papal patronage was quietly abandoned.[83] Jerome's outlook two centuries before had received papal approbation. It was an approval far from the spirit of contemporary Eastern monasticism of which we are told how Theodore, "a lay teacher of philosophy," had only one coat and a few books, slept in various churches, knew the Old and New Testaments by heart, and finally retired to be a monk in the monastery of Samala near Alexandria.[84] Centuries were to pass before the West regained the same equilibrium between Christianity and classical culture.

Monasticism was Gregory's life. Monks were favored. Some were granted "privileges" exempting them from episcopal control but in fact bringing their foundations under direct papal control. In his writings, Gregory's *Moral Discourses on Job*, begun when he was in Constantinople, took the form of homilies addressed to monks. The moral lessons which he drew from the texts set the tone for the homiletic type of preaching that was to be the hallmark of the Latin sermon for generations. The learning he showed in his *Dialogues* and *Homilies* was, as has been said, "simple, straightforward and accessible to ordinary people,"[85] emphasizing moral goodness rather than dogmatic issues. There was to be no revival of a Latino-Greek culture such as the Ostrogothic era had seen and which Boethius and Cassiodorus had tried to maintain. Cultural and liturgical links with the East were wearing thin. Gregory denied that the Roman rites owed anything to the Eastern churches. Current practices, he claimed, were all ancient customs of the Roman church.[86] For the time being, his *Dialogues* found little echo in the East.

Mission: Italy

Asceticism, so strongly imprinted on Gregory's character, also was to effect profoundly the history of Western Europe. Whatever the grain of truth that lies behind the Angli/Angeli story,[87] there is little doubt that Gregory placed high among his aims the reconversion of the West and the barbarians living beyond bounds of civilization. His joy at the news of Recared's conversion in 587 was great. Within a few months of his election as pope, Gregory was urging his bishops to more vigorous missionary efforts among the Arian Lombards. "The iniquitous Autharith," their king since 584, had died in January 591,[88] and his successor Agilulf was married to a Bavarian Catholic queen, Theodolinda. Gregory placed high hopes on her influence. Like other Western churchmen he had deep forebodings about the approach of the day of judgment. "Every day, every moment we draw near the end," he wrote to some grandees in Sardinia.[89] He felt compelled to garner all souls that could be saved before that dread event. Heresy and heathenism alike must be rooted out. Thus he dealt severely with the Sardinian landowners who allowed paganism to persist among their peasants, and praised imperial officials who were active in suppressing it.[90] He was liberal in gifts of baptismal robes to converts from paganism and Judaism,[91] and he was tactful toward the Catholic queen of the Lombards. She was a strong Chalcedonian, and, like many others in Lombard Italy, feared that acceptance of the condemnation of the Three Chapters

887

threatened the integrity of the council's decision, a fear that contributed to keeping northern Italy loyal to the Lombards. She was right, of course, but nonetheless served the Catholic cause until her death in 624 as loyally and effectively as had Clotilde at the court of Clovis.

Anglo-Saxon England

Another Catholic queen had been less effective. Bertha, the Frankish princess who was King Ethelbert of Kent's consort, had brought a bishop with her as her chaplain. Yet her husband remained deeply suspicious of Christianity, as if it was some form of magic,[92] and evidence to date suggests that Romano-British Christianity was represented—except for the shrine of St. Alban at Verulamium—only by ruins and memories.[93] Even in London, where one might have expected the survival of a rudimentary Christian organization, none existed. Inhabitants there reverted to paganism after the death of Ethelbert and expelled Mellitus.[94] Gregory seems originally (in 595) to have regarded the conversion of Anglo-Saxon England as a long-term hope. He had in mind the purchase of Anglian slave boys, "to be given to God in his monasteries," as he wrote to the rector of the papal patrimony in Gaul. Though he does not say so explicitly, he may have intended that these eventually could be ordained as clergy and sent back to the British Isles to refound the church.[95] It appears that he knew nothing of Columba and his monks, and cooperation with these played no part in his plans. By 596, however, he had decided on more urgent measures and entrusted a mission to Augustine, a Sicilian from Messina, who was prior of the monastery of St. Andrew on the Caelian Hill. The destination of the mission was Kent and not Deira whence the Anglian slaves would have come. After a false start, not surprising in view of what was rumored of Britain in the empire of the sixth century, Augustine and his band of forty monks landed on the Isle of Thanet around Easter 597. Ethelbert gave them a cool but civil reception at his royal city of Canterbury.[96]

Augustine was not discouraged. Queen Bertha had been given a church dedicated to Saint Martin, outside Canterbury, for her own use, which, says Bede, "had been built while the Romans still occupied the island." The building had survived in a ruinous state, but there was evidently no significant native Christian community to use it.[97] By Pentecost (1 June), however, the situation had changed dramatically. Ethelbert was baptized. In November Augustine was consecrated bishop by the metropolitan of Arles, and on Christmas Day more than ten thousand of Ethelbert's subjects received baptism.[98]

Next year he sent two of his chief followers, Lawrence a presbyter and Peter a monk, back to Rome to request more helpers and directions. Meantime, he established an episcopal family (*familia*) in Canterbury to train English clergy for missionary work. There is not much news of further progress during the next three years. Early in 601, however, Gregory decided to reinforce Augustine with a second group of monks led by Abbot Mellitus. The object was evidently twofold, to give effect to the full restoration of Catholic Christianity in Britain on the basis of what was known about Romano-British provincial administration; there were to be archbishoprics at Canterbury and York, and bishoprics in a number of urban sites, including London. The second objective was to speed up the process of conversion. Here one detects a remarkable change of tactics by Gregory.[99] On 22 June he sent letters to Ethelbert and Queen Bertha, urging Ethelbert to "hasten to spread the Christian faith among peoples subject to [him] . . . to repress the worship of idols . . . to destroy the shrines," and to act like a second Constantine "who subjected the Roman empire along with himself to Almighty God and our Lord Jesus Christ."[100] The queen was compared flatteringly with the empress Helena and encouraged to "strengthen the mind of her husband, in the love of the Christian faith."[101] This was traditional Western missionary policy and was followed by Martin of Tours and others, designed to root out paganism by force with no concessions to the previous beliefs of the convert.

By 18 July, however, Gregory had come to other conclusions. Three years before, Augustine had sent him a list of questions relating to difficulties he foresaw blocking the way of success. Now the pope gave his answer. He wrote to Mellitus having, he says, "thought long and deeply" about the situation in Britain and come to the conclusion that "the sanctuaries of the idols among this nation should on no account be destroyed." The idols were to be removed but the buildings reconsecrated for Christian worship, and there followed detailed instructions covering matters such as prohibited degrees for marriages, relations with the bishops in Gaul, who had contributed little to Augustine's success, and the direction that Augustine should share offerings and live in common with his monks.[102]

The English church was to be organized on the monastic/episcopal pattern that Gregory had taken for his own. But at this stage full success eluded Augustine. Bishoprics were established at Rochester and London, but not at York until 627. In 603, however, Augustine failed to win the support of the Celtic bishops and monks in the West. These, in the persons of the monks of Bangor in North Wales, were more intent on fighting the Anglo-Saxons than providing them with the means of salvation. At meetings held at "Augustine's tree"—either Aust on the Severn or near Worcester—the British bishops rejected Augustine's authority.[103] Christianity was now associated with the secular authority of the kingdom of Kent, which proved to be short-lived. After Augustine's death (c. 605), and that of Ethelbert in 616, there were two decades when the future of Christianity in England seemed in doubt.[104] In the following years the main missionary work in England, as we have seen, was carried out by the Celtic missionaries from Iona and Lindisfarne. But Gregory's initiative was not forgotten, and his personal aura remained undiminished after his death. It contributed greatly to Anglo-Saxon England's future devotion to the papacy.

Gregory and Constantinople

Gregory's relations with the emperor and the patriarch of Constantinople were less dramatic but no less significant. Gregory was unhesitatingly and at times obsequiously loyal to the emperor *and* the imperial idea. Whether or not he felt himself in the right, his language was deferential. "I obey the emperor," he said on one occasion, "and have not kept silence as to my conscience towards God."[105] He was emphatically the emperor's subject and in 603 he himself ordered the statues of Phocas and Leontia for the chapel of the imperial palace on the Palatine after acclamation by "the whole clergy and senate," the latter perhaps simply a group of laymen attached to the clergy![106] He himself realized, however, that so far as the safety of his cities and their inhabitants was concerned he was to all intents and purposes on his own. Everywhere he saw "towns laid waste, forts overthrown, churches destroyed and the land depopulated." He alone could act. In 592 he dispatched a military commander to defend Naples, and in July of that year and in 595 he initiated parleys with "the hated Lombards." The general truce that lasted from 598 to 601 was negotiated and concluded by Abbot Probus acting for Gregory, this time with the agreement of the Byzantine governor (*exarch*). Force of circumstances had obliged Gregory to take up an independent stance in secular affairs, but in so doing he had enhanced greatly the political power of the papacy. Where defense was concerned Constantinople seemed far away.[107]

The rival claims of pope and patriarch were more immediate. The same scenarios of ecclesiastical rivalry and prejudice as in previous centuries were played out by different actors. The Illyrian provinces of the empire were to all intents and purposes lost to the Slavonic invaders. Many bishops had become refugees and their bishoprics had ceased to exist, but empire and papacy continued to dispute over the remains.[108] In 591, Gregory confirmed the election of a metropolitan of Justiniana Prima and nominated him apostolic vicar, but it was the emperor who provided most of the aid for the Illyrian bishops fleeing before the Avars and Slavs. In 601 Gregory had to face reality and accept an imperial nominee as coadjutor bishop, one who was capable of putting the city in a state of defense. As long as Illyricum lasted, the centuries-old dispute over ecclesiastical jurisdiction endured.[109]

The real bone of contention, however, concerned the use of the title "Ecumenical Patriarch" by the patriarch of Constantinople, John "the Faster." John assumed the title at a synod in Constantinople in 587/88, and Pope Pelagius II had promptly annulled its acts and forbidden his delegate (*apocrisiarius*) to take communion with the patriarch until the offending title was repudiated.[110] In fact, John was only using a title that had become customary since the time of his namesake (518–20), if not since Acacius's day. Its acceptance by a synod, however, provided it with a formality it may have lacked before. Pelagius died early in 590 and it was five years before Gregory could act. Then he was presented with a pretext by an appeal by two clerics from Asia Minor against a decision by John. The pope noticed that throughout the dispute John had referred to himself as "Ecumenical Patriarch." Gregory protested to the emperor. Once again, in language reminiscent of that used by Leo against the patriarch Anatolius, the pope criticized the "pride" of John, "his bones dried up by fasts, his spirit filled with pride." His was an offense "against the canons of the councils and the precepts of Christ."[111] He wrote in a fury to the patriarchs of Alexandria and Antioch accusing anyone who dared to assume such a title of being a "forerunner of Antichrist,"[112] and foretelling gloom and doom for church and empire if John refused to abandon it. The emperor Maurice was not impressed. He told Gregory that "there ought not to be ill-feeling between us because of a silly name."[113] What was a piece of non-sense to the emperor, however, was a profound matter of principle to the pope. It was "God's cause, not his own," he urged.[114] He believed that his authority as Peter's successor was at stake in the East, and further, that since the title had not been offered to the pope at Chalcedon, the authority of that council was being challenged yet again.

John died in September 595. His successor, Cyriacus (595–603), though more conciliatory toward Gregory, continued to use the title, and the Chalcedonian patriarchs in the East continued to accept it.[115] When Gregory died on 12 March 604, worn out by tremendous activity and exertion on behalf of Christendom and his own see, the issue was undecided. It was yet another of those matters to be carefully committed to the papal archives for use when the next dispute over ecclesiastical precedence between Rome and Constantinople occurred.

To an observer living around the year 600, the relations between Rome and Constantinople might appear to have reached an equilibrium. Personal relations were friendly, the issues in dispute no worse than during previous reigns. Indeed, the equilibrium was destined to last another century and a half, so long as the Byzantines held Ravenna, and it was to survive even the shock of the Iconoclastic controversy. But it was now an equilibrium between two different civilizations reflecting distinctive interpretations of the Christian faith. It was not a question of "deep alienation" bedeviling relationships.[116] Gregory's correspondence with the emperors Maurice and Phocas, and with indolent and indifferent Byzantine officials, is proof enough of this. It was, rather, a question of two different ways of life and thought that permeated every level of their respective societies growing apart, with resultant tensions, misunderstandings, and conflicting ecclesiastical claims.

The trends already observable at the time of Constantine's conversion had become irreversible. The Byzantine state church was based on principles of collegiality that conflicted with the monarchical ideas of church government represented by the papacy. Civil status rather than apostolic connections was the mark for promotion in the leading Byzantine bishoprics. East and West, too, had adopted contrasting attitudes toward classical culture as early as the second century, and here time had proved no healer. While some Western chroniclers, such as the Spaniard John of Biclar who had spent time in Constantinople, seem astonishingly well-informed about the religious affairs of the East, for others, including Gregory of Tours, the Byzantine world seldom featured.[117] On the other hand, Evagrius of Antioch, friend and chronicler of the emperor Maurice, gives the West scant attention. Byzantines and Syrians were now foreigners in the West living in their own quarters in whatever Western cities survived. Byzantine culture did not flourish in Italy after Justinian's Reconquest. Justinian's basilicas apart, even Ravenna produced no Greek work in more than two centuries of Byzantine occupation (540–750).[118] On the other hand, Latin was hardly understood in Constantinople. Gregory ruefully remarked that no one could be found to translate Latin into Greek or vice versa.[119] Whether one considers ideas of holiness and monasticism, of liturgy and church architecture—no Hagia Sophia with its dome of heaven was built in Rome—of education and the place of the laity in Christian society, one discerns progressive divergence and contrast. Devotion to the *Theotokos* and the cult of icons reflecting the religious feeling of Constantinople and the eastern Roman provinces found little echo in the West. And now the Slavs had forced yet more unassimilated peoples between Latin and Greek Christendom. These would challenge missionary endeavor by both, but would also provoke ecclesiastical wrangles in the succeeding centuries. In most aspects of ecclesiastical, political, and cultural life the parting of the ways had come about, though in 600 not everyone would have been ready to admit the fact.

BIBLIOGRAPHY

NOTE

The center of the stage is occupied by Pope Gregory. The older surveys of F. Homes Dudden, *Gregory the Great: His Place in History and Thought* (2 vols., New York: Longmans, Green & Co., 1905), and E. Caspar, *Geschichte des Papstums von den Anfängen bis zur Höhe der Weltherrschaft*, vol. 2 (2 vols., Tübingen, 1930–33), are still the best. Jeffrey Richards, *The Popes and the Papacy in the Early Middle Ages, 476–752* (Boston and London: Routledge & Kegan Paul, 1979) is attractively written but needs to be used with care. For Western Catholicism, M. L. W. Laistner, *Thought and Letters in Western Europe, A.D. 500 to 900* (new rev. ed., Ithaca, N.Y.: Cornell University Press; London: Methuen & Co., 1957), is to be recommended, and similarly for the church in North Africa at the end of the sixth century, R. A. Markus, "Reflections on Religious Dissent in North Africa in the Byzantine Period," in Studies in Church History 3, ed. G. J. Cuming, pp. 140–50 (Leiden: E. J. Brill, 1966). This, though I believe it is mistaken in its main thesis that the evidence for a Donatist revival in the time of Pope Gregory is inadequate, is an important study. For the emergence of Benedictine monasticism there have been many works of distinction, especially since Dom K. Hallinger's "Papst Gregor der Grosse und der hl. Benedikt," in *Commentationes in Regulam S. Benedicti,* ed. B. Steidle, Studia Anselmiana 42 (1957), pp. 231–319. See also Dom D. Knowles's essay in *Great Historical Enterprises* [and] *Problems in Monastic History* (Camden, N.J.: Thomas Nelson & Sons, 1964; London: Thomas Nelson & Sons, 1963); and also D. H. Farmer, ed. *The Disciples of Benedict* (Leominster: Fowler Wright Books, 1980). For Columba and the Celtic church, Ian Finlay's *Columba* (London: Gollancz, 1979), though lacking a necessary critical apparatus, is a useful and original survey of Columba's life in the setting of the relations between the kingdom of Ulster and the Picts.

For the Eastern church, Averil Cameron's essays collected under the title *Continuity and Change in Sixth-Century Byzantium* (London: Variorum Reprints, 1981) are essential reading. Peter Brown's essay, "Eastern and Western Christendom in Late Antiquity: A Parting of the Ways," in *The Orthodox Churches and the West,* ed. D. Baker, Studies in Church History 13 (Oxford: Basil Blackwell & Mott, 1976), pp. 1–24, is suggestive regarding the real nature of the differences that separated Eastern and Western Christendom in the second half of the sixth century, as is R. A. Markus, "Carthage-Prima Justiniana-Ravenna; An Aspect of Justinian's *Kirchenpolitik,*" *Byzantion* 49 (1979): 277–306.

Henry Chadwick, "John Moschus and His Friend Sophronius the Sophist," *JTS* n.s. 25 (April 1974): 41–74, is an excellent study of Byzantine religious attitudes at the turn of the seventh century, and similarly, E. A. S. Dawes and N. H. Baynes's translation and edition of *Three Byzantine Saints: Contemporary Biographies* (Oxford: Basil Blackwell & Mott, 1948).

For the Monophysites, useful information will be found in the later chapters of L. Duchesne, *L'Eglise au VIe Siècle* (Paris: Boccard, 1925), as well as in chap. 9 of the present author's *Rise of Monophysite Movement.*

For the Nestorians in Persia, see William G. Young, *Patriarch, Shah, and Caliph: A Study of the Relationships of the Church of the East with the Sassanid Empire and the Early Caliphates up to 820 A.D.* (Rawalpindi: Christian Study Centre, 1974).

For Gaul in this period, Samuel Dill's *Roman Society in Gaul in the Merovingian Age* (New York and London: Macmillan & Co., 1926) remains a standard work.

SOURCES

Bede, *Ecclesiastical History of the English People,* ed. Bertram Colgrave and R. A. B. Mynors, New York: Oxford University Press; Oxford: At the Clarendon Press, 1969; also *Opera historica,* ed. C. Plummer, Oxford, 1890.

Benedict of Nursia. *Benedicti Regula.* Edited by R. Hanslik. CSEL 75. Vienna, 1960.

———. *La Règle de Saint Benoît.* Edited by A. de Vogüe and J. Neufville, 7 vols. SC 181–86 and one volume "hors série," 1972–77.

Corippus. *In Laudem Justini.* Edited by J. Partsch. *MGH* AA III.2, pp. 115–56. Berlin, 1879.

Evagrius, *Historia Ecclesiastica*, ed. J. Bidez and L. Parmentier, London, 1898; and *PG* 86.2.2115–2886; Eng. trans. in *Theodoret and Evagrius,* Bohn's Ecclesiastical Library, pp. 251–467, London, 1854.

Pope Gregory, *Epistolae,* ed. P. Ewald and L. M. Hartmann, *MGH* Epistolae, vols. I and II, Berlin, 1887–93; *Dialogus* II (devoted to the life of Benedict), *PL* 66.125–204.

Gregory of Tours, *Historia Francorum*, ed. B. Krusch and W. Levison, *MGH* Script. rerum Meroving., 2d ed. 1951; *History of the Franks*, ed. and Eng. trans. O. M. Dalton, 2 vols., New York and London: Oxford University Press, 1927.

John of Biclar. *Chronicle.* Edited by Th. Mommsen. *MGH* AA XI, Chron. Minora II, pp. 211–20.

John the Deacon. *Life of Pope Gregory. PL* 75.60–242.

John of Ephesus, *Historia Ecclesiastica,* part 3, ed. and Latin trans. E. W. Brooks, CSCO Scriptores Syri III.3, Paris and Louvain, 1935–36; *Third Part of Ecclesiastical History,* Eng. trans. R. Payne Smith, New York: Oxford University Press, 1860.

———. *Lives of Eastern Saints.* Edited and Eng. trans. E. W. Brooks. *Patrologia Orientalis* 17–19. Paris, 1923–26.

John Moschus. *Pratum Spirituale (The Spiritual Meadow). PG* 87.3.2852–3112.

John of Nikiou. *Chronicon.* Edited and Eng. trans. by R. H. Charles. London, 1916.

Michael the Syrian. *Chronicle.* Edited by J. B. Chabot. 3 vols. Paris, 1899–1911.

Paul the Deacon. *Historia Langobardarum.* Edited by L. Bethmann and G. Waitz. *MGH* Script. rerum Langobard, pp. 47–187. Berlin, 1878.

———. *Life of Pope Gregory. PL* 75.41–59.

SECONDARY WORKS

Aigrain, R. "Les Rapports entre Rome et Constantinople, 590–610." In *Grégoire le Grand, les états barbares et la conquêté arabe (590–757),* ed. L. Bréhier and R. Aigrain, vol. 5 of *Histoire de l'Eglise,* ed. Fliche and Martin, chap. 2, pp. 55–77. Paris, 1947.

———. "Saint Grégoire le Grand: sa politique italienne." In *Grégoire le Grand,* ed. Bréhier and Aigrain, chap. 1, pp. 17–54.

Bardy, G. "S. Columban et la Papauté." *Mélanges columbaniens,* pp. 103–18. Luxeuil and Paris, 1951.

Baynes, N. H. "The Icons Before Iconoclasm." In *Byzantine Studies,* pp. 226–39.

———. "The *Pratum Spirituale.*" In *Byzantine Studies,* pp. 261–70.

———. "The Supernatural Defenders of Constantinople." In *Byzantine Studies,* pp. 248–60.

Bischoff, B. "Il Monachesimo irlandese nei suoi rapporti col il Continente." *Atti della Settimane di Studio* IV, pp. 121–38. Spoleto, 1957.

Cameron, Averil. "The Early Religious Policies of Justin II." In *Orthodox Churches,* ed. Baker, pp. 51–67.

Chadwick, N. K. *The Age of the Saints in the Early Celtic Church.* New York and London: Oxford University Press, 1961.

Chapman, J. *Saint Benedict and the Sixth Century.* New York and London: Sheed & Ward, 1929.

Goffart, W. "Byzantine Policy in the West Under Tiberius II and Maurice." *Traditio* 13 (1957): 73-118.

Goubert, P. *Byzance avant Islam*. Vol. 1: *Byzance et l'Orient sous les successeurs de Justinien*. Paris: Editions A. et J. Picard, 1951.

———. Ibid. Vol. 2.1: *Byzance et les Francs*. Paris: Editions A. et J. Picard, 1956.

Hood, Sinclair. "Isles of Refuge in the Early Byzantine Period." *ABSA* 65 (1970): 37-45.

Huxley, G. L. "The Second Dark Age of the Peloponnese." Λακωνικῶν Σπουδῶν (*Laconian Studies*) Athens, 3 (1977): 84-110.

Markus, R. A. "Country Bishops in Byzantine Africa." In *The Church in Town and Countryside*, ed. D. Baker. Studies in Church History 16, pp. 1-15. Oxford: Basil Blackwell & Mott, 1979.

———. "Gregory the Great and a Papal Missionary Strategy." In Studies in Church History 6, pp. 29-38. Oxford: Basil Blackwell & Mott, 1970.

———. "The Parting Ways." In *Christianity in the Roman World*, chap. 9, pp. 162-84. New York: Charles Scribner's Sons, 1975; London: Thames & Hudson, 1974.

Mayr-Harting, H. *The Coming of Christianity to Anglo-Saxon England*. London: B. T. Batsford, 1972.

Metcalfe, D. M. "The Slavonic Threat to Greece, circa 580: Some Evidence from Athens." *Hesperia* 31 (1962): 134-57.

Mingana, A. "The Early Spread of Christianity in Central Asia and the Far East: A New Document." *BJRL* 9.2 (July 1925): 1-80.

Morris, John. *The Age of Arthur: A History of the British Isles from 350-650*. New York: Charles Scribner's Sons, 1973.

Partner, P. *The Lands of St. Peter: The Papal State in the Middle Ages and the Early Renaissance*. Berkeley and Los Angeles: University of California Press, 1972.

Radford, C. A. Ralegh. "Justiniana Prima (Tsaritsin Grad): A 6th-Century City in Southern Serbia." *Antiquity* 28 (1954): 15-18.

Rand, E. K. *The Founders of the Middle Ages*. Cambridge, Mass.: Harvard University Press; London: Oxford University Press, 1928.

Schuster, I. *Saint Benedict and His Times*. Eng. trans. G. J. Roettger. London: B. Herder, 1951.

Spearing, E. *The Patrimony of the Roman Church in the Time of Gregory the Great*. Edited by E. M. Spearing. New York: Macmillan Co., 1918.

Tchalenko, G. *Villages antiques de la Syrie du Nord*, 3 vols., Paris: Geuthner, 1953-58; and see M. Rodinson's review article in *Syria* 38 (1961): 170-200.

Thompson, E. A. *The Goths in Spain*. New York: Oxford University Press; Oxford: At the Clarendon Press, 1969.

Vogüé, A. de. "Benedikt von Nursia." *TRE* vol. 5, pp. 538-49.

Wallace-Hadrill, J. M. "Rome and the Early English Church: Some Questions of Transmission." *Atti della Settimane di Studio* VII, pp. 519-48. Spoleto, 1960.

NOTES

1. Markus, *Christianity in Roman World*, p. 18.
2. See Averil Cameron, "Elites and Icons in Late Sixth-Century Byzantium," chap. 18 of *Continuity and Change*.
3. Brown, "Eastern and Western Christendom, pp. 2-7.

4. See Hood, "Isles of Refuge"; and for the Slavonic penetration of Greece in the 570s and 580s, see also Metcalfe, "Slavonic Threat to Greece," and Huxley, "Second Dark Age of Peloponnese."

5. "A great and populous city, blessed in every way"—so Procopius *De aedificiis (Buildings)* IV.1.24. The bishopric had archiepiscopal status (*Novel* XI of 535 and CXXXI.3 of 545) as the archbishopric over a number of Illyrian provinces, carved out of the jurisdiction of Thessalonica, and designed effectively to be the ecclesiastical center of the empire's Latin-speaking provinces in the Balkans. See Markus, "Carthage-Prima Justiniana-Ravenna," pp. 289–92.

6. See Radford, "Justiniana Prima (Tsaritsin Grad)." The latest coins from the site appear to date to the reign of Phocas (602–10). The life of the city seems to have been restricted to the years c. 540–625.

7. For Carthage in the late sixth century, see H. Hurst, "Excavations at Carthage 1976: Third Interim Report," *AJ* 57 (1977): 259–60, and "Second Interim Report," *AJ* 56 (1976): 194–96; and in the seventh century, see Simon Ellis, *Third Report of the Michigan University Save Carthage Project* (Tunis and Ann Arbor: ASOR, 1976), pp. 41–67. The study of the "Ecclesiastical Complex" provides a detailed description of the type of occupation encountered in a restricted area of the city in the last century of the Byzantine occupation.

8. See L. Genicot, *Contours of the Middle Ages,* Eng. trans. L. Wood and R. Wood (New York: Barnes & Noble; London: Routledge & Kegan Paul, 1967), p. 40. See also John of Biclar *Chron.* ad. ann 571.

9. Thus, Gregory of Tours, *History of Franks,* ed. Dalton, preface: "The study of literature has perished among us, and the man is no longer to be found who can commit to writing the events of the time" (though Gregory was by no means unskilled himself!).

10. For the plague, see Paul the Deacon, *Historia Langobardorum,* ed. Bethmann and Waitz, II.4 and IV.4. For the record of an underlying Italian preference at this time to "serve the Goths rather than the Greeks," see II.5. Lack of resistance connected also with plague and famine, II.26.

11. For the Lombard invasion, see L. M. Hartmann's "Italy Under the Lombards," in *Cambridge Medieval History,* ed. H. M. Gwatkin and J. P. Whitney, 8 vols. (New York: Macmillan Co., 1911), vol. 2, chap. 7, pp. 194–221.

12. For Gregory's early career, see Aigrain, "Grégoire le Grand."

13. See Young, *Patriarch, Shah, and Caliph,* pp. 38–39.

14. Mar Aba was originally a Magian and secretary to the Marsban (governor) of Beit Aramage in the district of Nabt. He was converted c. 520, studied at Nisibis, entered into controversy with the Monophysites at Edessa, and c. 540 was appointed Catholicos of the Nestorian church. See the *Chronicle of Séert* II.27–30, ed. A. Scher, *Patrologia Orientalis* 7 (Paris, 1911), pp. 154–71.

15. From *Histoire de Mar Aba,* ed. P. Bedjan (Paris, 1890–91), pp. 266–69; and Mingana, "Early Spread of Christianity," pp. 10–11.

16. See the Christian monument at Ch'ang-an, line 87. Cited from *Handbook of Source Materials for Students of Church History,* ed. W. G. Young (Indian Theological Library, publ. by The Christian Literature Society, Madras, 1969), p. 32. The missionaries still looked back to Syria as their home even in the eighth century.

17. Thus Michael the Syrian, *Chronicon* XI.1 (ed. Chabot, p. 316); and see L. Bréhier, *La Civilisation byzantine* (Paris, 1950), p. 350. The Lombards regarded

Maurice as "the first Greek emperor" (Paul the Deacon *Historia Langobardum* III.15).

18. Thus, the Byzantines made no move against Leovigild during Hermenegild's rebellion of 582–83, to extend their province in Spain; see Thompson, *Goths in Spain*, p. 69. For an emphasis on Justin's Western as well as anti-Monophysite attitude, see Cameron, "Early Policies of Justin II." However, I do not share her unfavorable opinion of the value of the *Chronicon* of Michael the Syrian ("a late chronicler with no real understanding of the sequence of events").

19. Michael *Chronicon* X.1. (ed. Chabot, p. 283).

20. For the Tritheists, see Duchesne, *L'Eglise au VIe siècle*, pp. 342–43; and Frend, *Rise of Monophysite Movement*, pp. 289–91.

21. John of Ephesus *Church History* III.2.10; and Michael *Chronicon* X.7; but as John makes clear, she abandoned her overt Monophysitism so as not to impede Justin's chances of succeeding his uncle; see Cameron, "Early Policies of Justin II," p. 53.

22. Michael *Chronicon* X.3.

23. Ibid., X.2; see Frend, *Rise of Monophysite Movement*, pp. 318–19.

24. Michael *Chronicon* X.25 (ed. Chabot, pp. 379–80).

25. John of Ephesus, *Historia Ecclesiastica* III.3.19 (ed. Brooks, p. 108).

26. The basic study is by Tchalenko, *Villages antiques*, vol. 1, p. 376, and compare ibid., pp. 181–82. See also Rodinson's critique of Tchalenko's method and conclusions in *Syria* 38.

27. For the details, see *Rise of Monophysite Movement*, pp. 328–31.

28. Michael *Chronicon* X.19.

29. Khosrow was bound to Maurice both by treaty and by his marriage to Maurice's daughter, Maria.

30. John of Nikiou, *Chronicle* CI.5, ed. Charles, but writing in Egypt c. 670, a generation after the Arab conquest.

31. On the success of the Chalcedonian mission to Makurrah, see John of Biclar, *Chronicle*, ad ann. 569, ed. Mommsen, p. 212.

32. John of Ephesus *Church History* IV.8.

33. Ibid., IV.53 (ed. Brooks, pp. 180–81).

34. There were one or two Chalcedonian outposts, for instance at Talmis, *CIG* IV.8647–49, later than Justinian's reign.

35. See H. Chadwick, "John Moschus" (an excellent survey).

36. Evagrius *Ecclesiastical History* IV.35. Compare John Moschus *Spiritual Meadow* 88; and see H. Chadwick, "John Moschus," p. 47.

37. See H. Chadwick, "John Moschus," pp. 56 and 64 and for anecdotes from the *Spiritual Meadow* illustrating the realism of popular thought on the liturgy in the Byzantine East, see Baynes, *"Pratum Spirituale,"* p. 263.

38. And in particular by the power of the Virgin; see Baynes, "Supernatural Defenders," and Cameron, "Elites and Icons."

39. I owe this information to Professor M. J. O'Kelly of the University of Cork.

40. See Finlay, *Columba*, pp. 214–15, and N. K. Chadwick, *Age of Saints*, pp. 49–52.

41. Thus, Abbot Colman's quotation of Anatolius of Laodicea's (Alexandrian) calculations to support the Celtic calculation of Easter, Bede *Ecclesiastical History* III.25 (also used by Columbanus *Letter* I); and for Anatolius's calculations, see

Eusebius *HE* VII.32.14–19, and Lake's note, Eusebius, *Ecclesiastical History* II, pp. 244–45; also, J. F. Kenney, ed., *Sources for the Early History of Ireland: An Introduction and Guide*, 2 vols. (New York: Columbia University Press; London: Oxford University Press, 1929), vol. 2, pp. 210–17, and R. Aigrain, "Les chrétientés celtiques," in *Grégoire le Grand*, ed. Bréhier and Aigrain, pp. 308–9 (remoteness from Rome thesis).

42. *Ecclesiastical History* III.4, "utpote quibus longe ultra orbem positis. . ." ("for being so isolated from the rest of the world").

43. For the suggestion that the transition should be placed in "the latter half of the sixth century," see C. Thomas, *The Early Christian Archaeology of North Britain* (New York and London: Oxford University Press, 1971), p. 47.

44. I have taken the account of Samson's career from Morris, *Age of Arthur*, chap. 19. An additional social and economic factor favoring monastic as against episcopal Christianity would be the ruin of what survived of the Romano-British towns after the end of Arthur's hegemony in Britain, c. 520; see ibid., p. 366.

45. See *De Excidio et Conquestu Britanniae* 110, ed. Th. Mommsen, *MGH* XII Chron. Min. III (Berlin, 1898), pp. 3–85, God preserving "paucissimos bonos pastores." Gildas was also highly esteemed by Columbanus, *Letter* I, *MGH* Epistolae III, ed. E. Dümmler and W. Gundlach (Berlin, 1892), p. 158.

46. For the narrative, see Finlay, *Columba*, chap. 5, though I believe the cause of Columba's departure from Ulster was, indeed, his excommunication by a synod for his share in causing the battle of Cul Dreimne in 561, against Diarmaid, the high king of Ireland.

47. Ibid., p. 122 (King Brude); and pp. 144–49 (Columba as a king-maker).

48. Bede *Ecclesiastical History* III.5 and 15 (Aidan); and 19 (Fursey, who eventually moved on to Gaul, a typical Celtic ascetic preacher). For the work of the Celtic missionaries in Anglo-Saxon England, see Morris, *Age of Arthur*, chap. 20; and F. M. Stenton, *Anglo-Saxon England*, 2d ed. (New York and London: Oxford University Press, 1947), pp. 118–21.

49. Paraphrased from Bede *Ecclesiastical History* III.5; and compare III.15 for Bede on Aidan's virtues and miracles.

50. For the Synod of Whitby, see ibid., III.25; and Finlay, *Columba*, chap. 12.

51. "Peregrinatio pro Christi amore"; Columbanus left Ireland because "coepit peregrinationem desiderare," Jonas of Susa, *Vita*, preface II (*MGH* Script. rerum Meroving. IV, ed. E. Dümmler [Berlin, 1902]), p. 70.

52. Luxeuil (Luxovium) was a former Gallo-Roman town, "now deserted and overgrown with thickets."

53. Columbanus, *Letter* II, ed. Dümmler, p. 160.

54. *Letter* I, "Pascha tenebrosum colis," ed. Dümmler, p. 157.

55. *Letter* I (ed. Dümmler, p. 157), and more picturesquely, "Better perhaps a live dog than a dead lion." Particularly barbed as he had just charged Gregory with relying on "the great Leo."

56. For Amandus's life and work, see E. de Moreau, *Saint Amand*, Museum Lessianum, Section missiologique VII, Bruges, 1927.

57. For Eustasius, see "Eustasius," in *DCB*, vol. 2, p. 381.

58. See the account of post-Columbanus foundations, by R. Aigrain, "Le monachisme occidental," in *Grégoire le Grand*, ed. Bréhier and Aigrain, pp. 505–42, esp. p. 515.

59. I have accepted Hanslik's dating, CSEL 75, p. xi. Practically the sole source of Benedict's life is Pope Gregory's *Dialogus* II, *PL* 66.126ff. See also Chapman, *St. Benedict,* and the bibliography of Benedictine studies in B. Altaner, *Patrology,* 7th ed. (New York and Freiburg: Herder & Herder, 1966), p. 482.

60. *Regula* 48/1, in *Benedicti Regula,* ed. Hanslik, p. 114.

61. For the relations between the two *Rules,* see Knowles, *Great Historical Enterprises,* pp. 138–95; but also Hanslik's comments, CSEL 75, pp. xli–xlvi (textual comparisons). Hanslik suggests that the *Regula Magistri* dates from 570/80 and was itself derived from a version of Benedict's *Rule* (p. xlvi, which was drawn up c. 540–47); compare also J. J. O'Donnell, *Cassiodorus* (Berkeley and Los Angeles: University of California Press, 1979), pp. 187–89 (Cassiodorus and the *Regula Magistri*).

62. For instance, by the patrician Liberius on an estate in Campania in c. 554, and Rustica, a lady of noble birth on her estate in Sicily in c. 578; see Pope Gregory, *Letter* IX.162 and 164, ed. Ewald and Hartmann, vol. II, pp. 162–64.

63. See O'Donnell, *Cassiodorus,* pp. 185, 192ff.

64. Gregory, *Dialogus* II, praefatio, *PL* 66.126, "Recessit igitur scienter nescius et sapienter indoctus."

65. *Regula S. Benedicti* (*Rule of St. Benedict*) 48/1.

66. The example is cited from M. Deanesly, *History of the Medieval Church, 590–1500,* 8th ed. (New York: British Book Centre; London: Methuen & Co., 1954), pp. 39–40.

67. *Rule,* prologue 46.

68. Ibid., LVIII/17, and compare prologue L, "usque ad mortem in monasterio perseverantes passionibus Christi per patientiam participemur."

69. Gregory *Letter* XI.55, "Nos nec graece novimus."

70. Ibid., VII.27 (see below, n. 119).

71. Not least in the monumental two-volume work by Dudden, *Gregory the Great;* see also Richards, *Popes and Papacy;* and the comprehensive bibliography of sources and secondary works to 1965 in Altaner, *Patrology,* pp. 466–72 (additions to 1977 in 8th ed. [1978], pp. 648–50).

72. *Homily in Ezekiel* II.6.22 (*PL* 76.1010–11); and compare 6.24.

73. Ibid., II.6.22 (*PL* 76.1010C); and compare Agnellus, *Liber Pontif. Eccles. Ravenn.* 95, *MGH* Script. rer. Langobard, p. 338 (end sixth cent.), "Little by little the Roman Senate disappeared," referring to the time of Patriarch Peter, 570–78.

74. Gregory, *Letter* I.2, ed. Ewald and Hartmann, *MGH* Ep. I.

75. See Richards, *Popes and Papacy,* pp. 342–64.

76. *Letter* II.1.

77. See Richards, *Popes and Papacy,* chap. 18; and Spearing, *Patrimony of Roman Church;* also Partner, *Lands of St. Peter,* pp. 1–10.

78. John the Deacon, *Life of Pope Gregory* II.53, *PL* 75.110.

79. Gregory *Letters* I, XVIII, XXXIX, XLIV, LXV, LXVII, LXIX, and LXX; he was rector from September 590 to July 592.

80. For Hilarus, see Gregory *Letter* I.73–75 addressed to Gennadius (exarch of Africa) and to the Numidian episcopate.

81. Gregory *Letter* VI.34. See Frend, *Donatist Church,* p. 312; and idem, "The Organisation of the Donatist and Catholic Churches in the North African Countryside." in *Settimane di studio del Centro italiano di Studi sull'alto medioevo,* vol.

28, pp. 601–37 (Spoleto, 1982); and for a different view, R. A. Markus, "Donatism: The Last Phase," in *Studies in Church History*, ed. C. W. Dugmore and C. Duggan (Camden, N.J., and London: Thomas Nelson & Sons, 1964), vol. 1, pp. 118–26.

82. Gregory *Letter* XI.34. Not an isolated view in the West at the turn of the seventh century. Compare Isidore of Seville, *Sententiarum libri* III.13.1, *PL* 83.685–86.

83. For Cassidorus's attempt in 535 to establish a school of Christian learning at Rome in concert with Pope Agapetus, see O'Donnell, *Cassiodorus*, pp. 108, 182–84; and Rand, *Founders of Middle Ages*, p. 241 (but it would hardly "have closely resembled Harvard College," even "in the old days"!).

84. John Moschus *Spiritual Meadow* CLXXI (*PG* 87.3, col. 3037). See H. Chadwick, "John Moschus," pp. 63–64.

85. Richards, *Popes and Papacy*, p. 259.

86. Gregory *Letter* IX.26.

87. Recorded in *The Earliest Life of Gregory the Great, by an Anonymous Monk of Whitby* (ed. and Eng. trans. B. Colgrave [Lawrence and London: University Press of Kansas, 1968]), chap. 9, written in the monastery of Whitby c. 704–14. See Mayr-Harting, *Coming of Christianity*, pp. 57–58.

88. Ibid., I.17, "nefandissimus Autharith."

89. Ibid., IV.23.

90. Ibid., and compare II.4 and IV.25 (conversion of the pagan Barbaricini).

91. In 598 Gregory sent fifty solidi to Bishop Peter to buy baptismal vestments for pagan converts in Corsica, *Letter* VIII.1.

92. Thus Bede *Ecclesiastical History* I.25. See also R. A. Markus, "The Chronology of the Gregorian Mission to England: Bede's Narrative and Gregory's Correspondence," *JEH* 14 (April 1963): 16–30, esp. p. 23.

93. Bede *Ecclesiastical History* I.7; and see my *"Ecclesia Britannica:* Prelude or Dead End?" *JEH* 30 (April 1979): 129–44, esp. pp. 143–44.

94. Bede *Ecclesiastical History* II.5.

95. Gregory *Letter* VI, 10 September 595; see R. Aigrain, "L'Angleterre chrétienne et les églises celtiques," in *Grégoire le Grand*, ed. Bréhier and Aigrain, chap. 10, pp. 277–328, esp. pp. 280–81. Young men of seventeen and eighteen were envisaged, "ut in monasteris dati Deo proficiant," and money was to be spent from the revenues of the papal estates in Gaul to clothe them. For Gregory it was a good use to which to put Gallic solidi which could not be spent in Italy (as being lighter than the currency circulating there).

96. Bede *Ecclesiastical History* I.25; and see Markus, "Chronology of Gregorian Mission to England," p. 23.

97. Bede *Ecclesiastical History* I.26. Above, p. 763.

98. Gregory writing to Eulogius, Chalcedonian patriarch of Alexandria, *Letter* VIII.29.

99. See Markus, "Gregory the Great," pp. 33–38.

100. *Letter* XI.37.

101. Ibid., XI.35.

102. Ibid., XI.56. On this famous letter, see Markus, "Gregory the Great," pp. 33–38; Wallace-Hadrill, "Rome and Early English Church," and Aigrain, "L'Angleterre chrétienne," pp. 286–87. Details were for Augustine himself.

103. Bede *Ecclesiastical History* II.2.

104. See ibid., II.5. Ethelbert's son Eadbald returned to heathenism, as did the kingdom of the east Saxons, briefly converted thanks to Ethelbert's influence c. 604.

105. Gregory *Letter* III.61; he regarded himself as "servus tuus" of the emperor.

106. Ibid., XIII.1 (accepting Richards's view of the "senate" in this instance, *Popes and Papacy*, p. 246), altogether a horrible episode.

107. On Gregory's relations with the Lombards, see Richards, *Popes and Papacy*, chap. 10.

108. For the progressive disappearance of Byzantine bishoprics in the Balkans, see L. Bréhier, "Les Slaves dans la péninsule des Balkans," in *Grégoire le Grand*, ed. Bréhier and Aigrain, pp. 145–50, esp. p. 147.

109. See Aigrain's chapter, "Les Rapports."

110. See ibid., pp. 61–62.

111. Gregory *Letter* V.37; for the application of the term by the Easterners to the popes in the early sixth century, see Ewald's note, *MGH* Epistolae, vol. I (= Gregory's *Letter*) pp. 322–23.

112. *Letter* VII.30.

113. Ibid., "frivoli nominis."

114. Ibid., V.37.

115. See Aigrain, "Les Rapports," p. 68, for examples.

116. See Brown, "Eastern and Western Christendom," p. 2, on this theme and its limitations.

117. But see also Averil Cameron, "The Byzantine Sources of Gregory of Tours," *JTS* n.s. 26 (October 1975): 421–26.

118. Thus, Cyril Mango, "La culture grecque e l'occident au VIIIe siècle," in *I Problemi dell'Occidente nel secolo VIIIe, Atti della Settimane di Studio* XX (Spoleto, 1973), pp. 683–721, esp. p. 684: "Jusqu'à sa chûte en 751, Ravenna est demeurée une ville de langue et culture latine."

119. Gregory *Letter* VII.27, "Hodie in constantinopolitana civitate qui de latino in graeco dictata bene transferant, non sunt." Compare *Letter* I.28.

The year 604 marks no great turning point in the history of Christianity. Gregory's immediate successors were short-lived and lacked his character and foresight. In 607 the question of the title of "Ecumenical Patriarch" was quietly shelved when the emperor Phocas confirmed the primacy of Rome by edict. Different titles were left to mean different things in the Latin and Greek areas of the empire. In the latter case, Phocas's reign featured one barbarity after another, while year by year the Avars from the west and the Persians from the east threatened the empire with premature extinction. The first decade of the seventh century saw the first of many supreme tests for the Byzantine world. But it survived and Christendom with it, as in previous eras when the persecutions had been overcome. Throughout the seventh and eighth centuries, perils were never absent for long. The sudden, cataclysmic irruption of the Arabs in the 630s deprived the church of many of its ancient homelands. The semifeudal society that had developed with the Byzantine *Reconquista* proved inadequate when confronted by the surge of Arab armies imbued with militant faith and, as time went on, by the tacit support of the subject populations of the southern and eastern Mediterranean. Visigothic Spain was lost as the result of a single battle in 711. The Arab and Berber host was not stopped until, in 732, it met another force sustained equally by popular fervor and religious enthusiasm. New and permanent conquests were made among the peoples of northern, central, and eastern Europe, until by the year 1000 the map of Christendom began to resemble the pattern of later centuries.

In this work we have tried to show how the foundations were laid. The enormous influence of the Judaism of the Second Commonwealth period on both the mission and the thought of early Christianity has still to be appreciated fully. It may be claimed that the divergent outlooks of the synagogues in the cities whence the Christian communities sprang influenced the growth of the rival theological traditions of Antioch and Alexandria, and perhaps also of Rome and Carthage. The fact of the Jewish Dispersion gave Christianity a basis vital for its future success. Torah religion, however, was not a philosophy and its appeal was limited to Jews and those who were prepared to become Jews. The ability of Christians during the second century to adapt to conditions of life and thought in the Mediterranean cities without surrendering the essential demands of a revealed faith secured for Christianity a place among the great religions of the empire. In this transformation into a Gentile religion, the Gnostic movement was the pioneer, orthodoxy the able imitator who reaped the ultimate benefit. Orthodoxy, however, had certain crucial advantages. The revelation of divine truth embraced right conduct as well as right worship in a single system of belief. Dualism was not and never can be a satisfactory interpretation of the universe, nor libertinism an acceptable basis for human relations, nor quietism a viable attitude to society on the part of organized religion. Eventually, the combination of Hebrew monotheism with Stoic and Platonic philosophy, and a moral sense beyond that conceived of by its rivals proved to be what the Greco-Roman world was seeking. The Christian promise of salvation was preached with conviction and a zeal that accepted martyrdom as part of the consequence of belief. Moreover, what impressed friendly though detached observers toward the end of the third century was the essentially "simple" character of the Christian message, intelligible to learned and unlearned alike, when compared with the extravagant mythology of some of its rivals such as Manicheism or Mithraism. Blood sacrifices, too, the one-time sovereign means of willing the favor of the divine powers, were ceasing to be popular. People turned to the "bloodless sacrifice" offered to the Christian God by his ministers. Such were among the factors that enabled Christianity to overcome the hold of religious tradition among the populations of the empire. Finally, the organization of the church, unique in the ancient world for its cohesion and universality and feared by pagan Apologists such as Celsus, was proof against the worst that the political and economic disasters of the third century could bring.

Once Constantine became convinced that the Christian God offered him greater success and security than did the immortal gods of Rome the change from paganism to Christianity occurred rapidly and smoothly. It was a new civilization, but one to which a growing proportion of the old ruling classes in Rome and the provinces adapted themselves. Ruling families in the pagan empire became ruling families in the Christian church. There was no revolution, no dispossession of one class by another. Apocalyptic movements seeking social reform were suppressed by force and denounced as heresy. The Theodosian state-church and its poet Prudentius summed up the political aspirations of the Christian rulers in both parts of the Mediterranean at the end of the fourth century. Fusion and absorption of the past into a new Christian civilization, leaving society much as it was, was the order of the day.

We have attempted to show how this equilibrium was destroyed in the first half of the fifth century. In the West, one result of both the reemergence (led by Augustine and Aurelius) of North Africa as a dominant formative influence on theological attitudes, and the tensions and uncertainties caused by the relentless pressure of the Germanic barbarians on the empire's frontiers was the acceptance of pessimistic and world-renouncing values as the mark of a true Christian. In the East, the steady development of contradictory theological interpretations of the mystery of the person of Christ and the rivalries between the major bishoprics prevented the achievement of religious consensus. Between East and West too there were, apart from linguistic and cultural differences, deepening contrasts in the way authority in the church was understood. In a Christendom that accepted the Council of Nicaea as the touchstone of orthodoxy, the claims of the papacy to jurisdictional and doctrinal supremacy as well as honorary precedence over the other patriarchates could only be resisted.

The Council of Chalcedon in 451 represented a great effort at reconciliation on all fronts, but it failed—despite the ingenuity of the compromise. The religious sense of the majority of Christians in the East rejected it. From then on, Christendom gradually fragmented into its Latin, Nestorian, Orthodox, and Monophysite segments, each becoming increasingly identified with its own geographic and cultural area. While Orthodox and Monophysites participated in the creative splendor of the religious art of the age of Justinian—even the Faras frescoes in distant Nobatia are an echo of that achievement—the Latin church entered the long era of cultural regression known as the Dark Ages, while the Nestorians moved east to initiate from the second half of the sixth century onward one of the great missionary epics of Christianity. By 600 the dramatis personae were established in their respective roles. Archaeological and literary evidence that we have access to enable certain markers to be established and the outlines of the story to be sketched. It will be for another generation of historians to fill in the details and ask new questions from an ever-increasing volume of evidence.

General Bibliography*

This general bibliography includes major works—not cited in chapters—spanning wider periods of history than can be related to single chapters.

Adams, W. Y. *Nubia: Corridor to Africa.* London: Allen Lane, 1977.

Atiya, A. S. *A History of Eastern Christianity.* London: Methuen & Co., 1968.

Baldwin, Barry. "A Bibliographical Survey: The Second Century from Secular Sources." *The Second Century* 1/3 (1981): 173–89.

Barraclough, G., ed. *The Christian World: A Social and Cultural History.* New York: Harry N. Abrams, 1981; London: Thames & Hudson, 1980.

Bell, H. I. *Egypt from Alexander the Great to the Arab Conquests: A Study in the Diffusion and Decay of Hellenism.* New York and London: Oxford University Press, 1948.

Blumenthal, H. J., and Markus, R. A., eds. *Neoplatonism and Early Christian Thought: Essays in Honour of A. H. Armstrong.* London: Variorum Reprints, 1981.

Brown, Peter. *Society and the Holy in Late Antiquity.* Berkeley and Los Angeles: University of California Press; London: Faber & Faber, 1982.

Cambridge Medieval History, vol. 4.1: *Byzantine Empire,* ed. J. M. Hussey and D. M. Nicol. New York and Cambridge: Cambridge University Press, 1966.

———, vol. 4.2: *Government, Church and Civilization,* ed. J. M. Hussey and D. M. Nicol. New York and Cambridge: Cambridge University Press, 1967.

Cameron, A. *Claudian: Poetry and Propaganda at the Court of Honorius.* London: Oxford University Press, 1961.

Campenhausen, H. von. *The Fathers of the Latin Church.* Eng. trans. M. Hoffmann. London: A. & C. Black, 1964.

Carrington, P. *The Early Christian Church.* 2 vols. New York and Cambridge: Cambridge University Press, 1957.

---

* Full bibliographies of sources and secondary works relating to the period will be found in B. Altaner and A. Stuiber, eds., *Patrology* (7th ed., New York: Herder & Herder, 1966; 8th enl. ed., 1978); and also in *Patrologia,* published by the Institutum Patristicum Augustinianum, Rome, 1975. See also Johannes Quasten, *Patrology,* 3 vols. (Westminster, Md.: Newman Press; Utrecht and Antwerp: Spectrum, 1950–60). See the supplemental bibliographies to both patrologies in Frances M. Young's *From Nicaea to Chalcedon: A Guide to the Literature and Its Background* (Philadelphia: Fortress Press; London: SCM Press, 1983), pp. 335–99.

Chadwick, H. *The Early Church*. Grand Rapids: Wm. B. Eerdmans, 1969; London: Hodder & Stoughton, 1968.

Chitty, D. J. *The Desert a City: An Introduction to the History of Egyptian and Palestinian Monasticism Under the Christian Empire*. Oxford: Basil Blackwell & Mott, 1966.

Cornell, T., and Matthews, J. *Atlas of the Roman World*. New York: Facts on File; Oxford: Phaidon Press, 1982.

Davis, R. H. C. *History of Medieval Europe: From Constantine to Saint Louis*. London: Longmans, Green & Co., 1957.

Downey, G. *A History of Antioch in Syria: From Seleucus to the Arab Conquest*. Princeton, N.J.: Princeton University Press; London: Oxford University Press, 1961.

Duchesne, L. *Histoire ancienne de l'Eglise*. 3 vols. Paris, 1909–24.

Fage, J. D., ed. *Cambridge History of Africa*, vol. 2: *From ca. 500 B.C. to A.D. 1050*. New York and Cambridge: Cambridge University Press, 1979.

Frend, W. H. C. *The Early Church*. Rev. ed. Philadelphia: Fortress Press; London: SCM Press, 1981.

_____. *Town and Country in the Early Christian Centuries*. London: Variorum Reprints, 1980.

Frohnes, H., and Knorr, U. W., eds. *Die alte Kirche*, Vol. 1 of Kirchengeschichte als Missionsgeschichte. Munich: Chr. Kaiser Verlag, 1974.

Geffcken, J. *The Last Days of Greco-Roman Paganism*. Eng. trans. S. MacCormack. New York and Oxford: Elsevier Science, 1978.

Gough, M. *The Early Christians*. New York: Frederick A. Praeger; London: Thames & Hudson, 1961.

Grabar, A. *L'Art paléochrétien et l'Art byzantine*. New York: State Mutual Book & Periodical Service; London: Variorum Reprints, 1979.

_____. *The Beginnings of Christian Art, 200–395*. Eng. trans. S. Gilbert and J. Emmons. London: Thames & Hudson, 1967.

Grant, R. M. *Christian Beginnings: Apocalypse to History*. London: Variorum Reprints, 1983.

Greenslade, S. L. *Schism in the Early Church*. New York: Harper & Brothers; London: SCM Press, 1953.

Halton, T. P., and Sider, R. D. "A Decade of Patristic Scholarship." Vol. 1, *The Classical World* 76.2 (November–December 1982): 67–127; and vol. 2, ibid., 76.6 (July–August 1983): 313–92.

Harnack, A. von. *Die Chronologie der altchristlichen Literatur bis Eusebius*. 2 vols. Leipzig: Hinrichs, 1897–1904. (2d ed. rev. by K. Aland, 1958.)

Jedin, H., and Dolan, J. P., eds. *From the Apostolic Community to Constantine*. Vol. 1 of History of the Church. New York: Crossroad Publishing, 1980.

_____. *The Imperial Church from Constantine to the Early Middle Ages*. Vol. 2 of History of the Church. New York: Crossroad Publishing, 1980.

Jones, A. H. M. et al., *The Prosopography of the Later Roman Empire*. 3 vols. Vol. 2: *From 395–527*, ed. J. R. Martindale. New York and Cambridge: Cambridge University Press, 1980.

Lot, Ferdinand. *The End of the Ancient World and the Beginnings of the Middle Ages*. Eng. trans. Philip Leon and Mariette Leon. New York: Harper Torchbooks, 1961.

Ostrogorski, G. *History of the Byzantine State*. Eng. trans. J. Hussey. New Brunswick, N. J.: Rutgers University Press, 1958; Oxford: Basil Blackwell & Mott, 1956.

Pelikan, J. *The Emergence of the Christian Tradition (100–600)*. Vol. 1 of The Christian Tradition: A History of the Development of Doctrine. Chicago and London: University of Chicago Press, 1971.

Prestige, G. L. *Fathers and Heretics: Six Studies in Dogmatic Faith*. New York: Macmillan Co.; London: SPCK, 1940.

Pringle, Denys. *The Defence of Byzantine Africa from Justinian to the Arab Conquest*. 2 vols. *BAR* International Series 99, nos. 1 and 2. 1981.

Rajak, Tessa. *Josephus: The Historian and His Society*. Philadelphia: Fortress Press, 1984; London: Gerald Duckworth & Co., 1983.

Schäferdiek, K., ed. *Die kirchliche Früh und beginnende Hochmittelalter*. Vol. 2 of Kirchengeschichte als Missionsgeschichte. Munich: Chr. Kaiser Verlag, 1974.

Seeck, O. *Geschichte des Untergangs der antiken Welt*. 6 vols. Stuttgart: Metzler, 1920–21.

Sherrard, P. *The Greek East and the Latin West: A Study in the Christian Tradition*. New York and London: Oxford University Press, 1959.

Sider, R. D. "Approaches to Tertullian: A Study of Recent Scholarship." *The Second Century* 2/4 (1982): 228–60.

Stein, E. *Histoire du Bas Empire*. Vol. 1: *De l'Etat romain à l'Etat Byzantin (284–476)*, ed. J. R. Palanque, Paris, 1959; Vol. 2: *De la disparition de l'Empire de l'Occident à la mort de Justinien*, Paris, 1949.

Vasiliev, A. A. *History of the Byzantine Empire, 324–1453*. 2d Eng. ed., rev. Madison: University of Wisconsin Press; Oxford: Basil Blackwell & Mott, 1952.

Werner, M. *The Formation of Christian Dogma: An Historical Study of Its Problem*. Eng. trans and ed. S. G. F. Brandon. New York: Harper & Brothers; London: A. & C. Black, 1957.

Wiles, M. F. *The Making of Christian Doctrine: A Study in the Principles of Early Doctrinal Development*. New York and Cambridge: Cambridge University Press, 1967; 3d ed. 1970.

Wolfson, H. A. *The Philosophy of the Early Fathers*. Vol. 1. Cambridge, Mass., 1958.

Zernov, N. *Eastern Christendom: A Study of the Origin and Development of the Eastern Orthodox Church*. London: Weidenfeld & Nicolson, 1961.

Conference Proceedings: *La Conversione al Cristianesimo nell'Europa dell'Alto medioevo*. Settimane di studio del Centro Italiano di Studi nell'Alto Medioevo, vol. 14. Spoleto, 1960.

APPENDIXES

Synopsis of Events

912

General History		Jewish and Christian History		Literature and Philosophy	
31 B.C.	Battle of Actium.	31 B.C.	First abandonment of Qumran settlement, due to earthquake.		
30 B.C.	Tribunician power for life bestowed on Octavian.				
27 B.C.	Octavian receives title of Augustus.				
20 B.C.	Parthians restore Roman standards and prisoners.	20 B.C.	Herod begins Second Temple.		
				19 B.C.	Virgil dies.
		c. 10 B.C.	Agrippa born.	10 B.C.–A.D. 40	Philo *flor.*
		c. 6 B.C.	Jesus Christ born.		
		4 B.C.	Herod dies.		
		4 B.C.–A.D. 6	Archelaus, ethnarch. Reoccupation of Qumran.		
		4 B.C.–A.D. 34	Philip, tetrarch of Iturea.		
		4 B.C.–A.D. 39	Herod Antipas, tetrarch of Galilee.		
		A.D. 6	Judea becomes Roman province; The Census; Judas the Gaulonite revolts. Rise of Zealotism.		
A.D. 9	Varus's legions defeated.				
14	Augustus dies; accepted among gods of the state.				

913

General History		Jewish and Christian History		Literature and Philosophy	
14–37	Tiberius, emperor.				
				A.D. 17	Livy dies.
		18–37	Caiaphas, high priest.		
		19	Expulsion of Jews from Rome.		
		26	Pontius Pilate appointed prefect of Judea.		
		26(?)	John the Baptist's ministry.		
		27–30(?)	Jesus' ministry.		
		30(?)	Crucifixion.		
		35(?)	Stephen martyred. Conversion of Paul.		
		36	Pilate recalled to face charges of maladministration.		
37–41	Caligula, emperor; anti-Jewish policy provokes Jewish unrest in Palestine.	37	Caiaphas deposed.	c. 37	Josephus born.
		38	Anti-Jewish riot in Alexandria.		
				c. 40–45	Simon Magus *flor.* in Samaria.
				40–65	Seneca *flor.*
41	Claudius, emperor.	41	Jewish embassy to Claudius. Agrippa I becomes king of Judea and Samaria.		

914

General History		Jewish and Christian History		Literature and Philosophy	
		42(?)	James martyred.		
43	Rome invades Britain.				
		44	Agrippa dies; Judea again a province.		
		46–48	Paul and Barnabas's missionary journey.		
		48	Council of Jerusalem.		
		49	Expulsion of Jews from Rome.		
		49–58	Paul's missionary journeys.		
				c. 50(?)	Book of Enoch compiled.
				50–62	Paul writes letters to the churches.
51–52	Gallio, proconsul of Achaia.				
		53–56	Paul in Ephesus.		
54–68	Nero, emperor.				
		60–62	Paul in Rome.	c. 60	Menander, Gnostic.
		62	James of Jerusalem murdered.		
		63(?)	Peter in Rome(?).		
64	Great fire in Rome.	64	Neronian persecution.		
				c. 65–70(?)	Pastoral epistles written.
		66–74	First Jewish War.		

915

General History		Jewish and Christian History		Literature and Philosophy	
68	Nero commits suicide.	68	Qumran settlement destroyed.		
68–69	Year of the four emperors.				
69–79	Vespasian, emperor; policy of Romanization and urbanization in provinces.				
		70	Jerusalem falls to Titus.		
		74	Masada captured.		
		c. 75	Imposition of "Fiscus Ju-daicus" (ruth-lessly enforced by Domitian).	c. 75	Josephus writes *Jewish War*.
				75–80	Synoptic Gospels completed in final form.
79	Vesuvius erupts, destroys Pompeii and Herculaneum.				
79–81	Titus, emperor.				
80	Colosseum dedicated.			80–90	Letter to the Hebrews writ-ten.
				80–120	Epictetus *flor.*
81–96	Domitian, emperor; development of imperial cult.				
				85–95	Catholic epistles written.

General History		Jewish and Christian History		Literature and Philosophy	
		89	Philosophers and astrologers banished from Rome.		
				c. 90	John's Gospel in final form; Johannine Epistles.
				c. 93	Josephus writes *Antiquities of the Jews*.
		95	Domitian's persecution. Flavius Clemens and Acilius Glabrio executed; Flavia Domitilla exiled.	95(?)	Book of Revelation written.
96–98	Nerva, emperor.				
98–117	Trajan, emperor.				
				c. 100	Josephus dies. *1 Clement* written.
				c. 100(?)	*Didache* written (or earlier). *The Gospel of Thomas* written.
				100–120	2 Peter written.
101–2	War against the Dacians.				
105–6	War against the Dacians.				
				c. 107	*Letters* of Ignatius written.
				c. 108	*The Letter of Polycarp to the Philippians* written.
112–13	Pliny's mission to Bithynia.	112–13	Pliny-Trajan correspondence.		

General History	Jewish and Christian History	Literature and Philosophy
114–17 Roman war against Parthia; Roman Empire reaches maximum extent.		
	115–17 Jewish uprisings in Cyprus, Egypt, Cyrenaica, and Mesopotamia.	115 Tacitus writes of Neronian persecution (*Annals* XV.44).
117–38 Hadrian, emperor.		
		120 Suetonius writes of Neronian persecution (*Nero* 16).
		c. 120 *The Shepherd of Hermas.*
	124 Rescript to Minucius Fundanus, proconsul of Asia, concerning Christians.	
		c. 125 Quadratus, earliest Apologist.
c. 129 Hadrian's Wall completed.		
	c. 130 Justin Martyr converts.	c. 130 *Barnabas* written. Basilides, Gnostic, *flor.* Date of earliest Gospel fragments found in Egypt. Papias (fragments).
	130–80 Alexandrian Gnostic school.	

General History	Jewish and Christian History	Literature and Philosophy
	132–35 Second Jewish War: Bar Kochba revolts. Aelia Capitolina founded.	
138–61 Antoninus Pius, emperor.		
		c. 140 Juvenal dies.
	140–60 Rescripts concerning Christians to Thessalonica, Larissa, Athens, and assembly of province of Achaia.	140–60 Marcion *flor.*
	c. 140–60 Valentinus *flor.*	
142 Antonine Wall built.		
		c. 143 Marcion writes *The Contradictions.*
	144 Marcion expelled from Roman community; begins missionary activity.	
		c. 145 Aristides, Apologist, *flor.*
		c. 150 *The Letter to Diognetus.*
	154–55 Polycarp in Rome; date of Easter. Discussions with Pope Anicetus.	

General History	Jewish and Christian History	Literature and Philosophy
		c. 155 Justin Martyr writes *First Apology*.
		c. 160 Justin Martyr writes *Second Apology*.
		160–80 Melito of Sardis *flor*.
		160–200 Galen *flor*.
161 Commodus born.		
161–80 Marcus Aurelius, emperor.		
165 Plague spreads from Mesopotamia to eastern provinces of empire and thence to Rome and the Rhineland.	165 Justin martyred.	c. 165 Ptolemy writes *Letter to Flora* (Gnostic view of Old Testament).
	165–70 Sporadic persecutions in province of Asia.	165–66 Lucian writes *On the Death of Peregrinus*.
	166(?) Polycarp martyred.	
	c. 166 The "Red Wall" shrine of St. Peter in Rome.	
167–80 Pressure by Germanic groups on Danube frontier.		c. 170 Heracleon, Gnostic, *flor*.
		Apuleius writes *Golden Ass*.
		171–80 Marcus Aurelius writes *Meditations*.
	172 Montanist movement in Phrygia.	

920

General History		Jewish and Christian History		Literature and Philosophy	
. 175	War against the Quadi on Danube frontier: episode of the "Thundering Legion."			c. 175	Hegesippus *flor.*
				175–80	Tatian *flor.*
		177	Pogrom at Lyons; Blandina and companions martyred.	177–80	Athenagoras writes *Supplication for the Christians.*
		178	Irenaeus, bishop of Lyons.	178	Celsus writes *True Reason* against Christians.
		180	Scillitan Martyrs at Carthage.	180	Theophilus of Antioch *flor.;* writes *To Autolycus.*
		c. 180	Catechetical School at Alexandria (Pantaenus).	c. 180	Apollinaris and Miltiades, anti-Montanist writers, *flor.*
80–92	Commodus, emperor (assassinated).			180–200	Clement of Alexandria *flor.*
. 185	Marcia, Christian mistress of Commodus.	185	Origen born.	c. 185	Irenaeus writes *Against Heresies.*
		189–99(?)	Victor, first Latin-speaking pope.		
		c. 195	The Easter Controversy: Irenaeus's intervention.		

921

General History	Rome, North Africa, the West	Alexandria, Antioch, the East
		189–232 Demetrius, bishop of Alexandria.
		190–209 Serapion, bishop of Antioch.
193 Septimius Severus proclaimed emperor (July).		
193–97 Severus defeats rivals in East and West.		
193–96 Siege of Byzantium.		
197 Sack of Lyons.		
199 Severus's Parthian campaign.	199(?)–217 Zephyrinus, bishop of Rome. Beginnings of catacomb art.	
		c. 200 Abercius inscription.
	200–220 Controversies in Carthage. Tertullian writes against pagans, Gnostics, Marcionites.	200–220 Bardesanes *flor.*
201 Decius born.		

Councils, Schisms, Heresies, Persecutions		Literature and Philosophy	
		c. 190	Clement of Alexandria writes *Miscellanies*.
?0–220	Monarchian controversies in Rome (Noetus, the Theodoti, Praxeas).	190–220	Tertullian *flor.*
		c. 195	Tertullian converts to Christianity.
197	Sporadic persecutions in Carthage.	197	Tertullian writes *Apology*.
?2	Severus issues rescript(?) against Jewish and Christian conversions.		
?2–6	Persecutions in North Africa (Perpetua and Felicitas), Rome, Alexandria, Antioch, Corinth. Clement quits Alexandria (202).		

General History		Rome, North Africa, the West		Alexandria, Antioch, the East	
203–4	Severus in Africa.			203	Origen, head of Catechetical School at Alexandria.
		c. 207	Tertullian joins Montanists; completes *Against Marcion*.		
208–11	Severus's campaign in Scotland.				
211	Severus dies at York (February).				
211–17	Caracalla, emperor.				
212	Geta murdered (February); Caracalla sole emperor.				
212 (214?)	*Constitutio Antoniniana* published.				
c. 214	Origen visits governor of Arabia.				
				215	Caracalla orders Egyptians expelled from Alexandria.
				215–19	Origen withdraws from Alexandria.
217	Caracalla murdered.				
217–18	Macrinus, emperor.				

Councils, Schisms, Heresies, Persecutions		Literature and Philosophy	
203	Leonides martyred.		
		205	Plotinus born.
		207–20	Tertullian's Montanist writings: *On Flight in Persecution; Concerning the Crown; On Single Marriage; On Modesty;* etc.
		210–36	Hippolytus of Rome *flor.*
211–13	Further sporadic outbreaks at Carthage (Scapula).		
		212	Tertullian writes *To Scapula.*
		213	Tertullian writes *Against Praxeas* against Monarchians.
		c. 215	Philostratus writes *Life of Apollonius of Tyana.*
216	Mani born near Basra.		

General History	Rome, North Africa, the West		Alexandria, Antioch, the East	
218–22 Elagabalus. Syrian sun worship in Rome.	218–22	Callistus, bishop of Rome.	c. 218(?)	Origen visits Rome.
	c. 219	Tertullian with Hippolytus attacks Pope Callistus's edict.		
222–35 Alexander Severus.	222–30	Urban, pope.		
224 Sassanian revolution in Persia.				
			c. 225	Origen writes *On First Principles;* embarks on *Hexapla.*
			c. 228	Origen begins *Commentary on Gospel of John.*
			229–30	Origen leaves Alexandria for Caesarea.
c. 230 First Persian War.	230–35	Pontian, pope.		
			232(?)	Origen visits Julia Mamaea at Antioch.
			c. 232	Christian church built at Dura-Europos.
			232–47	Heraclas, bishop of Alexandria.

Councils, Schisms, Heresies, Persecutions	Literature and Philosophy
c. 220 Agrippinus convenes Council of Carthage (rebaptism). Sabellius *flor.* in Pentapolis.	220–28(?) Ulpian, jurist, *flor.*
	220–30 Sextus Julius Africanus *flor.*
	c. 220–30 Minucius Felix *flor.* Dio Cassius *flor.;* writes *Roman History.*
c. 230 Artemon *flor.*	230–40 Herodian, historian, *flor.*
	232 Porphyry born.

General History	Rome, North Africa, the West	Alexandria, Antioch, the East
235 Increasing pressures on Rhine frontier from Germanic peoples. Alexander murdered at Mainz (22 March).		
235–38 Maximin of Thrace.	235–36 Antherus, pope.	
	236–50 Fabian, pope; development of Roman diaconate and catacombs.	236 Origen writes *Exhortation to Martyrdom*.
237–38 Persian offensive against Roman East.		237–42 Origen and Gregory Thaumaturgus establish contact in Caesarea.
238 Attacks by Goths and Carpi. Revolution in North Africa places Gordiani on throne.	238 Civil War in North Africa.	
238–44 Gordianus III.		
241 Sapor I, king of Persia.		
243–44 War against Persia.		243 Gregory returns to Cappadocia.
244–49 Philip the Arabian.		
	247 1000-year celebrations in Rome.	247–64 Dionysius, bishop of Alexandria.
248 Rome attacked by Goths. Decius restores Moesia and Pannonia to empire.		248 Origen writes *Against Celsus*. Anti-Christian pogrom in Alexandria.

Councils, Schisms, Heresies, Persecutions	Literature and Philosophy
	233–44 Plotinus at Alexandria.
235–36 Christian leaders persecuted.	
236 Pontian and Hippolytus die. Christians persecuted in Cappadocia.	
240 Mani's mission in Persia begins.	240–45 Origen writes and debates against Monarchians.

General History		Rome, North Africa, the West		Alexandria, Antioch, the East	
249–51	Decius, emperor.				
250	Gothic War. Constantius born.	250–51	Cyprian flees Carthage.	250	Dionysius of Alexandria flees. Babylas of Antioch executed (24 January [?]).
				c. 250	Antony born.
251	Decius killed by Goths (June).	251	Cyprian reasserts authority at council (April); problem of Lapsed Christians.		
		251–53	Cornelius, pope.		
252–53	Gallus, emperor; persecution briefly renewed.				
253–60	Valerian, emperor.				
254	Persian War renews.	254–57	Stephen, pope (May 254–August 257).	254	Origen dies at Tyre.
254–55	European provinces invaded by Goths; Heruli and other peoples invade Black Sea provinces and Greece.	254	Spanish congregations of Mérida and Leon appeal to Cyprian (autumn).		
		255–57	Rebaptism controversy.	255–72	Firmilian of Cappadocia *flor.*
256	Dura falls to Sassanians.				
		257–58	Sixtus II, pope.	257	Dionysius exiled to Kufrah.
259–74	Gallic Empire.				

Councils, Schisms, Heresies, Persecutions	Literature and Philosophy
250 Christian leaders arrested. Pope Fabian executed (22 January). General order to sacrifice circulated throughout provinces. *Libelli* in Egypt (June–July).	
251 Novatianist Schism.	251 Cyprian writes *On the Unity of the Catholic Church* in support of Cornelius (autumn).
256 Council of eighty-seven bishops at Carthage (1 September).	
257–60 Valerianic persecution: 1. Attack on clergy and corporate life of church. 2. Sixtus, Cyprian, Laurence, and others executed.	

General History		Rome, North Africa, the West		Alexandria, Antioch, the East	
260	Valerian captured near Edessa (June). Silver currency collapses.				
260–62	Antioch and Eastern provinces lost to Persians.	260–68	Dionysius, pope.	260–62	Civil War in Egypt.
260–68	Gallienus, emperor.			260–63	Two Dionysii (of Alexandria and Rome) debate over Sabellianism.
				261–72	Paul of Samosata, bishop of Antioch.
262–72	Palmyrene ascendancy in Roman East.				
				c. 263	Porphyry at Rome.
268–70	Claudius II, emperor.				
269	Goths defeated by Claudius at Nish.				
270	Claudius dies of plague.	270	Plague.	c. 270	Antony establishes himself in desert.
270–75	Aurelian, emperor: empire restored to Rhine, Danube, and Euphrates boundaries; Palmyrenes defeated.	270–75	Felix I, pope.		
272	Sapor I dies.			272	Church of Antioch appeals to Aurelian concerning Paul.
274	Aurelian builds new walls around Rome; dedicates temple to Sun-god.				

Councils, Schisms, Heresies, Persecutions		Literature and Philosophy	
260	Toleration.		
261	Rescript of Gallienus to Egyptian bishops.		
264	Council at Antioch directed against Paul.		
265	Council at Antioch directed against Paul.	c. 265	Dexippus, historian, *flor.*
268	Council at Antioch condemns Paul as heretic.		
		270	Plotinus dies.

General History		Rome, North Africa, the West		Alexandria, Antioch, the East	
		275	Eutychian, pope.		
276–82	Probus, emperor.				
276–93	Bahram II, king of Persia.				
				277	Mani executed at orders of King Bahram II (February).
				c. 280	Pierius of Alexandria.
				280–300	Manichees active in Egypt and Syria.
282–83	Carus, emperor.			282–300	Theonas, bishop of Alexandria.
283–84	Carinus, emperor.	283–96	Gaius, pope.		
284–305	Diocletian overthrows Carinus, becomes emperor (November).				
286	Maximian given rank of Augustus.				
288	Carausius revolts in Britain.				
293–303	Diocletian institutes reforms: 1. Tetrarchy established (Diocletian, Maximian as Augustus; Constantius, Galerius as Caesar). 2. Provinces decentralized. 3. Army reformed.			c. 293	Athanasius born.

Councils, Schisms, Heresies, Persecutions	Literature and Philosophy
5 Aurelian threatens persecution.	c. 275 Porphyry writes *Against the Christians*.
	c. 280 Commodian *flor.* Anatolius *flor.*
	290–305 Arnobius of Sicca *flor.*

General History	Rome, North Africa, the West		Alexandria, Antioch, the East	
	4. Currency re-formed.			
	5. Edict of Prices (301).			
	6. Taxation re-formed.			
296	Constantius re-stores Britain to empire.	296–304	Marcellinus, pope.	
			298	Persian War; Galerius victori-ous.
			c. 300	Gregory the Illu-minator; conver-sion of royal hous of Armenia.
			300–311	Peter, bishop of Alexandria.
303	Diocletian cele-brates *vicennalia* in Rome; becomes ill (November).			
304	Galerius assumes power.	304(?)	Marcellinus's apostasy.	
		304	Martyrs of Abiti-na.	
305	Diocletian and Maximian abdicate (May). Constantius, Gale-rius as Augustus; Severus, Max-iminus as Caesar.			

Councils, Schisms, Heresies, Persecutions		Literature and Philosophy	
297	Anti-Manichean measures by Diocletian; rescript to Julianus, proconsul of Africa.		
298–302	Christians in army forced to resign.		
		c. 300	Alexander of Lycopolis *flor.* Methodius of Olympus *flor.*
		300–318	Lactantius *flor.*
303	Great Persecution begins (23 February): *first edict:* books surrendered; buildings destroyed; Christians discriminated against. *second edict:* clergy imprisoned. *third edict:* clergy forced to sacrifice, freed on compliance. *fourth edict:* general sacrifice ordered (spring 304).	303–5	Hierocles and others attack Christians. Early work of Eusebius of Caesarea *(Chronicle).*
305–6	Intermission of persecution.	305	Porphyry dies.

937

General History		Rome, North Africa, the West		Alexandria, Antioch, the East	
306	Constantius dies at York. Constantine hailed as Augustus (25 July). Maxentius accomplishes successful *coup d'état* in Rome (26 October).	306–12	Toleration for Christians in Rome and Africa.	306	Fifth edict of persecution in East.
307	Severus dies. Licinius becomes Augustus.				
308	Conference at Carnuntum (November).	308–11	Period of confusion in Roman church. Rebellion in North Africa.	308	Sixth edict of persecution in East. Egyptian martyrs in Palestine.
				309–79	Sapor II reigns.
310	Maximian dies. Meletius of Antioch born.			310	Pamphilus martyred in Caesarea.
311	Galerius dies (5 May).				
		311–12	Mensurius of Carthage dies; Caecilian elected.	311–12	Maximin fails to defeat Armenia.
		311–14	Miltiades, pope.		
312	Constantine defeats Maxentius at Milvian Bridge outside Rome (28 October).				
312–25	Ossius's influence over Constantine.			312–28	Alexander, bishop of Alexandria.

Councils, Schisms, Heresies, Persecutions		Literature and Philosophy
06–10	Maximin renews persecution in East; seeks to reorganize pagan cult.	
c. 308	Meletian Schism begins.	308	Ephraem Syrus born.
309(?)	Council of Elvira.	
11	Galerius issues Edict of Toleration (30 April).	311	Ulphilas born. Eusebius writes *Ecclesiastical History* (first edition).
11–12	Maximin continues persecution in dominions, especially Egypt. Donatist Schism breaks out. Peter of Alexandria (25 November 311) and Lucian of Antioch (January 312) martyred.	
12	Anti-Caecilianist Council at Carthage.	

General History		Rome, North Africa, the West		Alexandria, Antioch, the East	
313	Constantine and Licinius meet at Milan; Edict of Milan grants universal toleration (February).				
314 (or 316)	War between Constantine and Licinius.	314–35	Sylvester, pope.		
315	Constantine celebrates *decennalia;* Arch of Constantine at Rome.				
		316	Constantine acquits Caecilian of all charges (November).		
317	Crispus, Constantine II as Caesar.				
				c. 318	Arian controversy begins.
324	Licinius defeated at Chrysopolis; Constantine becomes sole emperor (September).				
				325–26(?)	Eustathius, bishop of Antioch.
326	Crispus and Fausta murdered.				
				328	Alexander of Alexandria dies (April). Athanasius elected (June).

Councils, Schisms, Heresies, Persecutions		Literature and Philosophy	
313	Anti-Caecilianist appeal to Constantine (April).	313(?)	Lactantius writes *Divine Institutes*.
	Maximin defeated and dies (summer).		
	Council of Rome; Caecilian vindicated (October).		
314	Council of Arles (1 August).	c. 314	Lactantius writes *On the Deaths of the Persecutors*.
	Council of Ancyra.		
		315	Epiphanius of Salamis born.
321	Donatists granted contemptuous toleration.		
321–24	Persecution in Licinius's domains.		
324	Philogonius, bishop of Antioch; dies (December).	324 (late)	Eusebius writes *Ecclesiastical History* (second edition).
325	Council of Antioch (January).		
	Council of Nicaea (May–July).		
327	Council of Nicaea, second session (October [?]).		

General History	Rome, North Africa, the West		Alexandria, Antioch, the East	
			328–73	Athanasius, bishop of Alexandria.
330	Constantinople dedicated (May).			
332	Goths defeated by Constantine.			
335	Empire divided between Constantine's sons and nephews.	335–36	Marcus, pope.	
	Hannibalianus becomes "King of Armenia."			
	Constantine celebrates *tricennalia* at Jerusalem.			
		c. 336	Donatus holds Council on Rebaptism.	
337	Constantine baptized; dies (22 May).			

Councils, Schisms, Heresies, Persecutions		Literature and Philosophy
330–32	Athanasius takes strong action against Meletians.	
330–37	Pressures against pagan centers in East on Constantine's orders.	
331	Sopater, Neo-Platonist, executed.	
333	Porphyry's works proscribed.	
334	Council of Caesarea.	
335	Council of Tyre condemns Athanasius (July).	
	Athanasius exiled to Trier (7 November).	
	336	Eusebius writes *Tricennial Oration* in praise of Constantine.

943

General History		Rome, North Africa, the West		Alexandria/Egypt, Antioch, Jerusalem	
				330	Monasticism *flor.* in Egypt.
				333–42	Flacillus, bishop of Antioch.
337	Military *putsch;* Constantine II, Constans, Constantius II, emperors (9 September).			337	Athanasius returns to Alexandria from first exile (November).
337–43	War against Persia.	337–52	Julius I, pope.		
339	Ambrose of Milan born.			339–45	Gregory, intrusive bishop of Alexandria.
				339–46	Athanasius's second exile.
				339–66	Acacius, bishop of Caesarea.
340	Civil War between Constantine II and Constans; Constantine II killed near Aquileia.	340	First reference to Circumcellions in Africa.		
				341	Athanasius in Rome.
				342–45	Stephen, bishop of Antioch (deposed for moral failings).
				345–57	Leontius, bishop of Antioch.

Constantinople	Councils, Schisms, Heresies, Persecutions		Writers and Leaders	
336–38(?) Paul, bishop.				
	337–40	Christians persecuted in Persia.		
338–41 Eusebius of Nicomedia, bishop (translated from Nicomedia).			c. 338	Eusebius writes *Life of Constantine*.
	339	Council in Rome vindicates Athanasius and Marcellus of Ancyra.	339	Eusebius dies.
	340(?)	Council of Gangra.	340–70	Ephraem Syrus *flor*.
341–42 Paul restored.	341	Dedication Council of Antioch; second and fourth Creeds of Antioch.		
	342	Pagan sacrifices forbidden (1 November).		
342–46 Macedonius, bishop.	342 or 343	Council of Sardica.		
	344	*Macrostichos* Creed.		
			345	Firmicus Maternus *flor*.

General History		Rome, North Africa, the West		Alexandria/Egypt, Antioch, Jerusalem	
				346	Athanasius returns to Alexandria in triumph (21 October).
					Pachomius dies.
347	Theodosius born.	347	Paul and Macarius's mission to North Africa.	c. 347	John Chrysostom born in Antioch.
			Donatus exiled to Gaul.		
		348–61	Catholic ascendancy in North Africa.		
349	Persians besiege Nisibis.				
350	Constans killed by usurper Magnentius (January).			350	Cyril becomes bishop of Jerusalem.
351	Civil War; Battle of Mursa (September); Magnentius defeated.				
		352–66	Liberius, pope.		
353	Magnentius dies.				
354	Gallus Caesar executed.	354	Augustine born at Thagaste (November).		
354–56	Germanic peoples invade Gaul.				
355	Julian becomes Caesar (November)				
c. 355	Donatus dies in exile.	c. 355	Victorinus converts in Rome.		
	Paulinus of Nola born.				
355–58	Julian's Gallic campaigns.	355–58	Liberius exiled.		
				356	Antony dies, age 105.

Constantinople		Councils, Schisms, Heresies, Persecutions		Writers and Leaders	
46–51	Paul restored again.				
		347	Councils of Milan and Sirmium. First (abortive) deposition of Photinus.		
		348(?)	Council of Carthage.		
				350–90	Libanius *flor.*
51–60	Macedonius restored.	351	Second Council of Sirmium. Photinus deposed.		
		353	Council of Arles.		
				354	Calendar of Philocalus.
		355	Council of Milan.		
		356	Pagan cult banned on penalty of death.		

General History		Rome, North Africa, the West		Alexandria/Egypt, Antioch, Jerusalem	
		356–65	Felix, antipope.	356–61	George of Cappadocia, intrusive bishop (lynched, December 361).
				356–62	Athanasius's third exile.
357	Constantius visits Rome.			357–60	Eudoxius, bishop of Antioch; appointed to Constantinople (January 360).
		c. 358	Ossius of Córdoba dies.		
359	Persian War renewed; Amida lost (5 October). Gratian born.				
360	Julian, Augustus (February).			360	Eudoxius translated to Constantinople.
361	Constantius II dies (3 November); civil war averted.			361	Meletius, bishop of Antioch; later exiled.
361–63	Julian the Apostate; general toleration of all rival Christian creeds as well as paganism.				
		362	Donatists return from exile.	362	Athanasius returns (21 February).
					Confusion in Antioch; Paulinus consecrated "Old Nicene" bishop.
					Meletius returns from exile.
		362–91/92	Parmenian, Donatist bishop of Carthage.	362–63	Athanasius's fourth exile.

Constantinople		Councils, Schisms, Heresies, Persecutions		Writers and Leaders	
				356–60	Aetius the "godless deacon", *flor*.
				356–60	Hilary of Poitiers exiled to Phrygia.
357	Relics of St. Andrew and St. Luke brought to Constantinople (March).	357	Third Council of Sirmium ("The Blasphemy").		
		358	Council of Ancyra.	358	Basil of Ancyra *flor*.
		359	The "dated" creed (22 May). Council of Ariminum (summer). Council of Seleucia (27 September).		
360	Hagia Sophia dedicated.	360	Council of Constantinople (January).		
360–70	Eudoxius, bishop.			360–90	Apollinaris of Laodicea *flor*.
		362	Council of Alexandria. Julian restores paganism. Christian teachers restricted.		

General History	Rome, North Africa, the West	Alexandria/Egypt, Antioch, Jerusalem
363 War against Persia renews; Julian killed after brilliant initial victories (26 June). Jovian, emperor; gives up Nisibis and Roman influence in Armenia to Persia.		
364–75 Valentinian I, emperor in West.		364 Athanasius returns to Alexandria (February).
364–78 Valens, emperor in East.		
	365 Stilicho born.	365–66 Athanasius forced into fifth exile by Valens's pro-Arian policy.
		c. 365–78 Meletius exiled again.
366–67 Procopius usurps.	366–67 Ursinus, anti-pope.	
	366–84 Damasus, pope. Riots in Rome.	
367 Gratian, joint emperor in West.		
		370 Hypatia born in Alexandria.
371 Valentinian II born.	371 Damasus accused of murder; acquitted by emperor.	
	373 Ambrose consecrated bishop of Milan (7 December).	373 Athanasius dies (4 May).

Constantinople	Councils, Schisms, Heresies, Persecutions		Writers and Leaders	
	363	Synod of Antioch (October).		
	364	Council of Lampsacus.		
			365–85	Optatus of Milevis *flor.*
			367	Hilary of Poitiers dies.
	368	Council at Rome; Auxentius of Milan condemned.		
370–80	Demophilus, bishop (deposed as anti-Nicene).		370–79	Basil of Caesarea *flor.*
			370–90	Ausonius *flor.*
			c. 373	Ephraem Syrus dies.

General History	Rome, North Africa, the West	Alexandria/Egypt, Antioch, Jerusalem
		373–81 Peter, bishop of Alexandria.
		374–77 Jerome in desert of Chalcis.
375–78 Valens, Gratian, Valentinian II, emperors.		c. 375 Cyril born in Alexandria.
377 Arcadius born.		
378 Valens defeated and dies at hands of Visigoths at Adrianople (9 August).		
379 Theodosius I, emperor (January).		
	c. 380–85 Martin of Tours's mission in northern Gaul.	
		381–85 Timothy, bishop of Alexandria.
		381–404 Flavian, bishop of Antioch.
383 Magnus Maximus revolts. Gratian dies (August).	383 Jerome begins translation of Bible.	

Constantinople	Councils, Schisms, Heresies, Persecutions		Writers and Leaders	
			373–90	Gregory of Nazianzus, bishop of Sasima.
			374–95	Gregory, bishop of Nyssa.
	c. 375	Priscillianism begins in Spain.	375–90	Symmachus *flor.*
			375–90	Diodore of Tarsus *flor.*
	378	Gratian refuses title *Pontifex Maximus.*		
	380	Heresy proscribed (28 February).	380–85	Tyconius *flor.*
			380–90	Ammianus Marcellinus *flor.*
381 Gregory of Nazianzus appointed bishop; resigns. Meletius of Antioch dies.	381	Council of Constantinople. Council of Aquileia.		
381–97 Nectarius, bishop.				
	382	Council of Rome.		
	382–84	Altar of Victory debate.		
			383	Ulphilas dies.

General History		Rome, North Africa, the West		Alexandria/Egypt, Antioch, Jerusalem	
384	Honorius born.	384	Jerome leaves Rome for Palestine.		
384–85	Conflict between Ambrose and court of Valentinian II.	384–87	Augustine in Milan.		
		384–99	Siricius, pope.		
				385–412	Theophilus, bishop of Alexandria.
		386	Augustine returns to Catholic orthodoxy (August).	386–417	John, bishop of Jerusalem.
387	Maximus invades Italy.			387	Affair of the Statues of Antioch.
388	Maximus defeated at Aquileia (28 July).			388	Paulinus dies; strict Nicene and pro-Western bishop of Antioch.
		390	Massacre at Thessalonica. Ambrose enforces penance on Theodosius.		
		391–427	Aurelius, bishop of Carthage.	391	Serapeum destroyed by Theophilus.
392	Valentinian II dies (May).				
392–94	Eugenius revolts.			392–428	Theodore, bishop of Mopsuestia.
394	Theodosius's victory on Frigidus River (6 September).				

Constantinople	Councils, Schisms, Heresies, Persecutions	Writers and Leaders
	385 Priscillian and associates condemned and executed.	385–407 John Chrysostom *flor.*
		385–420 Jerome in Bethlehem.
		c. 390 Simeon Stylites born.
	391 Sacrifices prohibited.	
	392 Maximianist Schism in North Africa. Further antipagan and anti-heretical laws. Council of Capua.	
	393 Council of Hippo.	
	394 Donatist Council at Bagai (24 April).	

General History	Rome, North Africa, the West	Alexandria/Egypt, Antioch, Jerusalem
395 Theodosius dies (17 January). Empire divided between sons of Theodosius: Arcadius in East, Honorius in West.	**395** Augustine consecrated bishop of Hippo. Meropius Paulinus arrives at Nola.	
395–408 Stilicho administers West on behalf of Honorius.		**395–407** Didymus the Blind *flor.* in Alexandria.
	397 Ambrose of Milan dies.	
	c. 397 Ninian's mission north of Hadrian's Wall.	
397–98 Gildo's revolt in North Africa fails.		
398 Gildo and Bishop Optatus of Thamugadi executed.		
	399–401 Anastasius, pope.	
	399–412 Augustine's anti-Donatist campaign.	
	401–17 Innocent I, pope.	
402 Visigoths defeated at Pollentia.		

Constantinople	Councils, Schisms, Heresies, Persecutions		Writers and Leaders	
395 Home Synods begin.				
			395–400	Rufinus *flor.*
			395–404	Claudian, poet, *flor.*
			395–411	Sulpicius Severus *flor.*
			396–97	Augustine writes *Confessions.*
	397	Third Council of Carthage.		
	397–401	Origenist controversy.		
98–404 John Chrysostom, bishop.				
99–400 Gainas revolts.			399–407	Prudentius, poet, *flor.*
	400	Toledo I.		
	403	Synod of the Oak.	403	Epiphanius of Salamis dies.

General History		Rome, North Africa, the West		Alexandria/Egypt, Antioch, Jerusalem	
		405	Edict of Unity against Donatists.		
406	Vandals and other peoples invade Gaul.				
407	Constantine III usurps.				
408	Arcadius dies; Theodosius II, emperor in East. Stilicho murdered.				
409–10	Romans leave Britain.			409–15	Synesius, bishop of Ptolemais.
410	Alaric takes Rome (24 August).				
		411	Conference at Carthage (May–June). Pelagian controversy begins.		
		412	Donatists condemned and proscribed (January).	412–44	Cyril, bishop of Alexandria.
413	Heraclian revolts in North Africa.	413	Augustine writes *On the Spirit and the Letter*.	413–20	Alexander, bishop of Antioch.
415–21	Constantius III's campaigns in Gaul.			415	Hypatia murdered.
		417	Innocent I condemns Pelagians.		
		417–18	Zosimus, pope.		

Constantinople	Councils, Schisms, Heresies, Persecutions	Writers and Leaders
406–25 Atticus, bishop.		
407 John Chrysostom dies in exile.		
	410 Synod of Seleucia-Ctesiphon.	410–20 Paulus Orosius *flor.*
	411 Caelestius condemned at Carthage.	411–26 Augustine writes *City of God.*
		413–16 Rutilius Namatianus, poet, *flor.*
	415 Pagans barred from military and civilian offices. Synod of Diospolis exonerates Pelagius (December).	415–30 Augustine writes anti-Pelagian treatises. Julian of Eclanum *flor.*
	416 Anti-Pelagian councils at Carthage and Milevis.	
		417–34 John Cassian *flor.*

General History		Rome, North Africa, the West		Alexandria/Egypt, Antioch, Jerusalem	
		417–26	Case of Apiarius.		
418	Riots in Rome (March). Honorius banishes Pelagians (30 April). Visigoths settle in Gaul.	418	Zosimus writes *Tractoria* against Pelagians.		
		418–22	Boniface I, pope.		
				420–51	Shenoute of Atripe *flor*.
		422–32	Celestine, pope.	422–58	Juvenal, bishop of Jerusalem.
423	Honorius dies.				
423–25	John, usurping emperor.				
425–55	Valentinian III.	425–30	Honoratus at Lérins *flor*. Regime of Count Boniface.		
		c. 427	Revolts in North Africa.		
		427–30	Honoratus, bishop of Arles.		
				428–41	John, bishop of Antioch.
429	Vandals invade North Africa.				
		430	Augustine dies (August).		
		430–35	Vincent of Lérins *flor*.		

Constantinople	Councils, Schisms, Heresies, Persecutions		Writers and Leaders	
	418	Council of Thelepte.		
	419	Council of Carthage.		
	424	Synod of Dadisó in Persia.		
425–35 Memnon, bishop of Ephesus, *flor.*				
426 Sisinnius, bishop.				
428–31 Nestorius, bishop.				
	429–31	Nestorius versus Cyril (christological controversy).		
			430–40	Socrates, historian, *flor.* Sozomen, historian, *flor.*

General History	Rome, North Africa, the West	Alexandria/Egypt, Antioch, Jerusalem
431 Hippo falls to Vandals.	431 Paulinus of Nola dies.	
	432 Patrick's mission to Ireland.	
	432–40 Sixtus III, pope.	
	435–40 Bagaudae in Gaul.	435 Rabbula, bishop of Edessa, dies.
437 Valentinian III marries Eudoxia.		
438 *Codex Theodosianus* published.		
439 Carthage falls to Vandals (October).		
	440–61 Leo, pope.	
		441–49 Domnus, archbishop of Antioch (deposed).
442 Peace treaty between Rome and Vandals.		
		444 Cyril dies.
		444–51 Dioscorus, patriarch of Alexandria.
	445 Papacy authoritative in West.	
		446–49 Dioscorus attacks Flavian and Domnus.
447 Huns threaten Eastern Empire.		

Constantinople		Councils, Schisms, Heresies, Persecutions		Writers and Leaders	
431–34	Maximian, bishop.	431	Council of Ephesus I; Nestorius condemned.		
		433	Formula of Reunion.		
434–46	Proclus, bishop.				
				435–58	Theodoret of Cyrrhus *flor.*
				437	Proclus writes *Tome to the Armenians.*
				440	Salvian of Marseilles *flor.*
446	Flavian, bishop.	446–51	Christological controversy, second phase.		
		448	Eutyches condemned at Home Synod (November)		

963

General History	Rome, North Africa, the West	Alexandria/Egypt, Antioch, Jerusalem
	449 Leo writes *Tome* to Flavian.	449 Jerusalem's claim to patriarchate conceded by Dioscorus at Ephesus II.
		449–55 Maximus, archbishop of Antioch (deposed).
450 Marcian and Pulcheria begin reign.		
451 Attila's empire defeated by Aetius at Catalaunian Plains.	451–54 Dioscorus exiled to Gangra; dies.	451 Jerusalem confirmed as patriarchate.

Constantinople		Councils, Schisms, Heresies, Persecutions		Writers and Leaders
449	Flavian exiled, dies.	449	Ephesus II (= "Robber Council") restores Eutyches and condemns Flavian and Domnus.	
449–58	Anatolius, bishop.			
		451	Council of Chalcedon (October–November); Chalcedonian Definition.	
452	Nestorius dies in exile.			

General History	Rome, North Africa, the West	Alexandria/Egypt, Antioch, Jerusalem
450 Marcian, emperor; marries Pulcheria Augusta.		
		451–52 Anti-Chalcedonian riots in Alexandria and Jerusalem.
		451–57 Proterius, patriarch of Alexandria (murdered).
	452 Leo participates in embassy to Attila. Leo rejects twenty-eighth canon of Chalcedon.	452 Juvenal forced to flee Jerusalem.
453 Pulcheria dies.		453–58 Juvenal restored; dies.
	454 Theodoric born.	
455 Gaiseric captures Rome.		
455–56 Avitus, emperor in West; Gallo-Visigothic alliance.		
456–72 Ricimer, de facto ruler of West.		
457 Marcian dies.		
457–61 Majorian, emperor in West (executed, August 461).		457–60 Timothy Aelurus of Alexandria (deposed).
457–74 Leo I, emperor in East.		
		458–78 Anastasius, patriarch of Jerusalem.
		459 Simeon Stylites dies.
		460 Empress Eudoxia dies in Jerusalem.
		460–82 Timothy "Wobble Cap," of Alexandria, Chalcedonian.

Constantinople	Councils, Schisms, Heresies, Persecutions		Writers and Leaders	
			c. 450	Zosimus, historian, *flor.*
	457–58	Leo's "plebiscite" concerning Timothy Aelurus.		
58–71	Gennadius, patriarch.			
			460	Sidonius Apollinaris *flor.;* bishop of Clermont from 471.

General History	Rome, North Africa, the West		Alexandria/Egypt, Antioch, Jerusalem	
	461	Leo I, pope, dies. Patrick dies.		
	461–68	Hilarus, pope.		
	466	Clovis born.		
	466–84	Euric, king of Visigoths, advances Arian cause in Gaul.		
468 Leo I fails to defeat Vandals.	468–83	Simplicius, pope.		
			469	Confusion in Antioch. Peter the Fuller emerges as anti-Chalcedonian leader in Antioch.
474 Leo II, emperor.				
474–91 Zeno, emperor.				
475–76 Basiliscus usurps.			475–77	Timothy Aelurus restored.
476 Romulus Augustulus deposed; de facto end of empire in West.				
476–93 Odoacer, king of Italy.				
477 Gaiseric dies.				
477–84 Huneric, king of Vandals.				
			478–86	Martyrius, patriarch of Jerusalem.
			479	Stephen, patriarch of Antioch, murdered.

Constantinople	Councils, Schisms, Heresies, Persecutions	Writers and Leaders
471 Aspar murdered.		
471–89 Acacius, patriarch.		
	475 Ephesus III, anti-Chalcedonian.	
476 Basiliscus's anti-Chalcedonian policies frustrated by Acacius and Daniel Stylite.		

General History	Rome, North Africa, the West	Alexandria/Egypt, Antioch, Jerusalem
	c. 480 Monasticism begins in Celtic Britain.	
	Boethius born.	
	Benedict born.	
		481–84 Calendio, patriarch of Antioch.
		482 John Talaia, patriarch of Alexandria, Chalcedonian.
		482–90 Peter Mongo, patriarch of Alexandria, anti-Chalcedonian.
	483–92 Felix III, pope.	
	484 Acacius excommunicated by Council at Rome (July).	484 John Talaia dies.
		484–88 Peter the Fuller, patriarch of Antioch.
		485–521 Philoxenus, bishop of Mabbug (Hierapolis).
		486–94 Sallust, patriarch of Jerusalem.
		488 Severus decides on monastic vocation.
		488–98 Palladius, patriarch of Antioch.
		490–98 Athanasius II of Alexandria, anti-Chalcedonian.
491–518 Anastasius, emperor.		
	492–96 Gelasius, pope.	

Constantinople	Councils, Schisms, Heresies, Persecutions	Writers and Leaders
		480–88 Peter the Iberian *flor.*
482 Zeno writes *Henotikon* (28 July).		
	483–84 Huneric persecutes African Catholics.	
	484–519 Acacian Schism.	
489–90 Fravitta, patriarch.		
490–96 Euphemius, patriarch (deposed).		

General History	Rome, North Africa, the West		Alexandria/Egypt, Antioch, Jerusalem	
493–526 Theodoric the Ostrogoth, king of Italy.				
			494–516	Elias, patriarch of Jerusalem (deposed).
	495	"Tablettes Albertini" (North Africa).		
496–523 Thrasamund, king of Vandals.	496–98	Anastasius II, pope; attempts to end Acacian Schism.		
498 Isaurians expelled from Constantinople.	498–506	Laurentian Schism.	498–505	John Hemula, patriarch of Alexandria.
	498–514	Symmachus, pope.	498–512	Flavian II, patriarch of Antioch (deposed).
499(?) Clovis baptized.				
			500–512	Philoxenus of Mabbug wages anti-Chalcedonian campaign.
			500–532	St. Sabas acts in favor of Chalcedon in Palestine.
			502	Mission of the Nine Saints in Ethiopia.
			505–16	John of Nikiou, patriarch of Alexandria.
507 Franks defeat Visigoths at Vouillé.				

Constantinople	Councils, Schisms, Heresies, Persecutions		Writers and Leaders	
496–511 Macedonius, patriarch (deposed).				
c. 500 Theodora born.			500–527	Fulgentius of Ruspe *flor.*
	506	Council of Agde.		
507 Philoxenus in Constantinople.			507–38	Severus *flor.*
508–11 Severus in Constantinople.				
510 Anastasius writes *Typos*.			510–20(?)	Zacharias Rhetor *flor.*
			510–23	Boethius *flor.*

General History		Rome, North Africa, the West		Alexandria/Egypt, Antioch, Jerusalem	
		511	Council of Orléans reestablishes official status of Catholicism throughout Gaul. Clovis dies (November).		
				512–18	Severus, patriarch of Antioch (deposed).
513	Vitalian revolts.				
514–23	Hormisdas, pope.				
				516–18	Dioscorus II, patriarch of Alexandria.
				516–24	John, patriarch of Jerusalem.
518	Justin I, emperor; reverses religious policy of Anastasius.			518–20	Paul, patriarch of Antioch (resigns).
				518–35	Timothy IV, patriarch of Alexandria.
				518–38	Severus in exile in Alexandria.
519	Justin I ends Acacian Schism (March).	519–21	Scythian monks in Rome.	519–30	Monophysites persecuted in Antioch and throughout East except Egypt.
				520–26	Euphrasius, patriarch of Antioch (killed in earthquake).
		523	Boethius executed.		

Constantinople		Councils, Schisms, Heresies, Persecutions		Writers and Leaders	
511–18	Timothy, patriarch.	511	Council of Sidon.		
512	*Trisagion* riots.				
		513	Synod of Tyre.		
				514–84	Cassiodorus, statesman and writer, *flor.*
		517	Council of Epaul; Catholicism victorious in Burgundy.		
518–20	John, patriarch; first use of term "Ecumenical Patriarch."				
520–35	Epiphanius, patriarch.				
				521	James of Sarug, poet and Monophysite theologian, dies.

General History		Rome, North Africa, the West		Alexandria/Egypt, Antioch, Jerusalem	
523–30	Hilderic, king of Vandals, pro-Catholic and Byzantine.	523–26	John I, pope.		
				524–44	Peter, patriarch of Jerusalem.
		526	Embassy to Constantinople on behalf of Theodoric. Theodoric dies (30 August).		
526–34	Athalaric, king of Ostrogoths; Amalasuntha regent.	526–30	Felix IV, pope.	526–44	Ephraim, patriarch of Antioch.
527–65	Justinian, emperor.				
		529	Benedict founds Monte Cassino.		
		530	Dioscorus, pope.		
530–32	Persian War.	530–32	Boniface II, pope.		
533–34	Belisarius's expedition to North Africa ends Vandal kingdom.	533–35	John II, pope.		

Constantinople	Councils, Schisms, Heresies, Persecutions		Writers and Leaders	
	c. 524	Julianist Schism begins.		
	525	Council of Carthage; partial restoration of Catholicism.		
	527–30	Monophysite hierarchy emerges. Antiheretical laws promulgated by Justinian.		
	529	Athens Academy closes. Council of Orange.		
			530–40	Leontius of Jerusalem *flor.* Anthimus of Tralles, architect, *flor.*
			530–60	Procopius, historian, *flor.*
532	Nika riot.			
532–33	Conferences with Monophysite leaders.			
534	*Codex Justinianus* published.			

General History		Rome, North Africa, the West		Alexandria/Egypt, Antioch, Jerusalem	
535	Amalasuntha murdered. Gothic War begins.	535	Catholicism restored in North Africa.	535	Gaianus, patriarch of Alexandria, Julianist (deposed).
		535–36	Agapetus, pope.	535–66	Theodosius, patriarch of Alexandria.
536	Belisarius invades Italy. Rome falls to Belisarius.				
		536–37	Silverius, pope.		
				537	Theodosius exiled to Constantinople. Chalcedonian succession restored in Alexandria.
		537–54	Vigilius, pope.	537–40	Paul, patriarch of Alexandria (deposed).
540	Ravenna falls to Belisarius.				
				542	Theodora launches successful mission of Julian to Nubia.
542–50	Gothic recovery under Totila.			542–51	Zoilus, patriarch of Alexandria, Chalcedonian.
				544–74	Macarius, patriarch of Jerusalem.
546	Theodore Ascidas prompts promulgation of Edict of Three Chapters. Totila captures Rome (December).				
547	Totila loses Rome to Belisarius again (April).	c. 547	St. Benedict dies.		
		548	Vigilius issues *Judicatum* condemning Three Chapters.		

Constantinople	Councils, Schisms, Heresies, Persecutions	Writers and Leaders
		c. 535 Leontius of Byzantium *flor.*
535–36 Anthimus, patriarch, pro-Monophysite (deposed).		
536 Agapetus visits. Severus condemned by Home Synod.		
536–52 Menas, patriarch.		
537 Hagia Sophia dedicated.		
	540–43 Origenist controversy.	540 Gildas *flor.*
	542 James Baradaeus begins mission.	
	542–60 Monophysite church established throughout Byzantine Empire.	
547 Vigilius visits Constantinople.		
548 Theodora dies.		

General History		Rome, North Africa, the West		Alexandria/Egypt, Antioch, Jerusalem	
				551–70	Apollinaris, patriarch of Alexandria, Chalcedonian.
552	Totila defeated at Busta Gallorum.	552	Reparatus, archbishop of Carthage, deposed.		
553	Justinian acquires most of Andalusia.				
554	Narses ends Gothic resistance: "Pragmatic Sanction" organizes Byzantine Italy.	554	Vigilius's *Constitutum* accepts decision of Fifth General Council.		
		554–90	Schisms in West, particularly in northern Italy, directed against Fifth General Council.		
		555–61	Pelagius I, pope.		
				557–61	Monophysite hierarchy restored in Antioch with Sergius as patriarch.
				559–70	Anastasius, patriarch of Antioch (deposed).
		561–74	John III, pope.		
		563	Columba arrives on Iona.		
565–78	Justin II, emperor.				
				c. 566	Chalcedonian mission to Makurrah.

Constantinople	Councils, Schisms, Heresies, Persecutions		Writers and Leaders	
	550–70	Tritheist heresy in Monophysite church.	550–60	Agathias, historian, *flor.*
			550–85	John of Ephesus, Monophysite historian, *flor.*
552–65 Eutychius, patriarch (deposed).				
	553	Fifth General Council; Three Chapters condemned.		
			560–70	Corippus, poet, *flor.*
565–77 John Scholasticus, patriarch.				
566–67 John Scholasticus's discussions with Monophysites.				

General History	Rome, North Africa, the West	Alexandria/Egypt, Antioch, Jerusalem
567 Plague in Italy.		
568 Lombard invasion begins.		568 Colloquy at Callinicum.
		569 Longinus's mission to Alwah.
		570–91 Gregory, patriarch of Antioch, Chalcedonian.
572–73 Lombards take Spoleto and Benevento.		
	574–79 Benedict I, pope.	574–94 John, patriarch of Jerusalem.
		576–77 Peter, patriarch of Alexandria, Monophysite.
		Coptic hierarchy established in Alexandria.
c. 577 Slav invasions of Balkans begin in earnest.		
578–82 Tiberius II, emperor.		578–604 Damian, patriarch of Alexandria, Monophysite.
		Schism between Alexandrian and Antiochene Monophysites.
579 Persian War renews.	579–90 Pelagius II, pope.	
581 Al-Mundhir affair.		581–91 Peter of Callinicum, patriarch of Antioch, Monophysite.
		581–608 Eulogius, patriarch of Alexandria, Chalcedonian.
582–602 Maurice, emperor.		

Constantinople	Councils, Schisms, Heresies, Persecutions	Writers and Leaders
		570–650 Nestorian missions in East; China reached 635.
571 "Second Henotikon" fails to end schism.		
577–82 Eutychius, patriarch, restored.		
		580–94 Gregory of Tours, historian, *flor.*
582–95 John the Faster, patriarch.		

General History	Rome, North Africa, the West		Alexandria/Egypt, Antioch, Jerusalem	
	587	Recared, king of Visigoths, converts to Catholicism.		
	590–604	Gregory I, pope.		
	590–615	Columbanus's missions.		
591 Treaty between Rome and Persia.				
			593–98	Anastasius restored at Antioch.
			594–600	Amos, patriarch of Jerusalem.
			595–631	Athanasius "the Camel Driver," patriarch of Antioch, Monophysite.
	597	Gregory I's mission to Anglo-Saxons.		
			600–609	Hesychius, patriarch of Jerusalem.
601 War between Byzantium and Avars.				
602 Maurice and family murdered (November).				
602–10 Phocas, emperor. Persians invade Roman Empire in force.				
	603	Lombard heir baptized Catholic.		
614 Jerusalem falls to Persians.				

Constantinople	Councils, Schisms, Heresies, Persecutions	Writers and Leaders
		590–615 Columbanus *flor.*
595 Controversy over title "Ecumenical Patriarch."		
595–603 Cyriacus, patriarch.		

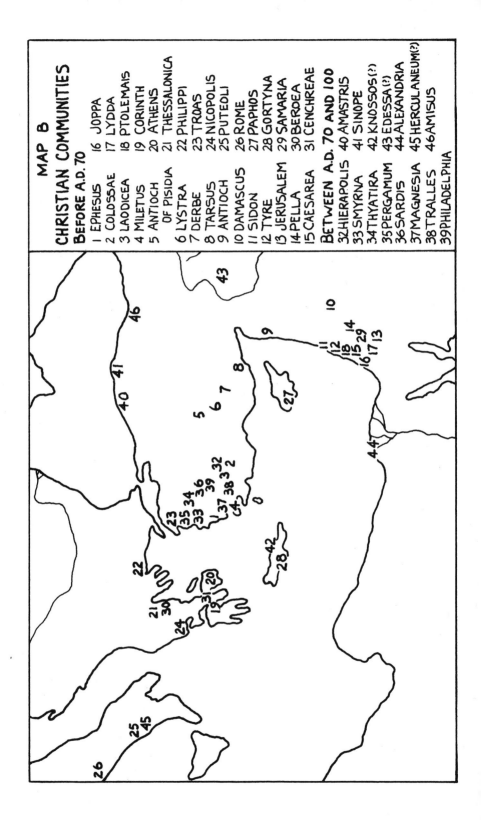

MAP B

CHRISTIAN COMMUNITIES

BEFORE A.D. 70

1 EPHESUS	16 JOPPA
2 COLOSSAE	17 LYDDA
3 LAODICEA	18 PTOLEMAIS
4 MILETUS	19 CORINTH
5 ANTIOCH	20 ATHENS
OF PISIDIA	21 THESSALONICA
6 LYSTRA	22 PHILIPPI
7 DERBE	23 TROAS
8 TARSUS	24 NICOPOLIS
9 ANTIOCH	25 PUTEOLI
10 DAMASCUS	26 ROME
11 SIDON	27 PAPHOS
12 TYRE	28 GORTYNA
13 JERUSALEM	29 SAMARIA
14 PELLA	30 BEROEA
15 CAESAREA	31 CENCHREAE

BETWEEN A.D. 70 AND 100

32 HIERAPOLIS	40 AMASTRIS
33 SMYRNA	41 SINOPE
34 THYATIRA	42 KNOSSOS (?)
35 PERGAMUM	43 EDESSA (?)
36 SARDIS	44 ALEXANDRIA
37 MAGNESIA	45 HERCULANEUM(?)
38 TRALLES	46 AMISUS
39 PHILADELPHIA	

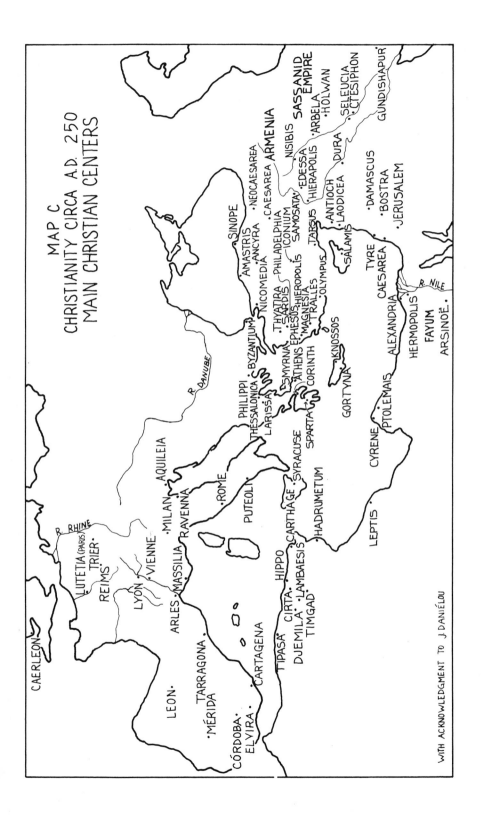

MAP C
CHRISTIANITY CIRCA A.D. 250
MAIN CHRISTIAN CENTERS

WITH ACKNOWLEDGMENT TO J.DANIÉLOU

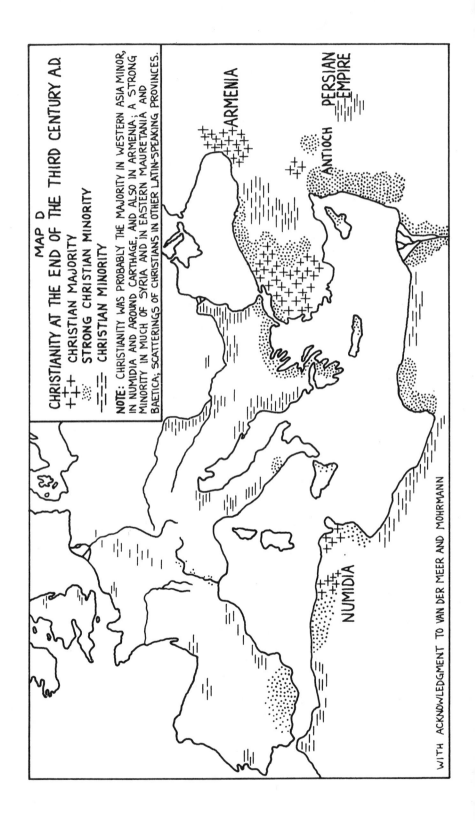

MAP D

CHRISTIANITY AT THE END OF THE THIRD CENTURY A.D.

+ + + CHRISTIAN MAJORITY
∴∴∴ STRONG CHRISTIAN MINORITY
≡≡≡ CHRISTIAN MINORITY

NOTE: CHRISTIANITY WAS PROBABLY THE MAJORITY IN WESTERN ASIA MINOR, IN NUMIDIA AND AROUND CARTHAGE, AND ALSO IN ARMENIA; A STRONG MINORITY IN MUCH OF SYRIA AND IN EASTERN MAURETANIA AND BAETICA, SCATTERINGS OF CHRISTIANS IN OTHER LATIN-SPEAKING PROVINCES.

ARMENIA

ANTIOCH

PERSIAN EMPIRE

NUMIDIA

WITH ACKNOWLEDGMENT TO VAN DER MEER AND MOHRMANN

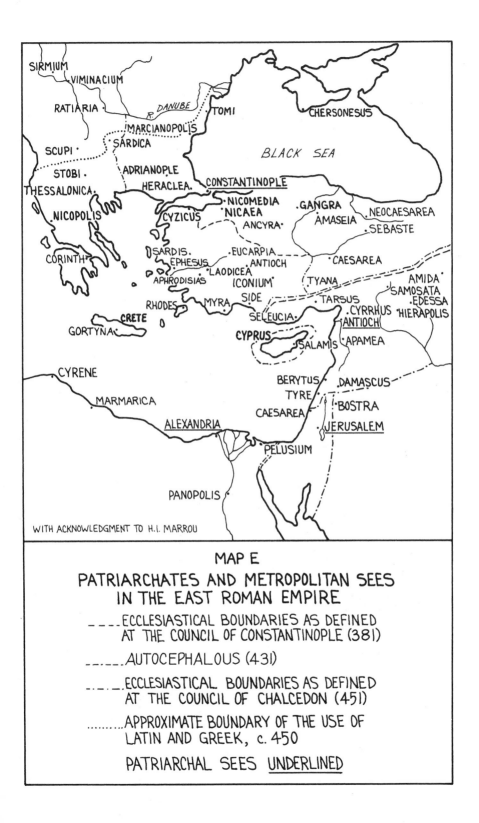

WITH ACKNOWLEDGMENT TO H.I. MARROU

MAP E
PATRIARCHATES AND METROPOLITAN SEES IN THE EAST ROMAN EMPIRE

_ _ _ _ ECCLESIASTICAL BOUNDARIES AS DEFINED
AT THE COUNCIL OF CONSTANTINOPLE (381)

_ _ _ _ _ AUTOCEPHALOUS (431)

_ _ · _ · _ ECCLESIASTICAL BOUNDARIES AS DEFINED
AT THE COUNCIL OF CHALCEDON (451)

.... APPROXIMATE BOUNDARY OF THE USE OF
LATIN AND GREEK, c. 450

PATRIARCHAL SEES UNDERLINED

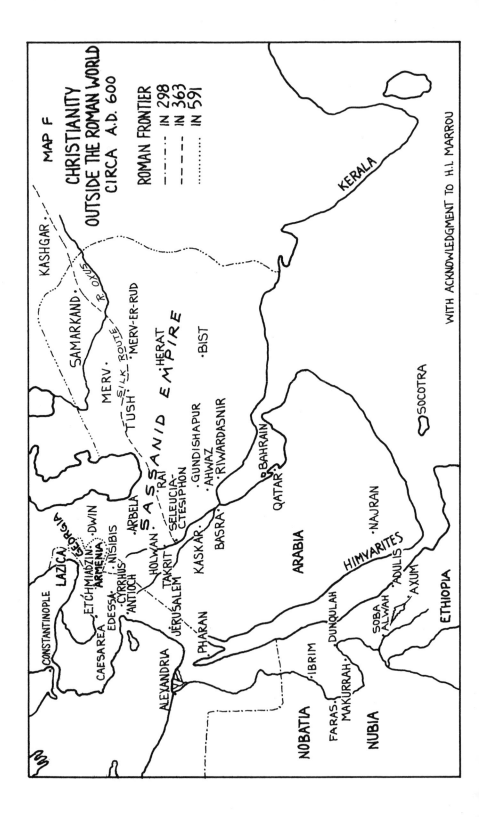

MAP F

CHRISTIANITY
OUTSIDE THE ROMAN WORLD
CIRCA A.D. 600

ROMAN FRONTIER
---·---·--- IN 298
---------- IN 363
·············· IN 591

WITH ACKNOWLEDGMENT TO H.I. MARROU

Names Index

Page references to illustrations are in italics (see p. x for descriptions of illustrations). References to maps are by map letter. Bishops of Rome have been indexed as "bishops" before c. 300 and "popes" thereafter. Bishops of the patriarchal sees of Alexandria, Antioch, Jerusalem, Constantinople, and Rome have been designated "bishops" to 431, "archbishops" from 431 to 449, and "patriarchs" thereafter. The date 449 is selected as it is the date that Juvenal of Jerusalem achieved patriarchal status.

Aaron (martyr), 449
Abbirgermaniciana, 356
Abelonii (North African sect), 686 n. 11
Abgar (king, "correspondent" of Jesus), 129
Abgar VIII the Great (king of Osrhoene), 295, 296, 306 n. 151
Abitina, 412, 447, 462, 489, 654
Ablabius, 528
Abraham, 13, 81 n. 53, 87, 94, 101, 115 n. 52, 121, 138, 215, 238, 240, 246, 275, 416, 500, 658, 669, 749, 751, 754
Abraham (monk), 576
Acacius (bishop of Caesarea), 356
Acacius (bishop of Melitene), 759
Acacius (patriarch of Constantinople), 808–10, 812, 813
Achaia, 101, 280, 379–80, 444, A, G
Achillas (bishop of Alexandria), 493
Acholius, 637, 638
Acilius Glabrio. See Glabrio
Acmonia, 40, 52 n. 124, 188 n. 12, A
Actium, 21
Adam, 103, 122, 136, 147, 197, 198, 213, 214, 246, 247, 316, 377, 416, 555, 635, 670, 673–74, 678, 679, 713, 753, 849; Apocalypse of, 203
Adamantius, 217
Adauctus, 444
Ad Decimum, 832, 860 n. 8
Aden, Gulf of, 286
Adeodatus, 665
Adiabene, 32, 33, 129, 295, G

Adige valley, 708
Adlectus, 278
Adonai, 178, 278
Adrianople, 617, 620, 635, E
Aedui, 709
Aegean Islands, 96, 130, 554, 847–48
Aegina, A, G
Aelafius, 486
Aelia Capitolina (Jerusalem), 162, 500
Aelianus, 512 n. 61
Aemilia-Liguria, 618, G
Aemilianus (deputy prefect of Egypt), 287, 326, 402
Aemilii, 717
Aeneid, 563, 828, 833
Aenon by Salim, 79 n. 36
Aetius (general), 801
Aetius ("godless deacon"), 537, 539, 541, 550 n. 99, 556, 583 n. 18, 601, 611 n. 34
Africa, A, G. See also North Africa; proconsular Africa
Agapetus (pope), 829, 843, 844, 864 n. 99
Agathias (historian), 828, 854, 862 n. 54
Agathopus (Gnostic), 372
Ager Sextii, 326
Agilulf (Lombard king), 887
Agis (temple), 554
Agonistici, 573
Agrippa I (king of Judea), 90, 113 n. 16
Agrippa II (king of Abilene) 50 n. 80, 148

991

Subject Index

Acacian Schism, 536, 790, 799, 807–13, 828, 844
Acta Martyrum (Acts of the Martyrs), 184, 327, 409, 417, 444, 707; Donatist Acta, 462, 654
Adoptionism, 344, 362 n. 41, 382, 385–87, 493, 532. See also Monarchians
Agape, 108, 141–42, 158 n. 105, 240, 408–9, 416, 559
Alienation (alienatio), 175, 346, 701, 710–11, 721, 722
Almsgiving, 157 n. 70; Christian, 133, 351, 421, 567, 569, 675; Jewish, 25
Alogi, 251, 254
Anchorites, 575, 631, 837. See also Monasticism
Angelology: Jewish, 197, 203, 235–36, 344; angels, 441, 534
Anhomoeans, 539, 540, 670
Antinomianism, 137
Antiphonal singing, 142, 706
Anti-Semitism, 241
Aphthartodocetism, 830
Apocalyptic, 29, 98, 120, 133, 143, 149, 194, 250, 255, 283, 309, 372, 422, 450, 542; Jewish, 143, 201
Apologetic literature, 36, 121, 179–80, 231, 234–50, 252, 283, 285–87, 290–91, 292–93, 370–71, 417–19, 421, 477–79, 483, 485, 526, 703, 716; Jewish, 36, 125–26, 236, 243, 252, 261 n. 24, 287, 340, 385, 418; pagan, 176, 177–80, 283, 291–92, 442–44, 477, 504, 604, 605–6
Apostates, 127, 147, 324, 354, 409, 410
Apostles, 87, 128, 135, 137, 140, 271, 311, 339, 351, 352, 401, 442, 530; apostolic succession, 140–41, 232, 249–50, 351, 403; relics, 877; tombs of the, 401, 563, 567
Aramaic, 22, 31, 33, 54, 56, 64, 129, 131, 145, 251, 403, 498, 560, 759
Archimandrite, 764, 765, 766
Arianism, 493, 503, 524, 531, 539, 540–41, 575, 620, 636, 637, 640,

718, 726, 745, 753, 755, 756; Germanic, 618–19, 640, 719, 726–27, 728, 743, 790–91, 792, 796–97, 800, 803, 805, 807, 813, 814, 821 n. 53, 822 n. 61, 832, 834, 854, 861 n. 33, 880, 881; in the West, 541, 620–21, 622, 718, 757, 767
Aristocracy, 501, 600, 702, 704, 707, 712–17, 721, 722, 724, 725, 733 n. 16, 734 n. 26, 794–95, 805–6, 838, 870, 886; and monasticism, 838, 881, 899 n. 62; and paganism, 600, 701–4, 716, 718
Art: Byzantine, 832, 835–37, 847; Christian, 280, 297, 306 n. 162, 367, 414–17, 422, 502, 555, 564–65, 582 n. 9, 652; Donatist, 560; funerary, 555, 564–65; Gnostic, 280–81; Jewish, 415–16, 449
Ascetics, 195–97, 217–18, 254, 421–24, 562, 567–68, 575–79, 597, 630–31, 653, 667–68, 677, 709, 710–21, 877; Manichean, 456, 653, 662–63, 711, 716
Astrology, 189 n. 4, 295, 297, 565, 566
Atheism, 148, 181, 182, 234, 241, 262 n. 57, 288, 477, 480, 526, 604
Atonement, 61, 69, 83 n. 96, 134, 206, 633

Baptism, 2, 58–60, 69, 103–4, 108, 134, 141–42, 233–34, 240, 251, 313, 315, 355–57, 368, 385–86, 407, 411, 416, 422, 430 n. 75, 433 n. 145, 450, 475, 654, 662, 677, 680, 693 n. 132, 709, 718, 792, 804; baptismal controversy, 284, 325, 352–57, 523; and Christianity, 699–729; Clement and, 390 n. 17; Cyprian and, 354–56, 654; Gnostic, 200, 210–11, 279, 411; as illumination, 233, 357, 390 n. 17; infant, 676–77, 695 n. 179; Manichean, 690 n. 68; Marcionite, 216; as "seal," 103, 108, 140, 355, 357; Tertullian and, 347. See also Rebaptism controversy

1013

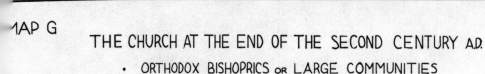

MAP G

THE CHURCH AT THE END OF THE SECOND CENTURY A.D.

- • ORTHODOX BISHOPRICS or LARGE COMMUNITIES
- ✕ GNOSTIC CENTERS
- ○ MARCIONITE BISHOPRICS AND CENTERS
- + MONTANIST CENTERS
- — OTHER CHRISTIAN CENTERS and REMAINS

BORDERS OF THE EMPIRE ·········· PROVINCIAL BORDERS ‑‑‑‑‑ LINGUISTIC DIVISION ‑·‑·‑·
LATIN/GREEK

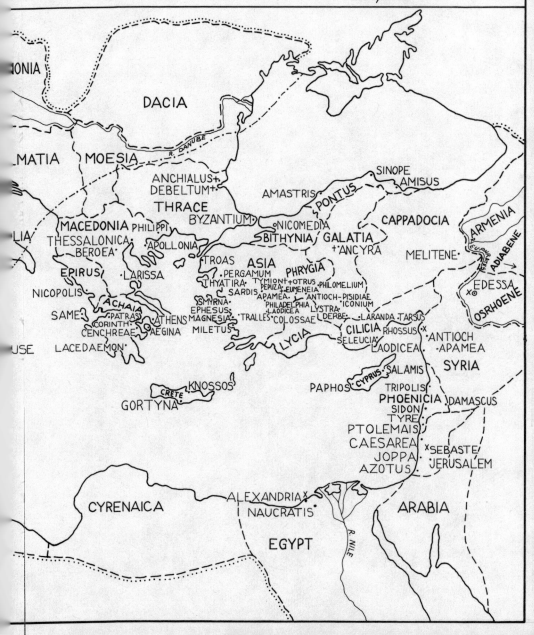

DACIA

ONIA

MATIA   MOESIA   R. DANUBE

SINOPE
AMISUS

ANCHIALUS+
DEBELTUM+
AMASTRIS   PONTUS

THRACE   BYZANTIUM   NICOMEDIA   CAPPADOCIA
MACEDONIA   PHILIPPI   BITHYNIA   GALATIA   ARMENIA
ILIA   THESSALONICA   APOLLONIA   +ANCYRA   ADIABENE
BEROEA·   MELITENE·
EPIRUS   TROAS   ASIA   PHRYGIA   EDESSA
·LARISSA   ·PERGAMUM   OSRHOENE
NICOPOLIS   THYATIRA·   TYMION+·OTRUS·PHILOMELIUM   ✕○
ACHAIA   SARDIS·   PEPUZA+·EUMENEIA   EDESSA
SAME·   PATRAS   SMYRNA·   APAMEA·   ·ANTIOCH-PISIDIAE
CORINTH·   EPHESUS·   PHILADELPHIA   ·ICONIUM   ·LARANDA·TARSUS
CENCHREAE·   ATHENS·MAGNESIA·   LAODICEA   LYSTRA·   RHOSSUS·✕
·AEGINA   MILETUS   TRALLES·COLOSSAE   ·DERBE   CILICIA   ANTIOCH
LACEDAEMON·   LYCIA   SELEUCIA   LAODICEA   ·APAMEA
USE   SALAMIS   SYRIA
CRETE   KNOSSOS   PAPHOS   CYPRUS   TRIPOLIS
GORTYNA   PHOENICIA·DAMASCUS
SIDON·
TYRE·
PTOLEMAIS·
CAESAREA·   ✕SEBASTE·
JOPPA·   ·JERUSALEM
AZOTUS·

CYRENAICA   ALEXANDRIA✕   ARABIA
I NAUCRATIS·

EGYPT   R. NILE